Anonymous

Poor Law Unions

A statement of the names of the several Unions and Poor law parishes in England

and Wales; and of the population, area, and rateable value thereof in 1881

Anonymous

Poor Law Unions
A statement of the names of the several Unions and Poor law parishes in England and Wales; and of the population, area, and rateable value thereof in 1881

ISBN/EAN: 9783337324957

Printed in Europe, USA, Canada, Australia, Japan

Cover: Foto ©Suzi / pixelio.de

More available books at **www.hansebooks.com**

A

STATEMENT

OF THE NAMES OF THE SEVERAL

UNIONS AND
POOR LAW PARISHES

IN

ENGLAND AND WALES;

AND OF THE

POPULATION, AREA, AND RATEABLE VALUE THEREOF IN 1881;

Together with the **POST TOWN** of each Parish, and the **PETTY SESSIONAL DIVISION** within which each Parish is included.

Presented to both Houses of Parliament by Command of Her Majesty.

LONDON:
PRINTED FOR HER MAJESTY'S STATIONERY OFFICE,
BY EYRE AND SPOTTISWOODE,
PRINTERS TO THE QUEEN'S MOST EXCELLENT MAJESTY.

And to be purchased, either directly or through any Bookseller, from
EYRE AND SPOTTISWOODE, EAST HARDING STREET, FLEET STREET, E.C., and
32, ABINGDON STREET, WESTMINSTER, S.W.; or
ADAM AND CHARLES BLACK, 6, NORTH BRIDGE, EDINBURGH; or
HODGES, FIGGIS, & Co., 101, GRAFTON STREET, DUBLIN.

1887.

[C.—5191.]　*Price 4s. 4d.*

MEMORANDUM.

This List of the Unions and Parishes under separate Boards of Guardians in England and Wales is so arranged as to show the Poor Law Parishes* of which each Union consists.

During recent years many alterations have been made in the areas of Parishes in consequence of the passing of the Divided Parishes and Poor Law Amendment Act, 1876, and the Acts amending that Statute; these alterations have been the result either of Orders issued by the Local Government Board or of the operation of Section 2 of the Divided Parishes and Poor Law Amendment Act, 1882, by virtue of which any part of a Parish which was isolated or detached from the other part or parts thereof, and which was wholly surrounded by another Parish, became, from and after the 25th of March, 1883, amalgamated with such other Parish. The Board are not in possession of complete information as to the alterations effected by the Act of 1882; hence changes of the former class only are shown in the List. These are indicated in foot-notes. They include alterations effected by Orders which came into operation on or before the 26th March, 1887.

The tabular portion of the List sets forth in six columns the following particulars :—

1. Name of Union or Separate Parish; and, in the case of a Union, date of formation and of any addition thereto; with the names of the Parishes included therein, arranged alphabetically under county divisions where the union is situated in more than one County, or in divisions between City and County where such exist; and the description of each place, viz., Parish, Township, Chapelry, &c.

2. Population of the Parish in 1881.

3. Its area in statute acres in 1881.

4. Its rateable value in 1881.

5. Post Town.

6. Petty Sessional Division.

(Col. 1.) As regards the names of the Parishes, it may be explained that, in consequence of the variations in this respect which are continually occurring, the Board have found it necessary in their Orders to observe some uniform rule, and in those documents they have for some time past followed the spelling of the name of a Parish as it appears in the Order declaring the Union in which it is contained. The same rule has been adopted in the present List except in cases where, as shown by notes at the head of the Union, the spelling of a name or names has been altered by Orders issued since the Declaration Order.

The descriptions of the several places correspond, as a rule, with those in the Census Report of 1871.

(Cols. 2 and 3.) As regards the population and area of the Parishes, the List follows the last Census Report. That Report refers to the Census taken on the 4th April, 1881, and consequently the figures as to area and population in the List refer to the Parishes as they then existed. It has not been found practicable to give precise information as to the changes in the area and population of Parishes effected by Orders

---

* A Poor Law Parish is a place for which a separate Poor Rate is, or can be, made, or a separate Overseer is, or can be, appointed.

a 2

under the Divided Parishes Acts which have come into operation since the 4th April, 1881, but the Board have inserted in foot-notes to the List references to the Orders by which the alterations were made.

(Col. 4.) The rateable value in 1881 is taken from the Parliamentary Return which was issued in 1882, with respect to the "Valuation to the Poor Rates of each Parish " in England for the parochial year 1881-1882."

(Cols. 5 and 6.) The post towns and petty sessional divisions have been taken from the lists of Guardians and paid officers furnished to the Board by the Clerks to the Guardians.

The meanings of the abbreviations used in the List are as follows :—

bor.	stands for	Borough, or Municipal Borough.
cha.	,,	Chapelry.
div.	,,	Division.
ham.	,,	Hamlet.
lib.	,,	Liberty.
lord.	,,	Lordship.
par.	,,	Parish.
pre.	,,	Precinct.
tow.	,,	Township.
ty.	,,	Tything.
u. p.	,,	United Parishes.
vill.	,,	Ville.

Local Government Board,
    September 1887.

In this List the letter (W.) following the name of a Parish or Place signifies that a Workhouse is locally situated in such Parish or Place.

Unions and Parishes, &c.	Population in 1881.	Area in Statute Acres in 1881.	Rateable Value in 1881.	Post Town.	Petty Sessional Division.
ABERAERON UNION.					
(Formed 8 May 1837 by Order dated 11 April 1837.)					
COUNTY OF CARDIGAN:			£		
Cilcennin (c) - - par.	503	3,405	1,202	Aberaeron - -	Aberaeron and Lower Ilar.
Cilie Aeron (c) - par.	329	1,914	758	do. - -	do.
Cydplwyf - parcel	233	In Llanina	330	do. - -	do.
Dihewid (a) - - par.	451	3,215	1,062	do. - -	do.
Henfynyw - - par.	1,015	2,261	1,825	do. - -	do.
Llanarth - - par.	2,003	15,044	4,149	do. - -	do.
Llanbadarn tref Eglwys par.	869	6,283	1,913	do. - -	do.
Llandewi Aberarth (W.) (b) } par.	1,361	3,595	2,383	do. - -	do.
Llandisilio Gogo - par.	1,187	10,221	2,627	do. - -	do.
Llanwchaeron (a) - par.	224	1,606	847	do. - -	do.
Llanfihangel Ystrad (c) par.	987	7,167	3,107	do. - -	do.
Llanina - - ham.	187	1,908	484	do. - -	do.
Llanllwchaiarn - par.	1,873	3,219	2,209	do. - -	do.
Llansaintfraed and Llannon (b) } par.	1,324	5,413	2,783	do. - -	do.
TOTAL of UNION -	12,543	65,704	25,679		
ABERGAVENNY UNION.					
(Formed 31 May 1836 by Order dated 27 April 1836.)					
COUNTY of HEREFORD:					
Tewddog - - ham.	89	2,101	579	Abergavenny -	Dore.
COUNTY of MONMOUTH:					
Abergavenny with Hardwicke and Lloyudu (W.) } par.	7,886	4,251	31,379	do. - -	Abergavenny.
Bettws Newydd - par.	109	1,129	1,085	Usk - -	Usk.
Bryngwn - - par.	294	1,481	2,098	Abergavenny -	Raglan.
Bwlch Trewyn - ham.	76	636	679	do. - -	Abergavenny.
Clytha - - ham.	293	1,840	2,784	do. - -	Raglan.
Llanarth - - tow.	243	1,978	3,032	do. - -	do.
Llanellan - - par.	366	2,527	2,205	do. - -	Abergavenny.
Llanfoist - - par.	1,463	3,260	11,656	do. - -	do.
Llangattock Lingoed par.	174	1,941	1,708	do. - -	do.
Llangattock nigh Usk par.	239	1,625	3,448	do. - -	do.
Llanover Lower and Higher - } par.	7193	4,742	17,076	do. - -	do. and Pontypool.
Llansaintfread - par.	24	290	374	do. - -	do.
Llanthewy Rytherch par.	353	2,201	2,757	do. - -	do
Llanthewy Skirrit - par.	115	1,060	1,025	do. - -	do.
Llantilio Patholey Ultra and Citra } par.	1,225	6,817	10,012	do. - -	do.
Llanvair Kilgiden - par.	293	1,808	3,031	do. - -	Pontypool.

(continued)

ABERAERON UNION:

(a) Two detached parts of Llanwchaeron were amalgamated with Dihewid, by Order which came into operation on 25 March 1884.

(b) A detached part of Llansaintfraed and Llannon known as "Gilfaeh," was amalgamated with Llandewi Aberarth,

ABERAERON UNION—continued.

by Provisional Order which came into operation on 25 March 1885.

(c) Parts of Cilcennin were amalgamated with Cilie Aeron and Llanfihangel Ystrad, and parts of Cilie Aeron and Llanfihangel Ystrad were amalgamated with Cilcennin, by Order which came into operation on 25 March 1886.

Unions and Parishes, &c.		Population in 1881.	Area in Statute Acres in 1881.	Rateable Value in 1881.	Post Town.	Petty Sessional Division.
ABERGAVENNY UNION—County of Monmouth—*continued.*				£		
Llanvapley - -	*par.*	105	845	1,471	Abergavenny -	Abergavenny.
Llanvetherine - -	*par.*	221	2,169	2,418	do. - -	do.
Llanvihangel Crucor- ney with Penbiddle	} *par.*	445	3,278	4,903	do. - -	do.
Llanvihangel nigh Usk	*par.*	108	388	667	do. - -	do.
Llanwenarth Citra -	*div.*	268	2,812	2,291	do. - -	do.
Llanwenarth Ultra -	*div.*	1,539	2,455	4,261	do. - -	do.
Lower Cwmyoye -	*div.*	231	3,507	2,383	do. - -	do.
Oldcastle - -	*par.*	50	934	636	do. - -	do.
Upper Cwmyoye -	*div.*	169	4,742	1,220	do. - -	do.
TOTAL of UNION -		23,571	60,850	115,178		
ABERYSTWITH UNION.						
(Formed 5 May 1837 by Order dated 19 April 1837.)						
COUNTY of CARDIGAN :						
Town and Liberties of Aberystwith (*a*)	} *cha.*	6,703	734	22,993	Aberystwith -	(Separate Commission of the Peace.)
Broncastellan -	*tow.*	141	505	589	do. - -	Upper Geneurglyn.
Caelan y Maesmor -	*tow.*	823	7,439	2,286	do. - -	do.
Clarach - -	*tow.*	227	1,702	1,846	do. - -	do.
Cwm Rheidol (*c*) -	*tow.*	1,128	7,824	2,333	do. - -	Lower Geneurglyn.
Cyfoeth y Brenin -	*tow.*	1,169	2,514	3,194	do. - -	Upper Geneurglyn.
Cynill mawr - -	*tow.*	539	3,748	2,576	do. - -	do.
Elerch - -	*tow.*	252	4,173	818	do. - -	do.
Henllys - -	*tow.*	399	5,144	2,339	do. - -	do.
Issayndre (*a*) - -	*tow.*	563	In Uchayn-dre.	1,597	do. - -	Lower Geneurglyn.
Llanafan - -	*par.*	628	2,588	2,405	do. - -	Upper Ilar.
Llanbadarn y Croyd-din Lower	} *tow.*	682	4,981	4,621	do. - -	do.
Llanbadarn y Croyd-din Upper (*c*)	} *tow.*	695	9,342	2,940	do. - -	do.
Llancynfelin - -	*par.*	905	6,556	3,088	do. - -	Upper Geneurglyn.
Llanddeinol - -	*par.*	228	2,077	1,376	do. - -	do.
Llanfihangel y Croyd-din Lower	} *tow.*	873	6,592	4,509	do. - -	do.
Llanfihangel y Croyd-din Upper, or Eg-lwys newydd	} *tow.*	1,694	15,961	3,772	do. - -	do.
Llanygwyryfon, or Llangrwyddon	} *par.*	522	3,846	2,012	do. - -	do.
Llanilar Upper and Lower	} *par.*	833	6,403	4,577	do. - -	do.
Llanrhystyd Haminiog	*tow.*	792	} 8,770 {	3,016	do. - -	Lower Ilar and Aber-ayron.
Llanrhystyd Mevenidd	*tow.*	585		2,808	do. - -	do.
Llanychaiarn -	*par.*	609	4,181	3,906	do. - -	Upper Ilar.
Melindwr (*b*) -	*tow.*	991	6,677	2,438	do. - -	Lower Geneurglyn.
Parcel Canol (*b*) -	*tow.*	564	4,325	2,073	do. - -	do.
Rhosdie - -	*par.*	168	1,307	578	do. - -	Upper Ilar.
Trefeirig - -	*tow.*	1,107	9,150	3,583	do. - -	Lower Geneurglyn.
Tyr y Mynach -	*tow.*	440	2,716	1,256	do. - -	Upper Geneurglyn.
Uchayndre - -	*tow.*	400	730	786	do. - -	Lower Geneurglyn.
Vainor Lower (W.) (*a*)	} *tow.*	598	1,148	2,490	do. - -	do.
Vainor Upper -	*tow.*	348	1,459	1,900	do. - -	do.
TOTAL of UNION -		25,606	132,592	94,735		

ABERYSTWITH UNION :

(*a*) The parts of Issayndre and Vainor Lower respectively, which were within the boundary of the municipal borough of Aberystwith, were respectively amalgamated with the town and liberties of Aberystwith by Orders which came into operation on 25 March 1883.

ABERYSTWITH UNION—*continued.*

(*b*) Two detached parts of Parcel Canol were amalgamated with Melindwr by Order which came into operation on 25 March 1885.

(*c*) A detached part of Llanbadarn y Croyddin Upper was amalgamated with Cwm Rheidol by Order which came into operation on 25 March 1886.

Unions and Parishes, &c.	Population in 1881.	Area in Statute Acres in 1881.	Rateable Value in 1881.	Post Town.	Petty Sessional Division.
ABINGDON UNION.					
(Formed 1 Jan. 1835 by Order dated 6 Dec. 1834.--Places marked thus * added 6 Oct. 1835 by Orders dated 12 Sept. 1835, as amended by Order dated 25 April 1836, and thus † added 29 Sept. 1858 by Order dated 19 July 1858).					
COUNTY of BERKS:		£			
*Appleford - - *cha.*	346	862	2,917	Abingdon - -	Abingdon.
*Appleton and Eaton - *par.*	573	2,077	3,116	do. - -	do.
†Bagley Wood - *par.*	14	639	203	do. - -	do.
Besselsleigh - *par.*	105	906	1,124	do. - -	do.
†Chandlings Farm - *par.*	3	76	85	do. - -	do.
Cumnor - - *par.*	1,011	5,962	6,756	Oxford - -	do.
*Draycot Moor - - *tow.*	225	1,054	1,685	Abingdon - -	do.
Drayton - - *par.*	622	1,851	3,561	do. - -	do.
*Frilford - - *tow.*	178	1,240	1,747	do. - -	do.
*Fyfield - - *par.*	337	1,603	2,401	do. - -	do.
*Garford - - *cha.*	164	1,055	1,975	do. - -	do.
*Kingston Bagpuze - *par.*	250	1,109	1,792	do. - -	do.
*Lyford - - *cha.*	133	775	1,290	Wantage - -	do.
Marcham - - *par.*	786	2,122	4,250	Abingdon - -	do.
*Milton - - *par.*	410	1,466	4,465	do. - -	do.
North Hinksey (*a*) - *par.*	527	876	2,217	Oxford - -	do.
Radleigh (*a*) - - *par.*	531	2,990	8,276	Abingdon - -	do.
Saint Helen, Abingdon (W.) (*a*) - } *par.*	6,410	3,275	21,290	do. - -	do. and Abingdon Borough.
Saint Nicholas, Abingdon - } *par.*	609	211	3,209	do. - -	do. do.
Seacourt - - *par.*	20	813	1,072	Oxford - -	Abingdon.
South Hinksey (*a*) - *par.*	956	651	3,954	do. - -	do.
*Steventon - - *par.*	924	2,401	7,039	Abingdon - -	do.
Sunningwell (*a*) - *par.*	327	1,454	3,264	do. - -	do.
*Sutton Courtney (*b*) *par.*	903	2,292	5,578	do. - -	do.
Sutton Wick - *ham.*	351	1,302	3,445	do. - -	do.
*Tubney - - *par.*	165	1,156	1,036	do. - -	do.
Wootton (*a*) - - *par.*	369	1,564	1,977	do. - -	do.
Wytham - - *par.*	198	1,165	1,488	Oxford - -	do.
COUNTIES of BERKS and OXFORD:					
*Culham - - *par.*	544	2,063	4,997	Abingdon - -	Bullingdon and Abingdon.
COUNTY of OXFORD.					
*Baldon Marsh - *par.*	300	829	1,380	Oxford - -	do.
*Baldon Toot - *par.*	217	1,565	2,093	do. - -	do.
*Binsey - - *par.*	63	387	959	do. - -	Oxford City.
*Burcott - - *ham.*	199	679	1,353	do. - -	Bullingdon.
*Chislehampton - *par.*	103	939	1,405	Wallingford - -	do.
*Clifton - - *par.*	347	1,245	1,896	Abingdon - -	do.
*Drayton - - *par.*	287	1,288	2,201	Oxford - -	do.
*Nuneham Courtney - *par.*	261	2,108	3,001	do. - -	do.
*Sandford - - *par.*	318	1,005	1,881	do. - -	do.
*Stadhampton - *par.*	268	623	1,353	Wallingford - -	do.
TOTAL of UNION - -	20,354	55,978	123,761		

ABINGDON UNION:

(*a*) By Orders which came into operation on 25 March 1885,—
Detached parts of North Hinksey and South Hinksey were amalgamated with Saint Aldate, in the City of Oxford;
Detached parts of Iffley and Hockmoor, in the Headington Union, were amalgamated with South Hinksey;
Detached parts of Radleigh, Sunningwell, and Wootton

ABINGDON UNION—*continued.*

respectively were amalgamated with South Hinksey;
and
Detached parts of Sunningwell, and Saint Helen, Abingdon, were amalgamated with Radleigh.
(*b*) By Order which came into operation on 25 March 1887,—
Detached parts of Sutton Courtney were amalgamated with East Hendred in the Wantage Union.

Unions and Parishes, &c.	Population in 1881.	Area in Statute Acres in 1881.	Rateable Value in 1881.	Post Town.	Petty Sessional Division.
ALCESTER UNION.					
(Formed 31 May 1836 by Order dated 7 May 1836.)					
COUNTY of WARWICK.			£		
Alcester - - *par.*	2,430	1,530	7,520	Redditch - -	Alcester.
Arrow - - *par.*	349	4,220	4,048	do. - -	do.
Aston Cantlow - *par.*	1,099	4,300	5,975	Birmingham -	Stratford on Avon.
Bidford - - *per.*	1,572	3,240	7,991	Stratford on Avon -	Alcester.
Coughton - - *tow.*	236	1,186	2,449	Redditch - -	do.
Exhall - - *par.*	234	780	1,230	do. - -	do.
Great Alne - - *par.*	435	1,753	3,359	do. - -	do.
Haseler - - *par.*	342	1,950	3,509	do. - -	do.
Ipsley - - *par.*	2,003	2,514	7,533	do. - -	do.
Kinwarton - - *par.*	58	480	848	do. - -	do.
Moreton Baggott - *par.*	86	1,160	1,467	do. - -	do.
Oversley (W.) - *ham.*	341	In Arrow	2,587	do. - -	do.
Salford - - *par.*	823	4,730	8,696	Evesham - -	do.
Sambourne - - *ham.*	531	1,884	3,081	Redditch - -	do.
Spernhall - - *par.*	88	1,090	1,235	do. - -	do.
Studley - - *par.*	2,477	4,262	10,340	do. - -	do.
Weethley - - *par.*	40	638	603	do. - -	do.
Wixford - - *par.*	107	530	1,155	do. - -	do.
COUNTY of WORCESTER.					
Abbots Moreton - *par.*	212	1,420	1,791	Redditch - -	Pershore.
Feckenham - - *par.*	4,352	6,787	15,542	do. - -	Redditch.
Inkberrow, or Ink-borough - *par.*	1,541	6,791	10,280	do. -	do.
Oldberrow - - *par*	74	1,185	1,531	Birmingham -	do.
TOTAL of UNION -	19,430	52,430	102,770		
ALDERBURY UNION.					
(Formed 12 Oct. 1835 by Order dated 28 Sept. 1835. —Places marked thus • added 25 Dec. 1858 by Order dated 12 Oct. 1858 ; and thus † added 16 April 1869 by Order dated 2 April 1869. Place marked thus ‡ added 25 Dec. 1869 by Order dated 30 Nov. 1869 ; and thus § added 30 Sept. 1883 by Order dated 22nd May 1883.)					
COUNTY of WILTS :					
Alderbury - - *par.*	667	2,265	2,968	Salisbury - -	Salisbury and Amesbury.
Britford (W.) (*b*) - *par.*	978	3,201	6,814	do. - -	do.
Clarendon Park (*b*) - *lib.*	217	4,313	4,265	do. - -	do.
Coombe Bisset (*b*) - *par.*	362	2,212	2,360	do. - -	do.
Downton (*b*) - - *par.*	3,378	12,495	15,511	do. - -	do.
• Earldoms - - *par.*	37	788	427	do. - -	do.
East Grimstead - *cha.*	120	951	1,432	do. - -	do.
Fisherton Anger - *par.*	4,783	348	17,193	do. - -	Salisbury and Amesbury and Borough of Salisbury.

(continued)

ALDERBURY UNION :

(*a*) Certain detached parts of West Dean were amalgamated with Winterslow by Order which came into operation on 25 March 1885.
(*b*) By Orders which came into operation on 25 March 1885,—
A detached part of Britford was amalgamated with Downton ;
Detached parts of Stratford Toney were amalgamated with Britford, Homington, and Coombe Bisset respectively :

ALDERBURY UNION—*continued.*

A detached part of Laverstoke and Ford was amalgamated with Clarendon Park ;

Detached parts of certain parishes in the Amesbury Union were amalgamated with Laverstoke and Ford, and Milford ;

A detached part of White Parish was amalgamated with Plaitford, in the Romsey Union.

Unions and Parishes, &c.		Population in 1881.	Area in Statute Acres in 1881.	Rateable Value in 1881.	Post Town.			Petty Sessional Division.
				£				

ALDERBURY UNION—County of Wilts—*continued.*

Homington (*b*)	*par.*	179	1,047	1,208	Salisbury	-	-	SalisburyandAme-bury.
Landford -	*par.*	263	1,720	1,594	do.	-	-	do.
' Langley Wood	*par.*	16	271	123	do.	-	-	do.
Laverstoke and Ford } (*b*) - - - }	*par.*	449	1,733	4,260	do.	-	-	do.
Milford (*b*) -	*par.*	2,106	1,363	9,941	do.	-	-	SalisburyandAmesbury and Borough of Salisbury.
‡No Man's Land	*par.*	134	14	125	do.	-	-	SalisburyandAmesbury.
Nunton and Bodenham	*par.*	296	1,214	1,515	do.	-	-	d(
Odstock	*par.*	148	1.295	1,170	do.	-	-	do
*Old Sarum -	*par.*	21	75	102	do.	-	-	do.
Pitton and Farley -	*cha.*	546	2,221	2,639	do.	-	-	do.
†Saint Edmund -	*par.*	4,160	61	11,019	do.	-	-	Borough of Salisbury.
†Saint Martin	*par.*	2,689	41	5,312	do.	-	-	do.
†Saint Thomas -	*par.*	2,035	378	11,982	do.	-	-	do.
Standlinch -	*par.*	94	713	885	do.	-	-	SalisburyandAmesbury.
Stratford Toney (*b*) -	*par.*	106	1,605	1,371	do.	-	-	do.
Stratford under the } Castle - - }	*par.*	318	1,501	3,063	do.	-	-	do.
Salisbury, the Close of } the Canons of the } Cathedral Church } of - - }	*lib.*	630	InSt.Thom.	3,941	do.	-	-	Borough of Salisbury.
§West Dean (*a*)	*par.*	313	3,540	3,809				
West Grimstead -	*par.*	238	1,509	1,656	do.	-	-	SalisburyandAmesbury.
West Harnham -	*par.*	288	1,179	2,309	do.	-	-	do.
White Parish (*b*) -	*par.*	1,100	6,127	6,809	do.	-	-	do.
Winterslow (*a*) -	*par.*	867	4,937	4,670	do.	-	-	do.
TOTAL of UNION		27,538	59,417	130,506				

ALNWICK UNION.

(Formed 15 Nov. 1836 by Order dated 20 Oct. 1836.)

COUNTY OF NORTHUMBERLAND.

Abberwick -	*tow.*	109	1,680	1,441	Alnwick	-	-	North Division of Coquetdale.
Acklington -	*tow.*	230	2,122	4,910	Acklington -	-	-	East Division do.
Acklington Park -	*tow.*	142	795	781	do. -	-	-	do. do.
Acton and Old Felton	*tow.*	106	1,401	1,596	Felton, R.S.O.	-	-	do. do.
Alnmouth -	*tow.*	535	296	2,325	do. -	-	-	do. do.
Alnwick (W.)	*par.*	7,410	16,749	34,985	do. -	-	-	do. do.
Amble -	*tow.*	2,016	1,218	5,634	Acklington -	-	-	do. do.
Bassington -	*tow.*	7	237	301	Alnwick -	-	-	do. do.
Beanly -	*tow.*	115	2,323	1,315	Eglingham -	-	-	North Division do.
Birling -	*tow.*	83	849	1,297	Acklington -	-	-	East Division do.
Bolton -	*tow.*	139	2,060	2,187	Alnwick -	-	-	North Division do.
Boulmer and Seaton } House - - }	*tow.*	222	395	766	Lesbury	-	-	East Division do.
Broompark -	*tow.*	58	471	641	Alnwick -	-	-	NorthDivision do.
Brotherwick -	*tow.*	20	186	1,085	Acklington -	-	-	East Division do.
Broxfield -	*tow.*	22	319	349	Alnwick -	-	-	do. do.
Brunton -	*tow.*	42	972	2,129	Chathill	-	-	do. do.
Buston High -	*tow.*	102	721	1,735	Lesbury -	-	-	do. do.
Buston Low -	*tow.*	95	899	2,865	do. -	-	-	do. do.
Craster -	*tow.*	221	648	1,157	do. -	-	-	do. do.
Crawley -	*tow.*	30	323	323	Alnwick -	-	-	North Division do.
Ditchburne, East and } West - - }	*tow.*	59	1,664	1,185	do. -	-	-	{ Bamburgh South Di- vision.
Doxford -	*tow.*	100	609	947	Chathill -	-	-	East Division of Coquetdale.
Dunstan -	*tow.*	277	1,731	1,863	Lesbury	-	-	do. do.

(*continued*)

Unions and Parishes, &c.			Population in 1881.	Area in Statute Acres in 1881.	Rateable Value in 1881.	Post Town.	Petty Sessional Division.

ALNWICK UNION—County of Northumberland—*continued.*

					£		
Edlingham	-	tow.	100	5,818	2,491	Alnwick - -	North Division of Coquetdale.
Eglingham	-	tow.	299	2,009	2,200	do. - -	do. do.
Elyhaugh	-	tow.	12	282	207	Felton - -	East Division do.
Embleton	-	tow.	643	2,077	5,796	Chathill - -	do. do.
Falloden	-	tow.	81	1,061	958	do. - -	do. do.
Felton	-	tow.	679	1,552	3,040	Felton - -	do. do.
Glanton	-	tow.	498	1,392	2,963	Glanton -	North Division do.
Gloster Hill	-	tow.	14	212	335	Acklington -	East Division do.
Greens and Glantlees	tow.		28	993	554	Felton - -	do. do.
Guizance	-	tow.	181	1,403	2,468	do. - -	do. do.
Harehope	-	tow.	50	520	472	Alnwick -	North Division do.
Hauxley	-	tow.	972	754	2,104	Acklington -	East Division do.
Hazon and Hartlaw	-	tow.	65	1,446	1,633	Felton - -	do. do.
Hedgley	-	tow.	86	709	632	Alnwick -	North Division do.
Howick	-	par.	311	1,638	2,679	Lesbury -	East Division do.
Learchild	-	tow.	30	474	410	Alnwick -	North Division do.
Lemmington	-	tow.	103	2,012	1,760	do. -	do. do.
Lesbury	-	tow.	960	4,042	9,438	Lesbury -	East Division do.
Littlehoughton	-	tow.	123	823	2,909	do. -	do. do.
Longhoughton	-	tow.	442	2,789	5,993	do. -	do. do.
Morwick	-	tow.	92	765	1,699	Acklington -	do. do.
Newton by the Sea	-	tow.	250	1,211	2,130	Chathill -	do. do.
Newton on the Moor	-	tow.	233	910	1,268	Acklington -	do. do.
North Charlton	-	tow.	159	2,808	2,361	Chathill -	do. do.
Rennington	-	tow.	294	1,773	2,495	Alnwick -	do. do.
Rock	-	tow.	240	2,053	2,775	do. -	do. do.
Shawdon	-	tow.	102	1,233	1,413	do. -	North Division do.
Shilbottle	-	tow.	428	3,000	3,189	do. -	East Division do.
Shipley	-	tow.	92	2,037	1,221	do. -	do. do.
South Charlton	-	tow.	127	1,885	1,767	Chathill -	do. do.
Stamford	-	tow.	138	1,662	3,946	Alnwick -	do. do.
Sturton Grange	-	tow.	116	1,114	2,143	Lesbury -	do. do.
Swarland	-	tow.	140	1,975	1,352	Felton -	do. do.
Titlington	-	tow.	82	2,267	1,003	Alnwick -	North Division do.
Togstone	-	tow.	232	1,079	2,460	Acklington -	East Division do.
Walkmill	-	tow.	5	128	378	do. -	do. do.
Warkworth	-	tow.	662	1,129	4,347	do. -	do. do.
Whittle	-	tow.	19	549	504	Felton -	do. do.
Woodhouse	-	tow.	21	567	456	Alnwick -	do. do.
TOTAL of UNION	-		21,318	98,879	157,829		

ALRESFORD UNION.

(Formed 31 Mar. 1835 by Order dated 9 Mar. 1835.—Places marked thus * added 11 Aug. 1835 by Order dated 23 July 1835. Place marked thus † added 25 Dec. 1858 by Order dated 18 Oct. 1858.)

COUNTY of SOUTHAMPTON :

Beaworth	-	par.	124	1,252	1,205	Alresford - -	Alresford.
*Bighton	-	par.	229	2,094	2,172	do. - -	do.
Bishops Sutton	-	par.	463	3,746	3,966	do. - -	do.
Bramdean	-	par.	262	1,237	1,686	do. - -	do.
Brown Candover	-	par.	266	2,110	2,100	do. - -	do.
*Cheriton	-	par.	613	3,064	3,063	do. - -	do.
Chilton Candover	-	par.	147	1,451	1,158	do. - -	do.
†Godsfield	-	par.	15	509	351	do. - -	do.
Hinton-Ampner	-	par.	383	2,379	2,620	do. - -	do.

(continued)

Unions and Parishes, &c.	Population in 1881.	Area in Statute Acres in 1881.	Rateable Value in 1881.	Post Town.	Petty Sessional Division

ALRESFORD UNION—County of Southampton—*continued.*

£

*Itchen Stoke - - *par.*	314	3,035	2,877	Alresford - -	Alresford.
Kilmeston - - *par.*	177	1,926	2,062	do. - -	do.
New Alresford (W.) *par.*	1,550	693	5,232	do. - -	do.
Northington - - *par.*	318	3,114	2,496	do. - -	do.
Old Alresford - *par.*	477	3,671	4,684	do. - -	do.
Ovington - - *par.*	116	1,309	1,204	do. - -	do.
Ropley - - *par.*	875	4,684	5,085	do. - -	do.
Swarraton - *par.*	129	755	662	do. - -	do.
*Tichborne - - *par.*	334	3,261	2,934	do. - -	do.
West Tisted - *par.*	175	2,356	1,970	do. - -	do.
TOTAL of UNION -	**6,967**	**42,637**	**47,527**		

ALSTON WITH GARRIGILL PARISH.

(Board of Guardians constituted 4 Mar. 1837 by Order dated 7 Feb. 1837.)

COUNTY of CUMBERLAND:

Alston with Garri-}*par.* gill (W.) - -	4,621	36,968	14,131	Alston - -	Leath Ward.

ALTON UNION.

(Formed 2 April 1835 by Order dated 9 Mar. 1835.—Place marked thus * added 26 May 1835 by Order dated 11 May 1835; thus † added 25 Dec. 1858 by Order dated 15 Oct. 1858; and Places marked thus‡ added 4 May 1869 by Order dated 21 April 1869.)

COUNTY of SOUTHAMPTON:

Alton (W.) - - *par.*	4,497	3,925	16,503	Alton - -	Alton.
*Bentley - - *par.*	704	2,299	4,192	Farnham - -	do.
Bentworth - - *par.*	558	3,763	3,765	Alton - -	do.
Binsted - - *par.*	1,466	6,920	8,113	do. - -	do.
Chawton - - *par.*	473	2,674	2,474	do. - -	do.
†Coldrey - - *par.*	22	194	356	Farnham - -	do.
East Tisted - *par.*	188	2,648	2,274	Alton - -	do.
East Worldham - *par.*	265	1,736	1,987	do. - -	do.
Faringdon - *par.*	585	2,357	2,720	do. - -	do.
Froyle - - *par.*	764	3,665	4,745	do. - -	do.
Hartley-Mandit - *par.*	99	1,404	1,037	do. - -	do.
‡Headley - - *par.*	1,628	6,923	5,653	Petersfield - -	do.
Holybourne - *par.*	591	1,405	2,561	Alton - -	do.
‡Kingsley - - *par.*	458	1,801	2,033	do. - -	do.
Lasham - - *par.*	201	1,797	1,438	do. - -	do.
Medsted - - *par.*	503	2,848	2,722	Alresford - -	do.
Neatham - - *ty.*	90	1,117	1,266	Alton - -	do.
Newton-Valence - *par.*	362	2,258	2,134	do. - -	do.
Selborne - - *par.*	1,215	7,016	5,522	do. - -	do.
Shalden - - *par.*	204	1,534	1,363	do. - -	do.
West Worldham - *par.*	79	471	636	do. - -	do.
Wield - - *par.*	246	2,104	1,578	Alresford - -	do.
TOTAL of UNION -	**15,198**	**61,759**	**75,672**		

Unions and Parishes, &c.	Population in 1881.	Area in Statute Acres in 1881.	Rateable Value in 1881.	Post Town.	Petty Sessional Division.

ALTRINCHAM UNION.

(Formed 25 Aug. 1836 by Order dated 2 Aug. 1836.)

County of Chester

			£		
Agden - - *tow.*	101	607	1,618	Altrincham -	Altrincham.
Altrincham - - *tow.*	11,250	662	56,476	do. -	do.
Ashley - - *tow.*	385	2,263	4,590	do. -	do.
Ashton upon Mersey *tow.*	3,326	1,622	22,781	Manchester -	do.
Aston by Budworth - *tow.*	449	2,957	5,118	Northwich -	Bucklow East.
Baguley - - *tow.*	736	1,806	7,061	Altrincham -	Altrincham.
Bexton - - *tow.*	94	635	1,514	Knutsford -	Bucklow East.
Bollen-Fee - - *tow.*	2,856	2,682	17,864	Wilmslow -	Prestbury.
Bollington - - *tow.*	272	617	1,774	Altrincham -	Altrincham.
Bowdon - - *tow.*	2,559	850	26,552	do. -	do.
Carrington - - *tow.*	438	2,337	4,019	Sale -	do.
Dunham-Massey - *tow.*	1,977	3,712	25,836	Altrincham -	do.
Etchells - - *tow.*	756	2,322	6,808	Manchester -	Stockport.
Fulshaw - - *tow.*	1,187	449	8,630	Wilmslow -	Prestbury.
Hale - - *tow.*	2,222	3,724	15,001	Altrincham -	Altrincham.
High Leigh - - *tow.*	850	4,522	9,405	Knutsford -	Bucklow East.
Lymm - - *par.*	4,665	4,375	26,214	Warrington -	Altrincham.
Martall with Little Warford - - *tow.*	268	1,799	2,930	Knutsford -	Bucklow East.
Mere - - *tow.*	512	2,519	5,530	do. -	do.
Millington - - *tow.*	266	747	1,816	Altrincham -	Altrincham.
Mobberley - - *par.*	1,462	5,206	10,444	Knutsford -	Bucklow East.
Nether Knutsford (W.) - - *tow.*	3,895	793	13,954	do. -	do.
Northen - - *tow.*	1,172	1,437	8,062	Manchester -	Stockport.
Ollerton - - *tow.*	287	1,224	2,374	Knutsford -	Bucklow East.
Over Knutsford - *tow.*	410	967	4,650	do. -	do.
Partington - - *tow.*	438	808	3,445	Sale -	Altrincham.
Peover Inferior - *tow.*	112	300	832	Knutsford -	Bucklow East.
Peover Superior - *tow.*	609	2,974	6,944	do. -	do.
Pickmere - - *tow.*	241	1,061	2,028	do. -	do.
Plumley - - *tow.*	366	1,695	3,238	do. -	do.
Pownal-Fee - - *tow.*	2,882	3,595	15,355	Wilmslow -	Prestbury.
Rosthern - - *tow.*	382	1,524	2,909	Knutsford -	Bucklow East.
Sale - - *tow.*	7,915	2,006	53,270	Manchester -	Altrincham.
Tabley Inferior - *tow.*	119	1,206	2,249	Knutsford -	Bucklow East.
Tabley Superior - *tow.*	452	2,671	5,637	do. -	do.
Tatton - - *tow.*	145	1,890	3,348	do. -	do.
Timperley - - *tow.*	2,211	1,638	16,947	Altrincham -	Altrincham.
Toft - - *tow.*	173	1,312	2,484	Knutsford -	Bucklow East.
Warburton - - *par.*	426	1,872	4,388	Lymm -	Altrincham.
Total of Union -	58,899	75,116	414,155		

ALVERSTOKE PARISH.

(Board of Guardians constituted 22 Oct. 1868 by Order dated 16 Sept. 1868.)

County of Southampton :

			£		
Alverstoke (W.) (a) - *par.*	21,581	3,865	62,526	Gosport - -	Fareham.

AMERSHAM UNION.

(Formed 25 March 1835 by Order dated 27 Feb. 1835.—Places marked thus* added 29 March 1838 by Order dated 24 Feb. 1838.)

County of Buckingham :

			£		
Amersham (W.) - *par.*	2,500	6,119	10,377	Amersham -	Burnham, Hundred of.
Beaconsfield - - *par.*	1,635	4,504	7,255	Maidenhead -	do.

(continued)

ALVERSTOKE PARISH :

(a) A detached part of Alverstoke was amalgamated with Rowner, in the Fareham Union, by Order which came into operation on 25 March 1886.

Unions and Parishes, &c.		Population in 1861.	Area in Statute Acres in 1881.	Rateable Value in 1861.	Post Town.	Petty Sessional Division.
AMERSHAM UNION—County of Buckingham—*continued.*				£		
Chalfont Saint Giles -	*par.*	1,261	3,726	5,110	Slough - -	Burnham, Hundred of.
Chalfont Saint Peter's	*par.*	1,456	4,758	7,385	do. - -	do.
Chenies - -	*par.*	388	1,759	2,259	Rickmansworth -	do.
Chesham - -	*par.*	6,502	12,746	22,509	Chesham - -	do.
Chesham-Bois -	*par.*	351	910	1,509	do. - -	do.
Coleshill - -	*ham.*	501	1,850	2,173	Amersham - -	do.
*Great Missenden -	*par.*	2,170	5,819	8,553	Great Missenden -	Borough and Hundred of Aylesbury.
*Lee - - -	*par.*	122	502	673	do. - -	do.
Penn - -	*par.*	1,100	3,992	4,585	Amersham - -	Burnham, Hundred of.
Seer Green - -	*cha.*	330	889	1,005	Beaconsfield -	do.
TOTAL of UNION -		18,319	47,574	73,393		

AMESBURY UNION.

(Formed 9 Oct. 1835 by Order dated 21 Sept. 1835.)

COUNTY of WILTS :

Allington - -	*par.*	84	957	1,177	Salisbury - -	Salisbury and Amesbury.
Amesbury (W.) -	*par.*	1,127	5,936	6,375	Amesbury - -	do.
Boscombe - -	*par.*	115	1,688	1,668	Salisbury - -	do.
Bulford - -	*par.*	346	3,612	2,348	Amesbury - -	do.
Cholderton - -	*par.*	164	1,695	1,300	Salisbury - -	do.
Durnford (*a*) -	*par.*	449	3,758	4,028	do. - -	do.
Durrington (*a*) -	*par.*	392	2,712	2,464	do. - -	do.
Figheldean (*a*) -	*par.*	464	5,429	4,730	Amesbury - -	Pewsey and Everleigh.
Idmiston (*a*) -	*par.*	583	5,616	5,174	Salisbury - -	Salisbury and Amesbury.
Maddington (*a*) -	*par.*	402	5,973	3,624	Devizes - -	do.
Milston - -	*par.*	155	2,265	1486	Amesbury - -	Pewsey and Everleigh.
Newton Toney -	*par.*	333	2,386	2,917	Salisbury - -	Salisbury & Amesbury.
Orcheston Saint George (*a*)	*par.*	193	2,363	2,105	Devizes - -	do.
Orcheston Saint Mary (*a*) - - -	*par.*	163	1,737	1,435	do. - -	do.
Rolleston (*a*) -	*par.*	32	865	645	do. - -	do.
Shrewton (*a*) -	*par.*	677	2,225	2,652	do. - -	do.
Tilshead - -	*par.*	473	3,990	3,072	do. - -	Devizes.
Wilsford cum Lake (*a*) - - -	*par.*	161	1,637	1,361	Salisbury -	Salisbury & Amesbury.
Winterborne Dantsey (*a*) - - -	*par.*	158	1,190	1,261	do. - -	do.
Winterborne Earls (*a*) - - -	*par.*	241	1,720	2,104	do. - -	do.
Winterborne Gunner (*a*) - - -	*par.*	171	1,530	1,496	do. - -	do.
Winterborne Stoke (*a*) - - -	*par.*	299	3,540	2,427	do. - -	do.
Woodford - -	*par.*	441	2,796	3,160	do. - -	do.
TOTAL of UNION -		7,623	63,650	59,012		

AMESBURY UNION.

(a) By Orders which came into operation on 25 March 1885,—

A detached part of Durnford was amalgamated with Wilsford cum Lake ;

A detached part of Durrington was amalgamated with Figheldean ;

Detached parts of Maddington were amalgamated with Winterborne Stoke :

A detached part of Orcheston Saint George, known as West Down, was amalgamated with Orcheston Saint

AMESBURY UNION—*continued.*

Mary, and a detached part of Orcheston Saint Mary was amalgamated with Orcheston Saint George ;

Detached parts of Shrewton were amalgamated with Rolleston and Winterborne Stoke respectively ;

Detached parts of Idmiston and Winterborne Dantsey were amalgamated with Laverstoke and Ford in the Alderbury Union ;

Detached parts of Winterborne Earls and Winterborne Gunner were amalgamated with Milford, in the Alderbury Union.

B

Unions and Parishes, &c.	Population in 1881.	Area in Statute Acres in 1881.	Rateable Value in 1881.	Post Town.	Petty Sessional Division.

AMPTHILL UNION.

(Formed 10 April 1835 by Order dated 17 March 1835.—Name of place marked thus * as altered by Order dated 13 July 1887.)

COUNTY of BEDFORD:

			£		
Ampthill (W.) - par.	2,257	1,928	9,694	Ampthill - -	Ampthill.
Clophill - par.	1,107	2,140	3,807	do. - -	do.
Cranfield - par.	1,447	3,500	5,826	Newport Pagnell -	do.
Flitton - par.	690	1,025	2,568	Ampthill - -	do.
Flitwick - par.	817	1,700	6,377	do. - -	do.
Hawnes - - par.	934	2,561	3,688	Bedford - -	do.
Higham-Gobion - par.	121	1,287	2,200	Ampthill - -	do.
Houghton-Conquest - par.	620	3,345	6,353	do. - -	do.
Lidlington - par.	657	2,520	4,454	do. - -	do.
Lower Gravenhurst - par.	79	1,240	1,204	do. - -	do.
Marston-Moretaine - par.	1,179	4,171	7,557	do. - -	do.
Maulden - par.	1,311	2,574	3,989	do. - -	do.
Milbrook - par.	276	1,450	4,597	do. - -	do.
Pulloxhill - par.	529	1,760	2,605	do. - -	do.
*Shillington - par.	2,226	5,030	8,557	Hitchin - -	do.
Silsoe - ham.	679	2,160	3,773	Ampthill - -	do.
Steppingley - par.	313	1,060	1,970	do. - -	do.
Upper Gravenhurst - par.	354	385	2,007	do. - -	do.
Westoning - par.	657	1,715	5,513	Woburn - -	do.
TOTAL of UNION -	16,253	41,551	86,739		

ANDOVER UNION.

(Formed 9 July 1835 by Order dated 23 June 1835.—Place marked thus * added 11 Aug. 1835 by Order dated 28 July 1835.)

COUNTY of SOUTHAMPTON:

Abbots Ann - par.	675	3,396	4,611	Andover - -	Andover.
Amport - par.	677	3,963	4,985	do. - -	do.
Andover (W.) - par.	5,653	8,662	23,860	do. - -	Borough of Andover.
Appleshaw - par.	265	713	1,476	do. - -	Andover.
Barton Stacey - par.	553	5,026	5,688	Stockbridge -	do.
Bullington - par.	157	1,635	1,700	Micheldever -	do.
*Chilbolton - par.	343	3,134	3,116	Stockbridge -	do.
Enham Knights - par.	163	791	1,332	Andover - -	do.
Faccombe - par.	221	2,668	1,778	Hungerford -	Kingsclere.
Foxcott - par.	54	953	1,120	Andover - -	Andover.
Fyfield - par.	186	978	1,241	do. - -	do.
Goodworth Clatford - par.	502	2,822	3,071	do. - -	do.
Grately - par.	256	1,551	2,198	do. - -	do.
Hurstborne Tarrant - par.	837	5,149	4,771	do. - -	do.
Kimpton - par.	278	2,794	2,456	do. - -	do.
Linkenholt - par.	72	1,073	641	Hungerford -	do.
Longparish - par.	675	5,317	5,376	Whitchurch (Hants)	do.
Monxton - par.	269	1,156	2,013	Andover - -	do.
Penton Grafton - par.	463	1,902	3,753	do. - -	do.
Penton Mewsey - par.	286	1,059	1,725	do. - -	do.
Quarley - par.	173	1,691	1,289	do. - -	do.
Shipton - par.	288	2,560	2,011	Marlborough -	do.
South Tidworth - par.	236	2,302	1,811	Andover - -	do.
Tangley - par.	219	1,570	1,588	Andover - -	do.
Thruxton - par.	321	1,877	2,016	do. - -	do.
Up Clatford - par.	739	2,209	3,820	do. - -	do.
Vernham Dean - par.	598	3,614	3,605	Hungerford -	do.
Wherwell - par.	541	3,645	4,971	Andover -	do.
TOTAL of UNION -	15,700	74,213	98,034		

Unions and Parishes, &c.	Population in 1881.	Area in Statute Acres in 1881.	Rateable Value in 1881.	Post Town.	Petty Sessional Division.

ANGLESEY UNION.

(Formed 1 June 1837 by Order dated 6 May 1837.—Places marked thus * added 21 July 1858 by Order dated 25 June 1858.)

COUNTY OF ANGLESEY:

			£		
Amlwch (W.) - par.	4,847	9,221	12,639	Amlwch - -	Second Division.
*Bodewryd - - par.	29	526	448	do. - -	do.
Coedana - - par.	214	1,627	1,325	Llanerchymedd, R.S.O.	do.
*Gwredog - - par.	38	936	813	do. - -	do.
Llanallgo - - par.	398	659	679	Moelfre - -	First Division.
Llanbabo - - par.	111	1,743	1,404	Garreglefn Rhosybol.	Second Division.
Llanbadrig - par.	1,061	4,097	3,896	Cemaes Amlwch -	do.
Llanbedr-Goch - par.	300	3,193	1,163	Pentraeth	First Division.
Llanddyfnan - par.	640	3,506	2,385	Llangefni - -	do.
Llandyfrydog - par.	528	3,819	3,091	Llanerchymedd, R.S.O	Second Division.
Llaneilian - - par.	948	2,398	2,143	Amlwch -	do.
Llanerchymedd - par.	63	15	99	Llanerchymedd. R.S.O	do.
Llanengrad - - par.	302	2,695	1,331	Tynygongl -	First Division.
Llanfair - Mathafarn- Eithaf } par.	680	1,949	1,388	do. - -	do.
Llanfairynghornwy - par.	278	2,135	1,525	Valley, R.S.O. -	Second Division.
Llanfechell - - par.	923	3,637	3,260	Rhosybol - -	do.
Llanflewyn - par.	79	1,265	1,031	Garreglefn Rhosybol.	do
Llanfihangel - trer - Beirdd } par.	322	1,570	1,472	Llangefni -	First Division.
Llangefni - - par.	1,563	2,426	4,596	do. - -	do.
Llangwyllog - par.	190	2,301	2,417	do. - -	do.
Llanrhwydrus - par.	116	1,143	1,037	Valley, R.S.O. -	Second Division.
Llanwenllwyfo - par.	403	1,756	1,664	Amlwch - -	do.
Llecheynfarwydd - par.	352	1,964	2,026	Llanerchymedd, R.S.O.	do.
Penrhos Lligwy - par.	385	2,894	1,774	Amlwch - -	First Division.
Rhod-y-geidio - par.	262	1,003	1,125	Llanerchymedd, R.S.O.	Second Division.
*Rhosbeirio - - par.	39	369	351	Rhosybol - -	do.
Tregayan - - par.	111	2,066	1,423	Llangefni -	First Division.
TOTAL of UNION -	15,182	60,913	56,505		

ASHBOURNE UNION.

(Formed 4 Jan. 1845, by Order of that date.—Places marked thus * added 2 Feb. 1869, by Order dated 13 Jan. 1869.)

COUNTY of DERBY:

Alkmonton (b) - tow.	95	739	1,188	Brailsford, Derby -	Sudbury.
Ashbourne - tow.	2,095	59	5,336	Ashbourne -	Ashbourne.

(continued)

ASHBOURNE UNION.

(a) By Orders which came into operation on 25 March 1886,—

A parish known as Masden Grange was amalgamated with Ilam ;

All the parts of a place known as Stydd were amalgamated with Yeaveley ;

All the parts of a place known as Calton in Blore, having in 1881, population 62, acreage 372, and rateable value 498l., and of a place known as Calton in Mayfield, having in 1881, population 64, acreage 376, and rateable value 526l., were united with certain detached parts of Croxden, in the Uttoxeter Union, and the parts so united were amalgamated with a place known as Calton in Waterfall, having in 1881, population 74, acreage 596, and rateable value 760l., the name of the last-mentioned place being altered to the Township of Calton ;

Detached parts of Mugginton and Turnditch, in the Belper Union, were amalgamated with Hulland Ward and Hulland respectively.

ASHBOURNE UNION—continued.

(b) By Provisional Order which came into operation on 25 March 1887,—

A detached part of Alkmonton, known as Paper Mills, was amalgamated with Longford ;

A detached part of Ellastone was amalgamated with Prestwood ;

A detached part of Hulland was amalgamated with Biggin ;

Certain parts of Mappleton were amalgamated with Mayfield and Okeover ;

Certain parts of Mayfield were amalgamated with Calwich, Clifton and Compton, Mappleton, and Snelston ;

A certain part of Offcote and Underwood was amalgamated with Clifton and Compton ;

Certain parts of Okeover were amalgamated with Mappleton and Thorpe ;

A detached part of Shirley was amalgamated with Hollington ;

Certain parts of Snelston were amalgamated with Calwich and Mayfield ; and

A detached part of Thorpe was amalgamated with Newton Grange.

Unions and Parishes, &c.		Population in 1881.	Area in Statute Acres in 1881.	Rateable Value in 1881.	Post Town.	Petty Sessional Division.
ASHBOURNE UNION—County of Derby—*continued*.				£		
Allow - - -	*tow.*	138	1,276	1,792	Ashbourne -	Ashbourne.
Ballidon - -	*tow.*	109	1,947	2,188	do. - -	do.
Bentley Fenny -	*par.*	248	1,038	1,824	do. - -	do.
Bentley Hungry -	*lib.*	82	1,086	1,806	Longford - -	Sudbury.
Biggin (b) - -	*tow.*	125	608	842	Ashbourne -	Wirksworth.
Bonsall - -	*par.*	1,354	2,447	3,368	Derby -	Matlock Bath.
Bradbourne - -	*tow.*	138	1,445	2,483	Wirksworth -	Ashbourne.
Bradley - -	*par.*	277	2,422	2,901	Ashbourne -	do.
Brailsford - -	*par.*	651	4,366	7,412	Derby -	Derby.
Brassington - -	*tow.*	690	4,221	5,017	Wirksworth -	Wirksworth.
Callow - -	*tow.*	93	1,259	1,527	do. -	do.
Carsington - -	*par.*	231	1,141	1,619	do. -	do.
Clifton and Compton (b)	*tow.*	1,016	1,051	4,276	Ashbourne -	Ashbourne.
Eaton and Alsop -	*tow.*	58	1,527	1,835	do. - -	do.
Edlaston and Wynston	*par.*	208	1,079	1,990	do. - -	do.
Hartington Nether Quarter - -	*tow.*	379	3,898	3,557	do. -	do.
Hartington Town Quarter - -	*tow.*	429	3,627	4,167	do. - - -	do.
Hognaston - -	*par.*	278	1,410	2,217	do. -	do.
Hollington (b) -	*tow.*	225	1,028	1,726	Brailsford -	do.
Hopton - -	*tow.*	123	1,450	1,407	Wirksworth -	Wirksworth.
Hulland (a) (b) -	*tow.*	202	955	1,278	Ashbourne -	Ashbourne.
Hulland Ward (a) -	*tow.*	382	1,559	1,723	do. -	do.
Hulland Ward Intacks - -	*tow.*	38	451	563	do. -	do.
Ible - -	*tow.*	50	424	542	Wirksworth -	Wirksworth.
Kirk Ireton -	*tow.*	485	1,528	2,243	do. -	do.
Kniveton - -	*par.*	272	2,077	3,106	Ashbourne -	Ashbourne.
Lea Hall - -	*tow.*	18	455	884	do. -	do.
Longford (b) -	*tow.*	408	2,983	5,438	Derby -	do.
Mappleton (b) -	*par.*	196	802	1,996	Ashbourne -	do.
Mercaston - -	*tow.*	86	1,157	2,009	Brailsford, Derby -	do.
Middleton by Wirksworth - -	*tow.*	929	991	1,739	Wirksworth -	Wirksworth.
Newton Grange (b) -	*tow.*	42	760	1,307	Ashbourne -	Ashbourne.
Offcote and Underwood (W.) (b) -	*lib.*	531	1,854	5,287	do. - -	do.
Osmaston - -	*par.*	234	1,267	2,276	do. - -	do.
Parwich - -	*par.*	470	3,264	4,207	do. - -	do.
Rodsley - -	*tow.*	136	820	1,400	do. - -	do.
Shirley (b) -	*tow.*	243	1,634	2,891	Wirksworth -	do.
Snelston (b) -	*par.*	319	2,197	3,768	Ashbourne -	do.
Sturston - -	*tow.*	750	962	3,027	do. - -	do.
Thorpe (b) -	*par.*	182	1,778	2,661	do. - -	do.
Tissington - -	*par.*	352	2,307	4,321	do. - -	do.
Yeaveley (a) -	*tow.*	226	1,394	2,411	do. - -	do.
Yeldersley - -	*tow.*	177	1,505	2,032	do. - -	do.
COUNTY OF STAFFORD :						
*Alstonefield -	*tow.*	471	2,938	4,419	Ashbourne -	Leek.
Blore with Swinscoe	*tow.*	217	1,886	2,572	do. -	do.
Calton (a) -	*tow.*	(a)	(a)	(a)	do. - -	do.
Calwich (b) -	*tow.*	125	763	1,502	do. - -	Uttoxeter.
Ellastone (b) -	*tow.*	280	795	1,832	do. - -	do.
Ilam (a) -	*par.*	229	3,571	4,648	do. - -	Leek.
Mayfield (b) -	*tow.*	1,215	1,859	6,239	do. - -	Uttoxeter.
Okeover (b) -	*par.*	81	874	1,480	Ashbourne -	do.
Prestwood (b) -	*tow.*	47	450	709	Denstone, Uttoxeter	do.
Ramshorn - -	*tow.*	101	1,509	1,596	Ashbourne - -	do.
Stanton - -	*tow.*	315	2,027	2,142	do. -	do.
Waterfal - -	*tow.*	415	1,625	2,391	Leek - -	Leek.
*Wetton - -	*par.*	327	2,129	3,212	Ashbourne - -	do.
Woodhouses -	*tow.*	19	253	366	do. - -	do.
Wootton - -	*tow.*	183	1,871	2,042	do. - -	Uttoxeter.
TOTAL OF UNION -		19,795 (a)	95,101 (a)	152,740 (a)		

ASHBOURNE UNION :
(a) (b) *See* notes, page 11.

Unions and Parishes, &c.	Population in 1881.	Area in Statute Acres in 1881.	Rateable Value in 1881.	Post Town.	Petty Sessional Division.

ASHBY DE LA ZOUCH UNION.

(Formed 28 June 1836 by Order dated 3 June 1836.— Places marked thus * added 30 Mar. 1837 by Order dated 2 Mar. 1837; thus † added 25 Dec. 1861 by Order dated 18 Oct. 1861; thus ‡ added 22 Mar. 1862 by Order dated 11 Mar. 1862; and thus § added 26 Mar. 1884 by Order dated 24 Mar. 1884.)

County of Derby:

Unions and Parishes, &c.	Population in 1881.	Area in Statute Acres in 1881.	Rateable Value in 1881. £	Post Town.	Petty Sessional Division.
Appleby - - par.	438	890	2,232	Atherstone -	Swadlincote.
Calke - - - par.	48	880	983	Derby - -	Repton.
Hartshorn - - par.	1,729	2,510	6,619	Burton on Trent	Swadlincote.
Measham (a) (b) - tow.	1,677	1,490	5,256	Atherstone -	do.
Oakthorp and Donisthorpe (a) (b) par.	370	715	4,435	Ashby de la Zouch	do.
Smisby - par.	289	1,220	2,098	Burton on Trent -	do.
*Stretton en le Fields (a) tow.	70	1,008	2,359	Ashby de la Zouch	do.
†The Boundary - par.	102	—	57	Burton on Trent -	do.
Ticknall (a) - - par.	935	2,590	4,545	Derby - -	Repton.
Willesley - - par.	57	910	1,154	Ashby de la Zouch	Swadlincote.

County of Leicester:

Unions and Parishes, &c.	Population in 1881.	Area in Statute Acres in 1881.	Rateable Value in 1881.	Post Town.	Petty Sessional Division.
Appleby - - par.	319	1,130	3,040	Atherstone -	Ashby de la Zouch.
Ashby de la Zouch (W.) (a) tow.	7,465	6,980	25,414	Ashby de la Zouch	do.
‡Bardon - - par.	74	1,710	1,233	Leicester -	do.
Blackfordby (a) - tow.	1,047	1,117	2,671	Burton on Trent -	do.
*Cole Orton (b) - par.	598	1,999	4,121	Ashby de la Zouch	do.
Heather - - par.	447	1,015	2,526	do. -	do.
Hugglescote and Donington - tow.	4,750	2,589	13,446	do. -	do.
Normanton - - tow.	162	1,920	2,067	do. -	do.
*Osgathorp - - par.	304	1,220	1,760	Loughborough -	do.
Packington (a) - par.	1,153	2,360	6,567	Ashby de la Zouch	do.
§Ravenstone with Snibstone (a) - par.	—	—	—	do. -	do.
Seals, Over and Nether (a) - tow.	1,338	4,890	11,172	do. -	do.

(continued)

ASHBY DE LA ZOUCH UNION.

(a) By Orders which came into operation on 25 March 1884,—

Detached parts of Seals, Over and Nether, were amalgamated with Blackfordby, and other detached parts were amalgamated with Oakthorp and Donisthorpe;

Detached parts of Measham were amalgamated with Oakthorp and Donisthorpe;

The part of Stretton en le Fields between the river Mease and Oakthorp and Donisthorpe was amalgamated with Oakthorp and Donisthorpe;

The part of Oakthorp and Donisthorpe which was in Leicestershire, contained a population of 1,124.

All the parts of Packington, which were in Derbyshire, were amalgamated with the parts of Packington, in Leicestershire;

A detached part of Ticknall was amalgamated with Stanton by Bridge, in the Shardlow Union; and

ASHBY DE LA ZOUCH UNION—continued.

A detached part of Ashby de la Zouch, known as "Alton Grange," a detached part of Packington, known as the hamlet of Snibstone, and the whole of a Parish known as Ravenstone, having in 1881, population 451, acreage 1,130, and rateable value 2,509l., were united to form one parish, which was designated the parish of Ravenstone with Snibstone.

(b) A detached part of Measham was united with a detached part of Newton Solney (in the Burton-upon-Trent Union), and the parts so united were amalgamated with Bradley, alias Bretby, in the Burton-upon-Trent Union, by Order which came into operation on 25 March 1885.

A detached part of Thringston was amalgamated with Cole Orton by Provisional Order which came into operation on 25 March 1885.

Unions and Parishes, &c.	Population in 1881.	Area in Statute Acres in 1881.	Rateable Value in 1881.	Post Town.	Petty Sessional Division.
			£		
ASHBY DE LA ZOUCH UNION—County of Leicester—continued.					
Snareston - - par.	318	1,325	2,630	Atherstone - -	Ashby de la Zouch.
Staunton Harrold - tow.	237 {	In Worthington	} 2,738	Ashby de la Zouch	do.
Swannington - - tow.	1,417 {	In Whitwick	} 5,557	Leicester - -	do.
Swepstone - - par.	526	2.287	4,476	Ashby de la Zouch	do.
*Thringston (b) - tow.	1,238 {	In Whitwick	} 2,786	Leicester - -	do.
Whitwick - - tow.	3,881	6,220	9,752	do. - -	do.
*Worthington - - tow.	970	3,400	3,546	Ashby de la Zouch	do.
TOTAL of UNION -	33,083 (a)	51,775 (a)	135,260 (a)		
ASHTON-UNDER-LYNE UNION. (Formed 3 Feb. 1837 by Order dated 17 Jan. 1837.) COUNTY of CHESTER :					
Duckingfield - - tow.	29,675	1,660	99,221	Duckingfield -	Hyde.
Godley - - tow.	1,392	645	9,201	Hyde, Manchester	do.
Hattersley - - tow.	263	1,059	3,093	Mottram - -	do.
Hollingworth - - tow.	2,658	2,086	10,333	Viâ Hadfield -	do.
Matley - - tow.	205	705	1,519	Hyde, Manchester	do.
Mottram - - tow.	2,913	1,084	9,459	Mottram - -	do.
Newton - - tow.	7,340	870	22,631	Hyde, Manchester	do.
Stavley - - tow.	7,363	2,344	32,889	Stalybridge -	do.
Tintwistle - - tow.	3,342	14,410	26,828	Viâ Hadfield -	do.
COUNTY of LANCASTER :					
Ashton-under-Lyne (W.) - par.	75,310	9,486	271,415	Ashton-under-Lyne	{ Salford Hundred and Ashton-under-Lyne.
Denton - - tow.	7,660	1,706	27,107	Denton - -	do.
Droylsden - - tow.	11,254	1,621	40,747	Droylsden -	do.
Haughton - - tow.	5,051	887	15,119	Denton - -	do.
TOTAL of UNION -	154,526	38,563	569,562		
ASTON UNION. (Formed 7 Nov. 1836 by Order dated 12 Oct. 1836.) COUNTY of WARWICK :					
Aston near Birmingham (W.) - par.	201,305	14,090	631,526	Birmingham -	{ Birmingham Division of the Hundred of Hemlingford.
Curdworth - - par.	318	} 3,170	3,974	do. - -	Coleshill Division.
Minworth - - ham.	354		7,773	do. - -	do.
Sutton Coldfield - par.	7,737	13,030	50,748	do. - -	Birmingham Division.
Whishaw - - par.	173	1,196	2,518	do. - -	Coleshill Division.
TOTAL of UNION -	209,887	31,486	696,539		

ASHBY DE LA ZOUCH UNION:

(a) (b). See notes, page 19.

Unions and Parishes, &c.	Population in 1881.	Area in Statute Acres in 1881.	Rateable Value in 1881.	Post Town.	Petty Sessional Division.

ATCHAM UNION.

(Formed 18 Nov. 1836 by Order dated 22 Oct. 1836.—Places marked thus * added 24 June 1871 by Order dated 5 June 1871 and thus † added 26 March 1885 by Order dated 20 March 1885.)

			£		
COUNTY of MONTGOMERY:					
Bauseley (d) - - tow.	341	} 1,390 {	2,415	Shrewsbury -	Deythur.
Criggion - - cha.	162		3,418	do. - -	do.
COUNTY of SALOP:					
Acton Burnel - tow.	237	3,141	2,368	Shrewsbury	Condover.
Alberbury with Car-deston (d) - - } par.	865	8,871	12,150	do. -	Ford.
Albrighton - - cha.	102	771	1,113	do. - -	Albrighton and Brinstree.
Astley - - cha.	236	1,204	2,619	do. - -	Albrighton.
Atcham (c) - - par.	412	3,762	7,926	do. -	Bradford, South, Hundred of, Wellington Division.
Battlefield - par.	91	1,025	1,595	do. - -	Albrighton.
Berrington (W.) (c) - par.	989	3,520	6,794	do. - -	Condover.
†Bicton (c) - par.					
Church Preen - par.	117	1,050	1,532	Church Stretton -	do.
Church Pulverbatch - par.	401	4,063	5,396	Shrewsbury	do.
Condover - par.	1,775	7,422	16,500	do. - -	do.
Cound - - tow.	477	} 5,530 {	5,834	do. - -	do.
Cressage (c) - cha.	259		2,943	do. - -	do.
Eaton Constantine (c) par.	234	874	1,430	Ironbridge -	Bradford, South, Hundred of, Wellington Division.
Fitz - - par.	291	1,512	3,180	Shrewsbury	Albrighton.
Ford (c) - - par.	373	1,773	2,752	do. - -	Ford.
Frodesley - par.	235	2,212	2,693	do. - -	Condover.
Great Hanwood - par.	310	590	1,720	do. - -	Ford.
Habberley - par.	137	795	1,197	do. - -	do.
Harley - - par.	178	1,955	2,144	do. - -	Condover.
*Holy Cross and Saint Giles } par.	2,783	1,580	18,327	do.	——
Hughley - - par.	110	1,225	1,001	Much Wenlock -	——
Kenley - - par.	217	1,897	1,732	Shrewsbury -	Condover.
Leighton (c) - par.	298	2,151	2,962	Ironbridge -	Bradford, South, Hundred of, Wellington Division.
Melverley - par.	188	1,418	3,016	Llanymynech, R.S.O.	Oswestry, Hundred of.
*Meole-Brace (c) - par.	1,208	In St. Chad	9,969	Shrewsbury	Condover.
Minsterley - cha.	926	In Westbury	5,356	do. -	Ford.
Montford - par.	500	3,137	5,192	do. -	Dimhill, Hundred of.

(continued)

ATCHAM UNION:

(a) A detached part of Worthin, in the Forden Union, was amalgamated with Pontesbury by Order which came into operation on 25 March 1884.

(b) All the parts of a parish known as Uffington were by Order which came into operation on 25 March 1885 amalgamated with a parish known as Haughmond Demesne, and the parish as so altered was designated the parish of Uffington.

(c) By Orders which came into operation on 25 March 1885,—

A detached part of Atcham known as " Uckington" was amalgamated with Wroxeter;

A detached part of Ford was amalgamated with Pontesbury;

A detached part of Leighton known as " Belswardine," was amalgamated with Cressage;

A detached part of Uppington was amalgamated with Eaton Constantine;

Certain parts of Saint Alkmond, Saint Julian, and Saint Chad were united and constituted a separate parish, which was designated the parish of Bicton;

ATCHAM UNION—continued.

Certain parts of Saint Julian and Saint Mary, and of the Parish of Saint Alkmond as it existed in 1881, were united and constituted a separate parish, which was designated the parish of Saint Alkmond; Saint Alkmond in 1881 had population 1,397, and rateable value 12,128l.

Certain parts of Saint Alkmond were amalgamated with Saint Mary;

All that part of Meole Brace comprised in the borough of Shrewsbury was amalgamated with Saint Julian;

Parts of Saint Chad were amalgamated with Berrington, Meole Brace, and Atcham;

Parts of Saint Julian were amalgamated with Saint Mary and Meole Brace by Order which came into operation on 25 March 1885.

(d) By Provisional Order which came into operation on 25 March 1886,—

A detached part of Bauseley and all the parts of a parish known as Alberbury were amalgamated with a parish known as Cardeston, and the latter parish, as altered, was designated Alberbury with Cardeston.

B 4

Unions and Parishes, &c.	Population in 1881.	Area in Statute Acres in 1881.	Rateable Value in 1881.	Post Town.	Petty Sessional Division.
ATCHAM UNION—County of Salop—*continued.*			£		
Pitchford - - par.	214	1,645	2,513	Shrewsbury -	Condover.
Pontesbury (*a*) (*c*) - par.	3,060	10,667	22,766	do. - -	Ford.
Preston Gubbals - par.	426	2,349	3,529	do. - -	Albrighton.
Ruckley - - tow.	90	In Acton Burnel.	1,516	do. - -	Condover.
†Saint Alkmond (*c*) - par.	(*c*)	(*c*)	(*c*)	do. - -	Albrighton.
ᵈSaint Chad (*c*) - par.	8,826	12,473	44,169	do. - -	Ford.
*Saint Julian (*c*) - par.	6,213	In St. Chad	23,130	do. - -	Condover and Ford.
*Saint Mary (*c*) - par.	9,953	3,979	40,316	do. - -	Albrighton.
Shincton - - par.	107	946	1,268	do. - -	Condover.
Shrawardine - - par.	193	1,951	3,530	do. - -	Pimhill, Hundred of.
Stapleton - - par.	256	1,836	4,129	do. - -	Condover.
Sutton - - par.	71	730	1,462	do. - -	do.
Uffington (*b*) - - par.	356 (*b*)	3,055 (*b*)	4,759 (*b*)	do. - -	Albrighton.
Uppington (*c*) - par.	191	755	1,292	Wellington (Salop)	Bradford, South, Hundred of, Wellington Division.
Upton Magna - par.	465	3,282	6,969	Shrewsbury -	do. do.
Westbury - - tow.	1,298	11,274	13,579	do. - -	Ford.
Withington - par.	259	1,144	2,090	Wellington (Salop)	Bradford, South, Hundred of, Wellington Division.
Woollaston - - cha.	315	In Albersbury with Cardeston.	4,104	Shrewsbury -	Ford.
Wroxeter (*c*) - par.	488	4,774	6,942	do. - -	Bradford, South, Hundred of, Wellington Division.
TOTAL of UNION -	47,236 (*c*)	123,728	323,376 (*c*)		

ATHERSTONE UNION.

(Formed 31 March 1836 by Order dated 16 March 1836.—Places marked thus * added 22 April 1851 by Order dated 5 April 1851.)

COUNTY of LEICESTER :					
Atterton (*a*) - ham.	59	In Witherley.	1,138	Nuneaton -	Market Bosworth.
Fenny Drayton - par.	139	1,280	2,151	do. - -	do.
*Ratcliffe Culey - cha.	228	} 2,820 {	2,397	Atherstone -	do.
Sheepy Magna (*a*) - par.	415		3,468	do. - -	do.
Sheepy Parva - par.	89	660	1,231	do. - -	do.
ᵖWitherley (*a*) - par.	457	1,570	2,670	do. - -	do.
COUNTY of WARWICK :					
Ansley - - par.	833	2,869	5,797	Atherstone -	Atherstone.
Atherstone (W.) - tow.	4,645	4,120	13,213	do. - -	do.
Baddesley Ensor - par.	932	1,100	2,898	do. - -	do.
Baxterley - - par.	360	874	2,832	do. - -	do.
Bentley - - ham.	224	1,830	2,288	do. - -	do.
Grendon - - par.	617	2,360	9,375	do. - -	do.
ᵖHartshill - - ham.	1,264	In Atherstone.	7,162	do. - -	do.

(*continued*)

ATCHAM UNION :

(*a*) (*b*) (*c*). *See* notes, page 15.

ATHERSTONE UNION.

(*a*) By Orders which came into operation on 25 March 1885 —

A detached part of Atterton was amalgamated with Witherley ; and

A detached part of Merivale was amalgamated with Sheepy Magna ; and

Other detached parts of Merivale were amalgamated with Orton on the Hill, in the Market Bosworth Union ; these parts were in Leicestershire, and contained a population of 77, an acreage of 1,050, and a rateable value of 2,850*l.*

Unions and Parishes, &c.		Population in 1881.	Area in Statute Acres in 1881.	Rateable Value in 1881.	Post Town.	Petty Sessional Division.

ATHERSTONE UNION—County of Warwick—continued.

£

Mancetter or Man-	tow.	436	In Ather-	7,087	Atherstone	Atherstone.
cester			stone.			
Merivale (a)	par.	112	1,011	2,555	do.	do.
Oldbury	ham.	61	In Ather-	968	do.	do.
			stone.			
Polesworth	par.	3,472	6,310	22,051	Tamworth	do.

| TOTAL of UNION | | 14,342 (a) | 26,744 (a) | 89,281 (a) | | |

AUCKLAND UNION.

(Formed 9 Jan. 1837 by Order dated 15 Dec. 1836.)

COUNTY of DURHAM :

						Darlington Ward :
Auckland Saint An-	tow.	2,289	1,274	13,516	Bishop Auckland	North West Division
drew						(Bishop Auckland).
Auckland Saint Helen	tow.	918	1,510	9,196	do. do.	do.
Auckland West	tow.	3,177	3,410	14,866	do. do.	do.
Bedburn North	tow.	2,426	2,858	11,725	Howden, Darlington	do.
Bedburn South (b)	tow.	345	7,409	3,160	Bishop Auckland	do.
Binchester (b)	tow.	52	583	3,409	Willington	do.
Bishop Auckland and						
Pollard's Lands (W.)	tow.	(c)	(c)	(c)	Bishop Auckland	do.
(c)						
Bolam	tow.	117	1,013	1,261	Darlington	do.
Byers Green (b)	tow.	2,452	1,082	7,521	Spennymoor	do.
Counden (c)	tow.	3,510	824	12,336	Bishop Auckland	do.
Counden Grange (c)	tow.	1,864	638	9,229	do. do.	do.
Crook and Billy Row	tow.	11,096	4,058	43,621	Darlington	do.
Eldon	tow.	1,389	1,421	8,162	do.	do.
Escombe (c)	tow.	3,982	1,063	12,575	Bishop Auckland	do.
Evenwood	tow.	2,954	5,433	16,077	do. do.	do.
Hamsterley (b)	tow.	493	2,967	2,975	do. do.	do.
Helmington Row (a)	tow.	4,040	1,302	11,631	Crook	do.
Hunwick and Hel-	tow.	2,086	1,594	13,690	Willington	do.
mington (b)						
Lynesack and Softly	tow.	2,347	6,375	10,135	Butterknowle, Darlington.	do.
(b)						
Merriugton	tow.	1,663	1,961	6,406	Ferryhill	do.
Middlestone	tow.	1,733	893	7,638	Bishop Auckland	do.
Midridge (b)	tow.	853	1,160	4,557	Darlington	do.
Midridge Grange (b)	tow.	64	950	3,196	do.	do.
Newfield	tow.	1,150	206	4,162	Willington	do.
Newton Cap (b)	tow.	1,349	1,681	11,044	do.	do.
Old Park	tow.	910	414	4,392	Spennymoor	do.
Shildon	tow.	6,946	598	16,940	Darlington	do.
Thickley East	tow.	1,758	168	10,139	Shildon, Darlington	do.
Westerton	tow.	463	699	5,735	Bishop Auckland	do.
Whitworth	tow.	6,187	1,568	19,190	Spennymoor	do.
Windlestone	tow.	244	1,188	2,089	Ferryhill	do.
Witton le Wear	tow.	2,469	3,179	17,260	Darlington	do.

| TOTAL of UNION | | 71,326 (c) | 59,779 (c) (d) | 317,833 (c) | | |

AUCKLAND UNION :

(a) Certain detached parts of Willington, in the Durham Union, were amalgamated with Helmington Row, by Provisional Order which came into operation on 25 March 1893.

(b) By Order which came into operation on 25 March 1885,—
A detached part of Byers Green was amalgamated with Binchester ;
Certain detached parts of Hamsterley were amalgamated with Lynesack and Softly, and another detached part was amalgamated with Bedburn South.
Two detached parts of Lynesack and Softly were amalgamated with Bedburn South, and three other parts with Hamsterley ;
A detached part of Midridge Grange was amalgamated with Midridge ; and

AUCKLAND UNION—continued.

A detached part of Newton Cap was amalgamated with Hunwick and Helmington.

(c) By Provisional Order which came into operation on 25 March 1886,—
A part of Bishop Auckland was amalgamated with Counden Grange ; and
The whole of a township known as Pollard's Lands (having in 1881 population 614, acreage 438, and rateable value 2,710l.), and parts of Counden Grange and Escombe were amalgamated with Bishop Auckland, the name of the latter being altered to Bishop Auckland and Pollard's Lands, (Bishop Auckland in 1887 had population 11,682 acreage 2,126, and rateable value 36,163l.)

(d) In this Union are included certain Common Lands containing in all 2,108 acres.

R 8372.

C

Unions and Parishes, &c.		Population in 1881.	Area in Statute Acres in 1881.	Rateable Value in 1881.	Post Town.	Petty Sessional Division.
AXBRIDGE UNION.						
(Formed 28 Jan. 1836 by Order dated 12 Jan. 1836.)						
COUNTY OF SOMERSET :				£		
Axbridge	par.	718	540	2,527	Weston super Mare	Axbridge.
Badgworth (a)	par.	281	1,815	5,488	do.	do.
Banwell	par.	1,717	4,829	17,040	do.	do.
Berrow	par.	442	6,563	5,457	Bridgwater	do.
Biddisham	par.	123	574	1,739	Weston super Mare	do.
Blagdon (a)	par.	911	3,535	5,723	Bristol	do.
Bleadon	par.	616	2,795	7,606	Weston super Mare	do.
Breane	par.	148	3,167	2,274	Bridgwater	do.
Brent Knoll (a)	par.	792	3,426	13,045	do.	do.
Burnham with Aston Morris	par.	3,645	4,302	23,980	do.	do.
Burrington (a)	par.	453	2,009	2,516	Bristol	do.
Butcombe (a)	par.	189	983	1,610	do.	do.
Chapel Allerton (a)	par.	249	1,169	3,001	Weston super Mare	do.
Charter House (a)	ville	79	2,410	1,132	Bristol	do.
Cheddar (a)	par.	2,366	6,998	14,457	Weston super Mare	do.
Christon	par.	57	571	1,054	do.	do.
Churchill	par.	733	2,397	5,664	Bristol	do.
Compton Bishop (W.)	par.	551	2,535	4,691	Weston super Mare	do.
Congresbury (a)	par.	1,185	4,443	14,213	Bristol	do.
East Brent (a)	par.	709	3,037	11,235	Bridgwater	do.
Hutton	par.	344	1,876	5,350	Weston super Mare	do.
Kewstoke (a)	par.	740	4,008	7,238	do.	do.
Locking	par.	122	1,016	2,262	do.	do.
Loxton	par.	134	1,203	2,721	do.	do.
Lympsham	par.	453	1,966	6,293	do.	do.
Mark (a)	par.	1,097	1,354	14,245	Bridgwater	do.
Nyland with Batcombe (a)	par.	43	590	1,963	Weston super Mare	Wells.
Puxton (a)	par.	125	613	1,971	Bristol	Axbridge.
Rowberrow (a)	par.	168	954	630	do.	do.
Shipham	par.	408	766	1,167	do.	do.
Uphill	par.	645	1,697	4,864	Weston super Mare	do.
Weare (a)	par.	650	2,146	6,045	do.	do.
Wedmore (a)	par.	3,060	9,986	26,842	do.	do.
Weston super Mare (a)	par.	12,884	2,770	61,853	do.	do.
Week Saint Lawrence (a)	par.	224	1,900	4,135	do.	do.
Winscombe	par.	1,259	4,140	9,101	do.	do.
Worle (a)	par.	965	1,810	7,442	do.	do.
Wrington with Broadfield	par.	1,551	5,786	10,532	Bristol	do.
TOTAL OF UNION		40,836	105,679	319,106		

AXBRIDGE UNION:

(a) By Orders which came into operation on 25 March 1885,—

A detached part of Burrington was amalgamated with Congresbury;

Several detached parts of Kewstoke were amalgamated with Worle, Congresbury, and Puxton;

Detached parts of Puxton were amalgamated with Congresbury;

A detached part of Rowberrow was amalgamated with Charter House;

Parts of Week Saint Lawrence were amalgamated with Puxton and Congresbury;

AXBRIDGE UNION—continued.

Detached parts of Weston-super-Mare and Worle were amalgamated with Kewstoke;

A detached part of Congresbury was amalgamated with Puxton;

Detached parts of Blagdon were amalgamated with Butcombe; and

A detached part of Blagdon was amalgamated with Winford in the Bedminster Union;

Alterations were made in the areas of Badgworth, Brent Knoll (formerly called South Brent), Chapel Allerton, East Brent, Mark, Weare, and Wedmore;

Detached parts of Cheddar, and Nyland with Batcombe, were amalgamated with Rodney Stoke, in the Wells Union.

Unions and Parishes, &c.	Population in 1881.	Area in Statute Acres in 1881.	Rateable Value in 1881.	Post Town.	Petty Sessional Division.

AXMINSTER UNION.

(Formed 16 April 1836 by Order dated 2 April 1836. — Place marked thus * added 25 Mar. 1863 by Order dated 23 Jan. 1861.)

COUNTY of DEVON :

			£		
Axminster (W.) (*a*) *par.*	2,849 (Devon) 23 (Dorset)	6,617 (Devon) 441 (Dorset)	15,911	Axminster - -	Axminster.
Axmouth - - *par.*	679	4,723	4,810	Axminster -	do.
Beer and Seaton - *par.*	2,343	2,821	8,128	do. - -	do.
Colyton (*b*) - - *par.*	2,330	7,196	11,236	do. - -	do.
Combe Pyne - - *par.*	128	796	768	do. - -	do.
Dalwood - - *par.*	406	1,709	2,572	Honiton - -	do.
Kilmington - - *par.*	501	1,760	3,421	Axminster -	do.
Membury (*a*) - *par.*	639	4,089	5,093	Chard - -	do.
Musbury - - *par.*	533	2,178	3,903	Axminster -	do.
*Roosdown - - *par.*	44	200	600	Lyme Regis -	do.
Shute - - *par.*	579	2,738	3,565	Axminster -	do.
Stockland - - *par.*	876	5,849	6,952	Honiton -	do.
Uplyme (*a*) - - *par.*	910	3,190	5,016	Lyme Regis -	do.
COUNTY of DORSET :					
Chardstock (*a*) - *par.*	1,328	5,800	7,602	Chard - -	Bridport.
Charmouth - - *par.*	626	518	2,518	Charmouth -	do.
Hawkchurch - - *par.*	590	4,130	4,700	Axminster -	do.
Lyme Regis - - *par.*	2,290	1,499	9,767	Lyme Regis -	Lyme Regis.
Thorncombe (*a*) - *par.*	1,095	4,896	7,223	Chard - -	Bridport.
TOTAL of UNION -	18,769	61,159	105,785		

AYLESBURY UNION.

(Formed 6 July 1835 by Order dated 13 June 1835. — Place marked thus* added 20 Aug. 1835 by Order dated 5 Aug. 1835.)

COUNTY of BUCKINGHAM :

Ashenden cum Pollecot *par.*	237	2,128	2,860	Thame - -	Ashenden.
Aston Abbots - *par.*	290	2,198	3,914	Aylesbury -	Cottesloe.
Aston Clinton - *tow.*	1,495	3,809	6,501	Tring - -	Aylesbury.
Aston Sandford - *par.*	59	679	928	Thame - -	do.
Aylesbury with Walton (W.) (*b*) - } *par.*	7,795	3,302	26,305	Aylesbury -	do.
Bierton with Broughton (*a*) (*b*) - } *par.*	812	2,412	5,120	do. - -	do.
Buckland (*b*) - - *par.*	863	1,555	2,559	Tring - -	do.

(*continued*)

AXMINSTER UNION.

(*a*) By Orders which came into operation on 25 March 1884,—
A detached part of Axminster known as the Tything of Beerhall in the County of Dorset was amalgamated with Thorncombe, and another part known as the tything of Shapwick was amalgamated with Uplyme;
A detached part of Chardstock was amalgamated with Membury; and
A detached part of Membury was amalgamated with Yarcombe, in the Chard Union.

(*b*) Certain detached parts of Colyton were amalgamated with Southleigh in the Honiton Union by Provisional Order which came into operation on 25 March 1885.

AYLESBURY UNION.

(*a*) By Orders which came into operation on 25 March 1885,—
A detached part of Bierton with Broughton was amalgamated with Hulcott; and

AYLESBURY UNION—*continued*.

A detached part of Wendover in the Wycombe Union was amalgamated with Bierton with Broughton.

(*b*) By Orders which came into operation on 25 March 1886,—
Detached parts of Aylesbury with Walton were amalgamated with Bierton with Broughton;
A detached part of Bierton with Broughton was amalgamated with Aylesbury with Walton;
Detached parts of Drayton Beauchamp were amalgamated with Buckland, and Wingrave with Rowsham;
Detached parts of Waldesdon were amalgamated with Woodham and Grendon Underwood;
All the parts of a place known as Quainton were amalgamated with Shipton Lee, the name being altered to Quainton; and
Detached parts of Brill and Long Crendon in the Thame Union, were amalgamated with Ludgershall and Wotton Underwood.

(*c*) By Provisional Order which came into operation on 25 March 1887,—
Certain detached parts of Stoke Mandeville in the Wycombe Union were amalgamated with Hartwell.

Unions and Parishes, &c.	Population in 1881.	Area in Statute Acres in 1881.	Rateable Value in 1881.	Post Town.	Petty Sessional Division.
			£		
AYLESBURY UNION—County of Buckingham—*continued.*					
Cheursley - - *par.*	235	913	1,518	Aylesbury - -	Ashenden.
Cholesbury - - *par.*	99	178	332	Tring - -	Chesham.
Creslow - - *par.*	10	887	1,725	Aylesbury - -	Cottesloe.
Cublington - - *par.*	259	1,223	2,140	Leighton Buzzard -	do.
Cuddington - - *par.*	176	1,308	2,589	Aylesbury - -	Aylesbury.
Dinton with Ford and Upton } *par.*	718	3,897	6,148	do. - -	do.
Drayton Beauchamp (*b*) *par.*	194	1,888	2,347	Tring - -	do.
*Grendon Underwood (*b*) *par.*	365	2,536	2,279	Aylesbury -	Ashenden.
Haddenham - - *par.*	1,443	3,274	6,513	Thame - -	Aylesbury.
Hilton - - *par.*	195	1,156	1,920	Tring - -	do.
Hardwicke - - *par.*	214	1,213	2,138	Aylesbury -	do.
Hartwell (*c*) - - *par.*	146	911	2,033	do. - -	do.
Hawridge - - *par.*	242	697	855	Berkhampstead -	Chesham.
Hulcott (*a*) - - *par.*	119	717	1,210	Aylesbury - -	Aylesbury.
Kingswood - - *ham.*	27	261	333	do. - -	Ashenden.
Ludgershall (*b*) - *par.*	395	2,562	2,936	do. - -	do.
Marston Fleet - *par.*	27	934	1,635	do. - -	Aylesbury.
Nether Winchendon - *par.*	257	1,554	2,640	do. - -	do.
Oving - - *par.*	385	990	2,041	do. - -	Winslow.
Pitchcott - - *par.*	35	925	1,709	do. - -	do.
Quainton (*b*) - *tow.*	865	5,346	8,416	do. - -	do.
Quarrendon - - *par.*	37	1,948	3,604	do. - -	Aylesbury.
Stone - - *par.*	1,368	2,568	4,998	do. - -	do.
Upper Winchendon - *par.*	188	1,202	2,221	do. - -	do.
Waddesdon (*b*) - *tow.*	1,375	5,346	9,525	do. - -	do.
Weedon - - *ham.*	433	1,788	3,463	do. - -	do.
Westcot - - *ham.*	245	1,411	1,697	do. - -	do.
Weston Turville - *par.*	824	2,323	4,333	Tring - -	do.
Whitchurch - - *par.*	725	1,718	3,875	Aylesbury -	Winslow.
Wingrave with Row-sham (*b*) - } *par.*	903	2,488	4,247	do. - -	Cottesloe.
Woodham (*b*) - - *ham.*	31	325	343	do. - -	Ashendon.
Wotton Underwood (*b*) *par.*	221	2,487	2,625	do. - -	do.
TOTAL of UNION -	24,607	73,617	142,575		

AYLSHAM UNION. (Formed 9 April 1836 by Order dated 26 March 1836.—Place marked thus * added by Order of 8 April 1836.) COUNTY of NORFOLK.					
Alby with Thwaite(*a*) *par.*	(*a*) 394	(*a*) 1,487	(*a*) 2,884	Hanworth -	South Erpingham.
Aylsham (W.) - *par.*	2,674	4,308	13,278	Aylsham -	do.
Banningham - - *par.*	245	920	1,971	do. -	do.
Belaugh - - *par.*	139	854	1,357	Norwich -	do.
Blickling - - *par.*	311	2,123	2,950	Aylsham -	do.
Brampton - - *par.*	182	521	1,159	Heringham -	do.
Burgh - - *par.*	219	789	1,833	Aylsham -	do.
Buxton - - *par.*	556	1,274	3,225	Hevingham -	do.
Calthorpe - - *par.*	204	1,048	1,928	Hanworth -	do.
Cawston - - *par.*	1,096	1,296	5,855	Norwich -	do.
Colby - - *par.*	241	1,115	2,215	Aylsham -	do.
Coltishall - - *par.*	952	1,180	3,961	Norwich -	do.

(*continued*)

AYLESBURY UNION :

(*a*) (*b*) (*c*) *See* Notes, page 19.

AYLSHAM UNION,

(*a*) All the parts of a parish known as Thwaite were amalgamated with a parish known as Alby, and the latter parish as so enlarged was designated the parish of Alby with Thwaite, by Order which came into operation on 25 March 1884.

Unions and Parishes, &c.		Population in 1881.	Area in Statute Acres in 1881.	Rateable Value in 1881.	Post Town.	Petty Sessional Division.
				£		
AYLSHAM UNION—County of Norfolk—*continued.*						
Corpusty	par.	379	1,018	1,618	Norwich - -	South Erpingham.
Erpingham -	par.	362	1,381	2,999	do. - -	do.
Foulsham -	par.	949	3,226	6,217	East Dereham -	Eynsford.
*Great Hautbois	par.	190	610	1,229	Norwich -	South Erpingham.
Guestwick -	par.	183	1,646	2,661	East Dereham -	Eynsford.
Hackford -	par.	803	754	3,217	Reepham - -	do.
Hevingham -	par.	764	2,855	3,951	Norwich -	South Erpingham.
Heydon -	par.	217	1,942	2,249	do. - -	do.
Hindolvestone -	par.	651	2,493	4,315	East Dereham -	Eynsford.
Ingworth -	par.	144	512	1,151	Norwich - -	South Erpingham.
Irmingland -	par.	5	714	940	Aylsham - -	do.
Itteringham -	par.	319	1,442	2,163	do. - -	do.
Lammas with Little Hautbois - }	u.p.	250	829	1,864	Norwich - -	do.
Little Barningham -	par.	203	1,224	1,420	do. - -	do.
Mannington -	par.	8	548	676	Aylsham - -	do.
Marsham -	par.	554	1,819	2,722	Norwich - -	do.
Oulton -	par.	379	1,849	2,530	Aylsham - -	do.
Oxnead -	par.	75	644	1,234	Norwich - -	do.
Reepham with Kerdiston - }	u.p.	527	2,250	4,860	do. - -	Eynsford.
Sall -	par.	194	1,802	3,305	Reepham - -	do.
Saxthorpe -	par.	331	2,113	2,730	Norwich - -	South Erpingham.
Scottow -	par.	430	2,120	1,298	do. - -	do.
Skeyton -	par.	313	1,264	2,423	do. - -	do.
Stratton Strawless -	par.	186	1,582	1,925	do. - -	do.
Swanton-Abbott -	par.	504	1,130	2,192	do. - -	do.
Themelthorpe -	par.	72	652	1,012	East Dereham -	Eynsford.
Thurning -	par.	170	1,584	2,249	do. - -	do.
Tuttington -	par.	198	830	1,730	Aylsham -	South Erpingham.
Whitwell -	par.	426	1,511	3,012	Reepham -	Eynsford.
Wickmere -	par.	243 }	1,697 {	1,962	Hanworth -	South Erpingham.
Wolterton -	par.	47 }		1,332	Aylsham -	do.
Wood-Dalling -	par.	484	2,444	4,052	Reepham -	Eynsford.
Wood-Norton -	par.	284	1,726	2,763	East Dereham -	do.
TOTAL OF UNION -		-18,057	68,123	125,617		

AYSGARTH UNION.						
(Formed 2 Feb. 1869 by an Order dated 6 Jan. 1869.)						
COUNTY of YORK, NORTH RIDING.						
Askrigg (a) -	tow.	624	4,907	3,884	Askrigg, Bedale -	Hang, West.
Aysgarth -	tow.	370	1,214	1,588	Aysgarth -	do.
Bainbridge (W.) (a) -	tow.	683	15,399	8,616	Bainbridge -	do.
Bishopdale -	tow.	87	4,735	2,382	Aysgarth -	do.
Burton-cum-Walden (a)	tow.	444	7,607	4,370	do. -	do.
Carperby-cum-Thoresby - }	tow.	298	4,915	3,428	do. -	do.
Hawes (a) -	tow.	1,890	16,021	13,113	Hawes -	do.
High Abbotside (a) -	tow.	493	6,319	5,834	Hawes, Bedale -	do.
Low Abbotside (a) -	tow.	130	2,036	2,309	Askrigg, do. -	do.
Newbiggen -	tow.	104	1,697	1,603	Aysgarth, Bedale -	do.
Thoralby (a) -	tow.	216	2,914	2,449	do. -	do.
Thornton Rust -	tow.	143	1,939	1,763	do. -	do.
TOTAL of UNION -		5,482	69,703 (b)	51,339		

AYSGARTH UNION:

(a) By Order which came into operation on 25 March 1886,—
  Detached parts of Bainbridge were amalgamated with Hawes and Askrigg ;
  A detached part of High Abbotside was amalgamated with Low Abbotside ; and
  Detached parts of Thoralby were amalgamated with Burton-cum-Walden.
(b) There are certain common lands comprised in this Union containing altogether 11,309 acres.

Unions and Parishes, &c.	Population in 1881.	Area in Statute Acres in 1881.	Rateable Value in 1881.	Post Town.	Petty Sessional Division.

BAKEWELL UNION.

(Formed 31 July 1838 by Order dated 5 July 1838. — Places marked thus * added 7 Dec. 1838 by Order dated 12 Nov. 1838; thus † added 25 Feb. 1845 by Order dated 25 Feb. 1845; and thus ‡ added 25 Mar. 1861 by Order dated 23 Feb. 1861.)

County of Derby :

£

Unions and Parishes, &c.	Population in 1881.	Area in Statute Acres in 1881.	Rateable Value in 1881.	Post Town.	Petty Sessional Division.
Abney and Abney Grange } ham.	77	1,350	748	Sheffield	Bakewell.
Aldwarke - tow.	52	967	825	Wirksworth	Wirksworth.
Ashford - tow.	675	2,554	5,096	Bakewell	Bakewell.
Bakewell (W.) - tow.	2,502	3,064	12,365	do.	do.
Baslow and Bubnell tow.	843	5,635	3,946	Chesterfield	do.
Beeley - tow.	362	3,237	1,578	Bakewell	do.
Birchover - tow.	76	866	1,156	do.	do.
†Blackwell - tow.	47	1,083	1,752	Buxton	do.
*Bradwell - tow.	1,019	2,174	2,459	Sheffield	Chapel en le Frith.
Brushfield - tow.	31	648	1,011	Buxton	Bakewell.
Calver - tow.	431	775	1,758	Sheffield	do.
‡Chatsworth - par.	60	1,292	1,791	Chesterfield	do.
Chelmorton - tow.	232	2,028	1,867	Buxton	do.
Cromford - tow.	1,074	1,324	4,000	Derby	Matlock.
Curbar - tow.	317	1,153	855	Sheffield	Bakewell.
Darley Dale - tow.	1,848	5,142	11,030	Matlock	Matlock.
Edensor - tow.	286	2,336	2,779	Bakewell	Bakewell.
†Elton - tow.	516	1,464	1,861	Derby	do.
Eyam - tow.	1,038	2,464	3,522	Sheffield	do.
Eyam Woodlands - tow.	237	1,091	1,113	do.	do.
Flagg - tow.	190	1,805	1,652	Buxton	do.
Foolow - ham.	223	986	1,073	Sheffield	do.
Froggatt - tow.	136	146	355	do.	do.
Grange Mill, alias Ironbrook Grange - } tow.	39	417	457	Wirksworth	do.
Gratton - tow.	38	910	907	Derby	do.
Grindlow - tow.	57	296	400	Sheffield	do.
Haddon Over - tow.	178	1,399	1,798	Bakewell	do.
Harthill - tow.	89	920	1,052	do.	do.
Hartington Middle Quarter - } tow.	335	4,816	3,787	Longnor	do.
Hassop - tow.	91	1,363	1,950	Bakewell	do.
Hathersage - tow.	828	3,229	3,281	Sheffield	do.
Hazlebadge - lord.	45	822	755	do.	do.
Highlow - lord.	44	421	331	do.	do.
Hucklow Great - ham.	173	1,113	1,517	do.	do.
Hucklow Little - ham.	175	589	701	do.	do.
Litton - ham.	727	1,639	2,941	do.	do.
Longston Great - tow.	187	3,028	6,438	Bakewell	do.
Longston Little - tow.	152	1,038	2,983	do.	do.
Matlock - par.	6,093	4,539	27,447	Matlock	Matlock.
Middleton by Youl- greave } tow.	218	2,956	3,053	Bakewell	Bakewell.
Money-ash - tow.	399	3,146	3,152	do.	do.
‡Nether Haddon - par.	11	1,499	3,555	do.	do.
Nether Padley - ham.	37	308	275	Sheffield	do.
*Offerton - ham.	26	619	351	do.	do.
*Outseats - tow.	191	4,501	2,314	do.	do.
Pilsley - tow.	231	465	741	do.	do.
†Rowland - tow.	68	303	740	do.	do.
Rowsley and Alport - tow.	284	700	1,716	Bakewell	do.
Sheldon - tow.	169	1,070	1,201	do.	do.
Stanton - tow.	762	1,824	2,681	do.	do.
Stoke - tow.	22	512	751	Sheffield	do.
Stoney Middleton - tow.	354	1,181	1,803	do.	do.
Taddington and Priestcliffe - } tow.	408	3,008	4,064	Buxton	do.
*Tansley - tow.	678	1,137	2,038	Derby	Matlock.
Tideswell - tow.	1,985	3,160	5,200	Stockport	Bakewell.
Wardlow Miers - tow.	163	643	713	Sheffield	do.

(continued)

Unions and Parishes, &c.		Population in 1881.	Area in Statute Acres in 1881.	Rateable Value in 1881.	Post Town.	Petty Sessional Division.

BAKEWELL UNION—County of Derby—continued.

				£		
Wensley and Snitterton, —	tnr.	679	2,007	3,549	Derby -	Matlock.
Whestone - -	ham.	73	1,394	1,195	Stockport -	Bakewell.
Winster - -	tnr.	836	1,123	2,410	Derby -	do.
†Youlgrave - -	tnr.	1,105	2,398	3,751	Bakewell -	do.
TOTAL of UNION -		30,522	104,377	166,620		

BALA UNION.

(Formed 10 Jan. 1837 by Order dated 15 Dec. 1836.)

COUNTY of MERIONETH :

Llandderfil (a) -	par.	1,059	7,794	5,108	Corwen -	Penllyn.
Llanfawr (a) -	par.	1,471	20,030	11,253	Bala -	do.
Llangower -	par.	258	5,600	2,243	do. -	do.
Llanuwchyllyn -	par.	1,078	12,000	5,392	do. -	do.
Llanycil (W.) -	par.	2,874	12,868	11,226	do. -	do.
TOTAL of UNION -		6,740	58,292	35,222		

BANBURY UNION.

(Formed 3 April 1835 by Order dated 17 March 1835.—Places marked thus * added 19 Oct. 1835 by Order dated 26 Sept. 1835 ; thus † 6 June 1836 by Order dated 10 May 1836 ; and Place marked thus ‡ 22 July 1847 by Order dated 22 July 1847.)

COUNTY of NORTHAMPTON :

†Appletree - -	ham.	58 }	1,270 {	985	Byfield -	Brackley.
†Aston le Wall (a) -	par.	101 }		1,861	do. -	do.
Chalcombe -	par.	447	1,694	3,537	Banbury -	do.
†Chipping Warden (a)	par.	396	1,987	3,290	do. -	do.
‡Edgcott -	par.	76	1,344	2,232	do. -	do.
†Lower Boddington -	par.	238	3,770	2,361	Byfield -	do.
Middleton Cheney (a) (b) -	par.	1,170	1,780	6,436	Banbury -	do.
†Upper Boddington -	par.	301 { In Lower Boddington. }		2,835	Byfield -	do.
Warkworth with Nethercote and Grimsbury (a) -	par.	2,467	2,370	11,101	Banbury -	do.

COUNTY of OXFORD :

Alkerton -	par.	159	742	1,254	Banbury -	Banbury South.
Banbury -	par.	3,600	81	18,898	do. -	{ Borough of Banbury (Separate Quarter Sessions).
Barford Saint John -	cha.	80	726	1,309	Deddington -	Banbury South.
*Barford Saint Michael	par.	298	1,102	2,139	do. -	Deddington South.
Bloxham -	par.	1,538	3,142	7,988	Banbury -	Banbury South.
Bodicott (a) -	cha.	687	1,291	4,127	do. -	do.

(continued)

BALA UNION :

(a) A detached part of Llanfawr was amalgamated with Llandderfil and parts of Llandderfil were amalgamated with Llanfawr by Order which came into operation on 25 March 1885.

BANBURY UNION :

(a) By Orders which came into operation on 25 March 1884,—

A detached part of Chipping Warden was amalgamated with Aston le Wall ;

BANBURY UNION—continued.

Two detached parts of Middleton Cheney were amalgamated with Warkworth with Nethercote and Grimsbury ;

A part of Warkworth with Nethercote and Grimsbury, situate on the right bank of the River Cherwell, was amalgamated with Bodicott ; and

A detached part of Byfield, in the Daventry Union, was amalgamated with Chipping Warden.

(b) Four detached parts of Marston Saint Lawrence, in the Brackley Union, were amalgamated with Middleton Cheney by Provisional Order which came into operation on 25 March 1885.

Unions and Parishes, &c.	Population in 1881.	Area in Statute Acres in 1881	Rateable Value in 1881.	Post Town.	Petty Sessional Division.

BANBURY UNION—County of Oxford—*continued.*

£

	Population in 1881.	Area in Statute Acres in 1881	Rateable Value in 1881.	Post Town.	Petty Sessional Division.
Bourton (Great and Little) - *ham.*	498	1,681	1,531	Banbury -	Banbury North.
Broughton - *par.*	158	975	2,081	do. - -	Banbury South.
Clattercott - *par.*	9	338	735	Leamington -	Banbury North.
Claydon - *cha.*	300	1,199	2,708	Banbury -	do.
Cropredy - *par.*	515	1,926	4,958	Leamington -	do.
Drayton - *par.*	162	926	1,729	Banbury - -	do.
East Adderbury - *tow.*	909	2,058	6,057	do. - -	Banbury South.
East Shutford - *tow.*	21	409	602	do. - -	Banbury North.
Epwell - *tow.*	259	1,140	1,820	do. - -	do.
Hanwell - *par.*	253	1,271	2,131	do. - -	do.
Hook Norton - *par.*	1,232	5,495	9,104	Chipping Norton -	Chaddlington.
Horley - *par.*	315	1,141	2,038	Banbury -	Banbury North.
Hornton - *par.*	500	1,473	2,729	do. - -	do.
Milcombe - *cha.*	221	1,255	2,110	do. - -	Banbury South.
Milton - *ham.*	131	810	1,752	do. - -	do.
Mollington - *cha.*	158	783	1,301	do. - -	Banbury North.
Neithrop (W.) - *tow.*	6,060	3,327	21,690	do. - -	do.
North Newington - *tow.*	418	1,108	1,968	do. - -	Banbury South.
Prescott - *lord.*	31	555	909	Leamington -	do.
Shenington - *par.*	385	1,628	2,623	Banbury -	Banbury North.
Sibford-Ferris - *tow.*	267	1,008	2,111	do. - -	do.
Sibford-Gower - *tow.*	431	1,758	3,220	do. - -	do.
*South Newington - *par.*	324	1,437	2,636	do. - -	Deddington.
Swalcliffe - *par.*	358	1,679	2,678	do. - -	Banbury North.
Tadmarton - *par.*	357	2,070	3,316	do. - -	do.
Wardington - *cha.*	623	2,572	5,368	do. - -	do.
West Adderbury - *tow.*	313	1,150	2,932	do. - -	Banbury South.
West Shutford - *tow.*	313	952	1,671	do. - -	Banbury North.
Wigginton - *par.*	265	1,187	1,982	do. - -	Banbury South.
Wroxton and Balscott - *par.*	662	2,543	4,929	do. - -	Banbury North.

COUNTY of WARWICK :

†Avon Dassett - *par.*	271	1,580	2,706	Leamington -	Burton Dassett.
†Farnborough - *par.*	376	1,953	4,177	Banbury - -	do.
*Mollington - *cha.*	117	620	995	do. - -	do.
†Radway - *par.*	255	1,530	2,440	Kineton -	Kineton.
†Ratley - *par.*	407	1,500	2,555	Banbury - -	Burton Dassett.
Shotteswell - *par.*	242	1,860	2,339	do. - -	do.
†Warmington - *par.*	388	1,750	3,570	do. - -	do.
TOTAL of UNION -	**30,120**	**78,015**	**193,563**		

BANGOR AND BEAUMARIS UNION.

(Formed 30 May 1837 by Order dated 4 May 1837.—Places marked thus * added 29 Sept. 1852 by Order dated 13 Sept. 1852.)

COUNTY of ANGLESEY :

Beaumaris - *par.*	1,907	1,220	5,543	Beaumaris - -	First Division of the County of Anglesey.
Llanddaniel Fab - *par.*	474	1,679	1,948	Llanfair-pwll-gwyn-gyll, Anglesey.	do.
Llanddona - *par.*	463	2,387	1,484	Beaumaris - -	do.
Llandegfan - *par.*	1,051	2,760	3,641	do. - -	do.
Llandysilio - *par.*	1,619	917	4,206	Menai Bridge -	do.
Llanedwen - *par.*	305	1,939	2,375	Llanfair-pwll-gwyn-gyll, Anglesey.	do.
Llanfaes - *par.*	234	2,297	2,661	Beaumaris -	do.
Llanfair-pwll-gwyn-gyll - *par.*	903	952	2,222	Llanfair-pwll-gwyn-gyll, Anglesey.	do.
Llanfinnan - *par.*	109	1,267	933	Llangefni, Anglesey	do.
Llanfihangel Esceifiog *par.*	903	2,889	3,398	Gaerwin, do.	do.
Llanfihangel-tyn-syl-wy - *par.*	48	833	586	Beaumaris, do.	do.

(continued)

Unions and Parishes, &c.		Population in 1881.	Area in Statute Acres in 1881.	Rateable Value in 1881.	Post Town.	Petty Sessional Division.
				£		
Bangor and Beaumaris Union—County of Anglesey—*continued.*						
*Llangadwaladr	par.	467	4,718	2,165	Llangefni, Anglesey	First Division of the County of Anglesey.
Llangoed	par.	609	1,343	1,702	Beaumaris, do.	do.
*Llangristiolus	par.	764	3,936	3,308	Llangefni, do.	do.
Llaniestyn	par.	177	1,663	1,397	Beaumaris, do.	do.
Llansadwrn	par.	382	2,891	2,849	Llanfair-pwll-gwyn-gyll, Anglesey.	do.
Penmon	par.	242	7,238	972	Beaumaris, Anglesey	do.
Penmynydd	par.	406	3,153	3,455	Llanfair-pwll-gwyn-gyll, Anglesey.	do.
*Pentraeth	par.	824	4,013	3,173	Pentraeth, Anglesey	do.
*Trefdraeth	par.	894	3,135	4,102	Llangefni do.	do.
County of Carnarvon :						
Aber	par.	442	8,833	4,086	Bangor	Isgorfai.
Bangor (W.)	par.	11,370	7,543	34,445	do.	do.
Llandegai	par.	3,587	16,100	31,169	do.	do.
Llanfair fechan	par.	2,041	6,521	8,273	do.	do.
Llanllechid	par.	8,291	18,111	12,152	do.	do.
Total of Union		38,512	108,338	142,335		

BARNET UNION.

(Formed 4 July 1835 by Order dated 15 June 1835.—Place marked thus * added 15 Mar. 1839 by Order dated 26 Feb. 1839.)

County of Hertford :						
Chipping Barnet (W.)	par.	4,283	1,488	18,334	Barnet	Chipping Barnet.
East Barnet	par.	3,092	1,699	22,718	New Barnet	do.
Elstree	par.	662	1,508	6,069	Elstree	do.
Ridge	par.	406	3,615	5,651	Barnet	do.
Shenley	par.	1,321	4,090	8,536	do.	do.
Totteridge	par.	657	1,605	4,429	Whetstone, N.	do.
County of Middlesex :						
*Finchley	par.	11,191	3,384	50,608	Finchley	Finsbury.
Friern-Barnet	par.	6,424	1,304	19,760	Whetstone, N.	do.
Hadley	par.	1,160	641	6,921	Barnet	South Mimms.
South Mimms	par.	4,002	6,386	23,076	do.	do.
Total of Union		34,098	25,720	166,102		

BARNSLEY UNION.

(Formed 15 Jan. 1850 by Order dated 28 Dec. 1849.)

County of York, West Riding :						
Ardsley	tow.	3,333	1,259	13,340	Barnsley	Barnsley.
Barnsley (W.)	tow.	29,790	2,386	88,637	do.	do.
Barugh	tow.	2,444	1,437	6,589	do.	do.
Billingley	tow.	198	862	1,568	do.	Doncaster.
Carlton	tow.	1,085	1,978	10,719	do.	Barnsley.
Cudworth	tow.	1,044	1,744	5,840	do.	do.
Darfield	tow.	2,616	2,017	12,362	do.	do.
Darton	tow.	2,960	1,378	6,735	do.	do.
Dodworth	tow.	2,989	1,916	16,324	do.	do.
Monk Bretton	tow.	2,918	2,221	14,144	do.	do.
Nether Hoyland	tow.	9,822	2,085	30,235	do.	do.
Notton	tow.	261	2,602	4,257	do.	do.
Royston	tow.	1,128	1,022	3,524	do.	do.
Stainbrough	tow.	529	1,719	9,143	do.	do.
Wombwell	tow.	8,451	3,851	41,902	do.	do.
Woolley	tow.	600	2,587	7,392	Wakefield	do.
Worsbrough	tow.	8,443	3,779	33,162	Barnsley	do.
Total of Union		78,611	31,843	305,873		

Unions and Parishes, &c.	Population in 1881.	Area in Statute Acres in 1881.	Rateable Value in 1881.	Post Town.	Petty Sessional Division.

BARNSTAPLE UNION.

(Formed 2 Dec. 1835 by Order dated 12 Nov. 1835.)

COUNTY of DEVON :

£

Unions and Parishes, &c.	Population in 1881.	Area in Statute Acres in 1881.	Rateable Value in 1881.	Post Town.	Petty Sessional Division.
Arlington - - *par.*	231	2,535	2,869	Barnstaple -	Braunton.
Ashford - - *par.*	162	359	1,164	do. - -	do.
Atherington - - *par*	518	3,326	3,374	do. - -	do.
Barnstaple (W.) (*b*) - *par.*	9,518	1.102	26,196	do. - -	(Separate Quarter Sessions.)
Berry-narbor - - *par.*	683	4,958	5,238	Ilfracombe -	Braunton.
Bishops Tawton (*b*) - *par.*	1,895	4,263	10,346	Barnstaple -	do.
Bittadon - - *par.*	51	1,018	891	do. -	do.
Bratton Fleming - *par.*	523	5,845	5,983	do. -	do.
Braunton - - *par.*	2,089	11,983	12,131	do. -	do.
Brendon - - *par.*	245	6,733	2,297	do. -	do.
Challacombe - - *par.*	223	5,343	2,864	do. -	do.
Combe Martin - *par.*	1,318	3,815	5,380	Ilfracombe -	do.
Countisbury - - *par.*	164	3,512	1,487	Barnstaple -	do.
East Down - - *par.*	360	3,643	4,122	do. -	do.
Fremington - - *par.*	1,235	6,810	7,836	do. -	do.
Georgeham (*a*) - *par.*	764	4,229	5,585	do. -	do.
Goodleigh - - *par.*	250	1,167	1,744	do. -	do.
Heanton Punchardon *par.*	439	3,020	4,234	do. -	do.
High Bray - - *par.*	207	4,273	3,228	do. -	do.
Horwood - - *par.*	112	860	956	do. -	do.
Ilfracombe - - *par.*	6,255	5,583	28,689	Ilfracombe -	do.
Instow - - *par.*	637	1,916	2,705	Barnstaple -	Braunton.
Kentisbury - - *par.*	349	3,129	3,805	do. -	do.
Landkey - - *par.*	597	3,162	4,824	do. -	do.
Linton - - *par.*	1,213	7,193	6,533	do. -	do.
Loxhore - - *par.*	211	1,530	1,585	do. -	do.
Martinhoe - - *par.*	192	2,549	1,183	do. -	do.
Marwood - - *par.*	808	5,396	5,757	do. -	do.
Morthoe (*a*) - - *par.*	430	4,621	3,552	do. -	do.
Newton Tracey - *par.*	125	336	582	do. -	do.
Paracombe - - *par.*	382	4,363	3,807	do. -	do.
Pilton - - *par.*	2,003	1,861	7,130	do. -	do.
Sherwill - - *par.*	408	4,762	4,452	do. -	do.
Stoke Rivers - *par.*	197	2,426	2,207	do. -	do.
Swymbridge - - *par.*	1,218	7,280	8,200	do. -	do.
Tawstock - - *par.*	1,062	6,582	8,142	do. -	do.
Trentishoe - - *par.*	84	1,571	982	do. -	do.
West Down - - *par.*	532	4,059	4,615	Ilfracombe -	do.
Westleigh - - *par.*	496	2,616	3,329	Bideford -	Bideford.
TOTAL of UNION -	38,206	149,729	210,024		

BARROW-IN-FURNESS PARISH.

(Board of Guardians constituted 19 April 1876 by Order dated 6 Mar. 1876. Formerly in the Ulverstone Union.)

COUNTY of LANCASTER :

Unions and Parishes, &c.	Population in 1881.	Area in Statute Acres in 1881.	Rateable Value in 1881.	Post Town.	Petty Sessional Division.
Barrow-in-Furness (W.) *par.*	47,259	10,967	195,092	Barrow-in-Furness	Barrow-in-Furness.

BARNSTAPLE UNION :

(*a*) A detached part of the parish of Morthoe was amalgamated with the parish of Georgeham by Order which came into operation on 25 March 1884.

(*b*) All the part of the parish of Bishops Tawton, situate in the municipal borough of Barnstaple, was amalgamated with the parish of Barnstaple, by Provisional Order which came into operation on 25 March 1885.

Unions and Parishes, &c.	Population in 1881.	Area in Statute Acres in 1881.	Rateable Value in 1881.	Post Town.	Petty Sessional Division.

BARROW-UPON-SOAR UNION.

(Formed 11 Sept. 1837 by Order dated 17 Aug. 1837.— Places marked thus * added 29 Sept. 1858 by Order dated 25 June 1858.)

COUNTY of LEICESTER :

Unions and Parishes, &c.	Population in 1881.	Area in Statute Acres in 1881.	Rateable Value (£) in 1881.	Post Town.	Petty Sessional Division.
Anstey (a) - *tow.*	1,279 {	In Thurcaston. }	3,654	Leicester -	Leicester.
*Anstey Pastures - *par.*	43	—	554	do. -	do.
Barkby - *tow.*	579	2,290	6,322	do. -	do.
Barkby Thorpe - *tow.*	47	In Barkby	800	do. -	do.
Barrow upon Soar (a) *tow.*	2,024	2,510	15,020	Loughborough	Loughborough.
*Beaumont Leys - *par.*	39	1,210	1,500	Leicester -	Leicester.
Beeby - *par.*	108	1,020	2,011	do. -	do.
Belgrave - *tow.*	7,260 }	2,230 {	26,730	do. -	do.
Birstall - *tow.*	487 }		3,740	do. -	do.
Cossington - *par.*	403	1,551	6,853	do. -	do.
Cropston - *tow.*	114 {	In Thurcaston. }	2,406	do. -	do.
Croxton South (a) - *par.*	251	1,760	2,329	do. -	do.
*Gilroe or Gilroes - *par.*	27	—	448	do. -	do.
*Leicester Abbey - *par.*	35	25	2,642	do. -	do.
Mountsorrell (a) - *tow.*	(a)	(a)	(a)	Loughborough	Loughborough.
Newtown Linford (a) } *par.*	479	3,990	3,994	Leicester -	Leicester.
(b) }					
Queeniborough - *par.*	549	1,390	5,189	do. -	do.
Quorndon - *tow.*	1,816	1,990	8,972	Loughborough	Loughborough.
Ratcliffe on the Wreake *par.*	106	880	1,585	Leicester -	Leicester.
Rearsby - *par.*	477	1,800	4,685	do. -	do.
Rothley (W.) (a) - *tow.*	1,048	(c) 2,170	4,065	Loughborough	Loughborough.
Seagrave - *par.*	360	2,470	3,074	do. -	do.
*Sherman's Grounds } *par.*	35	—	738	Leicester -	Leicester.
or Leicester Frith }					
Sileby - *par.*	2,033	2,190	11,813	Loughborough	Loughborough.
Swithland - *par.*	246	2,180	2,073	do. -	do.
Syston - *par.*	2,170	1,380	12,583	Leicester -	Leicester.
Thrussington - *par.*	604	2,200	4,013	Melton Mowbray	Melton Mowbray.
Thurcaston - *tow.*	223	2,060	1,958	Leicester -	Leicester.
Thurmaston North - *tow.*	420	In Barkby	3,232	do. -	do.
Thurmaston South - *tow.*	1,125	1,220	8,280	do. -	do.
Ulverscroft (a) - *par.*	91	—	1,753	Loughborough	Loughborough.
Walton on the Wolds *par.*	227	1,720	2,326	do. -	do.
Wanlip - *par.*	108	952	2,014	Leicester -	Leicester.
Woodhouse (a) - *tow.*	1,288	3,980	7,649	Loughborough	Loughborough.
TOTAL of UNION -	**26,431** (a)	**46,068** (a)	**165,125** (a)		

BARROW UPON SOAR UNION:

(a) By Orders which came into operation on 25 March 1884.—

A detached part of Barsby, in the Melton Mowbray Union, was amalgamated with Croxton South, and a detached part of Croxton South was amalgamated with Barsby ;

The several parts of a parish known as Rothley Temple (population 91, rateable value 1,173l.) were amalgamated with the respective parishes of Mountsorrell South and Rothley ;

The part of the township of Mountsorrell North situate on the east bank of the River Soar, was amalgamated with Barrow - upon - Soar; and the residue was amalgamated with Mountsorrell South, the name of the latter being altered to the township of Mountsorrell. (Mountsorrell North, population 1,272, rateable value 4,347l.) Mountsorrell South, population 1,015, acreage (including Mountsorrell North) 680, and rateable value 1,636l.)

BARROW UPON SOAR UNION—continued.

The several parts of a parish known as Broadgate, otherwise Bradgate Park (population 6, acreage 1,120, rateable value 2,010l.), were amalgamated with Ulverscroft, Anstey, and Newtown Linford respectively ;

Detached parts of the parish of Newtown Linford were amalgamated with Rothley and Ulverscroft :

A detached part of Newtown Linford was amalgamated with Markfield, in the Market Bosworth Union ; and

The several parts of a parish known as Mapplewell Longdale (population 20, rateable value 134l.) were amalgamated with Woodhouse.

(b) A detached part of Newtown Linford was amalgamated with Charley, in the Loughborough Union, by a Provisional Order which came into operation on 25 March 1885.

(c) Including the area known as Rothley Temple.

Unions and Parishes, &c.	Population in 1881.	Area in Statute Acres in 1881.	Rateable Value in 1881.	Post Town.	Petty Sessional Division.
BARTON REGIS UNION.					
(Formed as the Clifton Union 9 April 1836 by Order dated 26 Mar. 1836 ; the name of the Union altered 14 Mar. 1877 by Order dated 22 Feb. 1877.— Place marked thus * added 4 April by Order dated 1 April 1885.)					
BOROUGH of the CITY of BRISTOL and COUNTY of the same CITY :			£		
Clifton - - par.	28,695	915	185,077	Bristol - -	Bristol (Separate Quarter Sessions).
Saint James and Saint Paul Out - } par.	19,114	457	68,809	do. - -	do.
Saint Philip and Saint Jacob Out . } par.	50,108	765	128,583	do. - -	do.
COUNTY of GLOUCESTER :					
Filton (a) - - par.	296	1,040	2,628	do. - -	Lawfords Gate.
Henbury (a) (b) - par.	2,126	8,241	22,304	do. - -	do.
Horfield (a) · - par.	5,739	1,299	18,383	do. - -	do.
Saint George - - par.	26,433	1,831	62,524	do. - -	do.
*Shirehampton (a) - par.	In Westbury upon Trym.			do. - -	do.
Stapleton (W.) - par.	10,833	2,554	31,586	do. - -	do.
Stoke Gifford (a) - par.	342	2,323	4,069	do. - -	do.
Winterbourne (a) - par.	3,151	3,281	12,734	do. - -	do.
In the BOROUGH of the CITY of BRISTOL and COUNTY of the same CITY, and in the COUNTY of GLOUCESTER :					
Westbury-upon-Trym (a) } par.	19,209	5,456	{ 88,130 41,275 }	do. - -	Lawfords Gate and Bristol (Separate Quarter Sessions).
TOTAL of UNION -	166,136	28,162	666,102		
BARTON-UPON-IRWELL UNION.					
(Formed 30 Oct. 1849 by Order dated 9 Oct. 1849. Prior to 30 Oct. 1849 it formed part of the Chorlton Union.)					
COUNTY of LANCASTER :					
Barton - upon - Irwell (W.) - - } tow.	25,994	10,621	121,333	Patricroft - -	Salford Hundred.
Clifton - - tow.	2,578	1,194	26,673	Clifton - -	do.
Flixton - - tow.	1,776	1,564	11,274	Flixton - -	do.
Stretford - - tow.	19,018	3,255	118,760	Stretford - -	do.
Urmston - - tow.	2,242	993	14,414	Urmston - -	do.
Worsley - - tow.	21,207	6,928	82,626	Worsley - -	do.
TOTAL of UNION -	72,815	24,555	375,080		

BARTON REGIS UNION :

(a) By Orders which came into operation on 25 March 1885,—

A detached part of Filton was amalgamated with Horfield ;

A nearly detached part of Westbury upon Trym was amalgamated with Henbury ;

Two detached parts of Winterbourne were amalgamated with Stoke Gifford ;

BARTON REGIS UNION.—continued.

A part of Westbury upon Trym, known as the Tything of Shirehampton, which includes Dung Ball Island, was constituted a separate parish and designated the parish of Shirehampton ; and

A detached part of Winterbourne was amalgamated with Westerleigh in the Chipping Sodbury Union

(b) All the parts of Compton Greenfield were amalgamated with Henbury, by Provisional Order which came into operation on 25 March 1886.

Unions and Parishes, &c.	Population in 1881.	Area in Statute Acres in 1881.	Rateable Value in 1881.	Post Town.	Petty Sessional Division.

BASFORD UNION.

(Formed 2 May 1836 by Order dated 13 April 1836. Places marked thus * added 1 May 1878 by Order dated 17 April 1878.)

COUNTY of DERBY:

				£		
Codnor cum Loscoe	-	tow.	3,591	1,931	10,183	Derby	-	-	Smalley.
Codnor Park	-	par.	1,073	1,458	8,747	Alfreton	-	do.
Heanor	-	tow.	6,822	1,579	17,848	Nottingham	-	do.
Ilkestone	-	par.	14,122	2,526	35,560	do.	-	do.
Shipley	-	tow.	724	2,111	8,092	Derby	-	do.

COUNTY of NOTTINGHAM:

Annesley	-	par.	1,445	3,125	8,641	Nottingham	Nottingham.
Arnold	-	par.	5,745	4,670	14,908	do.	-	do.
Barton	-	par.	276	1,620	2,663	do.	-	do.
Basford (W.)	-	par.	18,137	2,720	49,496	do.	-	Borough of Nottingham.
Beeston	-	par.	4,479	1,440	13,806	do.	-	Nottingham.
*Bestwood Park (a)	-	par.	697	3,504	9,591	do.	-	do.
Bilborough	-	par.	199	1,090	2,040	do.	-	do.
Bradmore	-	par.	279	1,560	1,950	do.	-	do.
Bulwell	-	par.	8,375	1,210	17,883	do.	-	Borough of Nottingham.
Bunny	-	par.	262	2,000	3,326	do.	-	Nottingham.
Burton Joyce	-	tow.	668	970	2,960	do.	-	do.
Calverton	-	par.	1,246	3,320	4,848	do.	-	do.
Carlton	-	ham.	4,625	4,490	9,786	do.	-	do.
Clifton with Glapton	par.	382	1,980	3,967	do.	-	do.
Colwick	-	par.	113	1,255	6,666	do.	-	do.
Cossall	-	par.	244	987	3,983	do.	-	do.
Eastwood	-	par.	3,566	951	10,887	do.	-	do.
Felley	-	par.	31	413	306	do.	-	do.
Gamston	-	tow.	95	In West Bridgeford.	1,004	do.	-	Bingham.
Gedling	-	tow.	506	In Carlton	5,637	do.	-	Nottingham.
Gotham	-	par.	1,026	2,740	4,844	Derby	do.
Greasley	-	par.	8,867	7,220	37,906	Nottingham	-	do.
Hucknall Torkard	-	par.	10,023	3,270	24,379	do.	-	Mansfield.
Kirkby in Ashfield	-	par.	4,212	5,814	12,328	Mansfield	-	Nottingham.
Lambley	-	par.	803	2,170	3,904	Nottingham	-	Nottingham.
Linby	-	par.	320	1,188	6,784	do.	-	do.
Newstead	-	lib.	967	3,258	6,575	do.	-	do.
Nuthall	-	par.	1,466	1,586	8,197	do.	-	do.
Papplewick (a)	-	par.	331	1,902	1,877	do.	-	do.
Ruddington	-	par.	2,638	2,190	10,527	do.	-	Mansfield.
Selston	-	par.	4,373	3,318	13,892	Alfreton	-	Nottingham.
Stoke Bardolph	-	tow.	176	In Carlton	2,120	Nottingham	-	Nottingham.
Strelley	-	par.	252	1,069	2,622	do.	-	do.
Thrumpton	-	par.	163	1,080	2,362	Derby	-	do.
Trowell	-	par.	421	1,621	3,527	Nottingham	-	do.
West Bridgeford	-	tow.	293	1,720	2,879	do.	-	do.
Wilford	-	par.	1,106	1,450	9,327	do.	-	do.
Wollaton	-	par.	712	2,340	7,194	do.	-	do.
Woodborough	-	par.	889	1,910	4,153	do.	-	do.
TOTAL of UNION	-		116,940	93,176	420,175		

BASFORD UNION:

(a) Certain parts of the parish of Papplewick were amalgamated with the parish of Bestwood Park, by Order which came into operation on 25 March 1883.

Unions and Parishes, &c.	Population in 1881.	Area in Statute Acres in 1881.	Rateable Value in 1881.	Post Town.	Petty Sessional Division.

BASINGSTOKE UNION.

(Formed 18 May 1835 by Order dated 2 May 1835. — Places marked thus * added 25 Dec. 1861 by Order dated 27 Sept. 1861, and place marked thus † added 26 Mar. 1879 by Order dated 24 Feb. 1879.—The names of the places marked thus § are as altered by Order dated 18 June 1886.)

COUNTY of SOUTHAMPTON :

			£		
*Andwell - - *par.*	45	148	305	Basingstoke -	Basingstoke.
Basing (W.) - *par.*	1,310	5,635	10,664	do. - -	do.
Basingstoke - *par.*	6,681	4,172	31,763	do. - -	do.
Bradley - *par.*	75	974	872	Alresford -	do.
Bramley - *par.*	449	2,297	3,281	Basingstoke -	do.
Cliddesden *par.*	334	1,919	2,392	do. - -	do.
Dean - *par.*	145	1,586	2.801	Micheldever Station	do.
§Dummer with Kempshot (a) - }*par.*	(a) 390	(a) 2.774	(a) 3.306	Basingstoke -	do.
Eastrope, otherwise Eastrop - }*par.*	141	310	865	do. - -	do.
Ellisfield, otherwise Ilsfield - }*par.*	254	2,349	1,986	do. - -	do.
Farleigh-Wallop - *par.*	106	1,725	1,493	do. - -	do.
Hartley - Westpall, otherwise Hartley-Westpale }*par.*	236	1,420	1,997	do. - -	do.
Herriard - *par.*	406	2,978	2,812	do. - -	do.
Mappledurwell - *par.*	214	829	1,273	do. - -	do.
†Mortimer West End - *ty.*	384	2,292	2,055	Reading - -	do.
Nately Skewers - *par.*	248	521	1,020	Basingstoke -	do.
Newnham - *par.*	359	1,404	3,642	Winchfield -	do.
North Waltham - *par.*	415	1,958	2,178	Micheldever Station	do.
Nutley - *par.*	129	1,524	1,081	Basingstoke -	do.
Oakley, otherwise Church-Oakley }*par.*	297	1,630	2,687	do. - -	do.
Pamber - *par.*	694	2,185	2,063	do. - -	do.
Popham - *par.*	106	1,440	1,240	Micheldever Station	do.
Preston-Candover - *par.*	414	3,457	3,379	Basingstoke -	do.
Sherborne Saint John *par.*	639	3,972	4,860	do. - -	do.
Shirfield - *par.*	642	2,337	3,919	do. - -	do.
Silchester - *par.*	472	1,915	2,360	Reading - -	do.
Steventon - *par.*	288	2,155	4,062	Micheldever Station	Kingsclere.
Stratfield-Saye - *par.*	573	2,743	3,972	Winchfield -	Basingstoke.
Stratfield-Turgis - *par.*	197	1,042	1,546	do. - -	do.
Tunworth - *par.*	112	1,105	1,057	Basingstoke -	do.
Up-Nately - *par.*	117	1,149	1,195	do. - -	do.
Upton-Grey - *par.*	416	2,553	2,997	Winchfield -	do.
*Weston Corbett - *par.*	10	513	513	do. - -	do.
Weston Patrick - *par.*	157	1,186	865	do. - -	do.
West Sherborne, otherwise Monk's Sherbourn - }*par.*	473	2,985	3,911	Basingstoke -	do.
§Winslade (a) - *par.*	(a) 112	(a) 712	(a) 719	do. - -	do.
Woodmancot - *par.*	78	1,404	1,069	Micheldever Station	do.
Wooton St. Lawrence *par.*	996	4,406	7,493	Basingstoke -	do.
Worting - *par.*	160	1,145	2,534	do. - -	do.
TOTAL of UNION -	19,274	76,879	128,227		

BATH UNION.

(Formed 28 Mar. 1836 by Order dated 8 Feb. 1836. — Place marked thus * added 30 Sept. 1882 by Order dated 29 July 1882.)

COUNTY of SOMERSET :

Bath Easton - *par.*	1,637	1,863	10,513	Bath - -	Weston.
Bath Ford - *par.*	953	1,820	6,719	do. - -	do. *(continued)*

BASINGSTOKE UNION :

(a) By Order dated 8 December 1879, the part of Winslade known as Kempshot was transferred to Dummer.

Unions and Parishes, &c.	Population in 1881.	Area in Statute Acres in 1881.	Rateable Value in 1881.	Post Town.	Petty Sessional Division.
			£		
BATH UNION—County of Somerset—*continued.*					
Bath Hampton - *par.*	410	931	6,119	Bath - -	Weston.
Bathwick - - *par.*	5,167	573	35,030	do. - -	Bath.
Charlcomb (*a*) - *par.*	622	571	5,656	do. - -	Weston.
Charterhouse Hinton *par.*	548	2,890	4,306	do. - -	do.
Claverton - - *par.*	251	1,228	3,058	do. - -	do.
Combhay - - *par.*	181	1,091	1,566	do. - -	do.
Dunkerton (*b*) - *par.*	1,019	1,233	3,215	do. - -	do.
English Combe (*a*) - *par.*	524	1,852	3,116	do. - -	do.
*Freshford - - *par.*	615	561	3,086	do. - -	do.
Langridge (*a*) - *par.*	80	655	988	do. - -	do.
Lyncombe and Wid-⎫ *par.* combe (W.) ⎭	12,277	1,845	44,290	do. - -	Bath.
Moncton Combe - *par.*	1,495	720	5,877	do. - -	Weston.
Saint Catherine - *par.*	136	1,040	1,994	do. - -	do.
Saint James - - *par.*	5,043		21,387	do. - -	Bath.
Saint Michael - - *par.*	2,322	In Wal-⎫ cot.	22,833	do. - -	do.
Saint Peter and Saint ⎫ *par.* Paul - - ⎭	2,070	⎬	17,861	do. - -	do.
South Stoke - - *par.*	389	863	2,674	do. - -	Weston.
Swanswick - - *par.*	633	815	3,883	do. - -	do.
Twerton (*a*) - *par.*	4,833	971	16,971	do. - -	do.
Walcot (*a*) - - *par.*	21,980	1,023	128,011	do. - -	Bath.
Wellow - - *par.*	1,383	5,292	9,507	do. - -	Weston.
Weston (*a*) - - *par.*	3,606	2,650	21,697	do. - -	do.
Woolley - - *par.*	61	365	1,067	do. - -	do.
TOTAL of UNION -	71,241	30,882	384,724		

BATTLE UNION:
(Formed 10 June 1835 by Order
dated 22 May 1835.)
COUNTY of SUSSEX : -

Ashburnham (*b*) - *par.*	774	3,691	3,671	Battle - -	Battle division of Hastings Rape.
Battle (W.) - - *par.*	3,319	8,253	13,779	do. - -	do.
Bexhill - - *par.*	2,452	8,015	14,314	Hastings - -	Hastings. do.
Brightling (*b*) - *par.*	674	1,647	3,282	Hawkhurst -	Battle. do.
Catsfield (*b*) - *par.*	705	2,991	3,052	Battle - -	do. do.
Crowhurst - - *par.*	421	2,168	3,631	do. - -	do. do.
Dallington (*b*) - *par.*	522	2,894	1,959	Hawkhurst -	do. do.
Ewhurst - - *par.*	1,095	5,816	6,126	do. - -	do. do.
Hollington - - *par.*	1,752	2,463	8,964	St. Leonards on Sea	do. do.
Mountfield (*a*) - *par.*	622	3,900	5,195	Hawkhurst -	do. do.
Penhurst - - *par.*	106	1,455	705	Battle - -	do. do.
Sedlescomb - - *par.*	648	2,065	2,484	do. - -	do. do.
Westfield - - *par.*	1,051	4,314	5,133	do. - -	do. do.
Whatlington - - *par.*	378	1,260	2,080	do. - -	do. do.
TOTAL of UNION -	14,519	53,962	74,375		

BATH UNION :

(*a*) By Order which came into operation on 25 March 1885.—

    A detached part of Weston was amalgamated with the parish of Laugridge;

    A detached part of Walcot was amalgamated with Charlcomb; and

    A nearly detached part of English Combe was amalgamated with Twerton.

(*b*) By Provisional Order which came into operation on 25 March 1886, certain parts of Camerton, in the Clutton Union, were amalgamated with Dunkerton, and certain parts of Dunkerton were amalgamated with Camerton.

BATTLE UNION :

(*a*) By Provisional Order which came into operation on 25 March 1886,—

    A detached part of Etchingham, in the Ticehurst Union, was amalgamated with Mountfield.

(*b*) By Provisional Orders which came into operation on 25 March 1887,—

    Certain parts of Ashburnham and Dallington were amalgamated respectively with Ninfield and Warbleton, in the Hailsham Union ;

    Certain parts of Dallington were amalgamated with Ashburnham and Brightling ; and

    A detached part of Ninfield, in the Hailsham Union, was amalgamated with Catsfield.

Unions and Parishes, &c.		Population in 1881.	Area in Statute Acres in 1881.	Rateable Value in 1881.	Post Town.	Petty Sessional Division.

BEAMINSTER UNION.

(Formed 28 Mar. 1836 by Order dated 12 Mar. 1836.)

COUNTY of DORSET:

				£		
Beaminster	- par.	2,130	5,118	9,211	Beaminster	- Bridport.
Bettiscombe (a)	- par.	63	667	768	Crewkerne	- do.
Broadwinsor	- par.	1,256	6,214	8,142	Beaminster	- do.
Burstock	- par.	190	913	1,264	do. -	- do.
Cheddington	- par.	114	773	938	Crewkerne	- do.
Corscombe (a)	- par.	653	5,003	5,265	Dorchester	- do.
East Chelborough	- par.	113	948	1,037	do. -	- do.
Evershot (b)	- par.	500	1,409	1,997	do. -	- Dorchester.
Halstock	- par.	441	3,181	2,773	Yeovil	- Bridport.
Hooke (a) -	- par.	154	1,237	1,348	Beaminster	- do.
Mapperton -	- par.	103	804	1,225	do. -	- do.
Marshwood (a)	- par.	335	3,396	2,893	Crewkerne	- do.
Melbury Osmund	- par.	389	1,192	1,405	Dorchester	- Sherborne.
Melbury Sampford	- par.	70	1,024	1,114	do. -	- Dorchester.
Mosterton	- par.	321	958	1,453	Crewkerne	- Bridport.
Netherbury	- par.	1,584	6,225	10,953	Beaminster	- do.
North Poorton (a)	- par.	61	661	739	do. -	- do.
Pilsdon -	- par.	92	648	675	Bridport -	- do.
Poorstock (a)	- par.	821	4,078	4,824	do. -	- do.
Rampisham	- par.	290	2,030	2,385	Dorchester	- Dorchester.
South Perrott	- par.	303	1,451	1,996	Crewkerne	- Bridport.
Stoke Abbot (W.)	- par.	551	2,303	3,676	Beaminster	- do.
West Chelborough	- par.	62	578	607	Dorchester	- do.
Wraxall	- par.	97	952	1,086	do. -	- do.

COUNTY of SOMERSET:

Misterton	- par.	670	1,417	2,706	Crewkerne	- Crewkerne.
Seaborough	- par.	105	581	819	do. -	- do.
TOTAL of UNION	-	11,468	53,764	71,319		

BEDALE UNION.

(Formed 28 Mar. 1839 by Order dated 4 Mar. 1839. — Place marked thus * added 15 May 1850 by Order dated 24 April 1850; and places marked thus † added 29 Sept. 1869 by Order dated 10 Aug. 1869.)

COUNTY of YORK, NORTH RIDING.

Ainderby Miers with Holtby	tow.	73	953	1,344	Bedale	- Hang, East.
Aiskew -	tow.	831	2,035	5,959	do. -	- do.
Bedale (W.)	tow.	1,046	1,682	5,828	do. -	- do.
Burniston -	tow.	253	1,228	2,529	do. -	- Hallikeld.
†Burrell-with-Cowling	tow.	100	1,071	1,440	do. -	- Hang, East.
†Burton-upon-Ure (a)	tow.	152	2,289	2,661	Masham via Bedale	do.
*Carthorp -	tow.	325	2,112	3,353	Bedale	- Hallikeld.
†Clifton-upon-Ure	tow.	61	594	753	do. -	- Hang, East.
Crakehall -	tow.	484	1,885	3,702	do. -	- do.
Exilby, Leeming, and Newton	tow.	690	2,439	4,864	do. -	- do.
Firby -	tow.	84	685	1,151	do. -	- do. (continued)

BEAMINSTER UNION:

(a) By Orders which came into operation on 25 March 1881,—

A detached part of Corscombe was amalgamated with Hooke;

A nearly detached part of Poorstock was amalgamated with North Poorton; and

Certain detached parts of Whitchurch Canonicorum, in the Bridport Union, were amalgamated with Bettiscombe and Marshwood respectively.

(b) A detached part of Frome Vauchurch, in the Dorchester Union, was amalgamated with Evershot, by Order which came into operation on 25 March 1885.

BEDALE UNION:

(a) By Orders which came into operation on 25 March 1886,—

Detached parts of Burton-upon-Ure were amalgamated with Ilton with Pott and Swinton with Watermarsk;

Detached parts of Ilton with Pott were amalgamated with Ellingstring, in the Leyburn Union, and Swinton with Watermarsk;

Parts of Masham were amalgamated with Fearby and Ellingstring, in the Leyburn Union, and with Ilton with Pott and Swinton with Watermarsk;

A part of Swinton with Watermarsk was amalgamated with Healy with Sutton, in the Leyburn Union, and another part was amalgamated with Masham; and

A part of Well, known as "Gibdikes," was amalgamated with Snape.

(b) There are certain common lands comprised in the Union containing in the whole 8,810 acres.

Unions and Parishes, &c.	Population in 1881.	Area in Statute Acres in 1881.	Rateable Value in 1881.	Post Town.	Petty Sessional Division.
			£		
BEDALE UNION—County of York, North Riding—continued.					
Gatenby - - tow.	51	876	1,339	Bedale - -	Hallikeld.
Hackforth - - tow.	158	1,338	1,998	do.	Hang, East.
Hton with Pott (a) - tow.	128	2,310	1,525	Masham, viâ Bedale	do.
Killerby - - tow.	59	722	922	Catterick -	do.
Kirby Fleetham - par.	552	3,154	5,328	Bedale - -	do.
Kirklington with Upsland } tow.	249	1,987	3,566	Ripon - -	Hallikeld.
Langthorne - - tow.	127	833	1,170	Bedale - -	Hang. East.
Masham (a) - - tow.	1,071	2,347	4,895	Masham, viâ Bedale	do.
Rand Grange - - tow.	15	357	542	Bedale -	Hang, East.
†Rookwith - - tow.	53	995	1,033	do. -	do.
Sernton - - par.	359	2,115	4,746	do. - -	do.
Snape (a) - - tow.	469	In Well	4,538	do. - -	do.
Swainby with Allerthorpe } tow.	46	881	1,473	do. • -	Hallikeld.
Swinton with Watermarsk (a) } tow.	152	1,707	2,358	Masham, viâ Bedale	Hang, East.
Theakstone - - tow.	48	969	1,786	Bedale - -	Hallikeld.
†Thirn - - tow.	126	638	915	do. - -	Hang, East.
Thornton Watlass - tow.	183	1,482	2,244	do. - -	do.
Well (a) - - tow.	322	6,689	2,127	do. - -	do.
TOTAL of UNION -	8,270	46,373 (b)	76,089		

BEDFORD UNION.

(Formed 21 Sept. 1835 by Order dated 1 Sept. 1835.—Places marked thus * added 16 Nov. 1835 by Order dated 23 Oct. 1835; and thus † added 29 Sept. 1863 by Order dated 15 Aug. 1863.)

COUNTY of BEDFORD.

Unions and Parishes, &c.	Population in 1881.	Area in Statute Acres in 1881.	Rateable Value in 1881.	Post Town.	Petty Sessional Division.
Biddenham - - par.	308	1,760	3,893	Bedford -	Bedford.
Bletsoe - - par.	341	2,239	3,174	do. - -	Sharnbrook.
Bolnhurst - - par.	279	2,230	2,148	St. Neots -	do.
Bromham - - par.	327	1,798	5,490	Bedford -	Bedford.
Cardington - - par.	512	5,170	4,630	do. -	do.
Carlton - - par.	474	1,530	2,277	do. -	Sharnbrook.
Chellington - - par.	97	610	850	do. -	do.
Clapham - - par.	608	1,982	3,361	do. -	Bedford.
Colmworth - - par.	385	2,310	2,700	St. Neots -	Sharnbrook.
†Colworth Farm - par.	4	{In Sharnbrook. }	36	Bedford -	do.
Cople - - par.	459	2,109	3,718	do. - -	Bedford.
Eastcots - - tow.	713	{In Cardington. }	4,607	do. -	do.
Elstow - - par.	558	1,522	7,149	do. - -	do.
Felmersham cum Radwell } par.	489	2,400	6,084	do. - -	Sharnbrook.
Goldington - - par.	579	2,735	5,235	do. -	Bedford.
Great Barford - par.	788	2,830	4,758	St. Neots -	do.
Harrold - - par.	1,024	3,240	4,754	Bedford -	Sharnbrook.
Kempston - - par.	3,432	5,160	14,441	Bedford -	Bedford.
*Keysoe - - par.	710	3,653	4,420	St. Neots -	Sharnbrook.
Knotting - - par.	186	1,724	1,874	Bedford -	do.
*Melchbourne - - par.	219	2,574	3,360	do. - -	do.
Milton Ernest - par.	421	2,070	4,230	do. - -	do.
Oakley - - par.	295	1,740	5,741	do. - -	Bedford.
Odell - - par.	422	2,980	3,368	do. - -	Sharnbrook.
Pavenham - - par.	438	1,340	4,350	do. - -	do.
Ravensden - - par.	465	2,160	2,813	do. - -	Bedford.
Renhold - - par.	516	2,165	3,210	do. - -	do.
*Riseley - - par.	958	2,980	4,403	do. - -	Sharnbrook.
Roxton - - par.	551	2,880	4,862	St. Neots -	Bedford.
Saint Cuthbert - par.	1,334		5,205	Bedford -	
Saint John - - par.	537		1,204	do. -	Borough of Bedford
Saint Mary - - par.	3,565	2,127	14,672	do. - -	[Separate Quarter
Saint Paul - - par.	10,121		43,487	do. - -	Sessions].
Saint Peter (W.) - par.	3,976		11,371	do. - -	
Sharnbrook - - par.	826	2,880	7,723	do. - -	Sharnbrook.
Souldrop - - par.	238	1,290	4,016	do. - -	do.

Unions and Parishes, &c.		Population in 1881.	Area in Statute Acres in 1881.	Rateable Value in 1881.	Post Town.	Petty Sessional Division.
BEDFORD UNION—County of Bedford—*continued.*				£		
Stagsden	par.	548	3,386	3,889	Bedford -	Bedford.
Steventon	par.	624	1,950	2,829	do.	do.
Thurleigh	par.	603	3,480	3,889	do.	Sharnbrook.
Turvey	par.	916	3,944	6,230	do.	Bedford.
Wilden	par.	443	2,160	2,718	do.	do.
Wilhampstead	par.	820	3,027	4,795	do.	do.
Willington	par.	248	1,618	2,838	do.	do.
Wootton	par.	1,302	3,711	8,090	do.	do.
*Yielden	par.	243	1,912	2,295	Higham Ferrers -	Sharnbrook.
TOTAL of UNION -		42,932	97,106	247,607		
BEDMINSTER UNION.						
(Formed 11 April 1836 by Order dated 28 March 1836.)						
In the CITY AND COUNTY of BRISTOL and COUNTY of SOMERSET.						
Bedminster -	par.	44,759	4,161	121,513	Bristol -	Long Ashton (County part). Bristol (City part).
COUNTY of SOMERSET :						
Abbots Leigh -	par.	364	2,228	4,636	do.	Long Ashton.
Backwell -	par.	960	2,902	8,418	West Town, Somerset.	do.
Burrow Gurney	par.	302	2,026	6,944	Bristol -	do.
Brockley (b) -	par.	109	692	1,130	West Town, Somerset.	do.
Clapton (a) -	par.	196	1,066	2,130	Nailsea	do.
Clevedon	par.	4,869	4,067	28,575	Clevedon	do.
Dundry (a) -	par.	565	2,799	6,085	Bristol -	do.
Easton in Gordano or Saint George's (a)	par.	2,112	1,931	6,229	do.	do.
Flax Bourton	par.	175	621	3,319	do.	do.
Kenn (a) -	par.	289	1,018	2,888	do.	do.
Kingston Seymour	par.	293	3,422	7,361	do.	do.
Long Ashton (W.) -	par.	2,335	4,237	18,040	do.	do.
Nailsea (a) -	par.	1,852	2,771	9,918	Nailsea, Somerset -	do.
Portbury (a) -	par.	791	3,849	7,914	Bristol -	do.
Portishead -	par.	2,730	2,388	12,639	Portishead, Somerset.	do.
Tickenham -	par.	332	1,627	3,258	Nailsea, Somerset -	do.
Walton in Gordano -	par.	484	1,315	2,999	Clevedon -	do.
Weston in Gordano -	par.	177	733	986	Nailsea, Somerset -	do.
Winford (a) (c)	par.	947	2,991	6,692	Bristol -	do.
Wraxall (a) -	par.	897	3,773	7,358	Nailsea, Somerset -	do.
Yatton (a) -	par.	1,825	5,374	19,637	Yatton, Somerset -	do.
TOTAL of UNION -		67,405	57,068	291,215		
BEDWELLTY UNION.						
(Formed 26 Mar. 1849 by Order dated 24 Feb. 1849.)						
COUNTY of MONMOUTH.						
Aberystruth	par.	18,672	11,753	74,705	Blaina -	Bedwellty.
Bedwellty (W.) -	par.	37,168	16,244	99,876	Tredegar -	do.
TOTAL of UNION -		55,840	27,997	174,581		

BEDMINSTER UNION :

(a) By Orders which came into operation on 25 March 1884,—

A detached part of Kenn was amalgamated with Yatton, and another detached part with Nailsea ;

Detached parts of Portbury were amalgamated with Easton in Gordano or Saint George's, Wraxall, and Clapton ;

A detached part of Norton Hawkfield, in the Clutton Union, was amalgamated with Dundry ;

A detached part of the parish of Winford was amalgamated with the parish of Dundry ;

A detached part of Wraxall was amalgamated with Nailsea ;

BEDMINSTER UNION—*continued.*

A detached part of Yatton was amalgamated with Kenn ; and

A detached part of Winford was amalgamated with Nempnett, in the Clutton Union ;

(b) The two parts of a parish known as Chelvey, having, in 1881, population 42, acreage 1,077, rateable value 2,546*l.*, were amalgamated with Brockley by Provisional Order which came into operation on 25 March 1885.

(c) A detached part of Blagdon in the Axbridge Union was amalgamated with Winford by Order which came into operation on 25 March 1885.

Unions and Parishes, &c.	Population in 1881.	Area in Statute Acres in 1881.	Rateable Value in 1881.	Post Town.	Petty Sessional Division.
BELFORD UNION.					
(Formed 19 Nov. 1836 by Order dated 24 Oct. 1836. — Place marked * added 29 Sept. 1864 by Order dated 22 Aug. 1864.)					
COUNTY OF NORTHUMBERLAND.					
Adderstone - - tow.	273	2,693	4,468	Belford	Bamburgh Ward.
Bamburgh (a) - - tow.	345	1,200	2,569	do.	do.
Bamburgh Castle - tow.	51	6	173	do.	do.
Beadnell - - tow.	349	793	1,770	Chathill	do.
Belford (W.) - - tow.	924	2,863	4,670	Belford	do.
Bradford - - tow.	57	561	992	do.	do.
Budle - - - tow.	78	760	1,384	do.	do.
Burton - - tow.	118	1,085	1,435	do.	do.
Chathill - - tow.	66	137	1,459	Chathill	do.
Detchant - - tow.	109	2,178	2,186	Belford	do.
Easington - - tow.	152	862	2,844	do.	do.
Easington Grange - tow.	61	402	1,322	do.	do.
Elford - - - tow.	83	1,075	1,339	Chathill	do.
Ellingham - - tow.	225	3,176	2,751	do.	do.
Elwick - - tow.	64	878	1,002	Belford	do.
Fleetham - - tow.	61	570	784	Chathill	do.
Glororum - - tow.	50	460	695	Belford	do.
Lucker (a) - - tow.	(a)	(a)	(a)	do.	do.
Middleton - - tow.	145	1,231	2,189	do.	do.
*Monks House - - tow.	5	1	40	do.	do.
Mouson - - tow.	66	792	1,422	do.	do.
Newham - - tow.	243	2,690	4,065	Chathill	do.
Newstead - - tow.	136	2,054	1,504	do.	do.
Outchester - - tow.	99	1,055	1,599	Belford	do.
Preston - - tow.	59	454	811	Chathill	do.
Ratchwood - - tow.	8	154	102	do.	do.
Ross - - tow.	77	1,531	687	Belford	do.
Shoston (a) - - tow.	78	692	1,388	Chathill	do.
Spindleston - - tow.	123	460	1,110	Belford	do.
Sunderland - - tow.	996	1,169	4,046	Chathill	do.
Swinhoe - - tow.	145	1,575	2,804	do.	do.
Tughall - - tow.	88	1,533	2,420	do.	do.
Warenton - - tow.	127	1,585	1,504	Belford	do.
Warrenford (a) - tow.	21	190	210	Chathill	do.
TOTAL OF UNION -	5,452 (a)	37,165 (a)	57,744 (a)		
BELLINGHAM UNION.					
(Formed 20 Oct. 1836 by Order dated 23 Sept. 1836.)					
COUNTY OF NORTHUMBERLAND:					
Bavington, Great - tow.	47	1,576	1,364	Capheaton, Newcastle	Bellingham.
Bavington, Little - tow.	72	1,815	1,478	do.	do.
Bellingham (W.) (a) tow.	(b)	(b)	(b)	Bellingham	do.
Birtley - - par.	393	6,890	1,562	Wark on Tyne	do.
Cary Coats - - tow.	58	1,722	949	do.	do.
Catcherside - - tow.	12	614	422	Kirk Whelpington	do.
Chirdon (a) - - tow.	50	6,569	1,406	Bellingham	do.
Coldwell - - tow.	3	305	189	Cambo, Newcastle	do.
Corsenside - - par.	681	11,501	5,602	Woodburn, R.S.O.	do.
Crookdon - - tow.	5	358	216	Kirk Whelpington	do.
Fawns - - tow.	14	273	146	do.	do.
Harle, Little - - tow.	48	710	1,007	Newcastle	do.
Harle, West - - tow.	7	653	514	do.	do.
Hawick - - tow.	17	1,280	578	Capheaton, Newcastle	do.
Kirkharle - - tow.	100	2,102	2,390	Newcastle	do.
Kirkwhelpington - tow.	210	2,862	1,958	Kirk Whelpington	do.
Otterburn Ward - tow.	333	8,563	3,210	Newcastle	do.
Plashet and Tynehead tow.	440	29,271	5,965	Falstone, Newcastle	do.

(continued)

BELFORD UNION:

(a) By Orders which came into operation on 25 March 1897,—

A detached part of Shoston was amalgamated with Bamburgh; and

The two parts of a Township known as Lucker, having, in 1881, population 209, acreage 1,848, and rateable value 3,705l., were amalgamated with Hoppen and

BELFORD UNION—continued.

Warrenford. Hoppen as so altered to be designated Lucker (Hoppen bad in 1881, population 27, acreage 230, and rateable value 323l.)

BELLINGHAM UNION:

(a) (b) See notes, page 56.

E 2

Unions and Parishes, &c.		Population in 1881.	Area in Statute Acres in 1881.	Rateable Value in 1881.	Post Town.	Petty Sessional Division.
				£		
BELLINGHAM UNION—County of Northumberland—*continued.*						
Rochester Ward (*a*) -	*par.*	(*b*)	(*b*)	(*b*)	Otterburn, Newcastle	Bellingham.
Smalesmouth -	*tow.*	133	13,457	2,421	Bellingham -	do.
Sweethope -	*tow.*	8	1,025	458	Caphenton, Newcastle	do.
Tarset, West (*a*)	*tow.*	89	18,109	3,149	Bellingham -	do.
Thockrington -	*tow.*	57	2,451	1,101	Caphenton, Newcastle	do.
Thorneyburn -	*tow.*	120	2,832	1,578	Bellingham -	do.
Troughend Ward	*tow.*	256	26,477	6,701	Otterburn, Newensle	do.
Wark (*a*) -	*tow.*	(*b*)	(*b*)	(*b*)	Wark on Tyne -	do.
Wellhaugh -	*tow.*	315	33,807	5,413	Falstone, Newcastle	do.
Whelpington (West)	*tow.*	74	4,002	2,143	Kirkwhelpington -	do.
TOTAL of UNION -		3,542 (*b*)	179,287 (*b*)	55,256 (*b*)		

BELPER UNION.

(Formed 5 May 1837 by Order dated 8 April 1837. — Places marked thus * added 24 Oct. 1837, by Order dated 30 Sept. 1837.)

COUNTY of DERBY :						
Alderwasley (*a*) -	*tow.*	386	3,106	5,162	Wirksworth -	Belper.
*Alfreton -	*par.*	13,885	4,626	35,572	Alfreton -	Alfreton.
Allestree -	*par.*	586	990	5,167	Derby -	Derby.
Ashley Hay (*a*) -	*tow.*	218	1,143	1,839	Wirksworth -	Belper.
Belper (W.) -	*tow.*	9,875	3,185	27,765	Belper -	do.
Crich -	*tow.*	2,984	3,750	10,952	Derby -	do.
Denby (*a*) -	*par.*	1,394	2,415	7,947	do. -	Smalley.
Dethwick-Lea and Holloway	} *tow.*	1,036	1,826	4,515	Cromford, Derby -	Wirksworth.
Duffield (*a*) -	*tow.*	2,549	3,436	16,918	Derby -	Belper.
Hazlewood (*a*)	*tow.*	413	1,362	2,738	do. -	do.
Headge -	*tow.*	2,405	2,366	7,602	do. -	do.
Holbrooke -	*tow.*	1,025	888	2,347	Belper -	do.
Horseley -	*tow.*	383	1,296	2,631	Derby -	Smalley.
Horseley Woodhouse	*tow.*	906	627	2,061	do. -	do.
Ideridgehay and Alton (*a*) -	} *tow.*	235	1,032	2,001	do. -	Wirksworth.

(*continued*)

BELLINGHAM UNION :

(*a*) By Order which came into operation on 25 March 1886,—

All the parts of townships known as Bellingham, Charlton East Quarter, Charlton West Quarter, the greater part of the township of Tarretburn, and a part of the township of Nook, together with a certain part of Chirdon known as Tarsethall Haugh, were united and amalgamated with a township known as Leemailing, and the latter, as so altered, was designated the township of Bellingham ;

All the parts of townships known as Shitlington High Quarter, Shitlington Low Quarter, Wark, and the remaining part of Nook were united and amalgamated with the township known as Warksburn, and that township, as so altered, was designated Wark ;

The remaining part of the township known as Tarretburn was amalgamated with Tarset West ;

All the parts of a township known as Rochester Ward were amalgamated with a Parish known as Ramshope, and the latter, as so altered, was designated the Parish of Rochester Ward.

(*b*) The townships absorbed by the Order above-mentioned had in 1881,—

	Population.	Area.	Rateable Value.
			£
Bellingham -	728	2,352	2,084
Charlton East Quarter -	103	1,840	1,084
Charlton West Quarter -	161	1,908	958
Leemailing -	186	4,730	2,036
Nook -	79	3,065	1,342
Ramshope -	13	1,481	415
Rochester Ward -	339	21,819	5,415
Shitlington High Quarter	73	8,604	1,629
Shitlington Low Quarter	43	1,305	652
Tarretburn -	143	6,586	1,820
Wark -	513	3,408	2,247
Warksburn -	181	9,980	3,959

BELPER UNION :

(*a*) By Orders which came into operation on 25 March 1886,—

A detached part of Ashley Hay was amalgamated with Alderwasley ;

Detached parts of Duffield were amalgamated with Haslewood and Shottle and Postern ;

Detached parts of Haslewood were amalgamated with Duffield, Ideridgehay and Alton, and Shottle and Postern ;

A detached part of Kilburn was amalgamated with Denby ;

A detached part of Mackworth was amalgamated with Markeaton ;

Detached parts of Pentrich were amalgamated with Ripley ;

Detached parts of Turnditch were amalgamated with Hulland and Hulland Ward, in the Ashbourne Union ; and

The several parts of a township known as Mugginton, having in 1881, population 194, acreage 2203, and rateable value 3,337*l.*, were amalgamated with Hulland Ward, in the Ashbourne Union, and Weston Underwood.

Unions and Parishes, &c.	Population in 1881.	Area in Statute Acres in 1881.	Rateable Value in 1881.	Post Town.	Petty Sessional Division.
			£		
BELPER UNION—County of Derby—*continued.*					
Ireton Wood - - *tow.*	118	815	1,314	Derby - -	Wirksworth.
Kedlaston - - *par.*	120	959	2,031	do. - -	Derby.
Kilburn (*a*) - - *tow.*	1,157	927	3,942	do. - -	Belper.
Kirk Langley and Meynell Langley - } *par.*	679	2,552	5,077	do. - -	Derby.
Mackworth (*a*) - *tow.*	253	3,400	3,092	do. - -	do.
Mapperley - - *tow.*	432	982	3,390	do. - -	Smalley.
Markeaton (*a*) (W.) - *tow.*	758 {	In Mackworth. }	5,740	do. - -	Derby.
Morley - - - *tow.*	278	1,853	3,488	do. - -	Smalley.
Pentrich (*a*) - - *tow.*	887	1,883	5,759	Derby - -	do.
Quorndon - - *par.*	555	960	2,666	do. - -	Derby.
*Ravensdale Park - *ham.*	46	635	594	do. - -	do.
Ripley (*a*) - - *tow.*	7,298	2,188	21,889	do. - -	Smalley.
Shottle and Postern (*a*) *tow.*	449	3,789	4,936	Belper - -	Belper.
Smalley - - *tow.*	815	1,718	3,524	Derby - -	Smalley.
South Wingfield - *par.*	1,226	3,361	10,066	Alfreton - -	Alfreton.
Turnditch (*a*) - *tow.*	303	1,016	1,921	Derby - -	Belper.
Weston Underwood (*a*) *tow.*	175	1,413	2,566	do. - -	Derby.
Windley - - *tow.*	183	1,159	2,192	Derby - -	Belper.
Wirksworth - - *tow.*	3,678	3,020	12,621	Wirksworth -	Wirksworth.
TOTAL of UNION -	57,990 (*a*)	64,981 (*a*)	231,825 (*a*)		
BERKHAMPSTEAD UNION.					
(Formed 12 June 1835 by Order dated 21 May 1835.)					
COUNTY of BUCKINGHAM:					
Marsworth - - *par.*	455	1,266	5,938	Tring - -	Cottlesloe, First Division of the Three Hundred of.
Nettleden - - *ham.*	111	804	1,475	Hemel Hempstead	do. do.
Pightlesthorne, otherwise Pitstone (*b*) - } *par.*	433	1,655	3,727	Tring - -	do. do.
COUNTY of HERTFORD:					
Aldbury - - *par.*	912	2,058	6,738	Tring - -	Dacorum.
Berkhampstead Saint Peter's (W.) } *par.*	4,485	4,364	23,848	Berkhampstead -	do.
Little Gaddesden (*a*) *par.*	373	925	2,060	Hemel Hempstead	do.
Northchurch - - *par.*	2,135	3,908	17,320	Berkhampstead -	do.
Puttenham - - *par.*	121	744	1,034	Tring - -	do.
Tring - - *par.*	5,357	7,816	24,284	do. - -	do.
Wigginton - - *par.*	709	1,674	2,853	do. - -	do.
TOTAL of UNION -	15,091	25,241	89,277		

BERKHAMPSTEAD UNION:

(*a*) A detached part of Eddlesborough, in the Leighton Buzzard Union, was amalgamated with Little Gaddesden by Provisional Order which came into operation on 25 March 1885.

(*b*) Certain detached parts of Pightlesthorne, otherwise Pitstone, were amalgamated with Ivinghoe and Slapton, in the Leighton Buzzard Union, by Order which came into operation on 25 March 1884.

Unions and Parishes, &c.	Population in 1881.	Area in Statute Acres in 1881.	Rateable Value in 1881.	Post Town.	Petty Sessional Division.

BERWICK-UPON-TWEED UNION.

(Formed 21 Nov. 1836 by Order dated 26 Oct. 1836.)

COUNTY of the BOROUGH and TOWN of BERWICK-UPON-TWEED.

			£		
Berwick-upon-Tweed } par. (W.)	9,179	5,790	42,703	Berwick-upon-Tweed	Borough of Berwick-upon-Tweed.

COUNTY of the BOROUGH and TOWN of BERWICK-UPON-TWEED and COUNTY of NORTHUMBERLAND.

| Tweedmouth - - par. | 5,420 | 4,945 | 28,219 | do. - - | Borough of Berwick-upon-Tweed and Norham and Island-shires. |

COUNTY of NORTHUMBERLAND.

Ancroft (a) - - par.	1,523	9,958	20,780	Beal, Northumberland	Norham and Island-shires.
Cornhill - - par.	688	4,944	9,902	Cornhill, Northumd.	do.
Duddo - - tow.	181	1,887	2,525	Norham, do. -	do.
Filkington - tow.	107	1,464	1,745	do. do. -	do.
Grindon - - tow.	124	1,493	1,896	`do. do. -	do.
Holy Island (a) - par.	686	2,457	5,140	Beal, Northumd. -	do.
Horncliffe - - tow.	348	602	2,152	Berwick-upon-Tweed	do.
Kyloe - - par.	870	9,852	16,242	Beal, Northumd. -	do.
Loan End - tow.	147	859	2,775	Berwick-upon-Tweed	do.
Longridge - tow.	91	561	1,472	do. - -	do.
Norham - - tow.	920	2,343	6,668	Norham, Northumd.	do.
Norham Mains - tow.	128	1,100	2,237	do. do. -	do.
Shoreswood - tow.	245	1,212	1,844	do. do. -	do.
Thornton - tow.	117	1,375	2,003	Berwick-upon-Tweed	do.
Twizell - - tow.	274	2,273	4,276	Cornhill, Northumd.	do.
TOTAL of UNION -	21,048	53,115	152,579		

BEVERLEY UNION:

(Formed 15 Nov. 1836 by Order dated 26 Oct. 1836.)

COUNTY of YORK, EAST RIDING.

Aike - tow.	60	545	535	Hull - -	North Hunsley Beacon.
Beswick - tow.	247	2,028	3,135	do. - -	do. do.
Bishop Burton - par.	459	4,259	7,558	Beverley - -	do. do.
Brantingham - tow.	274	1,591	3,410	Brough, Yorks. -	South do.
Cherry Burton - par.	458	3,466	6,028	Beverley - -	North do.
Ellerker - tow.	296	2,144	8,467	Brough, Yorks. -	South do.
Elloughton with } Brough - } tow.	888	1,614	6,988	do. - -	do. do.
Eske - tow.	30	1,099	1,331	Beverley - -	North do.
Etton - - par.	498	3,729	5,853	do. - -	do. do.
Holme on the Wolds par.	164	1,517	1,966	do. - -	do. do.
Kilnwick - tow.	241	1,698	2,681	Hull - -	Bainton Beacon.
Leckonfield - tow.	320	3,629	5,765	Beverley - -	North Hunsley Beacon.
Leven - tow.	847	3,709	5,140	Hull - -	North Holderness.

(continued)

BERWICK-UPON-TWEED UNION:

(a) By Order which came into operation on 25 March 1887, a certain part of Holy Island, known as Goswick, was amalgamated with Ancroft.

Unions and Parishes, &c.		Population in 1881.	Area in Statute Acres in 1881.	Rateable Value in 1881.	Post Town.	Petty Sessional Division.
BEVERLEY UNION—County of York, East Riding—*continued.*				£		
Lockington	*tow.*	404	2,748	4,041	Hull	North Hunsley Beacon.
Lockington In } Kilnwick - -}	*tow.*	110	467	677	do.	do. do.
Lund	*par.*	460	3,078	4,300	Beverley	Bainton Beacon.
Meux	*tow.*	101	1,457	1,672	do.	North Hunsley Beacon.
Molescroft	*tow.*	178	1,359	3,840	do.	do. do.
North Newbald	*tow.*	648	3,982	5,896	Brough, Yorks.	do. do.
Routh	*par.*	164	2,385	2,828	Beverley	North Holderness.
Rowley	*par.*	593	6,423	8,976	do.	South Hunsley Beacon.
Saint Martin	*par.*	4,827	873	12,569	do.	North do.
Saint Mary (W.)	*par.*	4,221	579	15,209	do.	do. do.
Saint Nicholas	*par.*	2,377	960	8,148	do.	do. do.
Scorbrough	*par.*	66	1,385	2,522	Hull	do. do.
Skidby	*par.*	362	1,256	2,135	do.	South do.
South Cave	*tow.*	960	4,337	10,674	South Cave, R.S.O., Yorks.	do. do.
South Dalton	*par.*	263	1,814	3,273	Beverley	North do.
South Newbald	*tow.*	156	1,991	2,607	Brough, Yorks.	South do.
Stockhill	*tow.*	47	322	445	Beverley do.	North do.
Thearn	*tow.*	98	516	928	Beverley	do. do.
Tickton	*tow.*	369	779	1,961	do.	do. do.
Walkington	*par.*	978	3,725	5,869	do.	do. do.
Wawn or Waghan	*tow.*	299	3,983	5,253	Hull	do. do.
Weel	*tow.*	114	1,139	1,712	Beverley	do. do.
Woodmancey and } Beverley Parks - }	*tow.*	883	2,963	9,703	do.	do. do.
TOTAL of UNION		23,460	79,579 (*a*)	174,098		
BICESTER UNION.						
(Formed 1 Aug. 1835 by Order dated 11 July 1835.)						
COUNTY of BUCKINGHAM :						
Boarstall	*par.*	209	3,078	3,000	Brill, Thame	Ashendon.
COUNTY of OXFORD :						
Ambrosden	*par.*	160	605	917	Bicester	Ploughley.
Ardley	*par.*	161	1,493	1,653	do.	do.
Arncott	*ham.*	243	1,701	1,906	do.	do.
Blackthorn	*ham.*	314	2,031	2,784	do.	do.
Blechingdon	*par.*	602	2,654	4,316	Oxford	do.
Bucknell	*par.*	264	1,894	2,254	Bicester	do.
Caversfield	*par.*	140	1,498	2,038	do.	do.
Charlton	*par.*	290	822	1,585	Islip, Oxford	do.
Chesterton	*par.*	317	2,527	2,842	Bicester	do.
Cottesford	*par.*	240	1,506	1,800	Brackley	do.
Fencot and Moorcot	*ham.*	213	1,139	1,407	Islip, Oxford	do.
Fringford	*par.*	411	1,460	1,846	Bicester	do.
Fritwell	*par.*	556	1,879	3,167	Banbury	do.
Goddington	*par.*	60	1,019	1,335	Bicester	do.
Hardwicke	*par.*	60	385	369	do.	do.
Hethe	*par.*	375	1,102	1,424	do.	do.
Islip	*par.*	600	1,978	3,484	Oxford	do.
King's End, Bicester	*tow.*	329	1,457	2,899	Bicester	do.
Kirtlington	*par.*	718	3,582	4,898	Oxford	do.
Launton	*par.*	597	2,818	4,374	Bicester	do.

(*continued*)

BEVERLEY UNION :

(*a*) There are some common lands comprised in this Union containing an acreage of 336.

E 4

Unions and Parishes, &c.	Population in 1881.	Area in Statute Acres in 1881.	Rateable Value in 1881.	Post Town.	Petty Sessional Division.
BICESTER UNION—County of Oxford—*continued.*			£		
Lower Heyford - par.	518	1,764	3,341	Banbury - -	Ploughley.
Market End, Bicester (W.) - } tow.	2,977	2,283	8,913	Bicester - -	do.
Merton - - par.	169	1,932	2,060	do.	do.
Middleton Stoney - par.	293	1,853	2,386	do. - -	do.
Newton Purcell - par.	89	602	907	Buckingham - -	do.
Noke - - par.	118	808	1,179	Islip, Oxford -	Bullingdon.
Oddington - - par.	150	1,363	1,497	do. - -	Ploughley.
Piddington - - par.	281	2,354	2,671	Brill, Thame -	do.
Shelswell - - par.	42	822	1,173	Bicester - -	do.
Somerton - - par.	344	1,842	3,057	Banbury - -	do.
Souldern - - par.	515	1,496	3,433	do. - -	do.
Stoke Lyne - par.	551	3,901	3,930	Bicester - -	do.
Stratton Audley - par.	311	2,089	3,020	do. - -	do.
Tusmore - - par.	27	735	799	do. - -	do.
Upper Heyford - par.	384	1,628	2,622	Banbury - -	do.
Wendlebury - - par.	166	1,154	1,383	Bicester - -	do.
Weston on the Green par.	363	2,295	2,472	do. - -	do.
TOTAL of UNION -	14,157	65,549	95,171		

BIDEFORD UNION.

(Formed 1st Dec. 1835 by Order dated 11th Nov. 1835.)

Unions and Parishes, &c.	Population in 1881.	Area in Statute Acres in 1881.	Rateable Value in 1881.	Post Town.	Petty Sessional Division.
COUNTY of DEVON :					
Abbotsham - par.	469	1,758	2,503	Bideford - -	Bideford.
Alwington - par.	364	2,655	1,807	do. - -	do.
Bideford (W.) - par.	6,512	3,196	15,533	do. - -	Borough of Bideford, having separate Quarter Sessions.
Buckland Brewer (a) par.	737	6,157	3,848	do. - -	Bideford.
Bulkworthy (a) - par.	113	1,115	618	Brandis Corner, near Crediton.	do.
Clovelly - - par.	787	3,502	2,357	Bideford - -	do.
East Putford - - par.	157	2,380	969	Brandis Corner, near Crediton.	do.
Hartland - - par.	1,884	16,700	9,281	Bideford - -	do.
Landcross - - par.	84	331	509	do. - -	do.
Littleham - - par.	308	1,250	1,656	do. - -	do.
Monkleigh - - par.	540	2,177	2,200	Great Torrington -	do.
Newton Saint Petrock (a) - } par.	250	1,556	1,057	do. - -	do.
Northam - - par.	4,454	4,190	13,318	Bideford - -	do.
Parkham (a) - par.	802	5,908	3,870	do. - -	do.
Welcombe - - par.	209	1,751	1,045	Stratton, Cornwall	do.
West Putford - par.	232	2,620	1,479	Brandis Corner, near Crediton.	Holsworthy.
Woolfardisworthy - par.	699	5,798	3,108	Bideford - -	Bideford.
TOTAL of UNION -	18,581	62,944	65,158		

BIDEFORD UNION :

(a) By Provisional Orders which came into operation on 25 March 1885,—
  A detached part of Buckland Brewer was amalgamated with Parkham ;
  A detached part of Frithelstock, in the Torrington Union, was amalgamated with Bulkworthy ; and
  A detached part of Frithelstock, in the Torrington Union, was amalgamated with Newton Saint Petrock.

Unions and Parishes, &c.	Population in 1881.	Area in Statute Acres in 1881.	Rateable Value in 1881.	Post Town.	Petty Sessional Division.

BIGGLESWADE UNION.

(Formed 14th April 1835 by Order dated 18th Mar. 1835. —Places marked thus * added 29th Sept. 1858 by Order dated 10th Aug. 1858.)

County of Bedford:

Unions and Parishes, &c.	Population in 1881.	Area in Statute Acres in 1881.	Rateable Value in 1881.	Post Town.	Petty Sessional Division.
Arlsey - - - par.	1,908	2,370	14,340	Baldock - -	Biggleswade.
Astwick - - par.	49	570	920	do. -	do.
Biggleswade (W.) - par.	4,947	4,310	24,787	Biggleswade -	do.
Blunham - - par.	620	3,300	3,568	Sandy -	do.
Campton - - par.	555	1,120	1,924	Shefford -	do.
*Chicksands Priory - par.	43	2,120	1,741	do. - -	do.
Clifton - - - par.	1,458	1,420	3,985	Biggleswade -	do.
Cockayne-Hatley - par.	107	1,161	1,333	Sandy -	do.
Dunton with Millo - par.	477	2,840	3,285	Biggleswade -	do.
Edworth - - par.	112	1,099	1,508	Baldock - -	do.
Everton - - par.	216	975	2,394	Sandy -	do.
Eyworth - - par.	170	1,229	1,632	do. -	do.
Henlow - - par.	932	2,450	5,058	Biggleswade -	do.
Langford - - par.	1,242	2,100	9,496	do. -	do.
Meppershall - - par.	778	1,949	3,226	Shefford -	do.
Moggerhanger - ham.	404	In Blunham	3,455	Sandy -	do.
Northill - - par.	1,412	4,210	8,148	Biggleswade	do.
Old-Warden - - par.	498	3,330	4,417	do. -	do.
Potton - - par.	2,006	2,200	6,293	Sandy -	do.
Sandy - - par.	2,662	4,010	16,962	do. - -	do.
Shefford - - tow.	1,070	In Campton	2,086	Shefford -	do.
*Shefford Hardwick - par.	53 { In Chicksands Priory }		564	do. - -	do.
Southill - - par.	1,227	6,180	8,259	Biggleswade -	do.
Stotfold - - par.	2,892	2,323	5,621	Baldock -	do.
Sutton - - par.	295	2,230	3,126	Sandy - -	do.
Tempsford - - par.	535	2,350	7,706	do. - -	do.
Upper Stondon - par.	72	575	975	Shefford -	do.
Wrestlingworth - par.	638	1,620	2,321	Sandy - -	do.
Total of Union -	27,378	58,041	149,130		

BILLERICAY UNION.

(Formed 10 Oct. 1835 by Order dated 21 Sept. 1835. Place marked thus * added 24 Mar. 1862 by Order dated 21 Mar. 1862.)

County of Essex:

Unions and Parishes, &c.	Population in 1881.	Area in Statute Acres in 1881.	Rateable Value in 1881.	Post Town.	Petty Sessional Division.
Basildon - - cha.	157	1,638	1,616	Billericay - -	Sub-Division of Billericay.
Bowers-Gifford - par.	197	2,221	2,697	Wickford - -	do.
Brentwood - - ham.	4,653	459	16,284	Brentwood -	Brentwood.
Childerditch - par.	222	1,635	1,571	do. -	do.
Downham - - par.	247	2,229	2,617	Billericay - -	Sub-Division of Billericay.
Dunton - - par.	140	2,379	2,367	Brentwood -	Brentwood.
East Horndon - par.	504	1,529	2,190	do. - -	do.
Great Burstead (W.) par.	2,093	3,709	7,511	Billericay -	Sub-Division of Billericay.
Hutton - - - par.	451	1,699	3,547	Brentwood -	Brentwood.
Ingrave - - par.	524	1,822	2,780	do. -	do.
Laindon - - par.	320	2,192	2,232	Billericay -	Sub-Division of Billericay.
*Lee Chapel - - par.	12	490	408	do. -	do.
Little Burstead - par.	199	1,839	1,988	do. -	do.
Little Warley - par.	685	1,691	3,362	Brentwood -	Brentwood.
Mountnessing - par.	874	4,206	7,836	do. -	do.
Nevendon - - par.	136	993	1,291	Wickford -	Sub-Division of Billericay.
North Benfleet - par.	204	1,601	1,916	do. -	do.
Pitsea - - par.	203	1,765	2,237	do. -	do.
Ramsden Bell-House par.	396	2,699	2,994	Billericay -	do.
Ramsden Crays - par.	226	1,457	1,826	do. -	do.

(continued)

F

Unions and Parishes, &c.		Population in 1881.	Area in Statute Acres in 1881.	Rateable Value in 1881.	Post Town.	Petty Sessional Division.
				£		
BILLERICAY UNION—County of Essex—*continued.*						
Shenfield	par.	1,481	2,459	10,631	Brentwood -	Brentwood.
South Weald	par.	3,765	4,630	16,638	do. -	do.
Vange	par.	158	1,484	1,714	Romford -	Sub-Division of Billericay.
West Horndon	par.	75	1,396	1,275	Brentwood	Brentwood.
Wickford	par.	409	1,775	2,817	Wickford -	Sub-Division of Billericay.
TOTAL of UNION -		18,331	49,997	102,345		

BILLESDON UNION.

(Formed 6 April 1836 by Order dated 22 Mar. 1836.—Place marked thus * added 25 July 1837 by Order dated 30 June 1837 ; thus † added 5 Dec. 1837 by Order dated 10 Nov. 1837 ; and Places marked thus ‡ added 25 Dec. 1858 by Order dated 9 Nov. 1858. Spelling of name of Place marked § is as altered by Order dated 31 May 1887.)

COUNTY of LEICESTER :

Allexton	par.	48	1,000	1,590	Uppingham	East Norton.
Billesdon (W.)	tow.	839	4,430	4,693	Billesdon -	do.
Burton Overy	par.	424	1,660	4,248	Leicester -	Harborough.
Bushby	tow.	56	In Thurnby	1,143	do. -	Leicester.
§Carlton Curlieu	tow.	69	2,970	2,481	do. -	Harborough.
Cold Newton	tow.	185	In Lowesby	2,274	Billesdon	East Norton.
East Norton	par.	134	1,390	2,243	East Norton	do.
Evington	par.	450	1,360	5,473	Leicester -	Leicester.
Frisby	tow.	19	} 1,170 {	1,483	Billesdon -	East Norton.
Gaulby	tow.	88		1,576	do. -	do.
Glenn Magna	tow.	854	2,510	7,178	Leicester -	Leicester.
Goadby	tow.	103	In Billesdon	1,568	Tugby -	East Norton.
Halstead	tow.	309	1,432	2,694	Billesdon	East Norton.
Houghton	par.	415	2,450	3,453	Leicester -	Leicester.
Humberstone	par.	2,638	2,630	7,306	do. -	do.
Hungarton	par.	439	2,910	5,387	do. -	do.
Ilston on the Hill	tow.	311	{ In Carlton Curlieu. }	2,451	Billesdon	East Norton.
†Keyham	tow.	301	940	1,708	Leicester -	Leicester.
Kings Norton	tow.	52	1,990	1,615	Billesdon	East Norton.
‡Launde	par.	67	1,640	1,271	Tugby -	do.
Loddington	par.	147	1,840	3,353	do. -	do.
Lowesby	tow.	142	2,350	2,126	Billesdon -	do.
Marefield	tow.	19	170	958	do. -	do.
Newton Harcourt	tow.	185	In Wistow	4,227	Leicester -	Leicester.
‡Noseley	par.	70	880	2,149	Tugby -	East Norton.
Ouston	par.	189	2,460	4,101	Oakham -	Melton Mowbray.
Rolleston	tow.	68	In Billesdon	1,966	Billesdon -	East Norton.
Scraptoft	par.	120	1,450	2,832	Leicester -	Leicester.
Skeffington	par.	150	2,132	4,016	Skeffington	East Norton.
Stoughton	tow.	144	In Thurnby	3,002	Leicester	Leicester.
Stretton Magna	tow.	34	{ In Glenn Magna. }	1,142	do. -	do.
Stretton Parva	tow.	84	{ In Kings Norton. }	1,176	do. -	do.
*Thurnby	tow.	232	2,740	1,515	do. -	do.
Tilton	par.	235	1,510	2,958	Billesdon	East Norton.
Tugby	par.	344	1,830	3,747	Tugby -	do.
Whatborough	tow.	19	In Tilton	693	Billesdon	do.
Wistow	tow.	49	2,100	1,531	Leicester -	Leicester.
Withcot	par.	41	777	1,040	Uppingham -	East Norton.
TOTAL of UNION -		10,073	50,721	104,370		

Unions and Parishes, &c.	Population in 1881.	Area in Statute Acres in 1881.	Rateable Value in 1881.	Post Town.	Petty Sessional Division.
BINGHAM UNION.					
(Formed 27 April 1836 by Order dated 9 April 1836.—Places marked thus * added 29 Sept. 1858 by Order dated 12 Aug. 1858.)					
COUNTY of LEICESTER.			£		
Barkston - - *par.*	302	2,870	2,665	Bottesford, Notts -	Belvoir.
Plungar - - *par.*	252	1,310	1,401	do. - - -	do.
COUNTY of NOTTINGHAM :					
Aslacton - - *tow.*	404	In Whatton	3,904	Whatton, Notts -	Bingham.
Barnston cum Langar *par.*	425	3,442	7,146	Elton, Notts -	do.
Bingham (W.) - *par.*	1,673	3,054	10,637	Nottingham -	do.
Car-Colston - *par.*	276	1,200	2,773	Bingham, Notts -	do.
Clipston - - *tow.*	50	In Plumtree	878	Nottingham -	do.
Colston Bassett - *par.*	310	2,391	3,027	Bingham -	do.
Cotgrave - - *par.*	818	3,350	5,313	Nottingham -	do.
Cropwell Bishop - *par.*	636	1,380	2,349	Bingham -	do.
Cropwell Butler - *tow.*	540	In Tithby	3,191	Nottingham -	do.
East Bridgeford - *par.*	898	1,910	4,583	Radcliffe on Trent -	do.
Edwalton - - *par.*	113	813	1,895	Nottingham - -	Nottingham.
Elton - - - *par.*	76	980	1,435	do. - -	Bingham.
Flawborough - *tow.*	76	965	1,313	Orston, Notts -	Newark.
Flintham - - *par.*	381	2,450	3,598	Newark, Notts -	Bingham.
Granby - - *par.*	396	2,420	3,013	Elton, Notts -	do.
Hawksworth - - *par.*	158	720	1,375	Bingham, Notts -	do.
Hickling - - *par.*	498	2,930	3,956	Melton Mowbray -	do.
Holme-Pierpoint - *par.*	221	2,120	4,133	Radcliffe on Trent	do.
Keyworth - - *par.*	893	1,530	2,396	Nottingham -	Nottingham.
Kinoulton - - *par.*	331	2,950	3,434	do. - -	Bingham.
Knighton - - *par.*	115	924	1,380	Radcliffe on Trent	do.
*Lodge-on-the-Wolds *par.*	2	In Kinoulton	12	Nottingham -	do.
Normanton - - *tow.*	99	In Plumtree	1,973	do. - -	Nottingham.
Orston - - *par.*	484	1,910	4,360	do. - -	Bingham.
Owthorpe - - *par.*	131	1,700	1,395	do. - -	do.
Plumtree - - *tow.*	378	3,460	3,039	do. - -	Nottingham.
Radcliffe on Trent - *par.*	1,704	1,880	9,778	do. - -	Bingham.
Saxondale - - *tow.*	98	In Shelford	2,784	Bingham, Notts -	do.
Scarrington - *tow.*	208	910	1,458	Whatton, Notts -	do.
Screveton - - *par.*	179	1,150	1,827	Bingham, Notts -	do.
Shelford - - *tow.*	437	3,560	4,779	Radcliffe on Trent	do.
Shelton - - *par.*	116	740	1,769	Newark on Trent -	do.
Sibthorpe - - *par.*	130	880	1,413	do. - -	Newark.
Stanton on the Wold *par.*	107	1,220	1,528	Nottingham -	Bingham.
Thoroton - - *par.*	152	730	1,060	Bingham, Notts -	do.
Tithby - - *tow.*	81	3,610	921	do. - -	do.
Tollerton - - *par.*	124	1,240	1,981	Nottingham -	do.
Whatton - - *par.*	283	3,100	3,854	Bingham -	do.
Widmerpool - - *par.*	148	2,190	2,616	do. - -	do.
*Wiverton Hall - *par.*	18 { In Barnston cum Langar }		1,627	Elton, Notts -	do.
TOTAL of UNION -	14,721	68,019	123,949		
BIRKENHEAD UNION.					
(Formed 25 Mar. 1861 by Order dated 4 Mar. 1861 ; Places formerly in the Wirrall Union.)					
COUNTY of CHESTER :					
Bidstone-cum-Ford - *tow.*	270	1,713	3,201	Birkenhead -	Birkenhead.
Birkenhead - *tow.*	51,610	1,280	239,929	do. - -	do.
Claughton-cum-Grange - } *tow.*	2,934	439	28,757	do. - -	do.
Liscard - - *tow.*	11,612	982	74,926	do. - -	Liscard.
Noctorum - - *tow.*	121	330	1,248	do. - -	Birkenhead.
Oxton - - *tow.*	3,312	814	28,667	do. - -	do.

(continued)

Unions and Parishes, &c.	Population in 1881.	Area in Statute Acres in 1881.	Rateable Value in 1881.	Post Town.	Petty Sessional Division.
			£		
BIRKENHEAD UNION—County of Chester—*continued.*					
Poulton - cum - Sea - comb } tow.	7,640	830	55,143	Birkenhead - -	Liscard.
Tranmere (W.) - tow.	23,987	1,071	93,294	do. - -	Birkenhead.
Wallasey - - tow.	1,940	1,596	8,595	do. - -	Liscard.
TOTAL of UNION -	103,426	9,055	533,760		
BIRMINGHAM PARISH.					
(Under the 1 & 2 Will. 4, c. lxvii.)					
COUNTY of WARWICK :					
Birmingham (W.)- - par.	246,353	2,955	984,988	Birmingham -	Borough of Birmingham, having separate Quarter Sessions.
BISHOP STORTFORD UNION.					
(26 Mar. 1835 by Order dated 11 Mar. 1835.)					
COUNTY of ESSEX :					
Berdon - - par.	363	1,809	2,106	Bishop Stortford -	Saffron Walden.
Birchanger - - par.	468	1,066	3,268	do. - -	do.
Elsenham - - par.	468	1,852	3,156	do. - -	do.
Farnham - - par.	495	2,021	3,148	do. - -	do.
Great Hallingbury - par.	628	2,688	4,151	do. - -	Epping.
Henham - - par.	812	2,995	7,051	do. - -	Saffron Walden.
Little Hallingbury - par.	583	1,656	2,635	do. - -	Epping.
Manewden - - par.	721	2,531	3,777	do. - -	Saffron Walden.
Stansted Mount- } fitchet - par.	1,924	4,221	11,083	do. - -	do.
Ugley - - par.	401	2,122	2,657	do. - -	do.
COUNTY of HERTFORD :					
Albury - - par.	621	3,248	4,700	Ware - -	Albury.
Bishop Stortford (W.) par.	6,704	3,285	29,877	Bishop Stortford -	Bishop Stortford.
Braughin - - par.	1,022	4,368	6,946	Ware - -	Ware.
Little Hadham - par.	853	3,082	4,784	do. - -	Albury.
Much Hadham - par.	1,208	4,490	8,481	do. - -	do.
Pelham, Brent - par.	232	1,636	1,778	Buntingford -	do.
Pelham, Furneux - par.	571	2,585	4,122	do. - -	do.
Pelham, Stocking - par.	173	647	791	do. - -	do.
Sawbridgeworth - par.	3,049	6,639	17,645	Bishop Stortford -	Bishop Stortford.
Thorley - - par.	415	1,556	3,629	do. - -	do.
TOTAL of UNION -	21,801	54,471	126,085		
BLABY UNION.					
(Formed 6 Feb. 1836 by Order dated 21 Jan. 1836.—Places marked thus * added 25 Dec. 1861 by Order dated 5 Dec. 1861, and thus † added 15 Jan. 1862 by Order dated 30 Dec. 1861.)					
COUNTY of LEICESTER :					
Aylestone (a) - tow.	2,546	2,650	11,646	Leicester - -	Leicester.
Blaby - - tow.	1,303	3,300	4,676	do. - -	do.

(continued)

BLABY UNION :

(a) By Orders which came into operation on 25 March 1885.—
Certain detached parts of Aylestone were amalgamated with Glenn Parva and Lubbesthorpe ;
A detached part of Leicester Forest was amalgamated with Kirby Muxloe ;

BLABY UNION—*continued.*

Two detached parts of Narborough were amalgamated with Cosby ; and

Two detached parts of Croft were amalgamated with Broughton Astley, in the Lutterworth Union.

Unions and Parishes, &c.	Population in 1831.	Area in Statute Acres in 1831.ʼ	Rateable Value in 1831.	Post Town.	Petty Sessional Division.

BLABY UNION—County of Leicester—*continued.* £

Braunstone - - *tow.*	193	In Glenfield	3,231	Leicester - -	Leicester.
†Braunstone Frith - *par.*	12	—	397	do. - -	do.
Cosby (*a*) - - *par.*	1,004	2,550	4,742	do. - -	do.
Countesthorpe - *tow.*	1,103	In Blaby	4,004	Rugby - -	do.
Croft (*a*) - - *par.*	576	1,016	3,571	Leicester - -	Hinckley.
Enderby (W.) - *par.*	1,677	1,810	5,935	do. - -	Leicester.
Foxton - - *par.*	43	840	2,383	do. - -	do.
*Freaks Ground - *par.*	59	—	317	do. - -	do.
Glenfield - - *tow.*	632	4,890	2,470	do. - -	do.
*Glenfield Frith - *par.*	10	1,940	596	do. - -	do.
Glenn Parva (*a*) - *tow.*	742	In Aylestone	2,688	do. - -	do.
Huncote - - *tow.*	462 {	In Narborough }	2,314	do. - -	do.
Kilby - - *par.*	291	1,060	1,952	do. - -	do.
*Kirby Frith - *par.*	15 {	In Glenfield Frith }	516	do. - -	do.
Kirby Muxloe (*a*) - *tow.*	382	In Glenfield	4,341	do. - -	do.
Knighton - - *tow.*	1,827	1,020	17,699	do. - -	do.
*Knoll and Bassett House - } *par.*	18	—	369	Hinckley - -	Hinckley.
Leicester Forest (*a*) - *par.*	77	—	1,196	Leicester - -	Leicester.
Lubbisthorpe (*a*) - *tow.*	52	1,200	1,805	do. - -	do.
Narborough (*a*) - *tow.*	884	2,657	5,831	do. - -	do.
*New Found Pool - *par.*	56	—	466	do. - -	do.
*New Parks - - *par.*	72	—	1,804	do. - -	do.
Oadby - - *par.*	1,731	1,560	6,164	do. - -	do.
Potters Marston - *tow.*	20	280	1,231	Hinckley - -	Hinckley.
Thurlaston - - *par.*	533	2,980	5,176	do. - -	do.
*West Leicester Forest *par.*	48	—	413	Leicester - -	Leicester.
Whetstone - - *par.*	1,186	1,680	5,230	do. - -	do.
Wigston Magna - *par.*	4,299	2,780	20,621	do. - -	do.
TOTAL of UNION -	21,853	34,207	123,784		

BLACKBURN UNION.

(Formed 17 Jan. 1837 by Order dated 20 Dec. 1836.)

COUNTY of LANCASTER:

Balderstone - - *tow.*	487	1,808	2,739	Blackburn -	Lower Division, Hundred of Blackburn.
Billington - - *tow.*	1,410	3,139	6,943	do. - -	do.
Blackburn (W.) - *tow.*	91,958	3,681	272,513	do. - -	do.
Church - - *tow.*	4,850	528	15,758	do. - -	do.
Clayton-le-Dale - *tow.*	295	1,715	3,189	do. - -	do.
Clayton-le-Moors - *tow.*	6,695	1,059	17,240	do. - -	do.
Dinkley - - *tow.*	123	608	841	do. - -	do.
Eccleshill - - *tow.*	716	797	3,369	do. - -	do.
Great Harwood - *tow.*	6,287	2,863	18,014	do. - -	do.
Little Harwood - *tow.*	715	895	4,648	do. - -	do.
Livesay - - *tow.*	6,065	2,036	27,126	do. - -	do.
Lower Darwen - *tow.*	4,531	2,667	19,571	do. - -	do.
Mellor - - *tow.*	1,096	1,744	4,290	do. - -	do.
Osbaldeston - *tow.*	154	1,084	1,403	do. - -	do.
Oswaldtwistle - *tow.*	12,206	4,883	37,459	do. - -	do.
Over Darwen - *tow.*	27,626	5,134	81,313	do. - -	do.
Pleasington - *tow.*	459	1,701	5,303	do. - -	do.
Ramsgrave - - *tow.*	240	776	1,679	do. - -	do.
Rishton - - *tow.*	4,055	2,982	18,198	do. - -	de.
Salesbury - - *tow.*	184	1,215	1,791	do. - -	do.
Tockholes - - *tow.*	494	1,988	3,253	do. - -	do.
Wilpshire - - *tow.*	280	1,002	2,626	do. - -	do.
Witton - - *tow.*	4,356	700	9,063	do. - -	do.
Yate and Pickup-Bank - } *tow.*	682	850	2,213	do. - -	do.
TOTAL of UNION -	175,954	45,855	560,542		

Unions and Parishes, &c.	Population in 1881.	Area in Statute Acres in 1881.	Rateable Value in 1881.	Post Town.	Petty Sessional Division.

BLANDFORD UNION.

(Formed 5 Dec. 1835 by Order dated 20 Nov. 1835.)

County of Dorset :

			£		
Almer - - - *par.*	112	1,161	1,321	Blandford - -	Wimborne.
Anderson - - *par.*	64	570	682	do. - -	Blandford.
Blandford Forum (W.) (*b*) *par.*	3,791	862	10,214	do. - -	do.
Blandford Saint Mary (*c*) *par.*	364	1,583	2,350	do. - -	do.
Bryanston (*c*) - - *par.*	259	1,512	1,538	do. - -	do.
Charlton Marshall - *par.*	652	2,100	2,610	do. - -	do.
Durweston - - *par.*	376	1,763	1,864	do. - -	do.
Hilton - - *par.*	663	2,974	3,579	do. - -	do.
Iwerne Courtnay, alias Shroton *par.*	623	1,953	2,885	do. - -	Sturminster Newton.
Langton Long Blandford - *par.*	278	1,808	2,241	do. - -	Blandford.
Milbourne Saint Andrew - *par.*	309	1,717	1,769	do. - -	do.
Milbourne Styleham - *ham.*	258	—	896	do. - -	do.
Milton Abbas (*a*) - *par.*	873	1,392	5,285	do. - -	do.
Pimperne (*b*) (*c*) - *par.*	399	4,510	2,102	do. - -	do.
Spettisbury - - *par.*	530	2,148	3,018	do. - -	do.
Steepleton Preston (*c*) *par.*	73	773	618	do. - -	do.
Stourpain - - *par.*	563	2,305	2,238	do. - -	do.
Tarrant Crawford - *par.*	61	600	907	do. - -	Wimborne.
Tarrant Gunville - *par.*	348	3,425	2,479	do. - -	Blandford.
Tarrant Hinton - *par.*	237	2,279	1,930	do. - -	do.
Tarrant Keynston (*c*) *par.*	272	1,962	1,947	do. - -	do.
Tarrant Launceston - *par.*	86	} 3,818 {	1,230	do. - -	do.
Tarrant Monkton - *par.*	212		1,459	do. - -	do.
Tarrant Rawston - *par.*	48	696	554	do. - -	do.
Tarrant Rushton (*c*) - *par.*	170	1,221	1,301	do. - -	Wimborne.
Turnworth (*c*) - *par.*	115	1,560	1,060	do. - -	Blandford.
Winterborne Clenston (*c*) - *par.*	112	1,406	1,142	do. - -	do.
Winterborne Houghton *par.*	250	1,923	1,280	do. - -	do.
Winterborne Kingston - *par.*	520	2,508	2,671	do. - -	Wareham.
Winterborne Stickland (*c*) - *par.*	480	1,340	2,157	do. - -	Blandford.
Winterborne Tomson *par.*	40	710	526	do. - -	do.
Winterborne Whitchurch - *par.*	422	2,841	2,740	do. - -	do.
Winterborne Zelston - *par.*	145	823	1,241	do. - -	do.
Total of Union - -	**13,735**	**56,243**	**69,864**		

BLEAN UNION.

(Formed 26 April 1835 by Order dated 25 Mar. 1835.)

In the City and County of the City of Canterbury, and in the County of Kent :

Saint Dunstan - *par.*	1,719	342	6,117	Canterbury -	West or Home Division of Saint Augustine's, Kent, and City and Borough of Canterbury.
Hackington, alias Saint Stephens - *par.*	632	1,988	5,034	do. - -	

(continued)

BLANDFORD UNION :

(*a*) A detached part of Milton Abbas, known as "Liscombe," was amalgamated with Chesilborne, in the Cerne Union, and another detached part, known as "Holworth," was amalgamated with Owermoigne, in the Weymouth Union, by Provisional Orders [which came into operation on 25 March 1882.

(*b*) Two detached parts of Blandford Forum were amalgamated with Pimperne, by Order which came into operation on 25 March 1886.

BLANDFORD UNION—*continued.*

(*c*) By Provisional Order which came into operation on 25 March 1887,—
A detached part of Pimperne was amalgamated with Steepleton Preston ;
Certain parts of Tarrant Keynston were amalgamated with Tarrant Rushton ;
A detached part of Turnworth was amalgamated with Blandford Saint Mary ; and
Certain parts of Winterborne Clenston were amalgamated with Bryanston and Winterborne Stickland.

Unions and Parishes, &c.	Population in 881.	Area in Statute Acres in 1881.	Rateable Value in 1881.	Post Town.	Petty Sessional Division

BLEAN UNION—continued.

COUNTY of the CITY of CANTERBURY.

			£		
Precinct of Archbishop's Palace - }	178	4	795	Canterbury -	{ City and Borough of Canterbury.
Christ-church - *pre.*	223	20	1,492	do. - -	do.
Saint Gregory - *vill.*	1,306	10	1,852	do. - -	do.
Staplegate - *vill.*	259	1	436	do. - -	do.

COUNTY of KENT:

Chislett - *par.*	1,124	6,807	13,514	do. - -	West or Home Division of Saint Augustine's, Kent.
Herne, otherwise Hearne (W.) - } *par.*	4,110	4,938	21,951	do. - -	do.
Hoath - - *par.*	334	914	1,887	do. - -	do.
Reculver - *par.*	298	1,221	3,076	do. - -	do.
Saint Cosmus and Damian in the Blean } *par.*	687	2,334	4,003	do. - -	do.
Seasalter - *par.*	1,257	1,487	5,532	do. - -	do.
Sturry, otherwise Sturrey - } *par.*	1,175	3,151	5,975	do. - -	do.
Swalecliffe - *par.*	143	992	1,915	do. - -	do.
West-beer, otherwise Westbere - } *par.*	240	1,173	2,930	do. - -	do.
Whitstable - *par.*	4,882	3,601	16,688	do. - -	do.
TOTAL of UNION -	**18,867**	**28,983**	**93,197**		

BLOFIELD UNION.

(Formed Oct. 1835 by Order dated 16 Sept. 1835.)

COUNTY of NORFOLK:

Acle - *par.*	915	3,209	7,416	Norwich - -	Blofield and Walsham.
Beighton - *par.*	272	1,015	2,236	do. - -	do.
Blofield (a) - *par.*	1,136	2,334	5,951	do. - -	do.
Brundall (a) - *par.*	58	544	1,286	do. - -	do.
Buckenham-Ferry - *par.*	113	931	1,698	do. - -	do.
Burlingham Saint Andrew - } *par.*	178	750	1,801	do. - -	do.
Burlingham Saint Edmund (a) - } *par.*	74	661	1,436	do. - -	do.
Burlingham Saint Peter *par.*	64	405	1,003	do. - -	do.
Cantley - *par.*	266	1,850	3,663	do. - -	do.
Freethorpe - *par.*	400	869	2,287	do. - -	do.
Great Plumstead - *par.*	334	1,403	2,952	do. - -	do.
Halvergate - *par.*	482	2,675	5,487	do. - -	do.
Hasingham - *par.*	104	574	915	do. - -	do.
Hemblington - *par.*	236	739	1,458	do. - -	do.
Limpenhoe (a) - *par.*	199	1,075	2,247	do. - -	do.
Lingwood (W.) (a) - *par.*	399	661	1,734	do. - -	do.
Little Plumstead - *par.*	329	1,395	2,578	do. - -	do.
Moulton - *par.*	240	1,018	2,097	do. - -	do.
Postwick - *par.*	297	1,426	3,779	do. - -	do.
Ranworth with Panxworth - } *par.*	438	1,902	3,887	do. - -	do.
Reedham - *par.*	856	3,328	6,922	Great Yarmouth -	do.
Southwood (a) - *par.*	41	481	873	Norwich - -	do.
Strumpshaw (a) - *par.*	407	1,337	2,632	do. - -	do.

(continued)

BLOFIELD UNION:

(a) By Orders which came into operation on 25 March 1884,—
A detached part of Blofield was amalgamated with the parish of Wickhampton;
A detached part of Burlingham Saint Edmund was amalgamated with Lingwood;

BLOFIELD UNION—continued.

A detached part of Southwood was amalgamated with Limpenhoe; and
A certain part of a parish known as Bradestone, population 165, acreage 516, rateable value 1,236l., was amalgamated with Strumpshaw, and the remaining parts of that parish with Brundall.

F 4

Unions and Parishes, &c.	Population in 1881.	Area in Statute Acres in 1881.	Rateable Value in 1881.	Post Town.	Petty Sessional Division.
			£		
BLOFIELD UNION—County of Norfolk—*continued.*					
Thorpe (next Norwich) - } par.	1,887	1,795	6,761	Norwich - -	Blofield and Walsham.
Tunstal - - par.	106	1,612	2,782	do.	do.
Upton with Fishley - u.p.	531	2,169	1,413	do. -	do.
Walsham South, } par.	227		3,687	do. -	do.
Saint Lawrence }		3,149			
Walsham South, } par.	369		2,127	do. -	do.
Saint Mary }					
Wicklampton (a) - par.	148	1,605	2,777	do. -	do.
Witton - - par.	131	587	1,412	do. -	do.
Woodbastwick - par.	210	2,163	2,659	do. -	do.
TOTAL of UNION -	11,453 (a)	43,662 (a)	93,289 (a)		

BLYTHING UNION.					
(Formed 25 June 1835 by Order dated 1 June 1835.)					
COUNTY of SUFFOLK :					
Aldringham and } par. Thorpe - - }	524	1,783	1,756	Saxmundham -	Blything.
Bennere - - par.	207	1,660	2,451	Wangford -	do.
Blyford (a) - par.	195	947	1,244	Halesworth -	do.
Blythburgh (W.) - par.	821	4,116	4,689	do. -	do.
Bramfield - par.	628	2,546	4,581	do. -	do.
Brampton - par.	298	2,002	3,289	Wangford -	do.
Chediston (a) - par.	362	2,378	3,459	Halesworth -	do.
Cookley - par.	212	1,704	2,217	do. -	do.
Covehithe - par.	173	1,553	1,045	Wangford -	do.
Cratfield (a) - par.	495	2,085	3,460	Halesworth -	do.
Darsham - par.	434	1,550	3,315	Saxmundham -	do.
Dunwich - par.	250	1,465	788	do. -	do.
Easton Bavents - par.	43	381	152	Wangford -	do.
Frostenden - par.	386	1,310	2,275	do. -	do.
Halesworth (a) - par.	2,498	1,445	8,894	Halesworth -	do.
Haveningham - par.	316	1,659	2,783	Saxmundham -	do.
Henham - ham.	151	1,752	2,299	Wangford -	do.
Henstead, including } par. Hulver Hamlet - }	537	1,918	2,809	do. -	do.
Holton (a) - par.	441	1,130	2,664	Halesworth -	do.
Huntingfield - par.	357	2,134	3,012	do. -	do.
Kelsale (b) - par.	1,067	3,590	6,597	Saxmundham -	do.
Knodishall - par.	448	1,813	2,764	do. -	do.
Leiston - par.	2,439	4,610	9,116	do. -	do.
Linstead Magna - par.	123	1,304	1,842	Halesworth -	do.
Linstead Parva (b) - par.	159	554	877	do. -	do.
Middleton - par.	503	1,420	3,387	Saxmundham -	do.
Peasenhall (b) - par.	863	1,995	3,575	do. -	do.
Reydon - par.	307	2,727	3,575	Wangford -	do.
Rumburgh - par.	346	1,468	2,506	Halesworth -	do.

(continued)

BLOFIELD UNION :

(a) *See* note, page 47.

BLYTHING UNION :

(a) By Orders which came into operation on 25 March 1884,—

Two detached parts of Halesworth were amalgamated with Spexhall ;

A detached part of Blyford was amalgamated with Holton ;

A detached part of Holton was amalgamated with Blyford

BLYTHING UNION—*continued.*

A detached part of Ubbeston was amalgamated with Cratfield ; and

Two parts of Wissett were amalgamated with Chediston.

(b) By Provisional Orders which came into operation on 25 March 1885,—

A detached part of Withersdale, in the Hoxne Union, was amalgamated with Linstead Parva ;

A detached part of Silton was amalgamated with Peasenhall ; and

All the parts of a parish known as Carlton were amalgamated with Kelsale.

Unions and Parishes, &c.	Population in 1881.	Area in Statute Acres in 1881.	Rateable Value in 1881.	Post Town.	Petty Sessional Division.
			£		
BLYTHING UNION—County of Suffolk—*continued.*					
Sibton (b) - - par.	483	2,861	3,852	Saxmundham -	Blything.
Sotherton - - par.	180	1,085	1,541	Wangford -	do.
Southcove - - par.	157	1,214	1,426	do. -	do.
Southwold - - par.	2,107	566	6,307	do. -	do.
Spexhall (a) - - par.	204	1,484	2,246	Halesworth -	do.
Stoven - - par.	131	797	1,105	Wangford -	do.
Thoberton - - par.	593	1,954	2,945	Saxmundham -	do.
Thorington - - par.	104	1,800	1,812	do. -	do.
Ubbeston (a) - - par.	189	1,212	1,711	do. -	do.
Uggeshall - - par.	250	1,473	2,384	Wangford -	do.
Walberswick - - par.	289	1,960	1,062	do. -	do.
Walpole - - par.	394	1,750	2,463	Halesworth -	do.
Wangford - - par.	606	851	2,161	Wangford -	do.
Wenhaston - - par.	877	2,326	4,029	Halesworth -	do.
Westhall - - par.	431	2,316	3,816	Wangford -	do.
Westleton - - par.	835	6,103	5,674	Saxmundham -	do.
Wissett (a) - - par.	394	2,259	3,327	Halesworth -	do.
Wrentham - - par.	980	2,303	1,266	Wangford -	do.
Yoxford - - par.	1,060	2,724	5,811	Saxmundham -	do.
TOTAL of UNION -	25,817	92,097	150,359		

BODMIN UNION.

(Formed 10 May 1837 by Order dated 14 April 1837.)

COUNTY of CORNWALL:

Unions and Parishes, &c.	Population in 1881.	Area in Statute Acres in 1881.	Rateable Value in 1881.	Post Town.	Petty Sessional Division.
Blisland - - par.	556	6,338	4,012	Bodmin -	Trigg, Hundred of.
Bodmin (W.) - - bor.	5,061	2,797	12,062	do. -	Borough of Bodmin (separate Commission of the Peace).
Bodmin - - par.	394	3,417	2,998	do. -	Trigg, Hundred of.
Cardinham - - par.	582	9,534	4,692	do. -	West, Hundred of.
Egloshayle - - par.	1,549	5,682	7,521	Wadebridge -	Trigg, Hundred of.
Endellion - - par.	1,145	3,777	5,703	do. -	do.
Helland - - par.	195	2,493	2,063	Bodmin -	do.
Lanhydrock - - par.	186	1,786	1,473	do. -	Hundred of Powder, Tywardreath.
Lanivet - - par.	1,030	3,426	5,158	do. -	Trigg, Hundred of.
Lanlivery - - par.	1,388	6,779	7,593	Lostwithiel -	Hundred of Powder, Tywardreath.
Lostwithiel - - par.	931	106	1,985	do. -	Borough of Lostwithiel.
Luxulion - - par.	1,098	5,432	4,667	Bodmin -	Hundred of Powder, Tywardreath.
Saint Kew - - par.	1,102	7,563	8,986	Wadebridge -	Trigg, Hundred of.
Saint Mabyn - - par.	694	4,101	5,416	Bodmin -	do.
Saint Minver High-lands - } par.	586	5,335	6,034	Wadebridge -	do.
Saint Minver Low-lands - } par.	421	2,287	2,393	do. -	do.
Saint Tudy - - par.	521	3,283	4,317	Bodmin -	do.
Saint Winnow - - par.	1,131	6,217	6,249	Lostwithiel -	West, Hundred of.
Temple - - par.	38	843	252	Bodmin -	Trigg, Hundred of.
Warleggon - - par.	232	2,055	1,496	do. -	West, Hundred of.
Withiel - - par.	408	3,091	2,402	do. -	Pydar, Hundred of.
TOTAL of UNION -	19,248	88,372	97,772		

Unions and Parishes, &c.	Population in 1881.	Area in Statute Acres in 1881.	Rateable Value in 1881.	Post Town.	Petty Sessional Division.

BOLTON UNION.

(Formed 1 Feb. 1837 by Order dated 5 Jan. 1837.)

COUNTY of LANCASTER :

			£		
Bradshaw - - tow.	755	1,156	5,562	Bolton, Lanc.	Bolton (Lanc.).
Breightmet - - tow.	1,525	873	6,061	do. - -	do. do.
Darcy Lever - - tow.	1,994	499	8,453	do. - -	do. do.
Edgworth - - tow.	1,862	2,925	5,558	do. - -	do. do.
Entwistle - - tow.	341	1,668	4,075	do. - -	do. do.
Farnworth (W.) - tow.	20,708	1,502	64,121	do. - -	do. do.
Great Bolton - - tow.	45,694	826	188,826	do. - -	do. (Borough).
Great Lever - - tow.	3,673	867	22,870	do. - -	do. (Lanc.).
Halliwell - - tow.	12,551	2,480	46,052	do. - -	*do. do.
Harwood - - tow.	1,811	1,240	4,704	do. - -	do. do.
Heaton - - tow.	1,461	1,744	16,226	do. - -	do. do.
Horwick - - tow.	3,761	3,254	15,432	do. - -	do. do.
Kersley - - tow.	7,253	997	26,801	do. - -	do. do.
Little Bolton (a) - tow.	44,452	1,779	143,898	do. - -	do. (Borough).
Little Hulton - - tow.	5,714	1,707	22,788	do. - -	do. (Lanc.)
Little Lever - - tow.	4,413	807	16,317	do. - -	do. do.
Longworth - - tow.	106	1,654	1,972	do. - -	do. do.
Lostock - - tow.	782	1,520	6,691	do. - -	do. do.
Middle Hulton - tow.	2,051	1,517	7,981	do. - -	do. do.
Over Hulton - - tow.	984	1,316	8,581	do. - -	do. do.
Quarlton - - tow.	271	798	1,279	do. - -	do. do.
Rumworth - - tow.	4,932	1,244	16,031	do. - -	*do. do.
Sharples (a) - - tow.	3,710	3,999	19,734	do. - -	do. do.
Tonge with Haulgh - tow.	6,731	1,099	27,028	do. - -	*do. do.
Turton - - tow.	5,653	4,614	22,286	do. - -	do. do.
West Houghton - tow.	9,197	4,341	37,615	do. - -	do. do.
TOTAL of UNION -	192,405	46,426	746,942		*NOTE.—Parts only of these townships are in the Petty Sessional Division of Bolton (Lanc.), the other portions being within the limits of the Borough of Bolton, for which a separate Petty Session is held.

BOOTLE UNION.

(Formed 12 June 1837 by Order dated 17 May 1837.)

COUNTY of CUMBERLAND :

Birker and Austhwaite - - tow.	107	8,243	663	Holm Rook -	Bootle.
Bootle (W.) - - par.	810	6,786	6,470	Bootle -	do.
Corney (a) - - par.	210	4,440	2,352	do. -	do.
Drigg and Carlton - par.	567	3,978	5,222	Holm Rook -	Allerdale above Derwent.
Eskdale and Wasdale tow.	535	17,419	2,076	do. -	Bootle.
Irton with Santon - tow.	614	6,180	4,462	do. -	Allerdale above Derwent.
Millom (a) - - tow.	7,698	13,531	77,276	Millom -	Bootle.
Muncaster (a) - par.	638	6,496	4,093	Ravenglass -	do.
Ulpha - - tow.	294	13,092	2,276	Broughton in Furness	do.
Wabersthwaite (a) - par.	194	1,771	1,054	Bootle -	do.
Wickham (or Whicham) - par.	374	4,883	3,265	Silecroft -	do.
Whitbeck - - par.	184	4,482	3,075	Bootle -	do.
TOTAL of UNION -	12,225	91,301	112,284		

BOLTON UNION.

(a) Certain parts of Little Bolton were amalgamated with Sharples by Order which came into operation on 25 March 1885.

BOOTLE UNION :

(a) A detached part of Corney was amalgamated with Wabersthwaite, and a detached part of Millom was amalgamated with Muncaster, by Order which came into operation on 25 March 1886.

Unions and Parishes, &c.	Population in 1881.	Area in Statute Acres in 1881.	Rateable Value in 1881.	Post Town.	Petty Sessional Division.

BOSMERE AND CLAYDON UNION.

(Formed 8 Sept. 1835 by Order dated 22 Aug. 1835.— * This Parish was originally named Barking with Needham Market; by Order dated 29 December 1838, it was directed that Needham Market should be a separate Parish, but by Order of 21 July 1871 the Parishes of Barking, Darmsden, and Needham Market were directed to be described as the parish of Barking.)

COUNTY of SUFFOLK :

Unions and Parishes, &c.	Population in 1881.	Area in Statute Acres in 1881.	Rateable Value in 1881. £	Post Town.	Petty Sessional Division.
Akenham - - par.	115	998	1,634	Ipswich - -	Bosmere and Claydon.
Ashbocking - - par.	316	1,108	2,442	Needham Market -	do.
Ashfield with Thorpe par.	227	1,565	2,321	Debenham -	Plomesgate.
Badley - - par.	77	1,050	1,803	Needham Market -	Bosmere and Claydon.
Bailham or Bayleham par.	256	1,332	2,257	Ipswich - -	do.
Barham (W.) - - par.	470	1,806	3,217	do. - -	do.
*Barking (a) - - par.	1,841	3,161	7,834	Needham Market -	do.
Battisford - - par.	435	1,542	1,497	do. - -	do.
Bramford - - par.	1,339	3,226	8,263	Ipswich - -	do.
Claydon - - par.	530	950	2,279	do. - -	do.
Coddenham - - par.	815	2,719	4,618	Needham Market -	do.
Creeting Saint Mary (a) } par.	582	3,115	5,135	do. - -	do.
Crowfield - - par.	356	1,721	2,738	do. - -	do.
Debenham - - par.	1,179	3,271	6,388	Debenham -	Plomesgate.
Flowton - - par.	168	495	841	Ipswich - -	Bosmere and Claydon.
Framsden - - par.	785	2,837	4,931	Stonham Earl	Plomesgate.
Gosbeck - - par.	302	1,466	2,307	Needham Market -	Bosmere and Claydon.
Great Blakenham - par.	300	869	1,819	Ipswich - -	do.
Great Bricett - par.	243	915	1,406	Needham Market -	do.
Helmingham - - par.	339	2,438	3,931	Ipswich - -	do.
Hemingstone - par.	298	1,144	2,513	Needham Market -	do.
Henley - - par.	218	1,232	2,192	Ipswich - -	do.
Little Blakenham - par.	173	1,054	1,727	do. - -	do.
Mickfield - - par.	255	1,290	2,166	Stonham Earl	do.
Nettlestead (a) - par.	99	1,028	1,444	Ipswich - -	do.
Offton (a) - - par.	348	1,561	2,329	Needham Market -	do.
Pettaugh - - par.	196	794	1,313	Stonham Earl	Plomesgate.
Ringshall - - par.	331	2,116	2,831	Stowmarket	Bosmere and Claydon.
Somersham (a) - par.	403	1,027	1,383	Ipswich - -	do.
Stonham Aspal - par.	725	2,399	4,377	Stonham Earl	do.
Stonham Earl - par.	633	2,520	4,191	do. - -	do.
Stonham Parva - par.	309	1,193	2,239	do. - -	do.
Swilland - - par.	213	951	1,662	Ipswich - -	do.
Willisham (a) - par.	199	927	1,426	Needham Market -	do.
Winston - - par.	297	1,476	2,390	Debenham - -	Plomesgate.
TOTAL of UNION -	15,402	57,899	101,844		

BOSMERE AND CLAYDON UNION :

(a) By Orders which came into operation on 25 March 1884,—

A detached part of Barking was amalgamated with Creeting Saint Mary ;

A detached part of Nettlestead was amalgamated with Somersham ;

Detached and nearly detached parts of Offton were amalgamated with Nettlestead and Willisham ;

BOSMERE AND CLAYDON UNION—continued.

Detached parts of Willisham were amalgamated with Nettlestead, Offton, and Somersham ;

The several parts of Creeting All Saints and Creeting Saint Olave were amalgamated with Creeting Saint Mary ; and

A detached part of Elmsett, in the Cosford Union, was amalgamated with Offton.

Unions and Parishes, &c.	Population in 1881.	Area in statute Acres in 1881.	Rateable Value in 1881.	Post Town.	Petty Sessional Division.

BOSTON UNION.

(Formed 22 Sept. 1836 by Order dated 6 Sept. 1836. — Place marked thus * added 30 Mar. 1837 by Order dated 11 Mar. 1837; Places marked thus † added 22 Mar. 1862 by Orders dated 5 Mar. 1862 ; Place marked thus ‡ added 29 Sept. 1862 by Order dated 27 Aug. 1862 ; Places marked thus § added 25 Mar. 1866 by Order dated 15 Mar. 1866 ; and Place marked thus ¶ added 10 Feb. 1880 by Order dated 20 Jan. 1880 ; and names of Places marked || altered by Order dated 27 Nov. 1886.)

£

COUNTY of LINCOLN :					
Algarkirk - - par.	520	2,406	8,017	Spalding - -	Hundred of Kirton.
†Amber Hill - - par.	607	6,929	13	Boston - -	do.
Bennington - - par.	542	6,992	4,167	do. - -	Hundred of Skirbeck.
Bicker - - par.	723	3,720	5,116	Spalding -	Hundred of Kirton.
†Boston (W.) (a) - par.	14,937	2,801	42,992	Boston - -	Borough of Boston (Separate Commission of Peace).
Brothertoft - - tow.	253	1,805	1,362	do.	Hundred of Kirton.
Butterwick - - par.	533	4,068	2,608	do. - -	Hundred of Skirbeck.
†Carrington (a) - tow.	763	3,825	3,403	do. - -	Soke of Bolingbroke.
†Copping Syke - par.	23	—	779	do. - -	Hundred of Kirton.
Dogdyke (b) - - tow.	200	558	1,743	do. - -	Division of Langoe.
‡Drainage Marsh - par.	3	—	58	do. - -	Hundred of Kirton.
†Ferry Corner Plot - par.	45	—	137	do. - -	do.
Fishtoft - - par.	916	6,318	5,989	do. - -	Hundred of Skirbeck.
Fosdyke - - par.	477	1,856	3,932	Spalding -	Hundred of Kirton.
Frampton (b) - - par.	886	7,900	8,230	Boston -	do.
Frieston (a) - - par.	1,105	6,391	7,560	do. - -	Hundred of Skirbeck.
||Frithville - - tow.	656	4,057	3,850	do. - -	Spilsby.
†Gibbet Hills - par.	52	—	346	do. - -	Hundred of Kirton.
†Great Beats - - par.	8	—	71	do. - -	do.
†Great Brand End Plot par.	4	25	36	do. - -	do.
§Hall Hills - - par.	4	20	33	do. - -	do.
*Hart's Grounds - par.	79	1,110	777	do. - -	do.
Kirton - - par.	2,327	1,920	14,715	do. - -	do.
||Langriville (b) - tow.	505	2,511	2,891	do. - -	Soke of Horncastle.
Leake - - par.	2,120	9,514	10,244	do. - -	Hundred of Skirbeck.
Leverton (a) - - par.	593	6,560	4,889	do. - -	do.
†Little Beats - - par.	12	—	93	do. - -	Hundred of Kirton.
§Mown Rakes - - par.	12	—	151	do. - -	do.
†North Forty Foot Bank par.	198	3,990	143	do. - -	do.
†Pelhams Lands (a) - par.	160	1,059	1,234	do. - -	do.
‡Pepper Gowt Plot - par.	22	—	149	do. - -	do.
§Royalty Farm - par.	—	—	179	do. - -	do.
¶Seven Acres - - par.	—	7	20	do. - -	do.
†Shuff Fen - - par.	—	90	135	do. - -	do.
Sibsey - - par.	1,204	6,079	7,501	do. - -	Soke of Bolingbroke.
Simon Weir - - par.	17	—	15	do. - -	Hundred of Kirton.
Skirbeck - - tow.	2,550	2,659	12,211	do. - -	Hundred of Skirbeck.
Skirbeck Quarter - ham.	854	1,110	4,201	do. - -	Hundred of Kirton.
†South of the Witham - par.	2	—	141	do. - -	do.
Sutterton - - par.	920	3,587	8,866	Spalding -	do.
Swineshead (a) - - par.	1,622	5,781	11,031	do. - -	do.
§The Friths - - par.	—	—	211	Boston -	do.
Thornton le Fen - par.	346	541	1,847	do. - -	Soke of Horncastle.
Westville - - tow.	127	2,260	2,751	do. - -	Soke of Bolingbroke.
Wigtoft - - par.	672	3,300	5,293	Spalding -	Hundred of Kirton.
Wrangle - - par.	1,165	9,780	8,290	Boston -	Hundred of Skirbeck.
Wyberton (b) - par.	646	3,231	5,968	do. - -	Hundred of Kirton.
TOTAL of UNION -	39,410	127,793	204,418		

BOSTON UNION :

(a) By Provisional Orders which came into operation on 25 March 1882,—
A detached part of Boston was united with parts of Parishes in other Unions and amalgamated with Carrington ;
Parts of Frieston and Leverton were united with parts of Parishes in the Spilsby Union, and constituted the separate Parish of West Fen ; and
A detached part of Swineshead was amalgamated with Pelham's Lands.

BOSTON UNION—continued.

(b) By Orders which came into operation on 25 March 1884,—
A detached part of Coningsby, in the Horncastle Union, was amalgamated with Dogdyke ;
Two detached parts of Frampton were amalgamated with Langriville ;
A detached part of Wyberton was amalgamated with Langriville ; and
A detached part of Dogdyke was amalgamated with Coningsby, in the Horncastle Union.

Unions and Parishes, &c.		Population in 1881.	Area in Statute Acres in 1881.	Rateable Value in 1881.	Post Town.	Petty Sessional Division.
BOURN UNION.				£		
(25 Nov. 1835 by Order dated 10 Nov. 1835.)						
COUNTY of LINCOLN:						
Aslackby	par.	432	3,934	5,988	Falkingham	Aveland.
Aunby	ham.	63	In Bytham Castle.	614	Stamford	Biltisloe.
Baston	par.	774	3,520	1,561	Market Deeping	Ness.
Billingborough	par.	1,189	2,020	5,629	Falkingham	Aveland.
Birthorpe	ham.	57	In Semperingham.	886	do.	do.
Bourn (W.)	par.	3,760	9,352	23,475	Bourn	do.
Bytham Castle	par.	654	7,760	4,914	Stamford	Biltisloe.
Careby	tow.	168	1,454	3,942	do.	do.
Carlby (a)	par.	163	1,020	3,603	do.	Ness.
Corby	par.	783	2,726	5,887	Grantham	Biltisloe.
Counthorpe	ham.	73	In Bytham Castle.	3,448	do.	do.
Creeton	tow.	51	1,003	2,815	Stamford	do.
Deeping Market	par.	1,212	1,290	4,411	Market Deeping	Ness.
Deeping Saint James	par	1,648	6,470	10,250	do.	do.
Dowsby	par.	186	1,809	3,231	Falkingham	Aveland.
Dunsby	par.	223	2,695	4,258	Bourn	do.
Edenham	par.	563	6,844	9,215	do.	Biltisloe.
Folkingham	par.	576	1,861	3,702	Falkingham	Aveland.
Haconby	par.	412	3,220	4,209	Bourn	do.
Holywell	tow.	63	In Bytham Castle.	1,254	Stamford	Biltisloe.
Horbling	par.	501	2,620	5,542	Falkingham	Aveland.
Irnham	tow.	284	3,520	5,101	Bourn	Biltisloe.
Kirkby Underwood	par.	213	1,340	1,537	do.	Aveland.
Langtoft	par.	584	2,520	3,866	Market Deeping	Ness.
Laughton	par.	82	1,136	1,647	Falkingham	Aveland.
Little Bytham	par.	305	1,010	1,352	Grantham	Biltisloe.
Manthorpe	ham.	96	2,060	1,195	Bourn	Ness.
Morton	par.	950	3,390	8,324	do.	Aveland.
Pointon	ham.	438	In Semperingham.	5,016	Falkingham	do.
Rippingale	par.	551	2,740	5,996	Bourn	do.
Semperingham	tow.	85	3,480	3,470	Falkingham	do.
Swayfield	par.	253	1,300	5,527	Grantham	Biltisloe.
Swinestead	par.	349	1,330	2,011	Bourn	do.
Thurlby	par.	814	5,070	7,029	do.	Ness.
Toft cum Lound	ham.	168	In Manthorpe.	1,946	do.	Biltisloe.
Witham on the Hill	tow.	195	2,150	2,917	do.	do.
TOTAL of UNION		18,918	90,644	171,768		
BRACKLEY UNION.						
(Formed 8 June 1835 by Order dated 13 May 1835.)						
COUNTY of BUCKINGHAM:						
Biddlesden (a)	par.	125	2,052	2,602	Brackley	Buckingham.
Turweston	par.	305	1,295	2,118	do.	do.
Westbury (a)	par.	417	2,530	3,334	do.	do.

(continued)

BOURN UNION:

(a) By Order which came into operation on 25 March 1887, a detached part of Essendine, in the Stamford Union, was amalgamated with Carlby.

BRACKLEY UNION:

(a) By Orders which came into operation on 25 March 1884,—
The several parts of a parish, known as Saint James', Brackley, were amalgamated with the parish of Saint Peter's, Brackley;
A detached part of Saint Peter's, Brackley, was amalgamated with Syresham;
A detached part of Biddlesden, known as "Needle's Hole," and a detached part of Saint Peter's, Brackley, known as "Brackley Hatch," were united and amalgamated with Syresham; and
A detached part of Westbury was amalgamated with Biddlesden.

BRACKLEY UNION—continued.

(b) By Provisional Orders which came into operation on 25 March 1885,—
A detached part of Helmdon, known as Stocken Farm, was amalgamated with Astwell with Falcutt;
A detached part of Whitfield was amalgamated with Syresham;
Two detached parts of Marston Saint Lawrence were amalgamated with Thenford;
Four detached parts of Marston Saint Lawrence were amalgamated with Middleton Cheney, in the Banbury Union; and
The several parts of a parish known as Newbottle, population 514, acreage 2,990, rateable value 3,540l., were amalgamated with a parish known as Kings Sutton, having in 1881, population 1,218, acreage 3,956, and rateable value 10,718l., and the Parish of Kings Sutton, as so altered, was designated Kings Sutton with Newbottle.

Unions and Parishes, &c.	Population in 1881.	Area in Statute Acres in 1881.	Rateable Value in 1881.	Post Town.	Petty Sessional Division.

BRACKLEY UNION—*continued.*

COUNTY of NORTHAMPTON:

			£		
Astwell with Falcutt (b) *ham.*	62	(c)	1,801	Brackley	Brackley.
Aynhoe - - *par.*	562	2,330	5,256	Banbury	do.
Croughton or Crowton *par.*	605	2,620	2,874	do.	Buckingham.
Culworth - - *par.*	465	2,246	4,702	Banbury	Brackley.
Evenley - *par.*	501	3,104	4,036	Brackley	do.
Eydon - - *par.*	449	1,620	3,327	Banbury	do.
Farthinghoe - - *par.*	354	1,471	3,255	Brackley	do.
Greatworth or Gret-worth - - } *par.*	173	863	1,919	Banbury	do.
Helmdon (b) - *par.*	529	3,560	3,125	Brackley	do.
Hinton in the Hedges *par.*	153	2,070	1,971	do.	do.
Kings Sutton with Newbottle (b) - } *par.*	(b)	(b)	(b)	Banbury	do.
Marston Saint Law-rence (b) - } *par.*	416	1,230	4,200	do.	do.
Moreton Pinkney - *par.*	445	2,422	4,289	Byfield	do.
Radstone - - *par.*	116	810	1,306	Brackley	do.
Saint Peter's Brack-ley (W.) (a) - } *par.*	2,504	4,137	11,748	Banbury	do.
Steane - - *par.*	44	1,360	1,476	do.	do.
Stutchbury - *par.*	34	1,007	1,627	do.	do.
Sulgrave - - *par.*	459	4,100	3,498	do.	do.
Syresham (a) (b) - *par.*	800	4,060	3,446	Brackley	do.
Thenford (b) - *par.*	102	890	1,877	Banbury	do.
Thorpe Mandeville - *par.*	211	1,230	1,997	do.	do.
Whitfield (b) - *par.*	213	1,210	2,019	Brackley	do.

COUNTY of OXFORD:

Finmere - - *par.*	291	1,570	2,222	Buckingham	Bicester.
Mixbury - - *par.*	273	2,972	3,103	Brackley	do.
TOTAL of UNION -	10,008 (b)	52,759 (b)	83,128 (b)		

BRADFIELD UNION.

(Formed 2 Mar. 1835 by Order dated 12 Feb. 1835. Place marked thus * added 30 Sept. 1878 by Order dated 28 June 1878.)

COUNTY of BERKS:

Aldermaston - *par.*	528	3,742	4,479	Reading	Reading.
Ashampstead - *par.*	345	2,082	2,195	do.	do.
Bassildon - - *par.*	651	3,139	8,960	do.	do.
*Beech Hill - *ty.*	277	950	1,653	do.	do.
Beenham - *par.*	517	1,793	3,438	do.	do.
Bradfield (W.) - *par.*	1,161	4,359	6,574	do.	do.
Bucklebury - *par.*	1,142	6,168	5,749	Reading	Newbury.
Burghfield - *par.*	1,296	4,311	8,072	do.	Reading.
Englefield - *par.*	389	1,436	2,800	do.	do.
Fritsham - *par.*	209	977	1,761	Newbury	Newbury.
Grasicley - *ty.*	17	519	918	Reading	Reading.
Padworth - *par.*	268	1,211	2,242	do.	do.
Pangbourne - *par.*	737	1,940	7,328	do.	do.
Purley - *par.*	188	874	6,256	do.	do.
Stanford Dingley - *par.*	138	927	1,450	do.	Newbury.
Stratfield Mortimer - *par.*	1,018	3,032	6,002	do.	Reading.
Streatley - *par.*	648	3,656	4,390	do.	do.
Sulham - *par.*	145	699	1,232	do.	do.
Sulhampstead Abbots *par.*	302	1,417	2,396	do.	do.
Sulhampstead Ban-nister Lower End } *par.*	102	} 1,132	866	do.	do.
Sulhampstead Ban-nister - } *par.*	154	}	1,023	do.	do.
Tidmarsh - *par.*	190	785	1,626	do.	do.
Tilehurst - *par.*	4,408	5,259	24,345	do.	do.

(continued)

BRACKLEY UNION :
(a) (b) *See* notes, page 53.
(c) Area included in that of the Parish of Wappenham, in the Towcester Union.

Unions and Parishes, &c.	Population in 1881.	Area in Statute Acres in 1881.	Rateable Value in 1881.	Post Town.	Petty Sessional Division.
BRADFIELD UNION—County of Berks—*continued.*			£		
Ufton - - *par.*	315	2,189	2,518	Reading - -	Reading.
Wokefield - - *ty.*	137	666	1,047	do. - - -	do.
Yattendon - - *par.*	309	1,400	2,419	Newbury - -	Newbury.
COUNTIES of BERKS and OXFORD :					
Whitchurch - - *par.*	902	2,358	6,119	Reading - -	Henley.
COUNTY of OXFORD :					
Goring - - *par.*	1,027	4,611	10,530	Reading - -	Henley.
Maple Durham - *par.*	422	3,068	4,288	do. - -	do.
TOTAL of UNION -	17,972	64,700	132,976		

Unions and Parishes, &c.	Population in 1881.	Area in Statute Acres in 1881.	Rateable Value in 1881.	Post Town.	Petty Sessional Division.
BRADFORD UNION (WILTS).					
Formed 25 Mar. 1835 by Order dated 18 Feb. 1835, as amended by Order dated 1 June 1837.—Place marked thus * added 25 Mar. 1873 by Order dated 30 Jan. 1873, and altered in name and area on 24 Mar. 1885 by Order dated 19 Dec. 1884.)					
COUNTY of WILTS :					
*Atworth (*a*) - *par.*	(*a*)	(*a*)	(*a*)	Melksham -	Bradford.
Bradford (*a*) - - *par.*	8,259	11,310	37,029	Bradford on Avon-	do.
Broughton Gifford - *par.*	613	1,677	4,657	Melksham -	do.
Monkton Farley - *par.*	412	1,796	3,579	Bradford on Avon-	do.
Westwood (W.) (*a*) - *par.*	516	813	2,108	do. - -	do.
Winkfield with Rowley (*a*) (*b*) - - } *par.*	354	1,383	2,712	do. - -	do.
TOTAL of UNION - -	10,151	16,979	50,085		

Unions and Parishes, &c.	Population in 1881.	Area in Statute Acres in 1881.	Rateable Value in 1881.	Post Town.	Petty Sessional Division.
BRADFORD UNION (YORKS).					
(Formed 10 Feb. 1837 by Order dated 21 Jan. 1837.— Place marked thus * added 26 Mar. 1877 by Order dated 2 Mar. 1877.)					
COUNTY of YORK, WEST RIDING :					
*Bolton - - *tow.*	2,573	712	9,237	Bradford, Yorks -	Borough of Bradford (Separate Quarter Sessions).
Bowling - - *tow.*	28,738	1,561	91,880	do. - -	do.
Bradford - - *tow.*	68,372	1,595	462,654	do. - -	do.
Horton (W.) - *tow.*	46,045	2,033	192,506	do. - -	do.
Manningham - *tow.*	37,304	1,319	167,512	do. - -	do.
TOTAL of UNION - -	183,032	7,220	923,789		

BRADFORD UNION (WILTS) :

(*a*) Detached parts of Bradford (one of such parts being called Atworth or Atford), and the several parts of parishes known as Great Chalfield; having in 1881, population 34, acreage 700 rateable value 883*l.*, and Little Chalfield, having in 1881, population 44, acreage 560, rateable value 691*l.*, were united, and the parts so united were amalgamated with a parish known as Cottles, having in 1881, population 13, and rateable value 528*l.*, and Cottles, as so altered, was designated the parish of

BRADFORD UNION (WILTS)—*continued.*

Atworth, by Order which came into operation on 25 March 1885.
Parts of Bradford were amalgamated with Westwood, and parts of Westwood and of Winkfield with Rowley were amalgamated with Bradford, by Order which came into operation on 25 March 1885.
(*b*) A detached part of Farleigh Hungerford, in the Frome Union, was amalgamated with Winkfield with Rowley, by Order which came into operation on 25 March 1885.

Unions and Parishes. &c.	Population in 1881.	Area in Statute Acres in 1881.	Rateable Value in 1881.	Post Town	Petty Sessional Division.

BRAINTREE UNION.

(Formed 16 Dec. 1835 by Order dated 30 Nov. 1835. — Places marked thus * added 26 Mar. 1880 by Order dated 27 Feb. 1880.)

COUNTY of ESSEX :

			£		
Black Notley - par.	664	1,941	3,015	Braintree -	South Hinckford.
Bocking (W.) - par.	3,458	4,639	12,594	do. - -	do.
Bradwell near Cog-geshall } par.	251	1,183	1,893	do. - -	Witham.
Braintree - par.	5,182	2,282	15,364	do. - -	South Hinckford.
Cressing - par.	541	2,372	3,652	do. - -	Witham.
*Fairstead - par.	289	1,877	2,419	Witham -	do.
*Faulkbourn - par.	179	1,159	1,951	do. -	do.
*Feering - par.	759	3,254	7,400	Kelvedon -	do.
Finchingfield - par.	1,807	8,461	12,159	Braintree -	Freshwell.
*Great Coggeshall - par.	2,998	2,638	8,421	Great Coggeshall -	Witham.
Great Saling - par.	347	1,674	2,423	Braintree -	South Hinckford.
*Hatfield Peverell - par.	1,244	4,756	11,383	Chelmsford -	Witham.
*Kelvedon - par.	1,537	3,168	8,761	Kelvedon -	do.
*Little Coggeshall - par.	363	1,014	2,102	do. -	do.
*Mark's Hall - par.	42	813	1,010	do. - -	do.
Panfield - par.	322	1,498	2,168	Braintree -	South Hinckford.
Pattiswicke - par.	340	1,320	1,883	do. -	Witham.
Rayne - par.	404	1,708	2,761	do. -	South Hinckford.
*Rivenhall - par.	690	3,669	6,621	Witham -	Witham.
Shalford - par.	730	2,469	3,903	Braintree -	South Hinckford.
Stisted - par.	745	2,993	4,429	do. -	do.
*Terling - par.	856	3,228	4,625	Witham -	Witham.
Weathersfield - par.	1,453	4,226	7,067	Braintree -	South Hinckford.
White Notley - par.	461	2,245	3,380	Witham -	Witham.
*Witham - par.	2,966	3,706	14,882	do. -	do.
TOTAL of UNION - -	28,628	68,293	146,266		

BRAMLEY UNION.

(Formed 27 Dec. 1862 by Order dated 11 Dec. 1862. — Places marked thus * added 21 June 1869 by Order dated 31 May 1869.)

COUNTY of YORK, WEST RIDING :

*Armley (W.) - tow.	12,737	961	35,790	Leeds -	Borough of Leeds.
Bramley - tow.	11,055	2,505	40,571	do. - -	do.
*Farnley - tow.	3,608	2,084	15,517	do. - -	do.
Gildersome - tow.	3,470	993	9,857	do. - -	Leeds Division of the West Riding of Yorks.
*Wortley - tow.	23,530	1,054	66,285	do. - -	Borough of Leeds.
TOTAL of UNION -	54,400	7,597	168,020		

BRAMPTON UNION.

(Formed 17 June 1837 by Order dated 19 May 1837.—Places marked thus * added 25 Mar. 1861 by Order dated 20 Feb. 1861.)

COUNTY of CUMBERLAND :

Askerton - tow.	318	11,302	4,658	Brampton -	Brampton.
Brampton (W.) (a) - par.	3,438	10,269	17,336	do. -	do.
					(continued)

BRAMPTON UNION :

(a) By Orders which came into operation on 25 March 1863,—

Certain detached parts of Brampton and Waterhead were amalgamated with Midgeholme ;

BRAMPTON UNION—continued.

A detached part of Waterhead was amalgamated with Farlam East and West ; and

Two parts of Waterhead were amalgamated with Denton Nether.

Unions and Parishes, &c.		Population in 1881.	Area in Statute Acres in 1881	Rateable Value in 1881.	Post Town.	Petty Sessional Division.
				£		
BRAMPTON UNION—County of Cumberland—*continued.*						
Burtholm and part of Banks	*tow.*	299	4,783	2,433	Brampton - -	Brampton.'
*Carlatton - -	*par.*	67	1,462	1,003	do. - -	do.
Castlecarrock -	*par.*	296	3,031	2,153	do. - -	do.
Cumrew - -	*par.*	122	2,772	1,508	Carlisle -	do.
Cumwhitton, North-sceugh, and Moorthwaite	*par.*	497	5,824	4,378	do. - -	do.
Denton, Nether (*a*) -	*par.*	315	4,880	4,805	do. - -	do.
Denton, Upper -	*par.*	152	1,039	2,702	do. - -	do.
Farlam, East and West (*a*) -	*par.*	1,585	5,232	7,595	Brampton - -	do.
*Geltsdale Forest -	*par.*	11	5,245	620	Castlecarrock, Carlisle.	do.
Hayton, Fenton, Faugh, Little Corby, and Talkin	*par.*	1,420	7,845	11,054	Carlisle - -	do.
Irthington, Newby, Laversdale, and Newtown	*par.*	853	7,390	7,916	Brampton - -	do.
Kingwater - -	*tow.*	331	18,770	5,165	do. - -	do.
*Midgeholme (*a*) -	*par.*	142	720	516	do. - -	do.
Walton, High and Low	*par.*	395	3,811	3,997	do. - -	do.
Waterhead (*a*) - -	*tow.*	324	3,330	4,710	do. - -	do.
TOTAL of UNION -		10,565	97,705	82,549		

BRECKNOCK UNION.

(Formed 5 Oct. 1836 by Order dated 9 Sept. 1836.—Place marked thus * added 6 Jan. 1837 by Order dated 10 Dec. 1836, and thus † added 29 Sept. 1858 by Order dated 6 Aug. 1858.)

COUNTY of BRECKNOCK :

Aberyscir - -	*par.*	159	1,918	1,482	Brecon - -	Merthyr.
Battle - -	*par.*	136	1,544	1,867	do. - -	do.
Cantreff - -	*par.*	197	20,000	2,118	do. - -	Penkelly.
†Castle Inn - -	*par.*	29	—	186	do. - -	Merthyr.
Cathedine - -	*par.*	183	1,567	1,583	Bwlch, R.S.O. -	Talgarth.
Christs College -	*par.*	96	—	294	Brecon - -	Merthyr.
Cray - -	*ham.*	428	28,883	3,649	Senny Bridge, Brecon.	Defynnock.
Garth Brengy -	*par.*	142	2,001	1,403	Brecon - -	Merthyr.
Glyn - -	*ham.*	249	In Cray	1,565	Libanus, Brecon -	Defynnock.
Glyn Tawe - -	*ham.*	133	In Cray	987	Ystradgunlais -	do.
Llanddetty - -	*par.*	502	5,980	4,987	Bwlch, R.S.O. -	Penkelly.
Llanddew - -	*par.*	238	2,695	2,698	Brecon - -	Merthyr.
Llanddefailog fach -	*ham.*	195	2,000	1,681	do. - -	do.
Llanddefailog tre'r Graig	*par.*	39	540	383	do. - -	Talgarth.
Llandefalle - -	*par.*	584	8,509	4,545	do. - -	do.
Llandeilo 'r Fan -	*par.*	409	10,491	2,326	Sibanus, Brecon -	Defynnock.
Llanfigan - -	*par.*	549	12,642	5,372	Penkelly, Brecon -	Penkelly.
Llanfihangel feehan -	*cha.*	109	2,211	1,815	Brecon - -	Merthyr.
Llanfihangel Nant Bran	*par.*	386	9,161	2,645	Defynnock - -	do.
Llanfihangel Tal y llyn	*par.*	253	1,233	2,113	Bwlch, R.S.O. -	Talgarth.
Llanfillo - -	*par.*	215	3,305	2,634	Brecon - -	do.
Llanfrynach - -	*par.*	405	7,127	2,472	do. - -	Penkelly.
Llangasty Tal y llyn	*par.*	213	2,119	2,251	Bwlch, R.S.O. -	do.
Llangorse - -	*par.*	354	2,806	3,259	Talgarth, Brecon -	Talgarth.
Llanhamlach - -	*par.*	280	1,867	2,964	Brecon - -	Penkelly.
Llansaintfraed -	*par.*	206	2,247	2,864	do. - -	do.
Llanspyddyd -	*ham.*	144	1,691	1,912	do. - -	Defynnock.
Llanywern - -	*par.*	118	1,430	993	Bwlch, R.S.O. -	Penkelly.
Maescar - -	*ham.*	753	In Cray	4,162	Senny Bridge, Brecon.	Defynnock.

(*continued*)

Unions and Parishes, &c.		Population in 1881.	Area in Statute Acres in 1881.	Rateable Value in 1881.	Post Town.	Petty Sessional Division.
				£		
BRECKNOCK UNION—County of Brecknock—*continued.*						
Merthyr Cynog	*par.*	734	21,278	5,265	Brecon -	Merthyr.
Modrydd - -	*ham.*	125	4,774	1,119	Libanus, Brecon -	Defynnock.
Pen Pont - -	*ham.*	113	1,970	1,558	Brecon - -	do.
Saint Davids Upper and Lower Division or Llanfaes (W.) -	*par.*	1,647	2,789	5,385	do. -	Borough of Brecon.
Saint John the Evangelist - -	*par.*	1,891	2,932	6,131	do. - -	do.
Saint Mary's - -	*cha.*	2,887	705	12,614	do. -	do.
Senny - -	*ham.*	219	In Cray	2,165	Senny Bridge -	Defynnock.
Talachddu -	*par.*	148	1,818	1,468	Brecon -	Penkelly.
Trayan Glas -	*ham.*	496	22,295	3,294	Trecastle -	Defynnock.
Trayan Mawr	*ham.*	533	In Traian Glas	2,327	do. - -	do.
Trallwng -	*par.*	277	3,384	2,320	Brecon -	Merthyr.
*Trawscoed -	*ham.*	44	881	604	do. -	Talgarth.
Vennyfach -	*ham.*	130	In St. John	1,397	do. -	Merthyr.
Yselydach -	*ham.*	230	In Traian Glas	2,336	Senny Bridge -	Defynnock.
TOTAL of UNION -		17,178	196,793	115,193		

BRENTFORD UNION.

(Formed 30 June 1836 by Order dated 4 June 1836, as amended by Order dated 16 June 1836.—Place marked thus * added 25 Dec. 1851 by Order dated 21 Oct. 1861.)

COUNTY OF MIDDLESEX :

Acton - -	*par.*	17,126	2,305	82,912	Acton -	Kensington.
Chiswick - -	*par.*	15,975	1,245	70,626	Chiswick -	do.
Ealing - -	*par.*	25,436	3,821	144,797	Ealing -	Brentford.
Greenford (a) -	*par.*	538	2,078	7,472	Southall -	do.
Hanwell -	*par.*	5,178	1,067	20,383	Hanwell -	do.
Heston -	*par.*	9,754	3,823	39,483	Hounslow -	do.
Isleworth (W.)	*par.*	12,973	3,143	65,021	Isleworth -	do.
New Brentford	*tow.*	2,138	216	10,570	Brentford -	do.
Perrivale -	*par.*	31	633	1,741	Ealing -	do.
Twickenham -	*par.*	12,479	2,415	84,343	Twickenham -	do.
*Twyford Abbey	*par.*	75	281	1,530	Acton -	do.
TOTAL of UNION -		101,706	21,027	528,878		

BRIDGE UNION.

(Formed 20 April 1835 by Order dated 25 Mar. 1835.—Place marked thus * added 1 Aug. 1835 by Order dated 17 July 1835, thus † added 25 Dec. 1862 by Order dated 2 Dec. 1862, and thus ‡ added 30 June 1868 by Order dated 10 June 1868.)

CITY AND COUNTY OF THE CITY OF CANTERBURY AND COUNTY OF KENT :

Beaksbourne, otherwise Beakesbourne	*par.*	335	1,141	2,715	Canterbury -	West Division of the Lathe of Saint Augustine.
Holy Cross Westgate without -	*par.*	773	81	2,908	do. - -	City and Borough of Canterbury and West Division of the Lathe of Saint Augustine.
Fordwich -	*par.*	228	465	1,412	do. -	Fordwich and City and Borough of Canterbury.
Littlebourn -	*par.*	757	2,152	4,884	Sandwich - -	East Division of the Lathe of Saint Augustine, and City and Borough of Canterbury.
Nackington - -	*par.*	120	907	2,166	Canterbury -	West do. and do.
Patrixbourne -	*par.*	245	1,610	3,703	do. -	do. do. and do.
Thanington, otherwise Thanington -	*par.*	454	1,222	5,185	do. - -	do. do. and do.

(continued)

Unions and Parishes, &c.		Population in 1881.	Area in Statute Acres in 1881.	Rateable Value in 1881.	Post Town.	Petty Sessional Division.

BRIDGE UNION—*continued*.

COUNTY of KENT:

				£		
Adisham	- par.	449	1,853	3,623	Sandwich -	East Division of the Lathe of Saint Augustine.
Barham	- par.	1,012	4,698	6,060	Canterbury	do. do.
Bishopsbourne	- par.	353	2,024	2,930	do. -	do. do.
Bridge (W.)	- par.	857	1,170	3,279	do. -	West do.
*Chartham	- par.	2,173	4,569	9,018	do. -	do. do.
Harbledown	- par.	720	1,619	5,178	do. -	do. do.
Ickham	- par.	570	2,465	6,488	Sandwich -	East Division of the Lathe of Saint Augustine.
Kingstone, otherwise Kingston	} par.	293	1,555	2.270	Canterbury -	do. do.
Lower Hardres	- par.	284	1,180	2,035	do. -	West do.
‡Milton-next-Canterbury	} par.	13	404	548	do. -	do. do.
Petham	- par.	687	3,338	5,160	do. -	do. do.
†Saint Nicholas Hospital	} par.	31	70	471	do. -	do. do.
Stodmarsh	- par.	134	699	1,523	do. -	East do.
†The Mint	- par.	107	1	130	do. -	West do.
Upper Hardres	- par.	293	2,036	2.084	do. -	do. do.
Waltham	- par.	506	3,272	3.490	do. -	do. do.
Wickhambreaux	- par.	485	2,371	5,691	Sandwich -	East do.
Womenswould	- par.	226	1,408	1,572	Canterbury -	do. do.
TOTAL of UNION -		12,405	42,340	84,532		

BRIDGEND AND COWBRIDGE UNION.

(Formed 10 Oct. 1836 by Order dated 15 Sept. 1836.—Places marked thus * added 25 Dec. 1859 by Order dated 21 Nov. 1859, and thus † added 22 Mar. 1862 by Order dated 17 Mar. 1862.)

COUNTY of GLAMORGAN:

Bettws	- par.	1,025	5,023	4,983	Bridgend -	Bridgend.
Colwinstone	- par.	212	1,841	2,096	Cowbridge -	Cowbridge.
Cowbridge	- par.	1,229	85	3,735	do. -	do.
Cwmdu	- ham.	6,232	4,210	17,279	Maesteg -	Bridgend.
Eglwys Bewis	- par.	31	381	553	Cowbridge -	Cowbridge.
Ewenny (a) -	- par.	291	2,059	2,453	Bridgend -	Bridgend.
Flemingstone	- par.	55	701	968	Cowbridge -	Cowbridge.
Gilestone	- par.	52	367	734	do. -	do.
Higher Coychurch	- ham.	320	3,928	1,939	Bridgend -	Bridgend.
Higher Coyty	- ham.	515	2,937	3,689	do. -	do.
Higher Newcastle	- ham.	3,435	2,169	10,164	do. -	do.
Higher Tythegston	- ham.	1,514	2,231	5,660	do. -	do.
Kenfig	- par.	264	2,594	2,039	Taibach -	do.
Laleston	- par.	538	1,740	3,625	Bridgend -	do.
Lisworney -	- par.	160	982	1,361	Cowbridge -	Cowbridge.
Llanwit Major	- par.	992	5,122	9,077	do. -	do.
Llanblethian	- par.	724	3,263	5,613	do. -	do.
Llandough	- par.	117	727	1,097	do. -	do.
Llandow	- par.	128	1,119	1,593	do. -	Bridgend.
Llandyfodwg -	- par.	2,877	6,350	13,175	Bridgend -	do.
Llangan	- par.	200	1,200	1,818	do. -	do.
Llangeinor -	- par.	2,992	6,554	14,494	do. -	do.
Llanharan (a) -	- par.	534	3,080	6,827	Llantrissant -	Cowbridge.
Llanharry -	- par.	259	1,629	2,418	do. -	do.
Llanillid (a) -	- par.	105	1,641	1,480	Bridgend -	Bridgend.
						(*continued*)

BRIDGEND AND COWBRIDGE UNION :

(a) By Provisional Orders which came into operation on 25 March 1886,—
 A detached part of Saint Bride's Major was amalgamated with Ewenny; and
 A detached part of Llanillid was amalgamated with Llanharan.

Unions and Parishes, &c.		Population in 1881.	Area in Statute Acres in 1881.	Rateable Value in 1881.	Post Town.	Petty Sessional Division.

BRIDGEND AND COWBRIDGE UNION—County of Glamorgan—*continued.*

				£		
Llanmaes	par.	117	1,127	2,036	Cowbridge	Cowbridge.
Llanmihangle	par.	12	611	816	do.	do.
Llausanror	par.	187	1,819	1,901	do.	do.
Lower Coychurch	ham.	262	1,099	2,795	Bridgend	Bridgend.
Lower Coyty (W.)	ham.	3,281	1,680	16,186	do.	do.
Lower Llangonoyd	ham.	451	2,133	2,210	do.	do.
Lower Newcastle	ham.	1,061	870	4,262	do.	Newcastle.
Lower Tythegston	ham.	94	721	1,084	do.	Bridgend.
Marcross	par.	71	920	1,219	Cowbridge	do.
Merthyrmawr	par.	120	2,262	1,603	Bridgend	do.
Middle Llangonoyd	ham.	655	2,623	2,396	do.	do.
Monknash	par.	78	1,425	1,963	Cowbridge	do.
†Nash	par.	16	201	357	do.	Cowbridge.
Newton Nottage	par.	1,397	3,391	6,743	Bridgend	Bridgend.
Pencoyd	ham.	783	2,121	4,314	do.	do.
Penllino	par.	305	1,962	3,018	Cowbridge	Cowbridge.
Peterstone super Montem	tow.	211	2,106	2,249	Llantrissant	Bridgend.
Pyle	par.	938	1,637	4,351	Taibach	do.
*Saint Andrew Minor	par.	14	230	367	Bridgend	do.
Saint Athans	par.	378	1,531	2,816	Cowbridge	Cowbridge.
Saint Bride's, Major (a)	par.	674	5,437	5,100	Bridgend	Bridgend.
Saint Bride Minor	par.	917	1,919	2,685	do.	do.
Saint Donatts	par.	138	930	1,579	Cowbridge	Cowbridge.
Saint Hilary	par.	144	1,268	1,893	do.	do.
Saint Mary Church	par.	97	786	855	do.	do.
Saint Mary Hill	par.	171	1,419	1,429	Bridgend	Bridgend.
†Skerr	par.	11	361	111	do.	do.
†Stembridge	par.	7	38	57	Cowbridge	Cowbridge.
Wick	par.	363	1,439	2,064	Bridgend	Bridgend.
Ynysawdre	ham.	824	387	3,104	do.	do.
Ystradowen	par.	222	1,568	1,659	Cowbridge	Cowbridge.
TOTAL OF UNION		**38,920**	**107,984**	**202,115**		

BRIDGEWATER UNION.

(Formed 11 May 1836 by Order dated 16 April 1836.—Place marked thus * added 1 June 1866 by Order dated 2 May 1866.)

COUNTY OF SOMERSET :

Asholt (b)	par.	121	1,252	1,423	Bridgewater	Bridgewater.
Ashcot (c)	par.	718	2,272	3,350	do.	do.
Bawdrip	par.	393	1,889	4,232	do.	do.
Bridgewater (W.) (e) (f)	par.	12,704	3,539	Borough part 35,443 Extra part 12,948	do.	do.
Broomfield (f)	par.	420	4,274	3,565	do.	do.
Cannington (a) (c)	par.	1,369	4,980	10,641	do.	do.
Catcot	cha.	550	2,256	3,130	do.	do.

(continued)

BRIDGEND AND COWBRIDGE.

(a) *See note page 59.*

BRIDGEWATER UNION :

(a) A detached part of Cannington was amalgamated with Fiddington, by Order which came into operation on 25 March 1884.
(b) Detached parts of Asholt, Charlinch, and Goathurst, were united and amalgamated with Spaxton, by Order which came into operation on 25 March 1885.
(c) Two detached parts of Lyng were amalgamated with Stoke Saint Gregory, in the Taunton Union, by Order which came into operation on 25 March 1885.
(d) A detached part of Stogursey, in the Williton Union, was amalgamated with Huntspill, by Order which came into operation on 25 March 1885.
(e) By Provisional Order which came into operation on 25 March 1886, the several parts of the Hamlet of Edstock

BRIDGEWATER UNION—*continued.*

and Deer, having in 1881, population 23, and rateable value 153l., were amalgamated with Otterhampton and Cannington.

By Provisional Orders which came into operation on 25 March 1886, alterations were made in the areas of the following places, viz., Ashcot, Bridgewater, Cannington, Chedzoy, Chilton Trinity, Durleigh, Fiddington, Goathurst, Grointon, Huntspill, Lyng, Middlezoy, Nether Stowey, North Petherton, Othery, Otterhampton, Overstowey, Shapwick, Stockland Bristol, Wembdon, Weston Zoyland, and Woollavington.

(f) By Orders which came into operation on 25 March, 1887, -
A certain part of Broomfield was amalgamated with Enmore; and
Certain detached parts of Bridgewater were amalgamated with Durleigh.

Unions and Parishes, &c.		Population in 1881.	Area in Statute Acres in 1881.	Rateable Value in 1881.	Post Town.	Petty Sessional Division.
				£		
BRIDGEWATER UNION—County of Somerset—continued.						
Charlinch (b) -	par.	199	1,432	2,571	Bridgewater	- Bridgewater.
Chedzoy (e)	par.	356	1,655	3,885	do. - -	do.
*Chilton Common -	par.	—	30	75	do. - -	do.
Chilton Trinity (c) -	par.	169	1,543	3,599	do. - -	do.
Chilton upon Poldon	cha.	397	1,856	3,023	do. - -	do.
Coosington - -	par.	227	1,380	2,484	do. - -	do.
Durleigh (e) (f) -	par.	208	886	Borough part 333 Extra part 2,077	do.	- do.
Edington -	cha.	435	2,167	3,794	do. - -	do.
Enmore (f) -	par.	285	1,218	2,401	do. - -	do.
Fiddington (a) (e) -	par.	237	1,258	2,011	do. - -	Williton.
Goathurst (b) (e) -	par.	254	1,438	2,569	do. - -	Bridgewater.
Grointon (e) -	par.	133	845	1,681	do. - -	do.
Huntspill (d) (e) -	par.	1,920	9,289	20,246	do. - -	do.
Lyng (c) (e) -	par.	353	1,409	4,270	Taunton - -	do.
Michael Church -	par.	31	43	137	Bridgewater -	do.
Middlezoy (c) -	par.	565	2,520	5,005	do. - -	do.
Moorlinch -	par.	250	1,122	2,097	do. - -	do.
Nether Stowey (e) -	par.	731	1,080	2,884	do. - -	Williton.
North Petherton (e) -	par.	3,723	9,972	28,240	do. - -	Bridgewater.
Othery (e) -	par.	578	1,820	3,954	do. - -	do.
Otterhampton (e) -	par.	239	1,117	2,499	do. - -	do.
Overstowey (e) -	par.	512	3,647	2,648	do. - -	Williton.
Pawlet -	par.	531	3,566	10,188	do. - -	Bridgewater.
Puriton with Woollavington -	par.	753	1,632	6,122	do. - -	do.
Shapwick (e) -	par.	436	3,781	4,754	do. - -	do.
Spaxton (b) -	par.	916	3,009	5,126	do. - -	do.
Stowell -	ham.	177	973	1,961	do. - -	do.
Stockland Bristol (c)	par.	188	1,650	2,212	do. - -	do.
Sutton Mallet -	cha.	113	878	1,561	do. - -	do.
Thurloxton -	par.	161	551	1,316	do. - -	do.
Wembdon (e) -	par.	1,299	2,471	Borough part 248 Extra part 9,428	do. - -	do.
Weston Zoyland (e) -	par.	663	2,729	5,827	do. - -	do.
Woollavington (e) -	par.	336	1,725	3,926	do. - -	do.
TOTAL of UNION -		**33,650**	**91,163**	**229,431**		

BRIDGNORTH UNION.

(Formed 31 May 1836 by Order dated 7 May 1836.)

COUNTY of SALOP :

Acton Round -	par.	185	2,126	2,130	Bridgnorth -	Chelmarsh Division of Stottesdon.
Alveley -	par.	892	6,788	7,493	do. - -	do.
Astley Abbotts -	par.	623	3,228	5,599	do. - -	Do.
Aston Eyres -	tow.	89	In Morvill	1,700	do. - -	do.
Billingsley -	par.	125	1,285	1,242	do. - -	do.
Burwarton -	par.	146	1,239	1,542	do. - -	Cleobury Mortimer Division of Stottesdon.
Chelmarsh -	par.	478	3,259	4,877	do. -	Chelmarsh Division of Stottesdon.

(continued)

Unions and Parishes, &c.		Population in 1881.	Area in Statute Acres in 1881.	Rateable Value in 1881.	Post Town.	Petty Sessional Division.
				£		
BRIDGNORTH UNION.—County of Salop—*continued.*						
Chetton	par.	497	3,921	4,836	Bridgnorth	Bridgnorth Division of Stottesden.
Claverley	par.	1,700	8,143	17,249	do.	do.
Deuxhill	par.	45	487	611	do.	Chelmarsh Division of Stottesden.
Ditton Priors	par.	598	5,665	4,341	do.	Wenlock Franchise.
Eardington	tow.	263	1,301	3,379	do.	Chelmarsh Division of Stottesden.
Glazeley	par.	37	636	803	do.	do.
Middleton Scriven	par.	93	786	986	do.	do.
Monkhopton (a)	par.	169	2,258	2,293	do.	Wenlock Franchise.
Morville	par.	385	5,166	5,804	do.	Chelmarsh Division of Stottesden.
Neenton	par.	141	1,140	1,055	do.	do.
North Cleobury	par.	189	1,560	1,766	do.	do.
Oldbury	par.	257	808	3,283	do.	do.
Quatford	par.	197	512	1,189	do.	do.
Quatt	par.	547	2,674	4,376	do.	do.
Romsley	lib.	107	In Alveley	1,848	do.	do.
Saint Leonards (W.)	par.	2,859	500	9,204	do.	Borough of Bridgnorth (Separate Quarter Sessions).
Saint Mary Magdalen	par.	2,458	531	7,867	do.	do.
Sidbury	par.	49	1,277	1,328	do.	Chelmarsh Division of Stottesden.
Stanton Long (b)	par.	264	1,837	3,133	Much Wenlock	do.
Tasley	par.	77	1,031	1,517	do.	do.
Upton Cressett	par.	60	1,603	1,124	do.	do.
Worfield	par.	1,749	10,320	20,625	do.	Bridgnorth Division of Brimstree.
TOTAL of UNION		15,279	70,081	123,203		

BRIDLINGTON UNION. (Formed 28 Oct. 1836 by Order dated 4 Oct. 1836.) COUNTY of YORK, EAST RIDING :						
Argam	par.	39	559	645	Bridlington	Dickering.
Auburn	tow.	12	201	233	do.	do.
Burniston	tow.	198	2,418	3,519	Lowthorpe, Hull	do.
Bempton	par.	309	1,970	3,667	York	do.
Bessingby	par.	141	1,270	2,939	Carnaby, Hull	do.
Boynton	par.	156	2,615	3,113	Bridlington	do.
Bridlington and Quay (W.)	tow.	6,642	2,520	27,873	do.	do.
Buckton	tow.	151	1,984	2,930	Bempton, York	do.
Burton Agnes (a)	tow.	312	2,575	4,496	Hull	do.
Carnaby	tow.	180	1,944	3,071	do.	do.
Dringhoe, Upton, and Brough	tow.	157	1,705	2,290	Lowthorpe, Hull	North Holderness.
Easton	ham.	23	731	1,088	Bridlington	Dickering.
Flamborough	par.	1,390	3,084	1,800	Hull	do.
Fordon	tow.	57	1,464	1,112	Ganton, York	do.
Fraisthorp with part of Auburn	tow.	101	1,782	1,915	Carnaby, Hull	do.
Gransmoor (a)	tow.	84	1,253	1,629	Lowthorpe, Hull	do.
Grindale	tow.	179	2,429	2,904	Bridlington	do.
Haisthorp	tow.	123	1,390	2,561	Carnaby, Hull	do.
Hilderthorp	tow.	1,462	455	4,019	Bridlington Quay	do.
Hunmanby	tow.	1,351	6,988	11,120	Hunmanby, R.S.O.	do.

(continued)

BRIDGNORTH UNION :

(a) A detached part of Shipton, known as Skimblescott, in the Church Stretton Union, was amalgamated with Monkhopton, by Order which came into operation on 25 March 1883.

(b) Three detached parts of Holdgate, in the Ludlow Union, were amalgamated with Stanton Long, by Order which came into operation on 25 March 1884.

BRIDLINGTON UNION :

(a) A detached part of Burton Agnes was amalgamated with Gransmoor, and another detached part with Harpham, in the Driffield Union; and a detached part of Thornholm was amalgamated with Burton Agnes, by Order which came into operation on 25 March 1884.

Unions and Parishes, &c.		Population in 1881.	Area in Statute Acres in 1881.	Rateable Value in 1881.	Post Town.	Petty Sessional Division.
BRIDLINGTON UNION—County of York, East Riding—*continued*.				£		
Lissett	- tow.	90	1,150	1,580	Lowthorpe, Hull -	Dickering.
North Burton	- par.	543	3,910	4,643	Hunmanby, R.S.O.	do.
Reighton	- par.	254	1,818	2,556	Bempton, York -	do.
Rudston	- par.	604	5,551	6,585	Bridlington	do.
Sewerby and Marton	tow.	547	2,116	6,034	Hull -	do.
Skipsea	- tow.	398	1,595	2,483	Lowthorpe, Hull -	North Holderness.
Specton	- tow.	160	1,844	2,360	Bempton, York -	Dickering.
Thornholm (a)	- tow.	110	1,346	2,229	Burton Agnes, Hull	do.
Thwing	- par.	439	4,024	4,614	Hunmanby, R.S.O.	do.
Ulrome	- tow.	194	1,594	2,293	Lowthorpe, Hull -	do.
Willsthorp	- tow.	13	276	301	Bridlington	do.
Wold Newton	- par.	310	2,029	2,292	Ganton, York -	do.
TOTAL of UNION	-	16,762	66,592	123,927		
BRIDPORT UNION.						
(Formed 28 Mar. 1836 by Order dated 14 Mar. 1836.)						
COUNTY of DORSET :						
Allington (a)	- par.	1,709	591	5,610	Bridport -	Bridport.
Askerswell (a)	- par.	209	1,161	1,420	do. -	do.
Bothenhampton (a) -	par.	536	823	3,780	do. -	do.
Bradpole (W.)	- par.	1,567	966	6,629	do. -	do.
Bridport	- par.	3,936	62	12,248	do. -	do.
Burton Bradstock (a)	par.	946	2,680	5,081	do. -	do.
Catherston Leweston	par.	25	248	402	Charmouth	do.
Chideock	- par.	674	2,052	4,667	Bridport -	do.
Chilcombe -	- par.	40	465	648	do. -	Dorchester.
Litton Cheney (a)	- par.	458	3,817	4,852	Dorchester	do.
Loders (a) -	- par.	952	2,241	7,001	Bridport -	Bridport.
Punchknowle	- par.	473	2,160	2,397	do. -	Dorchester.
Shipton-Gorge (a) -	par.	312	1,528	1,724	do. -	Bridport.
Stanton Saint Gabriel	par.	71	1,242	1,087	Charmouth	do.
Swyre	- par.	213	1,146	1,179	Bridport -	Dorchester.
Symondsbury (a)	- par.	1,221	3,925	8,802	do. -	Bridport.
Walditch	- par.	192	285	1,220	do. -	do.
Whitechurch-Canonicorum (a)	} par.	1,053	6,113	8,767	Charmouth	do.
Wootton-Fitzpaine (a) par.		224	1,679	1,918	do.	do.
TOTAL of UNION	-	14,811	33,187	79,432		
BRIGHTON PARISH.						
(Under the 6 Geo. 4. c. clxxix.)						
COUNTY of SUSSEX :						
Brighton (W.)	- par.	99,091	1,625	542,850	Brighton -	Borough of Brighton (Separate Quarter Sessions).

BRIDPORT UNION :

(a) By Orders which came into operation on 25 March 1881

Detached parts of Whitechurch Canonicorum, were respectively amalgamated with Symondsbury and Wootton-Fitzpaine, and with Bettiscombe and Marshwood, in the Beaminster Union ;

A detached part of Bothenhampton was amalgamated with Symondsbury ;

BRIDPORT UNION—*continued*.

A detached part of Burton Bradstock was amalgamated with Shipton-Gorge ;

A detached part of Loders, known as " Loders West End," was amalgamated with Allington ; and

A detached part of Litton Cheney was amalgamated with Askerswell.

Unions and Parishes, &c.	Population in 1881.	Area in Statute Acres in 1881.	Rateable Value in 1884.	Post Town.	Petty Sessional Division.

BRISTOL INCORPORATION.

(Under the 3 Geo. 4. c. xxiv.; 1 Will. 4. c. iv.; 1 Vict. c. lxxxvi.; and 45 & 46 Vict. c. clxxx.)

CITY and COUNTY of BRISTOL:

			£		
All Saints - - par.	135	5	12,839		
Castle Precincts - par.	1,134	14	9,231		
Christ Church - par.	830	5	10,220		
Saint Augustine the Less - par.	9,167	155	51,436		
Saint Ewen - - par.	19	1	2,071		
Saint James - in par.	8,420	68	32,868		
Saint John - - par.	531	9	8,836		
Saint Leonard - par.	64	5	7,167		
Saint Mary-le-Port - par.	105	3	4,362		
Saint Mary Redcliffe par.	5,188	72	26,967	Bristol - -	Borough of Bristol (Separate Quarter Sessions).
Saint Michael - par.	4,899	98	24,908		
Saint Nicholas - par.	1,024	27	16,911		
Saint Paul - in par.	15,083	120	43,241		
Saint Peter (W.) - par.	912	11	9,962		
Saint Philip and Saint Jacob - in par.	3,560	31	11,747		
Saint Stephen - par.	1,994	30	20,077		
Saint Thomas - par.	650	18	16,050		
Temple - - par.	3,764	83	33,320		
TOTAL of INCORPORATION -	57,479	755	342,213		

BRIXWORTH UNION.

(Formed 9 July 1835 by Order dated 20 June 1835.—Places marked thus * added 21 April 1836 by Order dated 28 March 1836; thus † added 29 Sept. 1849 by Order dated 7 July 1849; thus ‡ added 25 Dec. 1861 by Order dated 26 Oct. 1861; and thus § added 25 Mar. 1862 by Order dated 25 Feb. 1862.)

COUNTY of NORTHAMPTON:

‡Althorp - - par.	91	In Brington	1,727	Northampton -	Northampton.
Boughton - - par.	321	1,850	3,506	do. -	do.
Brington - - par.	827	3,761	5,027	do. -	do.
Brixworth (W.) - par.	1,183	3,410	9,814	do. -	do.
Chapel Brampton - par.	233	1,330	2,218	do. -	do.
Church Brampton - par.	180	1,100	1,677	do. -	do.
*Cold Ashby - par.	339	1,940	3,316	Welford -	do.
Coton or Coaton - ham.	97	860	1,020	Northampton -	do.
Cottesbrooke - par.	214	2,780	4,580	do. -	do.
Draughton - - par.	161	1,477	2,182	do. -	Kettering.
East Haddon - par.	752	2,572	4,560	do. -	Northampton.
Faxton - - par.	55	2,120	2,680	do. -	Kettering.
Great Creaton (a) - par.	361	1,268	2,567	do. -	Northampton.
Guilsborough - par.	517	3,080	4,821	do. -	do.
Hanging Houghton - ham.	124	In Lamport	2,382	do. -	do.
Hannington - par.	187	1,270	1,736	do. -	do.
Harlestone - par.	569	2,530	4,213	do. -	do.
Haselbeech - par.	155	1,618	2,561	do. -	Little Bowden.
Holcot - - par.	377	1,670	2,349	do. -	Northampton.
Holdenby or Holmby par.	206	1,855	3,428	do. -	do.
Hollowell - ham.	211 {	In Guilsborough. }	1,913	do. -	do.

(continued)

BRIXWORTH UNION:

(a) The several parts of a hamlet, known as Little Creaton, were amalgamated with Great Creaton, by Order which came into operation 25 March 1884.

Unions and Parishes, &c.		Population in 1881.	Area in Statute Acres in 1881.	Rateable Value in 1881.	Post Town.		Petty Sessional Division.
				£			

BRIXWORTH UNION—County of Northampton—*continued*.

Unions and Parishes, &c.		Population in 1881.	Area in Statute Acres in 1881.	Rateable Value in 1881.	Post Town.		Petty Sessional Division.
Lamport	- - *par.*	165	1,440	3,215	Northampton	-	Northampton.
Maidwell	- *par.*	293	1,650	2,436	do.	-	Little Bowden.
§Mawsley	- *par.*	8	In Faxton	583	do.	-	Kettering.
Moulton	- *par.*	1,483	1,680	7,174	do.	-	Northampton.
‡Moulton Park	- *par.*	45	450	713	do.	-	do.
*Naseby	- *par.*	610	3,690	5,312	Welford	-	Little Bowden.
Old or Wold	- *par.*	362	1,650	3,383	Northampton	-	Northampton.
†Overstone	- - *par.*	181	1,940	3,202	do.	-	do.
Pisford or Pitsford	- *par.*	559	2,700	3,731	do.	-	do.
Ravensthorpe	- *par.*	411	1,330	2,659	do.	-	do.
Scaldwell	- - *par.*	337	1,060	2,514	do.	-	do.
Spratton	- - *par.*	817	2,332	5,791	do.	-	do.
Teeton	- - *ham.*	85	681	1,228	do.	-	do.
*Thornby	- - *par.*	211	1,212	2,373	do.	-	do.
Walgrave	- - *par.*	603	2,010	3,559	do.	-	do.
TOTAL of UNION	-	**13,336**	**60,376**	**116,156**			

BROMLEY UNION.

(Formed 19 May 1836 by Order dated 23 April 1836.—Place marked thus *, previously in Lewisham Union, added 1 April 1887 by Order dated 18 Feb. 1887.)

COUNTY of KENT :

Unions and Parishes, &c.		Population in 1881.	Area in Statute Acres in 1881.	Rateable Value in 1881.	Post Town.		Petty Sessional Division.
Beckenham	- - *par.*	13,045	3,881	108,425	Beckenham	-	Bromley.
Bromley	- *par.*	15,154	4,706	102,393	Bromley	-	do.
Chelsfield	- - *par.*	917	3,378	12,170	St. Mary's Cray	-	do.
Chislehurst	- - *par.*	5,311	2,748	46,251	Chislehurst	-	do.
Cudham	- - *par.*	1,029	5,925	6,173	Orpington	-	do.
Down	- *par.*	555	1,652	3,976	Beckenham	-	do.
Farnborough (W.)	- *par.*	1,451	1,429	7,076	do.	-	do.
Foot's Cray	- *par.*	1,908	805	13,709	Foot's Cray	-	do.
Hayes	- *par.*	691	1,282	5,456	Beckenham	-	do.
Keston	- *par.*	731	1,187	4,278	do.	-	do.
Knockholt	- *par.*	789	1,704	3,512	Sevenoaks	-	do.
*Mottingham	- *ham.*	779	612	5,853	Eltham	-	Blackheath and Lees ness.
North Cray	- *par.*	635	1,484	4,114	Foot's Cray	-	Bromley.
Orpington	- *par.*	3,050	3,517	17,670	Orpington	-	do.
Saint Mary's Cray	- *par.*	1,906	2,028	18,401	St. Mary's Cray	-	do.
Saint Paul's Cray	- *par.*	774	1,651	5,130	Chislehurst	-	do.
West Wickham	- *par.*	963	2,661	6,634	Beckenham	-	do.
TOTAL of UNION	-	**49,751**	**41,060**	**372,184**			

BROMSGROVE UNION.

(Formed 7 Nov. 1836 by Order dated 15 Oct. 1836, as amended by Order of 22 Sept. 1840 and 13 July 1841.—Place marked thus * added 1 Mar. 1863 by Order dated 19 Jan. 1863).

COUNTY of WORCESTER :

Unions and Parishes, &c.		Population in 1881.	Area in Statute Acres in 1881.	Rateable Value in 1881.	Post Town.		Petty Sessional Division.
Alvechurch	- - *par.*	1,618	6,747	12,635	Redditch	-	Redditch and North field.
Belbroughton	- *par.*	1,976	4,605	10,718	Stourbridge	-	Stourbridge.
Bentley Pauncefoot	- *tow.*	220	In Redditch	2,311	Bromsgrove	-	Bromsgrove.
Bromsgrove (W.) (*a*)	- *par.*	12,813	11,147	39,552	do.	-	do.
Clent	- - *par.*	972	2,365	6,201	Stourbridge	-	Stourbridge.
Cofton Hackett	- *par.*	188	1,261	2,521	Redditch	-	Northfield.
Frankley	- - *par.*	147	1,901	1,838	Halesowen	-	Halesowen.
*Grafton Manor (*a*)	- *par.*	55	1,414	1,898	Bromsgrove	-	Bromsgrove.
							(*continued*)

BROMSGROVE UNION :

(*a*) Detached parts of Dodderhill and Upton Warren, in the Droitwich Union, were amalgamated with Bromsgrove and Grafton Manor, by Provisional Order which came into operation on 25 March 1882.

L

Unions and Parishes, &c.		Population in 1881.	Area in Statute Acres in 1881.	Rateable Value in 1881.	Post Town.	Petty Sessional Division.
				£		
BROMSGROVE UNION—County of Worcester—*continued*.						
Hagley	*par.*	1,257	2,363	6,859	Stourbridge	- Stourbridge.
Hunnington	*tow.*	124	In Romsley	1,789	Halesowen	- Halesowen.
Pedmore	*par.*	500	1,474	4,338	Stourbridge	. - Stourbridge.
Redditch	*tow.*	7,740	5,541	24,128	Redditch	- Redditch.
Romsley	*tow.*	415	2,876	2,181	Halesowen	- Halesowen.
Stoke Prior	*par.*	2,354	3,820	18,230	Bromsgrove	- Bromsgrove.
Tutnall and Cobley	*ham.*	493	3,450	5,183	do. -	- do.
Webheath	*tow.*	1,042	In Redditch	4,274	Redditch -	- Redditch.
TOTAL of UNION -		31,914	48,967	141,659		

BROMYARD UNION.

(Formed 30 May 1836 by Order dated 5 May 1836.—Place marked thus * added 25 Dec. 1858 by Order dated 17 Nov. 1858, and thus † added 29 Sept. 1863 by Order dated 9 Sept. 1863.)

COUNTY of HEREFORD :

Avenbury (*a*) -	*par.*	371	3,233	4,147	Bromyard -	- Bromyard.
Bishop's Frome (*a*)(*b*)	*par.*	727	3,920	7,007	do. -	- do.
Bridenbury (*a*)	*par.*	84	545	837	do. -	- do.
Bromyard (*a*) -	*tow.*	1,477	3,368	3,908	do. -	- do.
Collington (*a*)	*par.*	103	985	1,116	do. -	- do.
Cradley	*par.*	1,746	5,966	9,797	Malvern -	- do. (part Malvern for convenience).
Edwin Ralph (*a*)	*par.*	163	1,590	1,531	Bromyard	- Bromyard.
Evesbach	*par.*	53	973	1,183	do. -	- do.
Felton (*a*) -	*par.*	105	1,699	2,013	do. -	- do.
Grendon Bishop	*par.*	169	} 1,689	{ 1,520	do. -	- do.
Grendon Warren	*par.*	23		476	do. -	- do.
Hampton Charles	*ham.*	98	492	503	Tenbury	- do.
Linton (W.) (*a*)	*tow.*	616	5,243	4,287	Worcester	- do.
Little Cowarne	*par.*	170	696	1,137	Bromyard -	- do.
†Lower Brockhampton	*par.*	66	In Linton	163	Worcester -	- do.
Moreton Jefferies	*par.*	43	703	959	Bromyard	- do.
Much Cowarne (*a*)	*par.*	498	3,706	5,595	do. -	- do.
Norton with Brockhampton (*a*)	*tow.*	492	In Linton	4,305	do. -	- do.
Ocle Pychard (*b*)	*par.*	291	1,507	3,319	Hereford -	- do.
Pencombe	*par.*	258	4,590	4,326	Bromyard -	- do.
*Saltmarsh -	*par.*	32	—	363	do. -	- do.
Stanford Bishop (*a*) -	*par.*	173	1,471	1,933	do. -	- do.
Stoke Lacy (*a*)	*par.*	286	2,005	2,625	do. -	- do.
Tedstone Delamere -	*par.*	251	1,677	2,020	Worcester -	- do.

(continued)

BROMYARD UNION :

(*a*) By Orders which came into operation on 25 March 1884,—
Four detached parts of Avenbury were amalgamated with Bridenbury; and another part was united with parts of Much Cowarne, and the parts so united were amalgamated with Stoke Lacy;
A detached part of Bishop's Frome was amalgamated with Stanford Bishop;
Detached parts of Bromyard were amalgamated with Winslow, Linton, and Stanford Bishop, and parts of Linton, Norton with Brockhampton, and Winslow were amalgamated with Bromyard;
A detached part of Edwin Ralph, known as Butterly, was amalgamated with Wacton;
Parts of Felton were amalgamated with Ullingswick, Bodenham, in the Leominster Union, and Sutton in the Hereford Union;

BROMYARD UNION—*continued*.

Detached parts of Wacton were amalgamated with Thornbury and Edwin Ralph respectively;
A detached part of Linton was amalgamated with Winslow;
A nearly detached part of Norton with Brockhampton was amalgamated with Winslow;
Two detached parts of Edwin Loach were amalgamated with Collington; and
Detached parts of Ullingswick were amalgamated respectively with Sutton and Marden, in the Hereford Union.

(*b*) By Orders which came into operation on 25 March 1887,—
A detached part of Bishop's Frome was amalgamated with Castle Frome, in the Ledbury Union; and
A detached part of Ocle Pychard was amalgamated with Sutton, in the Hereford Union.

Unions and Parishes, &c.	Population in 1881.	Area in Statute Acres in 1881.	Rateable Value in 1881.	Post Town.	Petty Sessional Division.
			£		
BROMYARD UNION—County of Hereford—*continued.*					
Tedstone Wafer - *par.*	79	683	684	Worcester -	Bromyard.
Thornbury (*a*) - *par.*	234	2,130	2,212	Bromyard - -	do.
Ullingswick (*a*) - *par.*	293	1,245	1,705	do. - -	do.
Upper Sapey - *par.*	323	2,190	2,584	Worcester - -	do.
Wacton (*a*) - *par.*	102	1,002	1,127	Bromyard -	do.
Whitbourne - *par.*	745	3,056	5,689	Worcester - -	do.
Winslow (*a*) - *tow.*	413 } In Bromyard }		4,630	Bromyard -	do.
Wolferlow - - *par.*	98	1,535	1,452	Tenbury - -	do.
COUNTY of WORCESTER :					
Acton Beauchamp - *par.*	199	1,529	2,137	Bromyard - -	Worcester.
Edwin Loach (*a*) - *par.*	44	534	633	do. - -	Bromyard.
Lower Sapey or Sapey Pritchard } *par.*	230	1,697	1,976	Worcester - -	Hundred House.
TOTAL of UNION -	11,055	61,659	89,989		
BUCKINGHAM UNION.					
(Formed 13 July 1835 by Order dated 18 June 1835. Place marked thus * added 25 Mar. 1865 by Order dated 18 Feb. 1865.)					
COUNTY of BUCKINGHAM :					
Addington - - *par.*	134	1,303	2,671	Winslow - -	Buckingham.
Adstock - - *par.*	352	1,166	2,012	do. - -	do.
Akeley - - *par.*	387	1,325	2,062	Buckingham -	do.
Barton Harthorn - *par.*	111	892	1,336	do. - -	do.
Beachampton - *par.*	217	1,528	2,321	Stony Stratford -	Stony Stratford.
Buckingham (W.) - *par.*	3,585	5,007	18,819	Buckingham -	Borough of Buckingham (Separate Quarter Sessions).
Charndon - - *ham.*	150	1,911	2,028	Bicester - -	Buckingham.
Chetwode - - *par.*	155	1,171	2,165	Buckingham -	do.
Edgecott - - *par.*	187	1,140	1,519	Aylesbury - -	do.
Foxcott - - *par.*	72	719	1,371	Buckingham -	do.
Hillersden - - *par.*	221	2,606	4,189	do. - -	do.
Leckhampstead - *par.*	340	2,571	4,060	do. - -	do.
Lillingstone Dayrell - *par.*	275	1,873	2,573	do. - -	do.
Lillingstone Lovell - *par.*	161	1,667	2,323	do. - -	do.
*Luffield Abbey - *par.*	8	216	296	Towcester - -	do.
Maids Morton - *par.*	418	1,366	3,311	Buckingham -	do.
Marsh Gibbon - *par.*	713	2,818	4,342	Bicester - -	do.
Middle Claydon - *par.*	225	2,640	4,001	Winslow - -	do.
Padbury - - *par.*	530	2,029	4,017	Buckingham -	do.
Pounden - - *ham.*	72	980	1,390	Bicester - -	do.
Preston Bissett - *par.*	341	1,523	2,915	Buckingham -	do.
Ratclive cum Chackmore } *par.*	367	1,184	2,562	do. - -	do.
Shalston - - *par.*	186	1,383	1,706	do. - -	do.
Steeple Claydon - *par.*	852	3,329	5,702	Winslow - -	do.
Stowe - - *par.*	338	3,088	1,678	Buckingham -	do.
Thornborough - *par.*	577	2,392	4,236	do. - -	do.
Thornton - - *par.*	67	1,317	2,347	Stony Stratford -	do.
Tingewick - - *par.*	787	2,178	4,108	Buckingham -	do.
Twyford - - *par.*	339	1,567	2,730	do. - -	do.
Water Stratford - *par.*	188	1,102	1,493	do. - -	do.
TOTAL of UNION -	12,418	54,021	99,283		

Unions and Parishes, &c.	Population in 1881.	Area in Statute Acres in 1881.	Rateable Value in 1881.	Post Town.	Petty Sessional Division.

BUILTH UNION.

(Formed 2 Jan. 1837 by Order dated 6 Dec. 1836 as amended by Order dated 16 Mar. 1853.)

COUNTY of BRECKNOCK :

Unions and Parishes, &c.	Population in 1881.	Area in Statute Acres in 1881.	Rateable Value in 1881.	Post Town.	Petty Sessional Division.
			£		
Altmawr - - par.	36	499	281	Builth - -	Builth.
Builth or Llanfair in Buallt (W.) } par.	1,455	712	4,845	do. -	do.
Crickadarn - - par.	330	4,331	2,362	Erwood R.S.O. -	Talgarth.
Gwaravog - - ham.	40	66	358	Garth, R.S.O. -	Builth.
Gwenddwr - - par.	369	7,381	2,906	Erwood R.S.O. -	do.
Llanafan-fawr - par.	647	7,971	3,570	Garth, R.S.O. -	do.
Llanafan fechan, or Llanfechan } par.	153	2,783	1,130	do. - -	do.
Llanddewi Abergwessin } par.	81	10,511	659	do. - -	do. do.
Llanddewi'r Cwm - par.	398	3,101	2,206	Builth - -	do.
Llanfihangel Abergwessin } par.	328	6,836	1,507	Garth, R.S.O. -	do.
Llanfihangel Bryn Pabuan } ham.	205	3,395	1,073	do. - -	do.
Llanganten - - par.	187	2,258	1,374	Builth - -	do.
Llangynog - - par.	48	1,429	382	do. - -	do.
Llanleonfel - - ham.	169	2,834	974	Garth, R.S.O. -	do.
Llanynis - - par.	134	2,250	966	Builth - -	do.
Llysdinam - - ham.	199	2,476	1,402	Newbridge on Wye	do.
Maesmynis - - par.	213	4,012	1,315	Builth - -	do.
Penbuallt - - ham.	538	5,423	2,038	Llangammarch, R.S.O.	do.
Rhosferig - - ham.	83	1,320	864	Builth - -	do.
Treflis - - ham.	518	6,325	2,534	Llangammarch, R.S.O.	do.
COUNTY of RADNOR :					
Aberedw - - par.	257	4,300	2,140	Builth - -	Colwyn.
Bettws Disserth - par.	109	1,885	760	do. - -	do.
Cregrina - - par.	96	1,595	915	do. - -	do.
Disserth and Trecoed par.	544	6,650	3,326	do. - -	do.
Llanbadarn y Garreg par.	47	900	503	do. - -	do.
Llandrindod - par.	303	2,689	2,307	Llandrindod -	Cefnllys.
Llanelwedd - - par.	204	2,020	2,173	Builth - -	Colwyn.
Llansaintfraed in Elvel par.	305	4,000	1,904	do. - -	do.
Llanfaredd - - par.	153	2,245	1,169	do. - -	do.
Rhulen - - par.	63	756	683	do. - -	do.
TOTAL of UNION -	8,182	102,953	48,656		

BUNTINGFORD UNION.

(Formed 29 June 1835 by Order dated 13 June 1835.)

COUNTY of HERTFORD :

Unions and Parishes, &c.	Population in 1881.	Area in Statute Acres in 1881.	Rateable Value in 1881.	Post Town.	Petty Sessional Division.
Anstey - - par.	391	2,150	2,060	Buntingford -	Buntingford.
Aspeden (a) - - par.	613	1,407	2,941	do. - -	do.

(continued)

BUNTINGFORD UNION :

(a) By Orders which came into operation on 25 March 1883,—

Certain detached parts of Laystone were amalgamated with Aspeden, Throcking, and Wyddial ;

BUNTINGFORD UNION—continued.

Two detached parts of Throcking were amalgamated with Laystone ; and
A parish known as Wakeley was amalgamated with Westmill.

Unions and Parishes, &c.		Population in 1881.	Area in Statute Acres in 1881.	Rateable Value in 1881.	Post Town.	Petty Sessional Division.
				£		
Buntingford Union—County of Hertford—*continued.*						
Broadfield	par.	19	375	388	Buntingford	Buntingford.
Buckland	par.	358	1,629	2,038	do.	do.
Cottered	par.	379	1,833	2,599	do.	do.
Great Hormead	par.	519	1,919	2,868	do.	do.
Laystone (W.) (*a*)	par.	1,071	2,242	4,796	do.	do.
Little Hormead	par.	127	1,067	1,376	do.	do.
Meesden	par.	189	1,009	1,071	do.	Great Hadham.
Rushden	par.	270	1,509	1,851	do.	Buntingford.
Sandon	par.	763	4,061	5,584	Royston	Royston.
Throcking (*a*)	par.	74	910	1,356	Buntingford	Buntingford.
Wallington	par.	191	2,043	2,320	Baldock	do.
Westmill (*a*)	par.	371	2,670	3,823	Buntingford	do.
Wyddial (*a*)	par.	202	1,224	1,904	do.	do.
Yardley	par.	495	2,421	3,454	do.	do.
Total of Union		6,032	23,472	41,338		

BURNLEY UNION.

(Formed 20 Jan. 1837 by Order dated 23 Dec. 1836.)

County of Lancaster :

Altham	tow.	395	1,440	3,718	Accrington	Accrington.
Barley with Wheatley Booth	tow.	314	2,625	2,034	Burnley	Colne.
Barrowford Booth	tow.	3,842	2,365	9,415	do.	do.
Briercliffe with Extwisle	tow.	1,147	4,227	7,311	do.	Burnley.
Burnley (W)	tow.	28,744	1,996	72,999	do.	do.
Cliviger	tow.	1,952	6,819	15,991	do.	do.
Colne	tow.	10,313	4,635	27,577	Colne	Colne.
Dunockshaw	tow.	212	389	809	Burnley	Bacup and Rawtenstall.
Foulridge	tow.	890	2,455	5,668	Colne	Colne.
Goldshaw Booth	tow.	355	2,034	2,318	Burnley	do.
Great and Little Marsden	tow.	16,725	4,089	42,584	do.	do.
Habergham Eaves	tow.	35,033	4,217	97,696	do.	Burnley.
Hapton	tow.	2,155	4,008	13,623	do.	do.
Heyhouses	tow.	77	322	420	Blackburn	do.
Higham with West Close Booth	tow.	751	1,534	2,830	Burnley	do.
Huncoat	tow.	930	990	4,714	Accrington	Accrington.
Ightenhill Park	tow.	205	760	4,886	Burnley	Burnley.
Old Laund Booth	tow.	332	431	797	do.	Colne.
Padiham	tow.	8,346	1,953	20,365	do.	Burnley.
Read	tow.	909	1,548	4,232	Blackburn	do.
Reedley Hollows, Filley Close, and New Laund Booths	tow.	667	1,446	5,939	Burnley	do.
Rough Lee	tow.	323	1,111	1,727	do.	Colne.
Simonstone	tow.	421	1,026	2,225	do.	Burnley.
Trawden	tow.	2,161	6,808	7,536	Colne	Colne.
Wheatley Carr	tow.	39	254	350	Burnley	do.
Worsthorn with Hurstwood	tow.	1,093	3,510	7,747	do.	Burnley.
Total of Union		118,334	63,672	365,514		

I 3

Unions and Parishes, &c.	Population in 1881.	Area in Statute Acres in 1881.	Rateable Value in 1881.	Post Town.	Petty Sessional Division.

BURTON-UPON-TRENT UNION.

(Formed 30 Mar. 1837 by Order dated 25 Feb. 1837, as amended by Order dated 7 Mar. 1837.— Places marked thus * added 31 May 1837 by Order dated 3 May 1837 ; thus † added 13 Aug. 1839 by Order dated 20 July 1839.)

COUNTY OF DERBY :

Unions and Parishes, &c.	Population in 1881.	Area in Statute Acres in 1881.	Rateable Value in 1881.	Post Town.	Petty Sessional Division.
			£		
Ash - ham.	75	703	1,381	Derby - -	Derby
*Barton Blount - par.	58	1,201	2,038	do. - -	Appletree.
*Bearwardcote (b) - tow.	35	457	821	do. - -	Derby.
Bradley alias Bretby (a) (b) - } cha.	336	In Repton	3,444	Burton on Trent -	Repton and Gresley.
Burnaston - - tow.	171	983	1,831	Derby - -	Derby.
Castle Gresley (b) - tow.	786 {	In Church Gresley }	3,353	Burton on Trent -	Swadlincote.
*Catton - - tow.	82	1,064	1,999	do. - -	do.
Cauldwell - - tow.	164 {	In Stapenhill }	2,179	do. - -	do.
Church Broughton (a) par.	588	2,363	1,701	Derby - -	Appletree.
Church Gresley (b) - tow.	5,422	6,700	17,042	Burton on Trent -	Swadlincote.
Coton in the Elms - tow.	495 {	In Lullington }	2,633	do. - -	do.
Dalbury - - par.	198	1,192	2,060	Derby - -	Derby.
Drakelow - - tow.	142 {	In Church Gresley }	2,643	Burton on Trent -	Swadlincote.
Eggington - - par.	408	2,289	8,467	do. - -	Derby.
Etwall (b) - - tow.	526	2,083	5,175	Derby - -	do.
Findern - - tow.	405 {	In Mickleover }	7,142	do. - -	do.
Foremark - - tow.	61	2,870	1,875	Burton on Trent -	Repton and Gresley.
Hatton (a) - - tow.	507	735	3,108	do. - -	Appletree.
Hilton (a) - - tow.	804	1,835	4,363	Derby - -	do.
Hoon - - tow.	51	789	1,533	do. - -	do.
Ingleby - - tow.	104 {	In Foremark }	1,510	do. - -	Repton and Gresley.
Linton - - tow.	1,193 {	In Church Gresley }	4,098	Burton on Trent -	Swadlincote.
Lullington - - tow.	250	2,083	3,294	do. - -	do.
Marston upon Dove - tow.	108	1,004	2,241	Derby - -	Appletree.
Mickleover - - tow.	1,413	2,378	6,299	do. - -	Derby.
Newton Solney (a) (b) par.	171	1,280	3,802	Burton on Trent -	Repton and Gresley.
†Osleston and Thurvaston - } tow.	335	1,732	3,058	Derby - -	Ashbourne.
Radburn - - par.	246	2,182	4,266	do. - -	Derby.
Repton - - par.	1,724	5,187	10,882	Burton on Trent -	Repton and Gresley.
Rosliston - - par.	459	1,197	2,431	do. - -	Swadlincote.
Stanton and Newhall tow.	4,257 {	In Stapenhill }	12,928	do. - -	do.
Stapenhill - - tow.	3,843	1,620	14,095	do. - -	do.
Sutton on the Hill - tow.	105	893	1,898	Derby - -	Appletree.
Swadlincote - - tow.	2,214 {	In Church Gresley }	7,916	Burton on Trent -	Swadlincote.

(continued)

BURTON-UPON-TRENT UNION :

(a) By Orders which came into operation on 25 March 1885,—
Certain parts of Church Broughton, including, a part known as Limbersitch, were amalgamated with Hatton ;
A part of Church Broughton known as Mackley Meadow Acre was amalgamated with Foston and Scropton ;
A detached part of Measham, in the Ashby de la Zouch Union, together with a detached part of Newton Solney, were amalgamated with Bradley alias Bretby ; and

BURTON-UPON-TRENT UNION—continued.

All the parts of a parish known as Hargate Manor, were amalgamated with Hilton ;

(b) By Provisional Order which came into operation on 25 March 1886, alterations were made in the areas of the following places, viz., Bearwardcote, Bradley alias Bretby, Castle Gresley, Church Gresley, Etwall, Newton Solney, Harton under Needwood, Burton Extra, Burton upon Trent, Dunstall, Horninglow, and Tatenhill.

Unions and Parishes, &c.		Population in 1881.	Area in Statute Acres in 1881.	Rateable Value in 1881.	Post Town.	Petty Sessional Division.
				£		
BURTON-UPON-TRENT UNION—County of Derby—*continued.*						
Trusley	*par.*	88	1,086	1,682	Derby	Derby.
Twyford and Stenson	*tow.*	219	1,800	6,723	do.	do.
Walton upon Trent	*par.*	440	2,309	5,464	Burton on Trent	Swadlincote.
Willington	*par.*	515	1,326	7,711	do.	Derby.
Winshill	*tow.*	2,917	1,150	10,960	do.	Repton and Gresley.
COUNTIES of DERBY and STAFFORD:						
Foston and	*tow.*	524 in Derby.	2,841 in Derby.	6,424 in Derby.	Derby	Appletree.
Scropton (*a*)	*par.*	98 in Stafford.	142 in Stafford.	959 in Stafford.	do.	
COUNTY of STAFFORD:						
Anslow	*tow.*	383	In Rolleston	2,626	Burton on Trent	Burton upon Trent.
Barton under Needwood (*b*)	*tow.*	1,789	In Tatenhill	17,786	do.	do.
Branston	*tow.*	991	In Burton upon Trent	11,525	do.	do.
Burton Extra (*b*)	*tow.*	12,582		44,013	do.	do.
Burton upon Trent (*b*)	*tow.*	9,348	6,580	102,048	do.	do.
Dunstall (*b*)	*tow.*	267	In Tatenhill	4,783	do.	do.
Hanbury	*tow.*	537	3,195	6,455	do.	do.
Horninglow (W.) (*b*)	*tow.*	10,717	In Burton-upon-Trent	33,660	do.	do.
Rolleston	*tow.*	757	3,647	5,938	do.	do.
Stretton	*tow.*	698	In Burton-upon-Trent	7,379	do.	do.
Tatenhill (*b*)	*tow.*	493	9,408	5,116	do.	do.
Tutbury	*par.*	2,306	4,001	12,544	do.	do.
Wichnor	*tow.*	173	In Tatenhill	4,800	Lichfield	do.
TOTAL of UNION		73,869	86,431	454,944		

BURY UNION.						
(Formed 8th Feb. 1837 by Order dated 19 Jan. 1837.)						
COUNTY of LANCASTER:						
Ainsworth	*tow.*	1,729	1,309	9,381	Bolton	Bury.
Ashworth	*tow.*	142	1,021	1,829	Rochdale	do.
Birtle cum Bamford (W.)	*tow.*	2,265	1,429	9,659	Bury	do.
Bury	*tow.*	39,283	2,330	163,086	do.	do.
Elton	*tow.*	11,947	2,553	54,609	do.	do.
Heap	*tow.*	17,686	2,938	82,151	Heywood	do.
Hopwood	*tow.*	4,440	2,126	28,703	do.	do.
Pilkington	*tow.*	13,144	5,469	69,418	Manchester	do.
Pilsworth	*tow.*	758	1,483	9,129	Bury	do.
Radcliffe	*par.*	16,267	2,533	74,552	Radcliffe	do.
Tottington Lower End	*tow.*	16,428	5,271	59,110	Ramsbottom	do.
Walmersley	*tow.*	5,519	5,065	36,115	Bury	do.
TOTAL of UNION		129,608	33,527	598,042		

BURY SAINT EDMUNDS INCORPORATION.						
(Under the 21 Geo. 2.)						
COUNTY of SUFFOLK:						
Saint James	*par.*	9,441	2,938	31,957	Bury St. Edmunds	Borough of Bury St. Edmunds Separate Quarter Sessions.
Saint Mary (W.)	*par.*	6,670		22,114	do.	
TOTAL of INCORPORATION		16,111	2,938	54,071		

Unions and Parishes, &c.		Population in 1881.	Area in Statute Acres in 1881.	Rateable Value in 1881.	Post Town.	Petty Sessional Division.
CAISTOR UNION.						
(Formed 13 Dec. 1836 by Order dated 23 Nov. 1836.)						
COUNTY of LINCOLN :				£		
Ashby cum Fenby	- par.	261	1,675	2,231	Great Grimsby	Bradley Haverstow.
Atterby	- tow.	109	In Bishop Norton	1,289	Kirton in Lindsey	Lawress.
Aylesby	- par.	112	2,110	2,629	Great Grimsby	Bradley Haverstow.
Barnoldby le Beck	- par.	212	1,460	1,761	do.	do.
Beelsby	- par.	171	2,189	3,552	do.	do.
Bigby	- par.	360	3,140	7,807	Brigg	Yarborough.
Bishop Norton	- tow.	356	4,240	3,175	Kirton in Lindsey	Lawress.
Bradley	- par.	99	1,648	1,747	Great Grimsby	Bradley Haverstow.
Brigsley	- par.	139	860	1,281	do.	do.
Buslingthorpe (a)	- par.	56	1,096	1,482	Market Rasen	Lawress.
Cabourn	- par.	174	2,860	3,126	Caistor	Bradley Haverstow.
Caistor (W.)	- tow.	1,867	6,490	7,683	do.	Yarborough.
Claxby	- par.	325	1,689	2,641	Market Rasen	Walsheroft.
Clee	- tow.	11,620	2,557	17,677	Great Grimsby	Bradley Haverstow.
Cleethorpe	- tow.	2,840	1,043	7,622	do.	do.
Clixby	- tow.	45	In Caistor	1,492	Caistor	Yarborough.
Croxby	- par.	127	1,628	1,924	do.	Walsheroft.
Cuxwold	- par.	101	1,563	2,068	do.	Bradley Haverstow.
East Ravendale	- tow.	108	1,430	1,658	Great Grimsby	do.
East Torrington	- par.	125	1,498	1,708	Wragby	Wraggoe.
Glentham	- par.	410	2,240	3,609	Market Rasen	Lawress.
Grasby	- par.	411	1,720	1,817	Caistor	Yarborough.
Great Coates	- par.	245	2,777	6,297	Uleeby	Bradley Haverstow.
Great Grimsby	- par.	28,503	1,737	78,524	Great Grimsby	do.
Habrough (a)	- par.	391	2,750	4,632	Uleeby	Yarborough.
Hatcliffe	- par.	203	1,370	1,878	Great Grimsby	Bradley Haverstow.
Hawerby with Beesby	par.	82	1,179	1,655	do.	do.
Heading	- par.	117	1,327	2,576	Uleeby	do.
Holton-le-Moor	- tow.	178	In Caistor	2,172	Caistor	Walsheroft.
Humberston	- par.	264	8,145	3,280	Great Grimsby	Bradley Haverstow.
Immingham (a)	- par.	270	3,715	6,130	Uleeby	Yarborough.
Irby	- par.	224	1,811	2,460	Caistor	Bradley Haverstow.
Keelby	- par.	712	1,861	3,086	Uleeby	Yarborough.
Kingerby	- par.	100	1,435	2,297	Market Rasen	Walsheroft.
Kirmond le Mire	- par.	138	1,051	1,148	do.	Wraggoe.
Laceby	- par.	1,017	2,065	4,616	Great Grimsby	Bradley Haverstow.
Legsby	- par.	336	2,886	3,253	Market Rasen	Wraggoe.
Limber Magna	- par.	489	5,180	7,069	Uleeby	Yarborough.
Limber Parva with Brocklesby (a)	par.	262	3,860	6,309	do.	do.
Linwood (a)	- par.	184	2,316	2,837	Market Rasen	Walsheroft.
Lissington (a)	- par.	259	1,526	1,906	Wragby	Wraggoe.
Little Coates	- par.	60	1,119	2,565	Great Grimsby	Bradley Haverstow.
Market Rasen	- par.	2,612	1,226	8,919	Market Rasen	Walsheroft.
Middle Rasen (a)	- par.	928	3,470	5,714	do.	do.
Nettleton	- par.	482	3,570	4,378	Caistor	Yarborough.
Newton by Toft	- par.	75	1,004	1,019	Market Rasen	Walsheroft.
Normanby on the Wold	par.	142	1,966	2,201	do.	do.
North Kelsey (a)	- par.	844	5,370	6,648	Brigg	Yarborough.
North Owersby	- par.	343	1,718	4,163	Market Rasen	Walsheroft.
North Willingham	- par.	211	1,990	2,677	do.	do.
Osgodby with Kirkby	par.	374	1,710	1,843	do.	do.
Riby	- par.	273	2,749	4,020	Great Grimsby	Bradley Haverstow.
Rothwell	- par.	260	2,690	3,417	Caistor	do.
Scartho	- par.	224	922	1,970	Great Grimsby	do.
Searby cum Owmby (a)	par.	217	1,860	3,487	Caistor	Yarborough.
Six Hills	- par.	175	1,962	2,287	Market Rasen	Wraggoe.
Snitterby	- par.	274	1,610	2,110	Kirton in Lindsey	Lawress.
Somerby	- par.	99	1,940	1,290	Brigg	Yarborough.
South Kelsey	- par.	615	4,380	5,287	Caistor	Walsheroft.
South Owersby	- par.	92	810	1,804	Market Rasen	do.
Stainton-le-Vale	- par.	158	2,450	3,167	Caistor	do.
Stallingborough	- par.	483	5,792	8,146	Uleeby	Yarborough.
Swallow	- par.	238	2,790	3,129	Caistor	Bradley Haverstow.
Swinhope	- par.	140	1,307	1,759	Great Grimsby	do.
Tealby	- par.	654	3,950	4,365	Market Rasen	Walsheroft.
Thoresway	- par.	258	2,730	3,507	Caistor	do.
Thorganby	- par.	144	1,568	1,961	Great Grimsby	do.

CAISTOR UNION :
(continued)

Unions and Parishes, &c.	Population in 1881.	Area in Statute Acres in 1881.	Rateable Value in 1881.	Post Town.	Petty Sessional Division.

CAISTOR UNION—County of Lincoln—*continued.*

			£		
Thornton-le-Moor - *par.*	96	1,503	1,790	Caistor - -	Walshcroft.
Toft - - *par.*	86	1,293	1,564	Market Rasen	do.
Usselby - - *par.*	54	1,110	1,125	do. - -	do.
Waddingham - - *par.*	715	3,720	4,538	Kirton in Lindsey	Manby.
Walesby - - *par.*	322	2,580	4,143	Market Rasen -	Walshcroft.
Waltham - - *par.*	743	2,464	3,927	Great Grimsby -	Bradley Haverstow.
West Rasen - - *par.*	251	2,720	4,134	Market Rasen -	Walshcroft.
West Ravendale - *tow.*	57 {	In East Ravendale }	1,016	Great Grimsby -	Bradley Haverstow.
Wold Newton - *par.*	165	2,060	2,592	do. - -	do.
TOTAL of UNION -	**66,899**	**174,152**	**339,182**		

CALNE UNION.

(Formed 25 March 1835 by Order dated 6 Feb. 1835.)

COUNTY of WILTS:

Blackland (*a*) - - *par.*	50	537	1,136	Calne - -	Calne.
Bowood - - *lib.*	92	969	1,062	do. - -	do.
Bremhill (*a*) (*b*) (*c*) - *par.*	1,163	5,920	9,839	do. - -	do.
Calne (W.) (*a*) - *par.*	5,191	8,079	25,305	do. - -	do.
Calstone Willington (*a*) *par.*	45	308	449	do. - -	do.
Cherhill (*a*) - - *par.*	290	1,817	2,458	do. - -	do.
Compton Basset (*a*) - *par.*	374	2,632	4,207	do. - -	do.
Heddington - *par.*	357	1,686	2,433	do. - -	do.
Highway - - *par.*	88	813	864	do. - -	do.
Hilmarton (*a*) - *par.*	756	4,182	6,389	do. - -	do.
Yatesbury - - *par.*	211	1,667	2,326	do. - -	do.
TOTAL of UNION -	**8,620**	**28,610**	**56,468**		

CAMBRIDGE UNION.

(Formed 2 April 1836 by Order dated 19 Mar. 1836.)

COUNTY of CAMBRIDGE:

All Saints - - *par.*	1,299		12,971	Cambridge -	Borough of Cambridge (Separate Quarter Session).
Holy Trinity - *par.*	2,007		8,897	do. - -	do.
Saint Andrew the Great (*a*) - } *par.*	2,390		14,918	do. - -	do.
Saint Andrew the Less (W.) (*a*) - } *par.*	21,078		60,953	do. - -	do.
Saint Benedict - *par.*	1,044	3,278	7,394	do. - -	do.
Saint Botolph (*a*) - *par.*	467		6,251	do. - -	do.
Saint Clements - *par.*	765		2,887	do. - -	do.
Saint Edward - *par.*	588		6,912	do. - -	do.
Saint Giles (*b*) - *par.*	3,010		13,706	do. - -	do.
Saint Mary the Great *par.*	600		5,318	do. - -	do.
Saint Mary the Less (*a*) *par.*	1,124		9,369	do. - -	do.
Saint Michael - *par.*	538		7,757	do. - -	do.
Saint Sepulchre - *par.*	453		2,876	do. - -	do.
TOTAL of UNION -	**35,363**	**3,278**	**160,209**		

CALNE UNION:

(*a*) By Order which came into operation on 25 March 1883.—Certain parts of Blackland were amalgamated with Calstone Willington and Calne;
A part of Bremhill was amalgamated with Calne;
Certain parts of Calne were amalgamated with Blackland, Calstone Willington, Cherhill, and Compton Basset;
Certain parts of Calstone Willington were amalgamated with Blackland, Calne, and Cherhill; and
A part of Compton Basset was amalgamated with Hilmarton.

(*b*) Certain parts of Christian Malford, in the Chippenham Union, were amalgamated with Bremhill; and a detached part of Bremhill was amalgamated with Tytherton Kelways, in the Chippenham Union, by Order which came into operation on 25 March 1884.

i R 8372.

CALNE UNION—*continued.*

(*c*) A detached part of Christian Malford, in the Chippenham Union, was amalgamated with Bremhill, by Order which came into operation on 25 March 1885.

CAMBRIDGE UNION:

(*a*) A detached part of Saint Andrew the Less was amalgamated with Saint Andrew the Great, and a detached part of Saint Botolph was amalgamated with Saint Mary the Less, by Order which came into operation on 25 March 1885.

(*b*) By Provisional Order which came into operation on 25 March 1886, the several parts which together constituted a parish known as Saint Peter, were amalgamated with the parish of Saint Giles.

Unions and Parishes, &c.	Population in 1881.	Area in Statute Acres in 1881.	Rateable Value in 1881.	Post Town.	Petty Sessional Division.

CAMELFORD UNION.

(Formed 1 Feb. 1837 by Order dated 5 Jan. 1837.)

COUNTY of CORNWALL :

			£		
Advent - - *par.*	223	4,059	1,902	Camelford -	Lesnewth.
Davidstow - - *par.*	406	6,756	4,178	do. -	do.
Forrabury - - *par.*	304	508	1,325	Boscastle -	do.
Lanteglos (with Camelford) (W.) - } *par.*	1,524	3,951	7,265	Camelford -	do.
Lesnewth - - *par.*	116	2,028	1,436	Boscastle -	do.
Michaelstow - - *par.*	222	1,636	1,843	Camelford -	do.
Minster - - *par.*	451	3,222	2,848	Boscastle -	do.
Otterham - - *par.*	163	3,262	1,090	Camelford -	do.
Saint Breward - *par.*	728	9,237	3,206	Bodmin -	Trigg.
Saint Clether - *par.*	215	2,960	2,275	Launceston -	Lesnewth.
Saint Juliot - *par.*	224	2,699	1,428	Boscastle -	do.
Saint Teath - *par.*	1,994	5,899	7,622	Camelford -	do.
Tintagel with Bossiney - } *par.*	894	4,350	4,882	do. -	do.
Trevalga - - *par.*	141	1,299	1,228	Boscastle -	do.
TOTAL of UNION -	7,605	51,866	42,528		

CANNOCK UNION.

(Formed as the Penkridge Union 29 Sept. 1836 by Order dated 5 Sept. 1836.—Place marked thus * added 18 Nov. 1836 by Order dated 24 Oct. 1836 ; and thus † added 1 July 1858 by Order dated 14 June 1858. Name of Union altered 14 Mar. 1877 by Order dated 5 Feb. 1877.)

COUNTY of STAFFORD :

Acton and Bednall - *tow.*	548	2,594	5,230	Stafford -	Penkridge.
Brewood - - *par.*	2,948	11,839	27,809	do. -	do.
Bushbury - - *par.*	1,770	3,120	17,370	Wolverhampton -	Seisdon North.
Cannock (W.) - - *tow.*	17,125	10,775	60,165	Stafford -	Penkridge.
Cheslyn-Hay - - *par.*	1,799	827	4,382	Walsall -	do.
Church Eaton - - *par.*	653	4,283	7,154	Stafford -	do.
Coppenhall - - *tow.*	86 }	In Penkridge {	1,625	do. -	do.
Dunston - - *tow.*	279 }		3,972	do. -	do.
Essington - - *tow.*	1,295	2,957	8,413	Wolverhampton -	Seisdon North.
Featherstone - *tow.*	76	488	873	do. -	Penkridge.
Great Wyrley - *tow.*	1,075	In Cannock	5,983	Walsall -	do.
Hatherton - *tow.*	426 }	2,789 {	3,499	Cannock -	do.
Hilton - - *tow.*	50 }		1,177	Wolverhampton -	Seisdon North.
Huntington - *tow.*	177	In Cannock	1,556	Penkridge -	Penkridge.
Kinvaston - *tow.*	12	233	802	Stafford -	do.
Lapley and Wheaton Aston - } *par.*	744	3,450	6,850	Penkridge -	do.
Norton - - *par.*	3,546	4,077	18,629	Cannock -	do.
Penkridge - *tow.*	2,536	18,020	24,837	Stafford -	do.
Saredon - - *tow.*	270 }	1,985 {	2,586	Wolverhampton -	do.
Shareshill - *tow.*	342 }		2,000	do. -	do.
*Stretton - - *cha.*	233	1,585	2,932	Penkridge -	do.
†Teddesley Hay - *par.*	130	2,625	2,590	do. -	do.
TOTAL of UNION -	36,122	71,947	210,434		

Unions and Parishes, &c.	Population in 1881.	Area in Statute Acres in 1881.	Rateable Value in 1881.	Post Town.	Petty Sessional Division.
CANTERBURY UNION.					
(Formed 26 Feb. 1881 by Order dated 11 Feb. 1881.)					
CITY and COUNTY of the CITY of CANTERBURY :					
All Saints - - par.	549	5	1,455	Canterbury -	City and Borough of Canterbury.
Black Prince's Chantry par.	5	—	—	do.	do.
East Bridge Hospital par.	36	—	—	do. - -	do.
Holy Cross West Gate par.	186	17	682	do. - -	do.
Old Castle - - par.	65	3	—	do. - -	do.
Saint Alphage - par.	1,060	10	3,042	do. - -	do.
Saint Andrew the Apostle } par.	120	4	3,857	do. - -	do.
Saint Augustine - par.	365	30	—	do. - -	do.
Saint George the Martyr par.	1,193	18	6,511	do. - -	do.
Saint John's Hospital par.	39	—	—	do. - -	do.
Saint Margaret - par.	539	8	2,609	do. - -	do.
Saint Martin - par.	212	638	1,472	do. - -	do.
Saint Mary Bredin(W.)par.	1,776	756	8,664	do. - -	do.
Saint Mary Bredman par.	267	1	2,010	do. - -	do.
Saint Mary Magdalen par.	387	1	1,684	do. - -	do.
Saint Mary North Gate par.	1,881	118	10,330	do. - -	do.
Saint Mildred - par.	2,361	99	7,295	do. - -	do.
Saint Paul - - par.	1,787	1,031	9,208	do. - -	do.
Saint Peter - par.	1,121	31	2,106	do. - -	do.
White Friars House - par.	2	2	—	do. - -	do.
TOTAL of UNION -	17,060	3,111	61,225		
CARDIFF UNION.					
(Formed 13 Sept. 1836 by Order dated 18 Aug. 1836.—Places marked thus * added 25 Dec. 1861 by Order dated 10 Oct. 1861.—Place marked thus † added 1 May 1883 by Order dated 21 April 1883.)					
COUNTY of GLAMORGAN :					
Barry - - par.	85	539	637	Cardiff -	Dynaspowis.
Bonvilstone - - par.	225	1,280	1,551	do. - -	do.
Cadoxton juxta Barry(e) par.	303	873	1,281	do. - -	do.
Cairau (c) - - par.	112	758	1,069	do. - -	Kibbor.
†Canton (b) - - par.	—	—	—	do.	do.
Cogan - - par.	755	616	1,635	do. - -	Dynaspowis.
*Highlight - - par.	16	405	254	do. - -	do.
Lancarvan - - par.	564	4,725	5,427	Cowbridge -	do.
Landaff (W.) (b) - par.	17,950	3,985	56,494	Landaff -	Kibbor.
Lavernock - - par.	81	649	761	Cardiff -	Dynaspowis.
Leckwith (b) - par.	177	1,342	3,221	do. - -	do.
Lisvane - - par.	228	1,416	1,956	do. - -	Kibbor.
Llandough (c) - - par.	510	712	6,602	do. - -	Dynaspowis.
Llanedarne - - par.	285	2,754	2,504	do. - -	Kibbor.
Llanilltern - - par.	118	1,075	1,131	do. - -	do.
Llanishen - - par.	469	3,052	7,780	do. - -	do.
Llantrythyd - - par.	159	1,433	1,703	Cowbridge -	Dynaspowis.
*Llanvythin - - par.	37	427	474	do. - -	do.
Merthyrdovan (d) - par.	102	1,359	939	Cardiff -	do.
Michaelstone le Pit - par.	108	800	866	do. - -	do.
Michaelstone super Ely (c) } par.	43	321	602	do. - -	do.
Pennarth (e) - par.	4,963	874	29,061	Penarth -	do.

(continued)

CARDIFF UNION :

(a) A detached part of Roath was amalgamated with Romney, and a detached part of Romney was amalgamated with Roath, by Orders which came into operation on 25 March 1883.

(b) All the parts of Landaff and Leckwith situate within the boundary of the municipal borough of Cardiff were together constituted a separate parish, and designated the parish of Canton, by Order which came into operation on 25 March 1883.

(c) By Provisional Order which came into operation on 25 March 1884,—

A detached part of Llandough was amalgamated with Pennarth ;

CARDIFF UNION—continued.

Detached parts of Saint Fagans were amalgamated respectively with Michaelstone super Ely and Cairau ; and

A detached part of Saint Bride super Ely was amalgamated with Peterstone super Ely.

(d) A detached part of Merthyrdovan was amalgamated with Saint Andrews, by Order which came into operation on 25 March 1885.

(e) There is some land known as "Sheeping Moors" common to Saint Andrews and Cadoxton juxta Barry, containing 181 acres.

Unions and Parishes, &c.	Population in 1881.	Area in Statute Acres in 1881.	Rateable Value in 1881.	Post Town.	Petty Sessional Division.
CARDIFF UNION—County of Glamorgan—*continued.*			£		
Pendoylon - - *par.*	393	3,579	4,129	Cardiff - -	Cowbridge.
Penmark - - *par.*	480	3,360	4,268	Cowbridge -	Dynaspowis.
Pentirch - - *par.*	2,102	3,939	9,565	Cardiff -	Miskin.
Peterstone super Ely } *par.* (*c*)	233	2,086	4,669	do. -	Dynaspowis.
Porthkerry - - *par.*	129	967	1,107	do. -	do.
Radyr - - *par.*	519	1,630	11,204	do. -	Kibbor.
Roath (*a*) - - *par.*	23,096	2,425	67,374	do. -	Borough of Cardiff.
Rudry - - *par.*	387	2,668	2,706	Caerphilly -	Caerphilly.
Saint Andrews (*d*), (*e*) *par.*	576	3,173 (*e*)	3,998	Cardiff -	Dynaspowis.
Saint Bride super Ely } *par.* (*e*)	78	686	1,289	do. -	do.
Saint Fagans (*e*) - *par.*	483	2,361	4,420	do. -	Kibbor.
Saint George - - *par.*	230	1,024	2,016	do. -	Dynaspowis.
Saint John Cardiff (W.)*par.*	16,614	988	88,625	do. -	Borough of Cardiff.
Saint Lythan - - *par.*	81	1,284	1,127	do. -	Dynaspowis.
Saint Mary Cardiff - *par.*	28,254	979	181,155	do. -	Borough of Cardiff.
Saint Nicholas - *par.*	349	2,172	2,780	do. -	Dynaspowis.
Sully - - - *par.*	203	1,387	1,871	do. -	do.
Vaen - - - *ham.*	251	862	2,048	Caerphilly -	Caerphilly.
Welch Saint Donatts *par.*	215	2,263	1,849	Cowbridge -	Cowbridge.
Wenvoe - - *par.*	405	3,035	3,512	Cardiff -	Dynaspowis.
Whitechurch - - *par.*	2,752	3,269	16,891	do. -	Kibbor.
COUNTY of MONMOUTH:					
Romney (*a*) - *par.*	445	3,375	5,632	do. -	Newport.
Saint Mellons - *par.*	599	2,574	5,998	do. -	do.
TOTAL of UNION -	106,164	79,481 (*c*)	555,440		

CARDIGAN UNION.

(Formed 9 May 1837 by Order dated 12 April 1837.)

COUNTY of CARDIGAN:					
Aberporth - - *par.*	479	2,200	1,139	Cardigan -	Lower Troedyraur.
Blaenporth - - *par.*	680	3,548	1,959	do. -	do.
Llandygwyd - - *par.*	921	5,595	3,879	Boneath, R.S.O. -	do.
Llangoedmore - *par.*	882	4,946	3,710	Cardigan -	do.
Llechryd - - *par.*	299	943	759	do. -	do.
Mount - - - *par.*	132	1,142	550	do. -	do.
Saint Mary's in the Borough of Car-digan } *par.*	2,727	2,517	5,823	do. -	Borough of Cardigan.
Tremaine - - *par.*	262	1,658	942	do. -	Lower Troedyraur.
Verwick - - *par.*	339	3,062	1,714	do. -	do.
COUNTY of PEMBROKE:					
Bayvil - - *par.*	140	1,344	913	Felindre, R.S.O. -	Kemes.
Bridell - - *par.*	291	2,179	1,348	Kilgerran, R.S.O. -	Kilgerran.
Cilgerran - - *par.*	1,118	2,672	2,046	do. -	do.
Dinas - - *par.*	786	2,328	1,542	Dinas Cross, R.S.O.	Kemes.
Eglwyserw - *par.*	452	3,661	2,095	Eglwyserw, R.S.O. -	do.
Llanfair Nant gwyn - *par.*	180	1,668	784	Boneath, R.S.O. -	do.
Llanfihangel Penbedw *par.*	291	2,410	1,224	Blaenllas, R.S.O. -	do.
Llantwyd - - *par.*	228	1,792	1,223	Kilgerran, R.S.O. -	do.
Llanychlwydog - *par.*	195	2,283	943	Letterstone, R.S.O. -	do.
Macnordewi - - *par.*	756	3,506	3,056	Boneath, R.S.O. -	Kilgerran.
Melinau - - *par.*	353	4,523	1,483	Eglwyswrw, R.S.O. -	Kemes.
Monnington or Eg-lwys Wythiel } *par.*	98	1,010	612	Cardigan -	do.
Moylgrove or Tre-wyddel } *par.*	422	2,442	1,434	do. -	do.
Nevern - - *par.*	1,307	14,637	5,877	Felindre, R.S.O. -	do.
Newport - - *par.*	1,504	4,714	3,220	Newport, Pembroke	do.
Saint Dogmel's (W.) *par.*	2,468	6,220	5,055	Cardigan -	Kemes and Borough of Cardigan.
Whitechurch or Eg-lwyswen } *par.*	299	2,481	1,453	Eglwyswrw, R.S.O. -	Kemes.
TOTAL of UNION -	17,612 (*a*)	85,484	54,483		

CARDIFF UNION:

(*a*) (*c*) (*d*) (*e*). See notes, page 77.

CARDIGAN UNION:

A place known as Penllyn, having a population of 3 persons, is stated to be locally included in this Union.

Unions and Parishes, &c.	Population in 1881.	Area in Statute Acres in 1881.	Rateable Value in 1881.	Post Town.	Petty Sessional Division.
CARLISLE UNION.			£		
(Formed 2 May 1838 by Order dated 7 Apr. 1838. — Place marked thus * added 25 Dec. 1862 by Order dated 7 Oct. 1862.)					
COUNTY of CUMBERLAND :					
Beaumont (b) - - par.	236	1,628	2,206	Carlisle - -	City of Carlisle (Cumberland Ward).
Burgh-by-Sands - par.	862	6,170	9,034	do. - -	do.
Saint Mary's Caldewgate, Carlisle - } tow.	13,679	1,700	30,369	do. - -	do.
Crosby upon Eden (b) par.	393	2,855	3,963	do. - -	do.
Saint Mary's Cummersdale, Carlisle - } tow.	848	2,015	6,015	do. - -	do.
Dalston (a) - - par.	2,418	12,459	19,455	do. - -	do.
*Eaglesfield Abbey - par.	64	5	462	do. - -	do.
Grinsdale - - par.	117	838	1,388	do. - -	do.
Kingmoor - - par.	479	1,169	2,408	do. - -	do.
Kirkandrews upon Eden - } par.	115	1,011	1,243	do. - -	do.
Orton - - par.	454	4,287	4,979	do. - -	do.
Rockcliffe - - par.	754	4,939	6,696	do. - -	do.
Saint Cuthbert's within Carlisle - } tow.	2,607	38	27,119	do. - -	do.
Saint Cuthbert's without Carlisle (W.) (b) } tow.	14,488	8,941	61,021	do. - -	do.
Saint Mary's Rickergate, Carlisle - } tow.	5,148	358	21,847	do. - -	do.
Saint Mary's within Carlisle - } tow.	3,342	34	15,559	do. - -	do.
Stanwix (b) - par.	2,877	6,251	19,373	do. - -	do.
Warwick and Aglionby - } par.	320	1,858	3,321	do. - -	do.
Weatherall - - par.	3,320	11,489	27,524	do. - -	do.
Wreay - - tow.	181	1,119	2,306	do. - -	do.
TOTAL of UNION -	52,762	69,164	266,588		
CARMARTHEN UNION.					
(Formed 2 July 1836 by Order dated 3 June 1836. — Place marked thus * added 27 Feb. 1837 by Order dated 2 Feb. 1837.)					
TOWN and COUNTY of the TOWN of CARMARTHEN and COUNTY of CARMARTHEN.					
Abergwilly (b) - par.	2,020	10,748	12,742	Carmarthen - -	Carmarthen.
Abernant - par.	734	6,321	4,114	do. - -	do.

(continued)

CARLISLE UNION :

(a) By Order which came into operation on 25 March 1886,—

A part of Dalston was amalgamated with Castle Sowerby in the Penrith Union, and a part of Castle Sowerby, was amalgamated with Dalston.

(b) By Provisional Order which came into operation on 25 March 1887,—

A part of Beaumont was amalgamated with Stanwix ;

Parts of Stanwix were amalgamated with Crosby upon Eden, and Saint Cuthbert's without Carlisle respectively ; and

A part of Saint Cuthbert's without Carlisle was amalgamated with Stanwix.

CARMARTHEN UNION :

(a) A part of Mydrim, known as "Vaenor Capel," was amalgamated with Merthyr, by Order which came into operation on 25 March 1884.

(b) A detached part of Abergwilly was amalgamated with Llanpumpsaint, by Provisional Order which came into operation on 25 March 1885.

(c) A detached part of Mydrim, known as Penweh, was amalgamated with Llanvihangel Abercowin, by Provisional Order which came into operation on 25 March 1885.

(d) A detached part of Newchurch was amalgamated with Carmarthen, by Provisional Order which came into operation on 25 March 1885.

Unions and Parishes, &c.		Population in 1881.	Area in Statute Acres in 1881.	Rateable Value in 1881.	Post Town.	Petty Sessional Division.
				£		

CARMARTHEN UNION —Town and County of, &c.—*continued.*

Unions and Parishes, &c.		Population in 1881.	Area in Statute Acres in 1881.	Rateable Value in 1881.	Post Town.	Petty Sessional Division.
Cynwyl in Elfet	par.	1,552	13,153	6,057	Carmarthen -	Carmarthen.
Carmarthen (W.) (d)	par.	10,511	1,996	33,348	do.	do.
Llanarthney	par.	1,856	10,994	9,338	do.	do.
Llandawk -	par.	24	613	534	St. Clears -	St. Clears.
Llanddarog -	par.	883	4,501	1,165	Llanarthney	Carmarthen.
Llandefaelog	par.	1,146	7,320	9,606	Kidwelly -	do.
Llandilo Abercowin -	par.	57	922	630	St. Clears -	St. Clears.
Llandowror -	par.	290	1,783	1,520	do.	do.
Llangain -	par.	338	2,660	2,616	Carmarthen	Carmarthen.
Llangendeyrne	par.	2,276	11,810	10,811	Kidwelly -	do.
Llangynnin -	par.	364	3,270	2,871	St. Clears -	Llanboidy.
Llangunnoch	par.	626	4,879	4,348	Carmarthen	Carmarthen.
Llangynor -	par.	1,091	5,795	7,151	do.	do.
Llanlawddog -	par.	598	7,013	3,110	Llanpumpsaint	do.
Llanpumpsaint (b)	par.	502	4,079	2,786	do.	do.
Llansadurnen	par.	177	1,644	1,647	St. Clears -	St. Clears.
Llanstephan -	par.	1,217	6,710	6,688	Llanstephen	Carmarthen.
Llanvihangel Aber-cowin (c) -	par.	811	5,180	6,477	St. Clears -	St. Clears.
*Llanwinio -	par.	880	7,169	4,551	Whitland, R.S.O. -	Llanboidy.
Llaugharne -	par.	148	} 14,703	{ 4,381	St. Clears -	St. Clears.
Llaugharne -	tow.	1,179		5,580	do.	do.
Merthyr (a) -	par.	262	2,218	2,183	Carmarthen	Carmarthen.
Mydrim (a) (c)	par.	906	6,905	7,581	St. Clears -	Llanboidy.
Newchurch (d)	par.	709	4,894	4,838	Carmarthen	Carmarthen.
Saint Clears -	par.	988	2,534	4,413	St. Clears -	St. Clears.
Saint Ishmael -	par.	1,297	8,081	6,893	Ferryside, R.S.O. -	Carmarthen.
Trelech ar Bettws -	par.	1,330	11,492	6,648	Llanfyrnach, R.S.O.	do.
TOTAL of UNION -		35,075	172,387	177,927		

CARNARVON UNION.

(Formed 1 June 1837 by Order dated 5 May 1837.)

COUNTY of ANGLESEY :

Unions and Parishes, &c.		Population in 1881.	Area in Statute Acres in 1881.	Rateable Value in 1881.	Post Town.	Petty Sessional Division.
Llanfair yn y Cwmmwd	par.	20	166	185	Bangor -	Menai Bridge.
Llangaffo (b) -	par.	106	1,590	1,815	do.	do.
Llangeinwen (b)	par.	917	5,388	4,519	do.	do.
Llanidan -	par.	1,379	4,645	5,158	do.	do.
Saint Peter's New-borough -	par.	1,012	7,410	2,082	do.	do.

COUNTY of CARNARVON :

Unions and Parishes, &c.		Population in 1881.	Area in Statute Acres in 1881.	Rateable Value in 1881.	Post Town.	Petty Sessional Division.
Bettws Garmon	par.	158	2,759	501	Carnarvon -	Carnarvon.
Clynnog -	par.	1,615	12,060	5,555	do.	do.
Llanbeblig (W.)	par.	11,995	6,792	30,523	do.	do.
Llanberis -	par.	3,033	10,431	15,302	do.	do.
Llanddeiniolen	par.	6,886	9,024	19,479	do.	do.
Llandwrog -	par.	4,436	9,516	10,823	do.	do.
Llanfaglan -	par.	258	1,884	1,147	do.	do.
Llanfair is Gaer (a)	par.	1,642	2,474	4,649	do.	do.
Llanllyfni -	par.	5,520	7,521	6,107	do.	do.
Llanrug (a) -	par.	3,075	4,516	5,102	do.	do.
Llanwnda -	par.	2,185	11,459	5,158	do.	do.
TOTAL of UNION -		43,997	97,635	118,435		

CARMARTHEN UNION :

(a) (b) (c) (d). *See* notes, page 79.

CARNARVON UNION :

(a) A detached part of Llanfair is Gaer was amalgamated with Llanrug, by Order which came into operation on 25 March 1883.

(b) A detached part of Llangeinwen was amalgamated with Llangaffo, by Provisional Order which came into operation on 25 March 1884.

Unions and Parishes, &c.	Population in 1881.	Area in Statute Acres in 1881.	Rateable Value in 1881.	Post Town.	Petty Sessional Division.

CASTLE WARD UNION.

(Formed 30 Sept. 1836 by Order dated 3 Sept. 1836.—Place marked thus * added 22 July 1843 by Order of same date.)

COUNTY of NORTHUMBERLAND :

			£		
Belsay - - - *tow.*	392	2,542	3,366	Newcastle - -	West Division, Morpeth Ward.
Berwick Hill - - *tow.*	99	1,665	1,889	Ponteland, Newcastle.	West Division, Castle Ward.
Bitchfield - - *tow.*	23	739	931	Belsay, Newcastle -	North-East Division, Tynedale Ward.
Black Callerton - *tow.*	156	1,384	1,991	Ponteland, Newcastle.	West Division, Castle Ward.
Black Hedden - *tow.*	51	1,668	2,106	Stamfordham -	North-East Division, Tynedale Ward.
Bolam - - *tow.*	80	1,119	1,261	Belsay, Newcastle-	West Division, Morpeth Ward.
Bolam Vicarage - *tow.*	10	139	249	do. do. -	do. do.
Bradford - - *tow.*	41	1,093	1,092	do. do. -	do. do.
Brenkley - *tow.*	45	925	2,061	Kenton, Newcastle	West Division, Castle Ward.
Capheaton - - *tow.*	180	2,318	3,012	Newcastle - -	Bellingham.
Cheeseburn Grange - *tow.*	101	819	1,066	do. - -	North-East Division, Tynedale Ward.
Coldcoats - *tow.*	47	1,079	818	Ponteland, Newcastle.	West Division, Castle Ward.
Coxlodge - - *tow.*	3,297	828	15,672	Newcastle -	do. do.
Dalton - - *tow.*	87	1,057	1,159	do. - -	do. do.
Darras Hall - - *tow.*	15	424	402	do. - -	do. do.
Dinnington - - *tow.*	229	791	1,677	Kenton, Newcastle	do. do.
Eachwick - *tow.*	58	984	1,348	Dalton, Newcastle	do. do.
East Brunton - - *tow.*	115	956	1,853	Kenton, Newcastle	do. do.
East Denton - - *tow.*	986	764	4,672	Newcastle - -	do. do.
East Heddon (*b*) - *tow.*	49	890	901	Wylam, R.S.O. -	do. do.
East Matfen - *tow.*	146	2,102	2,297	Newcastle - -	North-East Division, Tynedale Ward.
East Shaftoe - *tow.*	20	622	516	Belsay, Newcastle	West Division, Morpeth Ward.
Fawdon (*b*) - *tow.*	364	535	2,922	Kenton, Newcastle	West Division, Castle Ward.
Fenwick - *tow.*	100	1,647	2,270	Stamfordham -	North-East Division, Tynedale Ward.
Gallowhill - - *tow.*	34	628	806	Belsay, Newcastle -	West Division, Morpeth Ward.
Harlowhill - *tow.*	94	1,023	2,186	Stocksfield, R.S.O.	East Division, Tynedale Ward.
Harnham - *tow.*	48	701	1,049	Belsay, Newcastle -	West Division, Morpeth Ward.
Hawkwell - *tow.*	127	592	1,260	Stamfordham -	North-East Division, Tynedale Ward.
Heddon-on-the-Wall *tow.*	529	1,188	3,663	Wylam, R.S.O. -	West Division, Castle Ward.
Heugh - *tow.*	315	2,288	3,756	Stamfordham -	North-East Division, Tynedale Ward.
Higham Dykes - *tow.*	28	224	292	Newcastle - -	West Division, Castle Ward.
High Callerton - *tow.*	99	1,025	1,447	Ponteland, Newcastle	do. do.
Horton Grange - *tow.*	73	1,274	1,254	Dinnington -	do. do.
Houghton - *tow.*	173	617	1,321	Wylam, R.S.O. -	do. do.
Ingoe - *tow.*	188	2,137	2,377	Matfen, Newcastle	North-East Division, Tynedale Ward.
Kearsley - *tow.*	12	539	727	do. do. -	do. do.
Kenton - *tow.*	615	1,454	3,744	Newcastle - -	West Division, Castle Ward.
Kirkheaton - *par.*	170	2,061	1,901	Capheaton, Newcastle.	Bellingham. *(continued)*

(*b*) See note, page 82.

Unions and Parishes, &c.		Population in 1881.	Area in Statute Acres in 1881.	Rateable Value in 1891.	Post Town.	Petty Sessional Division.

CASTLE WARD UNION—County of Northumberland—*continued.*

Unions and Parishes, &c.		Population in 1881.	Area in Statute Acres in 1881.	Rateable Value in 1891. £	Post Town.	Petty Sessional Division.
Kirkley	*tow.*	173	1,861	2,444	Ponteland, Newcastle.	West Division, Castle Ward.
Little Callerton	*tow.*	16	592	596	do. do.	do. do.
Mason	*tow.*	1,001	1,241	3,255	Dinnington	do. do.
Milbourne	*tow.*	52	1,242	1,465	Higham, Newcastle	do. do.
Milbourne Grange	*tow.*	30	618	648	do.	do. do.
Nesbitt	*tow.*	37	858	1,092	Stamfordham	North-East Division, Tynedale Ward.
Newbiggen	*tow.*	60	537	933	Kenton, Newcastle	West Division, Castle Ward.
Newburn (*b*)	*tow.*	1,242	743	5,382	Scotswood on Tyne	do. do.
Newburn Hall (*b*)	*tow.*	819	869	3,056	do.	do. do.
Newham	*tow.*	43	1,349	1,520	Belsay, Newcastle	West Division, Morpeth Ward.
North Dissington	*tow.*	65	1,431	1,122	Dalton, Newcastle	West Division, Castle Ward.
North Gosforth	*tow.*	230	1,088	2,684	Newcastle	do. do.
Ogle	*tow.*	105	2,185	2,325	Ponteland, Newcastle.	West Division, Morpeth Ward.
Ouston	*tow.*	21	517	610	Stamfordham	North-East Division, Tynedale Ward.
Ponteland (W.)	*tow.*	447	1,898	3,854	Newcastle	West Division, Castle Ward.
Prestwick	*tow.*	186	854	1,995	Kenton, Newcastle	do. do.
Riplington	*tow.*	11	379	352	Ponteland, Newcastle.	West Division, Morpeth Ward.
Rochester	*tow.*	42	617	960	Wylam, R.S.O.	West Division, Castle Ward.
Ryall	*tow.*	72	2,133	2,695	Matfen, Newcastle	North-East Division, Tynedale Ward.
Shilvington	*tow.*	78	1,539	1,429	Ponteland, do.	West Division, Morpeth Ward.
Shortflatt	*tow.*	21	518	899	Belsay, do.	do. do.
South Dissington	*tow.*	60	1,348	1,342	Newcastle	West Division, Castle Ward.
South Gosforth (*b*)	*tow.*	829	468	5,230	Newcastle	do. do.
Stannington	*par.*	1,027	10,316	15,453	Cramlington	do. do.
Sugley	*tow.*	217	61	497	Scotswood on Tyne	do. do.
Throckley (*b*)	*tow.*	1,196	760	5,850	Newcastle	do. do.
Trewick	*tow.*	23	762	807	Belsay, Newcastle	do. do.
Twizell	*tow.*	31	775	850	Ponteland, Newcastle	do. do.
Wallbottle (*b*)	*tow.*	923	1,277	2,921	Newcastle	do. do.
Wallridge otherwise Waldridge	*tow.*	10	153	173	Matfen, Newcastle	North-East Division, Tynedale Ward.
West Brunton	*tow.*	107	1,143	1,970	Kenton, Newcastle	West Division, Castle Ward.
West Denton	*tow.*	458	329	1,533	Newcastle	do. do.
West Heddon	*tow.*	20	346	589	Wylam, R.S.O.	do. do.
West Matfen	*tow.*	309	2,001	2,950	Newcastle	North-East Division, Tynedale Ward.
West Shaftoe	*tow.*	26	502	564	Belsay, Newcastle	West Division, Morpeth Ward.
Whalton	*tow.*	345	2,126	3,399	Newcastle	West Division, Castle Ward.
Whitchester	*tow.*	40	817	1,004	Wylam, R.S.O.	do. do.
Whorlton, East and West (*a*)	*tow.*	109	846	1,101	Kenton, Newcastle	do. do.
Woodsington	*tow.*	73	610	816	Newcastle	do. do.
TOTAL of UNION		19,720	90,286 (*c*)	167,782		

CASTLE WARD UNION:

(*a*) The several parts of a township known as Butterlaw were amalgamated with Whorlton, East and West, by Order which came into operation on 25 March 1886.

(*b*) By Provisional Order which came into operation on 25 March 1887,—
A detached part of Fawdon was amalgamated with South Gosforth;

CASTLE WARD UNION—*continued.*

Detached parts of Newburn were amalgamated with East Heddon and Throckley respectively; and
A detached part of Newburn Hall was amalgamated with Wallbottle.

(*c*) There are some intermixed lands known as "Prestwick Carr" common to adjacent townships, containing 1,032 acres.

Unions and Parishes, &c.	Population in 1881.	Area in Statute Acres in 1881.	Rateable Value in 1881.	Post Town.	Petty Sessional Division

CATHERINGTON UNION.

(Formed 6 April 1835 by Order dated 10 March 1835.—Place marked thus * added 12 Oct. 1858 by Order dated 27 Sept. 1858.)

COUNTY of SOUTHAMPTON :

			£		
Blendworth - - par.	298	2,334	1,857	Horndean - -	Petersfield.
Catherington (W.) - par.	1,321	5,279	6,767	do. - -	do.
Chalton - - par.	208	1,749	2,066	do. - -	do.
Clanfield - - par.	279	1,403	1,042	do. - -	do.
Idsworth - - cha.	395	1,728	2,013	do. - -	do.
*Waterloo - - par.	246	652	1,430	Cosham - -	Fareham.
TOTAL of UNION -	2,747	13,145	15,175		

CAXTON AND ARRINGTON UNION.

(Formed 18 June 1835 by Order dated 1 June 1835.)

COUNTY of CAMBRIDGE :

Arrington - - par.	243	1,388	1,317	Royston - -	Arrington.
Bourn - - par.	807	4,065	4,324	Cambridge - -	Caxton.
Caldecot - - par.	118	833	660	do. - -	do.
Caxton (W.) - par.	568	2,000	2,125	do. - -	do.
Croxton - - par.	293	1,901	1,577	St. Neots, Hunts. -	do.
Croydon - - par.	478	2,711	2,502	Royston - -	Arrington.
East Hatley - - par.	129	1,176	791	Gamlingay, Sandy	do.
Elsworth - - par.	673	3,700	4,093	St. Ives, Hunts. -	Caxton.
Eltisley - - par.	465	1,922	1,574	St. Neots, Hunts. -	do.
Gamlingay - - par.	1,925	4,143	7,267	Sandy - -	Arrington.
Great Eversden - par.	269	1,200	1,672	Cambridge - -	Arrington.
Hardwicke - - par.	199	1,410	1,065	do. - -	Caxton.
Hatley Saint George par.	132	999	1,106	Gamlingay, Sandy	Arrington.
Kingston - - par.	286	1,807	1,673	Cambridge - -	Caxton.
Knapwell - - par.	188	2,000	1,288	St. Ives, Hunts. -	do.
Little Eversden - par.	212	670	1,177	Cambridge - -	Arrington.
Little Gransden - par.	243	1,896	1,799	St. Neots, Hunts. -	Caxton.
Longstow - - par.	278	1,412	1,514	Cambridge - -	do.
Orwell - - par.	802	1,850	3,289	Royston - -	Arrington.
Papworth Everard - par.	126	1,091	1,103	St. Ives, Hunts. -	Caxton.
Tadlow - - par.	202	1,717	1,332	Near Royston -	Arrington.
Toft - - par.	256	1,242	1,641	Cambridge - -	Caxton.
Wimpole - - par	355	2,428	2,939	Royston - -	Arrington.

COUNTIES of CAMBRIDGE and HUNTINGDON :

Papworth Saint Agnes par.	124 in Cambridge. 29 in Hunts.	1,302	1,258	St. Ives, Hunts. -	Caxton.

COUNTY of HUNTINGDON :

Great Gransden - par.	636	3,361	2,992	St. Neots, Hunts. -	Toseland.
Yelling - - par.	321	1,670	1,835	do. - -	do.
TOTAL of UNION -	10,357	49,897	53,043		

Unions and Parishes, &c.	Population in 1881.	Area in Statute Acres in 1881.	Rateable Value in 1881.	Post Town.	Petty Sessional Division.
CERNE UNION.					
(Formed 23 Dec. 1835 by Order dated 9 Dec. 1835. — Place marked thus * added 22 March 1862 by Order dated 11 March 1862.)					
COUNTY of DORSET :			£		
Alton Pancras - par.	247	2,243	2,197	Cerne - -	Cerne.
Batcombe - - par.	127	1,109	1,166	Maiden Newton -	do.
Buckland-Newton - par.	855	6,018	8,617	Cerne - -	do.
Cattistock - - par.	534	3,009	4,856	Dorchester -	do.
Cerne-Abbas (W.) - par.	925	3,063	4,315	Cerne - -	do.
Chesilborne (a) - par.	353	2,988	2,365	Dorchester -	do.
Frome Saint Quintin par.	188	1,025	1,617	do. - -	do.
Godmanston - par.	165	1,151	1,479	do. - -	do.
*Gore Wood - - par.	—	—	38	Cerne - -	do.
Hermitage (b) - par.	113	751	928	do. - -	do.
Hilfield (c) - - par.	133	1,581	1,477	do. - -	do.
Mappowder - - par.	226	1,887	2,837	Blandford -	do.
Melbury Bubb - par.	117	1,227	2,016	Dorchester -	do.
Melcombe Horsey - par.	183	2,151	2,158	do. - -	do.
Mintern Magna (b) - par.	322	2,064	2,662	Cerne - -	do.
Nether Cerne - par.	93	815	774	Dorchester -	do.
Piddletrenthide - par.	717	4,487	5,098	do. - -	do.
Pulham - - par.	269	2,370	3,145	Cerne - -	do.
Sydling Saint Nicholas par.	559	5,028	4,538	do. - -	do.
Up Cerne - - par.	76	1,103	1,161	do. - -	do.
Wootton Glanville - par.	237	1,665	2,526	Sherborne -	do.
TOTAL of UNION -	6,196	45,771	56,033		
CHAILEY UNION.					
(Formed 26 March 1835 by Order dated 28 February 1835.)					
COUNTY of SUSSEX :					
Barcomb - - par.	1,182	5,027	8,491	Lewes - -	Lewes Division of Lewes and Pevensey Rapes.
Chailey - - par.	1,522	5,944	6,658	do. - -	do.
Ditchelling - - par.	1,342	4,265	7,801	Hassocks Gate -	do.
East Chiltington (W) ham.	442	1,671	3,074	Lewes - -	do.
Hamsey - - par.	553	2,745	5,385	do. - -	do.
Newick - - par.	1,083	1,977	4,130	do. - -	do.
Plumpton - - par.	466	2,450	3,410	do. - -	do.
Ringmer - - par.	1,388	5,739	9,166	do. - -	do.
Street - - par.	183	1,281	1,661	do. - -	do.
Westmeston - - par.	326	2,436	2,594	do. - -	do.
Wivelsfield - - par.	1,916	3,142	4,607	Burgess Hill -	Cuckfield Division of Lewes and Pevensey Rapes.
TOTAL of UNION -	10,373	36,677	57,277		

CERNE UNION :

(a) A detached part of Milton Abbas, known as Liscombe, in the Blandford Union, was amalgamated with Chesilborne, by Provisional Order which came into operation on 25 March 1882.

(b) A detached part of Hermitage was amalgamated with Mintern Magna, by Order which came into operation on 25 March 1885.

(c) A detached part of Hilfield was amalgamated with Leigh, in the Sherborne Union, by Order which came into operation on 25 March 1885.

Unions and Parishes, &c.	Population in 1881.	Area in Statute Acres in 1881.	Rateable Value in 1881.	Post Town.	Petty Sessional Division.
CHAPEL-EN-LE-FRITH UNION.					
Formed 4 Dec. 1837 by Order dated 6 Nov. 1837.—Place marked thus * added 1 Sept. 1845 by Order dated 15 Aug. 1845.)					
COUNTY of DERBY.					
Aston - - *tow.*	96	710	646	Hope by Sheffield -	Chapel-en-le-Frith.
Bamford - - *tow.*	453	1,770	2,026	Bamford by Sheffield	do.
Brough and Shatton *tow.*	74	1,040	895	Hope by Sheffield -	do.
Buxton - - *tow.*	4,110	1,823	19,777	Buxton, Derbyshire	Buxton.
Castleton - - *tow.*	650	2,910	3,228	Castleton by Sheffield	Chapel-en-le-Frith.
Chapel en le Frith, including Browden's Edge, Bradshaw's Edge, and Coomb's Edge (W) }*par.*	4,170	9,752	18,009	Chapel-en-le-Frith-	do.
Chinley, Bugsworth and Brownside }*tow.*	1,233	3,831	7,006	do. for Chinley and Brownside. Whaley Bridge for Bugsworth. }Chapel-en-le-Frith.
Derwent - - *tow.*	187	3,533	1,395	Derwent by Sheffield	do.
Edale - - *tow.*	335	7,043	3,156	Hope by Sheffield -	do.
Fairfield - - *tow.*	2,817	3,975	18,279	Buxton -	Buxton.
Fernilee - - *tow.*	1,063	2,764	4,152	Whaley Bridge -	Chapel-en-le-Frith.
Hartington Upper Quarter }*tow.*	2,171	10,317	9,219	Buxton, Derbyshire	Buxton.
Hope - - *tow.*	332	2,819	3,036	Hope by Sheffield -	Chapel-en-le-Frith.
Hope Woodlands - *tow.*	220	20,614	3,651	do.	do.
Peak Forest - *par.*	499	5,299	5,220	Chapel-en-le-Frith-	do.
Thornhill - - *tow.*	118	610	801	Hope by Sheffield -	do.
Wormhill - - *tow.*	953	4,657	9,505	Buxton, Derbyshire	Buxton.
TOTAL of UNION -	19,484	83,497	110,001		
CHARD UNION.					
Formed 14 May 1836 by Order dated 20 April 1836.— Parish marked thus * added 5 April 1884 by Order dated 4 April 1884.)					
COUNTY of DEVON.					
Yarcombe (a) - *par.*	690	4,689	4,987	Honiton - -	Honiton.

(continued)

CHARD UNION:

a) A detached part of Membury, in the Axminster Union, was amalgamated with Yarcombe, by Order which came into operation on 25 March 1884.

b) By Provisional Order which came into operation on 25 March 1885,—
Detached parts of Ilton were amalgamated respectively with Ashill, Broadway, and Seavington Saint Mary, and a detached part of Seavington Saint Mary was amalgamated with Whitelackington ;
A detached part of Kingston was amalgamated with Dinnington ;
A detached part of Crewkerne was amalgamated with Wayford ;
Detached parts of Cricket Malherby was amalgamated with West Dowlish ; and
A detached part of Dowlish Wake was amalgamated with Knowle Saint Giles.

c) All the parts of a parish known as Stocklinch Magdalen, were united and amalgamated with all the parts of a parish, known as Stocklinch Ottersey, the parts so united and amalgamated were constituted one parish, to be designated the parish of Stocklinch, by Order which came into operation on 25 March 1884.

f) A detached part of Broadway was amalgamated with Ashill, and detached parts of Whitelackington were amalgamated with Broadway and Ilton, by Order which came into operation on 25 March 1885.

CHARD UNION—*continued.*

e) By Order which came into operation on 25 March 1885,—
A detached part of Barrington, in the Langport Union, was amalgamated with Broadway, and detached parts of Broadway were amalgamated with Curry Rivall and Swell in that Union ;
A detached part of Isle Abbots, in the Langport Union, was amalgamated with Ashill ;
A detached part of Shepton Beauchamp was amalgamated with Kingbury Episcopi, in the Langport Union ;
Detached parts of Beercrocombe, Fivehead, and Isle Abbots, in the Langport Union, were united with a detached part of Buckland Saint Mary, and as so united, were amalgamated with Curry Rivall, also in the Langport Union.

f) A detached part of Broadway was amalgamated with Hatch Beauchamp, in the Taunton Union, and a detached part of Whitelackington was amalgamated with Isle Abbots, in the Langport Union, by Order which came into operation on 25 March 1885.

g) A detached part of Cricket Saint Thomas was amalgamated with Winsham, by Order which came into operation on 25 March 1886.

h) Detached parts of Ilminster and Whitelackington were amalgamated with Broadway, by Order which came into operation on 25 March 1886.

i) A detached part of Puckington, in the Langport Union, was amalgamated with Ilminster, by Order which came into operation on 25 March 1886.

Unions and Parishes, &c.	Population in 1881.	Area in Statute Acres in 1881.	Rateable Value in 1881.	Post Town.	Petty Sessional Division
CHARD UNION—_continued._					
COUNTY of DORSET :			.£		
Wambrook _par._	263	1,857	2,126	Chard - -	Bridport.
COUNTY of SOMERSET :					
Ashill (b) (d) (e) - _par._	469	1,790	3,276	Ilminster -	Ilminster.
Broadway (b) (d) (e) (f) (h) _par._	446	2,072	2,973	do. - -	do.
Buckland Saint Mary (e) _par._	608	3,494	3,446	Chard - -	do.
Chaffcombe - _par._	206	999	1,143	do. - -	do.
Chard - - _bor._	2,411	} 5,449 {	1,978	do. - -	Chard Borough.
Chard (W.) - _par._	3,271		12,202	do. - -	Ilminster.
Chellington - _par._	228	881	1,404	Ilminster -	do.
Combe Saint Nicholas _par._	1,131	4,203	6,313	Chard - -	do.
Crewkerne (b) - _par._	4,986	5,331	18,928	Crewkerne -	Crewkerne.
Cricket Malherby (b) _par._	53	540	852	Ilminster -	Ilminster.
Cricket Saint Thomas (g) _par._	107	875	1,544	Chard - -	do.
Cudworth - _par._	110	1,077	1,415	Ilminster -	do.
Dinnington (b) - _par._	162	514	1,194	Crewkerne -	do.
Donyatt - _par._	382	1,223	2,286	Ilminster -	do.
Dowlish Wake (b) - _par._	345	1,282	1,715	do. - -	do.
Hinton Saint George _par._	681	1,500	4,033	Crewkerne -	Crewkerne.
Ilminster (h) (i) - _par._	3,281	4,050	14,567	Ilminster -	Ilminster.
Ilton (b) (d) - _par._	425	1,719	3,175	do. - -	do.
Kingston (b) - _par._	228	3,477	2,190	do. - -	do.
Knowle Saint Giles (b) _par._	105	540	905	Chard - -	do.
Lopen - - _par._	354	489	1,740	Crewkerne -	Crewkerne.
Merriott - - _par._	1,376	1,693	5,589	do. - -	do.
Seavington Saint Mary (b) - _par._	304	988	2,636	Ilminster -	Ilminster.
Seavington Saint Michael - _par._	229	280	891	do. - -	do.
Shepton Beauchamp (e) _par._	640	836	2,714	do. - -	do.
*Stocklinch (e) - _par._	210	498	1,352	do. - -	do.
Wayford (b) - _par._	224	1,618	3,128	Crewkerne -	Crewkerne.
West Dowlish (b) - _par._	47 { In Dowlish Wake }		965	Ilminster - -	Ilminster.
Whitelackington (b) (d) (f) (h) - _par._	284	1,165	3,000	do. - -	do.
Whitstaunton - _par._	208	1,960	2,000	Chard - -	do.
Winsham (g) - _par._	859	2,953	5,687	Crewkerne -	Crewkerne.
TOTAL of UNION -	25,353	60,342	125,654		
CHEADLE UNION.					
(Formed 31 May 1837 by Order dated 3 May 1837.)					
COUNTY of STAFFORD :					
Alton alias Alveton - _tow._	1,054	2,243	4,975	Cheadle - -	Cheadle.
Bradley in the Moors _par._	51	677	1,133	do. - -	do.
Cauldon - - _par._	322	1,494	3,511	Ashbourne -	do.
Caverswall - _par._	5,109	5,262	19,930	Stoke upon Trent -	do.
Cheadle (W.) - _par._	4,724	6,793	18,983	Cheadle - -	do.
Checkley and Tean - _par._	2,549	6,073	13,989	Stoke upon Trent -	do.
Cheddleton and Basford - _tow._	1,832	7,016	13,325	Leek - -	Leek.
Consall alias Cunsall _tow._	224	2,160	1,125	Stoke upon Trent -	Cheadle.
Cotton - - _tow._	648	2,263	3,139	Cheadle - -	do.
Denstone - - _tow._	441	686	1,905	Uttoxeter -	do.
Dilhorne - _par._	1,637	3,776	8,460	Stoke upon Trent -	do.
Draycott in the Moors _par._	406	3,907	5,231	do. - -	do.
Farley - - _tow._	478	2,342	3,941	Cheadle - -	do.
Ipstones - _par._	1,417	5,697	8,124	do. - -	Leek.
Kingsley and Whiston _par._	1,832	4,769	8,503	do. - -	Cheadle.
TOTAL of UNION -	22,724	55,158	119,274		

CHARD UNION :
(b) (c) (d) (e) (f) (g) (h) and (i)   _See_ notes, page 85.

Unions and Parishes, &c.	Population in 1881.	Area in Statute Acres in 1881.	Rateable Value in 1881.	Post Town.	Petty Sessional Division.

CHELMSFORD UNION.

(Formed 10 Aug. 1835 by Order dated 21 July 1835.— Places marked thus * added 21 Sept. 1835 by Order dated 27 Aug. 1835.)

COUNTY of ESSEX :

			£		
Boreham - - par.	992	3,801	9,733	Chelmsford -	Chelmsford.
Broomfield - - par.	855	2,224	5,447	do. -	do.
Butsbury - - par.	452	2,113	3,208	Ingatestone -	do.
Chelmsford (W.) - par.	9,885	2,858	37,859	Chelmsford	do.
Chignall Saint James par.	224	913	1,538	do. -	do.
Chignall Smealey - par.	131	476	673	do. -	do.
Danbury - - par.	978	2,975	4,607	do. -	do.
East Hanningfield - par.	404	2,504	3,091	do. -	do.
Fryerning - - par.	704	1,395	3,881	Ingatestone	do.
Good Easter - par.	520	2,087	2,966	Chelmsford	do.
Great Baddow - par.	2,055	3,910	10,230	do. -	do.
*Great Leighs - par.	753	3,146	4,831	do. -	do.
Great Waltham - par.	2,349	7,457	12,612	do. -	do.
Ingatestone - - par.	926	2,738	7,252	Ingatestone -	do.
Little Baddow - par.	541	2,756	3,970	Chelmsford -	do.
*Little Leighs - par.	125	1,079	1,801	do. -	do.
Little Waltham - par.	580	2,307	4,314	do. -	do.
Margaretting - par.	526	2,284	7,080	Ingatestone -	do.
Mashbury - - par.	142	822	1,058	Chelmsford -	do.
Pleshey - - par.	302	732	1,269	do. -	Dunmow.
*Rettendon - - par.	720	3,890	5,334	do. -	Chelmsford.
Roxwell - - par.	814	4,782	7,014	do. -	do.
Runwell - - par.	333	2,073	2,540	do. -	do.
Sandon - - par.	466	2,318	3,677	do. -	do.
South Hanningfield - par.	231	1,538	1,987	do. -	do.
Springfield - - par.	2,528	2,926	13,737	do. -	do.
Stock (a) - - par.	614	2,721	3,139	Ingatestone -	do.
West Hanningfield - par.	430	2,839	4,016	Chelmsford	do.
Widford - - par.	300	692	3,227	do. -	do.
*Woodham Ferris - par.	673	4,482	5,377	do. -	do.
Writtle - - par.	2,412	8,786	15,351	do. -	do.
TOTAL of UNION -	32,971	85,627	192,819		

CHELTENHAM UNION.

(Formed 16 Nov. 1835 by Order dated 30 Oct. 1835.— Place marked thus * added 16 May 1836 by Order dated 21 April 1836.)

COUNTY of GLOUCESTER :

Badgworth (a). - par.	1,004	3,927	9,623	Cheltenham -	Cheltenham.
Charlton Kings - par.	3,950	3,170	22,199	do. -	do.
Cheltenham (W.) - par.	43,972	4,203	223,832	do. -	do.

(continued)

CHELMSFORD UNION :

(a) A detached part of Orsett, in the Orsett Union, was amalgamated with Stock, by Order which came into operation on 25 March 1882.

CHELTENHAM UNION :

(a) Certain detached parts of Badgworth were amalgamated with Shurdington, by Order which came into operation on 25 March 1883.

(b) A detached part of Boddington, in the Tewkesbury Union, was amalgamated with Staverton, by Order which came into operation on 25 March 1883.

L 3

Unions and Parishes, &c.	Population in 1881.	Area in Statute Acres in 1881.	Rateable Value in 1881.	Post Town.	Petty Sessional Division.
			£		
CHELTENHAM UNION—County of Gloucester—*continued.*					
Cowley - - *par.*	300	1,831	2,451	Cheltenham and Gloucester.	Cheltenham.
Cubberley - - *par.*	326	3,421	3,521	do. - -	do.
Great Whitcombe - *par.*	159	918	2,019	Gloucester - -	do.
Leckhampton - *par.*	3,501	1,900	19,605	Cheltenham	do.
Prestbury - *par.*	1,402	3,022	12,859	do. - -	do.
Shurdington (*a*) - *par.*	215	383	1,631	do. - -	do.
Staverton (*b*) - *par.*	242	720	1,627	do. - -	do.
Swindon - *par.*	201	721	2,801	do. - -	do.
Uckington - *ham.*	145	880	1,607	do. - -	do
*Uphatherly - *par.*	88	810	1,386	do. - -	do.
TOTAL of UNION - -	55,505	25,909	305,164		

CHEPSTOW UNION.

(Formed 16 May 1836 by Order dated 18 April 1836.—Places marked thus ** added 24 Oct. 1836 by Order dated 28 Sep. 1836, thus † added 22 Mar. 1862 by Order dated 15 Mar. 1862, and thus ‡ added 29 Sep. 1862 by Order dated 27 Aug. 1862.)

Unions and Parishes, &c.	Population in 1881.	Area in Statute Acres in 1881.	Rateable Value in 1881.	Post Town.	Petty Sessional Division.
COUNTY of GLOUCESTER :					
*Alvington - *par.*	387	1,582	2,939	Lydney - -	Lydney.
*Aylberton - *ty.*	649	1,906	4,025	do. - -	do.
*Hewelsfield - *par.*	402	1,592	1,849	Coleford - -	do.
*Lidney - *tow.*	2,545	5,199	19,451	Lydney - -	do.
Llancaut - *par.*	14	218	241	Chepstow - -	do.
*Saint Briavels - *par.*	1,143	4,796	6,417	Coleford - -	Coleford.
Tidinham - *par.*	1,501	6,067	13,001	Chepstow - -	Lydney.
*Wollastone - *par.*	866	3,303	8,122	Lydney - -	do.
COUNTY of MONMOUTH :					
Caerwent with Crick *par.*	400	1,962	3,031	Chepstow -	Chepstow.
Caldicot - *par.*	1,401	3,158	6,715	do. - -	do.
Chapel Hill (*a*) - *par.*	411	1,267	1,720	do. - -	do.
Chepstow with Hardwick (W.) } *par.*	3,591	1,096	13,308	do. - -	do.
Dinham - *ham.*	44	670	507	do. - -	do.
East Newchurch (*a*) *dir.*	389	5,431	2,182	do. - -	do.
Howick - *ham.*	29	642	597	do. - -	do.
Ifton - *par.*	32	1,155	1,334	do. - -	do.
Itton - *tow.*	161	1,112	960	do. - -	do.
Kilgwrwg - *par.*	103	659	401	do. - -	do.
Little Tintern - *par.*	326	795	1,283	do. - -	do.
Llangwm Icha - *dir.*	43 }	3,159	575	Usk - -	Usk.
Llangwm Ucha - *dir.*	257 }		2,031	do. - -	do.
Llansoy - *par.*	147	1,415	1,167	do. - -	do.
Llanvair Discoed - *tow.*	146	1,316	1,038	Caerleon - -	Chepstow.
Llanvihangel Rogiatt *par.*	58	557	1,268	Chepstow - -	do.
Llanvihangel Tory-Mynedd } *par.*	163	1,186	953	do. - -	Trelleck.
Mathern and Saint Pierre (*b*) } *par.*	599	3,182	6,178	do. - -	Chepstow.
Mounton - *par.*	57	413	514	do. - -	do.
Penterry - *par.*	37	480	425	do. - -	do.
Port Skewett - *par.*	486	1,112	4,171	do. - -	do.
Rogiatt - *par.*	52	2,905	2,289	do. - -	do.
Saint Arvans (*a*) - *par.*	486	2,215	3,296	do. - -	do.
‡Saint Arvans Grange (*a*) } *par.*	13	520	579	do. - -	do.

(continued)

CHELTENHAM UNION :

(*a*) (*b*). *See notes, page 87.*

CHEPSTOW UNION :

(*a*) By Order which came into operation on 25 March 1885,—
Detached parts of Saint Arvans were amalgamated with Chapel Hill and Saint Arvans Grange ;

CHEPSTOW UNION—*continued.*

A detached part of West Newchurch was amalgamated with East Newchurch.

(*b*) By Provisional Order which came into operation on 25 March 1886, the several parts of a parish known as Mathern were amalgamated with a parish known as Saint Pierre and Runstone ; and the parish of Saint Pierre and Runstone, as so altered, was designated the parish of Mathern and Saint Pierre.

Unions and Parishes, &c.	Population in 1881.	Area in Statute Acres in 1881.	Rateable Value in 1881.	Post Town.	Petty Sessional Division.
			£		
CHEPSTOW UNION—County of Monmouth—*continued.*					
Saint Brides Nether-went } *tow.*	146	780	926	Chepstow -	Christchurch.
†Saint Kingsmark - *par.*	7	18	74	do. -	Chepstow.
Shire Newton - *par.*	773	3,511	3,953	do. - -	do.
Trelleck Grange - *par.*	126	1,817	1,618	do. - -	Trelleck.
Undy - - *par.*	439	3,717	4,835	Newport (Mon.) -	Christchurch.
West Newchurch (*a*) *div.*	124 { In East Newchurch }	1,138		Chepstow -	Chepstow.
Wolves Newton - *par.*	168	2,649	1,579	do. - -	Trelleck.
TOTAL of UNION - -	18,701	73,898	126,789		

CHERTSEY UNION.

(Formed 6 Nov. 1835 by Order dated 10 Oct. 1835.)

COUNTY of SURREY :

Bisley - - *par.*	651	922	1,452	Woking - -	Chertsey.
Byfleet - - *par.*	1,261	2,075	7,429	Weybridge -	do.
Chertsey (W.) - *par.*	9,215	10,777	37,594	Chertsey - -	do.
Chobham - - *par.*	2,489	9,579	9,550	Woking - -	do.
Horsell - - *par.*	900	2,937	4,148	do. - -	do.
Pyrford - - *par.*	343	1,881	2,756	do. - -	do.
Walton on Thames - *par.*	6,572	6,859	39,522	Walton on Thames	Kingston.
Weybridge - - *par.*	3,027	1,372	18,817	Weybridge -	Chertsey.
Windlesham and Bagshot } *par.*	2,669	5,692	9,382	Windlesham -	do.
TOTAL of UNION -	27,137	42,094	130,650		

CHESTER UNION.

(Formed 30 Sept. 1869 by Order dated 16 Sept. 1869.—*Places in the County of Chester, added 14 Mar. 1871 by Order dated 27 Feb. 1871.)

CITY of CHESTER and COUNTY of the same CITY :

Chester (*a*) - - *par.*	35,151	2,784	142,121	Chester -	City of Chester (having Separate Quarter Sessions).

*COUNTY of CHESTER :

Bache - - *tow.*	27	96	506	do. - -	Chester Castle.
Backford - - *tow.*	125	764	1,118	do. - -	do.
Blacon-with-Crabhall or Crabwall - } *tow.*	235	1,178	1,993	do. - -	do.

(*continued*)

CHESTER UNION :

(a) By Section 11 of the Chester Improvement Act, 1884, it is enacted that the area within the city of Chester should, for all purposes other than exclusively ecclesiastical purposes, become one parish, to be called the parish of Chester. The area referred to consisted of 11 Parishes, which were known by the following names, Holy and Undivided Trinity, Saint Bridget, Saint John-the-Baptist, Saint Martin, Saint Mary-on-the-Hill, Saint Michael, Saint Olave, Saint Oswald, Saint Peter, The Abbey Precincts, Spittle Boughton, and part of the parish of Great Boughton.

Unions and Parishes, &c.		Population in 1881.	Area in Statute Acres in 1881.	Rateable Value in 1881.	Post Town.	Petty Sessional Division.
CHESTER UNION—County of Chester—continued.				£		
Bridge Trafford	tow.	60	406	743	Chester - -	Chester Castle.
Capenhurst -	tow.	159	1,204	3,077	do. - -	do.
Caughall or Coughall	tow.	19	348	556	do. - -	do.
Chorlton-by-Backford	tow.	66	544	1,104	do. - -	do.
Christleton - -	tow.	835	1,506	5,511	do. - -	do.
Claverton - -	par.	—	264	464	do. - -	City of Chester.
Croughton or Crogh- } ton - - - }	tow.	29	281	471	do. - -	Chester Castle.
Doddleston - -	tow.	283	1,673	3,934	Wrexham -	do.
Dunham-on-the-Hill -	tow.	276	1,404	3,350	Chester -	Eddisbury.
Eaton - -	tow.	132	999	1,951	do. - -	Chester Castle.
Eccleston - -	tow.	323	1,392	2,345	do. - -	do.
Elton - -	tow.	197	1,143	2,046	do. - -	do.
Great Boughton (W.)	tow.	2,212	796	8,273	do. - -	do.
Great Saughall -	tow.	619	1,219	3,144	do. - -	do.
Great Stanney -	tow.	70	993	1,558	do. - -	do.
Hapsford - -	tow.	75	562	1,121	do. - -	Eddisbury.
Hoole (W.) -	tow.	3,062	750	10,459	do. - -	Chester Castle.
Ince - -	par.	331	1,739	3,382	do. - -	do.
Lea - -	tow.	68	697	2,714	do. - -	do.
Little Saughall -	tow.	92	482	828	do. - -	do.
Little Stanney -	tow.	157	831	1,574	do. - -	do.
Littleton - -	tow.	106	274	762	do. - -	do.
Lower Kinnerton -	tow.	112	537	836	do. - -	do.
Marlston-with-Leach	tow.	126	998	2,397	do. - -	do.
Mickle Trafford -	tow.	244	1,163	3,121	do. - -	do.
Mollington Banastre } or Little Molling- } ton - - - }	tow.	51	250	812	do. - -	do.
Mollington Tarrant } or Great Molling- } ton - - - }	tow.	237	832	2,019	do. - -	do.
Moston - -	tow.	19	303	1,319	do. - -	do.
Newton - by - Chester	tow.	268	441	3,445	do. - -	do.
Pickton - -	tow.	112	860	1,362	do. - -	do.
Poulton - -	tow.	161	1,105	1,776	Wrexham -	do.
Pulford - -	tow.	264	1,184	2,750	do. - -	do.
Shotwick - -	tow.	77	566	863	Chester -	do.
Shotwick Park -	par.	14	987	1,030	do. - -	do.
Stanlow - -	par.	18	254	413	do. - -	do.
Stoke - -	tow.	70	653	1,221	do. - -	do.
Thornton-le-Moors -	tow.	157	1,232	1,856	do. - -	do.
Upton - -	tow.	1,112	1,154	5,920	do. - -	do.
Wervin - -	tow.	92	743	1,164	do. - -	do.
Wimbolds Trafford -	tow.	97	591	1,000	do. - -	do.
Woodbank - -	tow.	59	180	367	Sutton -	do.
TOTAL of UNION -		48,002	38,662	239,409		

CHESTERFIELD UNION.						
(Formed 19 Oct. 1837 by Order dated 23 Sept. 1837. * Formerly consisted of Great Barlow and Little Barlow, which were consolidated by Provisional Order dated 2 May 1879, and continued in the Union.)						
COUNTY OF DERBY :						
Ashover - -	tow.	2,276	9,564	8,835	Chesterfield -	Alfreton.
*Barlow - -	tow.	920	3,921	8,180	do. -	Chesterfield.

(continued)

CHESTER UNION :

(b). See note, page 89.

CHESTERFIELD UNION :

(a) By a Provisional Order which came into operation on 25 March 1884,—
Certain detached parts of Brimmington were amalgamated with Tapton;
A detached part of Coal Aston was amalgamated with Unstone, and a detached part of Unstone was amalgamated with Coal Aston ;

CHESTERFIELD UNION—continued.

Detached parts of Morton were amalgamated with North Wingfield, Woodthorpe, and Pilsley ;
Detached parts of North Wingfield and Woodthorpe were amalgamated with Clayhune ; and
A detached part of Pilsley was amalgamated with North Wingfield.

(b) A detached part of Clown, in the Worksop Union, was amalgamated with Bolsover, by Order which came into operation on 25 March 1885.

Unions and Parishes, &c.		Population in 1881.	Area in Statute Acres in 1881.	Rateable Value in 1881.	Post Town.	Petty Sessional Division.

CHESTERFIELD UNION—County of Derby—*continued*.   £

Bolsover (b)	- tow.	2,281	4,917	8,392	Chesterfield -	Chesterfield.
Brackenfield -	- tow.	322	1,551	2,667	Alfreton - -	Alfreton.
Brampton -	- par.	6,385	8,156	19,189	Chesterfield -	Chesterfield.
Brimmington (a)	- tow.	3,457	1,389	8,809	do. - -	do
Calow	- tow.	563	1,339	2,097	do. - -	do.
Chesterfield (W.)	- tow.	12,221	328	42,004	do. - -	do.
Claylane (a)	- tow.	6,347	1,313	13,179	do. - -	Alfreton.
Coal Aston (a)	- tow.	909	1,287	2,922	Sheffield - -	Eckington.
Dronfield -	- tow.	5,169	2,389	18,189	do. - -	do.
Eckington -	- par.	11,094	7,125	36,218	Chesterfield -	do.
Haslaud -	- tow.	5,077	2,091	23,808	do. - -	Chesterfield.
Heath -	- par.	356	1,676	2,628	do. - -	do.
Holmesfield -	- tow.	492	4,699	2,949	do. - -	Eckington.
Killamarsh -	- par.	2,812	1,659	11,705	do. - -	do.
Morton (a) -	- tow.	879	1,258	9,175	Alfreton - -	Alfreton.
Newbold and Dunston	tow.	6,158	2,991	24,612	Chesterfield -	Chesterfield.
North Wingfield (a)	tow.	2,044	1,449	8,017	do. - -	do.
Pilsley (a) -	- tow.	1,821	1,591	10,997	do. - -	Alfreton.
Shirland and Higham -	} par.	3,415	2,956	11,198	Alfreton - -	do.
Staveley -	- tow.	8,194	6,872	38,340	Chesterfield -	Chesterfield.
Stretton -	- tow.	630	1,574	4,584	Alfreton - -	Alfreton.
Sutton cum Duck-manton -	} par.	477	4,369	5,631	Chesterfield -	Chesterfield.
Tapton (a) -	- tow.	183	655	4,417	do. - -	do.
Temple Normanton -	- tow.	198	520	1,079	do. - -	do.
Tupton -	- tow.	1,371	735	9,604	do. - -	do.
Unstone (a) -	- tow.	2,368	2,251	12,018	Sheffield - -	Eckington.
Walton -	- tow.	1,182	2,124	6,747	Chesterfield -	Chesterfield.
Wessington -	- tow.	609	973	1,715	Alfreton - -	Alfreton.
Whittington -	- par.	7,271	1,581	19,817	Chesterfield -	Chesterfield.
Wingerworth -	- par.	410	2,958	7,033	do. - -	do.
Woodthorpe (a)	- tow.	817	1,055	5,171	do. - -	do.
TOTAL of UNION	-	**98,741**	**89,852**	**392,256**		

CHESTER-LE-STREET UNION.

(Formed 12 Dec. 1836 by Order dated 16 Nov. 1836.)

COUNTY OF DURHAM :

Barmston -	- tow.	650	920	4,355	Washington Station	Gateshead.
Bidick South	- tow.	50	352	2,822	Fence Houses -	Houghton-le-Spring.
Birtley -	- tow.	3,540	1,429	10,274	Chester-le-Street -	Chester-le-Street.
Bourn Moor -	- tow.	1,355	512	7,009	Fence Houses -	Houghton-le-Spring.
Chester - le - Street (W.) (b) (c) (e)	} tow.	6,646	2,913	23,849	Chester-le-Street -	Chester-le-Street.
Cocken -	- tow.	184	465	1,714	Fence Houses -	Houghton le-Spring.
Edmondsley (e) (e) (g)	tow.	930	1,960	8,950	Chester-le-Street -	Chester-le-Street.
Haraton (a) -	- tow.	2,731	2,997	10,888	Washington Station	do.
Lambton -	- tow.	151	684	2,082	Fence Houses -	Houghton-le-Spring.

(*continued*)

CHESTER-LE-STREET UNION :

(a) A detached part of Usworth Great and Little was amalgamated with Haraton, by Order which came into operation on 25 March 1882.

(b) A detached part of Kimblesworth, in the Durham Union, was amalgamated with Chester-le-Street, by Order which came into operation on 25 March 1882.

(c) By an Order which came into operation on 25 March 1885,—
Detached parts of Chester-le-Street were amalgamated with Plawsworth and Witton Gilbert ;
A detached part of Edmondsley was amalgamated with Chester-le-Street ;
Detached parts of Pelton were amalgamated with Chester le-Street and Edmondsley ; and
A detached part of Plawsworth was amalgamated with Edmondsley ;

CHESTER-LE-STREET UNION—*continued.*

(d) A detached part of Plawsworth was amalgamated with Kimblesworth, in the Durham Union, by Order which came into operation on 25 March 1885.

(e) Parts of Chester-le-Street, and of Lanchester in the Lanchester Union, were amalgamated with Edmondsley, by Provisional Order which came into operation on 25 March 1886.

(f) A detached part of Tanfield, in the Lanchester Union, was amalgamated with Urpeth, by Provisional Order which came into operation on 25 March 1886.

(g) By Order which came into operation on 25 March 1887,—
Parts of Edmondsley and parts of Witton Gilbert were amalgamated with Lanchester and Satley in the Lanchester Union.

Unions and Parishes, &c.		Population in 1881.	Area in Statute Acres in 1881.	Rateable Value in 1881.	Post Town.	Petty Sessional Division.

CHESTER-LE-STREET UNION—County of Durham—
continued.

				£		
Lamesley	- tow.	4,670	7,178	23,335	Gateshead -	Chester-le-Street.
Lumley Great	- tow.	1,830	1,614	4,442	Fence Houses -	Houghton-le-Spring.
Lumley Little	- tow.	511	875	2,011	do. -	do.
Ouston	- tow.	854	613	2,590	Chester-le-Street -	Chester-le-Street.
Pelton (c) -	- tow.	4,130	1,161	13,017	do. -	do.
Plawsworth (c) (d)	- tow.	942	1,266	6,948	do. -	do.
Urpeth (f) -	- tow.	1,602	1,725	11,503	Chester-le-Street -	Chester-le-Street.
Usworth Great and Little (a) -	} tow.	4,606	2,134	18,091	Washington Station	Gateshead.
Waldridge -	- tow.	1,428	732	3,499	Chester-le-Street -	Chester-le-Street.
Washington -	- tow.	3,022	1,973	13,740	Washington Station	Gateshead.
Witton Gilbert (c) (g)	par.	3,130	3,249	12,100	Durham -	Durham.
TOTAL of UNION -		**43,352**	**34,812**	**184,121**		

CHESTERTON UNION.

(Formed 2 April 1836 by Order
dated 18 March 1836.—Place
marked thus * added 5 Feb.
1840 by Order of that date.)

COUNTY of CAMBRIDGE :

Barton -	- par.	323	1,812	2,981	Cambridge -	Cambridge.
Cherry Hinton	- par.	869	2,043	5,462	do. -	Bottisham.
Chesterton (W.)	- par.	5,706	2,729	17,881	do. -	Cambridge.
Childerley -	- par.	48	1,052	1,206	do. -	do.
Comberton -	- par.	576	1,925	3,106	do. -	do.
Coton -	- par.	325	1,130	1,605	do. -	do.
Cottenham -	- par.	2,458	7,107	16,963	do. -	do.
Dry Drayton	- par.	374	2,389	2,636	do. -	do.
Fen Ditton -	- par.	668	1,862	4,216	do. -	Bottisham.
Fulbourn -	- par.	1,769	5,221	8,063	do. -	do.
Girton -	- par.	484	1,674	3,227	do. -	Cambridge.
Grantchester -	- par.	1,147	1,591	5,436	do. -	do.
Great Shelford	- par.	972	1,900	8,096	do. -	do.
Great Wilbraham	- par.	547	2,800	4,985	do. -	Bottisham.
Harlton -	- par.	312	1,100	1,783	do. -	Arrington.
Harston -	- par.	808	1,480	4,064	do. -	Cambridge.
Haslingfield -	- par.	754	2,527	4,400	do. -	Arrington.
Hauxton -	- par.	232	568	1,389	do. -	Cambridge.
Histon (b) -	- par.	969	2,300	5,668	do. -	do.
Horningsey -	- par.	409	1,580	3,825	do. -	Bottisham.
Impington (b) -	- par.	398	1,200	3,468	do. -	Cambridge.
Landbeach -	- par.	510	2,490	3,753	do. -	do.
Little Shelford	- par.	516	1,200	2,781	do. -	do.
Little Wilbraham	- par.	112	1,300	3,344	do. -	Bottisham.
Long Stanton All Saints -	} par.	410	885	3,857	do. -	Cambridge.
Long Stanton St. Michael -	} par.	73	830	1,559	do. -	do.
Madingley -	- par.	236	1,763	2,125	do. -	do.
Milton -	- par.	554	1,378	4,960	do. -	do.
Newton -	- par.	226	984	1,666	do. -	do.
Oakington -	- par.	461	1,487	3,463	do. -	do.
Rampton (a) -	- par.	232	1,312	2,810	do. -	do.
Stapleford -	- par.	560	1,100	3,177	do. -	do.
Stow with Quy	- par.	351	1,820	3,180	do. -	Bottisham.
Teversham -	- par.	251	1,200	2,058	do. -	do.
Trumpington -	- par.	940	2,200	8,306	do. -	Cambridge.
Waterbeach -	- par.	1,508	5,556	17,743	do. -	do.
*Westwick -	- ham.	84	270	685	do. -	do.
Willingham (a)	- par.	1,577	4,663	11,981	do. -	do.
TOTAL of UNION -		**29,049**	**76,728**	**188,808**		

CHESTER-LE-STREET UNION :

(a) (c) (d) (f) (g). *See notes, page 91.*

CHESTERTON UNION :

(a) A detached part of Willingham was amalgamated with
Rampton, by Order which came into operation on
25 March 1884.

CHESTERTON UNION—*continued.*

(b) A detached part of Histon was amalgamated with Im-
pington, by Order which came into operation on
25 March 1886.

Unions and Parishes, &c.	Population in 1881.	Area in Statute Acres in 1881.	Rateable Value in 1881.	Post Town.	Petty Sessional Division.

CHICHESTER INCOR-PORATION.

(Under the 26 Geo. II.)

CITY and COUNTY of the CITY of CHICHESTER :

			£		
All Saints, *alias* the Pallant - } *par.*	327	12	1,521	Chichester -	City of Chichester (Separate Quarter Sessions).
The Close - - *pre.*	127	15	905	do. - -	do.
Saint Andrew - - *par.*	512	10	2,311	do. - -	do.
Saint Martin - - *par.*	242	4	670	do. - -	do.
Saint Olave - - *par.*	225	4	1,111	do. - -	do.
Saint Peter the Less *par.*	392	23	1,518	do. - -	do.

In the CITY and COUNTY of the CITY of CHICHESTER and COUNTY of SUSSEX :

Saint Bartholomew - *par.*	325	238	2,302	do. - -	do.
Saint Pancras - - *par.*	1,184	139	2,559	do. - -	do.
Saint Peter the Great, alias Sub-Deanery } *par.* (W.) - -	5,056	1,428	12,600	do. - ..	do.
TOTAL of INCORPORATION	8,390	1,873	25,590		

CHIPPENHAM UNION.

(Formed 1 Dec. 1835 by Order dated 17 Nov. 1835.)

COUNTY of WILTS :

Avon - - *par.*	19	156	103	Chippenham -	Chippenham.
Biddestone (*e*) " *par.*	426	2,418	3,056	do. - -	do.
Box (*b*) - - *par.*	2,304	4,591	15,869	do. - -	do.
Castle Combe - *par.*	495	1,494	2,722	do. - -	do.
Chippenham (W.) (*a*) } *par.* (*d*) -	5,192	7,455	24,007	do. - -	{ Chippenham and Borough of Chippenham.
Christian Malford (*c*) *par.*	777	3,101	8,339	do. - -	Chippenham.
Colerne - - *par.*	1,056	3,620	5,490	do. - -	do.
Corsham (*d*) - *par.*	3,747	6,498	21,981	do. - -	do.
Draycot Cerne (*a*) - *par.*	144	1,066	1,971	do. - -	do.
Grittleton - - *par.*	310	2,040	2,977	do. - -	do.
Hardenhuish (*a*) - *par.*	88	556	1,094	do. - -	do.
Kington Langley (*a*) *ty.*	553 }	4,136	{ 3,471	do. - -	do.
Kington Saint Michael *ty.*	457 }		3,483	do. - -	do.
Lacock (W.) - *par.*	1,171	3,639	9,097	do. - -	do.
Langley Burrell (*a*) - *par.*	1,129	1,694	9,270	do. - -	do.
Leigh Delamere - *par.*	105	1,227	1,521	do. - -	do.

(continued)

CHIPPENHAM UNION :

(*a*) By an Order which came into operation on 25 March 1884,—

Parts of Chippenham were amalgamated with Hardenhuish, Langley Burrell, and Pewsham, and parts of Langley Burrell were amalgamated with Chippenham.

A detached part of Draycot Cerne was amalgamated with Sutton Benger.

Parts of Hardenhuish were amalgamated with Langley Burrell, and parts of Langley Burrell were amalgamated with Hardenhuish.

A detached part of Kington Langley was amalgamated with Langley Burrell and Tytherton Kelways.

Detached parts of Slaughterford were amalgamated with a parish which was known as Biddestone Saint Nicholas (see note (*e*)), by Order which came into operation on 25 March 1884.

CHIPPENHAM UNION—*continued.*

(*b*) All the parts of a parish known as Ditteridge, were amalgamated with Box, by Order which came into operation on 25 March 1884.

(*c*) Detached parts of Christian Malford were amalgamated with Bremhill, in the Calne Union, and a detached part of Bremhill was amalgamated with Tytherton Kelways, by Orders which came into operation on 25 March 1884 and 1885 respectively.

(*d*) Certain detached parts of Chippenham and Corsham, and of Bremham, in the Devizes Union, were united and amalgamated with Pewsham, by Order which came into operation on 25 March 1884.

(*e*) All the parts of a parish which was known as Biddestone Saint Nicholas were amalgamated with Biddestone Saint Peter, and the latter as so altered was designated the parish of Biddestone, by Order which came into operation on 25 March 1885.

Unions and Parishes, &c.	Population in 1881.	Area in Statute Acres in 1881.	Rateable Value in 1881.	Post Town.	Petty Sessional Division.
CHIPPENHAM UNION—County of Wilts—*continued*.			£		
Littleton Drew - *par.*	201	971	1,235	Chippenham	Chippenham.
Nettleton - *par.*	405	1,959	3,034	do. -	do.
North Wraxhall - *par.*	454	2,127	3,004	do. -	do.
Pewsham (*a*) (*d*) - *par.*	367	1,314	2,301	do. -	do.
Seagry - *par.*	151	1,014	2,141	do. -	do.
Slaughterford (*a*) - *par.*	160 {	In Biddlestone	} 1,239	do. -	do.
Stanton Saint Quintin *par.*	295	1,820	2,123	do. -	do.
Sutton Benger (*a*) - *par.*	356	1,173	2,515	do. -	do.
Tytherton Kelways (*a*) (*c*) - } *par.*	26	140	418	do. -	do.
West Kington - *par.*	303	2,414	3,423	do. -	do.
Yatton Keynell - *par.*	520	1,749	3,213	do. -	do.
TOTAL of UNION -	21,211	58,405	139,406		
CHIPPING NORTON UNION.					
(Formed 18 Sept. 1835 by Order dated 1 Sept. 1835.—Places marked thus * added 25 Dec. 1858 by Order dated 22 Oct. 1858.)					
COUNTY OF OXFORD :					
Ascott - *par.*	401	1,839	3,972	Enstone -	Chadlington.
Bruern - *ville*	42	1,876	1,819	Chipping Norton -	do.
Chadlington - *tow.*	706	3,450	4,788	Enstone -	do.
Charlbury - *par.*	1,319	2,572	7,198	do. -	do.
Chastleton - *par.*	208	1,770	2,701	Moreton in Marsh	do.
Chilson - *tow.*	218	1,678	3,791	Enstone -	do.
Chipping Norton (W.) *tow.*	4,167	2,456	11,919	Chipping Norton -	Chipping Norton.
Churchill (*a*) - *par.*	505	2,818	4,822	do. -	Chadlington.
*Cornbury Park - *par.*	44	632	733	Enstone -	do.
Cornwell - *par.*	93	849	1,327	Chipping Norton -	do.
Enstone - *par.*	1,102	6,245	9,176	Enstone -	do.
Fawler - *tow.*	109	1,655	2,855	do. -	do.
Fifield - *par.*	216	1,160	1,262	Chipping Norton -	do.
Finstock - *tow.*	490	883	1,876	Enstone -	do.
Great Rollright - *par.*	388	2,414	3,295	Chipping Norton -	do.
Great Tew - *par.*	479	3,007	4,680	Enstone -	North Wootton.
Heythrop and Dunthrop (*b*) - } *par.*	250	1,689	2,690	Chipping Norton -	Chadlington.
Idbury (*a*) - *par.*	189	1,559	2,301	do. -	do.
Kingham - *par.*	617	1,877	4,928	do. -	do.
Langley - *tow.*	50	303	427	Witney -	do.
Leafield - *tow.*	712	901	1,929	do. -	do.
Little Rollright - *par.*	38	627	835	Chipping Norton -	do.
Little Tew - *par.*	277	1,579	2,148	Enstone -	North Wootton.
Lyneham - *tow.*	215	1,913	3,207	Chipping Norton -	Chadlington.
Milton - *tow.*	836	2,080	3,582	do. -	do.
Over Norton (*b*) - *ham.*	140	2,418	3,348	do. -	do.
Salford - *par.*	378	1,567	2,186	do. -	do.
Sarsden - *par.*	156	1,431	2,066	do. -	do.
Shipton - *tow.*	721	2,520	4,624	do. -	do.
Spelsbury - *par.*	540	1,304	4,697	Enstone -	do.
Swerford - *par.*	416	1,925	2,989	do. -	do.
*Whichwood - *par.*	213	3,782	4,175	Witney -	do.
COUNTY OF WARWICK :					
Barton in the Heath *par.*	189	1,540	2,230	Shipston-on-Stour -	Brailes.
Little Compton - *par.*	501	1,670	2,514	Moreton in Marsh	do.
Long Compton - *par.*	700	3,530	6,448	Shipston-on-Stour -	do.
TOTAL of UNION -	17,958	72,579	123,838		

CHIPPENHAM UNION :

(*a*) (*c*) (*d*). *See* notes, page 93.

CHIPPING NORTON UNION :

(*a*) A detached part of Churchill was amalgamated with Idbury, by Order which came into operation on 25 March 1884.

CHIPPING NORTON UNION—*continued*.

(*b*) A detached part of Over Norton was amalgamated with Heythrop and Dunthrop, by Order which came into operation on 25 March 1884.

Unions and Parishes, &c.		Population in 1881.	Area in Statute Acres in 1881.	Rateable Value in 1881.	Post Town.	Petty Sessional Division.

CHIPPING SODBURY UNION.

Formed 30 March 1836 by Order dated 11 Feb. 1836.)

COUNTY of GLOUCESTER :

				£		
Abson with Wick (*a*)	par.	878	2,308	4,432	Bath - -	Sodbury.
Acton Turville	par.	290	1,015	1,204	Chippenham -	do.
Alderley (*a*) - -	par.	93	898	1,767	Wotton under Edge	do.
Chipping Sodbury -	par.	1,067	107	2,127	Chipping Sodbury -	do.
Cold Ashton - -	par.	388	2,289	3,531	Chippenham -	do.
Dirham and Hinton -	par.	400	3,020	5,484	do. -	do.
Dodington - -	par.	140	1,196	2,112	Chipping Sodbury -	do.
Doynton - -	par.	402	1,728	3,354	Bath - -	Lawfords Gate.
Frampton Cotterell (*a*)	par.	1,983	2,125	4,835	Bristol - -	do.
Great Badminton -	par.	489	1,794	2,502	Chippenham -	Sodbury.
Hawkesbury (*a*) -	par.	1,948	9,770	12,694	do. -	do.
Horton - -	par.	367	3,582	4,469	Chipping Sodbury -	do.
Iron Acton - -	par.	1,156	2,952	6,181	Bristol -	Thornbury.
Little Sodbury -	par.	132	1,093	1,636	Chipping Sodbury -	Sodbury.
Marshfield -	par.	1,527	5,907	10,292	Chippenham -	do.
Old Sodbury -	par.	714	3,729	5,925	Chipping Sodbury -	do.
Pucklechurch (*a*) -	par.	1,292	2,149	10,574	Bristol - -	do.
Tormarton - -	par.	424	2,656	3,380	Chippenham -	do.
Wapley with Codrington - -	par.	275	2,598	3,905	do. -	do.
Westerleigh (*a*) (*b*) -	par.	1,285	4,116	10,390	Chipping Sodbury -	do.
West Littleton -	par.	101	1,013	1,283	Chippenham -	do.
Wickwar - -	par.	917	2,328	5,514	Charfield, R.S.O. -	do.
Yate (W.) - -	par.	1,255	1,081	10,520	Chipping Sodbury -	do.
TOTAL of UNION -		17,523	63,054	118,201		

CHORLEY UNION.

(Formed 26 Jan. 1837 by Order dated 31 Dec. 1836. — Place marked thus * added 2 June 1837 by Order dated 8 May 1837.)

COUNTY of LANCASTER :

Adlington - -	tow.	3,258	1,064	9,042	Chorley - -	Hundred of Leyland.
Anderton - -	tow.	317	1,229	6,338	do. -	do.
Anglezark - -	tow.	99	2,793	6,408	do. -	Hundred of Salford (Bolton Division).
*Bretherton - -	tow.	707	2,437	5,020	Preston -	Hundred of Leyland.
Brindle - -	par.	1,173	3,104	8,744	Chorley -	do.
Charnock Heath -	tow.	916	1,598	7,334	do. -	do.
Charnock Richard -	tow.	685	1,946	6,001	do. -	do.
Chorley (W.) -	par.	19,178	3,614	61,259	do. -	do.
Clayton-le-Woods -	tow.	582	1,431	3,296	do. -	do. (Leyland Division).
Coppul - -	tow.	1,826	2,280	12,531	do. -	do.
Croston - -	tow.	1,791	2,361	9,673	Preston -	do.
Cuerden - -	tow.	573	808	3,827	do. -	do. (Leyland Division). (*continued*)

CHIPPING SODBURY UNION :

(*a*) By Order which came into operation on 25 March 1885, —

Four detached parts of Alderley were amalgamated with Hawkesbury, and a detached part of Hawkesbury was amalgamated with Alderley :

A detached part of Frampton Cotterell was amalgamated with Westerleigh ; and

CHIPPING SODBURY UNION—*continued.*

A detached part of Pucklechurch was amalgamated with Abson with Wick, and a detached part of Westerleigh was amalgamated with Pucklechurch.

(*b*) A detached part of Winterbourne, in the Barton Regis Union, was amalgamated with Westerleigh, by Order which came into operation on 25 March 1885.

Unions and Parishes, &c.	Population in 1881.	Area in Statute Acres in 1881.	Rateable Value in 1881.	Post Town.	Petty Sessional Division.

CHORLEY UNION—County of Lancaster—*continued.*

Unions and Parishes, &c.	Population in 1881.	Area in Statute Acres in 1881.	Rateable Value in 1881. £	Post Town.	Petty Sessional Division.
Duxbury - - tow.	323	1,012	2,661	Chorley - -	Hundred of Leyland.
Eccleston - - tow.	900	2,090	4,879	do. - -	do.
Euxton - - tow.	1,147	2,934	10,311	do. - -	do.
Heapey - - tow.	369	1,464	4,547	do. - -	do.
Heskin - - tow.	382	1,212	2,618	do. - -	do.
Hoghton - - tow.	871	2,224	6,985	Preston - -	do.
Leyland - - tow.	4,961	3,726	24,475	do. - -	Hundred of Leyland (Leyland Division).
Mawdesley - - tow.	928	2,950	6,357	Ormskirk -	Hundred of Leyland.
Rivington - - tow.	330	2,768	11,819	Chorley - -	Hundred of Salford (Bolton Division).
Ulnes Walton - - tow.	386	2,106	5,563	Preston -	Hundred of Leyland.
Welsh Whittle - tow.	115	596	1,422	Chorley -	do.
Wheelton - tow.	1,570	1,696	5,850	do. -	do.
Whittle-le-Woods - tow.	1,937	1,355	6,069	do. - -	do.
Withnel - - tow.	2,106	3,628	10,949	do. - -	do.
TOTAL of UNION -	47,730	54,456	243,408		

CHORLTON UNION.

(Formed 3 Feb. 1837 by Order dated 14 Jan. 1837. — Place marked thus * added 30 March 1837 by Order dated 7 March 1837, and thus † added 9 Oct. 1837 by Order dated 13 Sept. 1837. Spelling of name of place marked thus § altered by Order dated 16 June 1886.)

COUNTY of LANCASTER:

Unions and Parishes, &c.	Population in 1881.	Area in Statute Acres in 1881.	Rateable Value in 1881.	Post Town.	Petty Sessional Division.
Ardwick - - tow.	31,197	509	121,157	Manchester -	City of Manchester.
Burnage - - tow.	818	666	5,910	do. - -	Hundred of Salford.
*Chorlton-cum-Hardy tow.	2,332	1,280	16,110	do. -	do.
Chorlton upon Medlock - - } tow.	55,598	646	278,013	do. - -	City of Manchester.
Didsbury - - tow.	4,601	1,553	34,533	do. - -	Hundred of Salford.
Gorton - - tow.	33,096	1,484	99,713	do. - -	do.
Hulme - - tow.	72,147	477	250,797	do. - -	City of Manchester.
Levenshulme - - tow.	3,557	606	18,891	do. - -	Hundred of Salford.
Mosside - - tow.	18,184	421	89,518	do. - -	do.
†Openshaw - - tow.	16,153	579	67,217	do. -	do.
§Rusholme - - tow.	9,227	971	61,438	do. - -	do.
Withington (W.) - tow.	11,286	2,502	92,690	do. - -	do.
TOTAL of UNION -	258,226	11,697	1,136,287		

CHRISTCHURCH UNION.

(Formed 28 July 1835 by Order dated 13 July 1835.)

COUNTY of SOUTHAMPTON:

Unions and Parishes, &c.	Population in 1881.	Area in Statute Acres in 1881.	Rateable Value in 1881.	Post Town.	Petty Sessional Division.
Christchurch (W.) - par.	12,989	21,264	67,715	Christchurch (a) -	Ringwood.
Holdenhurst - par.	15,646	5,935	106,614	Bournemouth (b) -	do.
Sopley - - par.	820	4,779	5,490	Ringwood -	do.
TOTAL of UNION -	29,455	31,978	179,819		

CHRISTCHURCH UNION:

(a) But, as to parts, Bournemouth or Ringwood.
(b) But, as to part, Christchurch.

Unions and Parishes, &c.	Population in 1881.	Area in Statute Acres in 1881.	Rateable Value in 1881.	Post Town.	Petty Sessional Division.

CHURCH STRETTON UNION.

(Formed 20 July 1836 by Order dated 25 June 1836.)

COUNTY of SALOP:

			£		Hundred of Munslow :
Acton Scott - - *par.*	221	1,889	2,139	Church Stretton -	Upper Division.
Cardington - - *par.*	576	6,713	6,147	do. -	do.
Church Stretton (W.) *par.*	1,683	10,716	12,239	do. - -	do.
					Hundred of Munslow :
Easthope - - *par.*	111	814	874	Much Wenlock -	Lower Division.
Eaton under Hay-⎱ *par.* wood (*a*) - ⎰	449	6,201	5,979	Church Stretton - {	Hundred of Munslow : Upper Division.
Hope Bowdler - *par.*	163	1,731	1,573	do. -	do.
Leebotwood - - *par.*	178	1,267	2,738	Shrewsbury -	Hundred of Condover.
Longnor - - *par.*	199	1,200	1,390	Leebotwood Shrews-bury.	do.
					Hundred of Munslow :
Rushbury (*a*) - *par.*	500	4,132	4,872	Church Stretton -	Upper Division.
Shipton (*b*) - - *par.*	185	2,032	2,502	Much Wenlock -	do.
Sibdon Carwood - *par.*	67	1,090	898	Craven Arms, Salop	Purslow.
Smethcott - - *par.*	283	2,705	2,571	Leebotwood Shrews-bury.	Hundred of Condover.
Wistanstow - - *par.*	960	5,160	9,543	Craven Arms, Salop	Purslow ; and Hundred of Munslow : Upper Division.
Woolstaston - - *par.*	97	843	948	Leebotwood Shrews-bury.	Hundred of Condover.
TOTAL of UNION - -	5,672	16,493	54,425		

CIRENCESTER UNION.

Formed 21 Jan. 1836 by Order dated 6 Jan. 1836.)

COUNTY of GLOUCESTER :

Ampney Crucis - *par.*	511	2,660	4,255	Cirencester -	Cirencester.
Ampney Saint Mary *par.*	129	1,170	1,397	do. -	do.
Ampney Saint Peter *par.*	173	533	1,055	do. -	do.
Badgington - - *par.*	181	1,106	1,442	do. -	do.
Barnsley - - *par.*	276	2,090	2,390	do. -	do.
Baunton - - *par.*	135	1,340	1,607	do. -	do.
Brimpsfield - - *par.*	369	2,611	2,810	Gloucester	do.
Cirencester (W.) - *par.*	7,737	4,749	27,665	Cirencester	do.
Coates - - *par.*	464	2,514	3,522	do. -	do.
Colesborne - - *par.*	286	2,200	1,788	Cheltenham	do.
Daglinworth - - *par.*	333	1,884	2,257	Cirencester	do.
Down Ampney - *par.*	345	2,541	3,361	Cricklade	do.
Driffield - - *par.*	119	1,310	1,541	Cirencester -	do.
Dunsborne Abbots - *par.*	289	3,290	2,024	do. -	do.
Dunsborne Lyre - *ty.*	129	1,730	1,975	do. -	do.
Edgeworth - - *par.*	130	1,566	1,465	do. -	do.
Elkstone - - *par.*	237	2,058	2,002	Cheltenham	do.
Fairford - - *par.*	1,525	4,012	7,244	Fairford -	Fairford.
Harnhill - - *par.*	71	689	1,181	Cirencester	do.
Hatherop - - *par.*	317	2,124	2,573	Fairford -	do.
Kempsford and Wel-⎱ *par.* ford ⎰	828	4,063	6,505	do. -	do.
Maisey Hampton - *par.*	332	1,020	2,379	do. -	do.

(*continued*)

CHURCH STRETTON UNION :

(*a*) A detached part of Eaton under Haywood, known as Longville in the Dale, was amalgamated with Rushbury, by Order which came into operation on 25 March 1883.

(*b*) A detached part of Shipton, known as "Skimblescott," was amalgamated with Monkhopton, in the Bridgnorth Union, by Order which came into operation on 25 March 1883.

M 4

Unions and Parishes, &c.	Population in 1881.	Area in Statute Acres in 1881.	Rateable Value in 1881.	Post Town.	Petty Sessional Division.
CIRENCESTER UNION—County of Gloucester—continued.			£		
North Cerney - - par.	617	4,158	5,009	Cirencester -	Cirencester.
Poulton - - par.	457	1,580	2,152	Fairford -	Fairford.
Preston - - par.	212	2,012	3,586	Cirencester -	Cirencester.
Quennington - - par.	380	1,630	2,407	Fairford -	Fairford.
Rendcomb - - par.	211	2,532	2,801	Cirencester -	Cirencester.
Rodmarton - - par.	382	4,010	3,040	do. -	do.
Sapperton - - par.	529	3,908	6,043	do. -	do.
Siddington - - par.	481	2,137	3,614	do. -	do.
Syde - - par.	42	614	600	do. -	do.
South Cerney - - par.	913	3,062	6,093	do. -	do.
Stratton - - par.	694	1,462	3,409	do. -	do.
Winston - - par.	231	1,437	1,589	do. -	do.
COUNTY of WILTS :					
Kemble - - par.	473	3,322	4,561	Cirencester -	Malmesbury.
Poole Keynes - par.	138	1,216	1,638	do. -	do.
Shorncote - - par.	37	526	676	Cricklade -	Cricklade.
Somerford Keynes - par.	322	1,573	2,395	do. -	do.
TOTAL of UNION - -	21,125	84,269	132,001		

CITY OF LONDON UNION (a).

(Formed 30 March 1837.—Places marked thus * added 30 Sept. 1869 by Order dated 10 Sept. 1869.)

CITY of LONDON and LIBERTIES thereof, and COUNTY of MIDDLESEX :					London City ; Guildhall :
Allhallows, Bread Street - - } par.	50	2·4	28,633	London, E.C. -	Mansion House.
Allhallows, Honey Lane - } par.	32	1·0	8,563	do. - -	do.
Allhallows, Lombard Street - - } par.	169	2·8	35,107	do. - -	do.
Allhallows, London Wall - } par.	535	8·5	43,512	do. - -	do.
Allhallows, Barking par.	716	9·8	51,881	do. - -	do.
Allhallows Staining - par.	175	4·2	44,692	do. - -	do.
Allhallows the Great par.	29	7·1	26,600	do. - -	do.
Allhallows the Less - par.	63	3·1	12,105	do. - -	do.
*Barnards Inn - par.	53	·6	1,023	do. - -	do.
*Bridewell Precinct - pre.	515	5·4	13,758	do. - -	do.
Christchurch, Newgate Street - } par.	1,359	12·2	51,415	do. - -	do.
*City Liberty of Saint Andrew, Holborn - } par.	2,917	19·6	57,268	do. -	do.
Saint Alban, Woodstreet - } par.	176	4·2	31,362	do. - -	do.
Saint Alpage, Sion College - } par.	31	4·2	29,958	do. - -	do.
Saint Andrew by the Wardrobe - } par.	175	7·2	20,723	do. - -	do.
Saint Andrew Hubbard par.	89	2·7	18,623	do. - -	do.

(continued)

CITY OF LONDON UNION :

(a) The Workhouse of the City of London Union is situate partly in the parish of Bromley Saint Leonard (Poplar Union) and partly in the hamlet of Mile End Old Town.

CITY OF LONDON UNION—continued.

(b) The Inner Temple and the Middle Temple are not included in the City of London Union, but by Orders of the Local Government Board, issued under the authority of Section 59 of the Valuation (Metropolis) Act, 1869, the Assessment Committee of that Union are required for the purposes of such Act, to act as the Assessment Committee for those places.

Unions and Parishes, &c.	Population in 1881.	Area in Statute Acres in 1881.	Rateable Value in 1881.	Post Town.	Petty Sessional Division.
CITY OF LONDON UNION—County of Middlesex—*continued.*			£		London, City ; Guildhall :
Saint Andrew Undershaft - *par.*	327	9·9	78,466	London, E.C.	Mansion House.
Saint Anne and Agnes, within, Aldersgate *par.*	158	3·0	8,461	do.	do.
Saint Anne, Blackfriars *par.*	943	12·5	30,622	do.	do.
Saint Antholin - *par.*	31	2·2	22,049	do.	do.
Saint Augustine - *par.*	151	1·6	13,604	do.	do.
Saint Bartholomew by the Royal Exchange *par.*	199	3·8	84,410	do.	do.
*Saint Bartholomew-the-Great - *par.*	2,373	9·3	22,819	do.	do.
*Saint Bartholomew-the-Less - *par.*	819	4·1	1,143	do.	do
Saint Bennet, Fink - *par.*	126	2·8	45,934	do.	do.
Saint Bennet, Gracechurch *par.*	51	2·0	21,451	do.	do.
Saint Bennet, Paul's Wharf - *par.*	73	6·0	27,997	do.	do.
Saint Bennet, Sherehog *par.*	24	1·1	16,641	do.	do.
Saint Botolph, Billingsgate - *par.*	99	2·3	13,804	do.	do.
*Saint Botolph without Aldersgate *par.*	2,399	20	78,381	do.	do.
*Saint Botolph without Aldgate - *par.*	6,269	39	79,730	do.	do.
*Saint Botolph without Bishopsgate *par.*	4,905	44	117,703	do.	do.
*Saint Bridget otherwise Saint Bride, Fleet Street *par.*	3,001	30·2	87,819	do.	do.
Saint Christopher-le-Stock - *par.*	38	2·8	21,240	do.	do.
Saint Clement, Eastcheap - *par.*	86	1·5	19,492	do.	do.
Saint Dionis Backchurch - *par.*	211	3·0	41,147	do.	do.
Saint Dunstan in the East - *par.*	412	11·8	91,623	do.	do.
*Saint Dunstan in the West - *par.*	1,584	12·8	50,077	do.	do.
Saint Edmund the King *par.*	106	2·8	46,811	do.	do.
Saint Ethelburga - *par.*	199	3·2	25,893	do.	do.
Saint Faith the Virgin, under Saint Paul's *par.*	403	5·5	37,735	do.	do.
Saint Gabriel, Fenchurch Street *par.*	111	2·7	30,809	do.	do.
Saint George, Botolph Lane *par.*	96	1·0	4,975	do.	do.
*Saint Giles without Cripplegate *par.*	3,863	41	124,277	do.	do.
Saint Gregory by Saint Paul's *par.*	730	12·0	57,218	do.	do.
Saint Helen, Bishopsgate - *par.*	289	8·4	48,515	do.	do.
Saint James, Duke's-place *par.*	622	3·3	5,562	do.	do.
Saint James, Garlick Hythe - *par.*	222	3·2	12,636	do.	do.
Saint John Baptist, Wallbrook - *par.*	57	2·0	14,952	do.	do.
Saint John Evangelist *par.*	5	·8	8,467	do.	do.
Saint John Zachary - *par.*	115	2·5	13,416	do.	do.
Saint Katherine, Coleman Street *par.*	277	6·7	31,279	do.	do.
Saint Katherine Cree Church, otherwise Christ Church *par.*	858	7·7	49,355	do.	do.
Saint Lawrence Jewry *par.*	162	5·3	48,653	do.	do.

(continued)

Unions and Parishes, &c.	Population in 1881.	Area in Statute Acres in 1881.	Rateable Value in 1881.	Post Town.	Petty Sessional Division.
City of London Union—County of Middlesex—*continued.*			£		London, City; Guildhall:
Saint Lawrence Pounteny - } *par.*	94	2·8	16,398	London, E.C. -	Mansion House.
Saint Leonard, Eastcheap - } *par.*	50	1·5	9,714	do.	do.
Saint Leonard, Foster-lane } *par.*	27	2·5	8,145	do. - -	do.
Saint Magnus - *par.*	169	3·5	11,938	do. - -	do.
Saint Margaret, Lothbury - } *par.*	124	4·0	48,396	do. -	do.
Saint Margaret Moses *par.*	55	1·2	15,188	do. - -	do.
Saint Margaret, New Fish Street } *par.*	106	2·0	10,581	do. - -	do.
Saint Margaret Pattens *par.*	67	1·5	12,906	do. -	do.
Saint Martin's, Ludgate *par.*	247	1·5	29,148	do. - -	do.
Saint Martin's Orgars *par.*	152	2·0	18,176	do. - -	do.
Saint Martin Outwich *par.*	132	3·9	40,334	do. -	do.
Saint Martin Pomroy, Ironmonger Lane - } *par.*	137	3·9	8,538	do. - -	do.
Saint Martin's Vintry *par.*	107	4·2	19,927	do. -	do.
Saint Mary Abchurch *par.*	142	2·3	23,271	do. - -	do.
Saint Mary Aldermanbury - } *par.*	168	4·6	33,629	do. - -	do.
Saint Mary Aldermary *par.*	121	2·2	19,360	do. -	do.
Saint Mary-at-Hill - *par.*	206	5·0	35,436	do. -	do.
Saint Mary Bothaw, Dowgate - } *par.*	101	1·6	11,877	do.	do.
Saint Mary Colechurch *par.*	36	1·4	13,280	do. -	do.
Saint Mary-le-Bow - *par.*	130	3·2	25,237	do. - -	do.
Saint Mary Magdalen, Milk-street - } *par.*	54	1·5	17,930	do. - -	do.
Saint Mary Magdalen, Old Fish Street - } *par.*	224	2·2	18,966	do. - -	do.
Saint Mary Mounthaw *par.*	3	1·0	7,307	do. - -	do.
Saint Mary Somerset *par.*	74	3·7	12,928	do. -	do.
Saint Mary Staining *par.*	33	1·2	9,675	do. - -	do.
Saint Mary Woolchurch Haw - } *par.*	29	2·3	22,604	do. - -	do.,
Saint Mary Woolnorth *par.*	290	2·5	39,804	do. -	do.
Saint Matthew, Friday Street - } *par.*	81	1·3	18,647	do. - -	do.
Saint Michael Bassishaw - } *par.*	215	5·2	20,566	do. - -	do.
Saint Michael, Cornhill *par.*	227	3·5	76,868	do. - -	do.
Saint Michael, Crooked Lane } *par.*	127	3·4	21,235	do. - -	do
Saint Michael-le-Quern *par.*	70	1·3	16,044	do. -	do.
Saint Michael, Paternoster Royal - } *par.*	101	2·3	10,671	do. -	do.
Saint Michael, Queen Hythe - } *par.*	189	3·5	18,829	do. - -	do.
Saint Michael, Wood Street - } *par.*	139	2·0	22,054	do. -	do.
Saint Mildred, Bread Street - } *par.*	24	1·4	11,892	do. -	do.
Saint Mildred the Virgin, Poultry - } *par.*	36	2·2	36,285	do. -	do.
Saint Nicholas Acons *par.*	116	1·6	23,744	do. -	do.
Saint Nicholas Cole Abbey - } *par.*	53	1·5	10,465	do. -	do.
Saint Nicholas Olave *par.*	94	1·3	3,621	do. -	do.
Saint Olave, Hart Street - } *par.*	255	10·3	58,970	do. -	do.
Saint Olave, Old Jewry *par.*	91 { In St. Martin Poinroy }		20,082	do. - -	do.
Saint Olave, Silver Street - } *par.*	82	3·1	23,769	do. -	do
Saint Pancras, Soper Lane - } *par.*	55	1·3	16,721	do. -	do.
Saint Peter, Cornhill *par.*	196	5·3	63,810	do. - -	do.

(continued)

Unions and Parishes, &c.		Population in 1881.	Area in Statute Acres in 1881.	Rateable Value in 1881.	Post Town.	Petty Sessional Division.
CITY OF LONDON UNION—County of Middlesex—*continued*.				£		London, City ; Guildhall :
Saint Peter-le-Poor, in Broad Street	*par.*	401	9·6	103,091	London, E.C. -	Mansion House.
Saint Peter, near Paul's Wharf	*par.*	19	2·8	12,899	do. - -	do.
Saint Peter, West Cheap	*par.*	22	1·6	23,530	do. - -	do.
*Saint Sepulchre, Newgate Street	*par.*	2,166	35·0	95,953	do. - -	do.
Saint Stephen, Coleman Street -	*par.*	1,799	26·7	116,068	d.. - -	do.
Saint Stephen, Wallbrook	*par.*	103	3·1	30,281	do. - -	do.
Saint Swithin, London Stone	*par.*	112	3·5	27,531	do. - -	do.
Saint Thomas the Apostle	*par.*	76	2·4	16,852	do. - -	do.
Saint Vedast alias Foster	*par.*	184	2·7	24,325	do. - -	do.
*Serjeants Inn, Fleet Street	*par.*	49	·6	1,930	do. - -	do.
*Thavies Inn -	*par.*	121	·5	2,380	do. - -	do.
Trinity the Less or Trinity the Holy -	*par.*	63	2·0	8,277	do. - -	do.
Whitefriars Precinct	*pre.*	467	7·8	13,345	do. - -	do.
TOTAL of UNION -		50,352	619·8			
Inner Temple (*b*) - -		156	13·4	22,321	do. -	London, City, Guildhall.
Middle Temple (*b*) - -				12,205	do. - -	Westminster.
				3,542,106		

CLEOBURY MORTIMER UNION.

(Formed 15 July 1836 by Order dated 20 June 1836.—Place marked thus * added 22 Mar. 1862 by Order dated 15 Mar. 1862.)

COUNTY OF SALOP :

		Population in 1881.	Area in Statute Acres in 1881.	Rateable Value in 1881.	Post Town.	Petty Sessional Division.
Aston Botterel -	*par.*	165	2,238	2,216	Bridgnorth -	Cleobury Mortimer.
Cleobury Mortimer (W.) - -	*par.*	1,581	7,127	9,144	Bewdley - -	do.
Coreley - -	*par.*	625	2,175	2,800	Tenbury -	Burford.
Farlow - -	*tow.*	346	2,135	1,733	Bewdley - -	Cleobury Mortimer.
Higley - -	*par.*	363	1,527	2,484	Bridgnorth -	Chelmarsh.
Hopton Wafers -	*par.*	133	1,560	2,035	Bewdley - -	Cleobury Mortimer.
Kinlet (*b*) - -	*par.*	432	6,692	6,173	do. - -	do.
Loughton - -	*cha.*	84	1,015	710	Bridgnorth - -	do.
Milsom - -	*par.*	121	1,025	1,122	Bewdley - -	do.
Neen Savage -	*par.*	331	3,779	4,664	do. - -	do.
Neen Solars - -	*par.*	199	1,779	2,101	do. - -	do.
Silvington - -	*par.*	48	493	413	do. - -	do.
Stottesden (*b*) -	*par.*	1,145	9,308	10,238	do. - -	do.
Wheathill - -	*par.*	107	1,115	1,377	Bridgnorth -	do.
*Woodhouse - -	*par.*	4 { In Cleobury Mortimer }		105	Bewdley - -	do.

(*continued*)

CITY OF LONDON UNION :

(*b*) See notes, page 98.

CLEOBURY MORTIMER UNION :

(*a*) A detached part of Bewdley, in the Kidderminster Union, was amalgamated with Rock, by Order which came into operation on 25 March 1882.

(*b*) A detached part of Stottesden, known as Kingswood Button Oak, was amalgamated with Kinlet, by Order which came into operation on 25 March 1883.

(*c*) A detached part of Abberley, in the Martley Union, was amalgamated with Rock, by Provisional Order which came into operation on 25 March 1885.

Unions and Parishes, &c.	Population in 1881.	Area in Statute Acres in 1881.	Rateable Value in 1881.	Post Town.	Petty Sessional Division.
CLEOBURY MORTIMER UNION—*continued.*					
COUNTY of WORCESTER :			£		
Bayton - - *par.*	418	2,360	3,064	Bewdley - -	Hundred House.
Mamble - - *par.*	231	2,258	2,174	do. - -	do.
Rock (*a*) (*c*) - - *par.*	1,514(*a*)	7,525	9,108	do. - -	do.
TOTAL of UNION -	8,138	54,411	61,694		
CLITHEROE UNION.					
(Formed 14 Jan. 1837 by Order dated 20 Dec. 1836, as amended by an Order dated 23 Feb. 1837.—Place marked thus * added 29 Sept. 1858 by an Order dated 18 Aug. 1858.)					
COUNTY of LANCASTER :					
Aighton - - ⎫				Whalley, Blackburn	⎧ Clitheroe.
Bailey and ⎬ *tow.*	1,663	6,300	8,133 ⎰	(*a*) - -	do.
Chaigeley ⎭				Clitheroe (*b*) - -	⎩ do.
Chatburn - *tow.*	771	894	3,337	Clitheroe - -	do.
Chipping - *tow.*	987	5,634	7,326	Preston - -	Clitheroe.
Clitheroe (W.) - *tow.*	10,176	2,375	32,286	Clitheroe - -	Borough of Clitheroe.
*Clitheroe Castle - *par.*	16	6	101	do. - -	do.
Downham - *tow.*	272	2,300	2,400	do. - -	Clitheroe.
Leagram - *tow.*	100	⎫ 4,664	1,994	Preston - -	do.
Little Bowland - *tow.*	106	⎭	3,168	do. - -	do.
Little Mitton - *tow.*	73	873	1,369	Whalley, Blackburn	do.
Mearley - *tow.*	30	1,509	1,205	Clitheroe - -	do.
Pendleton - *tow.*	1,312	2,826	5,384	do. - -	do.
Thorneley with ⎫ *tow.*	349	3,221	3,712	Preston - -	do.
Wheatley - ⎭					
Twiston ; - *tow.*	128	865	967	Clitheroe - -	do.
Whalley - *tow.*	895	1,603	5,506	Blackburn - -	do.
Wiswell - *tow.*	737	1,693	3,733	Whalley, Blackburn	do.
Worston - *tow.*	62	1,088	1,190	Clitheroe - -	do.
COUNTY of YORK, WEST RIDING :					
Bashall Eaves - *tow.*	263	3,806	3,638	Clitheroe - -	Bolton by Bowland.
Bolton by Bowland - *par.*	702	5,942	7,172	do. - -	do.
Bowland Forest High *tow.*	231	19,750	4,901	do. - -	do.
Bowland Forest Low *tow.*	304	5,497	4,553	do. - -	do.
Easington - *tow.*	299	9,199	5,096	do. - -	do.
Gisburn - *tow.*	527	1,997	4,135	do. - -	do.
Gisburn Forest - *tow.*	254	4,859	2,872	Gisburn, Clitheroe	do.
Mitton - *tow.*	171	1,720	2,191	Whalley, Blackburn	do.
Grindleton - *tow.*	623	3,777	5,107	Clitheroe - -	do.
Horton - *tow.*	94	2,019	2,691	Gisburn, Clitheroe	do.
Midhope - *tow.*	64	1,161	1,238	Clitheroe - -	do.
Newsholme - *tow.*	48	751	1,264	Gisburn, Clitheroe	do.
Newton - *tow.*	331	5,869	5,246	Clitheroe - -	do.
Paythorne - *tow.*	100	2,634	2,241	Gisburn, Clitheroe	do.
Rimmington - *tow.*	381	3,080	4,105	Clitheroe - -	do.
Sawley - *tow.*	178	2,104	2,815	do. - -	do.
Slaidburn - *tow.*	497	5,482	4,625	do. - -	do.
Waddington - *tow.*	447	2,073	2,966	do. - -	do.
West Bradford - *tow.*	311	1,955	2,487	do. - -	do.
TOTAL of UNION -	23,502	119,226	151,150		

CLEOBURY MORTIMER UNION—*continued.*
   (*a*) (*c*) See notes, page 101.

CLITHEROE UNION :
   (*a*) As to Aighton and Bailey
   (*b*) As to Chaigeley.

Unions and Parishes, &c.	Population in 1881.	Area in Statute Acres in 1881.	Rateable Value in 1881.	Post Town.	Petty Sessional Division.

CLUN UNION.

(Formed 18 July 1836 by Order dated 23 June 1836, as amended by Order dated 9 July 1836.)

COUNTY of MONTGOMERY :

			£		
Hyssington (c) - par.	315	2,382	2,161	Church Stoke -	Montgomery.
Snead (c) - - par.	43	644	807	do. - -	do.

COUNTY of SALOP :

Bishops Castle (W.) (f) par.	1,983	5,649	12,024	Bishops Castle	Clun and Purslow.
Clun - - par.	2,247	19,782	20,314	Aston on Clun	do.
Clunbury - - par.	986	5,404	9,712	do. -	do.
Clungunford (b) - par.	581	3,620	6,823	do. -	do.
Edgton (e) - par.	223	1,832	2,128	do. -	do.
Hopesay - - par.	631	4,060	6,167	do. - -	do.
Hopton Castle (b) - par.	117	2,552	2,563	do. -	do.
Lydbury North (d) - par.	976	7,830	10,266	Shrewsbury	do.
Lydham (c) - - par.	116	1,943	2,911	Bishops Castle	do.
Mainstone - - par.	187	4,931	2,939	do. -	do.
Mindtown (a) - par.	38	908	688	do. -	do.
More - - par.	200	3,533	3,241	do. -	do.
Norbury (a) - - par.	374	4,581	3,895	do. -	do.
Rutlinghope - par.	270	5,559	3,213	Shrewsbury	do.
Shelve (c) - par.	153	1,285	3,068	Minsterley -	Chirbury.
Wentnor - - par.	727	6,698	4,366	Bishops Castle	Clun and Purslow.
TOTAL of UNION -	10,167	83,196	97,286		

CLUTTON UNION.

(Formed 2 Feb. 1836 by Order dated 13 Jan. 1836.)

COUNTY of SOMERSET :

Camely - par.	522	1,633	3,203	Bristol -	Temple Cloud.
Camerton (i) - par.	1,361	1,748	5,983	Bath -	Weston.
Chelwood - par.	145	1,077	1,918	Bristol -	Temple Cloud.
Chew Magna (b) - par.	1,643	5,006	12,563	do. - -	do.
Chew Stoke - par.	696	2,092	5,814	do. -	do.
Chilcompton - par.	642	1,233	3,322	Bath -	Kilmersdon.

(continued)

CLUN UNION :

(a) A detached part of Norbury was amalgamated with Mindtown, by Order which came into operation on 25 March 1883.

(b) A detached part of Hopton Castle known as "Part of Lingen Meadow" was amalgamated with Clungunford, by Provisional Order which came into operation on 25 March 1884.

(c) All the part of Hyssington which was situate in the county of Salop was amalgamated with Shelve, and all the part of Snead which was situate in that county was amalgamated with Lydham, by Order which came into operation on 25 March 1884.

(d) The parishes known as Hill End, Old Church Moor, and Dinmore, were amalgamated with Lydbury North, by Order which came into operation on 25 March 1884.

(e) A parish which was known as Horderley Hall was amalgamated with Edgton, by Order which came into operation on 25 March 1884.

(f) All the parts of the area which was known as the parish of Bishops Castle were amalgamated with the area which was known as the borough of that name, and the borough was so altered that the parish of Bishops Castle, by Order which came into operation on 25 March 1885.

CLUTTON UNION :

(a) A detached part of Winford, in the Bedminster Union, was amalgamated with Nempnett, by Order which came into operation on 25 March 1884.

CLUTTON UNION—continued.

(b) Detached parts of Chew Magna were amalgamated with Stowey, and detached parts of Stowey were amalgamated with Chew Magna, by Order which came into operation on 25 March 1884.

(c) Part of Paulton and a detached part of Stone Easton were amalgamated with Mid-somer Norton, by Order which came into operation on 25 March 1884.

(d) Certain parts of Stone Easton were amalgamated with Chewton Mendip, in the Wells Union, and certain parts of Chewton Mendip were amalgamated with Stone Easton, by Orders which came into operation on 25 March 1884.

(e) A detached part of Norton Hawkfield was amalgamated with Dundry, in the Bedminster Union, by Order which came into operation on 25 March 1884.

(f) Detached parts of Paulton and Litton were amalgamated with Chewton Mendip, in the Wells Union, by Order which came into operation on 25 March 1884.

(g) All the parts of a parish which was known as Saint Thomas in Pensford were amalgamated with Stanton Drew, by Order which came into operation on 25 March 1884.

(h) Certain detached parts of Chewton Mendip, in the Wells Union, were amalgamated with Compton Martin, by Order which came into operation on 25 March 1884.

(i) Certain parts of Camerton were amalgamated with Dunkerton, in the Bath Union, and certain parts of Dunkerton were amalgamated with Camerton, by Provisional Order which came into operation on 25 March 1886.

Unions and Parishes, &c.	Population in 1881.	Area in Statute Acres in 1881.	Rateable Value in 1881.	Post Town.	Petty Sessional Division.

CLUTTON UNION—County of Somerset—continued.

Unions and Parishes, &c.	Population in 1881.	Area in Statute Acres in 1881.	Rateable Value in 1881. £	Post Town.	Petty Sessional Division.
Clutton (W.) - par.	1,019	1,636	4,137	Bristol - -	Temple Cloud.
Compton Martin (h) - par.	415	2,314	1,060	do. - -	do.
East Harptree - par.	655	2,770	4,846	do. - -	do.
Farmborough - par.	845	1,494	3,597	Bath - -	do.
Farrington Gurney - par.	535	923	2,893	Bristol - -	do.
High Littleton with Hallatrow - } par.	775	1,273	3,727	do. - -	do.
Hinton Blewett - par.	218	1,102	3,232	Temple Cloud	do.
Litton (f) - par.	217	1,171	3,475	Bath - -	do.
Midsomer Norton (c) par.	4,422	3,922	15,551	do. - -	Kilmersdon.
Nempnett (a) - par.	216	1,772	2,751	Bristol - -	Temple Cloud.
Norton Hawkfield (e) ville.	37	620	1,063	do. - -	do.
Norton Malreward - par.	142	1,067	2,127	do. - -	Keynsham.
Paulton (c) (f) - par.	2,122	1,056	5,029	do. - -	Temple Cloud.
Publow - par.	536	1,335	2,494	do. - -	Keynsham.
Radstock - par.	3,074	1,005	9,292	Bath - -	Kilmersdon
Stanton Drew (g) - par.	721	2,075	6,044	Bristol - -	Keynsham.
Stone Easton (c) (d) par.	357	1,374	3,309	Bath - -	Temple Cloud.
Stowey (h) - par.	127	814	1,797	Bristol - -	do.
Tim-bury - par.	1,425	1,148	5,737	Bath - -	do.
Ubley - par.	285	1,811	2,709	Bristol - -	do.
West Harptree - par.	399	2,850	4,314	do. - -	do.
Whitcomb - ty.	64	705	909	do. - -	do.
TOTAL of UNION -	23,615	47,026	125,896		

COCKERMOUTH UNION.

(Formed 1 Dec. 1838 by Order dated 5 Nov. 1838.— Places marked thus * added 25 Dec. 1858 by Order dated 20 Sept. 1858, and thus † added 25 Mar. 1862 by Order dated 24 Mar. March 1862. Names of places marked thus § as altered by Order dated 12 April 1887.)

COUNTY OF CUMBERLAND:

Unions and Parishes, &c.	Population in 1881.	Area in Statute Acres in 1881.	Rateable Value in 1881.	Post Town.	Petty Sessional Division.
§Above Derwent - tow.	924	14,750	9,107	Keswick	Keswick.
Bassenthwaite - par.	509	6,915	5,614	do. - -	do.
Bewaldeth and Snit-tlegarth } tow.	90	1,607	1,091	Cockermouth -	Derwent.
Blindbothel - tow.	81	1,261	1,262	do. - -	do.
Blinderake and Red-main } tow.	325	4,251	4,400	do. - -	do.
Borrowdale - tow.	449	16,666	3,169	Keswick -	Keswick.
§Bothel and Threap-land } tow.	392	3,389	3,651	Aspatria -	Derwent.
Brackenthwaite (a) - tow.	118	4,395	1,269	Cockermouth	do.
Bridekirk (a) - tow.	87	873	1,436	do. - -	do.
*Briery Cottages - tow.	92	46	271	Keswick -	Keswick.
Brigham - tow.	790	1,759	7,500	Carlisle -	Derwent.
Broughton Great (a) - tow.	1,121	3,069	4,931	do. - -	do.
Broughton Little (a) - tow.	798	1,026	2,834	do. - -	do.
Buttermere (a) - tow.	127	7,021	1,393	Cockermouth	do.
Camerton - tow.	239	785	1,720	Workington -	Workington.
Clifton Great (a) - tow.	974	989	4,299	do. - -	do.
Clifton Little (a) - tow.	489	1,089	3,133	do. - -	do.
*Cloffocks - par.	10	108	671	do. - -	do.
Cockermouth (W) - tow.	5,353	2,425	17,113	Cockermouth	Derwent.
§Crosscanonby - par.	8,296	2,889	32,904	Carlisle -	do.
Dean - par.	825	6,528	9,062	Cockermouth	do.
Dearham - tow.	2,246	2,149	6,937	Maryport -	do.
Dovenby (a) - tow.	227	1,935	3,306	Cockermouth	do.
Eaglesfield - tow.	258	1,998	2,936	do. - -	do.
Ellenborough and Ewerigg } tow.	2,883	996	12,751	Maryport -	do.
Embleton (a) - tow.	347	3,949	5,328	Cockermouth	do.
Flimby - par.	2,123	1,651	12,989	Maryport -	do.
Gilcrux - par.	514	2,018	5,007	Cockermouth	do.
§Greysouthen - tow.	690	1,616	4,779	Carlisle -	do. *(continued)*

CLUTTON UNION:
(a) (b) (c) (d) (e) (f) (g) (h) See notes, page 103.

Unions and Parishes, &c.		Population in 1881.	Area in Statute Acres in 1881.	Rateable Value in 1881.	Post Town.	Petty Sessional Division.

COCKERMOUTH UNION—County of Cumberland—*continued.* £

Isell, Old Park	- *tow.*	67	1,844	1,215	Cockermouth -	Derwent.
Keswick	- *tow.*	3,201	728	12,450	Keswick -	Keswick.
Lorton (*a*)	- *tow.*	397	5,318	3,585	Cockermouth -	Derwent.
Loweswater	- *tow.*	315	9,415	3,635	do. -	do.
Mosser	- *tow.*	76	1,190	1,243	do. -	do.
§Oughterside and Allerby	- *tow.*	500	2,194	3,860	Maryport -	do
Papcastle	- *tow.*	700	1,240	5,269	Cockermouth -	do..
Plumbland	- *par.*	650	2,568	6,541	Aspatria -	do.
Ribton	- *tow.*	18	616	685	Workington -	Workington.
§Saint John's Castle-rigg and Wythburn	*tow.*	675	19,700	8,001	Keswick -	Keswick.
Seaton	- *tow.*	2,904	2,626	26,405	Workington -	Workington.
Setmurthy (*a*)	- *tow.*	173	2,783	2,609	Cockermouth -	Derwent.
†Skiddaw	- *par.*	10	2,969	135	Keswick -	Keswick.
Stainburn	- *tow.*	227	1,228	2,238	Workington -	Workington.
Sunderland	- *tow.*	63	806	713	Cockermouth -	Derwent.
Tallantire	- *tow.*	217	1,992	2,498	do. -	do.
Underskiddaw	- *tow.*	526	6,026	7,751	Keswick -	Keswick.
Whinfell	- *tow.*	115	1,747	1,484	Cockermouth -	Derwent.
Winscales	- *tow.*	103	974	945	Workington -	Workington.
Workington	- *tow.*	14,361	3,355	43,923	do. -	do.
Wythop	- *tow.*	114	3,353	2,390	Cockermouth -	Derwent.
TOTAL of UNION -		56,789	170,155	308,468		

COLCHESTER UNION.

(Formed 19 Oct. 1835 by Order dated 30 Sept. 1835.)

COUNTY of ESSEX :

All Saints	- *par.*	912	285	1,015	Colchester -	Colchester.
Bere-Church	- *par.*	113	1,377	1,691	do. -	do.
Greenstead	- *par.*	752	1,501	3,685	do. -	do.
Holy Trinity	- *par.*	1,369	102	5,313	do. -	do.
Lexden	- *par.*	2,310	2,334	9,770	do. -	do.
Saint Botolph (W.)	- *par.*	5,707	905	15,979	do. -	do.
Saint Giles	- *par.*	4,803	1,502	11,516	do. -	do.
Saint James	- *par.*	2,336	238	5,345	do. -	do.
Saint Leonard	- *par.*	1,858	82	5,445	do. -	do.
Saint Martin	- *par.*	1,051	16	1,680	do. -	do.
Saint Mary at the Walls	*par.*	2,047	487	11,770	do. -	do.
Saint Mary Magdalen	*par.*	532	65	1,010	do. -	do.
Saint Michael Mile-end	*par.*	1,051	2,352	5,530	do. -	do.
Saint Nicholas	- *par.*	924	14	4,064	do. -	de.
Saint Peter	- *par.*	2,298	51	7,796	do. -	do.
Saint Runwald	- *par.*	308	13	2,525	do. -	do.
TOTAL of UNION -		28,374	11,324	97,167		

CONGLETON UNION.

(Formed 13 Jan. 1837 by Order dated 20 Dec. 1836, as amended by Order dated 3 April 1837.— Place marked thus * added 8 March 1867 by Order dated 21 Feb. 1867.)

COUNTY of CHESTER :

Alsager	- *tow.*	1,601	2,211	11,093	Stoke-on-Trent -	Northwich.
Arclid (W.)	- *tow.*	325	552	1,521	Sandbach -	do.
Bechton	- *tow.*	823	2,665	8,146	do. -	do.
Blackden	- *tow.*	142	749	2,117	Holmes Chapel -	do.
Bradwell	- *tow.*	662	2,114	5,930	Sandbach -	do. (*continued*)

COCKERMOUTH UNION.

(*a*) By Orders which came into operation on 25 March 1887.—
A detached part of Brackenthwaite was amalgamated with Lorton ;
A detached part of Broughton Little was amalgamated with Broughton Great ;
A detached part of Buttermere was amalgamated with Lorton ;
A detached part of Clifton Little was amalgamated with Clifton Great ;
A detached part of Dovenby was amalgamated with Bridekirk ; and
Detached parts of Setmurthy were amalgamated with Embleton.

Unions and Parishes, &c.		Population in 1881.	Area in Statute Acres in 1881.	Rateable Value in 1881.	Post Town.	Petty Sessional Division.
CONGLETON UNION—County of Chester—*continued.*				£		
Brereton cum Smeth-wick	} par.	613	4,599	9,102	Sandbach -	Northwich.
Buglawton -	tow.	1,550	2,911	9,221	Congleton -	do.
Church Hulme	tow.	658	905	4,035	Holmes Chapel -	do.
Church Lawton	par.	823	1,501	8,507	Scholar Green -	do.
Congleton -	tow.	11,116	2,572	31,963	Congleton -	Borough of Congleton.
Cotton	tow.	43	375	838	Holmes Chapel -	Northwich.
Cranage	tow.	442	1,969	3,887	do. -	do.
Davenport -	tow.	82	770	1,340	Congleton -	do.
Elton	tow.	549	1,084	4,756	Sandbach -	do.
*Goostrey-cum-Barn-shaw	} tow.	365	1,795	3,552	Holmes Chapel -	do.
Hassall	tow.	309	1,015	2,929	Sandbach -	do.
Hulme Walfield	tow.	113	1,058	2,222	Congleton -	do.
Kermincham	tow.	183	1,233	2,157	do. -	do.
Leese	tow.	107	548	1,094	Middlewich -	do.
Moreton cum Alcumlow	} tow.	117	1,095	2,459	Congleton -	do.
Moston	tow.	180	714	1,803	Sandbach -	do.
Newbold Astbury -	tow.	768	2,907	5,907	Congleton -	do.
Odd Rode	tow.	3,194	2,750	13,186	Scholar Green -	do.
Radnor	tow.	29	259	530	Congleton -	do.
Sandbach	tow.	5,493	2,694	19,555	Sandbach -	do.
Smallwood -	tow.	578	2,186	4,852	Scholar Green -	do.
Summerford	tow.	78	1,261	2,310	Congleton -	do.
Summerford Booths -	tow.	216	1,306	3,028	do. -	do.
Swettenham	tow.	176	1,010	2,224	do. -	do.
Tetton	tow.	161	1,050	2,684	Middlewich -	do.
Twemlow	tow.	163	885	2,700	Holmes Chapel -	do.
Wheelock	tow.	794	690	2,529	Sandbach -	do.
COUNTY of STAFFORD:						
Biddulph	par.	5,557	5,671	23,111	Congleton -	Leek.
TOTAL of UNION -		38,010	56,167	201,318		
CONWAY UNION.						
(Formed 11 April 1837 by Order dated 16 March 1837.—Place marked * constituted a separate Parish by Order dated 7 Feb. 1883, and added to the Union by Order dated 12 Sept. 1883.)						
COUNTY of CARNARVON:						
Caerhyn (a) -	par.	1,014	13,402	5,600	Conway -	Conway.
Conway (W.)	par.	2,381	2,437	7,254	do. -	do.
Dolygarrog -	tow.	117 { In Llanbedr y Cennin }		616	do. -	do.
Dwygyfylchi	par.	2,159	5,794	13,805	do. -	do.
Eglwys Rhos -	par.	1,478	3,735	15,188	do. -	do.
Eirias	tow.	788	957	3,935	Colwyn -	do.
Gyffin (b)	par.	587	3,705	3,873	Conway -	do.
*Llanbedr y Cennin (a)	par.	383	4,909	1,620	do. -	do.
Llandudno	par.	4,193	2,729	36,250	Llandudno -	do.
Llangelynin (b)	par.	160	2,017	1,787	Conway -	do.
Llangwstenin -	par.	599	1,314	1,274	do. -	do.
Llysfaen	par.	1,233	1,879	5,340	Abergele -	do.
COUNTY of DENBIGH:						
Llandrillo yn Rhos -	tow.	1,630	4,269	15,160	Colwyn Bay -	Isdulas.
Llanelian -	par.	481	3,187	3,085	Abergele -	do.
Llansainffraid	par.	1,158	5,281	7,983	Conway -	Uchdulas.
TOTAL of UNION -		18,361	55,915	123,770		

CONWAY UNION:
(a) A detached part of Llanbedr y Cennin known as Tal y Cain was amalgamated with Caerhyn, by Order which came into operation on 25 March 1884.

CONWAY UNION—*continued.*
(b) A detached part of Gyffin was amalgamated with Llangelynin, by Order which came into operation on 25 March 1882.

Unions and Parishes, &c.	Population in 1881.	Area in Statute Acres in 1881.	Rateable Value in 1881.	Post Town.	Petty Sessional Division.

COOKHAM UNION.

(Formed 20 July 1835 by Order dated 30 June 1835.)

COUNTY OF BERKS:

			£		
Bisham - - par.	703	2,178	5,000	Great Marlow and Maidenhead.	Maidenhead.
Bray - - par.	6,123	9,063	38,966	Maidenhead and Windsor and Bracknell.	do. ⎫ and, as to parts, the Borough of ⎬ Maidenhead.
Cookham (W.) - par.	6,851	6,548	34,849	Maidenhead -	do. ⎭
Hurley - - par.	1,132	4,159	7,545	do. and Twyford, Henley, and Great Marlow.	do.
Shottesbrook - par.	162	1,395	3,376	do. -	do.
Waltham, Saint Law- ⎫ par. rence - ⎭	853	3,610	7,027	Twyford and Wo- kingham.	Wokingham.
Waltham, White - par.	821	2,613	6,955	Maidenhead and Bracknell.	Maidenhead.
TOTAL OF UNION -	16,945	29,926	103,718		

CORWEN UNION.

(Formed 7 Jan. 1837 by Order dated 13 Dec. 1836.— Place marked thus * added 4 April 1837 by Order dated 9 March 1837.)

COUNTY OF DENBIGH:

Bryn Eglwys - par.	361	3,584	2,347	Corwen -	Llangollen.
Cerrig y Druidion - par.	1,157	15,159	4,891	do. -	Cerrig-y-druidion.
Glyn Traian, in the ⎫ div. Parish of Llangollen ⎭	918	7,830	5,523	Llangollen -	Llangollen.
Llanarmon dyffryn ⎫ par. Ceiriog - ⎭	287	9,295	1,911	do. -	do.
Llanfihangel glyn y ⎫ par. Myfyr (a) ⎭	126	7,830	2,105	Corwen -	Cerrig-y-druidion.
*Llangollen Traian ⎫ div. and Trevor Traian ⎭	5,163	14,566	18,515	Llangollen -	Llangollen.
Llangwm - - par.	933	10,077	5,166	Corwen -	Cerrig-y-druidion.
Llansaintffraid glyn ⎫ par. Ceiriog - ⎭	750	5,919	3,193	Llangollen -	Llangollen.
Llandisilio - - par.	986	8,252	5,232	do. -	do.

COUNTY OF MERIONETH:

Bettws-Gwerfil-Goch(a) par.	260	2,076	1,368	Corwen -	Corwen.
Corwen (W.) (b) - par.	2,708	12,646	11,511	do. -	do.
Gwyddelwern (b) - par.	1,415	9,127	6,328	do. -	do.
Llandrillo - - par.	767	28,200	5,190	do. -	do.
Llangar (b) - - par.	200	3,578	1,927	do. -	do.
Llansaintffraid glyn ⎫ par. dy-dwy - ⎭	172	693	597	do. -	do.
TOTAL OF UNION -	16,833	138,862	75,837		

CORWEN UNION:

(a) All that part of Bettws-Gwerfil-Goch which was situate in the county of Denbigh, was amalgamated with Llanfi-hangel glyn y Myfyr, and all that part of Llanfihangel glyn y Myfyr which was situate in the county of Merioneth, ceased to be part of that county, and formed part of the county of Denbigh, by Order which came into operation on 25 March 1885.

(b) Detached parts of Gwyddelwern were amalgamated with Corwen and Llangar respectively, by Provisional Order which came into operation on 25 March 1885.

Unions and Parishes, &c.		Population in 1881.	Area in Statute Acres in 1881.	Rateable Value in 1881.	Post Town.	Petty Sessional Division.
COSFORD UNION.						
(Formed 1 Aug. 1835 by Order dated 11 July 1835.)						
COUNTY of SUFFOLK :				£		
Aldham - -	par.	238	1,744	2,535	Ipswich - -	Cosford.
Bildeston (c) - -	par.	782	1,420	3,449	Bildeston -	do.
Boxford (a) (c) -	par.	659	1,820	3,513	Colchester -	Babergh.
Brent Eleigh -	par	220	1,617	2,501	Lavenham -	do.
Brettenham (c) -	par.	316	1,558	2,608	Ipswich -	Cosford.
Cheilesworth -	par.	245	861	2,129	do. -	do.
Cockfield - -	par.	931	5,626	6,009	Sudbury -	Babergh.
Edwardstone (b) -	par.	438	1,872	3,614	Colchester -	do.
Elmsett (a) - -	par.	432	1,973	3,375	Ipswich -	Cosford.
Groton (b) (c) -	par.	467	1,571	3,035	Colchester -	Babergh.
Hadleigh Parish -	par.	3,237	4,288	11,462	Hadleigh -	Cosford.
Hadleigh Hamlet -	ham.	205	In Boxford	906	Colchester -	do.
Hitcham (c) -	par.	897	4,117	6,553	Bildeston -	do.
Kersey - -	par.	495	1,510	3,207	Ipswich -	do.
Kettlebaston (c) -	par.	161	1,063	1,588	Bildeston -	do.
Lavenham -	par.	1,838	2,887	6,781	Lavenham -	Babergh.
Layham (a) -	par.	537	2,488	4,972	Hadleigh -	Cosford.
Lindsey (c) -	par.	224	1,246	2,181	Ipswich -	do.
Milden - -	par.	179	1,339	1,867	do. -	Babergh.
Monk's Eleigh -	par.	577	2,099	3,887	Bildeston -	do.
Naughton (c) -	par.	159	854	1,200	Ipswich -	Cosford.
Nedging (c) -	par.	173	837	1,307	do. -	do.
Polstead (a) (c) -	par.	820	3,402	5,706	Colchester -	Babergh.
Preston (b) (c) -	par.	300	1,931	2,960	Lavenham -	do.
Semer (W.) (c) -	par.	356	1,248	2,345	Ipswich -	Cosford.
Thorp Morieux (b) -	par.	416	2,457	3,593	Bildeston -	do.
Wattesham (c) -	par.	184	1,298	1,818	do. -	do.
Whatfield (c) -	par.	322	1,570	2,528	Ipswich -	do.
TOTAL of UNION -		15,820	52,696	100,629		
COVENTRY UNION.						
(Formed 26 March 1874 by Order dated 7 March 1874.)						
CITY of COVENTRY and COUNTY of WARWICK :						
Holy Trinity (a) -	par.	22,024	1,851	59,677	Coventry -	City of Coventry (Separate Commission of the Peace).
Saint Michael (W.) (a)	par.	23,092	3,661	76,088	do. -	do.
TOTAL of UNION -		45,116	5,512	135,765		

COSFORD UNION :

(a) By Orders which came into operation on 25 March 1884,—
A detached part of Assington, in the Sudbury Union, was amalgamated with Boxford ;

Detached parts of Layham were amalgamated with Shelley, in the Samford Union, and a detached part of Shelley was amalgamated with Layham ;

Detached parts of Polstead were amalgamated with Stoke (near Nayland) and Assington, in the Sudbury Union ;

A detached part of Elmsett was amalgamated with Offton, in the Bosmere and Claydon Union ;

(b) By Orders which came into operation on 25 March 1885,—
Parts of the parish of Great Waldingfield, in the Sudbury Union, were amalgamated with Edwardstone and Groton ; and

A detached part of Preston was amalgamated with Thorp Morieux.

(c) By Provisional Order which came into operation on 25 March 1885,—
A detached part of Bildeston was amalgamated with Naughton ;

COSFORD UNION—continued.

A detached part of Boxford was amalgamated with Polstead ;

Detached parts of Brettenham were amalgamated with Hitcham ;

A detached part of Groton was amalgamated with Boxford ;

A detached part of Kettlebaston was amalgamated with Preston ;

A detached part of Lindsey was amalgamated with Groton ;

Detached parts of Naughton were amalgamated respectively with Nedging and Whatfield ;

Parts of Semer were amalgamated with Whatfield, and parts of Whatfield were amalgamated with Semer ; and

A detached part of Wattesham was amalgamated with Hitcham.

COVENTRY UNION :

(a) Detached parts of Saint Michael were amalgamated respectively with Holy Trinity, and with Wyken, in the Foleshill Union, by Order which came into operation on 25 March 1884.

Unions and Parishes, &c.	Population in 1881.	Area in Statute Acres in 1881.	Rateable Value in 1881.	Post Town.	Petty Sessional Division.

CRANBROOK UNION.

(Formed 3 Nov. 1835 by Order dated 17 Oct. 1835.)

COUNTY of KENT:

			£		
Benenden - - par.	1,598	6,693	8,366	Staplehurst -	Lathe of Seray (Lower Division).
Cranbrook (W.) - par.	4,216	10,374	19,813	do. - -	do.
Frittenden - - par.	929	3,509	4,716	do. - -	do.
Goudhurst - - par.	2,764	9,798	15,244	do. - -	do.
Hawkhurst (a) (b) - par.	3,097	6,629	14,628	Hawkhurst -	do.
Sandhurst (a) - - par.	1,170	4,449	7,133	do. - -	do.
TOTAL of UNION -	13,774	41,452	69,900		

CREDITON UNION.

(Formed 19 April 1836 by Order dated 5 April 1836. — Place marked thus * added 22 Mar. 1862 by Order dated 13 Mar. 1862.)

COUNTY of DEVON:

Bow or Nymet Tracey (a) - } par.	815	2,710	4,461	Bow - -	Crediton.
Brushford - - par.	95	894	914	Wembworthy -	South Molton.
Chawleigh - - par.	671	5,020	4,818	Chumleigh -	do.
Cheriton Bishop - par.	591	4,875	4,001	Exeter - -	Crockernwell.
Cheriton Fitzpaine (a) (c) - } par.	769	5,382	7,579	Crediton -	Crediton.
Clanaborough (a) - par.	79	874	1,308	Bow - -	do.
Colebrooke (a) - par.	705	4,989	7,164	Copplestone -	do.
Coldridge - - par.	461	3,670	3,322	Wembworthy -	South Molton.
Crediton (W.) (a) (d) par.	5,747	12,309	28,941	Crediton -	Crediton.
Down Saint Mary (a) par.	325	2,229	3,089	Bow - -	do.
Eggesford - - par.	185	2,500	979	Wembworthy -	South Molton.
Hittesleigh (b) par.	117	1,155	881	Exeter - -	Crockernwell.
Kennerleigh - par.	106	732	773	Morchard Bishop -	Crediton.
Lapford (b) - - par.	641	3,819	4,372	do. - -	South Molton.
Morchard Bishop - par.	1,268	7,088	8,855	do. - -	Crediton.
Newton Saint Cyres - par.	849	4,305	10,506	Exeter -	do.
Nymet Rawland - par.	93	595	788	Morchard Bishop -	South Molton.
Poughill - - par.	260	1,663	1,994	Crediton -	Crediton.
Puddington - par.	208	1,261	1,221	Morchard Bishop -	do.
Sandford - - par.	1,485	7,793	11,929	Crediton -	do.
*Sherwood Villa - par.	2 { In Newton St. Cyres. }		61	Exeter - -	do.

(continued)

CRANBROOK UNION:

(a) A detached part of Sandhurst was amalgamated with Hawkhurst, by Provisional Order which came into operation on 25 March 1886.

(b) The detached part of Hawkhurst, in the county of Sussex, was amalgamated with Etchingham, in the Ticehurst Union, by Provisional Order which came into operation on 25 March 1886.

CREDITON UNION:

(a) By Orders which came into operation on 25 March 1884, —
    A detached part of Bow or Nymet Tracey, known as "Appledore," was amalgamated with Clanaborough;
    A detached part of Colebrooke was amalgamated with Crediton;
    A detached part of Cheriton Fitzpaine was amalgamated with Crawys Morchard, in the Tiverton Union;

CREDITON UNION—continued.

Detached parts of Cheriton Fitzpaine and Crediton were amalgamated with Shobrooke; and

A detached part of Down Saint Mary was amalgamated with Woolfardisworthy.

(b) By Provisional Orders which came into operation on 25 March 1885, —

A detached part of East Worlington, in the South Molton Union, was amalgamated with Woolfardisworthy;

A detached part of Lapford was amalgamated with Meshaw, in the South Molton Union; and

A detached part of Witheridge, in the South Molton Union, was amalgamated with Thelbridge;

A detached part of Hittesleigh was amalgamated with Drewsteignton, in the Okehampton Union, and a detached part of Drewsteignton was amalgamated with Hittesleigh.

Unions and Parishes, &c.	Population in 1881.	Area in Statute Acres in 1881.	Rateable Value in 1881.	Post Town.	Petty Sessional Division.

CREDITON UNION—County of Devon—*continued.*

			£		
Shobrooke (*a*) - - *par.*	641	3,835	6,197	Crediton - -	Crediton.
Stockleigh English - *par.*	65	1,110	1,269	do. - -	do.
Stockleigh Pomeroy - *par.*	174	1,239	1,652	do. - -	do.
Thelbridge (*b*) - *par.*	218	2,240	1,927	Morchard Bishop -	South Molton.
Upton Hellions - *par.*	125	819	1,494	Crediton - -	Crediton.
Washford Pine - *par.*	157	1,110	887	Morchard Bishop -	do.
Wembworthy - *par.*	433	2,411	1,970	Wembworthy -	South Molton.
Woolfardisworthy (*a*) (*b*) - } *par.*	176	1,815	1,695	Morchard Bishop -	Crediton.
Zeal Monachorum - *par.*	468	3,264	4,021	Bow - -	do.
TOTAL of UNION -	**17,929**	**91,866**	**129,071**		

CRICKHOWEL UNION.

(Formed 6 Oct. 1836 by Order dated 10 Sept. 1836.)

COUNTY of BRECKNOCK:

Crickhowel - - *par.*	1,333	1,911	5,638	Crickhowell -	Crickhowell.
Crickne fawr - - *ham.*	20 }	4,900	{ 250	do. - -	do.
Grwyne fechan - *ham.*	74 }		746	do. - -	do.
Llanbeder Ystradwy - *par.*	272	3,831	2,269	do. - -	do.
Llanelly - - *por.*	6,979	5,183	16,826	Crickhowell and Brynmawr.	do.
Llanfihangel or Saint Michael Cwm Dû - } *par.*	957	10,068	6,735	Crickhowell - -	do.
Llangattock (W.) - *par.*	4,731	9,597	10,393	Crickhowell and Brynmawr.	do.
Llangenau - - *par.*	505	2,783	3,667	Crickhowell -	do.
Llangynidir - - *par.*	3,625	13,908	8,039	do. - -	do.
Patricio - - *par.*	62	1,481	778	do. - -	do.
TOTAL of UNION -	**18,558**	**53,692**	**55,311**		

CRICKLADE AND WOOTTON BASSETT UNION.

(Formed 24 Nov. 1835 by Order dated 5 Nov. 1835. — Place marked thus * added on 25 Mar. 1882 by Order dated 29 Oct. 1881. — Place marked thus † added 26 Mar. 1884 by Order dated 24 Mar. 1884.)

COUNTY of WILTS:

Ashton Keynes (*a*) - *par.*	959	2,800	4,917	Cricklade -	Cricklade.
Braydon - - *ham*	48	1,181	1,210	Wootton Bassett -	do.
†Broad Town (*b*) - *par.*				do. - -	do.
Clyffe Pypard (*b*) - *par.*	777	3,985	6,374	do. - -	do.
Cricklade Saint Mary *par.*	397	122	993	Cricklade -	do.
Cricklade Saint Sampson - } *par.*	1,203	6,289	12,421	do. - -	do.
Eisey - - *par.*	158	2,516	3,417	do. - -	do.
Lattion - - *par.*	263	1,826	3,110	do. - -	do.

(*continued*)

CREDITON UNION:

(*a*) (*b*) *See* notes, page 109.

CRICKLADE AND WOOTTON BASSETT UNION:

(*a*) A detached part of Ashton Keynes was amalgamated with The Leigh, and a detached part of The Leigh was amalgamated with Ashton Keynes, by Order which came into operation on 25 March 1884.

(*b*) Certain parts of Clyffe Pypard, and of Broad Hinton in the Marlborough Union, were together constituted a separate parish, designated the Parish of Broad Town, by Order which came into operation on 25 March 1884.

Unions and Parishes, &c.	Population in 1881.	Area in Statute Acres in 1881.	Rateable Value in 1881.	Post Town.	Petty Sessional Division.
CRICKLADE AND WOOTTON BASSETT UNION—County of Wilts—*continued.*			£		
Lydiard Millicent - par.	886	2,321	4,818	Swindon - -	Cricklade.
Lydiard Tregooze - par.	660	5,142	9,605	do. - -	do.
Lyneham - par.	1,011	3,242	6,010	Chippenham	do.
*Marston Maisey - par.	185	1,331	2,045	Fairford - -	
Purton (W.) - par.	2,240	6,465	15,975	Wootton Bassett -	do.
The Leigh (*a*) - - cha.	295	1,460	2,498	Cricklade - -	do.
Tockenham - par.	149	761	1,907	Wootton Bassett -	do.
Wootton Bassett - par.	2,237	4,778	14,251	do. - -	Cricklade and Borough of Wootton Bassett.
TOTAL of UNION -	11,468	44,525	89,511		

CROYDON UNION.

(Formed 21 May 1836 by Order dated 26 April 1836, as amended by Order dated 26 Aug. 1836.)

COUNTY of SURREY :

Addington - par.	667	3,605	5,121	Croydon - -	Croydon.
Beddington - par.	2,485	3,128	17,908	do. - -	do.
Coulsdon - par.	2,589	4,314	33,037	Kenley - -	do.
Croydon (W.) (*a*) - par.	78,953	9,901	467,285	Croydon - -	do.
Merton - par.	2,480	1,765	19,236	Tooting - -	Wandsworth.
Mitcham (W.) - par.	8,960	2,915	39,756	Mitcham - -	Croydon.
Mordon - par.	694	1,475	7,530	Tooting - -	do.
Penge - ham.	18,650	770	151,035	Penge - -	do.
Sanderstead (*a*) - par.	382	2,261	6,900	Croydon - -	do.
Wallington - ham.	3,007	823	21,616	Carshalton -	do.
Woodmansterne - par.	306	1,591	3,325	Epsom - -	do.
TOTAL of UNION -	119,173	32,548	772,749		

CUCKFIELD UNION.

(Formed 26 Mar. 1835 by Order dated 10 Mar. 1835.)

COUNTY of SUSSEX :

Albourn - par.	306	1,763	2,232	Hurstpierpoint -	Bramber Rape (Upper Division).
Ardingley - par.	1,564	3,842	6,641	Haywards Heath -	Cuckfield (Lewes and Pevensey Rape).
Balcomb - par.	878	4,795	18,331	do. - -	do.
Bolney - par.	800	3,557	4,425	Hurstpierpoint -	do.
Clayton - par.	1,819	2,459	9,105	do. - -	do.
Cowfold - par.	1,042	4,501	5,178	Horsham - -	Bramber Rape (Lower Division).
Cuckfield (W.) - par.	4,964	11,275	29,122	Haywards Heath -	Cuckfield (Lewes and Pevensey Rape).
Horsted Keynes - par.	1,149	4,232	4,006	do. - -	do.
Hurst-Perpoint - par.	2,736	5,088	12,160	Hurstpierpoint -	do.
Keymer - par.	3,439	3,583	34,973	do. - -	do.
Lindfield - par.	2,080	5,763	12,203	Haywards Heath -	do.
New-Timber - par.	217	1,721	1,460	do. - -	Lewes (Lewes and Pevensey Rape).
Pieccombe - par.	343	2,286	8,946	do. - -	do.
Slaugham - par.	1,593	5,482	6,587	Crawley - -	Cuckfield (Lewes and Pevensey Rape).
Twineham - par.	292	1,937	2,354	Hurstpierpoint -	do.
TOTAL of UNION -	23,252	62,284	157,726		

CROYDON UNION :

(*a*) A detached part of Croydon was amalgamated with Sanderstead, by Order which came into operation on 25 March 1883.

Unions and Parishes, &c.		Population in 1881.	Area in Statute Acres in 1881.	Rateable Value in 1881.	Post Town.	Petty Sessional Division.
DARLINGTON UNION.						
(Formed 20 Feb. 1837 by Order dated 26 Jan. 1837.)						
COUNTY OF DURHAM:				£		Darlington Ward:
Archdeacon Newton	tow.	54	1,063	1,452	Darlington -	South-East Division.
Aycliffe Great (a) -	tow.	839	2,191	8,777	do.	do.
Barmpton - -	tow.	108	1,515	2,089	do. - -	do.
Blackwell - -	tow.	406	1,589	7,600	do. - -	do.
Brafferton - -	tow.	171	2,428	6,948	do. - -	do.
Burdon Great -	tow.	120	601	2,018	do. - -	do.
Coatham Mundeville (a) - - }	tow.	127	1,631	3,775	do. - -	do.
Cockerton - -	tow.	2,778	1,808	15,027	do. - -	do.
Coniscliffe High (a)	tow.	355	1,858	4,071	do. - -	do.
Coniscliffe Low (a)	tow.	164	1,320	2,255	do. - -	do.
Darlington (W.) -	tow.	33,128	3,351	145,311	do. - -	Darlington Borough. Darlington Ward:
Denton - -	tow.	84	987	1,536	do. - -	South-East Division. do.
Dinsdale Low -	par.	252	1,177	3,404	do. - -	do.
Haughton-le-Side -	tow.	103	1,065	11,355	do. - -	do.
Heighington (a) (b)	tow.	658	2,221	4,975	do. - -	do.
Houghton le Skerne	tow.	713	1,946	1,160	do. - -	do.
Hurworth - -	tow.	1,519	2,430	11,795	do. - -	do.
Killerby - -	tow.	89	634	1,067	do. - -	do.
Middleton Saint George	tow.	1,103	2,517	11,988	do. - -	do.
Morton Palms -	tow.	105	1,358	3,980	do. - -	do.
Neasham - -	tow.	421	1,634	2,887	do. - -	do.
Pierce Bridge -	tow.	206	973	2,457	do. - -	do.
Redworth - -	tow.	553	1,886	5,163	do. - -	do.
Sadberge - -	tow.	371	2,087	3,243	do. - -	do.
School Aycliffe (b) -	tow.	23	531	2,194	do. - -	do.
Sockburn - -	tow.	44	710	970	do. - -	do.
Summerhouse -	tow.	118	831	1,302	do. - -	do.
Walworth - -	tow.	182	2,156	2,883	do. - -	do.
Whessoe - -	tow.	256	1,413	6,608	do. - -	do.
COUNTY OF YORK, NORTH RIDING:						
Barton - -	tow.	515	2,449	4,346	do. - -	Gilling East Wapentake.
Cleasby - -	par.	178	1,205	2,303	do. - -	do. do.
Cliffe - -	tow.	72	707	1,177	do. - -	Gilling West Wapentake.
Croft - -	tow.	537	4,745	8,953	do. - -	Gilling East Wapentake.
Dalton - -	tow.	187	1,636	5,592	do. - -	do. do.
Eryholme - -	tow.	185	2,345	2,562	do. - -	do. do.
Girsby - -	tow.	68	1,227	1,241	do. - -	Yarm Division. -
Manfield - -	tow.	276	2,918	1,063	do. - -	Gilling East Wapentake.
Newton Morrel -	tow.	76	634	915	do. - -	do. do.
Over Dinsdale -	tow.	101	858	1,434	do. - -	Yarm Division.
Stapleton - -	tow.	151	998	1,720	do. - -	Gilling East Wapentake.
TOTAL OF UNION -		47,676	65,705	312,629		

DARLINGTON UNION:

(a) By Orders which came into operation on 25 March 1884,—

A detached part of Aycliffe Great, known as New House, was amalgamated with Coatham Mundeville;

A detached part of Coniscliffe Low, known as "Thornton Hall," was amalgamated with Coniscliffe High;

A detached part of Heighington was amalgamated with Woodham, in the Sedgefield Union;

DARLINGTON UNION—continued.

All the parts of a township known as Coatsaw Moor were amalgamated with Heighington.

(b) By Order which came into operation on 25 March 1885, a detached part of Heighington was amalgamated with School Aycliffe.

Unions and Parishes, &c.		Population in 1881.	Area in Statute Acres in 1881.	Rateable Value in 1881.	Post Town.	Petty Sessional Division

DARTFORD UNION.

(Formed 19 May 1836 by Order dated 23 April 1836.)

COUNTY of KENT:

				£		
Ash next Ridley	- par.	632	3,074	3,121	Wrotham - -	Upper Division of the Lathe of Sutton at Hone.
Bexley - - -	par.	8,793	5,328	43,610	Bexley - -	do.
Crayford - -	par.	4,347	2,457	19,531	Crayford - -	do.
Darenth - -	par.	1,536	2,222	6,791	Dartford -	do.
Dartford (W.) -	par.	10,163	4,251	38,929	do. - -	do.
East Wickham -	par.	1,182	895	4,386	Welling -	do.
Erith - - -	par.	9,812	3,860	47,757	Erith - -	do.
Eynesford - -	par.	1,700	3,541	6,701	Dartford - -	do.
Farningham -	par.	892	2,739	5,191	do. - -	do.
Fawkham - -	par.	237	1,198	1,568	do. - -	do.
Hartley - -	par.	251	1,210	2,633	do. - -	do.
Horton Kirby -	par.	1,541	2,840	10,495	do. - -	do.
Kingsdown -	par.	111	2,812	2,563	do. -	do.
Longfield - -	par.	328	605	2,206	Gravesend -	do.
Lullingstone -	par.	73	1,557	2,070	Dartford -	do.
Ridley - -	par.	65	834	770	Wrotham -	do.
Southfleet - -	par.	922	2,409	5,943	Gravesend -	do.
Stone - - -	par.	2,550	3,014	12,256	Dartford -	do.
Sutton-at-Hone -	par.	2,068	3,625	14,295	do. - -	do.
Swanscombe -	par.	4,511	2,140	20,498	do. - -	do.
Wilmington - -	par.	1,388	1,716	7,011	do. - -	do.
TOTAL of UNION -		53,435	52,330	258,358		

DAVENTRY UNION.

(Formed 29 Oct. 1835 by Order dated 12 Oct. 1835.)

COUNTY of NORTHAMPTON :

Ashby Saint Legers -	par.	261	2,050	5,429	Rugby - -	Daventry.
Badby - -	par.	530	2,370	3,596	Daventry - -	do.
Braunston -	par.	1,072	3,930	8,054	Rugby -	do.
Brockhall - -	par.	44	861	4,036	Weedon -	do.
Buckby, Long (a) -	par.	2,543	3,900	11,776	Rugby - -	do.
Byfield (a) -	par.	787	2,760	5,524	Byfield, R.S.O. -	do.
Canon's Ashby -	par.	55	1,410	2,572	do. - -	do.
Catesby - -	par.	98	1,990	2,994	Daventry - -	do.
Charwelton -	par.	182	2,332	3,662	do. -	do.
Daventry (W.) -	par.	3,859	4,090	14,925	do. -	Borough of Daventry.
Dodford - -	par.	212	1,180	5,467	Weedon -	Daventry.
Everdon - -	par.	565	1,900	4,746	Daventry - -	do.
Farthingstone -	par.	309	1,820	2,372	Weedon -	do.
Fawsley - -	par.	58	1,550	3,006	Daventry - -	do.
Floore or Flore -	par.	1,019	3,390	5,861	Weedon -	Northampton.
Hellidon - -	par.	317	810	2,461	Daventry -	Daventry.
Newnham - -	par.	413	1,910	3,710	do. - -	do.
Norton - -	par.	406	3,260	7,065	do. - -	do.
Preston Capes -	par.	221	2,280	3,397	do. - -	do.
Staverton - -	par.	384	2,240	3,758	do. - -	do.
Stowe Nine Churches (a) }	par.	267	1,865	4,543	Weedon -	do.
Watford (a) - -	par.	462	3,080	11,880	Rugby -	do.
Weedon Beck (a) -	par.	1,957	1,710	9,102	Weedon -	do.
Welton - -	par.	489	1,690	3,636	Daventry - -	do.

(continued)

DAVENTRY UNION :

(a) By Orders which come into operation on 25 March 1884,—

A detached part of Byfield was amalgamated with Chipping Warden, in the Banbury Union ;

DAVENTRY UNION—continued.

A detached part of Watford was amalgamated with Buckby, Long ;

A nearly detached part of Stowe Nine Churches was amalgamated with Weedon Beck.

Unions and Parishes, &c.	Population in 1881.	Area in Statute Acres in 1881.	Rateable Value in 1881.	Post Town.	Petty Sessional Division.

DAVENTRY UNION—County of Northampton—*continued.*

			£		
West Haddon - *par.*	882	2,900	5,686	Rugby - -	Daventry.
Whilton - - *par.*	354	1,270	4,415	Daventry - -	do.
Winwick - - *par.*	181	2,038	3,483	Rugby - -	do.
Woodford cum Membris - - *par.*	587	2,655	4,278	Byfield, R.S.O. -	do.
TOTAL of UNION -	18,511	63,301	151,134		

DEPWADE UNION.

(Formed 14 April 1836 by Order dated 28 Mar. 1836.)

COUNTY of NORFOLK:

Alburgh - - *par.*	602	1,512	2,771	Harleston -	Earsham.
Ashwellthorpe - *par.*	371	979	1,735	Wymondham -	Depwade.
Aslacton - - *par.*	301	1,194	1,905	Long Stratton	do.
Billingford (or Pirleston) - *par.*	194	1,820	1,642	Scole -	Earsham.
Brockdish (a) - - *par.*	434	1,069	2,165	do. -	do.
Bunwell - - *par.*	861	2,170	4,055	Attleborough	Depwade.
Burston - - *par.*	406	1,449	2,692	Diss -	Diss.
Carlton Rode - *par.*	772	2,631	4,668	Attleborough	Depwade.
Denton - - *par.*	484	2,437	3,972	Harleston -	Earsham.
Dickleburgh with Longmere - *par.*	829	2,343	4,116	Scole -	Diss.
Diss - - *par.*	3,846	3,627	12,903	Diss -	do.
Earsham (b) - *par.*	608	3,052	5,777	Bungay -	Earsham.
Forncett Saint Mary *par.*	275	728	1,312	Long Stratton	Depwade.
Forncett Saint Peter *par.*	616	1,828	3,734	do. -	do.
Fritton - *par.*	229	889	1,505	do. -	do.
Fundenhall - *par.*	318	1,347	2,385	Wymondham -	do.
Gissing - *par.*	454	1,981	3,753	Diss -	Diss.
Hapton - *par.*	195	695	1,298	Long Stratton	Depwade.
Hardwick - *par.*	197	855	1,316	do. -	do.
Hempnall - *par.*	881	3,636	5,787	Norwich -	do.
Morning-Thorpe - *par.*	119	1,001	1,785	Long Stratton	do.
Moulton Saint Michael *par.*	359	1,347	2,771	do. -	do.
Needham - *par.*	349	1,127	1,927	Scole -	Earsham.
Pulham Saint Mary Magdalen (W.) - *par.*	1,127	} 5,955	{ 4,938	Harleston -	do.
Pulham Saint Mary the Virgin - *par.*	822		4,960	do. -	do.
Redenhall with Harleston (a) *par.*	1,731	3,714	6,361	do. -	do.
Rushall - *par.*	209	1,170	1,737	Scole -	do.
Scole otherwise Osmondiston with Thorpe Parva and Frenze - *par.*	720	1,569	3,335	do. -	Diss.
Shelton - - *par.*	142	1,292	1,950	Long Stratton	Depwade.
Shimpling - *par.*	175	780	1,373	Scole -	Diss.
Starston - - *par.*	510	2,244	3,577	Harleston -	Earsham.
Stratton Long Saint Mary (a) - *par.*	622	1,517	2,985	Long Stratton	Depwade.
Stratton Saint Michael *par.*	261	1,050	1,989	do. -	do.
Tacolneston - *par.*	438	1,580	2,815	Wymondham -	do.
Tasburgh - *par.*	416	916	1,668	Long Stratton	do.
Tharston - - *par.*	375	1,582	3,036	do. -	do.

(*continued*)

DEPWADE UNION:

(*a*) By Provisional Orders which came into operation on 25 March 1885,—

A detached part of Brockdish was amalgamated with Thorpe Abbott's;

A detached part of Stratton Long Saint Mary was amalgamated with Wacton Magna;

DEPWADE UNION—*continued.*

All that part of Mendham, in the Hoxne Union, which was situate in Norfolk, was amalgamated with Redenhall with Harleston.

(*b*) By Order which came into operation on 25 March 1885, all that part of Earsham situate in Suffolk was amalgamated with Bungay Saint Mary, in the Wangford Union.

Unions and Parishes, &c.	Population in 1881.	Area in Statute Acres in 1881.	Rateable Value in 1881.	Post Town.	Petty Sessional Division.

DEPWADE UNION—County of Norfolk—*continued*. *£*

Thelveton - - *par.*	160	1,050	1,685	Scole - -	Diss.
Thorpe Abbott's (*a*) - *par.*	225	1,122	1,778	do. - -	Earsham.
Tibenham - - *par.*	629	3,286	5,187	Long Stratton -	Depwade.
Tivetshall Saint Margaret's - *par.*	339	1,668	3,402	Scole - -	Diss.
Tivetshall Saint Mary *par.*	299	1,125	1,901	do. - -	do.
Wacton Magna (*a*) - *par.*	233	1,014	1,718	Long Stratton -	Depwade.
Wortwell - - *par.*	416 { In Reddenhall with Harleston		1,911	Harleston -	Earsham.
TOTAL of UNION -	**23,582**	**72,681**	**131,342**		

DERBY UNION.

(Formed 30 Mar. 1837 by Order dated 25 Feb. 1837.)

COUNTY OF DERBY :

All Saints - - *par.*	3,821		26,353	Derby - -	Borough of Derby.
Litchurch - *tow.*	18,507		80,867	do. - -	do.
Little Chester - *tow.*	571		5,210	do. - -	do.
Saint Alkmund's - *par.*	13,680	3,324	42,231	do. - -	do.
Saint Michael's - *par.*	960		3,185	do. - -	do.
Saint Peter's - - *par.*	15,021		58,683	do. - -	do.
Saint Werburgh's - *par.*	26,071		76,591	do. - -	do.
TOTAL of UNION -	**78,631**	**3,324**	**293,420**		

DEVIZES UNION.

(Formed 3 Nov. 1835 by Order dated 16 Oct. 1835. — Place marked thus * added 25 Dec. 1861 by Order dated 27 Sept. 1861.)

COUNTY OF WILTS :

Alleannings - *par.*	193	5,483	4,656	Devizes - -	Devizes.
Allington - - *ty.*	137		1,210	do. - -	do.
Alton Barnes (*b*) - *par.*	156	1,053	1,390	Marlborough -	do.
Beechingstoke - *par.*	167	880	1,615	do. - -	do.
Bishops Cannings - *par.*	955	8,893	8,403	Devizes - -	do.
Bromham (*a*) - *par.*	1,162	3,593	6,636	Chippenham -	do.
Chirton - - *par.*	310	1,858	2,586	Devizes - -	do.
Chittoe (*a*) - - *ty.*	201	1,100	1,335	Chippenham -	do.
Earl Stoke - - *par.*	271	2,400	2,403	Devizes - -	do.
Easterton - - *ty.*	384	1,596	2,150	do. - -	do.
Etchilhampton - *ty.*	170 { In Alleannings		1,632	do. - -	do.
*Fullaway - - *par.*	11 { In Alleannings		296	do. - -	do.
Great Cheverell - *par.*	402	1,840	2,851	do. - -	do.
Little Cheverell - *par.*	222	1,930	1,408	do. - -	do.
Marden - - *par.*	203	1,278	1,857	do. - -	do.
Market Lavington (*a*) - *par.*	1,022	3,125	5,450	Market Lavington	do.

(continued)

DEVIZES UNION :

(*a*) By Orders which came into operation on 25 March 1884,—

  Detached parts of Bromham were amalgamated with Pewsham, in the Chippenham Union, and Chittoe :

  A detached part of Market Lavington was amalgamated with West Lavington, and a detached part of West Lavington was amalgamated with Market Lavington ;

  A detached part of Potterne was amalgamated with Worton ;

DEVIZES UNION—*continued*.

  Detached parts of Poulshot were amalgamated with Chittoe :

  A detached part of Saint James was amalgamated with Potterne.

(*b*) By Provisional Order which came into operation on 25 March 1885, a detached part of Alton Barnes was amalgamated with Alton Priors, in the Pewsey Union.

Unions and Parishes, &c.	Population in 1881.	Area in Statute Acres in 1881.	Rateable Value in 1881.	Post Town.	Petty Sessional Division.

DEVIZES UNION—County of Wilts—continued.

Unions and Parishes, &c.	Population in 1881.	Area in Statute Acres in 1881.	Rateable Value in 1881. £	Post Town.	Petty Sessional Division.
Marston - - ty.	164	In Potterne	1,791	Devizes -	Devizes.
Patney - - par.	142	830	1,367	do. -	do.
Potterne (a) - par.	1,151	4,956	9,507	do. -	do.
Poulshot (a) - par.	340	1,589	3,862	do. - -	do.
Rowde - - par.	1,192	2,665	7,087	do. -	Devizes and Borough of Devizes.
Saint James (W) (a) cha.	3,427	2,648	11,579	do. - -	do.
Saint John, Devizes - par.	1,940	} 639	} 11,033	do. - -	Borough of Devizes.
Saint Mary, Devizes par.	2,605		6,131	do. -	do.
Stanton Saint Bernard par.	327	1,979	2,610	Marlborough	Devizes.
Stert - - ty.	140	638	1,170	Devizes -	do.
Urchfont - - par.	1,057	6,235	10,016	do. - -	do.
West Lavington (a) - par.	1,406	6,283	9,426	do. -	do.
Worton (a) - - ty.	340	In Potterne	3,087	do. -	do.
TOTAL of UNION -	20,530	63,491	124,607		

DEWSBURY UNION.

(Formed 10 Feb. 1837 by Order dated 21 Jan. 1837.)

COUNTY of YORK, WEST RIDING :

Unions and Parishes, &c.	Population in 1881.	Area in Statute Acres in 1881.	Rateable Value in 1881.	Post Town.	Petty Sessional Division.
Batley - - tow.	27,505	2,039	80,506	Batley -	Borough of Batley.
Dewsbury (W.) - tow.	29,637	1,168	93,147	Dewsbury -	Borough of Dewsbury.
Gomersal - - tow.	13,153	3,254	39,520	Leeds -	Dewsbury Division of West Riding.
Heckmondwike - tow.	9,282	697	27,714	Normanton -	do.
Liversedge - - tow.	12,757	2,130	36,007	do. -	do.
Mirfield - - par.	15,872	3,765	57,866	do. -	do.
Morley - - tow.	15,011	2,765	50,751	Leeds -	do.
Ossett - - tow.	10,957	3,105	32,242	Wakefield -	do.
Soothill - - tow.	10,395	2,459	36,536	Dewsbury -	do.
Thornhill - - tow.	7,857	2,564	30,109	do. -	do.
Whitley Lower - tow.	986	1,038	3,131	do. -	do.
TOTAL of UNION -	153,712	25,284	487,529		

DOCKING UNION.

(Formed 1 Aug. 1835 by Order dated 17 July 1835 as amended by Order dated 3 Sept. 1835.— Place marked thus * added 29 Sept. 1865 by Order dated 24 July 1865.)

COUNTY of NORFOLK :

Unions and Parishes, &c.	Population in 1881.	Area in Statute Acres in 1881.	Rateable Value in 1881.	Post Town.	Petty Sessional Division.
Anmer - - par.	167	1,420	1,545	Lynn -	Freebridge Lynn.
Bagthorpe - - par.	85	750	796	do. -	Gallow.
Barmer (a) - - par.	52	890	1,182	do. - -	do.
Barwick - - par.	56	1,278	1,156	do. -	Smithdon.
Bircham-Newton - par.	100	1,128	995	do. - -	do.
Bircham-Tofts - par.	135	1,431	818	do. -	do.
Brancaster - - par.	770	5,777	1,586	do. - -	do.
Broomsthorpe - ham.	12	340	515	do. -	Gallow.

(continued)

DEVIZES UNION—continued.
(a) See notes, page 115.

DOCKING UNION :

(a) By Order which came into operation on 25 March 1885, a detached part of Syderstone was amalgamated with Barmer.

Unions and Parishes, &c.		Population in 1881.	Area in Statute Acres in 1881.	Rateable Value in 1881.	Post Town.	Petty Sessional Division.
DOCKING UNION—County of Norfolk—*continued.*				£		
Burnham Deepdale	- *par.*	96	1,061	1,172	Lynn - -	Brothercross.
Burnham Norton	- *par.*	139	3,896	1,883	do. - -	do.
Burnham Overy	- *par.*	617	2,548	3,693	do. - -	do.
Burnham Thorpe	- *par.*	354	2,328	3,387	do. - -	do.
Burnham Ulph and Sutton	} *par.*	319	1,452	1,979	do. - -	do.
Burnham Westgate	*par.*	968	3,047	5,995	do. - -	do.
*Choseley	- *par.*	10	—	752	do. - -	Smithdon.
Dersingham	- *par.*	1,011	3,472	4,929	do. - -	Freebridge Lynn.
Docking (W.)	- *par.*	1,409	5,113	8,606	do. - -	Smithdon.
East Rudham	- *par.*	781	3,891	4,705	Swaffham - -	Gallow.
Fring	- *par.*	174	1,710	2,283	Lynn - -	Smithdon.
Great Bircham	- *par.*	460	3,606	2,569	do. - -	do.
Great Ringstead	- *par.*	158	2,811	3,692	do. - -	do.
Heacham	- *par.*	998	1,853	7,015	do. - -	do.
Holme next the Sea	- *par.*	301	2,512	2,563	do. - -	do.
Houghton	- *par.*	198	1,195	1,274	Swaffham - -	Gallow.
Hunstanton	- *par.*	1,516	2,294	10,184	Lynn - -	Smithdon.
Ingoldesthorpe	- *par.*	309	1,395	2,499	do. - -	do.
North Creake	- *par.*	613	3,601	4,791	Fakenham - -	Brothercross.
Sedgeford	- *par.*	779	1,180	4,873	Lynn - -	Smithdon.
Shernborne	- *par.*	160	1,300	1,182	do. - -	do.
Snettisham	- *par.*	1,238	15,240	10,111	do. - -	do.
South Creake	- *par.*	976	4,146	6,252	Fakenham - -	Brothercross.
Stanhoe	- *par.*	437	1,489	2,335	Lynn - -	Smithdon.
Syderstone (*a*)	- *par.*	517	2,520	2,643	Fakenham - -	Brothercross.
Thornham	- *par.*	653	2,934	3,984	Lynn - -	Smithdon.
Titchwell	- *par.*	119	1,627	2,075	do. - -	do.
Waterden	- *par.*	44	763	997	Fakenham - -	Brothercross.
West Rudham	- *par.*	173	2,835	3,630	Swaffham - -	Gallow.
TOTAL of UNION	-	17,510	101,136	124,309		

DOLGELLY UNION.

(Formed 12 Jan. 1837 by Order dated 17 Dec. 1836.)

COUNTY of MERIONETH :						
Dolgelly (W.)	- *par.*	3,962	25,607	15,269	Dolgelley - -	Talybont.
Llanaber	- *par.*	2,155	12,679	10,053	Barmouth - -	Ardudwy-is-Artro.
Llanddwywe is graig	*tow.*	270	} 9,348 {	2,053	Dyffryn - -	do.
Llanddwywe uwch graig	} *tow.*	81		541	Dolgelley -	Talybont.
Llanegryn	- *par.*	699	6,819	3,892	Towyn - -	Estimaner.
Llanelltyd	- *par.*	421	6,736	2,357	Dolgelley -	Talybont.
Llaneuddwyn	- *par.*	953	7,777	3,890	Dyffryn - -	Ardudwy-is-Artro.
Llanfacreth	- *par.*	901	10,000	4,476	Dolgelley -	Talybont.
Llanfihangel y pennant	} *par.*	784	8,321	3,105	Abergynolwyn. Towyn.	Estimaner.
Llangelynin	- *par.*	1,143	11,004	5,782	Llwyngwril -	Ardudwy-is-Artro and Estimaner.
Llanymowddwy	- *par.*	183	15,290	2,701	Dinas Mawddwy -	Talybont.
Talyllyn (*a*)	- *par.*	2,045	15,182	7,648	Corris, R.S.O., Merioneth.	Estimaner.
COUNTIES of MERIONETH and MONTGOMERY :						
Mallwyd	- *par.*	1,283	16,450	5,292	Dinas Mawddwy -	Talybont.
TOTAL of UNION	-	15,180	115,213	67,362		

DOLGELLY UNION :

(*a*) By Order which came into operation on 25 March 1887, certain parts of Talyllyn were amalgamated with Towyn, in the Machynlleth Union.

P 2

Unions and Parishes, &c.	Population in 1881.	Area in Statute Acres in 1881.	Rateable Value in 1881.	Post Town.	Petty Sessional Division.

DONCASTER UNION.

(Formed 4 July 1837 by Order dated 7 June 1837, as altered by Order dated 28 Jan 1861.— Place marked thus * added 1 Mar. 1861 by the said Order dated 28 Jan. 1861, and thus † added 23 Aug. 1862 by Order dated 19 July 1862.)

Unions and Parishes, &c.	Population in 1881.	Area in Statute Acres in 1881.	Rateable Value in 1881.	Post Town.	Petty Sessional Division.
COUNTIES OF LINCOLN and NOTTINGHAM:			£		
Misson - - *par.*	683	6,129	8,471	Bawtry - -	Lower Strafforth and Tickhill.
COUNTY OF NOTTINGHAM:					
Finningley - - *tow.*	376	2,360	3,157	do. - -	do.
COUNTIES OF NOTTINGHAM and YORK, WEST RIDING:					
Awkley or Auckley - *tow.*	278	2,087	3,130	Doncaster -	do.
COUNTY OF YORK, WEST RIDING:					
Adwick le Street (*b*) *tow.*	268	2,067	4,776	do. -	do.
Adwick upon Dearne *par.*	253	1,112	10,059	Rotherham -	do.
Armthorpe - - *par.*	393	2,921	3,680	Doncaster -	do.
Askern (*b*) - - *tow.*	548	858	3,362	do. -	do.
Austerfield - - *tow.*	351	2,781	1,268	Bawtry -	do.
Balby with Hexthorpe - } *tow.*	3,422	1,613	21,031	Doncaster -	do.
Barmbrough (*b*) - *par.*	172	1,911	3,073	do. -	do.
Barnby upon Don, or Barnby Dunn (*b*) - } *tow.*	551	2,303	7,098	do. -	do.
Bawtry - - *tow.*	911	259	1,638	Bawtry -	do.
Bentley with Arksey *par.*	1,484	5,133	19,045	Doncaster -	do.
Bilham - - *tow.*	33	536	801	do. -	do.
Blaxton - - *tow.*	216	1,850	2,480	do. -	do.
Bolton upon Dearne *par.*	1,002	2,323	5,915	Rotherham -	do.
Braithwell - - *tow.*	362	1,918	2,857	do. -	do.
Brodsworth cum Pigburn and Scawsby - } *tow.*	346	2,120	1,202	Doncaster -	do.
Burghwallis (*b*) - *par.*	167	941	3,599	do. -	do.
Cadeby - - *tow.*	131	1,234	2,812	do. -	do.

(continued)

DONCASTER UNION:

(*a*) By Orders which came into operation on 25 March 1882,—
A detached part of Conisbrough was amalgamated with Dalton near Rotherham, in the Rotherham Union;
Six detached parts of Mexbrough were amalgamated with Swinton, in the Rotherham Union.

(*b*) By Provisional Order which came into operation on 25 March 1883,—
Three detached parts of Barmbrough were amalgamated with Hickleton;
A detached part of Barnby upon Don or Barnby Dunn was amalgamated with Thorpe in Balne;
Two detached parts of Burghwallis were amalgamated with Owston and Thorpe in Balne;
Two detached parts of Campsall were amalgamated with Askern and Moss;
A detached part of Conisbrough was amalgamated with Mexbrough;
Four detached parts of Kirk Bramwith and a detached part of Owston were amalgamated with Moss;
The two parts of a parish known as Langthwaite with Tilts, having in 1881 population 27, acreage 634, and rateable value 1,276*l.*, were amalgamated, one with Adwick-le-Street, and the other with Thorpe in Balne;
Four detached parts of Moss were amalgamated with Kirk Bramwith.

DONCASTER UNION—*continued.*

(*c*) By Provisional Order which came into operation on 25 March 1883, a part (called Trumfleet) of a parish known as Kirk Sandall and Trumfleet, having in 1881 population 240, acreage 1,141, rateable value 3,828*l.*, was amalgamated with Thorpe in Balne; and by Provisional Order which came into operation on 25 March 1886, the remaining parts of the parish were amalgamated with a township known as Long Sandall, having in 1881 population 126, acreage 1,198, rateable value 2,117*l.*, and Long Sandall, as so altered, was to be designated the township of Kirk Sandall.

(*d*) By Order which came into operation on 25 March 1885, a detached part of Stainton with Hellaby (note *f*) was amalgamated with Bramley, in the Rotherham Union.

(*e*) By Provisional Order which came into operation on 25 March 1886, the two parts of a township known as Stancil with Willingley and Wilsick, having in 1881 population 72, acreage 1,200, and rateable value 1,582*l.*, were amalgamated, one with Wadworth, and the other with Stainton with Hellaby (note *f*).

(*f*) By Order dated 27 July 1885, the parish of Stainton with Hellaby, as altered (notes *d* and *e*), was to be designated the parish of Stainton.

Unions and Parishes, &c.		Population in 1881.	Area in Statute Acres in 1881.	Rateable Value in 1881.	Post Town.	Petty Sessional Division
				£		

DONCASTER UNION—County of York, West Riding—*continued*.

Unions and Parishes, &c.		Population in 1881.	Area in Statute Acres in 1881.	Rateable Value in 1881.	Post Town.	Petty Sessional Division
Campsall (b)	tow.	306	1,730	2,887	Doncaster - -	Lower Strafforth and Tickhill.
Cantley - -	par.	559	5,590	9,205	do. -	do.
†Carr House and Elm-field - - }	par.	25	236	979	do. -	do.
Clayton with Frickley	par.	315	1,589	2,468	do. - -	do.
Conisbrough (a) (b)	par.	2,690	1,296	14,195	Rotherham -	do.
Daunaby or Denaby -	tow.	1,631	1,058	9,357	do. -	Upper Strafforth and Tickhill.
Doncaster (Borough of) (W.) - - }	tow.	21,139	1,691	97,025	Doncaster - -	Borough of Doncaster.
Edlington - -	par.	128	1,758	2,034	Rotherham -	Lower Strafforth and Tickhill.
Fenwick - -	tow.	196	2,371	4,723	Doncaster -	do.
Hampall or Hampole	tow.	123	1,301	2,748	do. -	do.
Hickleton (b) - -	par.	125	1,110	1,561	do. -	do.
Hooton Pagnell -	tow.	283	2,002	2,970	do. -	do.
Kirk Bramwith (b) -	tow.	176	1,335	2,369	do. -	do.
Kirk Sandall (c) -	tow.	—	—	—	do. -	do.
Loversall - -	tow.	177	2,172	3,077	do. -	do.
Marr - -	par.	180	1,821	2,694	do. -	do.
Melton High - -	par.	151	1,525	2,081	do. -	do.
Mexbrough (a) (b) -	tow.	6,319	1,293	20,170	Rotherham -	do.
Moss (b) - -	tow.	280	2,497	5,057	Doncaster -	do.
Norton - -	tow.	589	2,320	4,527	do. -	do.
Owston (b) - -	tow.	339	2,727	3,679	do. -	do.
Rossington - -	par.	354	3,051	8,107	do. -	do.
Skellow - -	tow.	164	932	2,029	do. -	do.
Sprotbrough - -	tow.	371	2,733	5,371	do. -	do.
Stainton (d) (e) (f) -	par.	224	2,857	3,059	Rotherham -	do.
Stotfold - -	tow.	7	257	251	Doncaster -	do.
Sutton near Don-caster - - }	tow.	92	763	1,188	do. -	do.
Thorpe in Balne (b) (c) - - }	tow.	181	2,211	1,544	do. -	do.
Thurnscoe - -	par.	249	1,672	2,712	Rotherham -	do.
Tickhill - -	tow.	1,830	5,579	11,811	do. -	do.
Wadworth (e) - -	par.	571	3,133	4,216	Doncaster -	do.
Warmsworth - -	par.	417	1,074	3,770	do. -	do.
*Wheatley - -	tow.	996	1,284	6,088	do. -	do.
TOTAL of UNION -		53,434 (b) (d) (e)	108,517 (b) (d) (e)	363,619 (b) (d) (e)		

DORCHESTER UNION.

(Formed 2 Jan. 1836 by Order dated 14 Dec. 1835.—Place marked thus * added 25 Dec. 1861 by Order dated 26 Oct. 1861.)

COUNTY of DORSET :

Unions and Parishes, &c.		Population	Area	Rateable Value	Post Town	Petty Sessional Division
All Saints - -	par.	912	42	3,720	Dorchester -	Dorchester.
Athelhampston -	par.	74	471	634	do. -	do.
Bradford Peverell -	par.	330	2,700	2,476	do. -	do.
Broadmayne - -	par.	511	2,540	1,447	do. -	do.
Burleston - -	par.	55	374	487	do. -	do.
Charminster (a) -	par.	1,516	4,095	5,862	do. -	do.
Chilfrome - -	par.	91	940	1,327	do. -	dc.

(continued)

DORCHESTER UNION :

(a) By Orders which came into operation on 25 March 1885,—
    A detached part of Fordington and two detached parts of Frampton were amalgamated with Charminster ;
    A detached part of Holy Trinity was amalgamated with Fordington ;
    A detached part of Piddletown was amalgamated were Piddlehinton ;
    A detached part of Frome Vauchurch was amalgamated with Evershot, in the Beaminster Union.

Unions and Parishes, &c.	Population in 1881.	Area in Statute Acres in 1881.	Rateable Value in 1881.	Post Town.	Petty Sessional Division.

DORCHESTER UNION—*County of Dorset—continued.*

Unions and Parishes, &c.	Population in 1881.	Area in Statute Acres in 1881.	Rateable Value £ in 1881.	Post Town.	Petty Sessional Division.
Compton Abbas - *par.*	66	846	1,081	Dorchester -	Dorchester.
Compton Vallence - *par.*	126	1,296	1,416	do. - -	do.
Dewlish - *par.*	457	2,090	2,610	do. - -	do.
Fordington (W.) (a) *par.*	4,095	2,749	12,972	do. - -	do.
Frampton (a) - *par.*	421	3,508	4,220	do. - -	do.
Frome Vauchurch (a) *par.*	121	614	1,175	do. - -	do.
Holy Trinity (a) - *par.*	1,565	1,369	6,987	do. - -	do.
Kingston Russell - *par.*	70	1,147	1,145	do. - -	do.
Littlebredy - *par.*	193	1,636	1,605	do. - -	do.
Longbredy - *par.*	227	2,117	2,806	do. - -	do.
Maiden Newton - *par.*	799	2,853	1,854	do. - -	do.
Piddlehinton (a) - *par.*	397	2,264	2,667	do. - -	do.
Piddletown (a) - *par.*	1,175	7,653	8,911	do. - -	do.
Saint Peter - *par.*	1,389	In All Saints	5,394	do. - -	do.
Stinsford - *par.*	339	1,999	3,270	do. - -	do.
Stratton - *par.*	299	1,683	2,915	do. - -	do.
Tincleton - *par.*	146	885	1,223	do. - -	do.
Toller Fratrum - *par.*	54	500	693	do. - -	do.
Toller Porcorum - *par.*	146	3,113	3,667	do. - -	do.
Tollpiddle - *par.*	305	2,039	2,511	do. - -	do.
Warmwell - *par.*	173	1,531	1,440	do. - -	do.
*Watercombe - *par.*	51	378	342	do. - -	do.
West Knighton - *par.*	312	2,339	2,872	do. - -	do.
West Stafford - *par.*	199	984	2,325	do. - -	do.
Whitcomb - *par.*	68	540	950	do. - -	do.
Winford Eagle - *par.*	150	1,370	2,012	do. - -	do
Winterborne Abbas - *par.*	198	1,500	1,400	do. - -	do.
Winterborne Came - *par.*	144	1,970	1,313	do. - -	do.
Winterborne Herringstone - *par.*	73	530	835	do. - -	do.
Winterborne Monckton - *par.*	83	631	1,055	do. - -	do.
Winterborne Saint Martin - *par.*	430	3,503	3,357	do. - -	do.
Winterborne Steepleton - *par.*	148	1,783	1,708	do. - -	do.
Woodsford - *par.*	183	1,742	1,793	do. - -	do.
TOTAL of UNION	18,394	70,354	109,477		

DORE UNION.

(Formed 27 Mar. 1837 by Order dated 25 Feb. 1837.)

COUNTY of HEREFORD :

Unions and Parishes, &c.	Population in 1881.	Area in Statute Acres in 1881.	Rateable Value in 1881.	Post Town.	Petty Sessional Division.
Abbey Dore (W.) - *par.*	535	5,390	5,574	Hereford -	Abbeydore.
Barton - *par.*	110	1,155	1,307	do. - -	do.
Craswall - *tow.*	306	17,833	2,151	do. - -	do.
Dulas - *par.*	82	815	900	do. - -	do.
Ewias Harold - *par.*	543	1,838	2,887	do. - -	do.
Kenderchurch - *par.*	58	783	2,374	do. - -	do.
Kentchurch - *par.*	353	3,286	4,183	do. - -	do.
Kilpeck - *par.*	224	2,135	2,798	do. - -	do.
Kingston (a) - *par.*	437	1,991	3,486	do. - -	do.
Llancillo - *par.*	62	1,085	2,280	Abergavenny	do.
Llanveyno - *tow.*	221	In Craswall	2,120	do. -	do.
Longtown - *tow.*	739	In Craswall	1,797	do. -	do.
Madley - *par.*	841	5,360	8,744	Hereford -	do.
Michaelchurch Escley *par.*	312	4,567	2,952	do. -	do.
Newton - *tow.*	192	In Craswall	1,330	do. -	do.

(continued)

DORCHESTER UNION—*continued.*

(a) *See* note, page 119.

DORE UNION :

(a) By Order which came into operation on 25 March 1884, a detached part of Thruxton was amalgamated with Kingston.

Unions and Parishes, &c.		Population in 1881.	Area in Statute Acres in 1881.	Rateable Value in 1881.	Post Town.	Petty Sessional Division

DORE UNION—County of Hereford—*continued.*

				£		
Orcop	- - par.	554	2,403	2,071	Tram Inn, R.S.O. Herefordshire.	Harewood End.
Peterchurch	- par.	639	5,089	5,518	Hereford -	Abbeydore.
Rollstone	- par.	129	1,678	1,952	do. - -	do.
Saint Devereux -	- par.	200	1,095	3,666	do. - -	do.
Saint Margarets	- par.	286	2,582	1,786	do. - -	do.
Thruxton (a) -	- par.	60	437	741	do. - -	do.
Tiberton	- par.	123	1,111	1,594	do. - -	do.
Treville	- par.	156	1,540	1,524	do. - -	do.
Turnastone	- par.	57	530	669	do. - -	do.
Vowchurch	- par.	325	2,690	3,262	do. - -	do.
Watterstone	- par.	114	1,241	1,971	Abergavenny -	do.
Wormbridge	- par.	99	720	1,109	Hereford - -	do.
COUNTY of MONMOUTH:						
Grosmont	- - par.	700	6,838	5,968	Hereford - -	Monmouth.
Llangua	- - par.	81	695	1,426	do. - -	do.
TOTAL of UNION -		8,568	74,917	81,113		

DORKING UNION.

(Formed 10 June 1836 by Order dated 14 May 1836.)

COUNTY of SURREY:

Abinger (a)	- - par.	1,172	7,513	7,601	Wootton -	Dorking.
Capel	- - par.	1,340	5,663	8,516	Dorking	do.
Dorking (W.)	par.	9,577	10,049	47,167	do. - -	do.
Effingham	- par.	585	3,183	4,504	Leatherhead -	do.
Mickleham	- par.	799	2,846	7,118	Dorking	do.
Newdigate	- par.	664	4,551	4,009	do. - -	do.
Ockley	- par.	623	3,008	3,708	do. - -	do.
Wootton	- par.	692	3,796	4,297	Wootton - -	do.
TOTAL of UNION -		15,152	40,609	87,220		

DOVER UNION.

Formed as the River Union 29 April 1835 by Order dated 10 April 1835. Name of Union changed 12 May 1837 by Order dated 27 April 1837.—Place marked thus * added 9 Sept. 1836 by Order dated 15 Aug. 1836, and Places marked thus † added 25 March 1884 by Order dated 19 Dec. 1883.)

COUNTY of KENT:

Alkham	- par.	575	3,203	4,091	Dover -	Dover, Elham Division.
Buckland, near Dover (W.) - - } par.		3,281	972	10,472	do. - -	Borough of Dover.
Capel-le-Ferne	- par.	186	1,582	2,209	Folkestone	Dover, Elham Division.
Charlton, near Dover	par.	6,683	381	21,095	Dover -	Borough of Dover.
Coldred	- par.	150	1,552	1,960	do. - -	Wingham.
Denton	- par.	137	1,184	1,418	Canterbury -	do.
†Dover Castle -	- par.	701	34	.—	Dover -	Borough of Dover.
†East Cliff	- par.	268	9	—	do. - -	do.
East Langdon	- par.	307	1,086	1,873	do. - -	Wingham.
Ewell	- par.	570	1,602	3,636	do. - -	do.
Guston	- par.	481	1,413	2,974	do. - -	do.
Hougham	- par.	5,919	2,917	23,437	do. - -	Borough of Dover.
						(continued)

DORKING UNION:

(a) By Order which came into operation on 25 March 1883, a detached part of Ockham, in the Guildford Union, was amalgamated with Abinger.

Unions and Parishes, &c.		Population in 1881.	Area in Statute Acres in 1881.	Rateable Value in 1881.	Post Town.	Petty Sessional Division.
DOVER UNION—County of Kent—*continued.*				£		
Lydden	par.	203	1,445	1,833	Dover	Wingham.
Oxney	par.	23	318	465	do.	do.
Poulton	par.	27	830	659	do.	do.
Ringswould	par.	853	1,601	3,910	do.	Borough of Dover.
River	par.	633	1,194	5,200	do.	Wingham.
Saint James the Apostle, Dover	par.	1,371	124	32.886	do.	Borough of Dover.
Saint Margaret at Cliffe	par.	612	1.865	3,102	do.	Wingham.
*Saint Mary the Virgin, Dover	par.	9,613	120	45,632	do.	Borough of Dover.
Sibertswould, otherwise Sibbertswold	par.	522	1,850	4,081	do.	Wingham.
West Cliffe	par.	123	1,180	1,704	do.	do.
West Langdon	par.	105	705	897	do.	do.
Whitfield	par.	317	913	1,949	do.	do.
Wootton	par.	153	1,028	1,763	Canterbury	do.
TOTAL of UNION		36,813	29,111	177,246		

DOWNHAM UNION.

(Formed 23 Aug. 1836 by Order dated 28 July 1836.—Names of places marked thus * as altered by Order dated 26 July 1887.)

In the COUNTY of CAMBRIDGE :						
*Welney (Cambs.) (a)	par.	199 {	Included in Welney (Norfolk) }	1,038	Wisbech	Clackclose and Wisbech.
COUNTY of NORFOLK :						
Barton Bendish	por.	437	1,390	4,859	Brandon	Hundred and Half-Hundred of Clackclose.
Bexwell	par.	79	1,177	2,045	Downham Market	do.
Boughton	par.	236	1,323	2,288	Brandon	do.
Crimplesham	par.	293	1,620	2,891	Downham Market	do.
Denver	par.	837	3,149	6,325	do.	do.
Downham Market (W.) (a)	par.	3,256	2,490	11,785	do.	do.
Fincham	par.	787	2,968	6,018	do.	do.
Fordham	par.	180	2,201	3,599	do.	do.
Hilgay (b)	par.	1,684	7,860	12,580	do.	do.
Holme (next Runcton)	par.	267	1,096	1,985	do.	do.
Marham	par.	752	3,966	5,006	do.	do.
Roxham	par.	23	—	878	do.	do.
Ryston	par.	35	1,199	1,058	do.	do.
Shouldham	par.	633	3,888	5,020	do.	do.
Shouldham Thorpe	par.	278	1,430	1,982	do.	do.
Southery (b)	par.	1,176	3,695	6,067	do.	do.
South Runcton	par.	153	831	1,333	do.	do.
Stoke Ferry (a)	par.	684	2,059	4,120	Brandon	do.

(continued)

DOWNHAM UNION :

(a) By Orders which came into operation on 25 March 1881,—

Detached or inconveniently situated parts of Stow-Bardolph and Wimbotsham were amalgamated with Downham Market, and detached parts of Downham Market were amalgamated with Stow-Bardolph ;

Detached parts of Wereham and Wretton were amalgamated with Stoke Ferry ;

Detached parts of Upwell (Cambridge) and Upwell (Norfolk), in the Wisbech Union, were amalgamated with Welney (Cambs.) and Welney (Norfolk), and a detached part of Welney (Norfolk) was amalgamated with Upwell (Norfolk).

DOWNHAM UNION—*continued.*

(b) By Order which came into operation on 25 March 1885, a part of Hilgay, on the right bank of the Little Ouse River, was amalgamated with Southery, and a part on the left bank of the river was amalgamated with Littleport, in the Ely Union.

Unions and Parishes, &c.	Population in 1881.	Area in Statute Acres in 1881.	Rateable Value in 1881.	Post Town.	Petty Sessional Division.
			£		
DOWNHAM UNION—County of Norfolk—*continued.*					
Stow-Bardolph (*a*) - par.	1,054	6,127	9,896	Downham Market -	Hundred and Half-Hundred of Clack-close.
Stradsett - - par.	139	1,318	2,029	do. - -	do.
Tottenhill - - par.	367	1,590	2,569	Lynn - -	do.
Wallington with } par. Thorpland - -	76	1,460	1,949	Downham Market -	do.
Watlington - - par.	619	1,709	4,492	do. - -	do.
*Welney (Norfolk) (*a*) par.	527	5,292	6,785	Wisbech - -	
Wereham (*a*) - par.	614	2,251	4.246	Brandon - -	do.
West Dereham - par.	560	3,440	5,170	do. - -	do.
*Wiggenhall Saint } par. Mary Magdalen -	696	4,248	7,960	Lynn - -	Freebridge Marshland.
Wiggenhall Saint } par. Germains - -	530	1,219	3,105	do. - -	do.
*Wiggenhall Saint } par. Mary the Virgin -	320	2,807	5,759	do. -	do.
Wiggenhall Saint } par. Peter - -	144	944	2,173	do. - -	do.
Wimbotsham (*a*) - par.	677	2,015	3,631	Downham Market -	Hundred and Half-Hundred of Clack-close.
Wormegay - - par.	472	2,788	3,716	Lynn - -	do.
Wretton (*a*) - par.	320	1,154	2,087	Brandon - -	do.
TOTAL of UNION -	19,404	83,687	149,724		

DRAYTON UNION.					
(Formed 3 Oct. 1836 by Order dated 7 Sept. 1836.—Place marked thus * added 30 May 1837 by Order dated 4 May 1837, and thus † added 29 Mar. 1839 by Order dated 9 Mar. 1838.)					
COUNTY of CHESTER:					
*Tittenley - - tow.	25	581	800	Market Drayton -	Nantwich.
COUNTY of SALOP:					
Adderley (*a*) - par.	434	4,037	7,718	do. - -	Bradford North (Drayton Division).
Cheswardine (*a*) - par.	1,071	5,740	11,549	do. - -	do.
Childs Ercall - par.	439	3,749	5,902	do. - -	do.
Drayton in Hales } par. (W.) - -	5,188	7,786	26,872	do. - -	do.
Hinstock - - par.	863	3,266	6,887	do. - -	do.
Hodnet - - par.	1,691	9,625	18,742	do. - -	do.
Moreton Say or Sea (*a*) par.	649	4,832	8,466	do. - -	do.
Norton in Hales - par.	373	1,878	3,878	do. - -	do.
Stoke upon Tern - par.	931	5,683	10,539	do. - -	do.
Woore - - cha.	850	4,457	8,026	Newcastle - under - Lyme.	do.
COUNTY of STAFFORD:					
†Ashley - - par.	806	2,821	5,123	Market Drayton -	Eccleshall.
Mucclestone - par.	763	4,252	7,125	do. - -	Pirehill North.
Tyrley - - tow.	766	6,589	10,255	do. - -	do.
TOTAL of UNION -	14,849	65,296	131,882		

DRAYTON UNION:

(*a*) By Orders which came into operation on 25 March 1883—
Detached parts of Cheswardine were amalgamated with Chetwynd, in the Newport (Salop) Union;
A detached part of Adderley was amalgamated with Moreton Say or Sea.

Q

Unions and Parishes, &c.	Population in 1881.	Area in Statute Acres in 1881.	Rateable Value in 1881.	Post Town.	Petty Sessional Division.

DRIFFIELD UNION.

(Formed 12 Oct. 1836 by Order dated 17 Sept. 1836.)

COUNTY of YORK, EAST RIDING :

			£		
Bainton - - tow.	100	2,981	4,138	Driffield - -	Bainton Beacon.
Beeford - - tow.	707	3,753	4,911	Lowthorpe, Hull -	do.
Bracken - - tow.	31	677	872	Kilnwick, Hull -	do.
Brigham (a) - - tow.	99	1,382	1,603	Hull - - -	do.
Butterwick - - tow.	105	1,779	1,624	Ganton, York -	Dickering.
Cottam - - tow.	113	2,586	2,382	Lowthorpe, Hull -	Bainton Beacon.
Cowlam - - par.	63	2,052	1,667	Sledmere, York -	do.
Eastburn - - tow.	23	843	1,055	Driffield - -	do.
Emswell with Little Driffield (b) - } tow.	168	2,398	3,155	do.	do.
Fimber - - - tow.	184	1,924	1,891	York - -	Buckrose.
Foston upon the Wolds - - } tow.	287	1,108	1,755	Hull - -	Bainton Beacon.
Foxholes with Boythorp - - } tow.	312	2,526	2,674	Ganton, York -	Dickering.
Garton on the Wolds par.	518	4,147	4,759	York - -	Bainton Beacon.
Gembling - - tow.	117	1,235	1,598	Hull - -	do.
Great Driffield (W.) (b) tow.	5,937	4,814	22,643	Driffield -	do.
Great Kelk - - tow.	180	1,173	1,431	Lowthorpe, Hull -	do.
Harpham (a) - - tow.	244	2,144	2,670	Hull - -	do.
Helperthorpe - - par.	189	2,593	2,361	Weaverthorpe, York	Buckrose.
Hutton Cranswick (a) tow.	1,237	4,814	7,160	Hull - -	Bainton Beacon.
Kilham - - par.	1,209	8,173	10,295	Lowthorpe, Hull -	do.
Kirkburn and Battleburn - - } ham.	150	1,387	1,843	Driffield - -	do.
Langtoft - - tow.	618	3,582	3,190	Lowthorpe, Hull -	do.
Little Kelk - - tow.	91	727	1,308	do. -	Dickering.
Lowthorp - - tow.	197	1,969	2,891	Hull - -	Bainton Beacon.
Luttons Ambo - par.	413	2,623	2,779	Wharram, York -	Buckrose.
Middleton - - par.	636	3,664	5,050	Hull - -	Bainton Beacon.
Nafferton (a) - tow.	1,230	4,899	8,931	do. - -	do.
Neswick - - tow.	72	987	1,564	Driffield -	do.
North Dalton - par.	489	4,636	5,331	Hull - -	do.
North Frodingham - par.	682	3,147	4,256	do. - -	do.
Rotsea - - tow.	43	805	977	Cranswick, Hull -	do.
Ruston Parva - par.	120	969	1,389	Lowthorpe, Hull -	do.
Skerne - - par.	176	2,757	3,655	Hull - -	do.
Sledmere with Croom tow.	501	7,041	6,517	York - -	do.
Southburn - - tow.	94	1,103	1,480	Driffield -	do.
Sunderlandwick (a) - tow.	58	823	983	do. - -	do.
Tibthorp - - tow.	281	2,885	3,202	do. -	do.
Towthorpe - - tow.	72	1,711	1,581	Wharram, York -	Buckrose.
Walton - - tow.	319	4,745	5,859	Cranswick, Hull -	Bainton Beacon.
Wansford (a) - par.	209	922	1,402	Hull - -	do.
Weaverthorp - - tow.	643	2,977	3,221	York - -	Buckrose.
Wetwang - - tow.	623	3,437	4,055	do. -	Bainton Beacon.
TOTAL of UNION -	**19,819** (b)	**110,898** (b)	**152,411** (b)		

DRIFFIELD UNION :

(a) By Orders which came into operation on 25 March 1884,—

A detached part of Burton Agnes, in the Bridlington Union, was amalgamated with Harpham ;

A detached part of Hutton Cranswick was amalgamated with Sunderlandwick ;

Detached parts of Nafferton were amalgamated with Brigham and Wansford.

(b) By Provisional Order which came into operation on 25 March 1885, three parts of a township which was known as Little Driffield were amalgamated with Great Driffield, and the remaining part was amalgamated with Emswell with Kelleythorpe, and the latter township was thenceforth to be designated Emswell with Little Driffield. (Little Driffield in 1881 contained population 218, acreage 388, and rateable value 1,012l.)

Unions and Parishes, &c.	Population in 1881.	Area in Statute Acres in 1881.	Rateable Value in 1881.	Post Town.	Petty Sessional Division.

DROITWICH UNION.

(Formed 11 Oct. 1836 by Order dated 16 Sept. 1836.— Places marked thus * added 25 Mar. 1860 by Order dated 13 Mar. 1860.)

COUNTY of WORCESTER :

			£		
Crowle - - par.	329	1,640	3,101	Worcester	- Worcester.
*Crutch - - par.	6	330	354	Droitwich	- Droitwich.
Dodderhill (a) (b) - par.	1,618	5,277	10,482	do. -	- do.
Doverdale - - par.	57	743	980	do.	- do.
Elmbridge - - cha.	337 { In Dodderhill }		3,118	do.	- do.
Elmley Lovett (b) - par.	345	2,381	1,757	do.	- do.
Hadsor (a) - - par.	120	946	1,709	do.	- do.
Hampton Lovett (a) (b) par.	187	2,018	3,638	do. -	- do.
Hanbury (a) - - par.	1,028	7,649	9,382	Bromsgrove	- do.
Hartlebury - - par.	2,271	5,493	14,812	Kidderminster	- Stourport.
Himbleton (b) - par.	459	2,450	3,224	Droitwich	- Droitwich.
Hinlip (a) - - par.	260	1,350	1,828	Worcester	- Worcester.
Huddington - - par.	86	890	1,076	Droitwich	- do.
Martin Hussingtree - par.	169	908	2,456	Worcester	- do.
North Claines (a) (d) per.	—	—	—	do. -	- do.
Oddingley - - par.	193	869	1,377	Droitwich	- Droitwich.
Ombersley - - par.	2,124	6,962	16,821	do. -	- Worcester.
Saint Andrew (a) (c) par.	961	504	5,203	do. -	- Borough of Droitwich.
Saint Nicholas (W.) } (a) (c) - - } par.	1,414	625	5,563	do. -	- do.
Saint Peter (a) (c) - par.	858	450	4,838	do. -	- do.
Salwarpe (a) - - par.	429	1,712	4,553	do. -	- Droitwich.
Stock and Bradley - cha.	224	1,142	2,361	Redditch -	- do.
Tibberton - - par.	347	1,320	2,394	Droitwich	- Worcester.
Upper Milton - ham.	833 { In Hartle- bury }		2,333	Stourport	- Stourport.
Upton Warren (a) - par.	316	2,358	3,980	Bromsgrove	- Bromsgrove.
Warndon (a) - par.	155	832	1,593	Worcester	- Worcester.
*Westwood Park - par.	11	1,380	1,170	Droitwich	- Droitwich.
TOTAL of UNION -	15,340 (c) (d)	50,259 (c) (d)	113,303 (c) (d)		

DROXFORD UNION.

(Formed 30 Mar. 1835 by Order dated 14 Mar. 1835.)

COUNTY of SOUTHAMPTON :

Bishops Waltham - par.	2,484	7,429	15,150	Bishops Waltham -	Droxford.
Corhampton (a) - par.	200	2,291	2,147	do. -	- do.

(continued)

DROITWICH UNION :

(a) By Provisional Order which came into operation on 25 March 1882.—

Detached parts of Dodderhill were amalgamated with Hadsor and Hanbury, and with Bromsgrove and Grafton Manor, in the Bromsgrove Union ;
Detached parts of Saint Andrew, Saint Peter, and Salwarpe were amalgamated with Saint Nicholas, and a detached part of Saint Nicholas was amalgamated with a parish known as In-Liberties (note b) ;
A detached part of Salwarpe was amalgamated with Hampton Lovett ;
Detached parts of Claines (note d) and Warndon were amalgamated with Hinlip ;
Detached parts of Upton Warren were amalgamated with Bromsgrove, and Grafton Manor, in the Bromsgrove Union.

(b) By Orders which came into operation on 25 March 1884,—

A detached part of Elmley Lovett was amalgamated with Hampton Lovett ;
The two parts of a parish which was known as Shell were amalgamated with Himbleton ;
An extra-parochial place which was known as Paper Mills was amalgamated with Dodderhill.

DROITWICH UNION—continued.

(c) By Provisional Order which came into operation on 25 March 1885,—
The four parts of a parish which was known as In-Liberties, having in 1881, population 528, and rateable value 1,690l. (note a), were respectively amalgamated with Saint Nicholas, Saint Peter, and Saint Andrew.

(d) So much of the parish of Claines as is included in the City of Worcester as extended by the Worcester Extension Act, 1885, was by that Act on and after the 30th September 1885, severed from the Droitwich Union, and added to the Worcester Union, under the name of South Claines. The part of Claines remaining in the Droitwich Union is by the Act designated the parish of North Claines (Claines in 1881 contained population 10,212, acreage 4,973, and rateable value 42,696l.)

DROXFORD UNION :

(a) By Orders which came into operation on 25 March 1884,—
A detached part of Corhampton was amalgamated with Exton ;
A detached part of Droxford was amalgamated with Botley, in the South Stoneham Union ;
A detached part of Soberton was amalgamated with Droxford.

Unions and Parishes, &c.		Population in 1881.	Area in Statute Acres in 1881.	Rateable Value in 1881.	Post Town.	Petty Sessional Division.
DROXFORD UNION—County of Southampton— *continued.*				£		
Droxford (W.) (*a*)	*par.*	2,285	6,950	11,264	Bishops Waltham -	Droxford.
Durley	*par.*	476	2,497	2,754	do.	do.
Exton (*a*)	*par.*	289	2,522	2,821	do.	do.
Hambledon	*par.*	2,047	9,417	11,426	Cosham, Hants	do.
Meon-Stoke	*par.*	474	2,055	1,998	Bishops Waltham -	do.
Soberton (*a*)	*par.*	1,097	5,887	5,774	do.	do.
Upham	*par.*	656	2,883	3,113	do.	do.
Warnford	*par.*	387	3,179	4,047	do.	do.
West-Meon	*par.*	802	3,774	4,466	Petersfield	do.
TOTAL of UNION	-	11,197	48,914	65,560		
DUDLEY UNION. (Formed 14 Oct. 1836 by Order dated 19 Sept. 1836. — Place marked thus * added 24 June 1866 by Order dated 7 May 1866.) COUNTY of STAFFORD :						
*Dudley Castle Hill	*par.*	19	In Dudley	14	Dudley	Dudley.
Rowley Regis	*par.*	27,385	3,670	72,113	Rowley Regis	Rowley Regis.
Sedgley (W.)	*par.*	36,574	7,743	80,805	Sedgley	North Division of the Hundred of Seisdon.
Tipton	*par.*	30,013	2,697	85,525	Tipton	Southern Division of the County of Stafford.
COUNTY of WORCESTER :						
Dudley	*par.*	46,233	3,930	118,906	Dudley	Dudley.
TOTAL of UNION	-	140,224	18,040	357,363		
DULVERTON UNION. (Formed 18 May 1836 by Order dated 23 April 1836 as amended by Order dated 4 May 1836.— Place marked thus * added 30 April 1856 by Order dated 7 April 1856.) COUNTY of DEVON :						
*Morebath	*par.*	414	3,449	4,210	Tiverton	Cullompton.
COUNTY of SOMERSET :						
Brompton Regis (*a*)	*par.*	756	8,810	6,818	Dulverton	Dulverton.
Brushford	*par.*	326	2,759	2,625	Tiverton	do.
Dulverton (W.) (*a*)	*par.*	1,373	8,337	7,854	Dulverton	do.
Exford	*par.*	456	5,699	3,455	Minehead	do.
Exton	*par.*	405	4,045	3,261	Dulverton	do.
Hawkridge (*b*)	*par.*	90	3,725	1,306	do.	do.
Huish Champflower (*a*)	*par.*	368	2,909	3,017	Wiveliscombe	Wiveliscombe.
Skilgate	*par.*	219	2,108	1,808	do.	Dulverton.
Upton	*par.*	278	3,779	2,992	do.	do.
Winsford	*par.*	485	8,656	4,848	Dulverton	do.
Withypoole (*b*)	*par.*	253	3,630	1,754	Minehead	do.
TOTAL of UNION	-	5,453	57,906	43,951		

DROXFORD UNION—*continued.*

(*a*) *See note, page 125.*

DULVERTON UNION :

a) By Orders which came into operation on 25 March 1884,—
A part of Brompton Regis was amalgamated with Dulverton ;

DULVERTON UNION—*continued.*

A detached part of Chipstable, in the Wellington (Som.) Union, was amalgamated with Huish Champflower.

(*b*) By Provisional Order which came into operation on 25 March 1885, a detached part of Hawkridge was amalgamated with Withypoole.

Unions and Parishes, &c.	Population in 1881.	Area in Statute Acres in 1881.	Rateable Value in 1881.	Post Town.	Petty Sessional Division.

DUNMOW UNION.

(Formed 26 Mar. 1835 by Order dated 12 Mar. 1835. — White Roothing, as a Parish, and Morrell Roothing, as a Hamlet, were added 13 May 1835 by Order dated 28 April 1835, but by an Order dated 25 Sept. 1865 were declared to be one Parish under the name of White Roothing.)

COUNTY of ESSEX :

			£		
Aythorpe Roothing - *par.*	237	1,394	1,719	Dunmow - -	Dunmow.
Barnston - - *par.*	166	1,472	1,896	do. - -	do.
Broxted - - *par.*	697	3,194	3,869	do. - -	do.
Chickney - - *par.*	42	713	804	do. - -	do.
Felstead - - *par.*	1,956	6,426	9,727	Chelmsford -	South Hinckford.
Great Bardfield - *par.*	948	3,761	6,453	Braintree -	Freshwell.
Great Canfield - *par.*	342	2,490	3,352	Dunmow - -	Dunmow.
Great Dunmow (W.) *par.*	3,005	6,740	13,611	do. - -	do.
Great Easton - *par.*	782	2,559	3,485	do. - -	do.
Hatfield Broad Oaks *par.*	1,946	8,810	12,718	Harlow - -	Harlow.
High Easter - - *par.*	799	4,832	5,800	Chelmsford -	Dunmow.
High Roothing - *par.*	447	1,815	2,589	Dunmow - -	do.
Leaden Roothing - *par.*	179	914	1,234	do. - -	do.
Lindsell - - *par.*	274	1,986	2,617	Chelmsford -	do.
Little Bardfield - *par.*	346	1,714	2,949	Braintree -	Freshwell.
Little Canfield - *par.*	295	1,492	2,104	Dunmow - -	Dunmow.
Little Dunmow - *par.*	338	1,728	2,472	do. - -	do.
Little Easton - *par.*	295	1,602	2,339	do. - -	do.
Margaret Roothing - *par.*	225	1,226	1,519	do. - -	do.
Saling Bardfield - *par.*	299	1,123	1,601	Braintree -	Freshwell.
Stebbing - - *par.*	1,118	4,382	6,822	Chelmsford -	Dunmow.
Takeley - - *par.*	824	3,188	4,302	Dunmow - -	do.
Thaxted - - *par.*	1,914	6,252	8,929	do. - -	do.
Tilty - - *par.*	93	1,053	1,295	do. - -	do.
*White Roothing - *par.*	423	2,539	2,985	do. - -	do.
TOTAL of UNION -	17,990	73,405	107,221		

DURHAM UNION.

(Formed 10 Jan. 1837 by Order dated 15 Dec. 1836. — Place marked thus * added 27 Jan. 1847 by an Order of the same date, and thus † added 24 Mar. 1862 by three Orders dated 20 Mar. 1862.)

COUNTY of DURHAM :

Brancepeth (*a*) (*b*) - *tow.*	432	3,750	24,448	Durham - -	Durham Ward.
Brandon and By-shottles (*a*) - } *tow.*	10,850	6,683	45,636	do. - -	do.
Broom - - *tow.*	719	1,086	7,475	do. - -	do.
Cassop - cum - Quar-rington (*e*) - } *tow.*	925	3,258	8,929	Ferryhill - -	do.

(*continued*)

DURHAM UNION :

(*a*) By Orders which came into operation on 25 March 1882,—
A detached part of Brandon and Byshottles was amalgamated with Brancepeth, and a detached part of Brancepeth was amalgamated with Stockley ;
A detached part of Pittington Hall Garth was amalgamated with Rainton West, in the Houghton-le-Spring Union ;
Two detached parts of Stockley were amalgamated with Willington, and a detached part of Willington was amalgamated with Stockley ;
A detached part of Kimblesworth was amalgamated with Chester-le-Street, in the Chester-le-Street Union.

(*b*) By Provisional Order which came into operation on 25 March 1883,—

DURHAM UNION—*continued.*

Detached parts of Willington were amalgamated with Helmington Row, in the Auckland Union.

(*c*) By Order which came into operation on 25 March 1885, a detached part of Plawsworth, in the Chester-le-Street Union, was amalgamated with Kimblesworth.

(*d*) By Orders which came into operation on 25 March 1886,—
A detached part of Elvet Borough and Barony was amalgamated with Framwellgate ;
A detached part of Ferryhill, in the Sedgefield Union, was amalgamated with Tudhoe.

(*e*) By Provisional Order which came into operation on 25 March 1887, all the parts of a township known as Cassop were amalgamated with Quarrington, and the latter as so altered was designated Cassop-cum-Quarrington.

Unions and Parishes, &c.	Population in 1881.	Area in Statute Acres in 1881.	Rateable Value in 1881.	Post Town.	Petty Sessional Division.
DURHAM UNION—County of Durham—*continued.*			£		
†Castle of Durham, Old Gaol Site, and their Precincts } *par.*	38	9	530	Durham - -	Borough of Durham.
Coxhoe - - *tow.*	2,455	1,058	4,515	Ferryhill - -	Durham Ward.
Crossgate (W.) - *tow.*	3,799	505	11,625	Durham - -	Durham Ward and Borough of Durham.
†Durham College - *par.*	66	28	1,037	do. - -	Borough of Durham.
Elvet Borough and Barony (*d*) } *tow.*	6,293	3,891	23,350	do. - -{	Durham Ward and Borough of Durham.
Framwellgate (*d*) - *tow.*	5,231	3,682	27,522	do. - -	do.
Gilligate - - *par.*	5,420	1,729	16,270	do. - -	do.
Hett - - *tow.*	338	1,279	2,842	do. - -	do.
Kimblesworth (*a*) (*c*) *par.*	1,132	625	3,002	Chester-le-Street	do.
†Magdalen Place - *par.*	27	27	501	Durham -	Borough of Durham.
North Bailey - - *par.*	334	14	2,034	do. -	do.
Pittington Hall Garth (*a*) - } *tow.*	2,206	2,191	13,748	do. -	Durham Ward.
Saint Nicholas - *par.*	2,134	73	13,979	Durham -	Borough of Durham.
Shadforth - - *tow.*	1,677	2,906	6,938	do. - -	Durham Ward and Castle Eden Ward.
Sherburn - - *tow.*	2,610	1,310	10,169	do. - -	Durham Ward.
Sherburn Hospital - *tow.*	196	740	3,194	do. - -	do.
Shincliffe - - *tow.*	969	1,379	8,933	do. - -	do.
South Bailey - - *par.*	110	4	798	do. - -	do.
Stockley (*a*) - - *tow.*	2,232	2,313	9,375	do. - -	do.
Sunderland Bridge - *tow.*	1,372	1,442	6,834	do. - -	do.
Tudhoe (*d*) - - *tow.*	7,585	1,785	21,918	Ferryhill - -	do.
*Whitwell House - *tow.*	135	642	2,429	Durham - -	do.
Willington (*a*) (*b*) - *tow.*	5,006	1,452	11,174	do. - -	do.
TOTAL of UNION -	64,321	41,191	289,205		
DURSLEY UNION. (Formed 4 April 1836 by Order dated 16 Feb. 1836.) COUNTY of GLOUCESTER:					
Cam (*a*) - - *par.*	1,758	2,946	8,190	Dursley - -	Dursley.
Coaley (*a*) - - *par.*	735	2,163	6,019	do. - -	do.
Dursley (W.) (*a*) - *par.*	2,344	1,059	6,629	do. - -	do.
Kingswood - - *par.*	932	2,350	5,495	Wotton-under-Edge	Wotton-under-Edge.
North Nibley (*a*) - *par.*	820	3,245	5,342	Dursley - -	do.
Nymphsfield (*a*) - *par.*	269	1,472	1,791	Stroud - -	Dursley.
Owlpen (*a*) (*b*) - *par.*	110	720	1,110	Dursley - -	do.
Slimbridge (*a*) - - *par.*	854	3,747	10,232	Stonehouse -	do.
Stinchcombe (*a*) (*c*) - *par.*	336	1,464	2,918	Dursley - -	do.
Uley (*a*) - - *par.*	1,043	1,192	3,859	do. - -	do.
Wotton-under-edge (*a*) - } *par.*	3,349	4,880	13,432	Wotton-under-Edge	Wotton-under-Edge.
TOTAL of UNION -	12,550	25,838	65,047		

Unions and Parishes, &c.		Population in 1881.	Area in Statute Acres in 1881.	Rateable Value in 1881.	Post Town.	Petty Sessional Division.
EASINGTON UNION. (Formed 25 Jan. 1837 by Order dated 30 Dec. 1836.) COUNTY of DURHAM :				*£*		Easington :
Burdon	*tow.*	104	1,135	3,060	Sunderland	North Division.
Castle Eden -	*par.*	880	1,940	7,961	Castle Eden	South Division.
Coldhesledon -	*tow.*	108	1,014	5,649	Sunderland -	North Division.
Dalton-le-Dale	*tow.*	118	812	4,834	do. -	do.
Dawdon	*tow.*	7,711	1,089	27,116	Seaham Harbour -	do.
Easington (W.)	*tow.*	1,260	5,058	8,331	Castle Eden	South Division.
Haswell	*tow.*	6,156	3,225	20,069	Fence Houses	do.
Hawthorn	*tow.*	282	1,506	5,230	Sunderland	North Division.
Hutton Henry	*tow.*	1,825	2,016	4,970	Castle Eden -	South Division.
Kelloe - -	*tow.*	937	1,596	4,126	Trimdon Grange -	do.
Monk Hesledon	*tow.*	2,421	2,522	6,514	Castle Eden	do.
Morton East	*tow.*	4,710	1,195	15,216	Sunderland -	North Division.
Nesbitt	*tow.*	10	333	178	Castle Eden -	South Division.
Seaham	*tow.*	2,989	1,518	14,091	Sunderland -	North Division.
Seaton and Slingley -	*tow.*	196	1,392	7,732	do. -	do.
Sheraton and Hulam	*tow.*	176	2,316	2,049	Castle Eden	South Division.
Shotton	*tow.*	2,131	3,701	5,163	do. -	do.
Thornley	*tow.*	3,132	1,148	7,718	Trimdon Grange -	do.
Wingate	*tow.*	5,949	1,176	15,389	Wingate, R.S.O. -	do.
TOTAL of UNION -		41,098	38,031	165,996		
EASINGWOLD UNION. (Formed 20 Feb. 1837 by Order dated 26 Jan. 1837.—Place marked thus * added 28 July 1837 by Order dated 1 July 1837.) COUNTY of YORK, North Riding :						
Aldwork -	*tow.*	223	2,337	2,830	Easingwold -	Bulmer West.
Alne -	*tow.*	492	2,262	6,684	do. -	do.
Angram Grange -	*tow.*	27	145	769	do. -	Birdforth.
Bradferton -	*tow.*	242	1,817	3,523	York -	Bulmer West.
Bransby with Stearsby	*par.*	300	3,077	3,919	Easingwold -	do.
Carlton Husthwaite -	*tow.*	168	819	1,399	Thirsk -	Birdforth.
Coxwold -	*tow.*	313	1,375	2,137	Easingwold -	do.
Craike -	*par.*	501	2,874	5,002	do. -	Bulmer West.
Dalby with Skewsby	*par.*	133	1,347	1,724	Terrington, York -	do.
Easingwold (W.)	*tow.*	2,014	7,000	13,624	Easingwold -	do.
Farlington (*a*)	*par.*	168	1,224	1,793	do. -	do.
Flawith -	*tow.*	71	609	971	do. -	do.
Huby -	*tow.*	494	4,658	5,333	do. -	do.
Husthwaite (*a*)	*tow.*	436	1,677	2,979	do. -	Birdforth.
Linton-upon-Ouze -	*tow.*	296	2,322	3,093	York -	Bulmer West.
Marton with Moxby (*a*)	*par.*	144	2,715	3,210	Easingwold -	do.
Myton upon Swale -	*par.*	189	1,672	3,846	York -	do.
Newborough -	*tow.*	147	2,318	3,051	Easingwold -	Birdforth.
*Newton upon Ouze -	*tow.*	592	1,734	4,934	York -	Bulmer West.
Oulston -	*tow.*	177	1,513	1,724	Easingwold -	Birdforth.
Raskelf -	*tow.*	478	4,281	10,787	do. -	Bulmer West.
Stillington -	*par.*	600	2,158	3,735	do. -	do.
Sutton on the Forest	*tow.*	576	5,997	6,607	do. -	do.
Tholthorp -	*tow.*	202	1,772	2,498	do. -	do.
Thormanby -	*par.*	135	1,002	1,696	do. -	do.
Thornton on the Hill (*a*)	*tow.*	92	1,448	2,130	do. -	Birdforth.
Whenby -	*par.*	111	1,042	1,471	Terrington, York -	Bulmer West.
Wildon Grange -	*tow.*	21	698	906	Easingwold -	Birdforth.
Yearsley -	*tow.*	161	2,792	2,179	do. -	do.
TOTAL of UNION -		9,533	65,015	104,683		

EASINGWOLD UNION :

(*a*) By Provisional Order which came into operation on 25 March, 1887,—
A detached part of Marton with Moxby was amalgamated with Farlington :
Certain parts of Thornton-with-Baxly were amalgamated with Husthwaite, the former as so diminished to be designated the Township of Thornton on the Hill.

Unions and Parishes, &c.	Population in 1881.	Area in Statute Acres in 1881.	Rateable Value in 1881.	Post Town.	Petty Sessional Division.

EASTBOURNE UNION.

(Formed 25 March 1835 by Order dated 24 Feb. 1835.)

COUNTY of SUSSEX :

Unions and Parishes, &c.	Population in 1881.	Area in Statute Acres in 1881.	Rateable Value in 1881.	Post Town.	Petty Sessional Division.
			£		
Alfriston - - par.	581	2,445	2,488	Polegate, R.S.O. -	Hailsham.
Eastbourne (W.) - par.	21,595	4,755	114,190	Eastbourne -	do.
East Dean - - par.	290	2,160	1,572	do. -	do.
Folkington - - par.	133	1,526	1,932	Polegate, R.S.O. -	do.
Friston - - par.	91	1,439	1,118	Eastbourne -	do.
Jevington - - par.	296	2,052	1,863	Polegate, R.S.O. -	do.
Littlington - - par.	89	904	779	do. -	do.
Lullington - - par.	16	1,157	772	do. -	do.
Pevensey - - par.	365	4,392	10,391	Hastings -	do.
Seaford - - par.	1,674	2,347	7,567	Seaford -	Lewes.
West Dean - par.	134	2,260	1,668	Eastbourne -	Hailsham.
Westham - par.	1,000	5,024	8,600	Hastings -	do.
Willingdon - par.	1,243	4,281	8,391	Polegate, R.S.O. -	do.
Wilmington - par.	246	1,788	2,299	do. -	do.
TOTAL of UNION -	27,756	36,539	163,630		

EASTHAMSTEAD UNION.

(Formed 27 July 1835 by Order dated 9 July 1835.)

COUNTY of BERKS :

Unions and Parishes, &c.	Population in 1881.	Area in Statute Acres in 1881.	Rateable Value in 1881.	Post Town.	Petty Sessional Division.
Binfield - par.	1,684	3,489	9,603	Bracknell -	Wokingham.
Easthamstead (W.) - par.	1,172	5,295	5,941	do. -	do.
Sandhurst - - par.	4,195	4,536	12,664	Wokingham -	do.
Warfield - - par.	1,986	3,435	9,829	Bracknell -	do.
Winkfield with Ascot par.	3,622	10,278	16,994	Windsor and Bracknell.	Maidenhead.
TOTAL of UNION -	12,659	27,033	55,034		

EASTRY UNION.

(Formed 27 April 1835 by Order dated 7 April 1835.—Places marked thus * added 6 April 1836 by Order dated 14 Mar. 1836; and thus † added 25 Mar. 1862 by Order dated 13 Feb. 1862.)

COUNTY of KENT :

Unions and Parishes, &c.	Population in 1881.	Area in Statute Acres in 1881.	Rateable Value in 1881.	Post Town.	Petty Sessional Division.
Ash near Sandwich - par.	2,198	7,021	20,773	Sandwich -	Wingham Division of Saint Augustine.
Barfreston - - par.	117	497	707	do. -	do.
Betshanger otherwise Betteshanger } par.	68	395	994	do. -	do.
Chillenden - - par.	138	202	535	do. -	do.
*Deal - - par.	8,500	1,111	26,697	Deal -	Borough of Deal.
Eastry (W.) - par.	1,380	2,733	7,627	Sandwich -	Wingham Division of Saint Augustine.
Elmstone - par.	61	439	1,380	do. -	do
Eythorn - par.	468	1,323	3,191	Dover -	do.
Goodnestone - par.	402	1,864	3,759	Sandwich -	do.
Great Mongeham - par.	469	886	3,172	Deal -	do.
Ham - - par.	57	321	829	Sandwich -	do.
Knowlton - - par.	36	430	800	do. -	do.
Little Mongeham - par.	172	1,147	1,648	Deal -	do.
Nonington - - par.	794	3,808	5,670	Sandwich -	do.
Northbourne - par.	947	3,659	7,167	Deal -	do.
Preston next Wing-ham } par.	449	1,492	4,193	Sandwich -	do.
Ripple - - par.	269	1,021	2,407	Deal -	do.

(continued)

Unions and Parishes, &c.		Population in 1881.	Area in Statute Acres in 1881.	Rateable Value in 1881.	Post Town.	Petty Sessional Division.
EASTRY UNION—County of Kent—*continued.*				£		
†Saint Bartholomew's Hospital -	*par.*	54	6	177	Sandwich - -	Borough of Sandwich.
*Saint Clement -	*par.*	843	555	3,351	do. -	do.
*Saint Mary the Virgin	*par.*	902	125	2,509	do. -	do.
*Saint Peter the Apostle	*par.*	1,047	40	3,338	do. -	do.
Shokden otherwise Shoulden	*par.*	386	1,816	4,369	Deal -	Wingham.
Staple next Wingham -	*par.*	521	1,009	3,276	Sandwich -	do.
Stourmouth -	*par.*	321	901	2,518	do. -	do.
Sutton by Dover -	*par.*	140	1,071	1,591	Deal -	do.
Tilmanstone - -	*par.*	362	1,149	2,279	Sandwich -	do.
Waldershare -	*par.*	132	1,020	1,955	Dover -	do.
Walmer - -	*par.*	4,309	867	13,336	do. -	Cinque Ports.
Wingham - -	*par.*	1,153	2,637	7,814	Sandwich -	Wingham.
Woodnesborough -	*par.*	936	2,940	8,582	do. -	do.
Word or Worth -	*par.*	443	3,930	6,940	do. -	do.
TOTAL of UNION -		28,074	46,395	153,582		
EAST AND WEST FLEGG INCORPORATION.						
(Under the 15 Geo. 3. c. XIII.)						
COUNTY of NORFOLK :						
Ashby-with-Oby -	*u.p.*	107	1,408	2,565	Great Yarmouth -	Flegg, East and West Flegg.
Billockby - -	*par.*	66	389	846	do. - -	do.
Burgh Saint Margaret and Saint Mary -	*par.*	553	1,655	3,599	do. - -	do.
Caistor - next - Yarmouth -	*par.*	1,572	3,017	7,196	do. - -	do.
Clippesby - -	*par.*	123	861	1,701	do. - -	do.
East Somerton -	*par.*	47	798	1,373	do. - -	do.
Filby - -	*par.*	578	1,425	3,113	do. - -	do.
Hemsby - -	*par.*	648	1,785	4,389	do. - -	do.
Martham - -	*par.*	1,097	2,614	6,000	do. - -	do.
Manthy -	*par.*	121	1,659	3,115	do. - -	do.
Ormesby Saint Margaret with Scratby	*u.p.*	1,126	} 2,761	{ 5,270	do. - -	do.
Ormesby Saint Michael	*par.*	287		2,143	do. - -	do.
Repps with Bastwick -	*par.*	261	1,229	2,353	do. - -	do.
Rollesby (W.) -	*par.*	557	1,653	3,173	do. - -	do.
Runham -	*par.*	911	1,715	4,702	do. - -	do.
Stokesby with Herringby -	*par.*	333	2,119	4,007	do. - -	do.
Thirne -	*par.*	213	660	1,393	do. - -	do.
Thrigby - -	*par.*	92	575	1,267	do. - -	do.
West Somerton -	*par.*	232	1,189	2,019	do. - -	do.
Winterton -	*par.*	790	1,515	1,755	do. - -	do.
TOTAL of INCORPORATION		9,714	29,087	63,239		
EAST ASHFORD UNION.						
(Formed 3 June 1835 by Order dated 15 May 1835.— Places marked thus * added 25 April 1836 by Order dated 30 Mar. 1836.)						
COUNTY of KENT :						
Aldington - -	*par.*	675	3,591	6,618	Hythe - -	Elham.
Bilsington - -	*par.*	382	2,844	4,380	Ashford -	Ashford

(continued)

Unions and Parishes. &c.		Population in 1881.	Area in Statute Acres in 1881.	Rateable Value in 1881.	Post Town.		Petty Sessional Division.
EAST ASHFORD UNION—*County of Kent—continued.*				£			
Bircholt	- par.	36	300	410	Ashford	-	Ashford
Bonnington -	- par.	135	1,113	1,883	Hythe	-	do.
Boughton Aluph	- par.	565	2,425	3,763	Ashford	-	do.
Brabourne	- par.	748	3,528	5,623	do.	-	do.
Brook	- par.	136	588	1,072	do.	-	do.
Challock	- par.	356	2,827	2,533	do.	-	do.
Chilham	- par.	1,419	4,398	10,430	Canterbury	-	do.
Crundale	- par.	275	1,593	1,895	do.	-	do.
Eastwell	- par.	113	896	1,520	Ashford	-	do.
Godmersham	- par.	358	3,106	5,033	Canterbury		do.
Hastingleigh	- par.	229	1,515	1,581	Ashford	-	do.
Hinxhill	- par.	138	717	1,378	do.	-	do.
Hurst (a) -	- par.	31	461	790	do.	-	Elham.
Kennington	- par.	741	1,391	4,828	do.	-	Ashford.
Mersham	- par.	722	2,680	6,349	do.	-	do.
Moldash	- par.	335	1,161	2,211	do.	-	do.
*Orlestone	- par.	412	1,832	2,807	do.	-	do.
*Ruckinge	- par.	396	3,148	4,345	do.	-	do.
Sevington	- par.	116	833	2,689	do.	-	do.
Smeeth	- par.	621	1,620	5,059	do.	-	do.
*Wareborne -	- par.	539	2,883	5,095	do.	-	do.
Willesborough (W.) -	par.	2,676	1,187	9,051	do.	-	do.
Wye	- par.	1,543	7,349	12,965	do.	-	do.
TOTAL of UNION	-	13,697	54,886	105,238			

EAST GRINSTEAD UNION.

(Formed 23 Sept. 1835 by Order dated 5 Sept. 1835.)

COUNTY of SURREY :

Lingfield	- par.	2,787	9,239	13,177	East Grinstead	-	Godstone.

COUNTY of SUSSEX :

East Grinstead (W.)	par.	6,968	15,130	26,116	East Grinstead	-	East Grinstead Division of Lewes and Pevensey Rapes.
Hartfield	- par.	1,558	10,387	8,260	Tunbridge Wells	-	do.
West Hoathly	- par.	1,547	5,340	6,330	East Grinstead	-	do.
Withyam	- par.	2,150	8,126	10,214	Tunbridge Wells	-	do.
Worth	- par.	3,571	13,331	24,726	Crawley	-	do.
TOTAL of UNION	-	18,581	61,553	88,823			

EAST PRESTON UNION.

(Formed 29 Sept. 1869 by Order dated 13 Aug. 1869.)

COUNTY of SUSSEX :

Angmering	- par.	982	4,557	6,571	Worthing	-	Arundel.
Arundel	- par.	2,748	1,969	9,336	Arundel	-	do.
Breadwater	- par.	11,817	2,735	56,033	Worthing	-	Worthing.
Burpham	- par.	286	2,725	2,358	Arundel	-	Arundel.
Clapham	- par.	233	1,807	1,499	Worthing	-	Worthing.
Clipping	- par.	270	2,010	3,194	Littlehampton	-	Arundel.
Durrington	- par.	181	900	1,492	Worthing	-	Worthing.
East Preston (W.) -	par.	420	467	1,613	do.	-	Arundel.
Ferring	- par.	232	948	2,099	do.	-	Worthing.
Ford	- par.	100	474	1,176	Arundel	-	Arundel.
Goring	- par.	528	2,014	5,124	Worthing	-	Worthing.
Heene	- par.	845	126	7,730	do.	-	do.
Houghton	- par.	196	1,739	885	Arundel	-	Arundel.
Kingston	- par.	34	425	931	Worthing	-	do.

(continued)

EAST ASHFORD UNION :

(a) A detached part of Newington, in the Elham Union, was amalgamated with Hurst, by Order which came into operation on 25 March 1886.

Unions and Parishes, &c.		Population in 1881.	Area in Statute Acres in 1881.	Rateable Value in 1881.	Post Town.	Petty Sessional Division.
EAST PRESTON UNION—County of Sussex—*continued.*				£		
Leominster -	par.	1,587	2,730	9,059	Arundel - -	Arundel.
Littlehampton	par.	3,926	925	15,310	Littlehampton -	do.
Patching -	par.	274	1,767	1,529	Worthing - -	Steyning.
Poling -	par.	180	790	1,189	Arundel - -	Arundel.
Rustington -	par.	360	945	2,998	Worthing - -	do.
South Stoke	par.	133	1,279	1,304	Arundel - -	do.
Tortington -	par.	165	1,116	2,158	do. - -	do.
Warningcamp	ty.	128	920	1,278	do. - -	do.
West Tarring	par.	733	1,192	4,017	Worthing - -	Worthing.
TOTAL of UNION -		26,364	31,869	139,483		

EAST RETFORD UNION.

(Formed 1 July 1836 by Order dated 7 June 1836.)

COUNTY of NOTTINGHAM:

Askham -	par.	219	1,302	3,266	Tuxford - -	Retford.
Babworth -	par.	731	6,165	12,164	Retford - -	do.
Barnby Moor	tow.	235	1,938	2,730	do. - -	do.
Bevercoates -	par.	32	790	754	Ollerton - -	do.
Bothamsel (a)	par.	264	1,630	2,678	Retford - -	do.
Clareborough (W.) -	par.	2,946	3,870	11,940	Retford - -	Retford and Borough of East Retford.
Clayworth -	tow.	439	3,080	3,318	Bawtry - -	Retford.
Cottam (e) -	tow.	107	900	1,017	Lincoln - -	do.
Darlton ' -	par.	150	1,507	2,078	do. - -	do.
Dunham -	par.	271	2,030	2,028	Newark - -	do.
East Drayton -	par.	214	1,543	2,280	Lincoln - -	do.
East Markham -	par.	752	2,820	8,479	Tuxford - -	do.
East Retford -	par.	3,414	288	10,306	Retford - -	Borough of East Retford.
Eaton -	par.	127	1,540	3,836	do. - -	Retford.
Elkesley -	par.	331	2,500	2,724	do. - -	do.
Everton -	tow.	654	4,679	5,130	Bawtry - -	do.
Fledborough -	par.	106	1,427	2,123	Newark - -	Newark.
Gamston (a) -	par.	252	2,000	5,398	Retford - -	Retford.
Gringley on Hill	par.	832	4,280	6,068	Bawtry - -	do.
Grove -	par.	126	1,257	1,708	Retford - -	do.
Haughton -	par.	51	1,001	1,048	Ollerton - -	do.
Hayton -	par.	255	2,700	3,082	Retford - -	do.
Headon cum Upton -	par.	224	2,300	2,663	Tuxford - -	do.
Laneham (c) -	par.	305	1,605	3,235	Lincoln - -	do.
Littleborough -	par.	64	290	642	do. - -	do.
Lound (a) (b) -	tow.	351	In Sutton	3,309	Retford - -	do.
Marnham (d) -	tow.	196	2,380	3,164	Newark - -	Newark.
Mattersea -	par.	342	2,210	3,165	Bawtry - -	Retford.
Normanton on Trent	par.	318	1,110	2,293	Newark - -	Newark.
North Leverton with Habblesthorpe (b) }	par.	412	2,090	4,160	Lincoln - -	Retford.
North Wheatley -	par.	389	2,181	2,767	Retford - -	do.
Ordsall -	par.	3,011	1,989	18,398	do. - -	Borough of East Retford.
Ragnall -	par.	183	In Dunham	1,913	Newark - -	Retford.

(continued)

EAST RETFORD UNION :

(a) By Order which came into operation on 25 March 1884,—
A detached part of Gamston was amalgamated with Bothamsel ;
A detached part of Lound was amalgamated with Sutton ; and
Three detached parts of Sutton were amalgamated with Lound.

(b) All the parts of a parish, known as Applesthorpe, were amalgamated with North Leverton, by Order which came into operation on 25 March 1884, and North Leverton as so altered was designated North Leverton with Habblesthorpe.

EAST RETFORD UNION—*continued.*

(c) A detached part of Laneham, situate on the east of the River Trent, was amalgamated with Kettlethorpe, in the Gainsborough Union, by Order which came into operation on 25 March 1884.

(d) All the part of Marnham situate to the east of the River Trent was amalgamated with South Clifton, in the Newark Union, by Provisional Order which came into operation on 25 March 1885.

(e) A detached part of Cottam was amalgamated with South Leverton, by Order which came into operation on 25 March 1885.

(f) A detached part of West Burton, in the Gainsborough Union, was amalgamated with Sturton, by Order which came into operation on 25 March 1886.

R 2

Unions and Parishes, &c.	Population in 1881.	Area in Statute Acres in 1881.	Rateable Value in 1881.	Post Town.	Petty Sessional Division.

EAST RETFORD UNION—County of Nottingham—*continued*.

Unions and Parishes, &c.	Population in 1881.	Area in Statute Acres in 1881.	Rateable Value in 1881.	Post Town.	Petty Sessional Division.
Rampton - - *par.*	357	2,155	3,608	Lincoln - -	Retford.
Rankskill - - *tow.*	376	1,261	4,288	Bawtry - -	do.
Scaftworth - - *par.*	106	In Everton	1,500	do. - -	do.
Scrooby - - *par.*	196	1,520	6,615	do. - -	do.
South Leverton (*e*) - *tow.*	403	1,630	3,822	Lincoln - -	do.
South Wheatley - *par.*	37	641	768	Retford - -	do.
Stokeham - - *par.*	43	564	843	Lincoln - -	do.
Sturton (*f*) - - *par*	529	1,610	6,963	do. - -	do.
Sutton (*a*) (*b*) - *tow.*	372	4,370	6,162	Retford - -	do.
Torworth - - *tow.*	223	1,140	3,522	Bawtry - -	do.
Treswell - - *par.*	185	1,561	2,362	Lincoln - -	do.
Tuxford - - *par.*	962	3,000	10,530	Tuxford - -	do.
West Drayton - - *par.*	75	1,300	707	Retford - -	do.
West Markham - *par.*	165	940	1,298	Tuxford - -	do.
West Retford - - *par.*	816	1,080	6,646	Retford - -	do.
Wiseton - - *tow.*	120 { In Clayworth }		1,602	Bawtry - -	do.
Total of Union -	23,271	91,594	201,390		

EAST STONEHOUSE PARISH.

(Board of Guardians constituted 3 Jan. 1837 by Order dated 30 Nov. 1836.)

County of Devon:

Unions and Parishes, &c.	Population in 1881.	Area in Statute Acres in 1881.	Rateable Value in 1881.	Post Town.	Petty Sessional Division.
East Stonehouse (W.) *par.*	15,041	190	36,664	East Stonehouse -	South Roborough.

EAST WARD UNION.

(Formed 31 Oct. 1836 by Order dated 7 Oct. 1836.)

County of Westmorland :

Unions and Parishes, &c.	Population in 1881.	Area in Statute Acres in 1881.	Rateable Value in 1881.	Post Town.	Petty Sessional Division.
Asby - - *par.*	496	8,497	4,028	Appleby - -	Appleby.
Broughs - - *tow.*	628	21,646	3,467	Kirkby Stephen -	do.
Brough Sowerby - *tow.*	133	In Broughs	1,729	do. - -	do.
Crosby Garrett - *tow.*	224	3,900	3,174	do. - -	do.
Dufton - - *par.*	414	16,848	3,726	Appleby - -	do.
Great Musgrave - *par.*	182	3,190	2,288	Kirkby Stephen -	do.
Hartley - - *tow.*	149	3,229	3,149	do. - -	do.
Helbeck - - *tow.*	56	In Broughs	641	do. - -	do.
Kaber - - *tow.*	200	4,533	3,219	do. - -	do.
Kirkby Stephen (W.) *tow.*	1,664	3,135	6,559	do. - -	do.
Kirkby Thore - *tow.*	513	2,502	4,248	Penrith - -	do.
Little Musgrave - *tow.*	71	1,208	1,046	Kirkby Stephen -	do.
Mallerstang - *tow.*	271	8,380	3,344	do. - -	do.
Murton - - *par.*	709	6,917	6,453	Appleby - -	do.
Milburn - - *tow.*	242	7,957	2,663	Temple Sowerby -	do.
Nateby - - *tow.*	175	2,195	1,509	Kirkby Stephen -	do.
Newbiggen - - *par.*	139	1,196	1,777	Temple Sowerby -	do.
Ormside - - *par.*	212	2,713	2,631	Appleby - -	do.
Orton - - *par.*	1,917	24,513	14,741	Tebay - -	do.
Ravenstonedale - *par.*	889	16,407	8,790	Kirkby Stephen -	do.
Saint Laurence Appleby } *par.*	1,456	6,058	6,538	Appleby - -	do.
Saint Michael Bondgate } *par.*	1,443	15,521	11,164	do. - -	do.
Smardale - - *tow.*	44	1,663	1,916	Kirkby Stephen -	do.
Soulby - - *tow.*	275	2,644	4,054	do. - -	do.
Stanemore - - *tow.*	494	In Broughs	7,840	do. - -	do.
Temple Sowerby - *tow.*	420	4,241	2,804	Temple Sowerby -	do.
Warcop - - *par.*	720	11,489	7,087	Penrith - -	do.
Wateby - - *tow.*	68	1,183	1,374	Kirkby Stephen -	do.
Wharton - - *tow.*	64	1,504	1,517	do. - -	do.
Winton - - *tow.*	250	4,570	2,883	do. - -	do.
Total of Union -	14,515	181,866	125,953		

EAST RETFORD UNION—*continued*.

(*a*) (*b*) (*e*) (*f*) See notes, page 133.

Unions and Parishes, &c.	Population in 1881.	Area in Statute Acres in 1881.	Rateable Value in 1881.	Post Town.	Petty Sessional Division.
ECCLESALL BIERLOW UNION.					
(Formed 3 July 1837 by Order dated 6 June 1837.—Place marked thus * added 6 May 1881 by Order dated 25 April 1881.)					
County of Derby :			£		
Beauchief - *lib.*	96	748	1,813	Sheffield - -	Hemsworth.
Dore - - *tow.*	874	3,593	4,839	do. - -	do.
Norton - - *par.*	3,759	4,437	15,587	do. - -	do.
Totley - - *tow.*	671	1,852	2,759	do. - -	do.
County of York, West Riding :					
Ecclesall Bierlow (W.) *tow.*	58,791	4,328	202,294	Sheffield - -	Borough of Sheffield.
*Heeley - - *par.*	8,747	305	19,690		
Nether Hallam - *tow.*	38,967	1,538	94,846	do. - -	do.
Upper Hallam - *tow.*	2,513	6,334	22,975	do. - -	do.
Total of Union -	114,418	23,135	364,803		
EDMONTON UNION.					
(Formed 3 Feb. 1837 by Order dated 7 Jan. 1837.)					
County of Essex :					
Waltham Abbey - *par.*	5,368	11,017	38,900	Waltham Cross -	Waltham Abbey.
County of Hertford :					
Cheshunt - - *par.*	7,735	8,480	48,423	do. -	Cheshunt.
County of Middlesex :					
Edmonton (W.) - *par.*	23,463	7,183	117,294	Edmonton -	Edmonton.
Enfield (W.) - - *par.*	19,104	12,653	99,961	Enfield -	Enfield.
Hornsey, including } Highgate - } *par.*	37,078	3,039	277,514	Hornsey - -	Finsbury.
Tottenham - - *par.*	46,456	4,612	224,667	Tottenham -	Edmonton.
Total of Union -	139,204	47,314	806,759		
ELHAM UNION.					
(Formed 3 June 1835 by Order dated 16 May 1835.—Places marked thus * added 23 April 1836 by Order dated 29 Mar. 1836 ; and thus † added 30 Sept. 1861 by Order dated 6 Sept. 1861.)					
County of Kent :					
Acrise - - *par.*	219	1,038	1,421	Folkestone -	Elham.
Cheriton (*a*) - - *par.*	* 4,053	1,754	16,815	Hythe - -	do.
					(continued)

Elham Union :

(*a*) By Orders which came into operation on 25 March 1886,—

The parts of Cheriton, Newington, and Saltwood within the Municipal Borough of Hythe, were amalgamated with Saint Leonard, Hythe ;

A detached part of Elmstead was amalgamated with Stelling ;

A detached part of Newington was amalgamated with Lympne ;

Elham Union—*continued.*

A detached part of Newington was amalgamated with Hurst, in the East Ashford Union ; and

A detached part of Sellinge was amalgamated with Dymchurch, in the Romney Marsh Union.

(*b*) A parish known as Folkestone, having in 1881 a population of 3,736, an acreage of 3,505, and a rateable value of 30,268*l.*, was amalgamated with the town of Folkestone and the parish of Hawkinge, by Order which came into operation on 25 March 1886.

Unions and Parishes, &c.	Population in 1881.	Area in Statute Acres in 1881.	Rateable Value in 1881.	Post Town.	Petty Sessional Division.
ELHAM UNION—County of Kent—*continued.*			£		
Elham - - par.	1,192	6,599	8,791	Canterbury -	Elham.
Elmstead (a) - - par.	433	2,726	3,372	Ashford -	do.
*Folkestone (b) - town	15,561	806	81,549	Folkestone -	Borough of Folkestone.
Hawkinge (b) - par.	113	522	739	do. -	Elham.
Lyminge (W.) - par.	854	4,617	5,405	Hythe -	do.
Lympne (a) - - par.	549	2,673	5,075	do. -	do.
Monks Horton - par.	148	1,084	1,791	do. -	do.
Newington (a) - par.	580	3,115	6,975	do. -	do.
Paddlesworth - - par.	50	561	566	Folkestone -	do.
Postling - - par.	139	1,563	1,988	Hythe -	do.
*Saint Leonard,Hythe(a) par.	3,522	795	11,896	do. -	Borough of Hythe.
Saltwood (a) - par.	693	2,590	7,333	do. -	Elham.
Sellinge (a) - par.	649	2,063	6,241	do. -	do.
Standford - - par.	294	1,192	3,198	do. -	do.
Stelling (a) - par.	293	1,374	1,822	Canterbury -	do.
†Stelling Minnis - par.	93	81	252	do. -	do.
Stouting - - par.	212	1,622	1,949	Hythe -	do.
Swingfield - - par.	386	2,639	2,970	Canterbury -	Wingham.
TOTAL of UNION -	30,033 (b)	39,414 (b)	170,148 (b)		

ELLESMERE UNION.

(Formed 14 Nov. 1836 by Order dated 18 Oct. 1836.—Places marked thus * added 30 Mar. 1837 by Order dated 4 Mar. 1837.)

COUNTY of FLINT :					
Bettisfield - - tow.	363	2,308	3,493	Whitchurch (Salop)	Hundred of Mealor.
Bronington - - tow.	674	4,692	5,088	do. -	do.
*Halghton - - tow.	411	2,368	3,521	do. -	do.
*Hanmer - - tow.	450	2,303	3,701	do. -	do.
*Overton - - par.	1,131	4,577	8,402	Overton, Ruabon -	do.
*Penley - - cha.	330	2,124	3,086	Ellesmere -	do.
*Tybroughton - - tow.	156	1,187	1,942	Whitchurch (Salop)	do.
*Willington - - tow.	318	1,950	3,147	do. -	do.
COUNTY of SALOP :					
Baschurch - - par.	1,426	8,491	20,408	Shrewsbury -	Hundred of Pimhill, Baschurch Division.
Ellesmere (W.) - par.	5,452	25,922	45,969	Ellesmere -	do.
Great Ness - - par.	657	5,279	6,677	Shrewsbury -	do.
Hardul Ease - cha.	531	2,444	6,198	do. -	Hundred of Albrighton.
Hordley - - par.	290	2,541	4,564	Ellesmere -	Hundred of Pimhill, Ellesmere Division.
Little Ness - - tow.	291 {	In Baschurch }	2,527	Shrewsbury -	Hundred of Pimhill, Baschurch Division.
Middle - - par.	676	4,691	6,446	do. -	do.
Petton - - par.	38	831	1,186	do. -	Hundred of Pimhill, Ellesmere Division.
Welsh Hampton - par.	514	1,515	2,861	Ellesmere -	do.
TOTAL of UNION -	13,708	73,226	129,216		

ELHAM UNION—*continued.*

(a) (b) See notes, page 135.

Unions and Parishes. &c.	Population in 1881.	Area in Statute Acres in 1881.	Rateable Value in 1881.	Post Town.	Petty Sessional Division.

ELY UNION.

(Formed 25 Mar. 1836 by Order dated 7 Mar. 1836.— Place marked thus * added 24 June 1862 by Order dated 6 June 1862, and thus † added 29 Sept. 1865 by Order dated 26 July 1865, and thus ‡ added 25 Mar. 1868 by Order dated 10 Mar. 1868.)

COUNTY OF CAMBRIDGE:

			£		
Coveney (a) - par.	488	2,181	4,355	Ely - -	Hundred of Ely and South Part of Hundred of Witchford.
Downham (b) - par.	1,965	9,789	18,651	do. - -	do.
*Ely College - par.	112	16,507	796	do. - -	do.
Ely Saint Mary's (W.) (a) (d) - par.	3,011		18,626	do. - -	do.
Ely Trinity (a) - par.	5,048		32,231	do. - -	do.
‡Grunty Fen (d) - par.	50	1,990	2,209	do. - -	do.
Haddenham - par.	1,739	8,912	16,183	do. - -	do.
Littleport (c) - par.	3,532	16,136	21,953	do. - -	do.
Mepal (b) - par.	378	1,452	3,190	do. - -	do.
Stretham - par.	1,076	5,310	9,442	do. - -	do.
Sutton - par.	1,525	6,970	12,065	do. - -	do.
Thetford - ham.	212	1,630	4,428	do. - -	do.
Wentworth (a) (b) (d) par.	143	1,437	2,746	do. - -	do.
Wilburton - par.	527	2,233	4,783	do. - -	do.
Witcham (a) (b) - par.	385	2,671	4,970	do. - -	do.
Witchford (a) (b) (d) par.	442	2,376	4,461	do. - -	do.
COUNTY OF NORFOLK:					
†Redmere - par.	39	1,113	191	Downham Market -	Hundred of Clackhouse.
TOTAL OF UNION -	20,702	81,007	164,580		

EPPING UNION.

(Formed 16 Jan. 1836 by Order dated 31 Dec. 1835.)

COUNTY OF ESSEX:

Chigwell - par.	5,431	5,009	30,794	Chigwell -	Epping.
Chingford - par.	1,387	2,791	8,395	Chingford -	do.
Epping - par.	2,343	5,319	13,776	Epping - -	do.
Great Parndon - par.	495	2,232	4,241	Harlow -	Harlow.
Harlow - par.	2,482	4,022	14,397	do. - -	do.
Latton - par.	232	1,618	1,136	do. - -	do.
Little Parndon - par.	122	522	1,919	do. - -	do.
Loughton - par.	2,851	3,961	15,873	Loughton -	Epping.
Magdalen Laver - par.	166	1,229	1,646	Ongar -	Ongar.
Matching - par.	598	2,417	3,397	Harlow -	Harlow.
Nazeing - par.	738	3,952	6,481	Waltham Abbey -	Epping.
Netswell - par.	332	1,552	3,487	Harlow -	Harlow.
North Weald Bassett par.	1,002	3,453	5,947	Epping -	Epping.
Roydon - par.	842	3,031	8,802	Roydon, Ware -	Harlow.
Sheering - par.	543	1,615	5,484	Harlow -	do.
Thoydon Bois - par.	875	2,198	5,408	Epping -	Epping.
Thoydon Garnon (W.) par.	1,315	3,168	7,099	do. - -	do.
TOTAL OF UNION -	21,754	48,099	141,309		

ELY UNION:

(a) By Orders which came into operation on 25 March 1884,—
  Detached parts of Ely Saint Mary's, Ely Trinity, and Witchford were united and amalgamated with Witcham; and
  Detached parts of Wentworth and Witcham were united and amalgamated with Coveney.
(b) By Order which came into operation on 25 March 1884,—
  A detached part of Witcham was amalgamated with Mepal; and

ELY UNION—continued.

  Detached parts of Downham, Wentworth, Witcham, and Witchford were amalgamated with Manea, in the North Witchford Union.
(c) A part of Hilgay, in the Downham Union, was amalgamated with Littleport, by Order which came into operation on 25 March 1885.
(d) By Order which came into operation on 25 March 1886, the parts of Ely Saint Mary's, Wentworth, and Witchford within the Drainage District of Grunty Fen, were amalgamated with Grunty Fen.

R 4

Unions and Parishes, &c.	Population in 1881.	Area in Statute Acres in 1881.	Rateable Value in 1881.	Post Town.	Petty Sessional Division.

EPSOM UNION.

(Formed 31 May 1836 by Order dated 5 May 1836.—Place marked thus * added 30 Sept. 1879 by Order dated 30 Aug. 1879.)

COUNTY of SURREY :

			£		
Ashstead - - par.	926	2,651	6,707	Epsom -	Epsom.
Banstead - - par.	3,826	5,557	12,330	do. -	do.
Carshalton otherwise } par. Casehorton - }	4,841	2,926	26,392	Carshalton -	Croydon.
Cheam - - par.	2,117	1,909	10,491	Sutton -	Epsom.
Chessington (b) - par.	243	1,250	2,164	Kingston -	do.
Cobham - - par.	2,319	5,332	14,970	Cobham -	Kingston.
Cuddington - par.	549	1,860	7,444	Worcester Park -	Epsom.
Epsom (W.) - - par.	6,916	4,424	39,402	Epsom -	do.
Ewell - - - par.	3,002	2,437	16,153	do. -	do.
Fetcham (a) - par.	472	1,804	4,094	Leatherhead -	do.
Great Bookham - par.	1,068	3,276	6,475	do. -	do.
*Headley - - par.	339	1,610	2,083	Epsom -	do.
Leatherhead (a) - par.	3,533	3,541	17,959	Leatherhead -	do.
Little Bookham - par.	214	949	1,658	do. -	do.
Stoke D'Abernon - par.	408	2,038	3,831	Cobham -	Kingston.
Sutton - - par.	10,334	1,836	55,723	Sutton -	Epsom.
TOTAL of UNION -	41,107	43,430	227,876		

ERPINGHAM UNION.

(Formed 11 April 1836 by Order dated 28 March 1836.—Place marked thus * added 9 Aug. 1836 by Order dated 14 July 1836.)

COUNTY of NORFOLK :

Aldborough - - par.	352	788	1,924	Norwich -	North Erpingham.
Antingham - - par.	258	1,509	2,412	North Walsham -	do.
Aylmerton - - par.	273	1,679	2,145	Norwich -	do.
Baconsthorpe - par.	293	1,360	2,010	Holt -	do.
Barningham Norwood par.	30	834	1,132	Norwich -	do.
Barningham Winter } par. (a) - }	101	833	1,250	do. -	do.
Beeston Regis - - par.	193	957	822	Cromer -	do.
Bessingham (a) - par.	136	514	1,066	Norwich -	do.
Bodham - - par.	302	1,688	2,288	Holt -	Holt.
Briston (a) - - par.	855	2,751	4,191	East Dereham -	do.
Cley next the Sea - par.	719	2,363	3,818	do. -	do.
Cromer - - par.	1,597	1,001	7,387	Cromer -	North Erpingham.
East Beckham - par.	55	782	761	Holt -	do.
Edgefield - - par.	479	2,435	3,274	East Dereham -	Holt.
Felbrigg - - par.	165	1,557	1,914	Norwich -	North Erpingham.
Gimingham - - par.	270	1,491	2,592	North Walsham -	do.
*Glandford with Bay- } par. field - }	106	1,163	1,588	East Dereham -	Holt.
Gresham - - par.	381	1,303	2,011	Norwich -	North Erpingham.
Gunton - - par.	73	945	1,406	do. -	do.
Hanworth - - par.	221	1,347	2,061	do. -	do.

(continued)

EPSOM UNION :

(a) A detached part of Leatherhead, known as "Brown's Farm," was amalgamated with Fetcham, by Order which came into operation on 25 March 1884.

(b) A detached part of Malden, in the Kingston Union, known as "Rushet," was amalgamated with Chessington, by Order which came into operation on 25 March 1884.

ERPINGHAM UNION :

(a) By Order which came into operation on 25 March 1884,—

A detached part of Bessingham was amalgamated with Barningham Winter ; and

Two detached parts of Stody were amalgamated with Briston.

Unions and Parishes, &c.		Population in 1881.	Area in Statute Acres in 1881.	Rateable Value in 1881.	Post Town.	Petty Sessional Division.
ERPINGHAM UNION—County of Norfolk—*continued.*				£		
Hempstead	*par.*	264	1,756	2,055	Holt - -	Holt.
Holt	*par.*	1,535	2,991	6,418	do. - -	do.
Hunworth	*par.*	214	838	926	East Dereham -	do.
Kelling	*par.*	211	2,211	1,890	Holt - -	do.
Knapton	*par.*	316	1,480	2,936	North Walsham -	North Erpingham.
Letheringsett	*par.*	280	853	1,812	Holt - -	Holt.
Matlask	*par.*	164	472	832	Norwich - -	North Erpingham.
Metton	*par.*	98	660	1,089	do. - -	do.
Mundsley	*par.*	377	674	1,928	North Walsham -	do.
Northrepps	*par.*	573	2,731	3,936	Norwich - -	do.
Overstrand	*par.*	227	508	762	do. - -	do.
Plumstead	*par.*	193	1,272	1,310	do. - -	do.
Roughton	*par.*	439	1,740	2,013	do. - -	do.
Runton	*par.*	506	1,418	1,852	Cromer - -	do.
Salthouse	*par.*	207	1,614	1,430	Holt - -	Holt.
Sherringham	*par.*	1,159	2,356	3,170	Cromer -	North Erpingham.
Sidestrands	*par.*	158	560	762	Norwich -	do.
Southrepps	*par.*	831	2,081	3,958	do. - -	do.
Stody (*a*)	*par.*	130	1,277	1,426	East Dereham -	Holt.
Suffield	*par.*	206	1,458	2,395	Aylsham -	North Erpingham.
Sustead	*par.*	116	522	1,049	Norwich - -	do.
Thornage	*par.*	327	1,266	2,214	East Dereham -	Holt.
Thorpe Market	*par.*	204	1,309	1,754	North Walsham -	North Erpingham.
Thurgarton	*par.*	231	961	1,980	Norwich - -	do.
Trimingham	*par.*	194	680	924	North Walsham -	do.
Trunch	*par.*	451	1,353	2,733	do. - -	do.
West Beckham (W.)	*par.*	300	785	1,334	Holt - -	do.
Weybourne	*par.*	232	1,680	1,965	do. - -	Holt.
TOTAL of UNION -		17,005	64,926	116,520		

ETON UNION.						
(Formed 25 Mar. 1835 by Order dated 25 Feb. 1835.)						
COUNTY of BUCKINGHAM :						
Boveny Lower	*lib.*	115	483	786	Windsor -	Burnham.
Burnham	*par.*	2,241	6,383	15,925	Maidenhead -	do.
Datchett	*par.*	1,202	1,387	7,887	Windsor -	Stoke.
Denham	*par.*	1,254	3,910	8,960	Uxbridge -	do.
Dorney	*par.*	319	1,560	2,824	Windsor -	Burnham.
Eton	*par.*	3,984	786	17,551	do. -	Stoke.
Farnham Royal	*par.*	1,042	1,663	6,139	Slough -	Burnham.
Fulmer	*par.*	428	1,895	3,191	do. -	Stoke.
Hedgerley	*par.*	132	1,097	1,396	do. -	do.
Hedgerley Dean	*ham.*	204	551	721	do. -	Burnham.
Hitcham	*par.*	395	1,484	3,298	Maidenhead -	do.
Horton	*par.*	861	1,367	4,979	Slough -	Stoke.
Iver	*par.*	2,309	6,467	21,464	Uxbridge -	do.
Langley Marish	*par.*	2,162	3,937	17,787	Slough -	do.
Stoke Poges	*par.*	2,150	3,465	11,081	do. -	do.
Taplow	*par.*	1,063	1,762	8,592	Maidenhead -	Burnham.
Upton with Chalvey (W.) }	*par.*	7,030	1,943	27,079	Slough -	Stoke.
Wexham	*par.*	172	748	1,591	do. -	do.
Wyrardisbury or Wraysbury }	*par.*	658	1,679	5,156	Staines -	do.
TOTAL of UNION -		27,721	42,597	166,410		

S

Unions and Parishes, &c.	Population in 1881.	Area in Statute Acres in 1881.	Rateable Value in 1881.	Post Town.	Petty Sessional Division.
EVESHAM UNION.					
(Formed 7 April 1836 by Order dated 26 Feb. 1836, as amended by Order dated 21 March 1836, and further amended by Order dated 7 March 1837. — Place marked thus * added 20 June 1836 by Order dated 25 May 1836.)			£		
COUNTY of GLOUCESTER :					
Ashton Underhill - par.	359	1,300	3,192	Tewkesbury -	Winchcombe.
Aston Somerville - par.	110	993	2,126	Broadway -	do.
Aston Sub-Edge - par.	121	755	1,695	Campden -	Campden.
Childs Wickham - par.	450	2,040	3,140	Broadway -	Winchcombe.
Cow Honeybourn - par.	367	1,360	3,189	do.	Campden.
Hinton - par.	180	2,239	2,566	Evesham -	Winchcombe.
*Pebworth - par.	691	3,050	5,108	Stratford-on-Avon	Campden.
Saintbury - par.	127	1,336	2,301	Broadway -	do.
Weston Sub-Edge - par.	341	2,632	5,706	do.	do.
Willersey - par.	393	1,344	2,428	do. -	do.
COUNTY of WORCESTER :					
Aldington - ham.	135	In Badsey	2,270	Evesham -	Evesham.
All Saints - par.	1,777 {	In Saint Lawrence, }	7,115	do. -	do.
Badsey - par.	442	1,770	2,736	do. -	do.
Bretforton - par.	565	1,683	4,044	do. -	do.
Broadway - par.	1,641	4,800	10,008	do. -	do.
Church Honeybourn - par.	116	1,312	2,385	Broadway -	do.
Church Lench - par.	387	2,523	3,269	Evesham -	do.
Cleve Prior - par.	284	1,580	2,388	do. -	do.
Great and Little Hampton (W.) - } par.	633	1,670	4,326	do. -	do.
Harvington - par.	490	1,238	3,010	do. -	do.
Hob Lench - ham.	42	870	868	do. -	do.
North and Mid Littleton (a) - } par.	277	1,610	2,501	do. -	do.
Norton and Lench Wick - } par.	412	2,614	4,356	do. -	do.
Offenham - par.	552	1,215	3,717	do. -	do.
Rouse Lench - par.	296	1,380	2,170	do. -	do.
Saint Lawrence - par.	2,024	2,338	6,741	do. -	do.
Saint Peter in Bengeworth - } par.	1,311 {	In Saint Lawrence, }	6,441	do. -	do.
Sedgbarrow - par.	300	1,042	1,730	do. -	do.
South Littleton (a) - par.	324	841	1,899	do. -	do.
Wickhamford - par.	123	1,242	1,507	do. -	do.
TOTAL of UNION -	15,270	46,797	104,932		
EXETER UNION.					
(Union constituted by "The City of Exeter Extension Act, 1877," and name given by Order dated 1 March 1878.)					
CITY AND COUNTY of EXON :					
Allhallows Goldsmith-street - } par.	273	2	5,759	Exeter -	City of Exeter.
Allhallows - on - the - Walls - } par.	986	7	2,927	do. -	do.
Bedford Circus - pre.	141	3	1,864	do. -	do.
Bradninch - pre.	75	4	630	do. -	do.
Close of Saint Peter's Cathedral - } pre.	401	16	3,585	do. -	do.

(continued)

EVESHAM UNION :

(a) By Provisional Order which came into operation on 25 March 1886, a detached part of South Littleton was amalgamated with North and Mid Littleton.

Unions and Parishes, &c.	Population in 1881.	Area in Statute Acres in 1881.	Rateable Value in 1881.	Post Town.	Petty Sessional Division.

EXETER UNION—*City and County of Exon—continued.*

Unions and Parishes, &c.	Population in 1881.	Area in Statute Acres in 1881.	Rateable Value in 1881.	Post Town.	Petty Sessional Division.
Holy Trinity - *par.*	3,704	50	12,597	Exeter	City of Exeter.
Saint David - *par.*	5,186	1,149	41,745	do.	do.
Saint Edmund - *par.*	1,307	20	4,446	do.	do.
Saint George the Martyr - *par.*	671	3	1,846	do.	do.
Saint John - *par.*	432	4	2,721	do.	do.
Saint Kerrian - *par.*	420	3	1,725	do.	do.
Saint Lawrence - *par.*	452	6	5,168	do.	do.
Saint Leonard - *par.*	1,659	158	11,408	do.	do.
Saint Martin - *par.*	188	2	5,143	do.	do.
Saint Mary Arches - *par.*	568	3	3,450	do.	do.
Saint Mary Major - *par.*	3,262	13	6,658	do.	do.
Saint Mary Steps - *par.*	1,370	14	3,823	do.	do.
Saint Olave - *par.*	785	6	3,900	do.	do.
Saint Pancras - *par.*	310	2	1,618	do.	do.
Saint Paul - *par.*	1,126	9	6,399	do.	do.
Saint Petrock - *par.*	193	2	3,955	do.	do.
Saint Sidwell (W.) - *par.*	13,840	388	49,294	do.	do.
Saint Stephen - *par.*	316	3	5,221	do.	do.
TOTAL of UNION -	37,665	1,867	185,891		

FALMOUTH UNION.

(Formed 13 June 1837 by Order dated 15 May 1837.)

COUNTY of CORNWALL :

Unions and Parishes, &c.	Population in 1881.	Area in Statute Acres in 1881.	Rateable Value in 1881.	Post Town.	Petty Sessional Division.
Budock (W.) - *par.*	2,488	3,733	11,795	Falmouth	Hundred of Kerrier : East Division.
Constantine - *par.*	1,925	8,022	9,561	Penryn	do.
Falmouth - *par.*	6,158	} 641	{ 18,988	Falmouth	do.
Falmouth - *bor.*	5,973		9,052	do.	Borough of Falmouth.
Mabe - *par.*	679	2,569	3,974	Penryn	Hundred of Kerrier : East Division.
Mawnan - *par.*	522	2,117	3,049	Falmouth	do.
Mylor - *par.*	2,207	3,599	6,678	do.	do.
Penryn - *bor.*	3,466 {	In St. Gluvias }	6,914	Penryn	Borough of Penryn.
Perranarworthal - *par.*	1,102	1,773	3,378	Truro	Hundred of Kerrier : East Division.
Saint Gluvias - *par.*	1,037	2,841	5,432	Penryn	do.
TOTAL of UNION -	25,557	25,295	78,821		

FAREHAM UNION.

(Formed 26 May 1835 by Order dated 11 May 1835.)

COUNTY of SOUTHAMPTON :

Unions and Parishes, &c.	Population in 1881.	Area in Statute Acres in 1881.	Rateable Value in 1881.	Post Town.	Petty Sessional Division.
Boarhunt (a) - *par.*	288	2,005	2,009	Fareham	Fareham.
Fareham (W.) - *par.*	7,183	6,386	29,106	do.	do.
Porchester - *par.*	772	1,379	1,417	do.	do.
Rowner (a) - *par.*	187	1,217	1,972	do.	do.
Southwick (a) - *par.*	664	4,237	5,218	do.	do.
Titchfield - *par.*	4,571	15,784	24,667	do.	do.
Wickham - *par.*	1,101	2,449	5,210	do.	do.
Widley (a) - *par.*	1,069	1,111	4,164	Cosham	do.
Wymmering (a) - *par.*	985	3,121	8,794	do.	do.
TOTAL of UNION -	16,820	37,689	85,617		

FAREHAM UNION:

(a) By Orders which came into operation on 25 March 1886,—
 Detached parts of Southwick were amalgamated with Boarhunt ;
 Detached parts of Widley were amalgamated with Southwick :

FAREHAM UNION—*continued.*

A detached part of Wymmering was amalgamated with Southwick ;
A detached part of Farlington, in the Havant Union, was amalgamated with Southwick ; and
A detached part of the Separate Parish of Alverstoke was amalgamated with Rowner.

Unions and Parishes, &c.	Population in 1881.	Area in Statute Acres in 1881.	Rateable Value in 1881.	Post Town.	Petty Sessional Division.

FARRINGDON UNION.

(Formed 2 Feb. 1835 by Order dated 1 Jan. 1835.— Place marked thus * added 25 Jan. 1836 by Order dated 1 Jan. 1836.)

COUNTY of BERKS :

			£		
Ashbury - - *par.*	684	5,609	7,324	Shrivenham -	Faringdon.
Balking - *tow.*	169	1,473	4,136	Faringdon -	do.
Bourton - - *tow.*	284	1,260	3,732	Shrivenham -	do.
Buckland - - *par.*	723	4,505	7,515	Faringdon -	do.
Buscott - - *par.*	371	2,887	6,244	do. -	do.
Charney - - *tow.*	222	1,209	2,158	Wantage -	do.
Coleshill (a) - - *par.*	309	2,014	3,867	Highworth -	do.
Compton and Knighton - - *par.*	120	1,466	2,245	Faringdon -	do.
Eaton Hastings - *par.*	133	1,570	2,221	do. - -	do.
Fearnham - - *tow.*	205	1,016	2,041	do. - -	do.
Great Coxwell - *par.*	289	1,435	2,414	do. - -	do.
Great Farringdon (W.) - - *par.*	3,141	5,897	16,067	do. - -	do.
Hatford - - *par.*	132	993	1,294	do. - -	do.
Hinton - - *par.*	287	2,017	2,945	do. - -	de.
Kingston Lisle and Fawler - - *tow.*	338	2,147	3,117	Wantage -	do.
Little Coxwell - *tow.*	250	887	1,720	Faringdon -	
Longcott - - *tow.*	393	1,894	3,263	do. - -	do.
Longworth - - *par.*	596	2,290	3,884	do. - -	do.
Pusey - - *par.*	117	1,040	1,348	do. - -	do.
Shillingford - *par.*	258	1,761	3,234	do. - -	do.
Shrivenham - *par.*	721	2,695	7,156	Shrivenham -	do.
Stanford - - *par.*	929	2,927	6,719	Faringdon -	do.
Uffington - - *par.*	566	3,205	5,850	do. -	do.
Watchfield - - *tow.*	362	1,517	2,534	Shrivenham -	do.
Woolstone - - *tow.*	201	2,012	3,088	Faringdon -	do.

COUNTY of GLOUCESTER :

*Lechlade (b) - - *par.*	1,176	3,625	7,718	Lechlade -	Fairford.

COUNTY of OXFORD :

Grafton - - *tow.*	64	625	1,085	Faringdon -	Bampton (West Division.)
Kelmscott - - *tow.*	101	1,037	1,520	Lechlade -	do.
Langford - - *tow.*	384	2,117	3,490	do. - -	do.
Little Farringdon - *tow.*	125	1,167	1,818	do. - -	Fairford.
Radcot - - - *tow.*	26	441	834	Faringdon -	Faringdon.
TOTAL of UNION -	13,676	64,738	122,611		

FARNHAM UNION.

(Formed 27 Feb. 1846 by Order of the same date. — Place marked thus * added 27 April 1846 by Order of the same date, and places marked thus † added 8 June 1869 by Order dated 28 May 1869.)

COUNTY of SOUTHAMPTON :

Aldershott - - *par.*	20,155	4,178	13,466	Aldershot, Hants -	Odiham.
Dockenfield - - *par.*	209	578	697	Frensham, Surrey -	Alton.

(continued)

FARRINGDON UNION :

(a) A detached part of Coleshill, known as Lynt Farm, was amalgamated with Inglesham, in the Highworth and Swindon Union, by Provisional Order which came into operation on 25 March 1883.

FARRINGDON UNION—continued.

(b) A detached part of Broughton Poggs, in the Witney Union, was amalgamated with Lechlade, by Order which came into operation on the 25 March 1886.

Unions and Parishes, &c.	Population in 1881.	Area in Statute Acres in 1881.	Rateable Value in 1881.	Post Town.	Petty Sessional Division.
FARNHAM UNION—*cont.*					
COUNTY of SURREY :			£		
†Ash - - - *par.*	1,930	6,324	7,739	Farnham - -	Guildford.
Farnham (W.) - - *par.*	11,058	10,118	40,257	do. - -	Farnham.
Frensham - - *par.*	2,079	8,807	8,207	do. -	do.
Frimley - - *ham.*	4,012	7,674	18,306	Farnborough Station, Hants.	do.
†Seal - - - *par.*	912	2,994	4,825	Farnham	do.
♦Waverley - - *ville.*	40	542	847	do. -	do.
TOTAL of UNION -	40,395	41,215	124,344		
FAVERSHAM UNION.					
(Formed 25 March 1835 by Order dated 24 Feb. 1835, as amended by Order dated 11 March 1835.)					
COUNTY of KENT :					Lathe of Scray :
Badlesmere - - *par.*	157	781	1,164	Faversham -	Upper Division.
Boughton under Blean *par.*	1,664	2,352	10,975	do. -	do.
Buckland - - *par.*	70	336	1,973	Sittingbourne -	do.
Davington - - *par.*	224	541	3,580	Faversham -	do.
Doddington - - *par.*	580	1,945	3,896	Sittingbourne -	do.
Eastling - - *par.*	181	1,034	2,888	Faversham -	do.
Faversham (W.) - *par.*	9,484	2,292	37,462	do. -	do.
Goodneston - - *par.*	80	341	967	do. -	Upper Division, and Borough of Faversham.
Graveney - - *par.*	252	1,992	4,669	do. -	Upper Division.
Hernhill - - *par.*	748	2,824	7,270	do. -	do.
Leaveland - - *par.*	129	381	668	do. -	do.
Linstead - - *par.*	1,284	1,826	6,562	Sittingbourne -	do.
Luddenham - - *par.*	236	1,327	5,304	Faversham -	do.
Newnham - - *par.*	312	1,285	2,156	Sittingbourne -	do.
Norton - - *par.*	171	903	2,339	Faversham -	do.
Oare - - - *par.*	512	647	2,167	do. -	do.
Ospringe - - *par.*	1,217	2,874	7,576	do. -	do.
Preston -next -Faversham - *par.*	2,340	1,571	12,725	do. -	do.
Selling - - - *par.*	817	2,454	6,850	do. -	do.
Sheldwich - - *par.*	638	1,948	4,069	do. -	do.
Stalisfield - - *par.*	340	2,293	2,361	do. -	do.
Stone next Faversham *par.*	66	757	2,474	do. -	do.
Teynham - - *par.*	1,790	2,474	13,688	Sittingbourne -	do.
The Ville of Dunkirk	742	5,338	3,816	Faversham -	do.
Throwley - - *par.*	622	3,256	4,456	do. -	do.
TOTAL of UNION -	24,956	44,672	152,058		
FESTINIOG UNION.					
(Formed 8 May 1837 by Order dated 6 April 1837.)					
COUNTY of CARNARVON :					
Dolbenmaen (a) - *par.*	2,407	21,146	6,808	Carnarvon - -	Eifionydd.
Trefllys - - *par.*	73	999	404	do. - -	do.
Ynyscynhaiarn - *par.*	5,506	6,546	10,577	do. - -	do.
COUNTIES of CARNARVON and MERIONETH :					
Beddgelert - - *par.*	1,330	26,716	3,851	do. - -	do.

(continued)

FESTINIOG UNION :

(a) By Provisional Order which came into operation on 25 March 1886, the several parts of the Parishes known as Llanfihangel y Pennant and Penmorfa, were amalgamated with Dolbenmaen.

Unions and Parishes, &c.		Population in 1881.	Area in Statute Acres in 1881.	Rateable Value in 1881.	Post Town.	Petty Sessional Division.

Festiniog Union—*continued.*

County of Merioneth :

				£		
Festiniog	-	11,274	16,456	69,394	Carnarvon	Ardudwyuwchartro.
Llanbedr	*par.*	300	7,312	1,542	do.	do.
Llandanwg	*par.*	990	4,964	2,296	do.	do.
Llandecwyn	*par.*	381	6,915	1,595	do.	do.
Llanfair	*par.*	409	5,196	2,078	do.	do.
Llanfihangel y Traethau (W.)	*par.*	3,014	7,567	5,594	do.	do.
Llanfrothen	*par.*	1,059	7,482	3,006	do.	do.
Maentwrog	*par.*	852	5,465	2,203	do.	do.
Trawsfynydd	*par.*	1,930	21,950	4,770	do.	do.
Total of Union	-	**29,525**	**138,714**	**114,118**		

FOLESHILL UNION.

(Formed 23 July 1836 by Order dated 28 June 1836.—Place marked thus * added 26 April 1851 by Order dated 8 April 1851.)

County of Warwick :

Ansty	*par.*	142	990	3,200	Coventry	Kirby Division.
*Bedworth	*par.*	5,376	2,157	14,266	do.	do.
Binley	*par.*	195	2,470	2,160	do.	do.
Exhall (*b*)	*par.*	881	1,990	7,501	do.	do.
Foleshill (W.) (*b*)	*par.*	7,727	2,594	18,659	do.	do.
Keresley	*ham.*	455	1,058	2,920	do.	do.
Shilton	*par.*	413	1,075	2,848	do.	do.
Sow	*par.*	1,324	2,505	7,519	do.	do.
Stoke	*par.*	1,447	936	5,582	do.	do.
Willenhall	*ham.*	121	440	1,755	do.	do.
Withybrook	*par.*	295	2,520	1,244	do.	do.
Wyken (*a*)	*par.*	121	670	1,818	do.	do.
Total of Union	-	**18,497**	**19,405**	**72,502**		

FORDEN UNION.

(Formed 25 Mar. 1870 by Order dated 26 Feb. 1870.)

County of Montgomery :

Aston	*tow.*	60	1,125	1,252	Churchstoke	Montgomery (Lower Division).
Berriew (*a*)	*par.*	1,838	12,010	15,152	Berriew, R.S.O.	Newtown (Lower Division).
Castle Caereinion (*a*)	*par.*	594	6,540	6,461	Welshpool	Caurse, Mathrafal, and Pool Borough.
Castlewright	*tow.*	166	1,332	1,418	Bishops Castle	Montgomery (Lower Division).
Churchstoke	*tow.*	1,263	8,787	10,760	Churchstoke	do.

(*continued*)

Foleshill Union :

(*a*) A detached part of Saint Michael, in the Coventry Union, was amalgamated with Wyken, by Order which came into operation on 25 March 1884.

(*b*) Certain nearly detached parts of Exhall were amalgamated with Foleshill, by Order which came into operation on 25 March 1885.

Forden Union :

(*a*) By Orders which came into operation on 25 March 1884,—
A detached part of a parish known as Cyfronydd (having in 1881 population 48, acreage 607, and

Forden Union—*continued.*

rateable value 821*l.*,) which was included in the municipal borough of Welshpool, was amalgamated with Pool Lower, and the remainder with Castle Caereinion.

A detached part of Castle Caereinion, known as Trehelig, and a part of Forden, were amalgamated with Pool Upper.

A detached part of Forden was amalgamated with Berriew.

A detached part of Worthin was amalgamated with Pontesbury, in the Atcham Union.

Unions and Parishes, &c.	Population in 1881.	Area in Statute Acres in 1881.	Rateable Value in 1881.	Post Town.	Petty Sessional Division.

FORDEN UNION—County of Montgomery—*continued.* £

Unions and Parishes, &c.	Population in 1881.	Area in Statute Acres in 1881.	Rateable Value in 1881.	Post Town.	Petty Sessional Division.
Cletterwood - - *tow.*	201	3,239	2,791	Welshpool -	Borough of Pool.
Forden (W.) (*a*) - *par.*	906	5,270	8,134	do. - -	Caurse.
Hope - - *tow.*	129 { In Cletterwood }	1,164	do. - -	Borough of Pool.
Leighton - - *tow.*	388	1,866	3,135	do. - -	Caurse.
Llandyssil - - *par.*	890	4,071	6,506	Montgomery -	Montgomery (Lower Division).
Llanmerewig - *par.*	146	978	1,600	Abermule -	Newtown (Upper Division).
Middletown - - *tow.*	102	736	922	Welshpool -	Caurse.
Montgomery - *par.*	1,194	3,323	7,557	Montgomery, R.S.O.	Borough of Montgomery.
Pool Lower (*a*) - *div.*	1,743	2,637	8,508	Welshpool -	Borough of Pool.
Pool Middle - - *div.*	2,544	3,557	6,906	do. - -	do.
Pool Upper (*a*) - *div.*	653 { In Pool Middle }	6,959	do. - -	do.
Rhosgoch - - *tow.*	39	1,193	604	do. - -	Caurse.
Trelystan - - *tow.*	81	1,190	1,033	do. - -	do.
Trewern - - *tow.*	358	1,860	3,274	do. - -	Borough of Pool.
Uppington - - *tow.*	85	1,002	1,029	do. - -	Caurse.
COUNTY of SALOP :					
Brompton and Rhiston } *tow.*	164	1,760	2,288	Churchstoke -	Chirbury.
Chirbury - - *par.*	1,477	11,041	13,581	Chirbury - -	do.
Worthin (*a*) - - *tow.*	3,209	13,760	16,334	Worthin - -	do.
TOTAL of UNION -	18,233	87,277	127,461		

FORDINGBRIDGE UNION.

(Formed 30 July 1835 by Order dated 15 July 1835. — Place marked thus * added 29 Sept. 1839 by Order dated 26 July 1839 ; thus † added 25 March 1861 by Order dated 18 March 1861, and its name fixed by Order of 23 Nov. 1868 ; and thus ‡ added 30 Sept. 1861 by Order dated 28 June 1861.)

COUNTY of SOUTHAMPTON :

Unions and Parishes, &c.	Population in 1881.	Area in Statute Acres in 1881.	Rateable Value in 1881.	Post Town.	Petty Sessional Division.
†Ashley Walk - *tow.*	294	8,474	764	Fordingbridge -	Ringwood.
Breamore - - *par.*	560	2,678	4,512	Salisbury - -	do.
Fordingbridge (W.) - *par.*	2,962	6,340	14,690	do. - -	do.
Hale - - *par.*	149	1,378	1,360	do. - -	do.
North Charford - *par.*	104	874	950	do. - -	do.
Rockbourne - *par.*	456	3,886	3,567	do. - -	do.
South Charford - *par.*	86	863	1,114	do. - -	do.
*Woodgreen - - *par.*	293 { In Ashley Walk. }	292	do. - -	do.
COUNTY of WILTS :					
Martin - - *par.*	507	4,566	3,561	do. - -	Salisbury.
South Damerham - *par.*	617	4,681	4,419	do. - -	do.
‡Toyd Farm - with - Allenford } *par.*	22	647	394	do. - -	do.
Whichbury - - *par.*	184	1,824	1,364	do. - -	do.
TOTAL of UNION -	6,234	36,211	36,987		

Unions and Parishes, &c.	Population in 1881.	Area in Statute Acres in 1881.	Rateable Value in 1881.	Post Town.	Petty Sessional Division.

FOREHOE INCORPORATION.

(Under the 16 Geo. 3, c. ix.; 23 Geo. 3, c. xxix.; 29 Geo. 3. c. iv; 54 Geo. 3, c. xliv.; and 3 & 4 Will. 4, c. cvii.)

COUNTY of NORFOLK :

			£		
Barford - - par.	315	1,052	2,612	Wymondham -	Forehoe.
Barnham Broom - par.	442	1,776	3,336	do.	do.
Bawburgh - - par.	419	1,440	2,241	Norwich -	do.
Bowthorpe - - par.	55	645	811	do. -	do.
Brandon Parva - par.	167	979	1,753	Wymondham -	do.
Carleton Forehoe - par.	130	772	1,233	do. -	do.
Colton - - par.	255	911	1,932	Norwich -	do.
Cossey (or Costessey) par.	960	3,040	4,519	do. -	do.
Coston - - par.	48	342	546	Wymondham -	do.
Crownthorpe - - par.	68	696	1,229	do. -	do.
Deopham - - par.	424	1,616	3,414	do. -	do.
Easton (a) - - par.	251	1,576	2,213	Norwich -	do.
Hackford - - par.	199	754	1,478	Wymondham -	do.
Hingham - - par.	1,554	3,649	9,297	Attleborough -	do.
Kimberley - - par.	181	1,460	2,501	Wymondham -	do.
Marlingford (a) - par.	226	674	1,219	Norwich -	do.
Morley Saint Botolph (b) - } par.	283	} 1,834	1,634	Wymondham -	do.
Morley Saint Peter (b) - } par.	135		2,149	do. -	do.
Runhall - - par.	192	834	1,461	do. -	do.
Welborne - - par.	190	732	1,617	East Dereham -	do.
Wicklewood (W.) - par.	730	1,564	3,308	Wymondham -	do.
Wramplingham - par.	181	845	1,724	do. -	do.
Wymondham - par.	4,506	10,613	28,409	do. -	do.
TOTAL of INCORPORATION	11,971	37,834	80,666		

FREEBRIDGE LYNN UNION.

(Formed 16 Nov. 1835 by Order dated 20 Oct. 1835.)

COUNTY of NORFOLK

Ashwicken - - par.	97	1,282	1,681	King's Lynn -	Hundred of Freebridge Lynn.
Babingley - - par.	58	849	1,002	do. -	do.
Bawsey - - par.	70	1,090	736	do. -	do.
Castle Acre - - par.	1,835	3,249	5,819	Swaffham -	do.
Castle Rising - par.	345	2,096	2,251	King's Lynn -	do.
Congham - - par.	331	2,850	3,450	do. -	do.
East Walton - - par.	183	2,659	2,005	do. -	do.
East Winch - - par.	401	2,530	3,732	do. -	do.
Flitcham with Apple-ton - } par.	466	4,200	4,682	do. -	do.
Gayton (W.) - par.	756	3,272	4,842	do. -	do.
Gayton-Thorpe - par.	162	2,355	1,756	do. -	do.
Gaywood - - par.	805	2,212	5,617	do. -	do.
Great Massingham - par.	885	4,112	5,053	Swaffham -	do.
Grimstone - - par.	1,132	4,240	4,591	King's Lynn -	do.
Harpley - - par.	425	2,193	2,958	Swaffham -	do.
Hillington - - par.	285	2,529	2,358	King's Lynn -	do.
Leziate - - par.	205	1,469	1,780	do. -	do.

(continued)

FOREHOE INCORPORATION :

(a) Part of Easton was amalgamated with Marlingford, by Order which came into operation on 25 March 1885.

(b) Certain detached parts of Morley Saint Botolph were amalgamated with Morley Saint Peter, by Order which came into operation on 25 March 1885.

Unions and Parishes, &c.		Population in 1881.	Area in Statute Acres in 1881.	Rateable Value in 1881.	Post Town.	Petty Sessional Division.
FREEBRIDGE LYNN UNION—County of Norfolk—*continued*.				£		
Little Massingham	*par.*	147	2,278	3,188	Swaffham	Hundred of Freebridge Lynn.
Middleton	*par.*	879	3,029	5,707	King's Lynn	do.
Mintlyn	*par.*	41	1,100	1,459	do.	do.
North Runcton	*par.*	242	2,239	2,929	do.	do.
North Wootton	*par.*	324	1,968	3,664	do.	do.
Pentney	*par.*	534	2,330	3,278	Swaffham	do.
Roydon	*par.*	186	1,351	921	King's Lynn	do.
Sanderingham	*par.*	81	1,172	1,206	do.	do.
Setchey	*par.*	118	780	1,815	do.	do.
South Wootton	*par.*	179	1,874	2,297	do.	do.
West Acre with Custhorpe	*par.*	415	3,400	3,437	Swaffham	do.
West Bilney	*par.*	223	2,750	2,635	King's Lynn	do.
West Newton	*par.*	329	1,230	1,583	do.	do.
West Winch	*par.*	408	1,170	2,960	do.	do.
Wolverton	*par.*	185	5,634	3,553	do.	do.
TOTAL of UNION		12,235	78,192	95,245		
FROME UNION.						
(Formed 26 March 1836 by Order dated 5 Feb. 1836. — Place marked thus * added 29 Sept. 1845 by Order dated 28 Aug. 1845.)						
COUNTY of SOMERSET:						
*Babington	*par.*	194	607	1,665	Bath	Kilmersdon.
Beckington (*a*)	*par.*	924	1,830	5,009	do.	Frome.
Berkeley (*a*)	*par.*	322	1,927	3,909	Frome	do.
Buckland Denham	*par.*	441	1,399	3,266	do.	do.
Cloford	*par.*	197	2,243	2,407	do.	do.
Elm (*a*)	*par.*	353	893	2,132	do.	do.
Farleigh Hungerford (*d*)	*par.*	184	901	1,737	Bath	Weston.
Forscote	*par.*	61	580	1,120	do.	Kilmersdon.
Frome (W.) (*a*)	*par.*	11,181	7,092	41,484	Frome	Frome.
Hardington	*par.*	38	831	1,007	do.	Kilmersdon.
Hemington	*par.*	581	3,046	1,130	Bath	do.
Kilmersdon (*a*) (*b*) (*c*)	*par.*	2,323	3,160	10,035	do.	do.
Laverton (*a*)	*par.*	123	1,034	1,771	do.	Frome.
Leigh upon Mendip	*par.*	461	1,125	2,613	do.	do.
Lullington	*par.*	131	687	1,218	Frome	do.
Marston Biggott (*a*)	*par.*	357	2,207	1,035	do.	do.
Mells (*a*)	*par.*	972	3,611	6,710	do.	do.
Norton Saint Philip	*par.*	551	1,527	3,271	Bath	Weston.

(*continued*)

FROME UNION :

(*a*) By Provisional Order which came into operation on 25 March 1885,—
  Detached parts of Berkeley were amalgamated with Beckington and Frome, and a detached part of Frome was amalgamated with Berkeley;
  A detached part of Elm was amalgamated with Whatley;
  A detached part of Laverton was amalgamated with Berkeley;
  A detached part of Marston Biggott was amalgamated with Frome;
  A detached part of Mells was amalgamated with Kilmersdon;
  Detached parts of Road were amalgamated with Woolverton and Tellesford;
  Detached parts of Tellesford were amalgamated with Road and Woolverton;
  Detached parts of Woolverton were amalgamated with Road and Tellesford; and

FROME UNION—*continued*.

The several parts of a Parish known as Standerwick (having in 1881 population 78, acreage 303, rateable value 754*l*.) were amalgamated with adjoining Parishes, namely, Beckington, Berkeley, and Frome.

(*b*) Detached parts of Stratton on the Foss, in the Shepton Mallet Union, were amalgamated with Kilmersdon, and parts of Kilmersdon were amalgamated with Stratton on the Foss, by Orders which came into operation on 25 March 1884 and 25 March 1885.

(*c*) Certain parts of Holcombe, in the Shepton Mallet Union, were amalgamated with Kilmersdon, and certain parts of Kilmersdon were amalgamated with Holcombe, by Order which came into operation on 25 March 1884.

(*d*) A detached part of Farleigh Hungerford were amalgamated with Winkfield with Rowley, in the Bradford (Wilts) Union, by Order which came into operation on 25 March 1885.

T

Unions and Parishes, &c.		Population in 1881.	Area in Statute Acres in 1881.	Rateable Value in 1881.	Post Town.	Petty Sessional Division.
				£		
FROME UNION—County of Somerset—*continued.*						
Nunney	par.	1,018	2,421	5,211	Frome	Frome.
Orchardleigh	par.	41	715	1,553	do.	do.
Road (a)	par.	570	928	3,254	Bath	do.
Rodden	par.	175	990	1,913	Frome	do.
Tellesford (a)	par.	85	757	1,150	Bath	Weston.
Wanstrow	par.	330	2,054	3,108	Frome	Frome.
Whatley (a)	par.	433	1,259	2,904	do.	do.
Witham Friary	par.	482	4,970	6,375	Bath	do.
Woolverton (a)	par.	129	736	1,197	do.	do.
Writhlington	par.	409	772	2,412	do.	Kilmersdon.
TOTAL of UNION		23,072	50,905	127,256		
FULHAM UNION.						
(Formed as the Kensington Union on 11 February 1837 by Order dated 12 January 1837, but certain Parishes having been separated the name of the Union was on 25 March 1845 by Order dated 14 March 1845 changed to the Fulham Union.)						
COUNTY of MIDDLESEX.						
Fulham (W.)	par.	42,900	1,716	190,136	London, W.	Kensington.
Hammersmith	par.	71,939	2,287	355,718	do.	do.
TOTAL of UNION		114,839	4,003	545,854		
FYLDE UNION.						
(Formed 27 Jan. 1837 by Order dated 31 Dec. 1836.)						
COUNTY of LANCASTER:						
Bispham with Norbreck (a)	tow.	714	1,644	5,143	Poulton	Kirkham.
Bryning with Kellamergh	tow.	114	1,061	1,804	Kirkham	do.
Carleton	tow.	377	2,012	5,118	Poulton	do.
Clifton with Salwick	tow.	418	3,189	7,400	Preston	do.
Elswick	tow.	242	1,037	1,732	Poulton	do.
Freckleton	tow.	1,134	2,417	5,652	Kirkham	do.
Greenhalgh with Thirleton	tow.	380	1,897	3,797	do.	do.
Hardhorn with Newton	tow.	120	2,651	7,615	Blackpool	do.
Kirkham (W.)	tow.	3,840	857	9,297	Kirkham	do.
Layton (a)	tow.	12,711	2,359	95,136	Blackpool	do.
Little Eccleston	tow.	197	1,280	1,952	Garstang	do.
Lytham	par.	5,268	5,310	32,654	Lytham	do.
Marton	tow.	2,303	1,707	11,365	Blackpool	do.
Medlar with Wesham	tow.	1,035	1,966	7,826	Kirkham	do.
Newton with Scales	tow.	267	1,523	3,302	Preston	do.
Poulton in the Fylde	tow.	1,225	914	6,168	Poulton	do.
Ribby with Wray	tow.	392	1,387	2,814	Kirkham	do.
Singleton	tow.	357	2,923	5,207	Poulton	do.
Thornton	tow.	7,589	6,387	33,923	Fleetwood	do.
Treales, Roseacre, and Wharles	tow.	560	4,100	7,828	Kirkham	do.
Warton	tow.	408	2,510	3,168	do.	do.
Weeton	tow.	425	2,973	6,646	do.	do.
Westby with Plumptons	tow.	534	3,598	8,506	do.	do.
TOTAL of UNION		40,910	59,032	274,113		

FROME UNION—*continued.*

(a) See note, page 147.

FYLDE UNION:

(a) A detached part of Bispham with Norbreck, known as Bispham Hawes, was amalgamated with Layton, by Order which came into operation on 25 March 1883.

Unions and Parishes, &c.	Population in 1881.	Area in Statute Acres in 1881.	Rateable Value in 1881.	Post Town.	Petty Sessional Division.
GAINSBOROUGH UNION.					
(Formed 19 Jan. 1837 by Order dated 22 Dec. 1836, as amended by Order dated 23 Mar. 1837.— Places marked thus * added 13 April 1837 by Order dated 23 Mar. 1837; and thus † added 25 Dec. 1863 by Order dated 3 Nov. 1863.)					
COUNTY OF LINCOLN :			£		
Blyborough - - *par.*	249	2,345	3,232	Kirton in Lindsey -	Gainsborough.
Blyton cum Warton (*d*) *par.*	705	2,830	6,894	Gainsborough -	do.
Brampton - - *tow.*	97	In Torksey	1,047	Lincoln -	Lincoln.
Burton Gate - *par.*	97	1,108	2,252	Gainsborough -	Gainsborough.
Coates - - *par.*	51	950	1,180	Lincoln -	Lincoln.
Corringham - - *par.*	714	6,279	7,679	Gainsborough -	Gainsborough.
Fenton - - *tow.*	268	3,280	2,059	Newark, Notts. -	Lincoln.
Ferry East (*c*) - *enc.*	146	In Scotton	1,026	Bawtry -	Gainsborough.
Fillingham - *par.*	307	3,980	4,175	Lincoln -	Lincoln.
Gainsborough (W.) - *tow.*	10,979	7,210	38,662	Gainsborough -	Gainsborough.
Gleutworth - *par.*	368	3,043	3,718	Lincoln -	Lincoln.
Grayingham - *par.*	167	1,675	2,265	Kirton in Lindsey -	Gainsborough.
†Greenhill and Redhill *par.*	26	250	685	Gainsborough -	do.
Harpswell - - *par.*	125	2,180	2,609	Kirton in Lindsey -	Gainsborough.
Harwick - - *tow.*	79	In Torksey	1,702	Lincoln -	Lincoln.
*Haxey (*c*) (*d*) - *par.*	1,982	8,470	12,512	Bawtry -	Epworth.
Heapham - - *par.*	141	1,250	1,449	Gainsborough -	Gainsborough.
Hemswell - - *par.*	373	2,890	3,533	Kirton in Lindsey -	do.
Kettlethorpe (*b*) - *tow.*	240	In Fenton	2,120	Newark -	Lincoln.
Kexby - - *tow.*	324	3,180	2,025	Gainsborough -	Gainsborough.
Knaith (*a*) - - *par.*	88	1,640	2,660	do. -	do.
Laughton - - *tow.*	295	4,598	3,643	do. -	do.
Lea - - *par.*	186	2,149	4,605	do. -	do.
Marton - - *par.*	439	1,310	3,100	do. -	do.
Morton - - *tow.*	917 { In Gainsborough }		2,552	do. -	do.
Newton on Trent - *par.*	313	1,390	2,676	Newark -	Lincoln.
Northorpe - - *par.*	182	1,816	3,722	Kirton in Lindsey -	Kirton in Lindsey.
*Owston with Kelfield (*c*) } *tow.*	1,322	5,350	7,625	Bawtry -	Epworth.
Pilham (*d*) - - *par.*	97	1,100	1,273	Gainsborough -	Gainsborough.
Scottar (*c*) - *par.*	1,070	4,630	7,182	Kirton in Lindsey -	do.
Scotton (*c*) - *tow.*	260	4,920	3,404	do. -	do.
Southorpe - - *par.*	39	590	1,080	do. -	do.
Springthorpe - *par.*	214	1,072	1,547	Gainsborough -	do.
Stockwith East - *tow.*	324 { In Gainsborough }		1,271	do. -	do.
Stowe - - *tow.*	361 } 4,620 {		4,101	Lincoln -	Lincoln.
Sturton and Bransby *tow.*	646		3,111	do. -	do.
Torksey - - *tow.*	160	3,170	2,352	do. -	do.
Upton (*a*) - - *tow.*	238	In Kexby	2,067	Gainsborough -	Gainsborough.
Walkerith - - *tow.*	87 { In Gainsborough }		626	do. -	do.
*West Butterwick (*d*) *tow.*	718 { In Owston with Kelfield }		4,286	Doncaster -	Epworth.
Wildsworth - *ham.*	130 { In Laughton }		1,550	Gainsborough -	Gainsborough.
Willingham - *par.*	460	2,170	3,038	do. -	do.
Willoughton - *par.*	520	2,460	3,420	Kirton in Lindsey -	do.

(*continued*)

GAINSBOROUGH UNION :

(*a*) A detached part of Knaith was amalgamated with Upton, by Order which came into operation on 25 March 1884.

(*b*) A part of Laneham, in the East Retford Union, was amalgamated with Kettlethorpe, by Order which came into operation on 25 March 1884.

(*c*) By Orders which came into operation on 25 March 1885,—

Detached parts of Scotton were amalgamated with Scottar ;

All the parts of Owston with Kelfield situate on the east side of the River Trent were amalgamated with Ferry East ; and

GAINSBOROUGH UNION—*continued*.

A detached part of Epworth, in the Thorne Union was amalgamated with Haxey.

(*d*) By Orders which came into operation on 25 March 1886,—

A detached part of West Butterwick was amalgamated with Haxey ;

A detached part of Pilham was amalgamated with Blyton cum Warton ; and

A detached part of West Butterwick was amalgamated with Sturton, in the East Retford Union.

Unions and Parishes, &c.		Population in 1881.	Area in Statute Acres in 1881.	Rateable Value in 1881.	Post Town.	Petty Sessional Division.

GAINSBOROUGH UNION—continued.

COUNTY of NOTTINGHAM:

				£		
Beckingham	par.	448	3,010	5,085	Gainsborough -	East Retford.
Bole	par.	208	1,250	3,032	do.	do.
Misterton	tow.	1,218	5,420	8,055	do. -	do.
Saunby	par.	113	1,373	2,744	do. - -	do.
Stockwith West	tow.	662 { In Misterton }	1,779	do. - -	do.
Walkeringham	par.	709	3,000	5,763	do. - -	do.
West Burton (d)	par.	56	710	2,263	Lincoln - -	do.
TOTAL of UNION -		**29,948**	**108,668**	**200,376**		

GARSTANG UNION.
(Formed 31 Jan. 1837 by Order dated 31 Dec. 1836.)

COUNTY of LANCASTER:

Barnacre with Bonds (W.) (a)	tow.	912	4,495	13,102	Garstang - -	Garstang.
Bilborough	tow.	197	852	2,566	do. -	do.
Bleasdale	tow.	410	7,298	3,755	do. -	do.
Cabus (a)	tow.	178	1,388	2,835	do. -	do.
Catteral (a)	tow.	612	1,742	4,385	do. -	do.
Claughton	tow.	548	3,786	7,664	do	do.
Clevely (a)	tow.	51	620	3,165	do. -	do.
Forton	tow.	595	1,279	2,722	do. -	do.
Garstang (a)	tow.	783	503	2,540	do. -	de.
Great Eccleston	tow.	628	1,469	3,183	do. -	do.
Hambleton	tow.	389	1,553	2,853	Poulton le Fylde	do.
Holleth	tow.	50	358	504	Garstang -	do.
Kirkland	tow.	314	974	2,150	do. -	do.
Myerscough	tow.	384	2,707	6,509	Preston -	do.
Nateby	tow.	393	2,087	3,601	Garstang -	do.
Nether Wyersdale (a)	tow.	606	1,215	6,272	do. -	do.
Out Rawcliffe	tow.	815	4,593	6,911	do. -	do.
Pilling (a)	tow.	1,620	6,060	9,390	Fleetwood -	do.
Preesall with Hackensall	tow.	848	3,393	6,199	Poulton le Fylde	do.
Sowerby with Inskip	tow.	542	2,979	1,525	Garstang -	do.
Stalmin with Stainall	tow.	501	2,583	4,450	Poulton le Fylde	do.
Upper Rawcliffe with Tarnacar	tow.	618	3,839	6,267	Garstang -	do.
Winmarleigh	tow.	381	2,342	3,239	do. -	do.
TOTAL of UNION -		**12,375**	**61,115**	**108,517**		

GATESHEAD UNION.
(Formed 12 Dec. 1836 by Order dated 15 Nov. 1836.)

COUNTY of DURHAM:

Chopwell	tow.	1,614	3,846	7,622	Lintz Green, Newcastle on Tyne	East Chester Ward.
Crawcrook	tow.	450	1,136	6,092	Ryton on Tyne -	do.
Gateshead (W.)	par.	65,041	3,011	219,919	Gateshead on Tyne	Borough of Gateshead.
Heworth	tow.	17,138	2,811	62,701	Newcastle on Tyne	East Chester Ward.
Ryton	tow.	3,036	1,201	11,571	Ryton on Tyne -	do.
Ryton Woodside	tow.	1,082	2,813	6,506	do. -	do.
Stella	tow.	743	286	2,451	Blaydon on Tyne -	do.
Whickham	par.	7,976	5,961	29,277	Whickham - -	do.
Winlaton	tow.	8,330	5,217	29,375	Blaydon on Tyne -	do.
TOTAL of UNION -		**105,410**	**26,282**	**378,544**		

GAINSBOROUGH UNION:

(d) *See note page 149.*

GARSTANG UNION:

(a) By Orders which came into operation on 25 March 1887,—
Certain parts of Barnacre with Bonds were amalgamated with Cabus and Garstang respectively;
A nearly detached part of Cabus was amalgamated with Garstang;

GARSTANG UNION—continued.

A detached part of Catteral was amalgamated with Barnacre with Bonds;
A detached part of Clevely was amalgamated with Nether Wyersdale;
Certain parts of Garstang were amalgamated with Barnacre with Bonds;
A detached part of Pilling was amalgamated with Cockersand Abbey in the Lancaster Union; and
A certain part of Eskel North and South, in the Lancaster Union, was amalgamated with Nether Wyersdale.

GLANFORD BRIGG UNION.

(Formed 18 Jan. 1837 by Order dated 22 Dec. 1836 as amended by Order dated 11 March 1861.—Places marked thus * added 30 Mar. 1837 by Order dated 15 Mar. 1837 ; and thus † added 25 Dec. 1861 by Order dated 18 Oct. 1861.)

COUNTY of LINCOLN :

Unions and Parishes, &c.		Population in 1881.	Area in Statute Acres in 1881.	Rateable Value in 1881. £	Post Town.	Petty Sessional Division.
Appleby	tow.	514	6,164	9,249	Doncaster	Winterton.
Ashby	tow.	1,462	7,470	3,861	Brigg	do.
Aulkborough	par.	399	2,875	3,936	Doncaster	do.
Barnetby le Wold	par.	849	1,630	7,240	Ulceby	Brigg.
Barrow	par.	2,711	5,990	12,762	Hull	Barton.
Barton-upon-Humber (a)	} par.	5,339	8,140	21,205	Barton on Humber	do.
Bonby	par.	406	2,410	4,182	do.	do.
Bottesford (a)	tow.	292	In Ashby	2,476	Brigg	Winterton.
Bromby	tow.	203 {	In Scunthorpe }	18,844	do.	do.
Broughton	par.	1,308	6,918	8,373	do.	Brigg.
Burringham	tow.	542	In Ashby	3,131	Doncaster	Winterton.
Burton-upon-Stather(a)	par.	971	3,860	5,474	do.	do.
Cadney cum Housham (a)	} par.	449	4,860	5,200	Brigg	Brigg.
Cleatham	tow.	114	In Manton	1,634	Kirton in Lindsey	Gainsborough.
Crosby (a)	tow.	304 {	In Scunthorpe }	8,370	Doncaster	Winterton.
Croxton	par.	120	1,630	3,681	Ulceby	Brigg.
East Butterwick (a)	tow.	316	680	1,893	Doncaster	Winterton.
East Halton	par.	647	5,190	4,269	Ulceby	Barton.
Elsham	par.	502	4,110	6,180	Brigg	Brigg.
Flixborough	tow.	229	2,650	2,752	Doncaster	Winterton.
Frodingham	tow.	1,663 {	In Scunthorpe }	22,589	do.	do.
Glanford Brigg	tow.	1,657	In Wrawby	3,962	Brigg	Brigg.
Goxhill	par.	1,181	8,790	9,360	Hull	Barton.
*Gunhouse	tow.	164 {	In West Halton }	1,078	Doncaster	Winterton.
Hibaldstow	par.	800	4,390	7,815	Kirton in Lindsey	Brigg.
Holm	tow.	72	In Ashby	779	Brigg	Winterton.
Horkstow	par.	274	2,085	3,697	Barton on Humber	Barton.
Kirmington	par.	401	1,815	3,242	do.	Brigg.
Kirton in Lindsey	par.	1,851	4,210	11,319	Kirton in Lindsey	Gainsborough.
Manton	tow.	139	1,630	1,097	do.	Winterton.
Melton Ross	par.	176	1,755	4,835	Ulceby	Brigg.
Messingham (a)	tow.	1,132	5,150	7,511	Kirton in Lindsey	Winterton.
†Newsteud	par.	59 {	In Cadney cum Housham }	588	Brigg	Brigg.
North Killingholme	tow.	225	7,225	2,918	Ulceby	Barton.
*Raventhorpe	ham.	26	In Appleby	494	Brigg	Winterton.
Redbourn	par.	367	3,919	4,588	Kirton in Lindsey	Brigg.
Roxby with Risby	par.	417	4,784	5,970	Doncaster	Winterton.
Saxby	par.	327	2,322	3,378	Barton on Humber	Barton.
Scawby with Sturton(a)	par.	1,519	3,930	8,134	Brigg	Brigg.
Scunthorpe	tow.	2,048	5,770	20,597	Doncaster	Winterton.
South Ferraby	par.	733	3,245	3,648	Barton on Humber	Barton.
South Killingholme (a)	tow.	549 {	In N. Killingholme }	3,757	Ulceby	do.
Thornton Curtis	par.	471	4,610	7,764	do.	do.
Twigmore	tow.	56	In Manton	780	Brigg	Winterton.
Ulceby	par.	961	3,790	7,352	Ulceby	Barton.
West Halton (a)	tow.	266	4,870	3,881	Doncaster	Winterton.
Whitton	par.	201	2,440	1,891	do.	do.
Winteringham	par.	671	5,675	5,642	do.	do.
Winterton	par.	1,601	3,628	7,327	do.	do.
Wootton	par.	580	2,980	5,125	Ulceby	Barton.
Worlaby	par.	500	2,910	6,608	Brigg	Brigg.

Unions and Parishes, &c.	Population in 1881.	Area in Statute Acres in 1881.	Rateable Value in 1881.	Post Town.	Petty Sessional Division.

GLENDALE UNION.

(Formed 18 Nov. 1836 by Order dated 22 Oct. 1836.—Names of Places marked thus * are as altered by Order dated 5 April 1886.)

COUNTY OF NORTHUMBERLAND :

Unions and Parishes, &c.	Population in 1881.	Area in Statute Acres in 1881.	Rateable Value in 1881. £	Post Town.	Petty Sessional Division.
Akeld - - - *tow.*	141	2,268	2,046	Wooler - -	Glendale Ward.
Brandon - - *tow.*	78	1,087	1,699	Alnwick - -	Coquetdale Ward, North Division.
Branxton - - *par.*	221	1,508	2,505	Coldstream - -	do.
Branton - - *tow.*	84	1,175	1,480	Alnwick - -	Glendale Ward.
Carham - - *par.*	1,125	10,712	20,791	Coldstream -	do.
Chatton - - *par.*	1,302	17,335	16,183	Belford -	do.
Chillingham - *tow.*	138	1,765	2,086	do. -	do.
*Coldsmouth and Thompsons Walls - } *tow.*	15	1,340	1,004	Coldstream -	do.
Coupland - - *tow.*	114	1,542	1,881	Wooler -	do.
Crookhouse - - *tow.*	21	480	435	do. -	do.
Doddington - - *tow.*	302	4,917	3,906	do. -	do.
Earl - - *tow.*	60	1,235	1,327	do. -	do.
East Lilburne - *tow.*	72	911	1,294	Alnwick -	do.
Ewart - - *tow.*	69	1,503	2,091	Wooler -	do.
*Fawdon and Clinch (a) *tow.*	47	2,110	1,372	Alnwick -	Coquetdale Ward, North Division.
Ford - - *par.*	1,584	11,727	18,163	Coldstream -	Glendale Ward.
Greys Forest - *tow.*	42	6,585	1,733	Wooler -	do.
Hebburn - - *tow.*	127	2,106	1,661	Alnwick -	do.
Hetchpool - - *tow.*	14	1,124	674	Wooler -	do.
Howtell - - *tow.*	118	1,163	1,844	Coldstream -	do.
Humbleton - - *tow.*	129	1,615	1,513	Wooler -	do.
Ilderton (a) - *tow.*	118	4,666	2,497	Alnwick -	do.
*Ingram, Linhope, Greenshawhill, and Hartside (a.) - } *tow.*	65	6,523	2,707	do. -	Coquetdale Ward, North Division.
Kilham - - *tow.*	156	2,870	2,530	Coldstream -	Glendale.
Kirknewton - *tow.*	82	2,026	1,592	Wooler -	do.
Lanton - - *tow.*	68	974	1,468	do. -	do.
Lowick - - *par.*	1,513	12,878	12,016	Beal -	do.
Middleton Hall - *tow.*	48	1,101	813	Wooler -	do.
Milfield - - *tow.*	176	1,510	2,415	do. -	do.
Nesbit (a) - - *tow.*	82	770	1,105	do. -	do.
New Bewick - *tow.*	85	1,140	1,319	Alnwick -	Coquetdale Ward.
Newton - - *tow.*	69	1,132	1,544	Belford -	Glendale Ward.
North Middleton - *tow.*	114	2,082	1,410	Alnwick -	do.
Old Bewick - *tow.*	159	5,519	2,183	do. -	Coquetdale Ward, North Division.
Paston - - *tow.*	172	2,355	2,858	Coldstream -	Glendale Ward.
Reavely - - *tow.*	53	2,310	1,048	Alnwick -	Coquetdale Ward, North Division.
Roddam - - *tow.*	83	1,201	855	do. -	Glendale Ward.
Rosedon (a) - *tow.*	64	1,565	1,519	do. -	do.
Selbys Forest - *tow.*	40	11,498	1,993	Wooler -	do.
South Middleton - *tow.*	49	1,611	1,221	Alnwick -	do.
West Lilburne - *tow.*	217	2,003	2,513	do. -	do.
Westnewton - *tow.*	56	1,119	1,195	Wooler -	do.
Wooler (W.) (a) *par.*	1,529	4,917	8,416	do. -	Coquetdale Ward, North Division.
Wooperton - *tow.*	88	930	1,061	Alnwick -	Glendale Ward.
Yeavering - *tow.*	44	868	781	Wooler -	
TOTAL OF UNION - -	10,933	147,809 (b)	142,180		

GLENDALE UNION :

(a) By Orders which came into operation on 25 March 1884,—

 A detached part of Fawdon, &c., known as Hartside, was amalgamated with Ingram, &c.;

 A detached part of Rosedon, known as "Flint Hill," was amalgamated with Ilderton; and

 A detached part of Wooler, known as Fenton, was amalgamated with Nesbit.

(b) There is an undivided Moor comprised in this Union, common to Lanton and Kirknewton, containing 7 acres.

Unions and Parishes, &c.	Population in 1881.	Area in Statute Acres in 1881.	Rateable Value in 1881.	Post Town.	Petty Sessional Division.

GLOSSOP UNION.

(Formed 5 Dec. 1837 by Order dated 7 Nov. 1837.)

COUNTY of DERBY :

			£		
Glossop, including Glossop Dale, Charlesworth, Chunal, Hadfield and Dinting, Padfield, Simondley, and Whitfield (W.) } *tow.*	21,393	18,432	63,931	Manchester	Glossop, Hundred of High Peak.
Ludworth and Chisworth } *tow.*	2,157	2,511	5,860	Stockport	do.
TOTAL of UNION	23,550	20,943	69,791		

GLOUCESTER UNION.

(Formed 30 April 1835 by Order dated 13 April 1835.—Places marked thus * added 14 Dec. 1835 by Order dated 19 Nov. 1835 ; thus † added 24 June 1859 by Order dated 4 May 1859 ; and thus ‡ added 26 March 1885 by Order dated 20 March 1885.— Names of Places marked thus § are as altered by Order dated 5 Feb. 1887.)

COUNTY of GLOUCESTER :

*Ashleworth - *par.*	501	1,710	3,659	Gloucester	Gloucester County.
Barnwood (e) - *par.*	761	1,471	5,561	do.	Gloucester.
*Brockworth - *par.*	445	1,847	3,151	do.	do.
Churchdown (e) - *par.*	686	4,076	6,763	do.	do.
Down Hatherly (e) - *par.*	193	930	2,114	do.	do.
Elmore (b) (e) - *par.*	352	1,486	2,573	do.	do.
Hempstead (e) - *par.*	714 { In South Hamlet }		6,726	do.	do.
Hucclecot - *ham.*	453 { In Churchdown }		3,442	do.	do.
Lassington - *par.*	62	535	978	do.	do.
‡Longford (e) - *par.*	—	—	—	do.	do.
Maismore (e) - *par.*	491	1,930	4,507	do.	do.
Matson (e) - *par.*	73	450	992	do.	do.
Norton - *par.*	429	1,870	3,220	do.	do.
Over Higham and Linton (a) (e) - } *ham.*	339	2,004	5,257	do.	do.
†Prinknash Park - *par.*	22	300	345	do.	do.
Quedgley (d) (e) - *par.*	474	1,453	5,564	do.	County of Gloucester (Wheatenhurst).
Sandhurst (e) - *par.*	462	2,227	4,788	do.	Gloucester.
Tuffley (e) - *ham.*	256 { In Barton St. Mary }		4,561	do.	do. *(continued)*

GLOUCESTER UNION :

(a) A detached part of Rudford, in the Newent Union, was amalgamated with Over Higham and Linton, by Order which came into operation on 25 March 1883.

(b) Detached parts of Minsterworth, in the Westbury Union, were amalgamated with Elmore, by Orders which came into operation on 25 March 1884.

(c) Detached parts of Hardwicke, in the Wheatenhurst Union, were amalgamated with Elmore, by Order which came into operation on 25 March 1884.

(d) Certain parts of Harescomb and Haresfield, in the Wheatenhurst Union, and Quedgley and Whaddon were amalgamated with Brockthrop, in that Union, and certain parts of Brockthrop, Haresfield, and Whaddon were amalgamated with Harescomb, by Provisional Order which came into operation on 25 March 1885.

(e) By Provisional Order which came into operation on 25 March 1885, alterations were made in the areas of the Parishes and Places of Barnwood, Churchdown, Down Hatherly, Hempstead, Maismore, Matson, North Hamlet, Quedgley, Saint Catherine's, Saint John Baptist, Saint Mary de Lode with Kingsholm Saint Mary, Saint Nicholas, Sand-

GLOUCESTER UNION—*continued.*

hurst, South Hamlet, Upton Saint Leonard's, Ville of Wotton, Whaddon, Over Higham and Linton, Barton Saint Mary, Barton Saint Michael, Longford Saint Catherine's, Longford Saint Mary, Tuffley, Twigworth, and Wootton Saint Mary.

By the operation of this Order, the new Parishes of Longford and Wotton Saint Mary (Without) were constituted, and the undermentioned Places were absorbed:—

	Population in 1881.	Area in 1881.	Rateable Value in 1881.
			£
Barton Saint Michael	3,338	500	6,661
Longford Saint Catherine's	335	200	2,082
Longford Saint Mary -	441 { In Wootton Saint Mary. }		2,077
North Hamlet -	509	do.	1,989
Ville of Wotton -	541	do.	1,021

Unions and Parishes, &c.	Population in 1881.	Area in Statute Acres in 1881.	Rateable Value in 1881.	Post Town.	Petty Sessional Division.

GLOUCESTER UNION—County of Gloucester—*continued*.

			£		
Twigworth - *ham.*	182 {In Wootton St. Mary}		1,313	Gloucester - -	Gloucester.
Upton Saint Leonard's (e) - } *par.*	1,430	2,975	6,752	do.	do.
Whaddon (d) (e) - *par.*	111	727	2,403	do. - -	do.
‡Wotton Saint Mary (Without) (e) - } *par.*	—	—	—	do. - -	do.

CITY of GLOUCESTER and COUNTY of the same CITY :

Barton, Saint Mary (e) *ham.*	10,480	1,470	23,241	do. - -	do.
Littleworth - *par.*	557	30	2,053	do. - -	County of Gloucester.
†Pool Meadow - *par.*	185 {In St. John Baptist}		421	do. - -	Gloucester.
Saint Aldate's - *par.*	708 {In St. John Baptist}		1,664	do. - -	do.
§Saint Catherine's (e) - *par.*	2,600 {In St. John Baptist}		10,135	do. - -	do.
Saint John Baptist (e) *par.*	3,694	680	9,948	do. - -	do.
Saint Mary de Crypt *par.*	879 {In St. John Baptist}		6,306	do. - -	do.
Saint Mary de Grace *par.*	175 {In St. John Baptist}		1,672	do. - -	do.
§Saint Mary de Lode (e) - } *par.*	2,231 {In St. John Baptist}		4,774	do. - -	
Saint Michael - *par.*	1,312 {In St. John Baptist}		8,194	do. - -	do.
Saint Owen - *par.*	623 {In St. John Baptist}		6,588	do. - -	do.
South Hamlet (e) - *par.*	3,521	1,311	18,204	do. - -	
The Holy Trinity - *par.*	493 {In St. John Baptist}		3,100	do. - -	do.

CITY of GLOUCESTER and COUNTY of the same CITY, and COUNTY of GLOUCESTER :

Saint Nicholas (e) - *par.*	2,833 {In St. John Baptist}		6,717	do. - -	do.
WoottonSaintMary(W.)*ham.*	2,969	2,040	9,150	do. - -	do.
TOTAL of UNION -	41,696 (e)	31,522 (e)	186,836 (e)		

GODSTONE UNION.

(Formed 31 Oct. 1835 by Order dated 7 Oct. 1835.)

COUNTY of SURREY :

Bletchingly (W.) - *par.*	1,856	5,621	11,159	Redhill - -	Godstone.
Catterham - *par.*	6,259	2,438	24,636	Caterham -	do.
Chelsham - *par.*	448	3,357	2,405	Croydon -	do.
Crowhurst - *par.*	426	2,119	3,053	East Grinstead -	do.
Farleigh - *par.*	88	1,051	740	Warlingham R.S.O.	do.
Godstone - *par.*	2,548	6,830	11,917	Redhill - -	do.
Horne - *par.*	698	4,594	3,768	East Grinstead -	do.
Limpsfield - *par.*	1,359	4,673	6,149	Redhill - -	do.
Oxted - *par.*	1,727	3,659	7,364	do. - -	do.
Tandridge - *par.*	605	3,928	5,365	do. - -	do.
Tatsfield - *par.*	168	1,304	953	Westerham -	do.
Titsey - *par.*	231	1,989	1,729	Redhill - -	do.
Warlingham *par.*	1,147	1,703	3,098	Warlingham R.S.O.	do.
Woldingham *par.*	132	684	511	Caterham Valley -	do.
TOTAL of UNION -	17,692	43,950	82,847		

GLOUCESTER UNION :
(d) (e) See notes page 155.

Unions and Parishes, &c.	Population in 1881.	Area in Statute Acres in 1881.	Rateable Value in 1881.	Post Town.	Petty Sessional Division.
GOOLE UNION.					
(Formed 24 Oct. 1837 by Order dated 29 Sept. 1837, as amended by the Snaith and Cowick Township Act, 1850 (13 & 14 Vict., cap. xlviii.)					
COUNTY of LINCOLN:			£		
Gowthorpe or Garthorpe (*r*) *tow.*	529	1,380	2,887	Goole -	Western Division of the Hundred of Manby, Parts of Lindsey.
Luddington (*c*) - *tow.*	628	2,300	3,650	do. - -	do.
COUNTY of YORK, WEST RIDING:					
Adlingfleet - - *tow.*	195	1,848	2,382	Goole - -	Lower Osgoldcross.
Armin - - - *tow.*	493	3,707	8,000	do. - -	do.
Eastoft (*a*) - - *tow.*	85	1,439	2,267	do. - -	do.
Fockerby (*a*) - *tow.*	81	910	1,451	do. - -	do.
Goole - - - *tow.*	4,823	4,838	18,257	do. - -	do.
Gowdall - - *tow.*	203	1,210	2,059	Selby - -	do.
Haldenby (*a*) - *tow.*	91	1,419	2,349	Goole - -	do.
Hook (W.) - *tow.*	6,364	2,001	16,749	Hook, R.S.O., Yorks	do.
Ousefleet - *tow.*	210	2,885	3,186	Goole - -	do.
Pollington - *tow.*	387	1,920	2,386	Selby - -	do.
Rawcliffe (*a*) - *tow.*	1,650	4,668	9,216	do. - -	do.
Snaith and Cowick (*a*) *tow.*	1,730	5,862	10,199	do. - -	do.
Swinefleet and Reedness (*b*) - *tow.*	(*b*) 1,727	5,555	9,669	Goole - -	do.
Whitgift - - *tow.*	362	1,501	2,357	do. - -	do.
TOTAL of UNION -	19,558	13,443	97,154		
GOWER UNION.					
(Formed 29 Sept. 1857 by Order dated 5 Sept. 1857.)					
COUNTY of GLAMORGAN:					
Bishopston - - *par.*	560	2,595	2,843	Swansea - -	Gower.
Cheriton - - *par.*	173	1,400	956	do. - -	do.
Ilston - - - *par.*	278	3,109	1,657	do. - -	do.
Knelston - - *par.*	94	548	506	do. - -	do.
Llandewy - - *par.*	108	2,010	1,198	do. - -	do.
Llangennith - *par.*	292	3,367	2,079	do. - -	do.
Llanmadock - *par.*	158	1,514	801	do. - -	do.
Llanrhidian Higher - *ham.*	3,226	4,709	6,697	do. - -	Swansea.
Llanrhidian Lower - *ham.*	474	5,592	2,888	do. - -	Gower.
Nicholaston - *par.*	75	488	420	do. - -	do.
Oxwich - *par.*	229	1,265	822	do. - -	do.
Oystermouth - *par.*	3,915	2,096	13,820	do. - -	Swansea.
Penmaen (W.) - *par.*	121	994	876	do. - -	Gower.
Pennard - - *par.*	269	2,855	2,003	do. - -	do.
Penrice - - *par.*	260	2,124	1,539	do. - -	do.
Port Eynon - *par.*	229	1,139	788	do. - -	do.
Reynoldson - *par.*	309	1,069	1,358	do. - -	do.
Rhoscilly - *par.*	332	2,707	1,165	do. - -	do.
TOTAL of UNION -	11,102	*40,481	42,436		

GOOLE UNION:

(*a*) By Order which came into operation on 25 March 1884,—

A detached part of Eastoft known as " Lover's Ground" was amalgamated with Thorne, in the Thorne Union;

A detached part of Fockerby was amalgamated with Haldenby; and

A detached part of Rawcliffe was amalgamated with Snaith and Cowick.

(*b*) All the parts of a township known as Swinefleet, were amalgamated with a township known as Reedness, by

‡ R 9372.

GOOLE UNION—*continued.*

Order which came into operation on 25 March 1884, the township to be designated Swinefleet and Reedness.

(*r*) Detached parts of Luddington were amalgamated one with Garthorpe, and one with Amcots in the Thorne Union, by Order which came into operation on 25 March 1885.

GOWER UNION:

* There is also a piece of land known as Cefn-y-bryn, common to Llanrhidian, Penmaen, Reynoldston, Nicholaston, and Penrice, containing 258 acres.

Unions and Parishes, &c.		Population in 1881.	Area in Statute Acres in 1881.	Rateable Value in 1881.	Post Town.		Petty Sessional Division.

GRANTHAM UNION.

(Formed 14 Jan. 1836 by Order dated 31 Dec. 1835.—Places marked thus * added 25 Dec. 1861 by Order dated 25 Nov. 1861, and thus † added 25 Mar. 1865 by Order dated 9 Mar. 1865.)

COUNTY of LEICESTER :

				£			
*Belvoir	- par.	141	170	1,614	Grantham	-	Belvoir.
Bottersford	- par.	1,331	5,010	10,970	Nottingham	-	do.
Croxton Kerial	- par.	548	3,900	4,219	Grantham	-	do.
Harston	- par.	165	1,009	1,497	do.	-	do.
Knipton	- par.	327	1,430	2,106	do.	-	do.
Muston	- par.	312	1,623	2,047	Nottingham	-	do.
Redmile	- par.	489	1,170	2,956	do.	-	do.

COUNTY of LINCOLN :

Ancaster	- par.	650	2,800	4,655	do.	-	Sleaford.
Barrowby	- par.	807	4,462	9,011	do.	-	Grantham County.
Basingthorpe	- par.	136	1,790	4,877	do.	-	do.
Belton	- par.	183	1,709	3,431	do.	-	do.
Bitchfield	- par.	167	1,344	1,904	do.	-	do.
Boothby Paguell	- par.	130	1,794	2,262	do.	-	do.
Braceby	- par.	115	903	1,257	Folkingham	-	do.
Burton Coggles	- par.	257	2,676	7,303	Grantham	-	Bourn.
Carlton Scroope	- par.	227	1,342	2,590	do.	-	Grantham County.
Colsterworth	- par.	986	3,000	5,312	do.	-	do.
Denton	- par.	547	2,600	4,484	do.	-	do.
Easton	- tow.	219	3,360	2,314	do.	-	do.
Grantham	- tow.	6,080 {	In Spittlegate }	17,924	do.	-	Grantham Borough.
†Grantham Grange	- par.	—	10	315	do.	-	do.
Great Gonerby	- par.	1,202	2,230	8,803	do.	-	Grantham County.
Great Ponton	- par.	477	2,930	6,817	do.	-	do.
Gunby (a)	- par.	110	666	1,096	do.	-	do.
Haceby	- par.	53	705	963	Folkingham	-	Sleaford.
Harlaxton	- par.	383	2,530	4,380	Grantham	-	Grantham County.
Harrowby	- tow.	336 {	In Spittlegate }	3,409	do.	- {	Grantham County and Borough.
Haydor	- tow.	363	3,140	3,576	do.	-	Sleaford.
Honington	- tow.	177	1,454	2,891	do.	-	Grantham County.
Hough on the Hill	- par.	619	3,600	6,651	do.	-	do.
Humby (a)	- ham.	104	In Ropsley	1,001	do.	-	do.
Ingoldsby	- par.	365	2,237	3,425	do.	-	do.
Kiesby	- tow.	62 {	In Lavington }	1,402	Bourn	-	Bourn.
Lavington or Lenton	tow.	178	4,193	2,489	Grantham	-	do.
Little Ponton	- par.	229	1,490	5,803	do.	-	Grantham County.
Londonthorpe	- par.	183	1,520	2,378	do.	-	do.
Manthorpe cum Little Gonerby	- tow.	3,567 {	In Spittlegate }	12,246	do.	- {	Grantham County and Borough.
Normanton	- par.	143	1,540	2,307	do.	-	Grantham County.
North Stoke	- tow.	156	1,910	3,437	do.	-	do.
North Witham (a)	- par.	238	2,373	2,781	do.	-	do.
Osgodby	- tow.	61 {	In Lavington }	1,365	Bourn	-	Bourn.
Pickworth	- par.	227	1,173	2,000	Folkingham	-	do.
Ropsley	- tow.	647	3,740	4,231	Grantham	-	Grantham County.
Sapperton	- par.	40	656	941	Folkingham	-	do.
Skillington	- par.	393	2,140	2,901	Grantham	-	do.
Somerby (a)	- par.	1,189	2,990	5,666	do.	-	Grantham County and Borough.
South Stoke	- tow.	134	In Easton	1,574	do.	-	Grantham County.
South Witham	- par.	410	3,230	2,446	do.	-	Bourn.
Spittlegate (W.)	- tow.	6,459	5,560	22,000	do.	-	Grantham County and Borough.
Stainby	- par.	163	1,550	2,166	do.	-	Grantham County.
							(continued)

GRANTHAM UNION :

(a) By Orders which came into operation on 25 March, 1887,—

'887.'
A detached part of North Witham was amalgamated with Gunby ;

GRANTHAM UNION—continued.

Detached parts of Somerby were amalgamated respectively with Ropsley and Little Humby, the name of the latter being changed to Humby.

Unions and Parishes, &c.	Population in 1881.	Area in Statute Acres in 1881.	Rateable Value in 1881.	Post Town.	Petty Sessional Division.
GRANTHAM UNION—County of Lincoln—*continued.*			*£*		
Stroxton - - *par.*	100	970	1,489	Grantham - -	Grantham County.
Welby - - *par.*	390	2,740	3,358	do. - -	do.
Woolsthorpe - - *par.*	598	2,600	3,261	do. - -	do.
Wyville cum Hungerton - }*par.*	116	1,670	1,799	do. - -	do.
TOTAL of UNION -	33,679	103,939	224,900		
GRAVESEND AND MILTON UNION.					
(Formed 9 Sept. 1835 by an Order dated 25 Aug. 1835.)					
COUNTY of KENT :					
Gravesend (W.) - *par.*	8,416	564	36,248	Gravesend -	Gravesend.
Milton - - *par.*	14,886	692	53,316	do. -	do.
TOTAL of UNION -	23,302	1,256	89,564		
GREAT OUSEBURN UNION.					
(Formed 8 June 1854 by Order dated 24 May 1854, as amended by Order dated 2 June 1854, and Places marked thus * added 11 September 1856 by Order of same date, and thus † added 21 June 1869 by Order dated 31 May 1869.)					
COUNTY of YORK, NORTH RIDING :					
Ellenthorpe - - *tow.*	68	611	1,150	Helperby, York -	Bulmer.
Helperby - - *tow.*	639	1,894	4,235	York - -	do.
Kirby Hill - - *tow.*	158	1,213	2,490	Boroughbridge -	Hallikeld.
Langthorpe - - *tow.*	341	1,026	2,635	do. - -	do.
Norton-le-Clay - *tow.*	100	1,092	1,870	do. - -	do.
Shipton - - *tow.*	430	2,009	6,404	York - -	Bulmer.
Thornton Bridge - *tow.*	55	1,091	1,590	Boroughbridge -	Hallikeld.
Tollerton - - *tow.*	512	2,109	8,348	Easingwold -	Bulmer.
Youlton - - *tow.*	58	803	1,186	do. - *	do.
COUNTY of YORK, NORTH and WEST RIDINGS :					
Humburton - - *tow.*	69	1,061	1,824	Helperby, York -	Hallikeld.
Lower Dunsforth - *tow.*	100	1,048	1,741	Ouseburn, York -	Claro.
Milby - - *tow.*	84	758	1,836	Helperby, York -	do.
Upper Dunsforth with Branton Green }*tow.*	109	1,009	2,167	Ouseburn, York -	do.
COUNTY of YORK, WEST RIDING :					
Acomb - - *tow.*	1,512	1,580	10,040	York - -	Ainsty.
Aldborough - - *tow.*	507	2,211	6,006	Boroughbridge -	Claro.
Allerton Mauleverer with Hopperton - }*tow.*	258	2,281	3,387	Knaresborough -	do.
Arkendale - - *tow.*	192	1,604	2,563	Leeds - -	do.
Boroughbridge - *tow.*	966	95	2,256	York - -	do.
Cattal - - *tow.*	178	1,123	2,133	do. - -	do.
*Clareton - - *tow.*	15	416	584	Knaresborough -	do.
*Coneythorpe - - *tow.*	79	392	667	do. - -	do.
Copgrove - - *par.*	88	860	1,353	Leeds - -	do.

(continued)

Unions and Parishes, &c.	Population in 1881.	Area in Statute Acres in 1881.	Rateable Value in 1881.	Post Town.	Petty Sessional Division.
GREAT OUSEBURN UNION—*continued.*					
COUNTY of YORK, WEST RIDING—*continued.*			£		
Great Ouseburn (W.) - *tow.*	499	1,568	3,549	York -	Claro.
†Great Ribston-with-Walshford - *tow.*	193	1,933	3,166	Wetherby - -	do.
Green Hamerton - *tow.*	295	1,206	2,472	York - -	do.
Hessay - - *tow.*	91	1,255	1,858	do. -	Ainsty.
†Hunsingore - *tow.*	183	1,159	2,081	Wetherby - -	Claro.
Kirby Hall - - *tow.*	35	427	1,073	Ouseburn, York -	do.
Kirk Hammerton - *tow.*	280	1,089	3,544	York -	do.
Knapton - *tow.*	104	870	1,452	Acomb, York -	Ainsty.
Little Ouseburn - *tow.*	240	706	1,733	York -	Claro.
Marton-with-Grafton *par.*	365	2,165	4,613	Ouseburn, York -	do.
Minskip - - *tow.*	219	1,114	2,935	Boroughbridge -	do.
Moor Monkton - *tow.*	249	3,067	3,675	York -	Ainsty.
Nether Poppleton - *par.*	293	1,278	4,702	do. -	do.
Nun Monkton - *par.*	261	1,775	3,312	do. -	Claro.
Rocliffe - *tow.*	243	1,861	2,449	Boroughbridge -	do.
Rufforth - *par.*	272	2,463	2,824	York -	Ainsty.
Skelton - *tow.*	299	926	2,128	Boroughbridge -	Liberty of Ripon.
Staveley - *par.*	327	1,425	2,843	Leeds -	Claro.
*Thornville - *tow.*	18	266	630	York -	do.
Thorpe-Underwoods - *tow.*	128	2,463	3,380	Ouseburn, York -	do.
Upper Poppleton - *tow.*	284	1,407	2,740	York -	Ainsty.
Westwick - *tow.*	13	423	517	Ripon -	Liberty of Ripon.
Whixley - *tow.*	521	2,374	4,847	York -	Claro.
Widdington - *tow.*	25	701	1,107	Nun Monkton, York	do.
TOTAL of UNION -	11,955	60,627	130,095		

GREAT YARMOUTH PARISH.

(Board of Guardians constituted 29 Mar. 1837 by Order dated 28 Feb. 1837.)

COUNTY of NORFOLK :

Great Yarmouth (W.) *par.*	37,151	1,510	97,267	Great Yarmouth -	Borough (Separate Quarter Sessions).

GREENWICH UNION.

(Formed 18 Nov. 1836 by Order dated 24 Oct. 1836.)

COUNTY of KENT :

Greenwich (W.) - *par.*	16,580	1,741	211,173	Greenwich -	Blackheath.
Saint Nicholas, Deptford - *par.*	7,901	111	44,157	Deptford - -	do.
COUNTIES of KENT and SURREY :					
Saint Paul, Deptford *par.*	76,752	1,575	361,922	do. - -	Blackheath (for Kent portion), Newington (for Surrey portion).
TOTAL of UNION -	131,233	3,427	617,252		

Unions and Parishes, &c.	Population in 1881.	Area in Statute Acres in 1881.	Rateable Value in 1881.	Post Town.	Petty Sessional Division.

GUILDFORD UNION.

(Formed 11 April 1836 by Order dated 24 Feb. 1836, as amended by Order dated 28 Feb. 1873.— Place marked thus * added 25 Dec. 1859 by Order dated 3 Oct. 1859, and thus † added 8 June 1869 by Order dated 28 May 1869.)

COUNTY OF SURREY :

Unions and Parishes, &c.	Population in 1881.	Area in Statute Acres in 1881.	Rateable Value in 1881.	Post Town.	Petty Sessional Division.
			£		
Albury - - par.	1,286	1,353	6,460	Guildford -	Guildford.
Compton - - par.	472	1,998	3,635	do.	do.
East Clandon - par.	275	1,448	1,989	do. -	do.
East Horsley - par.	291	1,832	2,147	Leatherhead -	do.
Godalming - par.	8,610	9,019	37,297	Godalming -	Guildford and Godalming.
Holy Trinity, Guildford (b) - } par.	(b)2,741	144	12,498	Guildford -	Borough of Guildford.
Merrow - - par.	595	1,629	3,908	do. -	Guildford.
Ockham (a) - par.	519	2,376	3,388	Woking -	do.
Purbright - par.	723	4,711	6,251	do. -	do.
†Puttenham - par.	438	1,950	2,441	Guildford -	do.
Saint Mary's, Guildford par.	1,751	35	7,642	do. -	Borough of Guildford.
Saint Nicholas, Guildford - - } par.	2,498	2,817	15,553	do.	{ Borough of Guildford and Guildford.
Send and Ripley - par.	1,855	5,182	9,337	Woking -	Guildford.
Shere (c) - par.	1,719	6,300	9,204	Guildford -	do.
Stoke (W.) - par.	6,706	2,329	25,146	do. -	Borough of Guildford and Guildford.
*The Friary - par.	447	13	1,775	do. -	Borough of Guildford.
Wanborrow - par.	288	1,879	2,198	do. -	Guildford.
West Clandon - par.	370	1,006	2,108	do. -	do.
West Horsley (a) - par.	597	3,022	3,558	Leatherhead -	do.
Wisley (a) - par.	186	1,339	1,284	Woking -	do.
Woking - par.	8,554	8,889	30,499	do. -	do.
Worplesdon - par.	1,715	5,289	12,141	Guildford -	do.
TOTAL OF UNION -	42,696	67,620	200,759		

GUILTCROSS UNION.

(Formed 6 Nov. 1835 by Order dated 8 Oct. 1835.)

COUNTY OF NORFOLK :

Unions and Parishes, &c.	Population in 1881.	Area in Statute Acres in 1881.	Rateable Value in 1881.	Post Town.	Petty Sessional Division.
Banham - par.	1,142	3,963	6,635	Attleborough -	Guiltcross and Shropham.
Blo' Norton - par.	243	1,132	1,844	Thetford -	do.
Bressingham - par.	509	2,354	3,744	Diss -	Diss.
Bridgham - par.	274	2,692	2,792	Thetford -	Guiltcross and Shropham.
East Harling - par.	1,062	2,572	4,287	do. -	do.
Eccles - par.	208	1,685	3,141	Attleborough -	do.
Fersfield - par.	288	1,386	2,160	Diss -	Diss.
Garboldisham - par.	641	2,705	3,758	Thetford -	Guiltcross and Shropham.
Gasthorpe - par.	94	864	629	do. -	do.
Kenninghall (W.) - par.	1,231	3,600	6,245	do. -	do.
New Buckenham - par.	548	324	1,415	Attleborough -	do.
North Lopham - par.	674	2,000	3,336	Thetford -	do.
Old Buckenham - par.	1,146	4,986	8,137	Attleborough -	do.

(continued)

GUILDFORD UNION :

(a) By Orders which came into operation on 25 March 1883,—
A detached part of Ockham was amalgamated with Abinger, in the Dorking Union ;
A detached part of Wisley was amalgamated with Ockham ; and
A detached part of West Horsley was amalgamated with Ockham.

GUILDFORD UNION—continued.

(b) A Parish known as the Bowling Green, was amalgamated with Holy Trinity, Guildford, by Order which came into operation on 25 March 1883.

(c) Detached parts of Ewhurst and Cranley, in the Hambledon Union, were amalgamated with Shere, by Order which came into operation on 25 March 1884.

Unions and Parishes, &c.	Population in 1881.	Area in Statute Acres in 1881.	Rateable Value in 1881.	Post Town.	Petty Sessional Division.
GUILTCROSS UNION—County of Norfolk—*continued.*		£			
Quidenham - *par.*	117	1,126	1,437	Thetford - -	Guiltcross and Shropham.
Riddlesworth - *par.*	96	1,157	795	do. - -	do.
Roydon - *par.*	612	1,329	2,770	Diss - -	Diss.
Shelfanger - *par.*	341	1,719	2,816	do. - -	do.
South Lopham - *par.*	529	1,937	3,170	Thetford -	Guiltcross and Shropham.
West Harling - *par.*	118	3,034	1,407	do. - -	do.
Wilby - *par.*	86	1,400	1,668	Attleborough -	do.
Winfarthing - *par.*	604	2,620	4,392	Diss -	Diss.
TOTAL of UNION -	10,563	44,585	66,578		
GUISBOROUGH UNION.					
(Formed 25 Feb. 1837 by Order dated 30 Jan. 1837.)					
COUNTY of YORK, NORTH RIDING :					
Brotton - *tow.*	3,753	2,076	28,417	Brotton, R.S.O. -	Langbaurgh East.
Common Dale - *tow.*	167	3,057	1,224	Grosmont, R.S.O. -	do.
Danby - *tow.*	1,304	6,289	7,022	do. - -	do.
Easington - *tow.*	644	3,767	5,888	Loftus, R.S.O. -	do.
Great Moorsham (*a*) *tow.*	392	4,238	2,706	Guisborough -	do.
Guisborough (W.) - *tow.*	6,616	7,014	31,471	do. - -	do.
Hutton Lowcras - *tow.*	233	1,560	1,888	do. - -	do.
Kilton (*a*) - *tow.*	431	1,724	6,778	Loftus, R.S.O. -	do.
Kirkleatham - *par.*	3,898	4,330	24,512	Redcar - -	do.
Liverton - *tow.*	669	2,454	2,729	Loftus, R.S.O. -	do.
Lofthouse - *par.*	4,318	3,737	21,054	do. - -	do.
Marsk (*a*) - *tow.*	5,113	3,970	25,658	Marske by the Sea	do.
Morton - *tow.*	62	1,006	1,503	Nunthorpe, R.S.O.	do.
Newton - *par.*	116	1,172	1,169	Ayton, Northallerton	Langbaurgh West.
Pinchingthorpe - *tow.*	117	858	1,574	do. - -	Langbaurgh East.
Redcar (*a*) - *tow.*	2,297	604	8,871	Redcar - -	do.
Skelton (*a*) - *tow.*	7,820	4,263	51,799	Skelton, R.S.O. -	do.
Skinningrove - *tow.*	1,775	188	3,911	Loftus, R.S.O. -	do.
Stranghow (*a*) - *tow.*	1,162	3,235	6,291	Skelton, R.S.O. -	do.
Tocketts - *tow.*	55	668	2,673	Guisborough -	do.
Upleatham (*a*) - *par.*	488	1,426	17,614	Marske by the Sea	do.
Upsall - *tow.*	137	514	2,273	Guisborough -	do.
Westerdale - *tow.*	266	9,881	2,413	Grosmont, R.S.O. -	do.
Wilton - *par.*	1,293	4,050	16,980	Redcar -	do.
TOTAL of UNION -	43,126	72,090 (*b*)	277,327		
HACKNEY UNION.					
(Formed 26 Jan. 1837 by Order dated 31 Dec. 1836.)					
COUNTY of MIDDLESEX :					
Hackney, Saint John (W.) } *par.*	163,681	3,297	797,895	Hackney, E. -	Metropolitan Police Court, Worship Street, E.C.
Stoke Newington Saint Mary - } *par.*	22,781	638	144,345	Stoke Newington, N.	Metropolitan Police Court, Clerkenwell, E.C.
TOTAL of UNION -	186,462	3,935	942,240		

GUISBOROUGH UNION :

(*a*) By Orders which came into operation on 25 March 1886,—

Parts of Kilton were amalgamated with Great Moorsham and Stranghow (called respectively in the Orders, Moorsholme and Stanghow) ;

Parts of Marsk were amalgamated with Redcar and Upleatham ;

GUISBOROUGH UNION—*continued.*

Parts of Skelton and Stranghow (called in the Order, Stanghow) were amalgamated with Kilton ; and Parts of Upleatham were amalgamated with Marsk and Redcar.

(*b*) Glaisdale Moor and Lealholme Moor, containing together 11,598 acres, are also comprised in this Union, and are common to Danby and Glaisdale.

Unions and Parishes, &c.		Population in 1881.	Area in Statute Acres in 1881.	Rateable Value in 1881.	Post Town.	Petty Sessional Division.
HAILSHAM UNION. (Formed 10 April 1835 by Order dated 25 Mar. 1835.) COUNTY of SUSSEX :				£		
Arlington	par.	585	5,231	6,523	Polegate, R.S.O, -	Hailsham.
Chiddingly	par.	881	4,481	4,096	Hawkhurst	do.
Hailsham	par.	2,964	5,330	13,308	Hailsham	do.
Heathfield	par.	1,995	8,032	7,473	Hawkhurst	do.
Hellingly (W.)	par.	1,616	6,050	7,575	do. -	do.
Hooe	par.	470	2,473	3,373	Battle	Battle.
Hurstmonceux (a)	par.	1,294	5,052	7,682	Hailsham -	Hailsham.
Laughton	par.	712	5,177	5,646	Hawkhurst	do.
Ninfield (b)	par.	603	2,575	2,927	Battle	Battle.
Warbleton (b)	par.	1,408	5,986	5,472	Hawkhurst	Hailsham.
Wartling (a)	par.	787	4,743	6,065	Hastings -	do.
TOTAL of UNION -		13,405	55,130	70,140		
HALIFAX UNION. (Formed 10 Feb. 1837 by Order dated 21 Jan. 1837.—Townships marked thus * added as separate Townships on 21 Dec. 1853 by Order of same date.) COUNTY of YORK, WEST RIDING :						
Barkisland	tow.	2,102	2,421	8,185	Halifax -	Wapentake of Morley.
*Clifton	tow.	2,181	2,207	14,098	Brighouse -	do.
Elland - with - Greet-land	tow.	13,007	3,448	48,217	Halifax -	do.
Fixby	tow.	503	935	2,564	do. -	do.
Halifax (W.)	tow.	42,633	999	177,600	do. -	Borough of Halifax.
*Hartshend	tow.	842	863	3,183	Normanton -	Wapentake of Morley.
Hipperholme - with - Brighouse -	tow.	12,660	2,598	49,471	Halifax -	do.
Midgley	tow.	3,084	2,629	11,626	do. -	do.
Norland	tow.	1,988	1,273	9,934	do. -	do.
Northowram	tow.	20,218	3,520	60,038	do. -	Wapentake of Morley and Borough of Halifax.
Ovenden	tow.	12,874	5,350	36,523	do. -	do.
Rastrick	tow.	8,039	1,371	23,379	Brighouse -	Wapentake of Morley.
Rishworth	tow.	1,110	6,548	4,103	Halifax -	do.
Shelf	tow.	2,754	1,302	7,915	do. -	do.
Skircoat	tow.	11,405	1,330	45,565	do. -	Wapentake of Morley and Borough of Halifax.
Southowram	tow.	8,813	2,546	29,598	do. -	do.
Sowerby	tow.	9,462	6,894	37,159	do. -	Wapentake of Morley.
Soyland	tow.	3,467	4,270	12,174	do. -	do.
Stainland and Old Lindley -	tow.	4,933	2,335	15,071	do. -	do.
Warley	tow.	8,365	4,025	32,752	do. -	do.
TOTAL of UNION -		170,440	56,864	629,155		

HAILSHAM UNION :

(a) By Orders which came into operation on 25 March 1886,—
A detached part of Wartling was amalgamated with Hurstmonceux.

(b) By Provisional Order which came into operation on 25 March 1887,—
A detached part of Ninfield was amalgamated with Catsfield, in the Battle Union ; and detached parts of Ashburnham and Dallington, in that Union, were amalgamated with Ninfield and Warbleton respectively.

Unions and Parishes, &c.		Population in 1881.	Area in Statute Acres in 1881	Rateable Value in 1881.	Post Town.	Petty Sessional Division.

HALSTEAD UNION.

(Formed 6 Nov. 1835 by Order dated 22 Oct. 1835.)

COUNTY of ESSEX :

				£		
Castle Hedingham -	par.	1,040	2,438	5,513	Halstead -	North Hinckford.
Colne Engain (a) -	par.	520	2,478	1,259	do.	South Hinckford.
Earl's Colne -	par.	1,594	2,978	7,001	do.	do.
Gosfield -	par.	613	3,033	4,686	do.	do.
Great Maplestead (a)	par.	394	1,966	3,362	do.	North Hinckford.
Great Yeldam (a) -	par.	599	1,838	3,629	do.	do.
Halstead (W.) -	par.	6,701	5,631	21,247	do.	South Hinckford.
Little Maplestead (a)	par.	261	1,067	1,755	do.	do.
Little Yeldam (a) -	par.	289	956	1,673	do.	North Hinckford.
Pebmarsh -	par.	516	2,062	3,453	Bures by Colchester	South Hinckford.
Ridgewell (a) -	par.	657	1,724	3,092	Halstead -	North Hinckford.
Sible Hedingham (a)	par.	1,926	5,407	9,082	do.	do.
Stambourne (a) -	par.	434	1,910	2,928	do.	do.
Tilbury juxta Clare (a) (b) -	par.	226	953	1,524	do.	do.
Toppesfield (a) -	par.	861	3,332	5,243	do.	do.
White Colne (a) -	par.	374	1,466	2,530	do.	South Hinckford.
TOTAL of UNION -		17,005	39,239	81,880		

HALTWHISTLE UNION.

(Formed 18 Oct. 1836 by Order dated 22 Sept. 1836.)

COUNTY of NORTHUMBER-LAND :

Bellister -	tow.	133	1,071	1,317	Haltwhistle -	Haltwhistle.
Blenkinsopp (a) -	tow.	750	5,022	6,456	do.	do.
Comnwood -	tow.	176	3,320	3,178	do.	do.
Featherstone -	tow.	347	2,993	3,366	do.	do.
Haltwhistle (W.) -	tow.	2,108	3,133	8,452	do.	do.
Hartleyburn -	tow.	526	3,535	2,606	do.	do.
Henshaw (a) -	tow.	509	11,325	6,653	do.	do.
Kirkhaugh -	par.	185	6,689	1,961	do.	do.
Knaresdale -	par.	521	15,593	4,249	do.	do.
Lambley and Ash-olme -	par.	712	3,060	2,737	do.	do.
Melkridge -	tow.	306	4,460	5,428	do.	do.
Plenmeller -	tow.	188	5,043	2,583	do.	do.
Ridley (a) -	tow.	204	4,443	3,532	do.	do.
Thirlwall -	tow.	584	8,016	7,195	do.	do.
Thorngrafton (a) -	tow.	293	3,177	3,699	do.	do.
Wall Town -	tow.	62	2,974	1,673	do.	do.
Whitfield -	par.	298	12,479	5,262	do.	do.
TOTAL of UNION -		7,902	96,333	70,317		

HALSTEAD UNION :

(a) By Provisional Order which came into operation on 25 March 1885,—

Detached parts of Colne Engain were amalgamated with White Colne ;

A detached part of Great Maplestead was amalgamated with Little Maplestead, and a detached part of Sible Hedingham was amalgamated with Great Maplestead ;

A detached part of Great Yeldam was amalgamated with Little Yeldam ;

A detached part of Little Yeldam was amalgamated with Tilbury juxta Clare ;

Detached parts of Stambourne and Toppesfield were amalgamated with Great Yeldam ;

Detached parts of Tilbury juxta Clare were amalgamated with Little Yeldam ;

Detached parts of Ridgewell were amalgamated with Stambourne and Tilbury Juxta Clare ;

HALSTEAD UNION—continued.

A detached part of Stambourne was amalgamated with Toppesfield ;

A detached part of Sible Hedingham was amalgamated with Toppesfield ; and

A detached part of Tilbury juxta Clare was amalgamated with Ashen, in the Risbridge Union.

(b) By Provisional Order which came into operation on 25 March 1885, a detached part of Ashen, in the Risbridge Union, was amalgamated with Tilbury Juxta Clare.

HALTWHISTLE UNION :

(a) By Order which came into operation on 25 March 1886,—

A detached part of Blenkinsopp was amalgamated with Henshaw ;

A detached part of Henshaw was amalgamated with Ridley ; and

A detached part of Ridley was amalgamated with Thorngrafton.

Unions and Parishes, &c.	Population in 1881.	Area in Statute Acres in 1881.	Rateable Value in 1881.	Post Town.	Petty Sessional Division.

HAMBLEDON UNION.

(Formed 25 Mar. 1836 by Order dated 22 Feb. 1836, as amended by Orders dated 7 January 1837 and 18 January 1884.)

COUNTY of SURREY :

£

Altold (b) - - par.	540	3,279	2,988	Billingshurst	Guildford.
Bramley (a) - - par.	1,271	4,106	8,223	Guildford -	do.
Chiddingfold (a) - par.	1,332	7,026	8,423	Godalming	do.
Cranley (a) - - par.	2,083	7,831	11,582	Guildford -	do.
Dunsfold (a) - - par.	749	4,451	4,161	Godalming	do.
Elstead - - par.	679	4,106	3,801	do.	Farnham.
Ewhurst (a) - - par.	892	5,534	5,747	Guildford -	Guildford.
Hambledon (W.) (a) - par.	542	1,588	2,296	Godalming	do.
Hascomb (a) - - par.	435	1,587	2,712	do. -	do.
Haslemere (a) - par.	1,111	1,856	6,092	Haslemere	do.
Peper Harrow - par.	151	1,320	1,339	Godalming	do.
Saint Martha Chilworth par.	212	1,072	2.663	Guildford -	do.
Shalford - - par.	1,574	2,606	9,217	do. -	do.
Thursley - - par.	1,020	4,378	4,611	Godalming	do.
Witley (a) - - par.	1,961	6,386	10,495	do. -	do.
Wonersh (a) - - par.	1,771	4,453	8,710	Guildford -	do.
TOTAL of UNION -	16,353	61,582	93,063		

HARDINGSTONE UNION.

(Formed 20 July 1835 by Order dated 25 June 1835.)

COUNTY of NORTHAMPTON :

Brafield on the Green (a) } par.	538	1,980	2,390	Northampton	Northampton.
Castle Ashby cum Chaddleston } par.	209	1,926	3,622	do. -	do,
Cogenhoe or Cooknoe (a) } par.	349	960	2,169	do. -	do.
Collingtree - par.	257	1,190	1,492	do. -	do.
Courteenhall (a) - par.	175	1,330	3,758	do. -	do.
Denton - - par.	547	1,970	1,678	do. -	do.
Great Houghton (a) - par.	330	1,783	4,378	do. -	do.
Hackleton - - par.	378 { In Piddington }	1,875		do. -	do.
Hardingstone - - par.	2,618	3,060	14,918	do. -	do.
Horton (a) - par.	78	2,790	2,222	do. -	do.
Little Houghton (a) - par.	510	1,070	3,852	do. -	do.

(continued)

HAMBLEDON UNION :

(a) By Order which came into operation on 25 March 1884,—
A detached part of Bramley was amalgamated with Dunsfold, and detached parts of Dunsfold were amalgamated with Wonersh and Bramley ;
A detached part of Chiddingfold was amalgamated with Haslemere, and a detached part of Witley was amalgamated with Chiddingfold ;
A detached part of Cranley was amalgamated with Shere, in the Guildford Union ;
Detached parts of Ewhurst were amalgamated with Shere, in the Guildford Union, and Wonersh ;
A detached part of Hambledon was amalgamated with Hascomb ; and
A detached part of Wonersh was amalgamated with Cranley.

(b) All the part of Alfold which was in the County of Sussex was amalgamated with Wisborough Green, in the Petworth Union, by Order which came into operation on 25 March 1884.

i R 3372.

HARDINGSTONE UNION :

(a) By Provisional Order which came into operation on 23 March 1884,--
A detached part of Brafield on the Green, known as Brafield Holme, was amalgamated with Little Houghton ;
Detached parts of Cogenhoe or Cooknoe were amalgamated with Horton ;
A detached part of Courteenhall was amalgamated with Road or Rode ;
A detached part of Great Houghton was amalgamated with Horton ; and
A detached part of Wootton was amalgamated with Courteenhall.

X

Unions and Parishes, &c.	Population in 1881.	Area in Statute Acres in 1881.	Rateable Value in 1881.	Post Town.	Petty Sessional Division.

HARDINGSTONE UNION—County of Northampton—*continued.*

			£		
Milton or Middleton Malzor - } *par.*	728	1,190	3,220	Northampton -	Northampton.
Piddington - - *par.*	508	1,980	1,781	do. - -	do.
Preston-Deanery - *par.*	107	1,470	2,358	do. - -	do.
Quinton - - *par.*	116	1,170	1,571	do. - -	do.
Road or Rode (*a*) - *par.*	720	1,600	7,678	do. - -	do.
Rothersthorpe - *par.*	240	1,200	2,022	do. - -	do.
Whiston - - *par.*	82	809	1,427	do. - -	do.
Wootton (W.) (*a*) - *par.*	817	1,420	4,611	do. - -	do.
Yardley Hastings - *par.*	1,179	3,510	4,083	do. - -	do.
TOTAL of UNION -	**10,486**	**32,408**	**70,205**		

HARTISMERE UNION.

(Formed 1 Sept. 1835 by Order dated 14 Aug. 1835.)

COUNTY of SUFFOLK :

Aspall - - *par.*	151	834	1,276	Stonham - -	Hartismere.
Bacton - - *par.*	642	2,204	4,364	Stowmarket - -	do.
Bottesdale - *ham.*	552	In Redgrave	2,792	Diss - -	do.
Braiseworth - *par.*	159	790	1,107	Eye - -	do.
Broome - - *par.*	261	843	1,691	Scole - -	do.
Burgate - - *par.*	287	2,076	2,775	Diss - -	do.
Cotton (*a*) - *par.*	506	1,921	2,917	Stowmarket - -	do.
Eye (W.) - *par.*	2,296	4,100	10,326	Eye - -	Borough of Eye.
Finningham (*a*) - *par.*	420	1,242	2,464	Stowmarket - -	Hartismere.
Gislingham - *par.*	552	2,251	4,033	Eye - -	do.
Mellis - - *par.*	471	1,344	2,842	Scole - -	do.
Mendlesham - *par.*	1,126	3,044	6,542	Stonham - -	do.
Oakley - - *par.*	276	1,289	1,895	Scole - -	do.
Occold - - *par.*	522	1,568	2,585	Eye - -	do.
Palgrave - - *par.*	748	1,474	3,133	Diss - -	do.
Redgrave - - *par.*	557	3,353	2,273	do. - -	do.
Redlingfield - *par.*	187	1,055	1,380	Eye - -	do.
Rickenhall Superior - *par.*	570	1,857	2,700	Diss - -	do.
Rishangles - *par.*	190	718	1,167	Eye - -	do.
Stoke Ash - *par.*	310	1,200	1,956	Stonham - -	do.
Sturston - - *par.*	190	775	1,195	Scole - -	do.
Thorndon All Saints - *par.*	639	2,692	4,331	Eye - -	do.
Thornham Magna - *par.*	285	1,324	2,210	do. - -	do.
Thornham Parva - *par.*	134	676	970	do. - -	do.
Thrandeston - *par.*	282	1,440	2,566	Scole - -	do.
Thwaite - - *par.*	146	882	1,273	Stonham - -	do.
Westhorpe - *par.*	213	1,322	1,943	Stowmarket - -	do.
Wetheringsett cum Brockford - } *par.*	1,034	3,783	6,013	Stonham - -	do.
Wickham Skeith - *par.*	505	1,770	3,043	do. - -	do.
Wortham (W.) - *par.*	948	2,726	4,427	Diss - -	do.
Wyverstone - *par.*	261	1,522	2,191	Stowmarket - -	do.
Yaxley - - *par.*	371	1,263	2,237	Eye - -	do.
TOTAL of UNION - -	**15,791**	**54,188**	**92,617**		

HARTLEPOOL UNION.

(Formed 25 Mar. 1859 by Order dated 15 Feb. 1859.)

COUNTY of DURHAM :

Brierton - *tow.*	37	762	752	West Hartlepool -	West Hartlepool.
Claxton - *tow.*	51	881	1,287	do. - -	do.
Dalton Piercy - *tow.*	82	1,006	1,000	do. - -	do.

(*continued*)

HARDINGSTONE UNION :

(*a*) See note, page 163.

HARTISMERE UNION :

(*a*) A detached part of Finningham was amalgamated with Cotton by Order which came into operation on 25 March 1881.

Unions and Parishes, &c.	Population in 1881.	Area in Statute Acres in 1881.	Rateable Value in 1881.	Post Town.	Petty Sessional Division.
HARTLEPOOL UNION—County of Durham—*continued.*			£		
Elwick - - *tow.*	228	1,537	2,027	Castle Eden -	West Hartlepool.
Elwick Hall - *par.*	166	4,440	3,350	do. - -	do.
Greatham - *tow.*	737	2,174	6,590	West Hartlepool -	do.
Hart - - *tow.*	291	2,465	5,154	Castle Eden -	do.
Hartlepool - *tow.*	12,361	137	27,812	Hartlepool - -	Hartlepool.
Seaton Carew - *tow.*	1,731	2,663	11,154	Seaton Carew -	West Hartlepool.
Stranton - *tow.*	20,143	2,831	120,168	West Hartlepool -	do.
Thorpe Bulmer - *tow.*	31	842	1,464	Castle Eden -	do.
Throston (W.) - *tow.*	3,752	1,636	16,256	Hartlepool - -	Hartlepool.
TOTAL of UNION - -	48,613	21,374	197,044		
HARTLEY WINTNEY UNION.					
(Formed 8 April 1835 by Order dated 20 March 1835. Places marked thus * added 5 May 1869 by Order dated 21 April 1869.)					
COUNTY of SOUTHAMPTON :					
Bramshill - - *ty.*	138	2,118	1,188	Winchfield - -	Odiham.
*Cove - - - *ty.*	785	1,972	3,418	Farnborough, Hants	do.
Crondall - *par.*	3,188	9,745	16,025	Farnham, Surrey -	do.
Dogmersfield - *par.*	293	1,732	1,965	Winchfield - -	do.
Elvetham - *par.*	469	3,305	4,017	do. - -	do.
Eversley - *par.*	688	3,141	3,574	do. - -	do.
*Farnborough - *par.*	6,266	2,331	12,169	Farnborough, Hants	do.
Grewell - *par.*	300	876	1,315	Odiham - -	do.
Hartley Wintney - *par.*	1,799	2,451	7,222	Winchfield -	do.
*Hawley - with - Minley - *ty.*	1,125	4,948	7,754	Farnborough, Hants	do.
Heckfield - *par.*	560	3,232	3,908	Winchfield -	do.
*Long Sutton - *par.*	310	2,290	2,422	Odiham - -	do.
Mattingly with Hazely - *ham.*	508	2,631	2,857	Winchfield -	do.
Odiham - *par.*	2,623	7,355	15,072	Odiham - -	do.
Rotherwick - *par.*	459	1,983	2,613	Winchfield -	do.
South Warnborough - *par.*	316	2,651	2,960	Odiham - -	do.
Winchfield (W.) - *par.*	366	1,582	4,243	Winchfield -	do.
*Yateley - *ty.*	1,133	3,222	4,726	Farnborough, Hants	do.
TOTAL of UNION - -	21,326	57,565	97,448		
HASLINGDEN UNION.					
(Formed 17 Jan. 1837 by Order dated 20 Dec. 1836.—The place marked thus * was formed by the readjustment and consolidation of the Townships of Old Accrington and New Accrington by Provisional Order dated 6 May 1878, which took effect on 29 Sept. 1878, from which date those Townships were continued in the Union as one Township under the name of Accrington.)					
COUNTY of LANCASTER :					
*Accrington - *tow.*	31,435	3,425	106,615	Accrington -	Accrington.
Coupe Lench, New Hall Hey and Hall-Carr - *tow.*	3,695	1,499	13,790	Waterfoot, near Manchester.	Rossendale.
Haslingden - *tow.*	14,298	4,342	53,926	Haslingden -	do.
Henheads - *tow.*	233	317	1,121	Accrington -	Accrington.
Higher Booths - *tow.*	6,239	4,412	23,751	Rawtenstall -	Rossendale.
Lower Booths (W.) - *tow.*	6,196	1,600	22,945	do. - -	do.
Musbury - *tow.*	1,010	1,714	5,551	Helmshore -	do.
New Church - *tow.*	28,261	5,858	90,230	Bacup and Newchurch.	do.
Tottington Higher End - *tow.*	3,926	3,545	22,992	Edenfield, Bury, Lancashire.	Bury.
TOTAL of UNION -	95,293	26,712	340,921		

Unions and Parishes. &c.	Population in 1881.	Area in Statute Acres in 1881.	Rateable Value in 1881.	Post Town.	Petty Sessional Division.
HASTINGS UNION.					
(Formed 20 July 1835 by Order dated 27 June 1835.)					
County of Sussex :			£		
All Saints - - *par.*	4,613	394	14,515	Hastings -	Borough of Hastings.
Fairlight - *par.*	482	2,884	3,076	do. -	Hastings, Division of Hastings Rape.
Guestling - - *par.*	802	3,578	4,896	do. -	do.
Ore (W.) - - *par.*	3,657	2,177	15,025	do. -	Borough of Hastings.
Pett - - *par.*	283	1,941	4,072	do. -	Hastings, Division of Hastings Rape.
Saint Andrew - *par.*	1,759	34	8,980	do. -	Borough of Hastings.
Saint Clements - *par.*	4,623	128	18,975	do. -	do.
Saint Leonards - *par.*	7,165	1,108	49,102	do. -	do.
Saint Mary Bulverhithe - *par.*	47	136	322	do. -	do.
Saint Mary in the Castle - *par.*	10,489	993	60,236	do. -	do.
Saint Mary Magdalen *par.*	12,238	363	95,097	do. -	do.
Saint Michael - - *par.*	352	3	3,188	do. -	do.
The Holy Trinity, otherwise the Dissolved Priory - *par.*	3,619	202	39,249	do. -	do.
TOTAL of Union -	50,129	13,941	316,733		
HATFIELD UNION.					
(Formed 4 July 1835 by Order dated 17 June 1835.)					
County of Hertford :					
Essendon - - *par.*	594	2,331	3,997	Hatfield -	Hertford.
Hatfield (W.) - *par.*	4,059	12,884	34,703	do. -	do.
Northaw - - *par.*	583	3,306	4,278	Barnet -	Cheshunt.
North Mimms - *par.*	1,266	4,966	14,704	Hatfield -	Hertford.
TOTAL of Union -	6,502	23,487	57,682		
HAVANT UNION.					
(Formed 27 May 1835 by Order dated 12 May 1835.)					
County of Southampton :					
Bedhampton - *par.*	709	2,127	5,809	Havant -	Fareham.
Farlington (a) - *par.*	1,223	2,124	8,189	do. -	do.
Havant (W.) - *par.*	3,032	2,786	14,075	do. -	do.
North Hayling - *par.*	268	1,390	2,641	do. -	do.
South Hayling - *par.*	1,066	2,582	6,077	do. -	do.
Warblington - *par.*	2,374	2,670	11,883	Emsworth -	do.
TOTAL of Union -	8,672	14,279	48,674		

HAVANT UNION :
(a) By Order which came into operation on 25 March 1886, a detached part of Farlington was amalgamated with Southwick, in the Fareham Union.

Unions and Parishes, &c.	Population in 1881.	Area in Statute Acres in 1881.	Rateable Value in 1881.	Post Town.	Petty Sessional Division.
HAVERFORDWEST UNION.					
(Formed 6 Jan. 1837 by Order dated 15 Dec. 1836.—Place marked * added 25 Dec. 1860 by Order dated 8 Oct. 1860, and places marked thus † added 1 Mar. 1862 by Order dated 20 Jan. 1862.)					
In the TOWN and COUNTY of the TOWN of HAVERFORDWEST :			£		
*Furzy Park and Port-field - } *par.*	271	820	1,058	Haverfordwest	- Haverfordwest.
Saint Mary - - *par.*	1,333	30	5,110	do. -	- do.
In the TOWN and COUNTY of the TOWN of HAVERFORD-WEST, and in the COUNTY of PEMBROKE :					
Prendergast - - *par.*	1,417	1,104	4,223	do.	- do.
Saint Martin - - *par.*	1,709	1,955	5,977	do. -	- Roose and Haverford-west.
Saint Thomas (including the hamlet of Saint Thomas)(W.) } *par.*	1,858	1,016	4,774	do. -	- do.
Usmaston - - *par.*	565	2,070	2,538	do.	- Dungleddy and Haver-fordwest.
COUNTY of PEMBROKE :					
Ambleston - - *par.*	494	3,956	2,542	Haverfordwest	Dungleddy.
Boulston - - *par.*	109	1,822	832	do. -	- do.
Brawdy - - *par.*	503	5,401	3,246	do.	- Dewsland.
Camrose - - *par.*	887	8,129	5,635	do. -	- Roose.
Castle Bythe - *par.*	196	2,537	1,022	do.	- Dungleddy.
Dale - - - *par.*	359	2,070	1,418	Milford Haven	- Roose.
East Walton - *par.*	195	1,893	1,521	Haverfordwest	- Dungleddy.
Fishguard - - *par.*	2,009	4,208	6,197	Fishguard -	- Kemes.
Freystrop - - *par.*	381	1,611	1,167	Haverfordwest	- Roose.
Granston - - *par.*	174	1,639	1,029	do. -	- Dewsland.
Haroldston - - *par.*	136	1,718	1,008	do. -	- Roose.
Haroldston Saint Issells - } *par.*	230	1,150	1,756	do. -	- do.
Hasguard - - *par.*	91	1,478	1,262	do. -	- do.
Haycastle - - *par.*	291	4,462	1,901	do. -	- Dewsland.
Henrysmoat - - *par.*	336	3,166	1,341	do. -	- Dungleddy.
Herbanston - - *par.*	358	1,433	2,348	Milford Haven	- Roose.
Hubberston - - *par.*	1,817	1,274	4,280	do. -	- do.
Johnston - - *par.*	209	1,295	875	Haverfordwest	- do.
Jordanston - - *par.*	153	1,876	1,232	Fishguard -	- Dewsland.
Lambston - - *par.*	200	1,761	1,302	Haverfordwest	- Roose.
Letterstone - - *par.*	410	2,216	1,527	do. -	- Dewsland.
Little Newcastle - *par.*	286	2,712	1,497	do. -	- Kemes.
Llandeloy - - *par.*	211	1,843	1,219	do. -	- Dewsland.
Llanfair nant y Goff - *par.*	167	2,597	1,371	Fishguard -	- do.
Llangum - - *par.*	871	1,935	2,104	Haverfordwest	- Roose.
Llanhowel - - *par.*	132	1,331	1,202	do. -	- Dewsland.
Llanllawer - - *par.*	88	1,202	672	Fishguard -	- Kemes.
Llanrian - - *par.*	824	3,683	3,712	Haverfordwest	- Dewsland.
Llanrythan - - *par.*	136	1,719	1,176	do. -	- do.
Llanstinian - - *par.*	166	1,579	1,334	Fishguard -	- do.
Llanwnda - - *par.*	1,003	5,701	3,555	do. -	- do.
Llanycharo - - *par.*	163	2,053	764	do. -	- Kemes.
Maenor Owen - *par.*	194	1,263	987	do. -	- Dewsland.
Marloes - - *par.*	412	2,577	2,606	Haverfordwest	- Roose.
Mathry - - *par.*	799	6,992	4,783	do. -	- Dewsland.
Morvil - - *par.*	143	2,551	788	do. -	- Kemes.
Nolton - - *par.*	154	1,504	1,023	do. -	- Roose.
Pontvan - - *par.*	45	695	316	Fishguard -	- Kemes.
Puncheston - - *par.*	245	1,725	911	Haverfordwest	- do.
Rock - - *par.*	536	4,603	2,901	do. -	- Roose.
Rudbaxton - - *par.*	521	4,142	3,000	do. -	- Dungleddy.
Saint Brides - *par.*	189	1,700	1,983	do. -	- Roose.
Saint David's - *par.*	2,053	11,185	9,194	Saint Davids	- Dewsland.
Saint Dogwell - *par.*	317	3,347	2,556	Haverfordwest	- do.
Saint Edrens - *par.*	92	916	634	do. -	- do.
Saint Elvis - *par.*	18	414	266	do. -	- do.

HAVERFORDWEST UNION :

(a) A detached part of Steynton was amalgamated with Walwens Castle, by Order which came into operation on 25 March 1882.

(continued)

X 3

Unions and Parishes, &c.		Population in 1881.	Area in Statute Acres in 1881.	Rateable Value in 1881.	Post Town.	Petty Sessional Division.
HAVERFORDWEST UNION—County of Pembroke—*continued.*				£		
Saint Ishmael - -	*par.*	480	3,123	3,649	Milford Haven -	Roose
Saint Lawrence -	*par.*	190	1,751	897	Haverfordwest -	Dewsland.
Saint Nicholas -	*par.*	234	2,141	1,285	Fishguard - -	do.
†Skokham Island -	*par.*	—	—	—	Milford Haven -	
Spittal - -	*par.*	403	2,674	2,141	Haverfordwest -	Dungleddy.
Steynton (*a*) - -	*par.*	3,223	7,108	12,194	Milford Haven -	Roose.
Talbenny - -	*par.*	214	1,517	1,466	Haverfordwest -	do.
†The Cathedral Close of Saint David's	*par.*	30 {	In St. David's }	112	St. Davids -	Dewsland.
Tretiarn - -	*par.*	112	1,205	641	Haverfordwest -	Roose.
Walwens Castle (*a*) -	*par.*	379	2,980	2,427	do. - -	do.
Westou - -	*par.*	717	7,078	4,326	do. - -	Dungleddy.
West Roheston -	*par.*	154	1,111	1,423	Milford Haven -	Roose.
West Walton - -	*par.*	367	1,333	1,688	Haverfordwest -	do.
Whitchurch - -	*par.*	829	3,138	3,003	do. -	Dewsland.
TOTAL of UNION -		33,791	167,217	152,957		
HAWARDEN UNION. (Formed 1 Feb. 1853 by Order dated 7 Jan. 1853.—Places marked thus * added 14 Mar. 1871 by Order dated 27 Feb. 1871.)						
COUNTY of FLINT:						
Hawarden (W.) -	*tow.*	7,087	15,000	40,894	Hawarden, Chester	Hawarden.
Higher Kinnerton -	*tow.*	405	1,825	4,277	Broughton, Chester	Hope.
*Hope - -	*par.*	3,890	9,442	17,523	Hope, Mold -	do.
*Merford and Hoseley (*a*)	*tow.*	314	604	2,246	Wrexham - -	do.
Saltney - -	*tow.*	2,300	2,302	23,084	Hawarden, Chester	Hawarden.
*Tryddyn - -	*tow.*	1,690	3,614	6,356	Tryddyn, Mold -	Hope.
TOTAL of UNION -		15,695	32,787	94,380		
HAY UNION. (Formed 26 Sept. 1836 by Order dated 31 Aug. 1836.)						
COUNTY of BRECON :						
Aberllunvy - -	*par.*	151	626	1,420	Three Cocks, R.S.O.	Talgarth.
Broullys - -	*par.*	301	2,109	3,217	Talgarth, R.S.O. -	do.
Glynfaeh, or Capel y flin - -	*ham.*	51	In Llanigon	619	Llandhoney, Abergavenny.	Hay.
Hay (W.) (*b*) (*c*) -	*par.*	2,154	2,602	8,798	Hay - -	do.
Llanelieu - -	*par.*	88	5,537	1,107	Talgarth - -	Talgarth.
Llanigon (*b*) -	*ham.*	359	9,256	3,953	Hay - -	Hay.
Llyswen - -	*par.*	198	2,067	1,468	Llyswen, R.S.O. -	Talgarth.
Pipton - -	*ham.*	105 {	In Tregoed and Felindre }	1,665	Three Cocks, R.S.O.	do.
Talgarth, including the Hamlets of Borough, Forest, Trefecca, and Pwll y wrach	*par.*	1,352	12,000	9,010	Talgarth - -	do.

(*continued*)

HAVERFORDWEST UNION :

(*a*) See note, page 167.

HAWARDEN UNION :

(*a*) Detached parts of Allington and Gresford, in the Wrexham Union, were amalgamated with Merford and Hoseley, and a detached part of Merford and Hosely was amalgamated with Allington, by Order which came into operation on 25 March 1885.

HAY UNION :

(*a*) The part of Glasbury on the right bank of the River Wye was amalgamated with Tregoed and Felindre, by Order which came into operation on 25 March 1884.

(*b*) A detached part of Llanigon was amalgamated with Hay and all that part of Llanigon on the left bank of the River Wye was amalgamated with Glasbury, by Order which came into operation on 25 March 1884.

(*c*) A part of Hay on the left bank of the River Wye was amalgamated with Llowes, by Provisional Order which came into operation on 25 March 1885.

Unions and Parishes, &c.	Population in 1881.	Area in Statute Acres in 1881.	Rateable Value in 1881.	Post Town.	Petty Sessional Division.
Hay Union—County of Brecon—*continued*.			£		
Tregoed and Feliudre (*a*) } *ham.*	318	5,816	3,003	Three Cocks, R.S.O.	Talgarth.
County of Hereford :					
Bredwardine - - *par.*	337	2,215	3,125	Hereford - -	Bredwardine.
Clifford - - *par.*	792	6,522	9,501	do. - -	do.
Cusop - - - *par.*	200	2,294	2,970	Hay - -	do.
Dorston - - *par.*	445	5,385	4,675	Hereford - -	do.
Whitney - - *par.*	258	1,483	2,902	do. - -	do.
County of Radnor :					
Boughrood - - *par.*	263	1,633	2,316	Llwyawen, R.S.O.	Painscastle.
Bryngwyn - - *par.*	247	4,536	2,475	Hay - -	do.
Clyro - - - *par.*	731	7,225	8,254	do. - -	do.
Glasbury (*a*) (*b*) - *tow.*	789	3,400	5,584	Glasbury - -	do.
Llanbedr Painscastle *par.*	246	3,877	2,325	Hay - -	do.
Llandeilo Graban - *par.*	251	3,059	2,379	do. - -	do.
Llandewi fach - - *par.*	103	2,297	1,277	do. - -	do.
Llanstephan - - *par.*	171	2,407	2,071	Llyswen, R.S.O. -	do.
Llowes (*c*) - - *par.*	312	3,319	3,128	Hay - -	do.
Total of Union -	10,222	89,695	87,632		
HAYFIELD UNION. (Formed 6 Dec. 1837 by Order dated 10 Nov. 1837.—Name of place marked thus * is as altered by Order of 4 March 1885.)					
County of Chester :					
Disley - - *tow.*	3,312	2,591	15,986	Disley, near Stockport.	Stockport.
County of Derby :					
Hayfield, including Great Hamlet, Kinder, Phoside } *tow.*	2,801	7,920	13,291	Hayfield, near Stockport.	Chapel-en-le-Frith.
Mellor - - *tow.*	1,242	2,362	7,252	Mellor, near Stockport.	Glossop.
*New Mills (W.) - *tow.*	5,379	5,078	22,845	New Mills, near Stockport.	Chapel-en-le-Frith.
Total of Union -	12,734	17,951	59,374		
HEADINGTON UNION. (Formed 15 Sept. 1835 by Order dated 29 Aug. 1835.—Place marked thus * added 5 July 1836 by Order dated 11 June 1836, thus † added 14 Oct. 1839 by Order dated 18 Sept. 1839, and thus ‡ added 25 June 1879 by Order dated 29 May 1879.)					
County of Oxford :					
Beckley - - *par.*	354	3,620	3,130	Oxford - -	Bullingdon.
Chippinghurst - *ham.*	15	314	644	Wheatley - -	do.
Cowley (W.) (*b*) (*c*) - *par.*	5,633	996	19,105	Oxford - -	do.

(continued)

HEADINGTON UNION :

(*a*) By Provisional Order which came into operation on 25 March 1883, Parishes known as Shotover, and Shotover Hill Place, were amalgamated with the Parish of Forrest Hill, and the name of the last-mentioned Parish, as so altered, was, by an Order dated 17 April 1883, changed to Forest Hill with Shotover.

(*b*) By Orders which came into operation on 25 March 1885,—

Certain parts of Cowley were amalgamated with Forest Hill with Shotover, and St. Clement (Oxford).

HEADINGTON UNION—*continued*.

Certain parts of St. Clement (Oxford) were amalgamated with Cowley; and

Certain parts of Iffley and Hockmoor were amalgamated with Littlemoor and Cowley and with South Hinksey, in the Abingdon Union.

(*c*) By Order which came into operation on 25 March 1886, a detached part of Iffley and Hockmoor was amalgamated with Cowley.

(*d*) There are about 845 acres of land included in the Union, common to different Parishes.

X 4

Unions and Parishes, &c.	Population in 1881.	Area in Statute Acres in 1881.	Rateable Value in 1881.	Post Town.	Petty Sessional Division.
			£		
HEADINGTON UNION—County of Oxford—*continued.*					
Cuddesdon - - *par.*	340	956	2,198	Wheatley	Bullingdon.
Denton - - *ham.*	138	545	1,095	do.	do.
Eldsfield - - *par.*	170	1,260	1,925	Oxford	do.
Forest Hill with Shot-over (*a*) (*b*) - *par.*	384	1,946	3,424	Wheatley	do.
Garsington - - *par.*	607	2,233	3,835	do.	do.
Headington (W.) - *par.*	2,776	2,172	7,835	Oxford	do.
Holton - - *par.*	237	1,717	2,528	Wheatley	do.
Horsepath - - *par.*	321	1,154	1,975	do.	do.
Ifley and Hockmoor (*b*) (*c*) - *par.*	990	1,138	4,832	Oxford	do.
† Littlemoor (*b*) - *ham.*	1,029	613	1,827	do.	do.
Marston - - *par.*	515	1,175	3,610	do.	do.
Saint Clement, Oxford (W.) (*b*) - *par.*	4,515	261	11,327	do.	Oxford City.
Saint Giles, Oxford - *par.*	8,584	936	12,169	do.	do. do.
†Saint John, Oxford - *par.*	137	9	3,042	do.	do. do.
Staunton St. John - *par.*	548	2,731	3,466	Wheatley	Bullingdon.
Stowood - - *par.*	18	578	472	Oxford	do.
Studley and Horton - *ham.*	213	1,287	1,523	do.	do.
*Studley and Horton - *ham.*	49	952	951	do.	Ashenden, Bucks.
Wheatley - - *par.*	1,020	990	3,285	Wheatley	Bullingdon.
Woodenton - - *par.*	67	657	1,261	Oxford	do.
TOTAL of UNION -	28,723	28,240 (*d*)	125,489		

HELMSLEY UNION.

(Formed as Helmsley Blackmoor Union 18 Feb. 1837 by Order dated 24 Jan. 1837 as amended by Orders dated 31 Jan. 1837 and 6 Mar. 1848.—Name altered by Order dated 15 Feb. 1887.—Places marked thus * added 4 Aug. 1837 by Order dated 10 July 1837, and thus † added 16 Sept. 1841 by Order of that date.—Spelling of names of places marked thus ‡ as altered by Order dated 15 June 1887.)

COUNTY OF YORK, NORTH RIDING:

Ampleforth (*a*) - *tow.*	—	—	—	Oswaldkirk	Ryedale.
Arden - cum - Arden-side - *tow.*	122	1,524	1,240	Helmsley	Birdforth.
Beadlam - - *tow.*	154	1,450	1,393	Nawton	Ryedale.
Bilsdale, Westside - *tow.*	148	2,920	1,139	Helmsley	Birdforth.
Byland-with-Wass (*a*) - *tow.*	205	2,568	1,970	Oswaldkirk	do.
Cawton - - *tow.*	67	1,056	1,569	Gilling	Ryedale.
Cold Kirby - - *par.*	164	1,617	1,374	Thirsk	Birdforth.
Colton - - *tow.*	131	1,087	1,030	Gilling	Ryedale.
*Dale Town - - *tow.*	61	1,773	904	Helmsley	Birdforth.
East Newton and Laysthorp - *tow.*	59	940	1,254	Oswaldkirk	Ryedale.
Gilling - - *tow.*	245	2,072	2,425	Gilling	do.
Grimston - - *tow.*	64	997	552	do.	do.
‡Harome - - *tow.*	439	2,359	3,118	Nawton	do.
Hawnby - - *tow.*	231	2,421	1,019	Helmsley	Birdforth.
Helmsley (W.) - *tow.*	1,550	8,812	6,331	do.	Ryedale.
Laskill Pasture - *tow.*	93	1,589	519	do.	do.
*Morton - - *tow.*	27	1,756	1,015	do.	Birdforth.
Old Byland - - *par.*	156	2,737	1,910	do.	do.
Oldstead - - *tow.*	122	1,380	1,274	Oswaldkirk	do.
Oswaldkirk (*a*) - *tow.*	197	2,195	2,532	do.	Ryedale.
Pockley - - *tow.*	188	3,440	1,449	Nawton	do.
‡Rivaulx - - *tow.*	227	5,311	2,294	Helmsley	do.
Scawton - - *par.*	132	2,876	1,424	Thirsk	do.
‡Spilesworth - - *tow.*	104	5,152	837	Helmsley	Birdforth.

(*continued*)

HEADINGTON UNION:

(*a*) (*b*) (*c*) (*d*) See notes, page 169.

HELMSLEY UNION:

(*a*) By Provisional Order which came into operation on 25 March 1887,—

The several parts of Townships known as Ampleforth Birdforth and Ampleforth Oswaldkirk were united with certain detached parts of Oswaldkirk and amalgamated with Ampleforth Saint Peter, and the

HELMSLEY UNION—*continued.*

last-mentioned place, as so altered, was designated the Township of Ampleforth.

The three Townships of Ampleforth Birdforth, Ampleforth Oswaldkirk, and Ampleforth Saint Peter had together, in 1881, population 703, acreage 2,389, and rateable value 3,167*l*.

The several parts of a Township known as Wass were amalgamated with Byland (Coxwold), and the latter, as so altered, was designated the Township of Byland-with-Wass.

Unions and Parishes, &c.	Population in 1881.	Area in Statute Acres in 1881.	Rateable Value in 1881.	Post Town.	Petty Sessional Division.

HELMSLEY UNION—County of York,
North Riding—*continued*.

				£		
Sproxton	-	*tow.*	165	2,869	1,984	Helmsley	-	Ryedale.
Stonegrave	-	*tow.*	140	915	1,471	Oswaldkirk	-	do.
Thorpe-le-Willows	-	*tow.*	25	471	690	do.	-	Birdforth.

| TOTAL of UNION | - | 5,216 (a) | 65,287 (a) | 42,717 (a) | | |

HELSTON UNION.

(Formed 12 June 1837 by Order dated 15 May 1837.)

COUNTY of CORNWALL:

Breage	-	*par.*	3,017	7,274	8,447	Helston	-	West Kirrier.
Crowan	-	*par.*	2,593	7,496	7,737	Camborne	-	East Penwith.
Cury	-	*par.*	434	2,822	3,148	Helston	-	West Kirrier.
Germoe	-	*par.*	588	1,331	1,710	Marazion	-	do.
Grade	-	*par.*	292	2,007	1,624	Helston	-	do.
Gunwalloe	-	*par.*	181	1,469	1,602	do.	-	do.
Helston (W.)	-	*bor.*	3,432	309	8,588	do.	-	Borough of Helston.
Landewednack	-	*par.*	585	2,050	2,107	do	-	West Kirrier.
Manaccan	-	*par.*	357	1,746	2,642	do.	-	do.
Mawgan (in Meneage)	*par.*	861	5,452	4,499	do.	-	do.
Mullion	-	*par.*	607	5,015	3,224	do.	-	do.
Ruan Major	-	*par.*	94	2,485	819	do.	-	do.
Ruan Minor	-	*par.*	292	704	729	do.	-	do.
Saint Anthony (in Meneage)	*par.*	217	1,419	1,732	do.	-	do.
Saint Keverne	-	*par.*	1,820	10,298	10,827	do.	-	do.
Saint Martin (in Meneage)	*par.*	397	2,371	2,293	do.	-	do.
Sithney	-	*par.*	3,330	5,826	8,631	do.	-	do.
Wendron	-	*par.*	4,584	13,259	12,319	do.	-	do.

| TOTAL of UNION | - | 23,684 | 73,333 | 82,678 | | |

HEMEL HEMPSTEAD UNION.

(Formed 12 June 1835 by Order dated 21 May 1835.)

COUNTY of HERTFORD:

Bovingdon	-	*par.*	1,054	3,958	8,067	Hemel Hempstead	-	Dacorum.
Flamstead	-	*par.*	1,846	6,004	9,682	Dunstable	-	do.
Flaunden	-	*par.*	240	919	1,134	Chesham	-	do.
Great Gaddesden	-	*par.*	938	4,140	6,114	Hemel Hempstead	-	do.
Hemel Hempstead (W.)	*par.*	9,064	7,184	41,183	do.	-	do.
King's Langley	-	*par.*	1,464	3,481	11,699	King's Langley, R.S.O.	do.

| TOTAL of UNION | - | 14,606 | 25,695 | 77,879 | | |

HEMSWORTH UNION.

(Formed 12 Aug. 1850 by Order dated 23 July 1850.— Place marked thus * added 20 Sept. 1851 by Order dated 28 Aug. 1851, and thus † added 29 Sept. 1858 by Order dated 7 Sept. 1858.)

COUNTY of YORK, WEST RIDING:

Ackworth	-	*par.*	2,222	2,643	8,100	Pontefract	-	Upper Osgoldcross.
Badsworth	-	*tow.*	226	1,546	2,672	do.	-	do.

(continued)

HELMSLEY UNION:
(a) See notes, page 170.

Unions and Parishes, &c.		Population in 1881.	Area in Statute Acres in 1881.	Rateable Value in 1881.	Post Town.	Petty Sessional Division.
HEMSWORTH UNION—County of York, West Riding—*continued.*				£		
Brierley	- tow.	484	2,590	3,223	Barnsley - -	Lower Staincross.
Great Houghton	- tow.	360	1,618	2,105	do. -	Lower Strafforth and Tickhill.
*Hamphall Stubbs	- tow.	24	239	512	Doncaster -	do.
Havercroft	- tow.	486	1,364	7,255	Wakefield	Lower Staincross.
Hemsworth (W.)	- par.	1,665	4,161	8,855	Pontefract	Upper Osgoldcross.
Hessle -	- tow.	119	645	809	Wakefield -	do.
Hill Top -	- tow.	101	242	283	do. -	do.
†Hunswick-with-Foulby and Nostal }	par.	575	1,141	3,390	do. -	do.
Kirk Smeaton	- par.	380	1,700	2,448	Pontefract	do.
Little Houghton	- tow.	190	670	2,525	Barnsley -	Lower Strafforth and Tickhill.
Little Smeaton	- tow.	215	1,238	1,685	Pontefract	Lower Osgoldcross.
North Elmsall	- tow.	287	2,118	3,637	do. -	Upper Osgoldcross.
Ryhill	- tow.	797	592	2,423	Wakefield -	Lower Staincross.
Shafton	- tow.	430	823	1,420	Barnsley -	do.
Skelbrooke	- tow.	134	1,147	1,566	Doncaster -	Upper Osgoldcross.
South Elmsall	- tow.	526	1,424	3,273	do. -	do.
South Hiendley	- tow.	366	1,292	1,884	Barnsley -	Lower Staincross.
South Kirkby	- tow.	634	2,360	5,066	Pontefract	Upper Osgoldcross.
Thorpe Audlin	- tow.	257	1,311	1,736	do. -	do.
Upton -	- tow.	259	1,113	1,312	do. -	do.
Walden Stubbs	- tow.	148	1,272	1,826	do. -	Lower Osgoldcross.
West Hardwick	- tow.	56	487	544	Wakefield -	Upper Osgoldcross.
Wintersett -	- tow.	165	1,065	1,765	do. -	Lower Staincross.
TOTAL of UNION	-	11,106	34,831	70,314		
HENDON UNION. (Formed 1 May 1835 by Order dated 11 April 1835.) COUNTY of MIDDLESEX :						
Edgware -	- par.	816	2,090	6,801	Edgware - -	Gore.
Great Stanmore	- par.	1,312	1,484	7,819	Stanmore - -	do.
Harrow-on-the-Hill -	par.	10,277	10,027	77,557	Harrow - -	do.
Hendon (W.) -	- par.	10,484	8,382	75,553	Hendon, N.W. -	do.
Kingsbury -	- par.	759	1,829	5,933	Kingsbury, N.W. -	do.
Little Stanmore	- par.	862	1,591	5,357	Edgware - -	do.
Pinner -	- par.	2,519	3,782	16,881	Pinner - -	do.
Willesden -	- par.	27,153	1,383	118,729	Willesden, N.W. -	Kensington and Marylebone Police Court District.
TOTAL of UNION	-	54,182	33,568	314,630		
HENLEY UNION. (Formed 15 June 1835 by Order dated 20 May 1835.— Places marked thus * added 24 June 1845 by Order dated 12 June 1845.) COUNTY of BERKS :						
Remenham -	- par.	617	1,573	5,291	Henley on Thames	Maidenhead.
COUNTY of BUCKINGHAM :						
*Fawley -	- par.	302	2,213	2,602	Henley on Thames	Hundred of Desborough, First Division.
*Hambledon -	- par.	1,502	6,598	9,371	do. -	do.
*Medmenham -	- par.	336	2,442	3,275	Great Marlow -	do.
COUNTY of OXFORD :						
Bix -	- par.	427	3,078	2,691	Henley on Thames	Henley.
Brightwell -	- par.	220	1,612	2,935	Tetsworth -	Watlington.
Britwell Prior -	- cha.	50	720	1,072	do. -	do.
Britwell Salome	- par.	158	884	1,510	do. -	do.
Caversham -	- par.	3,583	4,879	16,619	Reading -	Henley.
Checkendon -	- par.	383	3,077	3,776	Henley on Thames	do.

(continued)

Unions and Parishes, &c.		Population in 1881.	Area in Statute Acres in 1891.	Rateable Value in 1881.	Post Town.	Petty Sessional Division.
HENLEY UNION—County of Oxford—*continued.*				£		
Cuxham	*par.*	139	492	1,126	Tetsworth	Watlington.
Eye and Dunsden	*lib.*	863	3,151	4,749	Reading	Henley.
Harpsden	*par.*	226	2,024	3,149	Henley on Thames	do.
Henley (W.)	*par.*	3,692	1,758	15,373	do.	do.
Ipsden	*par.*	699	3,142	3,743	Wallingford, and Henley-on-Thames (as to Stoke Row).	do. Watlington.
Nettlebed	*par.*	657	1,172	2,195	Henley on Thames	
Nuffield	*par.*	215	2,104	2,090	do.	do.
Pishill	*par.*	170	793	735	do.	do.
Pyrton	*par.*	566	4,847	6,427	Tetsworth, and Henley-on-Thames (as to Upper Assendon and Stonor).	do.
Rotherfield Grays	*par.*	1,909	2,928	7,895	Henley on Thames	Henley and Borough of Henley-on-Thames.
Rotherfield Peppard	*par.*	484	2,194	3,831	do.	do.
Shiplake	*par.*	615	2,740	4,941	do.	do.
Swincombe	*par.*	364	2,708	2,251	do.	Watlington.
Watlington	*par.*	1,815	3,687	6,628	Tetsworth	do.
TOTAL of UNION		19,992	61,113	114,275		

HENSTEAD UNION.

(Formed 19 Dec. 1835 by Order dated 4 Dec. 1835.)

COUNTY OF NORFOLK :

Arminghall	*par.*	120	650	1,561	Norwich	Swainsthorpe.
Bixley	*par.*	160	760	1,416	do.	do.
Bracon-Ash	*par.*	282	974	1,743	do.	do.
Bramerton	*par.*	249	728	1,726	do.	do.
Caister Saint Edmunds	*par.*	143	1,044	1,839	do.	do.
Colney	*par.*	95	948	1,396	do.	do.
Cringleford	*par.*	225	980	2,140	do.	do.
Dunston	*par.*	73	816	1,420	do.	do.
East Carlton	*par.*	284	1,213	2,108	do.	do.
Flordon	*par.*	178	929	1,816	Long Stratton	do.
Framingham Earl	*par.*	139	560	984	Norwich	do.
Framingham Pigot	*par.*	234	608	1,426	do.	do.
Great Melton	*par.*	311	2,485	4,140	Wymondham	do.
Great or East Poringland with Little or West Poringland	*u.p.*	471	1,740	2,540	Norwich	do.
Hethel	*par.*	149	1,428	2,141	do.	do.
Hethersett	*par.*	1,123	2,674	6,438	Wymondham	do.
Holverstone	*par.*	18	480	604	Norwich	do.
Intwood	*par.*	35	617	1,139	do.	do.
Keswick	*par.*	148	729	1,745	do.	do.
Ketteringham	*par.*	210	1,680	3,199	Wymondham	do.
Kirby-Bedon	*par.*	269	625	2,861	Norwich	do.
Little Melton	*par.*	357	671	1,471	Wymondham	do.
Markshall or Mattishall Heath	*par.*	54	2,280	1,319	Norwich	do.
Mulbarton	*par.*	518	1,348	2,781	do.	do.
Newton Flotman	*par.*	284	1,173	2,488	Long Stratton	do.
Rockland	*par.*	442	1,360	2,392	Norwich	do.
Saxlingham Nethergate	*par.*	529	⎱ 2,111 ⎰	2,882	do.	do.
Saxlingham Thorpe	*par.*	146		1,050	do.	do.
Shotesham All Saints	*par.*	379		2,648	do.	do.
Shotesham Saint Mary and Saint Martin	*par.*	316	⎱ 3,544 ⎰	3,206	do.	do.
Stoke Holy Cross	*par.*	414	1,659	3,173	do.	do.
Surlingham	*par.*	486	1,767	2,897	do.	do.
Swainsthorpe (W.)	*par.*	291	821	1,909	do.	do.
Swardeston	*par.*	339	933	2,016	do.	do.

(continued)

Unions and Parishes. &c.	Population in 1881.	Area in Statute Acres in 1881.	Rateable Value in 1881.	Post Town.	Petty Sessional Division.
HENSTEAD UNION—County of Norfolk—*continued.*			£		
Trowse with Newton *par.*	610	1,153	3,386	Norwich - -	Swainsthorpe.
Whitlingham - *par.*	70	542	707	do. - -	do.
Wrenningham - *par.*	485	1,528	2,671	Wymondham -	do.
TOTAL OF UNION -	10,636	43,358	81,661		

HEREFORD UNION.

(Formed 28 April 1836 by Order dated 12 April 1836.—Places marked thus * added 22 May 1837 by Order dated 27 April 1837, thus † added 25 Dec. 1858 by Order dated 25 Oct. 1858, thus ‡ added 1 Jan. 1863 by Order dated 20 Dec. 1862, and thus § added 1 April 1884 by Order dated 29 March 1884). The name of the Place marked thus * * is as altered by Provisional Order dated 21 April 1875, which consolidated the Parishes of Sutton Saint Michael and Sutton Saint Nicholas.)

COUNTY OF HEREFORD :

Aconbury - - *par.*	159	1,591	1,163	Ross - -	Hereford.
*Allensmore - - *par.*	579	2,007	4,296	Tram Inn, R.S.O. Herefordshire.	do.
All Saints (e) (f) - *par.*	5,470	341	20,914	Hereford - -	Hereford City.
Bartestre - - *cha.*	199 { In Dormington }		884	do. - -	Hereford.
Boulston (e) - - *par.*	38	657	662	do. - -	Harewood End.
Breinton (e) - *par.*	465	1,629	4,200	do. - -	Hereford.
Burghill and Tillington (e) } *par.*	1,350	3,704	8,025	do. - -	do.
Callow - - *par.*	116	621	581	do. - -	do.
Clehonger (e) - *par.*	443	1,888	4,007	do. - -	do.
Credenhill (e) - *par.*	244	1,224	2,860	do. - -	do.
Dewsall - - *par.*	45	676	747	do. - -	Harewood End.
Dindor (e) - - *par.*	263	1,678	3,606	do. - -	Hereford.
†Dinmore (h) - *par.*	24	570	650	Leominster -	do.
Dormington - *par.*	108	1,381	1,365	Hereford -	do.
*Eaton Bishop (e) - *par.*	450	2,229	4,502	do. - -	do.
Fownhope (e) (e) - *par.*	1,038	4,723	7,078	do. - -	do. (continued)

HEREFORD UNION :

(a) By Provisional Order which came into operation on 25 March 1885,—
A detached part of Stoke Edith was amalgamated with Westhide ;
Detached parts of Stoke Edith were amalgamated with Yarkhill, in the Ledbury Union ;
A detached part of Weston Beggard was amalgamated with Yarkhill, in the Ledbury Union ; and
A detached part of Yarkhill, in the Ledbury Union, was amalgamated with Westhide.

(b) A detached part of Stoke Edith was amalgamated with Ashperton, in the Ledbury Union, by Order which came into operation on 25 March 1884.

(c) Certain detached parts of Fownhope were amalgamated with Brockhampton and Sellack, in the Ross Union, by Order which came into operation on 25 March 1884.

(d) Certain detached parts of Felton and Ullingswick, in the Bromyard Union, were amalgamated with Sutton and Marden respectively, by Order which came into operation on 25 March 1884.

(e) By Orders which came into operation on 25 March 1884,—
Part of Boulston, on the left bank of the River Wye, was amalgamated with Fownhope ;
Part of Dindor, on the left bank of the River Wye, was amalgamated with Hampton Bishop ;
Part of Eaton Bishop, on the left bank of the River Wye, was amalgamated with Stretton Sugwas ;
Part of Holm Lacy, on the left bank of the River Wye, was amalgamated with Fownhope ;
Part of Saint Owen, on right bank of the River Wye, was amalgamated with Saint Martin ;
A detached part of Burghill and Tillington was amalgamated with Credenhill ;
Detached parts of Marden were amalgamated with Sutton ;
Detached parts of Sutte were amalgamated with Marden ;

HEREFORD UNION—*continued.*

A detached part of Marden was amalgamated with Wellington ;
A detached part of Preston Wynne was amalgamated with Sutton ;
A detached part of Pipe and Lyde was amalgamated with Moreton on Lug ;
Detached parts of Saint John Baptist were amalgamated with All Saints, Tupsley, Saint Martin, and Clehonger ;
The part of Breinton within the Borough of Hereford was amalgamated with Huntington ;
The part of Tupsley not included in the Borough of Hereford was amalgamated with Hampton Bishop ; and
A detached part of Holmer and Shelwick was amalgamated with Breinton.

(f) A detached part of All Saints and a part of Holmer and Shelwick, within the Borough of Hereford, were united and constituted a separate Parish, and designated Holmer (Within), by Order which came into operation on 25 March 1884.

(g) Part of a Parish known as Upper Hullingham, having, in 1881, population 94, acreage 698, and rateable value 1,451*l.*, was amalgamated with Saint Martin, and the residue with Grafton, by Provisional Order which came into operation on 25 March 1885.

(h) By Orders which came into operation on 25 March 1887,—
The several parts of a Township known as Amberley, having, in 1881, population 34, acreage 377, and rateable value 725*l.*, were amalgamated with Bodenham, in the Leominster Union, and Marden and Sutton ;
A detached part of Dinmore was amalgamated with Wellington ; and
A detached part of Ocle Pychard, in the Bromyard Union, was amalgamated with Sutton.

Unions and Parishes, &c.		Population in 1881.	Area in Statute Acres in 1881.	Rateable Value in 1881.	Post Town.	Petty Sessional Division.
HEREFORD UNION—County of Hereford—*continued.*				£		
Grafton (*g*) -	*tow.*	110	440	1,387	Hereford -	Hereford.
Hampton Bishop (*e*)	*par.*	264	In Tupsley	2,932	do.	do.
†Haywood -	*par.*	180	1,395	3,242	do.	do.
Holmer and Shelwick (*e*) (*f*) -	*par.*	2,154	3,069	14,315	do.	do.
§Holmer (Within) (*f*)	*par.*	—	—	—		
Hom Lacy (*s*)	*par.*	321	3,192	5,292	do. -	do.
Huntington (*c*)	*tow.*	129 {	In Holmer and Shelwick }	1,470	do. -	Hereford City.
Kenchester -	*par.*	80	533	1,401	do. -	Hereford.
Little Birch -	*par.*	282	967	1,398	Tram Inn, R.S.O., Herefordshire.	Harewood End.
Little Dewchurch -	*par.*	328	1,652	2,306	Ross -	do.
Lower Bullingham -	*par.*	474	1,100	2,981	Hereford -	Hereford.
Lugwardine -	*par.*	755	2,097	6,498	do.	do.
Marden (*d*) (*e*) (*h*) -	*par.*	840	3,671	8,891	do. -	do.
Mordiford -	*par.*	570	1,478	2,593	do. -	do.
Moreton on Lug (*e*) -	*par.*	83	885	2,216	do. -	do.
Much Birch -	*par.*	528	1,287	2,651	Tram Inn, R.S.O., Herefordshire.	Harewood End.
Much Dewchurch -	*par.*	564	1,878	7,187	Hereford -	do.
Pipe and Lyde (*e*) -	*par.*	234	1,620	2,820	do. -	Hereford.
Preston Wynne (*e*) -	*cha.*	168 {	In Withington }	1,157	do. -	do.
Saint John Baptist (*c*) -	*par.*	1,382	436	9,122	do. -	Hereford City.
Saint Martin (*c*) (*g*) -	*par.*	1,426	770	6,426	do. -	do.
Saint Nicholas -	*par.*	1,624	554	8,297	do. -	do.
Saint Owen (*e*) -	*par.*	3,952	256	9,442	do. -	do.
Saint Peter (W.) -	*par.*	3,190	60	12,730	do. -	do.
Stoke Edith (*a*) (*b*) -	*par.*	282	2,852	2,928	do. -	Hereford.
Stretton Sugwas (*e*) -	*par.*	303	779	1,854	do. -	do.
**Sutton (*d*) (*e*) (*h*) -	*par.*	331	1,400	3,440	do. -	do.
‡The Vineyard -	*par.*	8	In Tupsley	103	do. -	Hereford City.
Tupsley (*c*) -	*tow.*	1,017	2,845	8,139	do. -	do.
Wellington (*c*) (*h*) -	*par.*	607	2,538	6,285	do. -	Hereford.
Westhide (*a*)	*cha.*	166 {	In Stoke Edith }	1,985	do. -	do.
Weston Beggard (*a*) -	*par.*	271	934	2,998	do. -	do.
Withington -	*par.*	772	2,392	6,351	do. -	do.
TOTAL of UNION -		34,398	68,999 (*g*) (*h*)	217,277 (*g*) (*h*)		

HERTFORD UNION.

(Formed 18 June 1835 by Order dated 3 June 1835.)

COUNTY OF HERTFORD :

All Saints -	*par.*	1,127	22	5,514	Hertford -	Hertford.
Aston -	*par.*	571	2,073	3,834	Stevenage -	Stevenage.
Bayford -	*par.*	273	1,745	2,735	Hertford -	Hertford.
Bengeo -	*par.*	2,335	3,054	8,966	do. -	do.
Bennington -	*par.*	578	2,949	4,891	Stevenage -	Stevenage.
Brantfield -	*par.*	249	1,609	2,359	Hertford -	Hertford.
Brickendon -	*lib.*	934	1,534	5,172	do. -	do.
Datchworth -	*par.*	626	1,960	3,408	Stevenage -	Stevenage.
Hertingfordbury -	*par.*	823	2,645	4,777	Hertford -	Hertford.
Little Amwell -	*lib.*	704	526	2,619	do. -	do.
Little Berkhampstead	*par.*	424	1,694	3,252	do. -	do.
Sacombe -	*par.*	260	1,534	2,269	Ware -	do.
Saint Andrew's -	*par.*	2,481	1,179	10,478	Hertford -	do.
Saint John's (W.) -	*par.*	2,987	2,138	11,794	do. -	do.
Stapleford -	*par.*	200	1,355	1,786	do. -	do.
Tewin -	*par.*	530	2,694	4,062	do. -	do.
Walkern -	*par.*	843	2,902	5,185	Stevenage -	Stevenage.
Watton -	*par.*	809	3,579	5,991	Hertford -	Hertford.
TOTAL of UNION -		16,751	35,282	89,095		

Unions and Parishes, &c.		Population in 1881.	Area in Statute Acres in 1881.	Rateable Value in 1881.	Post Town.	Petty Sessional Division.
HEXHAM UNION.						
(Formed 22 Oct. 1836 by Order dated 26 Sept. 1836.—Place marked thus * added 25 Dec. 1858 by Order dated 16 Oct. 1858.)						
COUNTY of NORTHUMBERLAND :				£		
Acomb	- tow.	1,056	2,897	6,748	Hexham	Tindale Ward.
Allendale	- par.	4,030	37,469	21,773	Allendale	do.
Aydon (a)	- tow.	95	780	1,061	Corbridge	do.
Aydon Castle	- tow.	17	415	459	do.	do.
Bearle (a)	- tow.	51	419	593	Stocksfield	do.
Bingfield	- tow.	65	2,082	2,220	Corbridge	do.
*Black Carts and Rye-hill	tow.	13 { In Humshaugh }		450	Humshaugh	do.
Blanchland, High Quarter (a)	tow.	293	5,006	1,559	Blanchland	do.
Broombaugh	- tow.	222	830	3,336	Riding Mill	do.
Broomley (a)	- tow.	389	3,611	5,135	Stocksfield	do.
Bywell	- tow.	56	435	449	do.	do.
Chollerton	- tow.	1,210	14,240	14,216	Wall	do.
Clarewood (a)	- tow.	38	825	1,016	Matfen	do.
Cocklaw	- tow.	180	3,764	4,221	Wall	do.
Corbridge (a)	- tow.	1,593	5,008	13,064	Corbridge	do.
Dilston (a)	- tow.	206	2,224	5,538	do.	do.
Dukeshagg	- tow.	4	115	60	Prudhoe	do.
Eltringham (a)	- tow.	451	355	5,093	do.	do.
Espersheels	- tow.	120	3,735	1,735	Riding Mill	do.
Fallowfield	- tow.	46	667	773	Wall	do.
Fotherly High	- tow.	68	1,657	785	Riding Mill	do.
Hallington	- tow.	99	1,713	2,431	Corbridge	do.
Halton	- tow.	50	841	1,434	do.	do.
Haughton	- tow.	115	1,839	1,799	Humshaugh	do.
Haydon	- tow.	2,365	14,339	22,897	Haydon Bridge	do.
Healey (a)	- tow.	106	2,182	858	Riding Mill	do.
Hedley (a)	- tow.	186	1,266	1,161	Stocksfield	do.
Hexham (W.)	- tow.	5,919	5,136	27,614	Hexham	do.
Hexham, High Quarter (b)	tow.	156	6,539	2,298	do.	do.
Hexham, Low Quarter	tow.	367	3,651	2,899	do.	do.
Hexham, Middle Quarter (b)	tow.	263	4,222	2,804	do.	do.
Hexham, West Quarter (b)	tow.	219	1,484	3,936	do.	do.

(continued)

HEXHAM UNION :

(a) By Orders which came into operation on 25 March 1887,—

Detached parts of Broomley were amalgamated with Healey and Mickley ;

Parts of Corbridge were amalgamated with Aydon and Dilston ;

A detached part of Eltringham was amalgamated with Mickley ;

Certain parts of Mickley were amalgamated with Broomley and Eltringham ;

A detached part of Newlands was amalgamated with Whittonstall ;

A detached part of Newton was amalgamated with Nafferton ;

Detached parts of Ovington were amalgamated with Nafferton and Stelling ; and

The several parts of the under-mentioned places, having, in 1881, the population, acreage and rateable

HEXHAM UNION—continued.

value shown, were amalgamated with other places a-stated,—

Places.	Population.	Area.	Rateable Value.	Places with which amalgamated.
Anick Sandhoe	153 216	158 1,629	1,052 2,572	Anick (name altered to Sandhoe).
Apperley Bywell Saint Andrew	19 16	429 102	280 537	Broomley, Mickley, Acomb (East) (name altered to Bywell), Bearle, Newton Hall.
Bywell Saint Peter	128	1,069	1,966	Acomb (East), Newton, Newton Hall.
Halton Shields Hedleywoodside	56 440	367 1,384	615 1,102	Clarewood, Ebchester (Lanchester Union), Hedley, Medomsley (Lanchester Union).
New Biggen	77	2,111	828	Blanchland, High Quarter.
Prudhoe Castle	844	796	7,910	Master's Close (name altered to Prudhoe Castle), Mickley.
Stocksfield Hall	113	330	1,160	Broomley, Mickley.

(b) There is some land known as Stinted Pasture Moor Land, and containing 4,909 acres, common to Hexham High Quarter, Middle Quarter, and West Quarter.

Unions and Parishes, &c.		Population in 1881.	Area in Statute Acres in 1881.	Rateable Value in 1881.	Post Town.	Petty Sessional Division.
HEXHAM UNION—County of Northumberland—*continued.*				£		
Horsley	- *tow.*	348	1,531	2,877	Wylam	Tindale Ward.
Humshaugh	- *tow.*	476	2,332	2,853	Humshaugh	do.
Mickley (*a*)	- *tow.*	1,371	1,206	3,853	Prudhoe	do.
Nafferton (*a*)	- *tow.*	60	804	758	Stocksfield	do.
Newbrough	- *tow.*	771	6,821	11,217	Fourstones	do.
Newlands (*a*)	- *tow.*	110	1,651	1,092	Stocksfield	do.
Newton (*a*)	- *tow.*	154	789	1,143	do.	do.
Newton Hall (*a*)	- *tow.*	138	710	1,161	do.	do.
Ovingham	- *tow.*	280	555	1,282	Prudhoe	do.
Ovington (*a*)	- *tow.*	533	1,133	2,569	do.	do.
Portgate	- *tow.*	72	664	712	Hexham	do.
Prudhoe	- *tow.*	3,041	1,457	9,934	Prudhoe	do.
Prudhoe Castle	- *tow.*	14	42	40	do.	do.
Riding	- *tow.*	213	1,036	3,516	Riding Mill	do.
Sandhoe	- *tow.*	61	556	1,118	Hexham	do.
Shotley, Low Quarter	- *tow.*	554	7,132	5,773	Black Hill	do.
Simonburn	- *tow.*	412	9,159	6,471	Humshaugh	do.
Slaley Out Quarter and Slaley Town	- *par.*	427	7,518	3,708	Slaley	do.
Spittle	- *tow.*	12	84	172	Wylam	do.
Stelling (*a*)	- *tow.*	47	242	408	Stocksfield	do.
Styford	- *tow.*	105	1,039	1,417	Riding Mill	do.
Thornborough	- *tow.*	75	782	844	Corbridge	do.
Wall	- *tow.*	398	1,699	2,966	Wall	do.
Warden	- *tow.*	882	3,281	8,231	Hexham	do.
Welton	- *tow.*	54	1,203	1,717	Stocksfield	do.
Whittington, Great	- *tow.*	219	1,494	1,886	Matfen	do.
Whittington, Little	- *tow.*	14	362	504	do.	do.
Whittle	- *tow.*	20	288	515	Wylam	do.
Whittonstall (*a*)	- *tow.*	156	2,176	1,597	Stocksfield	do.
Wylam	- *tow.*	959	974	5,069	Wylam	Castle Ward (West Division).
TOTAL OF UNION	-	32,024	191,766 (*b*)	245,878		

HIGHWORTH AND SWINDON UNION.						
(Formed 23 Nov. 1835 by Order dated 4 Nov. 1835.)						
COUNTY OF WILTS :						
Bishopstone	- *par.*	606	4,452	3,870	Shrivenham	Swindon.
Blunsden Saint Andrew (*b*)	- *par.*	93	1,431	1,772	Highworth	do.
Castle Eaton	- *par.*	323	1,979	3,408	Fairford	do.
Chiseldon	- *par.*	1,173	4,750	7,457	Swindon	do.
Draycot Foliat	- *par.*	46	702	912	do.	do.
Hannington	- *par.*	304	2,518	3,828	Highworth	do.
Highworth (*b*)	- *par.*	3,302	10,504	24,262	do.	do.
Hinton Parva (*b*)	- *par.*	247	1,815	3,111	Shrivenham	do.
Inglesham (*a*)	- *par.*	110	1,238	2,142	Lechlade	do.
Lyddington (*b*)	- *par.*	416	2,767	4,101	Swindon	do.
Rodbourne Cheney	- *par.*	1,978	2,728	9,002	do.	do.
Stanton Fitzwarren (*b*)	*par.*	192	1,360	3,082	Highworth	do.
Stratton Saint Margaret (W.)	- *par.*	3,959	2,620	16,558	Swindon	do.
Swindon (*b*)	- *par.*	19,904	3,136	86,648	do.	do.
Wanborough (*b*)	- *par.*	877	4,440	7,909	Shrivenham	do.
Wroughton	- *par.*	2,225	4,546	14,220	Swindon	do.
TOTAL OF UNION	-	35,755	50,986	193,182		

HIGHWORTH AND SWINDON UNION :

(*a*) A detached part of Coleshill, in the Farringdon Union, known as "Lynt Farm," was amalgamated with Inglesham by Provisional Order which came into operation on 25 March 1883.

(*b*) By Orders which came into operation on 25 March 1884,—

A detached part of Highworth was amalgamated with Blunsden Saint Andrew ;

HIGHWORTH AND SWINDON UNION—*continued.*

Detached parts of Stanton Fitzwarren were amalgamated with Highworth ;

A detached part of Wanborough was amalgamated with Hinton Parva ; and

A detached part of Lyddington was amalgamated with Swindon.

Unions and Parishes, &c.		Population in 1881.	Area in Statute Acres in 1881.	Rateable Value in 1881.	Post Town.	Petty Sessional Division.
HINCKLEY UNION.						
(Formed 9 Feb. 1836 by Order dated 22 Jan. 1836.— Places marked thus * added 30 April 1851 by Order dated 11 April 1851.)						
COUNTY of LEICESTER :				£		
Aston Flamville	- *tow.*	113	In Burbage	1,699	Hinckley	Market Bosworth.
Barwell	*tow.*	1,506	2,290	5,041	do.	do.
Burbage	*tow.*	1,691	4,670	7,225	do.	do.
Earl Shilton (*a*)	*tow.*	2,252	920	5,036	do.	do.
Elmsthorpe	*par.*	34	1,650	2,672	do.	do.
*Higham-on-the-Hill	*par.*	445	2,880	4,617	do.	do.
Sapcote	*par.*	693	1,380	2,745	do.	do.
Sharnford	*par.*	459	740	3,021	do.	do.
*Stoke Golding	*tow.*	551	In Hinckley	2,524	do.	do.
Stoney Stanton (*a*)	*par.*	993	1,750	4,258	do.	do.
COUNTIES of LEICESTER and WARWICK :						
Hinckley (W.)	- *tow.*	7,673	5,330	19,162	do.	do.
COUNTY of WARWICK :						
Burton Hastings (*a*)	*par.*	164	1,910	2,441	Nuneaton	Coventry.
Stretton Baskerville -	*par.*	45	760	1,456	do.	do.
*Wolvey (*a*) -	- *par.*	783	3,790	5,950	Hinckley	do.
TOTAL of UNION	-	17,402	28,070	67,847		
HITCHIN UNION.						
(Formed 15 June 1835 by Order dated 13 May 1835.— Place marked thus * added 1 Aug. 1835 by Order dated 18 July 1835.)						
COUNTY of BEDFORD :						
Holwell	- *par.*	215	592	2,454	Hitchin	Biggleswade.
COUNTY of HERTFORD :						
Baldock (*a*	- *par.*	2,326	261	5,797	Baldock	Baldock.
Bygrave (*a*) -	- *par.*	109	1,789	3,648	do.	do.
Caldicott	- *par.*	31	326	406	do.	do.
*Clothall (*a*) -	- *par.*	308	3,526	3,959	do.	do.
Codicote	- *par.*	1,191	2,532	4,785	Welwyn	Welwyn.
Graveley	- *par.*	380	1,838	2,729	Stevenage	Stevenage.
Great Wymondley	- *par.*	270	1,491	4,606	do.	Hitchin.
Hexton	- *par.*	200	1,485	1,916	Ampthill	do.
Hitchin (W.)	- *par.*	9,070	6,420	40,519	Hitchin	do.
Ickleford	- *par.*	563	1,035	2,308	do.	do.
Ippollitts	- *par.*	1,008	2,937	5,998	do.	do.
Kimpton	- *par.*	936	3,677	5,555	Welwyn	do.
King's Walden	- *par.*	1,135	4,392	5,785	do.	do.
Knebworth -	- *par.*	250	2,737	8,323	Stevenage	Stevenage.
Letchworth -	- *par.*	108	1,131	1,725	Baldock	Baldock.
Lilley	- *par.*	505	1,849	2,377	Luton	Hitchin.
Little Wymondley	- *par.*	401	1,007	3,609	Stevenage	do.

(continued)

HINCKLEY UNION :

(*a*) By Orders which came into operation on 25 March 1885,—
A detached part of Stoney Stanton was amalgamated with Earl Shilton ; and
A detached part of Wolvey was amalgamated with Burton Hastings.

HITCHIN UNION :

(*a*) All the parts of Bygrave, Clothall, Norton, Weston, and Willian which were comprised in the Urban Sanitary District of Baldock, were amalgamated with Baldock, by Order which came into operation on 25 March 1882.

Unions and Parishes, &c.		Population in 1881.	Area in Statute Acres in 1881.	Rateable Value in 1881.	Post Town.	Petty Sessional Division.
HITCHIN UNION—County of Hertford—*continued.*						
Newnham	par.	113	975	1,226	Baldock	Baldock.
Norton (a)	par.	250	1,753	2,389	do.	do.
Offley	par.	1,302	5,515	7,560	Hitchin	Hitchin.
Pirton	par.	1,125	2,761	4,056	do.	do.
Radwell	par.	101	743	1,162	Baldock	Baldock.
Saint Paul's Walden	par.	1,020	3,720	6,264	Welwyn	Hitchin.
Shephall	par.	221	1,156	1,653	Stevenage	Stevenage.
Stevenage	par.	3,116	4,545	19,171	do.	do.
Weston(a)	par.	897	4,511	5,899	Baldock	Baldock.
Willian (a)	par.	266	1,866	3,326	Hitchin	do.
TOTAL of UNION		27,417	66,600	159,205		

HOLBEACH UNION.

(Formed 7 Dec. 1835 by Order dated 23 Nov. 1835.—Place marked thus * added 24 June 1866 by Order dated 2 May 1866.)

		Population in 1881.	Area in Statute Acres in 1881.	Rateable Value in 1881.	Post Town.	Petty Sessional Division.
COUNTY of LINCOLN:						
Fleet (W.)	par.	1,331	6,667	11,838	Holbeach	Elloe.
Gedney (a)	tow.	1,884	} 25,257	17,544	do.	do.
Gedney Hill	ham.	344		3,161	Wisbech	do.
Holbeach	par.	5,190	35,220	39,367	Holbeach	do.
Lutton (a)	ham.	770	In Sutton Saint Mary	6,456	do.	do.
Sutton Saint Edmunds (a)	ham.	676	do.	9,335	Wisbech	do.
Sutton Saint James (a)	ham.	605	do.	4,752	do.	do.
Sutton Saint Mary (a)	ham.	4,901	25,146	21,471	do.	do.
Tydd Saint Mary	par.	928	4,845	8,000	do.	do.
Whaplode	par.	2,375	10,164	18,452	Spalding	do.
COUNTIES of LINCOLN and NORFOLK:						
*Central Wingland	par.	245	—	4,148	Wisbech	do.
TOTAL of UNION		19,249	107,209	144,824		

HOLBECK UNION.

(Formed 21 June 1869 by Order dated 31 May 1869.)

		Population in 1881.	Area in Statute Acres in 1881.	Rateable Value in 1881.	Post Town.	Petty Sessional Division.
COUNTY of YORK, WEST RIDING:						
Beeston	tow.	2,928	1,568	13,438	Leeds	Borough of Leeds.
Churwell	tow.	1,973	489	7,169	do.	Leeds Division of the West Riding of York.
Holbeck (W.)	tow.	19,150	611	52,618	do.	Borough of Leeds.
TOTAL of UNION		24,051	2,668	73,225		

HOLBEACH UNION:

(a) By Order which came into operation on 25 March 1884,—

Detached parts of Gedney were amalgamated with Lutton, and detached parts of Lutton were amalgamated with Gedney and Sutton Saint James; and

Detached parts of Sutton Saint Edmunds and Sutton Saint James were amalgamated with Sutton Saint Mary.

Unions and Parishes, &c.	Population in 1881.	Area in Statute Acres in 1881.	Rateable Value in 1881.	Post Town.	Petty Sessional Division.

HOLBORN UNION.

(Formed 27 April 1836 by Order dated 29 March 1836.—Place marked thus * added 16 May 1845 by Order of that date; thus † added 29 Sept. 1858 by Order dated 25 August 1858; thus ‡ added 24 June 1869 by Order dated 5 June 1869; and thus § added 26 March 1877 by Order dated 10 March 1877.)

County of Middlesex:

			£		
§Charterhouse - par.	149	10	11,898	E.C. - -	Finsbury.
†Furnival's Inn - par.	121	2	5,623	W.C. - -	Holborn.
Saint Andrew Holborn above Bars united with Saint George the Martyr (W.) - par.	28,874	112	183,778	do. - -	do.
†Saint James, Clerkenwell - par.	69,076	380	326,709	do. -	do.
‡Saint Luke, Middlesex par.	46,849	239	278,313	E.C. - -	Finsbury.
*Saint Sepulchre (a) - par.	2,404	20	40,958	W.C. - -	do.
†Staple Inn - par.	38	1	2,672	do. -	Holborn.
The Liberty of Saffron Hill, Hatton Garden, Ely Rents, and Ely Place -	3,980	30	63,165	do. -	do.
TOTAL of UNION -	151,491	794	913,116		

HOLLINGBOURN UNION.

(Formed 12 Oct. 1835 by Order dated 24 Sept. 1835.)

County of Kent:

Bicknor - - par.	37	633	546	Sittingbourne -	Bearstead.
Boughton Malherbe - par.	145	2,710	3,389	Maidstone	do.
Boxley - - par.	1,530	5,787	10,859	do. -	do.
Bredhurst - - par.	131	602	811	Chatham -	do.
Broomfield - - par.	160	1,449	1,641	Maidstone -	do.
Chart next Sutton Valence - par.	687	2,188	4,478	Staplehurst -	do.
Debtling - - par.	336	1,589	2,163	Maidstone -	do.
East Sutton - par.	388	1,596	2,818	Staplehurst	do.
Frinstead - par.	208	1,290	1,488	Sittingbourne	do.
Harrietsham - par.	679	2,185	3,769	Maidstone -	do.
Headcorne - par.	1,493	5,051	11,937	Ashford -	do.
Hollingbourn (W.) - par.	1,151	4,611	7,004	Maidstone -	do.
Hucking - par.	133	1,205	987	Sittingbourne	do.
Langley - par.	370	1,494	2,832	Maidstone -	do.
Leeds - par.	727	1,653	4,293	do. -	do.
Lenham - par.	1,987	6,966	10,507	do. -	do.
Otterden - par.	165	1,493	1,419	Faversham -	do.
Stockbury - par.	621	2,951	4,045	Sittingbourne	do.
Sutton Valence - par.	1,131	2,171	5,712	Staplehurst	do.
Thornham - par.	648	3,363	4,272	Maidstone -	do.
Ulcomb - par.	656	3,546	5,072	Staplehurst	do.
Witchling - par.	144	1,316	1,288	Sittingbourne	do.
Wormshill - par.	213	1,475	1,430	do. -	do.
TOTAL of UNION -	14,010	57,624	92,790		

HOLBORN UNION:

(a) This is only the part of Saint Sepulchre which is in Middlesex.

Unions and Parishes, &c.	Population in 1881.	Area in Statute Acres in 1881.	Rateable Value in 1881.	Post Town.	Petty Sessional Division

HOLSWORTHY UNION.

(Formed 31 Jan. 1837 by Order dated 5 Jan. 1837. — Place marked thus * added 24 June 1859 by Order dated 28 April 1859.)

COUNTY of CORNWALL :

			£		
North Tamerton - *par.*	469	5,261	2,664	Holsworthy - -	Stratton.

COUNTY of DEVON:

Abbots Bickington - *par.*	47	1,078	460	Brandis Corner -	Holsworthy.
Ashwater - - *par.*	849	8,587	3,427	Lifton -	do.
Black Torrington (*a*) *par.*	874	7,200	3,248	Highampton -	do.
Bradford (*a*) - *par.*	377	3,468	1,754	Brandis Corner -	do.
*Bradworthy - *par.*	887	9,586	3,800	Holsworthy	do.
Bridgerule East (*a*) - *par.*	158 { In Bridgerule West		1,150	do. - -	do.
Bridgerule West - *par.*	233	3,219	720	do. - -	do.
Clawton - *par.*	445	5,358	2,936	do. - -	do.
Cookbury - - *par.*	183	2,710	1,160	Brandis Corner -	do.
Halwell - - *par.*	317	3,126	1,328	Lifton -	do.
Hollacombe - *par.*	115	1,218	604	Holsworthy -	do.
Holsworthy (W.) - *par.*	1,716	8,836	6,805	do. -	do.
Luffincot (*b*) - *par.*	62	971	600	Launceston -	do.
Milton Damarel - *par.*	176	4,252	2,232	Brandis Corner -	do.
Panerasweek (*a*) - *par.*	318	3,782	1,888	Holsworthy -	do.
Pyworthy (*a*) *par.*	501	5,021	2,643	do. -	do.
Sutcombe (*a*) - *par.*	407	3,593	1,980	do. -	do.
Tetcot (*b*) - *par.*	263	2,181	1,200	do. -	do.
Thornbury - *par.*	311	2,772	1,554	Brandis Corner -	do.
TOTAL of UNION -	9,008	82,519	42,153		

HOLYHEAD UNION.

(Formed 29 Sept. 1852 by Order dated 13 Sept. 1852. — Place marked thus * added 29 Sept. 1852 by Order dated 21 Sept. 1852.)

COUNTY of ANGLESEY :

Aberffraw - *par.*	981	6,252	6,312	Aberffraw - -	Second Division.
Bodedern - *par.*	1,018	4,235	3,384	The Valley -	do.
Bodwrog - - *par.*	296	1,813	1,410	Llangefni - -	do.
Ceirchiog - *par.*	129	613	492	Bryngwran, The Valley.	do.
Cerrigceinwen - *par.*	483	1,582	1,335	Llangefni - -	First Division.
Heneglwys - - *par.*	438	2,062	1,678	do. -	do.
Holyhead - - *par.*	9,689	6,988	34,006	Holyhead - -	Second Division.
Llanbeulan - *par.*	223	2,945	2,329	Bryngwran, The Valley.	do.
Llanddeusaint - *par.*	452	2,011	1,818	Holyhead - -	do.
Llandrygarn - *par.*	323	2,430	2,024	Llangefni - -	do.
Llanfaethreth - *par.*	513	1,887	1,695	The Valley -	do.
Llanfaelog - *par.*	714	2,732	2,972	Holyhead - -	do.
Llanfaethly - *par.*	381	2,629	1,984	The Valley -	do.
Llanfair-yn-Neubwll *par.*	329	1,279	2,292	do. - -	do.
Llanfigael - *par.*	122	484	515	do. - -	do.
Llanfihangel-yn-Nho-wyn - - - } *par.*	174	1,404	1,734	do. - -	do.

(*continued*)

HOLSWORTHY UNION :

(*a*) By Provisional Orders which came into operation on 25 March 1884,—

A detached part of Black Torrington was amalgamated with Bradford ;

A detached part of Black Torrington was amalgamated with High Hampton, in the Okehampton Union ;

HOLSWORTHY UNION—*continued*.

A detached part of Bridgerule East was amalgamated with Pyworthy ; and

A detached part of Sutcombe was amalgamated with Panerasweek.

(*b*) A detached part of Tetcot was amalgamated with Luffincot, by Order which came into operation on 25 March 1883.

Unions and Parishes, &c.	Population in 1881.	Area in Statute Acres in 1881.	Rateable Value in 1881.	Post Town.	Petty Sessional Division.
HOLYHEAD UNION—County of Anglesey—continued.			£		
Llanfwrog - par.	193	2,017	1,448	The Valley -	Second Division.
Llangwyfan - par.	199	1,828	1,929	Aberffraw - -	do.
Llanllibio - par.	49	826	674	The Valley -	do.
Llanrhyddlad - par.	633	2,679	1,952	do. -	do.
Llantrisaint - par.	402	1,117	3,238	Llanerchymedd, R.S.O.	do.
Llanynghenedle (W.) par.	493	2,965	3,236	The Valley -	do.
Llechylched - par.	576	1,783	2,435	Bryngwran, The Valley.	do.
*Rhoscolyn - par.	442	2,580	1,426	Holyhead - -	do.
Trevalchmai - par.	707	1,700	1,483	Gwalchmai, The Valley.	do.
TOTAL of UNION -	19,959	62,169	83,801		
HOLYWELL UNION.					
(Formed 25 Feb. 1837 by Order dated 30 Jan. 1837.)					
COUNTIES of DENBIGH and FLINT :					
Nannerch - par.	346	2,875	2,631	Mold -	Caerwys.
COUNTY of FLINT :					
Caerwys - par.	805	2,737	3,804	Holywell - -	Caerwys.
Cilcen - - par.	936	6,570	6,684	Mold - -	Northop.
Flint - - par.	4,744	1,608	15,075	Flint - -	Borough of Flint.
Gwaenysgor - par.	273	817	1,060	Rhyl - -	Newmarket.
Halkin - par.	1,376	3,408	5,949	Holywell - -	Northop.
Holywell (W.) par.	9,963	7,808	41,535	do. -	Holywell.
Llanassa - par.	2,731	6,326	16,943	do. -	Newmarket.
Mold - - towc.	13,029	12,839	42,425	Mold - -	Mold.
Nerquis - - towc.	644	2,318	4,302	do. -	do.
Newmarket - par.	492	1,075	1,861	Rhyl - -	Newmarket.
Northop - par.	5,012	10,675	26,264	Flint - -	Northop.
Whitford - par.	4,136	8,247	22,641	Holywell - -	Holywell.
Yscciliog - par.	1,257	6,077	6,397	do. -	Caerwys.
TOTAL of UNION -	45,774	73,380	197,571		
HONITON UNION.					
(Formed 18 April 1836 by Order dated 4 April 1836.)					
COUNTY of DEVON :					
Awliscombe (b) - par.	534	2,569	3,675	Honiton -	Honiton.
Branscombe - par.	842	3,497	3,924	Sidmouth - -	do.
Broadhembury - par.	675	4,703	5,982	Honiton -	Cullompton.
Buckerell (b) - par.	255	1,559	3,163	do. -	Honiton.
Comb Rawleigh (b) - par.	230	1,747	2,570	do. -	do.
Cotleigh - par.	172	1,218	1,560	do. -	do.
Dunkeswell - par.	393	5,160	3,017	do. -	do.
Farway - par.	289	2,578	2,766	do. -	do.
Feniton - par	355	1,822	3,825	do. -	do.
Gittisham (b) - par.	444	2,067	3,269	do. -	do.

(continued)

HONITON UNION :

(a) Two detached parts of Colyton, in the Axminster Union, were amalgamated with Southleigh, by Provisional Order which came into operation on 25 March 1885.

(b) By Order which came into operation on 25 March 1881,—

Parts of Awliscombe were amalgamated with Gittisham and Buckerell;

HONITON UNION—continued.

Parts of Buckerell were amalgamated with Gittisham and Awliscombe, and

Parts of Gittisham were amalgamated with Buckerell.

A detached part of Comb Rawleigh was amalgamated with Monkton; and

A detached part of Offwell was amalgamated with Northleigh.

Unions and Parishes, &c.	Population in 1881.	Area in Statute Acres in 1881.	Rateable Value in 1881.	Post Town.	Petty Sessional Division.
			£		
HONITON UNION—County of Devon—*continued.*					
Harpford - - *par.*	273	1,518	1,979	Ottery St. Mary -	Ottery St. Mary.
Honiton (W.) - *par.*	3,358	3,066	11,298	Honiton - -	Honiton.
Luppitt - - *par.*	601	4,293	5,259	do. - -	do.
Monkton (*b*) - *par.*	121	1,233	1,523	do. - -	do.
Northleigh (*b*) - *par.*	216	994	1,240	do. - -	do.
Offwell (*b*) - *par.*	332	2,206	2,770	do. - -	do.
Ottery Saint Mary - *par.*	3,973	9,912	18,320	Ottery St. Mary -	Ottery St. Mary.
Payhembury - *par.*	427	2,698	4,001	do. - -	Cullompton.
Plymtree - - *par.*	436	2,185	3,432	Cullompton	do.
Salcombe Regis - *par.*	566	2,605	3,944	Sidmouth -	Ottery St. Mary
Sheldon - - *par.*	140	1,681	1,302	Honiton -	Honiton.
Sidbury - - *par.*	1,291	6,527	9,263	Sidmouth -	Ottery St. Mary
Sidmouth - - *par.*	3,475	1,600	13,362	do. - -	do.
Southleigh (*a*) - *par.*	222	2,579	2,030	Honiton -	Honiton.
Tallaton - - *par.*	462	2,365	1,337	Ottery St. Mary -	Ottery St. Mary.
Up Ottery - - *par.*	727	5,830	6,473	Honiton -	Honiton.
Venn Ottery - - *par.*	110	918	1,038	Ottery St. Mary -	Ottery St. Mary.
Widworthy - - *par.*	131	1,437	1,906	Honiton - -	Honiton.
TOTAL of UNION -	21,080	80,887	127,237		
HOO UNION.					
(Formed 9 Sept. 1835 by Order dated 22 Aug. 1835.)					
COUNTY of KENT :					
Allhallows - - *par.*	313	2,407	3,583	Rochester -	North Aylesford
Cooling (*a*) - *par.*	232	1,556	2,884	do. - -	do.
High Halstow - *par.*	376	3,212	4,076	do. - -	do.
Hoo (W.) - - *par.*	1,322	4,491	7,365	do. - -	do.
Saint James (Isle of Grain) } *par.*	283	3,177	4,093	do. - -	do.
Saint Mary - *par.*	309	1,946	3,214	do. - -	do.
Stoke - - *par.*	570	3,070	3,942	do. - -	do.
TOTAL of UNION -	3,405	19,859	29,157		
HORNCASTLE UNION.					
(Formed 16 Jan. 1837 by Order dated 20 Dec. 1836.— Place marked thus * added 20 May 1881 by Order dated 28 April 1881.)					
COUNTY of LINCOLN :					
Asgarby (*a*) - *par.*	70	658	1,108	Spilsby -	Spilsby.
Ashby Puerorum - *par.*	147	1,620	1,946	Horncastle -	Horncastle.
Ashby West - *par.*	382	1,074	3,788	do. - -	do.

(*continued*)

Hoo UNION :

(*a*) By Order which came into operation on 25 March 1887, a certain part of Frindsbury, in the Strood Union, was amalgamated with Cooling.

HORNCASTLE UNION :

(*a*) Detached parts of Asgarby, Miningsby, and Revesby were amalgamated with Carrington, in the Boston Union, by Provisional Order which came into operation on 25 March 1882.

(*b*) A detached part of Lusby was amalgamated with Stickford, in the Spilsby Union, by Provisional Order which came into operation on 25 March 1882.

HORNCASTLE UNION—*continued.*

(*c*) A detached part of Coningsby was amalgamated with Dogdyke, in the Boston Union, and a detached part of Dogdyke was amalgamated with Coningsby, by Orders which came into operation on 25 March 1884.

(*d*) A detached part of Tumby was amalgamated with Revesby, by Order which came into operation on 25 March 1884.

(*e*) Part of a Parish which, in 1881, was known as Haven Bank (having population 29, and rateable value 341*l.*), north of Great Beats, was amalgamated with Coningsby, and the remainder was amalgamated with Wildmore, by Order which came into operation on 25 March 1884.

(*f*) Detached parts of Coningsby, Haltham, Horncastle, Mareham-le-Fen, Moorby, and Wood Enderby were amalgamated with Wildmore, by Order which came into operation on 25 March 1884.

HORNCASTLE UNION—County of Lincoln—*continued.*

Unions and Parishes, &c.		Population in 1881.	Area in Statute Acres in 1881.	Rateable Value in 1881.	Post Town.	Petty Sessional Division.
				£		
Asterby	par.	213	620	1,112	Horncastle	Horncastle.
Bag Enderby	par.	71	617	750	Spilsby	do.
Barkwith East	par.	339	990	1,585	Wragby	Wragby.
Barkwith West	par.	119	500	996	do.	do.
Baumber	par.	391	3,200	3,736	Horncastle	Horncastle.
Belchford	par.	488	2,390	3,144	do.	do.
Benniworth	par.	381	2,994	3,282	Wragby	Wragby.
Bucknall	par.	336	2,471	2,307	Horncastle	Horncastle.
Cawkwell	par.	45	540	771	do.	do.
Claxby Pluckacre	par.	66	847	921	Boston	do.
Coningsby (c) (e) (f)	par.	1,332	5,022	5,836	do.	do.
Dalderby	par.	49	361	539	Horncastle	do.
Edlington	par.	213	2,900	3,349	do.	do.
Fulletby	par.	257	1,940	2,067	do.	do.
Gauthy	par.	100	1,444	959	Lincoln	do.
Goulceby	par.	250	1,440	1,249	Horncastle	do.
Greetham	par.	147	1,180	1,549	do.	do.
Hagworthingham	par.	484	2,430	2,747	Spilsby	do.
Haltham (f)	par.	179	2,380	1,445	Horncastle	do.
Hameringham	par.	175	1,370	1,141	do.	do.
Hatton	par.	178	1,831	1,471	Wragby	Wragby.
Hemingby	par.	402	2,430	2,527	Horncastle	Horncastle.
Horncastle (W.) (f)	par.	4,818	1,868	15,995	do.	do.
Horsington	par.	360	1,700	1,919	do.	do.
Kirkby on Bain	tow.	261	5,110	1,349	do.	do.
Kirkstead	par.	114	1,459	1,583	do.	do.
Langton	par.	203	980	1,125	do.	do.
Langton by Wragby	par.	296	2,249	2,341	Wragby	Wragby.
Lusby (b)	par.	96	585	1,263	Spilsby	Spilsby.
Mareham-le-Fen (f)	par.	736	1,560	2,395	Boston	Horncastle.
Mareham on the Hill	par.	153	1,211	1,593	Horncastle	do.
Martin	par.	70	755	990	do.	do.
Miningsby (a)	par.	132	496	1,810	Boston	do.
Minting	par.	347	2,543	2,439	Horncastle	do.
Moorby (f)	par.	98	830	926	Revesby, Boston	do.
Panton	par.	159	1,996	2,239	Wragby	Wragby.
Ranby	par.	132	1,240	1,411	do.	Horncastle.
Revesby (a) (d)	par.	565	4,200	5,778	Boston	do.
Roughton	par.	151	862	990	Horncastle	do.
Salmondby	par.	102	991	1,228	do.	do.
Scamblesby	par.	364	2,150	2,279	do.	do.
Scrafield	par.	53	670	780	do.	do.
Scrivelsby	par.	124	1,916	2,703	do.	do.
Somersby	par.	43	600	663	Spilsby	do.
Sotby	par.	191	1,500	1,586	Wragby	Wragby.
Stainton Market	par.	97	1,180	1,505	do.	Horncastle.
Stixwold	par.	227	2,250	3,006	Horncastle	do.
Sturton Great	par.	145	1,440	1,578	do.	do.
Tattershall	par.	481	} 4,578	2,615	Boston	do.
Tattershall Thorpe	tow.	301		2,496	do.	do.
Tetford	par.	590	2,210	2,282	Horncastle	do.
Thimbleby	par.	393	1,116	2,964	do.	do.
Thornton	par.	192	1,755	2,097	do.	do.
Torrington West	par.	160	1,109	1,129	Wragby	Wragby.
Toynton High	par.	133	1,054	1,207	Horncastle	Horncastle.
Toynton Low	par.	53	778	1,374	do	do.
Tumby (d)	tow.	319 {	In Kirkby on Bain }	3,470	Boston	do.
Tupholme	par.	93	1,795	1,401	Wragby	Wragby.
Waddingworth	par.	66	928	1,014	Horncastle	Horncastle.
*Wildmore (e) (f)	par.	689	3,701	5,098	Boston	do.
Wilksby	par.	35	558	671	do.	do.
Winceby	par.	64	842	948	Horncastle	do.
Wispington	par.	109	1,570	1,258	do.	do.
Wood Enderby (f)	par.	168	749	1,107	Boston	do.
Woodhall	par.	278	2,234	2,026	Horncastle	do.
Wragby	par.	508	1,594	2,396	Wragby	Wragby.
TOTAL of UNION		21,483 (e)	112,458	117,966 (e)		

HORNCASTLE UNION:

(a), (b), (c), (d), (e), (f), see notes page 185.

Unions and Parishes, &c.	Population in 1881.	Area in Statute Acres in 1881.	Rateable Value in 1881.	Post Town.	Petty Sessional Division.

HORSHAM UNION:

(Formed 14 Sept. 1835 by Order dated 27 August 1835.—Place marked thus * added 29 Sept. 1869 by Order dated 13 Aug. 1869 ; thus † added 14 Mar. 1870 by Order dated 16 Feb. 1870 ; and thus ‡ added 25 June 1880 by Order dated 14 May 1880.)

COUNTY of SUSSEX :

				£		
†Billingshurst	par.	1,611	6,862	7,977	Billingshurst -	Lower Bramber.
‡Crawley	par.	451	780	1,296	Crawley -	Cuckfield.
Horsham (W.)	par.	9,552	11,089	36,299	Horsham	Lower Bramber.
Ifield	par.	2,013	4,133	8,269	Crawley -	do.
Itchingfield	par.	434	2,519	3,299	Horsham - -	do.
Lower Beeding	par.	1,309	8,611	7,703	do. - -	do.
Nuthurst	par.	811	3,510	3,607	do. - -	do.
*Rudgwick	par.	1,122	6,022	5,086	do. - -	do.
Rusper	par.	539	3,123	2,832	do. - -	do.
Shipley	par.	1,114	7,778	7,019	do. - -	do.
Slinfold	par.	773	4,432	5,019	do. - -	do.
Warnham	par.	1,065	4,960	5,565	do. - -	do.
West Grinstead	par.	1,476	6,720	8,296	do. - -	do.
TOTAL of UNION -		22,300	70,539	102,267		

HOUGHTON-LE-SPRING UNION.

(Formed 20 Jan. 1837 by Order dated 23 Dec. 1836.)

COUNTY of DURHAM :

Eppleton Great	tow.	55	707	3,667	Hetton - le - Hole, Fence Houses.	Easington Ward (North Division).
Eppleton Little	tow.	38	337	1,566	do. - -	do.
Herrington East (b)	tow.	159	1,037	2,043	Sunderland	do.
Herrington West (b)	tow.	3,017	1,022	9,729	do. -	do.
Hetton-le-Hole	tow.	10,945	1,618	18,110	Hetton - le - Hole, Fence Houses.	do.
Houghton - le- Spring (W.)	tow.	6,041	4,551	21,123	Fence Houses -	do.
Moorhouse	tow.	71	277	2,909	Leamside, Fence Houses.	Durham Ward.
Moorsley	tow.	1,078	603	6,703	Fence Houses	Easington Ward (North Division).
Morton Grange	tow.	194	162	5,782	do. -	do.
Newbottle	tow.	4,740	1,454	14,137	do. - -	do.
Offerton (b)	tow.	137	847	3,357	Sunderland	Sunderland.
Painshaw	tow.	2,605	1,085	11,307	Fence Houses	Easington Ward (North Division).
Rainton East -	tow.	1,680	1,091	7,147	do. -	do.
Rainton West (a)	tow.	2,888	1,776	13,218	do. - -	do.
Silksworth	tow.	401	1,994	13,078	Sunderland	do.
Warden Law	tow.	96	498	3,017	Fence Houses	do.
TOTAL of UNION -		34,145	16,359	137,195		

HOUGHTON-LE-SPRING UNION :

(a) A detached part of Pittington, in the Durham Union, was amalgamated with Rainton West, by Order which came into operation on 25 March 1882.

HOUGHTON-LE-SPRING UNION—continued.

(b) By Order which came into operation on 25 March 1886, detached parts of Herrington East and Herrington West were amalgamated with Offerton, and a detached part of Offerton was amalgamated with Herrington West

Unions and Parishes, &c.		Population in 1881.	Area in Statute Acres in 1881.	Rateable Value in 1881.	Post Town.	Petty Sessional Division.

HOWDEN UNION.

(Formed 4 Feb. 1837 by Order dated 10 Jan. 1837.—Place marked thus * added 20 Feb. 1851 by Order dated 24 Jan. 1854; thus † added 25 Dec. 1859 by Order dated 14 Nov. 1859; and thus ‡ added 25 May 1882 by Order dated 13 May 1882.—Name of place marked thus § is as altered by Order dated 27th July 1881.)

COUNTY of YORK.
EAST RIDING.

Unions and Parishes, &c.		Population in 1881.	Area in Statute Acres in 1881.	Rateable Value in 1881.	Post Town.	Petty Sessional Division.
				£		
Asselby (a)	tow.	237	1,002	2,539	Howden	Howdenshire.
Aughton	tow.	137	1,952	2,455	York	Holme Beacon.
Balkholme (b)	tow.	73	1,060	1,513	Brough	Howdenshire.
Barmby on the Marsh (a)	tow.	308	1,558	1,274	Howden	do.
Belby	tow.	39	583	1,077	Brough	do.
Bellasize (a)	tow.	116	1,451	1,861	do.	do.
‡Bishopsoil (a)	par.	170	1,992	?	do.	do.
Blacktoft (a)	tow.	325	1,839	5,361	Howden	do.
Brackenholme with Woodall	tow.	100	1,341	1,387	do.	do.
Breighton	tow.	181	1,733	2,436	do.	do.
Broomfleet	tow.	243	1,571	6,654	Brough	South Hunsley.
Bubwith	tow.	514	1,551	3,215	Selby	Howdenshire.
†Cheapsides	tow.	37	7	66	Brough	do.
Cotness (a)	tow.	30	618	1,074	Howden	do.
Eastrington (a) (b)	tow.	381	2,051	6,089	Brough	do.
Ellerton Priory	par.	282	2,555	3,641	York	Holme Beacon.
Faxfleet	tow.	249	1,717	5,295	Howden	South Hunsley.
Foggathorpe	tow.	113	1,321	1,809	do.	Holme Beacon.
Gilberdike (a)	tow.	331	1,042	4,131	Brough	Howdenshire.
Grildthorpe	tow.	33	145	950	Howden	do.
Harlthorpe	tow.	81	758	881	Selby	Holme Beacon.
Hemingbrough	tow.	550	1,141	5,028	Howden	Howdenshire.
Holme upon Spalding Moor	par.	1,893	11,514	11,914	York	Holme Beacon.
Hotham	par.	372	2,808	3,574	Brough	South Hunsley.
Howden (W.)	tow.	2,198	3,098	12,772	Howden	Howdenshire.
Kilpin (b)	tow.	332	724	2,067	do.	do.
Knedlington (a)	tow.	93	394	1,776	do.	do.
Latham	tow.	68	1,434	1,249	do.	Holme Beacon.
Laxton (a)	tow.	238	1,119	3,411	do.	Howdenshire.
*Menthorpe with Bowthorpe	tow.	49	1,095	1,415	do.	Ouse and Derwent.
Metham (a)	tow.	60	954	1,239	do.	Howdenshire.
Newsham and Brind Wressel and Loftsome	par.	375	3,988	8,793	do.	do.
North Cave with Drewton Everthorpe	tow.	1,135	5,141	8,338	Brough	South Hunsley.
Portington and Cavil	tow.	95	1,236	2,734	Howden	Howdenshire.
Saltmarsh (b)	tow.	76	962	2,531	do.	do.
Scalby	tow.	176	1,398	3,256	Brough	do.
Skelton (b)	tow.	232	1,544	3,984	Howden	do.
Spaldington	tow.	296	3,542	3,547	do.	do.
Thorpe	tow.	56	265	568	do.	do.
§Wallingfen	par.	862	2,409	1777	Brough	South Hunsley.
Willitoft	tow.	43	1,628	876	Howden	Howdenshire.
Yokefleet (a)	tow.	108	1,265	2,460	do.	do.
TOTAL of UNION		13,287	75,726 (d)	146,017 (e)		

HOWDEN UNION:

(a) Certain detached parts of Asselby, Barmby on the Marsh, Bellasize, Blacktoft, Cotness, Eastrington, Gilberdike, Knedlington, Laxton, Metham, and Yokefleet were together constituted a Separate Parish, and designated the Parish of Bishopsoil, by Provisional Order which came into operation on 25 March 1882.

(b) Certain detached parts of Balkholme, Kilpin, Saltmarsh, and Skelton were united and amalgamated with East-

HOWDEN UNION—continued.

rington, by Provisional Order which came into operation on 25 March 1882.

(e) In 1884.

(d) The area of the Market Weighton Canal (42 acres), which is included in this Union, should be added to the total area.

Unions and Parishes, &c.		Population in 1881.	Area in Statute Acres in 1881.	Rateable Value in 1881.	Post Town.	Petty Sessional Division.
HOXNE UNION.				£		
(Formed 24 June 1835 by Order dated 30 May 1835.)						
COUNTY of SUFFOLK :						
Athelington	par.	118	487	831	Wickham Market	Stradbroke.
Badingham	par.	672	3,172	5,255	Framlingham	Framlingham.
Bedfield	par.	375	1,268	2,262	Wickham Market	do.
Bedingfield	par.	332	1,753	2,731	Eye	Stradbroke.
Brundish	par.	368	2,077	3,531	Framlingham	do.
Denham	par.	300	1,268	1,938	Wickham Market	do.
Dennington	par.	789	3,262	5,603	Framlingham	Framlingham.
Fresingfield	par.	1,147	4,560	7,773	Harleston	Stradbroke.
Horham	par.	339	1,433	2,526	Framlingham	do.
Hoxne (b)	par.	1,000	4,185	7,498	Scole	do.
Laxfield	par.	886	3,630	6,658	Framlingham	do.
Mendham (a) (b) (c)	par.	751	2,944	5,513	Harleston	do.
Metfield (b) (c)	par.	584	2,162	3,242	do.	do.
Monk Soham	par.	400	1,569	2,550	Wickham Market	Framlingham.
Saxtead	par.	338	1,202	2,180	do.	do.
Southolt	par.	134	798	1,227	do.	Stradbroke.
Stradbroke (W.)	par.	1,202	3,702	7,029	Wickham Market	do.
Syleham	par.	280	1,603	2,616	Scole	do.
Tannington	par.	206	1,602	2,636	Framlingham	Framlingham.
Weybred	par.	647	2,476	4,376	Harleston	Stradbroke.
Wilby (b)	par.	469	1,844	3,021	Wickham Market	do.
Wingfield	par.	463	2,441	3,770	Harleston	do.
Worlingworth	par.	643	2,446	3,982	Wickham Market	do.
TOTAL of UNION		12,443 (c)	51,884 (c)	88,748 (c)		
HUDDERSFIELD UNION.						
(Formed 10 Feb. 1837 by Order dated 21 Jan. 1837, as amended by Order dated 26 Jan. 1837.— Name of place marked thus * (formerly Cumberworth Half) is as altered by Provisional Order dated 23 Feb. 1876, which took effect on 29 Sept. 1876 and by which the Townships of Cumberworth and Cumberworth Half were re-adjusted, but were continued in the Union.						
COUNTY of YORK, WEST RIDING :						
Almondbury	tow.	13,977	2,636	27,848	Huddersfield	Huddersfield.
Austonley (a)	tow.	1,662	3,316	5,677	Holmfirth	Holmfirth.
Cartworth (a)	tow.	2,379	2,263	7,167	do.	do.
Cumberworth	tow.	1,471	1,185	3,614	Skelmanthorpe	Barnsley.
Dalton	tow.	7,900	1,341	22,002	Huddersfield	Huddersfield.
Farnley Tyas	tow.	614	1,785	2,521	do.	do.
Foolstone (a)	tow.	2,117	2,261	6,932	New Mill	do.
Golcar (W.)	tow.	7,653	1,593	24,275	Golcar	do.
Hepworth (a)	tow.	1,169	2,375	4,652	Hepworth	Holmfirth.
Holme (a)	tow.	678	1,728	2,787	Holmfirth	do.
Honley (W.)	tow.	5,070	2,435	16,289	Honley	Huddersfield.
Huddersfield	tow.	42,234	4,055	189,934	Huddersfield	do.
Kirkburton	tow.	3,407	1,286	8,523	Kirkburton	do.
Kirkheaton	tow.	2,747	1,674	9,488	Kirkheaton	do.
Lepton	tow.	3,019	1,863	6,537	Lepton	do.
Lingards	tow.	873	734	4,217	Lingards	do.
Linthwaite	tow.	6,068	1,320	16,929	Linthwaite	do.

(continued)

HOXNE UNION :

(a) All the part of Mendham, in the County of Norfolk, was amalgamated with Redenhall with Harleston, in the Depwade Union, by Provisional Order which came into operation on 25 March 1885.

(b) By Orders which came into operation on 25 March 1884.—

A detached part of Hoxne was amalgamated with Wilby ; and

A detached part of Metfield was amalgamated with Mendham.

B 3872.

HOXNE UNION—*continued.*

(c) By Provisional Order which came into operation on 25 March 1885.—

A certain detached part of a Parish known as Withersdale (having in 1881, population 158, acreage 880, and rateable value 1,396l.) was amalgamated with Linstead Parva, in the Blything Union ; a certain part was amalgamated with Metfield ; and all the remaining parts were amalgamated with Mendham.

HUDDERSFIELD UNION :

(a) See note, page 188.

A a

Unions and Parishes, &c.		Population in 1881.	Area in Statute Acres in 1881.	Rateable Value in 1881.	Post Town.	Petty Sessional Division.
HUDDERSFIELD UNION—County of York, West Riding—*continued.*				£		
Lockwood (W.)	- tow.	10,446	970	27,600	Lockwood - -	Huddersfield.
Longwood -	- tow.	4,661	1,334	12,792	do. - -	do.
Marsden in Almondbury -	} tow.	2,633	5,133	10,111	Marsden - -	do.
Marsden in Huddersfield -	} tow.	686	3,512	5,814	do. -	do.
Meltham -	- tow.	4,529	4,692	15,349	Meltham - -	do.
Netherthong -	- tow.	936	795	4,237	Netherthong -	do.
Quarmby-with-Lindley -	} tow.	7,284	1,491	16,964	{ Lindley-cum-Quarmby. }	do.
Scammonden -	- tow.	607	1,806	2,126	Scammonden -	do.
Shelley -	- tow.	1,687	1,568	4,108	Shelley - -	do.
Shepley -	- tow.	1,593	1,247	4,973	Shepley - -	do.
*Skelmanthorpe	- tow.	3,120	1,392	5,672	Skelmanthorpe -	do.
Slaithwaite -	- tow.	3,009	2,436	11,353	Slaithwaite -	do.
South Crosland	- tow.	3,048	1,834	10,738	Netherton -	do.
Thurstonland	- tow.	997	2,106	4,881	Thurstonland -	do.
Upperthong (*a*)	- tow.	2,436	3,206	7,772	Upperthong -	Holmfirth.
Whitley Upper	- tow.	909	2,053	4,665	Wakefield -	Huddersfield.
Wooldale (*a*)	- tow.	4,894	2,158	11,722	Holmfirth - -	Holmfirth.
TOTAL of UNION	-	156,513	71,586	520,275		
HUNGERFORD UNION.						
(Formed 1 May 1835 by Order dated 15 April 1835.—Place marked thus * added 18 July 1835, by Order dated 3 July 1835; thus † added 29 Sept. 1836, and thus ‡ added 29 Sept. 1858 by Order dated 24 July 1858.)						
COUNTY of BERKS :						
Avington -	- par.	109	1,185	1,175	Hungerford -	Hungerford.
East Garston	- par.	459	4,409	5,065	Swindon - -	Lamborne.
East Shefford	- par.	115	1,069	1,631	Hungerford -	Hungerford.
Inkpen -	- par.	692	2,885	3,543	Hungerford -	do.
Kintbury -	par.	1,683	7,778	13,477	do. - -	do.
Lambourne -	- par.	2,165	14,873	16,182	Swindon -	Lamborne.
West Shefford	- par.	485	2,213	3,187	do. - -	Hungerford.
West Woodhay	- par.	116	1,432	1,575	Newbury - -	do.
COUNTIES of BERKS and WILTS :						
Chilton Foliat	- par.	563	3,172	1,490	Hungerford	Marlborough.
Hungerford (W.)	- par.	2,965	5,836	13,925	do. -	Hungerford.
Shalbourn -	- par.	822	5,567	6,282	do. -	Marlborough.
COUNTY of SOUTHAMPTON :						
*Combe -	- par.	134	2,212	1,293	Hungerford -	Kingsclere.
COUNTY of WILTS :						
Aldbourn -	- par.	1,488	8,495	9,873	Swindon -	Marlborough.
Baydon -	- par.	299	3,060	2,728	do. -	do.
Buttermere -	- par.	129	1,502	1,184	Hungerford -	Everley.
Froxfield -	- par.	436	2,214	3,206	do. -	Marlborough.
Great Bedwin -	- par.	1,834	9,933	11,918	do. -	do.
Ham -	- par.	199	1,652	2,178	do. -	do.
‡Hippenscombe	- par.	42	911	372	do. -	Everley.
Little Bedwin	- par.	500	4,343	3,964	do. -	Marlborough.
Ramsbury -	- par.	2,329	9,742	13,386	do. -	do.
†Tidcombe -	- par.	238	2,367	2,076	Marlborough -	Everley.
TOTAL of UNION	-	17,802	97,180	123,010		

HUDDERSFIELD UNION :	HUDDERSFIELD UNION—*continued.*
(*a*) By Order which came into operation on 25 March 1886,— Detached parts of Austonley were amalgamated with Cartworth, Holme, and Upperthong ;	Detached parts of Cartworth, Foolstone, and Hepworth were amalgamated with Wooldale ; and Detached parts of Wooldale were amalgamated with Cartworth and Hepworth.

Unions and Parishes, &c.	Population in 1881.	Area in Statute Acres in 1881.	Rateable Value in 1881.	Post Town.	Petty Sessional Division.
HUNSLET UNION.					
(Formed 21 June 1869 by Order dated 31 May 1869.)					
COUNTY of YORK, WEST RIDING :			£		
Hunslet (W.) - *tow.*	46,942	1,152	119,746	Leeds -	Borough of Leeds.
Middleton in the Parish of Rothwell *tow.*	1,134	1,815	9,222	do. -	Agbrigg Wapontake.
Oulton-with-Woodlesford (a) *tow.*	2,344	1,361	13,007	do. - -	do.
Rothwell (a) - *tow.*	5,105	3,302	26,901	do. - -	do.
Templenewsam - *tow.*	2,661	4,086	19,695	do. - -	Lower Skyrack and Leeds Borough.
Thorpe Stapleton - *tow.*	29	294	397	do. - -	Skyrack Wapentake, Lower Division.
TOTAL of UNION -	58,215	12,010	188,968		
HUNTINGDON UNION.					
(Formed 19 Jan. 1836 by Order dated 18 Dec. 1835.)					
COUNTY of HUNTINGDON :					
Abbots Ripton with Wennington *par.*	392	3,956	11,875	Huntingdon -	Ramsey.
Alconbury - *par.*	689	3,700	5,039	do. -	Leightonstone.
Alconbury Weston - *par.*	413	1,540	2,551	do. - -	do.
All Saints - *par.*	403 { In St. John (Hunting-don.) }		2,111	do. - -	Huntingdon.
Barham - *par.*	64	700	952	do. -	Leightonstone.
Brampton - *par.*	1,203	2,411	9,967	do. -	do.
Buckworth - *par.*	223	1,950	3,070	do. -	do.
Conington - *par.*	292	3,089	8,459	Peterborough -	Norman Cross.
Coppingford - *par.*	89	1,030	761	Huntingdon -	Leightonstone.
Easton - *par.*	149	1,310	1,791	St. Neots -	do.
Ellington - *par.*	391	2,910	3,523	do. -	do.
Godmanchester - *par.*	2,188	4,970	17,982	Huntingdon -	Godmanchester.
Great Raveley - *par.*	203	2,040	2,459	do. -	Ramsey.
Great Stukeley - *par.*	417	2,990	9,979	do. -	Leightonstone.
Hartford - *par.*	379	1,720	3,451	do. -	do.
Hunerton - *par.*	186	2,150	2,456	do. -	do.
Kings Ripton - *par.*	183	1,210	1,421	do. -	Ramsey.
Leighton Bromswold *par.*	334	2,770	3,803	St. Neots -	Leightonstone.
Little Raveley - *par.*	47	760	1,014	Huntingdon -	Ramsey.
Little Stukeley - *par.*	295	1,500	2,553	do. -	Leightonstone.
Ramsey - *par.*	4,617	16,196	29,907	do. -	Ramsey.
Saint Benedict - *par.*	724 ⎫		2,022 ⎫	do. -	Huntingdon.
Saint John (W.) - *par.*	1,668 ⎬	1,116	6,613 ⎬	do. -	do.
Saint Mary - *par.*	1,433 ⎭		7,309 ⎭	do. - -	do.

(continued)

(continued)

HUNSLET UNION :

(a) A detached part of Oulton with Woodlesford was amalgamated with Rothwell, by Order which came into operation on 25 March 1884.

HUNTINGDON UNION :

(a) A detached part of Bury, in the Saint Ives Union, was amalgamated with Upwood, by Order which came into operation on 25 March 1884.

(b) By Provisional Order which came into operation on 25 March 1886, all the parts of Sawtry Saint Andrew were amalgamated with Sawtry All Saints ; the Parish of Sawtry All Saints as so altered to be designated Sawtry All Saints and Saint Andrew.

Unions and Parishes, &c.	Population in 1881.	Area in Statute Acres in 1881.	Rateable Value in 1881.	Post Town.	Petty Sessional Division.
HUNTINGDON UNION—County of Huntingdon—*continued.*			£		
Sawtry All Saints and St. Andrew (*b*) } *par.*	1,017 }	5,730 {	6,016	Peterborough -	Norman Cross.
Sawtry Saint Judith - *par.*	215 }		2,813	do. -	do.
Spaldwick - *par.*	355	1,690	2,743	St. Neots -	Leightonstone.
Steeple Gedding - *par.*	125	1,091	1,317	Oundle -	Norman Cross.
Upton - *par.*	125	970	1,292	Huntingdon -	Leightonstone.
Upwood (*a*) - *par.*	339	1,809	2,921	do. -	Ramsey.
Wolley - *par.*	89	1,420	931	do. -	Leightonstone.
Wood Walton - *par.*	284	3,718	9,721	Peterborough -	Norman Cross.
TOTAL of UNION -	19,561	76,446	168,855		
HURSLEY UNION.					
(Formed 11 Aug. 1835 by Order dated 27 July 1835.)					
COUNTY of SOUTHAMPTON :					
Farley Chamberlayne *par.*	157	1,795	1,745	Romsey -	Winchester.
Hursley (W.) - *par.*	1,389	10,726	12,508	Winchester -	do.
North Baddesley - *par.*	358	2,582	2,494	Romsey -	Romsey.
Otterbourne - *par.*	849	1,524	6,699	Winchester -	Winchester.
TOTAL of UNION -	2,753	16,627	23,446		
IPSWICH UNION.					
(Formed 9 Sept. 1835 by Order dated 24 Aug. 1835.—Places marked thus • added 24 June 1859 in pursuance of Orders dated 25 Aug.1858 and 16 May 1859.)					
COUNTY of SUFFOLK :					
Saint Clement - *par.*	8,976		24,832	Ipswich -	Borough of Ipswich.
Saint Helen - *par.*	4,207		9,591	do. -	do.
Saint Lawrence *par.*	480		5,865	do. -	do.
Saint Margaret (W)- *par.*	12,027		39,447	do. -	do.
Saint Mary at Elms - *par.*	1,111		3,332	do. -	do.
Saint Mary at the Quay *par.*	948		4,677	do. -	do.
Saint Mary at the Tower - } *par.*	787		7,711	do. -	do.
Saint Mary Stoke - *par.*	3,306	8,395 {	13,377	do. -	do.
Saint Matthew - *par.*	9,912		37,273	do. -	do.
Saint Nicholas - *par.*	1,917		7,068	do. -	do.
Saint Peter (W.) - *par.*	4,754		15,971	do. -	do.
Saint Stephen - *par.*	611		3,498	do. -	do.
•Shire Hall Yard - *par.*	291		679	do. -	do.
•Warren House - *par.*	12		20	do. -	do.
Westerfield - *par.*	317		3,160	do. -	do. and Needham Market.
Whitton - *par.*	631		4,912	do. -	do. do.
TOTAL of UNION -	50,320	8,395	181,113		

HUNTINGDON UNION :

(*a*), (*b*), see notes page 189.

Unions and Parishes, &c.	Population in 1881.	Area in Statute Acres in 1881.	Rateable Value in 1881.	Post Town.	Petty Sessional Division.

ISLE OF THANET UNION.

(Formed 20 April 1835 by Order dated 25 Mar. 1835 as amended by Order dated 9 April 1835.—Places marked thus * added 6 April 1836 by Order dated 11 Mar. 1836.)

COUNTY of KENT:

			£		
Birchington (including Gores-end) - } par.	1,393	1,681	8,076	Westgate-ou-Sea -	Margate.
Minster (W.) - par.	2,062	5,388	17,316	Ramsgate -	Ramsgate.
Monkton otherwise Moncton - } par.	372	2,370	5,973	do. - -	do.
*Saint George, Ramsgate - } par.	16,234	308	77,140	do. - -	do.
*Saint John the Baptist, Margate - } par.	18,226	3.919	92,925	Margate - -	Margate.
Saint Lawrence - par.	6,839	3,247	28,126	Westgate-on-Sea -	Ramsgate.
Saint Nicholas at Wade - } par	582	3,561	7,970	Margate - -	do.
Saint Peter's - par.	4,597	2,922	30,895	Ramsgate - -	Margate.
Sarr - vill.	184	669	2,066	Westgate-on-Sea -	Sandwich.
Stonar - par.	35	680	1,345	Sandwich - -	Ramsgate.
Wood, otherwise Acol par.	297	1,434	3,635	Westgate-on-Sea -	Margate.
TOTAL of UNION -	50,821	26,179	275,467		

ISLE OF WIGHT UNION.

(Formed 14 Sept. 1865 by Order dated 28 Aug. 1865.—Places marked thus * formed by "The Newchurch Parish Act, 1866.")

COUNTY of SOUTHAMPTON:

Arreton - par.	1,920	9,192	13,973	Newport, Isle of Wight.	Isle of Wight.
Binstead - par.	813	1,207	4,397	Ryde - -	do.
Bonchurch - par.	670	561	4,236	Ventnor -	do.
Brading - par.	7,952	8,273	41,079	Ryde - -	do.
Brixton - par.	530	3,114	4,001	Newport, Isle of Wight.	do.
Brook - par.	195	713	1,178	do. - -	do.
Calbourne - par.	693	5,539	5,077	do. - -	do.
Carisbrooke (W.) - par.	8,304	8,613	29,374	do. - -	Isle of Wight and Borough of Newport.
Chale - par.	681	2,222	4,379	Godshill - -	Isle of Wight.
Freshwater - par.	2,809	4,836	12,903	Yarmouth, Isle of Wight.	do.
Gatcombe - par.	228	1,401	2,318	Newport, Isle of Wight.	do.
Godshill - par.	1,302	6,628	12,679	Godshill - -	do.
Kingston - par.	69	914	1,118	Newport, Isle of Wight.	do
Mottiston - par.	143	1,100	1,323	do. - -	do.
*Newchurch - par.	1,356	4,627	9,628	Ryde - -	do.
Newport - par.	3,237	59	15,244	Newport, Isle of Wight.	Borough of Newport.
Niton - par.	801	1,335	4,894	Godshill, Isle of Wight.	Isle of Wight.
Northwood - par.	8,484	4,865	31,168	Cowes -	do.
Ryde - par.	12,817	3,812	80,233	Ryde - -	do. and Borough of Ryde.
Saint Helens - par.	4,343	1,896	21,407	do. - -	do. do.
Saint Lawrence - par.	240	328	1,388	Ventnor -	do.
Saint Nicholas - par.	351	966	2,276	Newport, Isle of Wight.	do. and Borough of Newport.

(continued)

Unions and Parishes, &c.	Population in 1881.	Area in Statute Acres in 1881.	Rateable Value in 1881.	Post Town.	Petty Sessional Division.

ISLE OF WIGHT UNION—County of Southampton—*continued.*

Unions and Parishes, &c.	Population in 1881.	Area in Statute Acres in 1881.	Rateable Value in 1881. £	Post Town.	Petty Sessional Division.
Shalfleet - *par.*	1,050	6,315	6,391	Yarmouth, Isle of Wight.	Isle of Wight.
Shanklin - *par.*	1,780	675	15,118	Ryde - -	do.
Shorwell - *par.*	646	3,613	5,129	Newport, Isle of Wight.	do.
Thorley - *par.*	189	1,581	1,990	Yarmouth, Isle of Wight.	do.
Ventnor - *par.*	5,739	458	32,253	Ventnor - -	do.
Whippingham - *par.*	4,528	4,638	17,232	Cowes - -	do. and Borough of Newport.
Whitwell - *par.*	706	1,909	4,550	Godshill, Isle of Wight.	do.
Wootton - *par.*	108	1,076	1,309	Newport, Isle of Wight.	do.
Yarmouth - *par.*	787	58	2,424	Yarmouth, Isle of Wight.	do.
Yaverland - *par.*	153	818	1,157	Ryde - -	do.
TOTAL of UNION -	73,633	93,342	391,846		

KEIGHLEY UNION.

(Formed 10 Feb. 1837 by Order dated 21 Jan. 1837.)

COUNTY of YORK, WEST RIDING :

Unions and Parishes, &c.	Population in 1881.	Area in Statute Acres in 1881.	Rateable Value in 1881.	Post Town.	Petty Sessional Division.
Bingley and Mickle- thwaite - *tow.*	18,437	10,336	55,463	Bingley - -	Keighley.
East and West Mor- ton - *tow.*	2,266	3,773	6,987	do. - -	do.
Haworth - *tow.*	6,873	8,114	26,892	Keighley -	do.
Keighley (W.) - *par.*	30,395	10,132	98,371	do. - -	do.
Steeton with East- burn - *tow.*	1,508	2,066	7,891	Steeton, Near Leeds	do.
Sutton - *tow.*	1,642	2,348	5,016	Crosshills, Near Leeds.	Skipton.
TOTAL of UNION -	61,121	36,769	200,620		

KENDAL UNION.

(Formed 15 July 1836 by Order dated 18 June 1836.—Place marked thus * added 14 Mar. 1850 by Order dated 28 Jan. 1850.)

COUNTY of LANCASTER :

Unions and Parishes, &c.	Population in 1881.	Area in Statute Acres in 1881.	Rateable Value in 1881.	Post Town.	Petty Sessional Division.
*Dalton - *tow.*	123	2,467	2,310	Burton, Westmor-land.	Lancaster.

COUNTY of WESTMORLAND :

Ambleside (*b*) - *tow.*	1,989	4,371	12,736	Windermere -	Ambleside.
Applethwaite - *tow.*	1,912	9,121	11,272	do. - -	do.

(continued)

KENDAL UNION :

(*a*) Four detached parts of Nether Graveship were amalgamated with Kendal by Provisional Order which came into operation on 25 March 1882.

(*b*) By Orders which came into operation on 25 March 1886. A detached part of Levens was amalgamated with Crosthwaite and Lyth ; and

KENDAL UNION—*continued.*

A detached part of New Hutton was amalgamated with Scalthwaitrigg Hay and Hutton i' th' Hay ; and the part of Rydal and Loughrigg included within the Local Government District of Ambleside was amalgamated with Ambleside.

Unions and Parishes, &c.		Population in 1881.	Area in Statute Acres in 1881.	Rateable Value in 1881.	Post Town	Petty Sessional Division.
KENDAL UNION—County of Westmorland— *continued.*				£		
Barbon	- tow.	275	4,261	2,899	Kirkby Lonsdale	Kirkby Lonsdale.
Beetham	- tow.	987	5,170	8,782	Milnthorpe	Kendal.
Burton	- tow.	675	1,473	4,381	Burton, Westmorland.	Kirkby Lonsdale.
Casterton	- tow.	581	4,324	4,251	Kirkby Lonsdale	do.
Crook	- tow.	279	2,119	2,210	Kendal	Kendal.
Crosthwaite and Lyth (b)	tow.	771	7,958	7,589	do.	do.
Dillicar	- tow.	122	1,121	3,190	Sedbergh	Kirkby Lonsdale
Docker	- tow.	69	1,373	2,025	Kendal	Kendal.
Farleton	- tow.	78	1,204	1,647	Burton, Westmorland.	do.
Fawcett Forrest	- tow.	56	3,935	1,020	Kendal	do.
Firbank	- tow.	207	2,985	2,451	Sedbergh	Kirkby Lonsdale.
Grasmere	- tow.	736	7,319	6,304	Ambleside	Ambleside.
Grayrigg	- tow.	228	3,753	3,494	Kendal	Kendal.
Haverbrack	- tow.	120	658	1,285	Milnthorpe	do.
Helsington	- tow.	349	3,327	4,101	do.	do.
Hincaster	- tow.	117	667	2,507	do.	do.
Holme	- tow.	779	1,648	3,635	Burton, Westmorland.	Kirkby Lonsdale.
Hugill	- tow.	392	2,901	2,947	Kendal	Kendal.
Huttonroof	- tow.	295	2,715	2,996	Kirkby Lonsdale	Kirkby Lonsdale.
Kendal (W.) (a)	- tow.	11,719	2,242	43,967	Kendal	Kendal.
Kentmere	- tow.	174	6,613	2,271	do.	do.
Killington	- tow.	248	4,938	3,059	Kirkby Lonsdale	Kirkby Lonsdale.
Kirkby Lonsdale	- tow.	1,733	3,254	9,406	do.	do.
Kirkland	- tow.	1,369	22	1,892	Kendal	Kendal.
Lambrigg	- tow.	168	1,803	2,988	do.	do.
Langdales	- tow.	726	9,511	3,477	Ambleside	Ambleside.
Levens (b)	- tow.	945	3,518	6,010	Milnthorpe	Kendal.
Longsliddale	- tow.	136	6,735	2,214	Kendal	do.
Lupton	- tow.	217	3,524	3,365	Burton, Westmorland.	Kirkby Lonsdale.
Mansergh	- tow.	239	2,668	2,835	Kirkby Lonsdale	do.
Meethop and Ulpha	- tow.	148	1,991	2,079	Grange, Carnforth	Kendal.
Middleton	- tow.	231	7,276	4,203	Kirkby Lonsdale	Kirkby Lonsdale.
Milnthorpe and Heversham (W.)	tow.	1,545	2,297	9,091	Milnthorpe	Kendal.
Natland	- tow.	287	1,155	4,596	Kendal	do.
Nether Graveship (a)	tow.	608	358	4,687	do.	do.
Nether Staveley	- tow.	324	2,563	2,636	do.	do.
New Hutton (b)	- tow.	120	2,591	2,012	do.	do.
Old Hutton and Holmescales	tow.	381	3,975	3,973	do.	do.
Over Staveley	- tow.	730	2,580	2,578	do.	do.
Patton	- tow.	63	637	917	do.	do.
Preston Patrick	- tow.	544	3,657	4,795	Burton, Westmorland.	do.
Preston Richard	- tow.	589	2,134	4,139	Milnthorpe	do.
Rydal and Loughrigg (b)	tow.	498	4,889	4,376	Ambleside	Ambleside.
Scalthwaitrigg Hay and Hutton i' th' Hay (b)	tow.	539	3,434	6,674	Kendal	Kendal.
Sedgwick	- tow.	247	495	2,152	do.	do.
Skelsmergh	- tow.	367	2,093	4,803	do.	do.
Stainton	- tow.	388	1,735	3,009	Milnthorpe	do.
Strickland Kettle	- tow.	613	2,349	5,557	Kendal	do.
Strickland Roger	- tow.	434	3,210	3,790	do.	do.
Troutbeck	- tow.	446	5,807	3,658	Windermere	Ambleside.
Underbarrow and Bradleyfield	tow.	464	5,122	5,660	Kendal	Kendal.
Undermillbeck	- tow.	2,236	4,183	12,836	Windermere	Ambleside.
Whelwell and Selside	tow.	244	3,388	3,050	Kendal	Kendal.
Whinfell	- tow.	173	4,346	2,347	do.	do.
Witherslack	- tow.	541	4,604	4,289	Grange, Carnforth	do.
TOTAL of UNION	-	41,574	196,267	283,423		

Unions and Parishes, &c.	Population in 1881.	Area in Statute Acres in 1881.	Rateable Value in 1881.	Post Town.	Petty Sessional Division.
KETTERING UNION. (Formed 23 Sept. 1835 by Order dated 3 Sept. 1835. — Place marked thus * added 1 Dec. 1862 by Order dated 23 Oct. 1862, and thus † added 25 Dec. 1863 by Order dated 5 Oct. 1863.)			£		
COUNTY OF NORTHAMPTON :					
*Barford - - - par.	6	—	4,095	Kettering - -	Kettering.
Barton Seagrave - par.	227	1,782	4,271	do. -	do.
†Beanfield Lawns - par.	8	In Corby	425	do. -	do.
Broughton - - par.	878	2,560	4,064	do. -	do.
Burton Lattimer - par.	1,630	2,640	8,034	do. -	do.
Corby - - par.	758	2,800	4,346	do. -	do.
Cottingham - par.	631	3,286	3,651	Rockingham R.S.O. Northants.	do.
Cranford Saint Andrew (a) - par.	197	} 2,420 {	2,468	Kettering - -	do.
Cranford Saint John (a) - par.	370		3,314	do. -	do.
Cransley - - par.	322	2,510	6,069	do. -	do.
Desborough - par.	2,060	2,410	11,885	Market Harborough	do.
East Carlton (a) - par.	87	1,598	3,270	Rockingham R.S.O. Northants.	do.
Geddington - par.	862	2,140	3,876	Kettering - -	do.
Glendon - - par.	63	1,490	2,678	do. -	do.
Grafton Underwood - par.	273	2,050	2,327	do. -	do.
Great Oakley - par.	213	2,810	3,112	do. -	do.
Harrington - par.	213	2,519	4,233	Kelmarsh -	do.
Kettering (W.) - par.	11,095	2,840	34,071	Kettering -	do.
Little Oakley - par.	128	724	859	do. -	do.
Loddington - par.	248	1,224	2,607	do. -	do.
Middleton (a) - tow.	314 {	In Cottingham }	3,087 {	Rockingham R.S.O. Northants.	do.
Newton - - par.	82	1,050	1,710	Kettering -	do.
Orton - - cha.	68	940	1,612	do. -	do.
Pytchley - - par.	561	2,833	6,736	do. -	do.
Rothwell - - par.	2,755	3,490	12,166	do. -	do.
Rushton, All Saints, and Saint Peter - par.	495	2,960	9,641	do. -	do.
Stanion - - par.	353	1,850	2,320	Thrapstone -	do.
Thorpe Malsor - par.	138	680	1,885	Kettering -	do.
Warkton - - par.	259	1,810	2,905	do. -	do.
Weekley - - par.	270	1,800	2,839	do. -	do.
TOTAL OF UNION - -	25,564	55,266	154,556		
KEYNSHAM UNION. (Formed 29 Mar. 1836 by Order dated 10 Feb. 1836.)					
COUNTY OF GLOUCESTER :					
Bitton (a) - - par.	2,788	3,379	13,103	Bristol - -	Lawford's Gate.
Hanham (a) (b) - cha.	1,633	1,210	6,133	do. -	do.
Mangotsfield - par.	5,707	2,607	16,512	do. -	do.
Oldland (a) (b) - ham.	7,241	2,602	16,939	do. -	do.
Siston - - par.	1,018	1,833	5,368	do. -	do.
COUNTY OF SOMERSET :					
Brislington - par.	1,767	2,393	14,933	do. -	Keynsham.
Burnet - - par.	69	608	993	do. -	do.

(continued)

KETTERING UNION :

(a) By Orders which came into operation on 25 March, 1885.—
   A detached part of East Carlton was amalgamated with Middleton ; and
   A detached part of Cranford Saint Andrew was amalgamated with Cranford Saint John.

KEYNSHAM UNION :

(a) By Orders which came into operation on 25 March 1884,—
   A detached part of Oldland was amalgamated with Keynsham ;
   A detached part of Bitton was amalgamated with Oldland ;
   Detached parts of Oldland were amalgamated with Bitton and Hanham, and detached parts of Hanham were amalgamated with Oldland and Bitton ;

(b) Certain parts of Oldland were amalgamated with Hanham, by Order which came into operation on 25 March 1885.

Unions and Parishes, &c.		Population in 1881.	Area in Statute Acres in 1881.	Rateable Value in 1881.	Post Town.	Petty Sessional Division.
KEYNSHAM UNION—County of Somerset—continued.				£		
Compton Dando	par.	328	1,974	2,952	Bristol -	Keynsham.
Corston	par.	385	1,190	4,204	do. -	Weston, Bath.
Kelston	par.	185	1,095	2,957	Bath -	do.
Keynsham (W.) (a)	par.	2,482	4,171	24,211	Bristol -	Keynsham.
Marksbury	par.	230	1,277	2,132	do.	do.
Newton Saint Loe	par.	352	1,578	6,318	do. -	Weston, Bath.
North Stoke	par.	190	778	1,228	Bath -	do.
Priston	par.	253	1,850	2,554	do. -	Keynsham.
Queen Charlton	par.	115	955	1,652	Bristol -	do.
Saltford	par.	137	880	6,157	do. -	do.
Stanton Prior	par.	96	841	1,481	do. -	do.
Whitchurch otherwise Felton	} par.	505	2,194	4,309	do. -	do.
TOTAL of UNION -		25,781	33,415	134,196		

KIDDERMINSTER UNION.

(Formed 14 Oct. 1836 by Order dated 20 Sept. 1836.)

COUNTY OF SALOP :

Dowles	par.	127	679	1,109	Bewdley -	Cleobury Mortimer.

COUNTY of STAFFORD :

Upper Areley	par.	731	3,912	5,367	do. -	Kidderminster for Police purposes, otherwise Brierley Hill.

COUNTY of WORCESTER :

Bewdley (a)	bor.	3,088	2,110	9,018	Bewdley -	Bewdley.
Broome	par.	129	716	1,698	Stourbridge -	Stourbridge.
Chaddesley Corbett	par.	1,429	5,914	12,956	Kidderminster -	Kidderminster.
Churchill	par.	169	921	1,813	do. -	Stourbridge.
Kidderminster Borough		22,299	} 10,685	64,484	do. -	Kidderminster.
Kidderminster, Foreign of the Parish of (W.)	}	5,376		{ 31,868	do. -	do.
Lower Mitton	ham.	3,358	861	11,149	Stourport -	Stourport.
Ribbesford	par.	83	2,549	1,434	Bewdley -	do.
Rushock	par.	185	1,218	2,046	Droitwich -	Kidderminster.
Stone	par.	625	2,450	6,760	Kidderminster -	do.
Wolverley	par.	3,343	5,532	15,576	do. -	do.
TOTAL of UNION - -		40,942	37,550	165,278		

KINGSBRIDGE UNION.

(Formed 22 June 1836 by Order dated 28 May 1836.— Spelling of names of places marked thus * is as altered by Order dated 17 Sept. 1887.)

COUNTY of DEVON :

Aveton Gifford (e)	par.	869	3,182	5,709	Kingsbridge -	Ermington.
Bigbury (b)	par.	451	3,167	3,686	do. -	do.

(continued)

KIDDERMINSTER UNION :

(a) A detached part of Bewdley was amalgamated with Rock, in the Cleobury Mortimer Union, by Order which came into operation on 25 March 1892.

KINGSBRIDGE UNION :

(a) A detached part of Halwell, in the Totnes Union, was amalgamated with Blackawton, by Order which came into operation on 25 March 1884.

(b) By Orders which came into operation on 25 March 1884,—
A detached part of Charleton was amalgamated with Buckland Toutsaints;
Detached parts of Kingston were amalgamated with Modbury and Bigbury;
A detached part of Stokenham was amalgamated with South Pool; and

KINGSBRIDGE UNION—continued.

Detached parts of West Alvington were amalgamated with Dodbrooke and Churchstow.

(c) Certain detached parts of Modbury were amalgamated with Ermington, in the Plympton Saint Mary Union, by Order which came into operation on 25 March 1884.

(d) A detached part of Morley, in the Totnes Union, was amalgamated with Woodleigh, by Order which came into operation on 25 March 1884.

(e) A detached part of Kingston was amalgamated with Aveton Gifford, by Order which came into operation on 25 March 1886.

(f) All the part of Stoke Fleming which was situated within the municipal borough of Dartmouth was amalgamated with St. Petrox, in the Totnes Union, by Order which came into operation on 25 March 1886.

Unions and Parishes &c.	Population in 1881.	Area in Statute Acres in 1881.	Rateable Value in 1881.	Post Town.	Petty Sessional Division.
			£		
KINGSBRIDGE UNION—County of Devon—*continued.*					
*Blackawton (*a*) - *par.*	1,059	5,646	7,601	Totnes - -	Stanborough and Coleridge.
Buckland Toutsaints } *par.* (*b*) - - - }	50	551	907	Kingsbridge -	do.
Charleton (*b*) - *par.*	548	2,779	3,861	do. - -	do.
Chivelstone - *par.*	426	2,806	3,254	do. - -	do.
Churchstow (W) (*b*) *par.*	368	1,877	3,352	do. - -	do.
Dodbrooke (*b*) - *par.*	1,204	464	3,079	do. - -	do.
East Allington - *par.*	516	3,646	4,124	Mounts Totnes -	do.
East Portlemouth - *par.*	302	2,143	2,010	Kingsbridge -	do.
Kingsbridge - - *par.*	1,527	150	4,309	do. - -	do.
*Kingston (*b*) (*c*) - *par.*	470	2,373	2,955	do. - -	Ermington.
Loddiswell - - *par.*	792	3,554	4,496	Kingsbridge -	Stanborough and Coleridge.
Malborough - - *par.*	2,434	5,310	9,081	do. - -	do.
Modbury (*b*) (*c*) - *par.*	1,513	6,258	12,106	Modbury -	Ermington.
Ringmore - - *par.*	250	1,128	1,915	Kingsbridge -	do.
Sherford - - *par.*	401	2,326	3,771	do. - -	Stanborough and Coleridge.
Slapton - - *par.*	618	3,430	4,822	do. - -	do.
South Huish - - *par.*	298	1,150	1,991	do. - -	do.
South Milton - - *par.*	349	1,556	2,581	do. - -	do.
South Pool (*b*) - *par.*	395	2,289	3,000	do. - -	do.
Stoke Fleming (*f*) - *par.*	765	3,332	6,243	Dartmouth -	do.
Stokenham (*b*) - *par.*	1,793	6,011	8,792	Kingsbridge -	do.
Thurlestone - - *par.*	364	1,898	2,744	do. - -	do.
*West Alvington (*b*) - *par.*	854	4,110	7,140	do. - -	do.
Woodleigh (*d*) - *par.*	198	2,319	2,476	Mounts Totnes -	do.
TOTAL of UNION -	18,844	73,455	116,009		
KINGSCLERE UNION.					
(Formed 3 June 1835 by Order dated 18 May 1835.)					
COUNTY of SOUTHAMPTON :					
Ashmansworth - *par.*	212	1,821	1,232	Newbury -	Kingsclere.
Baughurst - - *par.*	487	1,798	2,397	Basingstoke -	do.
Burghclere - - *par.*	753	5,270	5,935	Newbury -	do.
Crux Easton - *par.*	56	1,121	906	do. - -	do.
East Woodhay - *par.*	1,527	5,080	9,947	do. - -	do.
Ewhurst - - *par.*	34	477	802	Basingstoke -	do.
Hannington - *par.*	281	2,014	2,004	do. - -	do.
Highclere - *par.*	378	3,484	3,229	Newbury -	do.
Itchingswell - *par.*	415	2,349	2,933	do. - -	do.
Kingsclere (W.) - *par.*	2,770	13,117	15,221	do. - -	do.
Litchfield - *par.*	112	1,814	1,218	Micheldever Station	do.
Sydmonton - *par.*	191	2,145	1,815	Newbury -	do.
Tadley - - *par.*	1,017	2,079	2,321	Basingstoke -	do.
Woodcut - - *par.*	74	1,441	689	North Litchfield, Micheldever.	do.
Woolverton - *par.*	184	1,161	1,686	Basingstoke -	do.
TOTAL of UNION -	8,524	45,507	52,355		
KING'S LYNN UNION.					
(Formed 30 Sept. 1835 by Order dated 12 Sept. 1835.—Places marked thus * added 10 April 1837 by Order dated 17 Mar. 1837.)					
COUNTY of NORFOLK :					
*North Lynn (*a*) - *par.*	91	1,065	1,325	King's Lynn -	Freebridge Marshland. (continued)

KINGSBRIDGE UNION :

(*a*), (*b*), (*c*), (*d*), (*e*), (*f*), *see notes, page* 195.

KING'S LYNN UNION :

(*a*) Parts of Clenchwarton, in the Wisbeach Union, were amalgamated with North Lynn and West Lynn, by Order which came into operation on 25 March 1885.

Unions and Parishes, &c.	Population in 1881.	Area in Statute Acres in 1881.	Rateable Value in 1881.	Post Town.	Petty Sessional Division.

KING'S LYNN UNION—County of Norfolk—*continued*.

			£		
Saint Margaret's - *par.*	13,151	} 3,321 {	11,918	King's Lynn -	Borough of King's Lynn.
South Lynn or All Saints (W.) - *par.*	5,088		17,898	do. - -	do.
*West Lynn (*a*) - *par.*	576	1,619	4,895	do. - -	Freebridge Marshland.
TOTAL of UNION -	19,206	6,005	69,036		

KINGS NORTON UNION.

(Formed 12 Dec. 1836 and dated this 16 Nov. 1836.)

COUNTY of STAFFORD :

Harborne and Smethwick - *par.*	31,517	3,296	128,265	Harborne - -	Offlow, South Staffordshire.

COUNTY of WARWICK :

Edgbaston - - *par.*	22,760	2,606	179,328	Birmingham -	Borough of Birmingham.

COUNTY of WORCESTER :

Beoley - - *par.*	603	4,480	6,810	Redditch -	Northfield.
King's Norton - *par.*	34,071	12,132	155,852	King's Norton	do.
Northfield (W.) - *par.*	7,190	5,951	41,897	Northfield -	do.
TOTAL of UNION -	96,141	28,465	512,152		

KINGSTON UNION.

(Formed 4 June 1836 by Order dated 10 May 1836.)

COUNTY of MIDDLESEX :

Hampton - - *par.*	4,776	2,036	34,259	Hampton - -	Staines and Spelthorne.
Hampton Wick - *par.*	2,164	1,315	12,314	Kingston on Thames	do.
Teddington - - *par.*	6,599	1,214	39,840	Teddington - -	do.

COUNTY of SURREY :

East Moulsey - *par.*	3,289	781	20,441	Kingston on Thames	Kingston and Elmbridge.
Esher - *par.*	1,993	2,094	22,088	do. - -	do.
Ham with Hatch - *ham.*	1,855	1,913	11,296	do. - -	do.
Hook - - *ham.*	414	492	2,373	do. - -	do.
Kingston (W.) - *par.*	33,560	4,824	203,285	do. - -	do.
Long Ditton with Talworth - *par.*	2,315	2,102	20,855	do. - -	do.
Malden (*a*) - *par.*	525	1,294	4,524	Worcester Park -	do.
Thames Ditton - *par.*	2,956	2,981	24,673	Kingston on Thames	do.
West Moulsey - *par.*	661	737	9,799	do. - -	do.
Wimbledon - *par.*	15,950	3,220	135,829	Wimbledon -	Wandsworth.
TOTAL of UNION -	77,057	25,003	541,579		

KINGSTON-UPON-HULL INCORPORATION.

(Under 5 Geo. 4. c. XIII.)

COUNTY of YORK, East Riding :

Holy Trinity (W.) and Saint Mary - *a.p.*	78,222	1,054	313,717	Hull - -	Borough of Kingston upon Hull.

KINGSTON UNION :

(*a*) A detached part of Malden, known as " Rushet," was amalgamated with Chessington, in the Epsom Union, by Order which came into operation 25 March 1884.

Unions and Parishes, &c.	Population in 1881.	Area in Statute Acres in 1881.	Rateable Value in 1881.	Post Town.	Petty Sessional Division.

KINGTON UNION.

(Formed 25 Aug. 1836 by Order dated 20 July 1836.—Places marked thus * added 26 Mar. 1877 by Order dated 1 Mar 1877.)

County of Hereford :

			£		
Brilley - - par.	399	3,792	4,664	Whitney - -	Kington.
*Byton - - par.	168	916	1,214	Presteigne -	do.
*Combe - - tow.	78	599	1,034	do. -	do.
Eardisley (a) - par.	862	1,533	7,274	Eardisley -	do.
Huntington - par.	259	1,937	2,329	Kington -	do.
Kington (W.) - par.	2,952	8,313	15,894	do. -	do.
*Kinsham (b) - par.	92	1,581	1,969	Presteigne -	do.
*Knill - - par.	94	798	943	Kington -	do.
*Lingen - - par.	293	2,283	2,366	Presteigne -	Wigmore.
Lower Harton - tow.	72	900	1,062	Kington -	Kington.
Lyonshall or Lyn-hales } par.	869	1,658	8,534	do. -	do.
Pembridge - par.	1,318	7,077	12,661	Pembridge -	do.
*Rod, Nash, and Little Brampton - } tow.	174	1,934	2,478	Kington -	do.
*Stapleton - tow.	186	1,252	2,337	Presteigne -	do.
Staunton on Arrow - par.	340	2,925	3,811	Leominster -	do.
Titley - - par.	389	1,876	2,661	Titley -	do.
Willersley (a) - par.	8	230	432	Winforton -	Bredwardine.
*Willey - - tow.	123	2,095	1,644	Presteigne -	Wigmore.
Winforton - par.	120	1,099	2,349	Winforton -	Bredwardine.

County of Radnor :

Colva - - par.	149	2,293	1,903	Newchurch -	Colwyn.
Ednol - - tow.	53	} In Old Radnor and Burlinjobb {	627	Walton -	New Radnor.
Evenjobb, Newcastle, Barland, and Burca } tow.	316		2,923	do. -	do.
Gladestry - - par.	337	3,798	3,003	Kington -	do.
Glasewm - - par.	397	6,984	4,044	Builth -	Colwyn.
Harpton - - tow.	105	{ In Old Radnor and Burlinjobb }	1,488	Kington -	New Radnor.
Kinnerton, Salford, and Badland } tow.	205	do.	2,196	Walton -	do.
Llandegley - - par.	398	3,729	2,697	Penybont -	Cefnllys.
Llanfihangel Nant Melan - } tow.	129	9,350	3,170	New Radnor -	New Radnor.
Michaelchurch on Arrow } par.	115	1,936	1,538	Kington -	Painscastle.
Newchurch - par.	102	1,788	1,320	Hay -	do.
New Radnor - par.	472	3,101	3,363	New Radnor -	New Radnor.
Old Radnor and Burlinjobb - } tow.	332	10,798	2,551	Walton -	do.
Treworn and Gwithla tow.	105	1,834	1,456	do. -	do.
Walton and Womaston - } tow.	186	{ In Old Radnor and Burlinjobb }	2,100	do. -	do.
Total of Union -	12,197	94,762	110,035		

KIRKBY MOORSIDE UNION.

(Formed 6 March 1848, by Order of the same date.—Places marked thus * added 25 March 1849 by Order dated 3 March 1849.)

County of York, North Riding :

*Appleton-le Moors - tow.	300	1,323	1,358	Pickering -	Ryedale.
Bransdale West Side tow.	75	2,047	401	Kirkby Moorside -	do.

(continued)

KINGTON UNION :

(a) Two detached parts of Eardisley were amalgamated with Willersley, by Order which came into operation on 25 March 1884.

KINGTON UNION—continued.

(b) The several parts of a township known as Lower Kinsham were amalgamated with Upper Kinsham, and the parish thus altered was designated Kinsham, by Order which came into operation on 25 March 1886.

Unions and Parishes, &c.		Population in 1881.	Area in Statute Acres in 1881.	Rateable Value in 1881.	Post Town.	Petty Sessional Division.

Kirkby Moorside Union—County of York.
North Riding—continued

				£		
*East Ness (a)	tow.	104	1,105	2,245	Oswaldkirk, York	Ryedale.
Fadmore (a)	tow.	149	1,552	948	Kirkby Moorside	do.
Farndale East Side	tow.	370	6,166	1,510	do.	do.
Farndale Low Quarter	tow.	173	3,402	545	do.	do.
Farndale West Side	tow.	221	7,182	1,483	do.	do.
Gillamoor (a)	tow.	189	1,391	950	do.	do.
Great Edstone	tow.	113	1,286	1,561	do.	do.
Hutton-le-Hole	tow.	273	1,085	1,146	do.	do.
Kirkby Moorside (W.) (a)	tow.	1,843	4,506	6,670	do.	do.
Little Edstone	tow.	13	171	249	do.	do.
Muscoates (a)	tow.	71	983	1,051	do.	do.
Nawton (a)	tow.	550	1,216	1,381	York	do.
*Normanby	tow.	178	1,785	2,296	Kirkby Moorside	do.
North Holme	tow.	11	516	706	do.	do.
Nunnington	tow.	103	2,123	3,173	York	do.
*Salton	tow.	152	1,748	2,340	Oswaldkirk, York	do.
Skiplam (a)	tow.	67	2,572	1,207	Nawton, York	do.
*Thornton Riseborough (a)	tow.	35	620	830	Kirkby Moorside	do.
Welburn (a)	tow.	130	1,681	2,345	Oswaldkirk, York	do.
Wombleton (a)	tow.	291	1,187	1,474	Nawton, York	do.
Total of Union		5,514	45,977 (b)	35,869		

KNARESBOROUGH UNION.

(Formed 25 March 1854 by Order dated 15 March 1854 as amended by Order dated 22 March 1854.)

County of York, West Riding:

Bilton - with - Harrogate	tow.	9,279	4,121	63,500	Harrogate	Claro.
Brearton	tow.	162	1,562	2,200	Ripley	do.
Burton Leonard	par.	431	1,796	2,819	Leeds	do.
Cayton with South Stainley	par.	215	2,131	6,218	Ripley	do.
Farnham	tow.	155	1,044	1,612	Knaresborough	do.
Felliscliffe	tow.	326	2,628	2,739	Ripley	do.
Ferensby	tow.	117	424	842	Knaresborough	do.
Flaxby	tow.	81	718	1,177	do.	do.
Follifoot	tow.	496	1,860	7,650	Wetherby	do.
Goldsborough	tow.	211	1,785	2,414	Knaresborough	do.
Hampsthwaite	tow.	457	1,135	1,927	Ripley	do.
Haverah Park	tow.	64	2,245	1,426	Harrogate	do.
Killinghall	tow.	678	3,515	5,107	Ripley	do.
Knaresborough (W.)	tow.	5,065	3,013	20,892	Knaresborough	do.
Nidd	tow.	149	1,203	5,902	Ripley	Liberty of Ripon.
Pannal	par.	2,547	4,898	20,233	Harrogate	Claro.
Plumpton	tow.	166	2,131	2,417	Knaresborough	do.
Ripley	tow.	291	1,641	3,552	do.	do.
Scotton	tow.	291	1,127	2,049	do.	do.
Scriven-with-Tentergate	tow.	1,431	1,829	8,788	do.	do.
Walkingham Hill - with-Occaney	tow.	23	427	533	Burton Leonard. Leeds.	do.
Total of Union		22,635	41,236	163,997		

Kirkby Moorside Union:

(a) By Orders which came into operation on 25 March 1887,—
Detached parts of Fadmore were amalgamated with Gillamoor and Kirkby Moorside;
Detached parts of Gillamoor were amalgamated with Fadmore and Kirkby Moorside;
Detached parts of Kirkby Moorside were amalgamated with Fadmore and Gillamoor;
A detached part of Nawton was amalgamated with Wombleton;
Detached parts of Skiplam were amalgamated with Muscoates and Welburn;

Kirkby Moorside Union—continued.

A detached part of Thornton Riseborough was amalgamated with Middleton, in the Pickering Union;
Detached parts of Welburn were amalgamated with Muscoates; and
All the parts of a township known as West Ness were amalgamated with East Ness.

(b) There is some intermixed land containing 141 acres belonging to Welburn and Skiplam.

Unions and Parishes, &c.	Population in 1881.	Area in Statute Acres in 1881.	Rateable Value in 1881.	Post Town.	Petty Sessional Division.

KNIGHTON UNION.
(Formed 9 Nov. 1836 by Order dated 14 Oct. 1836. — Places marked thus * added 26 March 1877 by Order dated 1 March 1877.)

COUNTY OF HEREFORD:

			£		
Adforton, Stanway, Paytoe and Grange *tow.*	204	3,603	2,032	Leintwardine	Wigmore.
Brampton Bryan - *tow.*	275	2,926	3,058	Brampton Brian -	do.
Buckton and Coxwall *tow.*	175	1,430	1,684	Leintwardine	do.
Walford, Letton, and Newton - *tow.*	187	In Adforton, Stanway, Paytoe, and Grange	1,920	do. -	do.

COUNTY OF SALOP:

Bedstone (a) - *par.*	137	776	1,142	Bucknell -	Purslow.
Bettws y Crwyn - *par.*	542	8,664	3,965	Aston-on-Clun	do.
Bucknell (a) - *tow.*	521	2,730	3,133	Bucknell -	do.
Llanvair Waterdine - *par.*	556	7,720	5,836	Knighton -	do.
Stowe - *par.*	253	2,724	2,714	Brampton Brian -	do.

COUNTY OF RADNOR:

Bleddfa - *par.*	187	2,710	2,606	Knighton -	Knighton.
*Cascob - *par.*	102	3,136	1,360	Presteigne -	Radnor.
*Discoed - *tow.*	91	866	1,231	do. -	Presteigne.
Heyhop - *tow.*	270	Included in Llangynllo	1,615	Knighton -	Knighton.
Knighton (W.) - *par.*	1,905	2,461	7,496	do. -	do.
*Litton and Cascob - *tow.*	75	1,208	896	do. -	do.
Llananno - *par.*	296	1,400	1,677	Penybont -	Cefnllys.
Llanbadarn Fynydd - *par.*	601	8,965	2,757	do. -	do.
Llanbister - *par.*	815	14,837	5,378	do. -	Knighton.
Llandewi Ystradenny (a) *par.*	588	8,075	4,136	do. -	Cefnllys.
Llanfihangel Beguildy *par.*	994	16,645	7,110	Knighton	Knighton.
Llanfihangel Rhydithon *par.*	358	3,201	2,954	do. -	Cefnllys.
Llangynllo - *par.*	431	6,807	5,024	do. -	Knighton.
*Norton - *par.*	291	3,144	2,921	Presteigne -	Presteigne.
*Pilleth - *par.*	121	1,897	1,462	Knighton -	do.
*Presteigne - *tow.*	1,491	2,831	7,160	Presteigne -	do.
Stanage - *lord.*	151	2,388	2,007	Brampton Brian -	Knighton.
*Whitton - *par.*	165	1,549	1,560	Knighton	do.
TOTAL OF UNION -	11,782	115,720	84,834		

LAMPETER UNION.
(Formed 15 May 1837 by Order dated 13 April 1837. — Place marked thus * added 19 June 1837 by Order dated 25 May 1837.)

COUNTY OF CARDIGAN:

Bettws Bledrws (b) *par.*	202	2,216	1,146	Lampeter -	Upper Moyddon.
Cellan (a) - *par.*	452	3,645	1,234	do. -	do.
Lampeter or Llanbedr Pont-Stephen (W.) (a) *par.*	1,897	6,201	5,096	do. -	do.
Llanfair Clydogau - *par.*	536	4,815	1,824	do. -	do.
Llangybi (b) - *par.*	277	1,809	840	do. -	do.
Llanwenog - *par.*	1,560	10,720	4,506	Llanybydder	do.
Llanwnen - *par.*	299	2,180	1,100	Lampeter -	do.
Silian - *par.*	289	2,182	907	do. -	do.
Trefilan - *par.*	273	2,201	1,025	do. -	Lower Ilar.

(continued)

(continued)

KNIGHTON UNION:

(a) By Orders which came into operation on 25 March 1884, a detached part of Llandewi Ystradenny was amalgamated with Nantmel, in the Rhayader Union, and a detached part of Bucknell was amalgamated with Bedstone.

LAMPETER UNION:

(a) The parts of Pencarreg and Cellan on the right bank of the River Teifi were amalgamated with Lampeter or Llanbedr Pont-Stephen, by Orders which came into operation on 25 March 1884.

(b) A detached part of Bettws Bledrws was amalgamated with Llangybi, by Provisional Order which came into operation on 25 March 1885.

Unions and Parishes, &c.		Population in 1881.	Area in Statute Acres in 1881.	Rateable Value in 1881.	Post Town.	Petty Sessional Division.
LAMPETER UNION—*continued.*				£		
COUNTY of CARMARTHEN :						
*Llantihangel Rhos-y-Corn	} *par.*	639	9,012	2,006	Carmarthen -	Lower Carthinog.
Llanllwni - -	*par.*	785	6,624	2,311	do. - -	do.
Llanybydder - -	*par.*	1,266	10,031	2,790	Llanybydder -	do.
Llanycrwys - -	*par.*	426	3,379	1,262	Llandilo - -	Higher Carthinog.
Pencarreg (a) - -	*par.*	1,186	10,392	3,160	Lampeter - -	do.
TOTAL of UNION -		10,087	75,710	29,207		
LANCASTER UNION.						
(Formed 10 Dec. 1839 by Order dated 15 Nov. 1839.—Place marked thus * added 25 Dec. 1858 by Order dated 15 Oct. 1858, and thus † added 2 March 1869 by Order dated 17 Feb. 1869.)						
COUNTY of LANCASTER :						
Aldcliffe - -	*tow.*	94	1,016	1,703	Lancaster - -	Lonsdale South.
Ashton with Stodday	*tow.*	207	1,949	3,141	do. - -	do.
†Bolton-le-Sands (a) -	*tow.*	785	1,580	7,474	do. - -	do.
Bulk - -	*tow.*	117	1,158	3,619	do. - -	do.
Carnforth - -	*tow.*	1,879	1,459	11,671	Carnforth -	do.
Cockerham - -	*tow.*	761	5,562	10,042	Garstang -	do.
*Cockersand Abbey (a)	*par.*	36	346	497	Lancaster -	do.
Ellel North and South (a) -	} *tow.*	1,787	5,814	16,740	do. - -	do.
Heaton with Oxcliffe	*tow.*	136	2,036	3,412	do. - -	do.
†Heysham - -	*par.*	632	1,774	6,038	do. - -	do.
Lancaster (W.) -	*tow.*	20,663	1,494	71,815	do. - -	Borough of Lancaster.
Middleton - -	*tow.*	157	1,200	2,103	do. - -	Lonsdale South.
Overton - -	*tow.*	325	1,837	2,472	do. - -	do.
Over Wyersdale -	*tow.*	513	17,319	6,278	do. - -	do.
†Poulton Bare and Torrisholme	} *tow.*	3,931	1,725	27,078	do. - -	do.
Priest Hutton - -	*tow.*	213	1,085	2,301	Carnforth -	do.
Scotforth - -	*tow.*	2,263	2,880	12,802	Lancaster -	do.
Silverdale - -	*tow.*	489	1,168	3,152	Carnforth -	do.
Skerton - -	*tow.*	2,838	1,316	9,552	Lancaster -	do.
†Slyne-with-Hest (a) -	*tow.*	301	1,143	5,240	do. - -	do.
Thurnham - -	*tow.*	721	2,095	4,132	do. - -	do.
Warton with Lindith	*tow.*	1,471	2,824	10,032	Carnforth -	do.
Yealand Conyers -	*tow.*	309	1,582	3,744	do. - -	do.
Yealand Redmayne -	*tow.*	210	2,136	3,628	do. - -	do.
TOTAL of UNION -		40,838	62,408	228,705		
LANCHESTER UNION.						
(Formed 4 Jan. 1837 by Order dated 8 Dec. 1836.)						
COUNTY of DURHAM :					Chester Ward :	
Benfieldside (c) -	*tow.*	5,700	1,832	14,558	Blackhill -	West Division.
Collierly and Pontop (c)	*tow.*	3,856	1,998	15,684	Dipton - -	do.

(*continued*)

LANCASTER UNION :

(a) By Orders which came into operation on 25 March 1887,—
A detached part of Bolton-le-Sands was amalgamated with Slyne-with-Hest ;
A detached part of Ellel North and South was amalgamated with Nether Wyersdale, in the Garstang Union ; and
A detached part of Pilling, in the Garstang Union, was amalgamated with Cockersand Abbey.

LANCHESTER UNION :

(a) Certain parts of Lanchester were amalgamated with Edmondsley, in the Chester-le-Street Union, by Provisional Order which came into operation on 25 March 1886.

LANCHESTER UNION—*continued.*

(b) A detached part of Tanfield was amalgamated with Urpeth, in the Chester-le-Street Union, by Provisional Order which came into operation on 25 March 1886.

(c) By Orders which came into operation on 25 March 1887, changes were effected in the areas of all the parishes and townships in the Union except Hedleyhope ; and the township known as Billingside, having, in 1881, population 8, acreage 229, and rateable value 930l., was absorbed. (See also Chester-le-Street and Hexham Unions.)

Unions and Parishes, &c.		Population in 1881.	Area in Statute Acres in 1881.	Rateable Value in 1881.	Post Town.	Petty Sessional Division.
				£		
LANCHESTER UNION—County of Durham—*continued.*						
Conside and Knitsley	} tow.	6,746	2,715	22,380	Consett	Chester Ward : West Division.
(c)						
Cornsay (c)	tow.	2,327	3,088	16,764	Cornsay	do.
Ebchester (c)	par.	1,402	1,126	6,325	Ebchester	do.
Esh (c)	tow.	6,305	3,119	18,107	Esh	do.
Greencroft (c)	tow.	2,000	3,183	10,634	Annfield Plain	do.
Healeyfield (c)	tow.	357	1,282	1,706	Castleside	do.
Hedleyhope	tow.	1,504	1,653	5,210	Tow Law	do.
Ireston (c)	tow.	4,032	1,956	14,027	Leadgate	do.
Kyo Laws (c)	tow.	4,065	2,203	18,944	Annfield Plain	do.
Lanchester (W.) (a) (c)	tow.	4,038	15,235	21,294	Lanchester	do.
Langley (c)	tow.	143	2,172	5,695	Langley Park	do.
Medomsley (c)	tow.	4,133	5,057	21,731	Medomsley	do.
Muggleswick (c)	par.	841	13,086	4,808	Blackhill	do.
Satley (c)	tow.	122	{ In Lanchester }	590	Tow Law	do.
Tanfield (b) (c)	tow.	10,282	6,887	45,819	Stanley, R.S.O.	do.
TOTAL of UNION		57,853 (c)	66,892 (c)	244,276 (c)		

LANGPORT UNION.

(Formed 10 May 1836 by Order dated 15 April 1836.)

COUNTY of SOMERSET :

Unions and Parishes, &c.		Population in 1881.	Area in Statute Acres in 1881.	Rateable Value in 1881.	Post Town.	Petty Sessional Division.
Aller (a)	par.	473	3,651	6,809	Langport	Somerton.
Babcary	par.	322	2,393	3,836	Somerton	do.
Barrington (a)	par.	418	1,656	3,271	Ilminster	Ilminster.
Barton Saint David	par.	338	945	1,844	Somerton	Somerton.
Berecrocombe (a)	par.	136	871	1,271	Ilminster	Ilminster.
Charlton Mackrell (d)	par.	290	3,910	3,000	Somerton	Somerton.
Compton Dundon (d)	par.	574	2,571	4,164	do.	do.
Curry Mallet (a)	par.	483	1,650	2,807	Taunton	Ilminster.
Curry Rivall (a) (b)	par.	1,573	4,108	8,369	do.	do.
Drayton (a)	par.	472	2,165	3,968	do.	do.
Earnshill (a)	par.	7	375	644	do.	do.
Fivehead (a)	par.	416	1,721	2,829	do.	do.
High Ham (W.) (a)	par.	1,116	4,229	5,858	Langport	Somerton.
Huish Episcopi (a)	par.	661	2,314	4,311	do.	do.
Isle Abbots (a)	par.	348	1,935	2,949	Taunton	Ilminster.
Isle Brewers (a) (b)	par.	316	1,243	2,275	do.	do.
Kingsbury Episcopi (a) (b)	} par.	1,514	3,646	8,703	Ilminster	Ilminster.
Kingsdon (a) (b) (c)	par.	353	2,064	3,134	Somerton	Somerton.
Kington Manfield	par.	537	770	1,428	do.	do.
Kingweston (d)	par.	148	1,166	1,264	do.	do.
Langport	par.	897	171	2,510	Langport	do.
Long Sutton (a)	par.	876	3,955	7,459	do.	do.
Muchelney	par.	256	1,566	4,014	do.	do.
Pitney (a)	par.	321	1,500	1,699	do.	do.
Puckington (a) (b) (c)	par.	229	610	1,051	Ilminster	Ilminster.
Somerton (a) (c)	par.	1,917	6,925	12,321	Somerton	Somerton.
Swell (a)	par.	142	891	1,351	Ilminster	Ilminster.
TOTAL of UNION		15,133 (b) (d)	59,001 (b) (d)	103,139 (b) (d)		

LANCHESTER UNION :

(a), (b), (c), *see* notes, page 201.

LANGPORT UNION :

(a) By Orders which came into operation on 25 March 1885, and by Provisional Order which came into operation on 25 March 1886, changes were made in the areas of the following Parishes; Aller, Barrington, Berecrocombe, Curry Mallet, Curry Rivall, Drayton, Earnshill, Fivehead, High Ham, Huish Episcopi, Isle Abbots, Isle Brewers, Kingsbury Episcopi, Kingsdon, Long Sutton, Pitney, Puckington, Somerton, and Swell.

(b) By Orders which came into operation on 25 March 1885,—
Detached parts of Martock and Tintenhull, in the Yeovil Union, were amalgamated with Curry Rivall, Kingsbury Episcopi, and Kingsdon ; and

LANGPORT UNION—*continued.*

The several parts of a Parish known as South Bradon, having in 1881 population 25, acreage 390, and rateable value £677, were amalgamated with Isle Brewers, Puckington, and Kingsbury Episcopi.

(c) By Orders which came into operation on 25 March 1886,—
A detached part of Kingsdon was amalgamated with Somerton ; and
A detached part of Puckington was amalgamated with Ilminster, in the Chard Union.

(d) By Provisional Order which came into operation on 25 March 1887,—
The several parts of a Parish known as Charlton Adam, having, in 1881, population 416, and rateable value 2,930£., were amalgamated with Charlton Mackrell, Compton Dundon, and Kingweston.

Unions and Parishes, &c.	Population in 1881.	Area in Statute Acres in 1881.	Rateable Value in 1881.	Post Town.	Petty Sessional Division.

LAUNCESTON UNION.

(Formed 2 Feb. 1837 by Order dated 7 Jan. 1837.—Places marked thus * added 25 Dec. 1852 by Order dated 8 Dec. 1852. † Name as altered by Order dated 6 April 1887.)

COUNTY of CORNWALL:

			£		East Launceston :
Alternon - - par.	1,150	15,014	6,364	Launceston -	North Division.
Boyton - - ham.	383	4,154	2,230	do. - -	do.
Egloskerry - - par.	433	3,235	2,828	do. - -	do.
Laneast - - par.	259	2,487	1,692	do. - -	do.
Lawhitton - - par.	425	2,649	3,494	do. - -	do.
Lewannick - - par.	644	4,000	4,571	do. - -	do.
Lezant - - par.	739	4,560	5,253	do. - -	do.
North Hill - - par.	1,059	6,732	6,425	do. - -	do.
Saint Mary Magdalen (W.) } par.	2,430	1,136	7,775	do. -	Launceston Borough.
†Saint Stephens - par.	959	3,852	5,353	do.	East Launceston : North Division.
Saint Thomas the Apostle } par.	299	2,036	2,705	do. - -	do.
Saint Thomas Street - ham.	736	66	1,701	do. - -	Launceston Borough.
South Petherwin - par.	826	4,968	3,424	do. -	do.
Stoke Climsland - par.	2,100	8,732	7,749	Callington -	Callington.
Tremaine - - par.	87	1,045	669	Launceston -	East Launceston : North Division.
Treneglos - - par.	168	2,730	1,176	do.	Lesnewth.
Tresmeer - - par.	172	1,344	1,087	do. -	East Launceston : North Division.
Trewen - - par.	141	988	1,101	do. - -	do.
Warbstow - - par.	373	4,104	2,257	do. - -	Lesnewth.

COUNTY of DEVON :

*Broadwood Widger(a)(b)par.	684	8,780	4,622	Lifton -	Lifton.
*Northcott (c) - - ham.	80	802	458	Launceston -	Holsworthy.
North Petherwin - par.	857	8,157	4,958	do. -	Lifton.
*Saint Giles in the Heath } par.	275	3,044	1,716	do.	do.
*Virginstowe - - par.	121	1,274	921	do. - -	do.
Werrington (c) - par.	658	5,000	4,370	do. -	do.
TOTAL of UNION -	16,058	100,889	86,899		

LEDBURY UNION.

(Formed 2 June 1836 by Order dated 6 May 1836.)

COUNTY of HEREFORD :

Ashperton (a) (c) - par.	409	1,741	3,292	Ledbury -	Ledbury.
Aylton - - par.	90	825	1,335	do. -	do.
Bosbury - - par.	989	4,769	7,971	do. -	do.
Canon Frome - - par.	115	1,023	1,604	do. -	do.
Castle Frome (d) - par.	150	1,511	2,000	Bromyard -	do.

(continued)

LAUNCESTON UNION :

(a) A detached part of Lifton, in the Tavistock Union, was amalgamated with Broadwood Widger, by Order which came into operation on 25 March 1884.

(b) A detached part of Bratton Clovelly, in the Okehampton Union, was amalgamated with Broadwood Widger, by Provisional Order which came into operation on 25 March 1885.

(c) A detached part of Northcott was amalgamated with Werrington by Order which came into operation on 25 March 1897.

LEDBURY UNION :

(a) By Provisional Orders which came into operation on 25 March 1885, changes were made in the areas of the following Parishes, namely, Ashperton, Donnington

LEDBURY UNION—continued.

Ledbury, Munsley, Putley, Stretton Grandsome or Grandison, Woolhope, and Yarkhill.

(b) The two parts of a Parish known as Parkhold were amalgamated with Pixley, by Order which came into operation on 25 March 1884.

(c) By Orders which came into operation on 25 March 1884,—
A detached part of Stretton Grandsome or Grandison was amalgamated with Ashperton ;
A detached part of Stoke Edith, in the Hereford Union, was amalgamated with Ashperton : and
A detached part of Much Marcle was amalgamated with Upton Bishop, in the Ross Union.

(d) By Order which came into operation on 25 March 1887,—A detached part of Bishop's Frome, in the Bromyard Union, was amalgamated with Castle Frome.

C c

Unions and Parishes, &c.		Population in 1881.	Area in Statute Acres in 1881.	Rateable Value in 1881.	Post Town.	Petty Sessional Division.
LEDBURY UNION—County of Hereford—*continued.*				£		
Coddington -	par.	141	1,076	1,164	Ledbury -	Ledbury.
Colwall -	par.	1,438	3,771	9,328	Malvern -	do.
Donnington (*a*)	par.	89	808	1,668	Ledbury -	do.
Eastnor -	par.	394	3,186	1,238	do. -	do.
Eggleton -	tow.	133	630	959	do. -	do.
Ledbury (W.) (*a*) -	par.	4,226	8,191	25,454	do. -	do.
Little Marcle -	par.	146	1,218	1,762	do.	do.
Much Marcle (*c*) -	par.	858	4,940	7,970	Dymock -	do.
Munsley (*a*) -	par.	172	1,228	2,516	Ledbury -	do.
Pixley (*b*) -	par.	149	655	2,172	do. -	do.
Putley (*a*) -	par.	204	589	1,267	do. -	do.
Stretton Grandsome or Graudison (*a*) (*c*)	par.	110	710	1,891	do. -	do.
Tarrington -	par.	500	2,224	5,517	do. -	do.
Woolhope (*a*) -	par.	745	1,653	5,498	Hereford -	do.
Yarkhill (*a*) -	par.	443	1,666	3,548	do. -	do.
COUNTY of WORCESTER :						
Mathon -	par.	1,101	3,366	7,860	Malvern -	Great Malvern.
TOTAL of UNION -		12,605	48,783	99,344		

LEEDS UNION.

(Formed 21 June 1869 by Order dated 31 May 1869.)

COUNTY of YORK, West Riding :

Chapel Allerton -	tow.	4,324	2,811	21,556	Leeds -	Leeds.
Headingley-with-Burley	tow.	19,138	3,183	89,200	do. -	do.
Leeds (W.) -	tow.	160,109	2,736	632,531	do. -	do.
Potter Newton -	tow.	5,107	1,709	33,025	do. -	do.
Roundhay -	tow.	802	1,482	7,155	do. -	Wapentake of Morley.
Seacroft (*a*) -	tow.	1,367	1,834	6,783	do. -	do.
TOTAL of UNION -		190,847	13,755	790,250		

LEEK UNION.

(Formed 2 Dec. 1837 by Order dated 4 Nov. 1837.—Places marked thus * added 2 Feb. 1869 by Order dated 13 Jan. 1869.)

COUNTY of STAFFORD :

Bradnop and Caudery	tow.	445	3,568	4,380	Leek -	Leek.
*Butterton -	tow.	231	1,499	2,006	do. -	do.
Endon, Longsden and Stanley	tow.	1,560	5,457	11,131	Stoke upon Trent -	do.
Fawfield Head -	tow.	633	5,383	4,432	Ashbourne -	do.
*Grindon -	par.	364	3,274	4,549	Leek -	do.
Heathy Lea -	tow.	418	5,536	2,979	Buxton -	do.
Heaton -	tow.	328	2,689	3,137	Macclesfield -	do.
Hollings Clough -	tow.	348	1,842	1,103	Buxton -	do.
Horton and Horton Hay, Blackwood, and Crowborough	par.	1,201	4,975	7,068	Leek -	do.
Leek and Lowe (W.)	tow.	11,486	2,722	36,607	do. -	do.
Leek Frith -	tow.	821	7,542	7,596	do. -	do.
Longnor -	tow.	534	813	1,882	Buxton -	do.
Norton in the Moors -	par.	8,870	4,141	22,564	Stoke upon Trent -	Hundred of Pirehill (Northern Division).

(continued)

LEDBURY UNION :

(*a*), (*b*), (*c*), see notes, page 203.

LEEDS UNION :

(*a*) By Order which came into operation on 25 March 1885, a detached part of Shadwell, in the Wetherby Union, was amalgamated with Seacroft.

Unions and Parishes, &c.		Population in 1881.	Area in Statute Acres in 1881.	Rateable Value in 1881.	Post Town.	Petty Sessional Division
LEEK UNION—County of Stafford—*continued.*				£		
Onecote	- *tow.*	373	4,936	5,495	Leek -	Leek.
Quarnford	- *tow.*	136	3,141	1,372	Buxton -	do.
Rudyard	- *tow.*	72	1,435	1,994	Leek -	do.
Rushton James	- *tow.*	267	1,390	1,880	Macclesfield	do.
Rushton Spencer	- *tow.*	341	1,860	3,014	do. -	do.
Sheen	- *par.*	419	2,893	3,858	Ashbourne -	do.
Tittisworth	- *tow.*	1,517	1,659	5,101	Leek -	do.
Warslow and Elkston	*tow.*	574	3,597	3,572	Ashbourne -	do.
TOTAL of UNION -		31,238	70,352	135,720		

LEICESTER UNION.

(Formed 20 June 1836 by Order dated 20 May 1836.—Places marked thus * added 25 Dec. 1861 by Order dated 6 Nov. 1861.)

COUNTY of LEICESTER :

All Saints (a) -	- *par.*	6,371		18,133	Leicester -	Borough of Leicester.
*Augustine Friars	- *par.*	94		580	do. -	do.
*Black Friars -	- *par.*	2,108		4,880	do. -	do.
Saint Leonard -	- *par.*	3,046		6,485	do. -	do.
Saint Margaret (W.)(a) *par.*		78,805	3,200	262,246	do. -	do.
Saint Martin -	- *par.*	2,171		35,221	do. -	do.
Saint Mary -	- *par.*	26,110		101,192	do. -	do.
Saint Nicholas -	- *par.*	1,830		5,346	do. -	do.
The Castle View	- *par.*	153		544	do. -	do.
The Newarke	- *par.*	1,688		3,829	do. -	do.
TOTAL of UNION -		122,376	3,200	438,656		

LEIGH UNION.

(Formed 15 Feb. 1837 by Order dated 26 Jan. 1837.—Places marked thus * added 30 Sept. 1845 by Order of the same date.)

COUNTY of LANCASTER :

						Hundred of West Derby :
Astley	- *tow.*	2,669	2,685	11,789	Manchester -	Leigh Division.
Atherton (W.)	- *tow.*	12,602	2,426	13,424	do. -	do.
Bedford	- *tow.*	7,246	2,826	21,729	do. -	do.
Culcheth	- *tow.*	2,267	5,369	14,946	do. -	do.
*Golborne	- *par.*	4,502	1,679	20,750	Newton le Willows	Warrington.
*Kenyon	- *tow.*	233	1,685	8,125	Manchester -	Leigh.
Lowton	- *par.*	2,357	1,830	7,732	Newton le Willows	do.
Pennington	- *tow.*	6,640	1,483	21,420	Manchester -	do.
Tyldesly - with-Shak- } erley }	*tow.*	9,951	2,490	42,596	do. -	do.
West Leigh	- *tow.*	7,848	1,883	31,519	do. -	do.
TOTAL of UNION -		56,318	24,356	224,030		

LEICESTER UNION :

(a) A detached part of Saint Margaret was unamalgamated with All Saints, by Order which came into operation on 25 March 1885.

Unions and Parishes, &c.	Population in 1881.	Area in Statute Acres in 1881.	Rateable Value in 1881.	Post Town.	Petty Sessional Division.

LEIGHTON BUZZARD UNION.

(Formed 1 July 1835 by Order dated 12 June 1835.—Place marked thus * added 3 Mar. 1846 by Order of the same date.)

COUNTY of BEDFORD:

£

Unions and Parishes, &c.	Population in 1881.	Area in Statute Acres in 1881.	Rateable Value in 1881.	Post Town.	Petty Sessional Division.
Billington - - ham.	426	1,209	1,967	Leighton Buzzard -	Leighton Buzzard.
*Eaton Bray - - par.	1,520	2,117	4,275	Dunstable - -	do.
Egginton - - ham.	274	1,372	2,131	Leighton Buzzard -	do.
Heath and Reach - ham.	1,075	2,390	4,476	do. - -	do.
Leighton Buzzard (W.) } tow.	5,991	2,426	17,560	do. - -	do.
Stanbridge - ham.	512	1,514	2,519	do. - -	do.
COUNTY of BUCKINGHAM:					
Cheddington (a) - par.	744	1,429	6,116	Tring - -	Linslade.
Eddlesborough (b) - par.	1,598	4,647	9,287	Dunstable -	do.
Grove - - par.	17	437	1,623	Leighton Buzzard	do.
Ivinghoe (a) (b) (c) -- par.	1,380	5,618	8,242	Tring - -	do.
Linslade - - par.	1,724	1,693	12,588	Leighton Buzzard	do.
Mentmore - par.	314	1,575	5,509	do. - -	do.
Slapton (a) (b)(c) - par.	265	1,211	3,061	do. - -	do.
Soulbury - - par.	475	4,226	9,545	do. - -	do.
Stoke Hammond - par.	365	1,566	5,701	Bletchley Station -	Newport Pagnell.
Wing - - par.	1,636	5,703	10,244	Leighton Buzzard -	Linslade.
TOTAL of UNION -	18,316	39,433	104,844		

LEOMINSTER UNION.

(Formed 15 June 1836 by Order dated 17 May 1836.--Places marked thus * added 25 Dec. 1858 by Order dated 17 Nov. 1858.)

COUNTY of HEREFORD:

Unions and Parishes, &c.	Population in 1881.	Area in Statute Acres in 1881.	Rateable Value in 1881.	Post Town.	Petty Sessional Division.
Aymestrey - - par.	648	6,349	6,508	Leominster -	Wigmore.
Bodenham (a) (b) - par.	879	5,260	7,764	do. - -	Leominster.
Croft - - par.	36	1,057	1,558	do. - -	do.
Docklow (a) - par.	195	1,715	2,285	do. - -	do.
Eye - - tow.	279	In Luston	4,595	do. - -	do.
Eyton - - par.	111	964	1,884	do. - -	do.
Fordsbridge or } Hamlet of Ford } par.	17	321	409	do. - -	do.
*Hampton Wafer - par.	6	In Docklow	357	do. - -	do.
Hatfield (a) - par.	139	1,528	1,600	do. - -	do.
Hope under Dinmore par.	494	3,796	5,567	do. - -	do.
Humber - - par.	257	1,494	1,829	do. - -	do.
Kimbolton - par.	622	4,061	5,643	do. - -	do.
Kingsland - - par.	1,063	4,735	10,426	do. - -	do.
Laysters or Leysters par.	238	1,989	2,326	Tenbury -	do.
Leominster(Borough) (W.) } par.	4,939 }	8,086 {	16,031	Leominster -	Leominster Borough.
Leominster (Out-Parish)	1,105 }		17,134	do. - -	do.
Lucton - - par.	157	1,017	1,343	do. - -	Leominster.
Luston - - tow.	425	4,307	4,102	do. - -	do.

(continued)

LEIGHTON BUZZARD UNION:

(a) By Orders which came into operation on 25 March 1884,— A detached part of Cheddington was amalgamated with Ivinghoe, and detached parts of Ivinghoe were amalgamated with Cheddington and Slapton; and Detached parts of Pightlesthorne, otherwise Pistone, in the Berkhampstead Union, were amalgamated with Ivinghoe and Slapton.

(b) Detached parts of Eddlesborough were amalgamated with Little Gaddesden (in the Berkhampstead Union), Slapton, and Ivinghoe, by Provisional Order which came into operation on 25 March 1885.

(c) Detached parts of Slapton were amalgamated with Ivinghoe by Order which came into operation on 25 March 1886.

LEOMINSTER UNION:

(a) By Orders which came into operation on 25 March 1884,— A detached part of Felton, in the Bromyard Union, was amalgamated with Bodenham; and A detached part of Docklow was amalgamated with Hatfield.

(b) By Orders which came into operation on 25 March 1887,-- A detached part of Yarpole was amalgamated with Luston; and A detached part of Amberley, in the Hereford Union, was amalgamated with Bodenham.

Unions and Parishes, &c.		Population in 1881.	Area in Statute Acres in 1881.	Rateable Value in 1881.	Post Town.			Petty Sessional Division.
LEOMINSTER UNION.—County of Hereford—*conti*				£				
Middleton on the Hill	*par.*	392	2,921	3,212	Tenbury	-		Leominster.
Monkland	- *par.*	206	1,079	2,003	Leominster		-	do.
*New Hampton	- *par.*	11	452	116	do.	-	-	do.
Newton	- *tow.*	66	507	987	do.		-	do.
Orleton	- *par.*	575	2,603	5,032	Ludlow	-		do.
Puddlestone	- *par.*	287	1,743	2,052	Leominster		-	do.
Shobdon	*par.*	379	3,337	5,331	do	-	-	Wigmore.
Stoke Prior	*par.*	519	2,569	3,897	do.	-	-	Leominster.
Yarpole (*b*) -	- *par.*	603	2,523	3,776	do.		-	do.
TOTAL OF UNION	-	14,648	64,416	117,767				
LEWES UNION.								
(Formed 10 Aug. 1835 by Order dated 20 July 1835.—Place marked thus * added 25 Dec. 1858 by Order dated 27 Sept. 1858.)								
COUNTY of SUSSEX :								
All Saints -	- *par.*	1,962	50	9,859	Lewes		-	Lewes Division of Lewes and Pevensey Rape.
Saint John Baptist Southover } *par.*		1,462	546	7,192	do.	-	-	do.
Saint John under the Castle } *par.*		2,778	1,372	9,836	do.		-	do.
Saint Michael -	- *par.*	978	19	4,113	do.		-	do.
Saint Peter and Saint Mary, Westout, otherwise Saint Ann's (W.) } *par.*		1,945	1,838	9,079	do.		-	do.
Saint Thomas in the Cliffe } *par.*		1,664	33	6,370	do.		-	do.
South Malling	- *par.*	732	2,545	6,442	do.	-	-	do.
*The Castle Precincts	*par.*	26	4	364	do.	-		do.
TOTAL OF UNION	-	11,547	6,407	53,285				
LEWISHAM UNION.								
(Formed 28 Nov. 1836 by Order dated 2 Nov. 1836.)								
COUNTY of KENT :								
Eltham	- *par.*	5,048	3,782	47,598	Eltham	-	-	Blackheath and Little Lessness.
Lee	- *par.*	14,435	1,238	117,621	Lee	-	-	do.
Lewisham (W.)	- *par.*	53,065	5,774	376,087	Lewisham	-	-	do.
TOTAL OF UNION	-	72,548	10,794	541,306				
LEXDEN AND WINSTREE UNION.								
(Formed 1 Feb. 1836 by Order dated 13 Jan. 1836.—Place marked thus * added 14 May 1835 by Order dated 18 April 1836, and places marked thus † added 26 Mar. 1880 by Order dated 27 Feb. 1880.)								
COUNTY of ESSEX :								
Abberton	- *par.*	244	1,068	1,503	Colchester		-	Winstree and Lexden.
Aldham	- *par.*	433	1,847	3,212	do.	-	-	do.
Birch	- *par.*	873	3,105	4,540	do.	-	-	do.
Boxted	- *par.*	826	3,177	5,425	do.	-	-	do.
Chappel	- *par.*	363	1,176	2,309	do.	-	-	do.
Copford	- *par.*	710	2,492	4,564	do.	-	-	do.
Dedham	- *par.*	1,745	2,568	7,670	do.	-	-	do.
East Donyland	- *par.*	1,272	1,052	3,340	do.	-	-	do.
								(*continued*)

LEOMINSTER UNION :

(*b*) *See note on p.* 206.

Unions and Parishes, &c.	Population in 1881.	Area in Statute Acres in 1881.	Rateable Value in 1881.	Post Town.	Petty Sessional Division.
LEXDEN AND WINSTREE UNION—County of Essex—continued.			£		
Easthorpe - - par.	95	921	1,404	Colchester - -	Winstree and Lexden.
East Mersea - par.	283	1,989	2,632	do. - -	do.
Fingringhoe - - par.	659	2,890	3,826	do. - -	do.
Fordham - - par.	699	2,520	4,184	do. - -	do.
Great Horksley - par.	794	3,177	5,860	do. - -	do.
Great Tey - - par.	691	2,626	4,244	do. - -	Witham.
Great Wigborough - par.	421	2,527	2,806	Witham - -	Winstree and Lexden.
†Inworth - - par.	637	1,570	2,279	Kelvedon - -	Witham.
Langenhoe - - par.	234	2,084	2,322	Colchester -	Winstree and Lexden.
Langham - - par.	670	2,977	4,882	do. - -	do.
Layer Breton - par.	293	962	1,447	do. - -	do.
Layer-de-la-Hay - par.	687	2,594	3,735	do. - -	do.
Layer Marney - par.	258	1,995	2,243	do. - -	do.
Little Horksley - par.	199	1,039	2,284	do. - -	do.
Little Tey - - par.	67	491	748	Coggeshall -	Witham.
Little Wigborough - par.	91	1,223	1,147	Colchester -	Winstree and Lexden.
Marks Tey - - par.	411	1,225	3,577	do. - -	do.
†Messing - - par.	642	2,593	3,467	Kelvedon - -	Witham.
*Mount Bures (a) - par.	276	1,425	2,369	Colchester -	Winstree and Lexden.
Peldon - - par.	458	2,246	2,875	do. - -	do.
Salcott - - par.	239	274	479	do. - -	do.
Stanway (W.) - par.	1,004	3,436	6.306	do. - -	do.
Virley - - par.	86	640	743	Kelvedon - -	do.
Wakes Colne - par.	499	1,935	3,326	Halstead - -	do.
West Bergholt - par.	1,067	2,296	4,567	do. - -	do.
West Mersea - par.	1,092	3,193	4,024	Colchester -	do.
Wivenhoe - - par.	2,280	1,549	7,020	do. - -	do.
Wormingford - par.	477	2,322	3,965	do. - -	do.
TOTAL of UNION -	21,775	71,204	122,224		

LEYBURN UNION.

(Formed 22 Feb. 1837 by Order dated 28 Jan. 1837.)

COUNTY of YORK, North Riding :

Agelthorpe - - tow.	211	1,410	1,826	Bedale - -	Hang, West.
Akebar - - tow.	23	778	915	Catterick - -	do.
Arrowthorne - - tow.	62	671	747	do. - -	do.
Barden - - tow.	87	1,779	948	Bedale - -	do.
Bellerby - - tow.	311	3,063	2,359	do. - -	do.
Burton Constable - tow.	213	2,650	3,673	do. - -	do.
Caldbridge - - tow.	72	3,449	803	do. - -	do.
Carlton - - tow.	252	2,742	1,582	do. - -	do.
Carlton Highdale - tow.	247	10,133	2,677	do. - -	do.
Castle Bolton - - tow.	169	4,956	1,702	do. - -	do.
Ellingstring (a) - tow.	116	430	444	do. - -	Hang, East.
Ellingtons (a) - tow.	89	1,791	1,842	do. - -	do.
Fearby (a) - - tow.	222	891	1,099	do. - -	do.
Finghall - - tow.	99	562	749	do. - -	Hang, West.
Garriston - - tow.	30	670	627	do. - -	do.
Harmby - - tow.	182	1,111	1,476	do. - -	do.
Hauxwell, East - tow.	95	1,249	1,019	do. - -	do.
Hauxwell, West - tow.	40	892	673	do. - -	do.
Healy with Sutton (a) - tow.	244	4,893	2,491	do. - -	Hang, East.
Hornby - - tow.	90	1,591	2,164	do. - -	do.
Hunton - - tow.	111	1,910	2,311	Catterick -	Hang, West.
Hutton Hang - - tow.	31	591	730	Bedale -	do.
Leyburn - - tow.	972	2,515	4,702	do. - -	do.
Melmerby - - tow.	110	1,212	667	do. - -	do.
Middleham - - par.	818	2,154	4,795	do. - -	do.
Newton-le-Willows - tow.	338	1,858	2,948	do. - -	Hang, East.
Patrick Brompton - tow.	478	1,238	1,782	do. - -	do.

(*continued*)

LEXDEN AND WINSTREE UNION :

(*a*) Certain detached parts of Buers, in the Sudbury Union, were amalgamated with Mount Bures, and a part of Mount Bures was amalgamated with Bures, by Order which came into operation on 25 March 1884.

LEYBURN UNION :

(*a*) By Orders which came into operation on 25 March 1886, alterations were made in the areas of East Witton Within, East Witton Without, Ellingstring, Ellingtons, Fearby, Healy with Sutton, and Thornton Steward.

Unions and Parishes, &c.		Population in 1881.	Area in Statute Acres in 1881.	Rateable Value in 1881.	Post Town.	Petty Sessional Division.

LEYBURN UNION—County of York, North Riding—continued.

				£		
Preston -	tow.	362	2,577	1,877	Bedale -	Hang, West.
Redmire -	tow.	347	2,318	1,764	do. -	do.
Scrafton, West -	tow.	106	1,616	603	do. -	do.
Spennithorn -	tow.	200	1,303	2,105	do.	do.
Thornton Steward (a)	par.	240	2,158	2,811	do. -	do.
Wensley (W.) -	tow.	322	2,079	2,621	do. -	do.
Witton East, Within (a) -	tow.	240	2,610	2,280	do. -	do.
Witton East, Without (a) -	tow.	236	4,444	3,275	do. -	do.
Witton, West -	par.	560	3,874	4,081	do. -	do.
TOTAL of UNION -		**8,324**	**80,268**	**69,168**		

LICHFIELD UNION.

(Formed 21 Dec. 1836 by Order dated 25 Nov. 1836.—Place marked thus * added 6 July 1846 by Order dated 18 June 1846, and thus † added 1 July 1858 by Order dated 11 June 1858.)

CITY of LICHFIELD and COUNTY of the same CITY.

Saint Chad -	par.	2,205 ⎫		7,701 ⎫	Lichfield -	Lichfield.
Saint Mary -	par.	2,832 ⎬ 3,180		7,128 ⎬	do. -	do.
Saint Michael (W.) -	par.	3,012 ⎭		14,309 ⎭	do. -	do.
The Close -	par.	232 ⎫ In		1,272 ⎫	do. -	do.
†The Friary -	par.	9 ⎭ St. Michael		108 ⎭	do. -	do.

CITY of LICHFIELD and COUNTY of the same CITY and COUNTY of STAFFORD.

Pipe Hill -	tow.	173 { In Hammerwick }		1,472	Lichfield -	Offlow South.

COUNTY of STAFFORD:

Alrewas (a) -	par.	1,563	6,009	13,763	Burton-upon-Trent	Offlow North.
Armitage with Handsacre -	par.	1,283	1,921	7,295	Rugeley -	do.
Burntwood Edjall and Woodhouses -	tow.	6,270	4,417	20,077	Lichfield -	do.
Colton (b) -	par.	678	3,692	9,964	Rugeley -	Pire Hill South.
Curborough and Elmhurst -	tow.	201	2,080	3,770	Lichfield -	Offlow North.
Elford -	par.	426	2,070	5,226	Tamworth	do.
Farewell and Charley (a) -	par.	218	802	2,096	Lichfield -	Offlow South.
Fisherwick -	tow.	95 { In Hammerwick }		2,791	do. -	Offlow North.
†Freeford -	ham.	53	548	708	do. -	do.
†Fulfen -	par.	38 { In St. Michael }		1,328	do. -	do.
Hammerwick -	cha.	1,391	7,489	4,998	do. -	Offlow South.
Hamstall Ridware -	par.	383	3,124	4,026	Rugeley -	Offlow North.
†Haselor -	par.	29	584	2,087	Tamworth	do.
Kings Bromley -	par.	567	3,370	9,215	Lichfield	do.
†Kings Bromley Hays -	par.	13 { In King's Bromley }		660	do. -	do.
Longdon -	par.	1,366	4,511	8,111	Rugeley -	Offlow South.
Mavesyn Ridware -	par.	473	2,186	6,235	do. -	Offlow North.
*Ogley Hay -	par.	2,040	705	5,963	Walsall -	Offlow South.
Pipe Ridware -	par.	74	822	1,210	Rugeley -	Offlow North.
Rugeley -	par.	7,048	8,449	21,223	do. -	Cuttlestone East. (continued)

LICHFIELD UNION:

(a) By Order which came into operation on 25 March 1884.—
Detached parts of Farewell and Charley were amalgamated with Streethay and Alrewas; and
The several parts of parishes known as Fradley

LICHFIELD UNION—continued.

Orgreave, and Alrewas Hays were united with Alrewas.
(b) Certain detached parts of Colwich, in the Stafford Union, were amalgamated with Colton, by Order which came into operation on 25 March 1885.

Unions and Parishes, &c.	Population in 1881.	Area in Statute Acres in 1881.	Rateable Value in 1881.	Post Town.	Petty Sessional Division.
LICHFIELD UNION—County of Stafford—*continued.*			£		
Shenstone - - par.	2,488	8,451	14,922	Lichfield - -	Offlow South.
Streethay (*a*) - tow.	217 { In Hammerwick		4,167	do. - -	Offlow North.
Swinfen and Packington - } ham.	161	In Weeford	3,164	do. - -	Offlow South.
†Tamhorn - - par.	33	1,770	2,407	do. - -	Offlow North.
Wall - - - tow.	116 { In Hammerwick		1,323	do. - -	Offlow South.
Weeford - - tow.	244	4,556	3,302	do. - -	do.
Whittington - par.	2,009	2,921	9,647	do. - -	Offlow North.
Yoxall - - par.	1,301	4,961	9,236	Burton-upon-Trent	do.
TOTAL of UNION -	39,241	77,918	210,932		

LINCOLN UNION.

(Formed 28 Nov. 1836 by Order dated 5 Nov. 1836, which was amended as to the name of the parish marked thus §§ by Order dated 19 Dec. 1885.)—Place marked thus * added 30 March 1837 by Order dated 11 March 1837, thus † added 3 March 1855 by Order of the same date, thus ‡ added 1 July 1858 by Order dated 14 June 1858, thus § added 25 March 1859 by Order dated 11 February 1859, places marked thus ¶ added 25 Dec. 1861 by Order dated 16 Nov. 1861, thus ⁋ added 1 May 1862 by Order dated 5 April 1862, place marked thus ** added 1 Nov. 1862 by Order dated 29 Sept. 1862, thus †† added 29 Sept. 1864 by Order dated 29 July 1864, and thus ‡‡ added 14 April 1869 by Order dated 2 April 1869.)

CITY of LINCOLN and COUNTY of the same CITY :

§Castle Dykings - par.	181		331	Lincoln - -	City of Lincoln.
Saint Benedict - par.	628		5,169	do. - -	do.
Saint Botolph - par.	3,547		8,181	do. - -	do.
Saint John in Newport par.	500		842	do. - -	do.
Saint Margaret in the Close - } par.	415		3,900	do. - -	do.
Saint Mark - - par.	997		5,567	do. - -	do.
Saint Martin - par.	4,331		15,650	do. - -	do.
Saint Mary le Wigford par.	3,555		14,825	do. - -	do.
Saint Mary Magdalen in the Bail } par.	610		3,136	do. - -	do.
Saint Michael - par.	1,253		2,516	do. - -	do.
Saint Nicholas in Newport - } par.	4,462	3,891	10,215	do. - -	do.
Saint Paul in the Bail par.	820		1,749	do. - -	do.
Saint Peter at Arches par.	528		6,568	do. - -	do.
Saint Peter in Gowts par.	6,560		18,607	do. - -	do.
Saint Peter in East Gate (W.) - } par.	1,448		4,721	do. - -	do.
Saint Swithin - par.	7,328		25,763	do. - -	do.
‖The Bishop's Palace par.	6		64	do. - -	do.
‖The Cold Bath House par.	5		72	do. - -	do.
††The Holmes Common - } par.	18		672	do. - -	do.
‖The Monk's Liberty par.	79		1,968	do. - -	do.
‡‡The South Common - } par.	242		894	do. - -	do.

COUNTY of LINCOLN :

Aisthorpe - - par.	112	803	1,362	do. - -	Lindsey.
Apley - - par.	189	1,658	1,569	Wragby - -	do.
Auborn - - tow.	213	1,843	3,018	Lincoln - -	Kesteven.
Bardney - - par.	1,393	5,490	10,161	do. - -	Lindsey.
Barlings - - par.	469	2,630	2,940	Wragby - -	do.
Boothby - - par.	168	2,850	3,461	Lincoln - -	Kesteven.
Boultham - - par.	114	1,210	2,044	do. - -	do.
Bracebridge - par.	2,123	1,482	8,188	do. - -	do.
Branston - - par.	1,431	5,389	10,652	do. - -	do.

(continued)

Unions and Parishes, &c.	Population in 1881.	Area in Statute Acres in 1881.	Rateable Value in 1881.	Post Town.	Petty Sessional Division.

LINCOLN UNION—County of Lincoln—*continued.*

Unions and Parishes, &c.	Population in 1881.	Area in Statute Acres in 1881.	Rateable Value £ in 1881.	Post Town.	Petty Sessional Division.
Brattleby - - *par.*	148	1,220	1,648	Lincoln - -	Lindsey.
Broxholme - - *par.*	114	1,298	1,778	do. - -	do.
Bullington (b) - *tow.*	51	In Goltho	1,045	Wragby - -	do.
Burton (by Lincoln) - *par.*	282	2,325	3,687	Lincoln - -	do.
Caenby - - *par.*	129	1,430	2,523	Market Rasen -	do.
Cameringham - *par.*	156	1,806	2,314	Lincoln - -	do.
Canwick - - *par.*	246	1,999	4,815	do. - -	Kesteven.
Cold Hanworth - *par.*	89	707	835	do. - -	Lindsey.
**Coldstead - - *par.*	5	In Stainton	54	do. - -	do.
Coleby - - *par.*	435	2,600	4,228	do. - -	Kesteven.
Doddington - - *tow.*	156	4,044	2,422	do. - -	do.
Dunholme - - *par.*	403	2,190	4,380	do. - -	Lindsey.
Dunston - - *par.*	782	4,620	4,458	do. - -	Kesteven.
Eagle (a) - - *par.*	462 }	2,530	3,229	Newark - -	do.
* Eagle Hall - - *par.*	69 }		1,457	do. - -	do.
East Firsby - *tow.*	33 { In West Firsby }		638	Market Rasen -	Lindsey.
Faldingworth (c) - *par.*	310	1,820	2,745	do. - -	do.
Fiskerton - - *par.*	440	2,040	3,958	Lincoln - -	do.
Friesthorpe (c) - *par.*	61	586	681	Market Rasen -	do.
*Fulnetby (b) - *tow.*	73	2,330	1,101	Wragby - -	do.
Goltho - - *tow.*	106	2,540	1,088	do. - -	do.
‡Grange-de-Lings - *par.*	66	—	1,228	Lincoln - -	do.
Greetwell (b) - *par.*	86	1,113	2,657	do. - -	do.
Hackthorne - - *par.*	278	2,890	3,436	do. - -	do.
Haddington - *tow.*	82	910	1,482	do. - -	Kesteven.
Harmston - *par.*	345	2,690	4,681	do. - -	do.
Heighington (c) - *tow.*	747	5,190	4,673	do. - -	do.
Holton by Beckering-ham - *par.*	165	1,862	2,813	Wragby - -	Lindsey.
Ingham - - *par.*	596	1,750	3,329	Lincoln - -	do.
†Mere - - *par.*	84 { In Waddington }		2,164	do. - -	Kesteven.
Metheringham - *par.*	1,857	4,590	9,812	do. - -	do.
¶Morton - - *par.*	8	710	529	do. - -	do.
Navenby - - *par.*	957	2,110	6,152	do. - -	do.
Nettleham - - *par.*	958	3,270	6,868	do. - -	Lindsey.
§§Newball (b) - *tow.*	124	In Stainton	1,186	do. - -	do.
Nocton - - *par.*	628	5,340	6,711	do. - -	Kesteven.
Normanby - - *par.*	397	1,420	2,394	Market Rasen	Lindsey.
North Carlton - *par.*	163	1,795	2,481	Lincoln - -	do.
North Hyckham - *par.*	455	1,990	3,144	do. - -	Kesteven.
Owmby - - *par.*	266	1,650	2,884	Market Rasen -	Lindsey.
Potter Hanworth - *par.*	435	4,150	4,113	Lincoln - -	Kesteven.
Rand (b) - - *tow.*	66	In Fulnetby	1,255	Wragby - -	Lindsey.
Reepham - - *par.*	356	1,430	3,812	Lincoln - -	do.
Riseholme - - *par.*	68	1,370	1,272	do. - -	do.
Saxby - - *par.*	114	2,322	1,449	Market Rasen -	Lindsey.
Saxelby with Ingleby *par.*	1,191	4,270	9,168	Lincoln - -	do.
Scampton - - *par.*	230	2,147	3,261	do. - -	do.
Scothern - - *par.*	495	2,500	4,257	do. - -	do.
Skellingthorpe - *par.*	722	6,220	8,064	do. - -	Kesteven.
Skinnard - - *par.*	39	600	995	do. - -	do.
Snarford - - *par.*	102	1,120	1,150	Market Rasen -	Lindsey.
Snelland - - *par.*	133	1,261	1,614	Wragby - -	do.
South Carlton - *par.*	175	1,910	2,349	Lincoln - -	do.
South Hyckham - *par.*	103	1,160	1,254	do. - -	Kesteven.
Spridlington - *par.*	291	2,180	2,798	do. - -	Lindsey.
Stainfield - - *par.*	203	2,450	2,168	Wragby - -	do.
Stainton (by Langworth) - *tow.*	126	3,021	1,837	do. - -	do.
Sudbrooke - - *par.*	55	1,000	1,117	Lincoln - -	do.

(*continued*)

LINCOLN UNION :

(a) All the parts of a parish known as Eagle Woodhouse were amalgamated with Eagle, by Order which came into operation on 25 March 1886.

(b) By Provisional Order which came into operation on 25 March 1887,—
   A detached part of Bullington was amalgamated with Newball;
   A detached part of Rand was amalgamated with Fulnetby; and

LINCOLN UNION—*continued.*

A detached part of Willingham Cherry was amalgamated with Greetwell.

(c) By Orders which came into operation on 25 March 1887,—
   A detached part of Faldingworth was amalgamated with Friesthorpe; and
   A detached part of Waskingborough was amalgamated with Heighington.

i R 8372.

D d

Unions and Parishes, &c.	Population in 1881.	Area in Statute Acres in 1881.	Rateable Value in 1881.	Post Town.	Petty Sessional Division.

LINCOLN UNION—County of Lincoln—continued.

Unions and Parishes, &c.	Population in 1881.	Area in Statute Acres in 1881.	Rateable Value in 1881. £	Post Town.	Petty Sessional Division.
Swinethorpe - *par.*	42	980	1,208	Swinethorpe	Kesteven.
Thorpe in the Fallows } *par.*	70	640	846	Lincoln -	Lindsey.
Thorpe on the Hill - *par.*	286	1,820	2,868	do.	Kesteven.
Waddington - *par.*	878	4,671	8,304	do.	do.
Washingborough (c) *tow.*	729 { In Heighington }		6,956	do.	do.
Welton - - *par.*	682	3,690	6,009	do. -	Lindsey.
West Firsby - *tow.*	41	2,292	1,266	Market Rasen	do.
Whisby - *tow.*	118 { In Doddington }		1,931	Lincoln -	Kesteven.
Wickenby - - *par.*	269	1,997	2,604	Wragby -	Lindsey.
Willingham Cherry (b) *par.*	156	980	1,739	Lincoln -	do.
TOTAL of UNION -	64,512	158,792	378,480		

LINTON UNION.

(Formed 18 June 1835 by Order dated 2 June 1835.)

COUNTY of CAMBRIDGE:

Unions and Parishes, &c.	Population in 1881.	Area in Statute Acres in 1881.	Rateable Value in 1881.	Post Town.	Petty Sessional Division.
Babraham - - *par.*	267	2,350	2,865	Cambridge -	Linton.
Balsham - - *par.*	1,011	1,402	6,145	do. -	do.
Carlton (b) - - *par.*	337	2,200	2,987	Newmarket	do.
Castlecamps (a) - *par.*	888	2,703	3,477	Linton -	do.
Duxford - - *par.*	774	3,132	6,563	Cambridge -	do.
Great Abington - *par.*	279	1,500	2,246	do. -	do.
Great Bartlow - *par.*	115	370	697	Linton -	do.
Hildersham - - *par.*	245	1,499	2,096	Cambridge -	do.
Hinxton (b) - *par.*	343	1,503	3,226	Saffron Walden	do.
Horseheath - *par.*	545	1,849	2,803	Linton -	do.
Ickleton (b) - *par.*	657	2,672	5,549	Saffron Walden	do.
Linton (W.) - *par.*	1,753	3,775	7,153	Cambridge -	do.
Little Abington - *par.*	264	1,120	1,709	do. -	do.
Pampisford - *par.*	351	1,500	2,565	do. -	do.
Sawston - - *par.*	1,786	1,856	7,992	do. -	do.
Shudy Camps - *par.*	334	2,332	3,008	Linton -	do.
Weston Colville - *par.*	525	2,943	3,897	Cambridge -	do.
West Wickham - *par.*	455	2,937	3,720	do. -	do.
West Wratting - *par.*	591	3,441	4,869	do. -	do.
Whittlesford - *par.*	849	1,915	4,282	do. -	do.
COUNTY of ESSEX :					
Hadstock - - *par.*	416	1,731	2,569	Linton -	Saffron Walden.
Little Bartlow - *ham.*	200	1,241	1,228	do. -	do.
TOTAL of UNION -	13,015	48,971	81,645		

LISKEARD UNION.

(Formed 16 Jan. 1837 by Order dated 22 Dec. 1836.)

COUNTY of CORNWALL :

Unions and Parishes, &c.	Population in 1881.	Area in Statute Acres in 1881.	Rateable Value in 1881.	Post Town.	Petty Sessional Division.
Boconnoc - - *par.*	267	2,065	1,982	Lostwithiel -	West.
Broadoak - - *par.*	290	3,367	2,807	do. -	do.

(continued)

LINCOLN UNION :

(b), (c). See notes, page 211.

LINTON UNION :

(a) All that part of Helion's Bumpstead, in the Risbridge Union, which was situate in the County of Cambridge, was amalgamated with Castlecamps by Provisional Order which came into operation on 25 March 1885.

(b) A detached part of Ickleton was amalgamated with Hinxton, and a detached part of Brinkley, in the Newmarket Union,

LINTON UNION—*continued.*

was amalgamated with Carlton, by Orders which came into operation on 25 March 1886.

LISKEARD UNION

(a) All the parts of the Parishes of Liskeard and Saint Cleer, included in the Municipal Borough of Liskeard, were amalgamated with the Parish of the Borough of Liskeard, by Order which came into operation on 25 March 1881.

Unions and Parishes, &c.		Population in 1881.	Area in Statute Acres in 1881.	Rateable Value in 1881.	Post Town.	Petty Sessional Division.
LISKEARD UNION—County of Cornwall—continued.				£		
Callington	par.	1,925	2,192	6,491	Callington	East (Middle Division).
Duloe	par.	970	3,844	5,227	Liskeard	West.
East Looe	cha.	1,353	3,199	3,236	Looe	Borough of Liskeard.
Lanreath	par.	562	4,878	4,321	Duloe R.S.O.	West.
Lanselloes	par.	717	2,985	3,756	Polperro	do.
Lanteglos by Fowey	par.	1,339	3,320	5,305	Fowey	do.
Linkinhorne	par.	2,300	7,894	9,989	Callington	East (North Division).
Liskeard Borough (W.) (a)		4,053	801	14,427	Liskeard	Borough of Liskeard
Liskeard Parish (a)		1,481	7,422	11,661	do.	West.
Menheniot	par.	1,373	6,997	11,876	do.	do.
Morval	par.	664	3,562	4,398	Looe	do.
Pelynt	par.	672	4,683	4,680	Duloe R.S.O.	do.
Saint Cleer (a)	par.	2,865	11,263	10,309	Liskeard	do.
Saint Dominick	par.	826	3,226	4,408	Callington	East (Middle Division).
Saint Ive	par.	2,121	5,780	6,001	Liskeard	do.
Saint Keyne	par.	162	944	1,214	do.	West.
Saint Martin	par.	355 {	In East Looe. }	3,147	Looe	do.
Saint Neot	par.	1,303	13,997	7,459	Liskeard	do.
Saint Pinnock	par.	500	3,487	2,865	do.	do.
Saint Veep	par.	535	3,111	4,028	Lostwithiel	do.
South Hill	par.	506	3,459	3,327	Callington	East (Middle Division).
Talland	par.	780 }	2,665 {	3,696	Looe	West.
West Looe	tow.	868 }		1,369	do.	do.
TOTAL of UNION		28,787	107,441	137,979		

LIVERPOOL PARISH.

(Under the 5 & 6 Vict. c. lxxxviii.)

COUNTY of LANCASTER :

Liverpool (W.)	par.	210,164	2,470	2,128,762	Liverpool	Borough of Liverpool.

LLANDILO FAWR UNION.

(Formed 14 Dec. 1836 by Order dated 18 Nov. 1836.—Place marked thus * added 12 Aug. 1837 by Order dated 18 July 1837 and thus † added 24 May 1882 by Order dated 5 May 1882.)

COUNTY of CARMARTHEN :

*Bettws	par.	1,738	6,511	4,311	Ammanford	Llandilo.
Brechfa	par.	104	530	277	Carmarthen	do.
Llandybie	par.	3,560	10,796	11,312	Llanelly	do.
Llandilofawr (W.) (a)	par.	5,484	25,628	28,886	Llandilo	do.
Llandifeisant (a)	par.	196	1,551	2,255	do.	do.
Llanegwad	par.	1,638	12,330	9,620	Carmarthen	do.
Llanvihangel Aberbythych	par.	888	6,036	4,267	Llandilo	do.
Llanvihangel Kilfargen	par.	46	516	423	do.	do.
Llanfynydd	par.	1,019	10,744	6,329	Carmarthen	do.
Llangathen	par.	868	5,513	6,189	Llandilo	do.
Llansawl	par.	944	10,017	4,799	do.	Llansawl.
Talley	par.	839	7,167	5,217	do.	do.
†Quarter Bach (c)	par.	—	—	—	Brynamman	Llandilo.
TOTAL of UNION		17,324 (b)	97,339 (b)	83,885 (b)		

LLANDILO FAWR UNION :

(a) A detached part of Llandifeisant was amalgamated with Llandilo Fawr, by Order which came into operation on 25 March 1884.

(b) In 1881.

LLANDILO FAWR UNION—continued.

(c) A detached part of Llangadock, in the Llandovery Union, known as "Quarter Bach," was constituted a separate Parish by Order which came into operation on 25 March 1882.

Unions and Parishes, &c.	Population in 1881.	Area in Statute Acres in 1881.	Rateable Value in 1881.	Post Town.	Petty Sessional Division.

LLANDOVERY UNION.

(Formed 15 Dec. 1836 by Order dated 21 Nov. 1836.)

COUNTY of BRECKNOCK :

			£		
Llandulas - - par.	94	3,220	308	Llanwyrtyd, Builth	Builth.
Llanwyrtyd - - par.	848	11,335	3,067	do. - -	do.

COUNTY of CARMARTHEN :

Cilewm - - - par.	1,087	17,300	5,684	Llandovery - -	Landovery.
Convil Cayo - par.	1,979	41,785	8,904	Pumpsaint Llandilo	Cayo.
Llanddausant - par.	647	10,307	3,692	Llangadock	Llangadock.
Llandingat (W.) - par.	2,507	8,107	10,587	Llandovery -	Llandovery.
Llanfair ar y Bryn - par.	1,281	23,457	7,657	do. - -	do.
Llangadock (a) - par.	3,386	15,642	14,146	Llangadock - -	Llangadock.
Llansadwrn - - par.	944	7,064	5,446	do. - -	do.
Llanwrda - - par.	558	4,441	3,622	Llanwrda - -	Llandovery.
Myddfai - - par.	909	11,914	5,670	Myddfai Llandovery	do.
TOTAL of UNION -	14,246 (b)	154,572 (b)	68,783 (b)		

LLANELLY UNION.

(Formed 24 Oct. 1836 by Order dated 26 Sept. 1836.)

COUNTY of CARMARTHEN :

Llanedy - - par.	2,317	5,678	7,085	Llanelly -	Llanelly.
Llanelly (W.) - par.	27,779	17,692	80,733	do. - -	do.
Llangennech - par.	1,971	2,384	7,488	do. - -	do.
Llanon - - - par.	1,684	11,389	7,832	do. - -	do.
Pembrey - - par.	5,663	11,928	20,858	Burry Port -	do.
Kidwelly, Saint Mary (a) - par.	2,510	5,182	8,516	Kidwelly - -	Kidwelly.

COUNTY of GLAMORGAN :

Loughor - - par.	1,179	} 3,618	{ 7,417	Llanelly - -	Llanelly.
Loughor (Borough) - -	1,513		4,328	do. - -	do.
TOTAL of UNION -	44,616	61,201	144,257		

LLANFYLLIN UNION.

(Formed 15 Feb. 1837 by Order dated 19 Jan. 1837.—Place marked thus * added 29 Sept. 1856 by Order dated 29 Aug. 1856.)

COUNTY of DENBIGH :

Llanarmon mynidd Mawr } par.	152	2,218	1,186	Oswestry -	Chirk.
Llancadwalader - par.	203	2,771	1,501	do. - -	do.
Llangedwyn - par.	217	1,686	2,433	do. - -	do.
Llanrhaidr yn Moch-nant (a) } par.	1,383	13,497	7,844	do. - -	do.

COUNTY of MONTGOMERY :

Carreghova - - tow.	511	1,223	3,162	Oswestry - -	Deythur.
Garthbeibio - par.	286	7,200	1,189	Welshpool -	Mathrafal.
*Guilsfield - - par.	2,430	14,835	20,789	Welshpool -	Pool, Upper.
Hirnant - - par.	259	4,000	1,694	Oswestry - -	Llanfyllin.
Llandrinio - - par.	805	3,832	6,940	do. - -	Deythur.
Llandisilio - - par.	611	3,141	6,464	do. - -	do.
Llanerfyl - - par.	788	16,255	4,507	Welshpool -	Mathrafal.
Llanfair Carcinion - par.	2,286	16,157	12,021	do. - -	do. (continued)

LLANDOVERY UNION :

(a) A detached part of Llangadock, known as "Quarter Bach," was constituted a separate Parish, by Order which came into operation on 25 March 1882; the Parish was added to the Llandilo Fawr Union.

(b) In 1884.

LLANELLY UNION :

(a) All the parts of a parish known as Kidwelly were amalgamated with Kidwelly Saint Mary, by Order which came into operation on 25 March 1884.

LLANFYLLIN UNION :

(a) See note page 215.

Unions and Parishes, &c.		Population in 1881.	Area in Statute Acres in 1881.	Rateable Value in 1881.	Post Town.	Petty Sessional Division.
				£		

LLANFYLLIN UNION—County of Montgomery—*continued.*

Unions and Parishes, &c.		Population in 1881.	Area in Statute Acres in 1881.	Rateable Value in 1881.	Post Town.	Petty Sessional Division.
Llanfechan	- par.	630	4,462	6,490	Oswestry -	- Pool, Lower.
Llanfihangel	- par.	818	10,005	4,963	Llanfyllin -	- Llanfyllin.
Llanfyllin (W.)	- par.	1,774	7,923	8,782	do. - -	- do.
Llangadfan	- par.	923	16,929	4,285	Welshpool	Mathrafal.
Llangyniew -	- par.	486	4,513	4,243	do. - -	- do.
Llangynog	- par.	465	3,223	1,536	Oswestry -	Llanfyllin.
Llanrhaiadr yn Moch-nant (*a*) - - } par.		881	9,797	5,343	do. -	- do.
Llansaintffraid in the Hundred of Dey-thur - - } par.		437	} 6,065 {	4,402	do. -	- Deythur.
Llansaintffraid in the Hundred of Pool - } par.		802		6,406	do. -	Pool, Lower.
Llanwyddyn with Cowny - - } par.		453	20,190	2,388	Llanfyllin -	- Llanfyllin.
Myfod - - - par.		1,583	12,614	14,298	Welshpool	- do.
Pennant (*a*) - - par.		746	5,000	4,302	Oswestry -	- do.
TOTAL of UNION	-	**19,959**	**187,539**	**137,068**		

LLANRWST UNION.

(Formed 29 April 1837 by Order dated 3 April 1837.—Place marked thus * added 24 June 1858 by Order dated 22 June 1858.)

COUNTY of CARNARVON :

Bettws y Coed	- par.	784	3,537	2,656	Bettws y Coed	- Nant Conway.
Dolwyddelan	- par.	1,275	14,384	2,708	do. -	- do.
Eidda - -	- tow.	296	—	1,246	do. -	- do.
Llanrhychwyn	- par.	532	In Trefriew	1,692	Conway -	- do.
Maenan -	- tow.	403	2,902	2,111	Llanrwst -	- Conway.
Penmachno	- par.	1,787	11,208	3,672	Bettws y Coed	- Nant Conway.
*The Abbey -	- par.	24	—	232	Conway -	- do.
Trefriew	- par.	625	9,576	1,651	do. -	- do.
Tre Gwydir -	- tow.	433	7,621	1,522	Bettws y Coed	- do.

COUNTY of DENBIGH :

Eglwys Fach -	- tow.	1,126	7,902	5,327	Conway -	- Uwchddulas.
Gwernhowel	- par.	90	1,307	400	Bettws y Coed	- Uwchaled.
Gwytherin -	- par.	331	5,966	1,704	Llanrwst -	- Uwchddulas.
Llandogged	- par.	238	762	1,136	do. -	- do.
Llangerniew -	- par.	985	7,793	4,958	do. -	- do.
Llanrwst (W.)	- tow.	4,260	15,837	14,110	do. -	- do.
Pentre Voylas	- par.	487	10,747	2,176	Bettws y Coed	- Uwchaled.
Tir Evan	- tow.	277	8,937	908	do. -	- do.
Trebrys - -	- tow.	156	853	587	do. -	- do.
TOTAL of UNION	-	**14,109**	**109,332**	**48,796**		

LODDON AND CLAVERING UNION.

(Formed 7 May 1836 by Order dated 13 April 1836.)

COUNTY of NORFOLK :

Aldeby	- par.	612	3,056	5,227	Beccles -	- Loddon and Clavering.
Alpington	- par.	162	1,069	1,063	Burgh Apton, Norwich.	do.
Ashby	- par.	200	487	1,071	do. -	- do.
Bedingham	- par.	293	1,340	2,155	Bungay -	- do. (*continued*)

LLANFYLLIN UNION :

(*a*) By Provisional Order which came into operation on 25 March 1887,—
Certain parts of Pennant were amalgamated with Llangynog, Llanrhaidr yn Mochnant (Denbigh), and Llanrhaidr yn Mochnant (Montgomery).

Unions and Parishes, &c.		Population in 1881.	Area in Statute Acres in 1881.	Rateable Value in 1881.	Post Town.	Petty Sessional Division.
LODDON AND CLAVERING UNION—County of Norfolk—*continued.*				£		
Brooke	*par.*	706	2,135	3,823	Norwich - -	Loddon and Clavering.
Broome	*par.*	544	1,442	2,675	Bungay - -	do.
Burgh-Apton	*par.*	464	1,620	3,690	Norwich - -	do.
Burgh Saint Peter	*par.*	359	2,041	3,400	Beccles - -	do.
Carleton	*par.*	94	772	1,122	Loddon -	do.
Chedgrave	*par.*	368	1,432	2,456	do. -	do.
Claxton	*par.*	201	991	1,492	Burgh Apton, Norwich.	do.
Ditchingham	*par.*	1,075	2,083	5,426	Bungay -	do.
Ellingham	*par.*	310	1,379	2,174	do. - -	do.
Geldestone	*par.*	292	820	2,125	Beccles -	do.
Gillingham All Saints and Gillingham Saint Mary	*united pars.*	450	2,008	3,513	do. - -	do.
Haddiscoe	*par.*	390	2,071	4,258	Loddon - -	do.
Hales	*par.*	265	980	1,737	do. -	do.
Hardley	*par.*	243	1,469	2,350	do. - -	do.
Heckingham (W.)	*par.*	330	1,102	1,753	do. - -	do.
Hedenham	*par.*	281	1,770	2,759	Bungay -	do.
Hillington	*par.*	100	516	918	Framlingham, Norwich.	do.
Howe	*par.*	92	757	1,147	Brooke, Norwich -	do.
Kirby-Cane	*par.*	420	1,475	2,584	Bungay -	do.
Kirstead	*par.*	201	1,011	1,730	Brooke, Norwich -	do.
Langley	*par.*	308	2,723	4,352	Loddon - -	do.
Loddon	*par.*	1,145	3,020	6,307	Norwich -	do.
Mundham	*par.*	295	1,547	2,636	Brooke, Norwich -	do.
Norton-Subcourse	*par.*	359	1,882	2,937	Loddon - -	do.
Raveningham	*par.*	240	2,415	3,784	do. - -	do.
Seething	*par.*	392	1,630	2,906	Brooke, Norwich -	do.
Sisland	*par.*	71	466	727	do. - -	do.
Stockton	*par.*	116	1,051	4,711	Bungay -	do.
Thorpe (next Haddiscoe)	*par.*	93	824	1,343	Loddon -	do.
Thurlton	*par.*	419	1,170	2,270	do. - -	do.
Thurton	*par.*	199	771	1,347	Burgh Apton, Norwich.	do.
Thwaite	*par.*	120	676	1,139	Bungay -	do.
Toft-Monks	*par.*	397	2,238	3,944	Beccles -	do.
Topcroft	*par.*	357	1,875	3,149	Bungay -	do.
Wheatacre-All Saints	*par.*	144	1,163	1,866	Beccles -	do.
Woodton	*par.*	477	2,124	3,444	Bungay -	do.
Yelverton	*par.*	85 {	In Alpington }	994	Norwich -	do.
TOTAL of UNION -		13,702	59,401	105,804		
LONGTOWN UNION. (Formed 19 June 1837 by Order dated 25 May 1837.) COUNTY of CUMBERLAND :						
Arthuret (W.)	*par.*	2,611	12,956	15,360	Longtown -	Longtown.
Belbank	*tow.*	94	1,446	948	Brampton -	do.
Bewcastle	*par.*	889	28,563	11,649	do. -	do.
Hethersgill -	*tow.*	587	5,464	5,334	Kirklinton, Carlisle	do.
Kirkandrews, Middle Quarter	*tow.*	289	4,312	5,311	Longtown -	do.
Kirkandrews Moat	*tow.*	186	1,701	2,241	do. -	do.
Kirkandrews, Nether Quarter	*tow.*	369	4,878	6,324	do. -	do.
Kirklinton Middle	*tow.*	406	3,043	3,413	Carlisle -	do.
Nichol Forest	*tow.*	627	8,497	7,235	Longtown -	do.
Scaleby, East and West	*par.*	465	3,647	3,768	Carlisle -	do.
Solport Quarter	*tow.*	249	3,236	2,173	Longtown -	do.
Stapleton	*tow.*	372	4,744	3,553	Brampton -	do.
Trough	*tow.*	126	2,338	1,297	Longtown -	do.
West Linton -	*tow.*	441	3,420	3,977	Carlisle -	do.
TOTAL of UNION -		7,711	88,245	72,583		

Unions and Parishes, &c.	Population in 1881.	Area in Statute Acres in 1881.	Rateable Value in 1881.	Post Town.	Petty Sessional Division.
LOUGHBOROUGH UNION.					
(Formed 9 Sept. 1837 by Order dated 16 Aug. 1837.—Place marked thus * added 17 Oct. 1837 by Order dated 25 Sept. 1837, and thus † added 1 Mar. 1862 by Order dated 28 Jan. 1862.)					
COUNTY of LEICESTER :			£		
Belton - - - *par.*	645	1,900	4,583	Loughborough	-	Loughborough.
Burton on the Wolds *tow.*	356	4,720	3,665	do.	- -	do.
Charley (*a*) - - *par.*	43	500	740	do.	- -	do.
Cotes *tow.*	52 { In Burton on the Wolds }	1,032	do.	- -	do.
†Garendon - - *par.*	40	1,270	3,213	do.	- -	do.
Hathern - - *par.*	1,312	1,340	3,917	do.	- -	do.
Hoton - *tow.*	308 { In Burton on the Wolds }	2,786	do.	- -	do.
Knightthorpe - *tow.*	65 { In Loughborough }	1,325	do.	-	do.
Loughborough (W.) - *tow.*	14,681	5,460	48,637	do.	- -	do.
Prestwould - - *tow.*	83	In Burton	1,807	do.	- -	do.
Sheepshead - - *par.*	4,437	5,280	13,395	do.	- -	do.
Thorpacre with Dishley } *par.*	212	890	2,631	do.	- -	do.
Whatton Long - *par.*	702	2,050	3,866	do.	- -	do.
Wimeswould - *par.*	936	4,220	6,061	do.	- -	do.
Woodthorpe - *tow.*	57 { In Loughborough }	1,195	do.	-	do.
COUNTY of NOTTINGHAM :					
Corthingstock or Costock } *par.*	311	1,320	2,407	do.	- -	Nottingham.
East Leake - - *par.*	943	2,540	4,360	do.	- -	do.
Normanton upon Soar *par.*	322	1,500	6,653	do.	- -	do.
Rempstone - - *par.*	314	1,660	2,747	do.	- -	do.
Stanford - - *par.*	105	1,520	3,127	do.	- -	do.
Sutton Bonnington - *par.*	1,005	1,910	11,919	do.	- -	do.
*Thorpe in the Glebe *par.*	51	930	1,321	Nottingham	-	do.
West Leake - - *par.*	162	1,390	2,214	Loughborough	-	do.
Willoughby on the Wolds } *par.*	180	2,080	3,479	do.	- -	do.
Wysall - - *par.*	261	1,360	2,101	Nottingham	-	do.
TOTAL of UNION -	27,883	43,840	139,211			

LOUTH UNION.					
(Formed 12 April 1837 by Order dated 18 Mar. 1837, as amended by Order dated 26 Oct. 1849.—Places marked thus * added 29 Sept. 1858 by Order dated 26 June 1858, and place marked thus † added 25 Mar. 1859 by Order dated 26 Feb. 1859. Spelling of names of places marked ‡ as altered by Order dated September 1887.)					
COUNTY of LINCOLN :					
Aby with Greenfield - *par.*	352	1,440	1,978	Alford	-	Alford, Hundred of Calceworth.
Alvingham - - *par.*	267	1,940	2,352	Louth	-	Louth, Hundred of Louth Eske.

(continued)

LOUGHBOROUGH UNION :

(*a*) Detached parts of Newtown Linford (in the Barrow-upon-Soar Union), and Markfield (in the Market Bosworth Union) were amalgamated with Charley, by Provisional Orders which came into operation on 25 March 1885.

Unions and Parishes, &c.	Population in 1881.	Area in Statute Acres in 1881.	Rateable Value in 1881.	Post Town.	Petty Sessional Division.
LOUTH UNION—County of Lincoln—*continued.*			£		
Authorpe - - *par.*	159	921	1,262	Louth - -	Louth, Hundred of Louth Eske.
Beesby in the Marsh *par.*	145	1,180	1,372	Alford - -	Alford, Hundred of Calceworth.
Belleau - - *tow.*	65 {	In Claythorpe }	987	do. - -	do. do.
Biscathorpe - - *par.*	62	1,050	1,041	Louth - -	Louth, Hundred of Wraggoe.
Brackenborough - *par.*	67	890	928	do. - -	Louth, Hundred of Ludborough.
‡Burgh on Bain - *par.*	170	1,560	2,299	do. - -	Wragby, Hundred of Wraggoe.
Burwell - - *par.*	159	2,190	2,301	do. - -	Louth, Hundred of Louth Eske.
Calcethorpe - - *par.*	82	1,088	1,258	do. - -	do. do.
Carlton Castle - *par.*	21	500	498	do. - -	do. do.
Carlton Great - *par.*	261	2,190	3,102	do. - -	do. do.
Carlton Little - *par.*	169	1,006	1,365	do. - -	do. do.
Cawthorpe Little - *par.*	167	460	672	do. -	Louth, Hundred of Calceworth.
Claythorpe - - *tow.*	89	1,344	1,263	Alford -	Alford, Hundred of Calceworth.
Cockerington North - *par.*	267	1,750	2,249	Louth - -	Louth, Hundred of Louth Eske.
Cockerington South - *par.*	216	1,880	2,413	do. - -	do. do.
Conisholme - - *par.*	138	1,195	1,841	Great Grimsby -	do. do.
Covenham Saint Bartholomew (a) } *par.*	278	1,310	1,961	Louth -	Louth, Hundred of Ludborough.
Covenham Saint Mary (a) - } *par.*	128	950	1,285	do. - -	do. do.
Donington on Bain - *par.*	473	1,890	2,309	do. - -	Louth, Hundred of Gartree.
†East Wykeham - *par.*	37	560	643	Market Rasen -	Louth, Hundred of Louth Eske.
Elkington North - *par.*	89	991	1,204	Louth - -	do. do.
Elkington South - *par.*	356	3,019	4,358	do. - -	do. do.
Farforth with Maidenwell - } *par.*	143	1,940	2,271	do. - -	do. do.
Fotherby - - *par.*	237	1,400	1,920	do. - -	Louth, Hundred of Ludborough.
Fulstow - - *par.*	565	2,840	3,717	do. - -	Grimsby, Hundred of Bradley Haverstoe.
Gayton le Marsh - *par.*	248	2,166	2,842	Alford -	Alford, Hundred of Calceworth.
‡Gayton le Wold - *par.*	151	1,139	1,337	Louth -	Louth, Hundred of Louth Eske.
Grainsby - - *par.*	148	1,167	1,627	Great Grimsby -	Grimsby, Hundred of Bradley Haverstoe.
‡Grainthorpe (a) - *par.*	712	4,955	7,516	do. - -	Louth, Hundred of Louth Eske.
*Grimblethorpe - *par.*	11	591	700	Louth - -	do. do.
Grimoldby - - *par.*	363	1,729	2,660	do. - -	do. do.
Grimsby Little - *par.*	54	950	929	do. - -	Louth, Hundred of Ludborough.
Hagnaby with Hannay (a) - } *par.*	117	1,010	1,249	Alford -	Alford, Hundred of Calceworth.
Hainton - - *par.*	304	2,306	3,224	Wragby -	Wragby, Hundred of Wraggoe.
Hallington - - *par.*	112	860	1,787	Louth -	Louth, Hundred of Louth Eske.
*Haugh - - *par.*	26	640	674	Alford -	Alford, Hundred of Calceworth.
					(*continued*)

LOUTH UNION:

(*a*) By Orders which came into operation on 25 March 1887,—
    Detached parts of Covenham Saint Bartholomew and Covenham Saint Mary were amalgamated with Grainthorpe;
    Detached parts of Markby, in the Spilsby Union, were amalgamated with Hagnaby with Hannay;

LOUTH UNION—*continued.*

Certain parts of Saltfleetby All Saints were amalgamated with Saltfleetby Saint Peter's;
Certain parts of Saltfleetby Saint Clements were amalgamated with Saltfleetby All Saints and Saltfleetby Saint Peter's; and
Certain parts of Saltfleetby Saint Peter's were amalgamated with Saltfleetby All Saints.

Unions and Parishes, &c.	Population in 1881.	Area in Statute Acres in 1881.	Rateable Value in 1881.	Post Town.	Petty Sessional Division.
LOUTH UNION—County of Lincoln—*continued.*			£		
Hangham - par.	132	1,907	2,305	Louth -	Louth, Hundred of Louth Eske.
Holton le Clay - par.	283	1,430	2,068	Great Grimsby	Grimsby, Hundred of Bradley Haverstoe.
Keddington - par.	153	1,190	1,387	Louth -	Louth, Hundred of Louth Eske.
Kelstern with Lamb-croft - par.	235	2,700	3,141	do. -	do. do.
Legburne - par.	476	1,910	3,212	do. -	Louth, Hundred of Calceworth.
Louth (W.) - bor.	10,691 }	3,620	{ 37,581	do. -	Borough of Louth.
Louth Park - tow.	136 }		1,281	do. -	Louth, Hundred of Louth Eske.
Ludborough - par.	347	2,250	2,086	do. -	Louth, Hundred of Ludborough.
Ludford Magna - par.	390 }	3,310	{ 3,925	Market Rasen	Wragby, Hundred of Wraggoe.
Ludford Parva - par.	341 }		1,327	do. -	do. do.
Mablethorpe Saint Mary and Peter - par.	640	3,803	6,707	Alford -	Alford, Hundred of Calceworth.
Maltby le Marsh - par.	302	1,379	1,989	do. -	do. do.
Manby - par.	180	1,460	1,715	Louth -	Louth, Hundred of Louth Eske.
Marsh Chapel - par.	658	4,291	5,509	Great Grimsby	Grimsby, Hundred of Bradley Haverstoe.
Muckton - par.	96	1,025	1,120	Louth -	Louth, Hundred of Louth Eske.
North Coates - par.	266	4,101	3,545	Great Grimsby	Grimsby, Hundred of Bradley Haverstoe.
Ormsby North - par.	180	1,707	2,088	Louth -	Louth, Hundred of Ludborough.
Oxcomb - par.	28	1,021	1,236	Horncastle -	Horncastle, Hundred of Hill.
Raithby - par.	169	1,930	2,398	Louth -	Louth, Hundred of Louth Eske.
Reston North - par.	35	703	977	do. -	do. do.
Reston South - par.	238	710	1,156	do. -	Alford, Hundred of Calceworth.
Ruckland - par.	63	713	801	do. -	Louth, Hundred of Louth Eske.
Saint Mary and Saint Gabriel, Binbrooke - par.	1,157	6,070	7,437	Market Rasen	Market Rasen, Hundred of Walshcroft.
Saleby with Thores-thorpe - par.	223	1,770	2,048	Alford	Alford, Hundred of Calceworth
Saltfleetby All Saints (a) - par.	169	1,169	2,189	Louth	Louth, Hundred of Louth Eske.
Saltfleetby Saint Clements (a) - par.	133	2,205	1,735	do. -	do. do.
Saltfleetby Saint Peter's (a) - par.	327	2,003	3,158	do. -	do. do.
Skidbrooke with Saltfleet Haven - par.	415	3,455	3,696	Great Grimsby	do. do.
Somercoates North - par.	1,219	8,022	7,190	do. -	do. do.
Somercoates South - par.	435	2,507	4,191	do. -	do. do
Stenigot - par.	89	1,321	1,285	Louth -	Horncastle, Hundred of Gartree.
Stewton - par.	101	971	1,516	do. -	Louth, Hundred of Louth Eske.
Strubby with Wood-thorpe - par.	289	2,075	2,488	Alford -	Alford, Hundred of Calceworth.
Swaby - par.	414	1,160	2,080	do. -	do. do.
Tathwell - par.	422	4,314	5,176	Louth -	Louth, Hundred of Louth Eske.
Tetney - par.	807	8,325	7,225	Great Grimsby	Grimsby, Hundred of Bradley Haverstoe.
Theddlethorpe All Saints - par.	329	2,645	3,141	Louth -	Alford, Hundred of Calceworth.

(*continued*)

Unions and Parishes, &c.	Population in 1881.	Area in Statute Acres in 1881.	Rateable Value in 1881.	Post Town.	Petty Sessional Division.
LOUTH UNION—County of Lincoln—*continued.*			£		
Theddlethorpe Saint Helen's - } *par.*	414	3,530	3,329	Louth - -	Alford, Hundred of Calceworth.
Thoresby North - *par.*	745	2,485	4,023	do. - -	Grimsby, Hundred of Bradley Haverstoe.
Thoresby South - *par.*	159	932	1,376	Alford - -	Alford, Hundred of Calceworth.
Tothill - - *par.*	47	854	1,001	do. - -	do. do.
Trusthorpe - - *par.*	334	1,455	2,739	do. - -	do. do.
Utterby - - *par.*	275	1,564	2,250	Louth - -	Louth, Hundred of Ludborough.
Waith - - *par.*	60	780	1,042	Great Grimsby -	Grimsby, Hundred of Bradley Haverstoe.
Walmsgate - - *par.*	73	920	953	Louth - -	Louth, Hundred of Hill.
Welton le Wold - *par.*	334	2,520	3,443	do. -	Louth, Hundred of Louth Eske.
Willingham South - *par.*	330	1,900	2,664	Wragby -	Wragby, Hundred of Wraggoe.
Withcall - - *par.*	237	2,650	2,754	Louth - -	Louth, Hundred of Louth Eske.
‡Withern with Stain - *par.*	457	2,669	4,019	Alford - -	Alford, Hundred of Calceworth.
Worlaby - - *par.*	66	490	877	Louth - -	Horncastle, Hundred of Hill.
Wyham with Cadeby *par.*	139	1,880	1,909	do. - -	Louth, Hundred of Ludborough.
Yarborough - - *par.*	206	1,160	1,697	do. - -	Louth, Hundred of Louth Eske.
TOTAL of UNION -	33,852	170,708	250,788		

LUDLOW UNION.

(Formed 15 July 1836 by Order dated 20 June 1836.— Places marked thus * added 22 March 1862 by Order dated 11 March 1862 ; and place marked thus † added 26 March 1884, by Order dated 24 March 1884. Names of places marked thus ‡ are as altered by Order dated 17 Sept. 1887.)

Unions and Parishes, &c.	Population in 1881.	Area in Statute Acres in 1881.	Rateable Value in 1881.	Post Town.	Petty Sessional Division.
COUNTY of HEREFORD :					
Aston or Pipe Aston *par.*	49	920	387	Ludlow - -	Wigmore.
Burrington (*b*) - *par.*	201	2,580	1,857	do. - -	do.
Downton (*b*) - *par.*	180	1,201	1,557	do. - -	do.
Elton - - *par.*	113	1,470	1,329	do. - -	do.
Leinthall Starkes - *par.*	133	990	1,081	do. - -	do.
‡Richards Castle (Hereford) } *par.*	312	2,446	2,719	do. - -	Leominster.
Wigmore - - *par.*	417	3,441	3,204	Kingsland, Herefordshire -	Wigmore.
COUNTIES of HEREFORD and SALOP :					
Leintwardine (North Side) (*b*) - } *par.*	1,218	4,252	8,451	Leintwardine, Herefordshire.	Wigmore and Clun and Purslow.
Ludford - - *par.*	461	1,867	5,200	Ludlow - -	Leominster and Munslow, Lower Division. *(continued)*

LUDLOW UNION :

(*a*) By Orders which came into operation on 25 March 1884 :—

A detached part of Diddlebury was amalgamated with Abdon ;

A detached part of Holdgate was amalgamated with Diddlebury ;

A detached part of Stoke Saint Milborough was amalgamated with Heath ;

A detached part of Stanton Lacy was amalgamated with Bromfield ;

A detached of Tugford was amalgamated with Abdon ;

Detached parts of Diddlebury and Munslow were united and amalgamated with Hopton Cangeford ;

LUDLOW UNION—*continued.*

Three detached parts of Holdgate were amalgamated with Stanton Long, in the Bridgnorth Union ; and

A certain part of Stanton Lacy was amalgamated with Bitterley, and another part was constituted a separate parish, and called East Hamlet.

(*b*) A detached part of Downton was amalgamated with Leintwardine (North Side) and detached parts of Leintwardine (North Side) were amalgamated with Downton and Burrington, by Order which came into operation on 25 March 1885.

Unions and Parishes, &c.	Population in 1881.	Area in Statute Acres in 1881.	Rateable Value in 1881.	Post Town	Petty Sessional Division.

LUDLOW UNION—*continued.*

COUNTY OF SALOP :

			£		
Abdon (*a*) - - *par.*	154	1,134	1,005	Craven Arms -	Munslow, Lower Division.
Ashford Bowdler - *par.*	95	575	1,954	Ludlow	do.
Ashford Carbonel - *par.*	290	1,478	3,248	do. -	do.
Bitterley (*a*) - *par.*	988	6,591	7,601	Aston - -	Overs.
Bromfield (*b*) - *tow.*	565	6,112	9,947	Bromfield, Salop	Munslow, Lower Division.
Cainham - - *par.*	1,165	2,529	4,303	Ludlow -	Stottesden.
Clee Saint Margaret - *par.*	270	1,589	1,354	Bromfield, Salop -	Munslow, Lower Division.
Cold Weston - *par.*	30	670	305	do. -	do.
Culmington - *par.*	556	3,476	5,162	do. -	do.
Diddlebury (*a*) - *par.*	763	9,535	9,814	Craven Arms -	do.
†East Hamlet (W.) - *par.*					
Halford - - *cha.*	247	1,062	1,463	do. -	do
Heath (*a*) - *tow.*	39 {In Stoke Saint Milborough.}		602	Bromfield, Salop -	do.
Holdgate (*a*) - *par.*	183	1,896	1,854	Much Wenlock	Munslow, Lower Division.
Hope Baggot - *par.*	79	460	705	Ludlow - -	Stottesden.
Hopton Cangeford (*a*) *par.*	31	562	410	do. -	Munslow, Lower Division.
Ludlow - - *par.*	5,035	241	13,869	do. - -	Borough of Ludlow.
*Ludlow Castle - *par.*	5	—	48	do. -	Munslow, Lower Division.
Munslow (*a*) - *par.*	601	3,504	4,958	Craven Arms -	do.
Onibury - - *par.*	458	2,493	4,508	Onibury, Salop -	do.
‡Richards Castle (Salop) - } *par.*	448	2,425	5,678	Ludlow - -	do.
Stanton Lacy (W.) (*a*) } *par.*	2,178	7,114	13,819	Bromfield, Salop	do.
Stoke Saint Milborough (*a*) } *tow.*	468	5,750	4,905	Ludlow -	do.
Stokesay - - *par.*	744	3,567	7,251	Craven Arms -	do.
Tugford (*a*) - *par.*	110	1,320	1,606	do. - -	do.
TOTAL OF UNION -	18,589	83,250	132,154		

LUNESDALE UNION.

(Formed as the Lunedale Union 15 March 1869 by Order dated 17 Feb. 1869.—Name altered to Lunesdale 10 June 1869 by Order of that date.)

COUNTY OF LANCASTER :

Arkholme - with - Ca-wood - - } *tow.*	297	3,016	4,828	Kirkby Lonsdale, Carnforth.	Hornby.
Borwick - *tow.*	246	846	2,037	Carnforth - -	Lancaster.
Burrow-with-Burrow *tow.*	214	2,426	4,003	Kirkby Lonsdale -	Hornby.
Cantsfield - *tow.*	104	1,222	1,993	do. - -	do.
Caton - - *tow.*	1,085	8,396	8,337	Lancaster -	Lancaster.
Claughton - *par.*	100	1,581	2,396	do. - -	Hornby.
Gressingham - *tow.*	152	2,015	2,900	do. - -	do.
Halton - - *par.*	731	3,914	6,717	do. - -	Lancaster.
Hornby-with-Farleton (W.) (*a*) } *tow.*	480	3,012	5,219	do. - -	Hornby.
Ireby - - *tow.*	78	1,141	1,220	Kirkby Lonsdale -	do.
Leck - - *tow.*	271	4,636	3,380	do. - -	do.
Melling -with- Wray-ton } *tow.*	167	1,062	2,348	Carnforth - -	Lancaster.
Nether Kellet - *tow.*	279	2,082	3,115	do. - -	do.
Over Kellet - *tow.*	494	3,210	5,041	do. - -	do.

(continued)

LUDLOW UNION :

(*a*) (*b*) *See* notes, page 220.

LUNESDALE UNION :

(*a*) By Order which came into operation on 25 March 1887, all the parts of a Township known as Farleton were amalgamated with Hornby, and the latter as so altered was designated the Township of Hornby-with-Farleton.

Unions and Parishes, &c.	Population in 1881.	Area in Statute Acres in 1881.	Rateable Value in 1881.	Post Town.	Petty Sessional Division

LUNESDALE Union—County of Lancaster—
continued.

			£		
Quernmore - *tow.*	585	6,789	7,477	Lancaster - -	Lancaster.
Roeburndale - *tow.*	112	8,841	2,905	do. - -	Hornby.
Tatham - *par.*	534	8,547	7,355	do. - -	do.
Tunstal - *tow.*	104	1,076	2,162	Kirkby Lonsdale -	do.
Wennington - *tow.*	127	980	1,585	Lancaster - -	do.
Whittington - *par.*	316	4,416	6,386	Kirkby Lonsdale -	do.
Wray-with-Botton - *tow.*	626	6,526	5,274	Lancaster - -	do.
TOTAL of UNION	**7,132**	**75,734**	**86,678**		

LUTON UNION.

(Formed 16 April 1835 by Order dated 19 March 1835. Names of places marked * are as altered by Order dated 13 August 1887.)

COUNTY of BEDFORD :

Barton in the Clay - *par.*	1,061	2,270	3,490	Ampthill - -	Luton.
*Caddington (Beds) - *par.*	1,058	1,607	2,950	Luton - -	do.
Dunstable - - *par.*	4,627	453	12,616	Dunstable - -	Dunstable.
Houghton-Regis - *par.*	2,406	4,654	9,948	do. - -	Luton.
*Humbershoe - *ham.*	339	159	974	do. - -	do.
Luton (W.) - *par.*	26,140	15,435	110,263	Luton - -	Borough of Luton.
Streatley with Shar-peuhoe } *par.*	312	2,287	2,894	Dunstable - -	Luton.
*Studham (Beds) - *par.*	315	1,584	1,802	do. - -	do.
Sundon - - *par.*	376	2,160	5,446	do. - -	do.
Totternhoe - *par.*	707	2,321	3,090	do. - -	do.

COUNTY of HERTFORD :

*Caddington (Herts) - *par.*	1,146	2,996	5,531	Luton - -	Hemel Hempstead.
Kensworth - - *par.*	655	2,553	3,750	Dunstable - -	do.
*Studham (Herts) - *par.*	173	1,449	1,732	do. - -	do.

COUNTIES of BEDFORD and HERTFORD :

Whipsnade - - *par.*	185	1,088	1,174	do. - -	Luton.
TOTAL of UNION -	**39,500**	**41,016**	**165,660**		

LUTTERWORTH UNION.

(Formed 10 Dec. 1835 by Order dated 21 Nov. 1835.—Places marked thus * added 15 Feb. 1836 by Order dated 22 Jan. 1836 ; thus † added 6 Feb. 1837 by Order dated 12 Jan. 1837 ; and thus ‡ added 26 April 1851 by Order dated 8 April 1851. Name of place marked § as altered by Order dated 10 September 1887.)

COUNTY of LEICESTER :

Arnesby - - *par.*	421	1,510	2,752	Rugby - -	Lutterworth.
*Ashby Magna - *par.*	253	1,487	2,830	Lutterworth -	do.
Ashby Parva - *par.*	148	1,796	2,689	do. - -	de.
Bittesby - - *lib.*	37 { In Great Claybrook }		1,388	do. - -	do.
Bitteswell - *par.*	364	2,630	3,892	do. - -	do.
Broughton Astley (a) *par.*	708	1,930	6,068	Rugby - -	do.
Bruntingthorpe - *par.*	304	1,320	2,391	Lutterworth -	do.
Catthorpe - - *par.*	137	625	1,521	Rugby - -	do.

(continued)

LUTTERWORTH UNION :

(a) Certain detached parts of Croft, in the Blaby Union, were amalgamated with Broughton Astley, by Order which came into operation on 25 March 1885.

LUTTERWORTH UNION—*continued.*

(b) A detached part of Great Claybrook was amalgamated with Little Claybrook, by Order which came into operation on 25 March 1885.

Unions and Parishes, &c.		Population in 1881.	Area in Statute Acres in 1881.	Rateable Value in 1881.	Post Town.	Petty Sessional Division.

LUTTERWORTH UNION—County of Leicester—*continued.*

Unions and Parishes, &c.		Population in 1881.	Area in Statute Acres in 1881.	Rateable Value £ in 1881.	Post Town.	Petty Sessional Division.
Cottesbach	par.	138	1,227	2,329	Lutterworth	Lutterworth.
*Dunton Bassett	par.	409	1,860	2,739	do.	do.
Frowlesworth	par.	214	1,496	3,176	do.	do.
Gilmorton	par.	644	3,143	4,953	do.	do.
Great Claybrook (b)	tow.	433	4,717	2,500	do.	do.
Kimcote and Walton	par.	393	1,233	3,275	do.	do.
§Knaptoft	tow.	54	In Shearsby	1,933	Rugby	do.
Leire	par.	286	828	2,940	Lutterworth	do.
Little Claybrook (b)	tow.	64	In Great Claybrook	1,091	do.	do.
Lutterworth (W.)	par.	1,965	1,890	9,702	do.	do.
Misterton	par.	486	3,580	7,179	do.	do.
North Kilworth	par.	443	2,230	4,540	Rugby	do.
Peatling Magna	par.	194	1,900	3,242	Lutterworth	do.
Peatling Parva	par.	147	870	1,979	do.	do.
Shawell	par.	205	1,107	2,327	Rugby	do.
Shearsby	ham.	261	3,230	2,218	do.	do.
South Kilworth	par.	423	1,470	2,732	do.	do.
Swinford	par.	403	1,690	3,289	do.	do.
Ullesthorpe	ham.	523	In Great Claybrook	4,046	Lutterworth	do.
Walton in Knaptoft	ham.	174	In Shearsby	1,527	do.	do.
*Wigston Parva	tow.	65	In Great Claybrook	867	Hinckley	do.
Willoughby Waterless	par.	316	1,151	2,083	Lutterworth	do.
COUNTY of NORTHAMPTON:						
†Welford	par.	922	3,650	6,468	Rugby	Rugby.
COUNTY of WARWICK:						
Copston Magna	ham.	118		1,909	Hinckley	Coventry.
Monks Kirby	tow.	655	8,341	8,552	Lutterworth	Rugby.
‡Pailton	ham.	531		3,926	Rugby	do.
Stretton under Foss	ham.	314		4,130	do.	Coventry
Wibtoft	tow.	81	850	1,211	Lutterworth	Rugby.
Willey	par.	123	970	1,448	do.	do.
TOTAL of UNION		13,356	59,031	121,842		

LYMINGTON UNION.

(Formed 18 May 1835 by Order dated 27 April 1835.—The place marked thus *, which was constituted by Order dated 23 Nov. 1868, issued under "The New Forest Poor Act," was added 8 Feb. 1869 by Order dated 30 Jan. 1869. The place marked †, which was formerly comprised in Boldre Parish, but was constituted a separate Parish from and after 29 Sept. 1878 by Provisional Order dated 6 May 1878, and duly confirmed on 4 July 1878, was added 30 Sept. 1878 by Order dated 25 Sept. 1878.)

COUNTY of SOUTHAMPTON:

Boldre	par.	2,145	9,887	9,587	Lymington	Lymington and New Forest East.
Brockenhurst	par.	1,027	4,014	4,686	do.	do.
Hordle	par.	1,041	3,868	4,738	do.	do.
Lymington (W.)	par.	4,366	1,515	15,870	do.	Lymington and New Forest East and Borough of Lymington.
Milford	par.	1,745	4,696	7,727	do.	Lymington and New Forest.
Milton	par.	1,489	6,370	7,191	do.	do.
*Rinefield	tow.	40	7,360	899	do.	do.
†Sway	par.	798	2,208	2,387	do.	do.
TOTAL of UNION		12,651	39,948	53,085		

LUTTERWORTH UNION:

(b) See note, page 221.

Unions and Parishes, &c.		Population in 1881.	Area in Statute Acres in 1881.	Rateable Value in 1881.	Post Town.	Petty Sessional Division.

MACCLESFIELD UNION.

(Formed 26 Sept. 1836 by Order dated 3 Sept. 1836. Name of place marked thus * altered by Order dated 2 April 1881.)

COUNTY OF CHESTER :

				£		
Adlington	- tow.	858	3,899	9,229	Macclesfield -	Macclesfield.
Alderley Inferior	- tow.	573	2,852	7,724	Crewe - -	do.
Alderley Superior	- tow.	399	2,204	4,072	do. - -	do.
Birtles	- tow.	58	599	1,067	do. - -	do.
Bollington	- tow.	5,464	1,291	16,347	do. - -	do.
Bosley	- tow.	100	3,197	5,011	Congleton -	do.
Butteley	- tow.	552	1,811	4,780	Macclesfield -	do.
Capesthorne	- tow.	111	744	1,671	Crewe -	do.
Chelford	- tow.	313	1,182	4,978	do. - -	do.
Chorley	- tow.	1,961	1,338	18,082	Alderley Edge, Manchester.	do.
Eaton	- tow.	401	1,229	3,316	Congleton -	do.
Fallybroom	- tow.	35	242	653	Macclesfield	do.
Gawsworth -	- por.	588	5,704	10,026	do. -	do.
Great Warford	- tow.	351	1,313	3,525	Knutsford -	do.
Henbury with Pexhall	} tow.	431	1,934	1,361	Macclesfield	do.
Hurdsfield	- tow.	3,967	900	8,836	do. -	do.
Kettleshulme -	- tow.	329	1,232	1,846	Stockport -	do.
Lower Withington	- tow.	582	2,393	5,249	Crewe -	do.
Lyme Handley	- tow.	296	3,747	4,198	Stockport -	do.
Macclesfield Forest	tow.	207	3,499	2,916	Macclesfield -	do.
Macclesfield Town (W.)	} tow.	28,619	2,580	72,926	do. -	do.
Marton	- tow.	308	2,194	4,099	Crewe -	do.
Mottram Saint Andrews	} tow.	365	1,792	3,961	Macclesfield -	do.
Newton	- tow.	78	267	560	do. -	do.
North Rode	- tow.	263	1,566	4,185	Congleton -	do.
Old Withington	- tow.	155	1,115	2,009	Crewe -	do.
Pott-Shrigley	- tow.	385	1,706	2,795	Macclesfield	do.
*Poynton-with-Worth	tow.	2,166	2,966	12,343	Stockport -	do.
Prestbury	- tow.	292	746	2,484	Macclesfield -	do.
Rainow	- tow.	1,281	5,744	8,614	do. -	do.
Siddington	- tow.	406	2,159	4,428	Crewe -	do.
Snelson	- tow.	180	428	2,241	do. -	do.
Sutton	- tow.	6,084	5,456	23,138	Macclesfield	do.
Taxal	- tow.	313	3,799	2,441	Stockport -	Stockport.
Tytherington -	- tow.	312	938	6,233	Macclesfield -	Macclesfield.
Upton -	- tow.	185	480	2,570	do. -	do.
Whaley cum Yeardsley -	} tow.	1,272	1,323	5,291	Stockport -	Stockport.
Wildboar-Clough	- tow.	227	5,040	3,100	Macclesfield -	Macclesfield.
Wincell	- tow.	284	2,819	3,566	do. -	do.
Woodford	- tow.	362	1,464	3,071	Stockport -	do.
TOTAL OF UNION -		62,013	85,892	287,942		

MACHYNLLETH UNION.

(Formed 16 Jan. 1837 by Order dated 22 Dec. 1836.)

COUNTY OF CARDIGAN :

Scybor y coed	- tow.	521	11,264	2,905	Machynlleth -	Geneurglyn.

COUNTY OF MERIONETH :

Pennal (a)	- par.	667	7,461	3,253	do. -	Estimanor.
Towyn (a) -	- par.	3,365	26,372	15,604	do. -	do.

(continued)

MACHYNLLETH UNION.

(a) By Orders which came into operation on 25 March, 1887,—
A detached part of Darowen was amalgamated with Penegos
Certain parts of Isywarrie were amalgamated with Machynlleth and Pennal
Certain detached parts of Penegos were amalgamated with Darowen and Machynlleth ;

MACHYNLLETH UNION—continued.

A certain part of Pennal was amalgamated with Machynlleth ; and
Certain detached parts of Talyllyn in the Dolgelly Union were amalgamated with Towyn.

Unions and Parishes, &c.	Population in 1881.	Area in Statute Acres in 1891.	Rateable Value in 1881.	Post Town.	Petty Sessional Division.

MACHYNLLETH UNION—_continued._

COUNTY of MONTGOMERY:

			£		
Cemmes - - _par._	946	9,247	4,362	Machynlleth -	Machynlleth.
Darowen (_a_) - _par._	976	10,000	4,151	do. - -	do.
Isygarrig (_a_) - _tow._	397 {	In Machynlleth.	} 1,929	do. - -	do.
Llanbrynmair - _par._	1,575	19,006	6,423	do - -	do.
Llanwrin - - _par._	681	10,351	4,070	do. - -	do.
Machynlleth (W.) (_a_) _tow._	2,026	14,861	5,982	do. - -	do.
Penegos (_a_) - _par._	982	8,085	3,809	do. - -	do.
Uchygarreg - - _tow._	381 {	In Machynlleth.	} 2,255	do. - -	do.
TOTAL of UNION - -	12,517	116,647	54,743		

MADELEY UNION.
(Formed 6 June 1836 by Order dated 14 May 1836.)
COUNTY of SALOP :

Barrow - - _par._	313	2,329	2,828	Broseley - -	Borough of Wenlock.
Benthall - - _par._	450	866	1,905	lo. -	do.
Broseley - - _par._	1,158	2,006	10,616	do. - -	do.
Buildwas - - _par._	259	2,128	2,773	Iron Bridge -	Bradford South, Hundred of Wellington Division of Salop.
Dawley Magna - _par._	9,200	2,743	22,286	Dawley - -	do.
Linley - - _par._	83	663	763	Broseley - -	Borough of Wenlock.
Little Wenlock - _par._	555	2,697	3,835	Horsehay, Salop -	do.
Madeley (W.) - _par._	9,212	3,025	26,814	Iron Bridge -	do.
Much Wenlock - _par._	2,321	9,737	15,677	Much Wenlock -	do.
Posenhall - - _par._	27	960	516	Broseley - -	do.
Stirchley - - _par._	258	833	2,899	Shifnal -	Bradford South, Hundred of Wellington Division of Salop.
Willey - - _par._	148	1,415	2,150	Broseley -	Borough of Wenlock.
TOTAL of UNION - -	27,314	29,402	93,062		

MAIDSTONE UNION.
(Formed as the Coxheath Union 15 Oct. 1835 by Order dated 28 Sept. 1835.—Place marked thus * added 23 Nov. 1835 by Order dated 29 Oct. 1835 and thus † added 15 June 1836, by Order dated 17 May 1836. Name changed to that of the Maidstone Union on 15 June 1836 by the same Order.—Place marked thus ‡ added 25 Dec. 1860 by Order dated 8 Nov. 1860.)
COUNTY of KENT :

*Barming - - _par._	681	760	3,949	Maidstone -	Lath of Aylesford, East Division.
Berstead - - _par._	601	610	3,406	do. -	do.
Boughton Monchelsen }_par._	1,098	2,385	7,458	do. -	do.
East Farleigh (_b_) - _par._	1,668	2,038	9,603	do. -	do.
Hunton - - _par._	870	2,075	7,555	do. -	Lath of Aylesford, Upper South Division.
Linton (W.) (_a_) - _par._	874	1,393	5,054	do. -	Lath of Aylesford, East Division.
Loose (_b_) - _par._	1,465	983	7,388	do. -	do.
†Maidstone (_a_) - _par._	29,647	4,576	114,631	do. -	Borough of Maidstone.
Marden - - _par._	2,321	7,750	18,937	Marden -	Lath of Scray, Lower Division.

(_continued_)

MACHYNLLETH UNION :
(_a_) For notes see page 223.

MAIDSTONE UNION :
(_a_) A detached part of Maidstone, known as Loddington, was

MAIDSTONE UNION—_continued_.
amalgamated with Linton, by Order which came into operation on 25 March 1883.

(_b_) By Order which came into operation on 25 March 1887, a detached part of East Farleigh was amalgamated with Loose.

Unions and Parishes, &c.	Population in 1881.	Area in Statute Acres in 1881.	Rateable Value in 1881.	Post Town.	Petty Sessional Division.
MAIDSTONE UNION—County of Kent—*continued.*			£		
Nettlested - - *par.*	595	1,454	4,821	Maidstone -	Lath of Aylesford, Upper South Division.
Otham - *par.*	375	955	3,326	do. -	Lath of Aylesford, East Division.
Staplehurst - *par.*	1,637	5,897	13,656	Staplehurst -	Lath of Scray, Lower Division.
Testen - - *par.*	324	520	2,504	do. -	Lath of Aylesford, Upper South Division.
‡West Barming - *par.*	34	332	857	do. -	Lath of Aylesford, East Division.
West Farleigh - *par.*	384	1,107	4,488	do. -	Lath of Aylesford, Upper South Division.
Yalding - - *par.*	2,514	5,843	19,881	do. -	do.
TOTAL of UNION -	45,091	38,678	227,514		

MALDON UNION.

(Formed 14 Dec. 1835 by Order dated 26 Nov. 1835.—Places marked thus * added 26 Mar. 1880 by an Order dated 27 Feb. 1880.)

COUNTY of ESSEX:					
All Saints - - *par.*	1,143	57	4,417	Maldon -	Maldon.
Althorn - - *par.*	319	2,242	2,738	do. -	Dengie.
Asheldam - - *par.*	167	1,739	2,083	do. -	do.
Bradwell near the Sea *par.*	999	5,018	7,159	do. -	do.
Burnham - - *par.*	2,130	4,526	9,637	do. -	do.
Cold Norton - *par.*	185	1,692	1,537	do. -	do.
Creeksea - - *par.*	147	867	1,300	do. -	do.
Dengie - - *par.*	300	2,414	3,237	do. -	do.
Goldhanger - *par.*	524	2,131	3,410	Witham -	Witham.
*Great Braxted - *par.*	373	2,635	3,120	do. -	do.
Great Totham - *par.*	750	3,263	4,885	do. -	do.
Hazeleigh - *par.*	122	989	942	Maldon -	Dengie.
Heybridge - *par.*	1,677	1,854	6,001	do. -	do.
Langford - *par.*	231	1,078	1,915	do. -	Witham.
Latchingdon - *par.*	549	4,007	5,241	do. -	Dengie.
*Little Braxted - *par.*	117	622	791	Witham -	Witham.
Little Totham - *par.*	293	1,262	2,012	do. -	do.
Mayland - *par.*	246	2,067	2,515	Maldon -	Dengie.
Mundon - - *par.*	320	3,107	3,308	do. -	do.
North Fambridge *par.*	142	1,248	1,579	do. -	do.
Purleigh - *par.*	822	5,646	6,957	do. -	do.
Saint Lawrence - *par.*	212	2,023	2,362	do. -	do.
Saint Mary's - *par.*	1,383	1,368	3,838	do. -	Maldon.
Saint Peter's (W.) - *par.*	2,942	1,610	10,261	do. -	do.
Southminster - *par.*	1,311	6,316	10,537	do. -	Dengie.
Steeple - - *par.*	527	2,823	3,290	do. -	do.
Stow-Maries - *par.*	248	2,378	2,486	do. -	do.
Tillingham - *par.*	1,012	4,654	6,628	do. -	do.
Tollesbury - *par.*	1,435	6,155	7,962	do. -	Witham.
Tolleshunt D'Arcy - *par.*	823	3,110	4,821	do. -	do.
Tolleshunt Knights - *par.*	404	2,102	2,903	Kelvedon -	do.
Tolleshunt Major - *par.*	405	2,272	3,267	do. -	do.
*Ulting - - *par.*	163	1,162	1,797	Witham -	do.
*Wickham Bishop - *par.*	535	1,549	2,856	do. -	do.
Woodham Mortimer - *par.*	332	1,386	2,206	Maldon -	Dengie.
Woodham Walter - *par.*	524	2,621	4,005	do. -	do.
TOTAL of UNION -	23,812	89,993	143,956		

Unions and Parishes, &c.	Population in 1881.	Area in Statute Acres in 1881.	Rateable Value in 1881.	Post Town.	Petty Sessional Division.

MALLING UNION.

(Formed 12 Oct. 1835 by Order dated 25 Sept. 1835.)

COUNTY of KENT :

			£		
Addington - - *par.*	264	912	1,855	Maidstone - -	Upper South Aylesford.
Ailington - - *par.*	147	608	2,030	do. - -	do.
Aylesford - - *par.*	2,719	4,377	15,069	do. - -	do.
Birling - - *par.*	884	1,884	3,902	do. - -	do.
Burham - - *par.*	1,353	1,752	9,255	Rochester -	do.
Ditton - - *par.*	336	1,073	3,487	Maidstone -	do.
Ightham - - *par.*	1,254	2,611	5,831	Sevenoaks -	do.
Leybourne - - *par.*	277	1,523	3,517	Maidstone -	do.
Malling East - - *par.*	2,383	2,793	11,483	do. - -	do.
Malling West (W.) - *par.*	2,242	1,379	9,481	do. - -	do.
Mereworth - - *par.*	813	2,105	6,625	do. - -	do.
Offham - - *par.*	358	711	2,051	do. - -	do.
Peckham East - *par.*	2,068	3,403	12,635	Tunbridge -	do.
Peckham West - *par.*	459	1,577	3,360	Maidstone -	do.
Ryarsh - - *par.*	552	1,552	3,921	do. - -	do.
Shipbourne - - *par.*	507	1,922	3,488	Tonbridge -	Lower South Aylesford.
Snodland - - *par.*	2,826	1,880	9,113	Rochester -	Upper South Aylesford.
Stansted - - *par.*	408	1,974	2,438	Sevenoaks -	do.
Trottiscliffe - - *par.*	296	1,155	1,929	Maidstone -	do.
Wateringbury - *par.*	1,301	1,166	8,300	do. - -	do.
Wobldham - - *par.*	1,268	1,540	6,799	Rochester -	North Aylesford.
Wrotham - - *par.*	3,296	8,883	19,741	Sevenoaks -	Upper South Aylesford.
TOTAL of UNION - -	26,041	47,410	146,910		

MALMESBURY UNION.

(Formed 4 Dec. 1835 by Order dated 20 Nov. 1835.)

COUNTY of WILTS :

Abbey - - *par.*	150	In St. Paul	454	Malmesbury -	Malmesbury.
Alderton - - *par.*	125	1,587	1,770	Chippenham -	do.
Brinkworth (a) - *par.*	1,158	5,464	9,936	do. - -	do.
Brockenborough(W.) (a) - *par.*	370	2,552	3,326	Malmesbury -	do.
Charlton - - *par.*	612	5,054	5,024	do. - -	do.
Crudwell - - *par.*	753	4,899	6,537	do. - -	do.
Dauntsey (a) - *par.*	483	3,301	6,836	Chippenham -	do.
Easton Grey - *par.*	136	1,046	1,699	Malmesbury -	do.
Foxley (a) - - *par.*	73	735	850	do. - -	do.
Garsden - - *par.*	174	1,137	1,431	do. - -	do.
Great Somerford - *par.*	550	1,527	2,822	Chippenham -	do.
Hankerton - - *par.*	340	2,203	2,787	Malmesbury -	do.
Hullavington (a) - *par.*	626	3,121	4,131	Chippenham -	do.
Little Somerford (a) *par.*	379	1,376	2,953	do. - -	do.
Luckington (a) - *par.*	336	1,625	2,580	do. - -	do.
Minty (a) - - *par.*	718	3,681	6,643	Malmesbury -	do.
Norton (a) - - *par.*	101	1,001	1,220	do. - -	do.
Oaksey (a) - - *par.*	419	1,924	3,818	do. - -	do.

(continued)

MALMESBURY UNION :

(a) By Orders which came into operation on 25 March 1881,—
Detached parts of Dauntsey, Little Somerford, and Saint Paul, were amalgamated with Brinkworth ;
A detached part of Luckington was amalgamated with Sherston Magna, and a detached part of Sherston Magna was amalgamated with Luckington ;
Detached parts of Norton were amalgamated with Foxley and Hullavington ;

i R 8372.

MALMESBURY UNION—*continued*.

A detached part of Oaksey was amalgamated with Minty ;
Detached parts of Saint Mary Westport, were amalgamated with Saint Paul, and a detached part of Saint Paul was amalgamated with Brockenborough ;
All the parts of a parish, known as Bremilham (having in 1881, population 23, acreage 458, and rateable value £532), were amalgamated with Brockenborough, Foxley, and Saint Mary Westport.

F f

Unions and Parishes, &c.	Population in 1881.	Area in Statute Acres in 1881.	Rateable Value in 1881.	Post Town.	Petty Sessional Division.
MALMESBURY UNION—County of Wilts—*continued.*			£		
Saint Mary Westport, } *par.* (a)	1,867	2,036	4,733	Malmesbury -	Malmesbury.
Saint Paul (a) - *par.*	2,220	5,232	11,547	do. - -	do.
Sherston Magna (a) - *par.*	1,556	4,280	6,489	do. - -	do.
Sherston Pinckney - *par.*	122	950	1,234	do. - -	do.
Sopworth - - *par.*	195	1,011	1,411	Chippenham -	do.
The Lea *par.*	461	1,845	2,885	Malmesbury -	do.
TOTAL of UNION - -	13,924 (a)	57,587 (a)	93,116 (a)		
MALTON UNION. (Formed 12 Jan. 1837 by Order dated 17 Dec. 1836.)					
COUNTY of YORK, EAST RIDING :					
Acklam with Bar-} *tow.* thorp	287	2,358	3,057	{ North Grimston, York - -	} Buckrose.
Birdsall - - *par.*	321	4,030	4,091	do. -	do.
Burythorp - - *par.*	262	1,250	1,981	do. -	do.
Duggleby - - *tow.*	238	1,714	1,963	Wharram, York -	do.
Eddlethorp and } *tow.* Grange -	56	717	899	Malton -	do.
Firby - - *tow.*	42	526	749	Kirkham, York -	do.
Heslerton East - *tow.*	304	3,584	4,510	York -	do.
Heslerton, West - *tow.*	346	2,954	3,619	do. -	do.
Howsham - - *tow.*	177	2,150	2,789	Kirkham, York -	do.
Kennythorp - - *tow.*	50	542	700	Malton -	do.
Kirby Grindalyth - *tow.*	243	1,524	4,623	Wharram, York -	do.
Kirkham (Kirby } *tow.* Underdale) -	51	273	401	York -	do.
Knapton - - *tow.*	246	2,890	4,129	Rillington, York -	do.
Langton - - *tow.*	261	2,285	2,850	Malton -	do.
Leavening - - *tow.*	301	1,292	1,788	North Grimston, York.	do.
Leppington - - *tow.*	76	1,182	1,348	do. - -	do.
Menethorp - - *tow.*	65	583	1,102	Malton -	do.
North Grimston - *par.*	166	1,565	1,764	York -	do.
Norton - - *par.*	3,482	2,838	14,715	Malton -	do.
Raisthorp - - *tow.*	78	2,112	1,809	Wharram, York -	do.
Rillington - - *tow.*	877	2,170	4,309	York -	do.
Scagglethorp - - *tow.*	247	1,206	2,640	Rillington, York -	do.
Scampston - - *tow.*	241	2,412	3,636	do. -	do.
Settrington - - *tow.*	555	4,986	6,819	York -	do.
Thirkleby - - *tow.*	53	1,345	1,506	Wharram, York -	do.
Thorp Bassett - *tow.*	192	1,906	2,851	Rillington, York -	do.
Westow - - *tow.*	337	1,190	1,924	Kirkham, York -	do.
Wharram-le-Street - *par.*	137	2,072	2,259	York -	do.
Wharram Percy - *tow.*	57	1,459	1,557	do. -	do.
Wintringham - - *tow.*	324	5,340	6,305	Rillington, York -	do.
Yeddingham - *tow.*	137	582	954	Heslerton, York -	do.
COUNTY of YORK, NORTH RIDING :					
Amotherby - - *tow.*	280	1,831	2,560	Malton -	Malton.
Appleton-le-Street - *tow.*	178	1,633	1,864	do. -	do.
Aryholme and How-} *tow.* thorp	11	596	540	Hovingham, York	do.
Barton-le-Street - *tow.*	166	1,675	2,095	Malton -	do.
Barton-le-Willows - *tow.*	250	1,047	2,387	Kirkham, York -	East Bulmer.
Brawby - - *tow.*	174	1,013	1,386	Pickering -	Ryedale.
Broughton - - *tow.*	109	866	1,187	Malton -	Malton.
Bulmer - *tow.*	231	1,666	1,911	Welburn, York -	do.
Butterwick - - *tow.*	63	661	914	Barton - le - Street, Malton.	do.
Coneysthorpe - - *tow.*	185	1,205	923	Malton -	do.
Crambe - - *tow.*	148	1,169	3,167	Kirkham, York -	East Bulmer.
Foston - - *tow.*	90	922	1,966	York -	do.

(continued)

Unions and Parishes, &c.		Population in 1881.	Area in Statute Acres in 1881.	Rateable Value in 1881.	Post Town.	Petty Sessional Division.
MALTON UNION—County of York, North Riding—*continued.*				£		
Fryton	- tow.	93	1,131	1,304	Slingsby, York -	Malton.
Ganthorp -	tow.	123	730	685	Terrington, York -	do.
Great Habton	- tow.	165	951	1,252	Pickering - -	Pickering Lythe, West.
Henderskelf -	- tow.	132	1,706	1,645	Castle Howard, York	Malton.
Hildenly -	- tow.	43	304	359	Malton - -	do.
Hovingham -	- tow.	600	2,853	3,797	York - -	do.
Huttons Ambo	- par.	415	2,896	5,636	do. - -	do.
Little Habton	- tow.	52	472	598	Pickering - -	Pickering Lythe, West.
Malton Old (W.)	- par.	1,819	3,968	10,137	Malton - -	Malton.
Ryton -	- tow.	204	2,324	3,020	do. - -	Pickering Lythe, West.
Saint Leonard's and Saint Michael's (W.)	} par.	3,453	49	7,400	do. - -	Malton.
Scackleton -	- tow.	165	1,357	1,315	Hovingham, York	Bulmer, West.
Sheriff Hutton with Cornbrough	} hams.	819	5,352	6,235	York - -	do. East.
Slingsby -	- par.	596	2,570	3,600	do. - -	Malton.
Southholme -	- tow.	84	904	1,140	Slingsby, York -	do.
Stittenham -	- tow.	90	1,599	1,890	York - -	Bulmer, East.
Swinton -	- tow.	345	1,254	1,762	Malton - -	Malton.
Terrington and Wiganthorp	} tow.	562	3,223	3,886	York - -	do.
Thornton-le-Clay	- tow.	274	954	1,909	do. - -	Bulmer East.
Wath -	- tow.	11	371	267	Hovingham, York -	Malton.
Welburn -	- tow.	560	886	1,799	York - -	do.
Whitwell on the Hill	par.	203	1,571	3,021	do. - -	do.
TOTAL of UNION	-	23,031	115,652 (a)	177.243		

MANCHESTER TOWN-SHIP.

(Board of Guardians constituted 18 April 1850 by Order of that date.)

COUNTY of LANCASTER:

Manchester (W.)	- tow.	148,794	1,646	1,499.906	Manchester -	City of Manchester.

MANSFIELD UNION.

(Formed 29 June 1836 by Order dated 6 June 1836.—Place marked thus * added 23 May 1837 by Order dated 27 April 1837, and thus † added 25 Dec. 1861 by Order dated 6 Nov. 1861.)

COUNTY of DERBY:

Ault Hucknall	- par.	747	4,429	6,438	Chesterfield	Chesterfield.
Blackwell	- par.	2,195	1,739	10,327	Alfreton - -	Alfreton.
*Glapwell -	- tow.	94	774	916	Chesterfield	Chesterfield.
Pleasley (a)	- par.	1,152	3,293	7,323	Mansfield - -	do.
Scarcliffe -	- par.	618	3,954	4,090	do. - -	do.
South Normanton -	par.	3,205	1,934	10,550	Alfreton - -	Alfreton.
Tibshelf -	- par.	2,241	2,371	12,718	do. - -	do.
Upper Langwith (a)	par.	205	1,492	1,979	Mansfield	Chesterfield.
						(continued)

MALTON UNION:

(a) There is some intermixed Land in this Union, known as Sheriff Hutton Moor, which is stated to belong to the township of Sheriff Hutton with Cornbrough, and which contains 880 acres.

MANSFIELD UNION:

(a) By Provisional Order which came into operation on 25 March 1884,—

Two detached parts of Pleasley were amalgamated with Upper Langwith ;

Two detached parts of Hucknall under Huthwaite were amalgamated with Sutton in Ashfield, and detached parts of Sutton in Ashfield were amalgamated with Hucknall under Huthwaite and Fulwood.

Unions and Parishes, &c.	Population in 1881.	Area in Statute Acres in 1881.	Rateable Value in 1881.	Post Town.	Petty Sessional Division.
MANSFIELD UNION—*continued.*					
In the COUNTIES of DERBY and NOTTINGHAM :			£		
Pinxton - *par.*	2,317	1,253	8,205	Alfreton -	Alfreton.
COUNTY of NOTTINGHAM :					
Blidworth - *par.*	1,109	5,897	5,547	Mansfield -	Mansfield.
†Fulwood (*a*) - *par.*	5	174	196	do. -	do.
†Heywood Oakes - *par.*	33 {	In Blidworth	} 518	do. -	do.
Hucknall under Huthwaite (*a*) - *tow.*	2,028	1,228	5,353	do. -	do.
†Lyndhurst - *par.*	32	713	569	do. -	do.
Mansfield (W.) - *par.*	13,653	7,252	38,515	do. -	do.
Mansfield Woodhouse *par.*	2,618	4,834	8,630	do. -	do.
Skegby - *par.*	2,401	1,467	4,858	do. -	do.
Sokeholme - *tow.*	35	In Warsop	899	do. -	do.
Sutton in Ashfield (*a*) *tow.*	8,523	4,855	17,259	do. -	do.
Teversal - *par.*	415	2,725	8,642	do. -	do.
Warsop - *tow.*	1,329	6,710	7,519	do. -	do.
TOTAL of UNION -	44,958	57,094	161,951		
MARKET BOSWORTH UNION.					

(Formed 11 Feb. 1836 by Order dated 25 Jan. 1836.—Places marked thus * added 15 May 1851 by Order dated 29 April 1851 ; and thus † added 25 Dec. 1861 by Order dated 4 Oct. 1861.)

COUNTY of LEICESTER :					
Bagworth (*d*) - *tow.*	604	3,930	4,990	Leicester	Market Bosworth.
Barleston - *tow.*	708	1,039	2,213	do. -	do.
Barton in the Beans (*d*) *tow.*	136	In Nailston	1,200	Atherstone -	do.
Bilston - *tow.*	102	570	1,033	do. -	do.
Cadeby (*a*) - *tow.*	149	900	1,538	Hinckley -	do.
Carlton - *tow.*	274 {	In Market Bosworth	} 1,417	do. -	do.
Congerston (*a*) (*d*) - *par.*	132	1,020	1,172	Atherstone -	do.
Dadlington - *tow.*	170	870	1,814	Hinckley -	do.
Desford - *par.*	900	3,830	5,603	Leicester -	do.
†Gopsall - *par.*	24	600	1,181	Atherstone -	do.
Ibstock - *tow.*	2,335	2,257	10,587	Ashby de la Zouch	do.
Kirkby Mallory - *tow.*	190	2,190	3,177	Hinckley -	do.
Market Bosworth (W.) (*a*) - *tow.*	881	6,410	5,973	do. -	do.
Markfield (*a*) (*b*) - *par.*	1,605	2,534	4,115	Leicester -	Leicester.
Nailston (*d*) - *tow.*	389	2,486	4,389	Hinckley -	Market Bosworth.
Newbold Verdon (*d*) *par.*	729	2,400	3,507	Leicester -	do.
Norton - *tow.*	293	2,341	2,732	Atherstone -	do.
Odston - *tow.*	192	733	2,271	do. -	do.
Orton on the Hill (*c*) *par.*	275	2,290	2,415	do. -	do.
Osbaston - *tow.*	215	1,230	2,501	Leicester	do.
Peckleton - *par.*	267	1,583	3,637	Hinckley -	do.
Ratby - *par.*	1,615	5,410	9,377	Leicester -	Leicester.

(continued)

MARKET BOSWORTH UNION :

(*a*) By Orders which came into operation on 25 March 1884,—
A detached part of Newtown Linford, in the Barrow upon Soar Union, was amalgamated with Markfield ; Detached parts of Market Bosworth were amalgamated with Congerston and Cadeby.
(*b*) By Provisional Order which came into operation on 25 March 1885,—
A detached part of Markfield was amalgamated with Charley, in the Loughborough Union ;

MARKET BOSWORTH UNION—*continued.*

(*c*) By Order which came into operation on 25 March 1885, three detached parts of Merivale in the Atherstone Union were amalgamated with Orton on the Hill.
(*d*) By Order which came into operation on 25 March 1886,—
Detached parts of Nailston were amalgamated with Barton in the Beans and Congerston ;
Detached parts of Shackerston were amalgamated with Congerston ; and
A detached part of Bagworth was amalgamated with Newbold Verdon.

Unions and Parishes, &c.		Population in 1881.	Area in Statute Acres in 1881.	Rateable Value in 1881.	Post Town.	Petty Sessional Division.
MARKET BOSWORTH UNION—County of Leicester—*continued.*				£		
Shackerston (d)	tow.	288	1,920	2.227	Atherstone	Market Bosworth.
Shenton	tow.	210	In Market Bosworth	2,602	Nuneaton	do.
*Sibson	tow.	278	3,817	3,843	Atherstone	do.
Stanton under Bardon	tow.	259	InBagworth	2,006	Leicester	do.
*Stapleton	tow.	204	1,380	2,016	Hinckley	do.
*Sutton Cheyne	tow.	300	In Market Bosworth	2,160	do.	do.
Thornton	tow.	426	InBagworth	4,319	Leicester	do.
Twycross	par.	354	1,350	2,532	Atherstone	do.
Upton	tow.	103	In Sibson	2,065	Mincaton	do.
TOTAL OF UNION	-	14,611	53,090	100,912		

MARKET HARBOROUGH UNION.

(Formed 3 Dec. 1835 by Order dated 17 Nov. 1835. — Place marked thus * added 24 June 1863 by Order dated 13 May 1863.)

COUNTY OF LEICESTER :						
Bowden Magna (W.)	tow.	1,985	In Market Harborough	17,801	Market Harborough	Market Harborough.
Cranoe	par.	106	990	1,151	do.	East Norton.
East Langton (a)	tow.	242	In Tur Langton	3,573	do.	Market Harborough.
Fleckney	par.	770	1,630	2,788	do.	do.
Foxton	par.	348	2,020	3,789	do.	do.
Glooston	par.	105	660	1,422	do.	East Norton.
Gumley	par.	232	1,550	2,580	do.	Market Harborough.
Husband Bosworth	par.	831	3,870	7,099	Rugby	do.
Kibworth Beauchamp	tow.	1,123	3,220	6,967	Leicester	do.
Kibworth Harcourt	tow.	150	InKibworth Beauchamp	5,950	do.	do.
Laughton	par.	136	1,109	1,938	Rugby	do.
Lubbenham	par.	590	2,400	5,916	Market Harborough	do.
Market Harborough	tow.	2,418	3,120	6,293	do.	do.
Mowsley	tow.	208	1,710	2,333	Rugby	do.
Saddington	par.	185	1,050	3,318	Market Harborough	do.
Shangton	par.	74	1,500	1,819	Leicester	do.
Smeeton Westerby	tow.	390	InKibworth Beauchamp	2,971	do.	do.
Stonton Wyville	par.	88	1,190	2,062	Market Harborough	do.
Theddingworth	par.	246	2,220	3,138	Rugby	do.
Thorp Langton (a)	tow.	83	In Tur Langton	2,052	Market Harborough	do.
Tur Langton	tow.	279	4,280	2,915	Leicester	do.
Welham (a)	par.	68	1,109	2,260	Market Harborough	do.
West Langton (a)	tow.	60	In Tur Langton	5,472	do.	do.
COUNTY OF NORTHAMPTON :						
Arthingworth	par.	185	2,030	3,017	Northampton	Little Bowden.
Ashley	par.	296	1,190	2,725	Market Harborough	do.
Brampton	par.	120	2,259	3,333	do.	do.
Braybrooke	par.	360	3,060	10,099	do.	do.
Clipston	par.	696	2,800	5,152	Northampton	do.

(continued)

MARKET BOSWORTH UNION :

(d) *See note page 229.*

MARKET HARBOROUGH UNION :

(a) By Order which came into operation on 25 March 1885,
Four detached parts of East Langton were amalgamated with Thorp Langton ;
Parts of Thorp Langton were amalgamated with East Langton and Welham ;
Detached parts of West Langton were amalgamated with East Langton and Thorp Langton.

Unions and Parishes, &c.		Population in 1881.	Area in Statute Acres in 1881.	Rateable Value in 1881.	Post Town.	Petty Sessional Division
MARKET HARBOROUGH UNION—County of Leicester—*continued.*				£		
Dingley	*par.*	127	1,317	2,742	Market Harborough	Little Bowden.
East Farndon	*par.*	223	1,070	3,337	do.	do.
Hothorpe	*par.*	25 {	In Thed-dingworth }	1,475	Rugby	do.
Kelmarsh	*par.*	209	2,751	5,511	Northampton	do.
Little Bowden	*par.*	960	1,670	8,551	Market Harborough	do.
Marston Trussel	*par.*	206	1,640	2,654	do.	do.
Oxenden Magna	*par.*	232	1,620	3,072	do.	do.
Sibbertoft	*par.*	292	2,018	3,592	do.	do.
Stoke Albany	*par.*	322	1,661	2,951	do.	do.
Sulby	*par.*	80	700	2,808	Rugby	do.
Sutton Bassett	*par.*	116	720	1,454	Market Harborough	do.
*Thorpe Lubbenham	*par.*	6 {	In Marston Trussel }	935	do.	do.
Weston by Welland	*par.*	215	1,010	2,117	do.	do.
Wilbarston	*par.*	598	2,800	4,540	do.	do.
TOTAL OF UNION		16,285	64,094	165,705		
MARLBOROUGH UNION.						
(Formed 24 Nov. 1835 by Order dated 9 Nov. 1835. — Places marked thus * added 1 March 1862 by Order dated 22 Jan. 1862.)						
COUNTY OF WILTS :						
Avebury	*par.*	725	4,544	5,337	Calne	Marlborough and Ramsbury.
Berwick Basset	*par.*	134	1,388	1,500	Swindon	do.
Broad Hinton (*a*)	*par.*	550	3,659	5,912	do.	do.
*Clatford Park	*par.*	25 {	In West Overton }	141	Marlborough	do.
East Kennet	*par.*	85	808	899	do.	Marlborough and Ramsbury.
Fifield	*par.*	157 {	In West Overton }	1,232	do.	do.
Marlborough Saint Mary	*par.*	1,845	186 {	1,493	do.	Borough of Marlborough.
Marlborough Saint Peter and Saint Paul	*par.*	1,498		5,502	do.	do.
Mildenhall	*par.*	454	4,025	4,098	do.	Marlborough and Ramsbury.
*North Savernake	*par.*	108 {	In South Savernake, Brimslade, and Cadley }	1,329	do.	do.
Ogbourne Saint Andrew	*par.*	442	5,348	4,457	do.	do.
Ogbourne Saint George	*par.*	177	3,585	4,107	do.	do.
*Overton Heath	*par.*	24 {	In West Overton }	112	do.	do.
Preshute (W.)	*par.*	1,837	4,479	9,195	do.	do.
*South Savernake, Brimslade, and Cadley	*par.*	218	3,740	2,507	do.	do.
West Overton	*tow.*	673	5,400	4,517	do.	do.
Winterbourne Basset	*par.*	262	2,210	2,759	Swindon	do.
Winterbourne Monkton	*par.*	219	1,810	2,133	do.	do.
TOTAL OF UNION		9,733	41,212	60,230		

MARLBOROUGH UNION :

(*a*) A part of Broad Hinton was severed therefrom by Order which came into operation 25 March 1884.
See also Cricklade and Wootton Bassett Union.

Unions and Parishes, &c.		Population in 1881.	Area in Statute Acres in 1881.	Rateable Value in 1881.	Post Town.	Petty Sessional Division.

MARTLEY UNION.

(Formed 8 Oct. 1836 by Order dated 14 Sept. 1836. — Place marked thus * added 20 Jan. 1862 by Order dated 20 Dec. 1861.)

COUNTY of WORCESTER :

£

				£		
Abberley (c)	- par.	605	2,636	3,880	Stourport - -	Hundred House.
Alfrick (b) -	- tow.	450	In Suckley	2,599	Worcester -	Worcester.
Astley -	- par.	797	2,958	6,661	Stourport	Stourport.
Bransford (b)	- cha.	257	In Leigh	2,592	Worcester -	Worcester.
Broadwas (b) -	- par.	314	1,160	2,125	do. - -	do.
Clifton upon Teame -	par.	449	2,972	3,752	do. - -	Hundred House.
Cotheridge (b)	- par.	192	2,202	2,903	do. - -	Worcester.
Doddenham -	- par.	252	916	1,629	do. - -	do.
Great Witley	- par.	380	2,633	4,502	Stourport -	Hundred House.
Grimley -	- par.	715	2,459	5,021	Worcester -	Worcester.
Hillhampton -	- ham.	137	786	1,265	do. -	Hundred House.
Holt - -	- par.	239	1,951	2,894	do.	Worcester.
*Kenswick -	- par.	10 {	In Knight-wick }	608	do. - -	do.
King's Areley -	- par.	677	1,449	3,780	Stourport - -	Stourport.
King's Shelsley	- ham.	281 {	In Shellsey Beauchamp }	1,502	Worcester -	Hundred House.
Knightwick -	- par.	143	858	1,365	do. -	Worcester.
Leigh (b) -	- par.	4,621	6,129	25,044	Malvern -	Great Malvern.
Little Whitley	- cha.	214	960	1,648	Worcester -	Hundred House.
Lulsley (b) -	- tow.	160	In Suckley	1,795	do. -	Worcester.
Martley (W.) -	- par.	1,094	4,338	7,573	do. -	Hundred House.
North Hallow (a) -	par.	—	—	—	do. -	do.
Pensax -	- cha.	472	1,190	1,757	Tenbury -	do.
Shelsley Beauchamp -	par.	291	2,196	1,794	Worcester -	do.
Shelsley Walsh -	par.	40	468	769	do. -	do.
Shrawley -	- par.	462	1,877	3,487	Stourport -	do.
Stanford -	- par.	155	1,278	1,890	Worcester -	do.
Stockton -	- par.	123	893	1,537	Tenbury -	do.
Suckley -	- par.	623	5,184	3,972	Worcester -	Worcester.
Wickenford (b)	- par.	371	2,669	3,192	do. -	do.
TOTAL of UNION -		14,524 (a)	50,162 (a)	101,536 (a)		

MEDWAY UNION.

(Formed 7 Sept. 1835 by Order dated 20 Aug. 1835. — Place marked thus * added 2 May 1836 by Order dated 30 March 1836.)

COUNTY of KENT :

Cathedral Precincts -		125	7	745	Rochester -	City of Rochester.
Chatham (W.) -	- par.	26,889	4,444	90,513	Chatham -	Rochester.
Gillingham -	- tow.	20,644	4,317	61,295	do. - -	Northern Division of South Aylesford.
Grange -	- ham.	186	256	1,531	do. -	do.
*Lidsing -	- ville.	35	443	170	do. - -	do.

(continued)

MARTLEY UNION :

(a) So much of the parish of Hallow as was included in the City of Worcester, as extended by the Worcester Extension Act, 1885, was, by Section 95 of that Act, on and after the 30th of September, 1885, severed from the Martley Union, and added to the Worcester Union under the name of South Hallow. The part of Hallow remaining in the Martley Union is, by Section 96 of the Act, designated the parish of North Hallow. (Hallow in 1881 contained population 1,868, acreage 3,556, and rateable value 10,224l.)

(b) By Orders which came into operation on 25 March, 1884,—

The parts of Alfrick and Bransford north of the River

MARTLEY UNION—continued.

Teme, were amalgamated with Broadwas [and Cotheridge respectively ;

The parts of Broadwas and Cotheridge south of the River Teme, were amalgamated with Leigh and Bransford respectively.

A nearly detached part of Broadwas was amalgamated with Cotheridge ; and

A detached part of Cotheridge was amalgamated with Wickenford ; and

Detached parts of Lulsley were amalgamated with Alfrick.

(c) By Provisional Order which came into operation on 25 March, 1885, a detached part of Abberley was amalgamated with Rock, in the Cleobury Mortimer Union.

Unions and Parishes, &c.		Population in 1881.	Area in Statute Acres in 1881.	Rateable Value in 1881.	Post Town.	Petty Sessional Division.
MEDWAY UNION—County of Kent—*continued.*				£		
Saint Margaret	*par.*	10,200	2,492	31,582	Rochester - -	City of Rochester.
Saint Nicholas	*par.*	3,565	121	16,508	do. - -	do.
TOTAL of UNION -		61,614	12,080	202,614		

MELKSHAM UNION.

(Formed 2 Nov. 1835 by Order dated 30 Sept. 1835.)

COUNTY of WILTS :

Hilperton (*a*)	*par.*	822	1,078	3,342	Trowbridge -	Trowbridge.
Melksham	*par.*	1,412	12,572	25,835	Melksham -	Melksham.
Seend	*cha.*	919	In Melksham	7,915	do. - -	do.
Semington (W.) (*a*) -	*cha.*	479	1,238	3,099	Trowbridge -	do.
Trowbridge - -	*par.*	11,394	2,442	35,261	do. - -	Trowbridge.
Whaddon (*a*) - -	*par.*	51	438	891	do. - -	Melksham.
TOTAL of UNION -		18,077	17,768	76,376		

MELTON MOWBRAY UNION.

(Formed 26 March 1836 by Order dated 10 March 1836.—Places marked thus * added 25 Dec. 1858 by Order dated 9 Nov. 1858.)

COUNTY of LEICESTER :

Ab-Kettleby (*a*) -	*tow.*	230	In Holwell	1,460	Melton Mowbray -	Melton Mowbray.
Asfordby	*par.*	539	1,210	4,063	do. - -	do.
Ashby Folville (*a*) -	*tow.*	131	1,983	2,877	do. - -	do.
Barsby (*a*) -	*tow.*	254	1,030	1,422	Leicester - -	do.
*Bescaby	*par.*	9	—	1,376	Melton Mowbray -	do.
Branston	*par.*	247	960	2,404	Grantham - -	Belvoir.
Brooksby	*par.*	67	861	2,820	Leicester - -	Melton Mowbray.
Buckminster (*a*)	*tow.*	253	3,053	2,339	Grantham - -	do.
Burrough (*b*) -	*par.*	149	1,565	2,316	Melton Mowbray -	do.
Burton Lazars -	*tow.*	244	2,060	5,746	do. - -	do.
Coston -	*par.*	133	1,745	2,081	do. - -	do.
Dalby Magna -	*par.*	455	2,328	3,660	do. - -	do.
Dalby on the Woulds	*par.*	335	3,430	4,577	do. - -	do.
Dalby Parva -	*par.*	154	1,848	2,519	do. - -	do.
Eastwell -	*par.*	163	1,346	1,864	do. - -	Belvoir.
Eaton -	*par.*	351	2,170	2,499	Grantham - -	do.
Edmondthorpe	*par.*	209	1,753	3,301	Oakham - -	Melton Mowbray.
Freeby -	*tow.*	132	1,516	4,043	Melton Mowbray -	do.
Frisby on the Wreak	*par.*	396	1,080	4,504	Leicester - -	do.
Gaddesby -	*par.*	241	1,657	2,755	do. - -	do.
Garthorpe -	*par.*	120	1,711	1,745	Melton Mowbray -	do.
Goadby Marwood -	*par.*	155	1,618	2,345	do. - -	do.
Grimston -	*par.*	153	920	1,483	do. - -	do.

(continued)

MELKSHAM UNION :

(*a*) By Orders which came into operation on 25 March 1884,—
A detached part of Whaddon and a part of Semington were amalgamated with Hilperton; and
A detached part of Hinton, in the Westbury and Whorwellsdown Union, was amalgamated with Hilperton

MELTON MOWBRAY UNION :

(*a*) By Orders which came into operation on 25 March 1884,—
Three detached parts of Ab-Kettleby were amalgamated with Holwell ;

MELTON MOWBRAY UNION—*continued.*

A detached part of Ashby Folville was amalgamated with Barsby ;
A detached part of Barsby was amalgamated with Croxton South, in the Harrow-upon-Soar Union ;
A detached part of Wartnaby was amalgamated with Holwell ;
A part of Sewstern was amalgamated with Buckminster ; and
A detached part of Croxton South, in the Harrow-upon-Soar Union, was amalgamated with Barsby.

(*b*) By Order which came into operation on 25 March, 1887, a detached part of Somerby was amalgamated with Burrough.

Unions and Parishes, &c.	Population in 1881.	Area in Statute Acres in 1881.	Rateable Value in 1881.	Post Town.	Petty Sessional Division.
MELTON MOWBRAY UNION—County of Leicester —*continued.*			£		
Harby - - - *par.*	591	2,800	3,602	Melton Mowbray -	Belvoir.
Hoby - - *par.*	311	1,060	3,709	Leicester - -	Melton Mowbray.
Holwell (*a*) - - *tow.*	268	2,920	3,489	Melton Mowbray -	do.
Hose - - *par.*	438	2,140	3,953	do. - -	do.
Kirby Bellairs - *par.*	271	2,590	6,314	do. - -	do.
Long Clawson - *par.*	738	3,450	5,335	do. - -	do.
Melton Mowbray (W.) - - } *tow.*	5,820	5,680	25,685	do. - -	do.
Nether Broughton - *par.*	454	2,110	3,279	do. - -	do.
Pickwell - - *par.*	249	1,480	3,602	do. - -	do.
Ragdale - - *par.*	102	1,980	1,586	Leicester - -	do.
Rotherby - - *par.*	153	766	2,366	do. - -	do.
Saltby - - *par.*	272	2,680	2,373	Melton Mowbray -	Belvoir.
Saxby - - *par.*	120	1,430	4,164	do. - -	Melton Mowbray.
Saxelby - - *par.*	84	1,290	2,229	do. - -	do.
Sealford - - *par.*	684	2,520	4,579	do. - -	do.
Sewstern (*a*) - - *tow.*	201 {	In Buck- minster.	1,627	Grantham - -	do.
*Shoby - - *par.*	35	710	1,145	Melton Mowbray -	do.
Somerby (*b*) - *par.*	531	1,000	2,804	Oakham - -	do.
Sproxton - - *par.*	335	2,360	2,977	Melton Mowbray -	do.
Stapleford - - *par.*	114	3,960	3,301	do. - -	do.
Stathern - - *par.*	539	1,420	4,075	do. - -	Belvoir.
Stonesby - - *par.*	216	1,370	1,872	do. - -	Melton Mowbray.
Sysonby - - *tow.*	96	980	2,397	do. - -	do.
Thorpe Arnold - *par.*	147	1,742	2,625	do. - -	do.
Thorpe Satchville - *tow.*	169 }	2,420	2,214	do. - -	do.
Twyford - - *tow.*	426 }		2,019	do. - -	do.
Waltham on the Wolds - - } *par.*	595	2,870	3,641	do. - -	do.
Wartnaby (*a*) - *tow.*	165	610	1,660	do. - -	do.
Welby - - *tow.*	55 {	In Melton Mowbray.	1,555	do. - -	do.
Wycomb and Chad- well - - } *tow.*	107	1,730	1,147	do. - -	do.
Wyfordby - - *par.*	104	1,350	4,694	do. - -	do.
Wymondham - *par.*	655	2,852	6,674	Oakham - -	do.
COUNTY OF NOTTINGHAM :					
Over Broughton - *par.*	327	1,600	3,407	Melton Mowbray -	Bingham.
TOTAL of UNION -	20,492	98,077	190,301		

MERE UNION.

(Formed 14 Oct. 1835 by Order dated 29 Sept. 1835.)

COUNTY OF DORSET :					
Bourton (*a*) - - *cha.*	838	828	3,422	Bath - -	Shaftesbury.
Silton (*a*) - - *par.*	245	1,257	2,392	do. - -	do.
COUNTY OF SOMERSET :					
Kilmington - - *par.*	477	2,746	4,195	Bath -	Wincanton.
COUNTIES OF SOMERSET and WILTS :					
Maiden Bradley with Yarnfield (*b*) - } *par.*	591	4,334	4,882	Bath - -	{ Warminster and Win- canton.
Stourton with Gaspar *par.*	556	3,448	4,661	do. - -	Hindon and Win- canton.
					(*continued*)

MELTON MOWBRAY UNION :

(*a*) (*b*) *See notes page 233.*

MERE UNION :

(*a*) By Order which came into operation on 25 March, 1884, three detached parts of Silton were amalgamated with Bourton.

(*b*) By Provisional Order which came into operation on 25 March, 1885, a detached part of Maiden Bradley with

MERE UNION—*continued.*

Yarnfield was amalgamated with Horningsham, in the Warminster Union.

(*c*) By Provisional Order which came into operation on 25 March, 1885, all the parts of a parish known as Pertwood, having in 1881, population 38, acreage 450, and rateable value 311*l.*, were amalgamated with Sutton Veney in the Warminster Union, and East Knoyle.

(*d*) By Order which came into operation on 25 March, 1885, a detached part of Kingston Deverill was amalgamated with Hill Deverill, in the Warminster Union.

Unions and Parishes, &c.	Population in 1881.	Area in Statute Acres in 1881.	Rateable Value in 1881.	Post Town.	Petty Sessional Division.

MERE UNION—*continued*.

COUNTY of WILTS :

			£		
East Knoyle (c) - *par.*	877	5,558	6,936	Salisbury - -	Hindon.
Kingston Deverill (d) *par.*	278	2,060	1,991	Warminster -	do.
Mere (W.) - - *par.*	2,931	7,400	12,525	Bath - -	do.
Monkton Deverill - *par.*	127	1,735	1,221	Warminster -	do.
Sedgehill - - *par.*	192	1,175	2,009	Shaftesbury -	do.
West Knoyle - - *par.*	199	1,913	1,966	Bath - -	do.
TOTAL of UNION -	7,311 (c)	32,454 (c)	46,200 (c)		

MERIDEN UNION.

(Formed 29 March 1836 by Order dated 14 March 1836.)

COUNTY of WARWICK :

Allesley - - *par.*	968	4,225	8,732	Coventry - -	Coventry.
Berkswell - - *par.*	1,451	5,958	12,907	do. - -	do.
Church Bickenhill - *par.*	510	2,834	6,910	Birmingham -	Coleshill.
Coleshill - - *par.*	2,356	6,200	11,273	do. - -	do.
Corley - - *par.*	300	1,378	2,656	Coventry - -	Coventry.
Conndon - - *ham.*	277	1,046	2,867	do. - -	do.
Fillongley - - *par.*	1,049	4,731	7,460	do. - -	Coleshill.
Great Packington - *par.*	239	2,451	3,526	do. - -	do.
Hampton in Arden - *par.*	646	} 2,486	{ 6,310	Birmingham -	Solihull.
Kinwalsey - *ham.*	17		156	do. - -	do.
Lea Marston - *par.*	306	1,527	2,275	do. - -	Coleshill.
Little Packington - *par.*	119	1,110	1,475	Coventry - -	do.
Maxstoke - - *par.*	241	2,701	3,590	Birmingham -	do.
Meriden (W.) - *par.*	837	3,010	5,236	Coventry -	do.
Nether Whitacre - *par.*	587	2,210	4,512	Birmingham -	do.
Over Whitacre - *par.*	288	1,375	2,550	do. - -	do.
Sheldon - - *par.*	401	2,514	5,345	do. - -	Solihull.
Shustoke - - *par.*	433	2,014	7,907	do. - -	Coleshill.
TOTAL of UNION -	11,025	47,770	95,687		

MERTHYR TIDVIL UNION.

(Formed 3 Nov. 1836 by Order dated 10 Oct. 1836.)

COUNTY of BRECKNOCK :

Penderyn - - *par.*	1,598	12,765	8,459	Aberdare -	Penderyn, Brecon.
Vaenor - - *par.*	2,851	6,597	6,167	Merthyr Tidvil -	do.

COUNTY of GLAMORGAN :

Aberdare - - *par.*	35,533	16,619	145,188	Aberdare -	Miskin, Glamorgan : Upper Division.
Gelli-gaer - *par.*	11,592	16,772	65,269	Gelli-gaer -	Caerphilly Brithdir. Garthgyned, Ysgwyddgwyn : Upper Division.
Merthyr Tidvil (W.) *par.*	48,861	17,400	143,076	Merthyr Tidvil -	Caerphilly, Upper Division.
Rhigos - *ham.*	1,006	5,582	6,496	Aberdare -	Miskin, Glamorgan : Upper Division.
TOTAL of UNION -	101,441	75,735	374,655		

rishes, &c.	Population in 1881.	Area in Statute Acres in 1881.	Rateable Value in 1881.	Post Town.	Petty Sessional Division.
UGH UNION.			£		
1875 by Order c 1875.)					
ʀK, North					
G :					
- - *tow.*	6,297	2,252	39,207	Middlesbrough -	Langbaurgh, North.
- - *tow.*	103	1,118	1,396	Stockton - -	do.
·k - *tow.*	132	1,556	2,199	Yarm - -	Yarm.
(*a*) - *tow.*	18,736	2,136	84,210	Middlesbrough -	Borough of Middlesbrough, and Langbaurgh, North.
- *tow.*	113	1,116	1,547	Stockton - -	Yarm.
- *par.*	1,057	3,519	11,202	Middlesbrough	Borough of Middlesbrough, and Langbaurgh, North.
(*a*) - *tow.*	36,631	1,080	150,937	do. - -	do.
- *tow.*	7,714	1,462	23,345	do. - -	Langbaurgh, North.
- *tow.*	7,774	2,883	20,598	do. - -	do.
- - *tow.*	337	2,306	2,896	Stockton - -	Yarm.
- - *tow.*	10,795	1,695	37,694	do. - -	do.
ʋ) - *par.*	164	976	1,460	Middlesbrough	Langbaurgh, North.
'NION -	**89,853**	**22,099**	**376,691**		
URST UNION.					
835 by Order dated 16 April ırked thus * originally formed ·h of Woolavington, but by ler, dated 14 June, 1869 and 2 & 33 Vict. cap. cxxiii., ·ns readjusted and divided, ıg Fernhurst and Terwick y added to those parishes on), and the residue being conparishes under the names of ınd West Lavington. Places added 29 Sept. 1869 by Aug. 1869.)					
ʀTY of Sussex :					
- *par.*	269	1,910	4,602	Midhurst -	Lower Chichester Rape.
- *par.*	334	1,199	1,081	Petersfield -	do.
- *par.*	574	2,598	2,414	Midhurst - -	do.
- *par.*	85	825	660	do. -	do.
'.) - *par.*	1,016	4,010	4,487	do. -	do.
ı - *par.*	221	1,720	1,102	Petworth -	Lower Arundel Rape.
- *par.*	208	1,840	1,590	Petersfield -	Lower Chichester Rape.
- *par.*	1,091	4,950	3,514	do. -	do.
- *par.*	413	1,714	1,250	Petworth -	do.
- *par.*	1,274	7,946	8,440	Petersfield -	do.
- *par.*	148	2,184	1,889	Midhurst -	do.
- *par.*	523	2,247	2,053	do. -	do.
- *par.*	99	850	591	Liphook -	do.
- - *par.*	346	2,065	1,433	Haslemere -	do.
- *par.*	682	2,442	2,889	Petworth -	do.
- - *par.*	732	4,814	3,787	do. -	Lower Arundel Rape.
- *par.*	1,615	669	6,141	Midhurst	Lower Chichester Rape.
ıam - *ty.*	167	1,169	901	Haslemere -	do.
- *par.*	986	4,984	5,012	Petersfield -	do.
- *par.*	49	423	523	Petworth -	do.
ıam - *ty.*	124	1,502	938	Midhurst -	do.
- *par.*	541	2,493	2,785	do. -	do.
- *par.*	185	782	1,078	Petersfield -	do.
- *par.*	886	3,816	5,415	Petworth -	Lower Arundel Rape.
- *par.*	147	1,273	859	Petersfield -	Lower Chichester Rape.
- - *par.*	405	3,588	3,723	do. -	do.
n - *par.*	151	678	899	Midhurst -	do.
- *par.*	362	1,850	1,627	do. -	do.
Jnıon -	**13,933**	**66,571**	**68,686**		

MIDDLESBROUGH UNION :

(*a*) By Orders which came into operation on 25 March, 1887,—
    Detached parts of Middlesbrough were amalgamated with Linthorpe and West Acklam ;
    A detached part of Stockton, in the Stockton Union, was amalgamated with Thornaby.

Unions and Parishes, &c.	Population in 1881.	Area in Statute Acres in 1881.	Rateable Value in 1881.	Post Town.	Petty Sessional Division.

MILDENHALL UNION.

(Formed 12 Nov. 1835 by Order dated 29 Oct. 1835.—Place marked thus * added 28 Dec. 1835 by Order dated 5 Dec. 1835. Spelling of name of place marked thus † is as altered by Order dated 8 Sept. 1897.)

County of Suffolk :

			£		
Barton Mills - par.	468	2,050	3,066	Mildenhall -	Hundred of Lackford.
Cavenham - par.	186	2,630	1,099	do. -	do.
*Elveden otherwise } Elden - } par.	310	5,290	2,423	Thetford, Norfolk -	do.
Eriswell - par.	441	6,620	3,616	Brandon	do.
Freckenham - par.	371	2,520	2,915	Soham -	do.
Herringswell - par.	193	2,540	1,547	Mildenhall	do.
Icklingham Saint } James and All Saints } par.	425	6,560	3,595	do.	do.
Kentford - par.	196	798	1,132	Newmarket -	Hundred of Risbridge.
†Lakenheath - par.	1,877	10,550	11,632	Brandon - -	Hundred of Lackford.
Mildenhall Saint } Andrew's (W.) - } par.	3,764	13,710	19,937	Mildenhall -	do.
Tuddenham Saint } Mary - - } par.	377	2,644	2,090	do. -	do.
Wangford Saint Dennis par.	56	3,252	838	Brandon -	do.
Worlington - - par.	293	2,080	2,028	Soham - -	do.
Total of Union -	8,957	61,244	55,918		

MILE END OLD TOWN HAMLET.

(Board of Guardians constituted 25 Mar. 1857 by Order dated 13 Feb. 1857.)

County of Middlesex :

Mile End Old Town } (W.) - - } ham.	105,613	679	335,344	London, E. -	Tower.

MILTON UNION.

(Formed 25 Mar. 1835 by Order dated 24 Feb. 1835.)

County of Kent :

Bapchild - par.	412	1,085	4,090	Sittingbourne	Faversham.
Bobbing - par.	471	1,068	5,062	do. -	do.
Borden - par.	1,263	2,145	7,640	do. -	do.
Bredgar - par.	616	1,762	3,906	do. -	do
Halstow Lower - par.	721	1,555	6,191	do. -	do.
Hartlip - par.	380	1,422	3,370	do. -	do.
Iwade - par.	235	3,224	5,644	do. -	do.
Kingsdown - par.	77	704	1,095	do. -	do.
Milstead - par.	253	1,226	1,912	do. -	do.
Milton (W.) par.	4,219	2,558	22,415	do. -	do.
Murston - par.	878	1,294	9,013	do. -	do.
Newington - par.	1,038	2,115	10,126	do. -	do.
Rainham - par.	2,719	3,562	15,149	do. -	do.
Rodmersham - par.	428	1,234	3,361	do. -	do.
Sittingbourne - par.	7,856	1,004	25,469	do. -	do.
Tong - par.	314	1,632	5,779	do. -	do.
Tunstall - par.	269	1,200	3,115	do. -	do.
Upchurch - par.	1,121	3,122	10,459	do. -	do.
Total of Union -	23,270	31,912	143,826		

Unions and Parishes, &c.	Population in 1881.	Area in Statute Acres in 1881.	Rateable Value in 1881.	Post Town.	Petty Sessional Division.

MITFORD and LAUN-DITCH UNION.

(Formed 14 May 1836 by Order dated 18 April 1836.)

County of Norfolk :

			£		
Bawdeswell - par.	447	1,196	2,469	East Dereham -	Eynesford.
Beeston with Bitter-ing - par.	503	2,471	4,523	Swaffham -	{ Mitford and Laun-ditch.
Beetley - par.	341	1,770	3,050	East Dereham -	do.
Billingford - par.	315	1,820	2,559	do. -	Eynesford.
Bintree - par.	507	1,455	2,685	do. -	do.
Brisley - par.	345	1,201	2,284	do. -	Mitford and Laun-ditch.
Bylaugh - par.	105	1,546	1,253	do. -	Eynesford.
Colkerk - par.	431	1,482	2,746	Fakenham -	Mitford and Laun-ditch.
Cranworth - par.	239	1,126	1,746	Shipdham -	do.
East Bilney - par.	195	544	1,051	East Dereham -	do.
East Dereham - par.	5,640	5,222	27,492	do. -	do.
East Lexham - par.	191	1,190	1,620	Swaffham -	do.
East Tuddenham - par.	453	2,065	3,343	East Dereham -	do.
Elsing - par.	390	1,511	2,429	do. -	Eynesford.
Foxley - par.	220	1,620	2,429	do. -	do.
Garvestone - par.	336	802	1,880	Hingham -	Mitford and Launditch.
Gateley - par.	154	1,490	2,206	East Dereham -	do.
Great Dunham - par.	394	1,968	3,729	Swaffham -	do.
Great Fransham - par.	328	1,901	3,633	East Dereham -	do.
Gressenhall (W.) - par.	841	2,541	4,784	do. -	do.
Guist - par.	390	1,674	3,118	do. -	Eynesford.
Hardingham - par.	522	2,415	5,387	Hingham -	Mitford and Laun-ditch.
Hockering - par.	372	1,931	3,447	East Dereham -	do.
Hoo - par.	197	1,400	2,696	do. -	do.
Horningtoft - par.	210	1,405	2,193	do. -	do.
Kempston - par.	47	814	1,303	Swaffham -	do.
Letton - par.	114	1,274	1,793	Shipdham -	do.
Litcham - par.	801	1,932	3,865	Swaffham -	do.
Little Dunham - par.	293	1,835	3,132	do. -	do.
Little Fransham - par.	231	1,029	2,019	East Dereham -	do.
Longham - par.	324	1,304	1,876	do. -	do.
Lyng - par.	499	1,899	3,211	Norwich -	Eynesford.
Mattishall - par.	809	2,280	5,685	East Dereham -	Mitford and Launditch.
Mattishall Burgh - par.	145	604	1,293	do. -	do.
Mileham - par.	490	2,851	4,199	Swaffham -	do.
North Elmham - par.	1,090	4,631	7,809	East Dereham -	do.
North Tuddenham - par.	337	2,270	4,348	do. -	do.
Oxwick and Pattesley par.	76	1,039	1,565	Fakenham -	do.
Reymerston - par.	303	1,599	3,005	Hingham -	do.
Rougham - par.	389	2,627	3,833	Swaffham -	do.
Scarning - par.	666	3,470	6,392	East Dereham -	do.
Shipdham - par.	1,526	4,560	9,645	Thetford -	do.
South Burgh - par.	322	1,216	2,052	Shipdham -	do.
Sparham - par.	308	1,770	2,621	Norwich -	Eynesford.
Stanfield - par.	178	903	1,765	East Dereham -	Mitford and Launditch.
Swanton Morley - par.	690	2,714	5,309	do. -	do.
Thuxton - par.	101	1,102	2,155	Hingham -	do.
Tittleshall with God-wick - par.	514	3,361	4,810	Swaffham -	do.
Twyford - par.	58	529	1,062	East Dereham -	Eynesford.
Weasenham, All Saints par.	364	1,988	2,722	Swaffham -	Mitford and Launditch.
Weasenham, Saint Peter's - par.	268	1,423	2,063	do. -	do.
Wellingham - par.	132	1,066	1,527	do. -	do.
Wendling - par.	361	1,436	2,900	East Dereham -	do.
Westfield - par.	112	569	1,189	do. -	do.
West Lexham - par.	134	1,155	1,162	Swaffham -	do.
Whinberg - par.	226	1,211	2,436	East Dereham -	do.
Whissonsett - par.	608	1,344	2,829	do. -	do.
Wood Rising - par.	93	1,363	1,835	Shipdham -	do.
Worthing - par.	113	690	1,238	East Dereham -	do.
Yaxham - par.	489	1,596	3,759	do. -	do.
Total of Union -	27,367	105,233	203,159		

Unions and Parishes, &c.		Population in 1881.	Area in Statute Acres in 1881.	Rateable Value in 1881.	Post Town.	Petty Sessional Division.
MONMOUTH UNION.						
(Formed 11 July 1836 by Order dated 15 June 1836.—Place marked thus * added 30 March 1837 by Order dated 15 March 1837 ; thus † added by Order of 21 Feb. 1843 ; and thus ‡ added 25 Dec. 1861 by Order dated 5 Oct. 1861. Spelling of names of places marked thus § is as altered by Order dated 18 Aug. 1887.)						
COUNTY of GLOUCESTER :				£		
English Bicknor	par.	665	2,377	3,486	Coleford	Coleford.
Newland (a) (b)	tow.	4,812	8,743	17,380	do.	do.
Staunton	par.	121	1,517	2,108	do.	do.
†West Dean (a)	tow.	9,289	10,035	13,250	do.	do.
COUNTY of HEREFORD :						
Ganarew	par.	174	835	1,075	Monmouth	Harewood End.
*Garway	par.	534	3,625	2,993	Ross	do.
Llanrothal (a)	par.	91	1,630	1,270	Monmouth	do.
Welsh Bicknor	par.	99	8,502	1,176	Ross	Ross.
Welsh Newton	par.	225	1,821	1,452	Monmouth	Harewood End
Whitchurch (c)	par.	732	1,956	3,187	Ross	do.
COUNTY of MONMOUTH :						
Cwmcarvan (b)	par.	240	2,875	1,800	Monmouth	Trelleck.
§Dingestow	par.	185	1,972	1,741	do.	Raglan.
§Dixton Newton (a)	par.	772	3,839	4,977	do.	Monmouth.
Llandenny	par.	367	2,302	2,819	Usk	Raglan.
Llandogo	par.	583	1,821	1,859	Coleford	Trelleck.
§Llangattock Vibon Avel	par.	472	4,194	3,653	Monmouth	Skenfrith.
§Llangoven	par.	120	1,898	1,349	do.	Trelleck.
Llanishen (a)	par.	248	1,753	1,248	Chepstow	do.
§Llantilio Crossenny	par.	661	5,951	5,888	Abergavenny	Skenfrith.
Llanvihangel Ystern Lewern	par.	124	1,861	1,466	Monmouth	do.
Mitchel Troy (b)	par.	339	2,017	2,504	do.	Monmouth.
Monmouth with the Borough (W.)	par.	5,586	3,634	17,392	do.	do.
‡Parc Grace Dieu	par.	13	384	179	do.	Raglan.
§Penallt	par.	477	2,375	2,175	do.	Trelleck.
Penrose	par.	302	2,695	2,840	Raglan	Raglan.
Pen y Clawdd (a)	par.	68	614	474	Monmouth	do.
§Raglan	par.	722	4,083	5,870	Newport	do.
Rockfield (a)	par.	227	1,993	2,236	Monmouth	Monmouth.
Saint Maughan's	par.	179	1,304	1,424	do.	Skenfrith.
Skenfrith (a)	par.	624	4,720	3,620	do.	do.
Tregare	par.	281	2,416	2,293	do.	Raglan.
Trelleck	par.	752	5,001	2,842	do.	Trelleck.
Trelleck	tow.	124	566	626	do.	do.
§Wonastow	par.	135	1,615	1,391	do.	Monmouth.
TOTAL of UNION		30,340	102,927	120,043		

MONMOUTH UNION :

(a) By Order which came into operation on 25 March 1883,—
   A detached part of Newland was amalgamated with West Dean ;
   A detached part of Newland was amalgamated with Littledean, in the Westbury Union ;
   A detached part of Rockfield was amalgamated with Skenfrith ;
   A detached part of Dixton with the Hamlets of Dixton Hadnock and Dixton Newton was amalgamated with Llanrothal ;
   A detached part of Llanishen was amalgamated with Pen y Clawdd.

MONMOUTH UNION—continued.

(b) By Provisional Orders which came into operation on 25 March 1884,—
   Two detached parts of Newland were amalgamated with Ruardean, in the Ross Union ;
   A detached part of Mitchel Troy was amalgamated with Cwmcarvan.

(c) Two detached parts of Llangarran, in the Ross Union, were amalgamated with Whitchurch, and a part of Whitchurch was amalgamated with Llangarran, by Provisional Order which came into operation on 25 March 1885.

Unions and Parishes, &c.		Population in 1881.	Area in Statute Acres in 1881.	Rateable Value in 1881.	Post Town.	Petty Sessional Division.
MORPETH UNION.						
(Formed 27th Sept. 1836 by Order dated 1 Sept. 1836. Names of places marked thus * are as altered by Order dated 24 Jan. 1887.)						
COUNTY OF NORTHUMBERLAND:				£		
Ashington and Sheepwash	tow.	88	701	1,669	Morpeth - -	Morpeth
Bedlington - -	par.	11,510	8,436	53,666	Bedlington, R.S.O.	Bedlingtonshire
Benridge - -	tow.	60	1,092	874	Morpeth - -	Morpeth
Biggis Quarter -	tow.	261	2,925	2,362	do. - -	do.
Bockenfield - -	tow.	90	2,375	1,605	Felton - -	do.
Bothal Demesne -	tow.	2,091	3,191	9,017	Morpeth	do.
Bullers Green -	tow.	346	52	699	do. - -	do.
Bullocks Hall -	tow.	11	210	268	Acklington - -	do.
Cambo - -	tow.	90	691	875	Newcastle-on-Tyne	do.
Causey Park -	tow.	82	1,156	608	Morpeth - -	do.
Chevington East -	tow.	1,511	2,240	7,109	Acklington -	do.
Chevington West -	tow.	503	1,859	4,381	do. - -	do.
Cockle Park -	tow.	50	1,407	888	do. - -	do.
Corridge - -	tow.	8	335	445	Newcastle-on-Tyne	do.
Cresswell -	tow.	218	1,098	1,729	Morpeth	do.
Deanham - -	tow.	17	766	839	Newcastle-on-Tyne	do.
Earsdon - -	tow.	64	1,100	852	Morpeth -	do.
Earsdon Forrest -	tow.	24	762	420	do. - -	do.
*East and West Thirston with Shothaugh	tow.	264	1,998	2,457	Acklington -	do.
East Thornton -	tow.	49	1,037	931	Morpeth - -	do.
Edington - -	tow.	34	652	698	do. - -	do.
Ellington - -	tow.	225	2,257	2,260	do. - -	do.
Eshot - -	tow.	140	1,798	1,939	do. - -	do.
Fenrother - -	tow.	64	1,296	889	do. - -	do.
Freeholders Quarter -	tow.	106	899	700	do. - -	do.
Hadstone - -	tow.	81	1,175	2,272	do. - -	do.
Hartburn - -	tow.	32	109	140	do. - -	do.
Hartburn Grange -	tow.	60	1,207	959	do. - -	do.
Hebron - -	tow.	90	1,090	1,025	do. - -	do.
Hepscott - -	tow.	211	1,604	3,564	do. - -	do.
Highlaws - -	tow.	11	312	371	do. - -	do.
Highlaws, High and Low - -	tow.	89	1,369	1,367	do. - -	do.
High Angerton -	tow.	79	1,293	1,942	do. - -	do.
Hurst - -	tow.	27	402	896	do. - -	do.
Linmouth - -	tow.	12	342	364	do. - -	do.
Longhurst - -	tow.	842	1,769	4,407	do. - -	do.
Longshaws - -	tow.	21	797	492	do. - -	do.
Long Witton -	tow.	102	2,400	2,103	do. - -	do.
Lower Angerton -	tow.	53	1,069	1,637	do. - -	do.
Meldon - -	tow.	160	1,028	1,511	do. - -	do.
Mitford - -	tow.	224	1,898	2,193	do. - -	do.
Molesdon - -	tow.	41	827	476	do. - -	do.
Morpeth (W.) -	tow.	5,068	547	11,659	do. - -	Borough of Morpeth.
*Morpeth Castle -	tow.	232	1,522	7,964	do. - -	Morpeth.
Netherwitton -	tow.	215	3,930	2,485	do. - -	do.
Newbiggen on the Sea - -	tow.	1,388	339	4,384	do. - -	do.
Newminster Abbey -	tow.	158	724	1,745	do. - -	do.
Newton Park -	tow.	12	370	230	do. - -	do.
Newton-under-wood	tow.	61	906	1,255	do. - -	do.
North Middleton -	tow.	74	1,146	2,016	do. - -	do.
North Seaton -	tow.	1,943	1,465	5,125	do. - -	do.
Nunriding - -	tow.	33	661	417	do. - -	do.
Old Moor - -	tow.	68	957	2,085	do. - -	do.
Pegswood - -	tow.	968	1,236	3,982	do. - -	do.
Pigdon - -	tow.	45	1,125	821	do. - -	do.
Riddells Quarter -	tow.	127	2,174	1,112	do. - -	do.
Rivergreen - -	tow.	28	529	541	do. - -	do.
South Middleton -	tow.	16	639	500	do. - -	do.
Spittle Hill -	tow.	23	157	408	do. - -	do.
Stanton - -	tow.	91	2,272	1,429	do. - -	do.
Thropple - -	tow.	35	960	802	do. - -	do.

(continued)

Unions and Parishes, &c.	Population in 1881.	Area in Statute Acres in 1881.	Rateable Value in 1881.	Post Town.	Petty Sessional Division.
MORPETH UNION—County of Northumberland—*continued.*			£		
Todridge - - *tow.*	6	60	116	Morpeth - -	Morpeth.
Tranwell and High Church - } *tow.*	100	1,236	2,045	do. - -	do.
Tritlington - - *tow.*	132	1,279	1,089	do. - -	do
Ulgham - - *tow.*	722	3,742	9,904	do. - -	do.
Wallington Demesne *tow.*	166	1,850	2,553	do. - -	do.
West Thornton - *tow.*	75	1,065	1,470	do. - -	do.
Whitridge - - *tow.*	4	201	173	do. - -	do.
Widdrington - - *tow.*	1,038	4,702	6,874	do. - -	do.
Witton Shields - *tow.*	10	371	342	do. - -	do.
Woodhorn - - *tow.*	177	1,485	2,247	do. - -	do.
Woodhorn Demesne - *tow.*	21	312	880	do. - -	do.
TOTAL of UNION - -	36,077	97,186 (a)	203,582		
MUTFORD AND LOTH-INGLAND INCOR-PORATION. (Under the 4 Geo. 3, c. lxxxix, and 3 Will. 4, c. xlix.) COUNTY of SUFFOLK :					
Ashby - - *par.*	110	1,109	1,185	Lowestoft -	Mutford and Lothing-land.
Barnby - - *par.*	260	1,099	1,722	Beccles -	do.
Belton - - *par.*	624	2,059	3,481	Great Yarmouth -	do.
Blundeston - *par.*	714	1,573	3,821	Lowestoft -	do.
Bradwell - - *par.*	540	2,383	4,584	Great Yarmouth -	do.
Burgh Castle - *par.*	518	1,496	3,223	do. -	do.
Carlton Colville - *par.*	1,309	2,804	6,374	Lowestoft -	do.
Corton - - *par.*	552	1,495	2,600	do. -	do.
Flixton - - *par.*	60	602	945	do. -	do.
Fritton - - *par.*	253	1,562	2,187	Great Yarmouth -	do.
Gisleham - - *par.*	301	1,344	2,445	Lowestoft -	do.
Gorleston - - *par.*	9,008	2,175	28,585	Great Yarmouth -	Great Yarmouth.
Gunton - - *par.*	88	1,072	1,057	Lowestoft -	Mutford and Lothing-land.
Herringfleet - *par.*	224	1,720	1,615	do. -	do.
Hopton - - *par.*	320	1,267	2,580	Great Yarmouth -	do.
Kessingland - *par.*	1,229	1,691	4,153	Lowestoft -	do.
Kirtley - - *par.*	2,941	579	13,445	do. -	do.
Lound - - *par.*	440	1,264	3,049	do. -	do.
Lowestoft - - *par.*	16,755	1,685	54,958	do. -	do.
Mutford - - *par.*	394	1,574	2,663	Beccles -	do.
Oulton (W.) - *par.*	1,202	1,997	4,508	Lowestoft -	do.
Pakefield - - *par.*	884	771	2,462	do. -	do.
Rushmere - - *par.*	145	759	1,392	do. -	do.
Somerleyton - *par.*	597	1,410	3,229	do. -	do.
TOTAL of INCORPORATION -	39,478	35,490	156,213		
NANTWICH UNION. (Formed 18 Feb. 1837 by Order dated 24 Jan. 1837, as amended by Order dated 6 Feb. 1837. —Place marked thus * added 21 July 1837 by Order dated 24 June 1837.—Name of Parish marked thus † altered by Order dated 21 Oct. 1884.) COUNTY of CHESTER :					
Acton - - *tow.*	227	725	1,768	Nantwich -	Nantwich.
Alpraham - - *tow.*	438	1,624	3,253	Tarporley -	Eddisbury.

(continued)

MORPETH UNION :

(a) There is an undivided moor containing 23 acres, and a moor known as Horsley Moor, containing 192 acres, common to Biggis Quarter, Freeholders Quarter, Riddells Quarter, and Fenrother.

Unions and Parishes, &c.		Population in 1881.	Area in Statute Acres in 1881.	Rateable Value in 1881.	Post Town.	Petty Sessional Division.
NANTWICH UNION—County of Chester—*continued.*				£		
Alvaston	tow.	57	621	498	Nantwich	Nantwich.
†Aston juxta Mondrum	tow.	183	1,257	2,278	do.	do.
Audlem	tow.	1,520	2,388	6,877	do.	do.
Austerson	tow.	61	950	1,166	do.	do.
Baddiley	par.	285	1,981	3,207	do.	do.
Baddington	tow.	147	1,446	2,122	do.	do.
Bartherton	tow.	25	428	614	Nantwich	do.
Barthomley	tow.	372	1,961	3,799	Crewe	do.
Basford	tow.	77	671	4,190	Nantwich	do.
Breston	tow.	328	1,965	3,905	Tarporley	Eddisbury.
Bickerton	tow.	325	1,694	2,062	Whitchurch, Salop	Broxton.
Blakenhall	tow.	193	1,640	5,276	Nantwich	Nantwich.
Bridgemere	tow.	134	1,130	1,516	do.	do.
Brindley	tow.	185	1,098	1,664	do.	do.
Bromhall	tow.	127	1,332	1,903	do.	do.
Buerton	tow.	471	2,981	1,296	do.	do.
Bulkeley or Buckley	tow.	172	975	1,407	Malpas	Broxton.
Bunbury	tow.	881	1,161	3,141	Tarporley	Eddisbury.
Burland	tow.	657	1,568	2,962	Nantwich	Nantwich.
Burwardsley	tow.	410	1,058	1,641	Tarporley	Eddisbury.
Calveley	tow.	279	1,546	3,149	do.	do.
Checkley with Wrine-hill	tow.	170	1,433	3,706	Nantwich	Nantwich.
Cholmondeley	tow.	285	2,657	3,268	Malpas	Broxton.
Cholmondstone	tow.	187	1,749	2,813	Over	Nantwich.
Chorley	tow.	166	1,400	1,838	Nantwich	do.
Chorlton	tow.	78	839	4,411	do.	do.
Cool Pilate	tow.	60	715	1,035	do.	do.
Coppenhall Church	tow.	2,879	1,535	10,528	Crewe	do.
Coppenhall Monks	tow.	24,385	1,336	70,004	do.	do.
Crewe	tow.	423	2,033	8,317	do.	do.
Dodcot cum Wilkesley	tow.	654	5,802	8,717	Whitchurch, Salop	do.
Doddington	tow.	47	597	937	Nantwich	do.
Eaton	tow.	465	1,344	2,781	Tarporley	Eddisbury.
Eddleston	tow.	81	640	1,402	Nantwich	Nantwich.
Egerton	tow.	127	942	1,195	Malpas	Broxton.
Faddiley	tow.	234	1,207	1,961	Nantwich	Nantwich.
Hankelow	tow.	219	672	1,535	do.	do.
Haslington	tow.	1,814	3,789	7,138	Crewe	do.
Hatherton	tow.	322	1,666	2,742	Nantwich	do.
Haughton	tow.	131	1,098	1,686	Tarporley	Eddisbury.
Henhull	tow.	143	509	1,160	Nantwich	Nantwich.
Hough	tow.	275	987	1,850	do.	do.
Hunsterston	tow.	193	1,570	1,808	do.	do.
Hurleston	tow.	124	1,376	2,379	do.	do.
Lea	tow.	70	427	595	do.	do.
Leighton	tow.	172	1,266	1,816	Middlewich	do.
Minshull Church	par.	377	2,345	3,631	do.	do.
*Minshull Vernon	tow.	329	2,737	8,351	do.	Northwich.
Nantwich (W.)	tow.	7,495	703	16,108	Nantwich	Nantwich.
Newhall	tow.	712	4,159	6,382	do.	do.
Peckforton	tow.	208	1,754	2,230	Tarporley	Eddisbury.
Poole	tow.	146	762	1,440	Nantwich	Nantwich.
Ridley	tow.	98	1,458	1,752	Tarporley	Eddisbury.
Rope	tow.	81	613	1,259	Nantwich	Nantwich.
Rushton	tow.	334	1,797	2,807	Tarporley	Eddisbury.
Shavington with Gresty	tow.	1,067	1,154	3,365	Nantwich	Nantwich.
Sound	tow.	274	1,080	1,791	do.	do.
Spurston	tow.	451	1,821	2,855	Tarporley	Eddisbury.
Stapely	tow.	602	1,249	3,072	Nantwich	Nantwich.
Stoke	tow.	197	661	1,361	do.	do.
Tarporley	tow.	1,350	1,164	4,433	Tarporley	Eddisbury.
Tilston Fernall	tow.	149	889	1,756	do.	do.
Tiverton	tow.	520	1,705	3,286	do.	do.
Utkington	tow.	520	1,889	3,538	do.	do.
Walgherton	tow.	166	883	1,294	Nantwich	Nantwich.
Wardle	tow.	152	1,062	1,912	Tarporley	Eddisbury.
Warmingham	tow.	320	2,121	3,692	Sandbach	Northwich.
Weston	tow.	519	1,944	3,863	Crewe	Nantwich.
Wettenhall	tow.	214	1,976	2,535	Over	Eddisbury.

(continued)

Unions and Parishes, &c.		Population in 1881.	Area in Statute Acres in 1881.	Rateable Value in 1881.	Post Town.	Petty Sessional Division.
NANTWICH UNION—County of Chester—*continued.*				£		
Willaston	- *tow.*	1,986	1,010	5,165	Nantwich -	Nantwich.
Wistaston	- *par.*	407	1,472	3,192	do. -	do.
Woodcot	- *tow.*	33	162	344	do. -	do.
Woolstanwood	- *tow.*	117	612	1,376	do. -	do.
Worleston	- *tow.*	338	1,151	2,650	do. -	do.
Wrenbury with Frith	*tow.*	509	2,184	3,573	do. -	do.
Wybunbury	- *tow.*	595	870	2,080	do. -	do.
TOTAL of UNION	-	61,566	113,165	309,409		

NARBERTH UNION.						
(Formed 6 Jan. 1837 by Order dated 17 Dec. 1836.—Places marked thus * added 25 Aug. 1837 by Order dated 31 July 1837. Names of places marked thus † are as altered by Order dated 4 Feb. 1887).						
COUNTY of CARMARTHEN:						
Castle-dyran	- *ham.*	87	666	635	Narberth -	Llanboidy.
Cily Maenlwyd	- *ham.*	487	3,505	2,030	do. -	do.
Cyffic	- *par.*	452	4,556	2,315	do. -	do.
Eglwyscymmin	- *par.*	245	3,740	1,523	do. -	Saint Clears.
*Eglwysfair a Churig	- *cha.*	243	2,618	1,063	do. -	Llanboidy.
Egremont	- *par.*	114	1,006	738	do. -	do.
Henllan Amgoed	- *ham.*	145	1,033	912	do. -	do.
Llanboidy	- *par.*	1,548	10,666	6,912	Saint Clears -	do.
†Llandissilio East	- *dir.*	611	4,719	3,418	Narberth -	do.
Llangan East	- *par.*	734	4,758	3,834	do. -	do.
*Llanglydwen	- *par.*	298	1,834	908	do. -	do.
†Llanfallteg East	- *dir.*	318	1,448	1,214	do. -	do.
Marros	- *par.*	145	2,574	696	do. -	Saint Clears.
Pendine	- *par.*	169	1,578	564	Saint Clears -	do.
COUNTY of PEMBROKE:						
Amroth	- *par.*	733	2,878	2,371	Narberth -	Narberth.
Begelly	- *ham.*	558	2,447	2,041	do. -	do.
Bletherstone	- *par.*	244	2,366	1,705	do. -	Dungleddy.
Clarbeston	- *par.*	153	1,588	1,263	do. -	do.
Coadcanlass	- *par.*	84	843	527	do. -	Narberth.
Crinow	- *par.*	65	352	603	do. -	do.
Cronwear	- *par.*	212	1,690	1,149	do. -	do.
East Williamston	- *cha.*	493	1,431	1,383	do. -	do.
*Grondre	- *ham.*	59	210	207	do. -	Dungleddy.
Jeffreyston	- *par.*	494	2,357	2,184	do. -	Narberth.
Llampeter Velfrey	- *par.*	975	5,667	6,090	do. -	do.
Llanddewi Velfrey	- *par.*	602	4,022	4,398	do. -	do.
Llandilo	- *par.*	97	1,132	297	do. -	Kemes.
†Llandissilio West	- *dir.*	404	1,748	1,623	do. -	Dungleddy.
*†Llangan West	- *par.*	34	194	235	do. -	Narberth.
Llangolman	- *par.*	264	2,912	1,185	do. -	Kemes.
Llanhaden	- *par.*	538	4,490	3,603	do. -	Narberth.
†Llanfallteg West	- *dir.*	72	418	527	do. -	Dungleddy.
Llanycefn	- *par.*	379	2,684	1,916	do. -	do.
Llys y fran	- *par.*	194	1,466	1,022	Haverfordwest -	do.
Loveston	- *par.*	126	1,233	749	Narberth -	Narberth.
Ludchurch	- *par.*	215	1,607	808	do. -	do.
Maenlochog	- *tow.*	480	2,754	959	do. -	Dungleddy.
Mertletwy	- *par.*	374	3,331	2,167	do. -	Narberth.
Monachlogdo	- *par.*	481	6,166	1,294	do. -	Kemes.
Mounton	- *par.*	33	330	207	do. -	Narberth.
Mynwer	- *par.*	49	1,957	1,051	do. -	do.
Newmoat	- *par.*	305	3,101	1,959	do. -	Dungleddy.

(continued)

Unions and Parishes, &c.	Population in 1881.	Area in Statute Acres in 1881.	Rateable Value in 1881.	Post Town.	Petty Sessional Division.
NARBERTH UNION—County of Pembroke— *continued.*			£		
Newton - - *par.*	43	721	556	Narberth - -	Narberth.
North Narberth - *dir.*	1,654	6,084	5,644	do. - -	do.
Reynelton - - *par.*	71	525	316	do. - -	do.
Robeston Wathon - *par.*	319	1,345	1,544	do. - -	do.
Saint Issells - - *par.*	1,968	3,830	6,259	do. - -	do.
Slebech - - *par.*	363	4,586	2,636	do. - -	Dungleddy.
South Narberth (W.) *dir.*	680 {	In North Narberth }	3,000	do. - -	Narberth.
*Vorlan - - *ham.*	30 {	In Maen-lochog }	192	do. - -	Dungleddy.
Yerbeston - - *par.*	100	1,252	649	do. - -	Narberth.
TOTAL of UNION -	19,511	124,418	91,116		

NEATH UNION.

(Formed 2 Sept. 1836 by Order dated 6 Aug. 1836.— Place marked thus * added 24 Nov. 1836 by Order dated 29 Oct. 1836.)

Unions and Parishes, &c.	Population in 1881.	Area in Statute Acres in 1881.	Rateable Value in 1881.	Post Town.	Petty Sessional Division.
COUNTY of BRECON:					
Ystradfellte - *par.*	587	19,025	3,708	Penderyn, Aberdare	Penderyn.
COUNTY of GLAMORGAN:					
Aberafon - - *par.*	4,681	1,331	8,513	Port Talbot -	Borough of Aberavon.
Baglan Higher - *ham.*	143	1,718	450	Briton Ferry -	Neath.
Baglan Lower - *ham.*	529	2,393	3,806	do. - -	do.
Blaengwrach - *cha.*	267	2,871	3,279	Neath - -	do.
Blaenhonnda (W.) - *ham.*	2,363	3,739	10,600	do. - -	do.
Britonferry - - *par.*	6,061	1,522	13,369	Briton Ferry -	do.
Clyne - - *ham.*	285	2,184	2,307	Resolven, Neath -	do.
Coedfrank - - *ham.*	3,522	3,681	9,266	Skewen, Neath -	do.
Duffryn Clydach - *ham.*	1,222	1,725	5,799	do. - -	do.
Dylais Lower - *ham.*	331	5,228	1,850	Crynant, Neath -	do.
Dylais Upper - *ham.*	849	6,261	2,103	do. - -	do.
Glyncorwg (a) - *ham.*	1,288	8,221	4,950	Maesteg, Bridgend	do.
*HigherLlangonoyd(a) *ham.*	2,444	6,526	7,460	do. - -	Bridgend.
Llantwit Lower - *ham.*	2,890	4,301	6,950	Neath - -	Neath.
Margam - - *par.*	5,708	18,347	23,449	Port Talbot -	do.
Michaelstone super Afon Lower } *ham.*	4,924	1,019	10,021	do. - -	Bridgend.
Michaelstone super Afon Upper } *ham.*	569	4,088	1,065	do. - -	do.
Neath Higher - *ham.*	1,320	3,601	4,164	Glyn-Neath, nr. Neath	do.
Neath Lower - *ham.*	261	2,101	750	Resolven, Neath -	Neath.
Neath Middle - *ham.*	193	3,270	1,588	Glyn-Neath, nr. Neath	do.
Neath (Parish and Town) (W.) } *par.*	10,347	1,161	29,480	Neath - -	do.
Resolvend - - *ham.*	1,293	4,671	4,946	Resolven, Neath -	do.
TOTAL of UNION -	52,077	108,984	159,873		

NEATH UNION:

(a) By an Order which came into operation on 25 March 1885, all the part of Higher Llangonoyd, situate outside the Maesteg local Government District, was amalgamated with Glyncorwg.

Unions and Parishes, &c.	Population in 1881.	Area in Statute Acres in 1881.	Rateable Value in 1881.	Post Town.	Petty Sessional Division.

NEWARK UNION.

(Formed 24 Mar. 1836 by Order dated 9 Mar. 1836.—Places marked thus * added 9 May 1836 by Order dated 12 April 1836 ; thus † added 29 Sept. 1836 by Order dated 15 Sept. 1836 ; thus ‡ added 25 Dec. 1860 by Order dated 2 Nov. 1860; and thus § added 30 Sept. 1861 by Order dated 6 July 1861.)

COUNTY of LINCOLN :

Unions and Parishes, &c.	Population in 1881.	Area in Statute Acres in 1881.	Rateable Value in 1881.	Post Town.	Petty Sessional Division.
			£		
Barkston - - *par.*	499	2,083	4,204	Grantham -	Spittlegate.
Bassingham - *par.*	725	1,940	4,788	Newark - -	Lincoln.
Beckingham - *par.*	346	2,200	3,340	do. - -	Spittlegate.
§Bennington Grange - *par.*	14 { In Long Bennington }		223	do. -	do.
Brant Broughton - *par.*	679	2,932	5,902	do. -	do.
Carlton le Moorland - *par.*	310	2,610	3,542	do. - -	Lincoln.
Caythorpe - - *par.*	897	4,210	8,757	Grantham -	Sleaford.
Claypole (W.) - *par.*	678	3,370	7,928	Newark -	Spittlegate.
Doddington - - *par.*	225	2,160	3,804	Grantham -	do.
East and West Allington *par.*	331	2,070	3,154	do. -	do.
Fenton - - *par.*	84	1,220	1,766	Newark -	do.
Foston - - *par.*	357	2,180	3,163	Grantham -	do.
Fulbeck - - *par.*	645	3,900	5,927	do. - -	do.
Honghan - - *par.*	271	2,590	8,312	do. - -	do.
Long Bennington - *par.*	910	4,420	6,427	do. - -	do.
Marston - - *par.*	307	2,430	3,134	do. - -	do.
North Scarle - - *par.*	515	1,955	2,602	Newark -	Lincoln.
Norton Disney - *par.*	171	2,305	2,196	do. - -	do.
Sedgebrook - - *par.*	221	1,642	3,805	Grantham -	Spittlegate.
Stapleford (a) - *par.*	154	2,930	2,256	Newark -	Lincoln.
Stragglethorpe - *par.*	90	1,150	1,209	do. - -	Spittlegate.
Stubton - - *par.*	132	860	2,390	do. - -	do.
Swinderby - - *par.*	503	1,640	2,794	Lincoln -	Lincoln.
Syston - - *par.*	224	1,613	3,175	Grantham -	Spittlegate.
Thurlby - - *par.*	118	1,802	2,203	Newark -	Lincoln.
Westborough - *par.*	181	890	2,965	Grantham -	Spittlegate.

COUNTY of NOTTINGHAM :

Unions and Parishes, &c.	Population in 1881.	Area in Statute Acres in 1881.	Rateable Value in 1881.	Post Town.	Petty Sessional Division.
*Alverton - - *ham.*	17 { In Kilving- ton. }		607	Orston, Nottingham	Newark.
Balderton - - *par.*	1,075	4,050	9,342	Newark -	do.
Barnby (a) - - *par.*	218	1,703	2,818	do. - -	do.
Besthorpe - - *tow.*	192	510	1,970	do. - -	do.
†Broadholme - *tow.*	95	In Thorney	748	Lincoln -	do.
Coddington - *par.*	521	1,850	2,713	Newark -	do.
Cotham - - *par.*	130	1,210	2,131	do. - -	do.
Farndon (a) - *par.*	698	1,710	5,482	do. - -	do.
Girton - - *par.*	150	1,075	1,439	do. - -	do.
†Harby - - *tow.*	352	5,050	1,526	do. - -	do.
Hawton - - *par.*	286	2,160	4,141	do. - -	do.
Kilvington - - *ham.*	24	900	931	Orston, Nottingham	do.

(continued)

NEWARK UNION :

(a) By Orders which came into operation on 25 March 1884,—
A detached part of Farndon was amalgamated with Newark ;
A detached part of Winthorpe was amalgamated with Holme, in the Southwell Union ;
All that part of Flawford which was situate in the County of Nottingham, was amalgamated with Barnby ; and
All that part of Flawford which was situate in the County of Lincoln was amalgamated with Stapleford. (Flawford in 1881 contained population 14, acreage 272, and rateable value 163l.)

(b) By Provisional Order which came into operation on 25 March 1885, all the part of Marnham (in the East Retford Union), situate east of the River Trent, was amalgamated with South Clifton.

Unions and Parishes, &c.		Population in 1851.	Area in Statute Acres in 1881.	Rateable Value in 1881.	Post Town.	Petty Sessional Division.
NEWARK UNION—County of Nottingham—*continued.*				£		
Langford	- par.	167	2,182	2,929	Newark - -	Newark.
†Mering -	- par.	3	458	862	do. - -	do.
Newark (W.) (*a*)	- par.	14,683	2,018	47,799	do. - -	Borough of Newark.
†North Clifton	- tow.	184	In Harby	1,632	do. - -	Newark.
North Collingham	- par.	928	1,820	6,151	do. - -	do.
*South Clifton (*b*)	- tow.	270	In Harby	1,882	do. - -	do.
South Collingham	- par.	776	2,763	5,281	do. - -	do.
South Searle	- tow.	156	1,510	1,130	do. - -	do.
*Spalford -	- tow.	89	In Harby	783	do. - -	do.
Staunton	- tow.	95	1,410	2,016	Orston, Nottingham	do.
†Thorney -	- tow.	162 }	4,140 {	2,056	Lincoln - -	do.
†Wiggesley	- tow.	91 }		923	Newark - -	do.
Winthorpe (*a*)	- par.	256	680	1,789	do. - -	do.
TOTAL of UNION	-	30,602 (*a*)	94,331 (*a*)	209,347 (*a*)		
NEWBURY UNION.						
(Formed 7 April 1835 by Order dated 23 Mar. 1835.)						
COUNTY of BERKS :						
Boxford -	- par.	568	2,819	4,295	Newbury - -	Newbury.
Brimpton	- par.	427	1,705	3,450	Reading -	do.
Chieveley -	- par.	1,164	5,328	8,057	Newbury - -	do.
Enborne -	- par.	413	2,501	3,811	do. - -	do.
Greenham -	- ty.	1,586	2,564	6,756	do. - -	do. and Borough of Newbury.
Hampstead-Marshall	par.	249	1,852	2,514	do. - -	do.
Leckhamstead -	ty. & cha.	311	1,777	2,452	do. - -	do.
Midgham -	- ty.	298	1,436	3,165	Reading - -	do.
Newbury (W.)	- par.	7,017	1,242	22,202	Newbury - -	Borough of Newbury.
Sandleford -	- par.	34	520	651	do. - -	Newbury.
Shaw cum Donnington	par.	703	1,996	4,127	do. - -	do.
Speen - -	- par.	3,592	3,862	16,606	do. - -	do. and Borough of Newbury.
Thatcham -	- par.	2,882	7,865	15,706	do. - -	do.
Wasing -	- par.	80	690	765	Reading - -	do.
Welford -	- par.	943	5,228	6,945	Newbury and Lambourn, R.S.O.	do.
Winterbourne -	ty. & cha.	340	2,112	3,410	do. - -	do.
Woolhampton	- par.	493	719	2,585	Reading - -	do.
COUNTY of SOUTHAMPTON :						
Newtown -	- par.	227	479	820	Newbury - -	Kingsclere.
TOTAL of UNION	-	21,327	44,695	108,317		
NEWCASTLE-IN-EMLYN UNION.						
(Formed 31 May 1837 by Order dated 5 May 1837. — Places marked thus * added 23 April 1838 by Order dated 28 Mar. 1838.)						
COUNTY of CARDIGAN :						
Bangor -	- par.	181	1,392	948	Llandyssil - -	Llandysil.
Bettws Evan -	- par.	392	2,640	1,296	New Castle Emlyn	Penbriwpial.
Brongwyn -	- par.	269	1,620	1,090	do. - -	do.
Henllan -	- par.	117	387	244	Llandyssil -	do.
Llandyfriog -	- par.	794	2,867	2,194	New Castle Emlyn	do.
Llandyssil -	- par.	2,971	17,556	7,825	Llandyssil - -	Llandyssil.
Llanfair Orllwyn	- par.	425	1,744	1,112	do. - -	Penbriwpial.
Llanfair Treflygon	- par.	79	648	325	New Castle Emlyn	do.

(*continued*)

NEWARK UNION.

(*a*) (*b*) See notes, page 245.

Unions and Parishes, &c.		Population in 1881.	Area in Statute Acres in 1881.	Rateable Value in 1881.	Post Town.	Petty Sessional Division.
NEWCASTLE-IN-EMLYN UNION—County of Cardigan—continued.				£		
Llangranog	par.	786	4,383	1,942	Llandyssil - -	Penbriwpal.
Llangynllo	par.	581	3,650	1,744	do. - -	do.
Penbryn	par.	1,391	8,347	4,006	Rhydlewis, R.S.O.	do.
Troed yr aur	par.	836	4,660	2,582	do. - -	do.
COUNTY OF CARMARTHEN :						
Cenarth (W.)	par.	1,696	6,429	3,918	New Castle Emlyn	New Castle Emlyn.
Llanfihangel ar Arth	par.	1,959	15,993	5,542	Carmarthen -	Llanfihangel-ar-Arth.
Llangeler	par.	1,610	7,999	4,111	Llandyssil - -	New Castle Emlyn.
Penboyr	par.	1,284	6,876	2,738	Velindre, Carmarthenshire.	do.
COUNTIES OF CARMARTHEN and PEMBROKE :						
Cilrhedyn	par.	968	7,856	2,733	New Castle Emlyn	New Castle Emlyn.
COUNTY OF PEMBROKE :						
*Capel Coleman	par.	117	770	162	Boncath, R.S.O. -	Cilgerran.
*Castellan	cha.	172	899	357	Blaenffos, R.S.O. -	do.
Clyde	par.	1,114	8,120	2,670	Llanfyrnach, R.S.O.	do.
Llanfyrnach	par.	1,006	6,328	3,226	do. - -	Eglwysurw.
Penrydd	tow.	236	2,182	652	do. - -	Cilgerran.
TOTAL OF UNION -		19,014	113,346	51,787		
NEWCASTLE UNDER LYME UNION.						
(Formed 3 April 1838 by Order dated 1 March 1838.)						
COUNTY OF STAFFORD :						
Audley	par.	11,505	8,727	40,895	Newcastle - under - Lyme.	Pirehill North.
Balterley	tow.	253	1,231	2,265	Crewe - -	do.
Betley	par.	821	1,463	3,473	do. - -	do.
Chapel Chorlton	tow.	380	1,983	5,915	Newcastle - under - Lyme.	do.
Keel	par.	1,048	2,613	6,887	do. - -	do.
Madeley	par.	2,457	5,861	18,869	do. - -	do.
Maer	par.	393	2,750	5,830	do. - -	do.
Newcastle under Lyme (W.) - }	par.	17,493	621	39,879	do. - -	{ Borough of Newcastle-under-Lyme.
Whitmore	par.	311	2,015	4,559	do. - -	Pirehill North.
TOTAL OF UNION -		34,661	27,270	126,572		
NEWCASTLE UPON TYNE UNION.						
(Formed 26 Sept. 1836 by Order dated 29 Aug. 1836.)						
CITY AND COUNTY OF NEWCASTLE-UPON-TYNE :						
All Saints	tow.	26,549	280	125,927	Newcastle-upon-Tyne	Newcastle-upon-Tyne.
Byker	tow.	21,011	879	46,607	do. - -	do.
Elswick (W.)	tow.	34,612	807	119,250	do. - -	do.
Heaton	tow.	1,466	909	10,123	do. - -	do.
Jessmond	tow.	6,109	700	40,048	do. - -	do.
Saint Andrew's	tow.	18,731	1,440	125,019	do. - -	do.
Saint John's	tow.	5,709	87	81,410	do. - -	do.
Saint Nicholas	par.	4,319	14	46,648	do. - -	do.
Westgate	tow.	26,823	225	92,184	do. - -	do.
COUNTY OF NORTHUMBERLAND :						
Benwell	tow.	4,736	1,302	21,531	do. - -	Castle Ward (West Division).
Fenham	tow.	157	134	2,741	do. - -	do.
TOTAL OF UNION -		150,252	7,107	711,488		

Unions and Parishes, &c.		Population in 1881.	Area in Statute Acres in 1881.	Rateable Value in 1881.	Post Town.	Petty Sessional Division.

NEWENT UNION.

(Formed 23 Sept. 1835 by Order dated 7 Sept. 1835.)

COUNTY of GLOUCESTER:

				£		
Bromsberrow	-	par.	266	1,803	2,451	Ledbury -	Newent.
Corse	-	par.	513	2,190	3,044	Gloucester	do.
Dymock	-	par.	1,529	6,875	11,055	Newent	do.
Hartpury	-	par.	803	3,618	5,514	Gloucester -	Gloucester.
High Leadon	-	ham.	96	In Rudford	1,152	Newent -	Newent.
Kempley	-	par.	281	1,564	1,707	Ross -	do.
Newent (W.)	-	par.	2,889	7,803	15,230	Gloucester -	do.
Oxenhall (a)	-	par.	231	1,887	2,816	Newent -	do.
Pauntley (a)	-	par.	216	1,967	2,445	do. -	do.
Preston	-	par.	61	884	1,097	Ledbury -	do.
Rudford (a)	-	par.	124	1,204	1,030	Gloucester -	do.
Taynton	-	par.	568	2,501	3,578	do. -	do.
Tibberton	-	par.	363	1,400	2,731	do. -	do.
Up Leadon	-	par.	232	1,207	1,982	Newent	do.

COUNTY of HEREFORD:

Aston Ingham	-	par.	518	2,378	2,919	Ross -	Ross.
Linton	-	par.	927	2,775	4,132	do. -	do.

COUNTY of WORCESTER:

Redmarley D'Abitot	-	par.	1,000	3,778	5,850	Newent -	Upton-on-Severn.
Staunton	-	par.	413	1,447	2,317	Gloucester -	do.
TOTAL of UNION	-		11,030	45,281	71,080		

NEWHAVEN UNION.

(Formed 2 Feb. 1835 by Order dated 1 Jan. 1835.—Places marked thus * added 18 April 1835 by Order dated 19 March 1835.)

COUNTY of SUSSEX:

Bishopstone	-	par.	277	1,801	2,302	Lewes -	Lewes Division of Pevensey Rape.
Denton	-	par.	486	1,016	1,755	do. -	do.
East Blatchington	-	par.	213	735	1,285	Seaford -	do.
Falmer	-	par.	577	1,393	5,720	Lewes -	do.
Heighton	-	par.	89	930	690	do. -	do.
*Iford	-	par.	181	2,200	2,475	do. -	do.
*Kingston	-	par.	120	1,676	2,004	do. -	do.
Newhaven (W.)	-	par.	4,009	933	9,393	do. -	do.
Ovingdean	-	par.	136	1,630	2,860	Brighton	do.
Piddinghoe	-	par.	225	2,347	2,071	Lewes -	do.
Rodmell	-	par.	233	1,936	2,194	do. -	do.
Rotting Dean	-	par.	1,673	3,154	6,763	Brighton -	do.
Southease	-	par.	100	850	1,130	Lewes -	do.
Stanmer	-	par.	129	1,341	1,105	do. -	do.
Tarring Neville	-	par.	65	933	1,081	do. -	do.
Telscombe	-	par.	94	1,181	1,112	do. -	do.
TOTAL of UNION	-		8,607	27,056	43,940		

NEWENT UNION:

(a) By Orders which came into operation on 25 March 1883,—

A detached part of Pauntley was amalgamated with Oxenhall; and

A detached part of Rudford was amalgamated with Over Higham and Linton, in the Gloucester Union.

Unions and Parishes, &c.	Population in 1881.	Area in Statute Acres in 1881.	Rateable Value in 1881.	Post Town.	Petty Sessional Division.

NEWMARKET UNION.

(Formed 30 Dec. 1835 by Order dated 14 Dec. 1835.)

COUNTY of CAMBRIDGE :

£

Unions and Parishes, &c.	Population in 1881.	Area in Statute Acres in 1881.	Rateable Value in 1881.	Post Town.	Petty Sessional Division.
All Saints, Newmarket *par.*	1,364	320	7,039	Newmarket "	Newmarket, Cambs.
Ashley cum Silverly - *par.*	485	2,143	3,472	do. -	do.
Borough Green - *par.*	404	2,217	3,715	do. -	do.
Bottisham - *par.*	1,555	4,700	10,397	Cambridge -	Bottisham.
Brinkley (b) - *par.*	297	1,500	2,324	Newmarket -	Newmarket, Cambs.
Burwell - *par.*	1,949	7,232	19,921	Cambridge -	do.
Cheveley - *par.*	632	2,527	4,686	Newmarket -	do.
Chippenham - *par.*	646	4,205	5,575	Soham -	do.
Dullingham - *par.*	835	3,210	5,423	Newmarket -	do.
Fordham - *par.*	1,191	4,050	8,728	Soham -	do.
Isleham - *par.*	1,697	5,211	10,077	do. -	do.
Kennett - *par.*	174	1,425	1,784	Newmarket -	do.
Kirtling - *par.*	821	3,016	4,676	do. -	do.
Landwade - *par.*	28	120	210	do. -	do.
Snailwell - *par.*	186	2,014	3,464	Newmarket "	do.
Soham - *par.*	3,980	12,706	31,533	Soham -	do.
Stechworth - *par.*	608	2,824	4,785	Newmarket -	do.
Swaffham Bulbeck - *par.*	744	3,000	6,679	Cambridge -	Bottisham.
Swaffham Prior - *par.*	1,078	5,297	9,417	do. -	do.
Westley - *par.*	179	1,102	2,013	Newmarket -	Newmarket, Cambs.
Wicken - *par.*	844	3,812	7,954	Soham -	do.
Wood Ditton - *par.*	1,546	4,899	10,465	Newmarket -	do.
COUNTY of SUFFOLK :					
Dalham - *par.*	419	1,840	3,328	Newmarket -	Newmarket, Suffolk.
Exning (W.) - *par.*	1,791	5,710	15,324	do. -	do.
Gazeley - *par.*	835	5,899	8,509	do. and Bury Saint Edmunds (as to part) and Mildenhall (as to part).	do.
Lidgate - *par.*	417	1,780	2,773	Newmarket -	do.
Moulton - *par.*	505	3,134	5,026	do. -	do.
Ousden (a) - *par.*	307	1,200	2,195	do. -	do.
Saint Mary's, Newmarket - *par.*	2,730	250	11,232	do. -	do.
TOTAL of UNION -	28,247	97,373	212,727		

NEWPORT UNION (MON.)

(Formed 1 August 1836 by Order dated 5 July 1836. Spelling of name of place marked thus* is as altered by Order dated 24 Sept. 1887.)

COUNTY of GLAMORGAN :

Unions and Parishes, &c.	Population in 1881.	Area in Statute Acres in 1881.	Rateable Value in 1881.	Post Town.	Petty Sessional Division.
Llanvedow - *ham.*	304 *	2,453	2,264	Cardiff -	Newport, Monmouth.
Rhydgwern - *ham.*	248	722	793	Newport (Mon.) -	do.
COUNTY of MONMOUTH :					
Bedwas - *par.*	1,531	4,195	5,859	Caerphilly -	Bedwellty.
Bettws - *par.*	86	1,132	1,492	Newport (Mon.) -	Newport (Mon.)
Bishton - *par.*	154	1,211	3,388	do. -	Christchurch.
Caerleon - *tow.*	1,099	2,937	4,380	Caerleon -	Caerleon.
*Christchurch with Caerleon ultra Pontem - *par.*	6,524	5,757	31,438	Newport (Mon.) -	Christchurch.
Coedkernew - *par.*	165	765	977	Castletown, Cardiff	Newport (Mon.)
Duffryn - *ham.*	263 { In Rogerstone }		1,178	Newport (Mon.) -	do.
Goldcliff - *par.*	228	14,262	4,110	do. -	Christchurch.
Graig - *ham.*	949 { In Rogerstone }		4,284	do. -	Newport (Mon.) (continued)

(continued)

NEWMARKET UNION :

(a) By Order which came into operation on 25 March 1884, a detached part of Ousden, known as "Little Ousden," was amalgamated with Hargrave, in the Thingoe Union.

NEWMARKET UNION—*continued.*

(b) By Order which came into operation on 25 March 1886, a detached part of Brinkley was amalgamated with Carlton, in the Linton Union.

Unions and Parishes, &c.			Population in 1881.	Area in Statute Acres in 1881.	Rateable Value in 1881.	Post Town.	Petty Sessional Division.
NEWPORT UNION—County of Monmouth—continued.					£		
Hentlis	-	par.	334	2,622	2,733	Newport (Mon.) -	Newport (Mon.)
Kemeys Inferior	-	par.	127	1,676	1,731	Caerleon - -	Caerleon.
Llandevenny -	-	ham.	56	252	1,175	Newport (Mon.) -	Newport (Mon.)
Llangattock (juxta Caerleon) -	}	tow.	253	In Caerleon	3,075	Caerleon - -	Caerleon.
Llangston with Llanbedo	}	par.	174	1,314	1,673	Newport (Mon.) -	Newport (Mon.)
Llanhennock	-	par.	223	1,506	1,832	Caerleon - -	Caerleon.
Llanmartin with Llanbedar	}	par.	175	941	1,306	Newport (Mon.) -	Christchurch.
Llanvaches	-	par.	223	2,108	1,813	do. - -	do.
Llanvihangel Llantarnam	}	par.	3,991	4,092	14,902	do. - -	Caerleon.
Llanwern	-	par.	14	701	2,225	do. - -	Christchurch.
Lower Machin	-	ham.	1,036	2,000	4,033	do. - -	Newport (Mon.)
Magor	-	tow.	440	2,720	4,430	do. - -	Christchurch.
Malpas	-	par.	320	988	3,958	do. - -	Newport (Mon.)
Marshfield	-	par.	520	1,270	2,593	Castletown, Cardiff	do.
Michaelstone Vedow	ham.		201	1,134	1,160	Newport (Mon.) -	do.
Mynyddyslwyn	-	par.	8,827	16,077	38,889	Newport (Mon.) -	Bedwellty.
Nash -	-	par.	239	3,563	5,572	do. - -	Christchurch.
Newport	-	tow.	10,423 {	In St. Woollos }	50,634	do. - -	Newport (Mon.)
Penhow	-	par.	245	1,784	1,771	do. - -	Christchurch.
Peterstone	-	par.	156	3,234	5,419	Castletown, Cardiff	Newport (Mon.)
Redwick	-	cha.	260	7,794	5,176	Newport (Mon.) -	Christchurch.
Risca -	-	par.	3,971	1,879	11,149	do. - -	Newport (Mon.)
Rogerstone	-	ham.	1,302	6,955	7,467	Tydu, Newport (Mon.)	do.
Saint Brides -	-	par.	249	3,594	4,589	Castletown, Cardiff	do.
Saint Woollos (W.) -	tow.		23,509	3,584	101,749	Newport (Mon.) -	do.
Tredunnock	-	par.	154	1,393	1,626	Caerleon - -	Caerleon.
Upper Machin	-	ham.	1,448	2,485	4,843	Newport (Mon.) -	Newport (Mon.)
Willerick	-	par.	28	406	1,198	do. - -	do.
Witston	-	par.	93	1,073	2,099	do. - -	Christchurch.
TOTAL of UNION			70,542	110,579	354,022		

NEWPORT UNION (SALOP).

(Formed 5 Oct. 1836 by Order dated 9 Sept. 1836.—Places marked thus * added 20 Dec. 1836 by Order dated 24 Nov. 1836.)

COUNTY of SALOP :

Cherrington	-	tow.	183	1,086	1,954	Newport (Salop) -	Newport, Bradford.
Chetwynd (a)	-	par.	815	4,730	9,383	do. - -	do.
Chetwynd-Aston	-	tow.	456	1,248	3,561	do. - -	do.
Church-Aston		tow.	805	715	3,741	do. - -	do.
Edgmond	-	par.	939	4,199	8,115	do. - -	do.
Lilleshall	-	par.	3,844	6,140	18,568	do. - -	do.
Longford	-	par.	95	1,258	2,457	do. - -	do.
Newport (W.)	-	par.	3,044	566	9,127	do. -	do.
Tibberton	-	tow.	392	1,494	3,037	do. - -	do.
Woodcote	-	cha.	190	1,983	3,414	do. - -	do.

(continued)

NEWPORT UNION (Salop) :

(a) By Order which came into operation on 25 March 1883, detached parts of Cheswardine, in the Drayton Union, were amalgamated with Chetwynd.

(b) By Order which came into operation on 25 March 1885, detached parts of Gnosal were amalgamated with Bradley and Haughton, in the Stafford Union.

Unions and Parishes, &c.	Population in 1881.	Area in Statute Acres in 1881.	Rateable Value in 1881.	Post Town.	Petty Sessional Division.

NEWPORT UNION—*continued.*

COUNTY OF STAFFORD :

			£		
*Adbaston - *par.*	539	4,638	6,001	Newport (Salop) -	Pier Hill, South Stafford.
Forton - *par.*	541	3,740	6,382	do. -	Cuttlestone, West Stafford.
Gnosal (b) - *par.*	2,379	10,377	19,782	Stafford -	do.
*High Offley - *par.*	811	2,761	5,452	Newport (Salop) -	Pier Hill, South Stafford.
*Norbury - *tow.*	212	2,107	2,950	do. -	Cuttlestone, West Stafford.
*Weston Jones *tow.*	106	1,259	1,993	do. -	do.
TOTAL of UNION -	15,352	48,501	105,917		

NEWPORT PAGNELL UNION.

(Formed 26 Sept. 1835 by Order dated 10 Sept. 1835.— Places marked thus * added 25 Dec. 1861 by Order dated 21 Nov. 1861.)

COUNTY of BUCKINGHAM :

Astwood (b) - *par.*	222	1,286	1,706	Newport Pagnell -	Newport Pagnell.
Bletchley - *tow.*	514	1,308	2,639	Bletchley Station -	do.
Bow Brickhill - *par.*	460	1,848	3,142	do. -	do.
Bradwell - *par.*	2,460	917	5,945	Stony Stratford -	do.
*Bradwell Abbey - *par.*	28	447	1,987	do. -	Stony Stratford.
Broughton - *par.*	159	937	1,806	Newport Pagnell -	Newport Pagnell.
Castle Thorpe - *par.*	329	1,372	9,155	Stony Stratford -	Stony Stratford.
Chicheley - *par.*	181	2,071	2,740	Newport Pagnell -	Newport Pagnell.
Clifton Reynes - *par.*	203	1,454	2,487	do. -	do.
Cold Brayfield - *par.*	85	744	1,333	do. -	do.
Emberton (b) - *par.*	645	1,953	3,599	do. -	do.
Fenny Stratford - *tow.*	2,147	1,040	9,073	Bletchley Station -	do.
Gayhurst (b) - *par.*	91	1,012	1,438	Newport Pagnell -	do.
Great Brickhill - *par.*	557	2,383	4,295	Bletchley Station -	do.
Great Lindford - *par.*	437	1,836	3,832	Newport Pagnell -	do.
Great Woolstone - *par.*	81	514	699	Bletchley Station -	do.
Hanslope - *par.*	1,584	5,801	17,543	Stony Stratford -	do.
Hardmead (b) - *par.*	92	1,145	986	Newport Pagnell -	do.
Haversham - *par.*	237	1,634	4,591	do. -	do.
Lathbury (b) - *par.*	121	1,394	2,365	do. -	do.
Lavendon (b) - *par.*	783	2,615	3,680	do. -	do.
Little Brickhill - *par.*	241	1,367	2,221	Bletchley Station -	do.
Little Lindford - *par.*	69	727	1,238	Newport Pagnell -	do.
Little Woolstone - *par.*	81	631	971	Bletchley Station -	do.
Loughton - *par.*	324	1,536	9,468	do. -	Stony Stratford.
Middleton or Milton Keynes } *par.*	244	1,909	3,119	Newport Pagnell -	Newport Pagnell.
Moulsoe - *par.*	194	1,654	2,251	do. -	do.
Newport Pagnell (W.) *par.*	3,686	3,132	15,109	do. -	do.
Newton Blossomville *par.*	260	1,014	1,764	do. -	do.

(continued)

NEWPORT PAGNELL UNION :

(a) By Order which came into operation on 25 March 1885, a part of Wavendon was amalgamated with Aspley Heath, in the Woburn Union.

(b) By Provisional Order which came into operation on 25 March 1886,—
    A detached part of Astwood was amalgamated with North Crawley ;
    A detached part of Emberton was amalgamated with Hardmead ;
    Detached parts of Lathbury were amalgamated with Gayhurst ;
    Detached parts of Lavendon were amalgamated with Ravenstone and Warrington.

Unions and Parishes, &c.	Population in 1881.	Area in Statute Acres in 1881.	Rateable Value in 1881.	Post Town.	Petty Sessional Division.
NEWPORT PAGNELL UNION—County of Buckingham—*continued.*			£		
Newton Longville - *par.*	471	1,735	2,685	Bletchley Station -	Newport Pagnell.
North Crawley (*b*) - *par.*	699	3,362	4,904	Newport Pagnell -	do.
Olney - - - *par.*	2,347	2,153	7,493	do. - -	do.
*Olney Park Farm - *par.*	15	206	212	do. - -	do.
*Petsoe Manor - - *par.*	8	411	468	do. - -	do.
Ravenstone (*b*) - *par.*	370	1,920	2,405	do. - -	do.
Shenley Church End *tow.*	184	1,662	2,693	Stony Stratford -	Stony Stratford.
Sherrington - - *par.*	604	1,805	3,342	Newport Pagnell -	Newport Pagnell.
Simpson - - *par.*	260	1,366	3,811	Bletchley Station -	do.
Stantonbury - *par.*	35	806	1,580	Newport Pagnell -	do.
Stoke Goldington - *par.*	808	2,352	3,314	do. - -	do.
Tyrringham with Fil- grave - - } *par.*	199	1,792	3,738	do. - -	do.
Walton - - *par.*	112	773	1,489	Bletchley Station -	do.
Warrington (*b*) - *ham.*	68	901	1,110	Newport Pagnell -	do.
Water Eaton - *ham.*	248	1,016	5,556	Bletchley Station -	do.
Wavendon (*a*) - *par.*	971	2,791	5,701	Woburn, Beds. -	do.
Weston Underwood - *par.*	352	1,873	3,007	Newport Pagnell -	do.
Willen - - *par.*	86	678	1,186	do. - -	do.
Woughton on the } Green - - } *par.*	231	1,224	3,236	Bletchley Station -	do.
TOTAL of UNION -	24,583	74,807	181,115		

NEWTON ABBOT UNION.

(Formed 20 June 1836 by Order dated 26 May 1836.)

COUNTY of DEVON:

Abbots' Kerswell - *par.*	435	1,461	3,621	Newton Abbot -	Teignbridge
Ashburton - - *par.*	2,891	6,966	12,724	do. - -	do.
Bickington - *par.*	239	1,375	2,325	do. - -	do.
Bishops Teignton - *par.*	1,145	4,748	8,834	Teignmouth -	do.
Bovey Tracey (*b*) - *par.*	2,127	7,262	10,841	Newton Abbot -	do.
Broad Hempstone (*a*) *par.*	567	2,047	5,378	Totnes -	do.
Buckland in the } Moor - - } *par.*	69	1,458	875	Newton Abbot -	do.
Chudleigh - - *par.*	1,927	6,037	10,181	do. - -	do.
Cockington - - *par.*	358	1,209	5,221	Torquay -	Paignton.
Coffinswell - *par.*	196	1,126	2,057	Newton Abbot -	Teignbridge.
Dawlish (*b*) - - *par.*	4,519	5,512	25,328	Dawlish -	do.
East Ogwell (*b*) - *par.*	267	1,249	2,118	Newton Abbot -	do.
East Teignmouth - *par.*	2,482	745	14,974	Teignmouth -	do.
Haccombe - with - } Combe (*b*) - } *par.*	14	363	543	do. - -	do.
Hennock (*b*) - *par.*	760	3,469	1,239	Newton Abbot -	do.
High Week (*b*) - *par.*	2,161	2,422	10,051	do. - -	do.

(*continued*)

NEWPORT PAGNELL UNION:

(*a*) (*b*) See notes. page 251.

NEWTON ABBOT UNION:

(*a*) By Orders which came into operation on 25 March 1884,—
A detached part of Staverton, in the Totnes Union, was amalgamated with Broad Hempstone;
A detached part of Trusham, known as "Middle Bramble and Lower Bramble," was amalgamated with Ashton, in the Saint Thomas' Union;
A nearly detached part of Ipplepen was amalgamated with Marldon, in the Totnes Union;
Detached parts of Kings Kerswell were amalgamated with Saint Mary Church;
All the parts of Stoke in Teignhead, comprised in the Urban Sanitary District of Teignmouth, were amalgamated with Saint Nicholas.

(*b*) By Provisional Orders which came into operation on 25 March 1885,—
A detached part of Hennock was amalgamated with Bovey Tracey;

NEWTON ABBOT UNION—*continued.*

A detached part of Ipplepen was amalgamated with Torbryan;
A detached part of Torbryan was amalgamated with High Week;
A detached part of North Bovey was amalgamated with Lustleigh;
A detached part of Lustleigh, known as "Pepperdown," was amalgamated with Moreton Hampstead;
A detached part of Woolborough, known as "Roydon," was amalgamated with East Ogwell;
All the parts of a parish, known as Denbury, were amalgamated with Torbryan;
All the parts of a parish, known as Combe in Teignhead, (having in 1881, population 423, acreage 2,407, and rateable value 3,599*l.*), were amalgamated with Haccombe and Stoke in Teignhead, and Haccombe was thenceforth to be called Haccombe-with-Combe;
A detached part of Kenton, in the Saint Thomas' Union was amalgamated with Dawlish.

Unions and Parishes, &c.	Population in 1881.	Area in Statute Acres in 1891.	Rateable Value in 1881.	Post Town.	Petty Sessional Division.
NEWTON ABBOT UNION—County of Devon—continued.			£		
Ideford - *par.*	284	1,471	2,139	Newton Abbot -	Teignbridge.
Ilsington - *par.*	1,060	7,563	7,080	do. -	do.
Ipplepen (*a*) (*b*) - *par.*	825	3,069	7,004	do. -	do.
Kings Kerswell (*a*) - *par.*	1,009	1,744	5,950	do. -	do.
Kings Teignton - *par.*	1,691	4,021	10,267	do. -	do.
Lustleigh (*b*) - *par.*	366	2,939	2,457	do. -	Crockernwell.
Manaton - *par.*	331	6,393	2,801	do. -	Teignbridge.
Moreton Hampstead (*b*) *par.*	1,572	7,656	8,664	do. -	Crockernwell.
North Bovey (*b*) - *par.*	439	5,654	3,340	do. -	do.
Saint Mary Church (*a*) *par.*	5,970	2,589	22,097	Torquay -	Paignton.
Saint Nicholas (*a*) - *par.*	1,245	790	3,224	Teignmouth -	Teignbridge.
Stoke in Teignhead } (*a*) (*b*) - } *par.*	648	2,531	5,033	do. -	do.
Teigngrace - *par.*	172	1,329	2,542	Newton Abbot -	do.
Torbryan (*b*) - *par.*	534	3,078	5,269	do. -	do.
Tor Mohun - *par.*	24,767	1,465	123,021	Torquay -	Paignton.
Trusham (*a*) - *par.*	174	749	1,003	Newton Abbot -	Teignbridge.
West Ogwell - *par.*	46	683	920	do. -	do.
West Teignmouth - *par.*	4,638	493	15,039	Teignmouth -	do.
Widecombe in the } Moor - } *par.*	814	10,614	5,292	Newton Abbot -	do.
Woodland - *cha.*	157	1,606	2,131	do. -	do.
Woolborough (W.) } (*b*) - } *par.*	7,662	1,231	22,180	do. -	do.
TOTAL of UNION -	74,573 (*b*)	115,117 (*b*)	376,763 (*b*)		
NEWTOWN AND LLANIDLOES UNION. (Formed 13 Feb. 1837 by Order dated 17 Jan. 1837.) COUNTY OF MONTGOMERY :					
Aberhafesp - *par.*	427	4,568	3,463	Newtown -	Newtown Upper.
Bettws - *par.*	572	5,305	4,909	do. -	do.
Carno - *par.*	876	10,982	3,910	do. -	Llanidloes Lower.
Kerry - *par.*	2,093	21,430	17,325	do. -	Newtown Upper.
Llandinam - *par.*	1,541	18,064	10,243	do. -	Llanidloes Lower.
Llangirrig - *par.*	1,605	50,000	6,826	Llanidloes	Llanidloes Upper.
Llanidloes - *par.*	4,939	15,404	21,038	do. -	do.
Llanllugan (*a*) - *par.*	289	3,945	1,698	Shrewsbury	Newtown Lower.
Llanllwchairn - *par.*	2,891	4,426	11,171	Newtown -	Newtown Upper.
Llanwnog (W.) - *par.*	1,717	10,701	8,218	do. -	Llanidloes Lower.
Llanwyddelan - *par.*	385	3,784	2,504	Shrewsbury	Newtown Lower.
Manafon (*a*) - *par.*	627	6,635	4,290	do. -	do.
Moughtrey - *par.*	508	5,025	2,725	Newtown -	do. Upper.
Newtown - *par.*	4,279	2,736	17,457	do. -	do. do.
Penstrowed - *par.*	129	1,220	1,661	do. -	Llanidloes Lower.
Tref Eglwys - *par.*	1,823	18,166	6,723	Llanidloes	Llanidloes Upper.
Tregynon - *par.*	708	6,760	4,793	Newtown -	Newtown Upper.
TOTAL of UNION -	25,439	189,151	128,954		
NEW FOREST UNION. (Formed 29 Aug. 1835 by Order dated 15 Aug. 1835.—The place marked thus * which was constituted by Order dated 16 March 1868, issued under the New Forest Poor Act, was added 24 June 1868 by Order dated 6 April 1868. Names of places marked thus † are as altered by Order dated 5 May 1887.) COUNTY OF SOUTHAMPTON :					
Beaulieu - *par.*	928	8,632	6,533	Southampton	Lymington and New Forest Division of Hythe. (*continued*)

NEWTOWN AND LLANIDLOES UNION :

(*a*) A detached part of Manafon, known as Dolgwnfelin, was amalgamated with Llanllugan, by Order which came into operation on 25 March 1884.

Unions and Parishes, &c.		Population in 1881.	Area in Statute Acres in 1881.	Rateable Value in 1881.	Post Town.	Petty Sessional Division.
NEW FOREST UNION—County of Southampton—continued.				£		
†Bramshaw (Hants) -	par.	464	3,502	1,830	Lyndhurst - -	Lymington and New Forest Division of Lyndhurst.
*Denny Lodge - -	tow.	293	11,708	2,815	do. - -	do.
Dibden - -	par.	502	2,230	4,316	Southampton -	Lymington and New Forest Division of Hythe.
Eling (W.) -	par.	6,032	18,612	27,173	Totton - -	Lymington and New Forest Division of Lyndhurst.
Exbury with Leap -	par.	344	2,122	2,234	Southampton -	Lymington and New Forest Division of Hythe.
Fawley - -	par.	1,594	6,843	9,765	do. - -	do.
Lyndhurst - -	var.	1,580	3,825	7,281	Lyndhurst -	Lymington and New Forest Division of Lyndhurst.
Minstead - -	par.	880	10,246	4,580	do.	do.
COUNTY OF WILTS :						
†Bramshaw (Wilts) -	par.	296	1,579	1,596	Lyndhurst - -	Lymington and New Forest Division of Salisbury.
TOTAL OF UNION -		13,221	69,329	68,123		

NEW WINCHESTER UNION.

(Formed 10 Aug. 1835 by Order dated 24 July 1835. — Place marked thus * added 30 April 1836 by Order dated 7 April 1836; thus † added 1 Feb. 1853 by Order dated 17 Jan. 1853; thus ‡ added 25 Mar. 1884 by Order dated 14 Nov. 1883).

COUNTY OF SOUTHAMPTON :

†Avington - -	par.	204	1,812	1,822	Winchester -	Winchester.
Bishops Stoke -	par.	1,537	3,431	9,143	Southampton -	do.
Chilcomb - -	par.	300	2,299	3,206	Winchester - -	do. (City and County).
*Compton - -	par.	275	2,110	5,071	do. - -	do.
Crawley - -	par.	455	3,607	3,807	do. - -	do.
Easton - -	par.	484	2,781	3,702	do. - -	do.
East Stratton -	par.	340	1,996	2,237	Micheldever -	do.
Headbourne Worthy	par.	242	1,813	2,970	Winchester -	do.
Hunton - -	cha.	69	1,074	1,112	Micheldever -	do.
Itchen Abbas -	par.	244	2,165	3,005	Alresford - -	do.
Kings Worthy -	par.	438	2,241	5,460	Winchester -	do.
‡Lainston - -	par.	15	120	—	do. - -	do.
Littleton - -	par.	194	1,302	1,927	do. - -	do.
Martyrs Worthy -	par.	249	2,016	3,219	do. - -	do.
Milland - -	ville.	255	137	1,097	do. - -	do. (City and County).
Micheldever -	par.	1,039	7,820	13,577	Micheldever -	Winchester.
Morestead - -	par.	130	1,538	1,103	Winchester -	do.
Owselbury - -	par.	848	5,413	7,135	do. - -	do.
Saint Bartholomew Hide - - }	par.	1,432	693	7,829	do. - -	{ do. (City and County).
Saint Faith - -	par.	2,772	1,264	16,876	do. - -	do. do.
Saint John - -	par.	1,258	76	2,534	do. - -	do. do.
Saint Lawrence -	par.	214	3	2,080	do. - -	City of Winchester.
Saint Mary Kalander	par.	1,247	16	4,580	do. - -	do.
Saint Maurice -	par.	2,490	52	7,774	do. - -	do.
Saint Michael -	par.	964	61	4,592	do. - -	do.
Saint Peter Cheesehill	par.	847	50	2,491	do. - -	Winchester (City and County).
Saint Peter Colbrook -	par.	840	23	1,933	do. - -	City of Winchester.
Little Saint Swithin -	par.	156	3	883	do. - -	do.
Saint Thomas - -	par.	4,216	91	20,990	do. - -	do.

(continued)

Unions and Parishes, &c.	Population in 1881.	Area in Statute Acres in 1881.	Rateable Value in 1881.	Post Town.	Petty Sessional Division.
NEW WINCHESTER UNION—County of Southampton—*continued.*			£		
Sparsholt - - *par.*	434	3,552	3,283	Winchester -	Winchester.
Stoke Charity - *par.*	117	1,841	2,321	Micheldever	- do.
Twyford - - *par.*	1,429	4,260	9,788	Winchester -	do.
Week (W.) - - *par.*	1,808	1,093	7,088	do. - -	do. (City and County).
Winnall - - *par.*	124	532	1,069	do. -	do. do.
Wonston - *par.*	692	5,493	5,863	Micheldever -	Winchester.
TOTAL of UNION -	28,397	62,778	171,567		
NORTHALLERTON UNION.					
(Formed 23 Feb. 1837 by Order dated 28 Jan. 1837. — Places marked thus * added 29 Sept. 1860 by Order dated 14 July 1860.)					
COUNTY of YORK, NORTH RIDING :					
Ainderby Steeple - *tow.*	222	1,158	2,885	Northallerton -	Allertonshire.
Appleton-upon-Wisk *tow.*	331	1,865	2,712	do. - -	Yarm.
Birkby - - *tow.*	64	1,203	2,925	do. - -	Allertonshire.
Borrowby - *tow.*	323	924	2,196	Thirsk - -	do.
Brompton - - *tow.*	1,295	3,942	12,149	Northallerton -	do.
*Coteliffe - - *tow.*	9	133	185	Thirsk - -	do.
Crosby - - *tow.*	40	833	1,064	Northallerton -	do.
Danby Wisk - *tow.*	287	3,364	3,617	do. - -	Gilling, East.
Deighton - - *tow.*	114	2,036	2,078	do. - -	Allertonshire.
East Cowton - *par.*	387	3,369	12,061	do. - -	Gilling, East.
East Harsley - *par.*	379	3,057	3,960	do. - -	Allertonshire.
Ellerback - - *tow.*	72	871	1,083	do. - -	do.
Great Langton - *tow.*	133	872	1,146	do. - -	Gilling, East.
Great Smenton - *tow.*	192	1,536	2,328	do. - -	Allertonshire.
Gueldable - - *tow.*	81	348	686	Thirsk - -	Birdforth.
Hornby - - *tow.*	258	1,828	2,165	Northallerton -	Allertonshire.
Hutton Bonville - *tow.*	114	1,546	4,332	do. - -	do.
Kiplin - - *tow.*	80	1,011	1,465	do. - -	Gilling, East.
Kirby Sigston - *tow.*	101	1,242	1,458	do. - -	Allertonshire.
Landmoth with Catto *tow.*	42	798	897	do. - -	do.
*Lazenby - - *tow.*	44	829	4,665	do. - -	do.
*Leake - - *tow.*	11	309	695	Thirsk - -	do.
Little Langton - *tow.*	96	1,006	1,431	Northallerton -	Gilling, East.
Little Smenton - *tow.*	75	1,001	1,268	do. - -	Allertonshire.
Morton - - *tow.*	273	1,540	2,656	do. - -	do.
Northallerton (W.) - *tow.*	3,692	3,650	23,504	do. - -	do.
North Otterington - *tow.*	75	819	4,640	do. - -	do.
Osmotherly - - *tow.*	920	3,196	3,836	do. - -	do.
Romanby - - *tow.*	114	2,060	10,304	do. - -	do.
Silton Nether - *tow.*	176	1,538	2,077	do. - -	Birdforth.
Silton Over - - *tow.*	44	1,235	1,288	do. - -	do.
South Cowton - - *tow.*	111	2,239	2,641	do. - -	Gilling, East.
Sowerby under Cotcliffe - *tow.*	49	812	1,019	do. - -	Allertonshire.
Thimbleby - - *tow.*	140	2,053	2,204	do. - -	do.
Thirntoft - - *tow.*	146	1,228	1,670	do. - -	do.
Thornton-le-Beans - *tow.*	211	1,691	2,568	do. - -	do.
Warlaby - - *tow.*	78	767	1,275	do. - -	do.
Welbury - - *par.*	190	2,401	4,901	do. - -	do.
West Harsley - *tow.*	65	1,505	1,832	do. - -	do.
West Rounton - *par.*	219	1,456	4,253	do. - -	do.
Whitwell - - *tow.*	51	1,113	1,123	Catterick - -	Gilling, East.
Winton - - *tow.*	89	1,366	1,466	Northallerton -	Allertonshire.
Yaflorth - - *tow.*	189	1,350	2,297	do. - -	do.
TOTAL of UNION -	11,884	67,000	145,014		

Unions and Parishes, &c.	Population in 1881.	Area in Statute Acres in 1881.	Rateable Value in 1881.	Post Town.	Petty Sessional Division.

NORTHAMPTON UNION.

(Formed 27 Aug. 1835 by Order dated 31 July 1835.— Place marked thus * added 24 June 1861 by Order dated 25 April 1861.)

COUNTY of NORTHAMPTON:

			£		
Abington - - par.	118	1,112	2,785	Northampton	- Northampton.
All Saints - - par.	9,314	In St. Giles	41,444	do. -	- { Borough of Northampton.
Bugbrooke - - par.	896	2,420	9,361	Weedon Beck	- Northampton.
Dallington - - par.	1,610	1,520	6,182	Northampton	- do.
Duston - - par.	2,497	1,760	10,939	do. -	- do.
Great Billing - par.	390	1,290	2,977	do. -	- do.
Harpole - - par.	829	1,560	4,594	Weedon Beck	- do.
Kingsthorpe - - par.	3,054	1,800	10,317	*Northampton	- do.
Kislingbury - par.	695	2,170	4,638	Weedon Beck	- do.
Little Billing - par.	78	856	1,759	Northampton	- do.
Lower Heyford - par.	810	1,690	6,617	Weedon Beck	- do.
*Priory of Saint Andrew or Town part (a) - } par.	16,470	} 1,342	36,768	Northampton	- { Borough of Northampton.
Saint Giles (W.) (a) par.	10,449		36,924	do. -	- do.
Saint Peter - - par.	1,665		3,833	do. -	- do.
Saint Sepulchre (a) - par.	13,983		35,331	do. -	- do.
Upper Heyford - par.	115	726	1,003	Weedon Beck	- Northampton.
Upton - - par.	720	979	2,483	Northampton	- do.
Weston Favell - par.	551	1,050	2,920	do. -	- do.
TOTAL of UNION -	64,244	20,275	221,775		

NORTHLEACH UNION.

(Formed 18 Jan. 1836 by Order dated 4 Jan. 1836. — Place marked thus * formerly consisted of two Townships, Shipton Oliffe and Shipton Sollars, which were consolidated by Order dated 23 February 1871.)

COUNTY of GLOUCESTER:

Aldsworth - - par.	386	3,460	2,941	Northleach	- Northleach.
Aston Blank - par.	300	2,250	2,183	do. -	- do.
Bibury - - par.	738	5,110	6,442	Fairford	- Fairford.
Cheddworth - par.	816	4,689	5,142	Northleach	- Northleach.
Coln Rogers - par.	107	1,508	1,499	do. -	- do.
Coln Saint Aldwins - par.	443	2,666	3,230	Fairford	- Fairford.
Coln Saint Dennis - par.	192	2,430	1,829	Northleach	- Northleach.
Compton Abdale (a) par.	210	2,215	1,953	Cheltenham	- do.
Dowdeswell (a) - par.	483	2,246	3,254	Andoversford	- do.
Eastington (W.) - ty.	375 {	In Northleach }	4,743	Northleach	- do.
East Leach Martin (a) par.	146	1,966	2,171	Lechlade -	- Fairford.
East Leach Turville (a) par.	435	2,630	3,060	do. -	- do.
Farmington - par.	260	2,470	2,229	Northleach	- Northleach.
Hampnett - - par.	165	1,406	1,745	do. -	- do.
Hazleton - - par.	196	1,190	1,508	Cheltenham	- do.
Little Barrington (a) par.	154	1,260	1,368	Burford, Oxon	- do.
Northleach - - par.	831	3,460	1,570	Cheltenham	- do.
Salperton - - par.	145	1,210	1,595	Hazleton do.	- do.

(*continued*)

NORTHAMPTON UNION:

(a) By Order which came into operation on 25 March 1885, detached parts of the Priory of Saint Andrew or Town part were amalgamated with Saint Giles and Saint Sepulchre.

NORTHLEACH UNION:

(a) By Order which came into operation on 25 March 1883,—

A detached part of Compton Abdale was amalgamated with Shipton;

A detached part of East Leach Martin was amalgamated with Southrop;

A detached part of Little Barrington was amalgamated with East Leach Turville; and

A detached part of Withington was amalgamated with Dowdeswell.

Unions and Parishes, &c.		Population in 1881.	Area in Statute Acres in 1881.	Rateable Value in 1881.	Post Town.	Petty Sessional Division.
NORTHLEACH UNION—County of Gloucester—continued.				£		
Sevenhampton	- par.	512	2,600	3,257	Andoversford	Northleach.
Sherborne	- par.	573	4,560	5,414	Northleach -	do.
Shipton (a) -	- par.	330	2,210	2,625	Andoversford	do.
Southrop (a) -	- par.	350	1,493	2,332	Lechlade -	Fairford.
Stowell	- par.	50	823	864	Northleach	Northleach.
Turkdean	- par.	298	1,890	1,866	do. -	do.
Windrush	- par.	228	1,834	1,961	Burford, Oxon	do.
Winson	- cha.	162	1,190	1,444	Fairford -	do.
Withington (a)	- par.	626	5,830	5,168	Andoversford	do.
Wittington -	- par.	225	1,422	1,807	do. -	do.
Yanworth -	- cha.	139	1,340	1,052	Northleach	do.
TOTAL of UNION -		9,884	67,358	76,582		
NORTHWICH UNION. (Formed 20 Oct. 1836 by Order dated 26 Sept. 1836.) COUNTY OF CHESTER :						
Acton -	- tow.	597	1,177	9,859	Northwich -	Eddisbury.
Allostock	- tow.	501	3,017	6,058	Knutsford -	Northwich.
Anderton	- tow.	343	526	6,451	Northwich -	Leftwich.
Barnton	- tow.	1,538	760	7,535	do. -	do.
Birches	- tow.	8	160	207	Knutsford -	do.
Bostock	- tow.	198	1,156	2,618	Northwich and Middlewich	Northwich.
Byley cum Yatehouse	tow.	137	1,065	2,179	Middlewich	do.
Castle-Northwich	- tow.	2,126	135	5,351	Northwich -	Leftwich.
Clive -	- tow.	165	182	3,166	Winsford -	Northwich.
Cogshall	- tow.	90	520	1,191	Northwich -	Leftwich.
Comberbach	- tow.	310	370	1,191	do. -	do.
Crowton (a) -	- tow.	463	1,408	2,978	Northwich -	Eddisbury.
Croxton -	- tow.	49	575	1,952	Middlewich	Northwich.
Cuddington -	- tow.	408	1,151	3,280	Northwich -	Eddisbury.
Darnhall	- tow.	167	1,741	4,123	Winsford -	do.
Davenham -	- tow.	585	496	2,843	Northwich -	Leftwich.
Delamere -	- tow.	578	1,969	2,714	do. and Chester	Eddisbury.
Eaton	- tow.	17	456	3,919	do. -	Leftwich.
Eddisbury -	- tow.	246	2,085	2,111	do. and Chester	Eddisbury.
Hartford	- tow.	1,451	1,070	11,076	do. -	Leftwich.
Hulse	- tow.	41	311	644	Knutsford -	do.
Kinderton cum Hulme	tow.	541	1,691	4,129	Middlewich	Northwich.
Lach Dennis	- tow.	62	398	786	Knutsford -	Leftwich.
Leftwich (W.)	- tow.	2,864	968	9,594	Northwich -	do.
Little Budworth	- par.	541	2,908	4,982	Tarporley -	Eddisbury.
Little Legh	- tow.	455	1,595	5,274	Northwich -	Daresbury.
Lostock Gralam	- tow.	777	1,732	5,539	Knutsford -	Leftwich.
Low Oulton -	- tow.	47	959	1,313	Tarporley -	Eddisbury.
Marbury	- tow.	26	384	1,260	Northwich -	Leftwich.
Marston	- tow.	969	1,113	8,226	do. -	do.
Marton	- tow.	695	2,754	1,309	do. -	Eddisbury.
Middlewich	- tow.	1,325	37	2,750	Middlewich	Northwich.
Moresbarrow cum Parme	} tow.	27	410	713	do. -	do.
Moulton	- tow.	1,113	484	7,286	Northwich -	Leftwich.
Newhall	- tow.	19	236	407	do. -	do.
Newton	- tow.	1,962	1,118	7,094	Middlewich	Northwich.
Northwich -	- tow.	1,022	13	5,815	Northwich -	Leftwich.
Oakmere	- tow.	408	2,962	3,598	do. -	Eddisbury.
Occleston	- tow.	101	751	1,325	Middlewich -	Northwich.
Onston	- tow.	93	329	862	Northwich -	Eddisbury.
Over -	- tow.	6,534	4,527	26,591	Winsford -	do.
Peover Nether	- tow.	211	969	1,992	Knutsford -	Leftwich.
Ravenscroft -	- tow.	20	127	510	Middlewich -	Northwich.
Rudheath -	- tow.	501	2,218	5,864	Northwich and Middlewich.	Leftwich.
Shipbrook -	- tow.	67	564	1,630	do. -	do.
Shurlack	- tow.	179	313	1,180	do. -	do.
Sproston -	- tow.	141	874	2,017	Middlewich	Northwich.
Stanthorne	- tow.	193	1,113	2,940	do. -	do.

(continued)

NORTHWICH UNION :

(a) By Order which came into operation on 25 March 1882, a detached part of Narley, in the Runcorn Union, was amalgamated with Crowton.

Unions and Parishes, &c.		Population in 1881.	Area in Statute Acres in 1881.	Rateable Value in 1881.	Post Town.	Petty Sessional Division.

NORTHWICH UNION—County of Chester—*continued.*

				£		
Stublach	- - *tow.*	37	355	615	Middlewich -	Leftwich.
Sutton	- - *tow.*	32	201	505	do. - -	Northwich.
Wallerscoat -	- *tow*	11	128	384	Northwich - -	do.
Weaverham -	- *tow.*	1,699	3,623	16,228	do. -	Eddisbury.
Weever	- *tow.*	139	968	1,360	Winsford - -	do.
Wharton	- - *tow.*	3,507	1,253	23,136	do. -	Northwich.
Whatcroft -	- *tow.*	57	682	2,191	Northwich -	do.
Wimboldsley	- *tow.*	93	982	6,797	Middlewich -	do.
		1,172	974	7,983	Northwich and	Leftwich.
Wincham -	*tow.*				Knutsford.	
Winnington	- *tow.*	681	678	6,485	do. - -	do.
Witton cum Twam-brook - -	} *tow.*	5,704	622	17,342	do. - -	do.
Total of Union	-	41,046	62,613	283,388		

NORTH BIERLEY UNION.

(Formed 16 Sept. 1848 by Order of that date.—Place marked thus * added 21 June 1869 by Order dated 3 June 1869.)

County of York, West Riding :

Allerton	- - *tow.*	3,685	1,849	10,707	Bradford - -	Bradford.
Calverley with Fars-ley - -	} *tow.*	8,206	3,180	29,519	Leeds - -	do.
Clayton (W.)	- *tow.*	7,080	1,741	16,848	Bradford - -	do.
Cleckheaton -	- *tow.*	10,653	1,755	35,457	Normanton -	do.
Drighlington	- *tow.*	4,214	1,136	10,762	Bradford -	do.
*Eccleshill -	- *tow.*	7,037	1,220	19,757	do. - -	do.
Heaton	- *tow.*	3,107	1,323	13,691	do. -	do.
Hunsworth	- *tow.*	1,516	1,380	10,694	do. -	do.
Idle	- *tow.*	13,375	2,462	40,701	do. - -	do.
North Bierley	- *tow.*	15,620	3,312	44,409	do. -	do.
Pudsey	- *tow.*	15,459	2,546	42,614	Leeds -	do.
Shipley	- *tow.*	15,093	1,406	52,624	Shipley -	do.
Thornton	- *tow.*	9,633	4,785	24,664	Bradford -	do.
Tong	- *tow.*	5,591	2,657	19,038	do. - -	do.
Wike	- *tow.*	5,315	967	12,874	do. - -	do.
Wilsden	- *tow.*	2,966	2,638	9,811	Bingley - -	Keighley.
Total of Union	- -	128,550	34,390	391,200		

NORTH WITCHFORD UNION.

(Formed 9 May 1836 by Order dated 13 April 1836.)

County of Cambridge :

						Hundred of Witchford :
Benwick	- - *par.*	811	3,096	5,401	March - -	Northern Division.
Chatteris -	- *par.*	4,712	15,090	29,581	Chatteris -	do.
Doddington (W.)	- *par.*	1,358	7,159	12,602	March -	do.
Manea (*a*)	- *cha.*	1,151	4,768	8,915	Chatteris -	do.
March	- *par.*	6,190	19,141	47,545	March - -	do.
Welches Dam -	- *par.*	150	2,980	3,036	Chatteris -	do.
Wimblington	- *par.*	1,089	7,589	13,576	March -	do.
Total of Union	- -	15,464	59,823	120,656		

NORTH WITCHFORD UNION :

(*a*) By Orders which came into operation on 25 March 1884, detached or nearly detached parts of Downham, Wentworth, Witcham, and Witchford, in the Ely Union, were amalgamated with Manea.

K k

Unions and Parishes, &c.	Population in 1881.	Area in Statute Acres in 1881.	Rateable Value in 1881.	Post Town.	Petty Sessional Division.
NORWICH UNION.					
(Constituted by "The Norwich Poor Act, 1863," 26 & 27 Vict. cap. xciii.)					
In the CITY of NORWICH and COUNTY of the same CITY :			£		City of Norwich :
All Saints - - par.	378		1,617	Norwich - -	Separate Quarter Sessions.
Earlham - - ham.	238	In Heigham	1,551	do. - -	do.
Eaton - - ham.	1,237		7,454	do. - -	do.
Heigham (W.) - ham.	24,031	5,877	53,666	do. - -	do.
Hellesdon - - ham.	683	805	2,597	do. - -	do.
Lakenham - - ham.	6,378		15,796	do. - -	do.
Pockthorpe - - ham.	1,948		3,210	do. - -	do.
Saint Andrew - - par.	767		8,120	do. - -	do.
Saint Augustine - par.	1,812		3,228	do. - -	do.
Saint Benedict - par.	1,996		3,874	do. - -	do.
Saint Clement - - par.	5,190		8,557	do. - -	do.
Saint Edmund - par.	726		1,217	do. - -	do.
Saint Etheldred - par.	632		1,977	do. - -	do.
Saint George of Cole- gate - - par.	1,630		4,486	do. - -	do.
Saint George of Tombland - par.	779		4,388	do. - -	do.
Saint Giles - - par.	1,438		5,523	do. - -	do.
Saint Gregory - - par.	783		3,857	do. - -	do.
Saint Helen - - par.	557		1,008	do. - -	do.
Saint James - - par.	1,557		1,783	do. - -	do.
Saint John of Mad- dermarket - - par.	403		4,969	do. - -	do.
Saint John of Sepul- chre - - par.	2,909		4,314	do. - -	do.
Saint John of Timber- hill - - par.	1,208	In Heigham	2,755	do. - -	do.
Saint Julian - - par.	1,890		3,250	do. - -	do.
Saint Lawrence - par.	613		2,151	do. - -	do.
Saint Margaret - par.	699		1,406	do. - -	do.
Saint Martin at Oak par.	2,745		3,184	do. - -	do.
Saint Martin at Palace par.	755		4,255	do. - -	do.
Saint Mary at Coslany par.	1,281		2,318	do. - -	do.
Saint Mary in the Marsh - - par.	507		3,251	do. - -	do.
Saint Michael at Cos- lany - - par.	843		2,402	do. - -	do.
Saint Michael at Plea par.	168		4,038	do. - -	do.
Saint Michael at Thorn par.	1,747		2,813	do. - -	do.
Saint Paul - - par.	2,690		3,300	do. - -	do.
Saint Peter Hungate par.	387		869	do. - -	do.
Saint Peter of Mancroft par.	2,246		20,310	do. - -	do.
Saint Peter per Mountergate (W.) par.	2,938		9,023	do. - -	do.
Saint Peter of South- gate - - par.	565		3,578	do. - -	do.
Saint Saviour - - par.	1,572		2,920	do. - -	do.
Saint Simon and Jude par.	351		1,084	do. - -	do.
Saint Stephen - - par.	1,115		11,693	do. - -	do.
Saint Swithin - - par.	774		2,091	do. - -	do.
Thorpe - - ham.	2,864	730	13,976	do. - -	do.
Town Close - lib.	300		3,075	do. - -	do.
Trowse Millgate, Car- row, and Bracon- dale - - ham.	503	In Heigham	6,919	do. - -	do.
TOTAL of UNION - -	87,842	7,472	257,113		

Unions and Parishes, &c.	Population in 1881.	Area in Statute Acres in 1881.	Rateable Value in 1881.	Post Town.	Petty Sessional Division.

NOTTINGHAM UNION.

(Formed 6 July 1836 by Order dated 10 June 1836.--Places marked thus * added 26 March 1880 by Orders dated 15 Sept. 1879.)

Town and County of the Town of NOTTINGHAM :

Unions and Parishes, &c.	Population in 1881.	Area in Statute Acres in 1881.	Rateable Value in 1881. £	Post Town.	Petty Sessional Division.
*Brewhouse Yard - *par.*	84	—	320	Nottingham -	Nottingham.
*Radford - - *par.*	20,954	1,000	44,784	do. - -	do.
Saint Mary (W.) - *par.*	101,906		420,082	do. - -	do.
Saint Nicholas - - *par.*	5,355	1,996	30,101	do. - -	do.
Saint Peter - - *par.*	4,387		29,993	do. - -	do.
*Sneinton - - *par.*	15,473	720	38,994	do. - -	do.
*Standard Hill and Limits of the Castle *par.* of Nottingham	1,942	—	22,176	do. - -	do.

Town and County of the Town of NOTTINGHAM and COUNTY of NOTTINGHAM :

*Lenton - - *par.*	9,162	1,576	33,487	do. - -	do.
TOTAL of UNION - -	159,263	5,292	619,937		

NUNEATON UNION.

(Formed 6 April 1836 by Order dated 22 Mar. 1836.)

COUNTY of WARWICK :

Arley - - - *par.*	207	1,929	4,003	Coventry - -	Coleshill.
Astley - - - *par.*	244	2,550	3,560	Nuneaton - -	Coventry.
Bulkington - - *par.*	1,590	4,510	18,623	Rugby - -	do.
Caldecote - - *par.*	109	686	3,361	Nuneaton - -	Atherstone.
Chilvers-Coton (W.) *par.* (a)	3,005	3,730	11,877	do. - -	do.
Nuneaton (a) - *par.*	8,465	6,112	42,882	do. - -	do.
Weddington - *par.*	81	911	2,767	do. - -	do.
TOTAL of UNION - -	13,701	20,128	87,073		

OAKHAM UNION.

(Formed 29 April 1836 by Order dated 13 April 1836.— Place marked thus * added 25 Dec. 1861 by Order dated 18 Oct. 1861.)

COUNTY of LEICESTER:

Cold Overton - *par.*	80	1,657	2,316	Oakham - -	Melton Mowbray.
Knossington - *par.*	291	1,443	2,222	do. - -	do.

COUNTY of RUTLAND :

Ashwell - - *par.*	245	1,799	4,328	do. - -	Oakham.
Barrow - - *ham.*	120	In Cottesmore	1,475	do. - -	do.
Braunston - - *par.*	387	3,250	2,582	do. - -	do.
Brooke - - *par.*	107	1,560	2,195	do. - -	do.
Burley - - *par.*	296	3,390	5,270	do. - -	do.
Cottesmore - - *tow.*	409	2,120	3,936	do. - -	do.
Edith Weston - *par.*	350	1,723	2,796	Stamford - -	do.
Egleton - - *par.*	124	1,450	2,061	Oakham - -	do.
Empingham - - *par.*	823	2,780	6,386	Stamford - -	do.
Exton - - *tow.*	652	4,860	5,308	Oakham - -	do.
Greetham - - *par.*	583	2,800	3,696	do. - -	do. (continued)

NUNEATON UNION :

(a) By Order which came into operation on 25 March 1885, a detached part of Chilvers-Coton, known as " Sinnie," or " Sinny Fields," was amalgamated with Nuneaton.

Unions and Parishes, &c.		Population in 1881.	Area in Statute Acres in 1881.	Rateable Value in 1881.	Post town.	Petty Sessional Division.
CAKHAM UNION—County of Rutland—*continued.*				£		
Gunthorpe	*ham.*	23	In Oakham Lordshold	878	Oakham	Oakham.
Hambleton	*par.*	245	1,154	4,306	do.	do.
Horn	*tow.*	33	In Exton	986	do.	do.
Langham	*par.*	676	3,250	5,706	do.	do.
*Leighfield	*par.*	34	In Oakham Lordshold	3,118	Uppingham	do.
Lyndon	*par.*	103	902	1,669	Oakham	do.
Manton	*par.*	312	1,290	3,073	do.	do.
Market Overton	*par.*	388	2,840	2,983	do.	do.
Martinsthorpe	*par.*	9	533	993	do.	do.
Normanton	*par.*	79	2,450	1,375	Stamford	de.
Oakham Deanshold with Barleythorpe	*ma-nors.*	957	In Oakham Lordshold	3,441	Oakham	do.
Oakham Lordshold (W.)	*ma-nor.*	2,247	3,130	7,745	do.	do.
Stretton	*par.*	196	1,934	2,309	do.	do.
Teigh	*par.*	132	1,267	2,267	do.	do.
Thistleton	*par.*	133	1,420	1,749	do.	do.
Tickencote	*par.*	103	1,256	1,678	Stamford	do.
Whissendine	*par.*	732	3,870	6,845	Oakham	do.
Whitwell	*par.*	109	602	874	do.	do.
TOTAL of UNION		10,978	55,030	96,566		

OKEHAMPTON UNION.

(Formed 20 April 1836 by Order dated 6 April 1836.)

COUNTY of DEVON :						
Ashbury	*par.*	48	1,700	740	Exbourne	Hatherleigh.
Beaworthy	*par.*	296	3,806	1,386	do.	do.
Belstone	*par.*	156	1,500	1,205	Okehampton	do.
Bondleigh (*a*)	*par.*	189	1,784	1,535	North Tawton	South Molton.
Bratton Clovelly (*c*)	*par.*	601	8,316	4,018	Lewdown	Lifton.
Bridestow (*a*)	*par.*	612	5,661	4,357	Bridestow	do.
Broadwood Kelly (*c*)	*par.*	291	2,666	2,051	Winkleigh	Hatherleigh.
Chagford	*par.*	1,450	7,492	7,409	Exeter	Crockernwell.
Drewsteignton (*c*)	*par.*	805	6,937	6,951	do.	do.
Exbourne	*par.*	376	2,121	2,687	Exbourne	Hatherleigh.
Germansweek	*par.*	266	2,594	1,290	Lewdown	Lifton.
Gidleigh	*par.*	124	3,449	856	Exeter, viâ Chagford	Crockernwell.
Hatherleigh	*par.*	1,492	7,048	5,742	Hatherleigh	Hatherleigh.
High Hampton (*b*)	*par.*	297	3,039	1,470	do.	do.
Honey Church (*a*)	*par.*	51	607	474	Sampford Courtnay	do.
Iddesleigh	*par.*	444	2,952	2,792	Winkleigh	do.
Inwardleigh	*par.*	514	6,281	2,841	Exbourne	do.
Jacobstowe	*par.*	221	2,856	1,674	do.	do.
Meeth	*par.*	232	2,179	1,688	Hatherleigh	do.
Monk Okehampton (*c*)	*par.*	215	1,488	1,265	Winkleigh	do.
North Lew	*par.*	762	7,247	3,712	Exbourne	do.
North Tawton	*par.*	1,868	5,811	9,441	North Tawton	Hatherleigh.
Okehampton (W.)	*par.*	2,292	9,552	10,051	Okehampton	do.
Sampford Courtnay	*par.*	892	7,962	5,524	Sampford Courtnay	do.
Sourton	*par.*	514	5,018	3,219	Bridestow	Lifton.
South Tawton	*par.*	1,251	10,879	6,957	Okehampton	Crockernwell.
Spreyton	*par.*	383	3,606	2,439	do.	do.
Throwleigh	*par.*	317	1,943	2,045	do.	do.
TOTAL of UNION		16,962	126,797	93,861		

OKEHAMPTON UNION :

(*a*) By Orders which came into operation on 25 March 1884,—
A nearly detached part of Bondleigh was amalgamated with Honey Church ;
A detached part of Bridestow was amalgamated with Coryton, in the Tavistock Union.

(*b*) By Provisional Order which came into operation on 25 March 1884,—
A detached part of Black Torrington, in the Holsworthy Union, was amalgamated with High Hampton.

OKEHAMPTON UNION—*continued*.

(*c*) By Provisional Orders which came into operation on 25 March 1885,—
Certain detached parts of Monk Okehampton were amalgamated with Broadwood Kelly ;
A detached part of Bratton Clovelly was amalgamated with Broadwood Widger, in the Launceston Union ;
A detached part of Drewsteignton was amalgamated with Hittesleigh, in the Crediton Union ; and a detached part of Hittesleigh was amalgamated with Drewsteignton.

Unions and Parishes, &c.	Population in 1831.	Area in Statute Acres in 1831.	Rateable Value in 1831.	Post Town.	Petty Sessional Division.

OLDHAM UNION.

(Formed 3 Feb. 1837 by Order dated 14 Jan. 1837.)

COUNTY of LANCASTER:

			£		
Alkrington - - tow.	380	798	2,201	Middleton -	Oldham.
Chadderton - - tow.	16,899	3,082	67,785	Oldham - -	do.
Crompton - - tow.	9,797	2,864	33,099	do. - -	do.
Middleton - - tow.	10,346	1,930	25,364	Manchester -	Rochdale.
Oldham (W.) - - tow.	111,343	4,730	324,390	Oldham - -	Borough of Oldham.
Royton - - - tow.	10,582	1,372	33,661	do. - -	Oldham.
Thornham - - tow.	1,800	1,936	9,056	Shaw, near Oldham	Rochdale.
Tonge - - - tow.	7,254	392	17,943	Middleton -	Oldham.
TOTAL of UNION -	168,461	17,101	513,499		

ONGAR UNION.

(Formed 8 April 1836 by Order dated 25 Mar. 1836 and amended by Order dated 4 Mar. 1837.)

COUNTY of ESSEX:

Abbotts Roothing - par.	231	1,618	1,997	Ongar - -	Ongar.
Beauchamp Roothing par.	231	1,262	1,602	do. - -	do.
Berners Roothing - par.	86	1,073	1,088	do. - -	do.
Blackmore - par.	571	2,588	4,168	Ingatestone -	do.
Bobbingworth - par.	303	1,642	2,394	Ongar - -	do.
Chipping Ongar - par.	992	511	3,857	do. - -	do.
Doddinhurst - par.	401	1,917	2,980	Brentwood -	Brentwood.
Fyfield - par.	468	2,450	3,715	Ongar - -	Ongar.
Greenstead - par.	88	683	1,148	do. - -	do.
High Laver - par.	477	1,891	2,633	do. - -	do.
High Ongar - par.	1,063	4,520	7,844	do. - -	do.
Kelvedon Hatch - par.	375	1,684	2,772	Brentwood -	do.
Lambourne - par.	856	2,470	4,922	Romford -	do.
Little Laver - par.	110	962	1,305	Ongar - -	do.
Moreton - par.	453	1,475	2,277	do. - -	do.
Navestock - par.	834	4,518	6,001	Romford -	do.
Norton Mandeville - par.	94	775	1,112	Ingatestone -	do.
Shelley - par.	200	609	1,143	Ongar - -	do.
Shellow Bowels - par.	110	469	678	do. - -	do.
Stanford Rivers (W.) par.	975	4,414	6,327	Romford -	do.
Stapleford Abbotts - par.	492	2,365	3,337	do. - -	do.
Stapleford Tawney - par.	222	1,657	2,368	do. - -	do.
Stondon Massey - par.	261	1,126	1,949	Brentwood -	do.
Thoydon Mount - par.	148	1,564	2,100	Epping - -	Epping.
Willingale-Doe - par.	423	1,771	2,588	Ongar - -	Ongar.
Willingale-Spain - par.	207	1,216	1,526	do. - -	do.
TOTAL of UNION -	10,671	47,230	73,831		

ORMSKIRK UNION.

(Formed 31 Jan. 1837 by Order dated 5 Jan. 1837.)

COUNTY of LANCASTER:

Altcar - - par.	550	4,083	7,022	Liverpool -	Southport.
Aughton - - par.	3,145	4,610	23,958	Ormskirk -	Ormskirk.
Bickerstaffe - - tow.	2,260	6,414	19,230	do. -	do.
Birkdale - - tow.	8,705	2,215	47,288	Southport -	Southport.
Bispham - - tow.	280	926	1,910	Ormskirk -	Leyland.
Burscough - - tow.	2,290	4,960	17,587	do. -	Ormskirk.
Down Holland - tow.	748	3,473	6,133	do. -	do.
Formby - - tow.	3,908	6,619	20,928	Liverpool -	Southport.
Halsall - - tow.	1,368	6,995	12,173	Ormskirk -	Ormskirk.
Hesketh with Bec-censall - - } per.	863	4,736	5,996	Preston -	Leyland.
Lathom - - tow.	4,161	8,694	30,180	Ormskirk -	Ormskirk.

(continued)

Unions and Parishes, &c.		Population in 1881.	Area in Statute Acres in 1881.	Rateable Value in 1881.	Post Town.			Petty Sessional Division.

ORMSKIRK UNION—continued.

				£				
Lydiate	- - *tow.*	1,071	1,995	6,716	Ormskirk	-	-	Ormskirk.
Maghull	- - *tow.*	1,429	2,098	11,746	Liverpool	-	-	do.
Melling	- - *tow.*	802	2,118	7,060	do.	-	-	do.
North Meols	- - *tow.*	33,763	8,467	211,422	Southport	-	-	Southport.
Ormskirk (W.)	- *tow.*	6,651	573	17,412	Ormskirk	-	-	Ormskirk.
Rufford	- - *par.*	903	3,120	7,277	do.	-	-	Leyland, Hundred of (Old Division).
Scarisbrick	- - *tow.*	2,232	8,397	20,136	do.	-	-	Ormskirk.
Simonswood	- - *tow.*	465	2,645	7,086	Liverpool	-	-	do.
Skelmersdale	- *tow.*	5,707	1,941	33,845	Ormskirk	-	-	do.
Tarleton	- *par.*	1,900	5,553	9,519	Preston	-	-	Leyland.
TOTAL of UNION	-	83,212	90,662	524,654				

ORSETT UNION.

(Formed 10 Oct. 1835 by Order dated 22 Sept. 1835.)

COUNTY of ESSEX:

Aveley	- - *par.*	972	2,965	6,174	Romford	-	-	Orsett.
Bulphan	- *par.*	284	1,713	2,120	do.	-	-	do.
Chadwell Saint Mary's	*par.*	587	1,879	4,090	do.	-	-	do.
Corringham	- - *par.*	491	2,744	3,937	do.	-	-	do.
East Tilbury	- *par.*	405	2,134	3,775	do.	-	-	do.
Fobbing	- *par.*	429	2,588	4,371	do.	-	-	do.
Gray's Thurrock	*par.*	5,327	1,382	14,250	do.	-	-	do.
Hornden on the Hill	*par.*	592	2,649	4,585	do.	-	-	do.
Langdon-Hills	- *par.*	286	1,801	1,842	do.	-	-	do.
Little Thurrock	- *par.*	451	1,348	3,024	do.	-	-	do.
Mucking	- *par.*	251	2,217	3,857	do.	-	-	do.
North Ockendon	- *par.*	329	1,709	3,013	do.	-	-	do.
Orsett (W.) (a)	- *par.*	1,496	4,220	8,392	do.	-	-	do.
South Ockendon	- *par.*	1,194	2,936	5,835	do.	-	-	do.
Stanford-le-Hope	- *par.*	827	2,119	4,797	do.	-	-	do.
Stifford	- *par.*	286	1,597	2,763	do.	-	-	do.
West Thurrock	- *par.*	1,026	3,000	9,800	do.	-	-	do.
West Tilbury	- *par.*	347	1,866	3,370	do.	-	-	do.
TOTAL of UNION	-	16,480	41,167	89,995				

OSWESTRY INCORPORATION.

(Under the 31 Geo. 3, c. xxiv.)

COUNTY of DENBIGH:

Chirk	- - *par.*	2,171	4,773	16,498	Ruabon	-	-	Chirk Hundred.
Llansilin	- *par.*	1,645	15,188	12,479	Oswestry	-	-	do.

COUNTY of SALOP:

Kinnerley	- *par.*	1,200	5,891	10,980	Oswestry	-	-	Oswestry Hundred.
Knockin	- *par.*	264	1,610	2,416	do.	-	-	do.
Llanyblodwell	- *par.*	949	5,133	7,295	do.	-	-	do.
Llanymynech (such part as lies within the Hundred of Oswestry)	*par.*	492	1,341	3,808	do.	-	-	do.
Oswestry (W.)	- *par.*	1,076	14,346	29,220	do.	-	-	Borough of Oswestry.
Oswestry Town and Liberties	*hor.*	7,847	1,888	28,741	do.	-	-	Oswestry Hundred.
Ruyton	- *par.*	1,113	4,698	9,329	Shrewsbury	-	-	Pimhill Hundred. (continued)

ORSETT UNION:

(a) By Order which came into operation on 25 March 1882, a detached part of Orsett was amalgamated with Stock, in the Chelmsford Union.

Unions and Parishes, &c.	Population in 1881.	Area in Statute Acres in 1881.	Rateable Value in 1881.	Post Town.	Petty Sessional Division.

OSWESTRY INCORPORATION—County of Salop— continued.

			£		
Saint Martin's - *par.*	2,815	5,485	14,887	Oswestry -	Oswestry Hundred.
Syllatin - - *par.*	1,134	5,601	10,186	do. -	do.
*Sychtyn - - *tow.*	191	1,459	1,490	do. -	do.
West Felton - - *par.*	1,065	6,108	14,016	do. -	do.
Whittington - - *par.*	2,111	8,501	23,282	do. -	do.
TOTAL OF INCORPORATION	27,073	82,028	184,657		

OUNDLE UNION.

(Formed 1 Dec. 1835 by Order dated 13 Nov. 1835.)

COUNTY of HUNTINGDON :

Elton - - *par.*	805	3,250	6,043	Peterborough	Norman Cross.
Great Gidding - *par.*	485	2,050	2,908	Oundle -	Oundle.
Little Gidding - *par.*	56	713	690	do. -	do.

COUNTIES of HUNTINGDON and NORTHAMPTON :

Luddington in the Brook - - *par.*	86	580	932	Oundle -	Oundle.
Lutton - - *par.*	187	1,509	1,780	do. -	do.
Thurning - - *par.*	186	961	1,465	do. -	do.
Winwick - - *par.*	298	1,710	1,816	do. -	do.

COUNTY of NORTHAMPTON :

Apethorpe - - *par.*	214	2,630	2,355	Wansford -	Oundle.
Armston - - *ham.*	26 {	In Polebrooke }	873	Oundle -	do.
Ashton (a) - - *ham.*	120	In Oundle	2,236	do. -	do.
Barnwell All Saints - *par.*	137	1,680	2,150	do. -	do.
Barnwell Saint Andrew *par.*	257	1,740	2,673	do. -	do.
Benefield (a) - *par.*	472	5,100	5,978	do. -	do.
Blatherwick (a) - *par.*	142	1,975	2,830	Wansford -	do.
Bulwick - - *par.*	325	1,910	2,966	do. -	do.
Cotterstock - - *par.*	162	690	1,217	Oundle -	do.
Deene (a) - - *par.*	224 }	3,152 {	2,867	Wansford -	do.
Deenethorpe (a) - *ham.*	204 }		2,139	do. -	do.
Fotheringhay - *par.*	225	2,110	4,272	Oundle -	do.
Glapthorne - - *par.*	367	1,370	1,718	do. -	do.
Great Weldon (a) - *par.*	292	2,350	2,751	Wansford -	Kettering.
Hemington - - *par.*	157	1,240	1,369	Oundle -	Oundle.
King's Cliffe - *par.*	1,278	4,460	6,148	Wansford -	do.
Lilford cum Wigsthorpe - *par.*	157	1,940	2,548	Oundle -	do.
Little Weldon (a) - *ham.*	454	1,330	2,556	Wansford -	Kettering.
Nassington - *par.*	713	1,660	4,404	do. -	Oundle.
Oundle (W.) (a) - *par.*	2,953	5,300	13,806	Oundle -	do.
Pilton - - *par.*	123	1,473	1,798	do. -	do.
Polebrooke - - *par.*	125	2,730	2,356	do. -	do.

(*continued*)

OSWESTRY INCORPORATION :

* The township of Sychtyn is included in the Ecclesiastical Parish of Llansilin, and is not separately named in the Act 31 Geo. iii. c. xxiv. It has separate Overseers, and is shown separately in the Census Tables.

OUNDLE UNION :

(a) By Orders which came into operation on 25 March 1885,—
A detached part of Little Weldon was amalgamated with Great Weldon ;
A detached part of Deenethorpe was amalgamated with Deene ;
A detached part of Fineshade, in the Uppingham Union, was amalgamated with Blatherwick ;
Detached parts of Oundle were amalgamated with Benefield and Ashton.

Unions and Parishes, &c.	Population in 1881.	Area in Statute Acres in 1881.	Rateable Value in 1881.	Post Town.	Petty Sessional Division.
OUNDLE UNION—County of Northampton—*continued.*			£		
Southwick - - *par.*	262	1,320	4,650	Oundle - -	Oundle.
Stoke Doyle - *par.*	119	1,500	2,147	do. - -	do.
Tansor - - *par.*	252	2,050	2,586	do. - -	do.
Thorpe Achurch - *par.*	143	1,580	2,668	do. - -	do.
Wadenhoe - - *par.*	234	1,150	1,328	do. - -	do.
Warmington - *par.*	685	3,150	6,198	do. - -	do.
Wood Newton - *par.*	478	1,590	2,408	Wansford - -	do.
Yarwell - - *par.*	383	1,830	1,979	do. - -	do.
TOTAL of UNION - -	14,086	69,783	111,608		
OXFORD INCORPORA-TION. (Under the 17 & 18 Vict. c. ccxix. as amended by the 38 & 39 Vict. c. clxviii.) COUNTIES of BERKS and OXFORD :					
Saint Aldate (with the Liberty of Grand-pont) (a) - } *par.*	1,800		8,101	Oxford - -	City of Oxford (b).
COUNTY of OXFORD :					
All Saints - - *par.*	372		6,738	do. - -	do.
Holywell (otherwise called Saint Cross) } *par.*	821		5,749	do. - -	do.
Oxford University, Colleges and Halls } *par.*	428	1,506	36,066	do. - - {	The Chancellor's Court of the University.
Saint Ebbe - - *par.*	5,297		13,299	do. - -	do.
Saint Martin - *par.*	295		6,007	do. - -	do.
Saint Mary Magdalen *par.*	2,067		12,586	do. - -	do.
Saint Mary the Virgin *par.*	272		3,799	do. - -	do.
Saint Michael - - *par.*	696		9,807	do. - -	do.
Saint Peter le Bailey *par.*	887		5,151	do. - -	do.
Saint Peter in the East - } *par.*	593		4,749	do. - -	do.
Saint Thomas - *par.*	8,374		23,417	do. - -	do.
TOTAL of INCORPORATION	21,902	1,506	135,469		
PADDINGTON PARISH. (Board of Guardians constituted 25 Mar. 1845 by Order dated 11 Mar. 1845.) COUNTY of MIDDLESEX :					
Paddington (W.) (a) *par.*	107,248	1,251	1,189,864	Paddington, London, W.	Parish of Paddington : Hundred of Ossulston.

OXFORD INCORPORATION :

(a) By Order which came into operation on 25th March 1885, detached parts of North Hinksey and South Hinksey, in the Abingdon Union, were amalgamated with Saint Aldate, Oxford.

PADDINGTON PARISH :

(a) By Order dated 14 June 1883, the boundaries of the parish were re-adjusted in pursuance of Section 9 of the Willesden Local Board Act, 1876.

Unions and Parishes, &c.		Population in 1881.	Area in Statute Acres in 1881.	Rateable Value in 1881.	Post Town.	Petty Sessional Division.

PATELEY BRIDGE UNION.

(Formed 15 Feb. 1837 by Order dated 28 Jan. 1837 as amended by an Order dated 7 Feb. 1837.— Place marked thus * added 20 Oct. 1837 by Order dated 26 Sept. 1837, and Places marked thus † added 20 Feb. 1854 by Order dated 24 Jan. 1854.)

COUNTY of YORK, West Riding:

					£		
Bewerley	-	tow.	1,184	5,771	4,831	Pateley Bridge -	Claro.
†Birstwith	-	tow.	490	1,802	2,976	Ripley, Leeds -	do.
†Bishop Thornton	-	tow.	479	3,135	3,535	do. -	Liberty of Ripon.
†Clint	-	tow.	392	1,946	3,126	do. -	Claro.
Dacre	-	tow.	641	5,382	5,476	Leeds -	do.
Down Stonebeck	-	tow.	331	12,516	4,214	Pateley Bridge	do.
Fountain's Earth	-	tow.	322	6,744	3,596	do. -	do.
Hartwith-with-Wins-ley	-	tow.	1,062	5,360	6,482	Dacre, Leeds -	do.
High and Low Bishopside (W.) -		tow.	2,566	6,005	8,404	Pateley Bridge	Liberty of Ripon.
Menwith - with - Dar-ley		tow.	575	2,859	3,097	Ripley, Leeds	Claro.
Thornthwaite - with - Padside		tow.	247	3,480	1,707	do. -	do.
Thurcross	-	tow.	313	6,529	1,974	Otley, Leeds	do.
Upper Stonebeck	-	tow.	283	12,505	4,177	Pateley Bridge	do.
*Warsill	-	tow.	59	1,029	481	Ripley -	Liberty of Ripon.
TOTAL of UNION	- -		8,944	75,063	54,076		

PATRINGTON UNION.

(Formed 23 Sept. 1836 by Order dated 31 Aug. 1836.—Places marked thus * added 31 July 1837 by Order dated 5 July 1837.)

COUNTY of YORK, East Riding:

*Burton Pidsea	-	par.	352	2,303	3,421	Hull -	Middle Holderness.
Easington	-	tow.	382	2,319	3,216	do. -	South do
Halsham	-	par.	228	2,907	3,325	do. -	do. do.
Hilston	-	par.	39	553	603	do. -	Middle do.
Hollym	-	tow.	248	2,119	2,699	do. -	South do.
Holympton	-	tow.	216	1,903	2,302	do. -	do. do
Keyingham	-	par.	635	3,549	6,010	do. -	do. do.
Kilnsea	-	par.	198	911	644	do. -	do. do.
Otteringham	-	par.	568	4,304	6,703	do. -	do. do.
Out Newton	-	tow.	43	676	708	do. -	do. do.
Owstwich	-	tow.	89	1,336	1,636	do. -	Middle do.
Owthorne	-	tow.	510	1,052	3,018	do. -	South do.
Patrington (W.)	-	par.	1,360	3,741	7,427	do. -	do. do.
Paghill or Paul	-	tow.	545	4,956	7,474	do. -	do. do.
Rimswell	-	tow.	119	1,233	1,576	do. -	do. do.
Rooss	-	tow.	534	2,528	3,660	do. -	Middle do.
Ryhill cum Camer-ton -		tow.	275	1,571	2,578	do. -	South do.
*Skeckling cum Burst-wick -		tow.	422	4,338	6,130	do. -	do. do.
Skeffling	-	par.	166	1,834	2,096	do. -	do. do.
South Frodingham	-	tow.	63	1,205	1,309	do. -	do. do.
Sunk Island	-	par.	419	6,914	9,879	do. -	do. do.
Thorngumbauld	-	tow.	267	1,657	2,416	do. -	do. do.
Tunstall	-	par.	120	1,346	1,537	do. -	Middle do.
Waxholme	-	tow.	94	542	682	do. -	South do.
Welwick	-	par.	341	3,515	4,427	do. -	do. do.
Winestead	-	par.	163	2,108	2,834	do. -	do. do.
Withernsea	-	tow.	332	746	1,940	do. -	do. do.
TOTAL of UNION	-		8,758	62,166	90,280		

Unions and Parishes, &c.		Population in 1881.	Area in Statute Acres in 1881.	Rateable Value in 1881.	Post Town.	Petty Sessional Division.

PEMBROKE UNION.

(Formed 6 Jan. 1837 by Order dated 13 Dec. 1836.)

COUNTY of PEMBROKE:

Unions and Parishes, &c.		Population in 1881.	Area in Statute Acres in 1881.	Rateable Value in 1881. £	Post Town.	Petty Sessional Division.
Angle	par.	458	2,320	2,275	Pembroke	Castlemartin.
Bosheston	par.	174	1,664	994	do.	do.
Burton	par.	934	3,472	2,492	Haverfordwest	Roose.
Carew	par.	933	5,405	5,503	Pembroke	Castlemartin.
Castle Martin	par.	393	4,811	3,601	do.	do.
Cosheston	par.	566	1,990	2,690	do.	do.
Gumfreston	par.	91	1,644	1,637	Tenby	Narberth.
Hodgeston	par.	65	735	694	Pembroke	Castlemartin.
Lamphey	par.	307	1,985	3,165	do.	do.
Lawrenny	par.	288	2,502	1,889	do.	Narberth.
Llanstadwell	par.	3,017	3,307	8,996	Neyland	Roose.
Manorbier	par.	631	3,623	5,187	Tenby	Castlemartin.
Mouncton	par.	1,657	4,351	5,589	Pembroke	do.
Nash	par.	104	398	808	do.	do.
Penally	par.	535	2,832	3,018	Tenby	do.
Pwlcrochan	par.	190	1,709	1,816	Pembroke	do.
Redbarth	par.	90	305	270	Tenby	Narberth.
Roscerowther	par.	212	2,390	2,273	Pembroke	Castlemartin.
Rosemarket	par.	366	1,740	1,331	Haverfordwest	Roose.
Saint Florance	par.	338	2,528	3,157	Tenby	Castlemartin.
Saint Mary, Pembroke (W.)	} par.	11,869	2,435	30,347	Pembroke	do.
Saint Mary, Tenby	in lib.	4,750	} 2,242	{ 19,278	Tenby	Tenby.
Saint Mary, Tenby	out lib.	198		1,066	do.	Narberth.
Saint Michael), Pembroke	} par.	1,340	1,853	4,625	Pembroke	Castlemartin.
Saint Petrox	par.	121	1,000	1,202	do.	do.
Saint Twinell	par.	171	1,418	1,431	do.	do.
Stackpole	par.	295	2,990	2,558	do.	do.
Upton	par.	16	333	373	do.	do.
Warren	par.	149	1,211	1,108	do.	do.
TOTAL OF UNION		30,258	63,393	119,373		

PENISTONE UNION.

(Formed 27 July 1849 by Order dated 12 July 1849.)

COUNTY of YORK, West Riding:

Unions and Parishes, &c.		Population in 1881.	Area in Statute Acres in 1881.	Rateable Value in 1881.	Post Town.	Petty Sessional Division.
Cawthorne	par.	1,166	3,708	6,541	Barnsley	Barnsley.
Denby	tow.	1,559	2,885	6,013	Huddersfield	do.
Gunthwaite	tow.	70	953	939	Penistone, Sheffield	do.
High Hoyland	tow.	232	853	1,064	Barnsley	do.
Hoyland Swaine	tow.	750	2,024	2,778	Penistone, Sheffield	do.
Hunshelf	tow.	1,401	2,465	9,808	Deepcar	do.
Ingbirchworth	tow.	335	1,104	2,550	Penistone	do.
Kexborough	tow.	610	1,543	2,831	Barnsley	do.
Langsett	tow.	271	4,916	2,488	Penistone, Sheffield	do.
Oxspring	tow.	350	1,203	4,033	do.	do.
Penistone	tow.	2,254	1,133	10,938	do.	do.
Silkstone	tow.	1,433	1,497	5,521	Barnsley	do.
Thurgoland	tow.	1,953	2,221	5,925	Sheffield	do.
Thurlstone (W.)	tow.	2,851	8,117	21,667	Penistone, Sheffield	do.
West Clayton	tow.	1,435	1,140	4,686	Huddersfield	do.
TOTAL OF UNION		16,673	35,762	87,782		

Unions and Parishes, &c.	Population in 1881.	Area in Statute Acres in 1881.	Rateable Value in 1881.	Post Town.	Petty Sessional Division.

PENRITH UNION.

(Formed 26 Dec. 1836 by Order dated 30 Nov. 1836. Spelling of names of places marked * is as altered by Order dated 18 August 1887.)

COUNTY of CUMBERLAND:

Unions and Parishes, &c.	Population in 1881.	Area in Statute Acres in 1881.	Rateable Value in 1881.	Post Town.	Petty Sessional Division.
			£		
*Ainstable - - par.	453	4,433	4,569	Carlisle - -	Leath Ward.
Berrier and Murrah - tow.	103	2,552	1,402	Penrith - -	do.
*Bowscale - - tow.	32	1,262	122	do. - -	do.
Castle Sowerby (a) - par.	765	8,605	6,489	do. - -	do.
Catterlen - - tow.	116	1,561	1,581	do. - -	do.
*Croglin - - par.	251	7,112	2,809	Carlisle - -	do.
Culgaith - - tow.	347	2,911	3,792	Penrith - -	do.
Dacre - - par.	965	7,397	11,826	do. - -	do.
Edenhall - - par.	270	3,429	3,776	Carlisle - -	do.
Gamblesby (a) - tow.	269	4,687	2,720	do. - -	do.
Glassonby (a) - tow.	165	2,287	2,637	do. - -	do.
Great Salkeld (a) - par.	501	3,774	5,064	Penrith - -	do.
Greystoke, Johnby, Little Blencow, Motherby, and Gill - - } tow.	608	7,511	5,352	do. - -	do.
Hesket in the Forest par.	1,965	16,399	26,243	Carlisle - -	do.
Hunsonby and Winskill - - } tow.	284	1,687	2,198	do. - -	do.
Hutton and Thomas Close - } par.	244	2,462	2,819	Penrith - -	do.
Hutton John - tow.	47	689	726	do. - -	do.
Hutton Roof - - tow.	167	2,643	1,692	do. - -	do.
Hutton Soil - - tow.	384	4,349	4,216	do. - -	do.
Kirkland and Blencarn - } tow.	175	4,066	2,142	do. - -	do.
Kirkoswald - - tow.	595	5,737	5,646	Carlisle - -	do.
Lazonby - - tow.	650	8,378	7,792	do. - -	do.
Little Salkeld (a) - tow.	126	1,149	1,959	do. - -	do.
*Langwathby (a) - par.	341	2,012	4,077	do. - -	do.
Matterdale (a) - tow.	364	7,288	2,191	Penrith - -	do.
Melmerby - - par.	286	5,362	3,005	Carlisle - -	do.
*Middlesceugh and Braithwaite - } tow.	145	2,092	1,768	do. - -	do.
Mosedale - - tow.	46	2,418	362	Penrith - -	do.
Mungrisdale - - tow.	180	6,593	1,274	do. - -	do.
Newton - - tow.	171	1,013	2,264	do. - -	do.
Ousby - - par.	243	7,472	3,524	do. - -	do.
Penrith (W.) - par.	9,268	7,587	43,569	do. - -	do.
Plumpton Wall - tow.	345	3,052	3,727	do. - -	do.
Renwick - - par.	258	4,299	2,043	Carlisle - -	do.
Skelton - - par.	726	7,417	7,065	Penrith - -	do.
Skirwith - - tow.	276	5,249	3,165	do. - -	do.
Staffield - - tow.	247	5,636	4,227	Carlisle - -	do.
Threlkeld - - tow.	419	5,956	2,372	Keswick - -	do.
Watermillock (a) - tow.	445	9,735	3,987	Penrith - -	do.
TOTAL of UNION -	23,242	188,261	198,192		

PENRITH UNION:

(a) By Orders which came into operation on 25 March 1886,—

Certain parts of Matterdale were amalgamated with Watermillock ;

Certain parts of Great Salkeld were amalgamated with Little Salkeld and Langwathby ;

A part of Little Salkeld was amalgamated with Great Salkeld ;

A detached part of Glassonby was amalgamated with Gamblesby ;

A detached part of Castle Sowerby was amalgamated with Dalston, in the Carlisle Union, and a detached part of Dalston was amalgamated with Castle Sowerby.

Unions and Parishes, &c.	Population in 1881.	Area in Statute Acres in 1881.	Rateable Value in 1891.	Post Town.	Petty Sessional Division.
PENZANCE UNION.					
(Formed 10 June 1837 by Order dated 13 May 1837.— Place marked thus * added 25 Dec. 1861 by Order dated 19 Nov. 1861.)					
COUNTY of CORNWALL :			£		
Gulval - - par.	1,623	4,355	7,500	Penzance -	Penwith: West Division.
Ludgvan - - par.	2,632	4,541	7,898	do.	do.
Madron (W.) - par.	2,647	5,589	13,468	do.	do.
Marazion - cha.	1,294	719	3,925	Marazion -	do.
Morvah - par.	184	1,271	1,244	Penzance -	do.
Paul - - par.	6,005	3,442	11,754	do.	do.
Penzance - tow.	12,499	337	35,719	do.	Borough of Penzance.
Perranuthno - par.	896	1,103	2,784	Marazion -	Penwith : West Division.
Saint Buryan - par.	1,364	6,975	9,680	Penzance -	do.
Saint Erth - par.	2,049	4,012	8,822	Hayle	Penwith: East Division.
Saint Hilary - par.	957	2,922	4,240	Marazion	do. West Division.
Saint Ives - par.	6,445	1,890	13,825	St. Ives	Borough of St. Ives.
Saint Just - par.	6,409	7,033	14,958	Penzance	Penwith: West Division.
Saint Levan - par.	584	2,406	3,640	do.	do.
*Saint Michael's Mount par.	84	21	279	Marazion -	do.
Sancreed - par.	937	4,608	5,159	Penzance	do.
Sennen - par.	737	2,299	3,069	do.	do.
Towednack - par.	644	2,842	2,566	St. Ives	do.
Uny Lelant - par.	1,720	3,524	6,358	Lelant	East Division
Zennor - par.	601	4,360	3,230	St. Ives	West Division.
TOTAL of UNION -	50,311	64,879	160,118		
PERSHORE UNION.					
(Formed 14 Oct. 1835 by Order dated 28 Sept. 1835.— Place marked thus * added 7 Dec. 1835 by Order dated 13 Nov. 1835 ; and places marked thus † added 29 Sept. 1836 by Order dated 12 Sept. 1836.)					
COUNTY of WORCESTER :					
Abberton - par.	92	1,001	1,090	Pershore -	Pershore.
Besford - cha.	148	In Defford	2,069	do.	do.
Birlingham - par.	352	1,210	3,649	do.	do.
Bishampton - par.	428	2,140	2,606	do.	do.
†Bredicot - par.	67	397	821	Worcester	Worcester.
Bricklehampton - cha.	187	In Defford	1,872	Pershore -	Pershore.
Broughton Hackett - par.	160	390	632	Worcester -	Worcester.
Charlton - ham.	304 {	In Cropthorne }	2,618	Pershore -	Pershore.
Churchill - par.	70	924	875	Worcester	Worcester
Cropthorne - par.	320	2,000	2,841	Pershore -	Pershore.
Defford - cha.	438	5,810	3,148	do.	do.
*Dormstone - par.	101	830	631	Worcester	do.
Eckington - par.	673	2,260	5,346	Pershore	do.
Elmley Castle - par.	372	2,057	3,025	do.	do.
Fladbury - par.	454	4,290	3,906	do.	do.
Flyford Flavell - par.	165	750	698	Worcester	do.
Grafton Flyford - par.	229	1,610	1,766	do.	do.
Great Comberton - par.	211	960	1,798	Pershore -	do.
Hill and Moor - ham.	337	In Fladbury	2,334	do.	do.
Holy Cross in Pershore, (W.) (b) } par.	2,598	2,950	11,550	do.	do.
Kington - par.	136	1,000	914	Worcester -	do.

(continued)

Unions and Parishes, &c.		Population in 1881.	Area in Statute Acres in 1881.	Rateable Value in 1881.	Post Town.	Petty Sessional Division.
PERSHORE UNION—County of Worcester— *continued.*				£		
Little Comberton	par.	287	770	1,650	Pershore -	Pershore.
Naunton Beauchamp	par.	134	1,025	1,192	do.	do.
Netherton	ham.	66 {	In Cropthorne }	921	do. -	do.
North Piddle	par.	153	810	812	Worcester -	do.
†Norton juxta Kempsey (b)	} par.	830	1,811	4,332	do. -	Worcester.
Peopleton	par.	274	1,474	2,404	Pershore -	Pershore.
Pinvin	cha.	291 {	In Saint Andrew }	1,801	do.	do.
Pirton	par.	183	1,669	2,523	Worcester	do.
Saint Andrew in Pershore (b)	} par.	1,036	4,120	6,304	Pershore -	do.
†Spetchley	par.	160	779	1,466	Worcester	Worcester.
Stoulton (b)	par.	370	1,952	2,920	do.	do.
Strensham	par.	195	1,800	3,565	Tewkesbury	Pershore.
Throckmorton	cha.	148	1,560	1,599	Pershore	do.
Upton Snodsbury	par.	369	1,661	2,477	Worcester	Worcester.
White Ladies Aston	par.	312	1,230	1,985	do.	do.
†Whittington (a) (b)	cha.	373	989	2,708	do. -	do.
Wick	cha.	265	In Defford	3,408	Pershore -	Pershore.
Wyre Piddle	cha.	262	In Fladbury	1,235	do. -	do.
TOTAL of UNION	-	13,560	52,269	97,834		

PETERBOROUGH UNION.

(Formed 3 Dec. 1835 by Order dated 14 Nov. 1835. — Place marked thus * added 10 Dec. 1841 by Order of that date, and places marked thus † added 25 Mar. 1861 by Order dated 18 Mar. 1861.)

COUNTY of CAMBRIDGE :

*Thorney	par.	2,055	17,590	26,708	Peterborough -	Isle of Ely at Whittlesey.
COUNTIES of CAMBRIDGE and HUNTINGDON :						
Stanground (a)	par.	1,308	2,290	8,272	do. -	Hundred of Norman Cross.
COUNTY of HUNTINGDON :						
Alwalton	par.	318	1,040	1,679	do. -	Hundred of Norman Cross.
Caldecot	par.	39	778	1,121	Stilton -	do.
Chesterton	par.	172	1,330	2,010	Peterborough	do.
Denton	par.	75	890	1,997	Stilton -	do.
Farcet (a)	cha.	710	3,408	7,531	Peterborough	do.
Fletton	par.	1,841	780	18,352	do. -	do.
Folksworth	par.	201	867	1,331	Yaxley -	do.
Glatton	par.	249	2,100	2,962	Stilton -	do.
Haddon	par.	140	1,214	1,591	Yaxley	do.
Holme	cha.	629	4,300	8,775	Stilton -	do.
Morborne	par.	84	1,174	1,439	Yaxley	do.
Overton Longville	par.	261	2,400	4,670	Peterborough	do.
Overton Waterville	par.	309	1,350	2,306	do. -	do.

(continued)

PERSHORE UNION :

(a) By Order which came into operation on 25 March 1884, a detached part of Saint Peter the Great, in the Worcester Union, was amalgamated with Whittington.
(b) By Provisional Order which came into operation on 25 March 1885,—
    A detached part of Norton juxta Kempsey was amalgamated with Whittington ;
    A detached part of Stoulton was amalgamated with Norton juxta Kempsey;
    A detached part of Saint Andrew in Pershore, known as "Crab Common," was amalgamated with Holy Cross in Pershore.

PETERBOROUGH UNION :

(a) By Order which came into operation on 25 March 1886, certain detached parts of Stanground were amalgamated with Farcet.
(b) By Provisional Order which came into operation on 25 March 1887,—
    Detached parts of Maxey were amalgamated with Northborough ;
    Detached parts of Glinton were amalgamated with Newborough and Northborough ; and
    Detached parts of Peakirk were amalgamated with Glinton.

Unions and Parishes, &c.	Population in 1881.	Area in Statute Acres in 1881.	Rateable Value in 1881.	Post Town.	Petty Sessional Division.
PETERBOROUGH UNION—County of Huntingdon—*cont.*			£		
Stilton - - - *par.*	615	1,620	3,603	Stilton - -	Hundred of Norman Cross.
Washingley - - *par.*	97	1,260	1,664	do. - -	do.
Water Newton - *par.*	116	863	1,097	Wansford - -	do.
Woodstone - - *par.*	915	1,050	3,348	Peterborough -	do.
Yaxley - - - *par.*	1,355	1,290	13,088	do. - -	do.
COUNTY OF LINCOLN :					
Crowland - - *par.*	2,929	12,780	25,392	Crowland - -	Elloe.
COUNTY OF NORTHAMPTON :					
Ailesworth - - *ham.*	333	In Castor	1,718	Peterborough -	Liberty of Peterborough.
†Borough Fen - - *par.*	149	3,130	3,930	do. - -	do.
Castor - - - *par.*	661	7,020	4,800	do. - -	do.
Deeping Gate - *ham.*	212	In Maxey	1,304	Market Deeping -	do.
Etton - - - *par.*	137	1,270	3,319	do. - -	do.
Eye - - - *par.*	1,305	2,670	6,298	Peterborough -	do.
Glinton (*b*) - - *par.*	391	1,380	1,323	Market Deeping -	do.
Gunthorpe - - *ham.*	63 {	In Werrington }	401	Peterborough -	do.
Helpstone - - *par.*	711	1,860	7,807	Market Deeping -	do.
Marholm - - *par.*	166	1,790	2,879	Peterborough -	do.
Maxey (*b*) - - *par.*	380	2,280	3,930	Market Deeping -	do.
†Minster Close Precincts - } *par.*	277 {	In Saint John the Baptist }	1,783	Peterborough -	do.
Newborough (*b*) - *par.*	699	4,040	8,258	do. - -	do.
Northborough (*b*) - *par.*	212	710	1,504	Market Deeping -	do.
Paston - - *par.*	112 {	In Werrington }	1,533	Peterborough -	do.
Peakirk (*b*) - - *par.*	245	630	2,596	Market Deeping -	do.
Saint John the Baptist, in the City of Peterborough (W.) } *par.*	19,846	6,310	81,066	Peterborough -	do.
Sutton - - - *cha.*	92 }	In Castor {	1,285	do. - -	do.
Upton - - - *cha.*	72 }		1,554	do. - -	do.
Walton - - - *ham.*	216 {	In Werrington }	4,750	do. - -	do.
Werrington - - *ham.*	777	3,150	6,422	do. - -	do.
TOTAL of UNION -	41,504	100,514	291,299		
PETERSFIELD UNION.					
(Formed 27 April 1835 by Order dated 2 April 1835.—Place marked thus * added 4 May 1869 by Order dated 21 April 1869.)					
COUNTIES of SUSSEX and SOUTHAMPTON :					
*Bramshott - - *par.*	1,476	6,526	7,281	Liphook - -	Petersfield.
COUNTY of SOUTHAMPTON :					
Buriton - - *par.*	1,153	6,435	9,162	Petersfield -	do.
Colemore - - *par.*	100	1,472	974	Alton - -	do.
East-Meon - - *par.*	1,559	11,377	9,827	Petersfield -	do.
Empshot - - *par.*	158	761	1,247	do. - -	do.
Froxfield - - *par.*	691	4,909	4,181	do. - -	do.
Greatham - - *par.*	285	2,031	2,006	do. - -	do.
Hawkley - - *par.*	302	1,446	2,180	do. - -	do.
Lyss, otherwise Lyss Turney } *par.*	1,215	3,620	6,234	do. - -	do.
Petersfield (W.) - *par.*	1,646	237	4,896	do. - -	do.
Priors Dean - - *par.*	165	1,596	1,185	do. - -	do.
Privett - - *par.*	257	1,279	1,149	Alton - -	do.
Sheet - - - *ty.*	648	1,583	3,611	Petersfield -	do.
Steep - - - *par.*	600	2,658	4,642	do. - -	do.
TOTAL of UNION -	10,255	45,930	58,575		

PETERBOROUGH UNION :
(*b*) For notes, *see* p. 289.

Unions and Parishes, &c.		Population in 1881.	Area in Statute Acres in 1881.	Rateable Value in 1881.	Post Town.	Petty Sessional Division.

PETWORTH UNION.

(Formed 14 Sept. 1835 by Order dated 28 Aug. 1835.—Places marked thus * added 29 Sept. 1869 by Order dated 13 Aug. 1869.)

COUNTY of SUSSEX :

				£		
*Barlavington	par.	182	1,198	1,128	Petworth -	Petworth.
*Bignor	par.	154	1,344	1,195	Pulborough	do.
*Burton	par.	73	814	766	Petworth -	do.
*Bury	par.	517	3,495	3,493	Pulborough	do.
*Coates	par.	61	347	552	do. -	do.
*Duncton	par.	268	1,360	1,194	Petworth -	do.
*Egdean	par.	76	739	654	do. -	do.
*Fittleworth	par.	696	2,362	2,949	Pulborough	do.
Kirdford	par.	1,710	12,497	7,741	Billingshurst	do.
*North Chapel	par.	794	3,923	2,941	Petworth -	do.
Petworth (W.)	par.	2,942	6,129	12,551	do. -	do.
*Stopham	par.	156	864	1,264	Pulborough	do.
*Sutton	par.	310	2,064	1,759	do. -	do.
Wisborough - Green (W.) (a)	par.	1,656	8,565	7,380	Billingshurst	do.
TOTAL of UNION		9,595	45,701	45,576		

PEWSEY UNION.

(Formed 8 Dec. 1835 by Order dated 24 Nov. 1835.—Places marked thus * added 30 Sept. 1879 by Order dated 17 July 1879.)

COUNTY of WILTS :

Alton Priors (a) (b)	cha.	198	2,630	1,390	Marlborough	Everley and Pewsey.
Burbage	par.	1,317	4,013	4,808	do. -	Marlborough.
Charlton	par.	145	1,706	1,262	do.	Everley and Pewsey.
*Chute	par.	430	3,181	2,626	Andover -	do.
*Chute Forest	par.	159	1,930	1,850	do. -	do.
Collingbourn Ducis	par.	426	3,431	2,701	Marlborough	do.
Collingbourn Kingston	par.	696	7,400	5,867	do. -	do.
Easton	par.	323	2,080	2,126	do. -	do.
Enford (b)	par.	860	7,880	5,650	do. -	do.
Everley	par.	354	3,275	2,597	do. -	do.
Fittleton	par.	347	3,175	2,245	do. -	do.
Hewish (b)	par.	129	754	750	do. -	do.
*Ludgershall	par.	491	1,773	2,199	Andover	do.
Manningford Abbots	par.	102	919	1,340	Marlborough	do.
Manningford Bohun	ty.	233	1,305	1,656	do. -	do.
Manningford Bruce	par.	251	1,088	1,392	do. -	do.
Milton-Lilbourne	par.	599	3,502	3,723	Pewsey	do.
Netherhaven (b)	par.	582	5,160	3,322	Marlborough	do.
North Newnton (b)	par.	374	1,381	2,086	do. -	do.
*North Tidworth	par.	248	3,069	2,043	do. -	do.
Pewsey (W.)	par.	1,895	4,791	7,467	Pewsey	do.
Rushall	par.	195	2,164	1,817	Marlborough	do.
Uphaven	par.	484	3,329	3,244	do. -	do.
,Wilcot (b)	par.	563	2,668	2,957	do. -	do.
Wilsford	par.	204	1,692	1,603	do. -	do.
Woodborough	par.	397	1,015	1,650	do. -	do.
Wootton Rivers	par.	389	1,179	1,671	do. -	do.
TOTAL of UNION		12,403	76,490	72,042		

PETWORTH UNION :

(a) By Order which came into operation on 25 March 1884, the part of Alfold, in the Hambledon Union, situate in the County of Sussex, was amalgamated with Wisborough-Green.

PEWSEY UNION :

(a) By Provisional Order which came into operation on 25 March 1885, a detached part of Alton Barnes, in the Devizes Union, was amalgamated with Alton Priors.

(b) By Order which came into operation on 25 March 1885,— Detached parts of Alton Priors, Hewish, and North Newnton, were amalgamated with Wilcot; and A detached part of Netherhaven was amalgamated with Enford.

Unions and Parishes, &c.	Population in 1881.	Area in Statute Acres in 1881.	Rateable Value in 1881.	Post Town.	Petty Sessional Division.

PICKERING UNION.

(Formed 10 Jan. 1837 by Order dated 15 Dec. 1836.)

COUNTY of YORK, North Riding:

			£		
Aislaby (b) - - tow.	134	925	1,203	Pickering -	Pickering Lythe West.
Allerston - par.	444	10,043	3,802	do. -	do. East.
Barugh-Ambo - tow.	261	1,461	2,035	do. -	Pickering Lythe West.
Cowthorn - tow.	25	1,133	387	do. -	do. do.
Cropton (b) - tow.	353	4,337	1,952	do. -	do. do.
Ebberston (a) - tow.	592	6,094	3,705	York -	do. East.
Hartoft (b) - tow.	144	4,026	691	Pickering -	do. West.
Kingthorp - tow.	50	1,209	1,114	do. -	do. do.
Kirbymisperton - tow.	270	1,791	2,422	do. -	do. do.
Lastingham - tow.	184	417	648	do. -	Ryedale.
Levisham - par.	105	2,975	1,936	do. -	Pickering Lythe West.
Lockton - tow.	400	7,423	2,112	do. -	do. do.
Marton (b) - tow.	193	677	1,029	Kirby Moorside -	do. do.
Middleton (b) - tow.	285	2,156	1,849	Pickering -	do. do.
Newton (b) - tow.	247	2,397	2,054	do. -	do. do.
Pickering (W.) (b) - tow.	3,959	16,037	15,880	do. -	do. do.
Pickering Marshes (b) tow.	270	2,335	2,637	do. -	do. do.
Rosedale, Eastside - tow.	393	5,394	1,969	do. -	do. do.
Rosedale, West-side - tow.	309	1,080	1,989	do. -	Ryedale.
Sinnington (b) - tow.	315	2,215	3,297	do. -	Pickering Lythe West.
Spaunton - tow.	90	1,284	1,202	do. -	Ryedale.
Thornton-Dale (b) - par.	1,258	8,274	7,114	do. -	Pickering Lythe West.
Wilton - tow.	168	1,784	1,863	do. -	do. do.
Wrelton (b) - tow.	229	1,888	1,343	do. -	do. do.
TOTAL of UNION -	10,678	87,355 (c)	64,233		

PLOMESGATE UNION.

(Formed 5 Oct. 1835 by Order dated 21 Sept. 1835.—Places marked thus * added 22 Mar. 862 by Orders dated 11 Mar. 1862.)

COUNTY of SUFFOLK :

Aldeburgh - par.	2,106	1,832	7,471	Saxmundham -	Aldeburgh Borough.
Benhall - par.	623	2,156	4,139	do. -	Saxmundham.
Blaxhall - par.	513	1,975	3,163	Wickham Market -	Woodbridge.
Brandeston - par.	401	1,224	2,482	do. -	Framlingham.
Bruisyard - par.	239	1,126	1,775	Saxmundham -	do.
Butley - par.	383	1,978	2,126	Wickham Market -	Woodbridge.
Campsea Ash - par.	383	1,813	3,755	do. -	do.
Chillesford - par.	233	1,853	1,655	do. -	do.
Cransford - par.	184	1,189	1,810	do. -	Framlingham.
Cretingham - par.	303	1,638	2,783	do. -	do.
Earl Soham - par.	607	1,944	3,708	do. -	do.
Easton - par.	415	1,462	2,585	do. -	do.
Eyke - par.	380	2,749	2,719	Woodbridge -	Woodbridge.
Farnham - par.	185	1,177	2,109	Saxmundham -	Saxmundham.
Framlingham - par.	2,518	4,657	12,278	Wickham Market -	Framlingham.

(continued)

PICKERING UNION :

(a) Certain detached parts of Ebberston were amalgamated with Snainton, in the Scarborough Union, by Order which came into operation on 25 March 1886.

(b) By Orders which came into operation on 25 March 1887,—
Certain parts of Aislaby were amalgamated with Hartoft, Middleton, and Wrelton ;
Certain detached parts of Cropton were amalgamated with Middleton ;
Certain parts of Middleton were amalgamated with Hartoft ;
A detached part of Newton was amalgamated with Pickering ;
Detached parts of Pickering were amalgamated with Newton and Pickering Marshes ;
A detached part of Sinnington was amalgamated with Marton ;

PICKERING UNION—continued.

Detached parts of Wrelton were amalgamated with Cropton and Middleton ;
All the parts of a Township known as Farmanby were amalgamated with Thornton-Dale ; and
A detached part of Thornton Risebrough, in the Kirkby Moorside Union, was amalgamated with Middleton.

(c) There is some Moor Land comprised in this Union containing 7,561 acres common to Spaunton, Appleton-le-Moor, Lastingham, Hutton-le-Hole, and Rosedale West.
Wheeldale Moor containing 2,708 acres is comprised in this Union.
Other Lands containing altogether 1,413 acres common to Thornton-Dale and Farmanby are also comprised in this Union.

Unions and Parishes, &c.	Population in 1881.	Area in Statute Acres in 1881.	Rateable Value in 1881.	Post Town.	Petty Sessional Division

PLOMESGATE UNION—County of Suffolk—*continued.*

			£		
Freston - - *par.*	385	1,846	2,142	Saxmundham	Saxmundham.
*Gedgrave - - *par.*	66	1,809	2,012	Wickham Market	Woodbridge.
Great Glemham - *par.*	344	1,910	2,750	Saxmundham -	Framlingham.
Hacheston - - *par.*	435	1,726	3,142	Wickham Market -	do.
*Havergate Island - *par.*	6	264	200	do. - -	Woodbridge.
Haselwood - - *par.*	85	1,937	1,496	Saxmundham -	Saxmundham.
Hoo - - *par.*	104	1,185	1,680	Wickham Market -	Framlingham.
Iken - - *par.*	324	2,597	2,608	do. - -	Woodbridge.
Kenton - - *par.*	254	1,208	1,836	Stonham -	Framlingham.
Kettleburgh - *par.*	290	1,435	2,266	Wickham Market -	do.
Letheringham - *par.*	202	1,134	1,750	do. - -	do.
Little Glemham - *par.*	271	1,268	2,193	do. - -	do.
Marlesford - - *par.*	334	1,277	2,476	do. - -	do.
Mouewden - - *par.*	220	1,088	1,706	do. - -	do.
Orford - - *par.*	1,117	2,702	3,725	do. - -	Woodbridge.
Parham - - *par.*	446	2,212	3,521	do. - -	Framlingham.
Rendham - - *par.*	367	1,721	2,589	Saxmundham -	do.
Rendlesham - - *par.*	354	2,020	2,750	Woodbridge -	Woodbridge.
Saxmundham - *par.*	1,318	1,101	5,567	Saxmundham -	Saxmundham.
Snape - - *par.*	508	2,100	2,658	Wickham Market -	do.
Sternfield - - *par.*	232	1,105	1,683	Saxmundham -	do.
Stratford Saint Andrew *par.*	192	793	1,353	do. - -	Framlingham.
Sudborne - - *par.*	578	5,429	5,216	Wickham Market -	Woodbridge.
Swefling - - *par.*	290	1,120	2,069	Saxmundham -	Framlingham.
Tuustall - - *par.*	615	2,863	3,929	Wickham Market -	Woodbridge.
Wantisden - - *par.*	110	2,126	1,370	do. - -	do.
Wickham Market (W.) *par.*	1,469	1,174	4,178	do. - -	do.
TOTAL OF UNION -	20,479	75,923	123,442		

PLYMOUTH INCORPORATION.

(Under 6 Anne, c. VI. ; 32 Geo. 2, c. LIX ; 26 Geo. 3, c. XIX. ; and 53 Geo. 3, c. LXXIII.)

COUNTY of DEVON :

Charles (W.) - *par.*	27,213	900 }	193,845 {	Plymouth -	Plymouth.
Saint Andrew - *par.*	46,581	568 }		do.	do.
TOTAL OF INCORPORATION	73,794 (a)	1,468 (a)	193,845		

PLYMPTON SAINT MARY UNION.

(Formed 10 Oct. 1836 by Order dated 14 Sept. 1836, as amended by Order dated 10 Oct. 1836.—Place marked thus * added 25 Dec. 1861 by Order dated 11 Nov. 1861, and thus † added 31 Jan. 1863 by Order dated 7 Jan. 1863.)

COUNTY of DEVON :

Bickleigh - - *par.*	362	2,365	2,830	Roborough -	Midland Roborough.
Brixton (a) - - *par.*	686	2,945	5,696	Plympton -	Ermington and Plympton.
†Chelson Meadow - *par.*	5	177	495	Plymstock -	do.
Compton Gifford - *par.*	2,305	612	13,143	Plymouth -	Midland Roborough.
Cornwood - - *par.*	1,165	10,680	6,836	Ivybridge -	Ermington and Plympton.

(continued)

PLYMOUTH INCORPORATION :

(a) Drake's Island which is included in the Incorporation contains an acreage of 6. and a population of 64, and Plymouth Breakwater and Lighthouse contain an acreage of 17, and a population of 5.

PLYMPTON SAINT MARY UNION :

(a) By Orders which came into operation on 25 March 1884,—
Two detached parts of Modbury, in the Kingsbridge Union, were amalgamated with Ermington ;
A detached part of Ermington was amalgamated with Holbeton ;
A detached part of Holbeton was amalgamated with Newton Ferrers ; and
A detached part of Yealmpton was amalgamated with Brixton

Unions and Parishes, &c.		Population in 1881.	Area in Statute Acres in 1881.	Rateable Value in 1881.	Post Town.	Petty Sessional Division.

PLYMPTON SAINT MARY UNION—County of Devon —*continued.*

				£		
Egg Buckland	par.	1,131	3,331	9,275	Plymouth - -	Midland Roborough.
Ermington (a)	par.	2,205	4,952	11,196	Ivybridge - -	Ermington and Plympton.
Harford -	par.	182	2,050	2,789	do. - -	do.
Holbeton (a) -	par.	1,097	4,748	7,095	do. - -	do.
*Laira Green	par.	138	131	3,098	Plymouth - -	Midland Roborough.
Newton Ferrers (a) -	par.	705	3,001	4,017	Plympton -	Ermington and Plympton.
Plympton Maurice, alias Saint Maurice	par.	1,146	232	2,854	do. -	do.
Plympton Saint Mary (W.) - -	par.	3,513	10,211	22,483	do. - -	do.
Plymstock - -	par.	3,169	3,559	10,064	Plymstock -	do.
Revelstoke - -	par.	550	1,541	2,225	Plympton - -	do.
Saint Budeaux	par.	1,986	2,619	7,235	Plymouth -	Midland Roborough.
Shaugh Prior -	par.	607	8,707	6,450	Roborough -	do.
Tamerton Foliot -	par.	1,147	4,775	6,972	Plymouth -	do.
Wembury - -	par.	551	3,131	4,884	do. -	Ermington and Plympton.
Weston Peverell, or Pennycross	par.	509	1,252	6,042	do. -	Midland Roborough.
Yealmpton (a) -	par.	932	3,371	6,839	Yealmpton -	Ermington and Plympton.
TOTAL of UNION -		24,181	74,543	142,518		

POCKLINGTON UNION.

(Formed 22 Oct. 1836 by Order dated 29 Sept. 1836.)

COUNTY of YORK, East Riding:

Allerthorp - -	tow.	150	1,578	1,849	Pocklington, York	Wilton Beacon.
Barmby on the Moor	par.	437	2,578	4,014	York - -	do.
Bielby - -	tow.	220	1,737	2,153	Everingham, York	do.
Bishop Wilton with Bellthorpe	tow.	556	4,574	4,854	Wilberfoss, York -	do.
Bolton - -	tow.	119	911	1,625	do. - -	do.
Bugthorpe - -	par.	239	1,917	2,423	Stamford Bridge, York.	do.
Burnby - -	par.	121	1,701	2,729	Hayton, York -	do.
East Cottingwith -	tow.	259	1,251	2,160	Wheldrake, York -	Holme Beacon.
East Stamford Bridge	tow.	399	1,122	2,842	York - -	Wilton Beacon.
Everingham -	par.	263	2,980	3,162	do. - -	Holme Beacon.
Fangfoss with Spittle	par.	172	1,109	2,027	Wilberfoss, York -	Wilton Beacon.
Fridaythorpe -	par.	320	1,919	1,924	Wharram, York -	Buckrose.
Full Sutton -	par.	127	881	1,393	Stamford Bridge, York.	Wilton Beacon.
Goodmanham	par.	312	3,026	4,923	Market Weighton -	Holme Beacon.
Great Givendale and Grimthorpe	par.	81	1,314	1,314	Pocklington, York	Wilton Beacon
Huswell - -	par.	57	1,126	948	York - -	Holme Beacon.
Hayton - -	tow.	215	1,900	3,017	do. - -	Wilton Beacon.
High Catton -	tow.	191	1,697	2,743	Stamford Bridge, York.	do.
Huggate - -	par.	553	7,001	6,512	Pocklington, York	do.
Kilnwick Percy -	par.	118	1,580	2,116	do. - -	do.
Kirby under Dale -	par.	300	5,123	5,119	Stamford Bridge, York.	do.
Londesborough -	tow.	360	4,236	4,594	Market Weighton -	Holme Beacon.
Low Catton -	tow.	148	1,346	1,775	Stamford Bridge, York.	Wilton Beacon.
Market Weighton and Arras	tow.	1,881	5,880	11,898	Market Weighton -	Holme Beacon.
Melbourne - -	tow.	462	3,148	3,576	Pocklington, York	Wilton Beacon.
Millington with Little Givendale	par.	184	2,509	2,398	do. - -	do.
Newton upon Derwent	tow.	196	1,713	2,765	Wilberfoss, York -	do.

(continued)

PLYMPTON SAINT MARY UNION—*continued.*
(a) See note, page 293.

Unions and Parishes, &c.		Population in 1881.	Area in Statute Acres in 1881.	Rateable Value in 1881.	Post Town.	Petty Sessional Division.
POCKLINGTON UNION—County of York, East Riding—*continued.*				£		
North Cliff (*a*)	- *tow.*	121	1,304	1,230	Brough, East Yorks	Holme Beacon.
Nunburnholme	- *tow.*	248	1,858	2,219	Hayton, York -	Wilton Beacon.
Ousthorp -	- *tow.*	12	331	635	Pocklington, York	do.
Pocklington (W.)	- *tow.*	2,733	2,570	11,155	do. - -	do.
Sancton and Hough-ton (*a*) - -	} *tow.*	370	3,171	3,351	Brough, East Yorks	Holme Beacon.
Serayingham -	- *tow.*	114	1,560	1,866	Kirkham, Yorks -	Buckrose.
Seaton-Ross -	- *par.*	475	3,426	3,697	Everingham, York	Holme Beacon.
Shipton -	- *tow.*	428	1,474	2,746	Market Weighton -	do.
Skirpenbeck -	- *par.*	153	1,645	2,378	Stamford Bridge, York.	Wilton Beacon.
South Cliff	- *tow.*	95	2,127	1,526	Brough, East Yorks	Holme Beacon.
Storwood -	- *tow.*	84	1,222	1,429	Wilberfoss, York -	Wilton Beacon.
Sutton upon Derwent	*par.*	342	3,681	5,005	do. - -	do.
Thixendale -	- *tow.*	254	3,811	3,181	Wharram, York -	do.
Thornton -	- *tow.*	158	2,314	2,139	Pocklington, York	do.
Thorp in the Street -	*tow.*	38	676	966	Market Weighton -	Holme Beacon.
Waplington -	- *tow.*	22	813	656	Pocklington, York	Wilton Beacon.
Warter -	- *par.*	604	7,875	6,635	do. - -	do.
Wilberfoss -	- *tow.*	411	1,472	2,139	York -	do.
Yapham with Melton-by - -	} *tow.*	235	1,888	3,061	Pocklington, York	do.
Youlthorpe with Gowthorp - -	} *tow.*	85	1,180	1,136	Wilberfoss, York -	do.
TOTAL of UNION -		15,461	110,611 (*b*)	144,016		
PONTARDAWE UNION.						
(Formed 26 Mar. 1875 by Order dated 11 Mar. 1875.)						
COUNTY of BRECKNOCK :						
Ystradgynlais Higher	*ham.*	522 }	21,954 {	2,040	Ystradgynlais -	Ystradgynlais.
Ystradgynlais Lower	*ham.*	3,592 }		8,436	do. -	do.
COUNTY of GLAMORGAN :						
Killybebill -	- *par.*	1,910	3,982	5,415	Pontardawe, Swansea Valley.	Pontardawe.
Llanguick (W.)	- *par.*	9,110	12,553	19,596	do. - -	do.
Mawr -	- *ham.*	1,071	9,217	7,834	Llangefelach, Swansea.	Swansea.
Rhyndwyclydach	- *ham.*	3,529	7,704	10,630	Pontardawe -	Pontardawe.
Ynisymond -	- *ham.*	421	1,512	4,216	do. - -	do.
		20,185	56,922	58,167		
PONTEFRACT UNION.						
(Formed 15 Feb. 1862 by Order dated 23 Jan. 1862.—Places marked thus * added 24 June 1869 by Order dated 31 May 1869.)						
COUNTY of YORK, West Riding :						
*Ackton -	- *tow.*	706	968	6,312	Pontefract -	Wakefield.
Balne -	- *tow.*	358	2,866	4,511	Selby -	Snaith.
*Beal, otherwise Beng-hall - -	} *tow.*	414	1,876	3,323	Ferrybridge -	do.
Birkin -	- *tow.*	180	2,160	2,752	do. - -	Selby.
*Brotherton -	- *tow.*	1,159	933	4,059	do. - -	do.
*Burton Salmon -	*tow.*	273	956	2,910	Milford Junction -	Selby, Lower.

(*continued*)

POCKLINGTON UNION :

(*a*) By Order which came into operation on 25 March 1884, a detached part of Sancton and Houghton was amalgamated with North Cliff.

(*b*) Odland-Ings common to Thornton and Melbourne, and containing 13 acres, is comprised in this Union.

Unions and Parishes, &c.		Population in 1881.	Area in Statute Acres in 1881.	Rateable Value in 1881.	Post Town.	Petty Sessional Division.
PONTEFRACT UNION—County of York, West Riding—continued.				£		
Byram-with-Poole	- tow.	68	823	1,012	Ferrybridge -	Selby, Lower.
*Carleton -	- tow.	334	589	2,521	Pontefract - -	Pontefract, Lower. (W.R.)
*Castleford -	tow.	10,530	564	27,800	Normanton -	do.
Cridling Stubbs	- tow.	200	1,355	1,998	Knottingley -	Goole.
*Darrington -	- tow.	523	3,111	3,656	Pontefract - -	Pontefract. (W.R.)
East Hardwick	- tow.	228	527	942	do. - -	do. do.
Egborough -	- tow.	306	2,010	3,421	Snaith -	Goole.
*Fairburne -	- tow.	509	1,428	2,811	South Milford -	Selby, or Sherburn.
*Featherstone	- tow.	3,247	1,380	13,510	Pontefract -	Pontefract. (W.R.)
*Ferry Frystone	- tow.	1,131	1,168	15,848	Ferrybridge -	do. do.
*Glass Houghton	- tow.	1,049	1,079	7,047	Normanton -	do. do.
Heck - -	- tow.	226	1,677	3,771	Snaith -	Snaith.
Hensall	- tow.	358	1,177	3,677	do. -	do.
Hillam - -	- tow.	327	1,527	2,581	Milford Junction -	Selby.
Kellington -	- tow.	309	1,761	3,115	Ferrybridge -	Goole.
Knottingley -	- tow.	5,069	1,481	13,062	Normanton - -	Pontefract. (W.R.)
*Methley -	- par.	1,074	3,492	20,202	Leeds -	Wakefield.
Monk Frystone	- tow.	506	1,771	3,827	Milford Junction -	Selby.
Monk Hill	- tow.	86	5	200	Pontefract - -	Borough of Pontefract.
Pontefract -	- tow.	6,385	2,381	19,904	do. - -	do.
*Pontefract Park	- tow.	66	1,395	3,378	do. - -	do.
*Purston Jaglin	- tow.	706	1,021	2,665	do. - -	do.
Snydale -	- tow.	1,242	1,060	6,400	Normanton -	Wakefield.
Stapleton -	- tow.	120	1,633	1,423	Pontefract -	Pontefract. (W.R.)
*Sutton -	- tow.	39	632	992	Nr. Birkin, Ferry-bridge.	Selby.
Taushelf (W.)	- tow.	2,311	297	5,543	Pontefract -	Borough of Pontefract.
Whitley -	- tow.	409	1,843	2,391	Whitley Bridge -	Goole.
*Whitwood -	- tow.	4,102	1,082	17,674	Normanton -	Wakefield.
Womersley	- tow.	376	3,991	4,584	Pontefract -	Pontefract. (W.R.)
		47,876 -	52,019 (a)	219,825		
PONT-Y-POOL UNION. (Formed 23 May 1836 by Order dated 25 April 1836.) COUNTY of MONMOUTH:						
Glascoed	- ham.	221	1,733	1,435	Pontypool - -	Pontypool.
Goytrey -	- par.	672	3,348	5,323	do. - -	do.
Gwehellog -	- ham.	277	2,819	3,186	Usk - -	Usk.
Gwernesney -	- par.	44	545	647	do. -	do.
Kemeys Commander	- par.	76	508	685	do. - -	do.
Llanbadock -	- par.	391	3,465	4,112	do. - -	do.
Llandegveth -	- par.	81	789	954	Caerleon -	Caerleon.
Llangeview -	- par.	155	1,454	1,860	Usk - -	Usk.
Llangibby -	- par.	485	4,413	4,931	Newport, Mon. -	Caerleon.
Llanhiddel -	- par.	1,383	2,009	5,566	do. - -	Pontypool.
Llanllowell	- par.	73	796	804	Usk - -	Usk.
Llanthewy Vach	- par.	165	1,359	1,077	Caerleon -	Caerleon.
Llantrissent	- par.	255	2,762	2,398	Usk - -	Usk.
Llanvihangel Pont-y-Moyl	} par.	373	1,651	5,219	Pontypool - -	Pontypool.
Lower Llanvrechva -	dir.	1,181 {	In Upper Llan-vrechva.	4,705	do. - -	Caerleon.
Manhilad -	- par.	314	2,031	2,683	do. - -	Pontypool.
Monkswood -	- par.	176	1,126	965	Usk - -	Usk.
Panteague -	- par.	3,321	3,454	15,278	Pontypool - -	Pontypool.
Trevethin with Pont-y-pool	} par.	19,906	11,329	50,740	do. - -	do.
Trostrey -	- par.	142	1,261	1,278	Usk - -	Usk.
Upper Llanvrechva (W).	} dir.	4,177	4,329	13,795	Pontypool - -	Pontypool.
Usk - -	- tow.	1,470	404	5,461	Usk - -	Usk.
TOTAL of UNION -		35,338	51,597	133,102		

PONTEFRACT UNION:
(a) Water Frystone containing 2,018 acres is comprised in this Union.

Unions and Parishes, &c.	Population in 1881.	Area in Statute Acres in 1881.	Rateable Value in 1881.	Post Town.	Petty Sessional Division.

PONTYPRIDD UNION.

(Formed 27 Dec. 1862 by Order dated 27 Nov. 1862.)

COUNTY OF GLAMORGAN :

			£		
Eglwysilan - - par.	8,938	13,852	36,416	Pontypridd (a) -	Pontypridd and Hundred of Caerphilly.
Llanfabon - - par.	2,660	5,440	11,312	Cardiff - -	Hundred of Caerphilly.
Llantrisaint - - par.	13,368	17,060	53,087	Llantrisant, for part Pontypridd, do.	Hundred of Miskin, Lower Division.
Llantwitvairdre (W.) par.	5,829	5,412	41,053	Pontypridd -	do.
Llanwonno - - par.	18,652	13,109	100,707	do. (b) - -	do.
Ystradyfodwg - par.	44,016	19,441	200,731	do. - -	do.
TOTAL of UNION -	93,493	74,314	443,005		

POOLE UNION.

(Formed 2 Oct. 1835 by Order dated 18 Sept. 1835.—Name of place marked * as altered by Order dated 16 June 1887.)

TOWN and COUNTY of the TOWN of POOLE :

Hamworthy - - par.	668	1,086	2,659	Poole -	Poole.
Longfleet (W.) - ty.	2,207	1,289	5,920	do. -	do.
Parkston - - ty.	2,256	2,576	7,782	Parkstone -	do.
Poole - - par.	7,179	160	15,013	Poole -	do.

COUNTY of DORSET :

Canford Magna - par.	1,107	8,053	6,105	Wimborne -	Wimborne.
*Kinson - - ty.	3,745	4,715	8,738	do. -	do.
Lytchett Matravers - par.	692	3,329	4,474	Poole -	do.
Lytchett Minster - par.	848	3,344	4,065	do. -	do.
TOTAL of UNION -	18,702	24,552	54,756		

POPLAR UNION.

(Formed 20 Dec. 1836 by Order dated 25 Nov. 1836.)

COUNTY of MIDDLESEX :

Bromley (W.) - - par.	64,359	608	196,062	London, E. -	Metropolitan Police District, and Tower.
Poplar including Blackwall (W.) - } par.	55,077	1,164	335,563	do. -	do.
Stratford le Bow (W.) par.	37,074	563	138,851	do. -	do.
TOTAL of UNION	156,510	2,335	670,176		

PORTSEA ISLAND UNION.

(Formed 18 July 1836 by Order dated 24 June 1836.—Place marked thus * added 26 March 1862 by Order dated 5 March 1862.)

COUNTY of SOUTHAMPTON :

*Great Salterns - par.	33	346	449	Portsmouth -	Fareham.
Portsea (W.) - - par.	120,022	4,190	404,945	do. -	Portsmouth.
Portsmouth - - par.	7,967	130	37,128	do. -	do.
TOTAL of UNION -	128,022	4,666	442,522		

PONTYPRIDD UNION :

(a) Except for the Town of Caerphilly, the post town of which is Cardiff.
(b) Except for Mountain Ash, the post town of which is Mountain Ash.

M m 3

Unions and Parishes, &c.	Population in 1881.	Area in Statute Acres in 1881.	Rateable Value in 1881.	Post Town.	Petty Sessional Division.

POTTERSPURY UNION.

(Formed 20 May 1835 by Order dated 16 April 1835.—Places marked thus * added 28 Sept. 1835 by Order dated 4 Sept. 1835.)

COUNTY of BUCKINGHAM :

			£		
*Calverton (a) - - par.	550	2,011	3,281	Stony Stratford -	Stony Stratford.
*Stony Stratford Saint Mary Magdalen or East Side ⎫par.	727	69	2,292	do. - -	do.
*Stony Stratford Saint Giles or West Side (a) ⎫par.	1,216	55	2,718	do. - -	do.
*Woolverton - - par.	3,611	2,325	23,452	do. - -	do.

COUNTY of NORTHAMPTON :

Alderton (a) - - par.	117	910	1,208	Towcester -	Towcester.
Ashton - - par.	324	1,290	4,455	do. -	do.
Cosgrove (a) - - par.	636	1,760	3,510	Stony Stratford -	do.
Furtho (a) - - par.	20	480	1,094	do. - -	do.
Grafton-Regis (a) - par.	169	1,510	2,090	do. - -	do.
Hartwell - - par.	501	1,850	4,215	Northampton -	do.
Passenham - par.	1,128	2,230	5,777	Stony Stratford -	do.
Paulers-Pury - par.	1,141	2,961	4,972	Towcester -	do.
Potters-Pury (a) - par.	1,079	2,820	2,988	Stony Stratford -	do.
Wicken - - par.	108	2,280	3,275	do. - -	do.
Yardley-Gobion (W.) ham.	604 ⎰ In Potters-Pury. ⎱		2,558	do. - -	do.
TOTAL of UNION -	12,231	22,551	67,910		

PRESCOT UNION.

(Formed 31 Jan. 1837 by Order dated 5 Jan. 1837. — Place marked thus * added 22 Feb. 1817 by Order of that date.)

COUNTY of LANCASTER :

Bold - - tow.	880	4,183	11,939	St. Helens, Warrington, and Widnes.	Prescot Division.
Crouton - - tow.	468	1,148	4,299	Prescot - -	Prescot.
Ditton - - tow.	1,412	1,938	10,533	Widnes - -	do.
Eccleston - - tow.	18,026	3,569	52,266	St. Helens and Prescot.	Prescot and St. Helens (Borough).
Hale - - tow.	571	2,612	4,009	Liverpool - -	Childwall.
Halewood - - tow.	1,857	3,988	17,300	do. - -	do.
*Huyton with Roby - tow.	4,060	3,054	38,806	do. - -	Prescot.
Knowsley - - tow.	1,248	5,058	11,655	Prescot - -	do.
Little Woolton - tow.	1,159	1,388	13,765	Liverpool - -	Childwall.
Much Woolton - tow.	4,541	795	20,987	do. - -	do.
Parr - - tow.	11,278	1,633	25,983	St. Helens -	St. Helens (Borough).
Prescot - - tow.	5,546	270	12,435	Prescot - -	Prescot.
Rainford - - tow.	3,745	5,872	18,658	St. Helens -	St. Helens.
Rainhill - - tow.	2,219	1,640	14,778	Prescot - -	Prescot.
Speke - - tow.	513	3,734	7,756	Liverpool - -	Childwall.
Sutton - - tow.	12,695	3,725	87,057	St. Helens -	St. Helens (Borough).
Tarbock - - tow.	629	2,413	6,291	Prescot -	Prescot Division.
Whiston (W.) - tow.	2,705	1,783	19,393	do. - -	do.
Widnes with Appleton ⎫tow.	24,935	3,339	101,307	Widnes - -	do.
Windle - - tow.	19,473	3,150	78,885	St. Helens -	St. Helens, and St. Helens (Borough).
TOTAL of UNION -	117,960	55,592	561,192		

POTTERSPURY UNION :

(a) By Order which came into operation on 25 March 1883,—
A detached part of Alderton was amalgamated with Grafton-Regis ;
A detached part of Calverton, known as Stratford Bridge Meadows, was amalgamated with Stony Stratford Saint Giles or West Side.

POTTERSPURY UNION—continued.

A detached part of Cosgrove was amalgamated with Potters-Pury ;
A detached part of Furtho was amalgamated with Cosgrove.

Unions and Parishes, &c.		Population in 1881.	Area in Statute Acres in 1881.	Rateable Value in 1881.	Post Town.	Petty Sessional Division.

PRESTON UNION.

(Formed 31 Jan. 1837 by Order dated 31 Dec. 1836.—Place marked thus * added 30 Mar. 1837 by Order dated 11 Mar. 1837.)

COUNTY of LANCASTER:

Unions and Parishes, &c.		Population	Area	Rateable £	Post Town	Petty Sessional Division
Alston	- tow.	1,589 {In Hothersall}		7,798	Preston -	Blackburn.
Barton	- tow.	368	2,707	6,662	do.	Preston.
Broughton	- tow.	590	2,367	9,037	do. -	do.
Cuerdale	- tow.	58	684	1,205	do.	Walton le Dale.
Dilworth	- tow.	2,116	1,248	7,403	do. -	Blackburn.
Dutton	- tow.	259	1,899	2,146	do. -	do.
Elston	- tow.	43	962	1,283	do. -	Preston.
Farington	- tow.	2,017	1,860	12,282	do.	Chorley.
Fishwick	- tow.	2,142	693	8,660	do. -	Preston.
Fulwood (W.)	- tow.	3,725	2,117	16,792	do.	do.
Goosnargh	- tow.	1,197	8,673	12,461	do. -	do.
Grimsargh and Brockholes	} tow.	369	1,937	4,373	do. -	do.
Haighton	- tow.	215	1,078	1,912	do. -	do.
Hothersall	- tow.	132	3,079	1,880	do. -	do.
Howick	- tow.	62	754	1,632	do. -	Chorley.
Hutton	- tow.	389	2,745	5,137	do. -	do.
Lea, Ashton, Ingol, and Cottam	} tow.	2,913	3,188	18,129	do.	Preston.
Little Hoole	- tow.	440	1,223	2,664	do. -	Chorley.
Longton	- tow.	1,413	3,659	8,076	do. -	do.
Much Hoole	- tow.	581	1,776	3,455	do. -	do.
Penwortham	- tow.	1,612	2,270	10,733	do. -	do.
Preston	- tow.	91,578	2,127	270,732	do. -	Preston.
Ribbleton	- tow.	575	649	3,643	do. -	do.
Ribchester (W.)	- tow.	1,282	2,211	4,910	Blackburn -	Blackburn.
Samlesbury	- tow.	752	4,379	8,533	Preston -	Walton le Dale.
Walton-le-Dale	- tow.	9,286	4,683	38,987	do.	do.
*Whittingham	- tow.	2,158	3,192	5,974	do. -	Preston.
Wood Plumpton	- tow.	1,239	4,971	12,565	do. -	do.
TOTAL of UNION -		129,160	67,431 (a)	488,864		

PRESTWICH UNION.

(Formed 13 April 1850 by Order of that date.—Place marked thus * added 25 Dec. 1858 by Order dated 30 Oct. 1858.)

COUNTY of LANCASTER:

Unions and Parishes, &c.		Population	Area	Rateable	Post Town	Petty Sessional Division
*Beswick	- tow.	7,957	96	18,104	Manchester -	Manchester.
Blackley	- tow.	6,075	1,810	19,706	do. -	Salford.
Bradford	- tow.	16,121	288	41,593	do. -	Manchester.
Cheetham	- tow.	25,721	919	128,620	do. -	do.
Crumpsall (W)	- tow.	8,154	733	33,149	do. -	Salford.
Failsworth	- tow.	7,912	1,073	32,444	do. -	do.
Great Heaton	- tow.	376	875	3,191	do. -	do.
Harpurhey	- tow.	4,810	193	15,762	do. -	Manchester.
Little Heaton	- tow.	828	532	2,816	do. -	Salford.
Moston	- tow.	3,466	1,297	17,119	do. -	do.
Newton	- tow.	31,240	1,585	99,262	do. -	do.
Prestwich	- tow.	8,627	1,917	39,517	do. -	do.
TOTAL of UNION -		121,287	11,318	451,283		

PRESTON UNION:

(a) Ribbleton Moor, in which the townships of Grimsargh and Brockholes have interests, and which contains 168 acres, is comprised in this Union.

Unions and Parishes, &c.	Population in 1881.	Area in Statute Acres in 1881.	Rateable Value in 1881.	Post Town.	Petty Sessional Division.

PWLLHELI UNION.

(Formed 3 June 1837 by Order dated 8 May 1837; amended as regards the spelling of the name of the Parish marked thus * by Order dated 20 Dec. 1886.)

COUNTY of CARNARVON :

Unions and Parishes, &c.	Population in 1881.	Area in Statute Acres in 1881.	Rateable Value in 1881. £	Post Town.	Petty Sessional Division.
Aberdaron - - *par.*	1,202	7,078	3,920	Pwllheli - -	Pwllheli.
Abererch - - *par.*	1,726	5,962	5,465	do. - -	do.
Bodferin - - *par.*	42	511	223	do. - -	do.
Bodvean - - *par.*	282	2,572	1,140	do. - -	do.
Bottwnog - - *par.*	126	487	424	do. - -	do.
Brynerocs - - *par.*	829	3,646	1,785	do. - -	do.
Carngiwch - - *par.*	133	1,344	390	do. - -	do.
Ceidio - - *par.*	94	1,081	855	do. - -	do.
*Criccieth - - *par.*	1,213	1,678	2,551	do. - -	Criccieth.
Denio (W.) - *par.*	2,767	728	5,116	do. - -	Pwllheli.
Edeyrn - - *par.*	561	1,380	1,104	do. - -	do.
Llanaelhaiaru - *par.*	1,422	6,698	2,891	do. - -	Carnarvon.
Llanarmon - - *par.*	657	3,753	2,616	do. - -	do.
Llanbedrog - *par.*	541	2,548	1,656	do. - -	Pwllheli.
Llandegwning - *par.*	101	1,488	953	do. - -	do.
Llandudwen - *par.*	67	1,331	1,041	do. - -	do.
Llaneugan - - *par.*	1,408	4,354	3,614	do. - -	do.
Llanfaelrhys - *par.*	186	1,679	808	do. - -	do.
Llanfihangel Bachellaeth - *par.*	280	2,915	1,425	do. - -	do.
Llangian - - *par.*	1,087	4,835	3,015	do. - -	do.
Llangwnadle - *par.*	245	1,243	853	do. - -	do.
Llangybi - - *par.*	563	4,519	2,315	do. - -	Carnarvon.
Llaniestyn - *par.*	918	4,256	2,875	do. - -	Pwllheli.
Llannor - - *par.*	948	5,553	3,882	do. - -	do.
Llanystindwy - *par.*	1,151	6,780	4,898	do. - -	Criccieth.
Meyllteyrn - *par.*	275	1,519	1,075	do. - -	Pwllheli.
Nevin - - *par.*	2,003	1,575	2,630	do. - -	do.
Penllech - - *par.*	231	2,187	1,249	do. - -	do.
Penrhos - - *par.*	96	555	376	do. - -	do.
Pistill - - *par.*	909	3,940	1,444	do. - -	do.
Rhiw - - *par.*	350	1,653	753	do. - -	do.
Tydweiliog - - *par.*	363	2,241	1,405	do. - -	do.
TOTAL of UNION -	22,779	92,098	65,356		

READING UNION.

(Formed 10 August 1835 by Order dated 21 July 1835.)

COUNTY of BERKS :

Unions and Parishes, &c.	Population in 1881.	Area in Statute Acres in 1881.	Rateable Value in 1881.	Post Town.	Petty Sessional Division.
Saint Giles, with Whitley - *par.*	21,558	2,760	70,646	Reading -	Borough of Reading.
Saint Lawrence - *par.*	4,674	328	34,311	do. - -	do.
Saint Mary, with Southcot (W.) *par.*	17,262	1,867	61,757	do. - -	do.
TOTAL of UNION -	13,491	1,955	166,714		

Unions and Parishes, &c.		Population in 1881.	Area in Statute Acres in 1881.	Rateable Value in 1881.	Post Town.	Petty Sessional Division.
REDRUTH UNION—County of Cornwall—continued.				£		
Gwinear	par.	1,569	4,647	6,415	Hayle	Penwith (East Division).
Gwithian	par.	614	2,420	2,159	Camborne	do.
Illogan (W.)	par.	8,723	8,493	24,822	Redruth	do.
Phillack	par.	4,254	2,938	9,213	Hayle	do.
Redruth	par.	9,335	4,006	24,492	Redruth	do.
Stythians	par.	1,823	4,361	6,392	Perran-ar-Worthal	Kerrier.
TOTAL of UNION		46,128	40,426	118,028		
REETH UNION.						
(Formed 27 April 1840 by Order dated 2 April 1840.)						
COUNTY of YORK, North Riding:						
Arkengarthdale	par.	999	14,566	7,797	Reeth	Gilling, West.
Ellerton Abbey	tow.	44	1,665	1,144	Richmond, Yorks	Hang, West.
Grinton	tow.	377	8,182	4,247	do.	do.
Marrick	par.	307	6,206	4,163	do.	Gilling, West.
Melbecks	tow.	1,165	7,974	6,323	Reeth	do.
Muker	tow.	837	30,192	7,491	do.	do.
Reeth (W.)	tow.	988	5,699	5,766	do.	do.
TOTAL of UNION		4,717	74,484	36,931		
REIGATE UNION.						
(Formed 25 March 1836 by Order dated 26 Feb. 1836.)						
COUNTY of SURREY:						
Betchworth	par.	1,779	3,743	11,204	Reigate	Reigate.
Buckland	par.	401	1,855	4,119	do.	do.
Burstow	par.	1,200	4,760	7,952	Crawley	do.
Chaldon	par.	185	1,614	1,651	Caterham	do.
Charlwood	par.	1,359	7,093	11,563	Crawley	do.
Chipstead	par.	644	2,420	3,713	Redhill	do.
Gatton	par.	222	1,296	3,283	Reigate	do.
Horley	par.	2,385	7,320	31,490	Crawley	do.
Kings Wood	lib.	387	1,821	2,714	Epsom and Reigate	do.
Leigh	par.	523	3,419	4,092	Reigate	do.
Merstham	par.	903	2,599	17,244	Redhill	do.
Nutfield	par.	1,093	3,401	9,722	do.	do.
Reigate Borough		3,274	435	14,501	Reigate	Borough of Reigate.
Reigate Foreign (W.)		15,388	5,580	83,919	Reigate and Redhill	do.
Walton on the Hill	par.	616	2,608	4,734	Epsom	Epsom.
TOTAL of UNION		30,359	49,994	212,021		
RHAYADER UNION.						
(Formed 10 Oct. 1836 by Order dated 19 Sept. 1836. Spelling of names of Parishes marked thus * is as altered by Order dated 17 Sept. 1887.)						
COUNTY of BRECKNOCK:						
Llanwrthwl	par.	488	18,851	2,275	Rhayader	Builth.
COUNTY of RADNOR:						
*Abbey cwm Hir or Gollan and Cefn Pawl	par.	485	10,965	2,573	Penybont, Radnorshire.	Cefnllys.
Cefnllys	par.	673	4,135	3,798	do.	do.

(continued)

Unions and Parishes, &c.	Population in 1881.	Area in Statute Acres in 1881.	Rateable Value in 1881.	Post Town.	Petty Sessional Division.
RHAYADER UNION—County of Radnor—*continued.*			£		
*Llansantffraid Cwm- deuddwr } par.	741	32,000	3,149	Rhayader - -	Rhayader.
Llanbadarn fawr - par.	610	3,646	2,385	Penybont, Rad- norshire.	Cefullys.
Llanfihangel Helygen or fach } par.	88	1,459	661	{ Nantmel, Rhaya- der.	Rhayader.
Llanyre - - par.	700	5,901	2,832	Newbridge on Wye, Radnorshire.	do.
Nantmel (W.) (*a*) - par.	1,231	16,387	6,807	Rhayader	do.
Rhayader Gwy - par.	890	188	1,715	do. - -	do.
Saint Harmons - par.	832	12,000	3,514	do. - -	do.
TOTAL OF UNION -	6,741	105,532	29,709		

RICHMOND UNION.

(Formed 6 June 1836 by Order
dated 11 May 1836.)

COUNTY of SURREY :

Barnes - - par.	6,001	910	46,262	Barnes, S.W. -	Richmond.
Kew - - par.	1,670	298	14,075	Kew, S.O. Surrey -	do.
Mortlake - par.	6,330	1,883	42,223	Mortlake, S.W. -	do.
Petersham - par.	566	652	8,119	Petersham, Surrey	do.
Richmond (W.) - par.	19,066	1,210	132,768	Richmond, do. -	do.
TOTAL of UNION -	33,633	1,983	213,447		

RICHMOND UNION.

(Formed 24 Feb. 1837 by Order
dated 31 Jan. 1837.— Place
marked thus * added 25 Dec.
1859 by Order dated 18 Nov.
1859.)

COUNTY of YORK, North
Riding :

Aldbrough - tow.	400	1,807	3,019	Darlington -	Gilling, West.
Appleton - tow.	104	1,631	2,781	Catterick - -	Hang. East.
Aske - - tow.	211	1,764	1,681	Richmond, Yorks -	Gilling, West.
Bolton-upon-Swale - tow.	77	854	1,298	Catterick - -	Gilling, East.
Brough - - tow.	120	1,177	1,714	do. - -	Hang. East.
Brompton-on-Swale - tow.	360	1,700	3,313	Richmond, Yorks -	Gilling, East.
Caldwell - tow.	175	1,589	2,221	Darlington -	Gilling, West.
Carkin Forcett - tow.	206	2,270	4,366	do - -	do.
Catterick - tow.	650	1,738	3,989	Catterick -	Hang. East.
Colbourn - - tow.	102	1,357	1,786	Richmond, Yorks -	do.
Dalton - - tow.	206	2,706	3,323	Richmond	Gilling, West.
Downholme - tow.	112	1,506	843	do. - -	Hang. West.
Easby - - tow.	123	1,282	2,867	do. - -	Gilling, West.
East Layton - tow.	156	1,072	1,811	Darlington -	do.
Ellerton-upon-Swale - tow.	172	1,635	2,199	Catterick -	Gilling, East.
Eppleby - - tow.	417	1,118	2,206	Darlington	Gilling, West.
Gayles - - tow.	125	2,575	2,167	Richmond, Yorks -	do.
Gilling - - tow.	872	4,877	7,375	do. - -	do.
Hipswell - - tow.	269	2,647	2,282	do. - -	do.
Hudswell - - tow.	181	3,028	2,519	do. - -	do.
Kirby Ravensworth - tow.	81	227	393	do. - -	do.
Marske - - par.	268	6,759	4,210	do. - -	do.
Melsonby - - tow.	532	2,743	4,334	Darlington -	do.
Middleton Tyas - tow.	540	3,202	5,177	Richmond, Yorks -	Gilling, East.
Moulton - - tow.	273	3,042	3,216	do. - -	do.
New Forest - tow.	49	3,002	1,027	do. - -	Gilling, West.
					(*continued*)

RHAYADER UNION :

(*a*) By Order which came into operation on 25 March 1884,
a detached part of Llandewi Ystradenny, in the Knighton
Union, was amalgamated with Nantmel.

Unions and Parishes, &c.		Population in 1881.	Area in Statute Acres in 1881.	Rateable Value in 1881.	Post Town.	Petty Sessional Division.

RICHMOND UNION (Yorks)—County of York, North Riding—(continued).

				£		
Newsham	- tow.	275	3,407	3,683	Barnard Castle	Greta Bridge.
North Cowton	- tow.	283	1,396	2,104	Northallerton -	Gilling, East.
Ravensworth	- tow.	268	2,248	2,889	Richmond, Yorks -	Gilling, West.
Richmond (W.)	- par.	4,502	2,520	16,061	do. -	Borough of Richmond.
*Saint Martin	- par.	79	270	849	Richmond, Yorks -	Gilling, West.
Scorton	- tow	407	2,733	1,418	Catterick - -	Gilling, East.
Scotton	- tow.	116	1,407	1,537	Richmond, Yorks -	Gilling, West.
Skeeby	- tow.	159	835	1,527	do. - -	do.
Stainton	- tow.	44	1,877	469	do. - -	Hang, West.
Stanwick Saint John	tow.	56	1,397	1,794	Darlington -	Gilling, West.
Tunstall	- tow.	244	1,283	2,184	Catterick - -	Hang, East.
Uckerby	- tow.	38	779	851	do. - -	Gilling, East.
Walburn	- tow.	30	1,660	1,015	Richmond, Yorks -	Hang, West.
West Layton	- tow.	76	746	1,331	Darlington -	Gilling, West.
Whaston	- tow.	103	1,235	1,149	Richmond, Yorks -	do.
TOTAL of UNION	-	**13,158**	**81,101**	**114,078**		

RINGWOOD UNION.

(Formed 29 July 1835 by Order dated 14 July 1835 as amended by Order dated 23 Nov. 1868.— Place marked thus * added 1 March 1869 by Order dated 12 Feb. 1869.)

COUNTY of SOUTHAMPTON :

*Broomy	- tow.	127	1,729	519	Ringwood	Ringwood.
Burley	- tow.	633	11,275	3,817	do. - -	do.
Ellingham	- par.	284	2,559	2,740	do. - -	do.
Harbridge	- par.	371	4,214	2,974	do. - -	do.
Ibsley	- par.	243	1,793	1,494	do. - -	do.
Ringwood (W.)	- par.	3,830	10,365	20,711	do. - -	do.
TOTAL of UNION	-	**5,488**	**31,935**	**32,255**		

RIPON UNION.

(Formed 25 Oct. 1852 by Order dated 6 Oct. 1852.—Places marked thus * added 2 May 1853 by Order dated 5 April 1853 ; thus † added 25 Dec. 1853 by Order dated 13 Dec. 1853 ; place marked thus ‡ added 29 Sept. 1865 by Order dated 19 Aug. 1865 ; and thus § added 29 Sept. 1873 by Order dated 20 Sept. 1873.)

COUNTY of YORK, North Riding :

†Asenby	- tow.	171	1,178	2,509	Thirsk - -	Hallikeld.
†Baldersby	- tow.	290	1,830	1,560	do. -	do.
†Cundall-with-Leckby	tow.	178	2,049	3,266	Boroughbridge	do.
†Dishforth	- tow.	302	1,765	1,019	Thirsk -	do.
East Tanfield -	- tow.	41	1,295	1,534	Bedale -	do.
§Howgrave	- par.	39	290	456	Ripon -	do.
§Hutton Conyers	- tow.	136	3,212	5,219	do. -	do.
†Marton-le-Moor	- tow.	169	1,678	2,763	do. -	do.
Melmerby	- tow.	305	1,138	3,156	Thirsk -	do.
Middleton Quernhow	tow.	83	764	2,015	do. -	do.
Norton Conyers	- tow.	98	1,011	1,609	Ripon -	do.
†Rainton-with-Newby	tow.	394	1,576	3,622	Thirsk -	do.
Sutton with How-grave	tow.	85	593	1,166	Ripon -	do.
Wath	- tow.	253	766	2,471	do. -	do.
West Tanfield -	- par.	517	3,286	4,459	Bedale -	do.

(continued)

Unions and Parishes, &c.	Population in 1881.	Area in Statute Acres in 1881.	Rateable Value in 1881.	Post Town.	Petty Sessional Division.

RIPON UNION—_continued._

COUNTY of YORK,
West Riding:

£

Unions and Parishes, &c.		Population in 1881.	Area in Statute Acres in 1881.	Rateable Value in 1881.	Post Town.	Petty Sessional Division.
Aismunderby - with - } Bondgate	tow.	815	1,085	3,786	Ripon	{ City of Ripon and Liberty of Ripon.
Aldfield	tow.	125	1,269	1,187	do.	Kirkby Malzeard.
Azerley	tow.	683	1,018	5,419	do.	do.
†Bishop Monckton	tow.	483	2,186	5,031	do.	Liberty of Ripon.
Bishopton	tow.	101	386	1,643	do.	do.
Bridge Hewick	tow.	71	911	1,510	do.	do.
Clotherholme	tow.	12	339	425	do.	do.
Copt Hewick	tow.	233	661	1,829	do.	do.
Eavestone	tow.	36	1,143	689	do.	do.
Givendale	tow.	39	848	1,508	Boroughbridge	do.
Grantley	tow.	159	772	1,212	Ripon	do.
Grewelthorpe	tow.	516	4,521	4,842	do.	Kirkby Malzeard.
Ingerthorpe	tow.	49	512	1,337	Ripley	Liberty of Ripon.
Kirkby Malzeard	tow.	616	3,363	4,301	Ripon	Kirkby Malzeard.
Laverton	tow.	305	6,697	2,913	do.	do.
Lindrick	tow.	99	1,438	2,296	do.	do.
‡Markingfield Hall	par.	16	616	581	do.	Liberty of Ripon.
*Markington	tow.	464	3,179	4,819	Ripley	do.
†Newby-with-Mulwith	tow.	85	796	1,496	Boroughbridge	do.
North Stainley with } Sleningford	tow.	412	4,244	5,893	Ripon	do.
Nunwick-with - How- } grave	tow.	38	938	1,937	do.	do.
Ripon (W.)	tow.	6,641	1,561	30,020	do.	City of Ripon.
Sawley	tow.	372	3,284	3,589	do.	Liberty of Ripon.
Sharow	tow.	380	723	4,648	do.	do.
Skelding	tow.	28	990	600	do.	Kirkby Malzeard.
Studley Roger	tow.	148	986	1,478	do.	do.
Sutton Grange	tow.	52	1,022	737	do.	Liberty of Ripon.
Whiteliffe - with - } Thorpe	tow.	262	1,262	3,977	do.	do.
Winksley	tow.	116	729	864	do.	Kirkby Malzeard.
TOTAL of UNION		16,447	72,940 (a)	144,120		

RISBRIDGE UNION.

(Formed 3 Nov. 1835 by Order dated 15 Oct. 1835. — Place marked thus * added 25 Dec. 1858 by Order dated 16 Oct. 1858.)

COUNTY of ESSEX :

Unions and Parishes, &c.		Population in 1881.	Area in Statute Acres in 1881.	Rateable Value in 1881.	Post Town.	Petty Sessional Division.
Ashen (b)	par.	228	1,514	2,285	Sudbury, Suffolk	Castle Hedingham.
Birdbrook (b)	par.	581	2,422	3,628	Halstead, Essex	do.
Helion's Bumpstead (b)	par.	774	3,282	4,300	Haverhill, Suffolk	Bardfield.
Ovington (b)	par.	132	716	1,030	Sudbury, do.	Castle Hedingham.
Steeple Bumpstead (b)	par.	1,045	3,423	5,788	Haverhill, do.	do.
Sturmer (a) (c)	par.	374	999	1,736	Halstead, Essex	do.

(continued)

RIPON UNION :

(a) There are certain lands comprising 280 acres which are common to the townships of Grewelthorpe, Kirkby Malzeard, Laverton, and Azerley.

RISBRIDGE UNION :

(a) By Orders which came into operation on 25 March 1884,—
A detached part of Cavendish, in the Sudbury Union, was amalgamated with Clare ;
A certain part of Sturmer was amalgamated with Whixoe.

(b) By Provisional Orders which came into operation on 25 March, 1885,—
A detached part of Ashen was amalgamated with Tilbury juxta Clare, in the Halstead Union;
A detached part of Birdbrook was amalgamated with Steeple Bumpstead ;

RISBRIDGE UNION—continued.

A detached part of Hundon was amalgamated with Whixoe ;
A detached part of Little Wratting was amalgamated with Haverhill ;
A detached part of Ovington was amalgamated with Ashen ;
A detached part of Whixoe was amalgamated with Stoke by Clare ;
A detached part of Withersfield was amalgamated with Haverhill ;
A detached part of Tilbury juxta Clare, in the Halstead Union, was amalgamated with Ashen ;
All the part of Helion's Bumpstead which was in the County of Cambridge, was amalgamated with Castlecamps, in the Linton Union.

(c) By Order which came into operation on 25 March 1885, a detached part of Sturmer was amalgamated with Haverhill.

Unions and Parishes, &c.	Population in 1881.	Area in Statute Acres in 1881.	Rateable Value in 1881.	Post Town.	Petty Sessional Division.
RISBRIDGE UNION—*continued.*			£		
COUNTIES of ESSEX and SUFFOLK :					
Haverhill (*b*) (*c*) - *par.*	3,685	2,545	7,420	Haverhill, Suffolk -	Clare.
Kedington (W.) - *par.*	935	2,323	1,289	do.	do.
COUNTY of SUFFOLK :					
Barnardiston - - *par.*	212	1,100	1,490	Haverhill, Suffolk -	Clare.
Clare (*a*) - - *par.*	1,704	2,228	5,911	Clare, do. -	do.
Cowling - - *par.*	678	3,025	4,489	Newmarket, do. -	Newmarket.
Deuerdiston, otherwise Deuston - *par.*	266	1,230	1,809	do. do. -	Clare.
Great Bradley - *par.*	359	2,280	3,223	do. do. -	do.
Great Thurlow - *par.*	387	2,623	2,925	Haverhill, do. -	do.
Great Wratting - *par.*	391	1,329	1,945	do. do. -	do.
Hundon (*b*) - *par.*	885	4,461	5,873	Clare, do. -	do.
Little Bradley - *par.*	95	957	1,449	Newmarket, do. -	do.
Little Thurlow - *par.*	338	1,470	2,332	Haverhill, do. -	do.
Little Wratting (*b*) - *par.*	267	936	1,414	do. do. -	do.
*Monks Risbridge - *par.*	—	92	153	do. do. -	do.
Poslingford with Chipley - *par.*	356	2,438	2,868	Clare, do. -	do.
Stansfield - - *par.*	115	1,989	2,754	do. do. -	do.
Stoke by Clare (*b*) - *par.*	734	2,361	3,923	do. do. -	do.
Stradishall - - *par.*	382	1,376	2,030	Newmarket, do. -	do.
Whixoe (*a*) (*b*) - *par.*	118	600	1,142	Halstead, Essex -	do.
Wickhambrook - *par.*	1,318	4,318	6,454	Newmarket, Suffolk	Bury St. Edmund's
Withersfield (*b*) - *par.*	575	2,509	3,595	do. do. -	Clare.
TOTAL of UNION -	17,234	53,976	86,264		
ROCHDALE UNION.					
(Formed 15 Feb. 1837 by Order dated 21 Jan. 1837.)					
COUNTY of LANCASTER :					
Blatchinworth and Calderbrook - *tow.*	7,891	4,781	32,483	Littleborough, Manchester.	Middleton Division of the Hundred of Salford.
Butterworth - - *tow.*	8,411	7,766	46,036	Rochdale, and do.	Middleton Division of the Hundred of Salford and Borough of Rochdale.
Castleton - - *tow.*	35,272	3,812	151,655	Rochdale - Castleton, Manchester; Heywood, Manchester	do.
Spotland - - *tow.*	40,140	14,174	150,171	Rochdale and Bacup, Manchester.	do.
Wardleworth - - *tow.*	19,711	766	72,420	Rochdale -	Borough of Rochdale.
Wuerdale and Wardle (W.) - *tow.*	10,487	3,523	33,886	do. and Wardle, Manchester.	Middleton Division of the Hundred of Salford and Borough of Rochdale.
TOTAL of UNION -	121,912	34,822	186,651		
ROCHFORD UNION.					
(Formed 10 Oct. 1835 by Order dated 19 Sept. 1835.—Places marked thus * added 30 Mar. 1837 by Order dated 21 Feb. 1837 ; thus † added 14 Dec. 1847 by Order of that date ; thus ‡ added 21 Mar. 1862 by Order dated 20 Mar. 1862 ; and thus § added 13 May 1881 by Order dated 26 April 1881.)					
COUNTY of ESSEX :					
Ashingdon - - *par.*	91	1,166	1,292	Rochford - -	Rochford.
Barling - - *par.*	366	1,288	2,587	do. -	do.

(continued)

RISBRIDGE UNION :
For notes (*a*), (*b*), (*c*), see p. 304.

N n 3

Unions and Parishes, &c.		Population in 1881.	Area in Statute Acres in 1881.	Rateable Value in 1881.	Post Town.	Petty Sessional Division.
ROCHFORD UNION—County of Essex—*continued.*				£		
Canewdon	- par.	714	5,239	6,723	Rochford	- Rochford.
§Canvey Island	- par.	282	4,385	--	Rayleigh -	- do.
Eastwood	- par.	499	3,236	5,339	Rochford -	- do.
*Foulness	- par.	706	6,162	8,981	Southend -	- do.
Great Stambridge	- par.	299	2,447	3,406	Rochford -	- do.
Great Wakering	- par.	1,294	2,775	6,512	Rochford -	- do.
Hadleigh	- par.	466	1,816	2,390	Rochford -	- do.
‡Havengore	- par.	31	299	304	Southend -	- do.
Hawkwell	- par.	269	1,365	1,949	Rochford -	- do.
Hockley	- par.	619	1,475	5,029	Rayleigh -	- do.
Leigh	- par.	1,761	1,547	3,740	Rochford -	- do.
Little Stambridge	- par.	164	605	1,450	do. -	- do.
Little Wakering	- par.	284	2,410	2,898	do. -	- do.
North Shoebury	- par.	196	1,103	2,257	Southend -	- do.
Paglesham	- par.	514	2,017	3,601	Paglesham -	- do.
Prittlewell	- par.	7,979	3,441	39,901	Rochford -	- do.
Rawreth	- par.	331	2,375	3,261	Rayleigh -	- do.
Rayleigh	- par.	1,327	2,906	5,674	do. -	- do.
Rochford (W.)	- par.	1,675	1,867	5,815	Rochford -	- do.
Shopland	- par.	86	1,054	1,678	do. -	- do.
†South Benfleet	- par.	681	1,948	3,610	Rayleigh -	- do.
Southchurch	- par.	770	1,732	4,132	Southend -	- do.
South Fambridge	- par.	91	1,192	1,245	Rochford -	- do.
South Shoebury	- par.	2,251	1,039	5,799	Southend -	- do.
Sutton	- par.	144	700	1,417	Rochford -	- do.
†Thundersley	- par.	516	2,515	2,456	Rayleigh -	- do.
TOTAL of UNION - -		24,406	63,132	133,509		
ROMFORD UNION.						
(Formed 31 May 1836 by Order dated 6 May 1836.)						
COUNTY of ESSEX :						
Barking	- par.	16,848	12,307	113,941	Barking -	- Half Hundred of Becontree.
Cranham	- par.	416	1,879	3,443	Romford -	- Hundred of Chafford.
Dagenham	- par.	3,411	6,556	22,222	do. -	- Half Hundred of Becontree.
Great Warley	- par.	1,413	2,891	6,956	Brentwood -	- Hundred of Chafford.
Havering-atte-Bower	par.	437	2,093	5,036	Romford -	- Liberty of Havering atte Bower.
Hornchurch	- par.	2,824	6,784	21,192	do. -	- do.
Rainham	- par.	1,253	3,253	10,128	do. -	- Hundred of Chafford.
Romford (W.)	- par.	9,050	7,224	44,232	do. -	- Liberty of Havering atte Bower.
Upminster	- par.	1,202	3,375	9,740	do. -	- Hundred of Chafford.
Wennington	- par.	196	1,301	3,563	do. -	- do.
TOTAL of UNION - -		37,050	47,663	240,453		
ROMNEY MARSH UNION.						
(Formed 14 Nov. 1835 by Order dated 30 Oct. 1835.)						
COUNTY of KENT :						
Blackmanstone	- par.	12	300	620	New Romney	Romney Marsh.
Brenzett	- par.	309	1,819	4,137	do. -	- Romney Marsh and County of Kent.
Brookland	- par.	434	1,886	4,584	do. -	- do.

(continued)

Unions and Parishes, &c.		Population in 1881.	Area in Statute Acres in 1881.	Rateable Value in 1881.	Post Town.	Petty Sessional Division.
ROMNEY MARSH UNION—County of Kent—*continued.*				£		
Burmarsh -	- *par.*	178	1,834	4,312	Folkestone -	Romney Marsh.
Dymchurch (*a*)	- *par.*	553	1,106	5,018	do. -	do.
Eastbridge -	- *par.*	54	1,150	2,653	do. -	do.
Fairfield -	- *par.*	53	1,206	2,446	New Romney -	County of Kent.
Hope, All Saints	- *par.*	31	1,493	3,265	do. -	do.
Ivychurch	- *par.*	259	4,567	9,862	do. -	Romney Marsh.
Lydd -	- *par.*	2,128	12,015	12,430	do. -	Borough of Lydd.
Midley -	- *par.*	63	2,161	4,457	do. -	County of Kent.
Newchurch -	- *par.*	325	3,139	6,812	do. -	Romney Marsh.
New Romney (W.) -	*par.*	1,026	2,561	6,306	do. -	Borough of the Town and Port of New Romney, Romney Marsh, and County of Kent.
Old Romney -	- *par.*	150	2,546	5,378	do. -	County of Kent.
Orgarswick -	- *par.*	5	402	883	Folkestone -	Romney Marsh.
Saint Mary's -	- *par.*	185	1,916	4,108	New Romney -	do.
Snargate -	- *par.*	149	1,600	3,198	do. -	Romney Marsh, and County of Kent.
Snave -	- *par.*	113	1,494	3,235	Ashford -	Romney Marsh.
West Hythe -	- *par.*	138	1,137	1,735	Folkestone -	Borough of Hythe and Romney Marsh.
TOTAL of UNION	-	6,165	44,335	83,466		

ROMSEY UNION.

(Formed 25 March 1835 by Order dated 3 Feb. 1835.—Places marked thus * added 11 Aug. 1835 by Order dated 27 July 1835; and thus † added 25 Dec. 1858 by Order dated 25 Oct. 1858.)

COUNTY of SOUTHAMPTON :

†Dunwood -	- *par.*	9	261	136	Romsey -	Romsey.
*East Dean -	- *par.*	179	1,074	1,559	Salisbury -	do.
*East Wellow -	- *par.*	319	2,494	2,308	Romsey -	do.
*Lockerley -	- *par.*	599	1,756	2,487	do. -	do.
*Mitchelmarsh	- *par.*	1,156	4,245	6,619	do. -	do.
*Mottisfont -	- *par.*	520	2,754	4,148	do. -	do.
*Nursling -	- *par.*	948	2,227	5,866	Southampton -	do.
Romsey Extra (W.) -	*par.*	3,549	9,861	19,828	Romsey -	do.
Romsey Infra	- *par.*	2,030	355	7,084	do. -	do.
*Sherfield English	- *par.*	283	1,848	2,208	do. -	do.
*Timsbury -	- *par.*	206	1,459	2,078	do. -	do.
COUNTY of WILTS :						
†Melchet Park	- *par.*	53	536	795	do. -	Salisbury.
*Plaitford (*a*)	- *par.*	174	1,218	957	do. -	do.
*West Wellow -	- *par.*	575	1,401	2,069	do. -	do.
TOTAL of UNION	-	10,600	31,489	58,142		

ROMNEY MARSH UNION :

(*a*) By Order which came into operation on 25 March 1886, a detached part of Sellinge, in the Elham Union, was amalgamated with Dymchurch.

ROMSEY UNION :

(*a*) By Order which came into operation on 25 March 1885, a detached part of White Parish, in the Alderbury Union, was amalgamated with Plaitford.

Unions and Parishes, &c.	Population in 1881.	Area in Statute Acres in 1881.	Rateable Value in 1881.	Post Town.	Petty Sessional Division.

ROSS UNION.

(Formed 12 April 1836 by Order dated 29 March 1836, as amended by Order dated 9 April 1836. — Place marked thus * added 19 Dec. 1836 by Order dated 23 Nov. 1836.)

COUNTY of GLOUCESTER :

			£		
*Ruardean (b) - - par.	1,295	1,593	3,682	Gloucester -	Little Dean.

COUNTY of HEREFORD :

Ballingham - - par.	149	901	1,597	Ross - -	Harewood End.
Brampton Abbots (c) par.	213	1,452	3,440	do. - -	Ross.
Bridstow (c) - - par.	685	2,199	5,400	do. - -	do.
Brockhampton (c) - par.	133	785	1,324	do. - -	do.
Foy - - par.	326	2,322	1,445	do. - -	do.
Goodrich (c) - par.	743	2,421	5,504	do. - -	do.
Harewood - par.	121	664	1,232	do. - -	Harewood End.
Hentland (c) - par.	575	2,905	5,214	do. - -	do.
Hope Mansell (b) - par.	215	1,173	2,078	do. - -	Ross
How Caple - par.	113	1,018	1,729	do. - -	do.
Kings Caple - par.	315	1,607	4,522	do. - -	Harewood End.
Lea (a) - par.	183	702	1,987	do. - -	Ross.
Llandinabo - par.	61	494	925	Hereford -	Harewood End.
Llangaran (c) (d) - par.	1,045	5,605	8,933	Ross -	do.
Llanwarne - par.	374	2,469	3,790	Hereford -	do.
Marstow (c) - par.	143	809	1,677	Ross -	do.
Pencoyd - par.	168	879	1,813	do. -	do.
Peterstow (c) - par.	332	1,544	3,143	do. -	do.
Ross (W.) - par.	4,786	3,118	23,170	do. -	Ross.
Saint Weonards - par.	629	4,536	5,765	do. -	Harewood End.
Sellack (c) - par.	337	1,540	3,454	do. -	do.
Sollers Hope - par.	83	1,152	1,240	do. -	Ross.
Tretire with Michaelchurch } par.	173	1,356	2,067	do. -	Harewood End.
Upton Bishop (c) - par.	696	3,391	5,108	do. -	Ross.
Walford (b) (c) - par.	1,179	4,241	8,367	do. -	do.
Weston under Penyard (a) } par.	828	3,142	8,789	do. -	do.
Yatton - tow.	190	1,409	2,019	do. -	do.
TOTAL of UNION -	16,090 (c)	55,517 (c)	122,414 (c)		

Ross Union :

(a) By Orders which came into operation on 25 March 1883,—

Two detached parts of a Tything, known as Lea Bailey, were amalgamated with Weston under Penyard ;

Three detached parts of Lea Bailey were amalgamated with Lea Upper ; and

All the parts of a Parish, known as Lea Lower, were amalgamated with Lea Upper.

(b) By Provisional Orders which came into operation on 25 March 1884,—

A detached part of Hope Mansell was amalgamated with Walford ;

Detached parts of Lea Bailey were amalgamated with East Dean, in the Westbury Union, and with Hope Mansell ;

Two detached parts of Newland, in the Monmouth Union, were amalgamated with Ruardean.

(c) By Orders which came into operation on 25 March 1884,

A detached part of Lea Bailey, known as Nackershole, was amalgamated with Walford.

Ross Union—continued.

By the operation of the several Orders relating to Lea Bailey, the Tything ceased to exist. Lea Bailey in 1881 had population 279, acreage 54, and rateable value 562l. ;

A detached part of Much Marcle, in the Ledbury Union, was amalgamated with Upton Bishop ;

Detached parts of Bridstow, Hentland, and Peterstow were united and amalgamated with Marstow ;

Detached parts of Goodrich were amalgamated with Llangaran and Marstow, and a detached part of Upton Bishop was amalgamated with Brampton Abbots ;

Detached parts of Fownhope, in the Hereford Union, were amalgamated with Brockhampton and Sellack.

(d) By Provisional Order which came into operation on 25 March 1883, detached parts of Llangaran were amalgamated with Whitchurch, in the Monmouth Union, and a nearly detached part of Whitchurch was amalgamated with Llangaran.

Unions and Parishes, &c.	Population in 1881.	Area in Statute Acres in 1881.	Rateable Value in 1881.	Post Town.	Petty Sessional Division.

ROTHBURY UNION.

(Formed 8 Oct. 1836 by Order dated 12 Sept. 1836.)

COUNTY of NORTHUMBERLAND:

			£		
Alnham - - tow.	131	9,403	2,488	Whittingham -	Coquetdale Ward : North Division.
Alwinton (a) - tow.	88	1,194	858	Rothbury -	do. West Division.
Barrow (a) - - tow.	11	1,010	120	do. - -	do. do.
Bickerton - - tow.	12	542	360	do. - -	do. do.
Biddlestone (a) - tow.	157	5,562	2,671	do. -	do. do.
Brinkburn (High Ward) - } tow.	119	1,878	1,288	Morpeth - -	do. do.
Brinkburn (Low Ward) - } tow.	51	592	556	do. - -	do. do.
Brinkburn (South Side) - } tow.	29	985	492	do. - -	Morpeth Ward : West Division.
Burradon - - tow.	121	1,540	1,357	Rothbury -	Coquetdale Ward : West Division.
Caistron - - tow.	29	401	548	do. - -	do.
Callaley and Yetlington tow.	249	3,990	3,868	Whittington -	Coquetdale Ward : North Division.
Cartington - - tow.	74	2,793	1,280	Rothbury -	Coquetdale Ward : West Division.
Clennel - - tow.	26	1,071	480	do. - -	do.
Contyards - - tow.	10	236	191	Netherwitton -	Morpeth Ward : West Division.
Debdon - - tow.	16	288	253	Rothbury -	Coquetdale Ward : West Division.
Dueshill - - tow.	17	2,534	553	do. - -	do.
Elsdon Ward - tow.	203	6,490	2,880	Elsdon -	Bellingham.
Ewersley - - tow.	19	946	801	Netherwitton -	Morpeth Ward : West Division.
Fairhaugh - - tow.	6	521	128	Rothbury -	Coquetdale Ward : West Division.
Fairnley - - tow.	5	216	180	Cambo -	do. do.
Fallolees - - tow.	8	1,503	434	do. - -	do. do.
Farnham - - tow.	58	931	695	Rothbury -	Coquetdale Ward : West Division.
Flotterton - - tow.	85	767	818	do. -	do. do.
Great Ryle - - tow.	70	2,042	1,296	Whittingham -	Coquetdale Ward : North Division.
Great Tosson, and Ryehill - } tow.	121	2,326	1,578	Rothbury -	Coquetdale Ward : West Division.
Greenleighton - - tow.	15	1,670	884	Cambo -	do. do.
Harbottle (a) - tow.	159	534	479	Rothbury -	do. do.
Hartington - - tow.	57	2,011	965	Cambo -	do. do.
Hartington Hall - tow.	26	1,001	933	do. - -	do. do.
Harwood - - tow.	28	3,960	1,142	do. - -	do. do.
Healey and Combhill tow.	27	852	488	Netherwitton -	Morpeth Ward : West Division.
Hepple - - tow.	78	3,605	898	Rothbury -	Coquetdale Ward : West Division.
Hepple Demesne - tow.	44	2,247	621	do. - -	do. do.

(continued)

ROTHBURY UNION :

(a) By Orders which came into operation on 25 March 1883,—

    Detached parts of Alwinton, Barrow, Biddlestone, Holystone, Linsheeles, and Peels, were united and amalgamated with Harbottle ;

    Detached parts of Biddlestone and Alwinton were amalgamated with Linbridge ;

    A detached part of Holystone was amalgamated with Harbottle.

Unions and Parishes, &c.		Population in 1881.	Area in Statute Acres in 1881.	Rateable Value in 1881.	Post Town.	Petty Sessional Division.
ROTHBURY UNION—County of Northumberland—*continued*.				£		
Hesleyhurst	- tow.	30	656	458	Rothbury - -	Coquetdale Ward; West Division.
Hollinghill	- tow.	86	5,049	1,448	do. -	do. do.
Holystone (a)	tow.	122	2,941	814	do. - -	do. do.
Kidland	- tow.	60	11,827	2,475	do. -	do. do.
Lee Ward	- tow.	74	1,739	922	Pauperhaugh -	do. do.
Linbridge (a)	- tow.	43	8,365	2,262	Rothbury -	do. do.
Linsheeles (a)	- tow.	80	14,846	4,253	do. - -	do. do.
Little Ryle	- tow.	41	528	469	Whittingham -	Coquetdale Ward: North Division.
Little Tosson	- tow.	31	547	471	Rothbury -	Coquetdale Ward: West Division.
Longframlington	- tow.	413	5,102	3,284	Longframlington -	do.
Lorbottle	- tow.	95	2,437	1,684	Whittingham -	Coquetdale Ward: North Division.
Monkridge Ward	- tow.	82	5,800	2,376	Elsdon - -	Bellingham.
Mount Healey	- tow.	36	437	500	Rothbury -	Coquetdale Ward: West Division.
Netherton (North Side)	tow.	49	762	703	do. - -	do. do.
Netherton (South Side)	tow.	109	731	855	do. - -	do. do.
Newtown -	- tow.	12	925	558	do. - -	do. do.
Nunny Kirk	- tow.	40	117	158	Netherwitton -	Morpeth Ward: West Division.
Pauperhaugh	- tow.	40	956	660	Morpeth -	Coquetdale Ward: West Division.
Peels (a)	- tow.	57	3,173	1,292	Rothbury -	do. do.
Prendwick	- tow.	50	1,414	887	Whittingham -	Coquetdale Ward: North Division.
Raw -	- tow.	43	717	472	Pauperhaugh -	Coquetdale Ward: West Division.
Ritton Colt Park	- tow.	40	1,071	956	Netherwitton -	Morpeth Ward: West Division.
Ritton White House -	tow.	23	648	639	do. - -	do. do.
Rothbury (W.)	tow.	1,247	3,366	5,910	Rothbury -	Coquetdale Ward: West Division.
Rothley	- tow.	119	2,822	1,973	Cambo -	do. do.
Screnwood	- tow.	25	1,061	863	Rothbury -	Coquetdale Ward: North Division.
Sharperton	- tow.	74	966	840	do. -	Coquetdale Ward: West Division.
Snitter	- tow.	139	1,084	1,411	do. -	do. do.
Thropton	- tow.	266	843	1,656	do. -	do. do.
Todburn	- tow.	19	694	269	Morpeth -	Morpeth Ward: West Division.
Trewhitt, High and Low - -	tow.	98	1,682	1,785	Rothbury -	Coquetdale Ward: West Division.
Unthank	- tow.	20	177	183	Whittingham -	Coquetdale Ward (North Division).
Warton	- tow.	57	650	926	Rothbury -	Coquetdale Ward (West Division).
Whittingham	- tow.	520	6,216	5,084	Whittingham -	Coquetdale Ward (North Division).
Whitton	- tow.	80	696	786	Rothbury -	Coquetdale Ward (West Division).
Wingates	- tow.	106	2,617	1,674	Morpeth -	Morpeth Ward: West Division.
Woodside Ward	- tow.	101	6,635	2,071	Elsdon -	Coquetdale Ward (West Division).
Wreighill	- tow.	3	412	492	Rothbury -	do. do.
TOTAL of UNION	-	6,703	166,350 (b)	87,105		

ROTHBURY UNION—*continued*.

(a) See notes, page 309.
(b) There are some lands intermixed with Rothbury and Snitter which comprise 23 acres. The Manorial Allotments consist of 1,534 acres.

Unions and Parishes. &c.	Population in 1881.	Area in Statute Acres in 1881.	Rateable Value in 1881.	Post Town.	Petty Sessional Division.

ROTHERHAM UNION.

Formed 1 July 1837 by Order dated 5 June 1837.)

COUNTY OF DERBY :

			£		
Beighton - - *par.*	2,071	3,136	12,222	Sheffield - -	Eckington.

COUNTY of YORK, West Riding :

Aston cum Aughton - *tow.*	2,352	3,006	16,495	Rotherham - -	Stratforth Upper and Tickhill.
Bramley (e) - - *tow.*	401	1,015	1,951	do. - -	do.
Brampton Bierlow (a) *tow.*	3,704	3,221	18,495	do. - -	do.
Brampton en le Mor-then } *tow.*	137	1,122	1,324	do. - -	do.
Brinsworth - - *tow.*	1,332	1,391	16,288	do. - -	do.
Catcliffe - - *tow.*	349	704	2,738	do. - -	do.
Dalton near Rother-ham (a) (b) - } *tow.*	108	1,976	2,543	do. - -	do.
Greasbrough - - *tow.*	3,811	2,456	13,897	do. - -	do.
Hooton Levett - *tow.*	95	519	972	do. - -	do.
Hooton Roberts - *par.*	235	1,056	1,932	do. - -	do.
Kimberworth - - *tow.*	16,043	3,760	57,803	do. - -	do.
Laughton en le Mor-then - - } *tow.*	663	3,878	5,414	do. - -	do.
Maltby - - *tow.*	795	4,086	5,645	do. - -	do.
Orgreave - - *tow.*	81	518	5,973	do. - -	do.
Ravenfield - - *par.*	172	1,235	1,727	do. - -	do.
Rawmarsh (d) - *par.*	10,179	2,578	39,317	do. - -	do.
Rotherham (W.) - *tow.*	16,257	1,271	59,420	do. - -	do.
Swinton (a) (d) - *tow.*	7,612	1,700	28,982	do. - -	do.
Thrybergh - - *tow.*	207	1,318	3,708	do. - -	do.
Tinsley - - *tow.*	1,003	1,672	14,453	Sheffield - -	Stratforth and Tickhill Upper.
Treeton with that part of Wales in Treeton Parish } *tow.*	482	1,165	4,648	Rotherham -	do
Ulley - - *tow.*	136	933	1,673	do. - -	do
Wath upon Dearne (a) *tow.*	3,012	1,724	21,750	do. - -	do.
Wentworth - - *tow.*	1,792	2,328	5,767	do. - -	do.
Whiston - - *tow.*	1,388	3,948	11,532	do. - -	do.
Wickersley - - *par.*	798	1,273	2,849	do. - -	do.
TOTAL of UNION -	75,515	53,062	359,548		

ROYSTON UNION.

(Formed 29 June 1835 by Order dated 13 June 1835.)

COUNTIES of CAMBRIDGE and HERTFORD :

Royston - *par.*	{ 440 In Cambridge 1,272 In Herts }	315	{ 1,376 In Cambridge 4,326 In Herts }	Royston - -	{ Arrington and Mel-bourn (for Cam-bridge). Odsey (for Herts).

COUNTY of CAMBRIDGE :

Abington Pigotts - *par.*	180	1,237	2,216	Royston -	Arrington and Mel-bourn.
Barrington - - *par.*	622	2,120	3,854	Cambridge -	do.

(continued)

ROTHERHAM UNION :

(a) By Orders which came into operation on 25 March 1882,—
Detached parts of Wath upon Dearne were amalgamated with Brampton Bierlow, and detached parts of Brampton Bierlow were amalgamated with Wath upon Dearne ;
A detached part of Conisbrough, in the Doncaster Union, was amalgamated with Dalton near Rotherham ;
Detached parts of Mexbrough, in the Doncaster Union, were amalgamated with Swinton.

ROTHERHAM UNION—continued.

(b) By Provisional Order which came into operation on 25 March 1883, a detached part of Ecclesfield, in the Wortley Union, was amalgamated with Dalton near Rotherham.

(c) By Order which came into operation on 25 March 1885, a detached part of Stainton with Hellaby, in the Doncaster Union, was amalgamated with Bramley.

(d) By Order which came into operation on 25 March 1886, a part of Rawmarsh was amalgamated with Swinton.

Unions and Parishes, &c.	Population in 1881.	Area in Statute Acres in 1881.	Rateable Value in 1881.	Post Town.			Petty Sessional Division.
ROYSTON UNION—County of Cambridge— *continued.*			£				
Bassingbourn (W.) - *par.*	2,121	3,275	7,551	Royston	-	-	Arrington and Melbourn.
Foulmire - *par.*	542	2,212	3,028	do.	-	-	do.
Foxton - *par.*	415	1,727	2,865	do.	-	-	do.
Guilden Morden - *par.*	959	2,506	3,870	do.	-	-	do.
Kneesworth - *ham.*	596	948	2,208	do.	-	-	do.
Littlington - *par.*	674	2,098	3,294	do.	-	-	do.
Melbourn - *par.*	1,803	4,688	7,825	do.	-	-	do.
Meldreth - *par.*	718	2,000	5,147	do.	-	-	do.
Shepreth - *par.*	373	1,269	2,547	do.	-	-	do.
Shingay - *par.*	90	754	1,072	do.	-	-	do.
Steeple Morden - *par.*	981	3,767	5,798	do.	-	-	do.
Thriplow - *par.*	463	2,489	3,006	do.	-	-	do.
Wendy - *par.*	136	947	1,485	do.	-	-	do.
Whaddon - *par.*	348	1,463	2,735	do.	-	-	do.
COUNTY of ESSEX :							
Great Chishall - *par.*	412	2,542	2,580	do.	-	-	Saffron Walden.
Heydon - *par.*	257	1,426	1,533	do.	-	-	do.
Little Chishall - *par.*	129	1,216	1,096	do.	-	-	do.
COUNTY of HERTFORD :							
Ashwell - *par.*	1,568	4,109	7,290	Baldock	-	-	Odsey.
Barkway - *par.*	782	3,251	3,996	Royston	-	-	do.
Barley - *par.*	615	2,725	3,125	do.	-	-	do.
Hinxworth - *par.*	297	1,463	1,688	Baldock	-	-	do.
Kelshall - *par.*	249	2,360	2,035	Royston	-	-	do.
Nuthampstead - *ham.*	217	1,960	1,501	do.	-	-	do.
Reed - *par.*	189	1,477	1,375	do.	-	-	do.
Therfield - *par.*	1,175	4,833	4,833	do.	-	-	do.
TOTAL of UNION -	18,623	61,186	95,255				
RUGBY UNION.							
(Formed 29 Mar. 1836 by Order dated 11 Mar. 1836.—Place marked thus * added 25 Mar. 1840 by Order dated 15 Feb. 1840; thus † added 22 April 1851 by Order dated 3 April 1851. Spelling of names of places marked thus ‡ as altered by Order dated 20 July 1887.)							
COUNTY of LEICESTER :							
‡Westrill and Starmore *par.*	15	1,620	2,460	Rugby		-	Lutterworth.
COUNTY of NORTHAMPTON :							
‡Barby (a) - *par.*	584	2,535	8,525	Rugby	-	-	Daventry.
Clay Coton - *par.*	98	974	2,100	do.	-	-	do.
Crick - *par.*	931	3,930	6,764	do.	-	-	do.
Elkington - *par.*	86	1,720	2,810	do.	-	-	do.
Kilsby (a) - *par.*	599	3,200	10,149	do.	-	-	do.
Lilbourne - *par.*	266	1,920	3,352	do.	-	-	do.
Stanford - *par.*	52	1,510	3,807	do.	-	-	do.
Yelvertoft - *par.*	499	2,080	1,523	do.	-	-	do.
COUNTY of WARWICK :							
Bilton - *par.*	1,696	2,243	8,758	Rugby	-	-	Rugby.
Birdingbury - *par.*	190	1,180	1,552	do.	-	-	Southam.

(continued)

RUGBY UNION :

(a) By Orders which came into operation on 25 March 1885,—
A Parish known as Monks Riding was amalgamated with Brinklow. Monks Riding contained no population. The area is included in that of Combe or Combe Fields, and the rateable value in that of Brinklow.
A detached part of Barby known as Barby Nortoft was amalgamated with Kilsby.

Unions and Parishes, &c.		Population in 1881.	Area in Statute Acres in 1881.	Rateable Value in 1881.	Post Town.	Petty Sessional Division.

Rugby Union—County of Warwick—continued.

Unions and Parishes, &c.		Population in 1881.	Area in Statute Acres in 1881.	Rateable Value in 1881. £	Post Town.	Petty Sessional Division.
Bourton	par.	294	2,520	2,792	Rugby	Rugby.
Brandon and Bretford	tow.	435	In Wolston	4,454	Coventry	Coventry.
†Brinklow (a)	par.	783	1,410	3,143	do.	Rugby.
Brownsover	tow.	90	872	2,397	Rugby	do.
Church Lawford	par.	266	1,865	3,153	do.	do.
Churchover	par.	323	1,440	2,921	do.	do.
Clifton upon Dunsmore	} par.	592	2,870	5,230	do.	do.
Combe or Combe Fields	} par.	174	4,210	7,657	Coventry	Coventry
Cosford	tow.	45 {	In Newbold-upon-Avon }	1,116	Rugby	Rugby.
Dunchurch	tow.	992	4,846	6,023	do.	do.
*Easenhall	tow.	205	1,112	1,265	do.	do.
Frankton	par.	215	1,636	2,480	do.	do.
Grandborough	par.	425	4,100	6,197	do.	Southam.
Harborough Magna	par.	343	1,580	2,462	do.	Coventry.
Hillmorton	par.	1,311	3,150	12,060	do.	Rugby.
Leamington Hastings	par.	461	3,244	5,232	do.	Southam.
Little Lawford	tow.	47 }	In Newbold {	1,141	do.	Rugby.
Long Lawford	tow.	683 }	upon Avon {	4,281	do.	do.
Marton	par.	374	910	2,308	do.	Southam.
Newbold upon Avon	par.	699	4,020	7,386	do.	Rugby.
Newnham Regis	par.	118	1,418	2,280	do.	do.
Newton and Biggin	tow.	241	1,160	2,146	do.	do.
Princethorpe	tow.	310 {	In Stretton upon Dunsmore }	1,979	do.	do.
Rugby (W.)	par.	9,891	2,190	51,184	do.	do.
Ryton upon Dunsmore	par.	455	1,650	3,604	Coventry	Coventry.
Stretton upon Dunsmore	} tow.	668	3,110	3,315	Rugby	Rugby.
Thurlaston	tow.	321 {	In Dunchurch }	2,606	do.	do.
Willoughby	par.	302	2,290	3,849	do.	do.
Wolfhampcote	par.	330	3,470	7,842	do.	Southam.
Wolston	par.	791	2,770	6,020	Coventry	Rugby.
Total of Union		**27,200**	**80,755**	**226,341**		

RUNCORN UNION.

(Formed 26 Aug. 1836 by Order dated 2 Aug. 1836.)

County of Chester:

Unions and Parishes, &c.		Population in 1881.	Area in Statute Acres in 1881.	Rateable Value in 1881.	Post Town.	Petty Sessional Division.
Acton Grange	tow.	173	969	3,820	Warrington	Bucklow Hundred.
Alvanley	tow.	321	1,513	2,740	Frodsham, Warrington.	Eddisbury Hundred.
Antrobus (a)	tow.	430	2,114	4,060	Northwich	Bucklow Hundred.
Aston by Sutton	tow.	285	1,408	4,436	Preston Brook, Warrington.	do.
Aston Grange	tow.	33	458	1,079	do. do.	do.
Bartington	tow.	96	310	987	Northwich	do.
Clifton or Rocksavage	} tow.	203	615	3,741	Runcorn	do.
Crowley	tow.	196	1,400	2,283	Northwich	do.
Daresbury	tow.	139	607	1,584	Warrington	do.
Dutton (W.) (b)	tow.	452	2,090	10,374	Preston Brook, Warrington.	do.
Frodsham Lordship		1,087	2,688	8,237	do. do.	Eddisbury.
Frodsham Township		2,489	2,389	10,325	do. do.	do.

(continued)

RUNCORN UNION:

(a) By Orders which came into operation on 25 March 1882,—
   A detached part of Antrobus was amalgamated with Seven Oaks, and a detached part of Seven Oaks was amalgamated with Antrobus;
   A detached part of Norley was amalgamated with Kingsley; and

RUNCORN UNION—continued.

   A detached part of Norley was amalgamated with Crowton, in the Northwich Union.

(b) By Order which came into operation on 25 March, 1884, all the parts of Halton situate within the Urban Sanitary District of Runcorn were amalgamated with Runcorn.

Unions and Parishes, &c.		Population in 1881.	Area in Statute Acres in 1881.	Rateable Value in 1881.	Post Town.	Petty Sessional Division.
Runcorn Union—County of Chester—*continued.*				£		
Great Budworth	- tow.	532	903	2,769	Northwich	Bucklow Hundred.
Halton (*b*)	- tow.	1,439	1,806	6,746	Runcorn	do.
Hatton	- tow.	365	1,049	2,573	Warrington	do.
Helsby	- tow.	812	1,320	5,197	Frodsham, Warrington.	Eddisbury.
Hull and Appleton	- tow.	2,067	3,422	11,269	Warrington	Bucklow Hundred.
Kekwick	- tow.	83	528	3,203	do.	do.
Kingsley (*a*)	- tow.	1,207	2,705	6,767	Frodsham, Warrington.	Eddisbury.
Kingswood	- tow.	235	1,918	2,136	do. do.	do.
Manley	- tow.	306	1,337	2,442	do. do.	do.
Moore	- tow.	398	916	4,560	Warrington	Bucklow Hundred.
Newton by Daresbury	tow.	189	785	1,876	Preston Brook, Warrington.	do.
Newton by Frodsham	tow.	119	442	1,262	Frodsham, Warrington.	Eddisbury.
Norley (*a*)	- tow.	721	1,416	3,633	do. do.	do.
Norton	- tow.	345	2,235	6,680	Runcorn	Bucklow Hundred.
Preston on the Hill	- tow.	560	1,154	4,663	Preston Brook, Warrington	do.
Runcorn (*b*)	- tow.	14,812	1,153	47,137	Runcorn	do.
Seven-Oaks (*a*)	- tow.	183	631	1,448	Northwich	do.
Stockham	- tow.	25	331	810	Runcorn	do.
Stretton	- tow.	396	1,133	2,707	Warrington	do.
Sutton	- tow.	377	1,189	6,682	Preston Brook, Warrington.	do.
Walton Inferior	- tow.	498	558	3,001	Warrington	do.
Walton Superior	- tow.	246	437	2,190	do.	do.
Weston	- tow.	1,684	898	11,659	Runcorn	do.
Whitley Inferior	- tow.	214	1,136	2,363	Northwich	do.
Whitley Superior	- tow.	306	1,020	2,838	do.	do.
TOTAL OF UNION	-	34,023	47,103	200,357		

RUTHIN UNION.

(Formed 1 Mar. 1837 by Order dated 4 Feb. 1837.)

County of Denbigh :

Aberwheeler	- tow.	409	3,356	3,927	Trefnant	Isaled, Denbigh.
Clocaenog Isa Ucha	- par.	421	7,182	3,305	Ruthin	Ruthin
Derwen	- par.	535	3,554	3,193	Corwen	do.
Efenechtyd	- par.	194	1,233	1,445	Ruthin	do.
Gyffylliog	- par.	479	8,181	2,876	do.	do.
Llanarmon	- par.	1,681	11,874	8,742	Mold	do.
Llanbedr dyffryn Clwyd	- par.	410	3,102	3,804	Ruthin	do.
Llandegla	- par.	343	3,475	1,472	Mold	do.
Llandyrnog	- par.	475	3,371	5,657	Denbigh	Isaled, Denbigh.
Llanelidan	- par.	766	5,223	6,291	Ruthin	Ruthin.
Llanfair dyffryn Clwyd	- par.	1,117	7,480	9,137	do.	do.
Llanferras	- par.	690	3,867	3,234	Mold	do.
Llanfwrog	- par.	1,342	3,209	5,893	Ruthin	do.
Llangwyfan	- par.	189	4,159	1,569	Trefnant	Isaled, Denbigh.
Llangynhafal	- par.	401	2,361	2,754	Ruthin	Ruthin.
Llanrhaiadr in Kinmerch	- par.	1,679	17,238	15,578	Denbigh	Isaled, Denbigh.
Llanrhydd (W.)	- par.	876	1,336	3,963	Ruthin	Ruthin.
Llanychan	- par.	86	584	1,607	do.	do.
Llanynys	- par.	700	5,107	8,559	Denbigh	do.
Nantglyn	- par.	289	5,454	2,014	do.	Isaled, Denbigh.
Ruthin	- par.	1,130	737	6,344	Ruthin	Ruthin.
TOTAL OF UNION	-	14,215	99,083	101,364		

RUNCORN UNION :
(*a*) (*b*) *See notes, page* 313.

Unions and Parishes, &c.	Population in 1881.	Area in Statute Acres in 1881.	Rateable Value in 1881.	Post Town.	Petty Sessional Division.
RYE UNION.					
(Formed 27 July 1835 by Order dated 7 July 1835.)					
COUNTIES of KENT and SUSSEX :			£		
Broomhill - *par.*	126	2,587	3,882	Rye -	Rye.
COUNTY of SUSSEX :					
Beckley - *par.*	1,230	5,620	6,697	do.	do.
Brede - *par.*	1,056	4,840	6,291	do. - -	do.
East Guldeford - *par.*	182	2,823	7,147	do.	do.
Icklesham - *par.*	867	4,934	9,153	do. - -	do.
Iden - *par.*	551	2,970	6,224	do. - -	do.
Northiam - *par.*	1,207	3,585	5,848	do. - -	do.
Peasemarsh - *par.*	837	3,772	5,919	do. - -	do.
Playden - *par.*	294	1,296	3,012	do. - -	do.
Rye (W.) - *par.*	4,667	2,462	15,338	do. - -	Borough (Separate Quarter Sessions).
Saint Thomas the Apostle Winchelsea - *par.*	613	965	3,113	do. -	Rye.
Udimore - *par.*	410	2,277	3,796	do. -	do.
TOTAL of UNION -	12,040	38,131	76,420		
SADDLEWORTH TOWNSHIP.					
(Board of Guardians constituted 4 May 1853 by Order of that date.)					
COUNTY of YORK, WEST RIDING :					
Saddleworth (W.) - *tow.*	22,299	18,797	63,272	Oldham	Saddleworth.
SAFFRON WALDEN UNION.					
(Formed 6 April 1835 by Order dated 21 Mar. 1835.)					
COUNTY of ESSEX :					
Arkesden - *par.*	420	2,367	2,949	Bishop's Stortford-	Walden
Ashdon - *par.*	830	3,779	5,347	Linton -	do.
Chrishall - *par.*	573	2,789	3,014	Royston -	do.
Clavering - *par.*	1,039	3,831	4,902	Bishop's Stortford	do.
Debden - *par.*	816	4,653	5,096	Saffron Walden -	do.
Elmdon - *par.*	614	3,276	4,056	do. - -	do
Great Chesterford - *par.*	913	2,917	5,091	Saffron Walden -	do.
Great Sampford - *par.*	555	1,737	2,970	Braintree -	Bardfield.
Hempstead - *par.*	631	3,591	1,293	Saffron Walden -	do.
Langley - *par.*	400	1,660	1,651	Bishop's Stortford -	Walden.
Littlebury - *par.*	795	3,537	7,546	Saffron Walden -	do.
Little Chesterford - *par.*	214	1,207	1,447	do. - -	do.
Little Sampford - *par.*	407	3,322	3,555	Braintree -	Bardfield.
Newport - *par.*	992	1,722	5,674	Bishop's Stortford-	Walden.
Quendon - *par.*	192	657	1,464	do. - -	do.
Radwinter - *par.*	842	3,876	4,606	Saffron Walden -	do.
Rickling - *par.*	452	1,392	2,012	Bishop's Stortford-	Walden.
Saffron Walden (W.) *par.*	6,060	7,502	23,481	Saffron Walden -	Borough of Saffron Walden.
Streethall - *par.*	43	629	687	do. - -	Walden.
Wendon Ambo - *par.*	359	1,430	3,612	do. - -	do.
Wendon Lofts - *par.*	56	799	996	do. - -	do.
Wicken Bonhunt - *par.*	162	850	1,130	Bishop's Stortford	do.
Widdington - *par.*	377	2,054	4,082	do. - -	do.
Wimbish - *par.*	846	4,920	5,345	Saffron Walden -	do.
TOTAL of UNION -	18,588	64,506	105,096		

Unions and Parishes, &c.		Population in 1881.	Area in Statute Acres in 1881.	Rateable Value in 1881.	Post Town.	Petty Sessional Division.

SAINT ALBAN'S UNION.

(Formed 23 May 1835 by Order dated 27 April 1835.)

COUNTY of HERTFORD :

				£		
Harpenden	par.	3,064	5,112	17,613	St. Albans	St. Albans.
Redbourn	par.	2,177	1,563	8,946	do.	do.
Saint Alban's, otherwise the Abbey	par.	4,097	166	10,614	do.	City of St. Albans.
Saint Michael (W.)	par.	2,256	6,558	12,457	do.	St. Albans and City.
Saint Peter	par.	6,779	6,673	28,291	do.	do. do.
Saint Stephen	par.	1,763	7,387	16,881	do.	do. do.
Sandridge	par.	841	5,753	12,224	do.	do. do.
Wheathampstead	par.	2,319	5,187	12,118	do.	St. Albans.
TOTAL of UNION		23,296	41,399	119,117		

SAINT ASAPH UNION.

(Formed 10 April 1837 by Order dated 14 Mar. 1837.)

COUNTY of DENBIGH :

Abergele	par.	3,172	9,439	27,555	Abergele	Isdulas.
Bettws yn Rhos	par.	734	6,588	5,007	do.	do.
Denbigh	par.	4,422	1,609	15,820	Denbigh	Borough of Denbigh.
Henllan	par.	2,815	14,825	21,892	Trefnant, Rhyl	Isaled.
Llandulas	par.	597	640	3,120	Abergele	Isdulas.
Llanfair Talhaiarn	par.	1,183	11,239	7,568	do.	Uwchdulas.
Llansannan	par.	1,109	15,545	7,523	do.	Uwchaled.
Llanyfydd	par.	878	7,606	7,063	Trefnant, Rhyl	do.
Saint George	par.	318	2,067	2,829	Abergele	Isdulas.

COUNTIES of DENBIGH and FLINT :

Saint Asaph (W.)	par.	3,177	11,346	23,042	Saint Asaph	Rhuddlan.

COUNTY of FLINT :

Bodfary	tow.	452	1,494	2,879	Trefnant, Rhyl	Caerwys.
Cwm or Combe	par.	418	3,883	4,567	Rhyl	Rhuddlan.
Dremeirchion	par.	654	4,034	5,043	Saint Asaph	do.
Dyserth	par.	966	2,084	4,942	Rhyl	Prestatyn.
Meliden with Prestatyn	par.	1,137	2,068	7,091	do.	do.
Rhuddlan and Rhyl	par.	7,426	4,730	44,776	do.	Rhuddlan.
TOTAL of UNION		29,458	98,191	190,717		

SAINT AUSTELL UNION.

(Formed 30 April 1837 by Order dated 15 April 1837.)

COUNTY of CORNWALL :

Creed	par.	244	2,666	3,403	Grampound	East Powder.
Fowey	par.	1,656	1,945	5,631	Fowey	Tywardreath Division of East Powder.
Gorran	par.	916	1,961	6,420	Saint Austell	East Powder.
Grampound	tow.	182	199	933	Grampound	do.
Mevagissey	par.	2,186	1,380	4,622	Saint Austell	do.
Roche	par.	1,684	6,471	6,981	do.	do.
Saint Austell (W.)	par.	11,286	12,125	44,824	do.	do.
Saint Blazey	par.	2,762	1,797	8,036	Par Station	Tywardreath Division of East Powder.
Saint Dennis	par.	1,235	7,240	6,455	Saint Austell	East Powder.
Saint Ewe	par.	906	5,953	6,522	do.	do.
Saint Mewan	par.	1,018	2,653	4,685	do.	do.

(continued)

Unions and Parishes, &c.		Population in 1881.	Area in Statute Acres in 1881.	Rateable Value in 1881.	Post Town.	Petty Sessional Division.
Saint Austell Union—County of Cornwall—continued.				£		
Saint Michael Carhayes	par.	129	862	1,242	Saint Austell -	South Powder.
Saint Sampson	par.	238	1,170	1,782	Par Station - -	Tywardreath Division of East Powder.
Saint Stephens (in Brannel)	par.	3,228	9,292	19,262	Grampound Road -	East Powder.
Tywardreath -	par.	2,129	3,252	6,559	Par Station -	Tywardreath Division of East Powder.
Total of Union -		30,186	58,266	127,357		
SAINT COLUMB MAJOR UNION.						
(Formed 9 May 1837 by Order dated 13 April 1837.)						
County of Cornwall :						
Colan - -	par.	243	2,049	2,364	Saint Columb Major	Hundred of Pydar.
Crantock - -	par.	344	2,436	3,072	Grampound Road -	do.
Cubert - -	par.	373	2,511	3,108	do. -	do.
Little Petherick -	par.	215	1,224	1,344	Saint Issey - -	do.
Mawgan (in Pyder) -	par.	708	5,525	5,237	Saint Columb Major	do.
Newlyn - -	par.	1,414	8,371	8,049	Grampound Road -	do.
Padstow - -	par.	2,191	3,341	8,017	Padstow - -	do.
Saint Breock -	par.	1,787	7,984	7,975	Wadebridge -	do.
Saint Columb Major (W.)	par.	2,739	12,884	15,169	Saint Columb Major	do.
Saint Columb Minor -	par.	2,775	5,780	11,928	Newquay - -	do.
Saint Enoder - -	par.	1,120	7,274	7,821	Grampound Road -	do.
Saint Ervan - -	par.	391	3,142	3,262	Saint Issey -	do.
Saint Eval - -	par.	265	2,916	2,760	do. -	do.
Saint Issey - -	par.	677	4,501	5,049	Bodmin - -	do.
Saint Merryn - -	par.	560	3,946	4,413	Padstow - -	do.
Saint Wenn - -	par.	541	4,695	3,268	Bodmin - -	do.
Total of Union -		16,343	78,579	92,836		
SAINT FAITH'S UNION.						
(Formed 4 Jan. 1836 by Order dated 21 Dec. 1835.)						
County of Norfolk :						
Alderford - -	par.	37	432	746	Norwich - -	Eynsford.
Attlebridge - -	par.	66	1,267	1,237	do. -	Taverham.
Beeston Saint Andrew	par.	39	626	1,353	do. -	do.
Booton - -	par.	203	1,040	1,831	do. -	South Erpingham.
Brandistone - -	par.	142	764	1,457	do. -	Eynsford.
Catton - -	par.	751	895	3,908	do. -	Taverham.
Crostwick - -	par.	159	690	910	do. -	do.
Drayton - -	par.	408	1,332	2,249	do. -	do.
Felthorpe - -	par.	463	2,286	1,688	do. -	do.
Frettenham (a) -	par.	220	1,581	2,548	do. -	do.
Great Witchingham -	par.	565	2,245	4,394	do. -	Eynsford.
Hainford - -	par.	629	1,600	2,862	do. -	Taverham.
Haveringland -	par.	116	2,062	1,967	do. -	Eynsford.
Hellesdon (part of, not included in the Liberties of Norwich)	par.	338	1,148	1,733	do. -	Taverham
Honingham - -	par.	343	2,563	3,740	do. -	Forehoe.
Horsford - -	par.	697	4,177	4,213	do. -	Taverham.

(continued)

SAINT FAITH'S UNION :

(a) By Order which came into operation on 25 March 1885, a detached part of Frettenham was amalgamated with Horstead with Staininghall.

P p

Unions and Parishes, &c.	Population in 1881.	Area in Statute Acres in 1881.	Rateable Value in 1881.	Post Town.	Petty Sessional Division.

SAINT FAITH'S UNION—County of Norfolk—cont.

			£		
Horsham Saint Faith (W.) and Newton Saint Faith - } par.	1,082	2,310	5,749	Norwich - -	Taverham.
Horstead with Stainingball (a) - } par.	565	2,733	3,970	do. - -	do.
Little Witchingham, otherwise Saint Faith } par.	41	738	1,341	do. - -	Eynsford.
Morton on the Hill - par.	143	977	1,034	do. - -	do.
Rackheath - - par.	302	1,980	3,306	do. - -	Taverham.
Ringland - - par.	326	1,210	1,470	do. - -	Eynsford.
Salhouse - - par.	622	2,060	2,938	do. - -	Taverham.
Spixworth - - par.	61	1,224	2,312	do. - -	do.
Sprowston - - par.	1,782	2,576	6,327	do. - -	do.
Swannington - par.	326	1,433	2,027	do. - -	Eynsford.
Taverham - - par.	207	2,099	2,556	do. - -	Taverham.
Weston - - par.	404	2,737	4,086	do. - -	Eynsford.
Wroxham - - par.	378	1,489	2,529	do. - -	Taverham.
TOTAL of UNION -	11,418	48,304	76,481		

SAINT GEORGE'S UNION.

(Formed 28 Mar. 1870 by Order dated 14 Mar. 1870. — Place marked thus * added 29 Sept. 1875 by Order dated 14 Sept. 1875.)

COUNTY of MIDDLESEX :

Saint George, Hanover Square (W.) } par.	89,573	1,119	1,679,299	London, W. or S.W.	Hanover Square.
Saint Margaret and Saint John the Evangelist, in the City of Westminster - } united pars.	} 59,926	815	599,237	London, S.W. -	Saint Margaret.
*The Close of the Collegiate Church of Saint Peter, Westminster - } par.	219	9	2,393	do. * -	Westminster Police Court, Rochester Row.
TOTAL of UNION -	149,748	1,943	2,280,929		

SAINT GEORGE IN THE EAST, PARISH.

(Board of Guardians constituted 25 Mar. 1836 by Order dated 6 Feb. 1836.)

COUNTY of MIDDLESEX :

Saint George in the East (W.) - } par.	47,157	243	199,237	London, E. -	Tower.

SAINT GERMANS UNION.

(Formed 14 Jan. 1837 by Order dated 20 Dec. 1836.)

COUNTY of CORNWALL :

					East, Hundred of:
Antony (W.) - par.	3,201	3,288	11,071	Torpoint -	South Division
Botusfleming - par.	215	1,146	1,923	Hatt,R.S.O.,Cornwall	do.
Landrake with Saint Erney - } par.	735	3,555	6,336	Saint Germans -	do.
Landulph - - par.	505	2,686	3,749	Hatt,R.S.O.,Cornwall	do.
Maker - - par.	3,052	2,382	7,915	Devonport -	do.
Pillaton - - par.	338	2,478	2,634	Saint Mellion -	Middle Division.
Quethiock - par.	485	4,531	5,373	Liskeard - -	do.

(continued)

Unions and Parishes, &c.	Population in 1881.	Area in Statute Acres in 1881.	Rateable Value in 1881.	Post Town.	Petty Sessional Division.

SAINT GERMANS UNION—County of Cornwall—continued.

			£		East, Hundred of :
Rame - - par.	852	1,261	2,453	Devonport	South Division.
Saint Germans - par.	2,307	10,097	15,798	Saint Germans -	do.
Saint John - - par.	185	728	1,080	Antony, near Devonport.	do.
Saint Mellion - - par.	309	2,985	2,182	Saint Mellion -	Middle Division.
Saint Stephens (by Saltash) - } par.	1,421	} 5,210	{ 12,733	Saltash - -	South Division.
Saltash - - town & cha.	2,563		{ 6,608	do. - -	Borough of Saltash.
Sheviock - - par.	562	2,381	3,128	Sheviock, Saint Germans.	South Division of the Hundred of East.
TOTAL of UNION -	16,720	42,728	83,483		

SAINT GILES, CAMBERWELL PARISH.

(Board of Guardians constituted 24 Nov. 1835 by Order dated 19 Oct. 1835.)

COUNTY of SURREY :

| Saint Giles, Camberwell (W.) - } par. | 186,593 | 4,150 | 803,413 | Camberwell, S.E. - | East Half of the Hundred of Brixton. |

SAINT GILES - IN - THE - FIELDS AND SAINT GEORGE, BLOOMSBURY, UNITED PARISHES.

(Board of Guardians constituted 24 April 1868 by Order dated 24 Mar. 1868.)

COUNTY of MIDDLESEX :

| Saint Giles-in-the-Fields (W.) and Saint George, Bloomsbury } | — | 15,382 | 245 | 358,418 | Bloomsbury, London. W.C. | Holborn. |

SAINT IVES UNION.

(Formed 18 Jan. 1836 by Order dated 23 Dec. 1835.—Spelling of names of places marked * as altered by Order dated 31 May 1897.)

COUNTY of CAMBRIDGE:

Boxworth - - par.	251	2,521	3,126	Saint Ives -	Cambridge.
*Conington - - par.	145	1,477	1,760	do. -	do.
Fen Drayton - par.	344	1,496	3,596	do. - -	do.
Lolworth - - par.	170	1,076	1,579	do. - -	do.
Over - - par.	1,073	3,700	8,591	do. - -	do.
Swavesey - - par.	1,171	3,891	8,261	do. - -	do.

COUNTY of HUNTINGDON :

| Bluntisham with Earith (a) (b) - } par. | 1,085 | 3,423 | 8,207 | Saint Ives - | Hurstingstone. |
| Broughton - - par. | 293 | 2,950 | 2,755 | Huntingdon - | do. |

(continued)

SAINT IVES UNION :

(a) By Orders which came into operation on 25 March 1884,—A detached part of Bury was amalgamated with Upwood, in the Huntingdon Union ; Detached parts of Colne were amalgamated with Somersham and Bluntisham with Earith ;

SAINT IVES UNION—continued.

(b) By Order which came into operation on 25 March 1885,—A detached part of Old Hurst was amalgamated with Woodhurst, and a detached part of Woodhurst was amalgamated with Bluntisham with Earith.

Unions and Parishes, &c.	Population in 1881	Area in Statute Acres in 1881.	Rateable Value in 1881.	Post Town.	Petty Sessional Division.
SAINT IVES UNION—County of Huntingdon—continued.			£		
Bury (a) - par.	319	1,615	3,222	Huntingdon -	Ramsey.
Colne (a) - par.	328	2,011	5,191	Saint Ives -	Hurstingstone.
*Fen Stanton - par.	1,067	2,100	7,679	do. -	do.
Hemingford Abbots - par.	389	2,990	3,880	do. -	do.
Hemingford Grey (W.) } par.	881	1,610	5,758	do. -	do.
Hilton - par.	353	1,280	2,367	do. -	do.
Holywell with Needingworth } par.	726	3,290	6,581	do. -	do.
Houghton - par.	510	1,610	2,920	Huntingdon -	do.
Old Hurst (b) - par.	124	1,350	1,294	do. -	do.
*Pidley cum Fenton - par.	418	3,739	5,366	do. -	do.
Saint Ives - par.	3,002	2,330	14,021	Saint Ives -	do.
Somersham (a) - par.	1,409	4,121	11,167	do. -	do.
Warboys - par.	1,676	8,100	12,610	Huntingdon -	Ramsey.
Wistow - par.	392	2,070	3,489	do. -	do.
Woodhurst (b) - par.	331	2,130	2,338	do. -	Hurstingstone.
*Wyton - par.	238	1,690	1,995	do. -	do.
TOTAL of UNION -	16,755	62,930	127,753		

SAINT JOHN HAMPSTEAD PARISH.

(Board of Guardians constituted 19 May 1848 by Order dated 3 May 1848.)

COUNTY of MIDDLESEX :

Saint John Hampstead (W.) - } par.	45,452	2,248	421,490	Hampstead, N.W.-	Holborn Division, Hundred of Ossulstone.

SAINT LEONARD, SHOREDITCH, PARISH.

(Board of Guardians constituted 17 Jan. 1868 by Order dated 18 Dec. 1867.)

COUNTY of MIDDLESEX :

Saint Leonard, Shoreditch (W.) - } par.	126,591	648	580,411	London, E. -	Tower.

SAINT LUKE, CHELSEA, PARISH.

(Board of Guardians constituted 8 July 1841 by Order dated 22 June 1841.)

COUNTY of MIDDLESEX :

Saint Luke, Chelsea (W.) - } par.	88,128	796	465,353	London, S.W. -	Kensington.

SAINT MARY ABBOTS KENSINGTON PARISH.

(Board of Guardians constituted 25 Mar. 1845 by Order dated 11 Mar. 1845.)

COUNTY of MIDDLESEX :

Saint Mary Abbots Kensington (W.) - } par.	163,151	2,190	1,648,187	Kensington, London, W.	Kensington.

SAINT IVES UNION:
(a) (b) See notes, page 319.

Unions and Parishes, &c.	Population in 1881.	Area in Statute Acres in 1881.	Rateable Value in 1881.	Post Town.	Petty Sessional Division.
SAINT MARY AND SAINT ANDREW WHITTLESEA, UNITED PARISHES. (Board of Guardians constituted 29 Sept. 1836 by Order dated 3 Sept. 1836.) In the Isle of Ely, in the County of Cambridge : Saint Mary and Saint Andrew Whittlesea (W.) }	6,455	25,131	£ 46,482	Peterborough -	Whittlesey and Thorney.
SAINT MARY, ISLINGTON, PARISH. (Board of Guardians constituted 8 July 1867 by Order dated 4 June 1867.) County of Middlesex : Saint Mary, Islington (W.) } par.	282,865	3,107	1,145,913	London, N. -	Finsbury.
SAINT MARY, LAMBETH, PARISH. (Board of Guardians constituted 28 Dec. 1835 by Order dated 19 Nov. 1835.) County of Surrey : Saint Mary, Lambeth (W.) } par.	253,699	3,942	1,288,231	Lambeth, S.E. as to part ; S.W. as to part.	East Half of the Hundred of Brixton.
SAINT MARYLEBONE PARISH. (Board of Guardians constituted 2 Aug. 1867 by Order dated 28 June 1867.) County of Middlesex : Saint Marylebone (W.) par.	154,916	1,506	1,383,987	London, W. -	St. Marylebone.
SAINT MATTHEW, BETHNAL GREEN, PARISH. (Board of Guardians constituted 25 Mar. 1836 by Order dated 12 Feb. 1836.) County of Middlesex : Saint Matthew, Bethnal Green (W.) } par.	126,961	755	357,879	Bethnal Green, E.	Tower.

Unions and Parishes, &c.		Population in 1881.	Area in Statute Acres in 1881.	Rateable Value in 1881.	Post Town.	Petty Sessional Division.

SAINT NEOTTS UNION.

(Formed 24 Sept. 1835 by Order dated 9 Sept. 1835.— Places marked thus * added 16 Nov. 1835 by Order dated 21 Oct. 1835.)

COUNTY of BEDFORD :

				£		
*Dean - -	par.	487	2,370	2,912	Kimbolton -	Bletsoe.
Eaton Socon (W.) -	par.	2,365	7,530	12,720	St. Neotts -	Bedford.
Little Barford -	par.	189	1,188	5,121	do.	do.
*Little Staughton -	par.	469	1,773	2,124	do.	Bletsoe.
*Pertenhall -	par.	337	1,533	2,151	Kimbolton -	do.
*Shelton -	par.	149	1,080	985	do. -	do.
*Tilbrook -	par.	392	1,680	2,206	do. -	do.

COUNTY of CAMBRIDGE :

Graveley -	par.	207	1,558	1,470	St. Neotts -	Caxton.

COUNTY of HUNTINGDON :

Abbotsley -	par.	161	2,110	2,029	St. Neotts -	St. Neotts.
Buckden -	par.	1,044	3,590	5,554	Huntingdon	do.
Catworth (a) -	ham.	638	3,570	3,231	Kimbolton -	Huntingdon.
Diddington -	par.	203	1,450	1,800	Huntingdon	St. Neotts.
Eynesbury -	par.	1,312	1,249	7,501	St. Neotts -	do.
Graffham -	par.	334	2,380	2,020	do. -	Huntingdon.
Great Paxton -	par.	261	1,120	7,304	do. -	St. Neotts.
Great Staughton	par.	1,090	5,910	7,780	do. -	do.
Hail Weston -	par.	318	1,553	2,138	do. -	do.
*Kimbolton -	par.	1,220	5,061	8,117	Kimbolton -	do.
Little Paxton -	par.	279	2,040	2,681	St. Neotts -	do.
*Midloe -	par.	35	850	762	do. -	do.
*Offord Cluney	par.	287	960	5,279	Huntingdon	do.
*Offord Darcey	par.	317	1,827	5,539	do. -	do.
Saint Neotts -	par.	3,136	4,750	18,370	St. Neotts -	do.
Southoe -	par.	272	1,860	2,054	Huntingdon	do.
*Stow - -	par.	149	In Catworth	1,061	Kimbolton -	Huntingdon.
*Swineshead -	par.	240	1,330	1,579	do. -	do.
Tetworth -	par.	206	1,416	2,118	St. Neotts -	Tetworth.
Toseland -	par.	188	1,320	1,322	do. -	St. Neotts.
Waresley -	par.	232	1,979	2,581	do. -	do.
TOTAL of UNION -		16,907	65,097	120,809		

SAINT OLAVE'S UNION.

(Formed 1 Feb. 1836 by Order dated 31 Dec. 1835, as amended by Order dated 9 Jan. 1836.— Places marked thus * added 1 Oct. 1869 by Order dated 27 Aug. 1869.)

COUNTY of SURREY :

Saint John, Horsley-down (W.) - }	par.	8,928	69	77,643	Southwark, London, S.E.	Newington.
*Saint Mary Magdalen, Bermondsey (W.) - }	par.	86,652	627	377,318	do. -	do.
*Saint Mary, Rother-hithe (W.) - }	par.	36,024	754	193,217	do. -	do.
Saint Olave (W.) -	par.	2,247	18	113,947	do. -	do.
Saint Thomas -	par.	781	8	13,205	do. -	do.
TOTAL of UNION -		134,632	1,506	775,330		

SAINT NEOTTS UNION :

(a) By Order which came into operation on 25 March 1885, all the parts of a Parish known as Great Catworth were amalgamated with the Hamlet of Little Catworth, and the latter as so altered was designated the Hamlet of Catworth.

Unions and Parishes, &c.	Population in 1881.	Area in Statute Acres in 1881.	Rateable Value in 1881.	Post Town.	Petty Sessional Division.
SAINT PANCRAS PARISH.					
(Board of Guardians constituted 10 June 1867 by Order dated 7 May 1867.)					
COUNTY of MIDDLESEX :					
Saint Pancras (W.) - *par.*	236,258	2,672	£ 1,522,882	London, N.W.	St. Pancras.
SAINT SAVIOUR'S UNION.					
(Formed 11 Feb. 1836 by Order dated 13 Jan. 1836.—Places marked thus * added 1 Oct. 1869 by Order dated 27 Aug. 1869.)					
COUNTY of SURREY :					
Christchurch (W.) - *par.*	13,663	77	88,441	Southwark, S.E. -	Newington.
*Saint George the Martyr, Southwark (W.) - *par.*	58,652	281	237,012	do. - -	do.
*Saint Mary, Newington (W.) - *par.*	107,850	631	398,025	do. - -	do.
Saint Saviour's - *par.*	14,999	127	216,345	do. - -	do.
TOTAL of UNION -	195,164	1,119	939,853		
SAINT THOMAS' UNION.					
(Formed 21 April 1836 by Order dated 7 April 1836, as amended by Order dated 19 May 1836.—Place marked thus * added 29 September 1858 by Order dated 30 June 1858.)					
COUNTY of DEVON :					
Alphington (a) - *par.*	1,115	2,471	8,121	Exeter -	Wonford.
Ashcombe - *par.*	198	1,932	2,116	Dawlish - -	do.
Ashton (a) - *par.*	195	1,709	1,878	Chudleigh -	do.
Aylesbear (a) - *par.*	857	2,918	3,655	Exeter -	Ottery St. Mary.
Bicton - *par.*	157	1,294	1,697	do. -	Woodbury.
Bramfordspeke (a) - *par.*	485	1,642	3,856	do. -	Wonford.
Bridford - *par.*	436	4,111	2,949	do. -	Crockernwell.
Broad Clist - *par.*	2,089	9,188	18,684	do. -	Wonford.
Christow - *par.*	588	3,218	3,216	do. -	do.
Clist Hidon (a) - *par.*	277	1,725	2,951	do. -	do.
Clist Saint Lawrence(a) *par.*	120	1,060	1,698	do. -	do.
Colaton Rawleigh - *par.*	751	3,737	4,958	Ottery St. Mary -	Woodbury.
Doddiscombsleigh - *par.*	256	2,391	2,329	Exeter -	Wonford.
*Dotton - *par.*	9	214	267	Ottery St. Mary -	Ottery St. Mary.
Dunchedlock - *par.*	116	950	1,362	Exeter -	Wonford.
Dunsford - *par.*	777	5,948	5,152	do. -	Crockernwell.
East Budleigh - *par.*	2,856	3,277	11,965	Budleigh Salterton -	Woodbury.
Exminster (a) - *par.*	2,169	5,817	12,955	Exeter -	Wonford.
Farringdon (a) - *par.*	301	2,015	3,429	do. -	Woodbury.
Heavitree - *par.*	4,561	3,483	24,222	do. -	Wonford.
Holcomb Burnel - *par.*	218	1,836	1,118	do. -	do.
Honiton Clist - *par.*	302	1,725	3,856	do. -	Woodbury.

(continued)

SAINT THOMAS' UNION :

(a) By Orders which came into operation on 25 March 1884,—

A detached part of Trusham, in the Newton Abbot Union, was amalgamated with Ashton ;

A detached part of Bramfordspeke, known as "Cowley Barton," was amalgamated with Upton Pine ;

A detached part of Clist Saint Lawrence was amalgamated with Clist Hidon ;

A detached part of Exminster was amalgamated with Ashton ;

A detached part of Exminster, known as "Knowle," was amalgamated with Ide ;

Detached parts of Farringdon were amalgamated with Sowton ;

SAINT THOMAS' UNION—*continued.*

A detached part of Kenn was amalgamated with Ide

A detached part of Kenton was amalgamated with Alphington ;

A detached part of Saint Thomas, known as "Oldridge," was amalgamated with Whitestone ;

A detached part of Woodbury, comprising "Great and Little Houndbere," was amalgamated with Aylesbear

(b) By Provisional Order which came into operation on 25 March 1885, a detached part of Kenton was amalgamated with Dawlish, in the Newton Abbot Union.

Unions and Parishes, &c.		Population in 1881.	Area in Statute Acres in 1881.	Rateable Value in 1881.	Post Town.	Petty Sessional Division.
SAINT THOMAS' UNION—County of Devon—continued.				£		
Huxham	par.	132	761	1,124	Exeter	Wonford.
Ide (a)	par.	658	1,435	3,603	do.	do.
Kenn (a)	par.	946	5,412	7,799	do.	do.
Kenton (a) (b)	par.	1,919	6,811	12,174	do.	do.
Littleham	par.	1,069	3,654	18,866	Exmouth	Woodbury.
Lympstone	par.	1,070	1,400	4,754	Exeter	do.
Mamhead	par.	199	1,165	1,887	do.	Wonford.
Nether Exe	par.	70	450	1,186	do.	do.
Otterton	par.	969	3,479	5,290	Budleigh Salterton	Woodbury.
Pinhoe	par.	541	1,735	4,951	Exeter	Wonford.
Poltimore	par.	288	1,710	3,184	do.	do.
Powderham	par.	280	1,947	4,109	do.	do.
Rewe	par.	284	1,340	3,809	do.	do.
Rockbeare	par.	472	2,375	3,619	do.	Ottery St. Mary.
Saint George Clist	par.	266	1,066	2,550	do.	Woodbury.
Saint Leonard	par.	{ In Heavitree	In Heavitree	} 140	do.	Wonford.
Saint Mary Clist	par.	168	582	1,282	do.	Woodbury.
Saint Thomas (W.) (a)	par.	6,161	3,700	23,411	do.	Wonford.
Shillingford Saint George	par.	71	397	818	do.	do.
Sowton (a)	par.	408	1,091	2,764	do.	Woodbury.
Stoke Canon	par.	426	1,217	3,890	do.	Wonford.
Tedborne Saint Mary	par.	611	4,433	3,620	do.	Crockernwell.
Topsham	par.	2,867	1,740	10,361	do.	Wonford.
Upton Pine (a)	par.	407	1,852	4,269	do.	do.
Whimple	par.	665	3,019	6,270	do.	Ottery St. Mary.
Whitestone (a)	par.	459	4,077	3,906	do.	Wonford.
Withecombe Rawleigh	par.	3,155	2,617	11,962	Exmouth	Woodbury.
Woodbury (a)	par.	1,787	7,804	11,198	Exeter	do.
TOTAL of UNION		48,244	129,983	285,560		
SALFORD UNION.						
(Formed 12 July 1838 by Order dated 15 June 1838.)						
COUNTY of LANCASTER :						
Broughton	tow.	31,534	1,426	169,964	Manchester	Borough of Salford.
Pendlebury (a)	tow.	8,162	1,031	42,694	do.	Manchester.
Pendleton (a) (W.)	tow.	40,246	2,254	180,289	do.	Borough of Salford.
Salford (W.)	tow.	101,584	1,329	393,989	do.	do.
TOTAL of UNION		181,526	6,040	786,936		
SAMFORD UNION.						
(Formed 26 Mar. 1849 by Order dated 24 Feb. 1849. Names of Places marked * are as altered by Order dated 8 September, 1887.)						
COUNTY of SUFFOLK :						
Arwarton	par.	174	1,306	1,959	Ipswich	Samford.
Belstead	par.	318	1,022	1,923	do.	do.
Bentley	par.	398	2,801	4,220	do.	do.
Brantham	par.	405	2,182	3,699	Manningtree	do.
Burstall	par.	206	766	1,211	Ipswich	do.

(continued)

SAINT THOMAS UNION :

(a) (b) See notes, page 323.

SALFORD UNION :

(a) By Order which came into operation on 25 March 1884, a detached part of Pendlebury was amalgamated with Pendleton.

SAMFORD UNION :

(a) By Orders which came into operation on 25 March 1884,—
Detached parts of Copdock were amalgamated with Washbrook ;
Detached parts of Washbrook were amalgamated with Hintlesham and Copdock ;
A detached part of Hintlesham was amalgamated with Washbrook ;
A detached part of Layham, in the Cosford Union, was amalgamated with Shelley, and a detached part of Shelley was amalgamated with Layham.

Unions and Parishes, &c.	Population in 1881.	Area in Statute Acres in 1881.	Rateable Value in 1881.	Post Town.	Petty Sessional Division.

SAMFORD UNION—County of Suffolk—*continued.*

	£				
*Capel Saint Mary - *par.*	567	1,910	3,240	Ipswich - -	Samford.
Chattisham - - *par.*	221	713	1,225	do. - -	do.
Chelmondiston - *par.*	861	1,627	2,635	do. - -	do.
Copdock (*a*) - - *par.*	321	954	2,010	do. - -	do.
East Bergholt - *par.*	1,191	3,063	7,006	Colchester -	do.
Freston - - *par.*	274	1,513	2,251	Ipswich - -	do.
Harkstead - - *par.*	360	2,266	2,940	do. - -	do.
Higham - - *par.*	176	880	1,803	Colchester -	do.
Hintlesham (*a*) - *par.*	569	2,828	3,995	Ipswich - -	do.
Holbrook - - *par.*	779	3,153	4,037	do. - -	do.
*Holton Saint Mary - *par.*	169	837	1,334	Colchester -	do.
Raydon - - *par.*	524	2,335	3,446	Hadleigh, Suffolk -	do.
Shelley (*a*) - - *par.*	121	928	1,210	do. - -	do.
Shotley - - *par.*	622	2,042	3,773	Ipswich - -	do.
Sproughton - - *par.*	621	2,393	4,592	do. - -	do.
*Stratford Saint Mary *par.*	506	1,161	3,274	Colchester -	do.
Stutton - - *par.*	528	2,725	3,873	Ipswich - -	do.
Tattingstone (W.) - *par.*	535	1,637	2,647	do. - -	do.
Washbrook (*a*) - *par.*	346	1,443	2,395	do. - -	do.
Wenham Magna - *par.*	234	1,123	1,798	Colchester -	do.
Wenham Parva - *par.*	65	931	1,435	do. - -	do.
Wherstead - - *par.*	264	2,154	3,471	Ipswich - -	do.
Woolverstone - *par.*	243	1,256	1,579	do. - -	do.
TOTAL of UNION -	11,598	48,549	78,984		

SCARBOROUGH UNION.

(Formed 10 Jan. 1837 by Order dated 15 Dec. 1836.)

COUNTY of YORK, EAST RIDING.

Folkton - - *par.*	488	5,498	5,082	Ganton, York -	Dickering.
Ganton with Bromp- ton - - }*par.*	339	3,982	4,750	York - -	Buckrose.
Muston - - *par.*	395	2,293	4,278	Hunmanby -	Dickering.
Sherburn - - *par.*	726	4,739	5,580	York - -	Buckrose.
Willerby - - *par.*	415	4,567	5,495	Ganton, York -	do.

COUNTY of YORK, EAST and NORTH RIDINGS.

Filey - - - *tow.*	2,337	833	9,366	Filey - -	Dickering, and, as to part, Pickering Lythe East.

COUNTY of YORK, NORTH RIDING :

Brompton (*a*) - *tow.*	854	5,317	6,035	York - -	Pickering Lythe East.
Broxa - - *tow.*	55	533	356	Scarborough -	do.
Burniston (*c*) - *tow.*	353	2,099	2,743	do. - -	do.
Cayton (*a*) (*b*) - *tow.*	609	3,504	7,097	do. - -	do.
Cloughton (*c*) - *tow.*	512	2,538	3,343	do. - -	do.
East Ayton - - *tow.*	399	2,492	2,620	Seamer, York -	do.
Falsgrave - - *tow.*	4,266	1,103	20,054	Scarborough -	Borough of Scarborough.
Gristhorpe - - *tow.*	203	1,202	2,286	Filey -	Pickering Lythe East.
Hackness - - *tow.*	203	2,457	1,796	Scarborough -	do.

(continued)

SCARBOROUGH UNION :

(*a*) By Orders which came into operation on 25 March 1886,—
All the parts of the Township known as Brompton were amalgamated with Sawdon, and the latter as so altered was designated Brompton ;
All the parts of the Township known as Cayton Deepdale and Killerby, were amalgamated with Osgodby ; See note (*b*) :
All the parts of the Township known as Newby were amalgamated with Throxenby ; and
Certain detached parts of Ebberston, in the Pickering Union were amalgamated with Snainton ;

(*b*) By Order dated 26 July, 1886, it was directed that the

SCARBOROUGH UNION—*continued.*

Township of Osgodby as altered by the addition of Cayton Deepdale and Killerby, should be termed the Township of Cayton.

(*c*) By Provisional Order which came into operation on 25 March 1887,—
A certain part of Burniston was amalgamated with Harwooddale ;
A detached part of Hutton Bushel was amalgamated with West Ayton ;
A detached part of Silpho was amalgamated with Harwooddale ; and
Certain parts of Scalby and Burniston were united and amalgamated with Cloughton.

i R 8372.

Q q

Unions and Parishes, &c.	Population in 1881.	Area in Statute Acres in 1881.	Rateable Value in 1881.	Post Town.	Petty Sessional Division.
SCARBOROUGH UNION—County of York, North Riding—*continued.*			£		
Harwooddale (*c*) - *tow.*	207	5,537	1,858	Scarborough	Pickering Lythe East.
Hutton Bushel (*c*) - *tow.*	500	3,787	3,586	York	do.
Irton - - *tow.*	148	1,260	1,058	Scarborough	do.
Lebberston - - *tow.*	157	1,277	2,499	Filey	do.
Scalby (*c*) - - *tow.*	600	2,730	4,384	Scarborough	do.
Scarborough (W.) - *tow.*	26,238	1,245	126,975	do.	Borough of Scarborough.
Seamer - - *tow.*	752	4,691	7,402	York	Pickering Lythe East.
Silpho (*c*) - - *tow.*	85	1,447	981	Scarborough	do.
Snainton (*a*) - *tow.*	775	4,836	5,452	Heslerton, York	do.
Stainton Dale - *tow.*	238	3,114	2,114	Scarborough	do.
Suffield with Everley *tow.*	137	1,911	1,635	do.	do.
Throxenby (*a*) - *tow.*	202	1,300	3,675	do.	do.
Troutsdale - - *tow.*	60	1,204	660	do.	do.
West Ayton (*c*) - *tow.*	458	2,264	2,851	Seamer, York	do.
Wykeham - - *par.*	554	8,248	4,802	York	do.
TOTAL of UNION -	43,265	88,098	250,813		
SCULCOATES UNION.					
(Formed 6 July 1837 by Order dated 10 June 1837.— Place marked thus * added 25 Dec. 1859 by Order dated 29 Oct. 1859 ; thus † added 22 Mar. 1862 by Order dated 13 Mar. 1862 ; and thus ‡ added 1 May 1878 by Order dated 16 April 1878.)					
COUNTY of YORK, EAST RIDING :					
Anlaby - - *tow.*	629	1,471	4,525	Hull	South Hunsley Beacon.
Cottingham - - *par.*	6,228	9,831	46,609	do.	do., and Borough of Hull.
Drypool - - *tow.*	4,427	185	22,396	do.	Borough of Hull.
*Garrison Side - *tow.*	164	80	17,797	do.	do.
†Haltemprice - *par.*	6	209	265	do.	South Hunsley Beacon.
Hedon - - *par.*	966	321	3,475	do.	Borough of Hedon.
Hessle - - *tow.*	2,557	2,695	18,275	do.	South Hunsley Beacon.
Kirk Ella - - *tow.*	342	1,147	3,124	do.	do.
Marfleet - - *par.*	183	1,285	3,123	do.	Borough of Hull.
Melton - - *tow.*	172	897	3,117	do.	South Hunsley Beacon.
‡Newington - *par.*	7,954	760	25,693	do.	Borough of Hull.
North Ferriby - *tow.*	473	1,008	5,137	do.	South Hunsley Beacon.
Preston - - *tow.*	881	5,012	11,676	do.	Middle Holderness.
Sculcoates (W.) - *par.*	45,425	746	160,039	do.	Borough of Hull.
Southcoates - *tow.*	16,309	1,296	32,325	do.	do.
Sutton and Stoneferry *par.*	11,551	1,760	43,294	do.	Borough of Hull and Middle Holderness.
Swanland - - *tow.*	438	2,871	6,970	do.	South Hunsley Beacon.
Wauldby - - *tow.*	44	1,021	1,276	do.	do.
Welton - - *tow.*	669	1,778	5,427	do.	do.
West Ella - - *tow.*	123	534	1,013	do.	do.
Willerby - - *tow.*	328	982	2,086	do.	do.
TOTAL of UNION -	99,868	38,889	417,672		
SEDBERGH UNION.					
(Formed 11 Jan. 1840 by Order dated 17 Dec. 1839.)					
COUNTY of YORK, WEST RIDING :					
Dent - - *tow.*	1,209	20,890	10,278	Sedbergh, R.S.O. -	Ewecross.
Garsdale - - *tow.*	602	12,172	4,510	do.	do.
Sedbergh (W.) - *tow.*	2,268	19,603	12,853	do.	do.
TOTAL of UNION -	4,079	52,665	27,641		

SCARBOROUGH UNION :

(*a*) (*c*) *See notes, page 325.*

Unions and Parishes, &c.		Population in 1881.	Area in Statute Acres in 1881.	Rateable Value in 1881.	Post Town.	Petty Sessional Division.
SEDGEFIELD UNION.						
(Formed 7 Feb. 1837 by Order dated 12 Jan. 1837.)				£		
County of Durham :						
Bishop Middleham	tow.	480	2.056	3,730	Ferryhill -	Durham Ward.
Bishopton	tow.	350	2,178	2,789	do. -	Stockton Ward, South-west Division.
Bradbury	tow.	193	2,110	7,420	do.	Stockton Ward, North east Division.
Butterwick	tow.	61	1,513	993	do. -	do.
Chilton	tow.	2,693	2,122	12,712	do. -	Darlington Ward, North-west Division.
Cornforth	tow.	2,553	1,758	10,169	do. -	Durham Ward (Dur ham).
Elstob	tow.	74	738	1,361	Stockton on Tees -	Stockton Ward, North-east Division.
Embleton	tow.	114	3,425	2,075	Ferryhill	do.
Ferryhill (b)	tow.	3,510	2,502	15.158	do. -	Durham Ward.
Fishburn	tow.	317	2,126	2,496	do. -	Stockton Ward, North-east Division.
Foxton and Shotton-	tow.	48	1,803	1.211	do. -	do.
Garmondsway Moor-	tow.	156	1,149	2,664	do. -	do.
Mainsforth	tow.	114	653	1,409	do. -	Durham Ward.
Mordon	tow.	171	1,571	3,042	do. -	Stockton Ward, North-east Division.
Newbiggin	tow.	39	852	637	do. -	Stockton Ward, South-west Division.
Preston-le-Skerne	tow.	135	2,681	7,945	Darlington -	Darlington Ward, South-east Division.
Sedgefield (W.)	tow.	2,601	5,259	8,178	Ferryhill -	Stockton Ward, North-east Division.
Stainton Great	tow.	98	1,258	1,250	Darlington -	do.
Stainton Little	tow.	70	1,145	895	Stockton on Tees -	Stockton Ward, South-west Division.
Stillington	tow.	50	1,153	3,217	Ferryhill -	do.
Thrislington	tow.	74	594	3,295	do. -	Durham Ward.
Trimdon	par.	3,057	2,494	9,270	do. -	Easington Ward, South Division.
Woodham (a)	tow.	145	3,807	7.077	do. -	Darlington Ward, South-east Division.
Total of Union -		17,103	45.307	108,993		
SEISDON UNION.						
(Formed 17 Oct. 1836 by Order dated 21 Sept. 1836.—Place marked thus * added 25 Dec. 1861 by Order dated 18 Oct. 1861.)						
County of Salop :						
Rudge	tow.	155	1,542	2,710	Wolverhampton -	Brimstree South.
Counties of Salop and Stafford :						
Bobbington	par.	404	2,676	3,950	Stourbridge -	Kingswinford and Wordsley.
County of Stafford :						
Codsall and Oaken -	par.	1,398	2,580	10,137	Wolverhampton -	Wolverhampton. (Hundred of Seisdon North.)
Enville	par.	773	4,925	7,305	Stourbridge -	Kingswinford and Wordsley.

(continued)

SEDGEFIELD UNION :

(a) By Order which came into operation on 25 March 1884, a detached part of Heighington, in the Darlington Union, was amalgamated with Woodham.
(b) By Order which came into operation on 25 March 1886, a detached part of Ferryhill was amalgamated with Tudhoe, in the Durham Union.

Unions and Parishes, &c.	Population in 1881.	Area in Statute Acres in 1881.	Rateable Value in 1881.	Post Town.	Petty Sessional Division.
SEISDON UNION—County of Stafford—continued.			£		
Himley - - par.	346	1,185	4,910	Dudley - -	Kingswood and Wordsley.
Kinfare or Kinver - par.	2,812	8,790	17,529	Stourbridge -	do.
Pattenham - - par.	955	2,500	5,835	Wolverhampton -	Wolverhampton (Hundred of Seisdon North).
Penn (Lower) - tow.	335	} 3,986	{ 4,340	do. - -	do. do.
Penn (Upper) - tow.	2,469		11,037	do. - -	do. do.
Tettenhall - - par.	5,474	7,600	31,065	do. - -	do. do.
Trysull and Seisdon (W.), - - } par.	567	3,110	5,341	do. - -	do. do.
Wombourn - - par.	1,986	4,680	10,330	do. - -	do. do.
*Woodford Grange - par.	8	180	330	do. - -	do. do.
TOTAL of UNION -	17,712	43,754	114,819		

SELBY UNION.

(Formed 15 Feb. 1837 by Order dated 26 Jan. 1837.—Places marked thus * added 18 Feb. 1856 by Order of the same date; place marked thus † added 1 Mar. 1862 by Order dated 22 Feb. 1862; and thus ‡ added 21 June 1869 by Order dated 31 May 1869. Spelling of names of places marked thus § as altered by Order dated 15 June 1887.)

Unions and Parishes, &c.	Population in 1881.	Area in Statute Acres in 1881.	Rateable Value in 1881.	Post Town.	Petty Sessional Division.
COUNTY of YORK, EAST RIDING :					
Barlby (a) - - tow.	513	1,482	8,668	Selby - -	Ouse and Derwent.
Cliffe (a) - - tow.	641	2,740	6,109	do. - -	do.
Kelfield - - tow.	343	1,835	2,758	York - -	do.
North Duffield - tow.	376	3,417	4,345	Selby - -	do.
Osgodby - - tow.	225	1,559	2,951	do. - -	do.
Riccall (a) - - par.	780	2,667	6,906	York - -	do.
Skipwith - - tow.	278	2,644	2,023	Selby - -	do.
South Duffield - tow.	193	1,686	1,975	do. - -	do.
COUNTY of YORK, WEST RIDING :					
Barlow - - tow.	208	2,372	3,107	Selby - -	Barkstone Ash Lower.
*Biggin - - tow.	124	724	815	South Milford -	do.
Brayton (a) - - tow.	529	1,919	6,200	Selby - -	do.
Burn - - tow.	341	2,482	5,679	do. - -	do.
Camblesforth (a) - tow.	280	1,596	1,801	do. - -	Barkstone Ash.
Carlton (a) - - tow.	747	4,220	6,341	do. - -	do.
Cawood - - par.	1,108	2,891	5,410	do. - -	do.
Drax (a) - - tow.	371	1,382	2,310	do. - -	do.
Gateforth - - tow.	180	2,062	2,332	do. - -	do.
Haddlesey Chapel - tow.	177	1,163	1,829	do. - -	do.
†Hambleton - - tow.	530	2,338	5,894	do. - -	do.
§Hirst Courtney - tow.	112	630	991	do. - -	do.
*Little Fenton - tow.	84	780	612	South Milford -	do.
Long Drax - - tow.	156	1,696	2,453	Selby - -	do.
Newland - - tow.	270	2,296	3,691	do. - -	do.
Selby (W.) (a) - par.	6,046	3,643	18,637	do. - -	do.
§Temple Hirst - tow.	110	758	2,555	do. - -	do.
Thorpe Willoughby - tow.	176	463	1,868	do. - -	do.
‡West Haddlesey - tow.	148	1,193	1,820	do. - -	do.
§Wistow (a) - - par.	769	4,316	6,181	do. - -	do.
TOTAL of UNION -	15,815	56,984	116,261		

SELBY UNION :

(a) By Orders which came into operation on 25 March 1885,—
 A detached part of Barlby, known as the Holmes, was amalgamated with Selby ;

Two detached parts of Carlton were amalgamated with Camblesforth;
A detached part of Riccall, known as the Ness, was amalgamated with Wistow ; and
Detached parts of Brayton and Drax were united and amalgamated with Cliffe.

Unions and Parishes, &c.		Population in 1881.	Area in Statute Acres in 1881.	Rateable Value in 1881.	Post Town.	Petty Sessional Division.

SETTLE UNION.

(Formed 20 Jan. 1837 by Order
dated 24 Dec. 1836.)

COUNTY of YORK, WEST
RIDING:

				£		
Airton	- tow.	203	2,558	2,730	Bell Busk, Leeds -	Staincliffe West.
Arncliffe (a)	- tow.	147	3,189	1,805	Skipton - -	do.
Austwick (a)	- tow.	473	7,450	5,618	Lancaster - -	Ewecross.
Bentham	- tow.	2,211	7,711	9,444	do. -	do.
Burton in Lonsdale	- tow.	626	1,555	3,171	Kirkby Lonsdale -	do.
Clapham with Newby	tow.	676	12,037	6,958	Lancaster - -	do.
Giggleswick (W.)	- tow.	976	4,338	6,835	Settle -	Staincliffe West.
Halton Gill	- tow.	86	7,862	2,286	Skipton - -	do.
Hanlith	- tow.	34	965	843	Bell Busk, Leeds -	do.
Hawkswith (a)	- tow.	51	3,028	1,266	Skipton - -	do.
Hellifield	- tow.	424	3,401	4,258	Leeds - -	do.
Horton in Ribblesdale	par.	526	17,257	8,432	Settle -	do.
Ingleton	- tow.	1,625	17,508	11,623	Kirkby Lonsdale -	Ewecross.
Kirby Malham	- tow.	145	1,145	1,019	Bell Busk, Leeds -	Staincliffe West.
Langcliffe	- tow.	683	2,552	3,839	Settle -	do.
Lawkland (a)	- tow.	301	5,812	5,085	Lancaster - -	Ewecross.
Litton	- tow.	78	3,924	1,539	Skipton -	Staincliffe West.
Long Preston	- tow.	706	3,578	6,107	Leeds - -	do.
Malham	- tow.	148	4,282	2,714	Bell Busk, Leeds -	do.
Malham Moor	- tow.	126	10,976	3,280	do. -	do.
Nappa	- tow.	21	579	689	Hellifield, Leeds -	do.
Otterburn	- tow.	39	1,127	1,280	Bell Busk, Leeds -	do.
Rathmell	- tow.	219	3,423	3,635	Settle -	do.
Scosthrop	- tow.	67	1,275	1,172	Skipton -	do.
Settle	- tow.	2,213	4,490	10,148	Settle -	do.
Stainforth	- tow.	207	3,696	3,786	do. -	do.
Swinden	- tow.	47	1,049	1,284	Hellifield, Leeds -	do.
Thornton in Lonsdale	tow.	320	7,485	4,933	Kirkby Lonsdale -	Ewecross.
Tosside	- par.	66	1,112	850	Settle -	Staincliffe West.
West Halton	- tow.	142	2,290	2,376	Hellifield, Leeds -	do.
Wigglesworth	- tow.	214	4,288	3,583	Settle -	do.
TOTAL of UNION -		13,800	151,942	122,885		

SEVEN OAKS UNION.

(Formed 29 Sept. 1836 by Order
dated 15 Sept. 1836, uniting the
several Parishes in the Pens-
hurst and Seven-Oaks Unions,
those Unions having been
formed respectively on the
13 April 1835 and 14 April
1835 by Orders dated 2 March
1835 and 3 March 1835.)

COUNTY of KENT:

Brasted	- par.	1,292	4,449	7,416	Sevenoaks - -	Lathe of Sutton at Hone : Lower Division.
Cheddingstone	- par.	1,292	5,981	7,844	Edenbridge - -	Lathe of Aylesford : Lower South Division.
Chevening	- par.	1,086	3,893	6,364	Seven Oaks -	Lathe of Sutton at Hone : Lower Division.
Cowden	- par.	644	3,260	4,414	Edenbridge - -	Lathe of Aylesford : Lower South Division.
Edinbridge	- par.	1,943	5,329	10,811	do. - -	do.

(continued)

SETTLE UNION :

(a) By Order which came into operation on 25 March
1884 :—
   A detached part of Arncliffe was amalgamated with
   Hawkswith ; and
   A detached part of Lawkland was amalgamated with
   Austwick.

Unions and Parishes, &c.		Population in 1881.	Area in Statute Acres in 1881.	Rateable Value in 1881.	Post Town.	Petty Sessional Division.
SEVEN OAKS UNION—County of Kent—*continued.*				£		
Halstead	par.	474	923	2,572	Sevenoaks	Lathe of Sutton at Hone : Lower Division.
Hever	par.	670	2,660	4,005	Edenbridge -	Lathe of Aylesford : Lower South Division.
Kemsing	par.	413	1,909	2,691	Sevenoaks -	Lathe of Sutton at Hone : Lower Division.
Leigh	par.	1,293	4,721	10,421	Tonbridge -	Lathe of Aylesford : Lower South Division.
Otford -	par.	1,388	2,806	12,330	Sevenoaks	Lathe of Sutton at Hone : Lower Division.
Penshurst	par.	1,673	4,568	10,326	Tonbridge -	Lathe of Aylesford : Lower South Division.
Seal	par.	1,609	4,445	8,116	Sevenoaks	Lathe of Sutton at Hone : Lower Division.
Seven Oaks	par.	8,035	6,805	55,417	do.	do.
Shoreham	par.	1,420	5,599	13,839	do.	do.
Sundridge (W.)	par.	1,627	4,141	6,894	do.	do.
Westerham	par.	2,301	5,804	12,161	Edenbridge -	do.
TOTAL of UNION -		27,190	67,293	175,621		

SHAFTESBURY UNION.

(Formed 12 Oct. 1835 by Order dated 26 Sept. 1835.)

COUNTY of DORSET :

Ashmore	par.	275	2,335	2,002	Salisbury -	Shaftesbury.
Compton Abbas (*a*) -	par.	402	1,516	2,471	Shaftesbury	do.
East Orchard (*a*)	par.	233	860	2,091	do.	do.
East Stour -	par.	451	1,675	3,434	Gillingham	do.
Fontmell Magna (*a*)	par.	731	2,853	4,427	Shaftesbury -	do.
Gillingham	par.	3,293	7,527	19,400	Gillingham	do.
Holy Trinity (*a*)	par.	988	In St. James	2,399	Shaftesbury	do.
Iwerne Minster	par.	667	2,919	5,038	Blandford	do.
Margaret Marsh	par.	68	525	787	Shaftesbury	do.
Melbury Abbas	par.	328	2,276	2,508	do.	do.
Motcomb	par.	1,111	4,841	10,810	do.	do.
Saint James (W.) (*a*)	par.	1,001	2,400	4,774	do.	do.
Saint Peter (*a*)	par.	895	In St. James	2,525	do.	do.
Shaston Saint Rumbold, alias Cann	par.	560	930	2,926	do.	do.
Stour Provost	par.	726	2,777	5,458	Gillingham	do.
Sutton Waldron	par.	189	1,013	1,777	Blandford	do.
Todber	par.	167	384	902	do.	do.
West Orchard -	par.	113	617	1,387	Shaftesbury	do.
West Stour -	par.	165	1,015	2,096	Gillingham	do.
TOTAL of UNION -		12,662	36,493	77,212		

SHAFTESBURY UNION :

(*a*) By Orders which came into operation on 25 March 1886,—
A detached part of Compton Abbas was amalgamated with East Orchard, and three other parts were amalgamated with Fontmell Magna ; and

A detached part of Saint Peter was amalgamated with Holy Trinity.

Unions and Parishes, &c.		Population in 1881.	Area in Statute Acres in 1881.	Rateable Value in 1881.	Post Town.	Petty Sessional Division.
SHARDLOW UNION.						
(Formed 30 March 1837 by Order dated 23 Feb. 1837 as amended by Order dated 2 May 1837. — Place marked thus * added 29 May 1837 by Order dated 2 May 1837; Places marked thus † added 15 Jan. 1862 by Order dated 24 Dec. 1861; and Place marked thus § added 26 March 1884 by Order dated 24 March 1884.)						
COUNTY of DERBY :				£		
§Alvaston and Boulton (a)	par.	1,506	2,110	8,168	Derby	Derby.
Aston	par.	568	1,710	5,991	do.	do.
Barrow -	tow.	299	1,010	2,772	do.	do.
Breadsall	par.	204	1,210	10,705	do.	do.
Breaston	tow.	530	2,410	8,030	do.	do.
Chaddesden -	par.	611	2,080	8,552	do.	do.
Chellaston	par.	498	810	2,902	do.	do.
Dale Abbey (a)	par.	108	1,806	2,995	Nottingham	Smalley.
Derby Hills -	lib.	45	270	515	Ashby de la Zouch	Repton and Gresley.
Draycott	par.	1,015	1,151	8,788	Derby	Derby.
Elvaston (a)	par.	562	2,760	6,605	do.	do.
Hopwell	ham.	32	617	1,218	do.	do.
Kirk Hallam (a)	tow.	81	739	1,613	do.	Smalley.
Little Eaton -	par.	916	490	4,901	do.	Derby.
Littleover	tow.	776	1,163	5,901	do.	do.
Long Eaton -	tow.	6,217	2,099	29,367	Nottingham	do.
Melbourne	par.	3,123	3,290	11,019	Derby	Repton and Gresley.
Normanton	par.	3,854	1,362	16,400	do.	Derby.
Ockbrook	par.	1,938	1,697	10,328	do.	do.
Osmaston (a)	par.	111	1,254	2,511	do.	do.
Risley	tow.	218	1,152	2,770	do.	do.
Sandiacre (a)	par.	1,630	1,253	8,911	Nottingham	Smalley.
Sawley (a)	tow.	1,379	1,860	8,393	do.	Derby.
Shardlow (W.) (a)	par.	869	1,580	1,916	Derby	do.
*Sinfen and Arleston -	tow.	55	In Barrow	1,365	do.	do.
†Sinfin Moor	par.	21	—	1,285	do.	do.
Spondon (a)	tow.	1,757	2,830	15,107	do.	do.
Stanley (a)	tow.	816	1,059	3,556	do.	Smalley.
Stanton by Bridge (a)	par.	157	1,770	2,165	do.	Repton and Gresley.
Stanton by Dale (a)	par.	623	1,167	6,847	Nottingham -	Smalley.
Swarkeston	par.	209	913	2,465	Derby	Derby.
West Hallam (a)	par.	590	1,357	4,722	do.	Smalley.
Weston	par.	292	1,820	4,600	do.	Derby.
COUNTY of LEICESTER :						
Breedon	tow.	717	3,010	6,521	Ashby de la Zouch	Ashby de la Zouch.
Castle Donington	par.	2,662	4,250	14,076	Derby	Loughborough.
Diseworth	par.	416	1,880	3,302	do.	do.
Hemington	tow.	380	2,135	3,259	do.	do.
Isley Walton -	tow.	26	} 2,260	804	do.	do.
Kegworth	par.	2,142 }		9,761	do.	do.
†Langley Priory	par.	22	660	823	do.	do.
Lockington (a)	tow.	175 {	In Hemington }	3,984	do.	do.

(continued)

(continued')

SHARDLOW UNION :

(a) By Orders which came into operation on 25 March 1884,—
A detached part of Alvaston was amalgamated with Elvaston ;
Detached parts of Dale Abbey were amalgamated with Stanley, Spondon, and Sandiacre :
A detached part of Kirk Hallam was amalgamated with West Hallam ;
A detached part of Osmaston was amalgamated with Spondon :

SHARDLOW UNION—continued.

Detached parts of Sandiacre and Stanton by Dale were amalgamated with Dale Abbey ;
All the parts of Alvaston (except the part above referred to) and of Boulton were united and amalgamated and constituted one Parish, and designated Alvaston and Boulton ;
A part of Sawley, known as Clyffe Meadow, was amalgamated with Lockington ;
A detached part of Ticknall, in the Ashby de la Zouch Union, was amalgamated with Stanton by Bridge.

Unions and Parishes, &c.	Population in 1881.	Area in Statute Acres in 1881.	Rateable Value in 1881.	Post Town.	Petty Sessional Division.
SHARDLOW UNION—*continued.*					
COUNTY OF NOTTINGHAM :			£		
Brincote - - *par.*	751	1,076	3,928	Nottingham -	S. Broxton, Notts.
Chilwell - - *tow.*	1,046	2,843	8,224	do. -	do.
Kirgston - - *par.*	196	1,200	6,663	Derby -	North Rushcliffe, Notts.
Ratcliffe on Soar - *par.*	146	970	7,151	do. -	do.
Stapleford - - *par.*	3,196	1,450	9,367	Nottingham -	S. Broxton, Notts.
Toton - - *tow.*	199	In Chilwell	9,452	do. -	do.
TOTAL OF UNION -	44,673	72,796	308,063		

SHEFFIELD UNION.					
(Formed 30 June 1837 by Order dated 5 June 1837. — Place marked thus * added 1 Aug. 1837 by Order dated 7 July 1837.)					
COUNTY OF YORK, WEST RIDING :					
Attercliffe cum Dar- } *tow.* nall - - -	26,965	1,297	69,609	Sheffield -	Borough of Sheffield and Upper Division of Strafforth and Tickhill.
Brightside Bierlow } *tow.* (W.) - -	56,719	2,821	216,510	do. -	do.
*Handsworth - - *par.*	7,645	3,638	25,118	do.	Upper Division of Strafforth and Tickhill.
Sheffield - - *tow.*	91,806	3,028	336,148	do. -	Borough of Sheffield and Upper Division of Strafforth and Tickhill.
TOTAL OF UNION -	183,135	10,784	647,385		

SHEPPEY UNION.					
(Formed 25 March 1835 by Order dated 25 Feb. 1835.)					
COUNTY OF KENT :					
Eastchurch - - *par.*	983	7,006	11,593	Sheerness -	Scray : Upper Division (Faversham).
Isle of Elmley - *par.*	205	1,973	3,000	do.	do.
Isle of Harty - - *par.*	157	2,770	4,434	do. -	do.
Leysdown - - *par.*	196	2,179	3,487	do. -	do.
Minster in Sheppey } *par.* (W.) - -	15,658	8,002	59,971	do.	do.
Queenborough - *par.*	982	298	4,801	do. -	Queenborough.
Warden - - *par.*	23	223	387	do. -	Scray: Upper Division (Faversham).
TOTAL OF UNION -	18,204	22,451	87,670		

Unions and Parishes, &c.		Population in 1881.	Area in Statute Acres in 1881.	Rateable Value in 1881.	Post Town.	Petty Sessional Division.

SHEPTON MALLET UNION.

(Formed 30 Dec. 1835 by Order dated 10 Dec. 1835.—Place marked thus * added 30 Sept. 1879 by Order dated 23 Sept. 1879.)

COUNTY of SOMERSET :

Parish		Population in 1881.	Area in Statute Acres in 1881.	Rateable Value £ in 1881.	Post Town.	Petty Sessional Division.
Ashwick -	par.	755	1,525	3,176	Oakhill, Bath -	Shepton Mallet.
Batcombe -	par.	619	3,229	8,255	Evercreech, do.	do.
Binegar (a) -	par.	267	1,216	2,706	Oakhill, do. -	Wells.
Croscombe (a)	par.	576	1,432	3,236	Wells -	Shepton Mallet
Ditcheat (b) (c)	par.	808	3,676	9,301	Evercreech, Bath -	do.
Doulting (a) -	par.	604	3,600	6,573	Shepton Mallet -	do.
Downhead -	par.	178	1,525	1,579	do. -	do.
East Cranmore	par.	131	1,054	1,548	do. -	do.
East Lydford (a)	par.	162	706	1,381	Somerton, Taunton	Somerton.
East Pennard (a)	par.	608	2,829	6,680	Shepton Mallet -	Shepton Mallet.
Emborough (a) (b)	par.	178	2,039	2,540	Stratton on Fosse, Bath.	Clutton
Evercreech -	par.	1,126	4,078	9,977	Bath -	Shepton Mallet.
Holcombe (a) -	par.	531	780	2,013	do.	Kilmersdon
Hornblotton (b)	par.	113	1,082	1,721	Castle Cary -	Shepton Mallet.
Lamyat -	par.	250	1,000	2,582	Evercreech, Bath -	do.
Milton Clevedon	par.	171	1,221	2,191	do. -	do.
Pilton (a) -	par.	1,113	5,593	10,829	Shepton Mallet -	do.
Pylle (a) -	par.	267	1,055	1,591	do. -	do.
Shepton Mallet (W.)(a)	par.	5,322	3,572	17,867	do. -	do.
Stoke Lane or Stoke Saint Michael -	par.	677	2,071	5,382	Oakhill, Bath	do.
Stratton on the Foss (a) (b) -	par.	277	1,148	1,772	Bath	Kilmersdon.
Upton Noble -	par.	216	677	1,176	Bruton -	Shepton Mallet.
*West Bradley (a)	par.	279	1,460	3,332	Glastonbury -	do.
West Cranmore	par.	284	1,811	2,709	Shepton Mallet -	do.
West Lydford (a)	par.	267	1,900	2,039	Somerton, Taunton	Somerton.
TOTAL of UNION -		15,779	50,282	110,189		

SHEPTON MALLET UNION :

(a) By Orders which came into operation on 25 March, 1884 :—

Certain parts of North Wootton, in the Wells Union, were amalgamated with Pilton ;

Certain detached parts of Emborough were amalgamated with Chewton Mendip, in the Wells Union ;

A detached part of Emborough was amalgamated with Binegar ;

A detached part of Binegar was amalgamated with Saint Cuthbert Out, in the Wells Union ;

Certain detached parts of Stratton on the Foss were amalgamated with Kilmersdon, in the Frome Union ;

A certain part of Stratton on the Foss was amalgamated with Holcombe, and certain parts of Holcombe were amalgamated with Stratton on the Foss and with Kilmersdon, in the Frome Union ;

Certain parts of Kilmersdon, in the Frome Union, were amalgamated with Holcombe and with Stratton on the Foss ;

Certain detached parts of Croscombe were amalgamated with North Wootton and West Pennard, in the Wells Union, and with Pilton ;

Certain parts of Shepton Mallet were amalgamated with Doulting, Pylle, Croscombe, and Pilton ;

Certain parts of Doulting were amalgamated with Shepton Mallet ;

SHEPTON MALLET UNION—continued.

Certain parts of Pilton were amalgamated with Croscombe and Shepton Mallet, and with North Wootton and West Pennard, in the Wells Union ;

Certain detached parts of Pylle were amalgamated with East Pennard ;

Certain detached parts of West Bradley were amalgamated with Baltonsborough and West Pennard, in the Wells Union ;

A detached part of East Lydford was amalgamated with West Lydford.

(b) By Orders which came into operation on 25 March, 1885 :—

A part of Kilmersdon, in the Frome Union, was amalgamated with Stratton on the Foss ;

A detached part of Emborough was amalgamated with Chewton Mendip, in the Wells Union ;

A part of Alford, in the Wincanton Union, with Ditcheat ;

Parts of Ditcheat were amalgamated with Alford, in the Wincanton Union, and Hornblotton ;

A part of Hornblotton was amalgamated with Alford.

(c) By Order which came into operation on 25 March, 1886 :—

A part of Ansford or Almsford, in the Wincanton Union, was amalgamated with Ditcheat.

Unions and Parishes, &c.		Population in 1881.	Area in Statute Acres in 1881.	Rateable Value in 1881.	Post Town.	Petty Sessional Division.

SHERBORNE UNION.

(Formed 24 Dec. 1835 by Order dated 10 Dec. 1835.— Place marked thus * added 25 Dec. 1858 by Order dated 30 Nov. 1858.)

COUNTY OF DORSET :

				£		
Beer Hackett	- par.	83	903	1,403	Sherborne, Dorset -	Sherborne.
Bradford Abbas	- par.	510	1,139	3,140	do. - -	do.
Castleton -	- par.	81	69	436	do. - -	do.
Caundle Bishop (c) -	par.	335	1,397	2,089	do. - -	do.
Caundle Marsh (c)	- par.	97	792	1,019	do. - -	do.
Caundle Purse	- par.	194	1,470	1,363	do. - -	do.
Chetnole (c)	- cha.	243	877	1,851	do. - -	do.
Clifton-Mabank	- par.	80	1,254	1,979	Yeovil, Somerset -	do.
Folke (c) -	- par.	268	1,722	2,550	Sherborne, Dorset	do.
Haydon (c) -	- par.	101	632	822	do. - -	do.
Holnest (c) -	- par.	101	2,062	1,920	do. - -	do.
Holwell -	- par.	417	2,356	3,796	do. - -	do.
Leigh (b) (c) -	- cha.	403	1,984	2,822	do. - -	do.
*Leweston -	- par.	40	540	480	do. - -	do.
Lillington -	- par.	140	1,807	1,843	do. - -	do.
Longburton	- par.	379	1,025	1,553	do. - -	do.
Nether Compton	- par.	387	892	1,914	do. - -	do.
North Wootton	- par.	69	619	690	do. - -	do.
Oborne -	- par.	143	593	1,301	do. - -	do.
Over Compton	- par.	142	788	1,736	do. - -	do.
Ryme Intrinsica (c) -	par.	203	1,003	1,314	do. - -	do.
Sherborne (W.)	- par.	5,636	6,467	24,020	do. - -	do.
Stockwood -	- par.	70	692	831	Dorchester, Dorset	do.
Thornford -	- par.	413	1,107	2,093	Sherborne, Dorset	do.
Yetminster (c)	- par.	711	1,460	3,478	do. - -	do.
COUNTY OF SOMERSET :						
Goathill -	- par.	45	300	389	do. - -	Wincanton.
Marston Magna (a) -	par.	305	1,068	3,111	do. - -	Yeovil.
Pointington -	- par.	116	1,020	1,497	do. - -	Wincanton.
Rimpton -	- par.	260	999	2,423	do. - -	Yeovil.
Sandford Orcas	- par.	255	1,091	2,498	do. - -	Wincanton.
Trent -	- par.	468	1,590	3,930	do. - -	Yeovil.
TOTAL of UNION -		12,695	40,018	80,327		

SHIFFNAL UNION.

(Formed 2 June 1836 by Order dated 9 May 1836. — Place marked thus * added 25 Dec. 1858 by Order dated 25 Nov. 1858.)

COUNTY OF SALOP :

Albrighton -	- par.	1,212	3,421	9,787	Wolverhampton -	Brimstree ; Shiffnal Division.
Badger -	- par.	145	920	1,527	Shifnal -	do.
Beckbury -	- par.	329	1,343	2,749	do. -	do.
Bonninghall, other-wise Bonningale }	par.	497	1,003	2,504	{ Albrighton, Wolverhampton }	do.

(continued)

SHERBORNE UNION :

(a) By Provisional Order which came into operation on 25 March 1885 :—

A detached part of Queen Camel, in the Wincanton Union, was amalgamated with Marston Magna.

(b) By Order which came into operation on 25 March, 1885 :—

A detached part of Hilfield, in the Cerne Union, was amalgamated with Leigh.

(c) By Order which came into operation on 25 March, 1886 :—

Parts of Caundle Bishop were amalgamated with Caundle Marsh and Folke ;

SHERBORNE UNION—continued.

A detached part of Haydon was amalgamated with Holnest ;

A detached part of Leigh was amalgamated with Chetnole ;

A detached part of Ryme Intrinsica was amalgamated with Yetminster ;

Parts of Yetminster were amalgamated with Chetnole and Ryme Intrinsica.

Unions and Parishes, &c.		Population in 1881.	Area in Statute Acres in 1881.	Rateable Value in 1881.	Post Town.	Petty Sessional Division.
SHIFFNAL UNION—County of Salop—*continued.*				£		
*Boscobel	par.	23	600	796	Bishops Wood, Stafford.	Brimstree, Shiffnal Division.
Donington	par.	393	2,611	5,747	Albrighton, Wolverhampton.	do.
Kemberton	par.	274	1,387	3,995	Shiffnal	do.
Ryton	par.	212	1,442	2,155	do.	do.
Shiffnal (W.)	par.	6,812	11,441	38,508	do.	do.
Stockton	par.	538	3,162	5,264	do.	do.
Sutton Maddock	par.	389	2,662	4,748	do.	do.
Tong	par.	498	3,464	6,535	do.	do.
COUNTIES of SALOP and STAFFORD:						
Sheriff Hales	par.	819	5,408	7,714	Newport, Salop	Bradford and Cuttlestone Hundreds.
COUNTY of STAFFORD:						
Blymhill	par.	503	2,925	4,698	Shiffnal	Hundred of Cuttlestone.
Patshull	par.	193	1,850	3,370	Burnhill Green, Wolverhampton.	Hundred of Seisdon.
Weston under Lizard	par.	284	2,398	3,910	Shiffnal	Hundred of Cuttlestone.
TOTAL of UNION		12,821	46,070	104,337		
SHIPSTON ON STOUR UNION.						
(Formed 8 Feb. 1836 by Order dated 18 Jan. 1836, as amended by Order dated 4 May 1836, by which the Place marked thus * was included in the Union as a separate parish.)						
COUNTY of GLOUCESTER:						
Admington	ham.	149	In Quenton	1,587	Stratford on Avon	Campden.
Batsford (b)	par.	109	932	2,021	Moreton in Marsh	Moreton in Marsh.
Bourton on Hill	par.	151	2,960	2,957	do.	do.
Chipping Campden	par.	1,861	1,660	9,057	Campden	Campden.
*Clopton	ham.	51	In Mickleton	996	Stratford on Avon	do.
Ebrington	par.	543	2,960	1,147	Campden	do.
Hidcot Bartram	ham.	87	In Mickleton	802	do.	do.
Lemington	par.	54	855	809	Moreton in Marsh	Moreton in Marsh.
Mickleton	par.	611	3,766	5,922	Campden	Campden.
Moreton in Marsh	par.	1,424	900	1,955	Moreton in Marsh	Moreton in Marsh.
Quenton	par.	498	1,800	3,922	Stratford on Avon	Campden.
Todenham	par.	321	2,477	2,940	Moreton in Marsh	Moreton in Marsh.
COUNTIES of GLOUCESTER and WARWICK:						
Ilmington	par.	787	4,000	5,274	Shipston on Stour	Shipston on Stour.
COUNTY of WARWICK:						
Barcheston (a)	par.	182	1,475	1,920	do.	do.
Brailes	par.	1,131	5,220	7,787	do.	do.
Burmington (a)	par.	183	808	1,159	do.	do.
Butlers Marston (b)	par.	264	1,620	1,669	Kineton	Kineton.
Cherrington	par.	248	890	1,366	Shipston on Stour	Shipston on Stour.
Church Tysoe	par.	998	4,710	6,150	Kineton	Kineton.
Compton Wyniate	par.	28	997	1,347	do.	Shipston on Stour.
Great Woolford (b)	par.	231	2,679	1,486	Shipston on Stour	do.

(*continued*)

SHIPSTON ON STOUR UNION:

(a) By Order which came into operation on 25 March, 1884, two detached parts of Burmington were amalgamated with Barcheston.
(b) By Orders which came into operation on 25 March, 1885,—
  A part of Butlers Marston was amalgamated with Oxhill;
  A nearly detached part of Great Woolford was amalgamated with Batsford.

Unions and Parishes, &c.		Population in 1881.	Area in Statute Acres in 1881.	Rateable Value in 1881.	Post Town.	Petty Sessional Division.
SHIPSTON ON STOUR UNION—County of Warwick—continued.				£		
Halford	par.	255	1,010	1,279	Shipston on Stour -	Shipston on Stour.
Honington	par.	225	2,141	2,603	do. - -	do.
Idlicote	par.	114	1,408	1,436	do. - -	do.
Little Woolford	ham.	218 {	In Great Woolford }	1,007	do. - -	do.
Oxhill (b)	par.	273	1,800	1,937	Kineton - -	Kineton.
Pillerton Hersey	par.	150	1,390	1,461	do. - -	do.
Pillerton Priors	par.	138	1,460	1,631	do. - -	do.
Stourton	ham.	189 {	In Whichford. }	1,387	Shipston on Stour -	Shipston on Stour.
Stratton on Fosse	par.	388	1,939	2,407	Moreton in Marsh -	do.
Sutton	par.	183	1,135	1,749	Shipston on Stour -	do.
Whatcote	par.	143	1,400	828	do. - -	do.
Whichford	par.	401	3,100	2,856	do. - -	do.
COUNTY OF WORCESTER:						
Blockley	par.	2,154	7,870	12,365	Moreton in Marsh -	Campden.
Shipston on Stour (W.)	par.	1,735	1,198	4,603	Shipston on Stour -	Shipston on Stour.
Tidmington	par.	50	754	1,045	do. - -	do.
Tredington	par.	1,041	5,285	6,737	do. - -	do.
TOTAL OF UNION	-	17,874	78,899	114,894		

SKIPTON UNION.

(Formed 14 Jan. 1837 by Order dated 20 Dec. 1836, as amended by Order dated 10 March 1837.—Places marked thus * added 30 March 1837 by Order dated 10 March 1837; thus † recognised as separate Parishes in the Union 23 Aug. 1853 by Order of that date; thus ‡ added as separate Parishes 23 Aug. 1853 by Order of that date; and thus § added 24 June 1861 by Order dated 31 May 1861.)

COUNTY OF YORK, WEST RIDING:

Addingham	tow.	2,163	3,198	5,971	Leeds - -	Skipton.
Appletreewick	tow.	281	7,689	3,087	Skipton - -	do.
Bank Newton	tow.	100	2,339	2,941	Gargrave, Leeds -	do.
Barden	tow.	391	7,338	1,913	Skipton - -	do.
Barnoldswick	tow.	1,028	2,129	7,717	Leeds - -	do.
* Beamsley-in-Adding-ham	} tow.	31	317	411	Skipton - -	do.
§ Beamsley-in-Skipton	tow.	184	1,843	1,203	do. - -	do.
‡ Boardley	tow.	41	2,893	1,147	do. - -	do.
Bolton Abbey	tow.	112	2,071	1,071	do. - -	do.
Bracewell	par.	105	2,025	2,473	do. - -	do.
Bradleys Both	tow.	514	1,951	2,654	Kildwick, Leeds -	do.
Brockden	tow.	110	1,782	1,336	Barnoldswick, Leeds	do.
Broughton	tow.	177	2,401	3,517	Skipton - -	do.
Buckden	tow.	297	16,076	1,861	do. - -	do.
Burnsall (a)	tow.	121	706	910	do. - -	do.
Calton	tow.	59	1,449	1,366	Bell Busk, Leeds -	do.
Carlton	par.	1,691	5,258	7,352	Skipton - -	do.
Coates	tow.	99	633	1,132	Barnoldswick, Leeds	do.
Cold Coniston	tow.	337	1,337	1,960	Bell Busk, Leeds -	do.
Coniston with Kilnsey	tow.	179	8,646	3,288	Skipton - -	do.
† Connoley	tow.	829	1,451	3,564	Leeds - -	do.
* Cowling	tow.	1,901	1,716	4,761	Crosshills, Leeds -	do.
Cracoe	tow.	127	2,134	1,810	Skipton - -	do.
Draughton	tow.	178	2,501	2,932	do. - -	do.
Elslack	ham.	82	1,717	2,191	Leeds - -	do.

(continued)

SKIPTON UNION:

(a) There is some land common to Burnsall and Thorpe, comprising 1,123 acres.

Unions and Parishes, &c.		Population in 1881.	Area in Statute Acres in 1881.	Rateable Value in 1881.	Post Town.	Petty Sessional Division.
SKIPTON UNION—County of York, West Riding —continued.						
Embsay with Eastby	tow.	1,167	1,460	1,201	Skipton -	Skipton.
Eshton -	tow.	64	1,111	1,631	Gargrave, Leeds -	do.
†Farnhill -	tow.	561	546	1,572	Kildwick, Leeds -	do.
Flasby with Winter-burn	tow.	128	1,340	3,769	Gargrave, Leeds -	do.
Gargrave -	tow.	1,287	2,541	6,602	do. do. -	do.
Glusburn -	tow.	1,629	1,525	5,598	Crosshills, Leeds -	do.
Grassington -	tow.	617	5,802	3,798	Skipton -	do.
Halton East -	tow.	277	1,076	1,455	do. -	do.
Hartlington -	tow.	82	1,352	968	do. -	do.
Hazlewood with Storiths	tow.	173	3,487	1,283	do. -	do.
Hebden -	tow.	313	3,583	1,871	do. -	do.
‡Hetton -	tow.	101	1,713	1,631	do. -	do.
Kettlewell with Starbotton	par.	378	8,413	3,929	do. -	do.
Kildwick -	tow.	160	871	1,292	Leeds -	do.
Linton -	tow.	127	1,204	1,528	Skipton -	do.
Marton Both	par.	235	2,805	3,177	do. -	do.
Rilston -	tow.	130	3,197	2,220	do. -	do.
Salterforth -	tow.	391	1,762	2,134	Leeds -	do.
§Silsden -	tow.	3,329	7,060	9,956	do. -	do.
Skipton (W.) -	tow.	9,091	4,245	23,670	Skipton -	do.
Thorlby with Stirton	tow.	157	3,099	3,632	do. -	do.
Thornton -	par.	2,322	5,431	9,096	Leeds -	do.
Thorpe (a) -	tow.	67	1,133	1,306	Skipton -	do.
Threshfield	tow.	167	2,646	1,756	do. -	do.
TOTAL of UNION -		37,120	158,068 (a)	171,236		

SKIRLAUGH UNION.

(Formed 5 July 1837 by Order dated 9 June 1837.)

COUNTY of YORK, EAST RIDING:

Aldbrough (a)	tow.	724	4,167	7,271	Hull -	Middle Holderness.
Atwick, Skirlington, and Arram	par.	320	2,298	2,748	do. -	North do.
Benningholme and Grange (a)	tow.	120	1,471	1,738	do. -	Middle do.
Bewholme and Nunkeeling	par.	272	2,315	2,706	do. -	North do.
Bilton -	tow.	91	1,204	1,426	do. -	Middle do.
Bonwick -	tow.	23	774	865	do. -	North do.
Brandsburton (a)	tow.	723	4,671	6,373	do. -	do. do.
Catfoss -	tow.	53	1,084	1,359	do. -	do. do.
Catwick -	par.	272	1,570	2,207	do. -	do. do.
Coniston -	tow.	103	602	863	do. -	Middle do.
Cowden Great and Little	tow.	119	1,579	1,905	do. -	do. do.
Danthorp -	tow.	63	736	1,033	do. -	do. do.
Dunnington -	tow.	87	844	1,173	do. -	North do.
East Newton -	tow.	30	1,440	786	do. -	Middle do.
Ellerby -	tow.	344	2,248	3,512	do. -	do. do.
Elstronwick -	tow.	98	1,155	1,654	do. -	do. do.
Fitling -	tow.	137	1,529	1,718	do. -	do. do.
Flinton -	tow.	103	1,399	1,730	do. -	do. do.
Ganstead -	tow.	96	809	1,518	do. -	do. do.

(continued)

SKIRLAUGH UNION:

(a) By Orders which came into operation on 25 March 1885,—
A detached part of Aldbrough known as "Scurshaws" was amalgamated with Withernwick;
A detached part of Hempholme was amalgamated with Brandsburton;
A detached part of South Skirlaugh was amalgamated with Benningholme and Grange

SKIRLAUGH UNION—continued.

So much of Long Riston as was comprised in the Highway Parish of Arnold was amalgamated with the township previously known as North Skirlaugh, Rowton, and part of Arnold, and such township was thereupon designated North Skirlaugh, Rowton, and Arnold.

(b) There is some land in this Union comprising 1,080 acres, and known as Arnold, stated to be common to Swine, Long Riston, and Rise.

Unions and Parishes, &c.		Population in 1881.	Area in Statute Acres in 1881.	Rateable Value in 1881.	Post Town.	Petty Sessional Division.

SKIRLAUGH UNION—County of York, East Riding—_continued._

Unions and Parishes, &c.		Population in 1881.	Area in Statute Acres in 1881.	Rateable Value £	Post Town.	Petty Sessional Division.
Garton with Grimston	tow.	157	1,823	2,218	Hull	Middle Holderness.
Goxhill	par.	76	838	1,229	do.	North do.
Great Hatfield	tow.	151	1,489	1,702	do.	do. do.
Hempholme (a)	tow.	120	1,352	1,570	do.	do. do.
Hornsea with Burton	par.	1,836	3,332	10,963	do.	do. do.
Humbleton	tow.	160	1,477	1,929	do.	Middle do.
Lelley	tow.	135	808	1,203	do.	do. do.
Little Hatfield	tow.	38	976	1,226	do.	North do.
Long Riston (a) (b)	tow.	367	1,834	3,578	do.	do. do.
Mappleton and Rowlston	tow.	178	1,954	2,692	do.	do. do.
Marton	tow.	96	946	1,250	do.	Middle do.
Moor Town	tow.	32	513	521	do.	North do.
North Skirlaugh, Rowton, and Arnold (W.) (a)	tow.	284	534	1,191	do.	do. do.
Rise (b)	tow.	202	2,034	2,587	do.	do. do.
Seaton and Wassand	tow.	418	1,744	2,752	do.	do. do.
Sigglesthorne	tow.	217	1,032	1,614	do.	North do.
South Skirlaugh (a)	tow.	293	1,101	1,946	do.	Middle do.
Sproatley	par.	331	1,372	2,084	do.	do. do.
Swine (b)	tow.	195	2,286	3,878	do.	do. do.
Thirtleby	tow.	55	755	1,015	do.	do. do.
West Newton with Burton Constable	tow.	147	2,068	2,316	do.	do. do.
Withernwick (a)	tow.	449	2,822	4,074	do.	North do.
Wyton	tow.	80	792	1,379	do.	Middle do.
TOTAL of UNION		9,795	65,777 (b)	97,965		

SLEAFORD UNION.

(Formed 20 Sept. 1836 by Order dated 5 Sept. 1836.—Places marked thus * added 25 Mar. 1861 by Order dated 30 Jan. 1861.)

COUNTY of LINCOLN :

Unions and Parishes, &c.		Population in 1881.	Area in Statute Acres in 1881.	Rateable Value in 1881.	Post Town.	Petty Sessional Division.
Anwick (a)	par.	348	1,820	2,571	Sleaford	Sleaford.
Asgarby (a)	par.	126	838	1,403	do.	do.
Ashby de la Laund	par.	169	2,880	3,048	Lincoln	do.
Aswarby	par.	129	1,548	2,439	Falkingham	do.
Aunsby	par.	138	1,183	1,488	Sleaford	do.
Billinghay	tow.	1,440	6,780	7,189	Lincoln	do.
Blankney	par.	658	6,000	8,837	do.	do.
Bloxholme	par.	97	1,298	1,919	do.	do.
Branswell	par.	173	3,470	2,939	Sleaford	do.
Burton Pedwardine	par.	202	2,380	2,254	do.	do.
*Byards Leap	par.	27 { In Leadenham }		251	do.	do.
Cranwell	par.	206	2,522	2,665	do.	do.
Culverthorpe	tow.	85	In Kelby	1,111	do.	do.
Dembleby	par.	72	1,071	1,369	Falkingham	do.
Digby	par.	304	2,392	3,432	Lincoln	do.
Dorrington	par.	398	680	2,639	do.	do.
Evedon	par.	73	1,333	1,891	Sleaford	do.
Ewerby	par.	451	2,520	4,476	do.	do.

(continued)

SKIRLAUGH UNION :

(a) (b) See notes, page 337.

SLEAFORD UNION :

(a) By Order which came into operation on 25 March, 1885,—
Detached parts of Asgarby were amalgamated with Howell ;
A detached part of Anwick was amalgamated with Ruskington.

Unions and Parishes, &c.		Population in 1881.	Area in Statute Acres in 1881.	Rateable Value in 1881.	Post Town.	Petty Sessional Division.
SLEAFORD UNION—County of Lincoln—*continued.*				£		
Great Hale	- *tow.*	708	5,110	7,006	Sleaford - -	Sleaford.
²Haverholme Priory -	*par.*	21	291	573	do. - -	do.
Heckington - -	*par.*	1,766	5,720	10,993	do. - -	do.
Helpringham - -	*par.*	941	2,600	6,111	do. - -	do.
Holdingham - -	*ham.*	120 { In New Sleaford }		1,638	do. -	do.
Howell (*a*) - -	*par.*	89	1,650	2,050	do. - -	do.
Kelby - - -	*tow.*	99	2,000	1,077	Grantham - -	do.
Kirkby Green -	*par.*	123	437	639	Lincoln - -	do.
Kirkby le Thorpe -	*par.*	256	1,570	3,983	Sleaford - -	do.
Lendenham - -	*par.*	646	2,260	6,697	Grantham - -	do.
Leasingham - -	*tow.*	366	2,939	3,270	Sleaford - -	do.
Little Hale - -	*tow.*	362 { In Great Hale }		4,071	do. - -	do.
Martin - -	*ham.*	822	9,190	6,237	Lincoln - -	do.
New Sleaford (W.) -	*tow.*	3,955	3,160	13,130	Sleaford - -	do.
Newton - -	*par.*	173	1,220	1,825	Falkingham -	do.
North Kyme - -	*tow.*	696	3,490	5,951	Lincoln - -	do.
North Rauceby -	*par.*	270	3,160	3,763	Sleaford - -	do
Old Sleaford - -	*par.*	526	1,150	2,587	do. - -	do.
Osbornby - -	*par.*	496	1,260	2,860	Falkingham -	do.
Quarrington - -	*par.*	361	1,620	3,145	Sleaford - -	do.
Roulston - -	*par.*	226	1,520	2,875	Lincoln - -	do.
Roxholme - -	*ham.*	139 { In Leasingham }		1,102	Sleaford - -	do.
Ruskington (*a*) -	*par.*	1,191	4,750	5,830	do. - -	do.
Scopwick - -	*par.*	390	3,190	4,085	Lincoln - -	do.
Scott Willoughby -	*par.*	36	556	869	Falkingham -	do.
Screddington - -	*par.*	341	1,850	2,887	do. - -	do.
Silk Willoughby -	*par.*	280	2,505	2,978	Sleaford - -	do.
South Kyme - -	*tow.*	530	4,868	7,734	do. - -	do.
South Rauceby -	*par.*	388	2,430	3,574	do. - -	do.
Spanby - -	*par.*	104	1,019	1,311	Falkingham -	do.
Stow cum Threcking-ham - - }	*par.*	143	2,270	2,324	do. - -	do.
Swarby - -	*par.*	171	910	1,385	Sleaford - -	do.
Swaton - -	*par.*	288	3,670	5,928	Falkingham -	do.
²Temple Bruer with Temple High Grange }	*par.*	201	3,910	1,428	Grantham - -	do.
Thorpe Tilney -	*ham.*	113	In Martin	2,563	Lincoln - -	do.
Timberland - -	*tow.*	503	In Martin	4,076	do. - -	do.
Walcot near Billing-hay - - }	*ham.*	594 { In Billinghay }		5,114	do. -	do.
Walcot near Falking-ham - - }	*par.*	149	1,747	2,431	Falkingham -	Bourn.
Welbourne - -	*par.*	550	3,270	5,969	Grantham - -	Sleaford.
Wellingore - -	*par.*	790	2,400	5,912	do. - -	do.
Wilsford - -	*par.*	689	2,860	4,601	do. - -	do.
TOTAL of UNION -		25,720	131,777	216,606		
SMALLBURGH UNION.						
(Formed 9 Oct. 1869 by Order dated 24 Sept. 1869.—Place marked thus * added 26 March 1884 by Order dated 7 March 1884.)						
COUNTY of NORFOLK :						
Ashmanhaugh -	*par.*	162	665	1,044	Neatishead -	Tunstead and Happing.
Bacton (*a*) - -	*par.*	464	1,770	2,964	North Walsham -	do.

(*continued*)

SMALLBURGH UNION :

(*a*) By Order which came into operation on 25 March 1885,—
A detached part of Bacton was amalgamated with Eding-thorpe ;
A detached part of Hickling was amalgamated with Sutton ;
A detached part of Waxham, known as " Little Waxham," was amalgamated with Horsey.

Unions and Parishes, &c.		Population in 1881.	Area in Statute Acres in 1881.	Rateable Value in 1881.	Post Town.	Petty Sessional Division.
SMALLBURGH UNION—County of Norfolk—continued.				£		
Barton Turf - -	par.	374	1,599	2,562	Neatishead - -	Tunstead and Happing.
Beeston Saint Law-rence - -	}par.	46	519	976	do. - -	do.
Bradfield - -	par.	228	757	1,223	North Walsham -	do.
Brumstead -	par.	122	789	1,471	Stalham, S.O. -	do.
Catfield - -	par.	631	2,393	3,853	do. - -	do.
Crostwight - -	par.	80	777	977	Smallburgh -	do.
Dilham - - -	par.	426	1,563	3,049	do. - -	do.
East Ruston -	par.	667	2,491	4,808	Stalham, S.O. -	do.
Edingthorpe (a) -	par.	190	710	1,248	North Walsham -	do.
Felmingham - -	par.	395	1,886	3,508	do. - -	do.
Happisburgh - -	par.	556	2,163	4,200	Stalham, S.O. -	do.
Hempstead - with - Eccles	}par.	173	1,301	2,056	do. - -	do.
Hickling (a) -	par.	824	4,334	6,167	do. - -	do.
Honing - -	par.	321	1,400	2,380	Smallburgh -	do.
Horning - -	par.	135	2,567	4,241	Norwich - -	do.
Horsey (a) -	par.	199	1,880	1,572	Great Yarmouth -	do.
Hoveton Saint John -	par.	295	1,511	2,151	Norwich - -	do.
Hoveton Saint Peter -	par.	138	952	1,619	Neatishead -	do.
Ingham - -	par.	152	1,503	2,941	Stalham, S.O. -	do.
Irstead - -	par.	148	1,065	1,400	Neatishead -	do.
Lessingham -	par.	176	639	1,329	Stalham, S.O. -	do.
Ludham - -	par.	796	2,977	6,299	Norwich - -	do.
Neatishead - -	par.	578	1,905	3,752	do. - -	do.
*North Walsham -	par.	3,231	4,252	13,355	do. - -	do.
Palling - -	par.	459	905	1,711	Stalham, S.O. -	do.
Paston - -	par.	252	1,415	2,613	North Walsham -	do.
Potter Heigham -	par.	414	2,527	3,856	Stalham, S.O. -	do.
Ridlington - -	par.	195	635	1,337	North Walsham -	do.
Sloley - -	par.	264	719	1,512	Scottow - -	do.
Smallburgh (W.) -	par.	504	1,247	2,813	Norwich - -	do.
South Ruston -	par.	89	471	970	Scottow - -	do.
Stalham - -	par.	852	1,792	4,479	Norwich - -	do.
Sutton (a) -	par.	378	1,383	2,596	Stalham, S.O. -	do.
Swafield - -	par.	178	826	1,610	North Walsham -	do.
Tunstead - -	par.	420	2,291	4,770	Norwich - -	do.
Walcott - -	par.	121	735	1,694	Stalham, S.O. -	do.
Waxham (a) -	par.	147	2,087	2,290	do. - -	do.
Westwick - -	par.	181	1,013	1,581	Norwich - -	do.
Witton - -	par.	253	1,746	2,603	North Walsham -	do.
Worstead - -	par.	765	2,603	5,082	Norwich - -	do.
TOTAL of UNION -		17,582	66,859	122,728		
SOLIHULL UNION.						
(Formed 3 June 1836 by Order dated 10 May 1836. — Place marked thus * added 27 Feb. 1857 by Order of that date.)						
COUNTY of WARWICK :						
Baddesley Clinton -	par.	134	1,329	1,767	Knowle - -	Solihull.
Barston - -	par.	322	1,866	3,889	Solihull - -	do.
*Bushwood - -	ham.	43	475	601	Henley in Arden -	Henley in Arden.
Elmdon - -	par.	210	1,127	2,424	Birmingham -	Solihull.
Knowle - -	ham.	1,514	8,266	12,370	Knowle - -	do.
Lapworth - -	par.	646	2,971	6,498	Hockley Heath -	Henley in Arden.
Nuthurst - -	ham.	108	750	1,072	do. - -	do.
Packwood - -	par.	291	1,655	3,090	Knowle - -	do.
Solihull (W.) -	par.	5,280	12,233	45,095	Solihull - -	Solihull.
Tanworth - -	par.	1,933	9,100	16,246	Hockley Heath -	Henley in Arden.
Temple Balsall -	ham.	1,151	In Knowle	10,131	Knowle - -	Solihull.
COUNTY of WORCESTER :						
Yardley - -	par.	9,745	7,355	51,206	Birmingham -	Solihull.
TOTAL of UNION -		21,377	47,127	154,389		

Unions and Parishes, &c.	Population in 1881.	Area in Statute Acres in 1881.	Rateable Value in 1881.	Post Town.	Petty Sessional Division.
SOUTHAM UNION.					
(Formed 30 April 1836 by Order dated 14 April 1836.—Places marked thus * added 29 Sept. 1860 by Order dated 19 July 1860.)					
County of Northampton :			£		
*Stoneton - par.	23	—	1,311	Leamington	Brackley.
County of Warwick :					
Bishop's Itchington - par.	710	3,026	5,497	do.	Southam.
Burton Dasset - par.	630	5,400	7,147	do.	Kineton.
Chadshunt - par.	46	1,366	2,099	Warwick	do.
*Chapel Ascote - par.	5 { In Bishop's Itchington. }		927	Rugby	Southam.
Chesterton - par.	192	3,510	4,058	Leamington	Warwick.
Fenny Compton - par.	587	2,330	4,686	do.	Southam.
Gaydon - par.	262	1,140	1,907	Warwick	Kineton.
Harbury or Harberbury - par.	1,196	2,060	8,333	Leamington	Southam.
*Hodnel - par.	28 } In Will's {		662	Rugby	do.
Ladbrooke - par.	250 } Pastures {		3,143	do.	do.
Lighthorne - par.	354	2,007	2,654	Warwick	Kineton.
Long Itchington - par.	1,149	4,510	7,693	Rugby	Southam.
*Lower Radbourn - par.	10	In Watergall	677	do.	do.
Lower Shuckburgh - par.	101	870	1,972	Daventry	do.
Napton on the Hill - par.	885	4,140	7,169	Rugby	do.
Priors Hardwicke - par.	280	1,600	2,788	Byfield	do.
Priors Marston - par.	576	3,630	5,850	do.	do.
Southam (W.) - par.	1,784	2,770	8,107	Rugby	do.
Stockton - par.	682	1,800	3,131	do.	do.
Ufton - par.	200	1,920	2,076	do.	do.
*Upper Radbourn - par.	17	In Watergall	718	do.	do.
Upper Shuckburgh - par.	49	910	1,737	Daventry	do.
*Watergall - par.	22	1,149	589	Leamington	do.
*Will's Pastures - par.	13	3,951	176	do.	do.
Wormleighton - par.	231	2,320	4,341	do.	do.
Total of Union	10,282	50,409	89,438		
SOUTHAMPTON INCORPORATION.					
(Under the 13 Geo. 3, c. 1, as altered by Provisional Order which was confirmed by 40 & 41 Vict. cap. ccxxvii.)					
Town and County of the Town of Southampton :					
All Saints - par.	11,055	263	52,727	Southampton	Borough and County of the Town of Southampton.
Holy Rhood - par.	1,507	18	10,318	do.	do.
Saint John - par.	613	5	2,082	do.	do.
Saint Lawrence - par.	313	6	4,892	do.	do.
Saint Mary (W.) - par.	37,558	1,017	128,072	do.	do.
Saint Michael - par.	1,943	15	4,694	do.	do.
Total of Incorporation	52,989	1,324	202,785		

Unions and Parishes, &c.	Population in 1881.	Area in Statute Acres in 1881.	Rateable Value in 1881.	Post Town.	Petty Sessional Division.

SOUTH MOLTON UNION.

(Formed 28 Nov. 1835 by Order dated 12 Nov. 1835.—Place marked thus * added 25 Dec. 1861 by Order dated 21 Nov. 1861, and thus † added 26 March 1885 by Order dated 20 March 1885. Spelling of Names of Places marked ‡ as altered by Order dated 31 May 1887.)

			£		
County of Devon :					
Bishops Nympton - *par.*	1,150	9,579	8,527	South Molton	South Molton.
Burrington - - *par.*	776	5,330	4,306	Chulmleigh -	do.
Charles - - *par.*	263	2,429	2,601	South Molton	do.
Cheldon - - *par.*	70	1,108	670	Chulmleigh -	do.
†Chittlehamholt (*b*) - *par.*	—	—	—	do. -	do.
Chittlehampton (*a*) (*b*) *par.*	1,473	8,720	9,399	South Molton	do.
Chulmleigh - - *par.*	1,385	8,815	7,671	Chulmleigh -	do.
Creacombe (*a*) - *par.*	63	1,050	593	Morchard Bishop -	do.
East Anstey - *par.*	234	3,245	1,925	Dulverton -	do.
East Buckland - *par.*	172	1,385	1,509	South Molton	do.
East Worlington (*b*) *par.*	401	5,046	3,343	Morchard Bishop -	do.
Filleigh - - *par.*	339	2,038	2,240	South Molton	do.
George Nympton - *par.*	196	2,240	2,146	do. -	do.
Kings Nympton - *par.*	626	5,539	4,571	Chulmleigh -	do.
Knowstone - - *par.*	416	4,989	3,506	South Molton	do.
‡Mariansleigh - *par.*	221	1,963	1,590	do. -	do.
Meshaw (*b*) - *par.*	162	1,751	1,283	do. -	do.
Molland - - *par.*	501	6,168	3,744	do. -	do.
North Molton - *par.*	1,517	14,351	12,524	do. -	do.
Rackenford - *par.*	362	3,938	2,719	Morchard Bishop -	do.
Romansleigh - *par.*	149	2,491	1,567	South Molton	do.
‡Rose Ash (*a*) - *par.*	507	5,082	3,652	do. -	do.
Satterleigh - *par.*	59	515	516	do. -	do.
South Molton (W.) - *par.*	3,340	6,264	14,163	do. -	do.
Twitchen - - *par.*	205	2,918	1,969	do. -	do.
Warkleigh - - *par.*	259	2,151	2,085	do. -	do.
West Anstey - *par.*	235	3,008	1,969	Dulverton	do.
West Buckland (*a*) - *par.*	369	1,772	1,765	South Molton	do.
Witheridge (*b*) - *par.*	1,025	9,048	7,168	Morchard Bishop -	do.
County of Somerset :					
*Exmoor - - *par.*	313	20,765	4,759	South Molton, Devon.	Dulverton.
Total of Union -	16,818	143,998	114,492		

SOUTH SHIELDS UNION.

(Formed 10 Dec. 1836 by Order dated 14 Nov. 1836, which was amended as to the name of the parish marked thus * by Order dated 26 August 1886.)

County of Durham :					
Boldon - - *par.*	3,097	4,031	22,696	Newcastle-on-Tyne	East Chester Ward.
Harton (W.) (*c*) - *tow.*	3,484	1,430	13,829	South Shields -	do.
*Hedworth, Monkton, and Jarrow (*c*) } *tow.*	37,719	4,225	130,725	Jarrow-on-Tyne -	do.
South Shields - *tow.*	7,710	90	41,295	South Shields -	Borough of South Shields.
Westoe - - *tow.*	49,165	1,749	162,054	do. -	do.
Whitburn (*c*) - *par.*	2,024	4,250	18,014	Sunderland -	East Chester Ward.
Total of Union -	103,199	15,775	388,613		

SOUTH MOLTON UNION :

(*a*) By Order which came into operation on 25 March, 1884.—A detached part of Chittlehampton known as "Leary" was amalgamated with West Buckland.
A detached part of Rose Ash known as "Frankhill" was amalgamated with Creacombe.

(*b*) By Provisional Orders which came into operation on 25 March, 1885.—
A detached part of East Worlington was amalgamated with Woolfardisworthy in the Crediton Union.
A detached part of Lapford in the Crediton Union, known as "Irishcombe" was amalgamated with Meshaw.
A detached part of Witheridge was amalgamated with Thelbridge in the Crediton Union.
A detached part of Chittlehampton known as "Chittlehamholt" was constituted a separate parish and designated the parish of Chittlehamholt.

SOUTH MOLTON UNION—continued.

Detached parts of Witheridge were amalgamated with East Worlington, and the two parts into which the parish known as West Worlington was divided, were amalgamated with East Worlington.

SOUTH SHIELDS UNION :

(*c*) By Order which came into operation on 25 March, 1887.—A detached part of Whitburn was amalgamated with Harton;
A detached part of Fulwell, in the Sunderland Union, was amalgamated with Hedworth, Monkton, and Jarrow; and
Detached parts of Monkwearmouth and Southwick, in the Sunderland Union, were amalgamated with Harton.

Unions and Parishes, &c.		Population in 1881.	Area in Statute Acres in 1881.	Rateable Value in 1881.	Post Town.	Petty Sessional Division

SOUTH STONEHAM UNION.

(Formed 25 Mar. 1835 by Order dated 14 Feb. 1835.—Places marked thus * added 18 May 1835 by Order dated 5 May 1835.)

COUNTY of SOUTHAMPTON :

				£		
Botley (a)	- - par.	1,077	1,836	5,008	Southampton -	Southampton.
Bursledon	- par.	651	775	2,310	do.	do.
*Chilworth	- - par.	227	1,540	1,170	do. - -	do.
Hamble	- par.	421	414	2,137	do. - -	do.
Hound	- - - par.	1,068	3,638	14,183	do. - -	do.
*Milbrook	- - par.	15,051	3,032	50,533	do. - -	do.
*North Stoneham	- par.	1,358	5,056	13,320	do. -	do.
Saint Mary's Extra - par.		5,448	1,180	18,303	do. - -	do.
South Stoneham (W.) par.		12.971	8,757	56,226	do. - -	do.
TOTAL of UNION -		41,275	26,528	163,190		

SOUTHWELL UNION.

(Formed 25 April 1836 by Order dated 8 April 1836.—Place marked thus * added 25 Dec. 1860 by Order dated 3 Nov. 1860.)

COUNTY of NOTTINGHAM :

Averham	- tow.	164	2,646	4,561	Newark - -	North Thurgarton.
Bathley	- tow.	169 {	In North Muskham }	2,006	do. -	do.
Bilsthorpe	- - par.	194	1,572	1,994	Ollerton - -	Southwell.
Bleasby	- par.	296	1,550	3,511	Southwell -	do.
Boughton	- par.	296	1,372	2,525	Ollerton -	Hatfield.
Budby	- tow.	129	2,122	1,002	do. - -	do.
Bulcote	- tow.	111	970	1,455	Nottingham -	South Thurgarton.
Carlton upon Trent - tow.		196	In Norwell	3,131	Newark -	North Thurgarton.
Caunton	- par.	101	3,345	4,110	do. -	do.
Caythorpe	- tow.	294 {	In Lowd-ham }	1,426	Nottingham -	South Thurgarton.
Clipstone	- tow.	256	3,910	3,631	Ollerton -	Mansfield.
Cromwell	- par.	154	1,170	4,479	Newark -	North Thurgarton.
Eakring	- par.	421	2,197	3,565	Ollerton -	Southwell.
East Stoke (a)	- par.	208	1,601	3,746	Newark -	North Thurgarton.
Edingley (a) -	- par.	297	1,800	3,466	Southwell -	Southwell.
Edwinstow	- tow.	931	5,936	5,865	Ollerton -	Hatfield.
Egmanton	- par.	235	2,220	2,866	Tuxford -	do.
Elston (a)	- par.	453	1,640	3,120	Newark -	North Thurgarton.
Epperstone	- par.	435	2,300	3,823	Nottingham -	South do.
Farnsfield	- par.	1,044	4,665	8,063	Southwell -	Southwell.
Fiskerton cum Morton (a) (b) - par.	}	(a)	(a)	(a)	Newark -	do.
Gonalstone	- par.	119	950	2,027	Nottingham -	South Thurgarton.
Grassthorpe	- tow.	75	510	1,767	Newark -	North do.
Gunthorpe	- tow.	323 {	In Lowd-ham }	2,715	Nottingham -	South do.
Halam	- par.	290	1,310	3,138	Southwell -	Southwell.
						(continued)

SOUTH STONEHAM UNION :

(a) By Order which came into operation on 25 March 1884, a detached part of Droxford, in the Droxford Union, was amalgamated with Botley.

SOUTHWELL UNION :

(a) By Orders which came into operation on 25 March. 1884,—

A detached part of Winthorpe, in the Newark Union, was amalgamated with Holme ;

A detached part of Edingley was amalgamated with Oxton ;

SOUTHWELL UNION—*continued*

A detached part of Syerstone was amalgamated with Elston ;

A part of Fiskerton on the right of the River Trent was amalgamated with East Stoke, and the remaining parts were amalgamated with Morton (see note (b)). Fiskerton had in 1881 population 283, acreage 1,043, and rateable value 2,983l. Morton had in 1881 population 109, acreage 498, and rateable value 1,670l.

(b) By Order dated 9 May 1884, it was directed that the parish of Morton, as altered by the addition of parts of Fiskerton, should be termed Fiskerton cum Morton.

Unions and Parishes, &c.		Population in 1881.	Area in Statute Acres in 1881.	Rateable Value in 1881.	Post Town.	Petty Sessional Division.

SOUTHWELL UNION—County of Nottingham—
continued.

Unions and Parishes, &c.		Population in 1881.	Area in Statute Acres in 1881.	Rateable Value in 1881. £	Post Town.	Petty Sessional Division.
Halloughton	par.	64	977	1,039	Southwell	Southwell.
Hockerton	par.	101	1,373	1,934	do.	do.
Holme (a)	par.	127	1,330	2,236	Newark	North Thurgarton.
Hoveringham	par.	328	1,050	2,227	Nottingham	Southwell.
Kelham	par.	151	1,857	6,435	Newark	North Thurgarton.
Kersall	tow.	59	In Kneesal	918	do.	do.
Kirklington	par.	220	1,976	3,032	Southwell	Southwell.
Kirton	par.	126	1,090	1,430	Ollerton	South Clay.
Kneesall	tow.	283	3,360	2,605	Newark	North Thurgarton.
Laxton with Moorhouse	par.	483	3,610	5,021	do.	South Clay.
Lowdham	tow.	740	3,010	4,732	Nottingham	South Thurgarton.
Maplebeck	par.	123	1,136	1,636	Newark	North do.
North Muskham	tow.	542	2,180	5,163	do.	do.
Norwell	tow.	417	3,505	4,885	do.	do.
Norwell Woodhouse	tow.	87	In Norwell	611	do.	do.
Ollerton	tow.	818	1,708	3,748	Ollerton	Hatfield.
Ompton	tow.	58	In Kneesalt	597	do.	do.
Ossington	par.	188	2,265	2,501	Newark	North Thurgarton.
Oxton (a)	par.	516	3,580	4,890	Southwell	South do.
*Park Leys	par.	4	310	315	Newark	North do.
Perlethorpe	tow.	132	1,740	1,383	Ollerton	Hatfield.
Rolleston	tow.	232	1,662	4,406	Newark	North Thurgarton.
Rufford	lib.	333	10,320	6,766	Ollerton	Hatfield.
South Muskham	par.	245	2,631	6,968	Newark	North Thurgarton.
Southwell	par.	2,866	3,805	17,233	Southwell	Southwell.
Staythorpe	tow.	44 {	In Averham }	1,562	Newark	North Thurgarton.
Sutton on Trent	par.	966	2,930	9,850	do.	do.
Syerstone (a)	par.	165	610	1,819	do.	do.
Thorpe	par.	90	698	1,607	do.	do.
Thurgarton	par.	328	2,770	4,764	Southwell	Southwell.
Upton (W.)	par.	499	1,860	3,522	do.	do.
Walesby	par.	282	1,260	1,792	Ollerton	Hatfield.
Wellow	par.	368	991	1,627	Newark	North Clay.
Weston	par.	348	1,090	5,898	do.	North Thurgarton.
Winkbourn	par.	132	2,240	2,211	Southwell	Southwell.
TOTAL of UNION		19,959 (a)	113,610 (a)	207,316 (a)		

SPALDING UNION.

(Formed 30 Nov. 1835 by Order dated 16 Nov. 1835.—Place marked thus * added 30 Sept. 1836 by Order dated 17 Sept. 1836; and thus † added 1 Mar. 1862 by Order dated 4 Jan. 1862. Spelling of Name of Place marked thus ‡ as altered by Order dated 2 July 1887.)

COUNTY of LINCOLN:

Unions and Parishes, &c.		Population in 1881.	Area in Statute Acres in 1881.	Rateable Value in 1881.	Post Town.	Petty Sessional Division.
Cowbit	par.	637	4,590	3,800	Spalding	Holland, Elloe.
†Deeping Saint Nicholas	par.	1,364	16,290	23,265	do.	Holland, Elloe, and Kesteven Ness.
*‡Donington	par.	1,666	6,180	10,363	do.	Holland, Kirton, and Skirbeck.
Gosberton	par.	2,104	8,820	14,374	do.	do.
Moulton	par.	2,248	13,785	19,085	do.	Holland, Elloe.
Pinchbeck	par.	2,995	11,640	24,896	do.	do.
Quadring	par.	900	4,210	6,527	do.	Holland, Kirton, and Skirbeck.
Spalding (W.)	par.	9,260	12,070	41,976	do.	Holland, Elloe.
Surfleet	par.	941	3,500	7,578	do.	Holland, Kirton, and Skirbeck.
Weston	par.	846	5,386	9,282	do.	Holland, Elloe.
TOTAL of UNION		22,961	86,471	161,146		

Unions and Parishes, &c.	Population in 1881.	Area in Statute Acres in 1881.	Rateable Value in 1881.	Post Town.	Petty Sessional Division.

SPILSBY UNION.

(Formed 13 April 1837 by Order dated 18 March 1837, which was amended as to the names of places marked thus † by Order dated 27 Nov. 1886.—Place marked thus * added 5 May 1882 by Order dated 21 April 1882.)

COUNTY OF LINCOLN : £

Addlethorpe - par.	243	2,006	3,567	Burgh, R.S.O. -	Spilsby.
Alford - par.	2,894	1,110	7,907	Alford - -	Alford.
Anderby - par.	279	1,845	2,059	do. - -	do.
Ashby - par.	124	1,210	1,255	Spilsby - -	Spilsby.
Aswarby - par.	58	741	1,205	do. - -	do.
Bilsby with Thurlby par.	510	2,820	4,126	Alford - -	Alford.
Bolingbroke (a) - par.	459	2,136	2,990	Spilsby - -	Spilsby.
Bratoft - par.	218	1,811	2,132	Burgh, R.S.O. -	do.
Brinkhill - par.	149	780	1,186	Spilsby - -	do.
Burgh in the Marsh - par.	1,136	4,233	8,366	Burgh, R.S.O. -	do.
Calceby - par.	62	618	817	Alford - -	Alford.
Candlesby - par.	247	850	1,510	Spilsby - -	Spilsby.
Claxby - par.	90	590	1,418	Alford - -	Alford.
Croft - par.	752	6,153	9,014	Wainfleet, R.S.O. -	Spilsby.
Cumberworth - par.	223	950	1,744	Alford - -	Alford.
Dalby cum Dexthorpe par.	152	1,020	1,865	Spilsby - -	Spilsby.
†Driby - par.	117	1,338	1,779	do. - -	do.
Enattville - tow.	359	1,260	4,542	Boston - -	do.
Farlesthorpe - par.	104	1,043	1,460	Alford - -	Alford.
Firsby - par.	235	910	2,398	Spilsby - -	Spilsby.
Friskney - par.	1,477	13,083	10,638	Boston - -	do.
Gunby - par.	80	606	1,033	Burgh, R.S.O. -	do.
Hagnaby (a) - par.	74	524	1,261	Spilsby - -	do.
Halton Holgate - par.	499	1,320	3,465	do. - -	do.
Hareby (a) - par.	42	589	1,042	do. - -	do.
Harrington - par.	123	1,052	1,464	do. - -	do.
Hogsthorpe - par.	719	3,325	5,522	Alford - -	Alford.
Holme North - par.	201	30	301	Wainfleet, R.S.O. -	Spilsby.
Hundleby (W.) (a) - par.	631	734	2,577	Spilsby - -	do.
Huttoft - par.	597	3,310	5,236	Alford - -	Alford.
Ingoldmells - par.	241	1,857	2,145	Burgh, R.S.O. -	Spilsby.
Irby in the Marsh - par.	178	1,090	1,102	do. - -	do.
Keal East - par.	395	1,860	2,770	Spilsby - -	do.
Keal West (a) - par.	369	1,500	3,377	do. - -	do.
Kirkby East - par.	354	1,670	2,729	do. - -	do.
Langton by Spilsby - par.	219	1,590	2,051	do. - -	do.
Markby (b) - par.	118	652	924	Alford - -	Alford.
Mavis Enderby (a) - par.	140	1,318	1,746	Spilsby - -	Spilsby.
†Midville - tow.	204	3,450	3,507	Boston - -	do.
Mumby with Chapel Mumby } par.	639	2,020	5,071	Alford - -	Alford.
Orby - par.	410	2,088	3,278	Burgh, R.S.O. -	Spilsby.
Ormsby South with Ketsby } par.	294	2,377	3,355	Alford - -	Alford.
Partney - par.	442	919	2,033	Spilsby - -	Spilsby.
Reithby (a) - par.	155	385	1,695	do. - -	do.
Rigsby with Ailsby - par.	112	1,040	1,396	Alford - -	Alford.
Sausthorpe - par.	141	728	1,264	Spilsby - -	Spilsby.
Scremby with Grebby par.	172	970	1,730	do. - -	do.
Skegness - par.	1,338	2,474	6,745	Boston - -	do.
Skendleby - par.	270	1,719	2,151	Spilsby - -	do.
Spilsby (a) - par.	1,482	1,671	5,918	do. - -	do.
Steeping Great - par.	266	1,721	2,418	do. - -	do.
Steeping Little - par.	272	1,190	1,871	do. - -	do.
Stickford (a) - par.	486	1,774	1,775	Boston - -	do.
Stickney - par.	689	4,220	3,833	do. - -	do.
Sutterby - par.	36	471	646	Spilsby - -	do.
Sutton in the Marsh - par.	360	2,096	3,418	Alford - -	Alford.

(continued)

SPILSBY UNION :

(a) By Provisional Orders which came into operation on 25 March 1882,—

A detached part of Hagnaby was amalgamated with Thorpe;

A detached part of Bolingbroke was amalgamated with Carrington, in the Boston Union ;

Certain detached parts of Hareby, Hundleby, Keal West, Mavis Enderby, and Reithby, together with detached parts of certain parishes in the Boston

SPILSBY UNION—continued.

Union, were constituted a separate parish, and designated the Parish of West Fen ;

Certain detached parts of Keal West, Spilsby, and of Lusby, in the Horncastle Union, were amalgamated with Stickford.

(b) By Order which came into operation on 25 March 1887.—

Certain detached parts of Markby were amalgamated with Hagnaby with Hannay in the Louth Union.

Unions and Parishes, &c.		Population in 1881.	Area in Statute Acres in 1881.	Rateable Value in 1881.	Post Town.	Petty Sessional Division.
SPILSBY UNION—County of Lincoln—*continued.*				£		
Thorpe (*a*) - -	par.	566	2,996	4,860	Wainfleet, R.S.O. -	Spilsby.
Toynton All Saints -	par.	338	2,768	2,557	Spilsby - -	do.
Toynton Saint Peter's	par.	333	2,289	2,641	do. - -	do.
Ulceby with Forth- ington - -	par.	176	2,220	2,593	Alford - -	Alford.
Wainfleet All Saints -	par.	1,349	1,598	5,114	Wainfleet, R.S.O. -	Spilsby.
Wainfleet Saint Mary	par.	705	13,019	9,022	do. - -	do.
Well and Derthorpe -	par.	124	2,110	1,854	Alford - -	Alford.
Welton in the Marsh with Boothby	par.	375	2,600	3,455	Spilsby - -	Spilsby.
*West Fen (*a*) - -	par.	322	2,426	—	Boston - -	do.
Willoughby - -	par.	617	4,280	7,881	Alford - -	Alford.
Winthorpe - -	par.	337	2,339	4,313	Skegness - -	Spilsby.
TOTAL of UNION -		27,887	110,689	207,447		

STAFFORD UNION.

(Formed 28 Sept. 1836 by Order dated 3 Sept. 1836.—Places marked thus * added 5 Dec. 1836 by Order dated 10 Nov. 1836 ; Place marked thus † added 29 Mar. 1838 by Order dated 13 Feb. 1838 ; and Places marked thus ‡ added 24 June 1858 by Order dated 28 May 1858.)

COUNTY of STAFFORD :						
Berkswich or Bas- wich (*b*)	tow.	606	2,013	8,347	Stafford - -	Stafford.
Bradley (*b*) -	par.	496	5,594	8,450	do. - -	do.
Brockton (*b*) -	tow.	224	2,361	1,733	do. - -	do.
Castle Church	par.	5,923	3,861	33,087	do. - -	do.
‡Chartley Holme	par.	39	1,707	1,611	do. - -	do.
Colwich (*b*) (*d*)	tow.	1,541	7,775	18,560	do. - -	do.
‡Cresswell -	par.	29	828	1,431	do. - -	do.
†Ellenhall (*b*)	par.	243	2,519	3,625	Eccleshall -	Eccleshall.
Fradswell -	tow.	199	1,442	2,673	Stafford -	Stafford.
*Gayton -	par.	236	1,515	2,819	do. - -	do.
Haughton (*b*)	par.	501	1,903	4,326	do. - -	do.
Hopton and Coton (*c*)	tow.	1,352	3,711	6,535	do. - -	do.
Ingestre -	par.	138	879	2,123	do. - -	do.
Marston (*a*) (*b*) -	tow.	664	1,487	3,392	do. - -	do.
Ranton -	par.	205	1,843	3,053	Eccleshall -	do.
Saint Mary and Saint Chad, Stafford (W.) (*c*)	un- pars.	14,399	365	35,303	Stafford -	Borough of Stafford.
Salt and Enson (*b*) -	tow.	427	1,677	2,770	Stone -	Stafford.
Seighford -	par.	756	4,741	15,198	Stafford -	do.
*Stowe (*b*) (*d*) -	par.	1,168	5,120	9,673	do. - -	do.
‡Tillington (*a*) -	par.	271	977	3,560	do. - -	do.
Tixall -	par.	226	2,369	1,163	do. - -	do.
*Weston on Trent -	par.	528	833	3,659	do. - -	do.
*Whitgreave -	tow.	150	1,201	1,939	Stone -	do.
‡Worston -	par.	7	172	1,287	Stafford -	do.
‡Yarlett -	par.	117	400	711	Stone -	do.
TOTAL of UNION -		30,545	57,326	180,628		

SPILSBY UNION :
(*a*) See note, page 345.

STAFFORD UNION :
(*a*) By Order which came into operation on 25 March 1884, a detached part of Marston was amalgamated with Tillington.
(*b*) By Orders which came into operation on 25 March 1885,—
A detached part of Brockton was amalgamated with Berkswich or Baswich ;
Detached parts of Colwich were amalgamated with Stowe, and with Colton, in the Lichfield Union ;
A detached part of Salt and Enson was amalgamated with Marston ;

STAFFORD UNION—*continued.*

All the parts of a Parish known as Ranton Abbey were amalgamated with Ellenhall ;
A detached part of Bradley was amalgamated with Haughton, and detached parts of Gnosal, in the Newport (Salop) Union were amalgamated with Bradley and Haughton.
(*c*) By Provisional Order which came into operation on 25 March 1886, all the part of Hopton and Coton included in the Municipal Borough of Stafford was amalgamated with Saint Mary and Saint Chad, Stafford.
(*d*) By Order which came into operation on 25 March 1886, detached parts of Colwich were amalgamated with Stowe.

Unions and Parishes, &c.		Population in 1881.	Area in Statute Acres in 1881.	Rateable Value in 1881.	Post Town.	Petty Sessional Division.
STAINES UNION.				£		
(Formed 28 June 1836 by Order dated 2 June 1836.)						
COUNTY of MIDDLESEX :						
Ashford - -	par.	1,484	1,402	9,771	Staines - -	Spelthorne.
Cranford -	par.	503	737	3,568	Hounslow - -	Uxbridge.
East Bedfont with Hatton -	par.	1,152	1,926	9,049	do. - -	Spelthorne.
Feltham - -	par.	2,909	1,790	10,612	do. - -	do.
Hanworth - -	par.	1,010	1,373	5,445	do. - -	do.
Harlington -	par.	1,538	1,165	11,122	do. - -	Uxbridge.
Harmondsworth -	par.	1,812	3,307	9,075	Slough - -	do.
Laleham - -	par.	544	1,301	4,331	Staines - -	Spelthorne.
Littleton - -	par.	126	1,038	2,196	do. - -	do.
Shepperton -	par.	1,285	1,492	8,786	Walton on Thames	do.
Staines - -	par.	1,628	1,843	25,968	Staines - -	do.
Stanwell (W.) -	par.	2,156	3,999	12,183	do. - -	do.
Sunbury - -	par.	1,297	2,659	23,273	Sunbury - -	do.
TOTAL of UNION -		23,774	24,332	136,879		
STAMFORD UNION.						
(Formed 17 Nov. 1835 by Order dated 2 Nov. 1835.)						
COUNTY of HUNTINGDON :						
Stibbington -	par.	538	1,530	3,410	Wansford -	Fletton.
COUNTY of LINCOLN :						
All Saints - -	par.	2,612	1,860	9,096	Stamford - -	Borough of Stamford.
Barholm - -	par.	179	1,230	1,758	do. -	Bourn.
Braceborough -	par.	184	2,230	2,987	do. - -	do.
Greatford - -	tow.	220	1,510	2,795	do. - -	do.
Saint George -	par.	2,092		5,780	do. - -	Borough of Stamford.
Saint John Baptist -	par.	1,262	In	3,098	do. - -	do.
Saint Mary -	par.	311	All Saints	1,839	do. - -	do.
Saint Michael -	par.	1,325		5,355	do. - -	do.
Stow - -	par.	23	355	546	do. - -	Bourn.
Tallington - -	par.	215	690	4,574	do. - -	do.
Uffington -	par.	462	3,996	7,887	do. - -	do.
West Deeping -	par.	285	1,170	2,589	Market Deeping -	do.
Wilsthorpe -	tow.	81	In Greatford	2,114	Stamford -	do.
COUNTY of NORTHAMPTON :						
Bainton (a) - -	par.	279	3,080	5,217	do. - -	Liberty of Peterborough.
Barnack (a) -	ham.	711	4,140	8,329	do. - -	do.
Colly Weston -	par.	433	1,690	2,684	do. - -	Oundle and Saint Martin's Stamford Baron.
Duddington - -	par.	359	1,100	2,257	do. - -	Oundle.
Easton - -	par.	981	3,170	6,581	do. - -	do.
Saint Martin (W.) -	tow.	1,172	2,170	8,215	do. - -	Borough of Stamford.
Southorpe - -	ham.	174	In Barnack	2,240	do. - -	Liberty of Peterborough.
Thornhaugh (a) -	par.	215	1,706	2,710	Wansford - -	do.
Ufford (a) - -	tow.	152	In Bainton	1,456	Stamford - -	do.
Wansford (a) -	par.	143	469	871	Wansford - -	do.
Wittering - -	par.	261	2,690	2,728	do. - -	do.
Wothorpe -	ham.	109 {	In Saint Martin }	1,709	Stamford - -	do.
						(continued)

STAMFORD UNION :

(a) By Orders which came into operation on 25 March 1887,—
The several parts of a place known as Ashton were amalgamated with Bainton ;
Certain detached parts of Bainton were amalgamated with Ufford ;
The several parts of a place known as Barnack were

STAMFORD UNION—*continued.*

amalgamated with Pilsgate and the latter as so altered was designated the Hamlet of Barnack ;
A detached part of Essendine was amalgamated with Carlby in the Bourn Union ; and
A detached part of Wansford was amalgamated with Thornhaugh.

Unions and Parishes, &c.	Population in 1881.	Area in Statute Acres in 1881.	Rateable Value in 1881	Post Town.	Petty Sessional Division.

STAMFORD UNION—*continued.*

COUNTY OF RUTLAND :

			£		
Casterton Magna - par.	321	1,590	2,820	Stamford - -	Oakham.
Casterton Parva - par.	178	1,450	1,969	do. - -	do.
Clipsham - - par.	223	1,055	2,143	Oakham - -	do.
Essendine (a) - par.	176	1,526	5,184	Stamford - -	do.
Ketton - - par.	1,116	2,740	9,484	do. - -	do.
Pickworth - - par.	169	3,680	2,021	do. - -	do.
Ryhall - - par.	713	2,070	3,918	do. - -	do.
Tinwell - - par.	224	1,651	2,727	do. - -	do.
Tixover - - par.	86	1,080	1,381	do. - -	do.
TOTAL of UNION -	**18,314**	**52,858**	**131,105**		

STEPNEY UNION.

(Formed 19 Dec. 1836 by Order dated 23 Nov. 1836.)

COUNTY OF MIDDLESEX :

Limehouse - - par.	32,041	243	129,722	London, E. -	Tower.
Ratcliffe - - ham.	16,107	111	63,233	do. - -	do.
Shadwell - - par.	8,170	68	55,637	do. - -	do.
Wapping - - par.	2,225	40	69,877	do. - -	do.
TOTAL of UNION -	**58,543**	**462**	**318,469**		

STEYNING UNION.

(Formed 25 July 1835 by Order dated 8 July 1835.—Place marked thus * added 29 Sept. 1869 by Order dated 13 Aug. 1869.)

COUNTY OF SUSSEX :

Aldrington - - par.	144	744	6,583	Brighton - -	Hove.
Ashurst - - par.	376	2,372	2,746	Steyning - -	Steyning.
Beeding - - par.	611	5,438	5,912	do. - -	do.
Bramber - - par.	186	851	1,478	do. - -	do.
Buttolphs - - par.	94	920	1,484	do. - -	do.
Coombes - - par.	71	1,280	1,320	Shoreham - -	do.
Edburton - - par.	341	2,647	2,274	Upper Beeding -	do.
Hangleton - - par.	79	1,120	939	Brighton - -	Hove.
Henfield - - par.	1,890	1,518	12,138	Henfield - -	Steyning.
Hove - - par.	20,804	786	194,432	Brighton - -	Hove.
Kingston by Sea - par.	262	778	1,706	do. - -	Steyning.
*Lancing - - par.	1,341	2,530	9,550	Worthing - -	do.
New Shoreham (W.) par.	3,505	116	9,740	New Shoreham -	do.
Old Shoreham - par.	248	1,920	3,752	do. - -	do.
Patcham - - par.	873	1,425	16,932	Brighton - -	Hove.
Portslade - - par.	3,749	1,968	15,834	do. - -	do.
Poynings - - par.	316	1,642	2,079	Upper Beeding -	do.
Preston - - par.	8,545	1,304	56,801	Brighton - -	do.
Shermanbury - par.	363	1,917	2,421	Henfield - -	Horsham.
Sompting - - par.	662	2,917	5,023	Worthing - -	Worthing.
Southwick - - par.	2,561	1,044	8,117	Brighton - -	Steyning.
Steyning - - par.	1,672	3,414	9,357	Steyning - -	do.
West Blatchington - par.	59	873	939	Brighton - -	Hove.
Woodmancote - par.	317	2,239	3,318	Henfield - -	Steyning.
TOTAL of UNION -	**19,089**	**47,760**	**378,175**		

STAMFORD UNION :

(a) See note, page 347.

Unions and Parishes, &c.	Population in 1881.	Area in Statute Acres in 1881.	Rateable Value in 1881.	Post Town.	Petty Sessional Division.
STOCKBRIDGE UNION.			£		
(Formed 6 June 1835 by Order dated 20 May 1835.—Place marked thus * added 25 Dec. 1858 by Order dated 16 Oct. 1858, and thus † added 1 August 1860 by Order dated 26 June 1860.)					
COUNTY OF SOUTHAMPTON :					
Ashley (a) - - par.	134	1,898	1,598	Stockbridge - -	Winchester.
Bossington (a) - par.	33	629	762	do. - -	Romsey.
Broughton (a) - par.	901	4,369	6,174	do. - -	do.
*East and West Buck-holt - } par.	47	1,140	927	do. - -	do.
East Tytherly (a) - par.	378	2,447	2,705	do. - -	do.
Frenchmore - - par.	36	379	275	do. - -	do.
Houghton - - par.	433	2,672	4,103	do. - -	do.
Kings Somborne (a) - par.	1,256	7,404	8,702	do. - -	Andover.
Leckford - - par.	288	2,267	2,592	do. - -	Winchester.
Little Somborne (a) - par.	75	1,527	1,099	do. - -	Andover.
Longstock - - par.	136	2,985	3,800	do. - -	do.
Lower Wallop - par.	789	7,301	7,919	do. - -	do.
Stockbridge (W.) (a) - par.	873	1,128	2,868	do. - -	do.
†Upper Eldon - par.	6	295	250	do. - -	Romsey.
Upper Wallop - par.	513	4,672	4,408	do. - -	Andover.
West Tytherly (a) - par.	422	2,377	2,560	Salisbury - -	Romsey.
TOTAL of UNION -	6,653 (a)	43,580 (a)	50,742 (a)		
STOCKPORT UNION.					
(Formed 3 Feb. 1837 by Order dated 17 Jan. 1837.—Places marked thus * added 1 April 1878 by Order dated 30 March 1878 ; Place marked thus † originally consisted of Cheadle Bulkeley and Cheadle Moseley, but these were re-adjusted and consolidated and continued in the Union under the name of Cheadle by Provisional Order dated 3 May 1879, which took effect on 29 Sept. 1879. Spelling of name of Place marked ‡ is as altered by Order dated 18 August 1887.)					
COUNTY of CHESTER :					
*Bosden - - par.	1,962	492	4,725	Stockport - -	Stockport.
Bramhall - - tow.	2,682	2,901	14,311	do. - -	do.
Bredbury - - tow.	3,734	2,536	21,370	do. - -	do.
Brinnington - tow.	5,994	778	21,805	do. - -	do.
†Cheadle - - tow.	12,263	4,488	60,088	do. - -	do.
*Handforth - - par.	736	1,311	5,807	Manchester as to part ; Stockport as to part.	do.
Hyde - - tow.	17,876	897	62,219	Manchester -	Hyde.
Marple - - tow.	4,421	3,053	20,471	Stockport - -	Stockport.
Norbury - - tow.	1,499	1,249	7,207	do. - -	do.
Offerton - - tow.	358	623	1,966	do. - -	do.
‡Romiley - - tow.	1,819	1,189	11,132	do. - -	do.
Stockport (W.) - tow.	33,167	1,324	99,239	do. - -	do.
Stockport Etchells - tow.	1,369	1,572	8,644	Manchester -	do.
Torkington - - tow.	244	823	1,842	Stockport - -	do.
Werneth - - tow.	3,129	1,571	13,970	Stockport as to part ; Manchester as to part.	Hyde.
COUNTY of LANCASTER :					
Heaton Norris - tow.	20,347	2,116	96,247	Stockport - -	Heaton Norris.
Reddish - - tow.	5,557	1,541	27,771	do. - -	do.
TOTAL of UNION -	117,157	28,464	478,814		

STOCKBRIDGE UNION :

(a) By Orders which came into operation on 25 March 1883,—

A detached part of Ashley, known as "Baileys Down," was amalgamated with Kings Somborne ;
Detached parts of Bossington and Broughton were amalgamated with East Tytherly ;
Certain parts of Broughton and Kings Somborne were amalgamated with Bossington ;
The part of the Parish of Crown Farm, known as "Crown Farm," was amalgamated with Bossington, and the remaining part known as "Dunmore" was amalgamated with East Tytherly (the Parish of Crown Farm in 1881 had population 6, acreage 119, and rateable value 143l.)

STOCKBRIDGE UNION—continued.

A detached part of Kings Somborne, known as "Upper Sandylown Farm," was amalgamated with Stockbridge ;
Certain parts of Kings Somborne were amalgamated with Little Somborne ;
All that part of the Parish of West Dean, situate in the County of Southampton was amalgamated with West Tytherly, and certain other parts situate in the County of Wilts were amalgamated with Winterslow, in the Alderbury Union ; the remainder of the Parish was on the 30 September 1883 added to the Alderbury Union (the Parish of West Dean had in 1881 population 313, acreage 3,540, and rateable value 3,809l.)

Unions and Parishes, &c.		Population in 1881.	Area in Statute Acres in 1881.	Rateable Value in 1881.	Post Town.	Petty Sessional Division.

STOCKTON UNION.

(Formed 22 Feb. 1837 by Order dated 28 Jan. 1837.)

COUNTY of DURHAM :

				£		
Aislaby (a)	tow.	125	2,318	3,167	Yarm -	Stockton Ward.
Billingham -	tow.	1,488	3,155	9,268	Stockton on Tees -	do.
Carlton	tow.	209	1,501	3,779	do. -	do.
Cowpen Bewley	tow.	997	2,835	13,148	Middlesbrough	do.
Egglescliffe	tow.	655	1,517	8,521	Yarm -	do.
Elton -	par.	113	1,444	1,215	Stockton on Tees -	do.
Grindon	tow.	345	3,511	3,947	do.	do.
Hartburn East	tow.	360	1,045	3,886	do. -	do.
Longnewton	tow.	268	1,312	6,936	Darlington -	do.
Newsham (a) -	tow.	64	1,090	1,255	Yarm -	do.
Newton Bewley	tow.	131	1,564	1,901	Stockton on Tees -	do.
Norton (a) -	par.	3,195	4,653	23,328	do. -	do.
Preston -	tow.	163	1,136	5,418	Darlington -	do.
Redmarshall -	tow.	91	875	751	Stockton-on-Tees -	do.
Stockton Town and Borough (W.) (a)	—	41,719	3,162	154,505	do. -	do.
Whitton -	tow.	681	781	5,370	Ferry Hill -	do.
Wolviston -	tow.	605	2,417	3,609	Stockton on Tees -	do.
TOTAL of UNION	-	51,209	37,379	250,004		

STOKE DAMAREL PARISH.

(Under the 54 Geo. 3, c. clxxii.)

COUNTY of DEVON :

Stoke Damarel (W.)	par.	48,939	1,760	99,715	Devonport -	Borough of Devonport.

STOKESLEY UNION.

(Formed 27 Feb. 1837 by Order dated 2 Feb. 1837.—Place marked thus * added 29 Sept. 1837 by Order dated 26 Aug. 1837, and thus † added 25 June 1875 by Order dated 1 June 1875.)

COUNTY of YORK, NORTH RIDING :

*Bilsdale Midcable	tow.	677	14,290	4,276	Northallerton -	Ryedale.
Carleton -	par.	253	1,358	2,096	do. -	Langbaurgh, West.
†Castle Leavington	tow.	44	1,071	1,267	Yarm -	Yarm.
Crathorne -	par.	217	2,598	3,209	do. -	do.
Easby -	tow.	136	1,210	1,398	Great Ayton, Northallerton.	Langbaurgh, West.
East Rounton	tow.	166	1,622	2,233	Welbury, Northallerton.	Yarm.
Faceby -	tow.	174	1,382	1,243	Northallerton -	Langbaurgh, West.
Great and Little Broughton	tow.	566	3,091	5,386	do. -	do.
Great Ayton -	tow.	1,754	3,580	7,458	do. -	do.
Great Busby -	tow.	98	1,404	2,013	do. -	do.
†High Worsall -	tow.	81	1,594	1,456	Yarm -	Yarm.
Hilton -	par.	135	1,392	1,480	do. -	do.
Hutton -	tow.	849	2,371	4,776	do. -	Langbaurgh, West.
Ingleby Arncliffe	par.	306	1,893	2,636	Northallerton -	do.
Ingleby Greenhow -	par.	391	7,002	4,688	do. -	do.
Kildale	par.	280	5,192	3,177	Grosmont -	do.
Kirby in Cleveland -	tow.	244	1,708	3,053	Northallerton -	do.
†Kirk Leavington	par.	197	2,202	4,077	Yarm -	Yarm.
Little Ayton with Tunstall -	tow.	101	1,378	1,468	Northallerton -	Langbaurgh, West.
Little Busby -	tow.	33	705	1,090	do. -	do. (continued)

(continued)

STOCKTON UNION :

(a) By Orders which came into operation on 25 March, 1887,—

A detached part of Aislaby was amalgamated with Newsham ;

STOCKTON UNION—continued.

A detached part of Stockton was amalgamated with Norton ; and

A part of Stockton known as " Mandale " was amalgamated with Thornaby in the Middlesbrough Union.

Unions and Parishes, &c.		Population in 1881.	Area in Statute Acres in 1881.	Rateable Value in 1881.	Post Town.	Petty Sessional Division.
STOKESLEY UNION—County of York, North Riding—*continued.*				£		
†Low Worsall - -	*tow.*	199	1,362	1,603	Yarm - -	Yarm.
Middleton upon Leven - -	*tow.*	87	1,144	1,281	do. - -	do.
Newby - -	*tow.*	115	1,254	1,367	Stockton on Tees -	Langbaurgh. West.
Nunthorpe - -	*tow.*	165	1,427	2,003	R.S.O., Yorkshire -	do.
†Pickton - -	*tow.*	108	1,003	3,905	Yarm - -	Yarm.
Potto - -	*tow.*	209	1,532	2,599	Swainby, North-allerton.	Langbaurgh, West.
Rudby in Cleveland -	*tow.*	81	889	1,221	Yarm - -	do.
Scutterskelfe -	*tow.*	65	1,008	1,513	Stokesley -	do.
Seamer - -	*tow.*	246	2,650	3,204	Yarm - -	do.
Sexhow - -	*tow.*	34	528	829	Hutton Rudby, Yarm.	do.
Stokesley (W.) -	*tow.*	1,802	1,818	7,595	Stokesley -	do.
Whorlton - -	*tow.*	681	6,812	4,719	Swainby, North-allerton.	do.
†Yarm - -	*par.*	1,485	1,229	5,926	Yarm - -	Yarm.
TOTAL of UNION -		12,009	79,708	96,247		

STOKE UPON TRENT PARISH.						
(Board of Guardians constituted 30 April 1836 by Order dated 31 Mar. 1836.)						
COUNTY of STAFFORD :						Hundred of Pirehill North :
Stoke upon Trent (W.) - -	*par.*	104,313	12,818	348,279	Stoke upon Trent -	Newcastle under Lyme Division.

STONE UNION.						
(Formed 3 Feb. 1838 by Order dated 3 Jan. 1838.)						
COUNTY of STAFFORD :						
Barlaston - -	*par.*	821	2,184	5,621	Stoke upon Trent -	Stone.
Chebsey - -	*tow.*	467	2,852	6,853	Eccleshall -	Eccleshall.
Cold Norton - -	*tow.*	36	1,319	2,541	Stone - -	do.
Eccleshall - -	*par.*	4,075	19,755	38,865	Eccleshall -	do.
Milwich - -	*par.*	547	3,042	4,228	Stone - -	Stone.
Sandon - -	*par.*	513	3,637	6,261	do. - -	Stafford.
Standon - -	*par.*	359	2,620	4,450	Eccleshall -	Eccleshall.
Stone (W.) - -	*par.*	13,155	20,146	48,722	Stone - -	Stone.
Swynnerton - -	*par.*	778	6,481	11,063	do. - -	Eccleshall.
Trentham - -	*par.*	8,383	7,445	27,362	Newcastle under Lyme.	Newcastle under Lyme.
TOTAL of UNION -		29,134	69,781	155,966		

STOURBRIDGE UNION.						
(Formed 13 Oct. 1836 by Order dated 19 Sept. 1836, as amended by Orders dated 18 Aug. and 12 Dec., 1842.)						
COUNTY of STAFFORD :						
Amblecote - -	*ham.*	2,808	689	12,130	Stourbridge -	Seisdon: South Division.
Kingswinford (W.) -	*par.*	35,767	7,315	96,492	Brierley Hill -	do.

(continued)

Unions and Parishes, &c.		Population in 1881.	Area in Statute Acres in 1881.	Rateable Value in 1881.	Post Town.	Petty Sessional Division.
STOURBRIDGE UNION—*continued.*				£		
COUNTY of WORCESTER :						
Cakemore (*a*)	- tow.	624 {	In Hales Owen }	4,301	Rowley -	Brimstree : Halesowen.
Cradley -	- tow.	5,284	732	16,678	Brierley Hill -	Halfshire : Lower Division of Stourbridge.
Hales Owen -	- tow.	3,338	4,408	6,746	Birmingham	Brimstree : Halesowen.
Hasbury -	- tow.	2,494		5,111	Halesowen	do.
Hawn -	- tow.	716	In	3,707	do. -	do.
Illy -	- tow.	80	Hales Owen	598	do. -	do.
Lapal -	- tow.	351		2,257	do. -	do.
Lutley - -	- tow.	181	430	968	Stourbridge -	Halfshire : Lower Division of Stourbridge.
Ridgacre (*a*) -	- tow.	749 {	In Hales Owen }	2,000	Birmingham	Brimstree : Halesowen.
Stourbridge -	- tow.	9,757	2,626	26,005	Stourbridge-	Halfshire : Lower Division of Stourbridge.
The Hill -	- tow.	2,447 {	In Hales Owen }	4,820	Hales Owen -	Brimstree : Hales Owen.
The Lye -	- tow.	6,323		10,205	Stourbridge -	Halfshire : Lower Division of Stourbridge.
Upper Swinford	- tow.	3,203	In Stourbridge	11,164	do. -	do.
Wollaston -	- tow.	2,414		5,300	do. -	do.
Wollescote -	- tow.	3,060		4,860	do. -	do.
TOTAL of UNION	-	79,596	16,200	213,315		

STOW UNION.

(Formed 24 Oct. 1835 by Order dated 5 Oct. 1835.—Places marked thus * added 25 Jan. 1836 by Order dated 2 Jan. 1836, and thus † added 17 Oct. 1836 by Order dated 22 Sept. 1836.)

COUNTY of SUFFOLK :

Unions and Parishes, &c.		Population in 1881.	Area in Statute Acres in 1881.	Rateable Value in 1881.	Post Town.	Petty Sessional Division.
Ashfield Magna	- par.	398	1,546	2,632	Bury St. Edmunds	Blackbourn.
Badwell Ash	- par.	445	1,860	3,124	do. -	do.
Beyton otherwise Beighton	} par.	342	625	1,517	do. -	{ Thingoe and Thedwastre.
Buxhall -	- par.	476	2,120	3,976	Stowmarket	Stow.
Combs (*a*) -	- par.	1,174	2,745	5,297	do. -	do.
Creeting Saint Peter or West	} par.	239	1,335	2,532	do. -	do.
Drinkstone -	- par.	463	2,172	3,707	Woolpit -	Thedwastre.
Elmswell -	- par.	761	2,066	4,046	do. -	Blackbourn.
Felsham (*a*) -	- par.	331	1,630	2,651	do. -	Thedwastre.
Gidding (*a*) -	- par.	102	521	876	do. -	do.
Gipping with Stowor market	} ham.	54	1,144	1,190	Stowmarket	Stow.
Great Finborough (*a*)	par.	413	1,631	2,693	do. -	do.
Harleston -	- par.	76	615	900	Woolpit -	do.
Haughley -	- par.	881	2,518	5,012	Stowmarket	do.
Hessett (*a*) -	- par.	428	1,568	2,605	Woolpit -	Thedwastre.
†Hinderclay -	- par.	306	1,458	2,322	Diss -	Blackbourn.
Hunston -	- par.	134	957	1,539	Bury St. Edmunds	do.
*Langham -	- par.	204	951	1,513	do. -	do.
Little Finborough (*a*)	par.	66	367	526	Stowmarket	Stow.
Norton - -	- par.	716	2,419	4,235	Bury St. Edmunds	Thedwastre.
Old Newton with Dagworth	} par.	685	2,348	4,824	Stowmarket	Stow.
One House (W.)	- par.	336	898	1,559	do. -	do.

(continued)

STOURBRIDGE UNION :

(*a*) By Order which came into operation on 25 March 1884,—
Certain parts of Warley Salop and Warley Wigorn, in the West Bromwich Union, were united and amalgamated with Ridgacre ;
Certain parts of Ridgacre were united with parts of other Parishes, in the West Bromwich Union, and went to form a new Parish which was added to that Union ;
Certain parts of Oldbury and Warley Wigorn, in the West Bromwich Union, were amalgamated with Cakemore.

STOW UNION :

(*a*) By Orders which came into operation on 25 March 1881,—
A detached part of Gidding known as Little Gidding was amalgamated with Felsham ;
Detached parts of Little Finborough were amalgamated with Combs and Great Finborough ;
A detached part of Bradfield Saint George, in the Thingoe Union, was amalgamated with Hessett.

Unions and Parishes, &c.	Population in 1881.	Area in Statute Acres in 1881.	Rateable Value in 1881.	Post Town.	Petty Sessional Division.
Stow Union—County of Suffolk—*continued.*			£		
Rattlesden - - par.	1,040	3,254	5,413	Woolpit - -	Thedwastre.
†Rickinghall Inferior - par.	367	1,510	3,138	Diss - -	Blackbourn.
Shelland - - par.	91	540	725	Woolpit - -	Stow.
Stowlangtoft - - par.	178	1,171	2,235	Bury St. Edmunds	Blackbourn.
Stowmarket - - par.	4,052	1,033	11,501	Stowmarket -	Stow
Stow Upland - par.	1,170	2,841	8,756	do.	do.
Thurston - - par.	695	2,200	4,188	Bury St. Edmunds	Thedwastre.
Tostock - - par.	354	915	1,955	do. - -	do.
*Walsham-le-Willows par.	1,181	2,800	5,491	do. - -	Blackbourn.
†Wattisfield - - par.	481	1,517	2,664	do. - -	do.
Wetherden - - par.	489	1,830	3,021	Stowmarket -	Stow.
Woolpit - - par.	1,034	1,877	3,786	Woolpit - -	Thedwastre.
Total of Union -	20,195	55,342	112,785		

STOW ON THE WOLD UNION.

(Formed 25 Jan. 1836 by Order dated 11 Jan. 1836.—Names of Places marked thus * as altered by Order dated 28 April 1887.)

Unions and Parishes, &c.	Population in 1881.	Area in Statute Acres in 1881.	Rateable Value in 1881.	Post Town.	Petty Sessional Division.
County of Gloucester :					
Addlestrop - - par.	165	1,285	1,935	Chipping Norton -	Stow.
Bledlington - - par.	367	1,110	2,278	do. -	do.
Bourton on Water - par.	1,157	2,282	4,817	Moreton in Marsh	do.
Broadwell - - par.	391	1,600	2,769	do. - -	do.
*Church Iccomb - par.	144	530	635	Stow on the Wold	do.
Clapton - - par.	133	783	978	Moreton in Marsh	do.
Condicote (a) - par.	169	890	1,191	Stow on the Wold	do.
Donnington - - ham.	153 { In Stow on the Wold }		1,313	Moreton in Marsh	do.
Eyford - - par.	56	1,389	1,382	do. - -	do.
Great Barrington - par.	453	2,997	3,080	Burford - -	do.
Great Rissington - par.	413	2,120	3,006	S.O., Bourton on the Water.	do.
*Iccomb - - ham.	9	440	696	Stow on the Wold	do.
Little Rissington - par.	231	1,300	1,978	S.O., Bourton on the Water.	do.
Longborough (a) - par.	572	2,770	3,910	Moreton in Marsh	do.
Lower Slaughter (b) par.	212	1,140	1,791	do. - -	do.
Lower Swell - - par.	407	1,670	2,942	Stow on the Wold	do.
Maugersbury (W.) - ham.	350 { In Stow on the Wold }		2,716	do. - -	do.
Naunton - - par.	530	3,106	3,152	Andoversford, Cheltenham.	do.
Notgrove - - par.	132	1,530	1,816	Cheltenham	do.
Oddington - - par.	502	1,660	3,103	Stow on the Wold	do.
Seizincote - - par.	51	1,413	1,417	Moreton in Marsh	do.
Stow on the Wold - par.	1,266	3,130	2,562	do. - -	do.
Upper Slaughter (b) par.	252	1,390	1,990	do. - -	do.
Upper Swell - - par.	77	1,160	1,236	Stow on the Wold	do.
Westcote - - par.	185	1,503	1,754	Chipping Norton -	do.
Wick Rissington - par.	170	1,140	1,848	Stow on the Wold	do.
County of Worcester :					
Dalesford - - par.	119	653	1,225	do. - -	do.
Evenlode - - par.	263	1,563	3,227	Moreton in Marsh	do.
Total of Union -	9,129	41,115	60,840		

Stow on the Wold Union :

(a) By Order which came into operation on 25 March 1883, a detached part of Condicote was amalgamated with Longborough:

Stow on the Wold Union—*continued.*

(b) By Provisional Order which came into operation on 25 March 1884, two detached parts of Lower Slaughter known respectively as Aston Mill and Fir Farm or Slaughter Hill Farm were amalgamated with Upper Slaughter.

Unions and Parishes, &c.	Population in 1881.	Area in Statute Acres in 1881.	Rateable Value in 1881.	Post Town.	Petty Sessional Division.

STRAND UNION.

(Formed 25 March 1836 by Order dated 22 Feb. 1836, as amended by Order dated 7 Mar. 1836. —Place marked thus * added 16 March 1868 by Order dated 13 March 1868.)

COUNTY of MIDDLESEX :

			£		
Saint Clement Danes *par.*	10,280	53	112,807	London, W.C.	Strand and Holborn.
Saint Mary-le-Strand *par.*	1,989	15	36,943	do. - -	do.
Saint Paul, Covent Garden *par.*	2,919	26	85,312	do. - -	Strand.
*Saint Martin-in-the-Fields *par.*	17,508	286	382,721	do. - -	do.
The Liberty of the Rolls —	516	12	35,453	do. -	Holborn.
The Precinct of the Savoy —	245	7	17,205	do. - -	do.
TOTAL of UNION -	33,487	399	700,441		

STRATFORD ON AVON UNION.

(Formed 30 May 1836 by Order dated 5 May 1836.)

COUNTY of GLOUCESTER :

Clifford Chambers - *par.*	378	2,500	2,792	Stratford on Avon	Campden.
Dorsington - - *par.*	94	910	1,015	do. - -	do.
Marston Sicca - *par.*	367	1,680	2,306	do. - -	do.
Preston on Stour - *par.*	273	1,990	2,454	do. - -	do.

COUNTIES of GLOUCESTER and WARWICK :

Wellford - - *par.*	684	3,550	4,249	do. - -	do.
Weston on Avon - *par.*	167	1,540	2,276	do. - -	do.

COUNTY of WARWICK :

Alveston - - *par.*	963	4,300	7,158	do. - -	Snitterfield.
Atherstone on Stour *par.*	93	1,060	1,643	do. - -	Stratford.
Bearley - *par.*	215	810	1,571	do. - -	Henley in Arden.
Beaudesert - *par.*	167	1,285	2,412	Henley-in-Arden -	do.
Billesley - *par.*	43	750	716	Alcester - -	Stratford on Avon.
Binton - *par.*	217	1,260	1,477	Stratford on Avon	do.
Charlecote (*a*) - *par.*	260	2,100	4,083	Warwick - -	Warwick.
Claverdon - *par.*	576	4,330	4,246	do. - -	Henley in Arden.
Combroke - *tow.*	216	In Kineton	1,249	do. - -	Kineton.
Compton Verney - *par.*	80	1,740	2,098	do. - -	do.
Eatington - *par.*	691	4,080	4,765	Stratford on Avon	Stratford on Avon.
Fulbrook - *par.*	86	650	1,168	Warwick - -	do.
Hampton Lucy or Bishops Hampton *par.*	408	3,050	6,392	do. - -	Snitterfield.
Kineton - *par.*	1,053	3,810	4,405	do. - -	Kineton.
Langley - *ham.*	152 {	In Claverdon }	1,390	Stratford on Avon	Henley in Arden.
Loxley - *par.*	322	1,620	1,896	Warwick - -	Snitterfield.
Luddington (*a*) *ham.*	104 {	In Old Stratford }	1,580	Stratford on Avon	Stratford on Avon.

(*continued*)

STRATFORD ON AVON UNION :

(*a*) By Orders which came into operation on 25 March 1886,—

A detached part of Old Stratford was amalgamated with Luddington :

A detached part of Wellesbourn Mountford was amalgamated with Charlecote.

Unions and Parishes, &c.	Population in 1881.	Area in Statute Acres in 1881.	Rateable Value in 1881.	Post Town.	Petty Sessional Division.

Stratford on Avon Union—County of Warwick—*continued*.

	£				
Moreton Morell - par.	259	536	1,948	Warwick - -	Warwick.
Newbold Pacy - par.	378	1,824	2,857	Leamington -	do.
Old Stratford (W.) (a) par.	4,169	6,385	21,918	Stratford on Avon	Stratford on Avon.
Preston Baggott - par.	175	1,302	2,274	Birmingham -	Henley in Arden.
Snitterfield - - par.	817	3,725	5,892	Stratford on Avon	Snitterfield.
Stratford on Avon bor.	4,079 {	In Old Stratford }	12,574	do. - -	Stratford on Avon.
Temple Grafton - par.	412	1,830	3,092	Alcester - -	do.
Wellesbourn Hastings par.	697	} 4,740 {	4,717	Warwick - -	Warwick.
Wellesbourn Mont- } ford (a) - } par.	702		4,464	do. - -	do.
Witchurch - - par.	205	1,912	2,284	Stratford on Avon	Stratford on Avon.
Wolverton - - par.	156	1,320	1,511	do. - -	Snitterfield.
Wooton Wawen - par.	2,312	8,700	15,266	Henley in Arden -	Henley in Arden.

County of Worcester :

Alderminster - - par.	493	3,167	3,403	Stratford on Avon	Shipston on Stour.
Total of Union -	22,496	78,576	145 871		

STRATTON UNION.

(Formed 28 Jan. 1837 by Order dated 3 Jan. 1837.—Places marked thus * separated from the Union on 7 Dec. 1852 by Order dated 22 Nov. 1852, and re-annexed on 8 Aug. 1853 by Order dated 22 July 1853.)

County of Cornwall :

*Jacobstow (a) - par.	428	4,554	2,460	Stratton - -	Stratton.
Kilkhampton - - par.	975	8,272	5,265	do. - -	do.
Launcells - - par.	551	6,179	4,019	do. - -	do.
Marhamchurch - par.	535	2,720	3,020	do. - -	do.
Moorwinstow - par.	810	7,956	5,202	do. - -	do.
Poughill - - par.	399	1,947	2,694	do. - -	do.
Poundstock - - par.	522	4,814	3,171	do. - -	do.
*Saint Gennys - par.	493	5,516	3,085	do. - -	Lesnewith.
Stratton (W.) - par.	1,797	2,837	6,749	do. - -	Stratton.
Week Saint Mary (a) par.	519	5,824	3,031	do. - -	do.
Whitstone - - par.	410	3,787	2,271	Holsworthy, Devon	do.
Total of Union -	7,439	54,106	40,967		

STROUD UNION.

(Formed as the North Aylesford Union on 7 Sept. 1835 by Order dated 21 Aug. 1835 ; name changed on 26 Dec. 1884 by Order dated 29 Nov. 1884.)

County of Kent :

Chalk (a) - - par.	341	1,971	5,724	Gravesend - -	North Aylesford.
Cliffe - - par.	2,245	5,696	15,002	Rochester - -	do.
Cobham - - par.	919	3,056	11,301	Gravesend - -	do.
Cuxtone - - par.	393	1,692	6,590	Rochester - -	do.
Denton - - par.	218	438	1,941	Gravesend - -	do.
Frindsbury (a) - par.	3,815	3,608	21,982	Rochester - -	North Aylesford and City of Rochester.
Halling - - par.	1,306	1,852	12,266	do. - -	do.
Higham (a) - - par.	1,344	2,074	11,094	do. - -	do.

(*continued*)

Stratton Union :

(a) By Orders which came into operation on 25 March 1884,—
A detached part of Week Saint Mary was amalgamated with Jacobstow, and a detached part of Jacobstow was amalgamated with Week Saint Mary.

Stroud Union :

(a) By Orders which came into operation on 25 March 1887,—
A detached part of Chalk was amalgamated with Higham ; and
A detached part of Frindsbury was amalgamated with Cooling, in the Hoo Union.

T t 4

Unions and Parishes, &c.	Population in 1881.	Area in Statute Acres in 1881.	Rateable Value in 1881.	Post Town.	Petty Sessional Division.
STROOD UNION—County of Kent—*continued.*			£		
Ifield - - *par.*	69	313	949	Gravesend - -	North Aylesford.
Luddesdown - - *par.*	268	1,095	2,000	do. - -	do.
Meopham - - *par.*	1,220	1,713	9,697	do. - -	do.
Northfleet - - *par.*	8,790	3,934	44,614	do - -	do.
Nursted - - *par.*	64	521	1,395	do. - -	do.
Shorne - - *par.*	879	3,234	8,324	do. - -	do.
Strood (W.) - - *par.*	5,566	1,491	22,697	Rochester -	North Aylesford and City of Rochester.
TOTAL of UNION -	27,437	37,489	175,476		
STROUD UNION.					
(Formed 2 April 1836 by Order dated 15 Feb. 1836.)					
COUNTY of GLOUCESTER :					
Avening with Nailsworth } *par.*	2,018	4,510	7,857	Stroud - -	Horsley.
Bisley (a) (b) - *par.*	5,169	7,927	14,273	do. - -	Stroud.
Cranham (b) - *par.*	384	1,859	1,767	do. - -	do.
Horsley - - *par.*	2,537	3,887	7,722	do. - -	Horsley.
King Stanley - *par.*	2,117	1,563	6,939	Stonehouse, Glos. -	Whitminster.
Leonard Stanley (a) - *par.*	775	1,189	4,148	do. - -	do.
Minchinhampton - *par.*	4,561	4,791	16,040	Stroud - -	Horsley.
Miserdine (b) - *par.*	430	2,434	3,171	Cirencester -	Stroud.
Painswick - - *par.*	4,044	5,614	17,008	Stroud - -	do.
Pitchcombe (a) - *par.*	157	278	542	do. - -	do.
Randwick (b) (c) - *par.*	1,128	604	2,860	do. - -	Whitminster.
Rodborough - *par.*	2,759	1,272	10,132	do. - -	Horsley.
Stonehouse (a) (b) - *par.*	3,251	1,786	13,996	Stonehouse. Glos. -	Whitminster.
Stroud (W.) (a) - *par.*	11,112	3,731	36,001	Stroud - -	Stroud.
Woodchester - *par.*	903	1,188	3,367	do. - -	Horsley.
TOTAL of UNION -	41,345	42,633	145,823		

STURMINSTER UNION.

(Formed 4 Dec. 1835 by Order dated 19 Nov. 1835.— Place marked thus * added 15 May 1862 by Order dated 7 May 1862.)

COUNTY of DORSET :

Caundle Stourton - *par.*	374	1,975	2,769	Blandford - -	Sturminster.
Child Okeford (a) - *par.*	846	1,752	4,343	do. - -	do.

(*continued*)

STROUD UNION :

(a) By Orders which came into operation on 25 March 1884,—
A formerly extra-parochial place known as Hayward's Field was amalgamated with Stonehouse ;
Certain detached parts of Stroud were amalgamated with Stonehouse and Bisley ;
A detached part of Leonard Stanley known as "Lorridge Farm" was amalgamated with Stinchcombe, in the Dursley Union, and another detached part was amalgamated with Alkington, in the Thornbury Union ;
A detached part of Standish, in the Wheatenhurst Union, and three detached parts of Brockthrop, in that Union, were amalgamated with Pitchcombe.

(b) By Provisional Orders which came into operation on 25 March 1885,—
Two detached parts of Bisley were amalgamated with Miserdine and Cranham ;
A detached part of Miserdine was amalgamated with Cranham ;
Four detached parts of Randwick were amalgamated with Stonehouse ;
Two parts of Randwick were amalgamated with Haresfield and Standish, in the Wheatenhurst Union.

STROUD UNION—*continued.*

(c) By Order which came into operation on 25 March 1886,—
Two detached parts of Randwick were amalgamated with Moreton Valence, in the Wheatenhurst Union.

STURMINSTER UNION :

(a) By Orders which came into operation on 25 March 1884,—
A detached part of Child Okeford was amalgamated with Okeford Fitzpaine ;
The two parts into which a parish known as Stock Gaylard was divided, were amalgamated with Lydlinch ;

(b) By Provisional Order which came into operation on 25 March 1885, a detached part of a parish, known as Belchalwell, was amalgamated with Fifehead Neville, and the remaining parts were amalgamated with Okeford Fitzpaine. (Belchalwell had in 1881, population 169, acreage 1,308, rateable value 1,836.)

Unions and Parishes, &c.	Population in 1881.	Area in Statute Acres in 1881.	Rateable Value in 1881.	Post Town.	Petty Sessional Division.
STURMINSTER UNION—County of Dorset—*continued.*			£		
Fifehead Magdalen - *par.*	144	976	2,551	Gillingham, Dorset	Sturminster.
Fifehead Neville (*b*) - *par.*	120	791	1,181	Blandford - -	do.
Hammoon - *par.*	76	677	1,761	do. - -	do.
*Hanford - *par.*	56	460	769	do. - -	do.
Haselbury Bryan - *par.*	714	2,359	4,467	do. - -	do.
Hinton Saint Mary - *par.*	296	982	2,147	do. - -	do.
Ibberton - *par.*	187	1,383	1,572	do. - -	do.
Lydlinch (*a*) - *par.*	415	3,295	5,039	do. - -	do.
Manston - *par.*	187	1,323	2,811	do. - -	do.
Marnhull - *par.*	1,396	3,751	9,211	do. - -	do.
Okeford Fitzpaine(*a*)(*b*) *par.*	602	2,633	4,127	do. - -	do.
Shilling Okeford - *par.*	566	2,223	3,374	do. - -	do.
Stalbridge - *par.*	1,816	5,681	12,256	do. - -	do.
Stoke Wake - *par.*	107	1,038	1,358	do. - -	do.
Sturminster Newton (W.) } *par.*	1,859	4,229	10,051	do. - -	do.
Woolland - *par.*	120	1,098	1,358	do. - -	do.
TOTAL of UNION -	9,881 (*b*)	36,626 (*b*)	71,445 (*b*)		
SUDBURY UNION.					
(Formed 21 Sept. 1835 by Order dated 8 Sept. 1835.— Places marked thus * added 25 Dec. 1858 by Order dated 16 Oct. 1858, and Place marked thus † added 26 Mar. 1884 by Order dated 24 Mar. 1884.)					
COUNTY of ESSEX :					
Alphamstone (*b*) - *par.*	249	1,596	2,248	Colchester -	South Hinckford.
Ballingdon - *par.*	729	850	3,074	Sudbury - -	Sudbury Borough.
Belchamp, Otten (*b*) - *par.*	335	1,771	2,590	Clare - -	North Hinckford.
Belchamp, Paul - *par.*	708	2,623	3,957	do. - -	do.
Belchamp, Walter (*b*) *par.*	617	2,190	3,830	Sudbury -	do.
Borley - *par.*	210	795	1,544	do. - -	do.
Bures (*a*) (*b*) - *ham.*	540	1,598	3,022	Colchester -	South Hinckford.
Bulmer (*b*) - *par.*	696	2,801	4,964	Sudbury -	North Hinckford.

(continued)

SUDBURY UNION :

a) By Orders which came into operation on 25 March, 1884,—
 • Certain detached parts of Assington and Stoke (near Nayland) were united with the several parts of parishes known respectively as Nayland and Wiston, otherwise Wissington, and such parts so united were formed into a separate parish to be designated Nayland with Wissington ;
 (Nayland, in 1881, had population 901, acreage 941, and rateable value 3,167*l.* ;
 Wiston, otherwise Wissington, in 1881, had population 191, acreage 1,485, and rateable value 2,405*l.* ;)
 Certain parts of Bures were amalgamated with Mount Bures, in the Lexden and Winstree Union, and parts of Mount Bures were amalgamated with Bures ;
 A detached part of Assington was amalgamated with Boxford, in the Cosford Union, and detached parts of Polstead, in that Union, were amalgamated with Stoke (near Nayland) and Assington ;
 A detached part of Cavendish was amalgamated with Clare, in the Risbridge Union.

(*b*) By Provisional Order which came into operation on 25 March 1885,—
 A detached part of Acton was amalgamated with Long Melford ;
 Detached parts of Assington were amalgamated with Great Cornard, Bures Saint Mary, and Little Cornard ;
 Detached parts of Belchamp Otten were amalgamated with Foxearth and Belchamp Walter ;
 A detached part of Bulmer was amalgamated with Twinstead ;

SUDBURY UNION—*continued.*

 Two detached parts of Chilton were amalgamated with Great Cornard ;
 Two detached parts of Glemsford were amalgamated with Cavendish and Boxted ;
 Two parts of Great Cornard were amalgamated with Little Cornard ;
 Three parts of Great Henny were amalgamated with Twinstead ;
 Certain parts of Great Waldingfield were amalgamated with Chilton, Acton, and Little Waldingfield ;
 Two detached parts of Lamarsh were amalgamated with Alphamstone and Bures ;
 Three detached parts of Liston were amalgamated with Foxearth ;
 A detached part of Middleton was amalgamated with Bulmer ;
 Certain detached parts of Newton (near Sudbury) were amalgamated with Little Cornard ;
 A detached part of Somerton was amalgamated with Boxted ;
 A detached part of Stoke (near Nayland) was amalgamated with Assington ;
 A detached part of Twinstead was amalgamated with Great Henny.

(*c*) By Orders which came into operation on 25 March 1885,—
 A detached part of Stansted was amalgamated with Shimpling ;
 Detached parts of Great Waldingfield were amalgamated with Edwardstone and Groton, in the Cosford Union :

Unions and Parishes, &c.		Population in 1881.	Area in Statute Acres in 1881.	Rateable Value in 1881.	Post Town.	Petty Sessional Division.
SUDBURY UNION—County of Essex—*continued.*				£		
Foxearth (*b*) -	par.	390	1,683	2,689	Long Melford -	North Hinckford.
Gestingthorpe -	par.	662	2,709	4,378	Halstead -	do.
Great Henny (*b*) -	par.	301	1,118	1,883	Sudbury -	South Hinckford.
Lamarsh (*b*) -	par.	274	1,268	2,250	Colchester -	do.
Liston (*b*) -	par.	123	613	1,211	Long Melford -	North Hinckford.
Little Henny -	par.	75	420	686	Sudbury -	South Hinckford.
Middleton (*b*) -	par.	165	889	1,662	do. -	do.
*North Wood -	par.	8	254	306	do. -	North Hinckford.
Pentlowe -	par.	293	1,898	2,756	Cavendish -	do.
Twinstead (*b*) -	par.	200	1,051	1,566	Sudbury -	South Hinckford.
Wickham Saint Paul	par.	354	1,225	1,991	Halstead -	do.
COUNTY of SUFFOLK :						
Acton (*b*) -	par.	579	2,811	1,085	Sudbury -	Babergh.
Alpheton -	par.	249	1,202	1,529	Long Melford -	do.
Assington (*a*) (*b*) -	par.	735	2,986	4,701	Sudbury -	do.
Boxted (*b*) -	par.	181	1,367	1,900	Bury St. Edmunds	do.
Bures, Saint Mary (*b*)	par.	868	2,516	5,381	Colchester -	do.
Cavendish (*a*) (*b*) -	par.	1,149	3,354	5,793	Cavendish -	do.
Chilton (*b*) -	par.	284	979	2,530	Sudbury -	do.
Glemsford (*b*) -	par.	2,490	2,295	6,059	Glemsford -	do.
Great Cornard (*b*) -	par.	803	1,567	3,782	Sudbury -	do.
Great Waldingfield (*b*) (*c*) -	par.	587	2,423	3,871	do. -	do.
Hartest -	par.	616	1,964	3,179	Bury St. Edmunds	do.
Hawkedon -	par.	278	1,461	1,988	Clare -	Risbridge.
Lawshall -	par.	799	2,969	3,019	Bury St. Edmunds	Babergh.
Little Cornard (*b*) -	par.	385	1,657	2,807	Sudbury -	do.
Little Waldingfield (*b*)	par.	415	1,574	2,330	do. -	do.
Long Melford (*b*) -	par.	3,293	5,185	11,669	Long Melford -	do.
†Nayland with Wissington (*a*) -	par.	—	—	—	Colchester -	do.
Newton (near Sudbury) (*b*) -	par.	442	2,197	3,397	Sudbury -	do.
*Saint Bartholomew -	par.	5	In Sudbury	272	do. -	do.
Shimpling (*c*) -	par.	491	2,698	3,337	Bury St. Edmunds	do.
Somerton (*b*) -	par.	116	1,040	1,393	do. -	do.
Stanstead (*c*) -	par.	369	1,162	1,825	Glemsford -	do.
Stoke (near Nayland) (*a*) (*b*) -	par.	1,150	5,277	8,935	Colchester -	do.
Town of Sudbury, and Liberties thereof (W.)	—	5,850	1,093	14,621	Sudbury -	Borough of Sudbury.
TOTAL of UNION -		29,063 (*a*)	77,162 (*a*)	145,919 (*a*)		
SUNDERLAND UNION.						
(Formed 13 Dec. 1836 by Order dated 17 Nov. 1836.)						
COUNTY of DURHAM :						
Bishopwearmouth (W.)	tow.	74,441	2,669	275,852	Sunderland -	Easington Ward (Sunderland Division).
Bishopwearmouth Pauns	tow.	195	6	1,772	do. -	do.
Ford -	tow.	2,631	1,029	12,231	do. -	do.
Fulwell (*a*) -	tow.	527	737	7,030	do. -	do.
Hylton -	tow.	1,533	2,593	11,558	do. -	do.
Monkwearmouth (*a*)	tow.	8,355	550	24,301	do. -	do.
Monkwearmouth Shore	tow.	17,765	287	43,565	do. -	do.
Ryhope -	tow.	6,024	1,585	26,401	do. -	do.
Southwick (*a*) -	tow.	8,178	1,013	21,231	do. -	do.
Sunderland -	par.	15,333	220	54,225	do. -	do.
Tunstall -	tow.	4,306	808	8,383	do. -	do.
TOTAL of UNION -		139,298	11,497	186,569		

SUDBURY UNION :

(*a*), (*b*), (*c*). See notes, page 357.

SUNDERLAND UNION :

(*a*) By Order which came into operation on 25 March 1887,—A detached part of Fulwell was amalgamated with

SUNDERLAND UNION—*continued.*

Hedworth, Monkton, and Jarrow, in the South Shields Union ; and

Detached parts of Monkwearmouth and Southwick were amalgamated with Harton, in the South Shields Union.

Unions and Parishes, &c.		Population in 1881.	Area in Statute Acres in 1881.	Rateable Value in 1881.	Post Town.	Petty Sessional Division.

SWAFFHAM UNION.

(Formed 1 Aug. 1835 by Order dated 16 July 1835.—Places marked thus * added 28th Sept. 1835 by Order dated 31 Aug. 1835, and place marked thus † added 14 Nov. 1836 by Order dated 20 Oct. 1836.)

COUNTY of NORFOLK:

				£		
Ashill	par.	656	2,990	5,411	Thetford	Wayland.
Beachamwell	par.	313	3,730	2,896	Swaffham	South Greenhoe.
Bodney	par.	103	2,605	1,212	Brandon	do.
*Buckenham-Tofts	par.	49	931	369	Mundford, R.S.O.	Grimshoe.
Caldecot	par.	49	930	389	Brandon	South Greenhoe.
Cockley-Cley	par.	207	1,312	1,701	Swaffham	do.
*Colvestone	par.	44	861	424	Brandon	Grimshoe.
Didlington	par.	95	1,854	1,405	do.	do.
East Bradenham	par.	326	2,340	3,820	Thetford	South Greenhoe.
Foulden	par.	459	3,395	3,522	Brandon	do.
Gooderstone	par.	187	2,781	3,218	do.	do.
Great Cressingham	par.	164	2,424	2,837	Thetford	do.
Hilborough	par.	337	3,101	2,626	Brandon	do.
Holme-Hale	par.	411	2,601	4,267	Thetford	do.
Houghton on the Hill	par.	48	601	998	Swaffham	do.
*Igburgh	par.	182	1,599	863	Mundford, R.S.O.	Grimshoe.
Langford	par.	51	1,405	793	do.	do.
Little Cressingham	par.	207	1,826	2,337	Thetford	South Greenhoe.
Narburgh	par.	435	3,545	3,792	Swaffham	do.
Narford	par.	144	2,396	1,565	do.	do.
Necton	par.	793	3,748	5,551	do.	do.
Newton (by Castle Acre)	par.	68	1,058	1,503	do.	do.
North Pickenham	par.	246	1,590	1,859	do.	do
Oxborough	par.	228	2,518	3,127	Brandon	do.
Saham Toney	par.	1,212	4,048	7,223	Thetford	Wayland.
Shingham	par.	71	935	546	Swaffham	South Greenhoe.
South Acre	par.	73	2,192	3,091	do.	do.
South Pickenham	par.	175	1,830	1,696	do.	do.
Sporle with Palgrave	par.	729	3,817	6,314	do.	do.
†Stanford	par.	169	2,608	1,155	Brandon	Grimshoe.
Swaffham (W.)	par.	3,643	7,550	16,279	Swaffham	South Greenhoe.
*Threxton	par.	80	1,097	1,109	Thetford	Wayland.
West Bradenham	par.	305	1,682	3,036	do.	South Greenhoe.
TOTAL of UNION		12,859	81,200	96,964		

SWANSEA UNION.

(Formed 23 Oct. 1836 by Order dated 1 Oct. 1836.—Places marked thus * added 25 June 1876 by Order dated 11 May 1876.)

COUNTY of GLAMORGAN:

Clase (Higher and Lower)	ham.	18,882	5,038	34,983	Swansea	Swansea Hundred and Borough of Swansea.
Llandilo Tal y Bont	par.	3,247	7,560	10,880	Llanelly	Swansea Hundred.
*Llansamlet Higher	par.	3,786	4,158	19,845	Swansea	Pontardawe.
*Llansamlet Lower	par.	4,606	2,297	15,622	do.	Swansea Hundred and Borough of Swansea.
Penderry (Higher and Lower)	ham.	2,792	5,734	9,136	do.	Swansea Hundred.
Saint John	par.	6,271	419	19,323	do.	Borough of Swansea.
Saint Thomas	ham.	5,324	440	18,020	do.	do.
Swansea (Town and Franchise (W.)	—	43,015	1,918	154,466	do.	do.
Swansea Higher and Lower (W.)	par.	7,078	4,522	19,867	do.	Swansea Hundred.
TOTAL of UNION		95,001	32,086	302,142		

Unions and Parishes, &c.		Population in 1881.	Area in Statute Acres in 1881.	Rateable Value in 1881.	Post Town.	Petty Sessional Division.

TADCASTER UNION.

(Formed 22 Feb. 1862 by Order dated 7 Feb. 1862. — Place marked thus * added 20 Feb. 1863 by Order dated 31 Jan. 1863; thus † added 6 March 1865 by Order of the same date; thus ‡ added 1 June 1865 by Order dated 6 May 1865; and places marked thus § added 21 June 1869 by Order dated 31 May 1869.)

COUNTY of YORK, West Riding:

Unions and Parishes, &c.		Population in 1881.	Area in Statute Acres in 1881.	Rateable Value in 1881. £	Post Town.	Petty Sessional Division.
Aberford - -	tow.	653	1,580	2,523	Leeds - -	Lower Skyrack.
§Acaster Selby -	tow.	115	1,573	2,580	Bolton Percy, R.S.O., Leeds.	Eastern Ainsty.
§Allerton Bywater -	tow.	1,565	945	5,328	Castleford - -	Lower Skyrack.
§Appleton Roebuck -	tow.	441	2,920	5,362	Bolton Percy, R.S.O., Leeds.	Tadcaster.
§Askham Bryan -	par.	303	1,895	3,276	York - -	Eastern Ainsty.
Austhorpe - -	tow.	313	858	4,799	Leeds - -	Lower Skyrack.
§Barkstone Ash -	tow.	358	1,164	2,699	Tadcaster - -	Upper Barkston Ash.
§Barwick-in-Elmet (a)	tow.	2,215	6,966	12,570	Leeds - -	Skyrack.
§Billorough - -	par.	199	1,447	2,664	York - -	Tadcaster.
§Bolton Percy -	tow.	244	2,341	5,594	Leeds - -	do.
‡Catterton - -	tow.	44	742	702	Tadcaster - -	do.
Colton - -	tow.	100	1,206	3,020	do. - -	do.
†East Tadcaster -	tow.	869	580	2,106	do. - -	do.
§Garforth - -	tow.	2,213	1,517	7,886	Leeds - -	Lower Skyrack.
§Great and Little Preston - -	tow.	1,526	1,037	4,301	Garforth Bridge, Leeds.	do.
Grimston - -	tow.	108	892	1,681	Tadcaster - -	Tadcaster.
*Healaugh - -	par.	237	2,770	3,510	do. - -	do.
Huddleston and Lumby - -	tow.	288	1,423	2,433	South Milford -	Upper Barkston Ash.
§Kippax - -	tow.	2,533	1,632	5,085	Leeds - -	Skyrack.
Kirkby Wharf-with-North Milford -	tow.	147	1,230	2,088	Tadcaster - -	Tadcaster.
§Kirk Fenton -	tow.	518	1,973	5,297	do. - -	Upper Barkston Ash.
Lead Hall - -	tow.	33	1,055	1,048	do. - -	do.
§Ledsham - -	tow.	271	1,968	2,196	South Milford -	do.
§Ledstone - -	tow.	221	1,986	4,656	Castleford - -	do.
Lotherton-cum-Aberford - -	tow.	443	1,094	1,701	Leeds - -	do.
§Micklefield - -	tow.	694	1,778	5,079	South Milford -	do.
Newthorpe - -	tow.	84	746	2,578	do. - -	do.
§Newton Kyme -	par.	158	1,371	3,072	Tadcaster - -	Tadcaster.
Oxton - -	tow.	46	658	1,194	do. - -	do.
Parlington - -	tow.	217	1,770	1,929	South Milford -	Lower Skyrack.
§Ryther - with - Oxendyke - -	tow.	292	2,724	4,680	Tadcaster - -	Lower Barkston Ash.
§Saxton-with-Scarthingwell - -	tow.	322	2,719	3,859	do. - -	Upper Barkston Ash.
§Sherburn - -	tow.	1,671	4,859	12,521	South Milford -	do.
§South Milford -	tow.	1,057	2,301	9,391	do. - -	do.
§Steeton - -	tow.	71	1,141	1,616	Tadcaster - -	Tadcaster.
Sturton Grange -	tow.	55	877	2,809	Garforth, Leeds -	Lower Skyrack.
Stutton-with-Huzlewood - -	tow.	346	2,795	3,898	Tadcaster - -	Tadcaster.
§Swillington - -	par.	823	2,627	8,454	Garforth Bridge, Leeds.	Lower Skyrack.
Towton - -	tow.	93	885	1,209	Tadcaster - -	Tadcaster.
§Ulleskelf - -	tow.	459	1,323	4,410	do. - -	do.
West Tadcaster (W.)	tow.	1,660	1,497	5,945	do. - -	do.
TOTAL of UNION -		23,955	72,865	167,749		

TADCASTER UNION

(a) By Order which came into operation on 25 March 1884, a detached part of Barwick-in-Elmet was amalgamated with Thorner, in the Wetherby Union.

Unions and Parishes, &c.	Population in 1881.	Area in Statute Acres in 1881.	Rateable Value in 1881.	Post Town.	Petty Sessional Division.

TAMWORTH UNION.

(Formed 25 March 1836 by Order dated 8 March 1836.—Places marked thus * added 30 March 1837 by Order dated 14 Feb. 1837. Name of Place marked thus † as altered by Order dated 23 August 1887.)

Unions and Parishes, &c.	Population in 1881.	Area in Statute Acres in 1881.	Rateable Value in 1881.	Post Town.	Petty Sessional Division.
COUNTY of DERBY :			£		
Chilcote - - *tow.*	94	1,325	2,050	Ashby-de-la-Zouch	Swadlincote.
COUNTIES of DERBY and STAFFORD :					
*Croxall - - *par.*	208	1,956	5,913	Lichfield - -	Swadlincote.
COUNTY of STAFFORD :					
*Canwell - - *par.*	38	290	927	Tamworth - -	Shenstone.
Clifton Campville - *tow.*	494	4,679	5,629	do. - -	Elford.
Drayton Bassett - *par.*	442	3,315	5,560	do. - -	Shenstone.
Edingale - - *par.*	181	900	1,301	do. - -	Elford.
Fazeley - - *tow.*	1,793	2,468	7,426	do. - -	Shenstone.
Harlaston - - *tow.*	279 { In Clifton Campville }		3,112	do. - -	Elford.
Hints - - *par.*	214	1,849	2,902	do. - -	Shenstone.
Statfold - - *par.*	61	450	781	do. - -	Elford.
Syerscourt - - *tow.*	43 { In Wigginton }		766	do. - -	do.
Thorpe Constantine - *par.*	57	953	1,830	do. - -	do.
Wigginton (W.) (a) - *tow.*	1,152	3,940	13,747	do. - -	Elford and Shenstone.
COUNTIES of STAFFORD and WARWICK :					
Tamworth - - *tow.*	4,891	200	10,900	Tamworth - -	Borough of Tamworth.
COUNTY of WARWICK :					
Amington and Stony Delph - } *tow.*	641	2,133	7,144	Tamworth - -	Atherstone.
Austrey - - *par.*	364	2,097	3,655	Atherstone -	do.
Bolehall and Glascote *tow.*	3,113	2,861	13,853	Tamworth -	do.
Kingsbury - - *par.*	1,574	9,070	19,803	do. - -	do.
Middleton - - *par.*	465	3,540	5,374	do. - -	Coleshill.
†Newton Regis (a) - *par.*	520	1,610	2,213	do. - -	Atherstone.
Seckington - - *par.*	101	806	1,370	do. - -	do.
Shuttington - - *par.*	207	980	3,442	do. - -	do.
Tamworth Castle - *lib.*	357 { In Amington and Stonydelph }		1,391	do. - -	do.
Wilnecote - - *tow.*	2,111 { In Bolehall and Glascote }		7,232	do. - -	do.
TOTAL of UNION -	19,400	45,422	128,321		

TAMWORTH UNION :

(a) By Orders which came into operation on 25 March 1887,—
All the parts of a Township known as Wigginton were amalgamated with Hopwas Hays, and the latter as so altered was designated the Parish of Wigginton ;
All the parts of a Parish known as No Man's Heath were amalgamated with Newton Regis.

Unions and Parishes, &c.		Population in 1881.	Area in Statute Acres in 1881.	Rateable Value in 1881.	Post Town.	Petty Sessional Division.

TARVIN UNION.

(Formed as the Great Boughton Union 17 May 1837 by Order dated 15 April 1837. Amended as to Place marked thus * by Order dated 16 Sept. 1844. —Place marked thus † added 25 Dec. 1861 by Order dated 11 Nov. 1861. Name of Union altered 14 Mar. by Order dated 9 Mar. 1871.)

COUNTY of CHESTER :

Unions and Parishes, &c.		Population in 1881.	Area in Statute Acres in 1881.	Rateable Value in 1881. £	Post Town.	Petty Sessional Division.
Aldersey	tow.	109	803	1,409	Handley	Broxton.
Aldford	tow	510	1,276	2,690	Chester	do.
Ashton	tow.	388	1,324	2,844	Kelsall	Eddisbury.
*Barrow	pur.	724	3,033	6,154	Chester	do.
Barton	tow.	121	530	966	Farndon	Broxton.
Broxton	tow.	521	2,131	4,374	Handley	do.
Bruen Stapleford	tow.	151	754	1,527	Tarporley	Eddisbury.
Buerton	tow.	64	673	1,140	Chester	Broxton.
Burton	tow.	70	346	714	Tarporley	Eddisbury.
Caldecott	tow.	55	631	859	Farndon	Broxton.
Carden	tow.	169	830	1,234	Malpas	do.
Chowley	tow.	39	798	1,236	Handley	do.
Churton	tow.	256	574	1,298	Chester	do.
Churton by Farndon	tow.	113	445	935	do.	do.
Churton Heath or Bruera	tow.	8	133	231	do.	do.
Clotton Hoofield	tow.	342	1,552	2,680	Huxley	Eddisbury.
Clutton	tow.	71	633	918	Handley	Broxton.
Coddington	tow.	115	1,421	2,139	do.	do.
Cotton Abbots	tow.	13	313	510	Christleton	Broxton.
Cotton Edmund's	tow.	48	600	938	do.	do.
Crewe	tow.	53	292	564	Farndon	do.
Dudden	tow.	176	662	1,341	Tarporley	Eddisbury.
Eddishall	tow.	18	479	642	do.	do.
Edgerley	tow.	7	121	182	Farndon	Broxton.
Farndon	tow.	556	1,069	2,782	Chester	do.
Foulk Stapleford	tow.	234	1,332	2,083	Hargrave	do.
Golborn Bellow	tow.	82	607	1,098	Tattenhall	do.
Golborn-David	tow.	90	660	1,098	Handley	do.
Gra.ton	tow.	—	395	428	Malpas	do.
Guilden-Sutton	par.	187	974	2,362	Chester	Chester Castle.
Handley	tow.	274	1,351	2,549	Handley	Broxton.
Harthill	par.	100	493	724	do.	do.
Hatton	tow.	143	1,465	3,453	Waverton	do.
Hockenhall	tow.	26	344	644	Tarvin	Eddisbury.
Horton	tow.	94	807	1,236	Malpas	Broxton.
Horton-cum-Peele	tow.	40	343	643	Chester	Eddisbury.
Huntington	tow.	120	1,448	1,891	do.	Chester Castle.
Huxley	tow.	236	1,555	2,593	Hargrave	Broxton.
Kelsall	tow.	638	1,241	3,149	Chester	Eddisbury.
Kingsmarsh	par.	54	858	1,233	Farndon	Broxton.
Lea Newbold	tow.	46	729	1,281	Chester	do.
Mouldsworth	tow.	183	886	1,607	do.	Eddisbury.
Newton by Tatten-hall	tow.	116	622	1,842	Tattenhall	Broxton.
†Pryors Hayes	par.	—	106	155	Tarvin	Eddisbury.
Rowton	tow.	187	591	2,117	Chester	Chester Castle.
Saighton	tow.	344	1,777	2,965	do.	do.
Stretton	tow.	97	938	1,465	Malpas	Broxton.
Tarvin	tow.	1,274	2,044	5,333	Chester	Eddisbury.
Tattenhall	tow.	1,089	2,925	7,256	do.	Broxton.
Tilston	tow.	360	799	1,706	Malpas	do.
Waverton	tow.	330	1,182	3,933	Chester	do.
Willington	par.	145	1,030	1,959	Tarporley	Eddisbury.
TOTAL of UNION		11,186	48,925	97,410		

Unions and Parishes, &c.	Population in 1881.	Area in Statute Acres in 1881.	Rateable Value in 1881.	Post Town.	Petty Sessional Division.
TAUNTON UNION.					
(Formed 12 May 1836 by Order dated 18 April 1836,—Places marked thus * added 26 March 1885 by Order dated 21 March 1885.—Names of Parishes marked thus † altered by Order dated 18 July 1885. Spelling of name marked thus § is as altered by Order dated 16 April 1887; and of name marked thus ‡ as altered by Order dated 9 August 1887.)					
COUNTY of DEVON :				£	
Churchstanton - _par._	738	4,980	5,543	Honiton - -	Honiton.
COUNTY of SOMERSET :					
Angersleigh (_a_) - _par._	36	403	849	Wellington -	Taunton.
Ash Priors (_a_) - _par._	191	635	1,252	Taunton - -	Bishop's Lydeard.
§Bickenhall (_a_) - _par._	155	1,004	1,456	do. - -	Taunton.
†Bishop's Hull (Within) (_a_) (_b_) - } _par._	—	—	—	do. - -	do.
*Bishop's Hull (Without) (_a_) (_b_) - } _par._	—	—	—	do. - -	do.
Bishop's Lydeard (_a_) _par._	1,196	4,686	11,381	do. - -	Bishop's Lydeard.
Cheddon Fitzpaine - _par._	295	960	2,754	do. - -	Taunton.
Combe Florey - - _par._	317	1,369	3,100	do. - -	Bishop's Lydeard.
Corfe (_c_) - - _par._	386	1,127	1,942	do. - -	Taunton.
Cothelstone (_a_) - _par._	133	906	1,408	do. - -	Bishop's Lydeard.
Creech Saint Michael (_a_) - } _par._	1,166	2,304	10,968	do. - -	Taunton.
Curland - - _par._	187	777	940	do. - -	do.
Durston - - _par._	222	1,022	3,548	do. - -	North Petherton.
Halse - - _par._	404	1,301	3,253	do. - -	Bishop's Lydeard.
Hatch Beauchamp (_a_) (_b_) - } _par._	359	1,120	2,748	do. - -	Ilminster.
Heathfield - - _par._	102	692	1,473	do. - -	Bishop's Lydeard.
Kingston (_a_) - _par._	942	3,477	9,570	do. - -	Taunton.

(_continued_)

TAUNTON UNION :

(_a_) By Orders which came into operation on 26 March 1884.—

Detached and nearly detached parts of Ash Priors were amalgamated with Bishop's Lydeard ;

A detached part of Bishop's Lydeard was amalgamated with Ash Priors ;

A detached part of Creech Saint Michael, known as Little Creech, was amalgamated with West Hatch ;

Two detached parts of Hatch Beauchamp were amalgamated with Bickenhall ;

A detached part of Kingston was amalgamated with Cothelstone ;

A detached part of Trull, known as "Shobley Grounds," was amalgamated with Angersleigh ;

Two detached parts of Wilton were amalgamated with Bishop's Hull ;

A detached part of Saint James was amalgamated with Kingston ;

A detached part of Saint Mary Magdalen was amalgamated with Stoke Saint Mary ;

A detached part of Bishop's Hull was amalgamated with Oake, in the Wellington Union.

(_b_) By Orders which came into operation on 25 March 1885,—

A part of Saint James outside the boundary of the Municipal Borough of Taunton was amalgamated with Staplegrove, and the remaining part outside such boundary was constituted a Separate Parish and designated Saint James (Without) ;

(Saint James had in 1881, population 7,067, acreage 1,455, and rateable value 27,867_l._) ;

All the part of Saint Mary Magdalen outside the boundary of the Municipal Borough of Taunton,

TAUNTON UNION—_continued._

was united with a part of Wilton outside such boundary, and was constituted a Separate Parish and designated Saint Mary Magdalen (Without) ;

All the part of West Monkton within the boundary of the Municipal Borough of Taunton was amalgamated with the part of Saint Mary Magdalen within the borough which it adjoined, and the parish of Saint Mary Magdalen as so altered was designated Saint Mary Magdalen (Within) ;

(Saint Mary Magdalen had in 1881, population 8,553, acreage 1,300, rateable value 34,367_l._)

All the part of Bishop's Hull outside the boundary of the Municipal Borough of Taunton, and all the part of Wilton outside such boundary, and which adjoins the part of Bishop's Hull, were united and constituted a Separate Parish and designated Bishop's Hull (Without) ;

(Bishop's Hull had in 1881, population 1,530, acreage 1,341, rateable value 11,554_l._) ;

A detached part of Broadway, in the Chard Union, was amalgamated with Hatch Beauchamp ;

Certain parts of North Curry and West Hatch were amalgamated with Stoke Saint Gregory, and certain parts of West Hatch and Stoke Saint Gregory were amalgamated with North Curry ;

A detached part of Swell, in the Langport Union, was amalgamated with Stoke Saint Gregory ;

A detached part of Hatch Beauchamp was amalgamated with Swell, in the Langport Union ;

Certain detached parts of Lyng, in the Bridgewater Union, were amalgamated with Stoke Saint Gregory.

(_c_) By Order which came into operation on 25 March 1887, a detached part of Corfe was amalgamated with Saint Mary Magdalen (Without).

Unions and Parishes, &c.		Population in 1881.	Area in Statute Acres in 1881.	Rateable Value in 1881.	Post Town.	Petty Sessional Division.
TAUNTON UNION—County of Somerset—*continued*.				£		
Lydeard Saint Lawrence	par.	525	2,697	4,522	Taunton - -	Bishop's Lydeard.
North Curry (b)	par.	1,600	5,556	15,815	do. - -	Taunton.
Norton Fitzwarren	par.	642	1,307	6,075	do. - -	do.
Orchard Portman	par.	57	635	938	do. -	do.
Otterford	par.	405	2,387	2,352	do.	do.
Pitminster	par.	1,382	5,120	12,227	Taunton -	do.
‡Ruishton	par.	467	1,003	3,793	do. -	do.
†Saint James (Within) (a) (b)	par.	—	—	—	do. - -	do.
*Saint James (Without) (a) (b)	par.	—	—	—	do. -	do.
Saint Mary Magdalen (Within) (a) (b)	par.	—	—	—	do. -	do.
*Saint Mary Magdalen (Without) (a) (b) (c)	par.	—	—	—	do. - -	do.
Staple Fitzpaine	par.	188	2,964	2,317	do. -	do.
Staplegrove (b)	par.	571	1,059	5,960	do. - -	do.
Stoke Saint Gregory (b)	par.	1,418	3,790	11,672	Taunton and Bridgewater -	do.
Stoke Saint Mary (a)	par.	229	923	2,215	Taunton -	do.
Thorn Falcon	par.	179	814	1,710	do. -	do.
Thurlbere	par.	133	949	1,199	do. -	do.
Tolland	par.	129	824	1,371	do. -	Bishop's Lydeard.
Trull (a)	par.	980	2,233	8,158	do. -	Taunton.
West Bagborough	par.	475	1,972	3,268	do. -	Bishop's Lydeard.
West Hatch (a) (b)	par.	415	1,681	2,901	do. -	Taunton.
West Monkton (b)	par.	1,027	3,079	10,884	do. -	do.
Wilton (a) (b)	par.	1,201	700	7,534	do. -	do.
TOTAL of UNION -		18,832 (b)	66,356 (b)	167,126 (b)		
TAVISTOCK UNION.						
(Formed 8 Oct. 1836 by Order dated 12 September 1836.— Place marked thus * added 24 June 1860 by Order dated 17 May 1860.)						
COUNTY of CORNWALL :						
*Calstock	par.	6,517	6,133	12,951	Tavistock - -	Callington East. Hundred of (Middle Division) :
COUNTY of DEVON :						
Beer Ferris	par.	1,898	6,838	6,906	Tavistock -	Tavistock.
Bradstone	par.	126	1,257	1,557	do. -	Lifton.
Brentor (b)	par.	130	1,212	933	Bridestowe	Tavistock.
Buckland Monachorum	par.	1,297	6,338	7,426	Plymouth -	Roborough.
Coryton (a)	par.	216	1,334	1,923	Lewdown -	Lifton.
Dunterton	par.	115	1,161	1,483	Tavistock -	do.
Kelly	par.	227	1,721	2,158	Lifton -	do.
Lamerton (b)	par.	1,155	7,232	8,688	Tavistock -	Tavistock.
Lew Trenchard (b)	par.	309	2,818	2,012	Lewdown -	Lifton.
						(*continued*)

TAUNTON UNION :

(a) (b) (c) See notes page 363.

TAVISTOCK UNION :

(a) By Orders which came into operation on 25 March 1884,—
 A detached part of Lifton, known as "Westwick," was amalgamated with Broadwood Widger, in the Launceston Union ;
 A detached part of Bridestow, known as "Longlands," in the Okehampton Union, was amalgamated with Coryton.

TAVISTOCK UNION—*continued*.

(b) By Provisional Order which came into operation on 25 March 1884,—
 A detached part of Lamerton was amalgamated with Brentor ;
 A detached part of Lew Trenchard was amalgamated with Thrushelton ;
 A detached part of Peter Tavy, known as "Sortridge," was amalgamated with Whitchurch ;
 A detached part of Tavistock, known as "Cudliptown," was amalgamated with Peter Tavy.

Unions and Parishes, &c.	Population in 1881.	Area in Statute Acres in 1881.	Rateable Value in 1881.	Post Town.	Petty Sessional Division.
TAVISTOCK UNION—County of Devon—*continued.*			£		
Lifton (a) - - par.	1,393	5,982	7,579	Launceston -	Lifton.
Lydford (including Dartmoor) par.	2,708	56,333	6,172	Bridestowe	Tavistock.
Mary Stow - par.	390	2,895	2,848	Lewdown -	Lifton.
Mary Tavy - par.	895	4,180	3,048	Tavistock -	Tavistock.
Meavy - - par.	284	3,289	1,949	Horrabridge	Roborough.
Milton Abbott - par.	880	6,617	9,300	Tavistock -	Tavistock.
Peter Tavy (b) - par.	309	3,560	2,449	do.	do.
Sampford Spiney - par.	408	1,721	1,629	Horrabridge	do.
Sheepstor - par.	90	3,595	953	do.	Roborough.
Stowford - par.	392	2,065	2,489	Lifton	Lifton.
Sydenham Damarel - par.	469	1,413	1,628	Tavistock -	Tavistock.
Tavistock (W.) (b) - par.	6,914	11,450	32,328	do.	do.
Thrushelton (b) - par.	427	3,711	2,517	Lewdown	Lifton.
Walkhampton - par.	574	10,540	3,090	Horrabridge	Roborough.
Whitchurch (b) - par.	1,067	5,979	5,371	Tavistock -	Tavistock.
TOTAL of UNION -	29,190	159,317	129,387		

TEESDALE UNION.

(Formed 18 Feb. 1837 by Order dated 24 Jan. 1837.—Names of places marked thus * are as altered by Order dated 31 Mar. 1887,)

COUNTY of DURHAM :

Barnard Castle (W.) (a) tow.	4,269	4,017	17,795	Barnard Castle -	Darlington Ward.
Cleatlam - tow.	125	1,125	1,766	Winston by Darlington.	do.
Cockfield (a) - tow.	1,205	1,765	7,263	Darlington -	do.
Egglestone (a) - tow.	747	8,073	4,000	Barnard Castle -	do.
Forest and Frith - tow.	757	17,708	4,013	Middleton in Teesdale.	do.
Gainford - tow.	897	2,346	6,721	Darlington	do.
Headlam - tow.	107	808	1,575	Gainford -	do.
Hilton - tow.	106	1,097	1,354	do. -	do.
Ingleton - tow.	246	847	1,868	Darlington	do.
*Langleydale with Shotton (a) - tow.	224	4,692	5,057	Barnard Castle -	do.
Langton - tow.	101	1,085	1,681	Gainford -	do.
Middleton (a) - tow.	2,292	10,497	13,138	Middleton -	do.
Morton Tynemouth - tow.	31	416	721	Darlington	do.

(continued)

TEESDALE UNION :

(a) By Orders which came into operation on 25 March 1884,—
A detached part of Barforth known as "Little Hutton" was amalgamated with Thorpe (in the Order termed Wycliffe) ;
A detached part of Cockfield was amalgamated with Woodland ;
Detached parts of Hunderthwaite were amalgamated with Romaldkirk ;
A detached part of Middleton was amalgamated with Holwick ;
Certain parts of Egglestone, Langleydale with Shotton, and Strenthan and Stainton, together with all the parts of Marwood (having in 1881, population 197, acreage 3,711, and rateable value 4,676l.) were amalgamated with Barnard Castle ;
A detached part of Newbiggen was amalgamated with Holwick.

Unions and Parishes, &c.		Population in 1881.	Area in Statute Acres in 1881.	Rateable Value in 1881.	Post Town.	Petty Sessional Division.
TEESDALE UNION—County of Durham—*continued.*				£		
Newbiggen (a)	tow.	616	4,660	2,417	Middleton	Darlington Ward.
*Raby with Keverstone	tow.	280	2,814	4,507	Darlington	do.
Staindrop	tow.	1,318	2,004	5,784	do.	do.
Streatlam and Stainton (a)	tow.	340	2,952	4,864	do.	do.
Wackerfield	tow.	128	751	1,399	do.	do.
Westwick	tow.	74	1,469	1,881	do.	do.
Whorlton	tow.	241	1,972	2,736	do.	do.
Winston	tow.	334	3,050	6,174	do.	do.
Woodland (a)	tow.	580	2,726	3,357	do.	do.
COUNTY of YORK, North Riding:						
Barforth (a)	tow.	135	2,027	2,779	Winston by Darlington.	Gilling, West.
Barningham	tow.	261	3,521	2,672	Barnard Castle	do.
Boldron	tow.	152	1,250	2,601	do.	do.
Bowes	tow.	672	16,958	14,090	do.	do.
Brignall	par.	131	2,116	2,468	do.	do.
Cotherstone	tow.	638	8,363	6,305	do.	do.
Egglestone Abbey	tow.	62	648	945	do.	do.
Gilmonby	tow.	108	2,472	1,816	do.	do.
Holwick (a)	tow.	231	5,788	2,533	Middleton in Teesdale.	do.
Hope	tow.	26	2,606	801	Barnard Castle	do
Hunderthwaite (a)	tow.	285	6,336	4,303	do.	do.
Hutton	tow.	182	1,305	2,072	Winston by Darlington.	do.
Lartington	tow.	206	5,436	3,881	Barnard Castle	do.
Lunedale	tow.	385	22,770	3,859	do.	do.
Mickleton	tow.	667	4,749	4,231	do.	do.
Ovington	tow.	150	520	970	Darlington	do.
Rokeby	par.	196	1,160	2,049	Barnard Castle	do.
Romaldkirk (a)	tow.	278	1,324	1,779	do.	do.
Scargil	tow.	106	5,170	2,452	do.	do.
Startforth	tow.	516	1,010	3,010	do.	do.
Thorpe (a)	par.	175	2,229	3,292	Darlington	do.
TOTAL of UNION		20,580 (a)	174,635 (a)	169,002 (a)		
TENBURY UNION. (Formed 27 Aug. 1836 by Order dated 2 Aug. 1836.)						
COUNTY of HEREFORD:						
Brimfield	par.	633	1,842	3,518	Brimfield, R.S.O., Herefordshire.	Leominster.
Little Hereford and Upton	par.	509	3,550	5,080	Tenbury	do.
Stoke Bliss	par.	164	1,148	1,557	do.	Bromyard.
COUNTY of SALOP:						
Burford (a)	tow.	128	6,672	3,756	do.	Burford.
Burraston and Watmore (a)	tow.	293	In Burford	2,096	do.	do.
Greet (a)	par.	97	1,010	1,557	do.	do.
Nash, Weston and Tilsop (a)	tow.	526	In Burford	3,183	do.	do.
Whitton (a)	tow.	88	do.	932	Tenbury as to part ; Ludlow, as to part.	do.

(*continued*)

TEESDALE UNION :
(a) See note page 365.

Unions and Parishes, &c.	Population in 1881.	Area in Statute Acres in 1881.	Rateable Value in 1881.	Post Town.	Petty Sessional Division.

TENBURY UNION—County of Hereford—continued.

COUNTY of WORCESTER:

			£		
Bockleton - - par.	220	2,737	3,017	Tenbury -	Tenbury.
Eastham (a) - - par.	337	3,846	3,260	do. - -	do.
Great Kyre - - par.	105	1,520	1,575	do. - -	do.
Hanley Child (a) - cha.	217	In Eastham	1,235	do. - -	do.
Hanley William - par.	130	1,155	1,270	do. - -	do.
Knighton on Teme with Newnham - } cha.	571 }	} 5,062	{ 1,260	do. - -	do.
Lindridge - - par.	651 }		{ 1,646	do. - -	do.
Little Kyre - - ham.	128	930	1,066	do. - -	do.
Orleton - - - cha.	89	In Eastham	892	do. - -	do.
Rochford - - par.	319	1,379	2,281	do. - -	do.
Tenbury (W.) - - par.	2,083	5,060	11,702	do. - -	do.
TOTAL of UNION -	7,588	35,941	56,716		

TENDRING UNION.

(Formed 16 Nov. 1835 by Order dated 2 Nov. 1835. — Places marked thus * added 26 Mar. 1838 by Order dated 6 Jan. 1838, and thus † added 26 Mar. 1880 by Order dated 27 Feb. 1880.)

COUNTY of ESSEX:

Alresford - - par.	259	1,436	2,121	Colchester -	Tendring.
Ardleigh - - par.	1,594	5,062	10,638	do. - -	do.
Beaumont with Moze par.	434	3,058	4,519	do. - -	do.
Bradfield - - par.	812	2,154	4,591	Manningtree -	do.
†Brightlingsea - - par.	3,311	2,873	9,852	Colchester -	Lexden and Winstree.
*Dovercourt - - par.	2,021	1,438	9,150	Harwich -	Harwich.
Elmstead - - par.	928	3,725	6,543	Colchester -	Tendring.
Frating - - par.	253	1,276	2,203	do. - -	do.
Frinton - - par.	55	469	802	do. - -	do.
Great Bentley - - par.	911	3,235	6,216	do. - -	do.
Great Bromley - - par.	724	2,996	5,705	do. - -	do.
Great Clacton - - par.	1,963	4,074	12,378	do. - -	do.
Great Holland - par.	402	2,104	3,976	do. - -	do.
Great Oakley - - par.	915	3,569	6,222	Harwich -	do.
Kirby - - par.	828	3,859	6,241	Colchester -	do.
Lawford - - par.	814	2,712	6,512	Manningtree -	do.
Little Bentley - - par.	309	2,094	3,427	Colchester -	do.
Little Bromley - - par.	374	1,841	3,189	Manningtree -	do.
Little Clacton - - par.	611	3,009	5,058	Colchester -	do
Little Holland - - par.	55	652	983	do. - -	do.
Little Oakley - - par.	320	1,218	2,034	Harwich -	do.
Manningtree - - par.	932	22	2,921	Manningtree -	do.
Mistley - - par.	1,540	2,125	7,707	do. - -	do.
Ramsey - - par.	757	4,059	7,411	Harwich -	do.
*Saint Nicholas Harwich - } par.	5,821	88	11,930	do. - -	Harwich.
Saint Osyth - - par.	1,405	8,877	13,785	Colchester -	Tendring.
Tendring (W.) - par.	848	2,874	5,231	do. - -	do.
Thorpe-le-Soken - par.	1,092	3,337	7,054	do. - -	do.

(continued)

TENBURY UNION :

(a) By Order which came into operation on 25 March 1884,—

Two detached parts of Burford were amalgamated with Greet;

A detached part of Eastham was amalgamated with Hanley Child;

Two detached parts of Nash, Weston and Tibsop, known as "Mayhill" and "Woodseaves," were amalgamated with Burraston and Watmore;

A detached part of Whitton known as "Folly Barn" was amalgamated with Greet.

Unions and Parishes, &c.		Population in 1881.	Area in Statute Acres in 1881.	Rateable Value in 1881.	Post Town.	Petty Sessional Division.
TENDRING UNION—County of Essex— *continued.*				£		
Thorrington	par.	366	1,966	2,906	Colchester - -	Tendring.
Walton-le-Soken	par.	1,371	2,146	7,646	do. -	do.
Weeley	par.	603	2,098	3,978	do.	do.
Wix - -	par.	622	3,129	6,045	Manningtree	do.
Wrabness -	par.	225	1,112	2,181	do. -	do.
TOTAL of UNION	-	33,475	84,490	191,455		
TENTERDEN UNION.						
(Formed 2 Nov. 1835 by Order dated 15 Oct. 1835.)						
COUNTY of KENT :						
Appledore	par.	648	3,007	6,041	Ashford -	Ashford.
Biddenden -	par.	1,352	7,191	7,460	Staplehurst -	Scray Lower.
High Halden -	par.	637	3,749	3,654	Ashford -	do.
Kenardington	par.	188	2,161	3,295	do. -	Ashford.
Newenden	par.	152	1,046	2,075	do. -	Scray Lower.
Old Ebony -	par.	177	2,215	4,156	Tenterden -	Tenterden Borough and Ashford.
Rolvenden	par.	1,286	5,753	8,684	Ashford -	Scray Lower.
Stone next Tenterden	par.	384	3,101	5,703	Tenterden -	Ashford.
Tenterden (W.)	par.	3,511	8,471	18,029	Ashford -	Tenterden Borough.
Wittersham -	par.	886	3,625	6,323	do. -	Ashford.
Woodchurch -	par.	1,240	7,002	8,289	do. -	do.
TOTAL of UNION	-	10,461	47,324	73,709		
TETBURY UNION.						
(Formed 31 Mar. 1836 by Order dated 13 Feb. 1836.)						
COUNTY of GLOUCESTER :						
Beverstone -	par.	190	2,360	2,544	Tetbury - -	Tetbury.
Boxwell with Leigh-terton	par.	253	2,266	2,806	Wotton-under-edge	do.
Cherington -	par.	210	1,886	2,408	Stroud -	do.
Didmarton (a) -	par.	442	2,068	3,441	Chippenham -	do.
Kingscote (a) -	par.	272	1,810	2,118	Wotton-under-edge	do.
Newington Bagpath (a) (b)	par.	207	2,131	2,291	do. -	do. -
Ozleworth -	par.	78	1,114	1,593	do. -	do.
Shipton Moyne	par.	420	2,298	3,702	Tetbury -	do.
Tetbury (W.) -	par.	3,237	4,582	13,955	do. -	do.
Weston Birt with Lasborough	par.	194	1,904	2,555	do. -	do.
COUNTY of WILTS :						
Ashley -	par.	99	946	1,216	Tetbury - -	Malmesbury.
Long Newnton -	par.	291	2,289	3,303	do. -	do.
TOTAL of UNION	-	5,893	25,648	41,935		

TETBURY UNION :

(a) By Orders which came into operation on 25 March 1883,—
    Certain detached parts of Newington Bagpath were amalgamated with Kingscote ;
    The two parts into which a parish known as Oldbury-on-the-Hill was divided were amalgamated with Didmarton ;
(b) By Provisional Order which came into operation on 25 March 1884, certain detached parts of Newington Bagpath were amalgamated with Owlpen, in the Dursley Union.

Unions and Parishes, &c.	Population in 1881.	Area in Statute Acres in 1881.	Rateable Value in 1881.	Post Town.	Petty Sessional Division.

TEWKESBURY UNION.

(Formed 16 Nov. 1835 by Order dated 31 Oct. 1835.)

COUNTY of GLOUCESTER :

			£		
Ashchurch - - *par.*	670	4,201	11,290	Tewkesbury -	Tewkesbury.
Boddington (*a*) - *par.*	412	930	3,975	Cheltenham -	Cheltenham.
Deerhurst - - *par.*	832	2,930	5,951	Tewkesbury -	Tewkesbury.
Elmstone Hardwicke *par.*	173	1,733	2,279	Cheltenham -	do.
Forthampton - - *par.*	413	2,440	1,009	Tewkesbury -	do.
Hasfield - - *par.*	246	1,160	3,338	Gloucester -	Gloucester.
Kemerton - - *par.*	484	1,590	2,909	Tewkesbury -	Tewkesbury.
Leigh - - - *par.*	337	1,720	3,267	Cheltenham -	do.
Oxenton - - *par.*	136	1,050	1,200	do. - -	do.
Stoke Orchard - *ham.*	168	1,331	2,883	do. - -	Cheltenham.
Tewkesbury (W.) - *par.*	5,100	2,619	19,371	Tewkesbury -	Borough of Tewkesbury.
Tirley - - *par.*	481	1,850	3,367	do. - -	Tewkesbury.
Tredington - - *par.*	110	870	1,855	do. - -	do.
Twyning (*b*) - - *par.*	857	3,155	6,749	do. - -	do.
Walton Cardiff - *par.*	60	650	1,146	do. - -	do.
Woolstone - - *par.*	62	787	1,355	Cheltenham -	Cheltenham.

COUNTY of WORCESTER :

Bredon - - - *par.*	1,092	3,140	9,165	Tewkesbury -	Pershore.
Chaceley - - *par.*	246	1,725	3,363	do. - -	Upton on Severn.
Conderton - - *ham.*	180 {	In Overbury }	1,107	do. - -	Pershore.
Norton by Bredon - *ham.*	210	1,100	2,483	do. - -	do.
Overbury - - *par.*	337	2,760	1,971	do. - -	do.
Pendock - - *par.*	236	1,163	1,721	do. - -	Upton on Severn.
Teddington (*a*) - *ham.*	102 {	In Overbury }	1,105	do. - -	Tewkesbury.
TOTAL of UNION -	12,094	39,204	96,159		

THAKEHAM UNION.

(Formed 14 May 1835 by Order dated 16 April 1835.—Place marked thus * added 9 Dec. 1848 by Order of that date ; Places marked thus † added 29 Sept. 1869 by Order dated 13 Aug. 1869.)

COUNTY of SUSSEX :

†Amberley - - *par.*	570	1,953	3,310	Arundel -	Arundel.
Ashington - - *par.*	253	1,288	1,426	Pulborough -	Steyning.
Coldwaltham - - *par.*	389	1,233	1,904	do. -	Petworth.
Findon - - *par.*	708	4,370	4,317	Worthing -	Steyning.
†Greatham - - *par.*	59	770	829	Pulborough -	Petworth.
Hardham - - *par.*	101	956	1,784	do. -	do.
†North Stoke - *par.*	103	929	1,041	Arundel -	Arundel.
Parham - - *par.*	88	1,281	882	Pulborough -	Petworth.
Pulborough - - *par.*	1,808	6,395	10,719	do. -	do.
*Rackham - - *ham.*	161	1,002	1,018	do. -	do.
Storrington - - *par.*	1,351	3,249	5,062	Storrington -	Steyning.
Sullington - - *par.*	200	2,218	2,010	do. -	do.
Thakeham (W.) - *par.*	539	3,000	3,085	Pulborough -	do.
Warminghurst - *par.*	97	1,105	964	do. -	do.
Washington - - *par.*	844	3,185	3,989	do. -	do.
West Chiltington - *par.*	659	4,007	3,859	do. -	Petworth.
†Wiggonholt - - *par.*	38	850	927	do. -	do.
Wiston - - *par.*	315	2,842	2,680	Steyning -	Steyning.
TOTAL of UNION -	8,285	40,636	49,806		

TEWKESBURY UNION :

(*a*) By Orders which came into operation on 25 March 1883.—

A detached part of Boddington was amalgamated with Staverton, in the Cheltenham Union ;

TEWKESBURY UNION—*continued.*

A detached part of Teddington was amalgamated with Alstone, in the Winchcomb Union.

(*b*) By Order which came into operation on 25 March 1884,—a detached part of Ripple, in the Upton-upon-Severn Union, was amalgamated with Twyning.

Unions and Parishes, &c.	Population in 1881.	Area in Statute Acres in 1881.	Rateable Value in 1881.	Post Town.	Petty Sessional Division.

THAME UNION.

(Formed 16 Sept. 1835 by Order dated 31 Aug. 1835. — Place marked thus * added 24 June 1845 by Order dated 12 June 1845 ; thus † added 25 April 1853 by Order of that date ; and thus ‡ added 22 March 1862 by Order dated 15 March 1862.)

Unions and Parishes, &c.	Population in 1881.	Area in Statute Acres in 1881.	Rateable Value in 1881.	Post Town.	Petty Sessional Division.
COUNTY of BUCKINGHAM :			£		
Brill (a) - par.	1,289	3,109	5,438	Thame - -	Ashendon.
Chilton - - par.	301	2,069	3,265	do. - -	do.
Dorton - par.	111	1,477	2,352	do. - -	do.
Long Creudon (a) - par.	1,179	3,461	5,572	do. - -	do.
Oakley (a) - par.	421	2,283	3,386	do. - -	do.
Shabbington (a) - par.	351	2,152	3,601	do. - -	do.
*Towersey - par.	342	1,380	2,137	do. - -	Aylesbury.
Worminghall - par.	303	1,510	1,593	do. - -	Ashendon.
COUNTIES of BUCKINGHAM and OXFORD :					
Ickford (a) - par.	371	1,275	2,676	Thame - -	Ashendon.
Kingsey (a) - par.	243	1,445	2,497	do. - -	Aylesbury.
COUNTY of OXFORD :					
Adwell - par.	55	443	651	Tetsworth - -	Watlington.
Albury - par.	31	674	1,263	Wheatley, Oxford -	Bullingdon.
Ascott - ham.	18	581	896	Wallingford -	do.
Aston and Kingston - par.	646	2,924	4,350	Tetsworth - -	Watlington.
‡Attington - par.	29	444	715	do. - -	Bullingdon.
Charlgrove (a) - par.	512	2,385	4,053	Wallingford -	Watlington.
†Chilworth - ham.	76	1,082	2,075	Tetsworth - -	Bullingdon.
Crowell - par.	121	996	1,002	do. - -	Watlington.
Easington (a) - par.	22	235	402	do. - -	do.
Emmington - par.	75	740	1,145	do. - -	do.
Great Haseley with Little Haseley } par.	681	3,255	5,602	do. - -	do.
Great Milton - tow.	609	1,444	2,819	do. - -	Bullingdon.
Lewknor with Post-comb (a) } par.	529	2,718	3,147	do. - -	Watlington.
Little Milton - par.	364	1,348	2,638	do. - -	Bullingdon.
Shirburn - par.	313	2,421	2,392	do. - -	Watlington.
South Weston - par.	97	485	797	do. - -	do.
Stoke Talmage - par.	106	869	1,175	do. - -	do.
Sydenham - par.	355	1,548	2,138	do. - -	do.
Tetsworth - par.	428	1,179	2,851	do. - -	Bullingdon.
Thame (W.) - par.	3,267	5,229	14,987	Thame - -	do.
Thumley - ham.	24	564	649	do. - -	do.
Tiddington (a) - ham.	178	457	978	Wheatley, Oxford -	do.
Warpsgrove - par.	19	335	615	Wallingford -	Watlington.
Waterperry - par.	167	1,936	2,734	Wheatley, Oxford -	Bullingdon.
Waterstock (a) - par.	130	678	1,456	do. - -	do.
Wheatfield (a) - par.	99	788	1,142	Tetsworth - -	Watlington.
TOTAL of UNION -	13,862	55,919	95,189		

THAME UNION :

(a) By Orders which came into operation on 25 March 1886,—

All the part of Ickford south of the River Thame was amalgamated with Waterstock ;

A detached part of Brill was amalgamated with Ludgershall, in the Aylesbury Union ;

A detached part of Long Creudon, known as "Titter-shall Wood," was amalgamated with Wotton Underwood, in the Aylesbury Union ;

A detached part of Kingsey was amalgamated with Illmire, in the Wycombe Union ;

THAME UNION—continued.

A detached part of Lewknor with Postcomb was amalgamated with Easington ;

A detached part of Shabbington, known as "Shabbington Wood," was amalgamated with Oakley ;

A detached part of Tiddington, known as "Tiddington Meadow," was amalgamated with Waterstock ;

A detached part of Wheatfield was amalgamated with Charlgrove.

Unions and Parishes, &c.	Population in 1881.	Area in Statute Acres in 1881.	Rateable Value in 1881.	Post Town.	Petty Sessional Division.

THETFORD UNION.

(Formed 23 Dec. 1835 by Order dated 8 Dec. 1835. — Places marked thus * added 22 Feb. 1836 by Order dated 29 Jan. 1836 ; place marked thus † added 24 Mar. 1862 by Order dated 20 Mar. 1862 ; and thus ‡ added 25 Mar. 1864 by Order dated 9 Mar. 1864. Names of places marked thus § are as altered by Order dated 29 July 1887.)

Unions and Parishes, &c.	Population in 1881.	Area in Statute Acres in 1881.	Rateable Value in 1881.	Post Town.	Petty Sessional Division.
COUNTY of NORFOLK :			£		
Brettenham - - par.	93	1,981	990	Thetford - -	Shropham.
§Cranwich - - par.	69	1,824	874	Brandon - -	Grimshoe.
Croxton - - par.	308	4,609	3,759	Thetford - -	do.
East Wretham - par.	173	6,442	1,702	do. - -	Shropham.
‡Feltwell Anchor - par.	47	—	121	Brandon - -	Grimshoe.
Feltwell Saint Mary and Saint Nicholas } par.	1,633	14,060	12,679	do. - -	do.
†Great and Little Snarehill } par.	52	In Rushford	896	Thetford - -	Guiltcross.
Hockwold with Wilton - - } par.	809	7,478	6,725	Brandon - -	Grimshoe.
Kilverstone - - par.	85	2,026	1,630	Thetford - -	Shropham.
Lynford - - par.	109	1,500	644	Brandon - -	Grimshoe.
Methwold - - par.	1,453	13,192	11,084	do. - -	do.
Mundford - - par.	285	2,050	1,220	do. - -	do.
Northwold - - par.	1,206	5,232	7,719	do. - -	do.
Santon - - par.	35	1,500	1,449	do. - -	do.
Sturston - - par.	66	2,000	911	Mundford - -	do.
§Thetford Saint Peter par.	1,182	2,370	7,855	Thetford - -	Borough of Thetford.
Weeting with Broomhill - - } par.	333	6,187	4,799	Brandon - -	Grimshoe.
West Toft - - par.	189	3,051	1,630	do. - -	do.
West Wretham - par.	140 {	In East Wretham }	1,466	Thetford - -	Shropham.
COUNTIES of NORFOLK and SUFFOLK :					
Brandon - - par.	2,309	6,918	8,840	Brandon - -	Lackford.
Rushford - - par.	169	6,118	1,534	Thetford - -	Guiltcross.
§Thetford Saint Cuthbert par.	1,628	306	4,296	do. - -	Borough of Thetford.
§Thetford Saint Mary (W.) - - } par.	1,222	4,620	3,976	do. - -	do.
COUNTY of SUFFOLK :					
Barnham - - par.	459	5,184	2,753	Thetford - -	Blackburn.
Barningham - - par.	421	1,586	2,817	Ixworth - -	do.
Coney Weston - par.	198	1,341	2,120	do. - -	do.
Euston (b) - - par.	234	3,659	2,825	Thetford - -	do.
Fakenham Magna (a) (b) } par.	215	2,276	2,224	Ixworth - -	do.
*Hepworth - - par.	527	1,677	3,205	Diss - -	do.
Honington - - par.	308	1,203	2,050	Ixworth - -	do.
Hopton - - par.	555	1,373	2,125	East Harling -	do.
§Knettishall - par.	76	1,024	754	do. - -	do.
Market Weston (b) - par.	294	1,083	1,673	do. - -	do.
Santon Downham - par.	101	3,860	1,165	Brandon - -	Lackford.
Sapiston - - par.	263	1,230	1,569	Ixworth - -	Blackburn.
*Thelnetham (b) - par.	384	1,773	2,815	East Harling -	do.
TOTAL of UNION -	17,630	120,733	114,894		

THETFORD UNION :

(a) By Order which came into operation on 25 March 1882, the two parts into which a Parish known as Rymer was divided were amalgamated with Fakenham Magna.

(b) By Order which came into operation on 25 March 1886,

THETFORD UNION—continued.

a detached part of Fakenham Magna, known as "Fakenham Wood," was amalgamated with Euston, and a detached part of Market Weston was amalgamated with Thelnetham.

Unions, and Parishes &c.	Population in 1881.	Area in Statute Acres in 1881.	Rateable Value in 1881.	Post Town.	Petty Sessional Division.

THINGOE UNION.

(Formed 21 Jan. 1836 by Order dated 7 Jan. 1836. — Place marked thus * added 9 Nov. 1836 by Order dated 14 Oct. 1836 ; and places marked thus † added 1 Mar. 1862 by Order dated 27 Jan. 1862. Names of places marked thus ‡ are as altered by Order dated 23 August 1887.)

COUNTY of SUFFOLK :

			£		
Ampton - - par.	97	736	799	Bury St. Edmunds	Thedwastry.
Bardwell - - par.	756	3,144	4,197	do. - -	Ixworth.
Barrow - - par.	910	2,065	4,483	do. - -	Thingoe.
Bradfield Combust (a) par.	155	818	1,311	do. - -	Thedwastry.
Bradfield Saint Clare par.	230	1,428	1,628	do. - -	do.
Bradfield Saint George (a) - } par.	443	1,984	2,952	do. - -	do.
Brockley (b) - - par.	316	1,565	2,036	do. - -	Thingoe.
Chedburgh - - par.	257	566	862	do. - -	Risbridge.
Chevington - - par.	556	2,429	3,342	do. - -	Thingoe.
†Chimney Mills - par.	8	} 2,217	40	do. - -	do.
Culford - - par.	299	}	1,679	do. - -	Blackbourn.
*Denham - - par.	143	1,267	1,804	do. - -	Risbridge.
Depden - - par.	227	1,595	2,159	do. - -	do.
Flempton - - par.	178	789	1,331	do. - -	Thingoe.
Fornham All Saints - par.	424	1,698	3,179	do. - -	do.
Fornham Saint Geneveve - - } par.	95	790	927	do. - -	Thedwastry.
Fornham Saint Martin par.	310	1,230	2,360	do. - -	do.
Great Barton - par.	819	4,030	5,481	do. - -	do.
Great Saxham - par.	239	1,428	2,226	do. - -	Thingoe.
‡Great Welnetham (a) par.	440	1,493	2,420	do. - -	Thedwastry.
†Hardwick - - par.	19	[in]Hawstead	314	do. - -	Thingoe.
Hargrave (a) - par.	420	1,108	2,339	do. - -	do.
Hawstead - par.	321	2,237	3,382	do. - -	do.
Hengrave - par.	199	1,044	1,534	do. - -	do.
Horningsheath - par.	662	2,200	3,833	do. - -	do.
Ickworth - - par.	95	1,259	1,667	do. - -	do.
Ingham - - par.	284	1,808	1,991	do. - -	Blackbourn.
Ixworth - - par.	1,004	2,248	4,437	do. - -	Ixworth.
Lackford - - par.	175	2,243	1,933	do. - -	Thingoe.
Little Saxham - par.	173	1,381	1,874	do. - -	do.
‡Little Welnetham - par.	156	592	1,005	do. - -	Thedwastry.
Livermere Magna - par.	275	1,649	1,796	do. - -	Ixworth.
Livermere Parva - par.	166	1,433	1,678	do. - -	Blackbourn.
Nowton - - par.	180	1,157	2,263	do. - -	Thingoe.
Pakenham - - par.	959	3,696	5,789	do. - -	Ixworth.
‡Rede - - par.	224	1,224	1,500	do. - -	Thingoe.
Risby - - par.	441	2,801	3,620	do. - -	do.
Rougham - par.	816	3,840	5,379	do. - -	Thedwastry.
Rushbrook - par.	135	1,060	1,547	do. - -	do.
Stanningfield (a) - par.	268	1,455	2,144	do. - -	do.
‡Stanton - - par.	842	3,251	5,286	do. - -	Ixworth.
Thorpe by Ixworth - par.	145	770	1,411	do. - -	do.
Timworth - par.	179	1,358	1,558	do. - -	Thedwastry.
Troston - par.	309	1,764	2,259	do. - -	Ixworth.
Westley - par.	160	1,216	1,938	do. - -	Thingoe.
West Stow - par.	188	2,926	1,233	do. - -	Blackbourn.
Whepstead (a) (b) - par.	625	2,670	4,084	do. - -	Thingoe.
Wordwell - - par.	44	2,299	1,047	do. - -	Blackbourn.
TOTAL of UNION -	16,386	82,461	114,387		

THINGOE UNION :

(a) By Orders which came into operation on 25 March 1884.—

  A detached part of Great Welnetham was amalgamated with Whepstead ;
  A detached part of Bradfield Combust was amalgamated with Stanningfield ;
  A detached part of Ousden, in the Newmarket Union, was amalgamated with Hargrave ;

THINGOE UNION—continued.

  A detached part of Bradfield Saint George was amalgamated with Hessett, in the Stow Union.

(b) By Provisional Order which came into operation on 25 March 1885,—

  A detached part of Brockley was amalgamated with Whepstead.

Unions and Parishes, &c.	Population in 1881.	Area in Statute Acres in 1881.	Rateable Value in 1881.	Post Town.	Petty Sessional Division.

THIRSK UNION.

(Formed 24 Feb. 1837 by Order dated 26 Jan. 1837.—Places marked thus * added 25 Aug. 1841 by Order of that date; and thus † added 29 Sept. by Order dated 22 Aug. 1859.)

COUNTY of YORK, NORTH RIDING :

Unions and Parishes, &c.	Population in 1881.	Area in Statute Acres in 1881.	Rateable Value in 1881.	Post Town.	Petty Sessional Division.
Ainderby Quernhow - *tow.*	116	532	£ 1,091	Thirsk - -	Hallikeld.
Bagby - - - *tow.*	279	1,979	4,037	do. - -	Birdforth.
Balk - - *tow.*	69	916	1,060	do. - -	do.
*Birdforth - - *tow.*	42	628	923	Easingwold	do.
Boltby (*a*) - - *tow.*	304	4,712	3,343	Thirsk - -	do.
Carlton Miniot - *tow.*	380	1,552	7,618	do. - -	do.
Catton - - *tow.*	133	842	2,319	do. - -	do.
Cowsby - - *tow.*	97	1,165	1,205	Northallerton -	do.
Dalton - - *tow.*	249	1,263	1,610	Thirsk -	do.
Elmer with Crakehall *tow.*	71	986	1,317	do. - -	do.
*Fawdington - - *tow.*	23	556	723	York -	do.
Felix Kirk - - *tow.*	113	1,190	1,798	Thirsk - -	do.
Holme - - *tow.*	51	550	1,072	do. - -	Hallikeld.
†Hood Grange - *tow.*	9	312	369	do. - -	Birdforth.
Howe - - *tow.*	49	401	681	do. - -	Hallikeld.
Hutton Sessay - *tow.*	131	739	1,147	do. - -	Birdforth.
Kepwick - - *tow.*	168	2,742	1,586	Northallerton	do.
Kilburn - - *tow.*	387	2,808	3,106	Easingwold -	do.
Kirby Knowle - *tow.*	114	1,579	1,380	Thirsk -	do.
Kirby Wisk - - *tow.*	223	1,108	2,135	do. - -	do.
Knayton - with - Bra- with *tow.*	344	1,906	3,699	do. - -	Allertonshire.
Maunby - - *tow.*	205	1,546	2,786	do. - -	Birdforth.
Newby Wisk - *tow.*	216	1,430	2,915	Northallerton -	Allertonshire.
Newsham-with- Breckenbrough *tow.*	210	1,914	6,792	Thirsk - -	Birdforth.
North Kilvington - *tow.*	87	935	1,422	do. - -	do.
Pickhill-with-Roxby - *tow.*	282	2,181	4,081	do. - -	Hallikeld.
Sand Hutton - - *tow.*	312	1,349	2,975	do. - -	Birdforth.
Sessay - - *tow.*	325	3,031	9,626	do. - -	do.
Sinderby - - *tow.*	114	559	1,583	do. - -	Hallikeld.
Skipton - - *tow.*	115	841	1,407	do. - -	Birdforth.
South Kilvington - *tow.*	261	1,083	2,157	do. - -	do.
South Otterington - *par.*	349	1,450	9,831	do. - -	do.
Sowerby - - *tow.*	1,743	2,614	12,961	do. - -	do.
Sutton-under-White- stone Cliffe *tow.*	299	1,908	2,950	do. - -	do.
Thirkleby - - *par.*	261	2,690	3,837	do. - -	do.
Thirlby (*a*) - - *tow.*	109	635	960	do. - -	do.
Thirsk (W.) - - *tow.*	3,337	3,251	18,426	do. - -	do.
Thornbrough - *tow.*	29	561	924	do. - -	do.
Thornton-le-Moor - *tow.*	335	1,527	3,092	Northallerton	do.
Thornton-le-Street - *tow.*	138	1,389	2,166	Thirsk -	do.
Topcliffe - - *tow.*	615	4,202	8,552	do. - -	do.
Upsall - - *tow.*	124	1,292	1,994	do. - -	do.
TOTAL of UNION -	12,848	64,893	146,665		

THORNBURY UNION.

(Formed 5 April 1836 by Order dated 17 Feb. 1836.)

COUNTY of GLOUCESTER :

Unions and Parishes, &c.	Population in 1881.	Area in Statute Acres in 1881.	Rateable Value in 1881.	Post Town.	Petty Sessional Division.
Alkington (*a*) - *ty.*	854	4,099	8,654	Berkeley - -	Berkeley.
Almondsbury - *par.*	2,188	7,020	13,308	Almondsbury, R.S.O., Gloucester.	Thornbury.
Alveston - - *par.*	811	2,554	4,523	Alveston, R.S.O., Gloucester.	do.
Aust (*b*) - - *ty.*	181	979	2,042	Bristol - -	do.
Berkeley - - *bor.*	870	57	2,331	Berkeley - -	Berkeley.
Brendstone - - *ty.*	145	1,228	2,347	do. - -	do.

(*continued*)

THIRSK UNION :

(*a*) By Order which came into operation on 25 March 1887, two detached parts of Boltby were amalgamated with Thirlby.

THORNBURY UNION :

(*a*) (*b*) See notes, page 371.

Unions and Parishes, &c.	Population in 1881.	Area in Statute Acres in 1881.	Rateable Value in 1881.	Post Town.	Petty Sessional Division.

THORNBURY UNION—County of Gloucester—continued.

			£		
Charfield - - *par.*	553	1,383	4,739	Gloucester - -	Wotton-under-Edge.
Cromhall Abbots and Cromhall Lygon - } *par.*	592	2,594	1,343	Falfield, R.S.O., Gloucester.	do.
Elberton - - *par.*	158	1,531	2,586	Almondsbury, R.S.O., Gloucester.	Thornbury.
Ham and Stone - *par.*	818	4,410	8,804	Berkeley - -	Berkeley.
Hamfallow - - *ty.*	1,038	2,870	6,025	do. - -	do.
Hill - - - *par.*	206	2,053	4,016	Falfield, R.S.O., Gloucester.	do.
Hinton - - *ty.*	1,313	1,914	9,005	Berkeley - -	do.
Littleton upon Severn *par.*	203	938	1,665	Thornbury - -	Thornbury.
Northwick with Red- wick - - } *ty.*	521	1,282	3,035	Bristol - -	do.
Olveston (b) - - *par.*	1,609	4,812	10,774	Almondsbury, R.S.O., Gloucester.	do.
Rangeworthy - *cha.*	247	896	1,760	do. - -	do.
Rockhampton (b) - *par.*	220	1,224	2,380	Falfield, R.S.O., Gloucester.	do.
Thornbury (W.) (b) - *bor.*	3,917	10,674	23,505	Thornbury - -	do.
Tortworth - - *par.*	199	1,578	2,632	Falfield, R.S.O., Gloucester.	Wotton-under-Edge.
Tytherington - - *par.*	445	2,236	4,304	do. - -	Thornbury.
TOTAL of UNION -	**17,088**	**56,332**	**122,778**		

THORNE UNION.

(Formed 24 July 1837 by Order dated 28 June 1837.)

COUNTY of LINCOLN :

Althorpe - - *tow.*	527	5,460	2,850	Doncaster -	West Manley.
Amcotts (b) - - *tow.*	397	In Althorpe	3,663	do. - -	do.
Belton (a) - - *par.*	1,719	8,530	12,048	do. - -	do.
Eastoft - - - *tow.*	527	In Crowle	2,569	Goole - -	do.
Epworth (a) (b) - *par.*	2,178	8,140	9,473	Doncaster -	do.
Keadby - - *tow.*	575	In Althorpe	4,184	do. - -	do.
Wroot - - *par.*	356	3,246	3,587	Rotherham -	do.

COUNTY of LINCOLN, and COUNTY of YORK, WEST RIDING :

Crowle - - *tow.*	2,826	7,350	14,270	Doncaster -	do.

COUNTY of YORK, WEST RIDING :

Fishlake (a) - - *tow.*	596	3,909	4,876	do. - -	Lower Strafforth and Tickhill.
Hatfield (a) - *tow.*	1,788	14,294	15,506	do. - -	do.
Stainforth (a) - *tow.*	782	3,483	7,601	do. - -	do.
Sykehouse (a) - *tow.*	426	4,281	5,523	Selby - -	do.
Thorne (W.) (a) - *par.*	3,484	12,409	21,095	Doncaster -	do.
TOTAL of UNION -	**16,181**	**71,101**	**107,245**		

THORNBURY UNION :

(a) By Order which came into operation on 25 March 1884,—
A detached part of Leonard Stanley, in the Stroud Union, was amalgamated with Alkington.

(b) By Order which came into operation on 25 March 1885,—
A detached part of Olveston, known as " Cote Farm," was amalgamated with Aust.
A detached part of Rockhampton was amalgamated with Thornbury.

THORNE UNION :

(a) By Order which came into operation on 25 March 1884,—
Detached parts of Stainforth were amalgamated with Fishlake, Hatfield, and Thorne.
Two detached parts of Belton were amalgamated with Epworth ;

THORNE UNION—continued.
Detached parts of Sykehouse were amalgamated with Fishlake and Thorne ;
Detached parts of Fishlake were amalgamated with Thorne ;
Detached parts of Hatfield were amalgamated with Fishlake, Thorne, and Stainforth ;
Detached parts of Thorne were amalgamated with Hatfield, Fishlake, and Stainforth ;
A detached part of Eastoft (in the Goole Union) known as Lover's Ground, was amalgamated with Thorne.

(b) By Orders which came into operation on 25 March 1885,—
A detached part of Epworth was amalgamated with Haxey, in the Gainsborough Union ;
A detached part of Luddington, in the Goole Union, was amalgamated with Amcotts.

Unions and Parishes, &c.	Population in 1881.	Area in Statute Acres in 1881.	Rateable Value in 1881.	Post Town.	Petty Sessional Division.

THRAPSTON UNION.

(Formed 30 Nov. 1835 by Order dated 13 Nov. 1835.)

COUNTY of HUNTINGDON :

			£		
Brington - - par.	169	1,190	1,212	Kimbolton -	Huntingdon.
Bythorn - - par.	256	1,503	1,951	Thrapston -	do.
Covington - - par.	149	1,290	1,751	Kimbolton -	do.
Keyston - - par.	237	2,535	3,218	Thrapston -	do.
Molesworth - - par.	211	1,710	1,707	do. -	do.
Old Weston - - par.	327	2,012	2,151	Kimbolton -	do.

COUNTY of NORTHAMPTON :

Aldwinkle Saint Peters (a) - } par.	540	2,450	3,845	Thrapston - -	Thrapston.
Brigstock - - par.	1,043	5,900	8,100	do. -	do.
Chelveston cum Caldecot - } par.	423	1,730	2,422	Higham Ferrers -	Wellingborough.
Clapton - - par.	211	1,946	1,727	Thrapston - -	Thrapston.
Denford - - par.	408	1,940	2,911	do. -	do.
Great Addington - par.	316	1,230	2,301	do. -	do.
Hargrave - - par.	356	2,400	1,879	Kimbolton -	do.
Islip - - - par.	571	1,570	4,351	Thrapston -	do.
Little Addington - par.	340	1,170	1,663	do. -	Wellingborough.
Luffwick or Lowick - par.	390	2,200	3,022	do. -	Thrapston.
Raunds - - par.	2,799	3,680	9,202	do. -	do.
Ringstead - - par.	950	1,981	1,626	do. -	do.
Slipton (a) - - par.	105	720	1,688	do. -	do.
Stanwick - - par.	653	1,830	4,077	Higham Ferrers -	Wellingborough.
Sudborough - - par.	284	1,781	2,328	Thrapston - -	Thrapston.
Thrapston (W.) - par.	1,366	990	6,446	do. -	do.
Titchmarsh - - par.	920	4,480	6,338	do. -	do
Twywell (a) - par.	501	1,400	3,035	do. -	do.
Woodford - - par.	1,500	1,750	6,427	do. -	do.
TOTAL of UNION -	15,115	51,188	88,408		

TICEHURST UNION.

(Formed 11 Sept. 1835 by Order dated 26 August 1835.)

COUNTIES of KENT and SUSSEX :

Frant - - - par.	3,481	8,991	27,889	Tunbridge Wells -	Frant.
Lamberhurst - - par.	1,866	5,479	9,226	Hawkhurst -	do.

COUNTY of SUSSEX :

Bodiham - - par.	324	1,604	2,200	Hawkhurst -	Burwash.
Burwash - - par.	2,285	7,452	9,868	do. -	do.
Etchingham (a) - par.	907	3,783	6,670	do. -	do.
Salehurst - - par.	2,133	6,565	11,120	do. -	do.
Ticehurst (W.) - par.	3,007	8,265	12,917	do. -	do.
Wadhurst - - par.	3,216	10,213	16,471	do. -	Frant.
TOTAL of UNION -	17,219	52,352	96,361		

THRAPSTON UNION :

(a) By Order which came into operation on 25 March 1885,—
    The two parts into which a parish known as Aldwinkle All Saints was divided were amalgamated with Aldwinkle Saint Peters ;
    A detached part of Twywell, known as "Curtley," was amalgamated with Slipton.

TICEHURST UNION :

(a) By Provisional Orders which came into operation on 25 March 1886,—
    A detached part of Etchingham was amalgamated with Mountfield, in the Battle Union ;
    The part of Hawkhurst (in the Cranbrook Union) situate in the County of Sussex, was amalgamated with Etchingham.

Unions and Parishes, &c.	Population in 1881.	Area in Statute Acres in 1881.	Rateable Value in 1881.	Post Town.	Petty Sessional Division.

TISBURY UNION.

(Formed 14 Oct. 1835 by Order dated 26 Sept. 1835.—Name of place marked thus * is as altered by Order dated 3 August 1887.)

COUNTY OF WILTS :

			£		
*Alvediston - - par.	236	2,531	2,256	Salisbury - -	Hindon.
Ansty (b) - - par.	293	840	1,503	do. - -	do.
Berwick Saint John (a) par.	385	3,669	3,167	do. - -	do.
Berwick Saint Leonard par.	60	970	950	do. - -	do.
Chicklade - - par.	97	1,039	1,083	do. - -	do.
Chilmark (b) - par.	551	3,154	3,018	do. - -	do.
Donhead Saint Andrew (a) par.	763	3,540	4,597	do. - -	do.
Donhead Saint Mary (a) par.	1,344	5,247	7,195	do. - -	do.
East Tisbury (b) - par.	894	7,355	5,704	do. - -	do.
Fonthill Bishop - par.	196	1,735	1,511	do. - -	do.
Fonthill Gifford - par.	478	1,961	2,338	do. - -	do.
Hindon - - par.	554	212	886	do. - -	do.
Semley - - par.	686	2,915	5,884	Shaftesbury	do.
Sutton Mandeville - par.	231	1,300	2,309	Salisbury - -	do.
Swallowcliffe - par.	291	1,344	1,734	do. - -	do.
Teffont Evias - par.	121	742	1,613	do. - -	do.
Teffont Magna - par.	292	—	1,667	do. - -	do.
Tollard Royal - par.	280	1,910	1,575	do. - -	do.
Wardour (b) - par.	755 {	In East Tisbury	4,882	do. - -	do.
West Tisbury (W.) - par.	796 {	In East Tisbury	5,865	do. - -	do.
TOTAL OF UNION -	9,306	40,491	59,737		

TIVERTON UNION.

(Formed 30 Nov. 1835 by Order dated 11 Nov. 1835.— Places marked thus * added 25 June 1836 by Order dated 30 May 1836; and place marked thus † added 25 Dec. 1858 by Order dated 22 Oct. 1858.)

COUNTY OF DEVON :

Bampton - - par.	1,858	7,785	9,270	Tiverton - -	Cullompton.
Bickleigh - - par.	233	1,835	2,491	do.	do.
Bradninch - - par.	1,705	4,351	11,131	Cullompton -	do.
Butterleigh - par.	120	479	878	do. - -	do.
Cadbury - - par.	265	1,899	2,501	Tiverton - -	do.
Cadleigh - - par.	210	2,191	2,340	do. - -	do.
*Clayhanger - par.	239	2,083	2,211	do. - -	do.
Cruwys Morchard (a) par.	608	5,766	4,628	do. - -	do.
Cullompton - - par.	2,938	7,370	19,870	Cullompton -	do.
Halberton (a) - par.	1,417	5,755	11,614	Tiverton - -	do.
†Highley Saint Mary par.	23	370	238	do. - -	do.
*Hockworthy (a) - par.	304	2,526	2,728	Wellington, Somerset	do.

(continued)

TISBURY UNION :

(a) By Order which came into operation on 25 March 1884, certain parts of Donhead Saint Andrew were amalgamated with Berwick Saint John and Donhead Saint Mary, and a detached part of Donhead Saint Mary was amalgamated with Donhead Saint Andrew.

(b) By Orders which came into operation on 25 March 1885,—

A detached part of Chilmark, known as " Chilmark Mill," was amalgamated with East Tisbury ;

A detached part of Ansty, known as " Sangers," was amalgamated with Wardour.

TIVERTON UNION :

(a) By Orders which came into operation on 25 March 1884,—

A detached part of Huntsham was amalgamated with Hockworthy ;

A detached part of Halberton, known as " the tything of Chief Lomau," was amalgamated with Uplowman ;

A detached part of Burlescombe (in the Wellington (Som.) Union), was amalgamated with Sampford Peverell ;

A detached part of Cheriton Fitzpaine, in the Crediton Union, was amalgamated with Cruwys Morchard.

(b) By Provisional Order which came into operation on 25 March 1885, the two parts into which a parish known as Calverleigh was divided were amalgamated with Loxbear.

Unions and Parishes, &c.		Population in 1881.	Area in Statute Acres in 1881.	Rateable Value in 1881.	Post Town.	Petty Sessional Division.
TIVERTON UNION—County of Devon—*continued.*				£		
Huntsham (*a*)	- par.	194	1,875	1,776	Tiverton - -	Cullompton.
Kentisbear	- par.	838	4,228	6,336	Cullompton -	do.
Loxbear (*b*) -	- par.	205	1,262	1,723	Tiverton -	do.
Oakford	- par.	496	5,161	3,407	do. - -	do.
Sampford Peverell (*a*)	par.	638	2,000	4,215	do.	do.
Silverton	- par.	1,266	4,714	11,017	Cullompton	do.
Stoodley	- par.	440	1,336	3,198	Tiverton -	do.
Templeton	- par.	158	1,895	1,215	do. - -	do.
Thorverton	- par.	922	4,036	7,317	Cullompton	do.
Tiverton (W.)	par.	10,462	17,191	43,593	Tiverton - -	Borough of Tiverton Quarter Sessions.
Uffculm	- par.	1,811	6,122	12,025	Cullompton	Cullompton.
Uplowman (*a*)	- par.	398	2,912	3,859	Tiverton - -	do.
Washfield	- par.	397	3,319	3,696	do. -	do.
Willand	- par.	337	989	4,146	Cullompton	do.
TOTAL of UNION	-	28,512	103,053	180,426		

TODMORDEN UNION.

(Formed 15 Feb. 1837 by Order dated 28 Jan. 1837.)

COUNTY of LANCASTER :

Todmorden-and- Walsden } *tow.*		9,237	7,007	41,427	Todmorden -	Middleton.

COUNTY of YORK, WEST RIDING :

Erringden	- *tow.*	1,865	3,012	13,195	Hebden Bridge	Todmorden.
Hepstonstall	- *tow.*	4,047	5,394	15,500	do. -	do.
Langfield (W.)	- *tow.*	5,063	2,784	20,265	do. - -	do.
Stansfield	- *tow.*	10,608	6,331	39,913	do. - -	do.
Wadsworth -	- *tow.*	4,707	11,224	17,025	do. - -	do.
TOTAL of UNION	-	35,527	35,752	147,355		

TONBRIDGE UNION.

(Formed 5 Nov. 1835 by Order dated 19 Oct. 1835.)

COUNTY of KENT :

Ashurst	- par.	222	900	2,102	Tunbridge Wells -	Tunbridge Wells.
Bidborough (*b*)	- par.	278	1,339	2,867	do. -	Tunbridge.
Brenchley	- par.	3,605	7,804	20,010	Staplehurst -	do.
Capel (*a*)	- par.	1,110	3,189	12,267	Tonbridge -	do.
Hadlow	- par.	2,471	5,934	17,751	do. - -	do.
Pembury	- par.	1,409	3,518	8,349	Tunbridge Wells -	Tunbridge Wells.
Speldhurst	- par.	5,042	3,990	39,148	do. -	do.
Tonbridge (W.) (*b*) -	par.	35,919	15,378	234,403	Tonbridge - -	Tonbridge and Tunbridge Wells.
COUNTIES of KENT and SUSSEX :						
Horsemonden	- par.	1,451	4,606	8,854	Staplehurst -	Cranbrook.
TOTAL of UNION	-	51,507	46,658	345,781		

TONBRIDGE UNION :

(*a*) By Order which came into operation on 25 March 1885, the three parts into which a parish, known as Tudely, was divided, were amalgamated with Capel.

(*b*) By Provisional Order which came into operation on 25 March 1886, a detached or nearly detached part of Tonbridge was amalgamated with Bidborough.

Unions and Parishes, &c.	Population in 1881.	Area in Statute Acres in 1881.	Rateable Value in 1881.	Post Town.	Petty Sessional Division.

TORRINGTON UNION.

(Formed 30 Nov. 1835 by Order dated 10 Nov. 1835.)

County of Devon:

			£		
Alverdiscot - - par.	272	2,273	1,968	Barnstaple -	Great Torrington.
Ashreigny or Rings Ashe - - } par.	675	5,663	4,049	Chumleigh - -	Chumleigh.
Beaford - - par.	790	3,203	2,641	Beaford -	Great Torrington.
Buckland Filleigh - par.	189	3,037	2,012	Highampton	do.
Dolton - - par.	750	3,553	3,843	Beaford -	do.
Dowland - - par.	159	1,735	1,201	do.	do.
Frithelstock (a) (b) - par.	559	4,382	3,230	Great Torrington -	do.
Great Torrington (W.) - } par.	3,445	3,456	8,699	do. -	do.
High Bickington (a) par.	689	4,194	3,335	Barnstaple -	do.
Huish - - par.	111	986	986	Beaford -	do.
Huntshaw - - par.	191	2,050	1,268	Bideford -	do.
Langtree (a) - par.	735	4,594	3,432	Great Torrington -	do.
Little Torrington - par.	531	2,880	3,202	do. -	do.
Merton - - par.	583	3,738	3,232	Beaford -	do.
Peters Marland (a) - par.	264	2,237	1,720	Great Torrington -	do.
Petrockstow - - par.	510	4,000	3,089	Crediton -	do.
Roborough - - par.	402	3,114	2,622	Great Torrington -	do.
Saint Giles in the Wood - } par.	906	4,827	3,974	do. -	do.
Shebbear - - par.	913	5,827	4,213	Highampton	do.
Sheepwash - - par.	415	1,971	1,951	do. -	Hatherleigh.
Wear Gifford - par.	446	1,587	2,197	Bideford -	Great Torrington.
Winkleigh - - par.	1,219	9,118	7,079	Crediton -	South Molton.
Yarnscombe (a) - par.	266	3,047	2,310	Barnstaple -	Great Torrington.
TOTAL OF UNION -	14,820	81,472	72,253		

TOTNES UNION.

(Formed 21 June 1836 by Order dated 27 May 1836.)

County of Devon :

Ashprington (a) - par.	450	2,790	6,033	Totnes -	Stanborough and Coleridge.
Berry Pomeroy - par.	1,004	4,525	9,559	do. -	do.
Brixham - par.	7,033	5,612	20,204	Brixham -	Paignton.
Buckfastleigh - par.	2,802	5,928	9,884	Buckfastleigh	Stanborough and Coleridge.
Churston Ferrers - par.	631	2,532	4,105	Brixham -	Paignton.
Cornworthy - - par.	418	2,721	3,827	Totnes -	Stanborough and Coleridge.
Dartington (a) - par.	632	3,248	7,120	Totnes -	do.
Dean Prior - par.	315	4,165	3,421	Buckfastleigh	do.
Diptford - - par.	663	4,154	5,694	Ivybridge -	do.

(continued)

TORRINGTON UNION :

(a) By Orders which came into operation on 25 March 1884,—
A detached part of Frithelstock was amalgamated with Langtree ;
A detached part of Langtree was amalgamated with Peters Marland ;
A detached part of High Bickington was amalgamated with Yarnscombe.

(b) By Provisional Orders which came into operation on 25 March 1885, detached parts of Frithelstock were amalgamated with Bulkworthy and Newton Saint Petrock, in the Bideford Union.

TOTNES UNION :

(a) By Orders which came into operation on 25 March 1884,—
A detached part of Ashprington was amalgamated with Halwell ;

TOTNES UNION—continued.

A detached part of Dartington was amalgamated with Rattery ;
A detached part of Harberton was amalgamated with Ashprington ;
A detached part of Staverton was amalgamated with Broad Hempstone, in the Newton Abbot Union ;
A detached part of Halwell was amalgamated with Blackawton, in the Kingsbridge Union ;
A detached part of Morley was amalgamated with Woodleigh, in the Kingsbridge Union ;
A nearly detached part of Ipplepen, in the Newton Abbot Union, was amalgamated with Marldon.

(b) By Orders which came into operation on 25 March 1886,—
All the part of Stoke Fleming (in the Kingsbridge Union) included in the Municipal Borough of Dartmouth, and a detached part of Townstall were amalgamated with Saint Petrox.

Unions and Parishes, &c.		Population in 1881.	Area in Statute Acres in 1881.	Rateable Value in 1881.	Post Town.	Petty Sessional Division.

Totnes Union—County of Devon—continued.

Unions and Parishes, &c.		Population in 1881.	Area in Statute Acres in 1881.	Rateable Value in 1881. £	Post Town.	Petty Sessional Division.
Dittisham - -	par.	600	3,138	4,629	Totnes -	Stanborough and Coleridge.
Halwell (a) - -	par.	347	3,666	4,430	do. - -	do.
Harberton (a) -	par.	1,384	5,735	12,420	do. - -	do.
Holne - -	par.	298	4,197	2,364	Ashburton -	Newton Abbot.
Kingswear - -	par.	488	97	1,633	Dartmouth -	Paington.
Little Hempstone -	par.	222	1,270	3,036	Totnes -	Stanborough and Coleridge.
Maridon (a) -	par.	509	2,327	5,130	do. -	Paington.
Morley (a) -	par.	106	1,187	1,386	do. -	Stanborough and Coleridge.
North Huish -	par.	350	2,662	4,682	South Brent -	do.
Paington - -	par.	4,613	5,092	27,639	Paington -	Paington.
Rattery (a) -	par.	391	2,823	4,387	Buckfastleigh -	Stanborough and Coleridge.
Saint Petrox (b) -	par.	876	75	2,530	Dartmouth -	Dartmouth.
Saint Saviour -	par.	2,340	85	5,409	do. -	do.
South Brent -	par.	1,298	9,474	11,398	South Brent -	Stanborough and Coleridge.
Staverton (a) -	par.	746	5,356	10,137	Totnes -	Newton Abbot.
Stoke Gabriel -	par.	642	3.075	5,570	do. -	Paington.
Totnes (W.) -	par.	3,525	1,043	11,597	do. -	Totnes.
Townstall (b) -	par.	2,425	1,758	8,024	Dartmouth -	Dartmouth.
Ugborough - -	par.	1,465	8,659	11,885	Ivybridge -	Ridgway.
TOTAL OF UNION -		36,574	97,911	207,933		

TOWCESTER UNION.

(Formed 20 May 1835 by Order dated 29 April 1835.)

COUNTY OF NORTHAMPTON:

Unions and Parishes, &c.		Population in 1881.	Area in Statute Acres in 1881.	Rateable Value in 1881.	Post Town.	Petty Sessional Division.
Abthorpe - -	par.	460	1,919	2,870	Towcester -	Towcester.
Adstone -	ham.	151	1,190	2,074	do. -	do.
Blakesley (a) -	par.	400	2,840	4,091	do. -	do.
Blisworth - -	par.	1,060	1,980	9,305	Blisworth, R.S.O. -	do.
Bradden - -	par.	129	1,000	1,740	Towcester -	do.
Cold Higham -	par.	359	1,660	2,594	do. - -	do.
Easton Neston with Hulcote }	par.	122	1,703	3,871	do. -	do.
Gayton - -	par.	575	1,711	10,397	Blisworth, R.S.O. -	do.
Green's Norton -	par.	872	2,490	1,630	Towcester -	do.
Litchborough -	par.	318	1,701	2,904	Weedon -	do.
Loys Weedon or Weedon Pinkney - }	par.	451	1,050	3,839	Towcester -	do.
Maidford - -	par.	270	1,930	1,781	do. -	do.
Pattishall (a) -	par.	930	2,460	5,352	do. -	do.
Plumpton - -	par.	30	1,800	1,112	do. -	do.
Shuttlehanger (a) -	ham.	403 { In Stoke Bruern }	2,110	1,963	do. -	do.
Silverstone - -	par.	1,153	2,110	3,477	do. -	do.
Slapton - -	par.	166	930	1,200	do. -	do.
Stoke Bruern (a) -	par.	458	2,560	2,318	do. -	do.
Tiffield - -	par.	245	2,530	1,999	do. -	do.
Towcester (W.) -	par.	2,834	2,790	12,001	do. -	do.
Wappenham (b) -	par.	464	2,980	3,529	do. -	do.
Whittlebury -	par.	493	2,870	4,423	do. -	do.
Woodend - -	ham.	231 { In Blakesley }		2,699	do. -	do.
TOTAL OF UNION -		12,581	42,216	90,172		

TOWCESTER UNION :

(a) By Orders which came into operation on 25 March 1893,—
A part of Stoke Bruern, known as "Stoke Meadow," was amalgamated with Shuttlehanger ;
A detached part of Pattishall was amalgamated with Blakesley.

TOWCESTER UNION—continued.

(b) In the area of this parish is included that of the hamlet of Astwell with Falcutt, in the Brackley Union.

Unions and Parishes, &c.	Population in 1881.	Area in Statute Acres in 1881.	Rateable Value in 1881.	Post Town.	Petty Sessional Division.
TOXTETH PARK TOWNSHIP.			£		
(Board of Guardians constituted 24 June 1857 by Order dated 13 May 1857.)					
COUNTY of LANCASTER:					
Toxteth Park (W.) - *tow.*	117,028	3,598	500,417	Liverpool - -	Kirkdale.
TREGARON UNION.					
(Formed 15 May 1837 by Order dated 18 April 1837.)					
COUNTY of CARDIGAN:					
Bettws Leiki - - *par.*	282	2,342	1,250	Llanio Road, R.S.O.	Penarth.
Blaen Penal or Llan Penal - *cha.*	557	4,105	1,300	Tregaron - -	do.
Caron (W.) - - *tow.*	1,731	} 39,138	2,780	do. - -	do.
Caron Uwch Clawdd or Strata Florida - *tow.*	692		5,090	Ystradmeirig R.S.O.	do.
Dothie Camddwr - *tow.*	105	7,467	500	Tregaron - -	do.
Dothie Piscottwr - *tow.*	94	7,769	450	do. - -	do.
Garth and Ystrad - *tow.*	94	853	750	Llanio Road R.S.O.	do.
Gartheli - - *cha.*	307	2,475	1,150	Talsarn R.S.O. -	do.
Gogoyan - - *tow.*	88	707	550	Llanio Road R.S.O.	do.
Gorwydd - - *tow.*	698	6,601	1,690	do. - -	do.
Gwnfil - - *tow.*	335	1,522	970	do. - -	do.
Gwnnws (Lower) (b) *tow.*	451	} 17,959	1,410	Ystradmeirig R.S.O.	Ilar.
Gwnnws (Upper) - *tow.*	679		1,710	do. - -	do.
Llanbadarn Odyn (a) *par.*	303	1,125	1,990	Llanio Road R.S.O.	Penarth.
Llanfihangel Lledrod (Lower) - - *tow.*	589	} 8,692	1,670	Aberystwyth -	Ilar.
Llanfihangel Lledrod (Upper) - - *tow.*	479		1,610	Ystradmeirig R.S.O.	do.
Llangeitho (a) - *par.*	668	2,150	1,530	Llanio Road R.S.O.	Penarth.
Llanio - - *tow.*	140	1,228	800	do. - -	do.
Nantewnlle - - *par.*	735	4,603	2,240	Talsarn R.S.O. -	do.
Prisk and Carvan - *tow.*	129	3,522	840	Llanio Road, R.S.O.	do.
Yspytty Ystrad Meiric *par.*	178	945	450	Ystradmeirig R.S.O.	do.
Yspytty Ystwith (b) *par.*	938	5,544	1,730	do. - -	do.
TOTAL of UNION -	10,272	122,050	32,460		
TRURO UNION.					Hundred of Powder :
(Formed 12 May 1837 by Order dated 17 April 1837.)					
COUNTY of CORNWALL:					
Cornelly - - *par.*	93	1,368	1,312	Grampound Road -	South Division.
Cuby - - *par.*	149	2,318	2,684	do. - -	do.
Feock - - *par.*	2,057	2,963	5,114	Truro - -	West Division.
Gerrans - - *par.*	892	2,646	4,493	Grampound Road -	South Division.
Kea - - *par.*	2,470	6,759	7,870	Truro - -	West Division.
Kenwyn - - *par.*	8,639	9,206	22,860	do. - -	do.
Ladock - - *par.*	937	5,828	5,257	Grampound Road -	do.

(*continued*)

TREGARON UNION :

(a) By Order which came into operation on 25 March 1882,—
A detached part of Llanbadarn Odyn was amalgamated with Llangeitho.
(b) By Provisional Order which came into operation on 25 March 1886,—
A detached part of Gwnnws (Lower) was amalgamated with Yspytty Ystwith.

Unions and Parishes, &c.	Population in 1881.	Area in Statute Acres in 1881.	Rateable Value in 1881.	Post Town.	Petty Sessional Division.
Truro Union—County of Cornwall— *continued.*			£		Hundred of Powder :
Lamorran - - *par.*	91	1,262	1,019	Probus R.S.O., Cornwall.	South Division.
Merther - - - *par.*	246	1,726	2,120	do.	do.
Perranzabuloe - *par.*	2,851	10,897	7,167	Truro - -	West Division.
Philleigh - - *par.*	269	2,420	2,777	Grampound Road -	South Division.
Probus - - *par.*	1,273	8,097	10,276	Probus - -	do.
Ruan Lanyhorne - *par.*	325	2,227	2,825	Grampound Road -	do.
Saint Agnes - *par.*	4,630	8,441	9,816	St. Agnes Scorrier	West Division.
Saint Allen - - *par.*	584	3,506	3,232	Truro - -	do.
Saint Anthony (in Roseland) - - } *par.*	120	753	918	Grampound Road -	South Division.
Saint Clements (W.)- *par.*	3,481	3,548	11,785	Truro - -	West Division.
Saint Erme - - *par.*	507	4,552	4,210	do. - -	do.
Saint Just (in Rose- land) } *par.*	1,447	2,650	4,572	Grampound Road -	South Division.
Saint Mary Truro - *par.*	2,766	51	9,554	Truro - -	City of Truro.
Saint Michael Pen- kevil - - } *par.*	153	1,213	1,154	Probus - {	Hundred of Powder (South Division).
Tregavethan - - *par.*	47	1,002	715	Truro - -	West Division.
Tregony - - *par.*	676	139	789	Grampound Road -	Hundred of Powder (South Division).
Veryan - - *par.*	1,270	5,716	6,787	do. -	do.
Total of Union -	**35,982**	**89,288**	**129,306**		

TYNEMOUTH UNION.

(Formed 5 Sept. 1836 by Order dated 10 Aug. 1836.)

County of Northum- berland :

Unions and Parishes, &c.	Population in 1881.	Area in Statute Acres in 1881.	Rateable Value in 1881.	Post Town.	Petty Sessional Division.
Backworth (*a*) - *tow.*	2,056	1,588	13,729	Newcastle-on-Tyne	East Castle Ward.
Bebside - - *tow.*	54	535	2,563	Morpeth - -	Bedlingtonshire.
Burradon - - *tow.*	1,110	545	3,112	Newcastle-on-Tyne	East Castle Ward.
Chirton - - *tow.*	11,248	2,285	56,997	North Shields -	do.
Cowpen - - *tow.*	10,003	1,738	27,405	Cowpen, R.S.O.	Bedlington.
Cramlington - *par.*	5,744	3,583	21,627	Cramlington, R.S.O.	West Castle Ward.
Cullercoats - *tow.*	1,365	15	3,012	Newcastle-on-Tyne	East Castle Ward.
Earsdon (*a*) - *tow.*	1,518	1,062	3,403	do. - -	do.
East Hartford - *tow.*	117	308	4,283	Cramlington, R.S.O.	Bedlington.
Hartley - - *tow.*	1,142	1,573	3,253	Newcastle-on-Tyne	East Castle Ward.
Holywell - - *tow.*	2,231	1,376	6,122	do. - -	do.
Horton - - *tow.*	2,144	2,341	15,066	Cramlington, R.S.O.	Bedlington.
Longbenton - *par.*	19,136	8,981	80,593	Newcastle-on-Tyne	West Castle Ward.
Monkseaton (*a*) - *tow.*	450	1,125	6,989	do. - -	East Castle Ward.
Murton (*a*) - *tow.*	446	684	1,656	do. - -	do.
Newsham and South Blyth - - } *tow.*	2,831	1,226	10,042	Blyth - -	Bedlington.
North Shields - *tow.*	7,250	36	18,435	North Shields -	East Castle Ward.
Preston - - *tow.*	1,707	778	9,839	do. - -	do.
Seaton Delaval - *tow.*	3,801	2,653	15,847	Newcastle-on-Tyne	do.
Seghill - - *tow.*	2,131	1,425	10,173	do. - -	do.
Tynemouth (W.) - *tow.*	22,518	1,189	79,131	North Shields -	East Castle Ward.
Wallsend - - *par.*	15,737	2,530	52,098	Newcastle-on-Tyne	do.
West Hartford - *tow.*	78	519	543	Cramlington, R.S.O.	Bedlington.
Whitley (*a*) - *tow.*	1,350	540	10,440	Newcastle-on-Tyne	East Castle Ward.
Total of Union -	**114,197**	**38,635**	**456,358**		

Tynemouth Union :

(*a*) By Orders which came into operation on 25 March 1882,—

  Detached parts of Backworth, Earsdon, Monkseaton, and Whitley were united and amalgamated with Murton ;

  Detached parts of Monkseaton and Whitley were amalgamated with Backworth and Earsdon.

Z z

Unions and Parishes, &c.	Population in 1881.	Area in Statute Acres in 1881.	Rateable Value in 1881.	Post Town.	Petty Sessional Division.

UCKFIELD UNION.

(Formed 25 March 1835 by Order dated 17 Feb. 1835.)

COUNTY of SUSSEX :

Unions and Parishes, &c.	Population in 1881.	Area in Statute Acres in 1881.	Rateable Value in 1881.	Post Town.	Petty Sessional Division.
Buxted - - par.	1,934	8,961	9,220	Uckfield - -	Uckfield.
East Hoathley - par.	857	2,622	3,230	Hawkhurst	do.
Fletching - - par.	2,213	8,522	8,816	Uckfield -	do.
Framfield - - par.	1,527	6,468	7,885	Hawkhurst	do.
Isfield - - par.	451	1,895	2,945	Uckfield -	do.
Little Horsted - - par.	300	2,384	2,639	do. -	do.
Maresfield - - par.	2,082	8,132	7,025	do. - -	do.
Mayfield - - par.	2,912	13,668	14,979	Hawkhurst -	Frant.
Rotherfield - - par.	4,334	14,731	16,143	Tunbridge Wells -	do.
Uckfield (W.) - par.	2,146	1,760	8,478	Uckfield - -	Uckfield.
Waldron - - par.	1,342	6,243	6,264	Hawkhurst	do.
TOTAL of UNION -	**20,098**	**75,386**	**87,644**		

ULVERSTONE UNION.

(Formed 26 Aug. 1836 by Order dated 2 Aug. 1836. — Place marked thus * added 29 Sept. 1858 by Order dated 31 Aug. 1858.)

COUNTY of LANCASTER :

Unions and Parishes, &c.	Population in 1881.	Area in Statute Acres in 1881.	Rateable Value in 1881.	Post Town.	Petty Sessional Division.
Adingham - - par.	1,152	4,812	10,052	Ulverstone - -	Lonsdale, North.
*Angerton - - par.	32	2,195	832	Broughton in Furness.	do.
Blawith - - tow.	158	2,995	1,392	Ulverstone -	do.
Cartmel Fell (a) - tow.	293	4,958	3,404	do. -	do.
Church Coniston - tow.	965	7,424	3,182	Ambleside - -	Hawkshead.
Claife - - tow.	547	4,579	5,143	do. - -	do.
Colton - - par.	1,783	14,322	12,705	Ulverstone -	Lonsdale, North.
Dalton - - tow.	13,339	7,223	130,656	Dalton in Furness -	do.
Dunnerdale with Seathwaite } tow.	299	10,258	2,551	Broughton in Furness.	do.
East Broughton (a) - tow.	1,251	3,425	11,339	Carnforth - -	do.
Egton with Newland tow.	998	3,661	7,884	Ulverstone -	do.
Hawkshead and Monk Coniston with Skelwith } tow.	1,205	10,129	9,687	Ambleside - -	Hawkshead.
Kirkby Ireleth - tow.	1,722	9,702	10,942	Broughton in Furness.	Lonsdale, North.
Lower Allithwaite (a) tow.	975	3,211	8,715	Carnforth - -	do.
Lower Holker (a) - tow.	1,093	2,387	7,225	do. - -	do.
Lowick - - tow.	376	2,261	2,496	Ulverstone -	do.
Mansriggs - - tow.	64	569	844	do. - -	do.
Osmotherly - - tow.	474	1,929	3,699	do. - -	do.
Pennington - - par.	1,698	2,845	29,345	do. - -	do.
Satterthwaite - - tow.	452	7,322	3,166	do. - -	Hawkshead.
Staveley (a) - - tow.	426	4,199	4,053	do. - -	Lonsdale, North.
Subberthwaite - tow.	149	1,237	962	do. - -	do.
Torver - - tow.	202	3,816	1,380	Ambleside - -	do.
Ulverstone (W.) - tow.	10,008	3,120	41,836	Ulverstone -	do.
Upper Allithwaite (a) tow.	713	2,682	4,390	Carnforth -	do.
Upper Holker (a) - tow.	849	7,140	8,293	do. - -	do.
Urswick - - par.	1,287	4,043	11,268	Ulverstone -	do.
West Broughton - tow.	1,171	7,298	9,095	Broughton in Furness.	do.
TOTAL of UNION -	**43,681**	**140,042 (b)**	**316,536**		

ULVERSTONE UNION :

(a) By Orders which came into operation on 25 March 1884, changes were made in the areas of Cartmel Fell, East Broughton, Lower Allithwaite, Lower Holker, Staveley, Upper Allithwaite, and Upper Holker.

(b) There are certain reclaimed and common lands in the Union comprising in the whole 1,082 acres.

Unions and Parishes, &c.	Population in 1881.	Area in Statute Acres in 1881.	Rateable Value in 1881.	Post Town.	Petty Sessional Division.

UPPINGHAM UNION.

(Formed 23 April 1836 by Order
dated 8 April 1836. — Place
marked this * added 25 Dec.
1861 by Order dated 18 Oct.
1861.)

COUNTY of LEICESTER :

			£		
Blaston - - *par.*	114	1,267	2,068	Uppingham - -	East Norton.
Bringhurst - - *tow.*	73	⎫	1,032	Leicester - -	do.
Drayton - - *tow.*	137	⎬ 3,650	1,298	do. - -	do.
Easton Magna - *tow.*	540	⎭	4,606	do. - -	do.
Hallaton - - *par.*	716	2,360	5,814	Uppingham - -	do.
Holt - - - *tow.*	88	⎰ In Medbourne ⎱	2,070	Market Harborough	do.
Horninghold - *par.*	126	1,205	1,898	Uppingham - -	do.
Medbourne - - *tow.*	556	2,560	3,465	Market Harborough	Market Harborough.
Slawston - - *par.*	184	1,510	2,843	do. - -	do.
Stockerston (*a*) - *par.*	56	973	1,497	Uppingham - -	East Norton.

COUNTY of NORTHAMPTON :

Fineshade (*a*) - *par.*	64	840	888	Wansford - -	Oundle.
Gretton (*a*) - *par.*	835	4,450	8,308	Kettering - -	Kettering.
Harringworth - *par.*	364	3,060	6,324	Stamford - -	Oundle.
Laxton - - *par.*	100	1,370	1,552	do. - -	do.
Rockingham - *par.*	227	890	1,740	Leicester - -	Kettering.
Wakerly - - *par.*	223	2,130	2,292	Stamford - -	Oundle.

COUNTY of RUTLAND :

Ayston - - *par.*	108	897	1,507	Uppingham - -	Rutlandshire.
Barrowden - - *par.*	600	2,073	3,131	Stamford - -	do.
*Beaumont Chase (*a*) - *par.*	32	—	295	Uppingham - -	do.
Belton - - *par.*	375	2,380	2,352	do. - -	do.
Bisbrooke - - *par.*	268	720	2,199	do. - -	do.
Caldecott - - *par.*	297	1,440	2,393	Leicester - -	do.
Glaston - - *par.*	220	1,145	3,431	Uppingham - -	do.
Lyddington (*a*) - *par.*	546	2,020	4,458	do. - -	do.
Morcot - - *par.*	480	1,343	2,871	do. - -	do.
North Luffenham - *par.*	452	1,999	3,827	Stamford - -	do.
Pilton - - *par.*	58	332	935	Uppingham - -	do.
Preston - - *par.*	273	980	2,484	do. - -	do.
Ridlington - - *par.*	234	2,027	3,106	do. - -	do.
Seaton - - *tow.*	319	2,050	3,675	Stamford - -	do.
South Luffenham - *par.*	344	1,417	2,520	do. - -	do.
Stoke Dry (*a*) - *tow.*	65	1,424	2,593	Uppingham - -	do.
Thorpe by Water (*a*) *ham.*	63	In Seaton	1,006	do. - -	do.
Uppingham (W.) (*a*) *par.*	2,549	1,210	9,385	do. - -	do.
Wardley - - *par.*	48	1,550	989	do. - -	do.
Wing - - *par.*	320	1,050	3,088	Oakham - -	do.

| TOTAL of UNION - | 12,029 | 52,322 | 103,920 | | |

UPPINGHAM UNION :

(*a*) By Orders which came into operation on 25 March
1885,—
  All that portion of Stoke Dry which was situate in
  the County of Leicester, and contained in 1881
  population 5, acreage 540, and rateable value 936*l.*,
  was amalgamated with Stockerston ;
  All that portion of Thorpe by Water which was situate
  in the County of Northampton was amalgamated
  with Gretton ;
  A detached part of Thorpe by Water was amalgamated with Lyddington ;

UPPINGHAM UNION—*continued.*

A detached part of Uppingham, known as "Preston
Leys" and "Preston Leys Plantation," was amalgamated with Beaumont Chase ;

A detached part of Fineshade, known as "Britain
Sale," was amalgamated with Blatherwick, in the
Oundle Union ;

A detached part of Uppingham was amalgamated with
Beaumont Chase.

Unions and Parishes, &c.	Population in 1881.	Area in Statute Acres in 1881.	Rateable Value in 1881.	Post Town.	Petty Sessional Division.
UPTON UPON SEVERN UNION.					
(Formed 16 Nov. 1835 by Order dated 29 Oct. 1835.)					
COUNTY of WORCESTER:			£		
Berrow - par.	373	2,180	2,780	Ledbury	Upton.
Birtsmorton - par.	289	1,268	1,907	Tewkesbury	do.
Bushley - par.	273	1,740	3,028	do.	do.
Castlemorton - par.	747	3,656	4,603	do.	do.
Croome D'Abitot - par.	182	1,148	1,755	Severn Stoke, Worcester.	do.
Earl's Croome (a) - par.	213	1,141	2,148	do.	do.
Eldersfield - par.	399	3,307	5,624	Tewkesbury	do.
Great Malvern (a) - par.	7,934	5,021	59,691	Great Malvern	Malvern.
Hanley Castle - par.	2,265	5,630	17,743	Worcester	Upton.
Hill Croome - par.	197	982	1,412	Severn Stoke, Worcester.	do.
Holdfast - ham.	77 { In Queenhill }		883	Upton upon Severn	do.
Kempsey - par.	1,447	3,105	8,585	Worcester	Worcester.
Little Malvern - par.	107	943	942	Malvern Wells	Malvern.
Longdon - par.	528	3,903	5,613	Tewkesbury	Upton.
Madresfield (a) - par.	264	1,192	2,021	Great Malvern	Malvern.
Newland - cha.	223 { In Great Malvern }		2,112	do.	do.
Powick - par.	2,635	5,194	10,784	Worcester	Worcester.
Queenhill - ham.	107	1,380	915	Tewkesbury	Upton.
Ripple (a) - par.	722	2,760	4,959	do.	do.
Severn Stoke - par.	693	3,269	6,001	Severn Stoke, Worcester.	do.
Upton upon Severn (W.) } par.	2,485	3,170	10,606	Upton upon Severn	do.
Welland - par.	874	2,027	4,191	Malvern Wells	do.
TOTAL of UNION	23,234	53,016	158,333		
UTTOXETER UNION.					
(Formed 29 May 1837 by Order dated 2 May 1837.—Places marked thus * added 14 June 1838 by Order dated 19 May 1838; thus † added 28 Feb. 1844 by Order of that date; and thus ‡ added 3 Feb. 1845 by Order of that date. Spelling of names of places marked thus § is as altered by Order dated 17 Sept. 1887.)					
COUNTY of DERBY:					
Boylstone - par.	224	1,361	2,640	Derby	Appletree.
†Cubley - par.	300	2,388	3,302	do.	do.
Doveridge - par.	696	4,377	10,094	do.	do.
‡Marston Montgomery par.	379	2,175	3,974	do.	do.
‡Norbury - par.	399	2,298	4,369	Ashbourne	do.
Somersall Herbert - par.	107	715	1,266	Derby	do.
Sudbury - par.	522	3,702	6,870	do.	do.
COUNTY of STAFFORD:					
Abbots Bromley - par.	1,460	9,391	11,771	Rugeley	Pire Hill.
*Blithfield - par.	299	3,219	5,408	do.	do.
§Bramshall - par.	142	1,328	2,081	Uttoxeter	Totmonslow South.
Crozden (a) - par.	181	2,644	2,781	do.	do.
Draycott in the Clay tow.	451 { In Murchington }		4,097	Sudbury, Derby	Offlow.

(continued)

UPTON UPON SEVERN UNION:
(a) By Orders which came into operation on 25 March 1881.—
Certain parts of Madresfield were amalgamated with Great Malvern;

UPTON UPON SEVERN UNION—*continued.*
Detached parts of Ripple were amalgamated with Earl's Croome, and with Twyning, in the Tewkesbury Union.

Unions and Parishes, &c.		Population in 1881.	Area in Statute Acres in 1881.	Rateable Value in 1881.	Post Town.	Petty Sessional Division.
UTTOXETER UNION—County of Stafford—*continued.*				£		
*Field -	- *tow.*	71	983	1,262	Uttoxeter -	Totmonslow South.
§Gratwich	- *par.*	72	865	1,143	do. - -	do.
Kingston -	- *par.*	280	2,009	2,659	do. -	do.
Leigh -	- *par.*	866	6,223	9,245	Stoke on Trent -	do.
Marchington	- *tow.*	453	6,155	4,750	Uttoxeter -	Offlow North.
Marchington Wood-lands }	*tow.*	319 {	In Marchington	} 3,876	do. - -	do.
Newborough -	- *tow.*	651	2,762	4,412	Derby -	Offlow.
Rocester -	- *par.*	1,220	2,623	8,060	Uttoxeter -	Totmonslow South.
Uttoxeter (W.)	- *par.*	4,981	8,973	26,976	do. - -	do.
TOTAL of UNION	-	14,073	64,491	121,036		
UXBRIDGE UNION.						
(Formed 29 June 1836 by Order dated 3 June 1836 as amended by Order dated 16 June 1836. * By Order dated 3 August 1883, the main part of Cowley was constituted a Separate Parish and added to the Union.)						
COUNTY of MIDDLESEX :						
*Cowley -	- *par.*	498	306	2,450	Uxbridge -	Uxbridge.
Harefield -	- *par.*	1,503	4,621	10,859	do. -	do.
Hayes -	- *par.*	2,891	3,311	14,710	do. - -	do.
Hillingdon (W.)	- *par.*	9,295	4.845	40,163	do. - -	do.
Ickenham -	- *par.*	376	1,458	3,076	do. -	do.
Northolt (*a*) -	- *par.*	495	2,230	5,370	Southall -	do.
Norwood -	- *pre.*	6,681	2,461	26,734	do. -	Brentford.
Ruislip -	- *par.*	1,455	6,585	12,309	Uxbridge	Uxbridge.
Uxbridge -	- *tow.*	3,346	99	13,194	do. - -	do.
West Drayton	- *par.*	1,009	878	5,827	do. - -	do.
TOTAL of UNION	-	27,550	26,794	134,692		
WAKEFIELD UNION.						
(Formed 10 Feb. 1837 by Order dated 21 Jan. 1837.— Places marked thus * added 14 March 1850 by Order dated 28 Jan. 1850 ; thus † added 24 June 1861 by Order dated 7 June 1861 ; thus ‡ added 1 July 1861 by Order dated 17 June 1861 ; thus § added 25 Dec. 1861 by Order dated 4 Oct. 1861 ; and places marked thus ‖ added 21 June 1869 by Order dated 31 May 1869.)						
COUNTY of YORK, WEST RIDING :						
‖Altofts -	- *tow.*	3,172	1,837	24,173	Normanton -	Abrigg Lower.
Alverthorpe and Thornes (*a*) }	- *tow.*	10,486	3,345	40,926	Wakefield - -	do.
Ardsley East	- *par.*	2,595	1,818	15,340	do. - -	do.
Ardsley West	- *par.*	3,471	2,327	12,429	do. - -	do.
Bretton West -	- *tow.*	350	2,098	2,923	do. -	Staincross Lower.
*Chevet -	- *tow.*	96	839	1,815	do. - -	do.
Crigglestone -	- *tow.*	2,777	3,130	12,964	do. - -	Agbrigg Lower.
						(*continued*)

UTTOXETER UNION :

(*a*) By Order which came into operation on 25 March 1886, certain detached parts of Croxden were united with parts of other Parishes to form the Parish of Calton, in the Ashbourne Union.

UXBRIDGE UNION :

(*a*) By Order which came into operation on 25 March 1887, a detached part of Northolt was amalgamated with Greenford in the Brentford Union.

WAKEFIELD UNION :

(*a*) By Order which came into operation on 25 March 1881, a detached part of Alverthorpe and Thornes was amalgamated with Wakefield.

Unions and Parishes, &c.		Population in 1881.	Area in Statute Acres in 1881.	Rateable Value in 1881.	Post Town.	Petty Sessional Division.
WAKEFIELD UNION—County of York, West Riding—_continued._				£		
‡Crofton - - -	_par._	702	1,520	4,979	Wakefield - -	Agbrigg Lower. -
Emley - -	_tow._	1,289	3,556	6,025	do. - -	do.
Flockton - -	_tow._	1,180	1,108	3,470	do. - -	do.
Horbury - -	_tow._	5,050	1,279	24,909	do. - -	do.
†Lofthouse-with-Carlton - -	_tow._	3,528	1,984	12,842	do. - -	do.
§Newland-with-Woodhouse-Moor -	_par._	49	311	4,338	do. - -	do.
‖Normanton - -	_tow._	8,038	1,227	30,529	Normanton -	do.
Snydall Magna -	_tow._	4,264	1,617	14,198	Wakefield - -	do.
Sharlestone - -	_tow._	1,890	1,199	8,983	do. - -	do.
Shitlington - -	_tow._	2,993	3,410	11,446	do. - -	do.
Stanley - cum - Wren thorpe (W.) -	_tow._	13,431	4,674	45,448	do. - -	do.
Thorp - -	_tow._	71	518	2,830	do. - -	do.
Wakefield (_a_) -	_tow._	22,173	758	102,366	do. - -	do.
Walton - -	_tow._	621	1,824	6,161	do. - -	do.
Warmfield - cum - Heath -	_tow._	977	1,580	6,607	do. - -	do
TOTAL of UNION -		**89,113**	**41,989**	**395,701**		

WALLINGFORD UNION.

(Formed 2 June 1835 by Order dated 18 May 1835 as amended by Order dated 21 Jan. 1861. —Place marked thus * added 29 Aug. 1835 by Order dated 14 Aug. 1835; and thus † added 24 March 1862 by Order dated 21 March 1862.)

Unions and Parishes, &c.		Population in 1881.	Area in Statute Acres in 1881.	Rateable Value in 1881.	Post Town.	Petty Sessional Division.
COUNTY of BERKS :						
Allhallows and Clapcot -	_par._	167	859	2,160	Wallingford -	Borough of Wallingford.
Aston Tirrold -	_par._	310	1,752	2,325	do. - -	Hundred of Moreton.
Aston Upthorpe -	_lib._	168	1,324	1,512	do. - -	do.
Brightwell - -	_par._	618	2,061	4,921	do. - -	do.
Cholsey - -	_par._	1,735	4,438	12,219	do. - -	do.
Dudcote - -	_par._	373	1,120	5,232	Dudcote R.S.O. -	do.
East Hagborne -	_tow._	1,108	1,758	5,309	do. - -	do.
Little Wittenham -	_par._	112	888	1,601	Abingdon - -	Abingdon.
Long Wittenham -	_par._	562	2,275	4,182	do. - -	do.
Moulsford - -	_par._	170	1,141	1,565	Wallingford -	Hundred of Moreton.
North Moreton -	_par._	325	1,102	2,167	do. - -	do.
†Precincts of Wallingford Castle -	_par._	23	31	292	do. - -	do.
Saint Leonard -	_par._	1,019	236	2,678	do. - -	Borough of Wallingford.
Saint Mary the More, (W.) -	_par._	1,236	97	3,872	do. - -	do.
Saint Peter - -	_par._	459	31	1,916	do. - -	do.
Sotwell - -	_par._	196	708	1,915	do. - -	Hundred of Moreton.
South Moreton -	_par._	328	1,350	5,725	do. -	do.
West Hagborne -	_lib._	162	1,057	2,141	Dudcote R.S.O. -	do.
COUNTY of OXFORD :						
Bensington - -	_par._	1,145	2,920	7,039	Wallingford -	Watlington.
Berrick Salome -	_par._	105	600	1,123	do. - -	do.
Crowmarsh Gifford -	_par._	304	661	1,791	do. - -	Henley.
*Dorchester - -	_par._	813	1,954	5,367	do. - -	Oxford.
Ewelme - -	_par._	602	2,495	4,157	do. - -	Watlington.
Mongewell - -	_par._	148	1,651	1,911	do. - -	Henley.
Newington - -	_par._	363	2,116	3,191	do. - -	Watlington.
Newnham Murren -	_par._	218	1,852	2,752	do. - -	Henley.
North Stoke - -	_par._	167	853	1,497	do. - -	do.
South Stoke - -	_par._	838	3,370	6,689	do. - -	do.
Warborough - -	_par._	680	1,697	4,779	do. - -	Watlington.
TOTAL of UNION -		**14,493**	**42,706**	**102,388**		

Unions and Parishes, &c.	Population in 1881.	Area in Statute Acres in 1881.	Rateable Value in 1881.	Post Town.	Petty Sessional Division.
WALSALL UNION.			£		
(Formed 10 Dec. 1836 by Order dated 14 Nov. 1836.)					
COUNTY of STAFFORD:					
Aldridge - - *tow.*	1,890	7,752	12,015	Walsall - -	Offlow South, Northern Division.
Bentley - - *tow.*	337	1,650	4,856	do. - -	do.
Darlaston - - *par.*	13,563	800	33,704	do. - -	do.
Great Barr - - *tow.*	1,127	In Aldridge	10,195	do. - -	do.
Pelsall - - *tow.*	2,928	1,194	11,329	do. - -	do.
Rushall - - *par.*	5,809	1,924	15,151	do. - -	do.
The Foreign of Walsall (W.) - - } *tow.*	50,801 }	8,182	119,704 }	do. - -	Walsall Borough.
Walsall - - *tow.*	7,652 }		30,421 }	do. - -	do.
TOTAL of UNION -	84,107	21,502	237,378		
WALSINGHAM UNION.					
(Formed 12 April 1836 by Order dated 29 Mar. 1836, as amended by Order dated 12 Oct. 1863. —Place marked thus * added 15 Aug. 1836 by Order dated 20 July 1836 ; thus † added 25 Dec. 1858 by Order dated 16 Sept. 1858 : thus ‡ added 10 Mar. 1869 by Order dated 23 Feb. 1869.)					
COUNTY of NORFOLK :					
*Alethorpe - - *par.*	4	239	359	Fakenham -	Gallow.
Bale or Baithley - *par.*	232	1,041	1,885	Dereham -	Holt.
Barney - - *par.*	311	1,389	2,236	do. -	North Greenhoe.
Binham - - *par.*	478	2,242	3,448	Wells -	do.
Blakeney - - *par.*	804	1,865	2,464	do. -	Holt.
Briningham - - *par.*	255	1,201	2,239	Dereham -	do.
‡Brinton - - *par.*	161	625	1,258	do. -	do.
Cockthorpe - - *par.*	80	514	763	Wells -	North Greenhoe.
Dunton - - *par.*	167	1,721	2,244	Fakenham -	Gallow.
East Barsham - *par.*	180	1,167	1,931	Dereham -	do.
East Rainham - - *par.*	145	1,635	2,733	Swaffham -	do.
Egmere - - *par.*	97	1,237	1,786	Wells -	North Greenhoe.
Fakenham - - *par.*	2,756	2,208	12,101	Fakenham -	Gallow.
Field Dalling - *par.*	330	1,619	2,708	Dereham -	Holt.
Fulmodeston with Croxton } *par.*	361	2,333	3,076	do. -	Gallow.
Great Ryburgh (a) - *par.*	693	1,170	1,697	Fakenham -	do.
Great Snoring (W.)- *par.*	467	1,645	3,354	do. -	North Greenhoe.
Great Walsingham - *par.*	452	2,170	4,231	Wells -	do.
Gunthorpe - - *par.*	221	1,087	2,019	Dereham -	Holt.
Helhoughton - - *par.*	335	1,637	2,110	Swaffham -	Gallow.
Hempton - - *par.*	566	560	1,655	Fakenham -	do.
Hindringham - - *par.*	588	3,313	6,464	Wells -	North Greenhoe.
Holkham - - *par.*	537	5,973	5,715	do. -	do.
Houghton Saint Giles in the Hole } *par.*	165	978	1,764	Dereham -	do.
Kettlestone - - *par.*	185	1,168	1,715	Fakenham -	Gallow.
Langham - - *par.*	321	1,950	2,875	Dereham -	Holt.

(*continued*)

WALSINGHAM UNION :

(*a*) By Provisional Order which came into operation on 25 March 1886, a detached part of Great Ryburgh was amalgamated with Stibbard.

Unions and Parishes, &c.	Population in 1881.	Area in Statute Acres in 1881.	Rateable Value in 1881.	Post Town.	Petty Sessional Division.
WALSINGHAM UNION—County of Norfolk—continued.					
Little Ryburgh - par.	181	740	1,394	Fakenham - -	Gallow.
Little Snoring - par.	276	1,524	2,320	do. - -	do.
Little Walsingham - par.	1,016	860	3,394	Wells - -	North Greenhoe.
‡Melton Constable - par.	118	2,710	2,395	Dereham - -	Holt.
Morston - - par.	168	3.825	1,401	do. - -	do.
North Barsham - par.	91	1,015	1.620	do. - -	Gallow.
Pensthorpe - - par.	20	753	1,013	Fakenham - -	do.
Pudding Norton - par.	32	810	1,238	do. - -	do.
†Quarles - - par.	22	600	750	Wells - -	North Greenhoe.
Saxlingham - - par.	140	1,498	2,006	Dereham - -	Holt.
Sculthorpe - par.	574	2,055	4.037	Fakenham - -	Gallow.
Sharrington - par.	216	863	1,579	Dereham - -	Holt.
Shereford - - par.	86	842	1.193	Fakenham - -	Gallow.
South Rainham Saint Martin - } par.	158	1,010	1,519	Swaffham - -	do.
Stibbard (a) - par.	458	1,468	2,643	Dereham - -	Holt.
Stiffkey - - par.	434	3,912	2,808	Wells - -	do.
Swanton Novers - par.	282	1,315	1.704	Dereham - -	do.
Tatterford - - par.	89	959	1,533	Fakenham - -	Gallow.
Tattersett - - par.	203	1,750	2,878	do. - -	do.
*Testerton - - par.	13	613	1,043	do. - -	do.
Thursford - - par.	322	1,350	2,225	Dereham - -	North Greenhoe.
Toft Trees - - par.	64	1,184	1,798	Fakenham - -	Gallow.
Warham All Saints - par.	243	1,774	1,390	Wells - -	North Greenhoe.
Warham Saint Mary par.	67	3,066	2,034	do. - -	do.
Wells next the Sea - par.	2,645	4,510	9,841	do. - -	do.
West Barsham - par.	99	1,571	2,033	Dereham - -	Gallow.
West Rainham - par.	336	1,370	2,132	Swaffham - -	do.
Wighton - - par.	512	2,932	3,972	Wells - -	North Greenhoe.
Wiveton - - par.	181	1,042	1,547	Dereham - -	Holt.
TOTAL of UNION -	19,943	90,677	143,693		

WANDSWORTH AND CLAPHAM UNION.

(Formed 25 Mar. 1836 by Order dated 10 Mar. 1836.)

COUNTY of SURREY:

Battersea (W.) - par.	107,262	2,170	492,610	Battersea - -	Wandsworth.
Clapham - - par.	36,380	1,137	226,307	Clapham - -	Newington.
Putney - - par.	13,235	2,235	116,867	Putney - -	Wandsworth.
Streatham - - par.	21,611	2,914	171,973	Streatham - -	Newington.
Tooting Graveny - par.	3,942	566	18,333	Tooting Graveny -	Wandsworth.
Wandsworth (W.) - par.	28,004	2,433	164,571	Wandsworth -	do.
TOTAL of UNION -	210,434	11,455	1,190,661		

WANGFORD UNION.

(Formed 25 June 1835 by Order dated 6 June 1835.)

COUNTY of SUFFOLK:

All Saints and Saint Nicholas, South Elmham - } par.	216	1,600	2,432	Halesworth -	Bungay.
Barsham - - par.	305	1,722	2,546	Beccles - -	Beccles.
Beccles - - par.	5,721	1,892	18,520	do. - -	do.
Bungay, Holy Trinity par.	1,816	462	6,012	Bungay - -	Bungay.
Bungay, Saint Mary (a) par.	1,763	1,530	4,282	do. - -	do.

(continued)

WALSINGHAM UNION:
(a) See note, page 387.

WANGFORD UNION:
(a) By Order which came into operation on 25 March 1885, a detached part of Earsham, in the Depwade Union, was amalgamated with Bungay, Saint Mary.

Unions and Parishes, &c.	Population in 1881.	Area in Statute Acres in 1881.	Rateable Value in 1881.	Post Town.	Petty Sessional Division.

WANGFORD UNION—County of Suffolk—*continued.*

Unions and Parishes, &c.	Population in 1881.	Area in Statute Acres in 1881.	Rateable Value in 1881.	Post Town.	Petty Sessional Division.
Ellough - - par.	153	1,097	1,506	Beccles - -	Beccles.
Flixton - - par.	176	1,761	2,557	Bungay - -	Bungay.
Homersfield - - par.	144	981	1,581	Harleston - -	do.
Mettingham - - par.	366	1,386	2,815	Bungay - -	do.
North Cove - - par.	230	1,242	1,930	Beccles - -	Beccles.
Redisham - - par.	181	733	976	Halesworth -	do.
Ringsfield - - par.	285	1,815	2,688	Beccles - -	do.
Saint Andrew, Ilketshall - par.	472	1,694	2,419	Bungay - -	Bungay.
Saint Cross, South Elmham or Sandcroft par.	216	1,110	2,056	Harleston - -	do.
Saint James, South Elmham - par.	232	1,530	2,080	Halesworth -	do.
Saint John, Ilketshall par.	73	742	1,117	Bungay - -	do.
Saint Lawrence, Ilketshall - par.	218	1,171	1,765	do. - -	do.
Saint Margaret, Ilketshall - par.	286	2,085	2,791	do. - -	do.
Saint Margaret, South Elmham - par.	145	710	1,017	Harleston -	do.
Saint Michael, South Elmham - par.	127	930	1,225	Bungay - -	do.
Saint Peter, South Elmham - par.	77	900	920	do. - -	do.
Shadingfield - par.	164	1,369	2,041	Wangford -	Beccles.
Shipmeadow (W.) - par.	214	820	1,410	Beccles -	do.
Sotterley - - par.	268	1,593	2,121	Wangford -	do.
Weston - - par.	265	1,550	2,210	Beccles -	do.
Willingham - - par.	159	1,023	1,267	Wangford -	do.
Worlingham - - par.	184	1,631	2,189	Beccles -	do.
TOTAL of UNION -	14,456	35,079	74,473		

WANTAGE UNION.

(Formed 4 April 1835 by Order dated 19 Mar. 1835.—Place marked thus * added 11 April 1836 by Order dated 19 Mar. 1836.)

COUNTY of BERKS :

Unions and Parishes, &c.	Population in 1881.	Area in Statute Acres in 1881.	Rateable Value in 1881.	Post Town.	Petty Sessional Division.
Aldworth - - par.	275	1,806	1,809	Reading -	Ilsley.
Ardington (a) - par.	383	1,820	3,532	Wantage -	Wantage.
Beedon - - par.	323	2,012	1,978	Newbury -	Newbury.
Blewberry - - par.	746	1,246	4,394	Didcot -	Wallingford.
Bright Waltham - par.	428	2,054	2,767	Wantage -	Newbury.
Catmere - - par.	86	710	737	do. -	Ilsley.
Chaddelworth - par.	412	3,100	3,632	do. -	Wantage.
Charlton - - ham.	253	1,884	3,416	do. -	do.
Childrey (a) - - par.	516	2,861	3,455	do. -	do.
Chilton - - par.	276	1,418	2,133	Steventon -	Ilsley.
Compton - - par.	632	3,863	4,090	Newbury -	do.
Denchworth - par.	229	1,011	2,470	Wantage -	Wantage.
East Challow (a) - cha.	397	1,353	3,818	do. -	do.
East Hanney (a) - tow.	493	2,120	3,710	do. -	do.
East Hendred (a) - par.	815	3,117	4,808	do. -	do.
East Ilsley - - par.	577	3,017	4,174	Newbury -	Ilsley.
East Lockinge (a) - par.	330	2,878	3,714	Wantage -	Wantage.
Farnborough - par.	187	1,886	1,923	do. -	Ilsley.

(*continued*)

WANTAGE UNION :

(a) By Orders which came into operation on 25 March 1887.—
Certain detached parts of East Hendred, East Lockinge, and West Lockinge were amalgamated with Ardington ;
A detached part of Letcomb-Bassett was amalgamated with East Challow ;
Certain detached parts of Letcomb-Regis were amalgamated with Childrey and East Challow ;
A detached part of Sparsholt was amalgamated with West Challow ;
Certain detached parts of Wantage were amalgamated with East Hanney ;

WANTAGE UNION—*continued.*

A detached part of West Challow was amalgamated with East Challow ;
Certain detached parts of West Hanney were amalgamated with East Hanney ;
A detached part of West Hendred was amalgamated with East Hanney ; and
Certain detached parts of Sutton Courtney in the Abingdon Union, were amalgamated with East Hendred.

i R 9372.

3 A

Unions and Parishes, &c.		Population in 1881.	Area in Statute Acres in 1881.	Rateable Value in 1881.	Post Town.		Petty Sessional Division.
WANTAGE UNION—County of Berks—*continued.*				£			
Fawley - -	par.	228	2,191	1,792	Wantage -	-	Wantage.
¹Goosey and Circourt	cha.	161	968	1,944	Faringdon		do.
Grove -	tow.	557	1,791	5,860	Wantage -	-	do.
Hamstead Norris -	par.	1,378	6,047	5,628	Newbury -	-	Newbury.
Harwell - -	par.	810	2,521	5,465	Steventon -		Wantage.
Letcomb-Bassett (a) -	par.	221	1,662	1,424	Wantage -	-	do.
Letcomb-Regis (a) -	tow.	453	2,459	2,845	do. -	-	do.
Peasemore -	par.	302	2,049	2,796	Newbury -	-	Newbury.
Sparsholt (a) -	par.	440	3,698	5,573	Wantage -	-	Wantage.
Upton - -	lib.	415	1,413	1,585	Didcot -	-	Wallingford.
Wantage (W.) (a) -	tow.	3,488	2,503	10,781	Wantage -	-	Wantage.
West Challow (a) -	cha.	172	739	1,772	do. -	-	do.
West Hanney (a) -	tow.	369	1,383	2,768	do. -	-	do.
West Hendred (a) -	par.	351	2,007	3,889	do. -	-	do.
West Ilsley -	par.	377	3,037	2,657	Newbury -	-	Ilsley.
West Lockinge (a) -	ham.	80	864	1,335	Wantage -	-	Wantage.
TOTAL of UNION -		17,160	76,848	114,707			
WARE UNION.							
(Formed 16 April 1835 by Order dated 31 March 1835.)							
COUNTY of HERTFORD:							
Broxbourne - -	par.	785	1,932	6,207	Hoddesdon -	-	Cheshunt.
Eastwick -	par.	95	822	1,390	Harlow -	-	Ware.
Gilston -	par.	272	985	1,934	do. -	-	do.
Great Amwell -	par.	2,517	2,482	16,379	Ware -	-	do.
Great Munden -	par.	439	3,102	4,397	do. -	-	Stevenage.
Hoddesdon -	ham.	2,681	2,603	12,199	Hoddesdon -	-	Cheshunt.
Hunsdon -	par.	526	1,975	3,902	Ware -	-	Ware.
Little Munden -	par.	408	2,247	3,616	do. -	-	Stevenage.
Standon -	par.	2,069	7,745	13,556	do. -	-	Ware.
Stanstead Abbots -	par.	1,219	2,628	8,549	do. -	-	do.
Stanstead Saint Margaret -	}par.	96	408	1,364	do. -	-	do
Thundridge -	par.	467	2,206	3,799	do. -	-	do.
Ware (W.) -	par.	5,745	4,705	26,693	do. -	-	do.
Widford -	par.	511	1,168	2,126	do. -	-	do.
Wormley -	par.	735	946	3,565	Hoddesdon -	-	Cheshunt.
TOTAL of UNION -		18,625	36,254	109,976			
WAREHAM AND PURBECK UNION.							
(The Purbeck Union and the Wareham Union, which were respectively formed 25 March 1836 by Orders dated 10 March 1836, were united and formed into one Union, under the name of the Wareham and Purbeck Union, 29 Sept. 1836 by Order dated 13 Sept. 1836.)							
COUNTY of DORSET :							
Affpiddle - -	par.	477	3,818	2,958	Dorchester -	-	Wareham.
Arne - -	par.	121	4,196	630	Wareham -	-	do.
Bere Regis -	par.	1,284	8,894	6,772	do. -	-	do.
Bloxworth -	par.	261	2,776	1,965	do. -	-	do.
Chaldon Herring -	par.	331	2,981	2,077	Dorchester -	-	do.
Church Knowle -	par.	562	2,920	3,281	Wareham -	-	do.
Coombe Keynes -	par.	129	2,001	1,123	do. -	-	do.
Corfe Castle -	par.	1,777	9,884	7,515	do. -	-	do.
East Holme -	par.	89	1,200	404	do. -	-	do.
East Lulworth -	par.	364	4,364	1,895	do. -	-	do.
East Stoke (a) -	par.	582	3,273	3,665	do. -	-	do. (*continued*)

WANTAGE UNION :

(a) See note, page 389.

WAREHAM AND PURBECK UNION :

(a) By Order which came into operation on 25 March 1887,—
Certain detached parts of East Stoke were amalgamated with Saint Martin and West Lulworth; and
A detached part of Saint Martin was amalgamated with Lady Saint Mary.

Unions and Parishes, &c.	Population in 1881.	Area in Statute Acres in 1881.	Rateable Value in 1881.	Post Town.	Petty Sessional Division.
WAREHAM AND PURBECK UNION—County of Dorset—*continued.*			£		
Holy Trinity - *par.*	818	2,670	2,385	Wareham -	Wareham.
Kimmeridge - *par.*	170	1,570	1,484	do.	do.
Lady Saint Mary (W.) (*a*) *par.*	1,476	823	3,799	do.	do.
Langton Matravers - *par.*	892	2,250	2,615	do.	do.
Morden - *par.*	809	6,574	4,402	do.	do.
Moreton - *par.*	309	2,311	2,046	Dorchester	do.
Saint Martin (*a*) - *par.*	730	4,873	3,281	Wareham -	do.
Steeple - *par.*	295	3,362	1,845	do.	do.
Studland - *par.*	607	7,814	2,294	do.	do.
Swanage alias Sand-wich - *par.*	2,357	3,163	6,435	do.	do.
Tonerspiddle - *par.*	119	1,983	877	Dorchester	do.
Tyneham - *par.*	275	2,915	1,720	Wareham -	do.
West Lullworth (*a*) - *par.*	339 { In East Lullworth }		1,749	do.	do.
Winfrith - *par.*	959	4,496	4,552	Dorchester	do.
Wool - *par.*	509	2,550	2,105	Wareham -	do.
Worth Matravers - *par.*	302	2,645	1,916	do.	do.
TOTAL of UNION -	16,946	96,309	76,090		

WARMINSTER UNION.

(Formed 2 Nov. 1835 by Order dated 15 Oct. 1835, as amended by Order dated 25 Nov. 1858.)

COUNTY of WILTS :

Bishopstrow (*a*) - *par.*	245	1,045	1,909	Warminster -	Warminster.
Boyton (*a*) - *par.*	303	3,956	3,542	Codford St. Mary -	do.
Brixton Deverill - *par.*	162	2,450	1,857	Warminster -	do.
Chiltern All Saints - *par.*	431	4,476	3,102	Codford St. Mary -	do.
Chiltern Saint Mary - *par.*	198	1,198	1,177	do.	do.
Codford Saint Mary - *par.*	310	2,123	2,032	do.	do.
Codford Saint Peter (*a*) *par.*	319	1,611	2,975	do.	do.
Corsley (*a*) - *par.*	1,019	2,580	5,287	Warminster	do.
Heytesbury (*a*) (*b*) - *par.*	928	5,030	5,521	Heytesbury	do.
Hill Deverill (*a*) (*b*)- *par.*	136	1,120	1,978	Warminster -	do.
Horningsham (*a*) (*c*)- *par.*	813	2,541	3,486	do.	do.
Imber - *par.*	339	3,033	2,531	Codford St. Mary -	do.
Knook (*b*) - *par.*	163	1,440	1,284	Upton Lovell	do.
Longbridge Deverill (*a*) *par.*	914	4,156	5,677	Warminster	do.
Norton Bavant (*a*) - *par.*	264	2,165	3,017	do.	do.
Sherrington (*a*) - *par.*	157	1,280	1,431	Codford St. Mary -	do.
Stockton - *par.*	235	2,000	2,305	do.	do.
Sutton Veney (*a*) (*c*) *par.*	715	3,580	4,574	Warminster	do.
Upton Lovell - *par.*	207	1,399	2,107	Upton Lovell	do.
Upton Scudamore (*a*) *par.*	312	2,503	3,819	Warminster	do.
Warminster (W.) (*a*) *par.*	5,640	6,370	20,872	do.	do.
TOTAL of UNION -	13,840	56,356	80,483		

WARMINSTER UNION :

(*a*) By Order which came into operation on 25 March 1884,—
Detached parts of Bishopstrow, Boyton, and Corsley, were amalgamated with Warminster ;
A detached part of Corsley was amalgamated with Upton Scudamore ;
A detached part of Heytesbury was amalgamated with the Sutton Veney ;
Detached parts of Hill Deverill and Longbridge Deverill were amalgamated with Horningsham ;
Detached parts of Norton Bavant were amalgamated with Corsley and Warminster ;
A part of Sherrington was amalgamated with Codford Saint Peter ;
Detached parts of Warminster were amalgamated with Bishopstrow and Sutton Veney ; and

WARMINSTER UNION—*continued.*

Detached parts of Bishopstrow and Norton Bavant were amalgamated with Sutton Veney.
(*b*) By Orders which came into operation on 25 March 1885,—
A detached part of Knook was amalgamated with Heytesbury ; and
A detached part of Kingston Deverill, in the Mere Union, was amalgamated with Hill Deverill.
(*c*) By Provisional Orders which came into operation on 25 March. 1885,—
A detached part of Maiden Bradley with Yarnfield, in the Mere Union, was amalgamated with Horningsham ; and
A part of a parish known as Pertwood, in the Mere Union, was amalgamated with Sutton Veney.

Unions and Parishes, &c.	Population in 1881.	Area in Statute Acres in 1881.	Rateable Value in 1881.	Post Town.	Petty Sessional Division.

WARRINGTON UNION.

(Formed 2 Feb. 1837 by Order dated 5 Jan. 1837. — Places marked thus * added 30 Sept. 1845 by Order of that date.)

COUNTY of CHESTER :

Unions and Parishes, &c.	Population in 1881.	Area in Statute Acres in 1881.	Rateable Value in 1881.	Post Town.	Petty Sessional Division.
*Grappenhall - - *tow.*	788	1,610	£ 6,186	Warrington	Daresbury.
*Latchford (*a*) - *tow.*	4,282	790	13,612	do. -	Daresbury and Borough of Warrington.
*Thelwall (*a*) (*b*) - *tow.*	496	1,420	5,548	do. -	Daresbury.
COUNTY of LANCASTER :					
Burtonwood - - *tow.*	1,268	4,193	13,347	Warrington	Warrington.
Cuerdley - - *tow.*	227	1,723	5,138	do. -	do.
Great Sankey - *tow.*	630	1,923	7,569	do. -	do.
Haydock - - *tow.*	5,863	2,409	18,971	St. Helens -	Newton.
Houghton, Middleton, and Arbury - } *tow.*	242	853	2,152	Warrington	do.
Newton in Mackerfield - } *par.*	10,580	3,103	42,117	Newton -	do.
Penketh - - *tow.*	1,239	1,059	6,323	Warrington	Warrington.
Poulton with Fearnhead - } *tow.*	742	1,320	5,415	do. -	do.
Rixton with Glazebrook - } *tow.*	881	2,988	8,009	Manchester -	do.
Southworth and Croft *par.*	1,032	1,884	4,963	Warrington	do.
Warrington (W.) (*a*) *tow.*	40,957	2,887	135,497	do. -	Warrington and Borough of Warrington.
Winwick - - *tow.*	487	1,440	9,958	Newton -	Warrington.
Woolstone with Martinscroft (*b*) - } *tow.*	504	1,566	4,395	Warrington	do.
TOTAL of UNION -	70,218	31,168	289,200		

WARWICK UNION.

(Formed 29 June 1836 by Order dated 4 June 1836. — Place marked thus * added 22 Mar. 1862 by Order dated 11 Mar. 1862.)

COUNTY of WARWICK :

Unions and Parishes, &c.	Population in 1881.	Area in Statute Acres in 1881.	Rateable Value in 1881.	Post Town.	Petty Sessional Division.
Ashow - - - *par.*	178	1,012	1,813	Kenilworth -	Kenilworth.
Baginton - - *par.*	209	1,667	2,905	Coventry -	do.
Barford - - *par.*	720	1,540	4,745	Warwick -	Warwick.
Beausall - - *ham.*	195	In Hatton	2,180	do. -	do.
Bishops Tachbrook and Tachbrook Mallory - } *par.*	595	3,446	6,432	Leamington	do.
Bubbenhall - - *par.*	263	1,290	1,965	do. -	Kenilworth.
Budbrooke - - *par.*	751	3,216	7,625	Warwick -	Warwick.
Cubbington - - *par.*	980	1,780	4,337	Leamington -	Kenilworth.
Eathorpe - - *tow.*	148	1,550	1,150	do. -	Southam.
*Guy's Cliffe - - *par.*	16	—	160	Warwick -	Warwick.
Haseley - - *par.*	226	1,152	1,874	do. -	do.
Hatton - - *par.*	967	4,099	2,764	do. -	do.
Honily - - *par.*	53	642	897	do. -	do.
Hunningham - - *par.*	267	1,170	2,203	Leamington -	Southam.

(*continued*)

WARRINGTON UNION :

(*a*) By Orders which came into operation on 25 March 1884,—
Detached parts of Thelwall, known as Westy Barn Field and the Old Warps, were amalgamated with Latchford ; and
A part of Warrington was amalgamated with Latchford.

(*b*) By Provisional Order which came into operation on 25 March 1885,
A part of Thelwall, known as "Wilgrave's Farm," was amalgamated with Woolstone with Martinscroft.

Unions and Parishes, &c.		Population in 1881.	Area in Statute Acres in 1881.	Rateable Value in 1881.	Post Town.	Petty Sessional Division.

WARWICK UNION—County of Warwick—
continued.

				£		
Kenilworth	- par.	4,150	6,160	20,060	Kenilworth -	- Kenilworth.
Leamington Priors	- par.	22,979	1,720	122,620	Leamington -	- Borough of Leamington.
Leek Wootton	- par.	403	1,860	4,683	Warwick -	- Kenilworth.
Lillington	- par.	938	1,321	15,891	Leamington -	- do.
Milverton	- par.	2,162	1,180	21,297	do. -	- do.
Norton Lindsey	- par.	145	568	943	Warwick -	- Warwick.
Offchurch	- par.	322	2,273	3,957	Leamington -	- Kenilworth.
Radford Semele	- par.	556	2,093	4,217	do. -	- do.
Rowington (a)	- par.	853	3,424	8,379	Warwick -	- Henley.
Saint Mary's, Warwick	} par.	6,387	} 5,512	{ 24,858	do. -	Borough of Warwick.
Saint Nicholas, Warwick (W.) -	} par.	5,397		23,158	do. -	- do.
Sherborne	- par.	201	1,110	2,107	do. -	- Warwick.
Shrewley	- ham.	367	In Hatton	2,767	do. -	- do.
Stivichall	- par.	74	860	1,954	Coventry -	- Kenilworth.
Stoneleigh	- par.	1,216	9,907	18,127	Kenilworth -	- do.
Wappenbury	- par.	82	In Eathorpe	1,264	Leamington -	- Southam.
Wasperton	- par.	245	1,619	2,491	Warwick -	- Warwick.
Weston under Wetherley	} par.	227	1,290	2,404	Leamington -	- Southam.
Whitnash	- par.	426	1,242	3,693	do. -	- Kenilworth.
Wroxall (a)	- par.	176	1,735	2,843	Warwick -	- Warwick.
TOTAL of UNION	-	52,874	66,741	328,733		

WATFORD UNION.

(Formed 23 May 1835 by Order dated 27 April 1835.)

COUNTY of HERTFORD :

Abbots-Langley	- par.	2,989	5,281	20,455	Watford, Herts -	Watford.
Aldenham	- par.	1,833	6,113	18,944	do. -	- do.
Bushey	- par.	4,788	3,218	19,690	do. -	- do.
Rickmansworth	- par.	5,511	10,020	25,785	do. -	- do.
Sarratt	- par.	700	1,540	2,796	do. -	- do.
Watford (W.)	- par.	15,507	10,780	68,560	do. -	- do.
TOTAL of UNION	-	31,328	36,952	156,230		

WAYLAND UNION.

(Formed 19 Sept. 1835 by Order dated 2 Sept. 1835.)

COUNTY of NORFOLK :

Attleburgh	- par.	2,244	5,260	14,266	Attleborough -	Hundred of Shropham.
Besthorpe	- par.	188	2,464	5,017	do. -	- do.
Breckles	- par.	130	1,860	1,097	do. -	- Hundred of Wayland.
Carbrooke	- par.	612	3,033	5,371	Watton -	- do.
Caston	- par.	544	1,557	2,921	Attleborough -	- do.
Great Ellingham	- par.	652	2,670	5,050	do. -	- Hundred of Shropham.
Griston	- par.	268	1,360	2,568	Watton -	- Hundred of Wayland.
Hargham	- par.	70	1,080	1,905	Attleborough -	- Hundred of Shropham.
						(continued)

Unions and Parishes, &c.	Population in 1881.	Area in Statute Acres in 1881.	Rateable Value in 1881.	Post Town.	Petty Sessional Division.
WAYLAND UNION—County of Norfolk—*continued.*			£		
Hockham - - *par.*	504	3,406	3,684	Thetford - -	Hundred of Shropham.
Illington - *par.*	84	1,298	1,108	do. - -	do.
Larling - *par.*	180	1,548	1,667	do. - -	do.
Little Ellingham - *par.*	318	1,540	2,658	Attleborough -	Hundred of Wayland.
Merton - - *par.*	170	1,362	1,575	Watton - -	do.
Ovington - *par.*	277	1,497	2,644	do. - -	do.
Rockland All Saints (W.) and Saint An-drew's (a) - *par.*	122	1,671	2,694	Attleborough -	Hundred of Shropham.
Rockland Saint Peter's *par.*	254	1,010	1,797	do. - -	Hundred of Wayland.
Roudham - - *par.*	167	2,085	3,428	Thetford - -	Hundred of Shropham.
Scoulton - *par.*	326	2,193	3,141	Watton - -	Hundred of Wayland.
Shropham - *par.*	133	2,678	3,564	Thetford - -	Hundred of Shropham.
Snetterton - *par.*	203	2,189	2,330	do. - -	do.
Stow-bedon - *par.*	324	1,692	2,049	Attleborough -	Hundred of Wayland.
Thompson - *par.*	360	2,890	2,993	Watton - -	do.
Tottington - *par.*	279	3,213	2,513	do. - -	do.
Watton - *par.*	1,407	1,807	7,388	do. - -	do.
TOTAL OF UNION -	10,716	51,063	83,458		
WEARDALE UNION.					
(Formed 3 Jan. 1837 by Order dated 10 Dec. 1836.)					
COUNTY OF DURHAM :					
Edmondbyers - *par.*	352	5,132	1,955	Black Hill Co., Durham.	Darlington Ward, Stanhope Division.
Hunstonworth - *par.*	502	8,042	2,676	Riding Mill on Tyne	do.
Stanhope (W.) - *par.*	8,793	61,195	39,907	Darlington -	do.
Wolsingham - *par.*	7,895	24,016	33,730	Wolsingham -	do.
TOTAL OF UNION -	17,542	98,385	78,268		
WELLINGBOROUGH UNION.					
(Formed 28 July 1835 by Order dated 9 July 1835.— Place marked thus * added 22 March 1862 by Order dated 17 March 1862.)					
COUNTY OF BEDFORD :					
Poddington or Pud-dington (a) - *par.*	615	3,580	4,249	Wellingborough -	Sharnbrook.
Wymington or Wim-mington - *par.*	488	1,710	7,721	Higham Ferrers -	do.
COUNTY OF NORTHAMPTON :					
Bozeat - - *par.*	1,189	2,100	3,708	Wellingborough -	Wellingborough.
Earls Barton - *par.*	2,337	1,760	7,538	Northampton -	do.
Easton Maudit - *par.*	172	1,764	1,981	do. - -	do.
Ecton - - *par.*	618	1,790	4,679	do. - -	do.

(*continued*)

WAYLAND UNION :
(a) *See* note, page 393.

WELLINGBOROUGH UNION :
(a) By Orders which came into operation on 25 March 1881,—
A detached part of Strixton was amalgamated with Wollaston ;
All the parts of a parish known as Farndish were amalgamated with Poddington or Puddington.

Unions and Parishes, &c.		Population in 1881.	Area in Statute Acres in 1881.	Rateable Value in 1881.	Post Town.	Petty Sessional Division.
WELLINGBOROUGH UNION—County of Northampton—*continued.*						
Finedon or Thingdon	*par.*	2,404	3,650	11,983	Wellingborough	Wellingborough.
Great Doddington	*par.*	592	1,310	3,326	do.	do.
Great Harrowden	*par.*	155	1,415	5,622	do.	do.
Grendon	*par.*	542	3,120	3,590	Northampton	do.
Hardwick	*par.*	125	1,260	1,112	Wellingborough	do.
Higham Ferrers	*par.*	1,168	2,260	4,859	Higham Ferrers	do.
*Higham Park	*par.*	16	596	630	do.	do.
Irchester	*par.*	1,699	1,980	13,248	Wellingborough	do.
Irthlingborough	*par.*	2,736	3,720	14,622	Higham Ferrers	do.
Isham	*par.*	381	1,150	5,705	Wellingborough	do.
Little Harrowden	*par.*	828	1,480	5,112	do.	do.
Mear's Asbby	*par.*	501	1,890	2,984	Northampton	do.
Newton Bromshold	*par.*	111	1,740	908	Higham Ferrers	do.
Orlingbury	*par.*	285	1,990	2,818	Wellingborough	do.
Rushden	*par.*	3,657	2,770	9,198	Higham Ferrers	do.
Strixton (*a*)	*par.*	75	889	1,283	Wellingborough	do.
Sywell	*par.*	236	2,031	3,083	Northampton	do.
Wellingborough (W.)	*par.*	13,794	4,490	42,722	Wellingborough	do.
Wilby	*par.*	405	1,120	2,340	do.	do.
Wollaston (*a*)	*par.*	1,510	3,610	7,653	do.	do.
TOTAL OF UNION		36,912	55,505	172,974		

WELLINGTON UNION.

(Formed 4 June 1836 by Order dated 12 May 1836.— Place marked thus * added 26 March 1884 by Order dated 24 March 1884.)

COUNTY OF SALOP :						
Boius Magna	*par.*	304	1,897	3,238	Wellington, Salop	Newport.
Ercall Magna (*a*)	*par.*	1,803	11,988	19,293	do.	Wellington.
Eyton on the Wild Moors (*a*)	*par.*	433	1,232	3,228	do.	do.
Kinnersley (*a*)	*par.*	214	1,828	3,023	do.	Newport.
Longdon upon Tern	*par.*	131	823	1,857	do.	Wellington.
Preston on the Wild Moors (*a*)	*par.*	225	923	1,805	do.	Newport.
Rodington (*a*)	*par.*	398	1,628	3,278	Shrewsbury	Wellington.
Upton Waters (*a*)	*par.*	195	761	1,720	Wellington, Salop	do.
Wellington (W.) (*a*)	*par.*	14,199	8,757	49,979	do.	do.
Wombridge	*par.*	3,113	698	10,149	do.	do.
Wrockwardine (*a*)	*par.*	5,471	4,608	20,722	do.	do.
*Wrockwardine Wood (*a*)	*par.*	—	—	—	do.	do.
TOTAL OF UNION		26,484	35,143	118,292		

WELLINGTON UNION (SALOP) :

(*a*) By Orders which came into operation on 25 March 1884,—

  Detached and nearly detached parts of Ercall Magna were amalgamated with Kinnersley and Rodington ;

  A detached part of Eyton on the Wild Moors, and two detached parts of Preston on the Wild Moors, were amalgamated with Wellington ;

  A detached part of Upton Waters, known as "Waters Upton Moor," was amalgamated with Ercall Magna ;

  Certain detached parts of Wellington were amalgamated with Eyton on the Wild Moors and Preston on the Wild Moors ;

WELLINGTON UNION (SALOP)—*continued.*

  A detached part of Wrockwardine, known as "The Moors," was amalgamated with Eyton on the Wild Moors ;

  Certain parts of Rodington and Wellington were united and amalgamated with Wrockwardine ;

  Certain detached parts of Eyton on the Wild Moors, Preston on the Wild Moors, and Wrockwardine were united and constituted a separate parish, and designated Wrockwardine Wood.

Unions and Parishes, &c.		Population in 1881.	Area in Statute Acres in 1881.	Rateable Value in 1881.	Post Town.	Petty Sessional Division.

WELLINGTON UNION.
(Formed 17 May 1836 by Order dated 23 April 1836.)

County of Devon :

				£		
Burlescombe (a)	par.	820	3,768	9,311	Wellington	Cullompton.
Clayhidon	par.	584	5,089	4,783	do.	do.
Culmstock	par.	863	3,494	5,111	Cullompton	do.
Hemyock	par.	898	5,437	5,376	do.	do.
Holcombe Rogus	par.	734	3,024	5,390	Wellington	do.

County of Somerset :

Ashbrittle (a)	par.	380	2,189	3,588	Wellington	Wellington.
Badialton	par.	126	941	1,516	Wiveliscombe	Wiveliscombe.
Bradford	par.	462	1,782	5,359	Taunton	Wellington.
Chipstable (a)	par.	327	2,252	2,594	Wiveliscombe	Wiveliscombe.
Fitzhead	par.	264	1,208	2,371	Taunton	Taunton.
Kittisford	par.	113	952	1,478	Wellington	Wellington.
Langford Budville (a)	par.	363	1,853	2,745	do.	do.
Milverton (a)	par.	1,735	5,175	10,387	Milverton	Wiveliscombe.
Nynehead (a)	par.	318	1,448	3,350	Wellington	Wellington.
Oake (a)	par.	108	865	1,801	Taunton	Taunton.
Raddington	par.	98	1,505	1,347	Wiveliscombe	Wiveliscombe.
Runnington (a)	par.	73	323	910	Wellington	Wellington.
Sampford Arundel	par.	364	1,144	3,181	do.	do.
Stawley (a)	par.	153	830	1,229	do.	do.
Thorn Saint Margaret	par.	118	805	1,052	do.	do.
Wellington (W.)	par.	6,360	5,195	25,344	do.	do.
West Buckland	par.	899	3,671	7,797	do.	do.
Wiveliscombe	par.	2,612	5,084	12,934	Wiveliscombe	Wiveliscombe.
TOTAL of Union		18,772 (a)	59,534 (a)	119,251 (a)		

WELLS UNION.
(Formed 1 Jun. 1836 by Order dated 11 Dec. 1835.)

County of Somerset :

Baltonsborough (a)	par.	703	2,472	6,800	Glastonbury (Som.)	Somerton.
Butleigh (a) (b)	par.	771	4,467	7,180	do.	do.

(continued)

WELLINGTON UNION (SOMERSET) :

(a) By Orders which came into operation on 25 March 1884,—

A part of Chipstable consisting of two farms called Chiteombe and Withy, was amalgamated with Huish Champflower, in the Dulverton Union ;

A detached part of Milverton was amalgamated with Ashbrittle ;

Detached parts of Ashbrittle, known as "Great Brimley and Little Brimley" and "Greenham," were amalgamated with Stawley ;

Two detached parts of Langford Budville were amalgamated with Runnington ;

A detached part of Nynehead, known as "White Heathfield," was amalgamated with Oake ;

A certain part of Burlescombe was amalgamated with Sampford Peverell, in the Tiverton Union ;

The several parts of a parish known as Hillfarrence, (having in 1881, population 422, acreage 920, and rateable value 3,290l.), were amalgamated with Nynehead, Milverton, and Oake ;

A detached part of Bishop's Hull, in the Taunton Union, was amalgamated with Oake ;

WELLS UNION :

(a) By Orders which came into operation on 25 March 1884,—

A detached part of Meare was amalgamated with Wookey, and an inconveniently situated part was amalgamated with Saint Cuthbert Out ;

Certain parts of Saint Cuthbert Out which were situated within the Municipal Borough of Wells, were amalgamated with Saint Cuthbert In ;

Two detached parts of North Wootton were amalgamated with West Pennard, and certain inconveniently situated parts were amalgamated with Pilton, in the Shepton Mallet Union ;

A detached part of Street was amalgamated with Saint Benedict and Saint John, Glastonbury, a detached

WELLS UNION—continued.

part of Saint Benedict and Saint John, Glastonbury was amalgamated with Butleigh ; and parts of Saint Benedict and Saint John, Glastonbury, outside the Municipal Borough of Glastonbury, were amalgamated with Meare and North Wootton ;

A detached part of Pilton, in the Shepton Mallet Union, was amalgamated with North Wootton ;

Certain parts of Stone Easton, Paulton, and Litton, in the Clutton Union, were amalgamated with Chewton Mendip ; and detached parts of Chewton Mendip were amalgamated with Compton Martin and Stone Easton in that Union ;

Certain detached parts of Emborough, in the Shepton Mallet Union, were amalgamated with Chewton Mendip ;

A detached part of Binegar, in the Shepton Mallet Union, was amalgamated with Saint Cuthbert Out ;

Detached parts of Croscombe, in the Shepton Mallet Union, were amalgamated with North Wootton and West Pennard ;

Certain parts of Pilton, in the Shepton Mallet Union, were amalgamated with West Pennard and North Wootton ;

Detached parts of West Bradley, in the Shepton Mallet Union, were amalgamated with West Pennard and Baltonsborough ;

(b) By Provisional Order which came into operation on 25 March 1885, a detached part of Butleigh was amalgamated with Walton.

(c) By Orders which came into operation on 25 March 1885, certain detached parts of Cheddar and Nyland with Batcombe, in the Axbridge Union, were amalgamated with Rodney Stoke.

A parish, known as Green Ore, was amalgamated with Chewton Mendip ;

A detached part of Emborough, in the Shepton Mallet Union, was amalgamated with Chewton Mendip.

Unions and Parishes, &c.	Population in 1881.	Area in Statute Acres in 1881.	Rateable Value in 1881.	Post Town.	Petty Sessional Division.
WELLS UNION—County of Somerset—_continued._			£		
Chewton Mendip (a) (c) _par._	760	5,809	8,880	Bath - -	Temple Cloud.
Dinder - - _par._	207	1,071	2,198	Wells (Som.) -	Wells.
Meare (a) - - _par._	1,409	8,269	17,490	Glastonbury (Som.)	do.
North Wootton (a) - _par._	279	1,536	3,002	Shepton Mallet -	do.
Priddy - - _par._	226	1,361	990	Wells (Som.) -	do.
Rodney Stoke (c) - _par._	323	2,345	4,722	Weston-super-Mare	do.
Saint Andrew - _lib._	420 { In St. Cuthbert Out		2,114	Wells (Som.) -	Borough of Wells.
Saint Benedict and Saint John, Glastonbury (a) - } _par._	3,828	7,083	23,729	Glastonbury (Som.)	Borough of Glastonbury, and Wells.
Saint Cuthbert In (W.) (a) - } _par._	3,338 { In St. Cuthbert Out		9,554	Wells (Som.) -	Borough of Wells and Wells Division.
Saint Cuthbert Out (a) - - } _par._	4,340	14,918	28,515	do. - -	do.
Street (a) - - _par._	2,514	2,913	9,713	Bridgwater -	Somerton.
Walton (b) - - _par._	535	2,502	3,797	do. - -	do.
Westbury - - _par._	594	2,968	6,287	Wells (Som.) -	Wells.
West Pennard (a) - _par._	749	3,063	8,331	Glastonbury (Som.)	do.
Wookey (a) - _par._	1,017	3,420	9,129	Wells (Som.) -	do.
TOTAL of UNION -	22,013	64,197	152,731		

WELWYN UNION.

(Formed 4 July 1835 by Order dated 15 June 1835.)

COUNTY of HERTFORD:

Ayot Saint Lawrence _par._	112	751	1,310	Welwyn -	Hundred of Broadwater.
Ayot Saint Peter - _par._	219	1,093	1,607	do. - -	do.
Digswell - - _par._	227	1,656	6,298	do. - -	do.
Welwyn (W.) - _par._	1,742	3,081	13,620	do. - -	do.
TOTAL of UNION -	2,300	6,581	22,835		

WEM UNION.

(Formed 16 Nov. 1836 by Order dated 20 Oct. 1836.)

COUNTY of SALOP:

Broughton - _par._	204	904	2,597	Shrewsbury -	Albrighton.
Clive - - _cha._	393	1,500	3,593	do. - -	do.
Grinshill - _par._	345	842	2,129	do. - -	do.
Lee Brockhurst - _par._	97	585	939	do. - -	Wem.
Loppington - - _par._	540	3,466	5,928	Wem - -	do.
Moreton Corbet - _par._	251	2,193	2,870	Shrewsbury -	do.
Prees - - _par._	3,068	13,743	22,874	Whitchurch (Salop)	Whitchurch.
Shawbury - - _par._	967	7,414	9,422	Shrewsbury -	Wem.
Stanton upon Hine Heath - - } _par._	667	5,662	7,983	do. - -	do.
Wem (W.) - _par._	3,751	13,898	30,900	Wem - -	do.
Weston and Wixhill-under-Red-Castle - } _cha._	282	2,243	3,062	Shrewsbury -	do.
TOTAL of UNION -	10,565	52,450	92,297		

Unions and Parishes, &c.	Population in 1881.	Area in Statute Acres in 1881.	Rateable Value in 1881.	Post Town.	Petty Sessional Division.

WEOBLEY UNION.

(Formed 9 April 1836 by Order dated 25 March 1836.—Places marked thus * added 23 Dec. 1836 by Order dated 1 Dec. 1836 ; and thus † added 3 July 1837 by Order dated 10 June 1837.)

COUNTY of HEREFORD :

			£		
Almeley - - *par.*	604	3,352	4,217	Eardisley -	Weobley
Birley (a) - - *par.*	159	1,001	1,234	Leominster -	do.
Bishopstone (a) - *par.*	247	776	1,181	Hereford -	do.
†Blakemere - - *par.*	171	1,127	1,280	do. - -	do.
Bridge Sollers - *par.*	71	768	1,083	do. - -	do.
Brinsop - - *par.*	160	1,364	1,792	do. - -	do.
Brobury - - *par.*	75	508	720	do. - -	do.
Byford - - *par.*	214	903	1,346	do. -	do.
Dilwyn (a) - - *par.*	1,046	6,067	7,898	Leominster -	do.
Eardisland (a) - *par.*	781	4,455	6,801	Pembridge, Herefordshire.	do.
Kinnersley - - *par.*	306	2,199	3,236	Letton, Hereford -	do.
*Letton - - *par.*	175	1,196	2,175	Hereford -	do.
Mansell Gamage - *par.*	145	1,323	1,827	do. - -	do.
Mansell Lacy (a) - *par.*	197	1,547	2,348	do. - -	do.
†Moccas - - *par.*	177	1,163	1,528	do. - -	do.
Monnington - *par.*	89	1,011	1,317	do. - -	do.
Norton, Canon - *par.*	326	2,111	2,843	Weobley - -	do.
†Preston upon Wye - *par.*	227	1,379	1,871	Hereford -	do.
Pyon, Canon - *par.*	701	3,706	4,571	do. - -	do.
Pyon, Kings - *par.*	439	2,407	2,896	Weobley, Hereford	do.
Sarnesfield (a) - *par.*	123	1,256	1,372	Kington -	do.
*Staunton on Wye - *par.*	526	2,320	3,382	Hereford -	do.
Stretford - - *par.*	43	424	616	Leominster -	do.
Weobley (W.) (a) - *par.*	882	3,309	5,370	Herefordshire -	do.
Wormsley - - *par.*	78	1,233	979	Canon Pyon, Hereford.	do.
Yazor - - *par.*	217	2,051	2,543	Hereford - -	do.
TOTAL of UNION -	8,179	48,959	66,456		

WESTBOURNE UNION.

(Formed 25 Mar. 1835 by Order dated 21 Feb. 1835.)

COUNTY of SUSSEX :

Bosham - - *par.*	1,255	3,178	8,060	Chichester -	Upper Division of the Rape of Chichester.
Chidham - - *par.*	266	1,524	3,200	Emsworth -	do.
Compton - - *par.*	289	1,864	1,339	Petersfield -	do.
East Marden - *par.*	91	938	572	Chichester -	do.
Funtington - - *par.*	1,108	3,763	7,012	do. -	do.
North Marden - *par.*	39	697	268	do. - -	do.
Racton - - *par.*	97	1,199	1,273	Emsworth -	do.
Stoughton - - *par.*	626	5,374	3,813	do. -	do.
Up-Marden - *par.*	336	2,943	2,266	Chichester -	do.
West Bourn (W.) - *par.*	2,450	4,520	10,901	Emsworth -	do.
West Dean - *par.*	732	4,802	3,327	Chichester -	do.
West Thorney - *par.*	131	1,238	1,749	Emsworth -	do.
TOTAL of UNION -	7,420	32,040	43,780		

WEOBLEY UNION :

(a) By Order which came into operation on 25 March 1884,——
Detached parts of Eardisland were amalgamated with Dilwyn and Weobley ;
A detached part of Mansell Lacy, known as " Bunshill," was amalgamated with Bishopstone ;
Detached parts of Sarnesfield were amalgamated with Birley.

Unions and Parishes, &c.	Population in 1881.	Area in Statute Acres in 1881.	Rateable Value in 1881.	Post Town.	Petty Sessional Division.

WESTBURY UNION.

(Formed 28 Sept. 1835 by Order dated 11 Sept. 1835.—Place marked thus * added 17 Feb. 1843 by Order of that date.)

COUNTY of GLOUCESTER :

			£		
Abinghall (c) - par.	268	770	1,610	Mitcheldean, R.S.O., Gloucestershire.	Newnham.
Awre - - - par.	1,179	4,330	12,453	Newnham - -	do.
Blaisdon (a) - par.	203	927	1,821	do. - -	do.
Bulley - - par.	152	951	1,670	Gloucester -	Gloucester.
Churcham - - par.	510	2,260	6,712	do. -	do.
*East Dean (a) (b) (c) tow.	12,629	12,487	39,738	Newnham -	Newnham.
Flaxley (a) - par.	1,278	1,749	4,017	do. -	do.
Huntley - - par.	416	1,409	2,378	Gloucester -	do.
Littledean (a) - par.	823	495	2,386	Newnham -	do.
Longhope - - par.	971	3,070	5,770	Gloucester -	do.
Minsterworth (c) - par.	418	1,938	6,308	do. -	Gloucester.
Mitcheldean - par.	711	627	2,862	do. -	Newnham.
Newnham - - par.	1,455	1,937	9,876	Newnham -	do.
Westbury (W.) (a) - par.	2,262	8,206	20,901	do. -	do.
TOTAL of UNION -	23,275 (b)	41,156 (b)	118,502 (b)		

WESTBURY AND WHORWELLSDOWN UNION.

(Formed 4 Nov. 1835 by Order dated 30 Sept. 1835.)

COUNTY of WILTS :

Bulkington - - ty.	173	973	2,133	Devizes -	Whorwellsdown.
East Coulston - par.	103	868	1,100	Westbury -	do.
Edington - - par.	927	5,705	6,881	do. -	do.
Hinton (a) - ty.	167	703	1,668	Trowbridge -	do.
Keevil - - par.	377	1,910	4,608	do. -	do.
North Bradley (b) - ty.	887	} 4,036	{ 5,482	do. -	Trowbridge.
Southwick (b) - ty.	999		5,407	do. -	do.
Steeple Ashton - ty.	697	2,808	6,691	do. -	Whorwellsdown.
West Ashton - - ty.	306	2,040	3,761	do. -	do.
Westbury (W.) - par.	6,014	12,027	34,172	Westbury -	Westbury.
TOTAL of UNION -	10,650	31,070	71,966		

WESTBURY UNION :

(a) By Orders which came into operation on 25 March 1883,—

A detached part of Blaisdon was amalgamated with Flaxley, and a detached part of Flaxley was amalgamated with Blaisdon ;
Detached parts of Flaxley and Westbury were amalgamated with Littledean ;
A detached part of Flaxley was amalgamated with East Dean ;
A detached part of Newland, in the Monmouth Union, was amalgamated with Littledean.

(b) By Provisional Order which came into operation on 25 March 1884,—

The three parts into which a parish, known as Hinders Lane and Dockham, (having in 1881, populat'on 280, acreage 8, and rateable value 421l.), was divided, together with a part of Lea Bailey, in the Ross Union, were amalgamated with East Dean.

WESTBURY UNION—continued.

(c) By Orders which came into operation on 25 March 1884,—

Parts of Minsterworth were amalgamated with Elmore, in the Gloucester Union ; and

A detached part of Abinghall was amalgamated with East Dean.

WESTBURY AND WHORWELLSDOWN UNION :

(a) By Order which came into operation on 25 March 1884, a detached part of Hinton was amalgamated with Hilperton, in the Melksham Union.

(b) By Order which came into operation on 25 March 1885, a detached part of Southwick was amalgamated with North Bradley.

3 B 2

Unions and Parishes, &c.	Population in 1881.	Area in Statute Acres in 1881.	Rateable Value in 1881.	Post Town.	Petty Sessional Division.

WESTMINSTER UNION.

(Formed 16 Mar. 1868 by Order dated 13 Mar. 1868 as amended by Order dated 31 Dec. 1868.)

COUNTY of MIDDLESEX :

Unions and Parishes, &c.	Population in 1881.	Area in Statute Acres in 1881.	Rateable Value in 1881.	Post Town.	Petty Sessional Division.
Saint Anne within the Liberty of Westminster } *par.*	16,608	54	£118,653	London - -	St. James's.
Saint James, West-minster (W.) } *par.*	29,941	162	668,913	do. - -	do.
TOTAL of UNION -	46,549	216	787,566		

WEST ASHFORD UNION.

(Formed 3 June 1835 by Order dated 14 May 1835.—Places marked thus * added 25 April 1836 by Order dated 30 Mar. 1836.)

COUNTY of KENT :

Unions and Parishes, &c.	Population in 1881.	Area in Statute Acres in 1881.	Rateable Value in 1881.	Post Town.	Petty Sessional Division.
*Ashford - - *par.*	9,693	2,850	44,632	Ashford - -	Ashford.
Bethersden - - *par.*	1,015	6,376	8,926	do. - -	do.
Charing - - *par.*	1,349	4,681	7,687	do. - -	do.
Egerton - - *par.*	871	2,786	4,454	do. - -	do.
Great Chart - - *par.*	744	3,276	8,929	do. - -	do.
Hothfield - - *par.*	323	1,829	5,046	do. - -	do.
Kingsnorth - - *par.*	606	3,252	4,871	do. - -	do.
*Little Chart - - *par.*	276	1,607	3,217	do. - -	do.
Pluckley - - *par.*	923	3,094	8,108	do. - -	do.
Shadoxhurst - - *par.*	192	1,972	1,508	do. - -	do.
Smarden - - *par.*	1,139	5,387	11,403	Staplehurst -	do.
Westwell (W.) - *par.*	995	5,223	6,818	Ashford - -	do.
TOTAL of UNION -	18,126	42,333	115,599		

WEST BROMWICH UNION.

(Formed 5 Nov. 1836 by Order dated 11 Oct. 1836.—Place thus * added 1 April 1884 by Order dated 29 Mar. 1884.)

COUNTY of STAFFORD :

Unions and Parishes, &c.	Population in 1881.	Area in Statute Acres in 1881.	Rateable Value in 1881.	Post Town.	Petty Sessional Division.
Handsworth - - *par.*	21,251	7,680	107,643	Handsworth -	West Bromwich.
Wednesbury - - *par.*	24,566	2,124	74,198	Wednesbury -	Wednesbury.
West Bromwich (W.) *par.*	56,295	5,719	157,920	West Bromwich -	West Bromwich.
COUNTY of WORCESTER :					
Oldbury (a) - - *tow.*	18,306	3,799	57,868	Oldbury - -	Oldbury.
*Warley (a) - - *par.*	—	—	—	do. - -	do.
TOTAL of UNION -	123,418 (b)	19,322 (b)	397,629 (b)		

WEST BROMWICH UNION :

(a) By Order which came into operation on 25 March 1884,—

Certain parts of Oldbury were amalgamated with Cakemore, in the Stourbridge Union ;

Certain parts of Warley Wigorn, were amalgamated with Cakemore and Oldbury ;

Certain parts of Warley Salop and Warley Wigorn, were amalgamated with Ridgacre, in the Stourbridge Union ;

WEST BROMWICH UNION—*continued.*

Certain parts of Oldbury and Ridgacre were united with the remaining parts of Warley Salop and Warley Wigorn, and all the parts so united were formed into a separate parish and designated the parish of Warley ;

(b) (Warley Salop had in 1881, population, 546, rateable value 2,661*l.*; Warley Wigorn had in 1881, population 2,199, rateable value 6,243*l.* The acreage of both these places was included with that of Oldbury).

Unions and Parishes, &c.		Population in 1881.	Area in Statute Acres in 1881.	Rateable Value in 1881.	Post Town.	Petty Sessional Division.
WEST DERBY UNION.						
(Formed 31 Jan. 1837 by Order dated 5 Jan. 1837. — Place marked thus * added 24 March 1862 by Order dated 20 Mar. 1862.)				£		
COUNTY OF LANCASTER :						
Aintree	- tow.	277	850	5,685	Liverpool	Kirkdale.
Allerton	- tow.	830	1,586	18,191	do. - -	Childwall.
Bootle cum Linacre	- tow.	27,374	1,104	143,617	do. - -	Bootle cum Linacre.
Childwall	- tow.	187	1,729	4,196	do. - -	Childwall.
*Croxteth Park	- pur.	39	959	2,089	do. - -	Kirkdale.
Everton (W.)	- tow.	109,812	693	291,855	do. -	Liverpool.
Fazakerley	- tow.	533	1,709	8,691	do. -	Kirkdale.
Garston	- tow.	10,271	1,625	64,573	do. - -	do.
Great Crosby	- tow.	9,373	2,168	61,774	do. - -	do.
Ince Blundell	- tow.	516	2,316	5,972	do. - -	do
Kirkby	- tow.	1,101	4,175	13,497	do. - -	do.
Kirkdale	- tow.	58,145	926	299,477	do. - -	Liverpool.
Litherland	- tow.	7,204	1,205	42,845	do. -	Kirkdale.
Little Crosby	- tow.	553	1,811	5,273	do. - -	do.
Lunt	- tow.	104	477	1,270	do. -	do.
Netherton	- tow.	386	1,126	3,710	do. - -	do.
Orrell and Ford	- tow.	637	727	4,972	do. - -	do.
Sephton	- tow.	382	1,234	3,614	do. - -	do.
Thornton	- tow.	275	774	2,451	do. - -	do.
Walton on the Hill (W.)	- tow.	18,715	1,944	90,288	do. -	do.
Wavertree	- tow.	11,097	1,838	80,638	do. - -	Childwall.
West Derby	- par.	101,162	6,203	403,320	do. - -	Liverpool and Kirkdale.
TOTAL of UNION	-	359,273	37,479	1,557,068		
WEST FIRLE UNION.						
(Formed 25 Mar. 1835 by Order dated 5 Feb. 1835.)						
COUNTY of SUSSEX :						
Alciston	- par.	194	2,088	1,516	Lewes -	Lewes.
Beddingham	- par.	418	2,888	3,698	do. -	do.
Berwick	- par.	173	1,104	1,841	Polegate, R.S.O. -	do.
Chalvington	- par.	127	749	983	Hawkhurst -	do.
Glynde	- par.	284	1,570	2,208	Lewes -	do.
Ripe	- par.	385	1,900	2,345	Hawkhurst -	do.
Selmeston	- par.	188	1,509	2,780	Polegate, R.S.O. -	do.
West Firle (W.)	- par.	573	3,429	4,893	Lewes -	do.
TOTAL of UNION	-	2,369	15,327	20,264		
WEST HAM UNION.						
(Formed 31 May 1836 by Order dated 6 May 1836.)						
COUNTY of ESSEX :						
East Ham	- par.	9,713	2,498	42,929	London, E. -	Stratford.
Little Ilford	- par.	993	768	6,148	do. - -	do.
Low Leyton (W.)	- par.	23,016	2,370	72,958	do. -	do.
Walthamstow	- par.	21,715	4,374	99,254	do. - -	do.
Wanstead (a)	- par.	9,414	2,002	42,751	do. -	do.
West Ham (a)	- par.	128,953	4,667	483,137	do. - -	West Ham.
Woodford Saint Mary	par.	7,154	2,146	39,629	do. - -	Stratford.
TOTAL of UNION	-	200,958	18,825	786,806		

WEST HAM UNION :

(a) By Order which came into operation on 25 March 1887, a certain part of Wanstead was amalgamated with West Ham.

Unions and Parishes &c.		Population in 1881.	Area in Statute Acres in 1881.	Rateable Value in 1881.	Post Town.	Petty Sessional Division.

WEST HAMPNETT UNION.

(Formed 25 Mar. 1835 by Order dated 21 Feb. 1835.—Place marked thus * added 24 Aug. 1858 by Order dated 29 July 1858; thus † 29 Sept. 1869 by Order dated 13 Aug. 1869.—Place marked thus § originally consisted of East Lavant and Mid Lavant, which were consolidated by Provisional Order dated 19 May 1873, which took effect on 29 September 1873.)

COUNTY OF SUSSEX :

£

Aldingbourn -	- *par.*	743	3,098	5,834	Chichester - -	Upper Division of Chichester Rape.
Appledram -	- *par.*	159	937	1,651	do. - -	do.
Barnham	- *par.*	184	872	1,818	Bognor - -	Upper Division of Arundel Rape.
Binderton -	- *par.*	100	1,337	1,036	Chichester - -	Upper Division of Chichester Rape.
Binsted	- *par.*	135	1,105	1,138	Arundel - -	Upper Division of Arundel Rape.
Birdham	- *par.*	455	1,817	3,305	Chichester - -	Upper Division of Chichester Rape.
Boxgrove -	- *par.*	708	3,677	5,056	do. - -	do.
Donnington -	- *par.*	188	1,038	1,940	do. - -	do.
Earnley -	- *par.*	132	1,143	1,899	do. - -	do.
Eartham -	- *par.*	154	1,539	1,182	do. - -	do.
East Dean -	- *par.*	343	4,654	1,687	do. - -	do.
Eastergate -	- *par.*	161	918	1,903	Arundel - -	Upper Division of Arundel Rape.
East Wittering -	- *par.*	230	1,176	2,107	Chichester - -	Upper Division of Chichester Rape.
Felpham -	- *par.*	565	1,883	4,278	Bognor - -	Upper Division of Arundel Rape.
Hunston -	- *par.*	176	1,013	1,751	Chichester - -	Upper Division of Chichester Rape.
§Lavant -	- *par.*	805	4,073	4,551	do. - -	do.
Madehurst -	- *par.*	190	1,891	1,279	Arundel - -	Upper Division of Arundel Rape.
Merston - -	- *par.*	96	718	1,279	Chichester - -	Upper Division of Chichester Rape.
Middleton -	- *par.*	14	370	644	Arundel - -	Upper Division of Arundel Rape.
New Fishbourne -	- *par.*	316	597	2,145	Chichester - -	Upper Division of Chichester Rape.
North Mundham -	- *par.*	401	1,892	3,677	do. - -	do.
Oving -	- *par.*	1,662	2,989	8,160	do. - -	do.
Pagham -	- *par.*	874	3,886	7,689	do. - -	do.
Rumbold's Wyke -	- *par.*	902	652	4,198	do. - -	do.
Selsey -	- *par.*	901	2,600	4,690	do. - -	do.
Sidlesham -	- *par.*	946	3,961	7,113	do. - -	do.
Singleton -	- *par.*	555	4,063	4,086	do. - -	do.
*Slindon -	- *par.*	507	2,957	2,500	Arundel - -	Upper Division of Arundel Rape.
†South Bersted -	- *par.*	4,166	2,750	16,023	Bognor - -	Upper Division of Chichester Rape.
Tangmere -	- *par.*	185	775	1,616	Chichester - -	do.
Upwaltham -	- *par.*	82	1,275	559	Petworth - -	do.
Walberton -	- *par.*	607	1,752	3,570	Arundel - -	Upper Division of Arundel Rape.
West Hampnett (W.)	*par.*	521	1,308	2,848	Chichester - -	Upper Division of Chichester Rape.
West Itchenor -	- *par.*	154	545	907	do. - -	do.
West Stoke -	- *par.*	95	871	914	do. - -	do.
West Wittering -	- *par.*	655	2,286	3,922	do. - -	do.
Yapton -	- *par.*	556	1,740	4,382	Arundel - -	Upper Division of Arundel Rape.
TOTAL of UNION	-	19,653	70,758	123,337		

Unions and Parishes, &c.		Population in 1881.	Area in Statute Acres in 1881.	Rateable Value in 1881.	Post Town.	Petty Sessional Division.
WEST WARD UNION.						
(Formed 6 Sept. 1836 by Order dated 13 Aug. 1836.)						
COUNTY of WESTMORLAND:				£		
Askham	- - *par.*	513	4,484	3,724	Penrith - -	West Ward.
Bampton	- *par.*	537	10,925	4,747	do. - -	do.
Barton	- - *tow.*	371	2,569	3,513	do. - -	do.
Bolton	- - *tow.*	404	2,791	3,290	Kirkby Thore -	do.
Brougham	- *par.*	296	6,226	5,291	Penrith -	do.
Cliburn	- *par.*	279	1,890	2,217	do. - -	do.
Clifton	- - *par.*	393	1,782	4,322	do. - -	do.
Crosby Ravensworth	*par.*	781	11,049	10,924	Shap - -	do.
Great Strickland	- *tow.*	283	2,339	2,171	Penrith - -	do.
Kings Meaburn	- *tow.*	177	2,388	1,605	Kirkby Thore -	do.
Little Strickland	- *tow.*	114	790	1,413	Penrith -	do.
Lowther	- - *par.*	470	3,674	5,954	do. - -	do.
Low Winder	- *tow.*	20	301	278	do. - -	do.
Martindale	- - *tow.*	142	8,024	1,725	do. - -	do.
Morland	- - *tow.*	371	1,754	2,008	do. - -	do.
Newby	- - *tow.*	245	2,986	2,515	do. - -	do.
Patterdale	- - *tow.*	710	16,735	6,291	do. - -	do.
Shap (W.)	- - *par.*	1,416	27,177	12,502	Shap -	do.
Sleagill	- - *tow.*	140	1,390	983	Penrith -	do.
Sockbridge	- *tow.*	218	1,159	2,056	do. - -	do.
Thrimby	- - *tow.*	53	1,574	2,862	do. - -	do.
Yanwath and Eamont Bridge - - } *tow.*		289	1,299	3,817	do. - -	do.
TOTAL of UNION	-	**8,225**	**113,306** (*a*)	**84,208**		
WETHERBY UNION.						
(Formed 15 Feb. 1861 by Order dated 1 Feb. 1861. — Place marked thus * added 25 Dec. 1861 by Order dated 21 Oct. 1861; and places marked thus † added 21 June 1869 by Order dated 31 May 1869.)						
COUNTY of YORK, WEST RIDING:						
Angram	- *tow.*	50	519	637	York - -	Tadcaster.
Bardsey-with-Rigton	*tow.*	320	2,748	3,523	Leeds - -	Wetherby.
Bickerton	- *tow.*	138	1,073	1,639	Wetherby -	do.
†Bilton	- - *tow.*	238	1,923	3,179	York - -	do.
†Bramham-with-Ogle-thorpe } *tow.*		1,146	4,108	7,614	Tadcaster -	do.
†Clifford-with-Boston	*tow.*	2,604	1,619	9,840	do. - -	do.
†Collingham (*b*)	- *tow.*	329	1,881	2,555	Leeds - -	do.
Cowthorp (*b*) -	- *par.*	124	1,370	1,684	Wetherby -	do.
†Dunkeswick -	- *tow.*	169	1,467	2,057	Harewood, Leeds	do.
East Keswick -	- *tow.*	447	1,288	2,386	Leeds - -	do.
†Harewood -	- *tow.*	716	3,654	5,532	do. - -	do.
						(*continued*)

WEST WARD UNION:

(*a*) There are certain common lands comprised in this Union, containing in the whole 8,634 acres.

WETHERBY UNION:

(*a*) By Order which came into operation on 25 March 1884,—

A detached part of Barwick in Elmet, in the Tadcaster Union, was amalgamated with Thorner.

(*b*) By Orders which came into operation on 25 March 1885,—

A nearly detached part of Collingham was amalgamated with Wothersome ;
A detached part of Thorpe Arch, known as "Hall Park," was amalgamated with Walton ;
A detached part of Tockwith was amalgamated with Cowthorp ;
A detached part of Shadwell, known as Roundhay Grange, was amalgamated with Seacroft, in the Leeds Union.

Unions and Parishes, &c.	Population in 1881.	Area in Statute Acres in 1881.	Rateable Value in 1881.	Post Town.	Petty Sessional Division.

WETHERBY UNION—County of York, West Riding—
continued.

£

Unions and Parishes, &c.	Population in 1881.	Area in Statute Acres in 1881.	Rateable Value in 1881.	Post Town.	Petty Sessional Division.
†Hutton Wandesley - tow.	117	1,230	1,503	York - -	Tadcaster.
Kearby-with-Nether-by } tow.	141	1,123	2.271	Wetherby - -	Wetherby.
Kirkby Overblow - tow.	266	2,358	3,612	do. - -	Upper Claro.
†Kirk Deighton - tow.	353	2,274	4,049	do. - -	Wetherby.
Linton - - tow.	160	1,265	2,466	Leeds - -	do.
Little Ribston - tow.	181	856	1,533	Wetherby - -	do.
†Long Marston - tow.	363	2.846	3,560	York - -	Tadcaster.
*Micklethwaite Grange tow.	103	668	1,160	Wetherby - -	Wetherby.
North Deighton - tow.	111	1,175	2,103	do. - -	do.
Rigton - - tow.	383	3,111	6,908	Otley - -	Upper Claro.
Scarcroft - - tow.	290	1,073	2,574	Leeds - -	Lower Skyrack.
†Shadwell (b) - - tow.	1,101	1,199	5,763	do. - -	do.
Sicklinghall - - tow.	227	1,494	2,334	Wetherby - -	Wetherby.
Spofforth-with-Stockeld - } tow.	856	5,466	9,186	do. - -	do.
†Thorner (a) - - tow.	938	2,316	5,817	Leeds - -	Lower Skyrack.
†Thorpe Arch (b) - par.	393	1,671	3,593	Tadcaster - -	Wetherby.
†Tockwith (b) - tow.	572	1,814	3,956	York - -	do.
†Walton (b) - - tow.	194	1,447	2,561	Tadcaster - -	do.
Weardley - - tow.	154	874	1,606	Harewood, Leeds -	do.
†Weeton - - tow.	323	1,377	4,258	do. - -	Otley.
Wetherby (W.) - tow.	1,886	1,601	9,585	Wetherby - -	Wetherby.
Wighill - - tow.	239	2,247	4,316	Tadcaster - -	do.
†Wigton - - tow.	299	1,294	1,365	Moortown, Leeds -	Lower Skyrack.
†Wike - - tow.	142	879	1,164	do. - -	do.
†Wilstrop - - tow.	80	1,079	1,215	Greenhammerton, York.	York.
Wothersome (b) - tow.	41	653	532	Tadcaster - -	Wetherby.
TOTAL of UNION -	16,194	65,940	129,639		

WEYMOUTH UNION.

(Formed 14 Jan. 1836 by Order dated 31 Dec. 1835.)

COUNTY of DORSET :

Unions and Parishes, &c.	Population in 1881.	Area in Statute Acres in 1881.	Rateable Value in 1881.	Post Town.	Petty Sessional Division.
Abbotsbury - - par.	979	5,616	5,012	Dorchester -	Dorchester.
Bincomb - - par.	223	977	1,067	do. -	do.
Broadway - - par.	761	1,029	3,009	do. - -	do.
Buckland Ripers - par.	154	1,237	1,560	do. - -	do.
Fleet - - - par.	138	967	903	Weymouth -	do.
Langton Herring - par.	255	1,202	835	do. - -	do.
Melcombe Regis - par.	7,020	103	30,515	do. - -	Weymouth and Melcombe Regis.
Osmington - - par.	380	2,307	2,842	do. -	Dorchester.
Owermoigne (a) - par.	423	3,891	2,709	Dorchester -	do.
Portisham - - par.	705	4,540	5,407	do. - -	do.
Portland - - par.	10,061	2,890	19,008	Weymouth -	do.
Poxwell - - par.	86	887	927	do. -	do.
Preston - - par.	689	2,679	4,603	do. - -	do.
Radipole - - par.	1,322	1,329	10,171	do. - -	do.
Upway - - par.	729	1,785	3,625	Dorchester -	do.
West Chickerell - par.	819	1,576	3,008	Weymouth -	do.
Weymouth (W.) - par.	3,630	77	7,506	do. - -	Weymouth and Melcombe Regis.
Wyke Regis par.	2.748	1,702	13,064	do. - -	Dorchester.
TOTAL of UNION -	32,022	34,794	115,771		

WETHERBY UNION :

(a) (b) *See* notes, page 403.

WEYMOUTH UNION :

(a) By Provisional Order which came into operation on 25 March, 1882, a detached part of Milton Abbas, known as "Holworth," in the Blandford Union, was amalgamated with Owermoigne.

Unions and Parishes. &c.		Population in 1881.	Area in Statute Acres in 1881.	Rateable Value in 1881.	Post Town.	Petty Sessional Division.
WHARFEDALE UNION.						
Formed 15 Feb. 1861 by Order dated 1 Feb. 1861.—Places marked thus * added 21 June 1869 by Order dated 31 May 1869.)						
COUNTY of YORK, WEST RIDING :				*£*		
*Addle-with-Eccup	- *tow.*	1,190	4,890	11,430	Leeds - -	Upper Skyrack.
Alwoodley -	- *tow.*	448	1,510	2,079	Moortown, Leeds -	do.
*Arthington -	- *tow.*	449	2,266	7,393	Leeds - -	Otley.
*Askwith	- *tow.*	260	3,393	3,379	Otley - -	do.
*Baildon -	- *tow.*	5,430	2,605	16,303	Shipley - -	do.
Blubberhouses	- *tow.*	77	3,736	1,465	Otley - -	do.
Bramhope -	- *tow.*	408	1,398	4,651	Leeds - -	do.
*Burley	- *tow.*	2,550	3,133	12,603	Burley in Wharfedale near Leeds.	do.
*Carlton -	- *tow.*	90	1,289	1,512	Yeadon, Leeds -	do.
Castley -	- *tow.*	87	521	1,508	Harewood, Leeds -	do.
Clifton-with-Norwood	*tow.*	335	3,627	5,681	Otley - -	do.
*Denton -	- *tow.*	147	3,240	3,144	do.	do.
Esholt -	- *tow.*	388	691	2,885	Shipley - -	do.
Farnley -	- *tow.*	139	1,959	5,167	Otley - -	do.
Fewston -	- *tow.*	323	2,186	4,029	do. - -	do.
Great Timble	- *tow.*	171	1,566	1,964	do. - -	do.
Guiseley -	- *tow.*	3,706	1,554	11,732	Leeds - -	do.
*Hawksworth	- *tow.*	215	2,462	3,170	Guiseley, Leeds -	do.
Horsforth -	- *tow.*	6,346	2,801	19,853	Leeds - -	Upper Skyrack.
*Ilkley -	- *tow.*	4,736	3,822	29,123	Ilkley - -	Otley.
Leathley -	- *tow.*	150	1,565	4,937	Otley - -	do.
Lindley -	- *tow.*	56	1,789	2,376	do. - -	do.
Little Timble	- *tow.*	31	504	2,867	do. - -	do.
*Menstone -	- *tow.*	662	1,126	3,568	Leeds - -	do.
*Middleton -	- *tow.*	151	2,658	2,129	Otley - -	do.
*Nesfield- with -Langbar -	*tow.*	177	1,925	1,852	Ilkley - -	East Staincliffe.
Newall-with - Clifton (W.) -	*tow.*	361	1,531	3,413	Otley -	Otley.
*Otley -	- *tow.*	6,806	2,370	23,553	do. - -	do.
Poole -	- *tow.*	574	951	3,909	Leeds - -	do.
*Rawden -	- *tow.*	3,407	1,559	15,029	do. -	Upper Skyrack.
Stainburn -	- *tow.*	174	3,157	2,589	Otley - -	Otley.
*Weston -	- *tow.*	127	1,509	2,048	do. - -	do.
Yeadon -	- *tow.*	6,534	1,723	17,223	Leeds - -	do.
TOTAL of UNION -		46,705	71,019	234,594		
WHEATENHURST UNION.						
(Formed 21 Sept. 1835 by Order dated 4 Sept. 1835.)						
COUNTY of GLOUCESTER :						
Arlingham -	- *par.*	626	2,461	4,060	Stonehouse, Gloucestershire.	Whitminster.
						(continued)

WHEATENHURST UNION :

(a) By Orders which came into operation on 25 March 1881,—
Detached parts of Eastington were amalgamated with Fretherne ;
Detached and inconveniently situated parts of Standish were amalgamated with Moreton Valence ;
A detached part of Standish was amalgamated with Longney ;
A detached part of Standish, known as Colthrep tything, was amalgamated with Haresfield ;
A detached part of Standish was amalgamated with Pitchcombe, in the Stroud Union ;
Certain parts of Moreton Valence were amalgamated with Standish ;

WHEATENHURST UNION—*continued.*

Two detached parts of Hardwicke, known as " Furleigh's End," were amalgamated with Elmore, in the Gloucester Union ;
Three detached parts of Brookthrop were amalgamated with Pitchcombe, in the Stroud Union ;
Certain parts of a parish, known as Saul, were amalgamated with Fretherne, and the remaining parts were amalgamated with Moreton Valence ;
By Order dated 9 April, 1884 Fretherne as altered was termed Fretherne with Saul. (Fretherne had in 1881 population 239, acreage 558, and rateable value 1,195*l.* Saul had in 1881 population 597, acreage 572, and rateable value 1,899*l.*)

Unions and Parishes. &c.	Population in 1881.	Area in Statute Acres in 1881.	Rateable Value in 1881.	Post Town.	Petty Sessional Division.
WHEATENHURST UNION—County of Gloucester—continued.			£		
Brockthrop (a) (b) - par.	151	2,294	2,021	Gloucester -	Gloucester.
Eastington (W.) (a) par.	1,520	2,042	5,505	Stonehouse, Gloucestershire.	Whitminster.
Frampton on Severn par.	965	2,322	6,238	do. - -	do.
Fretherne with Saul (a) par.	—	—	—	do. - -	do.
Frocester - par.	271	1,833	4,679	do. - -	do.
Hardwicke (a) - par.	645	2,378	5,089	Gloucester -	do.
Harescomb (a) (b) - par.	149	478	1,319	Stroud - -	Gloucester.
Haresfield (a) (b) - par.	572	2,155	7,238	Stonehouse, Gloucestershire.	Whitminster.
Longney (a) - par.	126	1,558	2,917	Gloucester -	do.
Moreton Valence (a)(c) par.	339	672	4,287	Stonehouse, Gloucestershire.	do.
Standish (a) (b) - par.	189	3,022	8,607	do. - -	do.
Wheatenhurst or Whitminster par.	364	1,267	2,613	do. - -	do.
TOTAL of UNION -	6,517 (a)	22,482 (a)	54,573 (a)		
WHITBY UNION.					
(Formed 9 Jan. 1837 by Order dated 13 Dec. 1836.)					
COUNTY of YORK, NORTH RIDING :					
Aislaby - - tow.	337	1,072	1,834	Whitby - -	Whitby Strand.
Barnby (b) - tow.	196	2,140	2,119	do. - -	do.
Barrowby - - tow.	88	682	730	Saltburn by the Sea	do.
Egton - - tow.	1,266	15,657	11,029	Grosmont, York -	do.
Ellerby - - tow.	83	759	830	Whitby - -	do.
Eskedaleside cum Ugglebarnby (c) : tow.	1,805	6,001	9,743	do. - -	do.
Fylingdales - tow.	1,448	6,325	7,243	Scarborough -	do.
Glaisdale - - tow.	1,103	4,967	7,224	Grosmont, York -	do.
Goadland or Goatland tow.	514	9,032	3,412	York - -	Pickering Lythe, West.
Hawsker with Stainsiker - tow.	962	3,813	7,661	Whitby - -	Whitby Strand.
Hinderwell - tow.	2,467	1,655	4,925	Saltburn by the Sea	do.
Hutton Mulgrave (b) tow.	55	1,086	870	Whitby - -	do.
Lythe (b) - tow.	1,182	3,770	4,391	do. - -	do.
Mickleby - - tow.	170	1,398	1,259	do. - -	do.
Newholm with Dunsley - tow.	400	2,196	3,047	do. - -	do.
Newton Mulgrave - tow.	80	2,345	1,261	Saltburn by the Sea	do.
Roxby - - tow.	186	3,251	1,901	do. - -	do.
Ruswarp - - tow.	4,839	1,740	25,552	Whitby - -	do.
Sneaton - - par.	232	1,851	2,391	do. - -	do.
Ugthorpe - tow.	241	2,417	1,974	do. - -	do.
Whitby (W.) - tow.	8,820	78	16,092	do. - -	do.
TOTAL of UNION -	26,474	75,235 (a)	115,488		

WHEATENHURST UNION—continued.

(a) See notes, page 405.

(b) By Provisional Orders which came into operation on 25 March 1885,—

Parts of Quedgley and Whaddon, in the Gloucester Union, and of Harescomb and Haresfield, were amalgamated with Brockthrop ;

Parts of Whaddon, Brockthrop, and Haresfield were amalgamated with Harescomb ;

Detached parts of Randwick, in the Stroud Union, were amalgamated with Standish and Haresfield ;

Parts of Harescomb were amalgamated with Hempstead, Quedgley, and Upton Saint Leonard's, in the Gloucester Union ;

Parts of Brockthrop were amalgamated with Quedgley and Whaddon, in the Gloucester Union ;

Part of Haresfield was amalgamated with Quedgley.

(c) By Order which came into operation on 25 March 1886,—

Certain detached parts of Randwick, in the Stroud Union, were amalgamated with Moreton Valence.

WHITBY UNION :

(a) There is some land comprised in this Union, known as Fylingdales Moor, which is common to Hawsker with Stainsiker and Fylingdales, and which contains 7,002 acres.

(b) By Order which came into operation on 25 March 1884, certain detached parts of Barnby and Lythe were amalgamated with Hutton Mulgrave.

(c) By Provisional Order which came into operation on 25 March 1885, the several parts of a township known as Ugglebarnby, were amalgamated with a township known as Eskdaleside, and the latter as so altered was designated Eskdaleside cum Ugglebarnby.

Unions and Parishes, &c.	Population in 1881.	Area in Statute Acres in 1881.	Rateable Value in 1881.	Post Town.	Petty Sessional Division.

WHITCHURCH UNION.

(Formed 1 June 1835 by Order dated 19 May 1835.— Place marked thus * added 6 March 1846 by Order of that date.)

COUNTY of SOUTHAMPTON :

			£		
Ashe - - par.	198	2,127	3,420	Whitchurch, Hants	King-clere.
Freefolk Manor - par.	143	1,594	1,425	do. - -	do.
Hurstborne Priors - par.	409	3,249	4,101	do. - -	Andover.
*Laverstoke - par.	182	1,966	2,789	do. - -	Kingsclere.
Overton - - par.	1,433	6,763	10,162	do. - -	do.
Saint Mary Bourne - par.	1,078	7,746	8,723	Andover - -	Andover.
Tufton - - par.	119	1,546	1,650	Whitchurch, Hants	Kingsclere.
Whitchurch (W.) - par.	1,866	6,367	12,324	do. - -	do.
TOTAL of UNION -	5,458	31,358	44,894		

WHITCHURCH UNION.

(Formed 1 Feb. 1853 by Order dated 7 Jan. 1853.)

COUNTY of CHESTER :

Agden - - tow.	93	547	855	Whitchurch, Salop	Broxton.
Bickley - - tow.	400	2,473	3,597	Malpas, Cheshire -	do.
Bradley - - tow.	115	890	1,366	Whitchurch, Salop	do.
Chidlow - - tow.	17	157	268	do. - -	do.
Chorlton - - tow.	102	468	1,110	Malpas, Cheshire -	do.
Cuddington - tow.	271	1,355	2,456	do. - -	do.
Duckington - tow.	62	671	986	do. - -	do.
Edge - - tow.	218	1,601	3,079	do. - -	do.
Hampton - - tow.	348	1,213	2,634	do. - -	do.
Larkton - - tow.	48	403	688	Malpas - -	do.
Macefen - - tow.	62	340	776	Whitchurch, Salop	do.
Malpas - - tow.	939	1,988	5,502	Malpas - -	do.
Marbury with Quoisley - tow.	346	2,166	1,516	Whitchurch, Salop	Nantwich.
Newton-juxta-Malpas tow.	16	226	331	Malpas - -	Broxton.
Norbury - - tow.	330	1,553	2,738	Whitchurch, Salop	Nantwich.
Oldcastle - - tow.	123	845	1,123	Malpas - -	Broxton.
Overton - - tow.	125	736	1,420	do. - -	do.
Stockton - - tow.	35	272	412	do. - -	do.
Tushingham - with - Grindley - tow.	221	1,351	2,665	Whitchurch -	do.
Wichaugh - - tow.	15	332	545	Malpas - -	do.
Wigland - - tow.	150	570	1,038	do. - -	do.
Wirswall - - tow.	116	973	1,830	Whitchurch -	Nantwich.
COUNTY of FLINT :					
Iscoyd - - tow.	111	2.662	4.714	Whitchurch, Salop	Hanmer.
COUNTY of SALOP :					
Ightfield - - par.	344	1,615	2,879	do. - -	Whitchurch.
Whitchurch (W.) - par.	6,279	14,870	44,188	Whitchurch -	do.
TOTAL of UNION -	11,216	40,307	91,519		

WHITECHAPEL UNION.

(Formed 16 Feb. 1837 by Order dated 21 Jan. 1837.)

COUNTY of MIDDLESEX :

Christ Church, Spital-fields - par.	21,340	73	77,837	London, E. -	Worship Street.
Mile End New Town (W.) - ham.	10,673	42	27,869	do. - -	do.

(continued)

Unions and Parishes, &c.		Population in 1881.	Area in Statute Acres in 1881.	Rateable Value in 1881.	Post Town.	Petty Sessional Division.
WHITECHAPEL UNION—County of Middlesex— *continued.*				£		
Norton Falgate Liberty	—	1,528	9	11,021	London, E. -	Worship Street.
Old Artillery Ground	*lib.*	2,516	5	8,240	do. -	do.
Saint Botolph, Aldgate Without, or East Smithfield Liberty	—	2,883	33	45,996	do. -	Thames.
Saint Catharine by the Tower -	*pre.*	104	15	17,706	do. -	Worship Street.
Saint Mary Matfellon, Whitechapel (W.) -	*par.*	30,709	170	167,647	do. -	Thames.
Tower of London, Old Without, and Tower Precinct -	—	1,161	27	5,183	do. -	do.
Trinity in the Minories -	*par.*	449	4	8,835	do. -	do.
TOTAL of UNION -		71,363	378	370,334		
WHITEHAVEN UNION.						
(Formed 5 Dec. 1838 by Order dated 9 Nov. 1838. — Place marked thus * added 25 Dec. 1861 by Order dated 19 Nov. 1861.)						
COUNTY of CUMBERLAND:						
Arleedon	*par.*	6,651	5,556	39,671	Carnforth -	Allerdale-above-Der-went.
Cleator	*par.*	10,420	2,947	91,721	do. -	do.
Distington	*par.*	1,289	3,065	5,922	Whitehaven -	do.
Egremont (a)	*par.*	5,976	2,749	37,687	Carnforth -	do.
Ennerdale and Kinniside	*tow.*	534	22,407	4,202	do. -	do.
Gosforth (a)	*par.*	1,227	8,260	7,814	do. -	do.
Haile	*par.*	293	2,672	2,595	Beckermet -	do.
Harrington	*par.*	3,019	2,360	18,511	Harrington -	do.
Hensingham (a)	*tow.*	2,064	2,250	16,460	Whitehaven -	do.
Lamplugh	*par.*	1,261	6,342	14,940	Cockermouth -	do.
Low Side Quarter	*tow.*	314	1,962	4,886	Carnforth -	do.
Moresby	*tow.*	957	2,141	5,611	Whitehaven -	do.
Nether Wasdale	*tow.*	191	8,574	913	Carnforth -	do.
Parton	*tow.*	1,479	52	5,077	Whitehaven -	do.
Ponsonby	*par.*	166	2,127	2,282	Calder Bridge -	do.
Preston Quarter (W.) (a)	*tow.*	6,997	3,156	36,856	Whitehaven -	do.
Rottington	*tow.*	67	613	759	do. -	do.
Saint Bees (a) -	*tow.*	1,142	1,814	6,772	Carnforth -	do.
Saint Bridgets (a)	*par.*	661	5,063	6,076	Beckermet -	do.
Saint John's Beckermet -	*par.*	623	2,946	4,894	do. -	do.
*Salter and Eskat	*par.*	196	638	21,027	Carnforth -	do.
Sandwith (a)	*tow.*	322	1,365	3,247	Whitehaven -	do.
Whiddicar	*tow.*	69	1,150	970	do. -	do.
Whitehaven -	*tow.*	13,374	176	41,471	do. -	do.
TOTAL of UNION -		59,292	90,715	380,396		

WHITEHAVEN UNION:

(a) By Orders which came into operation on 25 March 1882,—

A detached part of Egremont was amalgamated with Hensingham;

A detached part of Saint Bridgets was amalgamated with Gosforth;

A parish, known as Low Keekle, was amalgamated with Hensingham;

WHITEHAVEN UNION—*continued.*

A detached part of Sandwith was amalgamated with Hensingham;

Certain detached parts of Sandwith were amalgamated with Preston Quarter; and

Three detached parts of Saint Bees were amalgamated with Preston Quarter.

Unions and Parishes, &c.	Population in 1881.	Area in Statute Acres in 1881.	Rateable Value in 1881.	Post Town.	Petty Sessional Division.

WIGAN UNION.

(Formed 2 Feb. 1837 by Order dated 5 Jan. 1837.)

County of Lancaster:

			£		
Abram - - tow.	2,638	1,982	19,588	Wigan - -	Wigan.
Ashton in Mackerfield - } tow.	9,824	6,250	57,181	Newton-le-Willows	do.
Aspull - - tow.	8,113	1,905	27,016	Wigan	Bolton.
Billinge Chapel End - tow.	1,935	1,161	3,802	do. - -	Wigan.
Billinge Higher End tow.	1,402	1,571	3,689	do. - -	do.
Blackrod - - tow.	4,234	2,388	20,283	Chorley - -	Bolton.
Dalton - - tow.	491	2,104	3,550	Southport -	Wigan.
Haigh - - tow.	1,186	2,135	14,638	Wigan - -	do.
Hindley - - tow.	14,715	2,611	50,961	do. - -	do.
Ince - - tow.	16,007	2,320	57,816	do. - -	do.
Orrell - - tow.	4,299	1,618	10,869	do. - -	do.
Parbold - - tow.	529	1,150	5,004	Southport -	Chorley.
Pemberton - - tow.	13,762	2,894	47,720	Wigan - -	Wigan.
Shevington - - tow.	1,570	1,728	5,819	do. - -	Chorley.
Standish with Langtree - } tow.	4,261	3,265	22,209	do. - -	do.
Upholland - - tow.	4,435	4,685	21,301	do. - -	Wigan.
Wigan (W.) - - tow.	18,194	2,188	145,222	do. - -	Borough of Wigan.
Winstanley - - tow.	545	1,859	7,153	do. - -	Wigan.
Worthington - tow.	255	659	6,036	do. - -	Chorley.
Wrightington - tow.	1,520	3,916	9,215	do. - -	do.
Total of Union -	139,918	48,398	539,102		

WIGTON UNION.

(Formed 22 June 1837 by Order dated 27 May 1837 as amended by Order dated 16 Sept. 1841. —Place marked thus * added 28 Aug. 1837 by Order dated 1 Aug. 1837.)

County of Cumberland:

Abbey Quarter (b) - tow.	938	5,617	7,271	Carlisle - -	Allerdale-below-Derwent.
Aikton - - par.	789	6,172	7,734	Wigton - -	do.
All Hallows - par.	736	1,692	3,270	Mealsgate, Carlisle	do.
Allonby and West Newton - } tow.	868	3,751	5,788	Maryport - -	do.
Aspatria - - tow.	2,408	3,550	17,079	Aspatria - -	do.
Blencogo - tow.	190	1,778	2,442	Wigton - -	do.
Blennerhasset with Kirkland - } tow.	490	1,263	2,245	Mealsgate, Carlisle	do.
Boltons (b) - - tow.	908	8,456	9,654	Wigton - -	do.
Bowness - - par.	1,369	11,177	9,070	Carlisle - -	Cumberland Ward.
Broomfield - tow.	378	3,028	5,557	Aspatria - -	Allerdale-below-Derwent.
Caldbeck - - par.	1,176	13,742	6,763	Wigton - -	do.
Dundraw - - tow.	272	2,365	2,760	do. - -	do.
Hayton and Mealo - tow.	295	1,868	2,668	Maryport - -	do.
Holme Cultram, East Waver Quarter (b) } tow.	452	5,572	6,075	Silloth, Carlisle	do.
Holme Cultram, Saint Cuthbert Quarter (b) } tow.	748	6,301	6,146	Maryport - -	do.

(continued)

WIGTON UNION :

(a) Included in this Union is Skinburness Marsh, containing 1,178 acres, common to the Townships of Abbey Quarter, Holme Cultram, Saint Cuthbert Quarter and Holme Low Quarter.

(b) By Orders which came into operation on 25 March 1887,—
The several parts of a place known as Bolton, Low Side, were amalgamated with Bolton, High Side, and the latter was so altered was designated the Township of Boltons;
Certain parts of Abbey Quarter were amalgamated with Holme Cultram, East Waver Quarter; Holme Cultram, Saint Cuthbert Quarter; and Holme, Low Quarter;

WIGTON UNION—continued.

Certain parts of Holme Cultram, East Waver Quarter, were amalgamated with Abbey Quarter, and Holme, Low Quarter;
Certain parts of Holme Cultram, Saint Cuthbert Quarter, were amalgamated with Abbey Quarter, and Holme, Low Quarter;
Certain parts of Holme Cultram, Low Quarter, were amalgamated with Abbey Quarter and Holme Cultram, Saint Cuthbert Quarter;
A certain part of Waverton, High and Low, was with the several parts of a place known as Woodside Quarter amalgamated with Wigton, and the latter as so altered was designated the Township of Wigton-cum-Woodside.

Unions and Parishes, &c.	Population in 1881.	Area in Statute Acres in 1881.	Rateable Value in 1881.	Post Town.	Petty Sessional Division.
WIGTON UNION—County of Cumberland—*continued.*			£		
Holme, Low Quarter (b) *tow.*	2,092	6,160	11,712	Silloth, Carlisle -	Allerdale-below-Derwent.
Ireby, High - - *tow.*	109	2,733	2,479	Mealsgate, Carlisle	do.
Ireby, Low - - *tow.*	312	1,200	1,825	do. - -	do.
*Kirkbampton - *par.*	420	3,733	3,754	Carlisle -	Cumberland Ward.
Kirkbride - - *par.*	363	1,667	2,177	Kirkbride, Carlisle	Allerdale-below-Derwent.
Lanrigg and Mealrigg *tow.*	277	2,138	3,087	Aspatria - -	do.
Oulton Quarter - *tow.*	370	2,878	3,322	Wigton - -	do
Sebergham, High and Low Quarter- } *par.*	551	5,557	4,841	Carlisle - -	do.
Thursby - *par.*	533	3,142	5,066	do. - -	do.
Torpenhow and Whitrigg - } *tow.*	278	2,742	2,534	Mealsgate, Carlisle	do.
Uldale - *par.*	254	5,814	2,541	do. - -	do.
Waverton, High and Low (b) - } *tow.*	481	4,163	6,658	Wigton - -	do.
West Ward - *par.*	1,044	13,230	13,605	do. - -	do.
Wigton - cum - Woodside (W.) (b) } *tow.*	4,339	4,980	20,551	do. - -	do.
TOTAL of UNION -	23,440	136,469 (a)	179,574		
WILLITON UNION.					
(Formed 19 May 1836 by Order dated 25 April 1836.—Spelling of Names of places marked thus * is as altered by Order dated 3 May 1887.)					
COUNTY OF SOMERSET :					
Bicknoller (a) - - *par.*	327	1,390	1,908	Taunton - -	Williton.
Brompton Ralph - *par.*	124	2,690	3,569	do. - -	Milverton.
Carhampton (a) (b) (d) *par.*	645	5,724	7,062	do. - -	Dunster.
Clatworthy - *par.*	225	2,848	2,747	do. - -	Milverton.
Crowcombe - *par.*	440	3,176	3,849	do. - -	Williton.
*Culbone - *par.*	37	1,502	452	Minehead -	Dunster.
Cutcombe (a) (d) *par.*	564	7,231	4,622	Dunster -	do.
Dodington (a) (b) (d) *par.*	91	543	748	Bridgwater -	Williton.
Dunster (d) - *par.*	1,126	3,455	5,375	Taunton -	Dunster.
East Quantoxhead - *par.*	238	2,582	1,717	Bridgwater -	Williton.
Elworthy (d) - *par.*	155	1,635	1,811	Taunton -	do.
Holford (b) (d) - *par.*	157	796	1,059	Bridgwater -	do.
Kilton-with-Lilstock (d) *par.*	—	—	—	do. - -	do.

(continued)

WIGTON UNION :

(a) (b) See notes, page 409.

WILLITON UNION :

(a) By Orders which came into operation on 25 March 1883,—

A detached part of Carhampton, known as "Beasley," was amalgamated with Timberscombe;

A detached part of Luckham was amalgamated with Timberscombe;

A detached part of Minehead was amalgamated with Wootton Courtney;

Certain detached parts of Saint Decuman's, known as "Hayne" and "Kingsdown," were amalgamated with Nettlecombe;

A detached part of Stogumber was amalgamated with Sampford Brett;

A detached part of Stogumber, known as "Halsway," was amalgamated with Bicknoller;

Detached parts of Stringston were amalgamated with Dodington;

A detached part of Timberscombe, known as "East Lynch," was amalgamated with Selworthy;

A detached part of Timberscombe, known as "Stafford Rocks," was amalgamated with Cutcombe.

(b) By Provisional Orders which came into operation on 25 March 1884,—

A detached part of Carhampton, known as "Rodhuish," was amalgamated with Withycombe;

A nearly detached part of Holford, known as "Newhall," was amalgamated with Dodington;

A detached part of Monksilver, known as "Doniford," was amalgamated with Old Cleeve;

WILLITON UNION—*continued.*

A detached part of Monksilver was amalgamated with Stogumber;

A detached part of Porlock, known as the "Hamlet of Bossington," was amalgamated with Selworthy.

(c) By Order which came into operation on 25 March 1885,—

A detached part of Stogursey was amalgamated with Huntspill, in the Bridgwater Union.

(d) By Orders which came into operation on 25 March 1886,—

A detached part of Holford was amalgamated with Dodington;

A detached part of Luckham was amalgamated with Cutcombe;

A detached part of Saint Decuman's was amalgamated with Old Cleeve;

Certain parts of Stogumber were amalgamated with Elworthy;

Certain parts of Withycombe were amalgamated with Carhampton and Old Cleeve;

A detached part of Stringston, known as "Alfoxton," was amalgamated with Holford;

A detached part of Carhampton and a nearly detached part of Dunster were amalgamated with Timberscombe;

All the parts of a parish known as Kilton were amalgamated with Stringston, Holford, and Lilstock, and Lilstock was so altered was designated Kilton-with-Lilstock.

Kilton had in 1881 population 141, acreage 1,694, rateable value 1,734l. Lilstock had in 1881 population 94, acreage 1,160, and rateable value 762l.

Unions and Parishes, &c.		Population in 1881.	Area in Statute Acres in 1881.	Rateable Value in 1881.	Post Town.	Petty Sessional Division.
WILLITON UNION—County of Somerset— *continued.*				£		
Kilve	par.	222	1,770	1,493	Bridgwater	Williton.
Luckham (a) (d)	par.	371	4,126	3,178	do.	do.
Luxborough	par.	417	3,740	2,725	Taunton	do.
Minehead (a)	par.	1,774	4,581	7,350	do.	do.
Monksilver (b)	par.	264	1,005	1,603	do.	do.
Nettlecombe (a)	par.	295	2,800	4,071	do.	do.
Oare	par.	61	4,000	786	Lynton, North Devon.	Dunster.
*Old Cleeve (b) (d)	par.	1,670	5,413	8,085	Washford, Taunton	Williton.
Porlock (b)	par.	765	6,019	3,730	Taunton	Dunster.
Saint Deenman's (W.) (a) (d)	par.	3,233	4,281	11,172	Williton, Taunton	Williton.
Sampford Brett (a)	par.	217	932	2,108	do.	do.
Selworthy (a) (b)	par.	410	2,219	2,813	Minehead	Dunster.
Stogumber (a) (b) (d)	par.	1,242	5,777	8,595	Taunton	Williton.
Stogursey (c)	par.	1,262	8,803	9,831	Bridgwater	do.
Stoke Pero	par.	49	3,422	601	Minehead	Dunster.
Stringston (a) (d)	par.	114	1,193	1,380	Bridgwater	Williton.
Timberscombe (a) (d)	par.	357	1,902	2,645	Dunster	Dunster.
Treborough	par.	150	1,798	1,191	Washford, Taunton	Williton.
West Quantoxhead	par.	278	1,491	1,853	Bridgwater	Williton.
Withiel Florey	par.	262	2,485	2,066	Taunton	Milverton.
Withycombe (b) (d)	par.	279	1,787	2,056	do.	Dunster.
Wootton Courtney (a)	par.	320	3,145	2,226	Dunster	do.
TOTAL of UNION		**18,450** (d)	**106,351** (d)	**116,520** (d)		

WILTON UNION.

(Formed 13 Oct. 1835 by Order dated 23 Sept. 1835.—Place marked thus * added 25 Dec. 1858 by Order dated 16 Oct. 1858.—Spelling of names of places marked thus † as altered by Order dated 27 June 1887.)

COUNTY OF WILTS:

Unions and Parishes, &c.		Population in 1881.	Area in Statute Acres in 1881.	Rateable Value in 1881.	Post Town.	Petty Sessional Division.
†Barford Saint Martin (a)	par.	468	2,236	4,986	Salisbury	Salisbury and Amesbury.
Baverstock (a)	par.	122	1,168	1,736	do.	do.
Berwick, Saint James (a)	par.	189	2,531	2,317	do.	do.
Bishopstone	par.	627	4,452	5,171	do.	do.
Bower Chalk (b)	par.	420	2,966	2,533	do.	do.
Broad Chalk	par.	734	6,904	6,347	do.	do.
Burcombe (a)	par.	313	1,450	2,338	do.	do.
Compton Chamberlayne	par.	298	2,130	2,160	do.	do.
Dinton	par.	457	4,086	4,486	do.	do.
Ebbesborne Wake	par.	271	2,762	2,275	do.	do.
†Fifield Bavant (b)	par.	62	1,145	744	do.	do.
Fisherton Delamere	par.	295	2,861	2,798	Heytesbury	Warminster.
Fovant	par.	550	2,160	3,328	Salisbury	Salisbury and Amesbury.
Fugglestone Saint Peter	par.	1,023	1,818	7,368	do.	do.
Great Wishford	par.	358	1,679	2,468	do.	do.
*Grovely Wood	par.	48	In Barford Saint Martin's	708	do.	do.
Langford Steeple	par.	523	3,941	4,373	Heytesbury	do.
Little Langford	par.	82	1,011	1,076	Salisbury	do.
Netherhampton	par.	185	778	1,166	do.	do.

(continued)

WILTON UNION:

(a) By Order which came into operation on 25 March 1884,—
A detached part of Baverstock was amalgamated with Barford Saint Martin;
A detached part of Berwick Saint James was amalgamated with Stapleford;

WILTON UNION—continued.

A detached part of South Newton called "Ugford" was amalgamated with Burcombe.
(b) By Order which came into operation on 25 March 1885,—
A nearly detached part of Fifield Bavant was amalgamated with Bower Chalk.

Unions and Parishes, &c.	Population in 1881.	Area in Statute Acres in 1881.	Rateable Value in 1881.	Post Town.	Petty Sessional Division.
WILTON UNION—County of Wilts—*continued.*			£		
South Newton (W.) } *par.* (*a*)	675	3,502	5,316	Salisbury -	{ Salisbury and Ames- bury.
Stapleford (*a*) - *par.*	228	2,084	2,108	do. -	do.
Wiley - - - *par.*	487	2,279	3,471	Heytesbury -	Warminster.
Wilton - - - *par.*	1,826	1,852	6,936	Salisbury -	Salisbury and Ames- bury.
TOTAL of UNION -	10,250	55,795	76,504		
WIMBORNE AND CRANBORNE UNION.					
(The Wimborne Union, which was formed 28 Sept. 1835 by Order dated 14 Sept. 1835, and the Cranborne Union, which was formed 30 Sept. 1835 by Order dated 16 Sept. 1835, were united and formed into the Wimborne and Cranborne Union 29 Sept. 1836 by Order dated 19 Aug. 1836. — Place marked thus * added 29 Sept. 1858 by Order dated 6 Aug. 1858 ; and thus † added 25 March 1865 by Order dated 13 Feb. 1865.)					
COUNTY of DORSET :					
Chalbury (*b*) - *par.*	211	1,314	1,386	Wimborne -	Wimborne.
Chettle - - *par.*	130	1,113	1,080	Blandford -	Blandford.
Corfe Mullen (*b*) - *par.*	694	3,086	2,876	Wimborne -	Wimborne.
Cranborne (*b*) - *par.*	2,317	13,730	8,632	Salisbury -	do.
†East Woodyates - *par.*	Nil	{ In Pentridge }	167	do. -	do.
Edmondesham (*b*) - *par.*	230	1,671	1,631	do. -	do.
Farnham (*a*) - - *par.*	285	1,299	1,536	do. -	Blandford.
Gussage All Saints (*b*) *par.*	415	2,907	2,767	do. -	Wimborne.
Gussage Saint Michael } *par.* (*b*)	259	2,882	2,173	do. -	do.
Hampreston - *par.*	1,393	4,948	4,558	Wimborne -	do.
Hinton Martell (*b*) - *par.*	381	1,534	1,968	do. -	do.
Hinton Parva (*b*) - *par.*	93	439	488	do. -	do.
Horton - - *par.*	463	2,740	1,975	do. -	do.
Long Critchell - *par.*	163	1,869	1,388	Salisbury -	do.
More Critchell (*b*) - *par.*	367	1,705	1,994	Wimborne -	do.
Pentridge - - *par.*	234	1,764	1,260	Salisbury -	do.
Shapwicke (*b*) - *par.*	432	3,670	3,750	Blandford -	do.
Sixpenny Handley - *par.*	938	5,928	6,026	Salisbury -	do.
Sturminster Marshall } *par.* (*b*) - -	809	3,851	5,201	Wimborne -	do.
West Parley (*b*) - *par.*	336	3,407	1,008	do. -	do.
*West Woodyates - *par.*	33	1,290	553	Salisbury -	do.
Wimborne Minster } *par.* (W.) (*b*)	5,390	11,966	22,451	Wimborne -	do.
Wimborne Saint Giles } *par.* (*b*)	453	3,978	3,512	Salisbury -	do.
Witchampton (*b*) - *par.*	512	1,481	2,279	Wimborne -	do.
Woodlands - - *par.*	453	2,561	2,116	do. -	do.
TOTAL of UNION -	16,991	81,163	83,684		

WILTON UNION:

(*a*) See note, page 411.

WIMBORNE AND CRANBORNE UNION :

(*a*) By Order which came into operation on 25 March 1885, all the parts of a tything known as Farnham Tollard were amalgamated with Farnham.

(*b*) By Order which came into operation on 25 March 1886,—
A detached part of Chalbury, known as " Didlens," was amalgamated with Wimborne Minster ;
Detached parts of Cranborne were amalgamated with Wimborne Saint Giles and West Parley ;
A detached part of Gussage All Saints, known as " Painsmoor Copse," was amalgamated with Edmondesham, and another detached part, known as

WIMBORNE AND CRANBORNE UNION—*continued.*

" Manaton " or " Mannington," was amalgamated with Wimborne Minster ;
A detached part of Gussage Saint Michael, known as " Sutton," was amalgamated with Wimborne Saint Giles, and another detached part with More Critchell ;
Two detached parts of Hinton Martell were amalgamated with Hinton Parva ;
Two detached parts of Shapwicke were amalgamated with Witchampton ;
A certain part of Sturminster Marshall was amalgamated with Wimborne Minster ; and
A certain part of Wimborne Minster was amalgamated with Corfe Mullen.

Unions and Parishes, &c.	Population in 1881.	Area in Statute Acres in 1881.	Rateable Value in 1881.	Post Town.	Petty Sessional Division.
WINCANTON UNION.			£		
(Formed 30 Dec. 1835 by Order dated 9 Dec. 1835.)					
County of Dorset :					
Buckhorne Weston - par.	517	1,632	4,413	Wincanton - -	Shaston.
Kington Magna - par.	465	1,891	4,168	Gillingham - -	do.
County of Somerset :					
Abbas Combe and Temple Combe - par.	790	1,850	6,222	Templecombe -	Wincanton.
Alford (c) - par.	95	722	1,417	Castle Cary -	do.
Ansford or Almsford (d) par.	296	844	2,932	do. - -	do.
Blackford (b) - par.	140	578	1,397	Wincanton -	do.
Bruton (d) - par.	87	1,093	1,438	do. - -	do.
Bruton (a) (b) - par.	1,849	3,631	10,925	Bruton - -	do.
Castle Cary - par.	2,031	2,625	10,299	Castle Cary -	do.
Charlton Horethorne (b) par.	478	2,363	4,316	Sherborne -	do.
Charlton Musgrove (a) (b) (d) par.	409	2,153	1,448	Wincanton - -	do.
Compton Pauncefoot par.	185	672	1,613	North Cadbury, Bath	do.
Corton Dinham par.	339	1,371	2,545	Sherborne -	do.
Cucklington par.	269	2,865	3,261	Wincanton -	do.
Henstridge (b) par.	1,298	4,252	9,571	Blandford -	do.
Holton (b) (d) par.	169	491	1,297	Wincanton -	do.
Horsington (b) (d) par.	734	3,591	7,969	Templecombe	do
Lovington - par.	203	822	1,637	Castle Cary -	do.
Maperton (d) - par.	203	1,531	2,967	Wincanton -	do.
Milborne Port (b) par.	1,877	3,277	8,162	Sherborne -	do.
North Barrow par.	118	751	1,245	Castle Cary	do.
North Brewham (b) par.	227	2,026	3,133	Bruton -	do.
North Cadbury (b) par.	896	2,810	8,701	Bath -	do.
North Cheriton (b) (c) par.	228	1,088	2,597	Wincanton -	do.
Penselwood (b) par.	420	1,101	2,200	Bath -	do.
Pitcombe (b) par.	421	1,050	4,180	Castle Cary -	do.
Queen Camel (b) par.	542	2,498	5,092	Bath -	Yeovil.
Shepton Montague (a) (b) par.	326	2,424	3,235	Castle Cary -	Wincanton.
South Barrow par.	122	752	1,401	do. -	do.
South Brewham (a) (b) (c) par.	350	2,671	3,310	Bruton -	do.
South Cadbury par.	187	800	1,917	North Cadbury, Bath	do.
Sparkford - par.	253	950	2,630	Bath -	Yeovil.
Stoke Trister (b) (d) par.	121	1,090	2,949	Wincanton -	Wincanton.

(continued)

WINCANTON UNION :

(a) By Orders which came into operation on 25 March 1884,—
Detached parts of Shepton Montague and Wincanton were amalgamated with Charlton Musgrove.
The two detached parts into which a Parish known as Eastrip (see note c) was divided were amalgamated, one with Bruton, and the other with South Brewham.

(b) By Provisional Order which came into operation on 25 March 1885,—
A detached part of Bruton was amalgamated with Pitcombe ;
A nearly detached part of Charlton Horethorne was amalgamated with Stowell ;
A nearly detached part of Henstridge was amalgamated with Milborne Port ;
A detached part of North Brewham was amalgamated with South Brewham ;
A detached part of North Cadbury was amalgamated with Blackford ;
A detached part of North Cheriton was amalgamated with Holton ;
A detached part of Penselwood was amalgamated with Stoke Trister ;
A detached part of Queen Camel, known as Nether Adber, was amalgamated with Marston Magna, in the Sherborne Union :

WINCANTON UNION—continued.

Detached parts of Shepton Montague were amalgamated with Charlton Musgrove ;
Parts of Wincanton were amalgamated with Charlton Musgrove and Horsington.

(c) By Orders which came into operation on 25 March 1885, a Parish known as Four Towers was amalgamated with South Brewham.
(Four Towers and Eastrip (see note a) contained together in 1881, population 18, acreage 160, and rateable value 986l.)
A certain portion of Wincanton was amalgamated with North Cheriton ;
Certain parts of Alford were amalgamated with Ditcheat, in the Shepton Mallet Union, and certain parts of Ditcheat and Hornblotton, in that Union, were amalgamated with Alford.

(d) By Orders which came into operation on 25 March 1886,—
A detached part of Charlton Musgrove was amalgamated with Bratton ;
A detached part of Horsington was amalgamated with Stoke Trister ;
A detached part of Maperton was amalgamated with Holton ;
A detached part of Ansford or Almsford was amalgamated with Ditcheat, in the Shepton Mallet Union

Unions and Parishes, &c.		Population in 1881.	Area in Statute Acres in 1881.	Rateable Value in 1881	Post Town.	Petty Sessional Division.
WINCANTON UNION—County of Somerset— continued.						
Stowell (b) -	- par.	110	902	£ 2,129	Sherborne - -	Wincanton.
Sutton Montis or } Montagne - - }	par.	115	508	1,591	North Cadbury, Bath	do.
Weston Bamfylde -	par.	104	631	1,897	Sparkford -	do.
Wheathill -	par.	37	314	622	Somerton - -	do.
Wincanton (W.) (a) } (b) (c) }	par.	2,410	4,130	13,063	Wincanton - -	do.
Yarlington -	par.	228	1,207	2,673	do. - -	do.
TOTAL of UNION -		19,752 (c)	65,960 (c)	155,598 (c)		
WINCHCOMB UNION.						
(Formed 16 Jan. 1836 by Order dated 30 Dec. 1835 as amended by Order dated 7 Aug. 1840.)						
COUNTY of GLOUCESTER :						
Alderton and Dixon -	par.	415	1,750	2,539	Winchcomb -	Winchcomb.
Alstone (a) -	ham.	76	1,060	736	Tewkesbury	do.
Beckford -	par.	461	2,650	4,888	do. -	do.
Bishop's Cleve (a)	tow.	650	6,819	4,534	Cheltenham -	Cheltenham.
Buckland -	par.	283	2,270	2,947	Broadway -	Winchcomb.
Charlton Abbots (a) -	par.	115	2,190	929	Andoversford, near Cheltenham.	do.
Didbrook (a) -	par.	215	1,528	1,758	Winchcomb	do.
Dumbleton -	par.	439	2,100	3,951	Evesham -	do.
Gotherington -	ham.	388 { In Bishop's Cleve }		2,952	Cheltenham	Cheltenham.
Great Washbourne -	par.	82	470	864	Tewkesbury	Winchcomb.
Hailes -	par.	57	1,520	2,003	do. -	do.
Hawling (a)-	par.	154	1,846	1,729	Andoversford	do.
Little Washbourne -	ham.	22	In Alstone	629	Winchcomb -	do.
Lower Guiting (a) -	par.	619	3,380	4,296	do. -	do.
Pinnock in Hyde (a)	tow.	29	1,050	794	do. -	do.
Prescott (a) -	par.	60	430	770	do. -	do.
Rowell -	par.	32	1,640	745	do. -	do.
Snowshill -	par.	255	2,294	1,875	Broadway	do.
Southam (a) -	ham.	238 { In Bishop's Cleve }		4,710	Cheltenham -	Cheltenham.
Stanley Pott Large -	par.	58	960	825	Winchcomb	Winchcomb.
Stanway (a) -	par.	307	3,390	3,320	do. -	do.
Staunton (a) -	par.	269	1,650	1,942	do. -	do.
Sudeley -	par.	100	2,622	1,967	do. -	do.
Temple Guiting -	par.	517	6,180	5,476	do. -	do.
Toddington (a) -	par.	212	1,857	2,754	do. -	do.
Winchcomb (W.) (a) -	par.	2,834	5,700	13,252	do. -	do.
Woodmancot (a) -	ham.	381 { In Bishop's Cleve }		2,198	Cheltenham	Cheltenham.
Wormington -	par.	94	560	540	Evesham	Winchcomb.
COUNTY of WORCESTER :						
Cutsdean -	cha.	171	1,578	1,171	Broadway -	Chipping Campden.
TOTAL of UNION -		9,533	57,494	77,094		

WINCANTON UNION :

(a), (b), (c), See notes, page 413.

WINCHCOMB UNION :

(a) By Orders which came into operation on 25 March 1883,—

A detached part of Bishop's Cleve was amalgamated with Woodmancot ;

Detached parts of Woodmancot and Bishop's Cleve were amalgamated with Southam ;

A detached part of Didbrook, known as Wormington Grange, was amalgamated with Staunton, and another detached part was amalgamated with Stanway :

WINCHCOMB UNION—continued.

A detached part of Lower Guiting, known as "Chapel Farmcott," was amalgamated with Pinnock in Hyde, and another detached part, known as " Westfield," was amalgamated with Hawling ;

A detached part of Toddington was amalgamated with Winchcomb ;

A detached part of Winchcombe was amalgamated with Charlton Abbots, and another detached part, known as " Rushy Cockbury Farm," was amalgamated with Prescott ;

A detached part of Teddington, in the Tewkesbury Union, was amalgamated with Alstone.

Unions and Parishes, &c.		Population in 1881.	Area in Statute Acres in 1881.	Rateable Value in 1881.	Post Town.	Petty Sessional Division.
WINDSOR UNION.						
(Formed 7 Sept. 1835 by Order dated 29 Aug. 1835, as amended by Order dated 16 April 1880.)						
COUNTY of BERKS:						
Clewer	par.	9,296	2,034	36,219	Windsor	Borough of New Windsor, and Windsor,
New Windsor	par.	7,831	2,583	46,788	do.	Borough of New Windsor.
Old Windsor (W.)	par.	2,521	5,530	15,955	do.	Windsor.
Sunninghill	par.	3,039	3,135	21,746	Ascot	do.
COUNTY of SURREY:						
Egham	par.	8,692	7,786	36,116	Staines	Godley, Second Division (Chertsey).
Thorpe	par.	610	1,563	4,510	Chertsey	do. do.
TOTAL of UNION		31,992	22,631	161,364		
WINSLOW UNION.						
(Formed 9 June 1835 by Order dated 23 May 1835.)						
COUNTY of BUCKINGHAM:						
Drayton Parslow	par.	473	1,750	2,035	Bletchley	Winslow.
Dunton	par.	80	1,197	1,578	Winslow	do.
East Claydon	par.	311	2,396	2,937	do.	do.
Grandborough	par.	300	1,580	2,014	do.	do.
Great Horwood cum Singleborough	par.	712	3,271	1,618	do.	do.
Hogston or Hoggeston	par.	175	1,571	2,181	do.	do.
Hogshaw cum Full-brooke	par.	62	1,322	1,562	do.	do.
Little Horwood	par.	309	1,948	2,453	do.	do.
Mursley with Saldin	par.	363	2,975	3,807	do.	do.
Nash	ham.	340	1,247	1,655	Stony Stratford	do.
North Marston	par.	649	1,983	3,134	Winslow	do.
Shenly Brook End	ham.	219	1,659	1,880	Stony Stratford	Stony Stratford.
Stewkley	par.	1,361	3,982	6,459	Leighton Buzzard	Ivinghoe.
Swanbourne	par.	474	2,552	4,425	Winslow	Winslow.
Tattenhoe	par.	17	647	760	Stony Stratford	do.
Whaddon	tow.	405	2,525	3,141	do.	do.
Winslow cum Shipton (W.)	par.	1,663	1,920	7,262	Winslow	do.
TOTAL of UNION		7,943	34,525	51,301		
WIRRALL UNION.						
(Formed 16 May 1836 by Order dated 23 April 1836.—Spelling of names of places marked * is as altered by Order dated 7 July 1887.)						
COUNTY of CHESTER:						
Arrow	tow.	127	758	1,402	Birkenhead	Wirral.
Barnston	tow.	280	1,108	2,314	do.	do.
Brimstage	tow.	186	1,019	1,611	do.	do.
Bromborrow	tow.	1,335	1,555	11,175	do.	do.
Burton	tow.	257	1,927	2,792	Neston, Chester	do.
Caldey	tow.	187	754	1,444	Birkenhead	do.
Childer Thornton	tow.	624	746	4,308	Little Sutton, Chester.	do.
Eastham	tow.	639	1,604	7,137	Birkenhead	do.
*Frankby	tow.	185	571	1,634	do.	do.
Gayton	tow.	199	708	1,550	Neston	do.

(continued)

Unions and Parishes, &c.		Population in 1881.	Area in Statute Acres in 1881.	Rateable Value in 1881.	Post Town.	Petty Sessional Division.
WIRRALL UNION—County of Chester—*continued.*				£		
Grange	- - *tow.*	108	929	1,249	Birkenhead -	Wirral.
Greasby	- *tow.*	236	809	1,690	do. -	do.
Great Meolse	- *tow.*	402	695	1,611	do. -	do.
Great Neston	- *tow.*	2,119	1,405	8,472	Neston, Chester -	do.
Great Sutton	- *tow.*	336	1,155	3,052	Little Sutton, Chester.	do.
Heswall with Old-field	} *tow.*	876	1,335	3,462	Neston - -	do.
Higher Bebbington -	*tow.*	4,122	944	25,607	Birkenhead -	do.
Hoose	- *tow.*	1,208	108	3,044	do. - -	do.
Hooton	- - *tow.*	161	1,178	3,212	Little Sutton, Chester.	do.
Irby	- - *tow.*	154	842	1,207	Birkenhead -	do.
Landican	- *tow.*	75	626	1,055	do. - -	do.
Leighton	- *tow.*	259	641	1,838	Neston, Chester -	do.
*Ledsham	- *tow.*	82	825	1,842	Little Sutton, Chester.	do.
Little Meolse	- *tow.*	926	711	6,300	Birkenhead -	do.
Little Neston	- *tow.*	1,027	1,495	4,955	Neston, Chester -	do.
Little Sutton	- *tow.*	866	1,130	6,054	Little Sutton, Chester.	do.
Lower Bebbington -	*tow.*	4,050	1,054	21,054	Birkenhead -	do.
Moreton	- *tow.*	424	1,202	2,974	do. -	do.
Ness	- *tow.*	376	1,195	1,799	Neston, Chester -	do.
Nether Pool -	*tow.*	31	474	603	Little Sutton, Chester.	do.
Newton with Larton	*tow.*	68	498	631	Birkenhead -	do.
Over Pool -	*tow.*	86	457	567	Little Sutton, Chester.	do.
Pensby	- *tow.*	30	354	639	Birkenhead -	do.
Poulton cum Spittle (W.) - -	} *tow.*	399	980	4,387	do. - -	do.
Prenton	- *tow.*	111	640	1,295	do. -	do.
Puddington	- *tow.*	158	1,391	2,130	Neston, Chester -	do.
Raby	- *tow.*	239	1,477	2,836	do. -	do.
Saughall-Massey	- *tow.*	191	942	1,580	Birkenhead -	do.
Storeton	- *tow.*	241	1,372	2,770	do. -	do.
Thingwell	- *tow.*	162	377	838	do. -	do.
Thornton Hough	- *tow.*	456	1,535	1,214	Neston, Chester -	do.
Thurstaston	- *tow.*	113	942	1,621	Birkenhead -	do.
Upton or Overchurch	*par.*	622	943	4,023	do. -	do.
West Kirby	- *tow.*	1,118	482	5,924	do. -	do.
Whitby	- *tow.*	1,488	1,232	5,927	Little Sutton, Chester.	Chester.
Willaston	- *tow.*	462	1,994	4,178	do. -	Wirral.
Woodchurch -	*tow.*	127	338	953	Birkenhead -	do.
TOTAL of UNION	-	27,928	45,457	180,990		

WISBEACH UNION.

(Formed 28 May 1836 by Order dated 28 April 1836.—Places marked thus * added 31 Oct. 1836 by Order dated 5 Oct. 1836, as amended by Order dated 1 May 1837.)

COUNTY OF CAMBRIDGE :						
Elm	- - *par.*	1,795	11,105	20,473	Wisbech -	Wisbech.
Leverington	- *par.*	1,214	7,871	9,077	do. -	do.

(*continued*)

WISBEACH UNION :

(a) By Order which came into operation on 25 March 1884,—
A detached part of Upwell (Cambs.) was amalgamated with Welney (Cambs.), in the Downham Union ;
A detached part of Upwell (Norfolk) was amalgamated with Welney (Norfolk), in the Downham Union ;
A detached part of Welney (Norfolk), in the Downham Union, was amalgamated with Upwell (Norfolk) ;
(b) By Order which came into operation on 25 March 1885,—
Parts of Clenchwarton were amalgamated with West Lynn and North Lynn, in the King's Lynn Union ;

WISBEACH UNION—*continued.*

A detached part of Terrington Saint John's, known as New Common Marsh, was amalgamated with Terrington Saint Clement's ;
A detached part of Walpole Saint Andrew's was amalgamated with Walpole Saint Peter ;
(c) By Order which came into operation on 25 March 1886, a detached part of Walpole Saint Andrew's was amalgamated with Walpole Saint Peter's, and detached parts of Walpole Saint Peter's were amalgamated with Walpole Saint Andrew's.
(d) Part of the area of Emneth is returned with that of Outwell (Norfolk).

Unions and Parishes, &c.	Population in 1881.	Area in Statute Acres in 1881.	Rateable Value in 1881.	Post Town.	Petty Sessions Division.
WISBEACH UNION—County of Cambridge— continued.			£		
Newton - par.	483	3,056	5,591	Wisbech - -	Wisbech.
*Outwell (Cambs.) - par.	343	506	1,478	do. - -	do.
Parson Drove - cha.	710 {	In Leverington }	7,587	do. - -	do.
Tyd Saint Giles - par.	878	4,991	8,146	do. - -	do.
*Upwell (Cambs.) (a) par.	1,356 {	In Upwell, Norfolk. }	13,951	do. - -	do.
Wisbeach Saint Mary's par.	2,124	9,606	17,037	do. -	do.
Wisbeach Saint Peter's (W.) } par.	9,249	6,432	36,875	do. - -	Wisbech and Borough of Wisbech.
COUNTY OF NORFOLK :					
*Clenchwarton (b) - par.	668	3,505	5,734	Lynn -	Freebridge Marshland.
Emneth (d) - par.	1,001	3,449	7,209	Wisbech - -	do.
*Outwell (Norfolk) - par.	869	2,512	4,894	do. -	Downham Market.
*Terrington Saint Clement's (b) - } par.	2,028	} 34,236 {	18,320	Lynn -	Freebridge Marshland.
*Terrington Saint John's (b) } par.	673		5,265	do. -	do.
*Tilney All Saints - par.	565		5,231	do. - -	do.
*Tilney Saint Lawrence par.	722	} 7,511 {	6,816	do. - -	do.
*Tilney with Islington par.	291		3,026	do. - -	do.
*Upwell (Norfolk) (a) par.	2,082	16,454	17,396	Wisbech -	Downham Market.
Walpole Saint Andrew's (b) (c) } par.	687	3,494	5,310	do. - -	Freebridge Marshland.
Walpole Saint Peter's (b) (c) } par.	1,137	6,982	13,606	do. - -	do.
Walsoken - par.	2,697	4,656	12,721	do. - -	do.
West Walton - par.	860	5,219	10,356	do. - -	do.
TOTAL of UNION -	32,462	131,585	236,099		

WITNEY UNION.

(Formed 26 Mar. 1835 by Order dated 6 Mar. 1835.—Place marked thus * added 1 Mar. 1864 by Order dated 9 Feb. 1864.)

COUNTIES of GLOUCESTER and OXFORD :

Broughton-Poggs (a) par.	113	1,153	1,115	Lechlade -	Bampton West.

COUNTY of OXFORD :

Alvescott (a) - par.	362	2,119	2,784	Faringdon -	do.
Asthall and Asthall Leigh (a) - } par.	374	2,223	2,447	Burford, Faringdon	do.
Aston and Cote - hams.	711	2,997	1,770	Bampton, Faringdon	Bampton East.
Bampton with Weald (a) - } par.	1,395	4,491	8,494	Faringdon -	do.
Blackbourton (a) - par.	212	2,379	2,561	do. -	Bampton West.
Brighthampton (a) - ham.	74	665	892	Witney -	do. East.
Broadwell (b) - par.	845	3,550	4,414	Lechlade -	do. West.
Burford (a) - tow.	1,312	750	3,195	Faringdon -	do. do.
Chimney - ham.	28	668	580	Bampton, Faringdon	do. East.

(continued)

WITNEY UNION

(a) By Orders which came into operation on 25 March 1886,—

Detached parts of Alvescott and Kencott were amalgamated with Clanfield ;
Detached parts of Norton Brize and Blackbourton were amalgamated with Bampton with Weald ;
Detached parts of Brighthampton and Ducklington were amalgamated with Hardwicke ;
A detached part of Upton and Signet was amalgamated with Burford ;
Detached parts of Hardwicke were amalgamated with Standlake and Brighthampton ;
A detached part of Stanton-Harcourt was amalgamated with Northmoor ;

WITNEY UNION—continued.

A detached part of Fulbrook, known as Laws Grove, was amalgamated with Swinbrook, and another detached part with Asthall and Asthall Leigh ;
A detached part of Taynton was amalgamated with Swinbrook ; and
A detached part of Broughton Poggs was amalgamated with Lechlade, in the Farringdon Union.

(b) By Provisional Order which came into operation on 25 March 1887,—
The several parts of a place known as Filkins were amalgamated with Broadwell.

(c) There is some land included in this Union known as Burroway, which comprises 31 acres, and other land known as Langel Common, which comprises 9 acres.

Unions and Parishes, &c.		Population in 1881.	Area in Statute Acres in 1881.	Rateable Value in 1881.	Post Town.	Petty Sessional Division.
WITNEY UNION—County of Oxford—*continued.*				£		
Clanfield (a) -	par.	499	1,713	3,169	Faringdon - -	Bampton West.
Cogges - -	par.	694	2,285	3,211	Witney - -	do. East.
Crawley -	ham.	160	1,128	1,519	do. - -	do. do.
Curbridge (W.)	ham.	604	2,983	5,639	Faringdon -	do. do.
Ducklington (a)	par.	435	1,941	2,816	Witney - -	do. do.
Ensham	par.	2,076	5,446	10,837	Oxford - -	do. do.
Fulbrook (a) -	par.	349	1,951	2,611	Burford, Faringdon	do. West.
Hailey -	tow.	1,265	2,879	5,964	Witney - -	do. East.
Handborough -	par.	968	2,270	4,375	Woodstock -	Wootton South.
Hardwicke (a)	ham.	115	671	882	Witney - -	Bampton East.
Holwell -	cha.	120	1,063	1,156	Burford, Faringdon	do. West.
Kencott (a) -	par.	202	1,099	1,531	Lechlade -	do. do.
Lew - -	ham.	129	1,642	1,711	Faringdon -	de. do.
Minster-Lovell	par.	511	1,951	2,730	Witney - -	do. East.
North Leigh -	par.	648	2,423	4,079	do. - -	Wootton South.
Northmoor (a)	par.	299	2,048	2,886	Eynsham, Oxford -	Bampton East.
Norton Brize (a)	par.	639	3,277	1,605	Bampton,Faringdon	do. West.
*Osney Hill -	par.	8	77	61	Witney - -	Wootton South.
Ramsden -	tow.	435	920	1,452	Charlbury, Enstone	Bampton East.
Shifford -	ham.	70	775	1,022	Bampton,Faringdon	do.
Shilton -	par.	287	1,604	1,806	do. - -	do. West.
South Leigh -	par.	359	2,074	3,208	Witney - -	do. East.
Standlake (a) -	par.	708	2,346	3,939	do. - -	do. do.
Stanton-Harcourt (a)	par.	541	3,740	4,668	Eynsham Oxford -	do.
Swinbrook (a) -	par.	168	1,319	1,254	Burford, Faringdon	do. West.
Taynton (a) -	par.	323	2,338	2,093	do. - -	do.
Upton and Signet (a) - }	hams.	218	2,189	2,838	do. - -	do.
Westwell -	par.	136	1,445	1,259	do. - -	do.
Widford -	par.	49	552	582	do. - -	do.
Wilcote -	par.	10	319	344	Charlbury, Enstone	Wootton South.
Witney -	tow.	3,017	192	7,388	Witney - -	Bampton East.
Yelford -	par.	8	336	393	do. - -	do.
TOTAL of UNION -		21,535	78,000 (c)	123,613		
WOBURN UNION.						
(Formed 10 April 1835 by Order dated 16 Mar. 1835.—Place marked thus * formed out of a separate portion of Aspley Guise, and added 1 May 1884 by Order dated 29 April 1884.)						
COUNTY of BEDFORD:						
Aspley-Guise -	par.	1,145	1,936	5,165	Woburn - -	Woburn.
*Aspley Heath (a)	par.	—	—	—	do. -	do.
Battlesden -	par.	114	1,123	2,078	do. -	do.
Chalgrave -	par.	873	2,130	3,635	Leighton Buzzard -	do.
Eversholt -	par.	708	2,119	3,387	Woburn - -	do.
Harlington -	par.	536	1,815	5,867	Dunstable -	Ampthill.
Hockliffe -	par.	326	1,021	1,904	Leighton Buzzard -	Woburn.
Holcutt -	par.	54	880	1,221	Woburn -	do.
Husborn-Crawley -	par.	479	1,520	2,547	do. -	do.
Milton-Bryant -	par.	223	1,480	1,780	do. -	do.
Potsgrove -	par.	203	1,385	1,826	do. -	do.
Ridgmont -	par.	746	2,218	3,166	do. -	do.
Salford -	par.	221	900	1,335	do. -	do.
Tilsworth -	par.	250	1,510	1,687	Leighton Buzzard -	do.
Tingrith -	par.	167	916	1,551	Woburn -	do.
Toddington -	par.	2,159	5,390	13,601	Dunstable -	do.
Woburn (W.) -	par.	1,316	3,200	7,476	Woburn -	do.
TOTAL of UNION -		9,880	29,603	58,526		

<table>
<tr><td>WITNEY UNION:

(a) (b) (c) See notes page 417.</td><td>WOBURN UNION:

(a) By Order which came into operation on 25 March 1885, a detached part of Wavendon, in the Newport Pagnell Union, was amalgamated with Aspley Heath.</td></tr>
</table>

Unions and Parishes, &c		Population in 1881.	Area in Statute Acres in 1881.	Rateable Value in 1884.	Post Town.	Petty Sessional Division.

WOKINGHAM UNION.

(Formed 1 Aug. 1835 by Order dated 15 July 1835.—Names of places marked * are as altered by Order dated 27 May 1887.)

COUNTY of BERKS:

				£		
Arborfield	- *par.*	270	1,469	2,263	Reading -	The Forest.
Barkham	- *par.*	217	1,388	2,036	Wokingham -	do.
Broadhinton	- *lib.*	657	1,750	5,506	Twyford -	do.
Earleigh	- *lib.*	4,463	2,252	22,891	Reading -	do.
Finchampstead	- *par.*	665	3,943	4,791	Wokingham -	do.
Newland	- *lib.*	277	1,170	2,653	Reading -	do.
Ruscomb	- *par.*	375	1,294	6,713	Twyford -	do.
Sandford and Woodley	*lib.*	1,112	3,609	12,253	Reading -	do.
Shinfield	- *par.*	1,277	4,567	9,311	do. -	Reading.
Sonning	- *lib.*	494	1,246	3,799	do. -	The Forest.
*Swallowfield East	- *par.*	313	1,522	2,839	do. -	Reading.
*Swallowfield West	- *par.*	1,039	2,223	4,557	do. -	do.
Wargrave	- *par.*	1,882	4,462	13610	Henley on Thames	The Forest.
Whistley	- *lib.*	1,249	1,933	7,559	Twyford -	do.
Winnersh	- *lib.*	685	2,045	3,901	Wokingham -	do.
Wokingham (W.)	- *par.*	5,043	8,545	24,210	do. -	do.
TOTAL of UNION -		20,018	43,418	128,922		

WOLVERHAMPTON UNION.

(Formed 11 Oct. 1836 by Order dated 16 Sept. 1836.)

COUNTY of STAFFORD:

Bilston	- *tow.*	22,730	1,845	57,441	Bilston -	Bilston.
Wednesfield -	*tow.*	10,801	3,736	26,240	Wolverhampton -	Wolverhampton.
Willenhall -	*tow.*	18,461	2,168	37,766	Willenhall -	do.
Wolverhampton (W.)	*tow.*	75,766	3,396	241,238	Wolverhampton -	Borough (Separate Quarter Sessions).
TOTAL of UNION -		127,758	11,145	362,685		

WOODBRIDGE UNION.

(Formed 3 Oct. 1835 by Order dated 17 Sept. 1835. — Places marked thus * added 29 Sept. 1858 by Order dated 25 Aug. 1858 ; and place marked thus † added 25 Mar. 1865 by Order dated 4 Feb. 1865.—Name of place marked thus ‡ is as altered by Order dated 29 July 1887.)

COUNTY of SUFFOLK:

Alderton	- *par.*	533	2,575	4,105	Woodbridge -	Woodbridge.
*Alnesbourn Priory	- *par.*	59	463	552	Ipswich -	do.
Bawdsey	- *par.*	432	1,636	3,086	Woodbridge -	do.
Boulge	- *par.*	64	545	856	do. -	do.
Boyton	- *par.*	271	1,530	2,282	do. -	do.
Bredfield	- *par.*	432	1,067	2,313	do. -	do.

(*continued*)

WOODBRIDGE UNION :

(*a*) By Orders which came into operation on 25 March 1883,—
    A detached part of Kesgrave was amalgamated with Playford ;
    A detached part of Trimley Saint Mary was amalgamated with Trimley Saint Martin.

3 D

Unions and Parishes, &c.	Population in 1881.	Area in Statute Acres in 1881.	Rateable Value in 1881.	Post Town.	Petty Sessional Division.
WOODBRIDGE UNION—County of Suffolk—continued.			£		
Brightwell - - par.	68	1,114	882	Ipswich - -	Woodbridge.
Bromeswell - - par.	210	1,787	1,798	Woodbridge -	do.
Bucklesham - par.	321	1,835	2,869	Ipswich - -	do.
Burgh - - par.	256	1,201	2,058	Woodbridge -	do.
Capel Saint Andrew par.	190	2,330	1,171	do. -	do.
Charsfield - - par.	430	1,299	2,203	Wickham Market -	do.
Clopton - - par.	382	2,074	3,437	Woodbridge -	do.
Culpho - - par.	60	726	904	Ipswich -	do.
Dallinghoo - - par.	301	1,495	2,476	Wickham Market -	do.
†Dallinghoo Wield - par.	—	35	43	Woodbridge -	do.
‡Debach - - par.	121	464	797	do.	do.
Falkenham - - par.	274	1,751	3,034	Ipswich -	do.
Felixstow - - par.	864	1,933	5,847	do. -	do.
Foxhall - - par.	251	1,840	2,125	do. -	do.
Great Bealings - par.	287	1,036	1,906	Woodbridge -	do.
Grundisburgh - par.	813	1,897	3,796	do. -	do.
Hasketon - par.	481	1,680	3,251	do. -	do.
Hemley - - par.	97	740	1,175	do. -	do.
Hollesley - - par.	511	3,987	4,977	do. -	do.
Kesgrave (a) - par.	98	900	961	do. -	do.
Kirton - - par.	627	1,855	3,219	Ipswich -	do.
Levington - - par.	167	1,026	1,370	do. -	do.
Little Bealings - par.	236	798	1,554	Woodbridge -	do.
Martlesham - - par.	498	2,632	3,103	do. -	do.
Melton - - par.	1,400	1,429	5,249	do. -	do.
Nacton (W.) - par.	516	1,920	2,526	Ipswich -	do.
Newbourn - - par.	141	909	1,345	Woodbridge -	do.
Otley - - par.	630	2,157	3,893	Ipswich -	do.
Petistree - - par.	275	1,767	3,379	Wickham Market -	do.
Playford (a) - par.	239	1,296	1,960	Ipswich -	do.
*Purdis Farm - par.	29 { In Alnesbourn Priory }		415	do. -	do.
Ramsholt - - par.	138	1,804	2,371	Woodbridge -	do.
Rushmere - - par.	630	2,142	3,615	Ipswich -	do.
Shottisham - - par.	277	1,134	1,377	Woodbridge -	do.
*Stratton Hall Farm - par.	24	505	638	Ipswich -	do.
Sutton - - par.	567	5,418	4,579	Woodbridge -	do.
Trimley Saint Martin (a) - - par.	611	2,154	4,013	Ipswich -	do.
Trimley Saint Mary (a) - - par.	418	1,925	3,547	do. -	do.
Tuddenham - - par.	358	1,239	2,384	do. -	do.
Ufford - - par.	554	1,150	2,611	Woodbridge -	do.
Waldringfield - - par.	270	902	1,618	do. -	do.
Walton - - par.	1,272	2,023	6,139	Ipswich -	do.
Witnesham - - par.	515	1,996	3,883	do. -	do.
Woodbridge - par.	4,544	1,101	14,610	Woodbridge -	do.
TOTAL of UNION -	22,745	77,252	138,302		

WOODSTOCK UNION.

(Formed 13 July 1835 by Order dated 23 June 1835, as amended by Order dated 14 March 1837. — Place marked thus * added 1 Jan. 1862 by Order dated 17 Dec. 1861 ; and thus † added 29 Sept. 1864 by Order dated 16 Aug. 1864 as amended by Order dated 30 Nov. 1864. Spelling of name of place marked thus ‡ is as altered by Order dated 3 Aug. 1887.)

County of OXFORD:

Asterleigh - - par.	52	296	387	Woodstock -	Wootton, South.
Barton - - par.	915	2,983	4,580	Steeple Aston -	do. North.
Barton, Westcott - par.	236	974	1,556	do. -	do. do. (continued)

WOODBRIDGE UNION : (a) See note, page 419.

WOODSTOCK UNION : (a) There is some land comprised in this Union, containing 202 acres, common to the Parishes of Begbrooke and Yarnton.

Unions and Parishes, &c.		Population in 1881.	Area in Statute Acres in 1881.	Rateable Value in 1881.	Post Town.	Petty Sessional Division.

WOODSTOCK UNION—County of Oxford—*continued.*

				£		
Begbrooke	- - *par.*	68	577	1,412	Kidlington -	Wootton, South.
Bladon	- - *par.*	333	851	1,331	Woodstock - -	do. do.
*Blenheim Park	- *par.*	122	2,269	2,580	do. - -	do. do.
Cassington -	- *par.*	335	2,299	4,228	Kidlington - -	do. do.
Combe - -	- *par.*	541	1,417	2,922	Woodstock -	do. do.
†Cutteslowe -	- *par.*	23	282	602	Oxford - -	Bullingdon.
Deddington	- *par.*	1,958	4,243	11,042	Deddington - -	Wootton, North.
Duns Tew -	- *par.*	307	1,749	3,067	do. - -	do. do.
Glympton	- *par.*	158	1,259	1,603	Woodstock - -	do. South.
Gosford	- *ham.*	10	260	445	Kidlington -	do. do.
Hampton Gay -	- *par.*	40	684	1,203	do. - -	Bullingdon.
Hampton Poyle	- *par.*	105	807	1,302	do. - -	do. do.
Hensington (W.)	- *ham.*	280	695	1,488	Woodstock - -	Wootton, South.
Kiddington, Over and Nether - }	*par.*	223	1,894	2,584	do. - -	do. do.
Kidlington -	- *par.*	1,087	2,194	6,630	Kidlington -	do. do.
Middle Aston -	- *tow.*	94	898	1,421	Steeple Aston -	do. North.
Nether Worton	- *par.*	61	734	1,373	do. - -	do. do.
North Aston -	- *par.*	225	1,288	2,834	Deddington - -	do. do.
Over Worton	- *par.*	60	631	1,139	Steeple Aston -	do. do.
Rousham	- *par.*	156	1,068	2,039	do. - -	do. do.
Sandford -	- *par.*	485	2,292	3,321	do. - -	do. do.
Shipton upon Cherwell	*par.*	115	1,058	1,705	Kidlington or Oxford	do. South.
Steeple Aston	- *par.*	682	1,076	3,304	Steeple Aston - -	do. North.
Stonesfield	- *par.*	586	817	1,431	Woodstock - -	do. South.
Tackley	- *par.*	540	2,913	5,107	Oxford - -	do. do.
Thrupp	- *ham.*	139	813	1,527	Kidlington - -	do. do.
Water Eaton -	- *ham.*	128	1,501	2,503	Oxford - -	do. do.
Wolvercot -	- *par.*	733	1,158	3,741	do. - -	Bullingdon.
Woodstock	- *par.*	1,133	62	2,851	Woodstock - -	Wootton, South.
Wootton	- *par.*	1,081	4,274	6,370	do. - -	do. do.
‡Yarnton	- *par.*	279	1,493	3,972	do. - -	do. do.
TOTAL of UNION -		13,320	47,719 (*a*)	93,603		

WOOLSTANTON AND BURSLEM UNION.

(Formed 2 April 1838 by Order dated 27 Feb. 1838.)

COUNTY of STAFFORD :

Burslem	- *par.*	28,249	3,121	78,235	Burslem - -	Pirehill, Hundred of (Northern Division).
Woolstanton (W.)	- *par.*	47,216	10,816	123,077	Stoke-upon-Trent -	do.
TOTAL of UNION -		75,465	13,937	201,312		

WOOLWICH UNION.

(Formed 10 Mar. 1868 by Order dated 7 Mar. 1868.)

COUNTY of KENT :

Charlton-next-Woolwich - }	*par.*	8,764	1,236	52,147	Charlton - -	Blackheath.
Kidbrooke -	- *lib.*	2,166	750	21,261	Blackheath, S.E. -	do.
Plumstead (W.)	- *par.*	33,250	3,388	89,803	Plumstead -	Woolwich
Woolwich -	- *par.*	36,665	1,126	116,980	Woolwich - -	do.
TOTAL of UNION -		80,845	6,500	280,191		

Unions and Parishes, &c.			Population in 1881.	Area in Statute Acres in 1881.	Rateable Value in 1881.	Post Town.	Petty Sessional Division.

WORCESTER UNION.

(Formed 10 Oct. 1836 by Order dated 15 Sept. 1836.—Place marked thus * added 25 Mar. 1860 by Order dated 15 Mar. 1860; and thus † added 24 June 1860 by Order dated 10 May 1860.—Places marked thus ‡ added 30 Sept. 1885 by § 95 of the Worcester Extension Act, 1885.)

CITY of WORCESTER and COUNTY of the same CITY:

					£		
All Saints	-	par.	2,197	19	7,009	Worcester -	City of Worcester.
*Blockhouse	-	par.	2,093	13	3,954	do.	do.
†College Precincts	-	par.	100	8	753	do.	do.
Saint Alban	-	par.	248	3	1,011	do.	do.
Saint Andrew	-	par.	1,288	9	2,605	do.	do.
Saint Clement	-	par.	2,410	149	6,492	do.	do.
Saint Helen	-	par.	1,215	12	6,036	do.	do.
Saint John in Bedwardine	par.		4,551	3,775	23,683	do.	do.
Saint Martin (W.)	-	par.	5,081	1,392	22,796	do.	do.
Saint Michael in Bedwardine	par.		439	12	2,120	do.	do.
Saint Nicholas	-	par.	1,804	48	17,476	do.	do.
Saint Peter the Great (a)	par.		7,178	1,252	23,194	do.	do.
Saint Swithin	-	par.	714	7	6,563	do.	do.
‡South Claines	-	par.	—	—	—	do.	do.
‡South Hallow	-	par.	—	—	—	do.	do.
Whistones	-	ty.	2,976		10,250	Worcester	do.
TOTAL of UNION	-		32,291	6,690	133,942		

WORKSOP UNION.

(Formed 2 July 1836 by Order dated 8 June 1836.—Places marked thus * added 24 Mar. 1862 by Order dated 19 Mar. 1862.)

COUNTY of DERBY:

Barlborough	-	par.	1,678	3,453	10,496	Chesterfield	Eckington.
Clown (a)	-	par.	1,812	1,922	7,307	do.	do.
Elmton	-	par.	518	2,830	4,097	do.	do.
Whitwell	-	par.	1,809	5,231	9,545	do.	do.

COUNTY of NOTTINGHAM:

Blyth	-	tow.	618	1,294	3,529	Worksop	Retford.
Carburton	-	tow.	191	2,233	1,908	Ollerton	Worksop.
Carlton in Lindrick (a)	par.		1,016	3,980	6,013	Worksop	do.
Cuckney	-	tow.	555	5,510	1,876	Mansfield	do.
Harworth	-	par.	549	4,320	7,352	Tickhill, Rotherham	do.
Hodsock	-	lord.	220	4,098	6,042	Worksop	do.
Holbeck	-	tow.	247	In Cuckney	2,101	Cuckney, Mansfield	do.
Nether Langwith	-	tow.	376	In Cuckney	1,977	Mansfield	do.
Norton	-	tow.	256	In Cuckney	2,082	Cuckney, Mansfield	do.

(continued)

WORCESTER UNION:

(a) By Order which came into operation on 25 March 1884, a detached part of Saint Peter the Great was amalgamated with Whittington, in the Pershore Union.

WORKSOP UNION:

(a) By Orders which came into operation on 25 March 1885,—
A detached part of Carlton in Lindrick was amalgamated with Wallingwells;

WORKSOP UNION—continued.

Three detached parts of Harthill and Woodhall were amalgamated with Wales;
Two detached parts of Wallingwells were amalgamated with Carlton in Lindrick;
A detached part of Clown was amalgamated with Holsover, in the Chesterfield Union.

Unions and Parishes, &c.		Population in 1881.	Area in Statute Acres in 1881.	Rateable Value in 1881.	Post Town.	Petty Sessional Division.
WORKSOP UNION—County of Nottingham— *continued.*				£		
Styrrup	- tow.	585	2,950	5,017	Tickhill	Worksop.
*Welbeck	- par.	72	2,410	2,661	Worksop	do.
*Woodhouse Hall	- par.	129	In Cuckney	1,123	Cuckney, Mansfield	do.
Worksop (W.)	- par.	11,625	18,220	64,190	Worksop	do.
COUNTY of YORK, WEST RIDING:						
Dinnington	- tow.	259	1,650	2,188	Rotherham	Rotherham.
Firbeck	- tow.	249	1,297	2,079	Tickhill, Rotherham	do
Gilden Wells	- tow.	78	587	700	Worksop	do.
Harthill and Woodhall (a)	} par.	1,109	3,565	10,471	Sheffield	do.
Letwell	- tow.	117	1,329	1,648	Worksop	do.
North and South Anston	} par.	1,266	3,849	9,256	Rotherham	do.
Saint John's with Throapham	} tow.	96	1,062	1,281	Laughton, Rotherham	do.
Thorpe Salvin	- par.	356	2,295	5,254	Worksop	do.
Todwick	- par.	173	1,808	3,138	Sheffield	do.
Wales (a)	- par.	2,255	1,786	13,921	do.	do.
Woodsetts	- tow.	246	831	1,237	Worksop	do.
Counties of NOTTINGHAM, and YORK, WEST RIDING:						
Wallingwells (a)	- par.	32	742	912	do.	Worksop.
TOTAL of UNION	-	28,522	79,252	189,401		
WORTLEY UNION.						
(Formed 21 Aug. 1838 by Order dated 27 July 1838.)						
COUNTY of YORK, WEST RIDING:						
Bradfield	- tow.	11,170	38,425	45,333	Sheffield	Sheffield.
Ecclesfield (W.) (a)	- tow.	21,156	10,893	63,188	do.	do.
Tankersley	- tow.	2,128	2,463	17.129	Barnsley	Barnsley.
Wortley	- tow.	1,131	5,616	15,430	Sheffield	do.
TOTAL of UNION	-	35,585	57,397	141,080		
WREXHAM UNION.						
(Formed 30 Mar. 1837 by Order dated 28 Feb. 1837.—Place marked thus * added 1 Mar. 1862 by Order dated 7 Feb. 1862.)						
COUNTY of CHESTER:						
Shocklach Church	- tow.	135	1,278	1,769	Malpas	Broxton, Chester.
Shocklach Oviatt	- tow.	135	1,018	1,736	do.	do.
COUNTIES of CHESTER and FLINT:						
*Threapwood	- par.	285	248	906	Wrexham	Maylor.
						(continued)

WORTLEY UNION:

(a) By Provisional Order which came into operation on 25 March 1883, a detached part of Ecclesfield was amalgamated with Dalton, near Rotherham, in the Rotherham Union.

WREXHAM UNION:

(a) By Orders which came into operation on 25 March 1885,—
  Detached parts of Allington and Gresford were amalgamated with Merford and Hoseley, in the

WREXHAM UNION—continued.

Hawarden Union, and a detached part of Merford and Hoseley was amalgamated with Allington;
All the parts of a township known as Abenbury Fechan were amalgamated with Abenbury Vawr;
All the parts of a township known as Wrexham Abbott were amalgamated with Wrexham Regis;
A detached part of Esclusham Below was amalgamated with Wrexham Regis.

Unions and Parishes, &c.		Population in 1881.	Area in Statute Acres in 1881.	Rateable Value in 1881.	Post Town.	Petty Sessional Division.
WREXHAM UNION—continued.				£		
COUNTY of DENBIGH :						
Abenbury Vawr (a)	tow.	268	1,263	2,320	Wrexham -	Wrexham.
Acton	tow.	333	890	2,124	do. - -	do.
Allington (a)	tow.	824	3,617	7,526	do. - -	do.
Bersham (W.)	tow.	4,779	1,985	10,627	do. - -	do.
Bieston or Boreston	tow.	93	531	797	do. - -	do.
Borras Bovah	tow.	41	461	746	do. - -	do.
Borras Riffrey	tow.	45	341	536	do. - -	do.
Broughton	tow.	4,339	1,242	9,138	do. - -	do.
Brymbo	tow.	3,812	2,543	12,418	do. - -	do.
Burton	tow.	713	2,869	8,040	do. - -	do.
Dutton Cacca	tow.	85	423	623	do. - -	do.
Dutton Driffreth	tow.	127	625	991	do. - -	do.
Dutton-y-Bran	tow.	34	616	1,064	do. - -	do.
Earlas	tow.	49	720	896	do. - -	do.
Eithig	tow.	155	303	916	do. - -	do.
Esclusham Above	tow.	456	3,827	3,749	do. - -	do.
Esclusham Below (a)	tow.	1,023	1,767	8,716	do. - -	do.
Eyton	tow.	221	1,332	2,130	do. - -	do.
Gourton	tow.	27	334	598	do. - -	do.
Gresford (?)	tow.	951	1,031	6,699	do. - -	do.
Gwersylt	tow.	3,412	1,690	15,378	do. - -	do.
Holt	tow.	1,023	2,912	5,602	do. - -	do.
Llay	tow.	550	2,252	4,984	do. - -	do.
Markiviel	par.	564	3,397	5,220	do. - -	do.
Minera	tow.	1,490	1,393	5,058	do. - -	do.
Pickhill	tow.	180	1,220	2,381	do. - -	do.
Ridley	tow.	27	698	523	do. - -	do.
Royton	tow.	86	702	1,314	do. - -	do.
Ruabon	par.	15,194	13,918	44,132	Ruabon -	Ruabon.
Sesswick	tow.	110	675	1,300	Wrexham -	Wrexham.
Stansty	tow.	1,216	577	6,731	do. -	do.
Sutton	tow.	168	1,171	1,920	do. - -	do.
Wrexham Regis (a)	tow.	10,939	1,304	40,973	do. - -	do.
COUNTIES of DENBIGH and FLINT :						
Erbistock	par.	291	1,624	2,397	Ruabon -	Ruabon.
COUNTY of FLINT :						
Bangor	tow.	502	2,124	3,858	Wrexham -	Overton Maylor.
Worthenbury	par.	446	3,420	5,742	do. - -	do.
TOTAL of UNION	-	55,158	68,371	232,578		
WYCOMBE UNION.						
(Formed 25 Mar. 1835 by Order dated 24 Feb. 1835, as amended by Orders dated 5 May 1836 and 20 August 1863.)						
COUNTY of BUCKINGHAM :						
Bledlow with Bledlow Ridge (W.) }	par.	1,070	4,169	4,414	{ Princes Risborough and Stokenchurch }	Desborough, Second Division.
Bradenham (a)	par.	183	996	1,146	High Wycombe -	do.
						(continued)

WREXHAM UNION :

(a) See note, page 423.

WYCOMBE UNION :

(a) By Orders which came into operation on 25 March, 1885,—
The four parts into which a place, known as Lewknor-up-Hill, (having in 1881, population 201, acreage 7,001, rateable value 1,823l.), was divided, were amalgamated with Stoken Church and Great Marlow.
A part of Little Hampden and a part of Stoke Mandeville were amalgamated with Great Hampden, and the latter as so altered was designated Great and Little Hampden ; and the remainder of Little Hampden, together with all the parts of a parish, known as Little Kimble, was amalgamated with Great Kimble ; and the latter as so altered was designated Great and Little Kimble.

WYCOMBE UNION—continued.

Great Hampden in 1881, contained population 255, acreage 1,763, and rateable value 1,660l.
Little Hampden in 1881, contained population 46, acreage 515, and rateable value 428l.
Great Kimble in 1881, contained population 422, acreage 2,507, and rateable value 2,745l.
Little Kimble in 1881, contained population 161, acreage 850, and rateable value 1,208l.
A detached part of Saunderton was amalgamated with Bradenham ;
A detached part of Wendover was amalgamated with Bierton and Broughton, in the Aylesbury Union.
(b) By Order which came into operation on 25 March, 1886.—
A detached part of Kingsey, in the Thame Union, was amalgamated with Illmire.
(c) By Provisional Order which came into operation on 25 March, 1887,—
A detached part of Stoke Mandeville was amalgamated with Hartwell, in the Aylesbury Union.

Unions and Parishes, &c.	Population in 1881.	Area in Statute Acres in 1881.	Rateable Value in 1881.	Post Town.	Petty Sessional Division

WYCOMBE UNION—County of Buckingham—*continued*. £

Unions and Parishes, &c.	Population in 1881.	Area in Statute Acres in 1881.	Rateable Value in 1881.	Post Town.	Petty Sessional Division
Chipping Wycombe or High Wycombe } par.	8,320	6,266	22,554	High Wycombe -	Borough of Chipping Wycombe, and Desborough, Second Division.
Ellesborough - par.	608	3,595	4,586	Wendover -	Aylesbury.
Fingest - par.	333	1,285	1,535	High Wycombe -	Desborough, First Division.
Great and Little Hampden (a) - } par.	—	—	—	Great Missenden -	Aylesbury.
Great and Little Kimble (a) - } par.	—	—	—	Princes Risborough	do.
Great Marlow (a) - par.	4,763	6,245	19,244	Great Marlow -	Desborough, First Division.
Hedsor - par.	155	548	1,469	Maidenhead -	do.
Horsendon - par.	46	535	927	Princes Risborough	Aylesbury.
Hughenden - par.	1,803	5,828	7,251	High Wycombe -	Desborough, Second Division.
Ibmire (b) - par.	63	684	991	Princes Risborough	Ashendon.
Little Marlow - par.	976	3,328	5,298	Great Marlow -	Desborough, First Division.
Little Missenden - par.	1,113	3,215	4,001	Amersham -	Aylesbury.
Monks Risborough - par.	847	2,873	3,952	Princes Risborough	do.
Princes Risborough - par.	2,418	4,697	8,092	do. -	do.
Radnage - par.	427	1,369	1,732	Stokenchurch -	Desborough, Second Division.
Saunderton (W.) (a) par.	421	1,831	2,134	Princes Risborough	do.
Stoke Mandeville(a)(c) par.	497	1,773	2,833	Aylesbury -	Aylesbury.
Turville - par.	423	2,328	2,453	Henley on Thames	Desborough, First Division.
Wendover (a) - par.	1,902	5,832	7,954	Wendover -	Aylesbury.
West Wycombe - par.	2,390	6,533	8,765	High Wycombe -	Desborough, Second Division.
Wooburn - par.	2,431	3,133	9,664	Beaconsfield -	do.
Wycombe (Borough) bor.	4,834	129	12,327	High Wycombe -	Borough of Chipping Wycombe.
COUNTIES of BUCKINGHAM and OXFORD:					
Ipstone - par.	300	1,121	1,172	Stokenchurch -	Desborough, First Division.
COUNTY of OXFORD:					
Chinnor - par.	1,237	2,712	4,235	Tetsworth -	Watlington.
Stoken-Church (a) - par.	1,630	4,374	4,883	Stokenchurch -	do.
TOTAL of UNION -	39,193 (a)	75,399 (a)	143,612 (a)		

YEOVIL UNION.

(Formed 13 May 1836 by Order dated 19 April 1836.— Place marked thus * added 25 Dec. 1861 by Order dated 8 Oct. 1861.—Name of Parish marked thus † is as altered by Order dated 11 Aug. 1884.)

COUNTY of SOMERSET:

Unions and Parishes, &c.	Population in 1881.	Area in Statute Acres in 1881.	Rateable Value in 1881.	Post Town.	Petty Sessional Division
Ashington (a) - par.	58	554	1,200	Ilchester -	Yeovil.
Barwick - par.	534	784	2,406	Yeovil -	do.

(*continued*)

YEOVIL UNION:

(a) By Orders which came into operation on 25 March 1884,—

A detached part of Norton under Hamdon was amalgamated with Montacute;

A detached part of Odcombe was amalgamated with Brimpton;

Detached and nearly detached parts of Brimpton were amalgamated with Preston;

A detached part of Preston was amalgamated with Mudford;

A detached part of Limington was amalgamated with Ilchester or Ivelchester;

Detached parts of Ashington were amalgamated with Limington and Ilchester or Ivelchester;

A detached part of Stoke under Hamdon was amalgamated with Tintenhull;

All the parts of a parish, known as West Chinnock, were amalgamated with Middle Chinnock, and by Order dated 21 April 1884 the latter as so altered was designated West Chinnock.

(b) By Orders which came into operation on 25 March 1885,—

A detached part of Ilchester or Ivelchester was amalgamated with Tintenhull;

A detached part of Sock Dennis was amalgamated with Tintenhull;

A detached part of Tintenhull was amalgamated with Ilchester or Ivelchester;

Detached parts of Martock were amalgamated with Curry Rivall and Kingsbury Episcopi, in the Langport Union, and a detached part of Tintenhull was amalgamated with Kingsdon, in that Union.

3 E 3

Unions and Parishes, &c.		Population in 1881.	Area in Statute Acres in 1881.	Rateable Value in 1881.	Post Town.	Petty Sessional Division.
YEOVIL UNION—County of Somerset—continued.				£		
Brimpton (a)	par.	109	465	1,296	Yeovil	Yeovil.
Chilthorne Domer	par.	204	1,392	2,328	do.	do.
Chilton Cantelo	par.	123	631	1,675	Ilchester	do.
Chiselborough	par.	361	790	1,718	Ilminster	do.
Closworth	par.	121	1,071	1,324	Sherborne	do.
East Chinnock	par.	580	1,320	2,437	Yeovil	do.
East Coker	par.	1,029	2,121	5,211	do.	do.
Hardington Mande-ville	par.	633	2,631	3,204	do.	do.
Haselbury Plucknett	par.	592	2,069	3,476	Crewkerne	Crewkerne.
Ilchester or Ivel-chester (a) (b)	par.	683	653	2,108	Ilchester	Yeovil.
Limington (a)	par.	296	1,602	3,418	do.	do.
Lufton	par.	51	292	674	Yeovil	do.
Martock (b)	par.	3,005	7,302	18,821	Martock	do.
Montacute (a)	par.	859	1,485	3,631	Ilminster	do.
Mudford (a)	par.	382	2,035	4,390	Ilchester	do.
Northover	par.	91	436	1,157	do.	do.
North Perrot	par.	322	1,248	2,646	Crewkerne	Crewkerne.
Norton under Hamdon (a)	par.	539	642	1,915	Ilminster	Yeovil.
Odcombe (a)	par.	624	1,276	3,125	do.	do.
Pendomer	par.	69	1,090	1,427	Yeovil	do.
Preston (a)	par.	266	790	2,195	do.	do.
Pudimore Milton	par.	89	990	1,313	Ilchester	Somerton.
*Sock Dennis (b)	par.	28	880	1,933	do.	Yeovil.
South Petherton	par.	2,424	3,311	10,514	South Petherton	Ilminster.
Stoke under Hamdon (a)	par.	1,516	1,330	4,702	Ilminster	Yeovil.
Sutton Bingham	par.	52	549	1,080	Yeovil	do.
†Thorne	par.	110	410	1,047	do.	do.
Tintenhull (a) (b)	par.	403	1,828	3,951	do.	do.
West Camel	par.	281	1,953	3,059	Ilchester	Somerton.
West Chinnock (a)	par.	568	1,113	2,834	Ilminster	Crewkerne.
West Coker	par.	957	1,299	4,136	Yeovil	Yeovil.
Yeovil (W.)	par.	9,507	4,056	36,603	do.	do.
Yeovilton	par.	240	1,753	3,185	Ilchester	Somerton.
TOTAL of UNION		27,706	52,151	146,439		

YORK UNION.

(Formed 15 July 1837 by Order dated 19 June, 1837 as amended by Order dated 14 Oct. 1854.— Place marked thus * added 30 Sept. 1843 by Order of that date : places marked thus † added 6 Sept. 1854 by Order dated 18 Aug. 1854 ; and thus ‡ added 24 June 1861 by Order dated 30 May 1861 ; and thus § added 12 April 1884 by Order dated 9 April 1884. Spelling of names of places marked ǁ as altered by Order dated 6 July 1887.

CITY of YORK and COUNTY of the same CITY :

All Saints, North-street	par.	1,429	12	4,147	York	City of York.
All Saints, Pave-ment	tow.	334	5	3,728	do.	do.
‡Davy Hall	par.	13		186	do.	do.
Holgate	tow.	513	299	4,277	do.	do. (continued)

YEOVIL UNION :

(a) (b). See notes, page 425.

YORK UNION :

(a) By Order which came into operation on 25 March 1884, all the parts of Saint Lawrence, Heslington, were united

YORK UNION—continued.

and amalgamated with all the parts of Saint Paul's, Heslington, and such parts so united and amalgamated were constituted one parish, and designated Heslington.

(b) "The Green," containing 39 acres, is comprised in this Union, and is common to certain owners in Flaxton-upon-the-Moor.

Unions and Parishes, &c.		Population in 1881.	Area in Statute Acres in 1881.	Rateable Value in 1881.	Post Town.	Petty Sessional Division.
YORK UNION—In the City of York and County of the same City—*continued*.				£		
Holy Trinity, Goodramgate	*tow.*	451	3	1,567	York - -	City of York.
Holy Trinity, King's Court	*par.*	595	4	2,816	do. - -	do.
Holy Trinity, Micklegate	*tow.*	2,040	63	10,207	do. - -	do.
Minster Yard, with Beddern	*tow.*	670	20	2,562	do. - -	do.
Saint Andrew	*tow.*	281	3	791	do. - -	do.
Saint Crux	*par.*	822	7	4,174	do. - -	do.
Saint Cuthbert's, Saint Helen on the Walls, and All Saints, Peasholm	*un. tows.*	3,580	292	6,775	do. - -	do.
Saint Dennis	*tow.*	1,268	14	3,130	do. - -	do.
*Saint George	*tow.*	2,277	14	3,103	do. - -	do.
Saint Giles in the Suburbs	*tow.*	2,727	59	8,382	do. - -	do.
Saint Helen, Stonegate	*par.*	413	5	3,022	do. - -	do.
Saint John, Delpike	*tow.*	312	2	1,084	do. - -	do.
Saint John, Micklegate	*par.*	699	7	3,077	do. - -	do.
Saint Lawrence	*tow.*	3,009	75	9,395	do. - -	do.
Saint Margaret's	*tow.*	1,792	16	2,187	do. - -	do.
Saint Martin, otherwise St. Martin le Grand, Coney Street	*par.*	393	9	5,166	do. - -	do.
Saint Martin cum Gregory	*par.*	656	12	5,609	do. - -	do.
Saint Mary, Bishophill, the younger	*tow.*	6,693	763	27,740	do. - -	do.
Saint Mary, Bishophill, Senior	*tow.*	5,323	214	14,053	do. - -	do.
Saint Mary, Castle Gate	*par.*	827	34	3,441	do. - -	do.
Saint Maurice	*tow.*	5,440	98	12,293	do. - -	do.
Saint Michael - le - Belfry	*tow.*	937	12	3,972	do. - -	do.
Saint Michaels, Spurrier Gate	*par.*	415	5	4,271	do. - -	do.
Saint Nicholas	*par.*	1,617	167	5,118	do. - -	do.
Saint Olave, Mary Gate	*tow.*	1,114	50	5,438	do. - -	do.
Saint Peter - le - Willows	*tow.*	548	4	918	do. - -	do.
Saint Peter the Little	*tow.*	319	2	2,147	do. - -	do.
Saint Sampson	*par.*	615	5	3,926	do. - -	do.
Saint Saviour's	*tow.*	2,751	44	5,470	do. - -	do.
Saint Wilfred	*tow.*	179	5	2,778	do. - -	do.
The Liberty of Mint Yard		—	4	1,088	do. - -	do.
CITY of YORK and COUNTY of the same CITY and EAST RIDING of the COUNTY of YORK :						
Fulford or Gate Fulford	*tow.*	6,717	1,652	16,517	York -	Ouse and Derwent, and City of York.
CITY of YORK and COUNTY of the same CITY and NORTH RIDING of the COUNTY of YORK :						
Clifton (W.)	*tow.*	6,037	1,582	20,327	do. -	Bulmer, North-east, and City of York.
Heworth	*tow.*	746	1,312	5,528	do. -	do. do.

(*continued*)

Unions and Parishes, &c.	Population in 1851.	Area in Statute Acres in 1881.	Rateable Value in 1881.	Post Town.	Petty Sessional Division.
YORK UNION—*continued.*					
CITY of YORK and COUNTY of the same CITY and WEST RIDING of the COUNTY of YORK :			£		
Dringhouses - *tow.*	477	779	6,016	York	-	Ainsty, East, and City of York.
Middlethorpe - - *tow.*	131	629	2,085	do. - -	do. do.
COUNTY of YORK, EAST RIDING :					
Deighton - *tow.*	196	2,002	3,659	do. - -	Ouse and Derwent.
Dunnington - - *tow.*	741	2,243	5,251	do. - -	do.
Elvington - - *par.*	376	2,372	3,445	do. - -	do.
Escrick - - *tow.*	589	4,346	8,238	do. - -	do.
Fulford Water - *tow.*	30	355	1,233	do. - -	do.
Grimston - - *tow.*	58	797	1,464	do. - -	do.
§Heslington (*a*) - *par.*	477	2,645	4,720	do. - -	do.
Kexby - - *tow.*	136	1,892	1,894	do. - -	do.
Langwith - - *tow.*	42	793	697	do. - -	do.
Naburn - - *tow.*	569	2,636	9,032	do. - -	do.
Stamford Bridge, with Scoreby - } *tow.*	150	1,945	2,588	do. - -	do.
Stillingfleet, with Moreby - } *tow.*	366	2,605	1,168	do. - -	do.
Thorganby, with West Cottingwith } *par.*	398	2,938	4,317	do. - -	do.
Wheldrake - - *tow.*	596	4,517	6,207	do. - -	do.
COUNTY of YORK, NORTH RIDING :					
Benningbrough - *tow.*	74	1,092	1,355	do. - -	Bulmer, North-east.
Butter Crambe with Bossall - } *tow.*	171	2,692	3,593	do. - -	do.
Claxton - - *tow.*	210	839	1,332	do. - -	do.
Earswick - - *tow.*	148	1,164	968	do. - -	do.
Flaxton upon the Moor *tow.*	366	1,825	3,912	do. - -	do.
Gate Helmsley - *par.*	204	496	1,102	do. - -	do.
Harton - - *tow.*	136	2,002	2,156	do. - -	do.
Haxby - - - *tow.*	559	2,208	5,231	do. - -	do.
Holtby - - *tow.*	136	901	1,699	do. - -	do.
Huntington - - *tow.*	592	2,606	9,327	do. - -	do
Lillings Ambo - *tow.*	217	1,747	2,204	do. - -	do.
Murton - - *tow.*	176	844	2,411	do. - -	do.
Osbaldwick - - *tow.*	164	730	2,515	do. - -	do.
Overton - - *tow.*	67	1,332	3,168	do. - -	do.
Rockliff, or Rawcliffe *tow.*	89	738	1,595	do. - -	do.
Sand Hutton - *tow.*	245	2,242	2,331	do. - -	do.
†Skelton - - *tow.*	313	2,473	3,692	do. - -	do.
Stockton on the Forest - } *par.*	446	3,267	4,029	do. - -	do.
Strensall - - *tow.*	446	2,910	4,360	do. - -	do.
Towthorpe - - *tow.*	49	1,071	1,467	do. - -	do.
Upper Helmsley - *par.*	71	833	1,211	do. - -	do.
‖Warthill, Copyhold - *tow.*	158	} 1,003	} 1,182	do. - -	do.
‖†Warthill, Freehold - *tow.*	32		445	do. - -	do.
Wigginton - - *par.*	399	1,881	3,489	do. - -	do.
COUNTY of YORK, WEST RIDING :					
Acaster Malbis, or Akester Malbis } *tow.*	264	1,886	3,496	do.	-	Ainsty, East.
Askham Richard - *par.*	232	981	2,168	do. - -	do.
Bishopthorpe - - *tow.*	422	719	4,009	do. - -	do.
Copmanthorpe - *tow.*	311	1,656	5,291	do. - -	do.
TOTAL of UNION -	76,695	82,506¼ (*b*)	365,462		

YORK UNION :
(*a*) (*b*). *See* notes, page 426.

Memorandum of Alterations affecting the Particulars contained in the Statement of Poor Law Unions, &c., 1887.—[C. 5191.]

I.—ALTERATIONS IN AREAS EFFECTED UNDER THE DIVIDED PARISHES ACTS.

A.—LIST of CASES in which one PARISH has been entirely amalgamated with some other PARISH or PARISHES in the same UNION by ORDERS which came into operation from and after the 25th MARCH 1888.

Name of Union. 1.	Name of Parish absorbed. 2.	With what Parish or Parishes amalgamated. 3.
Alnwick - - -	Boulmer and Seaton House -	Loughoughton.
Ampthill - - -	Upper Gravenhurst -	Lower Gravenhurst. (Name changed to Gravenhurst.)
Anglesey - - -	Gwredog - - -	{ Llanerchymedd. { Rhod-y-geidio.
Chelmsford - -	Chignall Saint James -	{ Chignall Smealey. { (Name changed to Chignall.) { Broomfield. { Writtle.
Great Ouseburn - -	Clareton - -	Coneythorpe. (Name changed to Coneythorpe and Clareton.)
Hemsworth - -	Hill Top - - -	Hessle. (Name changed to Hessle and Hill Top.)
Lincoln - - -	{ Saint Mary le Wigford -	The Holmes Common. (Name changed to Saint Mary le Wigford with Holmes Common.)
	{ Castle Dykings -	Saint Paul in the Bail.
Morpeth - - -	Bullers Green -	{ Morpeth. { Newminster Abbey.
Northallerton - -	Gueldable - -	Borrowby.
Pwllheli - - -	Llanfaelrhys -	Rhiw. (Name changed to Rhiw with Llanfaelrhys.)
Romney Marsh -	West Hythe -	{ Saint Leonard, Hythe. { Burmarsh.
Spilsby - - -	Holme North -	Wainfleet All Saints.

B.—LIST of CASES in which PARTS of DIVIDED PARISHES were amalgamated with adjoining PARISHES, by ORDERS which came into operation from and after the 25th MARCH 1888.

Name of Divided Parish, and of the Union in which situate.		Name of Parish with which Parts were amalgamated, and of the Union in which situate.	
Union.	Parish.	Parish.	Union.
Alnwick	Alnmouth	Lesbury	Alnwick.
	Felton	Acton and Old Felton	
		Swarland	
	Lesbury	Alnmouth	
	Walkmill	Sturton Grange	
	Felton	East and West Thirston with Shothaugh.	Morpeth.
Alresford	Kilmeston	Beaworth	Alresford.
	Northington	Brown Candover	
	Tichborne	Cheriton	
Alton	West Worldham	East Worldham	Alton.
Altrincham	Pownal-Fee	Bollen-Fee	Altrincham.
		Fulshaw	
Ampthill	Westoning	Tingrith	Woburn.
Andover	Foxcott	Tangley	Andover.
	Hurstborne Tarrant	Vernham Dean	
	Penton Grafton	Tangley	
	Thruxton	Fyfield	
	Vernham Dean	Hurstborne Tarrant	
	Wherwell	Longparish	
Anglesey	Amlwch	Llanbadrig	Anglesey.
	Llanbedr-Göch	Tregayan	
	Llanfechell	Llanbabo	
	Llecheynfarwydd	Llanerchymedd	
Aston	Minworth	Curdworth	Aston.
Banbury	Cropredy	Wardington	Banbury.
Bangor and Beaumaris	Beaumaris	Llandegfan	Bangor and Beaumaris.
	Llanddona	Laniestyn	
		Llanfaes	
	Llandegfan	Beaumaris	
	Llanfaes	Llanddona	
		Llangoed	
	Llanfihangel-tyn-sylwy	Laniestyn	
		Llanfaes	
	Llangoed	Pentraeth	
	Penmon	Llanfaes	
Berkhampstead	Aldbury	Tring	Berkhampstead.
	Marsworth	Puttenham	
Bicester	Caversfield	Stratton Audley	Bicester.
	Fritwell	Somerton	
	Hethe	Hardwicke	
Blandford	Tarrant Crawford	Tarrant Rushton	Blandford.
Brackley	Mixbury	Hethe	Bicester.
Braintree	Great Saling	Saling Bardfield	Dunmow.
	White Notley	Langford	Maldon.

Name of Divided Parish, and of the Union in which situate.		Name of Parish with which Parts were amalgamated, and of the Union in which situate.	
Union.	Parish.	Parish.	Union.
Chelmsford	Broomfield	Writtle	Chelmsford.
	Good Easter	Mashbury	
	Little Waltham	Broomfield	
	Mashbury	Good Easter	
	Rettendon	East Hanningfield	
	Springfield	Broomfield	
	Writtle	Chignall Smealey	
		Downham	
	Runwell	Ramsden Bell-House	Billericay.
		South Hanningfield	
	South Hanningfield	Runwell	Chelmsford.
		Wickford	Billericay.
	Good Easter	High Easter	Dunmow.
		Margaret Roothing	
Chester	Bridge Trafford	Wimbolds Trafford	Chester.
	Great Saughall	Little Saughall	
		Woodbank	
	Little Saughall	Great Saughall	
	Stanlow	Great Stanney	
	Christleton	Waverton	Tarvin.
Clutton	Paulton	Midsomer Norton	Clutton.
Dunmow	High Easter	Good Easter	Chelmsford.
		Mashbury	
Eastbourne	Folkington	Jevington	Eastbourne.
		Willingdon	
	Wilmington	Folkington	
		Jevington	
East Ashford	Aldington	Saint Leonard, Hythe	Elham.
Farringdon	Kingston Lisle and Fawler.	Balking	Farringdon.
	Uffington	Compton and Knighton	
	Woolstone	Uffington	
Fordingbridge	Breamore	Fordingbridge	Fordingbridge.
	Fordingbridge	Breamore	
		Rockbourne	
Great Ouseburn	Thorpe - Underwoods	Great Ouseburn	Great Ouseburn.
	Moor Monkton	Nun Monkton	
Hemsworth	Brierley	Shafton	Hemsworth.
	Little Smeaton	Walden Stubbs	
	Wintersett	Hessle	
Hertford	Aston	Watton	Hertford.
	Little Berkhampstead	Bayford	
	Watton	Bennington	
	Little Amwell	Ware	Ware.
Hexham	Chollerton	Birtley	Bellingham.
Hollingbourn	Ulcomb	Headcorne	Hollingbourn.
	Witchling	Lenham	
		Otterden	
	Langley	Boughton Monchelsea	Maidstone.
	Thornham	Berstead	
Horncastle	Asterby	Gonleeby	Horncastle.
	Langton	Woodhall	
	Revesby	Mareham le Fen	
	Scrivelsby	Dalderby	
	Tattershall Thorpe	Tattershall	
	Thimbleby	Woodhall	
	Thornton	Woodhall	

Name of Divided Parish, and of the Union in which situate.		Name of Parish with which Parts were amalgamated, and of the Union in which situate.	
Union.	Parish.	Parish.	Union.
Knaresborough	Bilton-with-Harrogate - Knaresborough - Scriven-with-Tentergate -	Breartou - - Knaresborough - Bilton-with-Harrogate - Pannal - - Bilton-with-Harrogate - Knaresborough. Pannal - -	Knaresborough.
Leominster -	Humber - - Stoke Prior - -	Stoke Prior - - Humber - -	Leominster.
Lexden and Winstree	Great Wigborough -	Tolleshunt Knights -	Maldon.
Lincoln -	Saint Peter in East Gate - - The Monk's Liberty -	Saint Margaret in the Close. Saint Paul in the Bail - Saint Peter in East Gate	Lincoln.
Louth -	Carlton Little - Cockerington North Cockerington South Ludford Magna - Ludford Parva - Swaby - - Theddlethorpe All Saints.	Reston North - - Cockerington South - Cockerington North - Louth Park - - Ludford Parva - Ludford Magna - Belleau - - Theddlethorpe Saint Helen's.	Louth.
Macclesfield -	Wincell - -	Wildboar-Clough -	Macclesfield.
Maidstone -	Nettlested - - Boughton Monchelsea	Yalding - - Langley - -	Maidstone. Hollingbourn.
Maldon -	Purleigh - - Tollesbury - -	Danbury - - Virley - -	Chelmsford. Lexden and Winstree.
Malling -	Aylesford - - Burham - - Ditton - - Peckham East - Ryarsh - - Snodland - - Mereworth - Wateringbury -	Mereworth - - Aylesford - - Peckham West - Addington - - Birling - - Yalding - -	Malling. Maidstone.
Morpeth -	East and West Thirston with Shothaugh. Widdrington -	Bockenfield - - Ellington - -	Morpeth.
Nantwich -	Audlem - - Baddiley - - Checkley with Wrinchill. Dodcot cum Wilkesley. Haughton -	Haukelow - - Brindley - - Faddiley - - Blakenhall - - Acton - - Spurston - -	Nantwich.
New Winchester -	Chilcomb - - Kings Worthy - Milland - -	Morestead - - Saint Bartholomew Hide Chilcomb - -	New Winchester.
Northallerton	Thirntoft - - Yafforth - -	Danby Wisk - - Little Langton -	Northallerton.
Orsett -	Little Thurrock - Mucking - - South Ockendon - Stifford - -	Orsett - - Stanford-le-Hope - Aveley - - Stifford - - South Ockendon -	Orsett.

Name of Divided Parish, and of the Union in which situate.		Name of Parish with which Parts were amalgamated, and of the Union in which situate.	
Union.	Parish.	Parish.	Union.
Pickering -	Newton - - Pickering - -	Pickering - - Newton - -	} Pickering.
Poole -	Canford Magna - Lytchett Matravers -	Hampreston - Wimborne Minster Sturminster Marshall -	} Wimborne and Cranborne.
Richmond (Yorks.)	East Layton - Hipswell - Hudswell - Ravensworth - Uckerby - Whaston -	West Layton - Hudswell - Hipswell - Whaston - Scorton - Kirby Ravensworth -	} Richmond.
Romsey -	Mitchelmarsh - } Timsbury - - } Lockerley - -	Romsey Extra - - East Tytherly - -	Romsey. Stockbridge.
Sculcoates - -	Melton - -	Welton - -	Sculcoates.
Sleaford -	Holdingham - Old Sleaford -	New Sleaford - Quarrington -	} Sleaford.
Spalding -	Cowbit - - Pinchbeck - - Spalding - -	Spalding - - Spalding - - Cowbit - - Pinchbeck - -	} Spalding.
Spilsby -	Addlethorpe - Firsby - Hogsthorpe - Ingoldmells - Mumby with Chapel Mumby. Orby - Skendleby - Steeping Little - Toynton All Saints - Toynton Saint Peter's	Ingoldmells - Irby in the Marsh - Mumby with Chapel Mumby. Addlethorpe - Orby - - Hogsthorpe - - Addlethorpe - Welton in the Marsh with Boothby. Thorpe - Toynton Saint Peter's - Toynton All Saints -	} Spilsby.
Sudbury - -	Belchamp, Paul - {	Little Yeldam - Tilbury juxta Clare -	} Halstead.
Tarvin -	Cotton Abbots - Kingsmarsh -	Cotton Edmund's - Caldecott -	} Tarvin.
Taunton - -	Durston - -	Lyng - -	Bridgewater.
Tendring -	Frating - - Frinton - -	Thorrington - - Great Holland - -	} Tendring.
Thirsk - -	Bagby - -	Dalton - -	Thirsk.
Ware -	Hunsdon - Little Munden {	Eastwick - - Great Munden - Bennington - -	} Ware. Hertford.
West Ward -	Low Winder - Sleagill - Sockbridge {	Sockbridge - Morland - Barton - Low Winder -	} West Ward.
Wimborne and Cranborne	Sturminster Marshall Shapwicke - Hampreston { Wimborne Minster -	Shapwicke - Tarrant Rushton - Canford Magna Kingston - Canford Magna	Wimborne and Cranborne. Blandford. } Poole.

Name of Divided Parish, and of the Union in which situate.		Name of Parish with which Parts were amalgamated, and of the Union in which situate.	
Union.	Parish.	Parish	Union.
York	{ Dringhouses · Saint Michael-le-Belfry Saint Saviour's · }	Middlethorpe · Saint Giles in the Suburbs Saint Cuthbert's, Saint Helen on the Walls, and All Saints, Peasholm.	} York.

II.—ALTERATIONS IN NAMES OF PARISHES.

WANTAGE UNION.

CARMARTHEN UNION.

{ In addition to the alterations of names by Orders under the Divided Parishes Acts (see Column 3 of Table I., A.), the Order declaring the Wantage Union was amended by Order dated 20th January 1888, in pursuance of which the Parish described in the Declaration Order as "Bright Waltham" must henceforth be described as "Brightwalton"; and the Order declaring the Carmarthen Union was amended by Order dated 23rd April 1888, in pursuance of which the Parish described in the Declaration Order as "Carmarthen" must henceforth be described as "Saint Peter." }

III.—ALTERATION IN THE PARISHES IN THE TAMWORTH UNION.

TAMWORTH UNION.

{ An Order issued in 1886 under the Divided Parishes Acts directed the amalgamation of the several parts of the Township of Wigginton with the adjoining Parish of Hopwas Hays, and that the name of the latter Parish should be changed to Wigginton. This Order has been rescinded by a further Order dated 1st March 1888. The list of Parishes in the Tamworth Union must therefore be corrected thus:— }

1. *Insert under County Stafford :—*

| ‡ Hopwas Hays | · | par | · | 5 | In Wigginton | 172 | Do | · | Elford and Shenstone. |

2. *Correct the particulars of Wigginton, thus:—*

| Wigginton | · | · | tow | · | 1147 | 3940 | 13575 | Do. | · | Elford and Shenstone. |

3. Strike out the foot-note, with reference to Hopwas Hays and Wigginton.

4. Insert at the end of the heading of the Union the words "Parish marked thus ‡ added 25th March 1864 by Order dated 1st March 1864."

IV.—ALTERATION IN COUNTY.

WITNEY UNION.

{ The Parish of Broughton-Poggs is wholly in the County of Oxford. The Witney Union must therefore be described as in that County only. }

Local Government Board,
31st May, 1888.

Memorandum (No. 2) of Alterations affecting the Particulars contained in the Statement of Poor Law Unions, &c., 1887.—[C. 5191.]

I.—ALTERATIONS IN AREAS EFFECTED UNDER THE DIVIDED PARISHES ACTS.

A.—LIST of CASES in which one PARISH has been entirely amalgamated with some other PARISH or PARISHES by ORDERS which came into operation from and after the 25th MARCH 1889.

Name of Union. 1.	Name of Parish absorbed. 2.	With what Parish or Parishes amalgamated. 3.
Belper	Ireton Wood	{ Ideridgehay and Alton. { Kirk Ireton (Ashbourne Union).
Bridge	The Mint (formerly extra-parochial).	Harbledown.
Chelmsford	Ingatestone	Fryerning. (Name changed to Ingatestone and Fryerning.)
Rothbury	Brinkburn (South Side)	Brinkburn (High Ward).
	Debdon	Rothbury.
	Dueshill	Holystone.
	Hepple	{ Hepple Demesne. { (Name changed to Hepple.) { Woodside Ward.
	Little Tosson	{ Hepple Demesne. (*See above.*) { Great Tosson and Ryehill. { (Name changed to Tosson.)
	Lee Ward	{ Hesleyhurst. { Raw.
	Pauperhaugh	Raw.
Skipton	Beamsley-in-Addingham	{ Hazlewood with Storiths. { Beamsley-in-Skipton. { (Name changed to Beamsley.)
Wirrall	Newton with Larton	Grange.

B.—List of Cases in which Parts of Divided Parishes were amalgamated with adjoining Parishes, by Orders which came into operation from and after the 25th March 1889.

Name of Divided Parish, and of the Union in which situate.		Name of Parish with which Parts were amalgamated and of the Union in which situate.	
Union.	Parish.	Parish.	Union.
Alresford	Itchen Stoke	Avington	New Winchester.
Ashton-under-Lyne	Droylsden	Openshaw	Chorlton.
Banbury	Barford Saint Michael	Deddington	Woodstock.
Basford	West Bridgeford	Edwalton	Bingham.
Billericay	Bowers-Gifford	Pitsea	Billericay.
	Downham	Ramsden Bell-House	
	Laindon	Bowers-Gifford	
	Nevendon	Pitsea	
	Pitsea	Bowers-Gifford	
	Vange		
	Dunton	Corringham	Orsett.
	Laindon		
	Lee Chapel	Langdon-Hills	
	Little Warley	Corringham	
Bingham	Hawksworth	Thoroton	Bingham.
Bradfield	Burghfield	Saint Giles with Whitley	Reading.
	Tileburst	Saint Mary with Southcot	
Braintree	Cressing	Bradwell near Coggeshall	Braintree.
		Rivenhall	
	Feering	Kelvedon	
		Little Coggeshall	
	Great Coggeshall	Pattiswicke	
	Kelvedon	Little Coggeshall	
	Rivenhall	Cressing	
	Stisted	Bradwell near Coggeshall	
	Terling	Fairstead	
	White Notley	Black Notley	
Bridge	Adisham	Littlebourn	Bridge.
	Beaksbourne otherwise Beakesbourne.	Adisham	
	Ickham		
	Kingstone otherwise Kingston.	Womenswould	
	Wickhambreux	Littlebourn	
	Waltham	Hastingleigh	East Ashford.
Chelmsford	Chelmsford	Broomfield	Chelmsford.
		Writtle	
	Widford	Writtle	
Dunmow	Barnston	Great Dunmow	Dunmow.
	Great Bardfield	Little Bardfield	
	Great Dunmow	Barnston	
		High Easter	
	High Roothing	Barnston	
	Little Bardfield	Great Bardfield	
Holyhead	Aberffraw	Llangadwaladr	Bangor and Beaumaris.
Isle of Wight	Brixton	Shorwell	Isle of Wight.
	Saint Nicholas	Shalfleet	
	Shalfleet	Calbourne	
		Brook	
	Shorwell	Kingston	

Name of Divided Parish, and of the Union in which situate.		Name of Parish with which Parts were amalgamated and of the Union in which situate.	
Union.	Parish.	Parish.	Union.
Lexden and Winstree	Aldham	Great Tey	Lexden and Winstree.
	Birch	Easthorpe	
		Layer-de-la-Hay	
	Chappel	Mount Bures	
		Wakes Colne	
	Copford	Birch	
		Marks Tey	
	Easthorpe	Birch	
	Fingringhoe	East Donyland	
	Fordham	West Bergholt	
	Great Wigborough	Layer Marney	
		Messing	
	Layer-de-la-Hay	Peldon	
	Little Tey	Aldham	
		Great Tey	
	Little Wigborough	Great Wigborough	
	Marks Tey	Aldham	
		Easthorpe	
	Messing	Birch	
		Inworth	
	Mount Bures	Chappel	
		Wakes Colne	
	Virley	Layer Breton	
	Wakes Colne	Chappel	
	Wormingford	Little Horksley	
Llanrwst	Llanrhychwyn	Trefriew	Llanrwst.
		Tre Gwydir	
	Llanrwst	Llandogged	
	Trefriew	Llanrhychwyn	
Maidstone	Berstead	Thornham	Hollingbourn.
Maldon	Asheldam	Dengie	Maldon.
		Steeple	
	Goldhanger	Little Totham	
		Tolleshunt D'Arcy	
	Great Totham	Goldhanger	
	Langford	Ulting	
		Wickham Bishop	
	Mayland	Southminster	
	Saint Lawrence	Dengie	
	Saint Peter's	Saint Mary's	
	Stow-Maries	Purleigh	
	Tollesbury	Tolleshunt D'Arcy	
		Tolleshunt Knights	
	Tolleshunt Major	Tolleshunt D'Arcy	
Malton	Scamston	Thorp Bassett	Malton.
	Thornton-le-Clay	Foston	
	Yeddingham	Heslerton, West	
New Winchester	Easton	Avington	New Winchester.
	Itchen Abbas		
Northwich	Marston	Wincham	Northwich.
	Rudheath	Hulse	
		Lack Dennis	
		Stublach	
	Stublach	Rudheath	
	Rudheath	Cranage	Congleton.
		Twemlow	
Orsett	Fobbing	Corringham	Orsett.
Petworth	Bignor	Easebourne	Midhurst.
Pontefract	Heck	Hensall	Pontefract.
	Pontefract	Pontefract Park	
		Tanshelf	
Pwllheli	Edeyrn	Tydweiliog	Pwllheli.
	Nevin	Ceidio	

Name of Divided Parish, and of the Union in which situate.		Name of Parish with which Parts were amalgamated, and of the Union in which situate.	
Union.	Parish.	Parish.	Union.
Rothbury	Cartington Great Ryle Hollinghill Linbridge Snitter Great Tosson and Ryehill. (*See* Table A.)	Rothbury Alnham Hesleyhurst Kidland Cartington Rothbury Thropton Hepple Demesne (*See* Table A.)	Rothbury.
Skipton	Beamsley-in-Skipton (*See* Table A.)	Hazlewood with Storiths	Skipton.
Tynemouth	Preston	Chirton	Tynemouth.
Wirrall	Great Sutton Little Neston	Over Pool Raby	Wirrall.
Wokingham	Earleigh Shinfield	Saint Giles with Whitley.	Reading.

II.—ALTERATIONS IN NAMES OF PARISHES.

In addition to the alteration of names by Orders under the Divided Parishes Acts (see Column 3 of Table I., A.), the Orders declaring certain Unions have been amended in regard to the names of certain Parishes in such Unions. The following Table includes all the cases of this kind between the 31st May 1888 and the date of the present Memorandum.

Union.	Name of Parish as in Declaration Order.	Name of Parish as Amended.	Date of Amending Order.
Bingham	Knighton	Kneeton	9 Aug. 1888.
Bridgewater	Puriton with Woolavington	Puriton	16 July 1888.
Patrington	Owstwich	Owstwick	5 Feb. 1889.
Pickering	Pickering Marshes	Pickering Marishes	8 Feb. 1889.
Rotherham	Treeton with that part of Wales in Treeton Parish.	Treeton	17 July 1888.
Saint Thomas'	Holcomb Burnel	Holcombe Burnell	2 Aug. 1888.
Solby	Haddlesley Chapel	Chapel Haddlesey	27 July 1888.
Teesdale	Thorpe	Wycliffe with Thorpe	20th Sept. 1888.
Wareham and Purbeck	East Lullworth West Lullworth	East Lullworth West Lullworth	21 Feb. 1889.
Warrington	Woolstone with Martinscroft.	Woolston with Martinscroft.	10 July 1888.

III.—CHANGES EFFECTED IN PAROCHIAL AREAS IN PURSUANCE OF LOCAL ACTS.

1. The Barking Parish Act, 1888.

   From and after the 29th September 1888, the Parish of Barking, in the Romford Union, was for all lay and civil purposes divided into two separate and distinct Parishes, to be called the Parish of Barking and the Parish of Ilford. The new Parishes form part of the Romford Union.

2. The Lancaster Corporation Act, 1888.

   On and after the 1st September 1888, the boundaries of the Borough of Lancaster were extended so as to comprise parts of the Townships of Scotforth and Skerton, and from and after the same date the Borough as extended became a separate and distinct Township, under the name of the Township of Lancaster, for all civil, lay, and parochial purposes. The effect of the Act was thus to amalgamate certain parts of the Townships of Scotforth and Skerton with the Township of Lancaster.

IV.—ALTERATIONS IN UNIONS BY ADDITION OR SEPARATION OF PARISHES.

BRIDGEND AND COWBRIDGE AND NEATH UNIONS.

1. By Order dated 11th January 1888, the Hamlet of Higher Llangonoyd was separated from the Neath Union from and after the 27th March 1888; and by Order dated the 12th January 1888, that Hamlet was added to the Bridgend and Cowbridge Union on the 28th March 1888.

CHESTER UNION.

2. By Order dated 5th March 1889, the Parish of Chester Castle otherwise Gloverstone was added to the Chester Union on the 26th March 1889. The Parish, although locally situated in the County Borough of Chester, forms part of the County of Chester.

V.—CORRECTIONS.

AMPTHILL UNION.—The Parish of Shillington is partly in Bedford and partly in Hertford, there being four detached parts of the Parish in the last-named County. The Union therefore extends into two Counties.

AYLESBURY, BICESTER, and THAME UNIONS.—The Parishes in these Unions stated in the sixth column of the Statement to be in the Petty Sessional Division of "Ashendon" or "Ashenden," are in the Petty Sessional Division of "Brill."

CRICKHOWEL UNION.—" Crickne fawr " should be " Grwyne fawr."

FORDINGBRIDGE UNION.—The Parish of Whichbury is partly in Wilts and partly in Southampton.

GREAT OUSEBURN UNION.—Before the name of " Cattal " insert † and after the name add " tow." In lieu of the * before the name of "Thornville" insert †. Both these Townships were added to the Union on 21st June 1869 by Order dated 31st May 1869.

MARKET HARBOROUGH UNION.—At top of page 231 " County of Leicester—*continued* " should be " County of Northampton—*continued*."

NEWPORT PAGNELL UNION.—The Parish of Hanslope is partly in Buckingham and partly in Northampton. The Union therefore extends into two Counties.

NORWICH UNION.—Hamlet of Heigham. This Hamlet was, by the Norwich Poor Act, 1863, divided into two Districts or Hamlets, to be called North Heigham and South Heigham. The Board have recently decided that each of these Hamlets is a separate Poor Law Parish, and they should accordingly be so entered in place of Heigham. The population, &c. of each Hamlet cannot be given.

ROSS UNION.—The Tything of Lea Bailey should, for the present, be inserted as a Parish in the Ross Union. It was supposed that all the parts of the Tything had been added to other Parishes under the Divided Parishes Acts, but two parts not dealt with under those Acts were brought to the notice of the Board in 1888. These two parts have now been dealt with by Order, which, however, will not operate until after the 25th March 1890.

RUTHIN UNION.—The Parish of Llanarmon is partly in Denbigh and partly in Flint. The Union therefore extends into two Counties.

TADCASTER UNION.—Insert the note letter (a) after the Townships of Allerton Bywater and Kippax, and add to the note at the foot of page 360 the following words, "and detached parts " of Kippax were amalgamated with Allerton Bywater."

THAME UNION.—The Parish of Ickford is now wholly in Buckingham. *See* the note (a) in regard to the Parish.

WORKSOP UNION.—" Wallingwells " was added to the Union on 24th March 1862, by Order dated 19th March 1862. Therefore insert * before the name of the Parish of Wallingwells.

VI.—STATEMENT showing as regards Union and Parochial Areas the alterations in Counties effected by Sections 50 and 59 of the Local Government Act, 1888. The former Section provides (1) that the first Council elected under the Act for any Administrative County shall be elected for the County at large as bounded for parliamentary purposes, subject, amongst other things, to the proviso that where any Urban Sanitary District is situate partly within and partly without the boundary of such County the District shall be deemed to be within that County which contains the largest portion of the population of the District according to the Census of 1881 ; and (2) that the County Council elected under the Act shall have for the purposes of the Act authority throughout the Administrative County for which it is elected, and the Administrative County as bounded for the purpose of the election shall, subject to alterations made in manner provided by the Act, be for all the purposes of the Act the County of such County Council. Section 59 further provides that, subject as therein mentioned, a place which is part of an Administrative County for the purposes of the Act shall form part of that County for all purposes.

Union.	Parish.	Urban Sanitary District or Districts (formerly in two or more Counties) in which the Parish is wholly or partly included.	County or Counties in which the Parish was formerly included.	County or Counties in which the Parish is now included.
Abingdon	Culham (1)	Abingdon Borough	Berks and Oxford	Berks and Oxford.
	North Hinksey	Oxford L.G.D.	Berks	Do.
	South Hinksey	Do.	Do.	Do.
Alcester	Ipsley	Redditch L.G.D.	Warwick	Warwick and Worcester.
Ashton-under-Lyne	Ashton-under-Lyne	{ Stalybridge Borough } and Mossley Borough. }	Lancaster	Chester and Lancaster.
	Stayley	Do.	Chester	Do.
	Tintwistle	Mossley Borough	Do.	Do.
Banbury	Warkworth with Nethercote and Grimsbury.	Banbury L.G.D.	Northampton	Northampton and Oxford.
Barnet	Hadley	{ Barnet L.G.D. } East Barnet Valley } L.G.D. }	Middlesex	Hertford.
	South Mimms	Do.	Do.	Do, and Middlesex.
Bedwellty	Aberystruth	{ Brynmawr L.G.D. } { Ebbw Vale L.G.D. }	Monmouth	Brecknock and Monmouth. [The Union will, therefore, be in two Counties.]
Burnley	Cliviger	Todmorden L.G.D.	Lancaster	Lancaster and West Riding of Yorkshire. [The Union will, therefore, be in two Counties.]
Burton-upon-Trent	Stapenhill	Burton-upon-Trent Borough.	Derby	Derby and Stafford.
	Winshill	Do.	Do.	Do.
Cardigan	Saint Dogmel's	Cardigan Borough	Pembroke	Cardigan and Pembroke.
Conway	Eirias	Colwyn Bay and Colwyn L.G.D.	Carnarvon	Carnarvon and Denbigh.
Crickhowel	Llangattock	{ Brynmawr L.G.D. } { Ebbw Vale L.G.D. } { Ebbw Vale L.G.D. } { Rhymney L.G.D. } { Tredegar L.G.D. }	Brecknock	Brecknock and Monmouth.
	Llangynidir	Do.	Do.	Do. [The Union will, therefore, be in two Counties.]
Edmonton	Enfield	East Barnet Valley L.G.D.	Middlesex	Hertford and Middlesex.
Hayfield	Disley	New Mills L.G.D.	Chester	Chester and Derby.
Hinckley	Hinckley	Hinckley L.G.D.	Leicester and Warwick	Leicester.
Malton	Norton	Malton L.G.D.	East Riding of Yorkshire.	North Riding of Yorkshire.
Market Harborough	Little Bowden	Market Harborough, Great and Little Bowden L.G.D.	Northampton	Leicester and Northampton.
Newmarket	All Saints, Newmarket	Newmarket L.G.D.	Cambridge	Western Division of Suffolk.
	Wood Ditton	Do.	Do.	Cambridge and Western Division of Suffolk.
Oxford	Saint Aldate	Oxford L.G.D.	Berks and Oxford	Oxford. [The Union will, therefore, be wholly in one County.]
Peterborough	Fletton	Peterborough Borough	Huntingdon	Huntingdon and Soke of Peterborough.
	Woodstone	Do.	Do.	Do.
Risbridge	Haverhill	Haverhill L.G.D.	Essex and Suffolk	Western Division of Suffolk.
Saddleworth (Separate Township)		Mossley Borough	West Riding of Yorkshire.	Lancaster and West Riding of Yorkshire.

(1) The effect of the Act is to transfer a part of the Oxfordshire portion of Culham to Berks.

Union.	Parish.	Urban Sanitary District or Districts (formerly in two or more Counties) in which the Parish is wholly or partly included.	County or Counties in which the Parish was formerly included.	County or Counties in which the Parish is now included.
Saint Asaph	Aberacle	Rhyl L.A.D.	Denbigh	Denbigh and Flint.
Scarborough	Filey	Filey L.G.D.	East and North Ridings of Yorkshire.	East Riding of Yorkshire.
Stamford	Saint Martin	Stamford Borough	Northampton	Parts of Kesteven and the Soke of Peterborough.
Sudbury	Ballingdon	Sudbury Borough	Essex	Western Division of Suffolk.
Tamworth	Tamworth	Tamworth Borough	Stafford and Warwick	Stafford
Teesdale	Startforth	Barnard Castle L.G.D.	North Riding of Yorkshire.	Durham and North Riding of Yorkshire.
Thetford	Thetford Saint Cuthbert.	Thetford Borough	Norfolk and Suffolk	Norfolk.
	Thetford Saint Mary	Do.	Do.	Do.
Thorne	Crowle	Crowle L.G.D.	Lincoln and West Riding of Yorkshire.	Parts of Lindsey.
Ticehurst	Frant (1)	Tunbridge Wells Borough	Sussex and Kent	Eastern Division of Sussex and Kent.
Todmorden	Todmorden and Walsden.	Todmorden L.G.D.	Lancaster	West Riding of Yorkshire. [The Union will, therefore, be wholly in one County.]
Warrington	Latchford	Warrington Borough	Chester	Chester and Lancaster.

(1) The effect of the Act is to transfer a part of the Sussex portion of Frant to Kent.

VII.—STATEMENT showing the Unions and parts of Unions comprised in the several Administrative Counties of London, Cambridge, the Isle of Ely, the Parts of Holland, the Parts of Kesteven, the Parts of Lindsey, Northampton, the Soke of Peterborough, the Eastern Division of Suffolk, the Western Division of Suffolk, the Eastern Division of Sussex, and the Western Division of Sussex.

A.—THE ADMINISTRATIVE COUNTY OF LONDON.

THE following Unions and separate Parishes are now wholly or partly comprised in the Administrative County of London, as formed by the Local Government Act, and, except as regards the City of London and Croydon Unions, they are to be described as in the County of London, and not as in the County of Kent, or Middlesex, or Surrey, as formerly:—

City of London Union. (1.)
Croydon Union (partly, namely, the Hamlet of Penge). (2.)
Fulham Union.
Greenwich Union.
Hackney Union.
Holborn Union.
Lewisham Union.
Hamlet of Mile End Old Town.
Parish of Paddington.
Poplar Union.
Saint George's Union.
Parish of Saint George in the East.
Parish of Saint Giles, Camberwell.
United Parishes of Saint Giles-in-the-Fields and Saint George, Bloomsbury.
Parish of Saint John Hampstead.
Parish of Saint Leonard, Shoreditch.
Parish of Saint Luke, Chelsea.
Parish of Saint Mary Abbots Kensington.
Parish of Saint Mary, Islington.
Parish of Saint Mary, Lambeth.
Parish of Saint Marylebone.
Parish of Saint Matthew, Bethnal Green.
Saint Olave's Union.
Parish of Saint Pancras.
Saint Saviour's Union.
Stepney Union.
Strand Union.
Wandsworth and Clapham Union.
Westminster Union.
Whitechapel Union.
Woolwich Union.

(1.) The City of London Union is to be described as "in the City of London and the County "of London." The only part of this Union which is not in the City of London is the part of the Parish of Saint Botolph without Aldersgate, known as "Glasshouse Yard."
(2.) The Croydon Union is also partly in the County Borough of Croydon, and the County of Surrey.

A 4

This County comprises the following Unions and parts of Unions :

Cambridge.

Caxton and Arrington (part, viz., the 23 Parishes shown in the Statement [C. 5191.] as in Cambridge, together with the part of Papworth Saint Agnes in Cambridgeshire).

Chesterton.

Linton (part, viz., the 20 Parishes shown in the Statement as in Cambridge).

Newmarket (part, viz., the Parishes shown in the Statement as in Cambridge, *except* All Saints, Newmarket, and part of Wood Ditton. *See* "Newmarket L.G.D., Table VI.)

Royston (part, viz., the 16 Parishes shown in the Statement as in Cambridge, together with the part of Royston in Cambridgeshire).

Saint Ives (part, viz., the 6 Parishes shown in the Statement as in Cambridge).

Saint Neotts (part, viz., "Graveley").

C.—The Administrative County of the Isle of Ely.

This County comprises the following Unions and parts of Unions :—

Downham (part, viz., the Parish of Welney (Cambs.)).

Ely (part, viz., the 16 Parishes shown in the Statement as in Cambridge).

North Witchford.

Peterborough (part, viz., Thorney and the part of Stanground in Cambridgeshire).

Saint Mary and Saint Andrew Whittlesea (United Parishes).

Wisbeach (part, viz., the 9 Parishes shown in the Statement as in Cambridge).

D.—The Administrative County of the Parts of Holland.

This County comprises the following Unions and parts of Unions :—

Boston (part, viz., the part of the Parish of Leake, together with the 39 other Parishes, not comprised in the Parts of Kesteven and the Parts of Lindsey (*q.v.*)).

Holbeach (part, viz., the whole Union except the portion of Central Wingland in Norfolk).

Peterborough (part, viz., "Crowland ").

Spalding (part, viz., the whole Union except the portion of Deeping Saint Nicholas in the Parts of Kesteven).

E.—The Administrative County of the Parts of Kesteven.

This County comprises the following Unions and parts of Unions :—

Boston (part, viz., "Dogdyke.")

Bourn.

Grantham (part, viz., the 47 Parishes shown in the Statement as in Lincoln).

Lincoln (part, viz., the 29 Parishes which are shown in the last column of the Statement as in Kesteven).

Newark (part, viz., the 26 Parishes shown in the Statement as in Lincoln).

Sleaford.

Spalding (part, viz., part of Deeping Saint Nicholas).

Stamford (part, viz., the 13 Parishes shown in the Statement as in Lincoln, together with the portion of Saint Martin (now shown in Northampton) which is in the Borough of Stamford).

F.—The Administrative County of the Parts of Lindsey.

This County contains the following Unions and parts of Unions :—

Boston (part, viz., part of the Parish of Leake, together with the Parishes of Carrington, Frithville, Langriville, Sibsey, Thornton le Fen, and Westville).

Caistor.

Doncaster (part, viz., the part of the Parish of Misson which is in Lincolnshire).

Gainsborough (part, viz., the 43 Parishes shown in the Statement as in Lincoln).

Glanford Brigg.

Goole (part, viz., the 2 Parishes shown as in Lincoln).

Horncastle.

Lincoln (part, viz., the 48 Parishes which are shown in the last column of the Statement as in Lindsey).

Louth.

Spilsby.

Thorne (part, viz., the 7 Parishes shown in the Statement as wholly in Lincoln, together with the Parish of Crowle now shown as in two Counties).

G.—The Administrative County of Northampton.

This County contains the following Unions and parts of Unions :—

Banbury (part, viz., the nine Parishes shown in the Statement as in Northampton except the part of Warkworth with Nethercote and Grimsbury which is in the Banbury L.G.D. *See* Table VI.)

Brackley (part, viz., the 22 Parishes shown as in Northampton).

Brixworth.

Daventry.

Hardingstone.

Kettering.

Lutterworth (part, viz., " Welford ").

Market Harborough (part, viz., the 19 parishes shown in the Statement as in Northampton, except the part of Little Bowden which is in the Market Harborough, Great and Little Bowden L.G.D. *See* Table VI.)

Newport Pagnell (part, viz., a part of Hanslope).

Northampton (part, viz., the 13 Parishes not included in the County Borough of Northampton—q.v.).

Oundle (part, viz., the 30 Parishes shown as wholly in Northampton, together with the Northamptonshire parts of the 4 parishes shown as partly in Northampton).

Potterspury (part, viz., the 11 Parishes shown as in Northampton).

Rugby (part, viz., the 8 parishes shown as in Northampton).

Southam (part, viz., " Stoneton ").

Stamford (part, viz , Colly Weston, Duddington, and Easton).

Thrapston (part, viz., the 19 Parishes shown as in Northampton).

Towcester.

Uppingham (part, viz., the 6 parishes shown as in Northampton).

Wellingborough (part, viz., the 24 Parishes shown as in Northampton).

II.—The Administrative County of the Soke of Peterborough.

This County comprises parts of two Unions as follows :

Peterborough (part, viz., the 21 Parishes now shown in the Statement as in Northampton, together with the parts of Fletton and Woodstone (now shown in Huntingdon), which are included in the City of Peterborough.

Stamford (part, viz., the Parishes of Bainton, Barnack, Southorpe, Thornhaugh, Ufford, Wansford, Wittering, and Wothorpe, together with the part of Saint Martin not included in the Borough of Stamford).

I.—The Administrative County of the Eastern Division of Suffolk.

This County comprises the following Unions and parts of Unions :—

Blything.

Bosmere and Claydon (viz., the whole Union except the portion of Bramford in the County Borough of Ipswich).

Hartismere.

Hoxne.

Ipswich (part, viz., the parts of Westerfield and Whitton not included in the County Borough of Ipswich).

Mutford and Lothingland (part, viz., the whole Incorporation except Gorleston).

Plomesgate.

Samford (part, viz., the whole Union except the portions of Belstead and Sproughton in the County Borough of Ipswich).

Stow (part, viz., the Parishes of Buxhall, Combs, Creeting Saint Peter, Gipping, Great Finborough, Harleston, Haughley, Little Finborough, Old Newton with Dagworth, One House, Shelland, Stowmarket, Stow Upland, and Wetherden).

Wangford.

Woodbridge (part, viz., the whole Union except the portion of Rushmere in the County Borough of Ipswich).

J.—The Administrative County of the Western Division of Suffolk.

This County contains the following Unions and parts of Unions :—

Bury Saint Edmunds.

Cosford.

Mildenhall.

Newmarket (part, viz., the 7 Parishes now shown in the Statement as in Suffolk, together with the Parish of All Saints, Newmarket, and part of Wood Ditton, now shown in Cambridge).

Risbridge (part, viz., the 19 Parishes now shown as in Suffolk, together with the whole of the Parish of Haverhill (now shown as in two Counties), and the part of the Parish of Kedington in Suffolk).

Stow (part, viz., the 20 Parishes which are not included in the Eastern Division of Suffolk —q.v.)

Sudbury (part, viz., the 24 Parishes now shown as in Suffolk, together with the Parish of Ballingdon now shown as in Essex).

Thetford (part, viz., the 13 Parishes now shown as in Suffolk, together with the parts of Brandon and Rushford in Suffolk).

Thingoe.

K.—THE ADMINISTRATIVE COUNTY OF THE EASTERN DIVISION OF SUSSEX.

This County contains the following Unions and parts of Unions:—

Battle.
Chailey.
Cuckfield (part, viz., all the part not included in the Western Division of Sussex.—q.v.)
Eastbourne.
East Grinstead (part, viz., the 5 Parishes shown in the Statement as in Sussex).
Hailsham.
Hastings (part, viz., the Parishes of Fairlight, Guestling, and Pett, and the parts of the Parishes of Ore, Saint Leonards, and Saint Mary in the Castle not included in the County Borough of Hastings).
Horsham (Parish of Crawley or part of that Parish).
Lewes.
Newhaven.
Rye (part, viz., the whole Union except the portion of the Parish of Broomhill which is included in the County of Kent).
Steyning (part, viz., the Parishes of Aldrington, Hangleton, Hove, Patcham, Portslade, Poynings, and West Blatchington, part of the Parish of Edburton, and the part of the Parish of Preston not included in the County Borough of Brighton).
Ticehurst (part, viz., the whole Union except the portions of the Parishes of Frant and Lamberhurst which are included in the County of Kent).
Tonbridge (part, viz., the part of the Parish of Horsemonden which is not included in the County of Kent).
Uckfield.
West Firle.

L.—THE ADMINISTRATIVE COUNTY OF THE WESTERN DIVISION OF SUSSEX.

This County contains the following Unions and parts of Unions:—

Chichester.
Cuckfield (part, viz., the Parishes of Albourn and Cowfold and part of each of the Parishes of Bolney and Slaugham).
East Preston.
Horsham (part, viz., the whole Union, except the Parish of Crawley, subject to the question whether that Parish is not partly in the Western Division of Sussex).
Midhurst.
Petersfield (part, viz., the portion of the Parish of Bramshott which is included in Sussex).
Petworth.
Steyning (part, viz., part of the Parish of Edburton, together with all other Parishes in the Union (except Preston) which are not included in the Eastern Division of Sussex.—q.v.)
Thakeham.
Westbourne.
West Hampnett.

VIII.—STATEMENT showing the names of the constituent Parishes of the County Boroughs named in the Third Schedule to the Local Government Act, together with the Unions in which such Parishes are comprised.

County Boroughs.	Constituent Parishes.	Unions.
Barrow-in-Furness	Barrow-in-Furness	Barrow-in-Furness (Separate Parish).
Bath	Bathwick Lyncombe and Widcombe Saint James Saint Michael Saint Peter and Saint Paul Walcot	Bath.
Birkenhead	Birkenhead Claughton-cum-Grange Oxton Tranmere Higher Bebington (part)	Birkenhead. Wirrall.
Birmingham	Birmingham Edgbaston Aston (part)	Birmingham (Separate Parish). Kings Norton. Aston.
Blackburn	Blackburn Little Harwood Livesay (part) Lower Darwen (part) Witton (part)	Blackburn.

County Boroughs.	Constituent Parishes.	Unions.
Bolton	Great Bolton Little Bolton Halliwell (part) Rumworth (part) Tonge with Haulgh (part)	Bolton.
Bootle cum Linacre	Bootle cum Linacre	West Derby.
Bradford	Bolton Bowling Bradford Horton Manningham Allerton Heaton Calverley with Farsley (part) Pudsey (part)	Bradford. North Bierley.
Brighton	Brighton Preston (part)	Brighton (Separate Parish). Steyning.
Bristol	The 18 Parishes in the Bristol Incorporation. Clifton Westbury-upon-Trym (part) Saint James and Saint Paul Out Saint Philip and Saint Jacob Out Bedminster (part)	Bristol. Barton Regis. Bedminster.
Burnley	Burnley (part) Habergham Eaves (part)	Burnley.
Bury	Bury Birtle cum Bamford (part) Elton (part) Heap (part) Pilkington (part) Pilsworth (part) Radcliffe (part) Tottington Lower End (part) Walmersley (part)	Bury.
Canterbury	The 20 Parishes in the Canterbury Union. The 13 Parishes shown under the Blean or Bridge Unions as wholly or partly in the City of Canterbury are wholly or partly in the County Borough of Canterbury. Sturry (part)	Canterbury. Blean. Bridge. Blean.
Cardiff	Saint Mary, Cardiff Saint John, Cardiff Canton Roath (part)	Cardiff.
Chester	Chester	Chester.
Coventry	Holy Trinity (part) Saint Michael (part)	Coventry.
Croydon	Croydon	Croydon.
Derby	All Saints Saint Alkmund's (part) Saint Michael's Saint Peter's Saint Werburgh's Litchurch Little Chester Littleover (part) Normanton (part) Mackeaton (part)	Derby. Shardlow. Do. Belper.
Devonport	Stoke Damarel	Stoke Damarel (Separate Parish).
Dudley	Dudley	Dudley.

County Boroughs.	Constituent Parishes.	Unions.
Exeter - - -	The Parishes in the Exeter Union -	Exeter.
Gateshead - - {	Gateshead - - - - Heworth (part) - - -	} Gateshead.
Gloucester - -	The 15 Parishes shown under the Gloucester Union as wholly or partly in the City of Gloucester are wholly or partly in the County Borough of Gloucester.	Gloucester.
Great Yarmouth - {	Great Yarmouth - - -	Great Yarmouth (Separate Parish).
	Gorleston (part) - -	Mutford and Lothingland.
Halifax - - {	Halifax - - - - Northowram (part) - - - Ovenden (part) - - - Skircoat (part) - Southowram (part) - - -	} Halifax.
Hanley - - -	Stoke-upon-Trent (part) - - -	Stoke upon Trent (Separate Parish).
Hastings - {	All Saints - - - - Ore (part) - - - Saint Andrew - - - Saint Clement's - - - Saint Leonards (part) - - Saint Mary Bulverhithe - - Saint Mary in the Castle (part) - Saint Mary Magdalen - - Saint Michael - - - The Holy Trinity - - -	} Hastings.
Huddersfield - {	Almondbury - - - Dalton - - - Huddersfield - - - Lockwood - - - Quarmby-with-Lindley - - -	} Huddersfield.
Ipswich - {	The Parishes in the Ipswich Union except parts of Westerfield and Whitton.	Ipswich.
	Bramford (part) - - -	Bosmere and Claydon.
	Sproughton (part) - - - Belstead (part) - - -	} Samford.
	Rushmere (part) - - -	Woodbridge.
Kingston-upon-Hull - {	The Kingston-upon-Hull Incorporation	Kingston-upon-Hull.
	Drypool - - - Garrison Side - - - Marfleet - - - Newington - - - Sculcoates - - - Southcoates - - - Cottingham (part) - - - Hessle (part) - Sutton and Stoneferry (part) -	} Sculcoates.
Leeds - {	Chapel Allerton - - Headingley-with-Burley - Leeds - - - Potter Newton - - - Seacroft (part) - - -	} Leeds.
	Armley - - - Bramley - - - Farnley - - - Wortley - - -	} Bramley.
	Beeston - - - Holbeck - - -	} Holbeck.
	Hunslet - - - Templenewsam (part) - -	} Hunslet.

County Boroughs.	Constituent Parishes.	Unions.
Leicester	All Saints - Augostine Friars - Black Friars - Saint Leonard - Saint Margaret - Saint Martin - Saint Mary - Saint Nicholas - The Castle View - The Newarke -	}Leicester.
Lincoln	The Parishes shown under the Lincoln Union as in the City of Lincoln.	Lincoln.
Liverpool	Liverpool (part) - Everton - Kirkdale - West Derby (part) - Toxteth Park (part) -	Liverpool (Separate Parish). }West Derby. Toxteth Park (Separate Parish).
Manchester	Manchester - Beswick - Bradford - Cheetham - Harpurhey - Ardwick - Chorlton upon Medlock - Hulme - Rusholme - Mosside (part) - Withington (part) -	Manchester (Separate Township). }Prestwich. }Chorlton
Middlesbrough	Linthorpe (part) - Marton (part) - Middlesbrough - Normanby (part) - Ormesby (part) - West Acklam (part) -	}Middlesbrough.
Newcastle-upon-Tyne	All Saints - Byker - Elswick - Heaton - Jessmond - Saint Andrew's - Saint John's - Saint Nicholas - Westgate -	}Newcastle-upon-Tyne.
Northampton	All Saints - Priory of Saint Andrew or Town Part Saint Giles - Saint Peter - Saint Sepulchre -	}Northampton.
Norwich	The Parishes in the Norwich Union -	Norwich.
Nottingham	The Parishes in the Nottingham Union Basford - Bulwell - Carlton (part) - Wilford (part) -	Nottingham. }Basford.
Oldham	Oldham -	Oldham.
Plymouth	Charles - Saint Andrew (part) -	}Plymouth.
Portsmouth	Portsmouth - Portsea -	}Portsea Island

County Boroughs.	Constituent Parishes.		Unions.
Preston	As from 1st June 1889	Fishwick Grimsargh and Brockholes(part) Lea, Ashton, Ingol, and Cottam (part) Penwortham (part) Preston Ribbleton (part)	Preston.
Reading	Saint Giles, with Whitley Saint Lawrence Saint Mary, with Southcot		Reading.
Rochdale	Butterworth (part) Castleton (part) Spotland (part) Wardleworth Wuerdale and Wardle (part)		Rochdale.
Saint Helen's	Eccleston (part) Parr Sutton Windle (part)		Prescot.
Salford	Broughton Pendleton Salford		Salford.
Sheffield	Attercliffe cum Darnall Brightside Bierlow Sheffield Ecclesall Bierlow Heeley Nether Hallam Upper Hallam		Sheffield. Ecclesall Bierlow.
Southampton	All Saints Holy Rhood Saint John Saint Lawrence Saint Mary Saint Michael South Stoneham (part)		Southampton. South Stoneham.
South Shields	South Shields Westoe		South Shields.
Stockport	Brinnington (part) Cheadle (part) Heaton Norris (part) Stockport		Stockport.
Sunderland	Bishopwearmouth (part) Bishopwearmouth Panns Monkwearmouth (part) Monkwearmouth Shore Ryhope (part) Sunderland		Sunderland.
Swansea	Clase (part) Llansamlet Higher (part) Llansamlet Lower (part) Saint John Saint Thomas Swansea Town and Franchise		Swansea.
Walsall	Rushall (part) Walsall Foreign (part) Walsall Borough		Walsall.
West Bromwich	West Bromwich		West Bromwich.
West Ham	West Ham		West Ham.
Wigan	Wigan		Wigan.

County Boroughs.	Constituent Parishes.	Unions.
Wolverhampton -	Wolverhampton - - -	Wolverhampton.
Worcester - -	The Parishes in the Worcester Union, except *parts* of Saint John in Bedwardine, Saint Peter the Great, and Saint Martin.	Worcester.
York - - -	The Parishes shown under the York Union as wholly or partly in the City of York are wholly or partly in the County Borough of York.	York.

Memorandum (No. 3) of Alterations affecting the Particulars contained in the Statement of Poor Law Unions, &c., 1887.—[C. 5191.]

I.—ALTERATIONS EFFECTED IN UNION AND PAROCHIAL AREAS UNDER THE DIVIDED PARISHES ACTS.

Ross AND WESTBURY UNIONS.—From and after the 25th March 1890, the two parts of which the Tything of Lea Bailey (in the Ross Union) consisted, became amalgamated with adjoining Parishes in pursuance of an Order of the Local Government Board dated 10th January 1889. One of such parts became amalgamated with the Parish of Lea (in the Ross Union), and the other with the Parish of Blaisdon (in the Westbury Union).

II.—ALTERATIONS EFFECTED IN PAROCHIAL AREAS IN PURSUANCE OF AN ORDER OF A COUNTY COUNCIL, CONFIRMED BY THE LOCAL GOVERNMENT BOARD.

CALNE UNION.—By an Order of the County Council of Wilts, as confirmed by " The County of " Wilts (Calne, &c.) Confirmation Order, 1890," (dated the 6th March 1890), the following alterations of parochial areas in this Union were made from and after the 25th March 1890 :—

1. The portion of the Parish of Calne within the Borough of Calne was made a separate Parish, to be called Calne Within.

2. The Parishes of Blackland, Bowood, and Calstone Willington, the part of the Parish of Bremhill south of the Calne Railway (but exclusive of the Railway), and the part of the Parish of Calne outside the Borough of Calne, were amalgamated and formed into a separate Parish, to be called Calne Without.

3. The Parish of Highway was united with and made part of the Parish of Hillmarton.

The new Parishes of Calne Within and Calne Without were included by the Order in the Calne Union, and in the Calne Petty Sessional Division.

III.—ALTERATIONS EFFECTED IN PAROCHIAL AREAS IN PURSUANCE OF LOCAL ACTS.

NORWICH UNION.—In pursuance of section 88 (1) of the Norwich Corporation Act (52 & 53 Vict. c. clxxxvii.), the area included within the City of Norwich (i.e., the Norwich Union) from and after the 25th March 1890, became one Parish, to be called the Parish of Norwich.

SCARBOROUGH UNION.—In pursuance of section 9 of the Scarborough Improvement Act, 1889 (52 & 53 Vict. c. clxiv.), the Townships of Falsgrave and Scarborough from and after the 25th March 1890, ceased to be separate Civil Parishes, and the Parish of Scarborough (including the Precinct of Scarborough Castle), which consisted of the two Townships named, was made one Parish for all lay and civil purposes, and was constituted one of the Parishes forming the Scarborough Union in lieu of the said two Townships.

i 62276.   150.—6/90.   Wt. 5570.   E. & S.

IV.—ALTERATIONS EFFECTED IN UNION, PAROCHIAL, AND COUNTY AREAS IN PURSUANCE OF PROVISIONAL ORDERS UNDER THE LOCAL GOVERNMENT ACT, 1888.

ABINGDON AND WOODSTOCK UNIONS.—By Provisional Order dated the 30th March 1889, which was confirmed by the Local Government Board's Provisional Orders Confirmation Act, 1889, a part of the Parish of Wolvercot, in the County of Oxford and the Woodstock Union, was separated from that Parish and County, and was amalgamated with the County of Berks, and with the Parish of Wytham in the Abingdon Union. The Order came into operation on the 9th November 1889.

BANBURY UNION.—Parish of Warkworth with Nethercote and Grimsbury.—The Borough of Banbury Order, 1889 (dated the 4th June 1889), confirmed by the Local Government Board's Provisional Orders Confirmation (No. 15) Act, 1889, had the effect of transferring a further portion of this Parish to Oxfordshire. (*See* Memorandum No. 2, Part VI.). The Order came into operation on the 9th November 1889.

MALTON UNION.—The Parish of Norton (as part of the Malton Local Government District) was by operation of sections 50 and 59 of the Local Government Act, 1888, transferred to the North Riding of Yorkshire (*see* Memorandum No. 2, Part VI.) By Provisional Order dated the 29th March 1889, this Parish was taken out of the Local Government District on the 29th September 1889, and by Provisional Order dated the 30th March 1889, it was re-transferred to the East Riding of Yorkshire, and to the Buckrose Petty Sessional Division on the 29th September 1889 (*see* Local Government Board's Provisional Orders Confirmation (No. 3) Act, 1889).

TEESDALE UNION.—The portion of the Township of Startforth which was in the Barnard Castle Local Government District was by operation of sections 50 and 59 of the Local Government Act, 1888, transferred to the County of Durham (*see* Memorandum No. 2, Part VI.). By Provisional Order dated the 29th March 1889, this portion of Startforth was taken out of the Local Government District on the 29th September 1889, and by Provisional Order dated the 30th March 1889, it was re-transferred to the North Riding of Yorkshire on the 29th September 1889 (*see* Local Government Board's Provisional Orders Confirmation (No. 3) Act, 1889). The Township is in the Greta Bridge Petty Sessional Division, as are all the other North Riding Parishes of the Teesdale Union, except Barforth.

V.—ALTERATION IN NAME OF PARISH.

EAST PRESTON UNION.—The Order declaring this Union was amended by Order of the Local Government Board dated the 4th July 1889, in pursuance of which the Parish described in the Declaration Order as "Leominster" is to be described as "Lyminster."

VI.—SEPARATION OF PARISHES FROM UNION AND FORMATION OF NEW UNION.

By an Order of the Local Government Board dated the 5th March 1890, the Parishes of Ashby cum Fenby, Aylesby, Barnoldby le Beck, Beelsby, Bradley, Brigsley, Great Coates, Great Grimsby, Habrough, Hatcliffe, Hawerby with Beesby, Healing, Humberston, Immingham, Irby, Laceby, Little Coates, Scartho, Stallingborough, Waltham, and Wold Newton, and the Townships of Clee, Cleethorpe, East Ravendale, and West Ravendale, were separated from the CAISTOR UNION, from and after the 15th April, 1890; and by a further Order dated the 5th March 1890, the same Parishes and Townships were, from and after the 15th April 1890, formed into a new Union, to be termed the GRIMSBY UNION.

VII.—CORRECTIONS.

BATTLE AND RYE UNIONS.—In addition to the Parishes and parts of Parishes stated on page 12 of Memorandum (No. 2) to be included in the County Borough of Hastings, the following areas although detached from the main part of the Borough are included in it, viz.:—

1. The portion of the Parish of Bexhill (in the Battle Union) known as the Liberty of the Sluice.

2. The portion of the Parish of Icklesham (in the Rye Union) which was formerly a detached part of the Parish of Saint Leonards (in the Hastings Union) but which, together with the main portion of the Parish of Saint Thomas the Apostle, Winchelsea (in the Rye Union), became amalgamated with the Parish of Icklesham under the Divided Parishes and Poor Law Amendment Act, 1882.

The list of Unions, &c in the Administrative County of the Eastern Division of Sussex, as shown on page 10 of Memorandum (No. 2), requires correction accordingly as regards the Battle and Rye Unions.

DONCASTER UNION.—In pursuance of the Redistribution of Seats Act, 1885, taken in connexion with a Provisional Order of the Local Government Board dated 20th May 1886, the Parish of Misson was included for parliamentary purposes in a Division of the County of Nottingham, and consequently under sub-sections (1) and (2) of section 50 of the Local Government Act, 1888, this Parish is included wholly in the Administrative County of Nottingham. The list of Unions, &c. in the Administrative County of the Parts of Lindsey as shown on page 8 of Memorandum (No. 2) therefore requires correction by striking out the reference to the Doncaster Union and Misson.

HOWDEN UNION.—The Township of Knedlington is partly in the East Riding and partly in the West Riding of Yorkshire, there being a detached part of the Township in the last-named Riding. The Union therefore extends into two Counties.

NOTTINGHAM UNION and NOTTINGHAM COUNTY BOROUGH.—On page 13 of Memorandum (No. 2) all the Parishes in the Nottingham Union are returned as included in the County Borough of Nottingham. There is, however, a small part of the Parish of Lenton which is not included in the Borough, namely, the part between the towing path on the north bank of the River Trent and the boundary of the Parish along the middle of the river. The Union therefore is included partly in the County of Nottingham.

TAMWORTH UNION.—The Parish of Drayton Bassett is partly in the County of Stafford and partly in the County of Warwick, the portion in the latter County consisting of about 3 acres, with no population.

WOODSTOCK UNION.—Before the name of "Asterleigh" insert †.

VIII.—NEW ADMINISTRATIVE COUNTY.

In pursuance of the Isle of Wight (County) Order, 1889 (dated the 30th March 1889), which was confirmed by the Local Government Board's Provisional Orders Confirmation (No. 2) Act, 1889, the Isle of Wight became, on the 1st April 1890, a separate Administrative County, under the name of the Administrative County of the Isle of Wight.

The new County is conterminous with the Isle of Wight Union.

IX.—NEW COUNTY BOROUGH.

OXFORD.—By the City of Oxford Order, 1889 (dated the 29th March 1889), which was confirmed by the Local Government Board's Provisional Orders Confirmation Act, 1889, the City of Oxford as extended by the Order was, on the 9th November 1889, constituted a County Borough.

The Parishes wholly or partly included in the County Borough, with the Unions in which they are comprised, are as follows :—

All the Parishes in the Oxford Incorporation.

Binsey
North Hinksey (pt.) } in the Abingdon Union.
South Hinksey (pt.)

Cowley (pt.)
Headington (pt.)
Iffley and Hockmoor (pt.)
Marston (pt.) } in the Headington Union.
Saint Clement, Oxford
Saint Giles, Oxford
Saint John, Oxford

Wolvercot (pt.), in the Woodstock Union.

X.—ALTERATIONS OF AREAS OR CONSTITUENT PARISHES OF COUNTY BOROUGHS.

BURNLEY.—By the Burnley Corporation Act, 1889 (52 & 53 Vict. c. lv.), the boundaries of the County Borough were, on the 1st September 1889, extended by the addition of—

(1.) Further portions of the Township of Habergham Eaves.

(2.) A further portion of the Township of Burnley.

(3.) Part of each of the Townships of—

Briercliffe with Extwisle ;
Reedley Hollows, Filley Close, and New Laund Booths ; and
Ightenhill Park.

All the Townships named are in the Burnley Union.

NORWICH.—*See* Part III. of this Memorandum.

NOTTINGHAM.—*See* Part VII. of this Memorandum.

SWANSEA.—By the Swansea Corporation Act, 1889 (52 & 53 Vict. c. cxcix.), the boundaries of the County Borough were, on the 31st September 1889, extended by the addition of—

    (1.) Part of the Parish of Swansea, Higher and Lower.

    (2.) Part of the Township of Penderry (Higher and Lower); and

    (3.) A further part of the Township of Clase, Higher and Lower.

    The places named are all in the Swansea Union.

    Local Government Board,
       31st May 1890.

Memorandum (No. 4) of Alterations affecting the Particulars contained in the Statement of Poor Law Unions, &c., 1887.—[C. 5191.]

I.—ALTERATIONS EFFECTED IN UNION AND PAROCHIAL AREAS UNDER THE DIVIDED PARISHES ACTS.

UNITED PARISHES OF SAINT GILES IN THE FIELDS AND SAINT GEORGE, BLOOMSBURY, AND PARISH OF SAINT PANCRAS.—From and after the 25th March 1891 an isolated and detached part of Saint Giles in the Fields became amalgamated with the Parish of Saint Pancras, in pursuance of an Order of the Local Government Board dated the 20th December 1890.

II.—ALTERATIONS EFFECTED IN UNION AND PAROCHIAL AREAS IN PURSUANCE OF ORDERS OF COUNTY COUNCILS, CONFIRMED BY THE LOCAL GOVERNMENT BOARD.

Unions.	Counties.	Dates of Orders of County Councils.	Dates of Confirming Orders.	Dates *from and after* which the Orders operated.	Particulars of Alterations effected by the Orders.
Berwick-upon-Tweed.	Northumberland.	7 Nov. 1890	24 Feb. 1891	25 Mar. 1891	The part of the Parish of Tweedmouth outside the Municipal Borough of Berwick-upon-Tweed (known as the Township of Ord) was separated from that Parish and formed into a separate Parish to be known as the Parish of Ord. The new Parish is included in the Berwick-upon-Tweed Union and in the Norham and Islandshires Petty Sessional Division.
Boston	Parts of Holland.	23 April 1890	7 Mar. 1891	25 Mar. 1891	The Parishes of Gibbet Hills, Great Brand End Plot, Mown Rakes, and Royalty Farm, in the Boston Union, and another place known as Little Brand End Plot, not comprised in any Union, were amalgamated with the Parish of Swineshead.
Burton - upon - Trent and Lichfield.	Derby and Stafford.	17 May 1890 (Order of Joint Committee.)	4 Sept. 1890	29 Sept. 1890	The three detached portions of the Parish of Foston and Scropton (which together constituted the Staffordshire portion of that Parish) were amalgamated with adjoining places in Staffordshire, viz., Tatenhill, Tutbury, and Yoxall. The last-named Parish is in the Lichfield Union, and the others are in the Burton-upon-Trent Union.
Highworth and Swindon.	Wilts	7 Nov. 1889	24 Sept. 1890	29 Sept. 1890	The part of the Parish of Stratton Saint Margaret known as the Hamlet of Gorse Hill, and the part of the Parish of Rodbourne Cheney known as the Hamlet of Even Swindon, were amalgamated with the Parish of Swindon.

Unions.	Counties.	Dates of Orders of County Councils.	Dates of Confirming Orders.	Dates *from and after* which the Orders operated.	Particulars of Alterations effected by the Orders.
Loughborough	Leicester	13 Aug. 1890	23 Mar. 1891	25 Mar. 1891	A detached part of the Parish of Garendon was amalgamated with the Parish of Sheepshead; a detached part of the Township of Knightthorpe was amalgamated with the Township of Loughborough; and the remaining portions of Garendon and Knightthorpe, together with the Parish of Thorpacre-with-Dishley, were re-arranged so as to form the three new Parishes of Garendon, Knightthorpe, and Thorpeacre - with - Dishley. The new Parishes are included in the Loughborough Union and in the Loughborough Petty Sessional Division.
Patrington	East Riding of Yorkshire.	7 Nov. 1890	14 Mar. 1891	25 Mar. 1891	New Townships, under the names of Owthorne and Withernsea, were formed by a re-arrangement of the areas of the old Townships of those names. The new Townships are included in the Patrington Union and in the South Holderness Petty Sessional Division.
Pontefract	West Riding of Yorkshire.	9 April 1890	25 July 1890	25 Mar. 1891	The Townships of Byram-with-Poole and Sutton were united so as to form a new Parish to be known as the Township of Byram-cum-Sutton. The new Township is included in the Pontefract Union, and in the Lower Barkston Ash Petty Sessional Division.
Thingoe	Western Division of Suffolk.	7 Nov. 1890	24 Feb. 1891	25 Mar. 1891	The Parish of Southwood Park was added to the Parish of Hargrave. [Southwood Park does not appear in the Statement as it was thought to have become part of Hargrave under 31 & 32 Vict. c. 122. s. 27.]
Totnes	Devon	7 Aug. 1890	7 Jan. 1891	25 Mar. 1891	The Parishes of Saint Petrox, Saint Saviour, and Townstall were united so as to form a new Parish to be called the Parish of Dartmouth. The new Parish is included in the Totnes Union, and is co-extensive with the Borough of Clifton Dartmouth Hardness.

III.—ALTERATIONS EFFECTED IN UNION AND PAROCHIAL AREAS IN PURSUANCE OF LOCAL ACTS.

BELPER, DERBY, AND SHARDLOW UNIONS.—In pursuance of sections 38 and 39 of the Derby Corporation Act, 1890 (53 & 54 Vict. ch. liv.), the under-mentioned alterations of areas took effect on and after the 30th September 1890 :—

1. The part of the Parish of Littleover included in the Borough of Derby was severed from that Parish and from the Shardlow Union, and was added to the Derby Union, and amalgamated with the Parish of Saint Werburgh's in that Union.

2. The part of the Parish of Normanton included in the Borough of Derby was severed from that Parish and from the Shardlow Union. The said part was also, for all parochial purposes, formed into a separate and distinct Parish under the name of New Normanton, and was added to the Derby Union.

3. The part of the Township of Markeaton included in the Borough of Derby was severed from that Township and from the Belper Union. The said part was also, for all parochial purposes, formed into a separate and distinct Parish under the name of Rowditch, and was added to the Derby Union.

WEST DERBY UNION.—In pursuance of section 11 of the Bootle Corporation Act, 1890 (53 & 54 Vict. ch. ccxix.), which made an improved boundary line between the Borough of Bootle and adjoining areas, parts of the Township of Bootle cum Linacre were, on the 1st September 1890, transferred to the Townships of Litherland, Orrell and Ford, and Walton on the Hill, and parts of the Townships of Litherland, Orrell and Ford, and Walton on the Hill were, on the same date, transferred to the Township of Bootle cum Linacre. *See* Part IX. of this Memorandum.

IV.—ALTERATIONS EFFECTED IN UNION, PAROCHIAL, AND COUNTY AREAS IN PURSUANCE OF PROVISIONAL ORDERS UNDER THE LOCAL GOVERNMENT ACT, 1888.

GREAT YARMOUTH UNION.— *See* Part IX. of this Memorandum.

TAMWORTH UNION.—By the Borough of Tamworth Order, 1890 (dated the 3rd June 1890) confirmed by the Local Government Board's Provisional Orders Confirmation (No. 11) Act, 1890, the Borough of Tamworth, in the County of Stafford, was, on the 9th November 1890, extended by the addition of part of the Township of Bolehall and Glascote and of part of the Liberty of Tamworth Castle, in the County of Warwick. The boundary between the Counties of Stafford and Warwick was also altered so that the added areas were transferred to the County of Stafford, and consequently the Township and Liberty named are now each partly in the County of Stafford, and partly in the County of Warwick.

V.—ALTERATION IN NAME OF UNION AND OF PARISH.

ULVERSTON UNION.—The Order declaring the Ulverstone Union was amended by an Order of the Local Government Board dated the 7th February 1891, in pursuance of which the Township described in the Declaration Order as " Ulverstone " is to be described as " Ulverston;" and by a further Order of the same date the name of the " Ulverstone " Union was, on and after the 26th March 1891, changed to the " Ulverston " Union.

VI.—SEPARATION OF PARISH FROM UNION AND FORMATION OF NEW UNION.

In pursuance of an Order of the Local Government Board dated the 17th January 1891, the Parish of Gorleston ceased, from and after the 15th April 1891, to form part of the Mutford and Lothingland Incorporation; and, from and after the same date, the Parish of Great Yarmouth ceased to be under a separate Board of Guardians, and the said Parishes of Gorleston and Great Yarmouth were formed into a new Union to be termed the GREAT YARMOUTH UNION.

VII.—CORRECTIONS.

1. PONTEFRACT UNION.—The note at the foot of page 296 of the Statement in regard to Water Frystone should be omitted, the acreage of that place being added to that of Ferry Frystone Township. It is understood that the Township or Civil Parish of Ferry Frystone includes Water Frystone.

2. The Counties of the Eastern Division of Sussex and the Western Division of Sussex are to be described as the Counties of East Sussex and West Sussex, and the references to those Counties in Memorandum No. 2 or Memorandum No. 3 should be amended accordingly.

VIII.—NEW COUNTY BOROUGH.

GRIMSBY.—By the Borough of Grimsby Order, 1890 (dated the 9th June 1890), which was confirmed by the Local Government Board's Provisional Orders Confirmation (No. 15) Act, 1890, the Borough of Grimsby was, on the 1st April 1891, constituted a County Borough. The Borough comprises the Parish of Great Grimsby and part of the Township of Clee, in the Grimsby Union.

IX.—ALTERATIONS OF AREAS OR CONSTITUENT PARISHES OF COUNTY BOROUGHS.

BOOTLE.—By the Bootle Corporation Act, 1890 (53 & 54 Vict. ch. ccxix.), the name of the County Borough of Bootle-cum-Linacre was, on and after the 14th August 1890, changed to "Bootle," and an improved boundary line was, on the 1st September 1890, made between the Borough and the adjoining areas. As the changes took effect also for parochial purposes, the Borough consists of the Township of Bootle cum Linacre (as altered), in the West Derby Union. *See* Part III. of this Memorandum.

CANTERBURY.—By the City of Canterbury Order, 1890 (dated the 2nd June 1890), which was confirmed by the Local Government Board's Provisional Orders Confirmation (No. 9) Act, 1890, the boundary of the City and County of Canterbury and of the County Borough was, on the 9th November 1890, extended by the addition of a further portion of the Parish of Hackington, alias Saint Stephens, in the Blean Union, and of a further portion of the Parish of Thanington, otherwise Thanington, in the Bridge Union.

COVENTRY.—By the City of Coventry Order, 1890 (dated the 6th June 1890), which was confirmed by the Local Government Board's Provisional Orders Confirmation (No. 13) Act, 1890, the boundary of the City and County Borough of Coventry was, on the 9th November 1890, extended by the addition of further portions of the Parishes of Holy Trinity and Saint Michael, in the Coventry Union.

GREAT YARMOUTH.—By the Borough of Great Yarmouth Order, 1890 (dated the 6th June 1890), which was confirmed by the Local Government Board's Provisional Orders Confirmation (No. 13) Act, 1890, the boundary of the County Borough was, on the 9th November 1890, extended by the addition of the remaining part of the Parish of Gorleston (then in the Mutford and Lothingland Incorporation, but now in the Great Yarmouth Union) and of a part of the Parish of Runham, in the East and West Flegg Incorporation. The boundary between the Counties of Norfolk and Suffolk was also altered so that the whole of the County Borough should be situated in Norfolk. The County Borough now comprises the Parishes of Gorleston and Great Yarmouth and part of the Parish of Runham. *See* Part VI. of this Memorandum.

HUDDERSFIELD.—By the Borough of Huddersfield Order, 1890 (dated the 9th June 1890), which was confirmed by the Local Government Board's Provisional Orders Confirmation (No. 15) Act, 1890, the boundary of the County Borough was, on the 9th November 1890, extended by the addition of the Township of Longwood, in the Huddersfield Union.

LIVERPOOL.—By the Liverpool Corporation Act, 1890 (53 & 54 Vict. ch. clxix.), the boundary of the City and County Borough where it abuts on the River Mersey was, on the 4th August 1890, extended to the centre of the bed of that River, thus adding to the City and County Borough the parts of the Parish of Liverpool and the Township of Kirkdale not before included, and also a further part of the Township of Toxteth Park. The County Borough, therefore, now includes the whole of the Parish of Liverpool and the Townships of Everton and Kirkdale, and parts of the Townships of West Derby and Toxteth Park.

MANCHESTER.—By the City of Manchester Order, 1890 (dated the 10th June 1890), which was confirmed by the Local Government Board's Provisional Order (No. 16) Act, 1890, the boundary of the City and County Borough was, on the 9th November 1890, extended by the addition of—

1. The part of the Township of Droylsden, in the Ashton-under-Lyne Union, which was included in the Rural Sanitary District.
2. The Township of Openshaw and part of the Township of Gorton, in the Chorlton Union.
3. The Townships of Blackley, Crumpsall, Moston, and Newton, in the Prestwich Union.

WALSALL.—By the Walsall Corporation Act, 1890 (53 & 54 Vict. ch. cxxx.) the boundary of the County Borough was, on the 31st October 1890, extended by the addition of a further portion of the Parish of Rushall, in the Walsall Union.

Local Government Board,
19th April 1891.

Memorandum (No. 5) of Alterations affecting the Particulars contained in the Statement of Poor Law Unions, &c., 1887.—[C. 5191.]

I.—ALTERATIONS EFFECTED IN UNION AND PAROCHIAL AREAS IN PURSUANCE OF ORDERS OF COUNTY COUNCILS, CONFIRMED BY THE LOCAL GOVERNMENT BOARD.

Unions.	Counties.	Dates of Orders of County Councils.	Dates of Confirming Orders.	Dates *from and after which* the Orders operated.	Particulars of Alterations effected by the Orders.
Caistor and Glanford Brigg.	Parts of Lindsey.	7 Nov. 1890	22 Dec. 1891	25 Mar. 1892	Part of the Parish of Bigby, in the Caistor Union, parts of the Parishes of Broughton, and Scawby with Sturton, and of the Township of Wrawby, in the Glanford Brigg Union, were amalgamated with the Township of Glanford Brigg, in the last-named Union.
Elham and Romney Marsh.	Kent	15 April 1891	31 Aug. 1891	29 Sept. 1891	Parts of the Parish of West Hythe, in the Romney Marsh Union, were amalgamated with the Parish of Lympne, in the Elham Union. (It had been supposed that all the parts of the Parish of West Hythe had been added to other Parishes by orders issued by the Local Government Board under the Divided Parishes Acts. The parts dealt with by this Order were subsequently found to have been omitted.)
Howden	East Riding of Yorkshire.	27 July 1891	26 Feb. 1892	25 Mar. 1892	The Township of Cheapsides was amalgamated with the Township of Sealby.
Northwich	Chester	12 Nov. 1891	25 Feb. 1892	24 Mar. 1892	The Townships of Darnhall and Weever were united so as to form a new parish, to be known as the Parish of Darnhall. The new parish is included in the Northwich Union. The Townships of Wimboldsley and Occleston were united so as to form a new parish, to be known as the Parish of Wimboldsley. The new parish is included in the Northwich Union. The Townships of Shipbrook and Whatcroft were united so as to form a new parish, to be known as the Parish of Whatcroft. The new parish is included in the Northwich Union.

Unions.	Counties.	Dates of Orders of County Councils.	Dates of Confirming Orders.	Dates *from and after* which the Orders operated.	Particulars of Alterations effected by the Orders.
Northwich— (*cont.*)	Chester -	12 Nov. 1891	25 Feb. 1892 -	24 Mar. 1892	The Townships of Rudheath and Shurlack were united so as to form a new parish, to be known as the Parish of Rudheath. The new parish is included in the Northwich Union.
					The Parish of Little Budworth and the Township of Low Oulton were united so as to form a new parish, to be known as the Parish of Little Budworth. The new parish is included in the Northwich Union.
					The Townships of Wallerscoat and Winnington were united so as to form a new parish, to be known as the Parish of Winnington. The new parish is included in the Northwich Union.
					The Townships of Sproston and Moresbarrow cum Parme were united so as to form a new parish, to be known as the Parish of Sproston. The new parish is included in the Northwich Union.
					The Townships of Crowton and Onston were united so as to form a new parish, to be known as the Parish of Crowton. The new parish is included in the Northwich Union.
					The Townships of Newton and Sutton were united so as to form a new parish, to be known as the Parish of Newton. The new parish is included in the Northwich Union.
					The Townships of Byley cum Yatehouse, Croxton, and Ravenscroft were united so as to form a new parish, to be known as the Parish of Byley. The new parish is included in the Northwich Union.
					The Townships of Birches, Hulse, Lack Dennis, Newhall, and Stublach were united so as to form a new parish, to be known as the Parish of Lach Dennis. The new parish is included in the Northwich Union.
Pontefract	West Riding of Yorkshire.	8 July 1891 -	27 Jan. 1892 -	25 Mar. 1892 -	The Township of Monk Hill was amalgamated with the Township of Pontefract.
Stroud -	Gloucester -	6 July 1891 -	13 Feb. 1892 -	25 Mar. 1892 -	Part of the Parish of Avening with Nailsworth was constituted a civil parish to be known as the Parish of Nailsworth, and parts of the Parishes of Horsley and Minchinhampton were added thereto. The new Parish is included in the Stroud Union and in the Horsley Petty Sessional Division.

II.—ALTERATIONS EFFECTED IN UNION AND PAROCHIAL AREAS IN PURSUANCE OF LOCAL ACTS.

BARTON-UPON-IRWELL AND SALFORD UNIONS.—By Part IV. of the Manchester Ship Canal (Alteration of Works) Act, 1888 (51 & 52 Vict. ch. clxi.) and Part III. of the Salford Corporation Act, 1891 (54 Vict. ch. xiv.), by which, from and after the 1st of June 1892, the boundary line between the County Borough of Salford and adjoining areas was altered to follow the centre line of the River Irwell as altered by a certain portion of the Manchester Ship Canal, part of the Township of Stretford was on the same date added to the Township of Salford, part of the Township of Salford was added to the Township of Stretford, part of the Township of Barton-upon-Irwell was added to the Township of Pendleton, and part of the Township of Pendleton was added to the Township of Barton-upon-Irwell.

(The Townships of Barton-upon-Irwell and Stretford are in the Barton-upon-Irwell Union and in the County of Lancaster, and the Townships of Pendleton and Salford are in the Salford Union and in the County Borough of Salford.)

(*See also Part VIII. of this Memorandum.*)

BARROW-UPON-SOAR, BILLESDON, BLABY, AND LEICESTER UNIONS.—In pursuance of sections 57, 58, 59, 60, 61, 62, 63, and 64 of the Leicester Extension Act, 1891 (54 & 55 Vict. ch. c.), the under-mentioned alterations of areas took effect from and after the 25th of March 1892 :—

BARROW-UPON-SOAR UNION :—

The part of the Township of Belgrave not included in the County Borough of Leicester was severed from that Township and amalgamated with the Parish of Beaumont Leys in the Barrow-upon-Soar Union. The Township of Belgrave, as so altered, was severed from the Barrow-upon-Soar Union and added to the Leicester Union.

The part of the Parish of Leicester Abbey not included in the County Borough of Leicester was severed from that Parish and amalgamated with the Parish of Beaumont Leys in the Barrow-upon-Soar Union. The Parish of Leicester Abbey, as so altered, was severed from the Barrow-upon-Soar Union and added to the Leicester Union. The Parish of Freaks Ground was amalgamated with the Parish of Leicester Abbey. (*See* Blaby Union.)

BILLESDON UNION :—

The part of the Parish of Evington included in the County Borough of Leicester was severed from that Parish and from the Billesdon Union. The said part was constituted a separate Parish under the name of the Parish of North Evington, and was added to the Leicester Union.

The part of the Parish of Humberstone included in the County Borough of Leicester was severed from that Parish and from the Billesdon Union. The said part was constituted a separate Parish under the name of the Parish of West Humberstone, and was added to the Leicester Union.

BLABY UNION :—

The part of the Township of Aylestone not included in the County Borough of Leicester was severed from that Township and was amalgamated with the Township of Lubbisthorpe in the Blaby Union. The Township of Aylestone, as so altered, was added to the Leicester Union.

The part of the Township of Braunstone included in the County Borough of Leicester was severed from that Township and from the Blaby Union, and was amalgamated with the Parish of Saint Mary, in the Leicester Union.

The parts of the Township of Knighton not included in the County Borough of Leicester were severed from that Township and amalgamated, as regards one part, with the Township of Lubbisthorpe in the Blaby Union, and, as regards the other part, with the Parish of Oadby in the Blaby Union. The Township of Knighton, as so altered, was added to the Leicester Union.

The Parish of Freaks Ground was severed from the Blaby Union and amalgamated with the Parish of Leicester Abbey in the Leicester Union. (*See* Barrow-upon-Soar Union.)

The Parish of New Found Pool was severed from the Blaby Union and added to the Leicester Union.

LEICESTER UNION :—

The Parish of Saint Mary, in the Leicester Union, was enlarged by the addition of part of the Township of Braunstone (from the Blaby Union).

The following Places were added to the Union :—

The Township of Aylestone (from the Blaby Union).
The Township of Belgrave (from the Barrow-upon-Soar Union).
The Township of Knighton (from the Blaby Union).
The Parish of Leicester Abbey (from the Barrow-upon-Soar and Blaby Unions).
The Parish of New Found Pool (from the Blaby Union).
The Parish of North Evington (from the Billesdon Union).
The Parish of West Humberstone (from the Billesdon Union).

(*See also Part VIII. of this Memorandum.*)

III.—ALTERATION EFFECTED IN AREA OF COUNTY IN PURSUANCE OF A PROVISIONAL ORDER UNDER THE LOCAL GOVERNMENT ACT, 1888.

BIRMINGHAM.—By Art. V. of the City of Birmingham Order, 1891 (dated the 15th of May 1891), which was confirmed by the Local Government Board's Provisional Order Confirmation (No. 13) Act, 1891, the boundary between the County of Warwick and the Counties of Stafford and Worcester was, on the 9th of November 1891, altered so that the City of Birmingham should be wholly situate in the County of Warwick. (*See also Part VIII. of this Memorandum.*)

IV.—ALTERATIONS IN NAMES OF PARISHES.

The Orders declaring certain Unions have been amended, as regards the cases in the following table, in regard to the names of certain Parishes in such Unions :—

Union.	Name of Parish as in Declaration Order.	Name of Parish as amended.	Date of Amending Order.
Aysgarth	Newbiggen	Newbiggin	7th August 1891.
Bicester	Goddington	Godington	3rd September 1891.
Cardigan	Llandygwyd	Llandygwydd	6th July 1891.
Tregaron	Nantewnlle	Nantewnlle	6th July 1891.

V.—ALTERATIONS IN UNIONS BY SEPARATION OR ADDITION OF PARISHES.

NANTWICH AND TARVIN UNIONS.—By orders issued by the Local Government Board, dated respectively the 24th of February 1892 and the 25th of February 1892, the Townships of Beeston, Burwardsley, Eaton, Rushton, Tarporley, Tilston Fernall, Tiverton, and Utkington were, from and after the 25th March 1892, separated from the Nantwich Union, and added to the Tarvin Union.

BARROW-UPON-SOAR, BILLESDON, BLABY, AND LEICESTER UNIONS.—(*See Part II. of this Memorandum.*)

VI.—CORRECTIONS.

1. BRENTFORD UNION.—"Perrivale" should be "Perivale" in the Statement.

2. THE ADMINISTRATIVE COUNTY OF THE WESTERN DIVISION OF SUSSEX.—The reference on page 10, L. of Memorandum (No. 2) to the part of the Cuckfield Union contained in the Administrative County of the Western Division of Sussex should be corrected by the omission of the words "and part of each of the Parishes of Bolney and Slaugham."

VII.—NEW COUNTY BOROUGH.

NEWPORT.—By the Borough of Newport Order, 1891 (dated the 8th of May 1891), which was confirmed by the Local Government Board's Provisional Orders Confirmation (No. 9) Act, 1891, the Borough of Newport, in the County of Monmouth, was, on the 7th of November 1891, constituted a County Borough.

The County Borough comprises the whole of the Township of Newport, part of the Parish of Christchurch with Caerleon ultra Pontem, part of the Parish of Nash, and part of the Township of Saint Woollos.

VIII.—ALTERATIONS OF AREAS OR CONSTITUENT PARISHES OF COUNTY BOROUGHS.

BIRKENHEAD. — By section 6 of the Birkenhead Corporation Act, 1891 (54 & 55 Vict. ch. lxxxvii.), the boundary of the County Borough, where it abutted on the River Mersey, was, on the 3rd of July 1891, extended to the centre of the bed of that river, and made the same for parochial and municipal purposes.

BIRMINGHAM.—By Art. III. (1) of the City of Birmingham Order, 1891 (dated the 15th May 1891), which was confirmed by the Local Government Board's Provisional Order Confirmation (No. 13) Act, 1891, the boundary of the City and County Borough was, on the 9th November 1891, extended so as to include the following areas :—

1. The Local Government District of Balsall Heath, in the Parish of King's Norton, in the Kings Norton Union, and in the county of Worcester.
2. The Local Government District of Harborne, in the Parish of Harborne and Smethwick, in the Kings Norton Union, and in the County of Stafford.
3. The Local Government District of Saltley, in the Parish of Aston near Birmingham, in the Aston Union, and in the County of Warwick.
4. The part of the Parish of Aston near Birmingham, in the Aston Union, and in the County of Warwick, known as the hamlet of Little Bromwich.

By Article V. of the Order it was provided that, for the purposes of the Local Government Act, 1888, the County Borough should be included within the County of Warwick.
(See also Part III. of this Memorandum.)

LEICESTER.—By Section 21 of the Leicester Extension Act, 1891 (54 & 55 Vict. ch. c.), the boundary of the County Borough was, on the 31st October 1891, extended by the addition of the Parishes of Freaks Ground and New Found Pool, and parts of the Parishes or Townships of Aylestone, Belgrave, Braunstone, Evington, Humberstone, Knighton, and Leicester Abbey. (See also Part II. of this Memorandum.)

SALFORD.—By Part IV. of the Manchester Ship Canal (Alteration of Works) Act, 1888, and Part III. of the Salford Corporation Act, 1891, parts of the boundary line between the County Borough and the County of Lancaster were, from and after the 1st of June 1892, altered, and made to follow the centre line of the River Irwell as altered by a certain portion of the Manchester Ship Canal. (See also Part II. of this Memorandum.)

Local Government Board,
31st May 1892.

Memorandum (No. 6) of Alterations affecting the Particulars contained in the Statement of Poor Law Unions, &c., 1887.—[C. 5191.]

I.—ALTERATIONS EFFECTED IN UNION AND PAROCHIAL AREAS IN PURSUANCE OF ORDERS OF COUNTY COUNCILS, CONFIRMED BY THE LOCAL GOVERNMENT BOARD.

Unions.	Counties.	Dates of Orders of County Councils.	Dates of Confirming Orders.	Dates from and after which the Orders operated.	Particulars of Alterations effected by the Orders.
Christchurch and Ringwood.	Southampton	11 May 1891	26 April 1892	29 Sept. 1892	Part of the Parish of Christchurch, in the Christchurch Union, was amalgamated with the Parish of Ringwood, in the Ringwood Union.
Kingsbridge	Devon	29 Sept. 1892	4 Mar. 1893	25 Mar. 1893	The parishes of Dodbrooke and Kingsbridge were united to form one parish, to be known as the Parish of Kingsbridge and Dodbrooke. The new parish is included in the Kingsbridge Union.
Orsett	Essex	5 July 1892	24 Mar. 1893	25 Mar. 1893	The boundaries of the Parishes of Grays Thurrock and Little Thurrock were altered by the transfer of parts of the Parish of Grays Thurrock to the Parish of Little Thurrock, and of parts of the Parish of Little Thurrock to the Parish of Grays Thurrock.
Romford and West Ham.	Essex	6 Oct. 1891	25 Jan. 1893	25 Mar. 1893	The boundaries of the Parishes of East Ham and Barking were altered by the transfer of part of the Parish of East Ham to the Parish of Barking, and of part of the Parish of Barking to the Parish of East Ham.

II.—ALTERATIONS EFFECTED IN PAROCHIAL AREAS IN PURSUANCE OF LOCAL ACTS.

BLACKBURN UNION.—In pursuance of section 5 of the Blackburn Corporation Act, 1892 (55 & 56 Vict. ch. cxviii.), the several Townships and parts of Townships comprised within the County Borough of Blackburn, viz., the Townships of Blackburn and Little Harwood, and parts of the Townships of Livesay, Lower Darwen, and Witton, were, from and after the 25th March, 1893, amalgamated, and became for all purposes one Township under the name of the Township of Blackburn. The remaining parts of the Townships of Livesay, Lower Darwen, and Witton were, from and after the same date, constituted separate Townships for all purposes.

The newly constituted Township of Blackburn and the diminished Townships of Livesay, Lower Darwen, and Witton continue in the Blackburn Union. (*See also Part VI. of this Memorandum.*)

III.—ALTERATION IN THE NAME OF A UNION, AND ALTERATIONS IN THE NAMES OF PARISHES AND TOWNSHIPS.

EASTHAMPSTEAD UNION.—The Order declaring the Easthamstead Union was amended by an Order of the Local Government Board dated the 25th January, 1893, by which "Easthampstead" was substituted for "Easthamstead," as regards the name of the Union.

A corresponding substitution was, by the same Order, made as regards the name of the Parish in the Union bearing the same name. (*See below* *.)

WHARFEDALE UNION.—The Order, dated the 31st May, 1869, which added the Township of Addle-with-Eccup to the Wharfedale Union, was amended by an Order of the Local Government Board dated the 2nd June, 1892, in pursuance of which the Township is to be described as "Adel cum Eccup."

The Orders declaring certain Unions have been amended, as regards the cases in the following table, in regard to the names of certain Parishes or Townships in such Unions :—

Union.	Name of Parishes or Townships as in Declaration Order.	Name of Parishes or Townships as amended.	Date of Amending Order.
Abergavenny	Tewddog	Fwddog	7th February 1893.
Ashton-under-Lyne	Duckingfield	Dukinfield	20th July 1892.
Easthampstead	Winkfield with Ascot	Winkfield	21st December 1892.
*Easthampstead	Easthamstead	Easthampstead	25th January 1893.
Royston	Foulmire	Fowlmere	24th August 1892.
Stroud	Avening with Nailsworth.	Avening	16th May 1892.
Wirrall	Bromborrow	Bromborough	12th October 1892.

IV.—FORMATION OF NEW UNION.

MUTFORD AND LOTHINGLAND UNION.—By a Provisional Order of the Local Government Board dated the 5th May, 1892, which was confirmed by the Local Government Board's Provisional Order Confirmation (Poor Law) Act, 1892, the unrepealed portions of two Local Acts, under one of which the Guardians of the Poor within the Hundred of Mutford and Lothingland, in the County of Suffolk, were incorporated, were repealed from and after the 25th March, 1893. In consequence of the operation of the Provisional Order referred to, the Local Government Board, by an Order dated the 21st February, 1893, declared that the under-mentioned Parishes should, on and after the 26th March, 1893, be united for the administration of the laws for the relief of the poor, and form the Mutford and Lothingland Union, in the County of the Eastern Division of Suffolk ; viz., the Parishes of—

Ashby,	Flixton,	Lound,
Barnby,	Fritton,	Lowestoft,
Belton,	Gisleham,	Mutford,
Blundeston,	Gunton,	Oulton,
Bradwell,	Herringfleet,	Pakefield,
Burgh Castle,	Hopton,	Rushmere,
Carlton Colville,	Kessingland,	and
Corton,	Kirtley,	Somerleyton.

V.—ALTERATIONS IN UNIONS BY SEPARATION OR ADDITION OF PARISHES.

STROUD AND TETBURY UNIONS.—By Orders issued by the Local Government Board, dated respectively the 4th January, 1893, and the 5th January, 1893, the Parish of Avening was, from and after the 25th March, 1893, separated from the Stroud Union, and added to the Tetbury Union.

VI.—ALTERATIONS OF AREAS OR CONSTITUENT PARISHES OF COUNTY BOROUGHS.

BLACKBURN.—The County Borough of Blackburn, which formerly comprised the Townships of Blackburn and Little Harwood, and parts of the Townships of Livesay, Lower Darwen, and Witton, has become by operation of the Blackburn Corporation Act, 1892, co-terminous with the Township of Blackburn, as now constituted. (*See also Part II. of this Memorandum.*)

HALIFAX.—By Art. III. of the Borough of Halifax Order, 1892 (dated the 13th May, 1892), which was confirmed by the Local Government Board's Provisional Orders Confirmation (No. 10) Act, 1892, the boundary of the County Borough of Halifax was, on the 9th November, 1892, extended so as to include the Local Government District of Ovenden, in the Township of Ovenden, in the Halifax Union, and in the County of the West Riding of Yorkshire. The whole of the Township of Ovenden is now included in the County Borough.

Local Government Board,
    8th May 1893.

23 Nov 96.

Dear Sir,

There has been no Memorandum of Alterations affecting the particulars in C.5191, since Mem^m (No 7) of April 1894. When a further Mem^m is issued I will send copies

Yours truly

N. Walsh.

H. P. Morris Esq.

Memorandum (No. 7) of alterations affecting the particulars contained in the Statement of Poor Law Unions, &c., 1887.—[C. 5191.]

I.—ALTERATIONS EFFECTED IN UNION AND PAROCHIAL AREAS IN PURSUANCE OF ORDERS OF COUNTY COUNCILS, CONFIRMED BY THE LOCAL GOVERNMENT BOARD.

Unions or separate Parishes.	Counties.	Dates of Orders of County Councils.	Dates of Confirming Orders.	Dates *from and after* which the Orders operated.	Particulars of alterations effected by the Orders.
Anglesey	Anglesey	27 July 1893	9 Mar. 1894	25 Mar. 1894	Part of the Parish of Amlwch was amalgamated with the Parish of Llanerchymedd.
Ashby-de-la-Zouch.	Leicester	9 Nov. 1892	24 July 1893	29 Sept. 1893	The part of the Township of Hugglescote and Donington not included within the Local Government District of Coalville was amalgamated with the Parish of Bardon.
Burnley	Lancaster	3 Aug. 1893	6 Mar. 1894	25 Mar. 1894	The part of the Township of Great and Little Marsden included within the Local Government District of Colne was amalgamated with the Township of Colne.
Chard	Somerset	3 Jan. 1893	22 June 1893	29 Sept. 1893	The part of the Parish of Chard included within the Municipal Borough of Chard was amalgamated with the Parish of Chard borough.
Cheadle	Stafford	7 Feb. 1893	26 June 1893	29 Sept. 1893	The part of the Parish of Cheekley and Teau known as Foxt (in Cheekley) was amalgamated with the Parish of Ipstones.
Chesterfield	Derby	5 July 1893	20 Feb. 1894	25 Mar. 1894	The parts of the Parish of Brampton and of the Townships of Hasland, Newbold and Dunston, and Walton, included within the Municipal Borough of Chesterfield were amalgamated with the Township of Chesterfield.
Holborn; Saint Giles-in-the-Fields and Saint George, Bloomsbury (United Parishes); and Saint Pancras (Parish).	London	19 Dec. 1893	30 Mar. 1894	31 Mar. 1894	Parts of the Parish of Saint Andrew Holborn above Bars united with Saint George the Martyr, and of the United Parishes of Saint Giles-in-the-Fields and Saint George, Bloomsbury, were amalgamated with the Parish of Saint Pancras.
Nautwich	Chester	14 Feb. 1893	27 Nov. 1893	25 Mar. 1894	The parts of the Parish of Wistaston and of the Townships of Coppenhall Church and Shavington with Gresty included within the Municipal borough of Crewe were amalgamated with the Township of Coppenhall Monks.
South Stoneham.	Southampton	8 May 1893	27 Dec. 1893	25 Mar. 1894	The part of the Parish of South Stoneham included in the Ecclesiastical District of Eastleigh, excepting any part of the Tything of Boyatt, was separated from that Parish and formed into a separate Parish to be known as the Parish of Eastleigh. The new Parish is included in the South Stoneham Union, and in the Southampton Petty Sessional Division.

Unions.	Counties.	Dates of Orders of County Councils.	Dates of Confirming Orders.	Dates from and after which the Orders operated.	Particulars of alterations effected by the Orders.
Stroud	Gloucester	2 Dec. 1893	20 Mar. 1894	25 Mar. 1894	Part of the Parish of Stonehouse was separated from that Parish and formed into a new Parish to be known as the Parish of Cainscross, and part of the Parish of Stroud was added thereto. The new Parish is included in the Stroud Union, and in the Whitminster Petty Sessional Division.
Stroud and Wheatenhurst.	Gloucester	2 Dec. 1893	20 Mar. 1894	25 Mar. 1894	Part of the Parish of Standish in the Wheatenhurst Union, and parts of the Parishes of Stonehouse and Stroud in the Stroud Union were amalgamated with the Parish of Randwick in the last-named Union.
Wells	Somerset	27 June 1893	19 Feb. 1894	25 Mar. 1894	The boundaries of the Parishes of Saint Benedict and Saint John, Glastonbury, and Street were altered by the transfer of parts of the Parish of Street to the Parish of Saint Benedict and Saint John, Glastonbury, and of parts of the Parish of Saint Benedict and Saint John, Glastonbury, to the Parish of Street.
West Bromwich	Stafford	25 Oct. 1892	5 Dec. 1893	25 Mar. 1894	The part of the Parish of Handsworth outside the Local Government District of Handsworth was separated from that Parish and formed into a new Parish to be known as the Parish of Perry Barr. The new Parish is included in the West Bromwich Union, and in the Handsworth Petty Sessional Division.
Windsor	Berks	29 Oct. 1892	1 Aug. 1893	24 Mar. 1894	The part of the Parish of Old Windsor included within the Ecclesiastical District of Sunningdale was separated from that Parish and formed into a new Parish to be known as the Parish of Sunningdale. The new Parish is included in the Windsor Union, and in the Windsor Petty Sessional Division.

II.—ALTERATIONS EFFECTED IN PAROCHIAL AREAS IN PURSUANCE OF LOCAL ACTS.

PRESCOT UNION.—In pursuance of section 23 of the St. Helens Corporation Act, 1893 (56 & 57 Vict. ch. ccxv.), the several Townships and parts of Townships comprised within the County Borough of Saint Helens, viz., the Townships of Parr and Sutton, and parts of the Townships of Eccleston and Windle, were, from and after the 25th March, 1894, amalgamated, and became for all purposes one Township under the name of the Township of St. Helens. The remaining parts of the Townships of Eccleston and Windle were, from and after the same date, constituted separate Townships for all purposes.

The newly constituted Townships of St. Helens, Eccleston, and Windle are included in the Prescot Union. (*See also Part VII. of this Memorandum.*)

III.—ALTERATIONS EFFECTED IN AREAS OF COUNTIES IN PURSUANCE OF PROVISIONAL ORDERS ISSUED UNDER THE LOCAL GOVERNMENT ACT, 1888.

ABERGAVENNY UNION.—By Provisional Order dated the 18th May, 1893, which was confirmed by the Local Government Board's Provisional Orders Confirmation (No. 16) Act, 1893, the boundary between the counties of Hereford and Monmouth was altered by the transfer of the Hamlet of Fwddog from the County of Hereford to the County of Monmouth. The Hamlet was also included in the Abergavenny Special or Petty Sessional Division of the County of Monmouth. The Order came into operation on the 29th September, 1893. The Abergavenny Union is now wholly in the County of Monmouth.

BROMYARD UNION.—By Provisional Order dated the 16th May, 1893, which was confirmed by the Local Government Board's Provisional Orders Confirmation (No. 16) Act, 1893, the boundary between the Counties of Hereford and Worcester was altered by the transfer of the Parish of Edwin Loach from the County of Worcester to the County of Hereford. The Parish is included in the Bromyard Special or Petty Sessional Division of the County of Hereford. The Order came into operation on the 29th September 1893.

YORK UNION.—By Provisional Order dated the 18th May, 1893, which was confirmed by the Local Government Board's Provisional Orders Confirmation (No. 16) Act, 1893, the boundary of the City and County Borough of York was altered by the inclusion therein of a further part of the Township of Clifton. The Order came into operation on the 9th November, 1893. (*See also Part VII. of this Memorandum.*)

IV.—ALTERATION IN NAME OF UNION AND OF PARISH.

BOURNE UNION.—PARISH OF BOURNE.—The Order declaring the Bourn Union was altered by an Order of the Local Government Board, dated the 4th September, 1893, by which " Bourne " was substituted for " Bourn " both as regards the name of the Union and of the Parish.

V.—ALTERATIONS IN UNIONS BY SEPARATION OR ADDITION OF PARISHES.

CONGLETON AND LEEK UNIONS.—By Orders issued by the Local Government Board, dated respectively the 20th June, 1893, and the 21st June, 1893, the Parish of Biddulph in the County of Stafford was, from and after the 29th September, 1893, separated from the Congleton Union and added to the Leek Union. The Congleton Union is now wholly in the County of Chester.

VI.—CORRECTION.

MALLING UNION.—" Malling East," " Malling West," " Peckham East " and " Peckham West," in the Statement of Poor Law Unions, &c., 1887, should be respectively " East Malling," " West Malling," " East Peckham," and " West Peckham."

VII.—ALTERATIONS OF AREAS OR CONSTITUENT PARISHES OF COUNTY BOROUGHS.

ST. HELENS.—By section 7 of the St. Helens Corporation Act, 1893 (56 & 57 Vict. ch. ccxv.), the boundary of the County Borough was, on the 24th August, 1893, extended by the addition of portions of the Townships of Eccleston and Windle (in addition to the portions of those Townships already included therein), in the Prescot Union ; and by section 23 of the Act the whole area included within the Borough was, from and after the 25th March, 1894, formed into one Township, to be called the Township of St. Helens. (*See also Part II. of this Memorandum.*)

YORK.—By Art. III. of the City of York Order, 1893 (dated the 18th May, 1893), which was confirmed by the Local Government Board's Provisional Orders Confirmation (No. 16) Act, 1893, the boundary of the City and County Borough of York was, on the 9th November, 1893, extended by the addition of a further portion of the Township of Clifton, in the York Union, and in the County of the North Riding of Yorkshire. (*See also Part III. of this Memorandum.*)

Local Government Board,
25th April, 1894.